I BELIEVE DISCARDED

IN THE HOLY SPIRIT

YVES CONGAR

I BELIEVE IN
THE HOLY SPIRIT

TRANSLATED BY

DAVID SMITH

A Herder & Herder Book

THE CROSSROAD PUBLISHING COMPANY

NEW YORK

This printing: 2006

The Crossroad Publishing Company
16 Penn Plaza, 481 Eighth Avenue
New York, NY 10001

Original edition: *Je crois en l'Esprit Saint*
© Les Éditions du Cerf, 1979-80

English translation: Copyright © 1983 by Geoffrey Chapman,
a division of Cassell Ltd.

Printed in the United States of America

Library of Congress Cataloging-in-Publication Data

Congar, Yves, 1904–
    [Je crois en l'Esprit Saint. English]
    I believe in the Holy Spirit / Yves Congar ; translated by
David Smith
        p.   cm.
    Includes bibliographical references.
    "A Crossroad Herder book."
    ISBN 0–8245–1696–6 (pbk.)
    1. Holy Spirit.   I. Title.
BT121.2.C   1997
231'.3—dc21   97-28324
                                         CIP

To
Nicole Legrain and Nicolas Walty
without whom this work
would never have been published
with gratitude and in friendship

GENERAL INTRODUCTION

This work, which I have been wanting to write for years, is dedicated to the Holy Spirit. The present 'Renewal' movement, all too frequently known as 'charismatic renewal', will have a place in it, but it is not the source of my wish to embark on the work, which in fact preceded it. It simply gives to our undertaking a contemporary interest and even an urgency with which I am favourably disposed to comply.

What are our standpoint and our point of departure to be? What will be the conditions governing our approach? They will follow the classical rules of faith seeking understanding. Faith, after all, seeks to understand what it holds and experiences, and it owes what it holds to what it has received from inspired or canonical Scriptures. It is through these Scriptures that God speaks to us and communicates to us what we have to know if we are to respond to his loving plan for us. The Christian, however, is a man who has been preceded by others. Generations of believers have reflected about faith before us and they have also experienced the Spirit. We seek an understanding of faith not alone, but with them, and also with contemporary witnesses to Christian experience, since the Spirit blows today as he did yesterday.

This questioning of Christian experience is very necessary because revelation and knowledge of the Spirit are affected by a certain lack of conceptual mediation. The ideas available to us when we speak of the Father and the Son are fairly well defined and easy enough to understand. They refer to fatherhood and begetting on the one hand and the bond between parent and offspring on the other. These two terms point in fact to the first and second Persons; being relative terms, they characterize those two Persons as mutually related.

The term 'Spirit', however, has none of these associations. The whole terminology used to speak of the third Person is common and absolute. The word 'Spirit' is equally suitable for the Father and the Son, as is 'Holy', but they are not terms signifying a person. 'Procession' can also be used of the Word, the Son. There is no revelation in the objective sense of the Person of the Holy Spirit as there is of the Person of the Word, the Son, in Jesus and, through that Person, of the Person of the Father. In this context, it has been suggested that the Holy Spirit empties himself, in a kind of kenosis, of his own personality in order to be in a relationship, on the one hand, with 'God' and Christ and, on the other, with men, who are called to realize the image of God and his Son. 'In order to reveal himself, he did not, like Yahweh in the

Old Testament and Jesus in the New, use the personal pronoun "I".[1] The Holy Spirit is revealed to us and known to us not in himself, or at least not directly in himself, but through what he brings about in us.[2] On the other hand, whereas the activities of understanding can be perceived in him in a very translucent way and therefore defined, those of affection and love have not yet been similarly analysed.[3] These difficulties will be considered when we turn our attention to a theology of the third Person.

My intention in this work is to divide the whole study into three parts, each part occupying one volume. I have no carefully preconceived and detailed plan, but rather a project and an intention. This can be outlined as follows:

I. THE 'ECONOMY' AND THE EXPERIENCE OF THE SPIRIT
(A) According to the canonical Scriptures
(B) In the life of the Church through the ages

II. 'HE IS LORD AND GIVER OF LIFE'
(A) The Spirit animates the Church:
   The Church is made by the Spirit. He is the co-instituting principle of the Church
   The Holy Spirit makes the Church one. He is the principle of communion
   The Holy Spirit is the principle of catholicity
   The Spirit keeps the Church 'apostolic'
   The Spirit is the principle of holiness in the Church
(B) The breath of God in our personal lives:
   The Spirit and man in God's plan
   The gift of the Spirit in the messianic era
   'God has sent the Spirit of his Son into our hearts'
   Life in the Spirit and according to the Spirit
   The Holy Spirit and our prayer
   The Spirit and the struggle against the flesh. The spirit and freedom
   The gifts and the fruits of the Spirit
(C) The Renewal in the Spirit. Promises and questions
   The positive aspect of the charismatic renewal
   Questions:
   What title should be used?
   Spectacular charisms
   Baptism in the Spirit
   The Renewal and ecumenism
(D) 'In the unity of the Holy Spirit, all honour and glory'

III. THE 'THEOLOGY OF THE SPIRIT'
(A) The third Person. Circumincession

(B) The Spirit and the incarnate Word
(C) Appropriation?
(D) East and West:
   The *Filioque*
   The Epiclesis. The Eucharist and the Holy Spirit

I shall, then, begin my study in the classical manner by an investigation of the canonical Scriptures. For whatever the extent and the variety of the activity, and therefore the manifestations of the Spirit, the meaning of that activity and those manifestations is vouchsafed to us in an 'inspired' and therefore for us normative way in canonical Scripture. In this investigation, however, there will be no need to discuss the relationship between the history of salvation, which is coterminous with the history of mankind as such, and the history of revelation, or between what has been called 'transcendental revelation' and 'categorial revelation'.[4] All Catholic theologians agree that the canonical Scriptures bear witness to that revelation and that they act as our criteria in our evaluation of our experience of God.

But this is not all. The Scriptures comprise 46 documents in the Old Testament and 27 in the New, compiled over a period lasting more than a millennium by various authors or groups of authors, many of whom are unknown to us. They cannot simply be treated as a whole, without distinction. On the other hand, I cannot, in this context, undertake a complete study, which would call for a series of detailed monographs. I shall therefore follow the chronological order of the written documents of the Bible. This will enable us to distinguish not only a development and even a progress in the revelation of the Spirit, but also a certain diversity in the way in which the subject of the Spirit is presented by the different authors.

There is, of course, a problem here, raised by modern exegesis. Greatly improved methods are used today, but this has frequently meant the classical groups of proof-texts have been broken up. It has been shown, for example, that Luke's presentation of the activity of the Holy Spirit is different from Paul's, but very often what one exegete claims to have established is contradicted by another, and the original ideas contained in one monograph make the arguments in another seem outdated. It is obvious, then, that the Church cannot wait to live and confess its faith until the exegetes have reached complete agreement or until Luke and Paul or Mark and John are made to dovetail neatly into each other. The Church has never in fact yielded to the temptation to melt the four gospels down into a single one, but has always regarded the four evangelists as the animals of Ezekiel, each one walking straight ahead. It has spoken of the gospel as 'tetramorphic' and has included these four forms as they are in a 'canon', the unity of which corresponds to the unity of God himself.

It is in the image of God himself that the Church honours diversity in unity. It experiences and preserves that unity in its Tradition, which is the vital handing on of 'all that she herself is and all that she believes'.[5] There is always the risk that, because of this unity, the most prominent shades of meaning, which form the wealth of the documents from which the Church lives, will be blurred by Tradition. For this reason, we are encouraged to look for and affirm these subtle differences within the Church itself. In every family, each child has its own character and its own individual tastes. The Church is similarly the family and the home in which we live. The unity of the Church is fully Catholic.

With these comments in mind, I shall provide the reader with what is inevitably an elementary and incomplete series of experiences and manifestations of the Spirit. I shall do this firstly at the level of the revelation to which the Scriptures bear witness and then at the level of the life of the Church throughout its two millennia of history.

I have no illusions about what I am doing. The task that I am undertaking will strike some readers as too difficult and others, who are specialists, as too elementary. Each of the sub-sections of this work could be the subject of a full scholarly monograph. In many cases, such monographs already exist. I have read, used and cited many of them, but have only retained what is necessary for my own purpose.

My purpose is above all to know and to teach. I know that it is not enough to stop there. For the Christian, knowledge is there for the sake of communion and love. I believe intensely in the essential union of theological study and a life of praise—the doxology and practice of the liturgy in which, by celebrating them, we are in communion with the mysteries. It is arguable that I ought to have quoted the texts themselves more often, instead of simply giving the references. It is, of course, essential to go to them, read them and enjoy them. The Scriptures are the forecourt of the kingdom of God. It is also the Holy Spirit who takes us into this forecourt. May he help us to speak of him in the chapters that follow!

Each one of us has his own gifts, his own means and his own vocation. Mine are as a Christian who prays and as a theologian who reads a great number of books and takes many notes. May I therefore be allowed to sing my own song! The Spirit is breath. The wind sings in the trees. I would like, then, to be an Aeolian harp and let the breath of God make the strings vibrate and sing. Let me stretch and tune the strings—that will be the austere task of research. And then let the Spirit make them sing a clear and tuneful song of prayer and life!

NOTES

1. H. Mühlen, *Mysterium Salutis*, XIII (Paris, 1972), p. 182.
2. This was the opinion of St Bernard, *Sermo 88 de diversis*, 1 (*PL* 183, 706); *De Pentecoste sermo*, 1 (*ibid.*, 323).
3. See Thomas Aquinas, *ST* Ia, q. 37, a. 1; *Comp.*, c. 59.
4. See C. Geffré, 'Esquisse d'une théologie de la révélation', P. Ricœur *et al.*, *La Révélation* (Brussels, 1977), pp. 171–205.
5. Dogmatic Constitution on Revelation, *Dei Verbum*, 8, 1.

VOLUME I

THE HOLY SPIRIT
IN THE 'ECONOMY'

REVELATION AND
EXPERIENCE OF THE SPIRIT

CONTENTS

ABBREVIATIONS USED IN THIS BOOK

AAS   *Acta Apostolicae Sedis*
Anal. Greg.   *Analecta Gregoriana*
Anal. Praemonstr.   *Analecta Praemonstratensia*
Arch. Fr. Praedic.   *Archivum Fratrum Praedicatorum*
Bib   *Biblica*
Bibl. August.   *Bibliothèque augustinienne*
Bibl. Œcum.   *Bibliothèque œcuménique*
Bibl. théol.   *Bibliothèque théologique*
Bibl. Thom.   *Bibliothèque thomiste*
BWANT   *Beiträge zur Wissenschaft vom Alten und Neuen Testament*
BZ   *Biblische Zeitschrift*
CBQ   *Catholii Biblical Quarterly*
CC   *Corpus christianorum*
COD   J. Alberigo et al. (eds), *Conciliorum Œcumenicorum Decreta*
Denz.   1st ed. of *DS* (below)
Doc. cath.   *La documentation catholique*
DS   H. Denzinger, rev. A. Schönmetzer, *Enchiridion Symbolorum*
DTC   *Dictionnaire de théologie catholique*
ETL   *Ephemerides Theologicae Lovanienses*
Et. Théol. et Rel.   *Etudes théologiques et religieuses*
Fliche and Martin   A. Fliche and V. Martin, *Histoire de l'Eglise*
GCS   *Griechische christliche Schriftsteller*
Greg   *Gregorianum*
Jaffé (Loewenfeld)   P. Jaffé *et al.* (eds), *Regesta Pontificum Romanorum* (2nd ed. rev. S. Loewenfeld *et al.*)
JTS   *Journal of Theological Studies*
LTK   *Lexikon für Theologie und Kirche*
Mansi   J. D. Mansi (ed.), *Sacrorum Conciliorum nova et amplissima Collectio*
M-D   *La Maison-Dieu*
MOPH   *Monumenta Ordinis Fratrum Praedicatorum Historica*
NRT   *Nouvelle Revue théologique*
NTS   *New Testament Studies*
OED   *Oxford English Dictionary*
Or. Chr. Anal.   *Orientalia christiana analecta*
Or. Chr. Period.   *Orientalia christiana periodica*
PG   Migne, *Patrologia Graeca*
PL   Migne, *Patrologia Latina*
RAM   *Revue d'ascétique et de mystique*
RB   *Revue biblique*

RHE   Revue d'histoire ecclésiastique
RSPT   Revue des sciences philosophiques et théologiques
RSR   Recherches de science religieuse
RTAM   Recherches de théologie ancienne et médiévale
RThom   Revue thomiste
RTP   Revue de théologie et de philosophie
SC   Sources chrétiennes
SE   Sciences ecclésiastiques
ST   Summa Theologica
Strack and Billerbeck   H. L. Strack and P. Billerbeck, *Kommentar zum Neuen Testament aus Talmud und Midrasch*
TDNT   G. Kittel and G. Friedrich (eds), *Theological Dictionary of the New Testament* (Eng. tr.)
ThSt   Theological Studies
TZ   Theologische Zeitschrift
VS   La Vie spirituelle
WA   Weimar edition of Luther's *Werke*
ZKT   Zeitschrift für katholische Theologie
ZNW   Zeitschrift für neutestamentliche Wissenschaft

A NOTE ON 'EXPERIENCE'

I have given this volume the sub-title 'Revelation and Experience of the Spirit'. This refers to the ways that are offered to our objective knowledge of the Spirit, not to our subjective personal experience.

Revelation consists of what God himself has communicated to us through the history of his people as interpreted by the inspired prophets and wise men of Israel and later, in regard to the decisive event of Jesus Christ, the evangelists, the apostles and their spokesmen. My first task will therefore be to examine the Scriptures. If, however, it is true that God continues to act in history and in men's lives after the period that is usually called 'constitutive' and that he does so through the Spirit, then we surely have something to learn from the period that has followed the constitutive era, since it is rooted in that era. We should not interpret simplistically the idea that revelation closed with the death of the last apostle. God has certainly enabled us to know something since that time. Our experience of the Spirit has continued since then. It is as intense and urgent as it ever was in the past, even though what we can learn from the constitutive period continues to be normative. This is what constitutes the interplay between Scripture and living tradition. That is also why I shall retrace the history, not of the activity of the Spirit, which would be impossible, but of certain particularly meaningful aspects of the knowledge that has been gained and expressed of the Spirit. I shall not, strictly speaking, be retracing the history of dogma. I shall rather be following history in order to explore the idea that Christians have expressed about the activity of the Holy Spirit and in this I shall try to go beyond the dogma of the third Person.

By 'experience', I mean our perception of the reality of God as he comes to us, is active in us and operates through us, drawing us to him in communion and friendship, as one being exists for the other. This experience falls short of vision and does not do away with the distance that we are aware of in our knowledge of God himself, but overcomes it at the level of a presence of God in us as the beloved end of our life, a presence that makes itself felt in signs and in the effects of peace, joy, certainty, consolation, enlightenment and all that goes with love. The experience that the great mystics have described is a special and indeed exceptional degree of this perception of a presence of God who is given to us so that we can 'enjoy' his presence as a living object of knowledge and love. On this side of what is exceptional, there is what is ordinary—our experience of God's presence and activity in the appeals and signs that occur in our prayer, our practice of the sacraments of faith, the life of the Church and the love of God and our neighbour.

We can, of course, only become conscious of this experience and express it in terms or concepts that are our own. 'It is the Spirit himself bearing witness with our spirit that we are children of God' (Rom 8:16). We find ourselves in finding God. This is the religious experience *par excellence*,[1] an experience which, it cannot be doubted, brings its own certainty. This certainty is confirmed by the fact that our experience and the way that we express it is in accordance with that of the 'cloud of witnesses' mentioned by the author of the letter to the Hebrews (12:1) and that of all other believers. Although we have a practical assurance, we can never say with total certainty—unless we have a private revelation—that we are in a 'state of grace'. Short of a direct vision of God that is without any created concept, there is no way of perceiving God and his activity that does not make use of our own mental resources and is not involved with those resources.

The whole context of Christian life, our effective service of others in response to charity and to the appeals and demands that are contrary to our 'carnal' selves are evidence that all this does not come from ourselves, but from God. The theme of the gospels and St Paul of the struggle between the flesh and the Spirit corresponds to a reality that forms part of the Christian experience.

I shall not trace the course of that experience in the ways in which it is expressed as a living reality in spiritual writings and the lives of the saints. I shall try to interpret that reality theologically, not by studying or analysing the spiritual life, but rather by attempting to evolve a theology of the Holy Spirit and his rôle in the Church. In this context, I shall be concerned with theoretical aspects or objective dimensions of our knowledge of the Spirit.

NOTE

1. This is the definition given by J. Mouroux, *L'expérience chrétienne. Introduction à une théologie* (Paris, 1952), pp. 21, 25, 48, 369. This definition is also accepted by D. Mollat, *L'expérience de l'Esprit-Saint selon le Nouveau Testament*, 2nd ed. (Paris, 1973), p. 7, and M. J. le Guillou, *Les témoins sont parmi nous. L'expérience de Dieu dans l'Esprit-Saint* (Paris, 1976). For an idea of Christian experience other than that of Mouroux, see H. U. von Balthasar, *La Gloire et la Croix. Les aspects esthétiques de la Révélation* (Paris, 1965; Fr. tr. of *Herrlichkeit*), I, pp. 185–360. For experience of faith: P. Jacquemont, J.-P. Jossua and B. Quelquejeu, *Une foi exposée* (Paris, 1972), pp. 171–174. For a note on the use of the word 'experience', see *Revue Internationale Catholique Communio*, I, 8 (November 1976). The number of *Concilium* on 'Revelation and Experience' (113; March 1978) contains little that is strictly relevant to our subject.

PART ONE
THE CANONICAL SCRIPTURES

NOTE

Most biblical quotations are taken from the
Revised Standard Version (© Copyright 1946,
1952, 1957, 1971, 1973 by Division of Christian
Education of the National Council of Churches of
Christ in the United States of America); I have
sometimes replaced the word 'spirit' by 'breath'
(and occasionally other variants may appear in
parentheses).

1

THE OLD TESTAMENT

THE WORD[1]

The Hebrew word *rûaḥ*, which is almost always translated by the Greek *pneuma*, means breath, air, wind or soul. In the Old Testament especially, but also quite often in the New, to translate it as 'breath' gives a realism and an emphasis to the data reported and to the biblical texts that our word 'spirit' does not suggest so well. The translation 'breath' has been used by D. Lys (see note 1 below), M.-A. Chevallier and, in books that do not claim to be scholarly, but are nonetheless very solid, by Jean Isaac, A.-M. Henry, T. Maertens, G. A. Maloney and others.[2]

The word *rûaḥ* occurs 378 times in the Old Testament and these occurrences can be divided into three roughly equal groups. It is used in the first place to denote wind or a breath of air. Secondly, it is used for the force that vivifies man—the principle of life or breath and the seat of knowledge and feeling. Finally, it indicates the life of God himself, the force by which he acts and causes action, both at the physical and at the 'spiritual' level.

Rûaḥ-breath is not in any sense opposed to 'body' or 'corporeal'. Even in profane Greek and the language of philosophy, *pneuma* expresses the living and generating substance that is diffused in animals, plants and all things. It is a subtle corporeality rather than an incorporeal substance. The *rûaḥ*-breath of the Old Testament is not disincarnate. It is rather what animates the body. It is opposed to 'flesh', but then 'flesh' is not the same as 'body'. 'Flesh' is the purely earthly reality of man and is characterized by the fact that it is weak and corruptible: 'The Egyptians are men and not God; their horses are flesh and not spirit' Isaiah declared (31:3) in order to dissuade the Jews from looking to them for support. It was a question of knowing the source of real strength and life. In Gen 6:3, the way is prepared for the flood by God's declaration: 'My breath shall not abide in man for ever, for he is flesh'. Men were, in other words, living only according to their own earthly principle.

The Greeks thought in categories of substance, but the Jews were concerned with force, energy and the principle of action. The spirit-breath was for them what acts and causes to act and, in the case of the Breath of God, what animates and causes to act in order to realize God's plan. It always refers to a life-energy. Cardinal Daniélou expressed this idea perhaps a little

3

too insistently in stressing the opposition between Greek and Hebrew thought, but certainly in a very striking and pedagogically successful way:

> What do we mean when we speak of 'spirit' and say that 'God is spirit'? Are we speaking Greek or Hebrew? If we are speaking Greek, we are saying that God is immaterial. If we are speaking Hebrew, we are saying that God is a storm and an irresistible force. This is why, when we speak of spirituality, a great deal is ambiguous. Does spirituality mean becoming immaterial or does it mean being animated by the Holy Spirit?[3]

It is clear, then, that the real meaning of the word cannot be understood simply by consulting a dictionary. As James Barr pointed out in his criticism of Kittel's *Wörterbuch*, it is its use in a particular context, in which it refers to a given subject or intention, that determines the value of the word. *Rûaḥ-pneuma* can, for example, simply mean the wind (as in Jn 3:8; Acts 2:1–4, 6). Elsewhere, it can mean the breath of God that communicates life (Ex 15:8–10; Ps 33:6) and consequently man's breath, the principle and sign of life (Gen 7:22; Ps 104:29–30; also very frequently in Job). We also speak about man's 'last breath' and 'expiring'. It is also breath or animation that enables a task to be accomplished, especially if it is in some way the work of God. This was so in the case of Bezalel's task of furnishing the sanctuary (Ex 31:3ff.). It is, as we shall see later, even more true in the matter of leading the people of God, conducting their wars and prophesying.

The breath-spirit (the Spirit) is qualified in various ways according to the effects that it, as a principle, produces. The Old Testament speaks, for example, of the spirit of intelligence (Ex 31:3) and of the spirit of wisdom (Deut 31:3; 34:9) and of jealousy (Num 5:14; all these texts are in P[4]). It even speaks of 'an evil spirit from the Lord' (1 Sam 16:14; 18:10 = D; cf. Judg 9:23).[5] The most interesting way in which it is qualified, however, is when the spirit or breath is said to be *of God*, in other words, when it expresses the subject by whose power various effects are produced in the world or in man, and especially in those who receive the gifts of leadership or prophecy or who become religious men and so on.[6] Sometimes the 'spirit of the Lord' or the 'spirit of God' simply refers to God himself, as for example in Is 40:13; 63:10: 'But they rebelled and grieved his Holy Spirit'.

This quotation brings us to the term that is so important for us here, an expression that is also used in the penitential psalm, 51:11, the 'holy spirit'. The spirit is holy because it comes from God and its reality belongs to the sphere of God's existence. There is no need to find any other reason for the holiness of the spirit. God is holy because he is God, but in the case of this spirit (or Spirit), the Old Testament does not emphasize the value of sanctification very much, at least not in the sense of an inner principle of perfection in life; such holiness is rather the result of observing the Torah. The Spirit-Breath is first and foremost what causes man to act so that God's plan in history may be fulfilled.

THE ACTION OF THE BREATH OF YAHWEH

Certain external effects, for which there are parallels and similarities in other religions, such as shamanism, were attributed to the breath-spirit (the Spirit) at a given period and in the earliest documents. What is ascribed to the forces of nature in shamanism, however, is always attributed to God (Yahweh) in the Old Testament. New data were contributed by the authors of the prophetic books, penetrating more deeply into man's innermost self.

The Spirit has effects on man and brings about an experience of seeing and wisdom. The Yahwistic and Elohistic accounts of Balaam show him manipulated by Yahweh and, despite himself, pronouncing a divine oracle: 'Balaam lifted up his eyes and saw Israel encamping tribe by tribe. And the spirit of God came upon him and he took up his discourse and said: "The oracle of Balaam, the son of Beor, the oracle of the man . . . who sees the vision of the Almighty, falling down, but having his eyes uncovered . . ." ' (Num 24:2ff. = J).

Samuel was the first of the prophets, whose greatness cannot be disputed, but the editor who was working at the time of King Josiah and was responsible for 1 Sam 9:9 said: 'He who is now called a "prophet" was formerly called a "seer" '. The 'seer' Samuel is really a 'prophet'; he has an inspired way of speaking about what has to be done. He tells Saul, for example: 'You will meet a band of prophets . . . they will be in the grip of a prophetic trance. And the spirit (breath) of the Lord will come mightily upon you and you will enter into a trance with them and be turned into another man' (10:5–6). This is precisely what happened (see 10:10ff.). A similar occurrence is recorded later in the same book (19:20–24) in the case of the messenger sent by Saul to Samuel, who was at the head of a group of prophets in a prophetic trance: 'The Spirit (the breath) of God came upon the messengers of Saul and they also entered into a trance'. The same happened to Saul himself when he followed his messengers to the same place. Even in the fairly rudimentary conditions of this event, we become aware of what is always true even in the most exalted activities caused by the Spirit, that is, the effects on man and his psyche in cases of guidance and inspiration that are attributed to the Breath of God himself. God, in other words, never seizes hold of man without involving him completely, including his psychosomatic being.

At the same time, in texts of the same period as the one quoted and even earlier, the spirit (or Spirit) that comes from God gives a discernment and wisdom that are in accordance with what is normal. What these experiences have in common with the preceding ones, however, is that they guarantee that God's plan for his people will be carried out.[7] Pharaoh, for example, says of Joseph: 'Can we find such a man as this in whom is the Spirit of God?' (Gen 41:38 = E). There is also the case of the seventy elders to whom God distributed some of the spirit that was in Moses (Num 11:16ff., 25). They began to prophesy and, as Joshua was scandalized by such an unselective

5

extension of this privilege, Moses told him: 'Would that all the Lord's people were prophets, that the Lord would put his spirit (his breath) upon them!' (11:29). When Moses was in sight of the promised land and was about to die, however, God inspired him to act in order to secure his succession: 'Take Joshua the son of Nun, a man in whom is the breath (a man who is inspired)' (27:18).

The Heroes or 'Judges'

These were charismatic leaders or warriors aroused in turn by God in the critical circumstances in which Israel was placed, repeatedly and through its own fault, during the 150 years from the occupation of Canaan by Joshua until the insitution of the monarchy.

> Othniel: 'The spirit (breath) of the Lord came upon him. . .' (Judg 3:10).
> Gideon: 'The spirit (breath) of the Lord took possession of Gideon. . .' (6:34).
> Jephthah: 'The spirit (breath) of the Lord came upon Jephthah. . .' (11:29).
> Samson: 'And the spirit (breath) of the Lord began to stir him. . .' (13:25); 'And the spirit of the Lord came mightily upon him and he tore the lion asunder . . . and he had nothing in his hand' (14:6); 'And the spirit (breath) of the Lord came mightily upon him and he went down to Ashkelon and killed thirty men of the town . . .' (14:19).

Saul was the last of the judges and the first of the kings. When the monarchy was instituted, this type of unusual and sudden experience of being seized by the breath-spirit that has been encountered in the Old Testament up to this point ceases, at least in this form. After Saul, who was still living under the régime of such 'happenings' (1 Sam 10:6–13; 11:6), when Samuel anointed the youngest of Jesse's sons, 'the spirit of the Lord came mightily upon David *from that day forward*' (1 Sam 16:13). Something quite definitive, then, began with David, the course of which can be traced through the prophecy of Nathan (2 Sam 7) and the prophecy of Isaiah— 'There shall come forth a shoot from the stump of Jesse and a branch shall grow out of his roots. And the Spirit of the Lord shall rest upon him . . .' (Is 11:1–2)—to Jesus, the 'son of David', as is attested by Matthew's genealogy and the genealogy that Luke (3:31) places after his account of Jesus' baptism. We shall consider this later.

The Prophets

At least since the time of the baptismal creed formulated by Cyril of Jerusalem (*c*. 348), but even in the writings of Justin Martyr and Irenaeus, the Holy Spirit has been characterized in our confessions of faith as the one 'who has spoken through the prophets'. In opposition to Gnosticism and the teaching of Marcion, Christians wanted to stress that the Spirit by whom Jesus had been conceived and who animated the gospel was the same as the

Spirit who acted in the old dispensation.[8] But in the Targums, this Spirit is often called the 'spirit of prophecy' and although it may not have been attributed to a breath of God or an in-spiration during the ninth to the eighth centuries B.C.,[9] the prophetic word was thus attributed during the Deuteronomic period[10] and quite firmly during the exile, especially in Ezekiel (Ezek 2:2; 11:5; see also Is 48:16; 61:1), and then again in post-exilic Judaism (Zech 7:12; 2 Chron 15:1; 20:14; 24:20), in Hellenistic Judaism and in the rabbinical writings.[11] Was the intention perhaps to avoid a rather mechanical portrayal? Certainly Jeremiah never had recourse to an in-spiration of this kind.

Three prophetic books are particularly interesting in this context. They are Isaiah, Ezekiel and Joel. The word *rûah* occurs about fifty times in the book of Isaiah[12] and 46 times in Ezekiel. The first aspect of *rûah* that is expressed in Isaiah is common to the rest of the Bible. What exists in life that is worthy of the name comes from the breath of God. So, for example, the prophet declares: 'The Egyptians are men and not God; their horses are flesh and not spirit. When the Lord stretches out his hand . . .' (Is 31:3). It is God who communicates life. After proclaiming the fall of Samaria, the prophet contrasts its 'fading flower' with the 'crown of glory' that the Lord will be for his people: 'A diadem of beauty to the remnant of his people; and a spirit of justice to him who sits in judgement' (28:5–6).

It is in the midst of storm and danger that Isaiah announces the deliverance of his people and a future of hope—to Ahaz through the prophecy of the Emmanuel (7:10ff.) and to Hezekiah at the time of Sennacherib's invasion (37:21–35; 'And the surviving remnant of the house of Judah shall again take root downwards . . .'). During these dramatic events, Isaiah foretells that 'There shall come forth a shoot from the stump of Jesse and a branch shall grow out of his roots. And the Spirit of the Lord shall rest upon him, the spirit of wisdom and understanding, the spirit of counsel and might, the spirit of knowledge and the fear of the Lord and (he will inspire him with) the fear of the Lord . . .' (11:1ff.).

This is the Messiah. He will receive from the Spirit all the gifts that are necessary to rule according to justice. The result of this will be wonderful—nothing less than paradise regained (see 32:15–18). D. Lys regards it as legitimate to see the promised descendant of David as a new Adam.[13] He finds it surprising that there is no reference to anointing in the text, but says that 'the link between anointing and the spirit cannot fail to be established insofar as the mediator in Is 11 is the king and the one on whom the spirit rests is the Messiah'.

The first Servant song in Deutero-Isaiah—'I have put my Spirit on him' (42:1)—at once raises the important question: Is it a prophetic utterance about the Messiah[14] or is it concerned with Cyrus? If it is in fact, as it would

7

seem to be, concerned with Cyrus, then it is remarkable that it is the breath of God upon him which enables him to reveal and realize God's judgement, in other words, his plan or his justice, for the nations. All those who, in the Old Testament, carried out God's plan with regard to his people were called the servants (*'ebhedh*) of God. They include Abraham (Gen 26:24; Ps 105:6), Moses (Ex 14:31; Num 12:7; Deut 34:5; Josh 1:2, 7; 9:24; 11:15; 1 Kings 8:53; 2 Kings 21:8; Mal 3:22; Ps 105:26; Neh 1:7, 8; 9:14), Joshua (Josh 24:29; Judg 2:8), David (2 Sam 3:18; 7:5, 8; 1 Kings 3:6; 8:66; 11:13; 14:8; 2 Kings 20:6; Is 37:35; Jer 33:21ff., 26; Ps 18:1; 78:70), Elijah (2 Kings 9:36; 10:10), Isaiah (20:3), Zorobabel (2 Kings 9:36; 10:10), the prophets collectively (2 Kings 9:7; Jer 7:25; Amos 3:7) and finally, in Isaiah, the people of Israel (41:8; 42:19; 43:10; 44:1, 2, 21; 45:4; 48:20).[15] Here, however, the nations are involved: Israel has entered the history of the world and its empires, in and through which God also pursues his plan. It is the work of his breath and of that impulse of life and activity which is his Spirit. For Isaiah, the return is a new exodus, and the first deliverance under the leadership of Moses had taken place under the action of the Spirit (the psalm inserted into Is 63:7–14). From the very detailed study made by D. Lys and the less exhaustive one made by J. Isaac, it is clear that there is a continuity and a connection between the movement that God gives to the creatures of the cosmos by his breath and that which he puts into them to establish a personal relationship with him, in other words, between nature and grace.

This universal extension of election of which Israel is the centre is celebrated by Trito-Isaiah in chapters 60 and 61, which are addressed in particular to the exiles of Israel in the solemn declaration: 'The Spirit of the Lord God is upon me; the Lord has made a messiah of me; he has sent me to bring good tidings to the afflicted' (61:1). This messiah is not called Servant, but has several of the aspects of the Servant that are found in chapters 42, 49 and 50 and also has aspects, not of a king, but of a prophet. As we shall see when we consider the New Testament, Jesus himself provided an interpretation of this text: 'Today this scripture has been fulfilled in your hearing' (Lk 4:21).

Isaiah 11, which deals with the king-messiah, goes back to a period when the Davidic monarchy was still in existence in Jerusalem. Ezekiel saw the ruin of Jerusalem that he had foretold and the destruction of the Temple, from which he had 'seen' the Presence depart. He also saw the deportation of the people into Babylonia. The cult and those who celebrated it are dead, but, as Yahweh is more present than ever to his people, his Spirit will re-animate the dead bones and his breath will make living beings of them. He will do this by communicating himself within men's hearts. There are, in this context, the two incomparable chapters of Ezekiel, 36 and 37:

'I will sprinkle clean water upon you and you shall be clean from all your uncleannesses and from all your idols I will cleanse you. A new heart I will give you, and a new spirit I will put within you; and I will take out of your flesh the heart of stone and give you a heart of flesh. And I will put my breath (spirit) within you. . .' (36:25–27).

'Son of man, can these bones live?' And I answered, 'O Lord God, thou knowest'. Again he said to me, 'Prophesy to (pronounce an oracle against) these bones and say to them: O dry bones, hear the word of the Lord. Thus says the Lord God to these bones: Behold, I will cause breath to enter you and you shall live. . . .' So I prophesied (pronounced an oracle) as he commanded me, and the breath came into them and they lived and stood upon their feet (37:3–5, 10).

And finally:

'And I will not hide my face any more from them when I pour out my spirit upon the house of Israel, says (oracle of) the Lord God' (39:29).

The disaster of the invasion and the test of exile, interpreted by the greatest prophets, led to a vision of the Spirit-breath of God as purifying men's hearts, penetrating into them and making them a holy people of God. This was to be a new beginning, a new exodus, a new covenant and a people renewed. This message is proclaimed, for example, in Jer 31:31–34 (although the breath is not mentioned in this text). It is also to be found in the part of Isaiah belonging to the exile: 44:3–5 (verse 3 proclaims a resurrection of the scattered people: 'I will pour water on the thirsty land and streams on the dry ground; I will pour my Spirit upon your descendants and my blessing on your offspring') and 63:11–14. Finally, the same theme occurs, after the return from exile, in Hag 2:5; Zech 4:6; 12:10; and Neh 9:20.

It is a very important step. Through his breath-Spirit, God will be the principle of faithful life and holy life for Israel. But this gift is extended to all peoples in Joel's proclamation of eschatological events made about 350–340 B.C.: 'Afterwards I will pour out my Spirit on all flesh; your sons and your daughters shall prophesy, your old men shall dream dreams and your young men shall see visions. Even upon the menservants and maidservants in those days I will pour out my Spirit' (3:1–2). On the day of Pentecost, Peter was to proclaim that this had in fact happened.

The Wisdom Literature

During the four centuries that preceded Jesus' coming into our world, a body of Jewish writings now known as the Wisdom literature developed. This literature includes Job and the Proverbs (between 450 and 400 B.C.), numerous Psalms, Qôheleth or Ecclesiastes, Sirach or Ecclesiasticus (c. 187 B.C.) and, in Alexandria, where the Jews were in contact with Hellenistic thought, Wisdom (c. 50 B.C.). The sapiential literature of Hellenized Judaism constitutes a remarkable reflection on Wisdom. In it, Wisdom is brought so close to the Spirit that the two realities are almost identified, at least if they are viewed in their action.[16]

9

This Wisdom comes from God. She is his action for the benefit of his creatures, enabling them to go straight. There is an inclination in God to do good and to desire what is good. Wisdom therefore has a universal extension. In Wis 1:7 and 8:1, she—or the Spirit—even has a cosmic function, similar to the part that Wisdom played in Stoicism in holding the universe together. The real function of Wisdom, however, is to guide men in accordance with God's will. For this reason, she chose especially to reside in Israel, where she formed God's friends and prophets. She is 'the book of the covenant of the Most High God, the law which Moses commanded (us)' (Sir 24:23). The action of Wisdom is therefore very similar to that of the Spirit. They would be identical were it not for the fact that Wisdom does not have what the Spirit has, namely the character of a force or inner energy, the power to transform. C. Larcher has outlined the relationship between Wisdom and the Spirit in the following way:

> The two realities are identified in several ways. Wisdom possesses a spirit (7:22b) or she is a spirit (1:6). She acts in the form of a spirit (7:7b). She also has power at her disposal and the various functions of the Spirit in the Old Testament are attributed to her. She has, for example, a universal cosmic function. She arouses the prophets. She guides mankind and especially the chosen people. Finally, she acts as the great interior master of the souls of men. Wisdom and the Spirit are identified in so many respects that Wisdom appears above all as a sublimation of the part played by the Spirit in the Old Testament. This explains why some of the Fathers of the Church regarded Wisdom as prefiguring, not the Word, but the Holy Spirit.[17]

There was a great deal of reflection about wisdom in the ancient world and in Judaism, then, but it incorporated certain philosophical and especially Stoic ideas only in the book of Wisdom itself.[18] That book presents us with a view of the nature of wisdom: wisdom *is* a spirit who is a friend of men (1:6; cf. Job 32:8). At the very beginning of the book, a number of profound statements are made:

> Wisdom is a kindly spirit (a friend to man) and will not free a blasphemer from the guilt of his words; because God is witness of his inmost feelings, and a true observer of his heart and a hearer of his tongue. The spirit of the Lord has filled the world and that which holds all things together knows what is said (1:6, 7).

This verse has been included in the Church's liturgy as the introit for Pentecost. Later in the book of Wisdom we read:

> In her there is a spirit that is intelligent, holy, unique, manifold, subtle, mobile, clear, unpolluted, distinct, invulnerable, loving the good, keen, irresistible, beneficent, humane (loving to man), steadfast, sure, free from anxiety, all-powerful, overseeing all and penetrating through all spirits that are intelligent and pure and most subtle. For Wisdom is more mobile than any motion; because of her pureness she pervades and penetrates all things. For she is a breath of the power of God and a pure emanation of the glory of the Almighty; therefore nothing defiled gains

10

entrance into her. . . . Though she is but one, she can do all things and while remaining in herself, she renews all things; in every generation she passes into holy souls and makes them friends of God, and prophets. . . . She reaches mightily from one end of the earth to the other and she orders all things well (7:22–25, 27; 8:1).

Two aspects that were influential in the later theology of the Holy Spirit should be noted here. The first is that the Spirit is to some extent personalized. In the case of Wisdom, this personalization is progressively stressed from Prov 8:22–31 onwards: 'The Lord created me at the beginning of his work . . .'; Sir 1:1–10; 4:11–19; 15:1–10; 24:1–22. Sometimes this personification is no more than a form of literary expression. The strict monotheism of the Jewish religion, however, associated certain realities with God which were God himself but which at the same time represented in God various ways of acting, being or being present (with men): the Shekinah, Wisdom. What is said of this Wisdom in chapters 8 and 9 of the book of Wisdom expresses the *intimate* action of the Spirit of God and can be applied to the Spirit. Wisdom and Breath (Spirit) are often closely connected and do the same thing (see, for example, Wis 1:4–5; 7:22–23; 9:17). They are God for us and with us. Writing about Palestinian Judaism, that is, the apocryphal and rabbinical literature, Erik Sjöberg said:

The autonomy of the Spirit in Judaism is surprising. In Rabbinic writings the Spirit is often spoken of in personal categories. There are many instances of the Spirit speaking, crying, admonishing, sorrowing, weeping, rejoicing, comforting etc. Indeed, the Spirit can even be said to speak to God. For this reason it has often been thought that the Spirit is regarded in Judaism as a hypostasis, as a personal angelic being. . . . The decisive thing is that man stands here before a reality which comes from God, which in some sense represents the presence of God, and yet is not identical with God. . . . The Holy Spirit is a special divine entity which is sent by God and which acts independently within the limits set by the divine will.[19]

Wisdom also provides us with a very interesting reflection on the very idea of spirit. The spirit is characterized by its subtlety and purity, which enable it to enter everything and everyone and, while remaining unique, to be in everything and everyone as the principle of life, newness and holy conduct.[20] In his *Treatise on the Holy Spirit* (written in 375), Basil of Caesarea described the Spirit as having a nature that is not limited and not subject to change, 'intelligent, infinite in power, unlimited in greatness, not governed by time and the centuries and generous with his own goods'.[21] I am allowing myself to look ahead in quoting a patristic text at this point, but it is important to mark the continuity of thought and to emphasize the promises that are already present in the Old Testament. Even before the book of Wisdom, there are texts such as Ps 139:7–12; Job 28:20–27 (on Wisdom). Nor was it without good reason that oil later became a symbol of the Spirit in the New Testament, the patristic period and the Church's liturgy. What sport and athletics did in the ancient world, cars and machines do in the modern world: they enable us to appreciate the play of this substance that penetrates everywhere, spoils nothing and, on the contrary, facilitates the smooth functioning of each part.

* * *

In the Jewish Bible, the Breath-Spirit of God is the action of God. Through that Breath-Spirit, God reveals himself as active in animating and giving life at the level of what we call nature. Through the Breath-Spirit too, God led his people and raised up for them heroes and strong warriors, kings, leaders (such as Moses and Joshua), prophets and finally wise men. The Messiah who had been proclaimed was to bring all these functions together in himself and raise them to a higher level. As for the prophets, there were no more after Zechariah and Malachi.[22]

The 'economy' or God's plan, to which Scripture bears witness, moves forward in the direction of greater and deeper interiority. Eschatology will be the realization of absolute interiority: 'God all in all'. This progress is clear in the Old Testament. It reaches its conclusion in the New Testament, where it is connected with a more perfect revelation and experience of the Spirit. It is possible to establish a progressive commitment and at the same time a more complete revelation of God himself, as Father, Son and Holy Spirit. That is the plan of our creed. Creation is attributed to the Father. That creation is visible and shared. Revelation and redemption are ascribed to the Son and these are universal works inscribed in history. The Spirit is regarded as responsible for sanctification, inhabitation and intimacy and he 'inhabits our hearts'.

NOTES

1. Studies that I have consulted include: P. van Imschoot, 'L'action de l'esprit de Jahvé dans l'Ancien Testament', *RSPT*, 23 (1934), 553–587; *idem*, 'L'esprit de Jahvé source de vie dans l'Ancien Testament', *RB*, new series, 44 (1935), 481–501; *idem*, 'L'esprit de Jahvé et l'alliance nouvelle dans l'Ancien Testament', *ETL*, 22 (1936), 201–226; *idem*, 'Sagesse et Esprit dans l'Ancien Testament', *RB*, new series, 47 (1938), 23–49; E. Schweizer *et al.*, '*pneuma*', *TDNT*, VI, pp. 332–451 [this article was also published separately in English: *Spirit of God* (London, 1960), but references in this present book are to *TDNT*]; F. Büchsel, *Der Geist Gottes im Neuen Testament* (Gütersloh, 1926); E. Haulotte, 'L'Esprit de Yahvé dans l'Ancien Testament', *L'homme devant Dieu. Mélanges H. de Lubac*, I (*Théologie*, 56) (Paris, 1963), pp. 25–36; D. Lys, '*Rûach': le Souffle dans l'Ancien Testament* (Paris, 1962). Most of these studies contain ample bibliographies. Specialized studies are noted at the relevant points in the text.
2. J. Isaac, *La révélation progressive des Personnes divines* (Paris, 1960), pp. 103–209; A.-M. Henry, *L'Esprit Saint* (Paris, 1959); T. Maertens, *Le souffle de l'Esprit de Dieu* (Paris, 1959); G. A. Maloney, *The Breath of the Mystic* (Denville, 1974). It is worth noting that 277 times out of the total of 378 that it occurs in the Old Testament, *rûaḥ* is translated in the Greek Septuagint as *pneuma*. In most of the cases where another Greek word is used, the reference is to 'wind'.

3. J. Daniélou, 'L'horizon patristique', originally meant to be included in *Recherches actuelles* (*Le Point théologique*, 1) (Institut Catholique, Paris, 1971), pp. 22–23; the author withdrew this text from publication and I do not know whether it has appeared since then elsewhere. This raises questions with regard to the old catechisms. E. Germain, for instance, quotes Mgr de Harlay's catechism of 1687, in which he answers the question: 'What is God?' with 'He is a spirit'. She comments: 'When the Bible said: God is Spirit, its intention was to declare that God is the only Living Being who did not receive life. He is. But now—since the time of Cartesian idealism—being a spirit means not having a body': *Langages de la Foi à travers l'histoire* (Paris, 1972), p. 90.

4. P is the priestly code or account, which has been dated to after the exile; J is the Yahwistic document, dated to the ninth century, Judah; E is the Elohistic account, dated to the eighth century, Northern Kingdom; D is the Deuteronomistic account, *c.* 620, which is found not only in Deut, but also in Judg, Sam and Kings. This distinction between various documents or accounts must, of course, be accepted with caution and it does not mean that there were no earlier attempts to edit, at least partially.

5. There are many examples besides these in '*pneuma*', *TDNT*, VI, pp. 361–362.

6. See *ibid.*, pp. 362–367.

7. According to the Priestly tradition, those who made the holy garments (Ex 28:3) or who provided the furnishings for cultic purposes (31:3; 35:31) were given the spirit of God to enable them to do this.

8. See A. Orbe, *La unción del Verbo. Estudios Valentinianos*, III (*Anal. Greg.*, 113) (Rome, 1961), pp. 483–499; H.-J. Jaschke, *Der Heilige Geist im Bekenntnis der Kirche* (Münster, 1976), p. 144 and note 4, which gives references to texts from the first three centuries A.D.; see also pp. 233 ff., where the author discusses this idea in the writings of Irenaeus.

9. Is the 'pneumatophore', the 'man of the spirit', mentioned in Hos 9:7 the same as the 'prophet' in the same verse? They are certainly placed in parallel. The word 'spirit' appears in the Revised Standard Version with a small initial letter. The reference to the spirit of the Lord in Mic 2:3 is possibly a gloss.

10. There is no reference in the Deuteronomistic account itself to the Spirit; but see Num 24:2 (Balaam) and 2 Sam 23:2 (David speaking about himself).

11. See *pneuma*, *TDNT*, VI, pp. 381–383. See also Wis 9:17.

12. In Isaiah, the word *rûaḥ* has three different meanings: the breath of God carrying out his plan of salvation; an anthropological and biological reality; the Spirit of Yahweh (especially in the messianic texts and the songs of the Servant). See R. Koch, 'La théologie de l'Esprit de Yahvé dans le livre d'Isaïe', *Sacra Pagina*, ed. J. Coppens *et al.* (Paris and Gembloux, 1959), I, pp. 419–433.

13. See D. Lys, *op. cit.* (note 1), p. 89, note 1.

14. The Jerusalem Bible thinks this, whereas the French *Traduction Œcuménique* opts for Cyrus. R. Koch, 'Der Gottesgeist und der Messias', *Bib*, 27 (1946), 241–268, 276–403, also interpreted it, pp. 379ff., in the sense of the Messiah, opposing the view that the text had Cyrus in mind. It is also interesting to note that the Ethiopic Book of Enoch attributes the Spirit to the Messiah (49:3).

15. These references, which have all been checked, are taken from Koch, 'Der Gottesgeist', *op. cit.*, p. 384.

16. See, for example, P. van Imschoot, 'L'Esprit de Jahvé et l'alliance nouvelle', *op. cit.* (note 1), 201–220; *idem*, 'Sagesse et Esprit', *op. cit.* (*ibid.*), 23–49; D. Colombo, 'Pneuma Sophias ejusque actio in mundo in Libro Sapientiae', *Studii Biblici Franciscani Liber Annuus*, I (1950–51), 107–160; C. Larcher, *Etudes sur le Livre de la Sagesse* (Paris, 1969), especially pp. 329–414, 'La Sagesse et l'Esprit'; M. Gilbert, 'Volonté de Dieu et don de la Sagesse (Sg 9, 17 sv)', *NRT*, 93 (1971), 145–166.

17. C. Larcher, *op. cit.*, p. 411, with reference, in the case of the Fathers, to J. Lebreton, *Les origines du dogme de la Trinité*, 2nd ed. (Paris, 1928), II, p. 513 (Theophilus of Antioch), pp. 567f. (Irenaeus) and pp. 569–70 (Clementine Homilies).

18. A. M. Dubarle, *Les sages d'Israël* (Paris, 1946); *'pneuma'*, *TDNT*, VI, pp. 370–372; G. Verbeke, *L'évolution de la doctrine du pneuma du stoïcisme à S. Augustin. Etude philosophique* (Paris, 1945).
19. *'pneuma'*, *TDNT*, VI, pp. 387–388; cf. F. Büchsel, *op. cit.* (note 1), pp. 35, 134.
20. The Breath-Spirit of God leads or conducts believers so that they may carry out his plan. The Exodus is the classical example of this. See also Is 32:15–17; 63:7–14; Ps 143; Neh 9:20–21. Clement of Rome quoted the text of Prov 20:27: 'The spirit of man is the lamp of the Lord, searching all his innermost parts' in this form: 'The Spirit of the Lord is a lamp searching the depths of the heart' (21:2).
21. Basil, *De spir. sanct.* 9; cf. Gregory Nazianzen, *Orat. theol.* V, 29 (*PG* 36, 165).
22. 'The Jewish people believed that they were, from that time onwards (that is, as the Christian event came closer), deprived of the Spirit: "We do not see our signs; there is no longer any prophet and there is none among us who knows how long" (Ps 74:9)'; 'Those righteous men have joined their fathers and the prophets have fallen asleep' (Apoc. Bar. 85:1, 3). The Maccabaean historians and their contemporaries were already conscious of this disappearance of the Spirit (see, for example, 1 Macc 14:41); this tradition of the Spirit is found again in the second century A.D. in the rabbis: 'Since the death of Haggai, Zechariah and Malachi, the last of the prophets, the Holy Spirit has ceased in Israel' (Tosefta of the Talmudic treatise *Sota* 13:2): see J. R. Villalon, *Sacrements dans l'Esprit. Existence humaine et théologie existentielle (Théologie historique*, 43) (Paris, 1977), p. 351. At the time of Jesus, the idea was widespread among the Jews that there would be no more revelation of the Spirit until the eschatological era: see Strack and Billerbeck, IV. 2, pp. 1229ff. See also H. Gunkel, *Die Wirkungen des Hl. Geistes nach der populären Anschauung des apostolischen Zeit und der Lehre des Apostels Paulus*, 3rd ed. (1909), pp. 50ff.; F. Büchsel, *op. cit.* (note 1), pp. 123ff.

2

THE NEW TESTAMENT[1]

[*Note:* in this chapter the numbered notes are collected at the end of each section.]

Because of the chronological order of the New Testament texts, I ought to discuss the evidence provided by Paul first, then that found in Mark and Matthew, followed by that in Luke, both the gospel and Acts, and finally the witness of John. All the New Testament texts, however, including Paul, speak of Jesus as the one without whom everything lacks a foundation (1 Cor 3:11). It is therefore both legitimate and suitable to follow an order of realities rather than an editorial order and, since our knowledge of Jesus Christ comes above all from the gospels, it is also legitimate and suitable to begin with them.

If I were approaching this question purely as a study in exegesis and biblical theology, I would have to write a series of learned monographs. That, however, is not the aim of this book and, in any case, I lack the competence to write such monographs. All that needs to be done here is to make use of the relevant works and with their aid to disengage the meaning of the most important elements in the experience and revelation of the Spirit during the messianic period—the conception, baptism and activity of Jesus, Christian existence according to St Paul, the life of the early Church and the supreme witness borne by John.

*　　*　　*

THE BAPTISM, CONCEPTION AND LIFE OF JESUS

The Gospels

The Gospel is the communication to men of the fact that God's promises of salvation are fulfilled in Jesus. It opens with John the Baptist's call to conversion and the baptism of Jesus (see Mk 1:1ff.).[2] It is in this framework that Mark sets the 'beginning of the good news'. This is the beginning of the eschatological period characterized by the gift of the Spirit to a people of God with a universal vocation. At his baptism by John the Baptist, Jesus is marked out and dedicated as the one by whose words, sacrifice and activity the Spirit enters the history of mankind as a messianic gift and, at least as

15

arrha or earnest-money, as an eschatological gift. There is no doubt that the Spirit was active before Jesus' coming, under the old disposition. It was by the Spirit that Mary conceived Jesus, whose quality of 'son of God' is mentioned by Luke (1:35), in whose gospel it refers, not to Jesus' pre-existence, but to his conception by the Holy Spirit. Nevertheless neither Matthew nor Luke, both of whom speak of it, connect the fact that Jesus is to act through the Spirit and will finally communicate that Spirit with his birth. Both connect it with his baptism. Before it, Jesus did not appear as someone acting in the power of the Spirit, and his fellow-townsmen in Nazareth saw nothing exceptional in him.[3] The event of baptism cannot therefore be seen simply as a 'manifestation that played a subordinate part in the cycle of infancy'.[4] On the contrary, it opens an entirely new chapter. Jesus was indeed the Son of God and he was filled with the Spirit from the time that he was in Mary's womb. F. Büchsel, however, has noted (p. 167) correctly that a pneumatology inherited from the Old Testament and Judaism is used in the gospels.[5] The Spirit is received by an act of God which expresses his love and brings about a union with him. A first sending of the Spirit—Thomas Aquinas speaks of the 'mission' of the Holy Spirit—made the little Jesus who was brought to life in Mary's womb 'holy' and the 'Son of God' (= Messiah).[6] A new communication or mission was initiated in the event of his baptism, when he was declared the Messiah, the one on whom the Spirit rests, who will act through the Spirit and who, once he has become the glorified Lord, will give the Spirit. If he was consecrated at the time of his baptism to carry out his prophetic ministry, then he was able to pour out the Spirit when he was 'exalted at the right hand of God' (see Acts 2:33).

There is no need for us to examine the texts of each gospel exegetically here. The close unanimity of the witness that they bear is expressed at the same time as their differences. In the gospel of John, for example (1:32–34), Jesus, the Word made flesh, already possesses the Spirit, and the theophany of the Jordan is evidence given to John the Baptist. Jesus is baptized by John in the Jordan. Luke adds that he was baptized after a great number of people and that the Spirit descended while he was praying. The heavens opened and the Spirit descended upon Jesus (according to John, it remained on him) 'in the corporeal form of a dove'.

The dove was not a symbol of the Spirit in the Old Testament or the rabbinical writings.[7] Need we look for a different meaning from that of a pair of wings showing that a gift comes from heaven? The gift of the Spirit to the prophets was sometimes represented by a winged heavenly messenger.[8] The dove was a messenger and the message was given in heavenly words (*bath-qôl*). The dove was, however, a symbol of Israel, the chosen people.[9] It may therefore be a representation or the symbolic presence of that people and of the penitential movement with which Jesus wanted to be at one, since he was the new Adam and represented and embodied the new people of God (Mt 3:14–15). In addition, the titles 'Son of God' and 'Servant' were also applied to the whole people of God.[10] The dove might therefore represent it as the people to whom the Spirit was to come through the Messiah.

In the Christian tradition, the dove was to be the symbol of the Holy Spirit. This is clear from iconographical evidence and from a whole series of texts, including liturgical ones.[11] The part played in Augustine's ecclesiology by *columba* is well known—it is a name for the one, holy Church and for the Holy Spirit.[12]

As in the case of the annunciation to Mary (Lk 1:35), the Word and the Spirit came together. The Word, the testimony of the Father, is addressed to the crowd and to Jesus according to Matthew and Luke, to Jesus according to Mark. In the fourth gospel, John the Baptist testifies that he has seen the Spirit, in the form of a dove, descend and remain on Jesus, but he does not report the heavenly word. 'We see the Dove rest on the Lamb and we hear the Father, who has sent the Spirit, proclaim the beloved Son' (a monk of the Eastern Church, *Contacts*, 41, 1963).

The word is: 'This is my beloved Son, the one whom it has pleased me to choose (= the one with whom I am well pleased)' (Mt 3:17) or 'Thou art my beloved Son. . .' (Mk 1:11). It is not a call, as it would be in the case of the prophets or Paul, but a declaration that echoes in Jesus' mind and it is also the confirmation of a condition that qualifies Jesus in what he is. This word also includes a verse of Ps 2:7, which is a royal, messianic psalm: 'The Lord said to me, "You are my son, today I have begotten you" ', which is the way in which the Father's word is reported, in the so-called Western version, in Lk 3:22. It combines this verse with the first verse of the first Song of the Servant (Is 42:1): 'Behold my servant, whom I uphold, my chosen, in whom my soul delights; I have put my Spirit upon him'. This was the moment when Jesus was called and sent as the Messiah and that Messiah is described as having the characteristics of a prophet, as a king in the line of David and his house ('he shall be my son', 2 Sam 7:14) and also as the Servant. The characteristics of the Servant, called to mind by the reference to Is 42:1, are made explicit in the description of Jesus as the 'Lamb of God, who takes away the sin of the world' (Jn 1:29), the declaration made by Jesus in the synagogue in Nazareth (Lk 4:17–21) and Matthew's commentary on Jesus' healings (11:16ff.).

Jesus himself was fully conscious of being the one 'whom the Father consecrated and sent into the world' (Jn 10:36). This is a particularly difficult point to explain and even to express, since it concerns the growth in Jesus' human knowledge of his consciousness of his own quality and his mission. His baptism, his encounter with John the Baptist, the Spirit's coming to him and the Word that accompanied that coming were certainly all events of decisive importance in making explicit his human consciousness of his quality of the one who was chosen and sent and of the Son of God and the Servant and Lamb of God. There is fairly general agreement now that, because of the hypostatic union, the Word or Son of 'God' is the principle of

17

Jesus' existence and the metaphysical subject to which his actions are attributed, but that this union leaves the play of his faculties of knowing and willing a matter of his true and full humanity.[13] It is a fact that is borne out in Scripture that Jesus increased in wisdom and favour with God (Lk 2:52), that there were certain things that he did not know, that he may have been mistaken[14] and that he experienced difficulty in obeying his Father perfectly.[15] He carried out his mission from childhood to the cross under the rule of obedience (see Phil 2:6–8; see also Rom 5:19), which means that he was ignorant and not in control of the consequences of his actions. In what terms and how was he, at the level of his human experience, conscious of his ontological quality of the Son of God? The 'categorial' way of expressing and representing this consciousness is made explicit by the experiences, encounters and actions that take place in his life. He understood his mission by carrying it out. On the one hand, he discovered it as something that was already outlined in the Mosaic law, the prophets and the psalms.[16] On the other hand, he carried it out by receiving the miraculous works and prophetic words from his Father and living in obedience to God's will for him: 'In that same hour he rejoiced in the Holy Spirit and said, "I thank thee, Father, Lord of heaven and earth, that thou hast hidden these things from the wise and understanding and revealed them to babes" ' (Lk 10:21).

Jesus' acceptance of baptism by John the Baptist within the plan of fulfilling God's will (see Mt 3:13–15), the new coming of the Spirit to him and the words describing him as the royal Messiah, Servant and 'beloved Son' are all moments of decisive importance at the beginning of the mission that he had to carry out for us. The Spirit then leads him at once into the desert to confront the demon (Mt 4:1; Mk 1:12; Lk 4:1). Jesus' temptation is closely connected with his baptism and the declaration: 'Thou art (This is) my beloved Son'. The words 'If you are the Son of God' are repeated twice by the tempter, but Jesus is also the Servant, whom the Father has chosen to fight and to suffer and die on the cross. His temptation is a test of his obedience to God. We know that it ended in a decisive victory—Satan was bound and Jesus again and again cast him out by the 'finger' or the Spirit of God.[17]

After his baptism and his victory over the tempter, Jesus experienced the presence in himself of the Spirit, whose activity made it possible for him to make the kingdom of God present and therefore to eliminate the reign of the demon. That is also why Jesus was to heal so many people. His healing ministry is on several occasions linked in Matthew with his call to be the Servant (see 8:17 and Is 53:4; 12:15–21 and Is 42:1–4). It is possible to be mistaken about Jesus himself, 'being born in the likeness of men, being found in human form', but it is wrong to blaspheme or sin against the Spirit by not recognizing his work where the Spirit exerts his power.[18] His opponents' wrong and hostile interpretation of his power over evil and the evil one confirmed Jesus in the evidence that he had of working through the Spirit.

It would undoubtedly be claiming too much if we were to say that the baptism of Jesus contained the whole doctrine of his substitutive death,[19] but there can be no doubt—and it is stated quite explicitly in Mt 3:15—that Jesus came to be baptized and that he experienced the event with the intention of offering himself and being open to God's plan for him. This plan included firstly the type of the Servant and then the supreme offering of his life (see Heb 10:5–10). Jesus in fact saw his death as a 'baptism' (Mk 10:38; Lk 12:50). He offered himself to God as a spotless victim through the 'eternal spirit', that is, the Holy Spirit.[20] His sacrifice was the consequence of this baptism, and his glory was the consequence of his sacrifice. The baptism of the passion and glory are brought together in his reply to the sons of Zebedee (Mk 10:35ff.), who represent us all. Several exegetes have compared these texts, and their closeness confirms the fact that all those who believe in Jesus are concerned in his baptism, in which his destiny as the Messiah who suffers and is dedicated to glory is involved.[21] We are baptized in his death (Rom 6:3), but we are also baptized by one Spirit into one body (1 Cor 12:13).

It was also as one who was led by the Spirit that had come upon him at his baptism that Jesus undertook his evangelical ministry. All three synoptic gospels show that ministry as beginning with his victorious struggle against the demon. Luke brings together several aspects of Jesus' presence in Nazareth and adds the reading of Isaiah 61:1–2a (and 58:6): 'The Spirit of the Lord is upon me, because he has anointed me to bring good tidings to the afflicted . . .' and the declaration: 'Today this scripture has been fulfilled in your hearing' (4:21). The descent of the Holy Spirit on Jesus at his baptism is described as an anointing, that is, as a prophetic anointing for a mission to proclaim, and as a realization of, the good news of liberation from evil and the evil one.[22] Luke writes of the continuation of this process in the Acts of the Apostles. Pentecost was for the Church what his baptism was for Jesus, that is, the gift and the power of the Spirit, dedication to the ministry, mission and bearing witness.[23] In Acts 10:38–39, for example, we read: 'You know . . . how God anointed Jesus of Nazareth with the Spirit and with power; how he went about doing good and healing all that were oppressed by the devil, for God was with him. And we are witnesses to all that he did. . . .' Acts 4:24–30 is the prayer of the community of Jerusalem. It recalls Ps 2, the messianic psalm from which the heavenly word spoken at Jesus' baptism was taken: 'Thy holy servant Jesus, whom thou didst anoint'. The coming of the Spirit at Jesus' baptism, then, is clearly seen as his anointing for his messianic ministry. That anointing is both royal and prophetic.

The Patristic Tradition

We will leave our exegesis of the New Testament texts at this point and go on to a synthesis of the Tradition and a consideration of the dogmatic implications. Our first task, however, is ecclesiological and for this purpose we will examine a number of patristic statements.

In their attempts to explain the anointing of Christ at his baptism, the Fathers were troubled by three data in the context within which they thought and expressed themselves. The first of these was the climate of Stoic thought, according to which *pneuma* was seen as a force permeating the universe and holding it together, in such a way that it was associated with the *logos*. A cosmic function was ascribed to this *logos* which preceded the part that it played in the economy of salvation. The second datum was the need to maintain that Christ did not begin to be the Son of God and the Christ at the time of his baptism. Justin Martyr insisted on this in his reply to Trypho (*Dial*. 87–88), but he did not make a clear distinction between the Logos and the Pneuma. He also believed that Jesus possessed his power from the moment of his birth and that the descent of the Spirit at his baptism was simply a sign of his messianic quality.[24] The third datum was that certain Gnostics maintained that the Saviour on high descended on Jesus at the time of his baptism and that this was necessary since, in their opinion, his birth in the flesh could only have defiled him.[25]

Irenaeus refuted them firmly and clearly.[26] In an admirable statement, he says that this Jesus, the humanity of the Word, 'insofar as he is God receives from the Father, that is, God, the throne of the eternal royalty and the oil of anointing'. He quotes Ps 45:7–8 in this context and believes that this points to the incarnation.[27] The Spirit, however, had to be given to all of us[28] and that is why it descended on Jesus at his baptism. This happened so that he could communicate the Spirit to us. It was for this reason that the Word became Jesus Christ:

> St Matthew says, in connection with the baptism of the Lord: 'The heavens were opened and he saw the Spirit of God descending like a dove and alighting on him; and lo, a voice from heaven, saying, "This is my beloved Son, with whom I am well pleased" ' (3:16–17). It was, after all, not one who claimed to be the Christ who descended on Jesus, and it cannot be claimed that the Christ was other than Jesus. The Word of God, the Saviour of all men and the Lord of heaven and earth—that Word who is, as we have already shown, no other than Jesus—by having assumed a flesh and having been anointed with the Spirit by the Father, became Jesus Christ. As Isaiah said: 'There shall come forth a shoot from the stump of Jesse and a branch shall grow out of his roots. And the Spirit of the Lord shall rest upon him' (11:1–4). Elsewhere Isaiah announced his anointing and the reason why he was anointed: 'The Spirit of the Lord God is upon me, because the Lord has anointed me to bring good tidings to the poor' (61:1–2) . . . . It was therefore the Spirit of God that descended on him—the Spirit of that same God who had, through the prophets, promised to bestow anointing on him so that, receiving ourselves the superabundance of that anointing, we should be saved.[29]

Hippolytus was familiar with the works of Irenaeus and it should not surprise us to read, in his prayer for the consecration of a bishop: 'Pour out that power which comes from you, the sovereign Spirit that you have given to your beloved Son, Jesus Christ; that he gave to the holy apostles who founded the Church in every place'.[30]

There was, then, a lively awareness in the Church of the part played by the baptism of Jesus in the economy of salvation. Basil the Great wanted to show that the Spirit 'was with the flesh of the Lord' and therefore cited Jn 1:33; Lk 3:22 and Acts 10:38, which refer to the anointing at the time of Jesus' baptism.[31] Jesus had been filled and sanctified by the Spirit since the time of his conception, which had brought about the union of a humanity with the person of the eternal Son. He had, however, been 'anointed' by the Spirit at his baptism in order to be the Messiah, the minister of salvation and holiness. It was then that 'he appeared as the man who was able to make others holy'.[32] No other kind of 'anointing' occurs in Scripture.[33]

The Fathers were, however, impressed by the gifts of grace, salvation and deification that were made to humanity by the incarnation of God in the man Jesus. They traced the beginning of the new creation, which was paschal and pentecostal, back to the incarnation as such.[34]

A century after Irenaeus, Methodius of Olympus formulated statements that have been repeated again and again in the East. He said, for example, that through the incarnation, the mortal had been changed into immortal and the passible into impassible.[35] The struggle against Arianism and its by-products, and the necessary but difficult growth of Christological thought led to attempts to trace the saving and sanctifying activity of Jesus Christ back to the personal union of the Word with humanity in Jesus rather than to the descent of the Spirit on Jesus at his baptism. Athanasius,[36] for example, maintained that it was by the incarnation of the Logos that humanity was anointed by the Holy Spirit.[37] A similar view was held by Gregory Nazianzen,[38] Gregory of Nyssa († c. 394),[39] Augustine[40] and Cyril of Alexandria, who said: 'Christ filled his whole body with the life-giving power of the Spirit. . . . It was not the flesh that gave life to the Spirit, but the power of the Spirit that gave life to the flesh.'[41] At the end of the great Christological debates, Maximus the Confessor (580–662) stated that the hypostatic union was the basis of the individual nature of Christ.[42]

In the West, the Fathers expressed this consecration of Christ by the Spirit in terms of the grace of Christ as the Head, which made him the principle of salvation and sanctification for his body.[43] This view was formulated in the twelfth century in the theology of Christ the Head and his capital grace. This theology was very consistently, forcefully and systematically outlined by Thomas Aquinas. It teaches that sanctification by the Spirit and the fullness of grace were acquired from the outset of the hypostatic union and as a necessary consequence of that union. According to the Fathers, the coming of the Spirit in the form of a dove at the time of Jesus' baptism was a sign for John the Baptist.[44] Thomas Aquinas called it a 'visible mission', and such a mission is simply a sign given for the sake of others of an invisible mission that had previously been carried out fully.[45] The question in the *Summa* devoted to Jesus' baptism goes back to a theology that is both analytical and typological, not to say metaphorical, and certainly disappointing.[46]

Thomas derived his Christology from the Greek Fathers,[47] Augustine and the early Scholastic theologians. Möhler, the Roman School and Scheeben also used the same sources in their theological renewal in the nineteenth century. In all these theologies, the Church is linked to the incarnation and the Trinity because of the hypostatic union.[48] This is particularly clear in the case of Scheeben, who, despite his theology of the indwelling of the Holy Spirit, was more systematic. He went so far as to say, for example: 'When the Fathers say that Christ is anointed with the Holy Spirit, this means only that the Holy Spirit has descended into the humanity of Christ in the Logos from whom he proceeds, and that he anoints the humanity of Christ as the pouring out of the unction which is the Logos himself. Only God the Father can be regarded as the efficient principle of Christ's anointing because he alone communicates to the Son the divine dignity and nature which formally anoint the humanity that is assumed to the Son's person. . . . Christ is anointed not merely by divine deputation for the discharge of an office, nor even merely by the pouring out of the Holy Spirit. He is called divine, but not simply as God's friend and representative. He is the true Son of God and truly God.'[49]

Is this a satisfactory argument? Yes, as analytical theology, but as a concrete, historical theology going back to biblical sources, it is disappointing.

The Theology of Heribert Mühlen

Nearly twenty years ago, Heribert Mühlen of Paderborn undertook a wide-ranging renewal of this aspect of Catholic theology.[50] In numerous publications, he has explored the same themes and has developed them continuously and progressively in the following order:

1. The Holy Spirit can be presented in his relationship with the Father and the Son as 'the We in person'. This representation is valid not only at the level of the essential Trinity (the intra-divine level), but also at that of the 'economic' Trinity. In other words, it also applies to the involvement and the revelation of the divine Persons for the benefit of the world and men.

2. The greatest importance has to be attached to the anointing of Christ, at his baptism, by the Holy Spirit.

3. The Church has to be seen not as what Möhler called a 'continued incarnation', a formula that was later accepted by the Roman School, but rather as the presence and activity in the 'Church' of the same personal Spirit that anointed Jesus as the Messiah. The most suitable formula for a dogmatic definition of the mystery of the Church, then, would be 'only one Person, that of the Holy Spirit, in several persons, namely Christ and us, his believ-

ers'. This would 'define' the mystery of the Church as strictly, as precisely and as concisely as the mystery of the Trinity has been 'defined' as 'three Persons in one nature' and the mystery of the incarnation has been 'defined' as 'one Person in two natures'. Of course, the presence (or 'indwelling') and activity involved are a presence and an activity in *persons*, who preserve their freedom, including their freedom to sin, so that there is nothing of an 'incarnation' of the Spirit here in the way there is an incarnation of the Word in Jesus.

4. Mühlen provides another formula for the mystery of the Church, calling it a 'Great I' or a 'corporative personality'. It is not the Great I of the Holy Spirit, but it is the Great I of Christ, since the Spirit is the Spirit of Christ. He is communicated by Christ and he animates the body of Christ.

5. Mühlen has also applied these pneumatological and ecclesiological views to several contemporary movements and in particular to the movement of renewal in the Spirit, which we shall consider later, and to ecumenism. In the case of the latter, it can be used, he claims, either to justify the ecclesiological value of other churches or church communities[51] or to interpret ecumenical activity in the light of a future council (perhaps the next council?), which might be ecumenical in that sense of the word as well and as such an act of unity.[52]

We cannot at this point consider either these contemporary applications of pneumatology or Mühlen's original development of relationships within the Trinity in terms of interpersonal relationships.[53] We shall come back to these questions later. Here, we must limit ourselves to his theology of the anointing of Christ by the Spirit in its connection with the hypostatic union, in other words, the assumption of an individualized human nature by the Person of the Word or Son of God.

Mühlen's interpretation is fortunately quite close to the way in which Scripture speaks, that is, concretely and historically. Whereas 'Christus' was regarded by the Scholastic theologians simply as a proper noun or name that could be replaced equally well by 'Jesus' or 'the Lord', Mühlen gives it its full biblical value of 'the anointed one', in Hebrew *meŝîaḥ*, the 'Messiah', a term which points to the three biblical and classical functions of king, priest and prophet. 'Christ', then, is a name describing the part played and the mission carried out by Jesus of Nazareth. The preaching of the apostles and the disciples' confession of faith also point to this affirmation: Jesus is the Christ, the Messiah of God.[54] 'You know', Peter testified, what happened 'throughout all Judea, beginning from Galilee after the baptism which John preached: how God anointed Jesus of Nazareth with the Holy Spirit and with power' (Acts 10:38). I. de la Potterie was therefore able to conclude his study of the anointing of Christ with the words: 'The real and, in one sense, unique context within which the New Testament speaks of the anointing of Christ is that of baptism'. This does not present us with any difficulty if the term 'Christ-Messiah' is understood simply in the sense of a function and a ministry and if no more is attributed to his 'anointing' than the naming and the gifts of the power required for this mission. If, however, what occurred at his baptism was a declaration of this mission—Mühlen speaks of 'promulgation' in this context[55]—then Jesus was destined for it from the beginning. The revelatory and soteriological part played by Christ cannot be separated from what he was constituted to be from the beginning. The author of the Acts calls Jesus the 'Christ-Messiah' from the very beginning. He does this implicitly in the annunciation made to Mary (Lk 1:31–33) and explicitly in the annunciation to the shepherds (2:11) and the assurance given to Simeon (2:26). This has led W. Grundmann to comment that, when Peter proclaims: 'God has made him both Lord and Christ, this Jesus whom you crucified' (Acts 2:36), this is, on God's part, a revelation or manifestation in the quality of Christ-Messiah, even though Jesus was that from the moment of his conception.[56]

What is Mühlen's intention and what does he in fact base on the theology of the Trinity and Scripture? It is not that Christ was not made holy at the moment of his conception. It is rather that this sanctification should not be attributed to the hypostatic union as such, that is, the mission of the Word, but to the Holy Spirit. The mission of the Spirit is the consequence in time—'in the fullness of time'—of his eternal procession 'from the Father and the Son', as the term of their mutual love, first in Mary's womb and then in the Church, whose supernatural existence is connected with the Spirit of Jesus. This view is quite in accordance with the dogmatic explanation of the mystery, which attributes the hypostatic union to the Word, and the *formatio corporis* and the sanctification of the fruit conceived in Mary's womb to the Spirit (see Lk 1:35).[57] This sanctification is the gift, made in absolute fullness, of created graces, a fullness that is evoked by the quality of the Son of God in the absolute sense of the term. This is why Thomas Aquinas spoke of it in this way and quoted Is 42:1, applying the words to the Messiah: 'Behold my servant, whom I uphold, my chosen, in whom my soul delights; I have put my Spirit upon him'. Thomas distinguished two aspects, following one another not in time, but in logic and by nature, the first relating to the assumption of a human nature by the Word and the second to the Spirit who fills that man-God with gifts of grace.[58]

Ought we, then, not to recognize a similar order in the Church and, in these circumstances, make up for what Mühlen has failed to do by stressing the real connection between the Church and the incarnation as such? Was the institution of the Twelve by Jesus (see Mk 3:14) not followed by the sanctification and animation of the apostles by the Spirit of Pentecost? And was the institution of the sacraments and the delivery of the message of the gospel not followed by the making present of those gifts of the covenant by the Spirit? This is a very familiar theme in the patristic tradition (see below, note 2) and we shall return to it later, when we shall see that it can be applied to the theology of the sacraments and in particular to the two-sided sacrament of baptism/confirmation and to the consecration of the eucharistic gifts by the words of institution and the epiclesis. The essential thing is to respect the two missions, of the Word and of the Spirit, on the pattern of the succession which derives from the procession within the Trinity. It goes without saying that we speak of such matters as best we can. . . .

NOTES

1. For this chapter, see, in addition to '*pneuma*', *TDNT*, VI, esp. pp. 396–451; and F. Büchsel, *Der Geist Gottes im Neuen Testament* (Gütersloh, 1926): H. B. Swete, *The Holy Spirit in the New Testament. A Study of Primitive Christian Teaching* (London, 1909); M.-A. Chevallier, *L'Esprit et le Messie dans le bas-judaïsme et le Nouveau Testament* (Paris, 1958); *idem*, *Esprit de Dieu, paroles d'hommes* (Neuchâtel, 1966), pp. 7–17.
2. J. Dupont, ' "Filius meus es tu". L'interprétation du Ps. 2.7 dans le Nouveau Testament', *RSR*, 35 (1948), 522–543; I. de la Potterie, 'L'onction du Christ', *NRT*, 80 (1958), 225–252; C. Cranfield, 'The Baptism of our Lord. A Study of St Mark 1, 9–11', *Scottish Journal of Theology*, 8 (1955/1); A. Feuillet, 'Le baptême de Jésus d'après l'évangile selon S. Marc (1, 9–11)', *CBQ*, 21 (1959), 468–490; A. Légault, 'Le baptême de Jésus et la doctrine du Serviteur souffrant', *SE*, 13 (1961), 147–166; M. Sabbe, 'Le baptême de Jésus. Evangiles synoptiques', *De Jésus aux Evangiles. Mélanges J. Coppens*, ed. I. de la Potterie (Gembloux and Paris, 1967), II, pp. 184–211; H. Mentz, *Taufe und Kirche in ihrem ursprünglichen Zusammenhang* (Munich, 1968); F. Porsch, *Pneuma und Wort. Ein exegetischer Beitrag zur Pneumatologie des Johannesevangeliums (Frankfurter Theologische Studien, 16)* (Frankfurt a. M., 1974), pp. 19–51; J. Bornemann, *Die Taufe Christi durch Johannes in der dogmatischen Beurteilung der christlichen Theologen der vier ersten Jahrhunderte* (Leipzig, 1896); D. A. Bertrand, *Le baptême de Jésus. Histoire de l'exégèse aux deux premiers siècles (Beiträge zur Geschichte der biblischen Exegese, 14)* (Tübingen, 1973).
3. Hence their astonishment (see Lk 4:22; Mt 13:54–56; Mk 6:1ff.). See F. Büchsel, *op. cit.*, pp. 149ff.
4. D. A. Bertrand, *op. cit.*, p. 12.
5. The Holy Spirit is simply the spirit, the powerful breath of God that is creative and gives life and the force by which Jesus performs miracles and drives out demons (see Acts 10:38ff.; Mt 12:28; Lk 11:20). Jesus said: 'The Father who dwells in me does his works' (Jn 14:10). In the New Testament, 'God' is the Father. See K. Rahner, 'Theos in the New Testament' (Eng. tr.), *Theological Investigations*, I (London and Baltimore, 1961), pp. 79–148.
6. What is known as the hypostatic union is, as a 'work *ad extra*', the action of the three Persons and the result of this action is the union in the Person of the Son, the Word. It is, however, the Spirit who, by activating in Mary her capacity as a woman to conceive (and thereby supplying the 23 male chromosomes), produces the human being whom the Son, the Word, unites to himself, and thereby also the 'holy' fact. In this way, Jesus is Emmanuel, God with us, because he was of the Holy Spirit (and conceived by that Spirit). That is, dogmatically and theologically, the meaning of Lk 1:35. See, for example, Thomas Aquinas, *ST* IIIa, q. 32, a. 1, ad 1 and 2 ad 2, in which he explains a saying of 'Jerome's' (in reality, it was not Jerome, but Pelagius, *Libellus fidei ad Innocentium: PL* 45, 1716) and quotes 'John Chrysostom' (the unknown author of the *Opus imperf. in Mat.*, 1:20: *PG* 56, 634) and John Damascene (*De fide orthod.*, c. 2: *PG* 94, 985). The Ottawa edition of the *Summa* gives other references in the same sense to Hugh of Saint-Victor, Peter Lombard and Bonaventure.

25

7. See 'pneuma', TDNT, VI, p. 382. Many suggestions have been made to explain the meaning of the dove: see M. E. Isaacs, The Concept of Spirit (London, 1976), pp. 116f.
8. Targum on Is 6. See F. Lentzen-Deis, Die Taufe Jesu nach den Synoptikern. Literarkritische und gattungsgeschichtliche Untersuchungen (Freiburg, 1970), pp. 243 ff., 270.
9. See H. Sahlin, Studien zum dritten Kapitel des Lukasevangeliums (Uppsala, 1949), pp. 101–105; A. Feuillet, 'Le symbolisme de la colombe dans les récits évangeliques du baptême', RSR, 46 (1958), 524–544; F. Lentzen-Deis, op. cit., pp. 181, 265–270; L. E. Keck, 'The Spirit and the Dove', NTS, 17 (1970–71), 41–67; F. Porsch, op. cit. (note 2), pp. 28–31 (with a very full documentation).
10. See H. Mentz, op. cit. (note 2), p. 64.
11. It is forbidden to represent the Holy Spirit in human form: see M. Meschler, Le don de la Pentecôte (Paris, 1895), II, p. 226 and note 1. The divine Persons should only be represented by the characteristics for which there is scriptural evidence: see, for example, the decree of the Holy Office, 16 March 1928, AAS, 20 (1928), 103. The Holy Spirit could therefore be represented, for example, as a dove, as tongues of fire or as the finger of God (see below, note 17). In the East, adaptations were made to the theological needs of various periods. Representations have included the dove, tongues of fire, light, a luminous cloud or a ray and various human forms, such as the three Magi or Abraham's three visitors (Andrei Rublev). Geometrical shapes have also been used. See T. M. Provetakis, 'To hagion Pneuma eis tēn Orthodoxēn Zōgraphikēn', To Hagion Pneuma (Thessalonica, 1971), with 58 illustrations; see also RHE, 67 (1972), 675.
12. See my general introduction to Augustine's Traités antidonatistes, I, Bibl. August., Vol. 28 (Paris, 1963), pp. 104–109.
13. It is impossible to mention all the books and articles that have been written on this subject since P. Galtier's study in 1939. I would mention only three short bulletins: B.-D. Dupuy, RSPT, 47 (1963), 110–116; E. Gutwenger, Concilium, 11 (1966), 81–94; B. Sesboué, RSR, 56 (1968), 635–666. There are other, more advanced studies which can act as norms for us today. Among the most important of these is K. Rahner, 'Dogmatic Reflections on the Knowledge and Self-Consciousness of Christ' (Eng. tr.), Theological Investigations, V (London and Baltimore, 1966), pp. 193–215. C. V. Héris, 'Problème de Christologie. La conscience de Jésus', Esprit et Vie, 81 (1971), 672–679 (who criticizes J. Galot and makes a distinction between the metaphysical person and the personality) keeps to Thomistic principles, as does H.-M. Féret, 'Christologie médiévale de S. Thomas et Christologie concrète et historique pour aujourd'hui', Memorie Domenicane (1975), pp. 109–141.
14. See A. Vögtle, 'Exegetische Erwägungen über das Wissen und Selbstbewusstsein Jesu', Gott in Welt. Festgabe für K. Rahner (Freiburg, 1964), I, pp. 608–667; R. E. Brown, 'How much did Jesus know?' CBQ, 29 (1967), 315–345; O. Cullmann, Salvation in History (Eng. tr.; London, 1967), esp. pp. 209ff.
15. The agony (agōn = struggle), Mt 26:39 and 51; Mk 14:36; Lk 22:42; Heb 2:10 and 13; 4:15; 5:8.
16. The explanation that he gives to the disciples (Lk 24:27 and 44) is based (on infused knowledge, but also) on the circumstances in which the Father has given him the opportunity to verify that he was being spoken of (see, for example, Mt 11:5; Lk 5:17) or on his own prayerful meditation on the Scriptures (see, for example, Mk 12:10; Lk 4:12; 9:22; 20:41ff.).
17. See Lk 11:20 (finger); Mt 12:28 (Spirit); finger of God: Ex 8:19; 31:18; Deut 9:10; Ps 8:3.
18. See my article 'Le blasphème contre le Saint-Esprit (Mt 9, 32–34; 12, 22–32; Mc 3, 20–30; Lc 11, 14–23; 12, 8–10)', L'Expérience de l'Esprit. Mélanges Schillebeeckx (Le Point théologique, 18) (Paris, 1976), pp. 17–29; G. Fitzer, 'Die Sünde wider den Hl. Geist', TZ, 13 (1957), 161–182.
19. See O. Cullmann, The Christology of the New Testament (Eng. tr.; London, 1959), pp. 66–68; A. Légault, op. cit. (note 2).

20. Heb 9:14. H. Mühlen defends the interpretation as the Holy Spirit. Swete did not favour this interpretation: *op. cit.* (note 1), pp. 252–253. According to the Syriac Fathers of the fourth century A.D., Aphraates and Ephraem Syrus, Jesus was, at the time of his baptism, consecrated as a priest (deriving his royal quality from his Davidic descent). This priesthood, which was derived from Moses and Aaron (!), was then communicated by John. See R. Murray, *Symbols of Church and Kingdom. A Study in Early Syriac Tradition* (Cambridge, 1975), p. 179.

21. H. Mentz, *op cit.* (note 2), pp. 52 ff.; J. A. T. Robinson, ' "The One Baptism" ', *Scottish Journal of Theology*, 6 (1953), 257–274.

22. I. de la Potterie, *op. cit.* (note 2), who stresses, with Luke, the prophetic mission of Jesus.

23. This traditional idea has been systematically elaborated by J. Lécuyer in his contribution to *Etudes sur le sacrement de l'ordre* (*Lex orandi*, 22) (Paris, 1957), pp. 167–213, and *Le sacerdoce dans le mystère du Christ* (*Lex orandi*, 24) (Paris, 1957), pp. 313–338, especially p. 321, with the references in note 1.

24. See A. Houssiau, *La christologie de S. Irénée* (Louvain and Gembloux, 1955), pp. 172ff., 176–180; J. P. Martín, *El Espíritu Santo en los Orígenes del Cristianismo. Estudio sobre I Clemente, Ignacio, II Clemente y Justino Mártir* (*Biblioteca di Scienze Religiose*, 2) (Zürich, 1971), pp. 213–223.

25. For these ideas and their context, see A. Orbe's enormous work, *La unción del Verbo. Estudios Valentinianos*, III (*Anal. Greg.*, 113) (Rome, 1961); see also F.-M. Braun, *Jean le théologien*, III/I (Paris, 1966), p. 67.

26. Irenaeus, *Adv. haer.* III, 9, 3; 10, 4; 17. 1. For Irenaeus' theology of the anointing of Christ by the Spirit, see A. Houssiau, *op. cit.*, pp. 166–186; H.-J. Jaschke, *Der Hl. Geist im Bekenntnis der Kirche. Eine Studie zur Pneumatologie des Irenäus von Lyon* (Münster, 1976), pp. 148–252, especially pp. 208ff.

27. See *Adv. haer.* III, 6, 1 (*SC* 211, ed. A. Rousseau and L. Doutreleau, p. 67); 12, 7 (pp. 211–213); *Démonstration de la Prédication apostolique* (*SC* 62; Fr. tr. L.-M. Froidevaux), 47. In §§9 and 53, Irenaeus says that the Spirit of God rested 'on the Son of God, that is to say, the Word, in his coming as a man' (pp. 45 and 114). Did he have the incarnation or the manifestation in the Jordan in mind here or both? See, for example: 'these texts (Rom 14:15; Eph 2:13; Gal 2:13; 1 Cor 8:11) make it sufficiently clear that a "Christ" who was impassible never descended into a "Jesus", but that Jesus, who was the Christ in person, suffered for us and that he fell asleep and was raised again, descended and went up again. That Jesus was the Son of God who became the Son of man. This is moreover what his name indicates, since the name "Christ" means the one who is anointed, the one who anoints and the unction with which he has been anointed. The one who anoints is the Father, the one who is anointed is the Son and he was anointed in the Spirit, who is the unction. As the Word says through the mouth of Isaiah: "The Spirit of the Lord God is upon me, because he has anointed me" (61:1; Lk 4:18)' (*Adv. haer.* III, 18, 3 (*SC* 211, p. 351; *PG* 7, 934)).

28. *Adv. haer.* III, 17, 1, 3 and 4 (*SC* 211, pp. 329, 331: 'That is why this Spirit descended on the Son of God who had become the Son of man—it was in this way, with him, that he became accustomed to dwell in the human race, to rest on men, to live in the work modelled by God'); 3 (pp. 335ff.: 'the dew, which is the Spirit of God, spread over the whole of the earth. It was this Spirit who descended on the Lord, "the Spirit of wisdom and understanding, the Spirit of counsel and might, the Spirit of knowledge and the fear of the Lord" (Is 11:2–3). It is this same spirit that the Lord gave to the Church when he sent the Paraclete from heaven on the whole of the earth'); 4 (pp. 337ff.: 'It was therefore the Spirit who descended because of the "economy" of which we have been speaking').

29. *Adv. haer.* III, 9, 3 (*SC* 211, pp. 107–113).

30. Hippolytus, *Apostolic Tradition*, 3 (verse 215).

31. Basil, *De Spiritu Sancto* XVI, 39 (*PG* 32, 140C; *SC* 17bis (1968), pp. 386 and 387).

32. Cyril of Alexandria, *Comm. in Ioan.* lib. XI, c. 10 (*PG* 74, 549C).

27

33. See I. de la Potterie, 'L'onction du Christ. Etude de théologie biblique', *NRT*, 80 (1958), 225–252, who says, on p. 250: 'There is no text in the New Testament which refers to an anointing of Christ at the moment of his incarnation. According to the patristic and theological tradition, the hypostatic union is a consecration of Jesus' humanity by his divinity, but this idea cannot be found in any of the New Testament authors.'

34. S. Trooster, 'De Heilige Geest in de Menswording bij de Griekse Vaders', *Bijdragen*, 17 (1956), 117–151, who examined the teaching of Irenaeus, Clement of Alexandria, Origen, Athanasius, Didymus, Gregory of Nyssa, Gregory Nazianzen and Basil. For the anointing at the moment of conception and the hypostatic union, see also S. Tromp, *Corpus Christi quod est Ecclesia*, III: *De Spiritu Christi anima* (Rome, 1960), pp. 237ff. After Nicaea, the part played by the Spirit in the baptism of Jesus was toned down; see J. G. Davies, *The Spirit, the Church and the Sacraments* (London, 1954), pp. 20–26. The Fathers were especially conscious, in the baptism of Christ, of the 'mystery' that was at the foundation of Christian baptism; see P. T. Camelot, *Spiritualité du baptême (Lex orandi, 30)* (Paris, 1960), chapter X, pp. 257–281, which contains deep insights into its reference to the crucifixion, pp. 268f.

35. Methodius, *De res.* 3, 23, 4 (*GCS* 27, 421–422).

36. Athanasius, *Contra Arian.* 2, 61 and 70 (*PG* 26, 277A, 296B); 3, 34 (397B).

37. *Ibid.* 1, 50 (*PG* 26, 117Aff.).

38. Gregory Nazianzen, *Orat.* 10 in the presence of Basil (*PG* 35, 832A).

39. The Logos, becoming merged with the flesh, raised it to the properties of the Logos by the reception of the Holy Spirit that the Logos possessed even before creation: Gregory of Nyssa, *In illud 'Tunc ipse Filius'* (*PG* 44, 1320D); see also *In Cant. Cant., Hom.* 12 (*PG* 44, 1016).

40. Augustine, *De Trin.* XV, 26, 46.

41. Cyril of Alexandria, *Comm. in Ioan.* 6, 64 (*PG* 73, 604); see also *Comm. in Heb.* (*PG* 74, 961B); P. Galtier, 'Le Saint-Esprit dans l'Incarnation du Verbe d'après S. Cyrille d'Alexandrie', *Problemi scelti di Teologia contemporanea* (Rome, 1954), pp. 383–392. See also Cyril's eleventh anathematism: *DS* 262.

42. Maximus the Confessor, *Ambigua* (*PG* 91, 1040C). See also John Damascene, *De fide orthod.* lib. III, c. 3; lib. IV, c. 14 (*PG* 94, 989A and 1161A).

43. Ambrose, *Hexaemeron* 3, 17, 71 (*PL* 14, 186C; in 386–389); Augustine, *Enarr. in Ps.* 123, 1; 136, 22 (*PL* 37, 1640, 1774); *Comm. in Ioan.* 3, 8 (*PL* 35, 1399D), etc.

44. See Augustine, *De Trin.* XV, 26 (*PL* 42, 1093–94); *De Praed. Sanct.* 15, 31 (*PL* 44, 982); Cyril of Alexandria, *Comm in Ioan.* lib. II (*PG* 73, 209A–212D).

45. *In I Sent.* d. 16, q. 1 and 2; III, d. 13, q. 1, a. 2, q. 3, ad 3; *ST* Ia, q. 43, a. 7, ad 6.

46. *ST* IIIa, q. 39. In article 2, Thomas says: 'Christus spirituali baptismate non indigebat, qui a principio suae conceptionis gratia Spiritus Sancti repletus fuit'.

47. See I. Backes, *Die Christologie des hl. Thomas von Aquin und die griechischen Kirchenväter* (Paderborn, 1931).

48. J. A. Möhler, not in *Die Einheit* (1825), but in the successive editions (1832 onwards) of his *Symbolik*: see §36 (for the precise meaning of this, see H. Mühlen, *Una mystica Persona* (below, note 50), pp. 8ff.); see also C. Passaglia, *De Ecclesia Christi* (Regensburg, 1853), lib. III, cc. 1–5 and 41; J. B. Franzelin, *Theses de Ecclesia Christi* (Rome, 1887), Thesis 17, pp. 296ff.

49. M. J. Scheeben, *Mysterien des Christentums* (1865), §51; Eng. tr. *The Mysteries of Christianity* (St Louis and London, 1946), pp. 332–333 [based on 1941 Ger. ed.; not identical with translation here of Fr. tr. (1947), pp. 338–339].

50. H. Mühlen, *Der Heilige Geist als Person. Beitrag zur Frage nach dem Hl. Geiste eigentümliche Funktion in der Trinität bei der Inkarnation und im Gnadenbund. Ich-Du-Wir* (Münster, 1963); *Una mystica Persona. Die Kirche als das Mysterium der heilsgeschichtlichen Identität des Heiligen Geistes in Christus und den Christen* (Paderborn, 1964; refs are to 2nd ed., 1967). He has also written several other, less important works, which add nothing

essential to the theology of these major works. See also, however, *Die Erneuerung des christlichen Glaubens. Charisma-Geist-Befreiung* (Munich, 1974).

51. *Una mystica Persona, op. cit.*, pp. 369ff.; see also my study 'Le développement de l'évaluation ecclésiologique des Eglises non catholiques', *Revue de Droit canonique*, 25 (1975), 168–198, especially 186ff.

52. H. Mühlen, *Morgen wird Einheit sein. Das kommende Konzil aller Christen. Ziel der getrennten Kirchen* (Paderborn, 1974).

53. See, for example, the surveys made by B. Rey in *RSPT*, 49 (1965), 527–533, and A. Paatfort in *Angelicum*, 45 (1968), 316–327.

54. W. Grundmann, F. Hesse, M. de Jonge and A. S. van der Worde, '*chriō*', *TDNT*, IX, pp. 493–580 (with a lengthy bibliography); H. Mühlen, *Der Heilige Geist als Person, op. cit.* (note 50), pp. 176ff.

55. *Ibid.*, p. 187. Elsewhere, in *Una mystica Persona*, p. 219, Mühlen says: 'This form of activity of the Pneuma in the man Jesus is quite different from his prophetic anointing by the Holy Spirit, which is bestowed on him with others in mind. It is therefore possible to speak of a twofold aspect of the anointing of Jesus in the Holy Spirit—an anointing which reaches him in his own humanity and an anointing which is bestowed on him for others.' But, if this is not a separation, then surely it is at least to make too much of a distinction between the two? Personal grace and capital grace are strictly identical in Christ. See L. Lécuyer, 'Mystère de la Pentecôte et apostolicité de la mission de l'Eglise', *Etudes sur le sacrement de l'Ordre* (Paris, 1957), pp. 193–194.

56. W. Grundmann, '*chriō*', *TDNT*, IX, esp. pp. 531–532, 534–535.

57. Thomas Aquinas: 'Filio attribuitur ipsa carnis assumptio, sed Spiritui Sancto attribuitur formatio corporis quod assumitur a Filio': *ST* IIIa, q. 32, a. 1, ad 1. See also above, note 6.

58. See *ST* IIIa, q. 7, a. 13, especially the first and the third reason. See also H. Mühlen, *Una mystica Persona, op. cit.* (note 50), p. 248; the author also quotes the Encyclical *Mystici Corporis* in this sense on p. 252.

ST PAUL[1]

An experience of the Holy Spirit is narrated in the Acts of the Apostles, but it is not combined with any form of teaching. The writings of Paul and John, on the other hand, contain teaching about the Spirit. It would obviously be impossible and in any case out of place to look closely here at all the texts in which the word *pneuma* is used by Paul. (It occurs 146 times, including 117 times in the great early epistles.) We will confine our attention here to the most important and significant uses of the term and deal with them systematically. This treatment is fully justified in the case of the great epistles, since Paul's thought does not reveal any real development.

1. Luke shows the Spirit which anointed Jesus at Nazareth, and especially at his baptism in the Jordan, as having been sent to the Church to animate it and to thrust it forward in its bearing of witness and its mission. Paul, on the other hand, proclaims the Gospel of God, which was promised in the old dispensation and has now become a reality. This Gospel, he claims, concerns God's Son, 'who was descended from David according to the flesh and designated Son of God in power according to the Spirit of holiness by his resurrection from the dead, Jesus Christ our Lord' (Rom 1:3–4; cf. 8:11).

Paul did not know Christ according to the flesh. He was certainly acquainted with the incarnation (see Phil 2:6ff.) and the crucifixion, which was for him the condition of salvation, but, even if he had any knowledge of the Church that came about at Pentecost, he makes no reference to it in his writings. His experience of the Spirit is exclusively and directly related to the event of Easter and to the resurrection and glorification of Jesus as Christ and Lord.

2. This gift of the Spirit, which is dependent on the redemption through the crucifixion, fulfils the promise made to Abraham. This promise is connected with Abraham's faith and is fulfilled, not in the economy of the law, but in that of faith. According to Gal 3, the crucifixion took place 'that in Christ Jesus the blessing of Abraham might come upon the gentiles, that we might receive the promise of the Spirit through faith' (verse 14) This is done 'in Jesus Christ', who is the one 'offspring of Abraham' and who takes us into himself (verses 16ff.), so that we are also 'sons' in him (verse 26) and heirs. Our inheritance as sons is the content of the promise (verses 18 and 29). This is accomplished by faith and when we have been 'baptized into Christ' we shall 'put on Christ' (verse 27).

3. This blessing of Abraham and this Spirit as the object of the promise come from God and also reach the gentiles through preaching, which arouses faith. The Spirit acts first and foremost in this proclamation of the Gospel. Paul here bears witness to his own experience as a 'minister of Christ Jesus to the gentiles in the service of the Gospel of God, so that the offering of the gentiles may be acceptable, sanctified by the Holy Spirit' (Rom 15:16). Paul also bears witness in other letters:

> Our Gospel came to you not only in word, but also in power and in the Holy Spirit. . . . And you became imitators of us and of the Lord, for you received the word in much affliction, with joy inspired by the Holy Spirit (1 Thess 1:5–6; Paul's first epistle).

> My speech and my message were not in plausible words of wisdom, but in demonstration of the Spirit and of power, that your faith might not rest in the wisdom of men, but in the power of God. . . . And we impart this (the gifts of God's grace) in words not taught by human wisdom, but taught by the Spirit, interpreting spiritual truths in spiritual language (1 Cor 2:4–5, 13).

> O foolish Galatians! . . . Did you receive the Spirit by works of the law or by hearing with faith? (Gal 3:2).

God is the absolute principle of the Christian's being. He is the norm and the source. Man has to be open to his activity and to allow the norm and the source to do their work. That work is done through faith. The minister of the word does that work by emptying himself of all his own wisdom so that everything can be from God.

4. By faith and baptism,[2] the believer begins a life in and through the Spirit, serving 'in the life of the Spirit' (Rom 7:6; 8:2). He enters and follows the way of a holy life: 'God chose you from the beginning to be saved through sanctification by the Spirit and belief in the truth' (2 Thess 2:13; 1 Thess 4:7–8; cf. 5:23). This life under the rule of the Spirit is described in Rom 8. It is the life of sons of God: 'For all who are led by the Spirit of God are sons of God. For you did not receive the spirit of slavery to fall back into fear, but you have received the spirit of sonship. When we cry "Abba, Father!" it is the Spirit himself bearing witness with our spirit that we are children of God and, if children, then heirs, heirs of God and fellow-heirs with Christ' (Rom 8:14–17; Gal 4:5–7).

Clearly, our inheritance is eschatological. The Holy Spirit is given to us in the present time as a 'guarantee of our inheritance until we acquire possession of it' (Eph 1:14; cf. 4:30). 'He who has prepared us for this very thing (= this future) is God, who has given us the Spirit as a guarantee' (2 Cor 5:5; 2:21–22).

This guarantee or earnest-money is real and fruitful, so long as we make it bear fruit: 'If we live by the Spirit, let us also walk by the Spirit' (Gal 5:25). It is possible, 'having begun with the Spirit', to end 'with the flesh' (Gal 3:3). Paul develops the theme of the struggle between the flesh and the Spirit as a conflict between two choices and two ways of life in the epistles that are concerned with the idea of justification by faith. 'Walk by the Spirit and do not gratify the desires of the flesh, for the desires of the flesh are against the Spirit and the desires of the Spirit are against the flesh; for these are opposed to each other' (Gal 5:16–17; cf. 23–25; Rom 7:5–6; 8:1, 17). Paul also lists the fruits of the flesh and the fruits of the Spirit.[3] The first fruit of the Spirit is love. It is more than simply the first in the order of the list. It is the all-embracing and creative principle and is in fact all. 'He who loves has fulfilled the law' (Rom 13:8). Paul, however, goes even further than this and teaches that the holy life is a communication of the holiness of God. The love of which he speaks is the love of God which 'has been poured into our hearts through the Holy Spirit which has been given to us' (Rom 5:5). This Spirit also makes us sons of God.

The Spirit who made the humanity of Jesus (who was 'descended from David (and from Mary) according to the flesh', Rom 1:3; Gal 4:4) a completed humanity of the Son of God (through his resurrection and glorification, Rom 1:4; Eph 1:20–22; Heb 5:5) does the same with us, who are of the flesh from the moment of our birth, and makes us sons of God, sons in the Son and called to inherit with him and to say after him: 'Abba, Father!' (Rom 8:14–17). The Spirit makes us sons of God in accordance with a truth that the status of adoption, which corresponds to our condition as creatures, situates but does not contradict. As Paul affirms, 'You are sons' (Gal 4:6). In this way, God himself communicates himself to us, makes himself active in us and thus enables us to perform actions of 'Christ in us',

31

which are the actions of sons.[4] This is particularly expressed in the cry invoking the name of God in the form that Jesus himself did it and taught us to do it: 'Because you are sons, God has sent the Spirit of his Son into our hearts, crying "Abba, Father!" ' (Gal 4:6). In a very unpredictable way, in which he continues to be Master, the Holy Spirit 'helps us in our weakness . . . and intercedes for us with sighs too deep for words' (Rom 8:26). In other words, he prays in us. This is not a case of God replacing us. The Protestant fear of a 'mystical' merging together of God and man—a fear that, in certain authors, is almost a morbid obsession—has been fully allayed.[5] God's substance does not take the place of our substance. There is a communication of dynamism or of an active faculty and we continue to act. This is clear from the parallel passage in Rom 8:14–15: 'All who are *led by* the Spirit of God are sons of God. . . . You have received the spirit of sonship and . . . cry, "Abba, Father!" '

This fine distinction is important, because this is a question of what the Fathers of the Church called 'deification'. The biblical texts and, in this context, those of Paul in particular have a power that is inescapable: 'Christ is all in all' (Col 3:11) and he lives in us (see Gal 2:20; Phil 1:21); 'In Christ Jesus you are all sons of God . . . you have put on Christ' (Gal 3:26–27) and finally God will be 'everything to everyone' (1 Cor 15:28). It has to be recognized that we are and will be the subjects of a quality of existence and activities which go back to God's sphere of existence and activity. This is the ultimate content of the promise and the real fruit of the Spirit and the principle of our eschatological life (see 1 Cor 15:44ff.).

5. Our life in Christ—or his life in us—is ecclesial. The Spirit plays a decisive part in building up the Church.[6] 'By one Spirit we were all baptized into one body' (1 Cor 12:13). The Spirit and the body are not opposed to each other—they have recourse to each other.[7] The 'body' of which Paul is speaking here is a visible reality, but it is not a physical or material body. Whoever is united to the glorious body of Christ and is permeated with the Spirit through faith, baptism and the bread and wine of the Last Supper is spiritually—and therefore really—a member of Christ and forms a body with him at the level of the life of a son which promises God's inheritance.[8] The captivity epistles add to this concrete view, which is rather lacking in theoretical structure, a theology of the glorified Christ as the head of the body that is the Church (Eph 1:20–23) and even of Christ as enjoying an absolute cosmic primacy (Col 1:15–20).

The body of Christ formed by believers on earth has to be built up (1 Cor 3:9; Eph 2:20; 4:12). What is built in this way becomes a 'dwelling place of God in the Spirit' (Eph 2:22), a 'spiritual house' (1 Pet 2:5ff.; Phil 3:3), which is a temple where spiritual worship is offered to God. 'Do you not know that you are God's temple and that God's Spirit dwells in you?' (1 Cor 3:16; 6:19; 2 Cor 6:16). This rich and profound theme of the indwelling of the Holy Spirit in our bodies and the community that we form is the other side of the balance in a theology affirming God's immanence whilst avoiding confusion. The Spirit can be the principle of communication and communion between God and us and between us and our fellow-men, because of what he is as Spirit—sovereign and subtle, unique in all men and uniting persons without encroaching on their freedom or their inner lives. (See 2 Cor 13:13: *koinōnia tou hagiou pneumatos*; subjective genitive, indicating the communion or 'fellowship' of which the Spirit is the principle.)

Christ is similarly in me and is my life, but he remains himself and I continue to be myself. This indwelling or immanence is expressed in the depth of its intimacy by the fact that the Spirit is said to have been 'sent into our hearts' (see Gal 4:6; 2 Cor 1:22; 3:2, 3; Rom 5:5; cf. 2:29; 8:27; Eph 3:17; 2 Thess 3:5).

Paul also compares the fruit of his apostolate to a 'letter from Christ, written not with ink, but with the Spirit of the living God . . . on tablets of human hearts' (2 Cor 3:2–3).[9] In this image, he compares a ministry of the Spirit and its fruit in the Church with a ministry of writing letters. This gives an eschatological range to the Christian ministry—it reaches the definitive and absolute limit of the communication that God establishes between us and his good things and himself. This means that the minister has to be quite translucent and simply the means of an activity that goes beyond his own power and even the measure of his initial understanding of it.

This ministry of the Spirit is first and foremost something that has to be carried out by the apostle, who lays the foundation (1 Cor 3:10; Rom 15:20). Among the ministers whom God calls or 'places' are the apostles, whom Paul always places first (1 Cor 12:28; Eph 4:11). After these come the 'prophets' and these are followed by different 'gifts', 'ministries', 'ways of acting' or 'ways of working'. These are the terms that are employed as almost equivalent to those used by Paul in reference to the one Spirit, the one Lord or the one God, for example, in 1 Cor 12:4ff. It is, however, mainly to the Spirit that Paul traces back the various gifts which reveal his activity 'for the common good'. This chapter in the first letter to the Corinthians contains a truth and a contemporary value of remarkable importance for the modern Church, and we shall be examining it in depth at a later stage. Here, we shall restrict ourselves to a few paragraphs on the situation in the church of Corinth.

6. The situation in the church of Corinth can be outlined as follows.[10] Corinth was a great and intensely busy town, in which there were many cross-currents. Paul spent eighteen months there. The Christians of Corinth presented a spectacle of abundant vitality. They were 'enriched with all speech and all knowledge' and 'not lacking in any spiritual gift' (1 Cor 1:5, 7). This vitality, however, was full of dangers. Several of these Corinthian Christians believed that they were living in the last age and were therefore

beyond the stage of the difficult struggle between the spirit and the flesh.[11] They all rejoiced in the gifts of the Spirit, but did not care about serving the community or the unity of Christians. This is why there were sects and divisions among them: ' "I belong to Paul"—"I belong to Apollos"—"I belong to Cephas"—"I belong to Christ" ' (1 Cor 1:12), court cases between Christians (chapter 6) and individuals asserting themselves at meetings and even at eucharistic assemblies (11:17ff.). There were also anarchistic tendencies in the Corinthian community in the manifestations of the gifts of the Spirit, the *pneumatika* such as speaking in tongues and prophesying, in which members of the community took such delight.[12] They were intoxicated and almost bewitched by these manifestations of an external kind and, although they continued to ask questions about sexual morality (see, for example, 7:1), they were undoubtedly lax in their behaviour (see chapter 5; 6:12; 10:23).[13]

Paul discussed all this, both at the practical level and at the level of fundamental truths, although he made no attempt to restrain the Corinthians' exuberant manifestations of the Spirit. He insisted, however, that there could be no Church of the Spirit based either on individual inspiration or on a greedy personal enjoyment of the gifts of the Spirit. The apostle traces everything back in the first place to Christ. Christ is the 'all' of Christianity.[14] All the activity of the Spirit goes back to this 'all', which is the criterion of the active presence of that Spirit: 'No one speaking by the Spirit of God ever says "Jesus be cursed!" and no one can say "Jesus is Lord" except by the Holy Spirit' (12:3).

In the second place, he traces everything back to the Spirit himself as the sovereign subject. The Corinthians attached more importance to the gifts of the Spirit which they enjoyed than to the Spirit himself as the transcendent subject who is above all personal 'spiritual experience' and, by his gifts, builds up the Church as the Body of Christ.

In the third place, Paul teaches that the gifts of the Spirit and their use are for the 'common good' (12:7) and the building-up of the Body and that this is done by the diversity of the gifts given according to grace (*echontes de charismata kata tēn charin . . . diaphora*; Rom 12:6). He develops this idea in chapter 12, continuing it in chapter 13, in which he expatiates on charity (we should not allow the lyricism of this chapter to make us forget the critical aspect), and then returns to the *pneumatika* which the Corinthian Christians preferred—speaking in tongues and 'prophesying' (chapter 14).

He provides criteria for the healthy use of these gifts of the Spirit. He stresses that, if the Christian is too attached to his individual and immediate experience of the manifestations of the Spirit, he will place an excessive value on their external and extraordinary forms. In the first place, he maintains, they are not simply gifts among other gifts. They have to be appreciated according to the criterion of the 'common good' and, seen in this light, speaking in tongues is the last in importance. They have to use it as responsible men. This means, in concrete terms, that there are three demands: (a) discipline in the community (14:27–33); (b) the need for others to understand (14:14ff.)—speaking in tongues is not simply a means of self-expression; it is the expression of an intelligible word that is useful to the community; (c) discernment.[15]

We shall consider these questions more closely when we come to discuss the present-day movement of Renewal in the Spirit. At present, however, all that is necessary is to define more precisely the meaning of *charisma* in Paul's writings. With the exception of 1 Pet 4:10, which bears a remarkable resemblance to Paul, this word occurs seventeen times in the New Testament and always in the Pauline letters. For the most part, it is used in 1 Cor and Rom.

A great deal has been written about the charisms. I have myself consulted dozens of books and articles. Very many of them contain two serious defects. On the one hand, there is a false contrast in many of these publications, which is elevated to a false problem, between 'charisms' and 'institution' or institutional functions. This goes back to Harnack, Sohm and Troeltsch.[16] Theological problems of pneumatology and ecclesiology are reduced to the level of the sociology of religion. On the other hand, 'charism' is often regarded as a particular gift of the Spirit representing a special register of activities. (These two defects are, of course, closely linked.) I have myself at times accepted this view, which Chevallier calls the 'theory of charisms'. The same author has also remarked that 'to state, as Paul does here very forcefully, that the charisms *are* gifts of the pneuma has never meant that the *word* charisma *means* "gifts of the pneuma" '.[17]

If these charisms are connected with the Holy Spirit, as they are in 1 Cor 12:4–11, then they must refer in the first place, simply because of their name, to God's *charis* or grace. *Charisma* and *charis* are compared textually in 1 Cor 1:7; Rom 5:15 and 12:6. The last text is particularly illuminating: *echontes de charismata kata tēn charin dotheisan hēmin diaphora*, 'having gifts (charisms) that differ according to the grace given to us'. The charisms are differing gifts depending on one single grace. They are the gifts of salvation and of Christian life (see also Rom 5:15–16; 1 Cor 3:10) and of eternal life (Rom 6:23). As they correspond in the case of each Christian to his vocation, they closely resemble what has been called a 'grace of state', provided the idea of vocation is included in it (see 1 Cor 7:7).[18]

Paul says of these gifts or talents that come from God's grace firstly that they are distributed by the Spirit 'according to his will' and secondly that they are different. He gives several lists which do not coincide exactly with each other and which do not claim to be exhaustive. He says thirdly that the Spirit gives these various gifts 'for the common good', that is, so that they can be used to build up the community of the Church or the life of the Body of

Christ. Fourthly and finally, he raises above all these gifts the gift or charism of love, and puts in their proper place two 'gifts of the Spirit' or *pneumatika* (12:1 and 14:1) which the Corinthians valued very highly: speaking in tongues and prophecy.[19]

This way of understanding the charisms as different gifts of grace for the building-up of the Church (cf. 1 Pet 4:10) is also to be found in the apostolic Fathers,[20] John Chrysostom,[21] the language of the liturgy[22] and at times in the writings of the mediaeval theologians.[23]

Very soon, however, and too often even until quite recently, the charisms were seen as graces—*gratis datae* in the sense of the Scholastic tradition[24]— and even as extraordinary gifts of the kind that works miracles or causes healings. The apologists of the second and third centuries, such as Irenaeus and Origen,[25] Theodore of Mopsuestia and Theodoret at the end of the fourth and during the first half of the fifth centuries[26] tended to think this. Leo XIII at the end of the nineteenth century spoke of extraordinary and miraculous gifts when he spoke of charisms.[27] It was at this period too that German Protestant critics emphasized the fallacious contrast and even opposition between free charisms and institutional functions.[28] Most Catholics rejected this opposition, but unfortunately all too often accepted a contrast and a state of tension between charism and office.[29] This was all the more difficult to avoid in view of the fact that history pointed to the existence of tension between free inspiration and the institution, as we shall see later. A place has to be made for this in any true ecclesiology, but it is important not to let it influence Paul's teaching about charisms so much that it changes the real meaning of those gifts according to the apostle.

These charisms, in the sense in which Paul uses them, have made a remarkable return to modern Catholic theology. Pius XII spoke about them in the encyclical *Mystici Corporis*.[30] The Second Vatican Council recognized their value and gave them an important theological place.[31] Since then, in conjunction with a renewed theology of ministries, including that of the bishop and the priest, they have been reintroduced into ecclesiology as gifts or talents placed by the Spirit at the service of the building-up of the community and the Body of Christ.[32]

We do, however, still have further work to do in order to give the charisms their full place. Let me do no more than simply point to an essay by W. C. van Unnik, in which he explains the meaning of the liturgical formula: 'The Lord be with you—And with your spirit'.[33] This, the author claims, can be compared with statements made by Paul in Gal 6:18; Philem 25; 2 Tim 4:22. The words do not simply mean: 'And with you', which would be no more than an exchange of religious wishes helping to create the spiritual space of the celebration. They mean more than this. The formula 'The Lord is (be) with . . .' is frequently used in the Old Testament and it is often concerned with an action that has to be done according to God's plan and is connected with the presence of the Spirit in the one who has to perform this action. In the New Testament and early Christianity, the Spirit is particularly active in prayer and the worshipping assembly.[34] In the brief dialogue between the minister and the community recorded by Hippolytus (*Apostolic Tradition*, 4; 7; 22; 26), the presence of the Spirit has to be ensured so that the liturgical action can take place; hence the words: The Lord be with you, gifted as you are for that purpose with the charism of the Spirit. According to the Fathers, the necessary charism was conferred on the priest at ordination. Nothing, however, takes place automatically, and every spiritual activity requires an epiclesis.[35]

7. The Pneuma and Christ:
(a) The Pneuma, as given to us, relates entirely to Christ. Paul was so dedicated to Christ and so full of him that he was able, as Büchsel has pointed out (*op. cit.* (note 1 below), p. 303), to present what constituted his life without even mentioning the Spirit. It is a question of believing and then of confessing, with one's lips and in one's life, that 'Jesus is Lord' (Rom 10:9). It is the Spirit that enables us to do that: 'No one speaking by the Spirit of God ever says "Jesus be cursed!" and no one can say "Jesus is Lord" except by the Holy Spirit' (1 Cor 12:3)—this is a most important text and we shall be returning to it later.

The Spirit makes it possible for us to know, recognize and experience Christ.[36] This is not simply a doctrinal statement. It is an existential reality which comes from a gift and involves us in our lives. There is no 'Body of the Holy Spirit'—there is a 'Body of Christ'. Is the Spirit not the Spirit of Christ (Rom 8:9; Phil 1:19), the Spirit of the Lord (2 Cor 3:17) and the 'Spirit of his Son' (Gal 4:6)? Irenaeus pointed out that the Spirit brought about the *communicatio Christi* (or *commutatio*, as Sagnard writes), that is, the intimacy of union with Christ.[37] As regards the content of a work of the Spirit as opposed to a work of Christ, it is neither autonomous nor different.
(b) It has often been stressed that very many effects have been attributed either to Christ or to the Spirit and that the formulae 'in Christ' and 'in the Spirit' are indiscriminately applied to both.[38] It is not difficult to find a number of examples:

So that in him (Christ) we might become the righteousness of God (2 Cor 5:21)	Righteousness and peace and joy in the Holy Spirit (Rom 14:17)
Justified in Christ (Gal 2:17)	Justified in the name of the Lord Jesus Christ and in the Spirit of our God (1 Cor 6:11)
Those who are in Christ Jesus. . . . If Christ is in you (Rom 8:1, 10)	But you are not in the flesh, you are in the Spirit, if the Spirit of God really dwells in you (Rom 8:9)

37

Rejoice in the Lord (Phil 3:1)	Joy in the Holy Spirit (Rom 14:17)
The love of God in Christ Jesus (Rom 8:39)	Your love in the Spirit (Col 1:8)
The peace of God . . . will keep your hearts and your minds in Christ Jesus (Phil 4:7)	Righteousness and peace and joy in the Holy Spirit (Rom 14:17)
Sanctified in Christ Jesus (1 Cor 1:2, 30)	An offering . . . sanctified by the Holy Spirit (Rom 15:16; cf. 2 Thess 2:13)
Speaking in Christ (2 Cor 2:17)	Speaking by the Spirit (1 Cor 12:3)
Fullness of life in him (Christ) (Col 2:10)	Filled with the Spirit (Eph 5:18)
One body in Christ (Rom 12:5)— baptized into Christ (Gal 3:27)	By one Spirit we were all baptized into one body (1 Cor 12:13)
In whom (Christ) the whole structure . . . grows into a holy temple in the Lord (Eph 2:21)	Becoming a dwelling place of God in the Spirit (Eph 2:22)

In several texts, Christ and the Spirit are combined in the same statement: 1 Cor 6:11; 12:13; Rom 9:1.

It is important, however, to go further and consider four other texts:

The Gospel concerning his Son, who was descended from David according to the flesh and designated Son of God in power according to the Spirit of holiness by his resurrection from the dead, Jesus Christ our Lord (Kyrios) (Rom 1:3–4).[39]

The first man Adam became a living being (= an animal being endowed with life); the last Adam became a life-giving spirit (= a spiritual being giving life) (1 Cor 15:45).

If the Spirit of him who raised Jesus from the dead dwells in you, he who raised Christ Jesus from the dead will give life to your mortal bodies also through his Spirit which dwells in you (Rom 8:11).

This Jesus God raised up. . . . Being therefore exalted at the right hand of God and having received from the Father the promise of the Holy Spirit, he has poured it out (Acts 2:32–33).

These texts raise us to the eschatological level. Paul reveals the fantastic perspective at the end of time: 'When all things are subjected to him, then the Son himself will also be subjected to him who put all things under him, that God may be everything to everyone' (1 Cor 15:28). The means of achieving this, however, is for Jesus to be glorified in his humanity, in such a way that he has a humanity and an activity of the Son of God and that these are assumed by a divine condition.[40] It is the Spirit, as the content and the end of the Promise and therefore as an eschatological gift, who establishes 'Jesus', that is, Christ in his crucified humanity, in his condition as the 'Son of God in power' and as Kyrios. The Spirit permeates him and makes him a *Pneuma zōopoioun*, a spiritual being giving life. It is therefore not difficult to understand why Paul attributes activities and consequences in the Christian life either to Christ or to the Spirit, to such an extent that he apparently identifies the two.

(c) He says in fact: 'When a man turns to the Lord, the veil is removed (from the eyes of Moses' disciples). Now the Lord is Spirit and where the Spirit of the Lord is, there is freedom' (2 Cor 3:16–17). Ingo Hermann has devoted a whole monograph to a study of this text.[41] He dismisses those interpretations that claim that the Spirit is the Lord (since the Lord is Christ) or the Lord (Jesus) is made of spirit as of substance. The statement, he believes, has to be understood in the sense of existential experience. In other words, we experience the Lord Jesus as Spirit, or what we experience as Spirit is in reality the Lord Jesus glorified. As a whole, exegetes are in agreement that there is no identification in Paul between the Lord and the Pneuma and that the two are not confused in his writings. The evidence of this is that Paul speaks, in the text considered here, of the 'Spirit of the Lord': 'The distinction made in verse 17b between *kurios* (Lord) and *pneuma* shows clearly that the two persons are not identified in verse 17a, but that the mode of existence of the *kurios* is defined by the word *pneuma*. In speaking of *pneuma kuriou*, Paul is defining his mode of existence and pointing to the power in which he is coming forward to meet his community.'[42] The apostle, then, is pointing to the sphere of existence and activity of the glorified Lord. That sphere is the eschatological and divine sphere of the Spirit. This means that, from the functional point of view, the Lord and his Spirit perform the same work, but in the duality of their rôles.

There are some forty ternary and even Trinitarian formulae in Paul's writings, but there are no precise dogmatic statements about the Trinity of persons in a unity of substance. In any attempt to consider the question at the level and in the categories of the Trinitarian dogma (and the Christological dogma!) it is necessary to go back firstly to the biblical datum (John) of consubstantiality and circumincession, according to which the divine Persons are in each other,[43] and secondly to the idea of the raising of Jesus' humanity by his glorification to the quality of Lord and Son of God in power. I have already said a little about this.

8. The possible personality of the Spirit is discussed by Büchsel in part of chapter XVI of his book (see note 1 below). The Spirit is not a simple force in Paul's writings, but God himself insofar as he is communicated, present and active in others. The Spirit is God as love that is active in us (Rom 5:5). Is it

possible to go further than this and find indicators pointing in the direction of a personality of the Spirit in this Trinitarian manifestation and communication of God? In the following passage, V. Warnach (*op. cit.* (below, note 1), pp. 185–186) recognizes these indicators and gives them the greatest possible importance:

There are many passages which give us the sense of a personality that is unique to the divine Pneuma who 'searches . . . even the depths of God' (1 Cor 2:10ff.) or is 'sent into our hearts' (Gal 4:6). The Pneuma enters actively into the history of salvation or, in what he enables us to know of God's will to save us (1 Cor 2:10–14), establishes a 'fellowship' between God and ourselves and between us and our fellow-men (2 Cor 13:13). The Pneuma also 'bears witness with our spirit that we are children of God' (Rom 8:16) and cries in us: 'Abba, Father!' (Gal 4:6). Finally, the same Pneuma also intercedes for us with God (Rom 8:26ff.).

These are texts which cannot be understood as purely figurative and which must indicate that a subject acting in this way must be an autonomous, free person. This personal character is particularly obvious in 1 Cor 12:11, in which Paul shows the Spirit distributing the gifts of grace 'as he wills'. Paul also sees the divine Pneuma as a person when he speaks of his dwelling in believers (1 Cor 3:16; 6:19). God is present in the Pneuma as he is present in the Son, because he is God himself (1 Cor 3:16; cf. 14–25). As the Spirit 'which is from God' (1 Cor 2:12), he is a gift to us (Rom 5:5), not as a thing, but as someone who gives, since, in the Pneuma, God gives himself (1 Thess 4:8).

Finally, the triadic formulae in which the Pneuma is presented as equal to God (*ho Theos* = the Father) and Christ (see especially 1 Cor 12:4–6; 2 Cor 13:13) do not point to a simple community of activity, but indicate an equality of three Persons in being.

NOTES

1. Very many books and articles have been written on this subject, but I will mention only H. B. Swete, *The Holy Spirit in the New Testament* (London, 1909), I, chapters IV-VI, pp. 169–253; F. Büchsel, *Der Geist Gottes im Neuen Testament* (Gütersloh, 1926), chapters XIII–XVII, pp. 267–451; E. Schweizer, '*pneuma*', *TDNT*, VI, esp. pp. 415–437; P. Gächter, 'Zum Pneumabegriff des hl. Paulus', *ZKT*, 53 (1929), 345–408; H.-D. Wendland and V. Warnach have published under the same title 'Das Wirken des Hl. Geistes in den Gläubigen nach Paulus', *Pro Veritate. Ein theologischer Dialog. Festgabe L. Jaeger und W. Stählin*, ed. E. Schlink and H. Volk (Münster and Kassel, 1963), pp. 133–156 and 156–202; M.-A. Chevallier, *Esprit de Dieu, paroles d'hommes. Le rôle de l'Esprit dans les ministères de la parole selon l'apôtre Paul (Bibl. théol.)* (Neuchâtel, 1966), with an extensive bibliography.

2. 1 Cor 1:13f. shows that baptism accompanies accession to faith, even if Paul regarded himself as a minister of faith rather than as a minister of baptism. See also Gal 3:27; 1 Cor 6:11; 12:13; Rom 6:3; Tit 3:5–7; Col 2:12.

3. Gal 5:19–23; 2 Cor 6:6; Rom 6:19–22; 8:6, 12, 14, 17, also 15, 13; Eph 5:9. It is also in this context that those passages in which Paul speaks of 'a spirit of . . .' revelation, wisdom

(Eph 1:17), gentleness (1 Cor 4:21), faith (2 Cor 4:13) and adoption (Rom 8:15) should be situated. See Swete, *op. cit.* (note 1), p. 234.

4. See Phil 2:5, which can be translated literally as 'This think in you which also in Christ Jesus'.

5. E. Schweizer stresses the fact that Paul expressed himself in Greek categories and therefore substantially, but that he thought in biblical and Semitic ways and therefore 'forcefully' or dynamically: *'pneuma'*, *TDNT*, VI, pp. 424–432. This dynamism of God is in the Christian and is a part of him, but it does not come from him or from his own being; *ibid.*, pp. 428, 439 note 731, 441. In addition to the prayer that the Spirit makes us utter, there is also the prayer that he himself utters in us: see K. Niederwimmer, 'Das Gebet des Geistes, Rom. 8. 26', *TZ*, 20 (1964), 252–265.

6. This question has unfortunately been very little studied by exegetes. There is nothing about it, for example, in E. Schweizer's article *'pneuma'* in *TDNT*. It has aroused more interest among Catholic scholars, but these have been mainly dogmatic theologians, who have approached it from the angle of the mystical Body, rather than exegetes.

7. G. Martelet, 'Le mystère du corps et de l'Esprit dans le Christ ressuscité et dans l'Eglise', *Verbum Caro*, 45 (1958), 31; P.-A. Harlé, 'Le Saint-Esprit et l'Eglise chez S. Paul', *ibid.*, 74 (1965), 13–29.

8. The body of Christ permeated by the Spirit: Rom 1:4; 1 Cor 15:45; see also Phil 3:21; union with the body of Christ: 1 Cor 6:15–17; Col 3:1–4; baptism: 1 Cor 12:13; body and cup of the Last Supper: 1 Cor 11:23–29. See also P. Benoît, 'Corps, Tête et Plérôme dans les épîtres de la captivité', *RB*, 63 (1956), 5–44; also republished in *Exégèse et Théologie* (Paris, 1961), II, pp. 107–153.

9. See M.-A. Chevallier, *op. cit.* (note 1), Parts I and II; K. Prümm, *Diakonia Pneumatos: Der Zweite Korintherbrief als Zugang zur apostolischen Botschaft. Auslegung und Theologie*, II: *Theologie des 2. Korintherbriefes*, 2 vols (Rome, 1960 and 1962).

10. F. Büchsel: see below, note 13; L. Cerfaux, *L'Eglise des Corinthiens* (Paris, 1946); M.-A. Chevallier, *op. cit.*, pp. 22ff., 171ff.

11. Hence such statements as 1 Cor 4:8: 'Already you are filled! Already you have become rich! Without us you have become kings!'; 4:10: 'We are fools for Christ's sake, but you are wise in Christ. We are weak, but you are strong. You are held in honour, but we in disrepute'; 1:7: 'So that you are not lacking in any spiritual gift, as you wait for the revealing of our Lord Jesus Christ'.

12. *Pneumatika*: 1 Cor 12:1; 14:1. I have here followed M.-A. Chevallier's exegesis, *op. cit.*, pp. 148, 167, 172ff. Hence: 'Since you are eager for manifestations of the Spirit, strive to excel in building up the Church' (14:12); 'Come to your right mind' (15:34).

13. F. Büchsel devoted chapter XV, pp. 367–395, of his book (see note 1 above) to Paul's 'pneumatic' adversaries at Corinth. He saw them as 'inflated' with pride (the word *phusioun* occurs six times in 1 Cor) and intoxicated with freedom, although love was the supreme value. These adversaries were, Büchsel believed, Christians who had come from Judaism. They were not Judaizers, as in Galilee, but 'pneumatic' Christians. Those who 'belonged to Christ' (1:12) appealed, Büchsel thought (p. 392), to the Christ of goodness and anti-legalism. This, of course, is Büchsel's own interpretation.

14. 1 Cor is addressed to 'the church of God which is at Corinth, to those sanctified in Christ Jesus'. Christ, then, is the only foundation (3:11); he is all to us (1:30–31; 10:4; 15); he is the judge (4:4–5). We are his (3:23); we live in him and from him (1:9; 4:15–17; 6:11). He is Christ crucified and our wisdom is the wisdom of the cross (1:23ff; 2:2). The spiritual man is the man who has 'the mind of Christ' (2:16).

15. See 1 Cor 12:1–3, 10; 14:29; 2 Thess 5:15–22. For these three demands, see M.-A. Chevallier, *op. cit* (note 1), pp. 181ff. For the second, see also G. Sauter, 'Gewissheit oder vergewissernde Sicherung? Zum Verhältnis von Geist und Vernunft', *Erfahrung und Theologie des Heiligen Geistes*, ed. C. Heitmann and H. Mühlen (Hamburg and Munich, 1974), pp. 192–213.

16. See U. Brockhaus, *Charisma und Amt. Die paulinische Charismenlehre auf dem Hintergrund der frühchristlichen Gemeindefunktionen* (Wuppertal, 1972); M.-A. Chevallier, *op. cit.* (note 1), pp. 210–213.

17. *Ibid.*, p. 155.

18. This is fundamentally M.-A. Chevallier's explanation, *op. cit.*, pp. 139ff.; see also O. Kuss's disciple J. Hainz, *Ekklesia, Structuren paulinischer Gemeinde-Theologie und Gemeinde-Ordnung* (Regensburg, 1972), pp. 333–335, 338; H. Conzelmann, '*charisma*', *TDNT*, IX, pp. 402–406; B. N. Wambacq, 'Le mot "charisme" ', *NRT*, 97 (1975), 345–355. A.-M. de Monléon writes, in 'L'expérience des charismes, manifestations de l'Esprit en vue du bien commun', *Istina*, 21 (1976), 340–373, on p. 342: 'The word charisma . . . has a great breadth of meaning. With perhaps a special emphasis on the gratuitous nature of the gift, it points to the whole gift of grace made by God (Rom 5:15–16), from eternal life (6:23) to healing (1 Cor 12:30) and from the grace given in marriage (7:7) to the ministry (1 Tim 4:14).'

19. This is Chevallier's way of interpreting the *pneumatika*, *op. cit.*, pp. 148, 167; it is also Hainz's.

20. See the references in Chevallier, *op. cit.*, pp. 164ff.

21. See A.-M. Ritter, *Charisma im Verständnis des Joannes Chrysostomos und seiner Zeit. Ein Beitrag zur Erforschung der griechisch-orientalischen Ekklesiologie in der Frühzeit der Reichskirche* (Göttingen, 1972); cf. G.-M. de Durand, *RSPT*, 59 (1975), 460–464.

22. See, for example, the phrases *carismata coelestia* and *carismata gratiarum* in prayers of the period and the formulae 136 and 137 in G. Manz, *Ausdrucksformen der lateinischen Liturgiesprache* (Beuron, 1941), pp. 96–97.

23. I am thinking here of a text such as that by William of Auxerre: 'credidit Abel Christum fore plenum charismatibus . . . et ita per fidem in ipsum fluxit aliquid de plenitudine Christi sicut in nos per fidem': *Summa Aurea* lib. III, tr. 1, c. 4, sol. ad obj. Of all the charisms discussed by Paul, the Fathers and the mediaeval theologians believed that those of knowledge and wisdom were of permanent value in the Church: see S. Tromp, *Corpus Christi quod est Ecclesia*, III: *De Spiritu Christi anima* (Rome, 1960), pp. 342ff.

24. Even M. Zerwick does this in his excellent *Analysis philologica Novi Testamenti Graeci*, under Rom 12:6; 1 Cor 12:1; 14:1; in the last two places, he even identifies *pneumatika* and *charismata*.

25. See M.-A. Chevallier, *op. cit.* (note 1), p. 165; S. Tromp, *op. cit.* (note 23), pp. 336ff.

26. See A.-M. Ritter, *op. cit.* (note 21).

27. According to the Encyclical *Divinum illud munus* of 9 May 1897 on the Holy Spirit, 'Charisms are only extraordinary gifts obtained by the Holy Spirit in exceptional circumstances and destined above all to prove the divine origin of the Church. They do not form part of the structure of the Church, which is founded exclusively on the authority of the apostles, which is ordinarily the instrument that is both sufficient and adequate to satisfy everything that calls for the building up of the Church and the Church's life.' See also the letter *Testem Benevolentiae* of 22 January 1899 to the Archbishop of Baltimore.

28. See above, note 16.

29. The full history of this has still to be written. I will only mention a few important recent publications: J. Brosch, *Charismen und Ämter in der Urkirche* (Bonn, 1951); *idem*, 'Amt und Charisma', *LTK*, 2nd ed., I (1957), cols 455–457; I. Gomá Civit, *Ubi Spiritus Dei, illic Ecclesia et omnis gratia* (Barcelona, 1954); García Extremeño, 'Iglesia, Jerarquía y Carisma', *La Ciencia Tomista*, 89 (1959), 3–64; P. Rodríguez, 'Carisma e institución en la Iglesia', *Studium* (1966), pp. 489ff.

30. 17 and 47: *AAS*, 35 (1943), 200 and 215. See also D. Iturrioz, 'Carismas. De la encíclica "Mystici Corporis" al Concilio Vaticano', *Estudios Eclesiásticos*, 30 (1956), 481–494. The editor of the encyclical, S. Tromp, produced a 'systematic' study of the charisms: *op. cit.* (note 23), pp. 295–326.

31. See especially *Lumen Gentium*, 12 and *Apostolicam Actuositatem*, 3. See also H. Schür-

mann, 'Les charismes spirituels', *L'Eglise de Vatican II* (*Unam Sanctam*, 51b) (Paris, 1966), pp. 541–573; D. Iturrioz, 'Los carismas en la Iglesia. La doctrina carismal en la Const. "Lumen Gentium" ', *Estudios Eclesiásticos*, 43 (1968), 181–233; G. Rombaldi, 'Uso e significato di "Carisma" nel Vaticano II', *Greg*, 55 (1974), 141–162.

32. See my bulletins and those of H.-M. Legrand, the reviews of journals and the tables in the last ten years of *RSPT*, especially C. R. de Dias, H. Küng, G. Hasenhüttl, H. Mühlen, A.-M. Ritter etc.

33. W. C. van Unnik, 'Dominus vobiscum: The Background of a Liturgical Formula', *New Testament Essays. Studies in Memory of T. W. Manson*, ed. A. J. R. Higgins (Manchester, 1959), pp. 270–305.

34. In prayer: Rom 8:15ff., 26; 1 Cor 14:14ff., 25; Eph 5:18. In the assembly: *Apostolic Tradition*, 31, 35; *Didache* X, 7; Hermas (M. Dibelius, *Der Hirt des Hermas* (1928), Excursus, pp. 517ff., on pneumatology).

35. Van Unnik, *op. cit.*, pp. 273, 299, note 21, quotes John Chrysostom, *In 2 Tim., Hom.* 10, 3 (*PG* 62, 659), and Theodore of Mopsuestia, *Commentary on the Lord's Prayer and on the Sacraments of Baptism and the Eucharist* (ed. A. Mingana, Cambridge, 1933), pp. 90ff.

36. And Christ enables us to know the Father: see Irenaeus, *Dem.* 7; *Adv. haer.* IV, 25, 5; V, 36, 2 (*PG* 7, 1035, 1223; ed. W. W. Harvey, II, 216, 429).

37. *Adv. haer.* III, 24, 1 (*PG* 7, 966; Harvey, II, 131; F. Sagnard, *SC* 34, pp. 398–401). A. Rousseau and L. Doutreleau (*SC* 311, pp. 471, 472) have restored *communicatio* and translated it as 'communion with Christ'.

38. A. Deissmann has given very many examples, including some that are not very convincing: *Paul* (Eng. tr; London and New York, 1926), p. 140. It is interesting in this context to note that the wisdom of the disciples when on trial is attributed to Christ in Lk 21:12–15 and to the Holy Spirit in Mt 10:18–20 and Mk 13:10–12.

39. See J. Dupont, 'Filius meus es tu. L'interprétation du Ps II, 7 dans le Nouveau Testament', *RSR*, 35 (1948), 522–543; M.-E. Boismard, 'Constitué Fils de Dieu (Rm 1, 4)', *RB*, 60 (1953), 5–17; M. Hengel, *Jésus, Fils de Dieu (Lectio divina*, 94) (Paris, 1977), pp. 98ff.

40. See, for example, E. Schillebeeckx, *Christ the Sacrament of Encounter with God* (London and New York, 1963), esp. pp. 13ff., 33f., 65ff.; my own *Un peuple messianique* (Paris, 1975), pp. 35ff.; W. Thüsing, *Per Christum in Deum. Studien zum Verhältnis von Christozentrik und Theozentrik in den paulinischen Hauptbriefen* (Münster, 1965).

41. Ingo Hermann, *Kyrios und Pneuma. Studien zur Christologie der paulinischen Hauptbriefe* (Munich, 1961). C. F. D. Moule has taken up a very similar position in '2 Cor 3, 18ᵇ', *Neues Testament und Geschichte. Oscar Cullmann zum 70. Geburtstag*, ed. H. Baltensweiler and B. Reicke (Zürich, 1972), pp. 231–237. The identification is not at the ontological level, but, in the Christian experience, the same thing is expressed by 'Spirit of God', 'Spirit of Christ' and 'Christ'.

42. E. Schweizer, '*pneuma*', *TDNT*, VI, p. 419, with references. See also F. Büchsel, *op. cit.* (note 1), p. 409 (dynamic unity); M.-A. Chevallier, *op. cit.* (*ibid.*), pp. 95ff. (the spirit of the Kyrios introduces the Kyrios into the heart of man); B. Schneider, *Dominus autem Spiritus est* (Rome, 1951); L. Cerfaux, *Christ in the Theology of St Paul* (Eng. tr.; New York/ Edinburgh and London, 1959), pp. 284ff., esp. 293–296; J.-R. Villalon, *Sacrements dans l'Esprit* (Paris, 1977), pp. 286ff. I have not read J. D. G. Dunn, '2 Cor III, 17 "The Lord is the Spirit" ', *JTS*, new series, 21 (1970), 309–320. For the patristic and the modern interpretations, see J. Lebreton, *Les origines du dogme de la Trinité*, I (5th ed., Paris, 1919), pp. 567ff.; K. Prümm, 'Die katholische Auslegung von 2 Kor 3.17 in den letzten vier Jahrhunderten', *Bib*, 31 (1950), 316–345, 459–482; 32 (1951), 1–24.

43. See Jerome, *Epist.* 18, 4 (*PL* 22, 363); Cyril of Alexandria, *Comm. in Ioan.* lib. IX (*PG* 74, 261); L. Malevez, *NRT*, 67 (1945), 403–404; F. Malmberg, *Ein Leib, ein Geist* (Paderborn, 1960), pp. 150, 163.

SAINT LUKE: ACTS [1]

All the evangelists stress the existence of a dynamic continuity between Christ and the Church.[2] This continuity is the fulfilment of what God had promised from the beginning in accordance with his plan of grace.[3] It is especially noticeable in Luke's Acts, in which it appears under the sign of the Holy Spirit. This Spirit, who, according to Luke, brought Jesus to life in Mary's womb, also brings the Church into the world. The same Spirit who sent Jesus on his mission after his anointing in baptism also animates the apostolate 'from Jerusalem to the ends of the earth'. The central episode in this history is the gentiles' entry into the Church as sanctioned by the council which met at Jerusalem. Together with Cornelius and his family and the gentiles converted by Paul on his missions, they became the people of God. In other words, the *ethnē* became *laos* (Acts 15:14). The 'nations'—terrestrial realities of the 'flesh'—became a people—a reality of the economy of salvation.

In Acts, the Holy Spirit is the dynamic principle of the testimony that ensures the spread of the Church. This is why he appears at Pentecost, which undoubtedly marks the beginning. Luke's account incorporates a tradition that interpreted the event in the light of the values experienced at the Jewish feast of Pentecost. This was a festival of the harvest, the first-fruits of which had been offered on the day after the Passover. The two feasts were thus linked as feasts of the gift of the Law.

A knowledge derived from the Qumran texts, the readings used in the Jewish liturgy of the festival, and the texts of the Book of Jubilees and Philo Judaeus provides a good foundation for the theme of Pentecost as the feast celebrating the giving of the Law on Mount Sinai. On this basis, important comparisons can be made.[4] The tablets of the Law, for example, were written by the 'finger of God' (Ex 31:18). The same 'finger of God' is also used by Luke for the Holy Spirit (Lk 11:20).

Just as the new sanctuary is simply Jesus Christ who is open to all nations, the new Law is the Spirit bearing witness to Jesus for and in all peoples. The sign of tongues prophesies the catholicity of witness. The apostles (possibly all the disciples?) speak the tongues of other peoples and announce in those languages the marvels of God. The Fathers of the Church, many exegetes and probably Luke himself regarded this miracle of the Spirit as a reversal of the scattering of Babel (Gen 11:1-9).[5] It is not simply an extension or a universalization. The distinctive aspect of the Spirit is that, while remaining unique and preserving his identity, he is in everyone without causing anyone to lose his originality. This applies to persons, peoples, their culture and their talents. The Spirit also makes everyone speak of the marvels of God in his own language.[6]

To begin with, Christians celebrated Pentecost simply as the end of an Easter of fifty days. The mystery of Easter was conceived as a whole and

44

included the resurrection, the glorification (ascension) and the life of sons of God communicated by the Lord by the sending of his Spirit. It was not until the end of the fourth century that each element of this great single mystery was celebrated separately.[7] Pentecost did not thereby become a feast (of the Person) of the Holy Spirit.[8] There is in fact no feast of the Persons of the Trinity. Pentecost was and is a paschal feast. There is one single liturgical cycle, which is Christological and paschal. What is celebrated is the making present, through faith and the sacrament and in praise and thanksgiving, of the Christian mystery as such.

According to Acts, the part played by the Spirit is that of making present and spreading the salvation that has been gained in and through Christ and to do this by bearing witness. This salvation is always attributed to Christ. It is communicated 'in the name' of Christ, that is, in his power.[9] It is always Christ who acts. The Spirit animates his disciples so that they proclaim him. He guides them in the witness that they bear and is even concerned with the details of their movements and journeyings.[10] 'The Acts describe Christ's saving activity as it takes place in the communities. The communication of the Spirit to the disciples is therefore not a total replacement of Christ, but rather a transmission of his prophetic mission (in the full sense of the word), which consists of being the one who proclaims the message of God. . . . It is possible to say that Christ transmits to his apostles the presence of the Spirit that he received in the Jordan.'[11]

The Spirit intervenes at every decisive moment in the carrying out of God's plan to save. As Swete has noted, Pentecost did not simply give the apostles once and for all an understanding of the universal nature of the call to faith. This understanding was only gained after some time and several fresh interventions. There is, in other words, a history of the coming of the Spirit. In accordance with his plan (see 1:8), Luke refers to a series of various kinds of Pentecosts: in Jerusalem (2:4, 25–31), in Samaria (8:14–17), in the event which begins the missionary adventure with Cornelius and the 'Pentecost' at Caesarea (10:44–48; 11:15–17) and even the episode in Ephesus (19:1–6). A sign indicating the intervention of the Spirit is given at each of these important moments. This sign is a giving of praise to God in tongues and 'prophesying'.[12]

Jesus had proclaimed the coming of the Spirit as the gift of a power that would make witnesses who were full of confidence (parrēsia[13]) and as a baptism, not with water, but with the Holy Spirit (1:5; 11:16). The Twelve themselves and the 120 disciples mentioned by Luke seem never to have received baptism by water, except possibly from John the Baptist.[14] They were, as it were, plunged in the Spirit, who came upon them. From that time onwards, they practised a baptism of water in the name of Jesus, that is, in reference, through faith, to his saving Passover and his power as Lord.[15] This baptism was accompanied by the gift of the Spirit. All the texts point to a connection between the two. Apart from the case of Cornelius, in which the

Spirit had an absolute initiative, the gift of the Spirit follows the baptism of water, although the baptismal rite does not appear as the direct means (or rather the instrumental cause) of that gift.[16] Sometimes another rite is the instrument of the gift of the Spirit. This rite is usually the apostolic laying-on of hands (see 8:16; 19:5–7). One is, however, bound to ask whether the gift of the Spirit which figures in the Acts of the Apostles, where it is said to be the same as that given at Pentecost (11:17), is that of the Spirit as the principle of interior personal sanctification, or of the Spirit as the principle of dynamic testimony accompanied by a confidence that is borne out by the experience of speaking in tongues.

One is prompted to ask this question by the difference, as stressed by G. Haya-Prats, for example, between Acts and Paul.[17] The explanation that Haya-Prats gives for this is based on P. Gächter's summary. In the first place, Acts describes the intervention of the Spirit in the growth of the Church outwards, whereas Paul considers that intervention as it concerns each member inwardly. In the second place, in Acts, the activity of the Spirit is charismatic and the normal experience of any Christian, whereas for Paul that activity is as much the object of faith as it is of experience and he is aware of the fact that many Christians do not have that experience. In the third place, Christ sends his Spirit, according to Acts, to this disciples so that his work will be carried out. According to Paul, on the other hand, the Spirit realizes each Christian's being in Christ individually.

It is, of course, true to say that Luke does not provide a theology of the effects and fruits of the Spirit in the life of the Christian as Paul does ('Christ in us'), but that he shows the dynamism of faith and the growth of the Church. Even when he says that Christ gives the Spirit (2:33), it is still in the line of mission and prophecy (2:17ff.), not in that of the new life. Both were proclaimed in the Old Testament (the one in Joel 3, for example, and the other in Ezek 36:26ff.; Jer 31:31–34). Luke is firmly orientated in Acts towards mission, but is it really possible to separate the disciples' impulses for mission and the 'spiritual' life in this way? Is this not a question of letting the theme in the text predominate over the reality? It has been said, quite correctly, that the famous summary which describes the life of the Church (Acts 2:42) and the *koinōnia* (communion or 'fellowship') mentioned in that summary do not explicitly refer to the Holy Spirit. From the point of view of the reality of the situation, however, Acts 2:42 may well reflect the life of the Church as it emerged from Pentecost. If the Church was sent out into the world by the event of the Spirit, did the Spirit not animate its inner life as he animated its external life? Is there not a danger of saying that Luke has an Old Testament understanding of the Spirit, even a partial one? He may well be close to such a view, but can his understanding be reduced to that level?

Is the Holy Spirit, even with the article (in Greek), and repeated at that (before the noun and before the adjective), in Luke *the Person* of the Holy Spirit? We cannot attribute to the evangelist the explicit statement of the dogma of the Second Ecumenical Council (Constantinople I, in 381). All the same, Luke certainly goes beyond the Old Testament stage, at which 'God' gives his breath. At certain times, the Spirit acts himself in the Acts of the Apostles.

It is therefore possible to agree with Haya-Prats' statement at the end of his section 11 (pp. 82–90): 'A remarkable development in the direction of a personalization of the Holy Spirit that goes beyond a merely literary personification can be discerned in the Acts of the Apostles. The author's repeated attribution of definite and important interventions in the history of salvation to the Holy Spirit would seem to indicate that the Spirit was regarded in practice as the subject of such attribution and therefore as in some way different from Yahweh, even though the problem of such a distinction is not posed as such.'

NOTES

1. In addition to H. B. Swete, *The Holy Spirit in the New Testament* (London, 1909), pp. 63–109, and the article '*pneuma*', *TDNT*, VI, esp. pp. 404–415, the following can be consulted: H. von Baer, *Der Heilige Geist in den Lukasschriften* (*BWANT*, III/3) (Stuttgart, 1926); G. W. H. Lampe, 'The Holy Spirit in the Writings of Luke', *Studies in the Gospels. Essays in Memory of R. H. Lightfoot*, ed. D. E. Nineham (Oxford, 1955), pp. 145–200; J. H. E. Hull, *The Holy Spirit in the Acts of the Apostles* (London, 1967); J. Borremans, 'L'Esprit Saint dans la catéchèse évangélique de Luc', *Lumen Vitae*, 25 (1970), 103–122; E. Rásco, 'Jesus y el Espíritu, Iglesia e "Historia"': Elementos para una lectura de Lucas', *Greg*, 56 (1975), 321–367; G. Haya-Prats, *L'Esprit force de l'Eglise. Sa nature et son activité d'après les Actes des Apôtres (Lectio divina* 81) (Paris, 1975), with a very full bibliography.
2. This is very clear in the ecclesiological gospel of Matthew with its missionary conclusion. For John, see O. Cullmann, *The Johannine Circle* (Eng. tr.; London, 1976), esp. pp. 14f. For Mark, apart from 16:15ff., the summary 1:14–15 combines the mission of the Church and the ministry of Jesus: see *Traduction Œcuménique de la Bible*, note w; J. J. A. Kahmann, *Bijdragen*, 38 (1977), 84–98.
3. The Spirit = the Promise: Lk 24:49; Acts 1:4; 2:33; Gal 3:14; Eph 1:13. It is clear from the last two texts that the Spirit is the fulfilment of the promise made to Abraham insofar as it concerns all nations and comes to them through the apostolic word. See also Col 1:25.
4. See R. le Déaut, 'Pentecôte et tradition juive', *Spiritus*, 7 (1961), 127–144 or *Assemblées du Seigneur*, 51 (1963), 22–38; R. Cabié, *La Pentecôte. L'évolution de la Cinquantaine pascale au cours des cinq premiers siècles (Bibl. de Liturgie)* (Tournai and Paris, 1965); J. Potin, *La fête juive de la Pentecôte*, 2 vols (*Lectio divina*, 65) (Paris, 1971); K. Hruby, 'La fête de la Pentecôte dans la tradition juive', *Bible et Vie Chrétienne*, 63 (1965), 46–64; G. Haya-Prats, *op. cit.* (note 1), pp. 185ff. and notes, pp. 280ff.; E. Schweizer, '*pneuma*', *TDNT*, VI, pp. 410–411, who says: 'It is far more probable, however, that already in the pre-Lucan period the concept of the new covenant, of the renewal of the giving of the Law for world-wide Judaism, strongly influenced the account of the first coming of the Spirit. Undoubtedly pre-Christian are [the Book of Jubilees] and Philo's account of the divine voice at Sinai which evokes a special sound in each individual soul, turns into flame, and passes like a *pneuma* through a trumpet, so that it is heard by those both near and far off, and the sound goes forth even to the ends of the earth. . . . If even before 70 Pentecost was

regarded as the end of the passover which celebrates the exodus from Egypt, and if already in Deut 4:10, 9:10, 18:16 LXX the day of the giving of the Law is called *hē hēmera tēs ekklēsias* [the day of the assembly], such an interpretation is natural.'

5. We could add to the patristic references given in the conciliar decree *Ad Gentes Divinitus*, 4, with regard to this striking theme. See also the various liturgies (the Syrian and the Leonine liturgies especially) and the following exegetes: L. Cerfaux, 'Le symbolisme attaché au miracle des langues', *ETL*, 13 (1936), 256–259 (= *Recueil Lucien Cerfaux*, II, pp. 183–187); J. G. Davies, 'Pentecost and Glossolalia', *JTS*, new series, 13 (1952), 228–231. There may not be any allusion in the account in Acts to Babel, but there is certainly one to the rabbinical theology of the universal intelligibility of the Torah.

6. See, for example, H.-M. Legrand, 'Inverser Babel, mission de l'Eglise', *Spiritus*, 63 (1970), 323–346.

7. This was one of the most important discoveries made by the liturgical movement. See *Les questions liturgiques et paroissiales* (June 1925: Kreps); *ibid.* (1948), 60; *ibid.* (1949), No. 208; *ibid.* (1958), 101–131; D.-R. Pierret, *Ami du Clergé* (1935), 278ff.; J. Daniélou, *Bible et Liturgie* (Paris, 1951), pp. 249ff.; my own *La Pentecôte* (Chartres, 1956; Eng. tr. in *The Mystery of the Church* (London, 1960)); R. Cabié, *op. cit.* (note 4). The scholarly studies of O. Casel are indispensable; see especially *Jahrbuch für Liturgiewissenschaft*, 14 (1938), 1–71. Equally important are G. Kretschmar's studies: see especially *Zeitschrift für Kirchengeschichte*, 66 (1954–55), 209–253.

8. See Leo XIII, encyclical *Divinum illud munus* of 9 May 1897.

9. See Joel 3:5, included in Peter's address, Acts 2:21ff.; 4:12, 29–31; 16:18 (hence 19:13).

10. See Acts 16:6, 7 (verse 10 speaks of a vision); 19:1; 20:3 in the text of Codex D; 19:21; 20:22, 23; 21:4, 11.

11. See Haya-Prats, *op. cit.* (note 1), p. 52.

12. Speaking in tongues: 2:4, 11; 10:46; 19:6; prophesying: 2:17; 11:27; 20:23; 21:4, 11.

13. See Acts 2:29; 4:13, 29; 4:31; 14:3. See also Haya-Prats, *op. cit.*, pp. 102ff.

14. The question of the baptism of the apostles troubled Tertullian: *De bapt.* 12 and 13 (*SC*, 35, pp. 85–86). Clement of Alexandria, in a treatise that has been lost, but for a fragment (ed. O. Stählin, *GCS* III, p. 196) quoted by John Moschus, reports a legendary story: see H. A. Echle, 'The Baptism of the Apostles. A Fragment of Clement of Alexandria's Lost Work "Ipotyposeis" in the Pratum Spirituale of John Moschus', *Traditio*, 3 (1945), 365–368. John Moschus' imaginative account, according to which Jesus baptized Peter, who baptized Andrew, who in turn baptized James and John, was not entirely without foundation. His quotation from Clement of Alexandria's lost work can be found in the *Pratum Spirituale*, 176: *PG* 87/3, 3045. From the theological point of view, it is possible to think that contact with Jesus was, for the apostles, equivalent to baptism; the same applies, in exceptional cases, to the righteous: see O. Rousseau, 'La descente aux enfers. Fondement sotériologique du baptême chrétien', *RSR*, 40 (1952), 273–297. Paul, on the other hand, was baptized: see Acts 9:18.

15. 'In the name of' (*eis to onoma*) has a note of finality and indicates that the baptized person enters into the redemption of the Son, the effectiveness of the Spirit and communion with 'God': see H. Bietenhard, '*onoma*', *TDNT*, V, pp. 270ff. There are many texts mentioning baptism in the name of Jesus: see, for example, Acts 2:38; 8:12; 8:16; 8:37 (Western text); 10:48; 16:15, 30ff.; 19:5; 22:16. H. von Campenhausen has gone against the opinion of most exegetes and historians in favour of the liturgical existence of a baptism 'in the name of Jesus' and has shown that a formula of baptism is not indicated in the texts: 'Taufen auf den Namen Jesu', *Vigiliae Christianae*, 25 (1971), 1–16. See also H. de Lubac, *La foi chrétienne. Essai sur la structure du Symbôle des Apôtres* (Paris, 2nd ed., 1970), pp. 72ff.; I. Crehan, *Early Christian Baptism and the Creed* (London, 1950).

16. See 2:38; 8:15–17; 19:5, 6. H. von Baer, *op. cit.* (note 1), p. 180, believed that baptism of water and baptism of the Spirit were the same. H. Mentz, *Taufe and Kirche* (Munich, 1960), pp. 71, note 139, 75, 93, regarded baptism in the Spirit as baptism of water given on

the basis of faith in the kerygma of Jesus Christ. E. Haenchen, *Die Apostelgeschichte* (Göttingen, 14th ed., 1965), pp. 83–84, thought that baptism was the ordinary means of giving the Spirit. Haya-Prats, *op. cit.* (note 1), pp. 132–138, however has shown that, in Acts, the Spirit does not appear to be given by means of the baptism of water. I shall be dealing with baptism of the Spirit in Volume II.

17. Haya-Prats, *op. cit.*, pp. 28, 117–129, 206. Haya-Prats' quotation from Gächter will be found on p. 241, note 17. See also E. Schweizer, '*pneuma*', *TDNT*, VI, pp. 409–410; and E. Trocmé, 'Le Saint-Esprit et l'Eglise d'après le livre des Actes', *L'Esprit Saint et l'Eglise. L'avenir de l'Eglise et de l'Œcuménisme* (Paris, 1969), pp. 19, 27, 44.

THE JOHANNINE WRITINGS[1]

Jesus appears in the fourth gospel firstly as the one who gives the Spirit and then, in the discourses of the last evening, as the one who proclaims the sending of the Paraclete.

1. *Jesus gives the Spirit*

In the first place, he has the Spirit. Jn 3:34 can be translated either as: 'He whom God has sent utters the words of God, who gives (him) the Spirit not by measure' or as: '. . . and (he) gives the Spirit not by measure'. The first translation exalts Christ, who is word and who reveals God in comparison with the prophets.[2] This translation is in accordance with the testimony of John the Baptist: 'I saw the Spirit descend as a dove from heaven and it remained on him' (Jn 1:32). In addition, it makes the whole verse coherent—the fact that Jesus utters the words of God and does his work is based on his having received the Spirit without measure.

Jesus speaks of the Spirit in his dialogue with Nicodemus: 'Unless one is born of water and the Spirit, he cannot enter the kingdom of God. That which is born of flesh is flesh and that which is born of the Spirit is spirit. . . . The wind blows where it wills and you hear the sound of it, but you do not know whence it comes or whither it goes; so it is with everyone who is born of the Spirit' (3:5–6, 8).[3] The fact that the words 'of water and' do not come from Jesus' words to Nicodemus (at a time when they could only have called to mind the baptism of John the Baptist) does not detract in any way from the text as we have it or the fact that it refers to Christian baptism. We are not told that baptism confers the Spirit, but that, with the Spirit, it causes birth from on high or 'of God' (1:13; 1 Jn 3:9; 5:1), that is, the birth that introduces man into the kingdom of God. The Spirit is active in the whole of the process that leads to faith; he enables man to confess faith and to live by it.

In the dialogue with the Samaritan woman, Jesus says: 'Everyone who drinks of this water will thirst again, but whoever drinks of the water that I shall give him will never thirst; the water that I shall give him will become in him a spring of water welling up to eternal life' (4:13–14). The Spirit is involved here and Jesus gives him. The Spirit is described as the one who urges and animates the believer on to eternal life, in the way in which water coming from higher ground makes water rise to the same level. What we have here is 'living water', that is, a current or stream going from God the source to God the ocean without shores or banks. Jesus also says elsewhere: 'He who believes in me shall never thirst' (6:35). In other words, Christ also gives (eternal) life through faith in him (see also Jn 3:36; 5:21, 40; 6:33, 35; 10:10; 20:31). As in the Pauline writings, then, Christ and the Spirit both carry out the same work of salvation.

We must now consider another passage in the fourth gospel:

> (7:37) On the last day of the feast (of Tabernacles), the great day, Jesus stood up (in the Temple) and proclaimed (in a loud voice), 'If anyone thirst, let him come to me and let him drink (38) who believes in me. As Scripture has said, "Out of his heart shall flow rivers of living water".'(39) Now this he said about the Spirit, which those who believed in him were to receive; as yet the Spirit had not been given, because Jesus was not yet glorified.

This way of punctuating this passage is widely accepted nowadays. The 'rivers of living water' flow from the heart of the Messiah, not from the believer, who is invited to come and drink.[4] The situation is clearly indicated—it is at the feast of Tabernacles, when the priests went every morning to draw water from the spring of Siloam. They brought it back to the Temple singing the Hallel (Ps 113–118) and the verse from the book of Isaiah (12:3): 'With joy you will draw water from the wells of salvation', and poured it out as a libation on the altar of sacrifice. This was a purification rite and at the same time a prayer for the autumn rains. In the Bible and for the Israelites, however, the symbolism of the water was very rich in several ways, in that it pointed to purification and life or fertility. It also pointed to the Law, the word of God and the wisdom that these brought (Is 55:1ff., 10–11) and, in connection with the memory of the water from the rock in the desert during the exodus, an eschatological announcement of a new miracle (Isaiah) or a fertility flowing from the Temple in the form of living water from a spring. The people of God had experienced or were to experience this water. Jesus applies the promise of this water to himself. In the gospel of John, he is the temple (2:21) from which the prophet Ezekiel saw life-giving waters flowing (47:1–12; see also Rev 21:22; 22:1).[5] We have, then, a second image of the Spirit. He is not only the wind or breath—he is also water (see, for example, Is 44:3ff.; Ezek 47:1–12; in the Johannine writings, Rev 22:1, 17). In the East especially, water is what enables seed to produce life. It also quenches the thirst and purifies (baptism!).

What were Jesus' listeners able to understand of the appeal that he was making to them? The symbolism of the water was sometimes applied to the Spirit,[6] but it was not common or at once intelligible. Jesus claimed to fulfil all these images in himself and John, understanding this, says explicitly: 'He said this about the Spirit'. Various suggestions have been made to determine the passage or the passages in Scripture to which Jesus was referring. It is probable that there were several passages with a related meaning or intention—those concerning the Rock, those referring to the Temple and also those on the Torah as a source of life. Jesus claimed to be the truth of all these passages.

John adds to this passage: 'As yet the Spirit had not been given, because Jesus was not yet glorified'. Obviously this does not mean that the Holy Spirit did not exist at that time. The evangelist himself says elsewhere that not only Jesus, but also the disciples had (the) Spirit already.[7] There are also other examples in which a formula of this kind should clearly not be understood in an exclusive or negative sense.[8] The Johannine affirmation corresponds to the statement made by Luke or Paul, namely that the gift of the Spirit relating to the messianic period is made by Jesus glorified and raised to the state of Lord.

It is true that John speaks of a certain glory of Jesus that his disciples can perceive in the signs that he performed (see Jn 2:11; 12:4, 40; 18:28; cf. 1:14), but he insists again and again that Jesus' glorification is closely connected with his Passover and even more closely with his Passion (see Jn 12:23, 27–28; 13:31–32, 17:1; cf. 3:14; 12:32). Jesus' glory was not a worldly glory derived from the appreciation of men because of success according to the criteria of the world. It was a glory that he, as the only Son, had from the Father (1:14) by his obedience and his carrying out of his plan.[9] This included the cross, and the cross was followed by the resurrection and the glorification. As he was approaching his Passion, Jesus said: 'Now is the Son of man glorified and in him God is glorified; if God is glorified in him, God will also glorify him in himself and glorify him at once' (13:31–32). Later, he said: 'Father, the hour has come; glorify thy Son . . . . And now, Father, glorify thou me in thy own presence with the glory which I had with thee before the world was made' (17:1, 5). The glorification governing the sending of the Spirit by Jesus consists in his heavenly glory or his divine glory as the Son being communicated to his humanity as offered and sacrificed. John envisages this, in the book of Revelation, in the form of a Lamb standing and sacrificed (Rev 5:6). He shares his throne with God, and a river of living water flows from this throne (22:1). Later, we read: 'Let him who is thirsty come; let him who desires take the water of life without price' (22:17; cf. 21:6).

This is a description of the consummation in the heavenly Jerusalem. But what is there between the crucifixion and the glory? The giving of the Spirit by Jesus is indicated in the fourth gospel in four ways:

(a) John uses a phrase that is peculiar to him to speak of Jesus' death. Whereas Matthew says that he 'yielded up his spirit' (*aphēken to pneuma*;

27:50) and Mark (15:37) and Luke (23:46) say that he 'breathed his last' or 'expired' (*exepneusen*), thus using quite ordinary terms that have no theological intention, John says that Jesus 'bowed his head and gave up (handed over) his (the) spirit' (*klinas tēn kephalēn paredōken to pneuma*; 19:30). Jesus, in the fourth gospel, 'breathes out' over Mary and John, who are, as the Church, at the foot of his cross, and thus hands over the spirit. It is, of course, not possible to say that this is the Holy Spirit. John shows that the Holy Spirit is given on the evening of Easter (20:22). At the symbolic level, which is endowed in John's gospel with such intense significance, however, there is clearly a very close connection between the gift of the Spirit and Jesus' self-sacrifice. The phrase used in the gospel clearly expresses this connection and also translates what has already been said in 7:39 and 16:5–7. Several of the Church Fathers saw it in this light[10] and certain exegetes agree with this interpretation.[11] This is, finally, a further example of a term with a double intention of the kind that John liked to use. Jesus breathes his last breath and, through his death, which he willingly accepts, hands over the Spirit to his disciples.

(b) John speaks of the lance or spear thrust into Jesus' side or breast when he has just breathed his last breath 'and at once there came out blood and water' (19:34). F.-M. Braun believes that the water here symbolizes the Spirit and that John regarded this as the fulfilment of the anouncement made in 7:38–39.[12] The terms, however, are not exactly the same. In Jn 19:34, the word *pleura*, 'side' or 'chest', and not *koilia*, 'bosom' or 'belly', is used and there is no question of 'rivers of living water'. There is also no really close parallel with 1 Jn 5:6–8, since the Spirit is explicitly linked with the water in the latter text, whereas in Jn 19:34 the water does not mean the Spirit. It is, however, not possible to doubt that the text has a deep and important meaning, since it is clear that John or his disciple bears very solemn witness to this. This lends serious credibility to the tradition that has persisted since the time of Tertullian that the water and blood flowing from the side of Christ who had fallen asleep in death symbolizes the birth of the Church taken from the new Adam, just as Eve had been taken from the side of the first Adam who had similarly fallen asleep (see Gen 2:33). This is, according to this tradition, an affirmation of the unity of mankind expressed in the duality of man *and* woman and therefore in the duality of Christ *and* his Church. The Church, however, is taken from Christ and especially from his Passion. On the other hand, we should retain the exegetically more satisfying explanation given by both the Fathers and the Scholastics, that is, that the water and blood point to the two most important sacraments, baptism and the Eucharist, through which the Church is built up.[13]

(c) In John, Jesus promises another Paraclete. This teaching is only found in the fourth gospel. It is so important that the following sub-section is devoted entirely to it.

(d) The paschal gift of the Spirit to the Eleven (Thomas being absent) plays an important part in the Johannine account. Jesus says:

> 'Peace be with you. As the Father has sent me, even so I send you.' And when he had said this, he breathed on them and said to them, 'Receive the Holy Spirit. If you forgive the sins of any, they are forgiven; if you retain the sins of any, they are retained' (20:21–23).

Scholars have referred to the 'Johannine Pentecost', which is not the exact equivalent of the Pentecost described in the Acts.[14] According to the fourth gospel, Jesus was still not fully 'glorified' and had 'not yet ascended to the Father' (see verse 17). He had risen, but was still for a time with his disciples, where they were, although he was to take them to where he would be and return to them, at the same time sending his Spirit to them from the Father (15:26).[15]

Jesus communicates the Holy Spirit, but not the Paraclete, whom he had promised in Jn 14 and 16. The Spirit is not given personally (there is no article preceding *pneuma hagion*), but as a force that corresponds to the mission that is communicated.[16] This mission is, to be sure, superhuman and is the continuation of the mission of Christ himself, who was sent by the Father (see 17:18; 13:20). It has to be carried out here on earth in the Church in the time following the ascension, a Church in which there will always be sin. (This is clear from the first Johannine epistle.[17]) Jesus brought about and still brings about purification and remission of sins (Jn 1:29; 1 Jn 1:7, 9; 2:1–2; 3:5; 4:10). As the victim of propitiation, he communicates his breath to the apostles as energy active in the Church for the forgiveness of sins. This is, as it were, a beginning of this promised gift of another Paraclete. We must now turn to this promise and the wide-ranging mission of the Paraclete.

2. *The Promised Paraclete*

Jesus speaks explicitly in the fourth gospel of the Spirit in this context and sometimes of the 'Spirit of truth' (Jn 14:17; 15:26; 16:13). I prefer to keep to the simple Greek term 'Paraclete' (*Paraklētos*) as both Jerome and the Jews themselves did (*peraqlît*), because there is no suitable word in our language which adequately renders all the values of the Greek word: defender, counsel for the defence, helper, comforter (this word is used by both Swete and J. G. Davies; Luther used the German word *Tröster*), assistant, lawyer, advocate, solicitor, counsellor, mediator and one who exhorts and makes urgent appeals. All these meanings are present in the Greek *Paraklētos*.[18] With one exception, the term is used exclusively in the Johannine writings, where it occurs five times.

There are five passages in the farewell discourses (Jn 14–16 and 17) that are concerned with the Paraclete-Holy Spirit. The first is 14:16–17, where Jesus promises 'another Paraclete' who will be—and is already—with the disciples and in them. In the second text (14:26), we are told that the Paraclete will teach and recall to mind. The third passage is 15:26–27 (he will bear witness to Jesus). The fourth text (16:7–11) describes how he will establish the guilt of the world and the fifth (16:13–15) points out that he will lead the disciples into the fullness of truth. These passages have to be re-read and re-examined in detail. It is not possible to go into detailed exegesis here, but, in the absence of this, the survey that is provided by F. Porsch (*op. cit.* (note 1 below), pp. 237ff.) is rather meagre, but it is very instructive. It is given in translation below and followed by a brief elucidation.

THE RELATIONSHIP OF THE PARACLETE

(a) *with the Father*

He will give him (at the prayer of Jesus): 14:16.

He will send him (in Jesus' name): 14:26; cf. Lk 24:49. 'In Jesus' name' points to his value and importance in the economy of salvation (Porsch, pp. 90, note 47, 256). It also means that the Son, precisely as the Son, plays an active part in sending the Spirit in close association with the Father (I. de la Potterie, *op. cit.* (note 1 below), pp. 90–91).

The Spirit 'proceeds' from the Father: 15:26.

The Spirit will take (or receive) from what is Christ's, but also from what is the Father's: 16:14ff.

(b) *with the Son*

With regard to Jesus, the Spirit is the other Paraclete: 14:16.

He will be given (at the prayer of Jesus): 14:16.

He will be sent (in his name): 14:26.

He will teach the disciples and recall to their minds all that Jesus has said to them: 14:26.

He will bear witness to Jesus: 15:26.

He will glorify Jesus because he will take (receive) from what is his: 16:14, and he will communicate it to the disciples.

He will point out (say) what he hears (of Jesus): 16:13.

The glorified Jesus will send him: 15:26; 16:7.

Jesus' departure is presupposed at the coming of the Spirit: 16:7.

(c) *with the disciples*

They know him because he dwells with them: 14:17.

He will be with them for ever: 14:16.

He will be in them: 14:17.

He will teach them and recall to their minds all that Jesus has said to them: 14:26.

He will be given to them: 14:16.

He will be sent to them: 15:26; 16:7.

He will come to them: 16:7, 13.

He will guide them into all the truth: 16:13.

He will communicate (or unveil) all that is to come: 16:13, or all that he will receive from Jesus.

(d) *with the world*

The world neither sees him nor knows him and therefore cannot receive him: 14:17.

He will confound the world with regard to sin, righteousness and judgement: 16:8.[19]

THE NATURE, CHARACTERISTICS AND ACTIVITY OF THE PARACLETE

(a) *His relationships with the Pneuma (the Spirit)*

He is the Spirit of truth; he is the Holy Spirit.

(b) *He is the subject of the following actions*

He dwells with the disciples: 14:17; he will be in them: 14:17.
He comes: 16:7ff.; 16:13.
He receives what is Jesus': 16:14ff.
He proceeds from the Father: 15:26.
He listens (hears): 16:13.
He teaches: 14:26.
He calls to mind: 14:26.
He communicates (makes known): 16:13ff.
He speaks (reveals): 16:13.
He glorifies (Jesus): 16:14.
He guides into all the truth: 16:13.
He bears witness: 15:26.
He convinces of sin: 16:8.

(c) *He is the object of the following actions*

He is given: 14:16.
He is sent: 14:26; 15:26; 16:7.
He is neither seen nor known: 14:17.
He is not received: 14:17.

THE CLOSE CONNECTIONS BETWEEN THE PARACLETE AND JESUS
PARALLEL ACTIVITIES

There are far more statements about these connections than there are about the relationships between the Paraclete and the Father. The Paraclete should therefore be seen above all in his relationship with Jesus. It should be clear from the following conspectus how close this is. (G. Bornkamm (see note 18 below) should also be consulted in this context.)

The Paraclete	Jesus
given by the Father: 14:16	3:16
is with and in the disciples: 14:16ff.	3:22; 13:33; 14:20; 14:26
the world cannot receive him: 14:17	1:11; 5:53 (12:48)

The Paraclete	*Jesus*
it does not know him; only believers know him: 14:17	14:19; 16:16ff.
sent by the Father: 14:26	see chapters 5, 7, 8, 12
teaches: 14:26	7:14ff.; 8:20; 18:37
comes (from the Father into the world): 15:26; 16:13, 7	5:43; 16:28; 18:37
bears witness: 15:26	5:31ff.; 8:13ff.; 7:7
confounds the world: 16:8	(3:19ff.; 9:41; 15:22)
does not speak of himself; speaks only what he has heard: 16:13	7:17; 8:26, 28, 38; 12:49ff.; 14:10
glorifies (Jesus): 16:14	cf. 12:28; 17:1, 4
unveils (communicates): 16:13ff.	4:25 (16:25)
guides into all the truth—he is the Spirit of truth: 16:13	cf. 1:17; 5:33; 18:37; 14:6

The fact that the Spirit is the subject of a number of actions, that he is, after Jesus, 'another Paraclete' (14:16) and that the masculine form of the demonstrative is used in the text, even after the neuter word *Pneuma*,[20] clearly means that certain personal characteristics are attributed to him.[21] It is, however, probably impossible to draw any direct conclusions from the fourth gospel regarding the dogma of the Trinity. The evangelist says, it is true, that the Spirit proceeds from the Father: *ekporeuetai*, but *para tou patros*, 'from near the Father', not *ek* (15:26). He also says: 'he will take from what is mine', *ek tou emou lēmpsetai*, since 'all that the Father has is mine' (16:14, 15). The context, however, is one of a communication of truth, not one of eternal existence preceding the economy of salvation.[22] Of course, the Father is the first and absolute origin, both of the Spirit and of the Word. The relationships between the Paraclete and Christ are also extremely close in the economy of salvation. The revelation of the Father, as the source of faith and love, must be experienced by the disciples in a hostile world and in faithfulness to that revelation. This is the function of the Spirit-Paraclete, the Spirit of truth. He continues, after Jesus' departure, to do Jesus' work, that is, to welcome by faith the one who is sent by the Father to reveal the Father and to keep his words and his commandments. He enables us to bring about the new relationship between Jesus and his own after Jesus has withdrawn his tangible presence from us. This takes place in the baptism of water, the offering of flesh and blood and the keeping and the living penetration of Jesus' words. I. de la Potterie has shown in his very detailed studies that the part played by the Spirit relates to faith, which forms the living substance of our relationship with Jesus. F. Porsch has also pointed, in his equally detailed and exact book, to a constant relationship between the Spirit-Paraclete and the word of Jesus, especially in the life of the disciples and within the framework of the struggle in which they are engaged. The Spirit does not invent or introduce a new and different economy. He gives life to the flesh and words *of Jesus* (6:63). He recalls those words to mind and penetrates the whole truth: 'He will not speak on his own account, but whatever he hears he will speak. . . . He will glorify me'. According to Swete, Jesus is the way (*hē hodos*) and the Spirit is the guide (*ho hodēgos*) who enables man to go forward on that way (p. 162).

3. *The Spirit in the Disciples and in the Time of the Church*

The evangelist and the circle of his disciples belonged to a Church in which the Spirit was active. Their particular place was probably in Syria; they certainly lived and wrote in a Church which knew of the activity of Paul and the history recounted in Acts. The Spirit aroused in them a feeling of communion, by reason of which they were, through faith and love, in God, who was in them: 'By this we know that we abide in him (God) and he in us, because he has given us of his own Spirit' (1 Jn 4:13; cf. 3:24; Jn 14). The Spirit acts in the first place in order to make them believe that the Son was sent in human flesh and to make them know and to confess him. This involves their loving as he loved (1 Jn 4:14ff.; 3:23).

In order to achieve this, the Spirit adds his testimony to that of Jesus, who was sent from the Father in human flesh, and that testimony is made present in the Church by baptism and the Eucharist:

> This is he who came by water and blood, Jesus Christ, not with the water only, but with the water and blood. And the Spirit is the witness, because the Spirit is the truth. There are three witnesses, the Spirit, the water and the blood, these three agree (1 Jn 5:6–8).

An intention to oppose Cerinthus, who made a distinction between the Christ of baptism and the Christ of the Passion, and even to oppose Docetism, by affirming the elements of which man is made in his mother's womb, water and blood,[23] can be recognized in the above passage. If, however, the whole text is seen as part of the entire Johannine witness, it is easy to recognize in it the coming of Jesus in the water, through his baptism, his coming through the blood of his Passion, and the Spirit, given to us thanks to both comings. John is not, however, thinking simply of the historical and unique events of the baptism and the sacrificial death of Jesus. As O. Cullmann has pointed out,[24] in accordance with the intention of his gospel, the evangelist saw Jesus' gestures as the inauguration and institution of what was to take place in the Church in a sacramental form. Because of this, the Spirit acts in the one who hears the testimony in order to arouse faith in him; he then acts in or with the sacraments (for baptism, see Jn 3:5; for the Eucharist, see 6:27, 63). He also similarly acts in the word, with which he is, as John shows, constantly united (6:63) and in the worship that true worshippers give to God (4:23–24).[25]

The time of the Church is essentially a time of mission, bearing witness and kerygma. It is a remarkable fact that all the gospels end with the sending of the apostles on their mission and with the gift of the Holy Spirit, at least in the case of Luke and John (see Mt 28:15; Mk 16:15; Lk 24:47ff.; Acts 1:8; Jn 17:18; 20:20). In John, the Spirit is essentially the Spirit of truth and, as such, he bears witness to Christ together with the apostles.[26]

Throughout the time of the Church, there are disciples. The Spirit guides them in a knowledge of the whole truth and even announces or communicates to them what is to come (see 16:13). While they were still accompanying Jesus and still saw and heard him, the disciples had both faith and a lack of faith. They also had above all a lack of understanding. The Spirit will bring to mind the teachings of Jesus and will bring to maturity in them a testimony which will not be simply a repetition of material facts, but a communication and an understanding of their meaning.[27]

John admits that he understood the meaning of Jesus' words and actions only after his departure (see 2:22; 12:16; 14:26) and the whole of his gospel illustrates this gradual deepening of understanding after Easter. What we have here is simply the fullness of the Christian mystery and the economy of salvation resulting from the life and the passover of Christ. 'The things that are to come' means that the calling to mind of what Jesus said is accompanied by an unfolding of new responses in what is new in history. The Spirit takes the realization of the Christian mystery forward in the history of mankind. This is in accordance with the nature of the testimony as contained in Scripture—as R. Asting has shown, it is 'directed forward', *vorwärtsgerichtet*.

All believers are concerned in this. John writes to them: 'You have been anointed by the Holy One and you all know. . . . The anointing which you received from him abides in you and you have no need that anyone should teach you; as his anointing teaches you about everything . . .' (1 Jn 2:20, 27). According to the context, this 'anointing' is received from Christ and it consists of the word of Jesus assimilated in faith and subject to the action of the Holy Spirit.[28] In the book of Revelation, Jesus' testimony is called the 'spirit of prophecy' (19:10).[29] The 'prophets' occupy an important place in it,[30] whereas, in the Johannine writings, there is no reference to the 'charisms' and the 'spiritual gifts' that abounded in Corinth. Despite all tribulations, it is essential to preserve the 'testimony of Jesus' (1:2; 12:11; 17:6; 19:10; 20:4) and to resist the 'false prophet' who serves the idolatrous ambition of the beast (13; 16:13; 19:20; 20:10). The Spirit does not reveal himself. He appears in relation to Jesus. He is communicated by Jesus and intervenes with the churches—the Church—to warn them and to bring them back to the truth.[31] In them, he is constantly an inspiration from Jesus and an aspiration towards Jesus the Lord: 'The Spirit and the Bride say, "Come" '

(22:17). This, then, in a situation of tribulation and distress, is the struggle of faith, which corresponds to what the gospel and the first epistle of John tell us.[32]

The fourth gospel is remarkably coherent in its teaching about the Spirit. What it says about the Spirit relates entirely to the testimony given to Jesus and Jesus is entirely related to the Father. The passage that provides the best summary of this mystery is undoubtedly the meditation that the evangelist added to the testimony of John the Baptist:

> He who comes from above is above all; he who is of the earth belongs to the earth and of the earth he speaks; he who comes from heaven is above all. He bears witness to what he has seen and heard, yet no one receives his testimony; he who receives his testimony sets his seal to this, that God is true. For he whom God has sent utters the words of God, for it is not by measure that he gives the Spirit. . . . He who believes in the Son has eternal life . . . (3:31–36).

Jesus comes from heaven, from eternity. At his baptism, John the Baptist bears witness: 'He was before me. . . . I have borne witness that this is the Son of God' (1:30, 34). John baptizes him and sees the Spirit, as a dove, descend from heaven and remain on him, declaring: 'It is he who baptizes with the Holy Spirit' (1:33). The man Jesus, the Word made flesh, who shows a humanity that is so much a part of this earth that it is often denounced (see Jn 6:30, 42; 7:27ff.; 5:18; 10:33), lives, in that humanity, totally in reference to the Father, so that he is entirely from him, for him and towards him (*pros ton Theon*: 1:1; 1 Jn 1:2). He is the one who is sent. He is the revelation of the Father and the communication of eternal life. It is enough to cling to him through faith and to practise love. In order to achieve this, Jesus, before leaving our earth corporeally, sent his Spirit as living water into believers,,as the Paraclete to make their faith and their testimony firm and as one who is jointly effective in the word, the water of baptism, the Eucharist, bearing witness, the ministry of reconciliation: in a word, as the one who does his work, the task that he received from the Father, in the time of the Church. 'I will pray the Father and he will give you another Paraclete, to be with you for ever . . . the Paraclete, the Holy Spirit, whom the Father will send *in my name*' (14:16, 26).

This deeply Trinitarian Johannine view of the Christian mystery inspired the thinking of the earliest Fathers of the Church—Ignatius of Antioch in 107,[33] Justin about 150[34] and Irenaeus about 180 A.D.[35] It has also been a constant theme in the liturgy: to the Father (who gives absolute life), through Christ, in the Spirit. There are so many pronouncements made by the Fathers during the classical period that it would be impossible to refer to them all. Reference may, however, be made to several of the documents of the Second Vatican Council, which re-established links with this great tradition.[36]

NOTES

1. See, for example, H. B. Swete, *The Holy Spirit in the New Testament* (London, 1909), pp. 129–168 (Jn) and 267–279 (Jn and Rev); F. Büchsel, *Der Geist Gottes im Neuen Testament* (Gütersloh, 1926), chapter XIX, pp. 485–511; E. Schweizer, *'pneuma'*, *TDNT*, pp. 437–444 (Jn), 448–449 (1 Jn) and 449–451 (Rev); I. de la Potterie, various studies in *La vie selon l'Esprit. Condition du chrétien (Unam Sanctam*, 55) (Paris, 1965); F.-M. Braun, *Jean le théologien*, III: *Sa théologie*, 2 vols incorporating earlier articles (Paris, 1966 and 1972), especially II, pp. 37–56, 139–169, 180–181; F. Porsch, *Pneuma und Wort* (Frankfurt, 1974), with a bibliography containing some 700 titles.
2. The prophets had the Spirit only in a certain measure: see Strack and Billerbeck, II, p. 132. The interpretation that Jesus gave the Spirit (to the community) also has its supporters, including M.-J. Lagrange. It ensures a certain coherence with the rest of the fourth gospel: see 7:38–39; 19:34; 14:26; 15:26; 16:14; 20:22.
3. See P. van Imschoot, 'Baptême d'eau et baptême d'Esprit', *ETL*, 13 (1936), 653–664; F.-M. Braun, 'Le baptême d'après le 4ᵉ évangile', *RThom*, 48 (1948), 358–368 and *op. cit.*, II, pp. 139, 145; J. Guillet, 'Baptême et Esprit', *Lumière et Vie*, 26 (1956), 85–104; I. de la Potterie, ' "Naître de l'eau et naître de l'Esprit". Le texte baptismal de Jn 3, 5', *SE*, 14 (1962), 417–443, included in *op. cit.* (note 1), pp. 31–63, with full bibliography; Porsch, *op. cit.* (note 1), pp. 83–135.
4. Swete, *op. cit.* (note 1), pp. 142ff., still has the earlier punctuation. See, however, Braun, *op. cit.* (note 1), II, pp. 50–56; Porsch, *op. cit.*, pp. 53–81; H. Rahner, 'Flumina de ventre Jesu. Die patristische Auslegung von Joh VII, 37–39', *Bib*, 22 (1941), 269–302, 307–403; J.-E. Ménard, 'L'interprétation patristique de Jean VII, 38', *Revue de l'Université d'Ottawa, Section spéciale*, 25 (1955), 5*–25* (Origen believed that it referred to Christ, with reference to the rock in the desert, but then applied it to the Christian); J. Daniélou, 'Le symbolisme de l'eau vive', *RSR*, 32 (1958), 335–346; M.-E. Boismard, 'De son ventre couleront des fleuves d'eau vive', *RB*, 65 (1958), 523–546; P. Grelot, the same title and the same journal, 66 (1959), 369–374; A. Feuillet, 'Les fleuves d'eau vive de Jn VII, 38', *Parole de Dieu et sacerdoce. Etudes présentées à Mgr Weber* (Tournai and Paris, 1962), pp. 107–120; P. Grelot, 'Jean VII, 38: Eau du Rocher ou Source du Temple', *RB*, 70 (1963), 43–51.
5. Miracle of a new exodus: Is 35:6ff.; 41:13–20; 43:20. Water from the rock in the exodus: Ex 17:1–7; Num 20:1–3; Ps 78:16–20; 114:8; Is 48:21–22. Water flowing from the Temple: Ezek 47:1, 8–12; Zech 13:1; 14:8–9; Joel 4:18; Ps 46:5. See also J. Bonsirven, *Le judaïsme palestinien au temps de Jésus-Christ* (Paris, 1976), I, p. 432; A. Jaubert, *Approches de l'Evangile de Jean* (Paris, 1976), pp. 80, 140–146; my own *The Mystery of the Temple* (Eng. tr.; London, 1962), pp. 75–77. The following texts were included in the readings of the synagogue during the feast of Tabernacles: Is 43:20; 44:3; Jer 2:13; Zech 14:8; Deut 7:11–15; see Braun, *op. cit.* (note 1), II, p. 52.
6. Swete, *op. cit.* (note 1), p. 144, note 2 (talmudic texts); Strack and Billerbeck, II, p. 434; Porsch, *op. cit.* (note 1), pp. 63–65.
7. See 6:63; 14:17. Before Jesus' glorification, there is a mixture of faith and weak faith or understanding: see Porsch, *op. cit.*, p. 67.
8. Büchsel, *op. cit.* (note 1), p. 495, note 4, quotes texts here where a negation is at once compensated for by an affirmation: Jn 8:15–16; 3:32–33; 5:31; 6:63, 51. 16:12, contrasted with 15:15, could also be added to this list.
9. See Jn 5:36, 41, 44; 7:13; 8:50, 54; 12:43. See also Michael Ramsey, *The Glory of God and the Transfiguration of Christ* (London, 1949).
10. See Irenaeus, *Adv. haer.* IV, 31, 2 (*PG* 7, 1069–70); V, 1, 1 (*PG* 7, 1121). Caesarius of Arles, *Sermo* 40, 4 (*PL* 39, 1825) and Gregory the Great, *Moralia* XXXV, 8, 18 (*PL* 76, 759) compared Christ giving life to the Church on the cross by the seven gifts of the Spirit with Elijah leaning over the dead child and breathing seven times into him.

THE NEW TESTAMENT

11. See Porsch, *op. cit.* (note 1), pp. 327ff.

12. F.-M. Braun, 'L'eau et l'Esprit', *RThom*, 49 (1949), 5–30; *idem*, *op. cit.* (note 1), I, pp. 167ff.

13. I have personally collected more than a hundred pieces of evidence of the symbols of the Church or the sacraments. See S. Tromp, 'De nativitate Ecclesiae ex corde Iesu in cruce', *Greg*, 13 (1932), 489–527; J. Daniélou, *Sacramentum Futuri* (Paris, 1950), pp. 37ff., 172; H. Barré, *Bulletin de la Société française d'Etudes mariales*, 13 (1955), 61–97; E. Guldan, *Eva-Maria* (Cologne and Graz, 1966), pp. 33ff., 46ff., 75, 173ff. For the East (and especially the liturgy of the Eastern Church), see J. Ledit, *La plaie du côté* (Rome, 1970).

14. See Swete, *op. cit.* (note 1), pp. 165–168; Porsch, *op. cit.* (note 1), pp. 341–378. *La Pentecôte johannique (Jean XX, 19–23; Ac II)* is the title of a book by Mgr Cassien Besobrasoff (Valence, 1939).

15. See Jn 14:3 and M. Ramsey's commentary, *op. cit.* (note 9), pp. 73, 23, 26, 28.

16. See Swete, *op. cit.*, p. 166; Porsch, *op. cit.*, p. 343.

17. See 1:8–10; 2:1ff., 12; 5:16. See also Porsch, *op. cit.*, pp. 361ff.

18. For the word, see J. Behm, *'paraklētos'*, *TDNT*, V, pp. 800–814; J. G. Davies, 'The Primary Meaning of parakletos', *JTS*, new series, 4 (1953), 35–38; Porsch, *op. cit.*, pp. 227ff. D. Betz believed that the word was derived from *parakalein* and that it had a Jewish origin, having the meaning of bearing witness in front of a tribunal: see his *Der Paraklet* (Leiden and Cologne, 1963). See also H.-M. Drion, 'L'origine du titre de "Paraclet": à propos d'un livre récent', *SE*, 17 (1965), 143–149. C. K. Barrett, 'The Holy Spirit in the Fourth Gospel', *JTS*, new series, 1 (1950), 1–15, thought, however, that the word was related to *paraklēsis*, 'exhortation'. For an exegesis of the Johannine texts, see Porsch, *op. cit.*, pp. 215–324; Swete, *op. cit.*, pp. 148–164; F. Mussner, 'Die johanneischen Parakletssprüche und die apostolische Tradition', *BZ*, 5 (1961), 56–70; I. de la Potterie, *op. cit.* (note 1), pp. 85–105; R. E. Brown, 'The Paraclete in the Fourth Gospel', *NTS*, 13 (1967), 113–132; G. Bornkamm, 'Der Paraklet im Johannes-Evangelium', *Geschichte und Glaube. Erster Teil. Gesammelte Aufsätze*, III (Munich, 1968), pp. 68–89; G. Johnston, *The Spirit-Paraclete in the Gospel of John* (Cambridge, 1970), reviewed by E. Malatesta in *Bib*, 54 (1973), 539–550.

19. See T. Preiss, 'La justification dans la pensée johannique', *Hommage et Reconnaissance. Recueil ... K. Barth* (Neuchâtel and Paris, 1946), pp. 100–118; M.-F. Berrouard, 'Le Paraclet, défenseur du Christ devant la conscience du croyant (Jo XVI, 8–11)', *RSPT*, 33 (1949), 361–389; Porsch, *op. cit.*, pp. 275–289. This text is concerned with Jesus' trial, which continues in history: the Spirit will convince the world that it has sinned and still sins in its rejection and condemnation of Jesus, that Jesus' cause was just, that God declared it to be just when he raised him up and glorified him and finally that the unbelieving world and the demon that inspires that world have already been judged and declared guilty.

20. For *ekeinos*, see 14:26; 15:26; 16:8, 13.

21. These have been underestimated by certain authors, including, for example, G. Johnston, *op. cit.* (note 18). See, however, apart from E. Malatesta, *op. cit.* (*ibid.*): J. Goitia, 'La noción dinámica del pneuma en los libros sagrados', *Estudios Biblicos*, 16 (1957), 115–159; R. E. Brown, *The Gospel according to John*, II (Garden City, N.Y., 1970/London, 1971), esp. App. V.

22. See Porsch, *op. cit.* (note 1), pp. 273, 300ff.

23. This interpretation was suggested by G. Richter, 'Blut und Wasser aus der durchbohrten Seite Jesu', *Münchener Theologische Zeitschrift*, 21 (1970), 1–21. For Cerinthus and Gnosticism, see F.-M. Braun, *op. cit.* (note 1), I, p. 169; II, p. 148.

24. O. Cullmann, *The Johannine Circle* (Eng. tr.; London, 1976). See also Braun, *op. cit.* (note 1), II, pp. 148–149, 150–154; R. Bréchet, 'Du Christ à l'Eglise. Le dynamisme de l'Eglise dans l'évangile selon S. Jean', *Divus Thomas*, 56 (1953), 67–98; A. Feuillet, 'Le temps de l'Eglise d'après le IVᵉ évangile et l'Apocalypse', *M-D*, 65 (1961/1), 60–79.

61

25. I. de la Potterie, in the article quoted below, note 28, has pointed out that, in Jn 5:8, the Spirit is put before the water and the blood; he arouses faith, the anointing of faith that is nourished in the sacraments of baptism and the Eucharist. For this exegesis, see also W. Nauck, *Die Tradition und der Charakter des ersten Johannesbriefes* (Tübingen, 1957), pp. 147–182, 2nd excursus: 'Geist, Wasser und Blut'. A. Jaubert, *op. cit.* (note 5), pp. 147–154, has pointed to possible different meanings and has emphasized the sacramental meaning. In this context, he mentions the Syrian custom of anointing (the Spirit) before administering the sacraments of entry into the Church, namely baptism and the Eucharist.

26. Jn 15:26–27; Acts 5:32. The testimony of the Spirit is linked with that borne by the witness of the life and resurrection of Jesus: Acts 1:8, 21–22; 2:32; 3:15; 4:13; 10:39, 41; 13:31.

27. For the nature of this testimony, see G. Marcel, 'Le témoignage comme localisation de l'existentiel', *NRT* (March 1946), 182–191; J. Guitton, *La pensée moderne et le catholicisme.* VI: *Le problème de Jésus et les fondements du témoignage chrétien* (Aix-en-Provence, 1948), pp. 153–164, 174ff.; *idem, Jésus* (Paris, 1956), pp. 193–217. For the exegesis of this theme, see R. Asting, *Die Verkündigung des Wortes im Urchristentum. Dargestellt an den Begriffen 'Wort Gottes', 'Evangelium' und 'Zeugnis'* (Stuttgart, 1939), pp. 666–698; I. de la Potterie, 'La notion de témoignage dans S. Jean', *Sacra Pagina*, ed. J. Coppens *et al.* (Gembloux and Paris, 1959), II, pp. 193–208; A.-M. Kothgesser, 'Die Lehr-, Erinnerungs-, Bezeugungs- und Einführungsfunktion des johanneischen Geist-Parakleten gegenüber der Christusoffenbarung', *Salesianum*, 33 (1971), 557–598; 34 (1972), 3–51; H. Schlier, The Holy Spirit as Interpreter according to St John's Gospel' *Communio* (Eng. ed.), 2 (1973), 61–67; F. Porsch, *op. cit.* (note 1), pp. 67, 262ff., 289ff. and, for the 'things to come', p. 298. Finally, F. Mussner, *The Historical Jesus in the Gospel of St John* (Freiburg and London, 1967), pp. 59–67, is worth consulting, but J. Beutner's monograph, *Martyria. Traditionsgeschichtliche Untersuchungen zum Zeugnisthema bei Johannes* (Frankfurt, 1972), which is largely lexicographic, goes technically further than our question.

28. See I. de la Potterie, 'L'onction du chrétien par la foi', *Bib*, 40 (1959), 12–69, reissued in *La vie selon l'Esprit, op. cit.* (note 1), pp. 107–167. John's text is also cited in the conciliar Constitution *Lumen Gentium*, 12.

29. This text was quoted by the Second Vatican Council to illustrate the prophetic function of believers (*Lumen Gentium*, 35) and their priestly mission (*Presbyterorum Ordinis*, 2).

30. See 1:3; 10:7; 11:3, 18; 16:6; 18:20, 24; 22:6, 9. John himself prophesied as one seized by the Spirit: 1:10; 4:2.

31. The seven letters to the churches came from Christ, but six of them end with 'what the Spirit says to the churches'. The 'seven spirits' (1:4; 4:5) are the Spirit in his fullness. Jesus possesses them (3:1) and he gives living water (21:6; 22:1, 17).

32. Jn 16:8–11; 1 Jn 2:18–19, 22; 4:1 (false prophet); Rev 4:14 and *passim*.

33. Ignatius' imagery is derived from architecture: Eph 9:1.

34. Justin Martyr, *1 Apol.* LXV and LXVII on the Eucharist.

35. Irenaeus, *Adv. haer.* IV, 20, 5 and 34, 5; V, 36; *Dem.* 7 (*SC* 62, pp. 41–42: the whole of this text would be worth quoting here).

36. Dogmatic Constitution *Lumen Gentium*, 51; Decree *Ad Gentes divinitus*, 2.

PART TWO

IN THE HISTORY OF CHRISTIANITY

1

THE EXPERIENCE OF THE SPIRIT
IN THE EARLY CHURCH[1]

The apostles 'set out, filled with the assurance of the Holy Spirit, to proclaim the good news of the coming of the kingdom of heaven'.[2] In the beginning, the Church saw itself as subject to the activity of the Spirit and filled with his gifts. In the Church's understanding of itself, this was how the glorified Lord exercised his authority over the Church. 'As the hand moves over the zither and the strings speak, so does the Spirit of the Lord speak in my limbs and I speak through his love.'[3]

The charism that is most frequently discussed is prophecy. The *Didache* gives an important place to the ministry of prophets, provides criteria that enable its authenticity to be determined[4] and at the same time observes that those 'bishops' and deacons who are 'worthy of the Lord . . . carry out the ministry of prophets and teachers' (XV, 1). In the middle of the second century A.D., Justin Martyr claimed that prophecy and charismatic gifts still existed in the Church.[5] They would, it was believed, accompany the Church throughout the whole of its history until the end.[6]

The community at Corinth had been given a number of rules by Paul for the correct use of the *pneumatika* and, in the same way, Clement of Rome, in his epistle of *c.* 95 A.D., reminded the Corinthians of the 'abundant outpouring of the Holy Spirit' on them (II, 2; see also XLVI, 6) and gave them this rule: 'Let each one of us respect in his neighbour the charisms that he has received' (XXXVIII, 1). This was the same as saying 'respect your presbyters'. Prophecy declined to some extent in the early Church, at least in the form of more or less ecstatic mental exaltation, but this was not, as Harnack believed, because the canon of scriptures had been established, but rather because of an increasing emphasis on the authority of the bishops.[7] This does not imply a contrast between the 'charismatics' and the hierarchical ministers, still less an opposition, since the ministers were themselves charismatic. Ignatius of Antioch, for example, claimed that he called out his essential message under the action of the Spirit,[8] Polycarp of Smyrna was called a 'teacher who was both an apostle and a prophet'[9] and Melito of Sardis was said to 'live entirely in the Holy Spirit'.[10] That is why the increasing affirmation of the part played by the bishops did not in any way minimize the charismatic life of the Church. They were spiritual men in the sense in which Paul described them (1 Cor 2:10–15). Later, Irenaeus spoke of them in the same way: 'Those who have received the pledge of the Spirit and who behave correctly in everything are rightly called by the Apostle spiritual men'.[11] Elsewhere, he speaks of the obedience owed to the presbyters who have received 'with their succession to the episcopate, the certain charism of truth, according to the pleasure of the Father'.[12] This is the tradition which ended by applying this text of spiritual anthropology to authority in the Church,[13] the bishop being regarded as a spiritual man, endowed with charisms of the Spirit and especially with those of knowledge and teaching.

It was because of this abundance of charisms and the important part played by them in the Church—especially the charism of 'prophecy'—that Montanus received a sympathetic hearing when he first began to 'prophesy' about 172:

> It was at this time that the disciples of Montanus, Alcibiades and Theodotus began to acquire a reputation as prophets in the Phrygian region. The very many other wonders that had been worked up to that time in several churches by the divine charism persuaded many to believe that the wonder-workers were also prophets.[14]

The disciples of the Montanist sect were received more and more favourably: 'You have a duty to welcome the charisms!'[15] A serious crisis arose in the Church. The teachings and practices of the Montanists spread so rapidly that when the martyrs of Lyons were in prison in 177, their chief concern was the 'peace of the churches'. It was at this time that the first synods met. From 202 onwards, Tertullian was increasingly drawn towards the Montanists, finding an answer to the reasons which had at first deterred him from a Church in which women prophesied. The Montanists, however, were very ascetic and practised severe fasting. . . . The Catholics criticized both the ways in which the Montanist prophets expressed themselves—by convulsions, cries and the suspension of judgement, for example—and the manner of life and biased attitudes of these new prophets. They claimed, for example, that God spoke in them, that they were the living recipients and even the incarnation of the Paraclete[16] and that eschatological fulfilment and the descent of the heavenly Jerusalem were near at hand. There was, in their teaching, a notable connection between, on the one hand, an appeal to prophecy, sectarian protest and a call to ascetic practice and, on the other, a strong eschatological expectation, often with reference to Joel 3:1–5: 'I will pour out my spirit on all flesh; your sons and daughters will prophesy . . . before the great and terrible day of the Lord comes'.[17]

This 'new prophecy' had to be rejected by the Catholic Church, but a rejection of this kind was dangerous if it meant bulding up the life of the Church without charisms and without the Holy Spirit. This danger did not, however, materialize. Irenaeus, whom the Christians of Vienne and Lyons had sent in 177 to the Bishop of Rome, Eleutherus, to discuss with him the new prophetic movement, testified in 180 to the existence in the Church of miraculous charisms[18] and wrote, about ten years later, that 'we know that, in the Church, many of our brothers have prophetic charisms and, by virtue of the Spirit, speak all the languages, reveal, for the good of all men, all secrets and expose the mysteries of God. The Apostle calls them spiritual men, not through tearing and repressing their flesh, but through sharing the Spirit and only because of that.'[19] Similar statements are made again and again later. Miltiades' has already been mentioned (see above, p. 65, and below, note 6). In 248, Origen wrote: 'Among Christians, there are always marks of that Holy Spirit who appeared in the form of a dove. They drive out evil spirits, bring about cures and predict certain events according to the will of the Logos.'[20] In 375, Epiphanius of Salamis added to a quotation of the Montanists' claim regarding the 'duty to welcome the charisms' that 'the holy Church of God also welcomes them, but (in the Church) they are truly charisms, authenticated by the Holy Spirit and coming to the Church from the prophets, the apostles and the Lord himself'.[21]

It is important to mention here the place occupied by visions, warnings and suggestions attributed to the Spirit in the early Church. Cyprian said, for example, of a council held at Carthage in the spring of 252: 'It has pleased us, under the inspiration of the Holy Spirit and according to the warnings given by the Lord in many clear visions. . .'.[22] The life of Cyprian himself is studded with supernatural visions and warnings.[23] The early Church believed that its life was guided by God—not simply by his Word, but also by the inspirations and indications that he gave again and again. It is worth recalling Rudolf Sohm's arguments and his supporting documentation in this context.[24] In the same way, the long series of texts attributing the forces and influences in the life of the Church to an *inspiratio* or a *revelatio* are also worth consulting.[25] This is what we would now call the development of dogma and the teachings of the Church's councils, their canons, the decisions of the Church's teaching authority and the understanding of Scripture. It was the Spirit who disclosed the 'spiritual meaning' of Scripture and it was important to obtain a view of that meaning that would be worthy of the Spirit.[26]

There was, then, only one Church, which was both corporeal and spiritual, hierarchical and pneumatic, institutional and charismatic. As a Montanist, Tertullian made a sharp contrast between the Church of the Spirit and the Church of the bishops,[27] but this was based on a sectarian ecclesiology: the true Church ought, he believed, to be known by the sign of ecstasy.[28] Others would have said that it should be known by the sign of glossolalia. Those who expressed the Catholic Tradition situated the Spirit firmly within the Church. In his refutation of the Alogi, who, in their opposition to the Montanists, suppressed the gospel of John with its emphasis on the promise of the Paraclete, Irenaeus reaffirmed both the gospel and the prophetic Spirit.[29] At the end of Book III of his great work *Against Heresies*, he exalted the Spirit as the principle giving life to the Church and faith:

(Faith) is received from the Church and kept by us; it always makes us young again and, under the influence of the Spirit, like a costly drink contained in a precious vase, even renews the vase that holds it. The Church is entrusted with this gift of God, just as God entrusted breath to the flesh that he fashioned so that all members receive life from it. In this gift the intimacy of the gift of Christ, that is to say, the Holy Spirit, is contained. God established in the Church the apostles, the prophets, the doctors and all the other effects of the working of the Spirit in which those who do not run to the *ecclesia* do not share. . . . Where the Church (*ecclesia*) is, there is also the Spirit of God and where the Spirit of God is, there are also the Church and all grace. And the Spirit is truth.[30]

This Church is the Church Irenaeus knew, the Church of the succession of presbyters and of an assembly of brothers in communion with the faith of the apostles. He recognized that this Church and the Spirit conditioned each other and did so, as it were, at two different but interdependent points of entry. It was for this reason that he stressed not only that where the Spirit is there is also the Church, but also that where the Church is there is also the Spirit. The whole of the history we have to cover and the whole of the theology we must outline are contained within this dialectical tension which is too divine for us to be able to break it without betraying some aspect of it.

Hippolytus and Clement of Alexandria were writing at the same time as Tertullian. According to Hippolytus, the Holy Spirit ensured that the tradition of the apostles would be preserved.[31] The same Spirit refuted heresies and was handed on in the Church, in which there was not only a succession of ministers, but also a kind of succession or transmission of the Spirit.[32] This Church was to be found in the local assembly in which instruction was given by teachers. At least twice, Hippolytus insisted: *Festinet autem et ad ecclesiam ubi floret spiritus*—'Let us hasten to the assembly, where the Spirit produces fruit' (*Apos. Trad*. 31 and 35).

Clement called the Church of the Lord a 'spiritual and holy choir' and a 'spiritual body' (*sōma pneumatikon*) about 210, because 'the one who clings to the Lord is one spirit with him and a spiritual body'.[33] Cyprian's contemporary, Novatian, before his schism in 251, wrote one of the finest theological or ecclesiological statements about the Holy Spirit:[34]

(That Spirit, who enabled the disciples not to fear, in the name of the Lord, either the powers of the world or its torments) gives similar gifts, like jewels, to the Bride of Christ, the Church. He causes prophets to appear in the Church, instructs the Church's teachers, encourages tongues, obtains power and health, works wonders in the Church, brings about the discernment of spirits, helps those who govern the Church, inspires the Church's councils and dispenses the other gifts of grace. In this way, he perfects and completes the Church of Christ everywhere and in all things.

The same Spirit, in the form of a dove, came and remained with the Lord after his baptism, dwelling fully and totally in him, without any kind of limitation. He was then dispensed and sent out in superabundance so that the others might receive from him a pouring out of graces, the source of every gift of the Holy Spirit dwelling in Christ, in whom the Holy Spirit lives in great profusion. This is what was said in prophecy by Isaiah: 'The Spirit of the Lord shall rest upon him. . .' (11:2–3) and in the name of the Lord himself: 'The spirit of the Lord is upon me. . .' (61:1; Lk 4:17–19) and by David: 'Therefore God, your God, has anointed you with the oil of gladness above your fellows' (Ps 45:7).

Did the situation change—for the worse—after the peace of Constantine? It is true that the favour given to the Church by Constantine and his successors brought a certain relaxation. The fourth-century Fathers bear witness to this and complain of it.[35] The extraordinary and more or less miraculous charisms undoubtedly seem to have become rare at this time.[36] The monastic movement has often been represented as the successor of the martyrs and as a protest in favour of an eschatological form of Christianity that was opposed to the secular spirit of the age and against a Church that was too powerful, carnal and worldly. It is, of course, true that, as a way of life and an approach to reality and even in the form of authority that it favoured, monasticism was an original spiritual power that was relatively independent of what Tertullian called the Church of the bishops. In the course of our survey of the Church's history and the Holy Spirit, we shall encounter quite frequently evidence of this kind of duality with its resulting tension. It would, however, be historically incorrect, and it would also do injustice to the ideal, to speak of a complete dichotomy.

In the first place, many bishops were in fact monks or at least men who had been educated within the framework of the religious life and who had retained the attitudes and behaviour encouraged by that way of life. Many examples spring at once to mind: Basil the Great, John Chrysostom, Augustine, Martin of Tours, Germanus of Auxerre, Patrick, Eucherius of Lyons, Faustus of Riez, Lupus of Troyes, Caesarius of Arles, Martin and Fructuosus of Braga, Gregory the Great, Augustine of Canterbury, and Leander and Isidore of Seville. The hierarchy, as we term it, acting as the minister of the Spirit, drew its strength from its close and living relationship with monachism.[37] The bishop as the father of Christians and the monastic founder have the same quality of 'men of God', who are animated by the Spirit and in whom the Spirit dwells.[38] The term vir Dei or 'man of God' is the classic name for the man in whom the active presence of the Spirit is made manifest and who is filled with the Spirit. The virtue of God rests on him, animates him, acts through him and often goes beyond the limits of what is ordinary because of a discernment of spirits, a power over souls, prophetic lights and the gifts of knowledge. Such a man, in other words, has thaumaturgic abilities.

One cannot fail to recognize these qualities in such men as Martin of Tours (†397) and Patrick (†460). Did they not form part of a tradition? Patrick himself wrote in his autobiographical *Confession*:

I am bound to the Spirit and it is not I, but the Lord who asked me to come (§ 43).

Was it without God or according to the flesh that I came to Ireland? Who drove me here—bound by the Spirit—to see no one who was related to me? (Letter No. 10).

Once again I saw him praying in me and I was as it were inside my body and I heard him praying over me, that is, over the inner man, and he was praying powerfully there, with groans. And during the whole of that time I was dumbfounded and astonished and I wondered who it was praying in me, but at the end of the prayer he spoke as if he was the Spirit, and so I woke up and recalled that the Apostle had said: 'The Spirit helps us in our weakness; for we do not know how to pray as we ought, but the Spirit himself intercedes for us with sighs too deep for words' (§25–26).[39]

A disciple, Gildas (†570), wrote: 'May he speak for me, he who alone is true—the Holy Spirit'[40] and 'May the *sancti vates* reply for us, today as in the past, since they were the mouth and the organ of the Holy Spirit'.[41]

NOTES

1. H. Weinel, *Die Wirkungen des Geistes und der Geister im nachapostolischen Zeitalter bis auf Irenäus* (Freiburg, 1899); G. Bardy, *La théologie de l'Eglise de S. Clément de Rome à S. Irénée (Unam sanctam*, 13) (Paris, 1945), pp. 128–156.

2. Clement of Rome, *Cor* XLII, 3. In the Acts of the Apostles, the apostles seem to be moved by the Spirit (see W. Mundle, 'Das Apostelbild der Apostelgeschichte', *ZNW*, 27 [1928], 36–54) as are, in a more general way, all those who are engaged in building up the Church: Stephen (Acts 5:8; 7:55), Barnabas (11:24), Paul (13:9), etc. Thomas Aquinas' idea of the apostles was that of persons who were permeated with and fashioned by the Spirit; see A. Lemonnyer, 'Les Apôtres comme docteurs de la foi d'après S. Thomas', *Mélanges thomistes* (Le Saulchoir, 1923), pp. 153–173.

3. *Odes of Solomon*, VI, in Syria, c. 90 A.D. These odes bear witness to great joy through the action of the Spirit.

4. See *Didache*, XI, 8–12; XIII. Similar criteria, based on manner of life, are contained in the *Shepherd of Hermas*, which appeared in the middle of the second century: see especially chapter 43 (Precept XI). For the important part played by prophecy in the apostolic and the sub-apostolic periods, see P. de Labriolle, *La crise montaniste* (Paris, 1913), pp. 112–123.

5. Justin, *Dial*. 82; G. Bardy, *op. cit*., p. 132. For the gifts of the Spirit, see *Dial*. 39, 2–5; 88, 1.

6. Miltiades, an opponent of Montanism, quoted by Eusebius, *Hist. Eccl.* V, XVII, 4.

7. See J. L. Ash, 'The Decline of Ecstatic Prophecy in the Early Church', *ThSt*, 37 (1976), 227–252.

8. Ignatius, *Philad*. 7.

9. *Mart. Polycarpi*, XVI, 2.

10. See Eusebius, *Hist. Eccl.* V, 24, 2, 5, quoting Polycrates.

11. Irenaeus, *Adv. haer*. V, 8, 2 (*PG* 7, 1142; ed. W. W. Harvey, II, p. 339); IV, 33 (*PG* 7, 1072ff.; Harvey, II, p. 256).

12. *Adv. haer*. IV, 26, 2 (*PG* 7, 1053; Harvey, II, p. 236). For the interpretations of this text, see my *L'Eglise une, sainte, catholique et apostolique (Mysterium Salutis*, 15) (Paris, 1970), p. 210, note 73.

13. See A. M. Koeniger, 'Prima sedes a nomine iudicatur', *Beiträge zur Geschichte des christlichen Altertums und der byzantinischen Literatur. Festgabe A. Ehrhard* (Bonn, 1922), pp. 273–300.

14. Eusebius, *Hist. Eccl.* V, III, 4; Fr. tr. P. de Labriolle, *Les sources de l'histoire du Montanisme. Textes grecs, latins, syriaques* (Fribourg and Paris, 1913), p. 68; *idem, La crise montaniste, op. cit.* (note 4); R. A. Knox, *Enthusiasm* (Oxford, 1950), pp. 25–49; H. Kraft, 'Die altkirchliche Prophetie und die Entstehung des Montanismus', *TZ*, 11 (1955), 249–271. For the latest stage in research into this subject, see F. Blanchetière, 'Le montanisme originel', *RSR*, 52 (1978), 118–134, and 53 (1979), 1–22.

15. In Epiphanius, *Panarion*, XLVIII, 1: see P. de Labriolle, *La crise montaniste, op. cit.*, p. 136.

16. P. de Labriolle, *La crise montaniste, op. cit.*, pp. 130ff. For an appeal to the fourth gospel and the book of Revelation, see pp. 190ff.

17. P. de Labriolle, *ibid.*, p. 541. In note 1, this author quotes Priscillian. A recent book on the latter is H. Chadwick, *Priscillian of Ávila. The Occult and the Charismatic in the Early Church* (Oxford, 1976). Priscillian, who was the Bishop of Avila from 381 until 385, was in favour of asceticism and encouraged charismatic prophetism among men and women. He was accused of sorcery and Manichaeanism and was tortured and executed by order of the emperor at Trier in 385. St Martin protested against this use of constraint.

18. Irenaeus, *Adv. haer.* II, 32, 4: 'It is impossible to say how many charisms the Church receives throughout the whole world from God in the name of Jesus Christ who was crucified under Pontius Pilate'.

19. *Adv. haer.* V, 6, 1 (*PG* 7, 1137; Harvey, II, p. 334). To complete Irenaeus' testimony, it is worth quoting once again his *Adv. haer.* III, 11, 9, against Marcion: 'Those people who maintain that there are false prophets and who use it as an excuse to reject the Church's grace of prophecy are very unfortunate, since they behave like men who, because of people who act as hypocrites, even refrain from having relationships with their brothers' (see A. Rousseau and L. Doutreleau, *SC* 211, p. 173); see also IV, 20, 6 (*SC* 100, p. 642). In the *Demonstration of the Apostolic Preaching*, the same author writes: 'Others do not accept the gifts of the Holy Spirit and reject the prophetic charism by which man, when he is watered, bears God's life as a fruit' (*Dem.* 99; Fr. tr. L.-M. Froidevaux, *SC* 62, p. 169). What was most necessary and most permanent in the Church for Origen was the charism of discernment (*In Num.*, Hom. XXVII, 11; ed. W. A. Baehrens, p. 272). This was so even when 'most of the other charisms have ceased' (*In Prov.* c. 1; *PG* 13, 25A). See also I. Hausherr, *Direction Spirituelle* (see note 38 below), p. 46.

20. Origen, *Contra Cels.* I, 46.

21. *Panarion*, XLVIII, 1; see P. de Labriolle, *Les sources, op. cit.* (note 14), 88, p. 115. It is not certain whether Epiphanius was referring here to undisputed contemporary facts.

22. Cyprian, *Ep.* LVII, 5 (ed. W. von Hartel, p. 655).

23. See A. von Harnack, 'Cyprian als Enthusiast', *ZNW*, 5 (1902), 177–191; A. d'Alès, *La théologie de S. Cyprien* (Paris, 1922), pp. 77–83.

24. See my 'Rudolph Sohm nous interroge encore', *RSPT*, 57 (1973), 263–294.

25. See my *Tradition and Traditions* (Eng. tr.; London and New York, 1966), Part One, Excursus B, pp. 119–137, which deals with the permanence of *revelatio* and *inspiratio* in the Church and provides a bibliography. Among dozens of texts, the following, taken from the Council of Carthage (256 A.D.) is worth noting: '(Deus) cuius inspiratione ecclesia eius instruitur' (*Sent.* 28; Hartel, p. 447).

26. See the works of H. de Lubac, *Histoire et Esprit. L'intelligence de l'Ecriture d'après Origène* (Paris, 1950), pp. 104ff., 295–335 and *passim*; and *Exégèse médiévale. Les quatre sens de l'Ecriture*, 4 vols (Paris, 1959–1964).

27. Tertullian, *De pud.* XXI, 17–18 (after 217); see also K. Adam, *Der Kirchenbegriff Tertullians* (Paderborn, 1907).

28. *Contra Marc.* IV, 22 (in 207–208).

29. Irenaeus, *Adv. haer.* III, 11, 9 (*PG* 7, 890; Harvey, II, pp. 50–51; *SC* 34, pp. 203ff.).

30. *Adv. haer.* III, 24, 1 (*PG* 7, 966; Harvey, II, p. 131; *SC* 34, pp. 399ff.). A. Benoît has given this explanation of Irenaeus' text: 'Because the Spirit is given to the Church, Irenaeus was

able to say that where the Spirit was there was the Church. And since there is only one Church, he was able to reverse the statement and say that where the Church was there was also the Spirit': see *L'Esprit Saint et l'Eglise* (Paris, 1969), p. 133. It is, however, important to define the content of the term 'Church' as used by Irenaeus. The Church was, for him, what contained the faith handed down from the apostles by the succession of ministers and made present and renewed again and again by the Spirit. This Church was the whole Church, but also the Church made concrete in the local community. P.-M. Gy understands this passage to refer to the *ecclesia*, i.e. the local assembly in which it is necessary to share in order to participate in the gifts of the Spirit: see his 'Eucharistie et "ecclesia" dans le premier vocabulaire de la liturgie chrétienne', *M-D*, 130 (1977), 19–34, especially 31.

31. In the Prologue to the *Apostolic Tradition*, written in 215 and continuing a treatise on the charisms, Hippolytus ends with these words: 'The Holy Spirit conferring on those whose faith is correct the perfect grace to know how those who are at the head of the Church must teach and preserve everything' (Fr. tr. B. Botte, *SC* 11, p. 26).

32. *Philosophoumena* I, *Praef.* 6 (after 222): 'No one will dispute all this (the teaching of the philosophical sects)—only the Holy Spirit handed down in the Church. The apostles were the first to receive the Spirit and they communicated it to those whose faith was correct. We, who are their successors, who share in the same grace of the priesthood and teaching and who are considered to be the guardians of the Church, do not close our eyes and do not suppress our words. . . . Each one of us will fulfil our tasks in our own time and we shall share in all the graces that the Holy Spirit will grant to us.'

33. Clement of Alexandria, *Strom.* VII, 14 (*PG* 9, 522; ed. O. Stählin, p. 62).

34. Novatian, *De Trin. lib.* XXIX (*PL* 3, 943–946; L. Y. Fausset, *Cambridge Patristic Texts* (1909), pp. 105–111).

35. See the references in my *Vraie et fausse réforme dans l'Eglise*, 2nd ed. (Paris, 1969), pp. 155–156.

36. John Chrysostom made a connection between the gift of tongues, which was, in his opinion, at an end, and the crude nature of the earliest Christians: see his *Hom*. 3, 4, on the Acts of the Apostles; 'the time of miracles is over', *Hom.* 40, 2, on the Acts: see P. Rancillac, *L'Eglise manifestation de l'Esprit chez S. Jean Chrysostome* (Dar Al-Kalima, Lebanon, 1970), pp. 124, 142; A.-M. Ritter, *Charisma im Verständnis des Joannes Chrysostomus und seiner Zeit* (Göttingen, 1972). A more certain faith has no need of external signs: *In 1 Cor. Hom.* 29, 12, 1 (*PG* 61, 239); *Hom.* 1 on Pentecost, 4; cf. Gregory the Great, *Mor. in Job* XXXIV, 3, 7 (*PL* 76, 721A-C).

37. See O. Casel, 'Die Mönchesweihe,' *Jahrbuch für Liturgiewissenschaft*, 5 (1925), pp. 1–47.

38. See O. Casel, 'Benedikt von Nursia als Pneumatiker', *Heilige Überlieferung. Festgabe I. Herwegen* (Münster, 1938), pp. 96–123; B. Steidle, ' "Homo Dei Antonius". Zum Bild des "Mann Gottes" im Alten Mönchtum', *Antonius Magnus Eremita, 356–1956* (*Studia Anselmiana*, 38) (Rome, 1956), pp. 148–200; A. Mandouze, *Saint Augustin. L'aventure de la raison et de la grâce* (Paris, 1968, pp. 168ff.; P. Rousseau, 'The Spiritual Authority of the "Monk-Bishop". Eastern Elements in Some Western Hagiography of the Fourth and Fifth Century', *JTS*, new series, 22 (1971), 380–419. For monks in the early Church, see I. Hausherr, *Direction spirituelle en Orient autrefois* (*Or. Chr. Anal.*, 144) (Rome, 1955), pp. 39–55: 'Spirituel'.

39. Translation based on Fr. tr. of Patrick's *Confession* and the letter to Coroticus by G. Dottin, *Les livres de saint Patrice* (Paris, 1908). See also J. Chevalier, *Essai sur la formation de la nationalité et les réveils religieux au Pays de Galles des origines à la fin du sixième siècle* (Lyons and Paris, 1923), pp. 396ff.

40. Gildas, *De Excidio Britanniae*, c. 62.

41. *ibid.*, c. 37.

2

TOWARDS A THEOLOGY AND A DOGMA
OF THE THIRD PERSON

There is no lack of comprehensive histories and detailed monographs on this subject.[1] It would be presumptuous and even foolish to try to provide in a few pages a worthwhile outline of the development of this quite complex teaching and the various forms that it has taken in the course of its history. All that can be done here is to present a number of aspects of reflection about the Christian experience of the Spirit in the Church.

In a well-known text, Gregory Nazianzen, who died in 390 after having been Patriarch of Constantinople, pointed to the gradual progress of the revelation of the mystery of God through the Old Testament to the New and in Christian reflection itself:

> The Old Testament preached the Father openly and the Son more obscurely, while the New revealed the Son and hinted at the deity of the Spirit. Now the Spirit dwells in us and reveals himself more clearly to us. For it was not right, while the deity of the Father had still not been confessed, to preach the Son openly and, before the deity of the Son had been acknowledged, to force us to accept the Holy Spirit—and I speak too boldly here—into the bargain. . . . (It was much more suitable that) by gradual advances and, as David said, by partial ascents, moving forward and increasing in clarity, the light of the Trinity should shine on those who had already been given lights (*Orat. XXXI Theol.* V, 26).[2]

Although several important expressions of this doctrine were known at the beginning, they were insufficient and they were not accepted everywhere. For Hermas, for example, about 148–150, the Holy Spirit was the Son of God.[3] Justin Martyr, writing at the same period, also seems to identify, in an inadequate way, the Pneuma and the Logos. Even more surprising is the confusion that exists in writings (wrongly) attributed to Cyprian, in Lactantius and in a creed attributed to the Council of Sardica (343).[4] From about that time onwards, however, a Trinitarian faith was confessed in the celebration of baptism. When exactly did Christians begin to baptize 'in the name of the Father, of the Son and of the Holy Spirit'? This was certainly being done at the time when Matthew was editing his gospel, but were the words that he attributed to the risen Lord spoken by Jesus? Exegetes think not and have given various reasons for their conviction.[5] The Trinitarian affirmation, however, was generally accepted from the time of St Paul. It is found in its

Matthaean form in the *Didache* (VII, 1) and in Justin.[6] In Irenaeus, it is expanded into a confession of faith containing a form of catechesis:

> In the first place, (faith) urges us to remember that we have received baptism for the remission of sins in the name of God the Father and in the name of Jesus Christ the son of God incarnate who died and rose again and in the Holy Spirit of God.[7] . . . That is why, when we are born again, baptism takes place through these three articles and gives us the grace of new birth in God the Father by means of his Son in the Holy Spirit.[8]

In the East, orthodox teachers reacted against the heresy of Macedonius and the Pneumatomachi[9] or 'enemies of the Holy Spirit'. These believed that the Spirit was a power or an instrument of God that had been created in order to act in us and the world. They therefore remained, in their idea of the Spirit, at the level of 'economy' and did not reach the level of 'theology', that is to say, what, at the level of God himself and in his being, is the presupposition of a deifying activity in man. Among those who reacted against this heresy were Athanasius, Basil of Caesarea and Gregory Nazianzen. In his *Letters to Serapion*, written between 356 and 362, Athanasius concluded from the baptismal formula that the Spirit shared the same divinity as the Father and the Son in the unity of the same substance.[10]

Basil (†379) resumed Athanasius' argument and developed the traditional position still further. On 5 (or 7) September 374, the feast of St Eupsychus, at Caesarea in Cappadocia, he pronounced this doxology: 'Glory to the Father, with the Son, with the Holy Spirit'. Criticized for this ambiguous innovation, since the usual form of the doxology, which Basil also used, was 'Glory to the Father, through the Son, in the Holy Spirit', he wrote a treatise on the Holy Spirit in 374–375.[11] In it, he showed that his new doxology was justified by Scripture and tradition. His argument followed the pattern that it had taken in several letters written at about the same time,[12] namely that it is necessary to be baptized according to the form that has been received, to believe as one has been baptized and to praise God as one believes. Basil avoided calling the Spirit explicitly God, just as Athanasius had avoided this. He did so for two reasons. The first is that, when one speaks of God, one has to remain faithful to the terms defined in Scripture and the second is that it is better to adapt oneself to the weakness of those whom one is combating and to make it easy for them to be converted by not providing an opportunity for a new cavil. An affirmation that the Spirit is worthy of the same honour and the same adoration as the Father and the Son is, however, a confession that the three are of the same substance and a way of confounding the Pneumatomachi, just as the Arians had been confounded by the faith expressed at Nicaea.

One hundred and fifty bishops met at the Council convoked at Constantinople by the emperors Gratian and Theodosius I and completed the Nicene Creed by adding an article on the Holy Spirit in the tradition of Basil and Athanasius. According to this so-called Niceno-Constantinopolitan Creed of 381, the Spirit was neither 'God' nor 'consubstantial' with the Father and the Son, but was the 'Lord and life-giver, proceeding from the Father, object of the same worship and the same glory with the Father and the Son'.[13] In a letter sent in the course of the following year to Pope Damasus and other Western bishops, the bishops, meeting again at Constantinople, set out the work of the Council by using the words *ousia mia, aktistō kai homo-ousiō kai sunaidiō triadi*, 'one substance, the uncreated Trinity, consubstantial and eternal'.[14] That, then, is our faith, proclaimed every Sunday in the Creed that comes from Athanasius, Basil and the 150 Fathers of the Council of Constantinople. At about the same time, Pope Damasus also formulated the same faith. In 374, he expressed it in his letter *Ea gratia* to the Eastern bishops and in 382 (the most commonly accepted date) he convoked a synod at Rome, which formulated exactly the same faith as that of the Fathers of Constantinople in 24 canons.[15]

Seen in the perspective of the Eastern Fathers, but also in the light of our present understanding, this affirmation is concerned not only with the truth of God, but also with the truth about man and his absolute destiny. If the Spirit is not God in substance, then we cannot be truly deified, Athanasius declared in 356.[16] Gregory Nazianzen repeated this in 380, with reference to the baptismal formula.[17] With or without reference to baptism, this argument about our sanctification is common to all the Fathers, but especially to the Greek Fathers, who claimed that the Holy Spirit is God, because he carries out what only God can carry out.[18]

It was, however, in the West, thanks especially to Tertullian (†222–223), that the vocabulary and therefore the concepts used in the Christian confession of faith were fully developed, even though Tertullian's theology remained, in the long run, unsatisfactory.[19] He also referred to baptism, in which we confess our faith in the Spirit as a 'third' in one God.[20] He was responsible for what have been called 'those well-known terms *Trinitas, tres personae* and *una substantia*, which he formulated and which became commonplaces in the dogma of the Trinity, and for such imaginative expressions as *Deum de Deo* and *lumen de lumine*, which we still use in confessing our faith'.[21]

The Latin terms *substantia* and *persona* used by Tertullian were readily intelligible, although the second expresses the rôle played and tends to favour the modalism. (In Tertullian, it has the juridical meaning of 'responsible individual'.) The Greek word *hupostasis* was translated literally into Latin as *sub-stantia*: for the Latin Fathers, substance was the same as essence. In the final anathema of Nicaea, *ousia* and 'substance' were also identified, but this was done by calling the latter 'hypostasis'.[22] At a local council at Alexandria in 362, the Cappadocians meant by 'hypostases' the specific characters of the divine persons and spoke of one substance, *ousia*, or nature, *phusis*, in three hypostases or three persons, *prosōpois*. Jerome

75

was quite confused by this.[23] Nonetheless, this vocabulary was finally recognized by the Second Council of Constantinople in 553.[24] It was difficult to find words that were adequate to express a mystery—that of God in his most intimate being—which transcends all created intelligence and understanding. Hilary of Poitiers, one of the great early authors writing about the faith, apologized for having to speak about this question and said that heresy obliged him *illicita agere, ardua transcendere, ineffabilia loqui*—'to do what is not permitted, to rise to the heights and to express what is inexpressible'.[25] The mystery of the Trinity of God is undoubtedly a principle of life, contemplation and praise, but the theological study of the Trinity consists to a great extent of a reflection about the vocabulary and the grammar used to express it; as will also be the case in the *Summa* of a mystic like Aquinas. Now, however, we must return to our special theme, the Spirit.

The struggle against and the victory over the Pneumatomachi seem to have had an influence on two liturgical developments. The first of these is the epiclesis or invocation of the Holy Spirit over the bread and wine. This epiclesis certainly existed already. (See, for example, the anaphora of Hippolytus, and *Catechesis* V, 7 of Cyril of Jerusalem, dating from 348–349; *SC* 126, p. 155.) It gained more and more ground towards the middle and end of the fourth century and subsequently, when the anaphoras of Serapion and Basil of Caesarea, the *Catechesis* of Cyril of Jerusalem or his successor John, and the liturgy attributed to John Chrysostom appeared. We shall be considering the problem of the epiclesis from the liturgical and theological points of view in Volume III. Secondly, whereas the early Christians celebrated the single mystery of salvation and the new life gained and communicated by Christ during the fifty days beginning with Easter, they began, in the course of the fourth century, to make a distinction between the feasts of the Resurrection, the Ascension and Pentecost.[26] Accounts of pilgrimages to Jerusalem detail the separate feasts; there was a wish to give liturgical solemnity to dogmas defined in opposition to heresies. Pentecost was certainly never a feast *of the Holy Spirit*, The mysteries of the Word made man were celebrated and the divine persons were not isolated—the Spirit was 'co-adored and conglorified with the Father and the Son'. This does not mean that Christians did not pray to him as a separate Person, in the same way that they prayed to Christ. According to J. A. Jungmann, this practice was favoured by reaction against the Arians.

No attempt is made here to provide a history of the pneumatological dogma. Certain Fathers have, of course, to be mentioned in this context. These include Hilary of Poitiers (†367), Cyril of Jerusalem (†386), Didymus the Blind (†c. 398), Ambrose (†397), who wrote a treatise *De Spiritu Sancto*, in which he developed the orthodox doctrine of the Tri-unity of God and the divinity of the third Person, and finally Cyril of Alexandria (†444). It is also important to speak of Syrian Christianity and to include Antioch and, at Edessa or Nisibis, Ephraem Syrus (†373), who was called the 'lyre of the Holy Spirit'.[27] In this Syrian tradition, which was for the most part expressed in lyrical verse and especially in hymns, the Church, together with the orientation of its ministries, its sacramental life and the fulfilment of its mission as expressed in Mt 28:18–20, is linked not so much to the incarnate Word as to the Spirit of Pentecost. It is the Spirit that brings the Church to birth and acts in the three sacraments of initiation—baptism, chrismation and the Eucharist. The epiclesis is here an invocation that the reality of the resurrection may be brought about in the celebrating community.

In 393, Augustine (354–430), who was at the time still a simple priest, presented his treatise *De fide et symbolo* to a local council. In it, he said:

> Many books have been written by scholarly and spiritual men on the Father and the Son. . . . The Holy Spirit has, on the other hand, not yet been studied with as much care and by so many great and learned commentators on the scriptures that it is easy to understand his special character and know why we cannot call him either Son or Father, but only Holy Spirit.[28]

From that time onwards, Augustine became intensely interested in the theology of the Holy Spirit. His ideas on this subject are found scattered throughout the whole of his later work, but they are most fully developed in *De Trinitate*, which he began in 399 and did not finish until 419. In this treatise, he reflects about the whole of the Trinitarian mystery at a depth and breadth that are unequalled elsewhere.[29] We shall deal only with what concerns the Holy Spirit. Augustine has an original doctrine of the third Person and the part played by that Person in our lives, the powerful simplicity of which we do not want to betray because of the recurrent constraints of space.

Oddly enough, Augustine had at first criticized his idea of the Spirit, at least in the form in which he met it, in his treatise of 393,[30] but he had other encouraging reasons for pursuing the theme. Thirty years previously, Marius Victorinus, whose conversion had impressed him and to whom he owed his knowledge of the 'books of the Platonists', had written:

> Adesto, sancte spiritus, patris et filii copula.
> Tu cum quiescis, pater es, cum procedis, filius,
> In unum qui cuncta nectis, tu es sanctus spiritus.

> Help us, Holy Spirit, you who connect the Father and the Son!
> When you are resting, you are the Father; when you proceed, the Son;
> in binding all in one, you are the Holy Spirit.[31]

Augustine takes as his point of departure the fact that some attributes are common both to the Father and to the Son; these neither contrast them nor distinguish them. Are goodness and holiness, then, the Holy Spirit? Augustine hardly dares to say this;[32] they are the properties of essence. Augustine, however, does not accept this essence or common nature as his starting-point to go on to the Persons. One only has to read his work to set aside this popular idea, which is still encountered here and there. The Bishop of Hippo is firmer and more precise in his commentary on Jn 16:13, a whole section of which he includes in his *De Trinitate*.[33] The Father, he says, is only the Father of the Son and the Son is only the Son of the Father, but the Spirit is the Spirit of both. According to Mt 10:20 and Rom 8:11, he is the Spirit of the Father and, according to Gal 4:6 and Rom 8:9, he is the Spirit of the Son (that is, of Christ). Although he is quite distinct, the Spirit is therefore what is common to the Father and the Son. He is their shared holiness and their love. The unity of the Spirit is established by the bond of peace:

> Whether he is the unity of the other two Persons or their holiness or their love (*charitas*), whether he is their unity because he is their love, and their love because he is their holiness, it is clear that he is not one of the two (other Persons). . . . The Holy Spirit is therefore something that is common to the Father and the Son, whatever he is. This communion, however, is both consubstantial and coeternal. If the term 'friendship' is suitable, then let us use it, but it would be more exact to speak of 'charity'. . . . They are therefore no more than three: the one loving him who has his being from him, the other loving him from whom he has his being, and that love itself. And if that love is nothing, how can God be Love (see 1 Jn 4:8 and 16)? And if he is not substance, how can God be substance?[34]

Augustine insists on the unity of substance and therefore also on equality in that substance. It is not hard to imagine how difficult it was for him to make an effective transition from the essential to the 'notional', that is, to the 'personal' level. In fact, God is charity (or love), but, Augustine asks, 'Is it the Father who is charity, is it the Son, is it the Holy Spirit or is it the Trinity?' He also asks the same question with regard to the other attributes that are at once common to the three Persons and unique to the Father (*memoria*) or the Son (*intelligentia*). 'It is important to recognize that the Persons—all three and each one separately—possess these perfections, each one in his own nature' (*De Trin*. XV, 17, 28). There is a general or essential meaning and a distinctive or personal meaning with which the terms Love (Charity) and Spirit are used. 'God' is Spirit (Jn 4:24), the Father is Spirit and the Son is Spirit. In some scriptural texts, however, the term Love is applied to the Holy Spirit and Augustine mentions and explains 1 Jn 4:7–19 and Rom 5:5 in this context (*De Trin*. XV, 17, 31). There are also other places in Scripture where the same word is used either in a general sense or in a limited and particular sense; 'the Law' or 'Prophet' are examples of this (*De Trin*. XV, 17, 30).

God is Spirit, the Father is Spirit and the Son is Spirit. Just as both are called and each one is called 'Spirit', the same word can also be applied, Augustine believes, to the one who is not one of them, but in whom is manifested *communitas amborum*, the 'community of both' (*In Ioan. ev.* XCIX, 7). Being common to both, the Spirit receives as his own the names that are common to them: 'Spirit' and 'Holy' (*De Trin.* XV, 19, 37).

The Spirit, then, is Spirit and Love of the first two Persons. He must therefore be said to proceed from those Persons, but in the first place from the Father, since the Son derives his being from the Father, although he is also, with the Father, the origin of the Spirit.[35] Augustine cites several texts in Scripture which show that the Spirit also proceeds from the Son. One is Jn 20:22: 'He breathed on them and said to them: "Receive the Holy Spirit"'. Two others are taken from Luke: 6:19 and 8:4–6: 'Power came forth from him'. Augustine gives various examples showing that this *virtus* is the Spirit. He also quotes Jn 15:26; 17:15 and 5:26. It is clear, then, that there is, for him a continuity between 'economy' and 'theology'; this conviction is a characteristic of his Trinitarian theology. For him, the *Filioque* is an obvious necessity, as it was also for Ambrose, who had quite explicitly affirmed it though his theology of the Trinity had been so inspired by the Greek Fathers that he even took whole sections from their writings.

Augustine also discusses Jn 15:26: *qui de Patre procedit*, 'who proceeds from the Father', but does not find it a difficulty. Jesus, he claims, said this in the sense in which he said: 'My teaching is not mine, but his who sent me' (Jn 7:16). He provides an admirable commentary on the latter text (*In Ioan. ev.* XCIX, 8 and 9; cf. *De Trin.* XV, 27, 48). This goes back to the Spirit proceeding in the first place (*principaliter*) from the Father, since the Father gave the Son life in him and the power to communicate that life. Augustine sums up his teaching in the following way:

> According to Holy Scripture, this Holy Spirit is neither only the Spirit of the Father nor only the Spirit of the Son, but is the Spirit of both. Because of this, he is able to teach us that charity which is common both to the Father and to the Son and through which they love each other.[36]

It is clear that the images that Augustine used for the Trinity continued to preoccupy him throughout his treatise. The third term employed in Books VIII to XV of *De Trinitate* is *amor* (or *voluntas*).[37] Although he sees the Spirit as a mutual love (*invicem*), he does not apply the idea of friendship in a special way to the theology of the Trinity. He is clearly not deceived by the value of psychological images, and dissimilarities occur in his writing together with similarities (*De Trin.* XV, 21, 40ff.). Images are nonetheless useful theological tools which he does not hesitate to employ, because they help to point to the difference between the procession of the Word and that of the Spirit and between 'being begotten' and 'proceeding'.[38]

Augustine frequently calls the Holy Spirit 'Gift (of God)'[39] and refers in this context to Scripture (Acts 2:37–38; 8:18–20; 10:44–46; 11:15–17; Eph 4:78). It is true that the Spirit is only 'given' when there are creatures who are capable of 'possessing' and enjoying him, but at the same time he also proceeds eternally as 'giveable' and, in this sense, as Gift, so that this can be regarded as one of his attributes and one of his proper names. When the Spirit is given to us, he unites us to God and each other by the same principle that seals the unity of Love and Peace in God himself. It is not enough to speak here of the created gift of grace, even though it is in effect through that gift that the Spirit is given to us.[40] The Spirit, however, is given as the principle of the Church's unity:

> In our way of speaking, the Holy Spirit is not only the Spirit of the Father and the Son who have given him to us, but also ours, given to us who have received him. It is as in the words 'the deliverance of the Lord' (Ps 3:8), which is the salvation given and our salvation given to us who receive it. The Holy Spirit is therefore the one of God who gives him to us, and ours for us who receive him.[41]
>
> It is because he is common both to the Father and to the Son that they wanted us to have communion with each other and with them, that is to say, through the Holy Spirit, who is God and gift of God.
>
> It is in the Holy Spirit that we are reconciled with God and that we have our delight. . . . It is through the Holy Spirit that the people of God (the Church) are gathered together in unity. . . . Since the remission of sins can only be given in the Holy Spirit, it can only be given in that Church which has the Holy Spirit. . . . The society of unity of the Church of God, outside which there is no remission of sins, is the work of the Holy Spirit, although the Father and the Son clearly collaborate in this, because the Holy Spirit himself is in a sense the society of the Father and the Son. . . . The Spirit is possessed in common by the Father and the Son, because he is the only Spirit of both.[42]

This brings us to the very heart of Augustine's ecclesiology. As I have pointed out elsewhere,[43] Augustine saw the Church as existing at two levels or in two orbs or circles. The first of these is the *communio sacramentorum*, which is the work of Christ, and the second is the *societas sanctorum*, which is the work of the Holy Spirit. Augustine calls this heart of his teaching about the Church *ecclesia in sanctis, unitas, caritas, Pax*. He also calls it *Columba*, since its principle is the Holy Spirit, who performs in the Church that function that is carried out in the body by the soul.[44] This idea can be expressed in contemporary language by saying that there is the *institution* of the Church which comes from Christ, the Word, the sacraments and the ministry, but that, if this institution is to bear the Christian fruit of salvation and communion with God, there must also be the *event* of the Holy Spirit. The word 'event' expresses in this case the values of not being given in advance, of contemporaneity and penetration. If, however, the Church is seen as a whole, the Spirit always dwells in it. Augustine often refers to the Church as the Temple of the Holy Spirit.[45] His view of the Church is also very profound in a truly theo-logical sense; he wants us to believe that God aims to bring us together and unite us to himself by the same Spirit, who is the bond between the Father and the Son, that is, *in Spiritu Sancto, quo in unum Dei populus congregatur*.[46]

80

The part played by the Holy Spirit in the Church and in our personal lives of grace is of the very greatest importance. Augustine became acquainted with the work of the 'Platonists' through Marius Victorinus. It was to them that he owed the idea of *regressus*, that is, the return of the soul to its source. (Centuries later, Thomas Aquinas was to build up his synthesis on the basis of the idea of *egressus* and *reditus*.) The Spirit was seen by Augustine as the end and the seal of intra-divine fertility, who communicates that fertility to us and is also the principle of our return to the Father through the Son. He is also at the deepest level the longing that impels us towards God and causes us to end in him: *donec requiescat in Te*!

NOTES

1. Apart from articles in dictionaries, see J. Lebreton, *Les origines du dogme de la Trinité*, I (Paris, 1919); II: *Histoire du dogme de la Trinité* (Paris, 1928); H. B. Swete, *The Holy Spirit in the Ancient Church* (London, 1912); T. Ruesch, *Die Entstehung der Lehre vom Heiligen Geist* (Zürich, 1953); G. L. Prestige, *God in Patristic Thought* (London and Toronto, 1936; repub. London, 1952); G. Kretschmar, *Studien zur frühchristlichen Trinitätstheologie* (Tübingen, 1956); *idem*, 'Le développement de la doctrine du Saint-Esprit du Nouveau Testament à Nicée', *Verbum Caro*, 88 (1962), 5–55; H. Opitz, *Ursprünge frühchristlicher Pneumatologie* (Berlin, 1960). For the Stoic context, see G. Verbeke, *L'evolution de la doctrine du Pneuma du stoïcisme à S. Augustin* (Paris, 1945); M. Spanneut, *Le Stoïcisme des Pères de l'Eglise de Clément de Rome à Clément d'Alexandrie* (Paris, 1957). For the Gnostic context, see A. Orbe, *La teología del Espíritu Santo (Estudios Valentinianos*, IV) (Rome, 1960).
2. *PG* 36, 161; cf. Anselm of Havelberg, *Dialogi* I, 6 (*PL* 188, 1147D; *SC* 118, p. 62).
3. See the *Shepherd of Hermas*, cc. 41; 58; 59, 5–6; 78, 1 (numbering of chapters according to R. Joly, *SC* 53 [1958]); see also Justin, *1 Apol.* 39.
4. See P. Smulders, 'Esprit Saint', *Dictionnaire de Spiritualité*, IV/2, col. 1274.
5. See E. Schweizer, *'pneuma'*, *TDNT*, VI, pp. 401, esp. note 440, 451, note 842.
6. Justin, *1 Apol.* 61, 3, not quoting Mt 28:19; nor do the texts of Irenaeus' *Demonstration* quoted below, whereas, fifteen years before this, Irenaeus referred explicitly to Mt 28:19 as the Lord's words: see *Adv. haer.* III, 17, 1 (*PG* 7, 929; ed. W. W. Harvey, II, p. 92). See also *1 Apol* 67 for the Eucharist.
7. *Dem.* 3 (Fr. tr. L.-M. Froidevaux, *SC* 62, p. 32 [Paris, 1959]). See also *Adv. haer.* III, 17, 1 (*SC* 211, pp. 328ff.).
8. *Dem.* 7 (*SC* 62, p. 41). The text continues: 'Those who have the Spirit of God are led to the Word, that is, to the Son, but the Son presents (them) to the Father and the Father obtains incorruptibility (for them). Without the Spirit, then, it is not (possible) to see the Son of God and, without the Son, no one can approach the Father, since knowledge of the Father (is through) the Son and knowledge of the Son (is) through the Holy Spirit. As for the Spirit, it is according to whether it pleases the Father that the Son dispenses (him) as a minister to whom the Father wishes and as he wishes': see also chapter 99. For Irenaeus' pneumatology, see A. d'Alès, 'La doctrine de l'Esprit Saint chez S. Irénée', *RSR*, 14 (1924), 496–538; H.-J. Jaschke, *Der Heilige Geist im Bekenntnis der Kirche. Eine Studie zur Pneumatologie bei Irenäus von Lyon im Ausgang vom altchristlichem Glaubensbekenntnis* (Münster, 1977).
9. P. Meinhold, 'Pneumatomachoi', Pauly-Wissowa, *Real-Encyclopädie der classischen*

Altertumswissenschaft, XXI/1 (1951), cols 1066–1101; W. D. Hauschild, *Die Pneumatomachen* (Hamburg, 1967). The error of the Pneumatomachi was attributed to Macedonius, who was Bishop of Constantinople from 342 to 360. According to the Pneumatomachi, the being and the activity of the Holy Spirit were not those of a divine Person.

10. Athanasius, *Ad Ser. Ep.* I, 28 (*PG* 26, 593 and 596); *Ep.* III, 6 (*PG* 26, 633; the Spirit is not a different substance, *allotrioousion*); IV, 7 (*PG* 26, 648; Fr. tr. J. Lebon, *SC* 15 (1947)). The same argument is also found about 380 in Italy, in Faustinus, *De Trin.* VII, 3 (*PL* 13, 78). Hilary of Poitiers made a connection, in 355–356, between his confession of the three Persons and the text of Mt 28:19; see *De Trin.* II, 1 (*PL* 10, 50–51).

11. Basil of Caesarea, *De spir. sanct.* (Fr. tr. B. Pruche, *SC* 17bis (1968)). To the bibliography given in this translation, pp. 243ff., should be added the following contributions to *Verbum Caro*, 89 (1968): B. Bobrinskoy, 'Liturgie et ecclésiologie trinitaire de S. Basile', 1–32; J.-M. Hornus, 'La divinité du Saint-Esprit comme condition de salut personnel selon Basile', 33–62; T.-F. Torrance, 'Spiritus creator', 63–85; P. C. Christou, 'L'enseignement de S. Basile sur le Saint-Esprit', 86–99.

12. *Ep.* 125, 3 (*PG* 32, 549; in 373); 159, 2 (*PG* 32, 620–621; in 373); 226, 3 (*PG* 32, 849; in 375).

13. The text will be found in *DS*, 150 and in *Conciliorum Œcumenicorum Decreta* (= *COD*), J. Alberigo *et al.*, 3rd ed. (Bologna, 1973), p. 24 with a short history and bibliography, pp. 21–23. This creed was only presented as such and as having come from the 150 Fathers of the Council in 381 by the Council of Chalcedon (451): see the bibliography in *COD*, *op. cit.*

14. *COD*, pp. 25–30.

15. For the letter *Ea gratia*, see *DS*, 145; Synod, *DS*, 152–177. I am following dates given in *DS*, although C. Pietri, *Roma Christiana* (Rome, 1976), pp. 828ff., dates these texts to 377.

16. Athanasius, *Ad Ser. Ep.* I, 22ff. (*PG* 26, 584ff.; *SC* 15, pp. 127ff.).

17. Gregory Nazianzen, *Orat. theol.* V, 28 (*PG* 36, 165). W. Jaeger, who specialized in the study of Gregory of Nyssa, showed that, in Christian teaching, humanity is completed in the holiness of which the Spirit is the principle. See *Gregor von Nyssa's Lehre vom Heiligen Geist, aus dem Nachlass* (ed. H. Dörries, Leiden, 1966).

18. See Gregory Nazianzen, *Orat. theol.* V, 28 (*PG* 36, 165); Didymus, *De Trin.* II, 7 (*PG* 39, 560–600); Cyril of Alexandria in N. Charlier, 'La doctrine sur le Saint-Esprit dans le "Thesaurus" de S. Cyrille d'Alexandrie', *Studia Patristica*, II, pp. 187ff.; G. M. de Durand has edited and Fr. tr. Cyril's *Dialogues on the Trinity*, Vol. I, *SC* 231; Theodore of Mopsuestia, *Hom. cat.* 9, 15; Augustine, *Ep.* 238, 21 (*PL* 33, 1046).

19. R. Piault, 'Tertullien a-t-il été subordinatien?' *RSPT*, 47 (1963), 181–204; J. Moingt, 'Théologie trinitaire de Tertullien', *RSR*, 54 (1966), 337–369; *idem*, *Théologie trinitaire de Tertullien*, 3 vols and one volume of tables (*Théologie*, 68, 69, 70) (Paris, 1966)—a total of 1,094 pages!

20. Tertullian, *Adv. Prax.* 8–9 (*PL* 2, 163–164; *CC* 2, 1168–1169).

21. Piault, *op. cit.*, 204.

22. *DS*, 126.

23. *Ep.* 15 to Pope Damasus (*PL* 22, 356–357): 'Speaking of three hypostases. . . . The entire school of profane literature recognizes only ousia as hypostasis. Who, I ask you, would speak of three substances?' An echo of this can be found in Thomas Aquinas, *ST* Ia, q. 29, a. 3, ad 3; q. 30, a. 1, ad 1. Augustine was more serene and also went deeper: 'To speak of what cannot be expressed, we have to express as we can what cannot be explained. The Greeks among us (*a nostris Graecis*) used the terms "one essence, three substances", whereas the Latins spoke of "one essence or substance, three persons" ' (*De Trin.* VII, 4, 7; cf. 6, 11; *Bibl. August.*, XV, pp. 527, 541; cf. p. 584).

24. *DS*, 421.

25. Hilary, *De Trin.* II, 2 (*PL* 10, 51), in 355.

26. See O. Casel, 'Art und Sinn des ältesten christlichen Osterfeier', *Jahrbuch für Liturgiewissenschaft*, 14 (1938), 1, 78; J. Daniélou, *Bible et Liturgie (Lex Orandi*, 11) (Paris, 1951), pp. 429–448; G. Kretschmar, 'Himmelfahrt und Pfingsten', *Zeitschrift für Kirchengeschichte*, 66 (1954–1955), 209–253; see especially R. Cabié, *La Pentecôte. L'évolution de la cinquantaine pascale au cours des cinq premiers siècles* (Tournai and Paris, 1965), with a bibliography, pp. 11–14. See also 'Esprit Saint', *Dictionnaire de Spiritualité*, IV/2, col. 1285.

27. See Emmanuel-Pataq Siman, *L'expérience de l'Esprit par l'Eglise d'après la tradition syrienne d'Antioche (Théologie historique*, 15) (Paris, 1971); cf. P. Rancillac, *L'Eglise, manifestation de l'Esprit chez S. Jean Chrysostome* (Dar Al-Kalima, Lebanon, 1970).

28. Augustine, *De fid. et symb.* IX, the beginning of 18 and 19 (*PL* 40, 190 and 191).

29. *De Trin.*: *PL* 42; Latin text, with Fr. tr. and explanatory notes by M. Mellet and T. Camelot in *Bibl. August.*, Vol. 15 (1955): by P. Agaësse and J. Moingt, Vol. 16 (1955). For the Trinitarian theology of Augustine, see the classic studies by M. Schmaus (1927), I. Chevalier (1940) and O. du Roy (1956). For his pneumatology, see F. Cavallera, 'La doctrine de saint Augustin sur l'Esprit Saint à propos du "De Trinitate" ', *RTAM*, 2 (1930), 365–387; 3 (1931), 5–19; I. Chevalier, *S. Augustin et la pensée grecque. Les relations trinitaires* (Fribourg, 1940); 'La théorie augustinienne des relations trinitaires. Analyse explicative des textes', *Divus Thomas*, 18 (1940), 317–384; M. Nédoncelle, 'L'intersubjectivité humaine est-elle pour S. Augustin une image de la Trinité?' *Augustinus Magister* (Paris, 1954), I, pp. 595–602; O. du Roy, 'L'expérience de l'amour et l'intelligence de la foi trinitaire selon S. Augustin', *Recherches augustiniennes*, 2 (1962), 415–445; P. Smulders, 'L'Esprit Saint chez les Pères', *Dictionnaire de Spiritualité*, IV/2, cols 1279–1283; F. Bourassa, *Questions de théologie trinitaire* (Rome, 1970); B. de Margerie, *La Trinité chrétienne dans l'histoire (Théologie historique*, 31) (Paris, 1975), pp. 159–172; E. Bailleux, 'L'Esprit du Père et du Fils selon saint Augustin', *RThom*, 77 (1977), 5–29.

30. *De fid. et symb.* IX, 19 (*PL* 40, 191): 'Some have dared to believe that the communion between the Father and the Son, that is, if I may say it, the deity that the Greeks call *theoteta*, may be the Holy Spirit. . . . This deity that they also want to understand of the mutual love of the two and of the charity that they (the Father and the Son) have for each other is, according to them, called the Holy Spirit.' Later, in his treatise *De haeresibus*, Augustine was to say that these 'some' were Semi-Arians and Macedonians who denied the personality of the Holy Spirit: see B. de Margerie, *op. cit.*, p. 161, note 180.

31. First hymn, lines 3–5 (Fr. tr. P. Hadot, *SC* 68 (Paris, 1960), pp. 620–621); cf. the Third Hymn, lines 245–246 (*ibid.*, pp. 650–651). Victorinus, however, has his own theology of the Trinity, which does not contain any idea of a procession on the part of the Holy Spirit.

32. *De Civ. Dei*, XI, 24 (*PL* 41, 337ff.).

33. *In Ioan. ev.* XCIX, 6–9 (*PL* 35, 1888–1890); *De Trin.* XV. 27, 48.

34. *De Trin.* VI, 5, 7; this translation is slightly changed, but is based on the Fr. tr. of Mellet and Camelot (see above, note 29). The text can be compared with the following, among others: 'Ecce tria sunt ergo, amans, et quod amatur, et amor' (*De Trin.* VIII, 14; *PL* 42, 960); 'Spiritus est Patris et Filii, tamquam charitas substantialis et consubstantialis amborum' (*In Ioan. ev.* CV, 3; *PL* 35, 1904).

35. 'I say "in the first place" (*principaliter*) because it is established that the Holy Spirit also proceeds from the Son. But the Father gives this privilege to the Son. It is not that the Son ever existed without having it, but everything that the Father has ever given to his only Word has been given to him by begetting him. He has therefore begotten him in such a way that their shared Gift proceeded also from the Son and that the Holy Spirit is spirit of the other two Persons' (*De Trin.* XV, 17, 29; cf. 26, 45–47).

36. *De Trin.* XV, 17, 27 (*Bibl. August.*, Vol. 16, p. 501).

37. Table in *Bibl. August.*, Vol. 16, pp. 586ff.; cf. pp. 593ff.

83

38 *De Trin*. XV, 27, 50: '(What is) suggested is the outline of a distinction between birth and procession, since to understand by thinking is not the same as desiring or even enjoying by the will' (*Bibl. August*., Vol. 16, p. 563).

39. *De Trin*. V, 11, 12; 12, 13; 15, 16; VII, 4, 7; XV, 17, 29; 18, 32; 19, 33; 27, 50. F. Cavallera, *op. cit*. (note 29), pp. 368–370, has given a full account of this.

40. 'It is, I think, for a good reason that the Lord speaks in the gospel of John so many times and in such a striking way of unity—his unity with the Father or our unity among ourselves—without ever saying that we and they are one, but always saying (Jn 17:20) "that they may all be one *even as* we are one" ' (*De Trin*. VI, 3, 4; *Bibl. August*. Vol. 16, p. 479); 'It is what we are commanded to imitate in the order of grace' (*De Trin*. VI, 5, 7; Vol. 16, p. 485). J. Moingt has rightly insisted on this aspect of Augustine's teaching, but, in my opinion, has not gone far enough in exploring his thought in *Bibl. August*., Vol. 16, pp. 655–656.

41. *De Trin*. V, 14, 15 (*Bibl. August*., Vol. 16, p. 459).

42. *Sermo* 71, 12, 18; 12, 19 and 17, 28; 20, 33 (*PL* 38, 454; 455 and 459; 463–464). This sermon has been dated to about 419.

43. See my general introduction to *Traités antidonatistes*, *Bibl. August*., Vol. 28 (Paris, 1963), pp. 100–124.

44. *In Ioan. ev*. XXVI, 6, 13 (*PL* 35, 1612–1613); XXVII, 6, 6 (*PL* 35, 1618); *Sermo* 267, 4 (*PL* 38, 1231); 268, 2 (*PL* 38, 1232–1233). The last text is quoted, together with those of John Chrysostom, Didymus, Thomas Aquinas, Leo XIII and Pius XII, to illustrate this theme in the Dogmatic Constitution *Lumen Gentium*, 7, 7, on the Church.

45. See D. Sanchis, 'Le symbolisme communautaire du Temple chez S. Augustin', *RAM*, 37 (1961), 3–30, 137–147.

46. *Sermo* 71, 12, 18–20, 33 (*PL* 38, 454–464); *De Trin*. XV, 21, 41 (*PL* 42, 1087).

THE THEME OF THE HOLY SPIRIT AS THE MUTUAL LOVE OF THE FATHER AND THE SON[1]

The story of this theme is studded with the reflections of various great Christian thinkers who have followed one another and have been acquainted with the work of their predecessors, which they may have accepted or corrected. These great thinkers were all members of the Western Church, since there is hardly any evidence of this theme in the Eastern Church.[2] In this chapter, we shall consider above all Anselm, Achard and Richard of Saint-Victor, Bonaventure and Thomas Aquinas.

Anselm (1033–1109) wrote his *Monologion* about 1070, when he was the Abbot of Bec, and his *De Processione Spiritus Sancti* after the Council of Bari, in which he took part in 1098 with the Greeks, as Archbishop of Canterbury, during one of his periods of exile. Just as it would be controversial to call Augustine an 'essentialist', so too would it be restricting the theological legacy of Augustine to only one aspect of his teaching if Anselm were to be called an Augustinian. Anselm does not treat of the Holy Spirit as the mutual Love of the Father and the Son. What he does is to extend the anthropological analogy, but he does this not in the psychological, but in the metaphysical sense that came naturally to him.[3] In the *Monologion*, he deduces the existence of a Word and a Love from the perfection that it is necessary to attribute to the *Summus Spiritus*. It is, according to Anselm, not possible to deny that this Supreme Spirit is capable of an act of understanding and therefore of saying; the Word thus expressed is perfect similarity and therefore also consubstantial and the Son. But the one who remembers himself and knows himself necessarily also loves himself, and this forms the basis for the existence of the third Person (*Mon.* 49). In this Supreme Spirit, however, Memory is the Father and Understanding is the Son. It is therefore evident that Love proceeds from both (*Mon.* 51) and does so as from a single principle (*Mon.* 53). H. F. Dondaine observed correctly that 'there is a difference of perspective between Augustine and Anselm. In the case of the latter, the friendship of the Father and the Son is no longer the principle by which the second divine procession is explained. This friendship is only a secondary consideration and is seen as an aspect assumed by divine Love, when this is considered in the Father and the Son. Anselm introduces the third Person first and foremost as the Love of the Supreme Spirit proceeding from his memory and his thought (*Mon.* 50).'

In *De Processione*, Anselm develops the argument outlined by Augustine—an argument which Thomas Aquinas was later to recognize as having an absolute value in favour of the *Filioque* that could not be refuted. This is that, in God, everything is one at the point where there is no opposition in relationship.

It would be impossible to overestimate the genius of Anselm, but it has to be said that his deduction is too closely related to that of faculties or properties from an essence. How is it that he, as a man of prayer, was not able to express more clearly the demands made by the personalization of the three Persons, whom he calls the *tres nescio quid* (*Mon.* 78)?

One of the greatest mystics and theologians of the Middle Ages, William (†1148), who left Liège to become Abbot of Saint-Thierry near Rheims, wrote, in 1119–1120, a treatise *De contemplando Deo* (*SC* 61, Paris, 1959). In it, he comments on these words in Jesus' high priestly prayer (Jn 17:22–23, 26): 'The glory which thou hast given me I have given to them, that they may be one even as we are one, I in them and thou in me, . . . that the love with which thou hast loved me may be in them and I in them'. In this meditation, which is written in the form of a prayer, William reaches the greatest depths of knowledge of our communion with the mystery of God. Here is this prayer, based on F. Bourdeau's French translation in *Les quatre saisons, Automne* (Paris, 1977):

> You love yourself, O most lovable Lord, in yourself, when, from the Father and the Son, the Holy Spirit proceeds—the Holy Spirit who is the love of the Father for the Son and the love of the Son for the Father, such a sublime love that it is the unity of both, such a deep unity that, of the Father and the Son, the substance is one.
>
> And you love yourself in us, when, having sent the Spirit of your Son into our hearts, by the sweetness of the love and the warmth of the good will that you inspire in us, crying 'Abba, Father', you cause us to love you with a great love. You also love yourself in us so much that we, who hope in you and cherish your name of Lord, . . . who dare to believe by the grace of your Spirit of adoption that everything that belongs to the Father is also ours and who are your adopted sons, call you by the same name that your only natural son used for you!
>
> In this way, such a firm bond, such a clinging and such a strong taste of your sweetness comes about that our Lord, your Son, called it 'unity', when he said: 'that they may be one in us'. And this unity has such dignity and glory that he added: 'As I and you are one'. O joy, O glory, O wealth, O pride—for wisdom also has its pride! . . .
>
> We therefore love you, or rather you love yourself in us, we loving with affection, you loving with effectiveness, making us one in you by your own unity, or rather by your own Holy Spirit, whom you have given to us. . . .

Adorable, terrible and blessed one, give him to us! Send your Spirit and everything will be created and you will renew the face of the earth. . . . May the dove bearing the olive branch come! . . . Sanctify us with your holiness! Unite us with your unity!

Richard, Prior of Saint-Victor in Paris, who died in 1175, wrote a treatise *De Trinitate* (*SC* 63, Paris, 1959; Fr. tr. G. Salet), although it has been established that his teaching follows that of Achard of Saint-Victor.[4] His approach is also very similar to that of Anselm, in that he introduces reasons that are not only probable, but also necessary,[5] but he ends by building up a very different structure, which is much more directly linked to prayer and personal experience. He also claims that we must attribute to God what we regard as supreme in our scale of values (*De Trin.* 1, 20). That supreme value is love, *caritas*. This idea makes it possible for the two affirmations that faith and prayer make us confess to be combined: *tres*, three, and yet *unus*, one (see the Creed *Quicumque*). For *caritas* calls for a multiplicity of subjects— there is a transition here from essentialism to personalism, and Richard works out a new definition of the person. But even this is not saying enough, for we have to go further and speak of a charity that is perfect, since that is what we have to attribute to God (3, 2 and 5). This perfect charity requires a *consortium amoris* (3, 11), that is, a loving together of a third and an enabling together of that third to share in the happiness of the first two. The Spirit is therefore postulated as the *condilectus* of the Father and the Son (3, 11 and 19; 6, 6; Salet translates this word as 'a common friend': see p. 192, note 2; he also calls it 'a third equally loved'). It is clear, then, that Richard of Saint-Victor follows Augustine (whom he quotes 87 times[6]) and Anselm (whom he quotes 44 times), but, instead of speaking of understanding and will, he deduces everything from love. The prayerful confession of faith— *tres* who are *unus*—is translated into 'one Love and three lovers'.

As it is not my aim to outline a history of the theology of the Trinity here, I shall not discuss the teachings of Alexander of Hales, although I would not want to overlook the importance of his *Summa*. It would not, however, be possible to leave out Alexander's disciple Bonaventure, who combined in his work the precise formulations of his master and an inheritance from Augustine and Richard of Saint-Victor.[7] He was undoubtedly in sympathy with Richard's theology of unselfish and communicative love. This is clear from his statement: 'Mutual love is more perfect than love of oneself. Mutual love that communicates itself is even more perfect, since the one who is not inclined to communicate has a flavour of desire' (*In I Sent.* d. 10, a. 1, q. 1). J.-G. Bougerol has defined Bonaventure's understanding of this love in the following way: 'Essential love or the love with which each person loves himself and with which each person loves the other two is *complacentia*. Notional love or the love in which the Father and the Son are united in spirating the Holy Spirit is the love of *concordia* or *dilectio*. Personal love is produced by the Holy Spirit, by means of liberality, of the *concordia* of the Father and the Son.'[8] The Spirit is the *nexus* or bond between the two. For us, he is Gift. As Bonaventure himself says: 'Spirit, Love and Gift all refer to the same reality, but to different aspects of it. They are different names for the same emanation. "Spirit" expresses that emanation mainly by reference to the power that produces it. "Love" expresses it mainly with regard to its mode of emanation, that is, as a *nexus*. "Gift" expresses it with regard to the relationship which is the consequence of it, . . . (because) it is made to unite us (*connectare*)' (*In I Sent*. d. 18, a. 1, q. 3, ad 4). The Spirit is the principle of our return to God.

Throughout the whole of his career as a theologian, Thomas Aquinas was open to the idea, which had come down to him from a long and deeply rooted tradition, of the Holy Spirit as the bond of love between the Father and the Son.[9] What part did Thomas make the Spirit play in his attempt to account intellectually for the mystery of the Trinity, which was not accessible to natural reason and transcended all human explanation, even within the framework of faith? It was, in his opinion, only possible to look for an *intellectus* of what faith enables us to hold by using the resources available to human reason. The theme of mutual love meant a great deal to the religious and poetical aspects of man and there is undoubtedly a deep relationship between prayer and poetry, but Thomas did not believe that this theme had sufficient intellectual force to provide a basis for organizing the treatise on the Trinity. He did not employ it in his *Contra Gentiles*, his *Compendium Theologiae* or the very important articles at the beginning of the *Summa*: Ia, q. 27, a. 3 ('Is there in God another procession other than the begetting of the Word?') and a. 4 ('Is the procession of love in God a begetting?'). This theme can, however, be found in the *Summa* in Thomas' statements concerning the procession from the Father *and* the Son (q. 36, a. 4, ad 1), his attempts to explain that, as the bond between the two, the Spirit was not a term, but a *medius* (q. 37, a. 1, ad 3) and finally his attempts to elucidate certain traditional expressions (q. 37, a. 2; q. 39, a. 8). He preserved Augustine's analogy derived from the structure of the spirit[10] and given special emphasis by Anselm, whose train of thought Thomas followed. There is a clear expression of the Augustinian image of the Trinity in his *Compendium Theologiae*:

> Three aspects of man can be considered here: man existing in his nature, man existing in his intellect and man existing in his love. These three aspects are, however, not one, since thinking here is not being, nor is loving; and only one of the three is a subsisting reality, that is, man existing in his own nature. In God, however, being, knowing and loving are one, with the result that God existing in his own natural being, God existing in his intellect and God existing in his love are only one, each of the three being one subsisting reality.[11]

Presented in this way, this view has rather too philosophical a character, however valuable it may otherwise be, and shows the spirit as three times in itself. If this statement had been made by Hegel, it would have aroused great interest! It might also lead us to believe that Thomas thought of the Persons on the basis of essence, as modes or faculties. This, however, is not the case, as A. Malet, E. Bailleux and others have shown. Everything active in God was, for Thomas, done by Persons (*actiones sunt suppositorum*). The essential knowledge and love of self exist only as hypostasized in personal subjects, which can be distinguished only by the opposition in the relationships which constitute them. These relationships are established in the divine substance, which is absolute existence, and are therefore themselves subsisting, in other words, they make the Persons exist according to the divine substance, the first *sub ratione intellectus*, under the aspect of knowledge (although the Word is *spirans amorem*: see *Comm. in ev. Ioan.* c. 6, lect. 5, no. 5) and the second *sub ratione voluntatis*, under the aspect of will or love. 'The Person in God signifies the relationship in the mode of substance.'[12] In these conditions, as Thomas explained in his *Summa*:

It is necessary to state that the Holy Spirit proceeds from the Son. If he did not proceed from him, it would not be possible to distinguish the one from the other. This goes back to our previous arguments. In fact, it is not possible to say that the divine Persons can be distinguished one from the other by any absolute thing. If this were so, it would follow that the three were not a single essence, since every absolute attribute in God belongs to the unity of essence. It is clear, then, that the divine Persons can only be distinguished from each other by their relationships. These relationships, however, can be used to distinguish the Persons only insofar as they are opposed. The evidence of this is that the Father has two relationships; he is related by the one to the Son and by the other to the Spirit. As these relationships are not opposed to each other, however, they do not constitute two Persons, but only belong to one Person, that of the Father. If, then, it is only possible to find in the Son and the Holy Spirit these two relationships, each of which refers to the Father, these relationships will not be mutually opposed, just as the two relationships between the Father and each of them are not opposed. Just as the Father is only one Person, then, it would follow that the Son and the Holy Spirit would only be one Person possessing two relationships opposed to the two relationships of the Father. This, however, is a heresy, since it destroys faith in the Trinity. It is therefore necessary for the Son and the Holy Spirit to refer to each other by opposed relationships. In God, however, the only opposed relationships there can be are relationships of origin, and these opposed relationships of origin are, on the one hand, relationships of principle and, on the other, of term resulting from that principle. It is therefore necessary to say either that the Son proceeds from the Holy Spirit—but no one says this—or that the Holy Spirit proceeds from the Son—which is what we confess.

The explanation that we have given above of their respective procession is in accordance with this teaching. It has been said that the Son proceeds according to the mode that is peculiar to the intellect, as Word, and that the Holy Spirit proceeds according to the mode that is peculiar to the will, as Love. Love, however, has of necessity to proceed from the word, since we can love nothing but what we can apprehend in a conception of the mind. On this basis, then, it should be clear that the Holy Spirit proceeds from the Son (*ST* Ia, q. 36, a. 2).[13]

I have carefully re-read, in chronological order, the various accounts of Thomas Aquinas of the Trinity and the studies that have been devoted to this subject (see below, note 9) and the most acceptable explanations and conclusions have, in my opinion, been provided by H. F. Dondaine. I give a few extracts from his study:[14]

To defend the territory acquired by Anselm in his synthesis, Thomas relegates mutual love to the second level. It is not invoked to introduce the second procession in q. 27, it is recalled as a traditional datum which has to be taken into account in theory in q. 37 and it is taken into account exactly as it is by Anselm in ad 3. . . .

Thomas often has recourse to this aspect of the Holy Spirit as the *nexus duorum*. His aim is to safeguard Augustine's datum (whatever may be the case with Richard of Saint-Victor) and he does not forget that the Holy Spirit is the bond of love uniting the Father and the Son. *It is clear, however, that he does not regard this as a suitable context in which to introduce the mystery of the third Person*; to do this would expose him to the danger of anthropomorphism and those inequalities and oppositions which caused Richard's disciples to stumble.[15]

In fact, the metaphor of love as the 'bond between lovers' cannot be raised above the image. What two friends have in common to unite them is not the reality experienced in their act of love. Each experiences his own act, which makes two loves, two acts of loving. What they have in common is the object and their common good. . . . But it is to this one object, their community in good, that they adapt their two hearts and their two wills by two loves. It is useless to change the image by speaking, for example, about a single breath, one kiss,[16] one balm or one single liquor distilled from the two. These images are not capable of grasping the mystery of the origin of the Holy Spirit in an intelligible way. It is clear that this mystery contains only one act, only one spiration and only one 'loving' that is common to both loving Persons, but this is so *because of the unity of essence*, not because of friendship as such. . . .

It is therefore illuminating and very interesting to present the Holy Spirit as the friendship of the Father and the Son or the mutual Love of the Father and the Son. This view can, however, not be used metaphysically, since it does not provide a consistent analogy for our understanding of the Person of the Holy Spirit. The other way of presenting the Holy Spirit, that is, as the Love which God bears for his Goodness or the Love that proceeds from the divine Knower and Lover, and from his Word, is much plainer, but it is more certain, and Thomas preferred it to introduce in a rational way the procession of the third Person.

NOTES

1. In addition to F. Bourassa, *Questions de théologie trinitaire* (Rome, 1970) and B. de Margerie, *La Trinité chrétienne dans l'histoire* (*Théologie historique*, 31) (Paris, 1975), see H. F. Dondaine, 'Saint Thomas et la Procession du Saint-Esprit', *S. Thomas d'Aquin, Somme Théologique. La Trinité*, II (Paris, 1946), pp. 387–409; A. Malet, *Personne et*

amour dans la théologie trinitaire de saint Thomas d'Aquin (Bibl. Thom., XXXII) (Paris, 1956).

2. Almost the only Greek author who can be quoted here is Epiphanius of Salamis, *Ancoratus*, VII, 'Sundesmos tēs Triados' (*PG* 43, 28B).

3. R. Perrino, *La dottrina trinitaria di S. Anselmo nel quadro del suo metodo teologico e del suo concetto di Dio (Studia Anselmiana*, 29) (Rome, 1952); A. Malet, *op. cit.*, pp. 55–59.

4. A. M. Ethier, *Le* De Trinitate *de Richard de Saint-Victor* (Paris and Ottawa, 1939); G. Dumeige, *Richard de Saint-Victor et l'idée chrétienne de l'amour* (Paris, 1952); A. Malet, *op. cit.*, pp. 37–42; O. González, *Misterio Trinitario y existencia humana. Estudio histórico teológico en torno a San Buenaventura* (Madrid, 1966), pp. 295–363. For Achard of Saint-Victor, see J. Ribaillier's edition of Richard's *De Trinitate* (1958); J. Chatillon, *Théologie et spiritualité dans l'œuvre oratoire d'A. de St-Victor* (Paris, 1969).

5. Richard of Saint-Victor, *De Trin.* 1, 4. M.-D. Chenu has observed, correctly, that 'the *necessariae rationes*, following St Anselm, continued to influence the school': see his *Introduction à l'étude de S. Thomas* (Paris, 1950), p. 158.

6. Richard also resumes and defines more precisely Augustine's argument about the Holy Spirit as the Love of the Father and the Son: *Quomodo Spiritus Sanctus est Amor Patris et Filii (PL* 196, 1011–1012).

7. J.-F. Bonnefoy, *Le Saint-Esprit et ses dons selon S. Bonaventure* (Paris, 1929); A. Malet, *op. cit.* (note 1), pp. 42–48 (Alexander), 48–53 (Bonaventure); O. González, *op. cit.* (note 4). To these works can also be added monographs by J. Kaup (1927), Z. Alszeghy (1946) and P. Prentice (1951) on Bonaventure's theology of love. Our knowledge of the Franciscan school is continuously being increased by historical research. The following recent works are worth consulting: W. H. Principe, 'St. Bonaventure's Theology of the Holy Spirit with Reference to the Expression "Pater et Filius diligunt se Spiritu Sancto" ', *S. Bonaventura: 1274–1974*, IV (Grottaferrata, 1974), pp. 243–269; *idem*, 'Odo Rigaldus, a Precursor of St Bonaventure on the Holy Spirit as Effectus formalis in the Mutual Love of the Father and Son', *Mediaeval Studies*, XXXIX (1977), 498–505.

8. J. F. Bougerol (ed.), *Lexique Saint Bonaventure* (Paris, 1969), pp. 16ff., 'Amor', with references.

9. See the following texts, among others: *In I Sent*. d. 10, q. 1, a. 3; d. 32, q. 1, a. 1, ad 4 (in 1254); *De Pot.* q. 9, a. 9, ad 2; q. 10, a. 2, ad 15 ('cum enim Spiritus Sanctus sit amor mutuus et nexus duorum, oportet quod a duobus spiretur') and a. 4, ad 10; a. 5, ad 11 (in 1256?); *Resp. ad 108 art.* a. 25 ('procedit ut nexus duorum'; in 1265–1266); *ST* Ia, q. 36, a. 4, ad 1 ('Si considerentur supposita spirationis, sic Spiritus Sanctus procedit a Patre et Filio un sunt plures. Procedit enim ab eis ut amor unitivus duorum'); q. 37, a. 1, ad 3 (the whole); q. 39, a. 8, where Thomas considers the opinions of several of the doctors of the Church (in 1267). See also J. Slipyi, *De Principio Spirationis in SS. Trinitate* (Lwow, 1926); M.-T. L. Penido, ' "Cur non Spiritus Sanctus a Patre Deo Genitus". S. Augustin et S. Thomas', *RThom*, 13 (1930), 508–527; *idem*, *Le rôle de l'analogie en théologie dogmatique (Bibl. Thom.*, XV) (Paris, 1931), pp. 295–311, also published in *ETL*, 8 (1931), 5–16 under the title 'La valeur de la théorie psychologique de la Trinité'; *idem*, 'Gloses sur la procession d'amour dans la Trinité', *ETL*, 14 (1937), 33–68; H. F. Dondaine, *op. cit.* (note 1); A. Malet, *op. cit.* (*ibid.*); C. Vagaggini, 'La hantise des *rationes necessariae* de S. Anselme dans la théologie des processions trinitaires de S. Thomas', *Spicilegium Beccense*, I (*Congrès internationale du IXᵉ centenaire de l'arrivée d'Anselme au Bec*) (Paris, 1959), pp. 103–139; E. Bailleux, 'Le personnalisme de S. Thomas en théologie trinitaire', *RThom*, 61 (1961), 35–38; F. Bourassa and B. de Margerie, *op. cit.* (note 1).

10. *De Pot.* q. 9, a. 5: 'Ad manifestationem aliqualem hujus quaestionis, et praecipue secundum quod Augustinus eam manifestat'.

11. Chapter 50, translated by Dondaine, *op. cit.*, II, p. 406, note 1; cf. *C. Gent.* IV, 26.

12. *In I Sent*. d. 23, a. 3, sol.; or 'the relationship as it subsists in the divine nature': *ST* Ia, q. 29, a. 4; q. 39, a. 1.

13. Cf. *C. Gent*. IV, 24; *De Pot*. q. 10, a. 5; *Comm. in ev. Ioan*. c. 15, lect. 6.
14. H. F. Dondaine, *op. cit*. (note 1), II, pp. 397–401.
15. The danger, to which Dondaine pointed, of anthropormophism in the theme of the Spirit as the mutual love of the Father and the Son can be illustrated by several of the formulae found in the otherwise deep and edifying books of Yves Raguin: see especially *La Profondeur de Dieu* (Collection *Christus*, 33) (1973) and *L'Esprit sur le Monde* (Collection *Christus*, 40) (1975). Some of these formulae, seen from the point of view of the strict theology of the Trinity, are not exact and to some extent ambiguous; see, for example, 'life of relationships in God' (*La Profondeur*, p. 137); 'the persons are centres of action and consciousness; this consciousness is a consciousness that is totally mutual' (p. 138); 'the Father is Father in the depths of the Son; the Son is Son in the depths of the Father; this relationship is the Love of both, which is called the Spirit' (p. 159); 'in the Trinity, it is the relationship which we call the Holy Spirit that is the ultimate depth of God; that Spirit is both the relationship that unites the Father to his Son and the ultimate intimacy of that relationship' (*L'Esprit*, p. 16); 'the relationship of the Father and the Son is united in the Spirit' (p. 7); 'between these three, if it is possible to speak of "three", what matters is not the number, but the fact that there is, in their total identity, a constant relationship of knowledge and love' (p. 27). In all these texts, the word 'relationship' is used in the sense in which it occurs in human psychology, whereas, in the doctrine of the Trinity, it has a technical and metaphysical meaning. Human interpersonal experience is transferred to God without being subjected to a necessary and purifying process of criticism. What Raguin says, however, in *La Profondeur*, p. 148, is quite correct: 'I do not claim that we project our mode of being on to that of the ultimate reality; all that I am claiming is that our mode of being provides us with a vocabulary by which we can express what is inexpressible'. There is, however, an obvious danger of anthropomorphism if our mode of being is projected as it is.
16. See Bernard, *Sermo 8 on the Canticle*, 2 (*PL* 183, 810ff.); *Sermo 89 de diversis* (*PL* 183, 707).

4

ST SIMEON THE NEW THEOLOGIAN
AN EXPERIENCE OF THE SPIRIT

[*Note:* For convenience, this not being a scholarly study, I give in this chapter two-figure references in parentheses: the volume number in the series *Sources chrétiennes* and the page number of the translation; a third figure, appearing occasionally, is the line number.]

St Simeon was one of the greatest Christian mystics. He was born in 949. He became a monk, first at Studion and then at St Mamas, where he became hegumenos in 982. He often refers to Simeon the Pious (†987) as the one who revealed the way of the spirit to him. He experienced great difficulties and strong opposition because of this reference, his exacting enthusiasm and his determination to tell others about his spiritual experiences. He gave up the hegumenate and was sent in 1009 to the opposite bank of the Bosporus, where he died on 12 March 1022. He left behind a considerable body of writings.[1]

The title 'New Theologian' refers to his having had and having communicated a (new) experience of God. In accordance with the categories that we use, we would say that Simeon was essentially a spiritual writer. His teaching is the result of his spiritual experience, which was extremely intense. He gives several accounts of it, using quite staggering language.[2] He describes, for example, how, as something of an elegant man of the world, he met his spiritual father and followed him with docility. In the following passage, he is addressing Christ:

You did not leave me lying, defiling myself in the mud, but by the bowels of mercy you sent for me and made me rise up out of this swamp. . . . You seized hold of me and dragged me out of it. . . . You entrusted me to your servant and disciple; I was covered in dirt and my eyes, ears and mouth were blocked with mud. . . . While he washed and purified himself again and again at every spring and every fountain, I saw nothing and went past them almost every time. If he had not taken me by the hand and left me near the spring, I would never have been able to find the source of the water. But as he showed it to me and often let me cleanse myself in it I would take not only the pure water into my hands but also the mud and slime and make my face dirty. . . .

One day, I was on the way and running towards the spring when once again you, who had only recently taken me out of the mud, came to meet me on the path. For

93

the first time, you dazzled my weak sight with the immaculate splendour of your face. . . . From that time onwards, more and more frequently, when I was beside the spring, you, who are without pride, did not scorn to come down (to me), but came close to me and took hold of my head, bathed it in the waters and enabled me to see more and more clearly the light of your face. . . . You came in this way and left again and gradually you appeared more and more clearly. You flooded me with those waters and gave me the grace better to see a purer light.

You were close to me, you washed me, so it seemed to me, in the waters, you flooded me with them and plunged me into them again and again. I saw the lightning shining around me and the rays of your face mixed with the waters and I was stupefied, finding myself sprinkled with luminous water. . . . You took me and, going up to heaven again, you raised me up with you, either in my body or out of my body, I do not know. . . . Then, after a little time, when I was here below, on high the heavens opened and you deigned to show me your face, like a sun without a shape. . . .

After having shown yourself in this way again and again and concealed yourself again and again. . . . I saw the lightning flashes of your face and its brilliance. . . . You showed yourself to me in this way after you had entirely purified my understanding in clarity by the light of the Holy Spirit (*Cat.* XXXVI, Thanksgiving 2 (113, 335–349)).

One day he (= Simeon) stood up and said: 'O God, show me, a sinner, your favour'. He said this in his spirit rather than with his lips, when suddenly a divine light shone down from on high on him in great profusion and completely filled the place where he was standing. The young man could not understand what was happening. He did not know whether he was in a house or whether he was beneath a roof. All that he could see everywhere was light. . . . He was entirely present to this immaterial light and it seemed to him that he had himself become light. Forgetting the whole world, he was overwhelmed with tears and with inexpressible joy and happiness. His understanding rose up to heaven and discovered another light there, even brighter than the one that was close to him (*Cat.* XXII (104, 273)).

In this account of his spiritual experience, Simeon moves from water to light, that is, from the act of washing, which represents the ascetic effort, to the breaking-in of light, which he calls the 'light of the Holy Spirit'. Light plays a very important part in his mystical experience.[3] This mysticism is entirely pneumatic and entirely Christological. Prayers to the Holy Spirit are rare in the Eastern Church.[4] Simeon introduces his hymns with such a prayer: 'Come, true light! Come, eternal life!. . . Come, light that never sets! . . . Come, you whom my wretched soul has desired and still desires! Come, only one, to one who is alone, since you can see that I am alone! . . . Come, you who have yourself become desire in me and have made me long for you—you who are absolutely inaccessible! Come, my breath and my life! . . .' (156, 151ff.).

For Simeon, the Holy Spirit is the principle of all spiritual life. Need we quote references? All Simeon's writings proclaim it: 'It is by the Holy Spirit that everyone experiences the resurrection, by which I do not mean the ultimate resurrection of the body. . . . I am speaking about the resurrection that takes place every day of dead souls, a spiritual regeneration and resurrection, occurring in a spiritual fashion.'[5] He believed that the end and the goal of the Incarnation was the communication of the Holy Spirit (*Cat.* VI (104, 45ff.); *Hymn* XV (156, 287, 121ff.); XLIV (196, 81, 145 and 95, 342); LI (p. 193); *Cent.* 3, 88 (51, 108–109)). This is in accordance with both the economy and the sequence of processions in God and it also explains a number of elements in the patristic and liturgical tradition. The end of the economy corresponds to the fullness of intra-Trinitarian life and is nothing less than our own deification: 'Who, if he has the grace of the Spirit in his heart, does not possess, dwelling in him, the revered Trinity which enlightens him and makes him god?' (*Hymn* XIX, 53–55 (174, 99); XLIV, 266–271 (196, 89ff.); L, 153ff. (p. 169); LI, 95ff. (p. 193)).

This life of the spirit, which is entirely pneumatological, is also entirely Christological. Again, what need of quoting references when everything proclaims it? The appearances are Christological and the face is the face of Christ. 'Christ is the principle, the means and the end. He is in all' (*Cent.* 3, 1 (51, 80); cf. *Cat.* XX (104, 333)). The spiritual life comes about by Christ's invitation (*Cat.* VI (104, 41); XX (pp. 331ff.)). Here too, the economy determines the order of Christian progress—it is necessary to go through the Passion in order to reach the resurrection of which the Spirit is the agent, and to follow the way of asceticism in order to achieve union.[6]

It is at this point that Simeon's own distinctive positions become clear. His pneumatology is to some extent autonomous, not with regard to Christ but with regard to the hierarchy and the sacraments. Simeon writes: 'In holy baptism, we receive the remission of our faults, we are delivered from the old curse and we are made holy by the presence of the Holy Spirit, but we do not yet have perfect grace according to the promise "I will dwell in them and I will go there", because that is the privilege of those believers who are confirmed in faith and who have proved this by their works'.[7] Again: 'By baptism and in divine communion with my fearful mysteries, I give life to all. And when I say "life" I mean my divine Spirit' (*Hymn* LV, 145–147 (196, 265)). The sacrament as such, however, is only a symbol, a statement, a beginning or an initiation. It must be followed by a baptism of the Spirit before it can be made effective, fruitful and true. 'If one is not baptized in the Holy Spirit, one cannot become a son of God or a co-heir of Christ' (*Cat.* XXXIII (112, 259)). It is worth quoting here a number of very clear statements made by Simeon in *Ethical Treatise* X and *Hymn* LV:

> Our salvation is not to be found only in the baptism of water. It is also to be found in the Spirit; just as it is not exclusively in the bread and wine of communion that we are given remission of our sins and enabled to share in life. . . . May no one venture to say: 'Since holy baptism, I have received Christ and I possess him'. Let him, on the contrary, learn that not all those who are baptized receive Christ through baptism, but only those who are strengthened in faith and (who reach)

perfect knowledge, or those who have been prepared by purification and are therefore well disposed to come to baptism (*Ethical Treatise* X (129, 273, 283)).

> Those who received your baptism in early infancy and who have throughout their lives lived unworthily of you will be more severely condemned than those who have not been baptized. . . . O Saviour, you gave repentance for a second purification and you established as its end the grace of the Spirit that we first received at baptism, since it is not only 'by water' that grace comes, according to your words, but rather 'by the Spirit', in the invocation of the Trinity. Since we were baptized as unknowing children and as beings who were still imperfect, we receive grace also very imperfectly (*Hymn* LV, 28–39 (129, 255ff.); cf. 61ff. (p. 259)).

Just as the sacrament alone is insufficient in itself, so too is faith which is mere belief, faith based on catechetical formulae. Faith calls for works[8], and these are above all works of 'repentance' (the baptism of tears, which plays such an important part in Simeon's teaching[9]) and works of effective charity. It is then that the fruits of the Spirit follow, as the signs of his indwelling (*Ethical Treatise* IX (129, 241)). For Simeon, then, possession of the Spirit and animation by the Spirit were normally the object of experience. This is an essential aspect of his spiritual teaching.

> Once again I find myself grappling with those who say that they have the Spirit of God in an unconscious manner and who imagine that they have possessed him since their baptism. They may be convinced that they have this treasure, but they do not recognize its importance. I have to deal with those who confess that they felt nothing at their baptism and who believe that the gift of God has dwelt in them in an unconscious and intangible manner and that it is still subsisting even now in that way in their souls.[10]

> If someone were to say that each one of us believers receives and possesses the Spirit without knowing it or being conscious of it, he would be blaspheming by making Christ lie when he said: 'In him there will be a spring of water welling up to eternal life' (Jn 4:14) and: 'He who believes in me, out of his heart shall flow rivers of living water' (7:38) (*Ethical Treatise* X (129, 297)).

> The Lord who has favoured us with good things that transcend our senses will also give us a new sensitivity that transcends our senses through his Spirit, so that his gifts and his favours, which transcend our senses, will be supernaturally perceived in a clear and pure way by our very senses, and through them all.[11]

The Spirit is light. Simeon's mystical experience was above all an experience of light and an experience of the Spirit. 'As for the power and effectiveness of his most holy Spirit, otherwise known as his light, no one can speak about it if he has not first seen the light with the eyes of his soul and has not become aware in himself of its illuminations and its effective powers.'[12] Simeon makes use of a comparison which is very striking and which also throws light on the part played by the Spirit in his relationship with Christ as the Son of God. The following text contains this image and also a very important problem that we shall consider without delay:

What can I say to those who like to hear themselves praised, who want to be appointed as prelates and superiors (*hēgoumenoi*) and who want to be given (the confidence) of others' thoughts (*logismoi*) and to be considered worthy to be entrusted with the task of binding and loosing? When I see them and know that they have no understanding of the divine and necessary things and that they neither instruct others nor lead them to the light of knowledge, I recognize that this is just what Christ himself said to the scribes and Pharisees: 'Woe to you lawyers, for you have taken away the key of knowledge; you did not enter yourselves and hindered those who were entering' (Lk 11:52). What is this 'key of knowledge' if it is not the grace of the Holy Spirit given by faith, which, by illumination, really brings about a state of knowledge and indeed of full knowledge? . . .

And I would also say that the door is the Son: 'I am the door' (Jn 10:7, 9) and that the key of the door is the Holy Spirit: 'Receive the Holy Spirit. If you forgive the sins of any, they are forgiven; if you retain the sins of any, they are retained' (Jn 20:22–23). What is more, the house is the Father: 'In my Father's house are many rooms' (Jn 14:2). Pay great attention, then, to the spiritual meaning of the word. If the key does not open—for 'to him the gatekeeper opens' (Jn 10:3)—then the door will not be open; but if the door is not open, no one will enter the Father's house. Christ himself said: 'No one comes to the Father, but by me' (Jn 14:6).

Now that it is the Holy Spirit who first opens our spirit (see Lk 24:45) and teaches us about the Father and the Son, is what he himself has said (*Cat.* XXXIII (113, 255ff.)).

This very important text, which I have had to quote at some length, continues with scriptural citations from Jn 16:13 and 15:26; 16:13 and 14:26; 16:7; 14:15–17 and 20; and finally concludes with the promise: 'John baptized with water, but . . . you shall be baptized with the Holy Spirit' (Acts 1:5; 11:16). Simeon's comment on this text is: 'This is normal, since, if one is not baptized in the Holy Spirit, one cannot become a son of God or a co-heir of Christ' (*Cat.* XXXIII (p. 259)). He then continues by developing the idea of the activity of the Spirit as the key that opens for us our life as children of God:

If the Holy Spirit is called the key, then it is above all through and in him that our spirit is enlightened and that we are purified, illuminated by the light of knowledge, baptized from on high, born anew (see Jn 3:3, 5) and made children of God. Paul himself said: 'The Spirit himself intercedes for us with sighs too deep for words' (Rom 8:26) and 'God has sent the Spirit of his Son into our hearts, crying Abba! Father!' (Gal 4:6). It is therefore he who shows us the door and that door is light (*Cat.* XXXIII (p. 261)).

These texts are very clear, but they also raise important questions. The relationship between the Spirit, Christ the Son and the Father is defined biblically and traditionally as a return to a principle. The comparison with the key and the door brings together, in a very remarkable way, pneumatology and Christology and shows them to be inseparable and as together forming access to the Father. The problem raised by the beginning of this series of texts is this: If it is the Spirit that opens, who in fact has the 'power of the keys'? Is it the monk or spiritual man, or is it the priest or ordained hierarchical minister?

This question is similar to that raised by the sacraments. We have already considered Simeon's idea of baptism as an introduction to the state of being a member of Christ and a child of God, but as a dead reality if it is not given life in the Spirit. The same applies to his conception of the Eucharist. He believed in what we would call the Real Presence, but he also insisted that communion should be what Thomas Aquinas called a *manducatio spiritualis*, that is, a partaking with an understanding that was full of the Spirit (*Ethical Treatise* X (129, 293); XIV (339); *Hymn* XXVI, 151ff. (174, 269)). If it were only a question of receiving a confession of thoughts (*logismoi*), there would be no problem—it would be the task of the spiritual father. The practice of confessing and entrusting oneself to a spiritual father was an essential aspect of the search for God in monasticism.[13] Simeon lived this out heroically and speaks about it frequently and forcefully in several of his writings.[14] What we have here, however, is the forgiveness of sins and the exercise of the power of the keys and that is an episcopal or presbyteral function. It is not that Simeon is denying the sacrament of order. He had himself been ordained and he took the charism of his ordination into account.[15] He was anxious, however, to castigate those who wanted to appoint themselves to such a sublime responsibility (*Ethical Treatise* VI (129, 149ff.); III (122, 433ff.)) and those who were not possessed and even crushed by it: 'Is there not and does it not seem to you that there is something fearful in this encroachment upon the apostolic dignity, brother? Can you really regard it as unimportant when you come close to the inaccessible light and become a mediator between God and men?' (*Cat*. XVIII (104, 287); XXXIII (113, 255)).

Without the Spirit, the sacrament is empty, and the same applies to the office of hegumenos and that of the priest: 'As for guiding others or teaching them the will of God, he would not be capable of doing this any more than he would be worthy to receive (the confidence of) others' thoughts—even if he were chosen by men to be a patriarch—until he possessed the light shining in him' (*Cat*. XXXIII (113, 251)). Simeon believed that it was not possible to communicate the Spirit by means of an external, visible and social process as such, even though it might be canonical, and therefore to open the door, bind or loose, in this human way with the key of the Spirit. This can only be given by the Spirit himself to the one who has opened himself or has responded to his coming by doing penance or practising ascesis. The same applies to the celebration of the holy mysteries:

> Those who have not preferred him (Christ) to the whole world and who have not regarded it as a glory, an honour and great wealth simply to adore him, to officiate and merely to be in his presence are also unworthy of the spotless vision, the joy, the happiness and all the good things in which they will never share unless they are

repentant and . . . do everything zealously what my God has said. Only then, and even so with great fear and respect, if God commanded it, could they be in touch with the sacred realities! Not all those people have the right to officiate after all. Even if (someone) had received the whole grace of the Spirit, . . . so long as God did not give him a guarantee by his choice and his command by illuminating him with his divine light and embracing him with the desire of his divine love, it would not seem to me to be reasonable for him to offer the divine (sacrifice) and to be in touch with such untouchable and fearful mysteries.[16]

In the treatise *Peri exomologēseōs*, which was until recently attributed to John Damascene, but which K. Holl has, in his new edition, restored to Simeon,[17] the latter says that he 'does not deny that the power to bind and loose was handed on from Christ to the apostles and from the apostles to the bishops and priests of the Church, but affirms that the latter are unable to exercise it because of their fallen moral state. In order to be reconciled to God's holiness, it is necessary to be holy. In order to give the Holy Spirit, it is necessary to have the Spirit because of the purity of one's own life. At the present time, those who satisfy these conditions are the monks and even then only those who live in accordance with their profession, not those who *gegonasi monachoi pampan amonachoi* (monks who have become totally non-monks).'[18]

Simeon's decisive scriptural text here is Jn 20:22–23; 'Receive the Holy Spirit. If you forgive the sins of any, they are forgiven; if you retain the sins of any, they are retained.' Only those who have the Spirit and manifest him in their lives, he insists, can bind and loose. Only holy monks, even if they have not been ordained, are therefore able to exercise this ministry. Simeon's own spiritual father received ordination, not from men, but from God!

There were many antecedents pointing in this direction—if not Origen,[19] then certainly Anastasius of Sinai (†after 700), who taught that it was right to confess one's sins to spiritual men.[20] Pseudo-Dionysius, despite his letter to Demophilus, also inclined towards a spiritual interpretation that was outside, if not opposed to, the hierarchy, in the sacramental and juridical sense of the term, since, for him the hierarchy was one of purification and mystical illumination.[21]

Simeon's position was also certainly followed. His disciple and biographer (or hagiographer), Nicetas Stethatos, did not deny that the words of the gospel 'you are the salt of the earth. . . . You are the light of the world' (Mt 5:13–14) referred to priests, but summarized Simeon's teaching in the following way:

Am I perhaps insisting too much? Is it possible for someone without the rank of bishop to go beyond the bishops of knowledge of God and wisdom? In this case, I would repeat what I have just said: the brilliance of episcopal dignity also shines on the man who has been given the power to manifest the Spirit by the word. In fact, if someone, even though he may not have been ordained a bishop by men, has received, whether he is a priest, a deacon or a monk, the grace from on high of the apostolic dignity . . . he is in effect the bishop with God and the Church of Christ who has been manifested in that Church under the influence of the Holy Spirit as God's spokesman, rather than the man who has received episcopal ordination from men and has still to be initiated into the mysteries of the kingdom of God. . . . I believe, then, that the man who has been purified as a result of sharing abundantly in the Holy Spirit . . . is the bishop. . . . In these conditions, he possesses the knowledge of these mysteries, he is the one who is the hierarch and the bishop, even if he has not received from men the ordination making him a hierarch and a bishop.[22]

It is hardly surprising that Nicetas, who had, it seems, just completed his *Life of Simeon*, came into conflict with Cardinal Humbert of Silva Candida, whom he met during the latter's dramatic mission to Constantinople in 1054 to talk with the Patriarch Michael Cerularius. Humbert may have adopted a rigid attitude, but he can hardly be blamed for saying to Nicetas: 'Every state or profession must remain within the limits of its investiture and its degree, so that it does not overturn the whole order of dignity in the Church'.[23]

What were the results, and the success, of Simeon's position, as taken up by Nicetas Stethatos, in the Eastern Church? In the *Admonitio* at the head of his edition of the treatise *De confessione*, which had until then been attributed to John Damascene (*PG* 95, 279–282), Lequien quoted texts for and against, and K. Holl has also produced testimony, such as that of John of Antioch in the twelfth century, that confession of sins, *epitimiai* and absolution to a great extent became the prerogative of monks until the middle of the thirteenth century.[24] Holl's thesis encountered a great deal of criticism and was even rejected. His leading critics were M. Jugie,[25] I. Hausherr[26] and H. von Campenhausen.[27] The texts should be re-examined now and the whole question reconsidered.

I would now like to look at a rather different question, although I do not claim that I can elucidate it satisfactorily. Augustine also attributed the remission of sins to the Holy Spirit, to the dove, the Church united by charity and the Spirit.[28] He frequently pointed out that, in these conditions, it is the Christian community, the *ecclesia*, that binds and looses.[29] One text which synthesizes this idea is: 'Has enim claves non unus homo, sed unitas accepit ecclesiae. . . . Columba ligat, columba solvit; aedificium supra petram ligat et solvit.'[30] In this context of unity and charity, Augustine goes so far as to tell believers: 'Audeo dicere, claves ista habemus et nos. Et quid dicam? Quia nos ligamus, nos solvimus? Ligatis et vos, solvitis et vos.'[31]

Augustine's theology in this case is different from that of Simeon, which can be compared with certain statements made by Tertullian as a Montanist.[32] For Augustine, binding and loosing was the task, not of spiritual men, but of the *ecclesia* as *caritas*, *pax* and *unitas* through the Holy Spirit: 'Pax ecclesiae dimittit peccata . . . columba tenet, columba dimittit; unitas tenet, unitas dimittit'.[33] In addition, the united activity of the saints who together form the *columba* is closely connected with the sacraments celebrated by the ordained ministers of the Church. The bond between what proceeds from Christ (the sacrament and the ordained minister) and what proceeds from the Holy Spirit (the spiritual fruit of salvation), is, moreover, expressed in this close connection.[34] Augustine would not have separated the two orders of reality as much as Simeon did and he would not have given such autonomy to the spiritual reality (or to spiritual men). Some of Simeon's arguments are reminiscent of those of the Donatists and even of a statement by Cyprian, who said: 'Quomodo autem mundare et sanctificare aquam potest qui ipse immundus est et apud quem Sanctus Spiritus non est?'[35] We may therefore conclude that Simeon did not sufficiently emphasize the importance of the sacrament of ordination, which is derived from the saving activity of the incarnate Word. On the other hand, he overemphasized a certain autonomy of the Spirit and of experience of the Spirit with regard to this sacrament of order, which forms part of the structure of the Church.

NOTES

1. The works of Simeon the New Theologian include *PG* 120; the treatise *Peri exomolog-ēseōs*, ed. K. Holl, *Enthusiasmus und Bussgewalt beim griechischen Mönchtum. Eine Studie zu Symeon dem Neuen Theologen* (Leipzig, 1898), pp. 110–127. Several of his works have appeared in a critical edition and translated into French in *Sources chrétiennes*. These include his *Catéchèses*, with an introduction, text and notes by Basile Krivochéine and tr. J. Paramelle: *SC* 96, 104, 113 (Paris, 1963, 1964, 1965); *Chapitres théologiques, gnostiques et pratiques*, tr. J. Darrouzès: *SC* 51 (Paris, 1957) (the 'Centuries'); *Traités théologiques et éthiques*, ed. and tr. J. Darrouzès: *SC* 122 and 129 (Paris, 1966 and 1967), with a valuable introduction; *Hymnes*, crit. ed. by J. Koder, tr. J. Paramelle and L. Neyrand: *SC* 156, 174, 196 (Paris, 1969, 1971, 1973). There have been several important studies of Simeon. These include I. Hausherr and G. Horn, *Un grand mystique byzantin: Vie de Syméon le Nouveau Théologien par Nicétas Stéthatos* (*Orient. Chr.*, XII) (Rome, 1928); S. Gouillard, 'Syméon', *DTC*, XIV/2, cols 2941-2959; B. Krivochéine, 'The Writings of St Symeon the New Theologian', *Or. Chr. Period.*, 2 (1954), 298–328; L. Bouyer in *Histoire de la Spiritualité chrétienne*, 2: *La spiritualité du Moyen Age* (Paris, 1961), pp. 662–675. There are quotations and comments in M.-J. Le Guillou, *Les témoins sont parmi nous. L'expérience de Dieu dans l'Esprit-Saint* (Paris, 1976), but they do not appear in any systematic form. An article by A. L. van der Aalst which I know only by name is 'Ambten, Charisma bij Simeon de nieuwe theoloog', in *Het Christelijk Oosten*, 22 (1970), 153–172.

2. Especially in the 'Catecheses' or instructions given to his monks: see, for example, *Cat.* XXII (104, 367ff.); XXXV and XXXVI (the two Thanksgivings: 113, 305ff., 331ff.); *Hymn* XVIII (174, 77ff.).

3. See *Cat.* XXXV (Thanksgiving 1: 113, 313ff.). Simeon's experiences of light are reported in Nicetas' *Life of Simeon*, Nos. 5, 26 and 69; see I. Hausherr and G. Horn, *op. cit.* (note 1).

4. A. Renoux noted this in 'L'office de la génuflexion dans la tradition arménienne', *Le Saint-Esprit dans la liturgie* (*XVIᵉ Semaine de Saint-Serge*) (Rome, 1977), pp. 149–163.

The Armenian liturgy includes a prayer to each of the three Persons at Pentecost; the text of the prayer to the Holy Spirit can be found on pp. 161ff.

5. *Cat.* VI (104, 45ff.; cf. p. 23: 'The kingdom of heaven consists of sharing in the Holy Spirit'); *Cat.* XXXIII (113, 249ff.); XXXV (307 and 325).

6. *Cat.* VI (104, 45); XIII (pp. 191ff.); *Hymn* LI, 89ff. (196, 593). It is worth noting how far removed Simeon's teaching here is from quietism. The coming of God, of his Spirit is as much an act of pure grace as it demands from us the keeping of the commandments, the effort and the striving of asceticism: see *Hymn* XIII (156, 257ff.); *Cat.* XII, XXII and XXVI and B. Krivochéine's Introduction (96, 35–40).

7. *Cent.* 3, 45 (51, 93); cf. 1, 36 (p. 50): 'In the first baptism, the water is the symbol of tears and the oil of anointing prefigures the inner anointing of the Spirit; in the second baptism, however, there is no symbol of truth—it is the truth itself'.

8. See *Hymn* XVII, 558–560; L, 172–176; LII, 69–77; *Cat.* VII and XIII (104, 61 and 201); *Ethical Treatise* X (129, 295): 'You see that those who do not possess the Spirit acting and speaking in them are unfaithful'.

9. This theme appears again and again in Nicetas' *Life* and very often in Simeon's own work; see *Cat.* IV (96, 48ff.); *Cent.* 1, 64, 67, 69–71; 2, 45, 46, 49, 50; 3, 34. See also I. Hausherr, *Penthos. La doctrine de la componction dans l'Orient chrétien (Or. Chr. Anal.*, 132) (Rome, 1944); M. Lot-Borodine, 'Le mystère du don des larmes dans l'Orient chrétien', *Suppl. de la Vie Spirituelle* (September, 1936).

10. *Ethical Treatise* V (129, 79ff.); *ibid.* (p. 105): ' "How do you know, much loved friend of Christ, that you will resemble him? Tell us how you know!"—"By the Spirit that he has given us!" he said (1 Jn 3:24). "It is through him that we know that we are children of God and that God himself is in us" '.

11. *Cent.* 2, 3 (51, 72). Following J. Darrouzès (p. 34) it is worth noting these brief texts: 'The indwelling of divinity in three Persons in those who are perfect, which comes about in a way that can be perceived by the mind' (*Cent.* 1, 7 (p. 42)); 'The soul no longer has the firm assurance that it will be united for ever to its God . . . if it does not have the pledge of his grace and does not possess this consciously' (3, 47 (p. 94)); 'The Son of God, God himself, came to earth so that he might unite us consciously to himself through his holy and consubstantial Spirit' (3, 58 (p. 97)); 'The man who has consciously received in himself the God who gives knowledge to men (3, 100 (p. 112)). J. Darrouzès, however, notes that the word *agnōstōs* occurs twice: 'Simeon therefore must have believed that God could act and even teach without our being conscious of it' (p. 104, note 1).

12. *Ethical Treatise* V (129, 99); cf., for the Spirit as light, IX (p. 225); XI (p. 381); *Cat.* XXXIV (113, 301). For antecedents in the writings of the Greek Fathers, see S. Gribomont, 'Esprit', *Dictionnaire de Spiritualité*, IV/2, cols 1269ff.

13. I. Hausherr, *Direction spirituelle en Orient autrefois (Or. Chr. Anal.*, 144) (Rome, 1955). For Russian Orthodoxy, see K. Holl, *op. cit.* (note 1), p. 154; I. Smolitsch, *Leben und Lehre der Starzen* (Vienna, 1936); *idem, Das altrussische Mönchtum (11.-16. Jahrhundert). Gestalter und Gestalten* (Würzburg, 1940).

14. See, for example, *Hymn* IV, 25ff. (156, 193); V, 11 (p. 201); Simeon's personal case, *Cat.* XXXVI (Thanksgiving 2: 113, 337).

15. *Cat.* XXXIV (113, 283); see also no. 16 of his treatise on Confession (*PG* 95, 304): he desired to be ordained.

16. *Hymn* XIX, 147–165 (174, 107ff.); *Ethical Treatise* XV: 'Is it necessary to speak, in the case of men of this kind (the false hesychasts), of the power to bind and loose, while those who have in them the Paraclete, who remits sins, are afraid to do the slightest thing that might be contrary to the judgement of the one who is in them and who speaks through them? But who would be so foolish . . . as to speak and do the works of the Spirit without having received the Paraclete and to deal with the affairs of God without the judgement of God?' (129, 459).

17. K. Holl, *op. cit.* (see note 1), edition of the text, pp. 110–127. This treatise was also edited

by M. Lequien; his edition appears in *PG* 95, 283–304, together with a Latin translation by Thomas Gale, the Dean of York. This is the version that I have read. I. Hausherr's summary (*op. cit.*, note 13) is not full, but it is exact.

18. I. Hausherr, *op. cit.* (note 13), p. 107, provides a summary of the argument of the treatise.
19. This is so, whatever may be said by W. Völker, *Der Wahre Gnostiker nach Clemens Alexandrinus* (1952), p. 172. See also K. Rahner, 'La doctrine d'Origène sur la pénitence', *RSR*, 37 (1950), 47–97, 252–286, 422–456; B. Poschmann, *Poenitentia secunda* (Bonn, 1949), pp. 462ff.
20. Anastasius of Sinai, *Quaestiones et Responsiones*, q. VI, 1; *PG* 89, 369ff.
21. See J. Stiglmayr, 'Die Lehre von den Sakramenten und der Kirche nach dem Ps.-Dionysios', *ZKT*, 22 (1898), 246–303.
22. Nicetas Stethatos, 'De la Hiérarchie', chapter V, nos. 32–40: *Opuscules et Lettres*, Fr. tr. J. Darrouzès, *SC* 81 (Paris, 1961), pp. 335–345.
23. Quoted by I. Hausherr, *op. cit.* (note 1), p. lxxix, in accordance with C. Will, *Acta et Scripta quae de Controversiis Ecclesiae Graecae et Latinae saeculo XI° composita exstant* (1861), p. 137. *PL* 143, 973–984 contains a treatise written by Nicetas criticizing the Latins for their use of unleavened bread (indicating an absence of life and of the Spirit), fasting on Saturday and insistance on priestly celibacy. *PL* 143, 983–1000 contains Cardinal Humbert's violent reply to this, which begins by insulting Nicetas and calling him *stultior asino* and also includes him among various heretics. In his account of his mission of 1054, however, he says that Nicetas had retracted, had been restored to communion and had even become a *familiaris amicus*.
24. K. Holl, *op. cit.* (note 1). See also H. Koch, 'Zur Geschichte der Bussdisziplin und Bussgewalt in der orientalischen Kirche', *Historisches Jahrbuch*, 21 (1900), pp. 58–78; J. Hörmann, *Untersuchungen zur griechischen Laienbeicht* (Donauwörth, 1913); J. T. McNeill, *A History of the Cure of Souls* (London, 1952), pp. 370ff.
25. M. Jugie, *Theologia dogm. Christian. Oriental.*, III (Paris, 1930), p. 365.
26. I. Hausherr, *op. cit.* (note 13), pp. 106–107.
27. *H. von Campenhausen, Kirchliches Amt und geistliche Vollmacht in den ersten drei Jahrhunderten* (Tübingen, 1953), p. 287, note 1.
28. With reference to Jn 20:22, *Sermo* 99, 9 (*PL* 38, 600); *Sermo* 71, 13, 23: 'Spiritu Sancto in ecclesia peccata solvuntur' (*PL* 38, 457). The *columba* is the *ecclesia sancta*: *De bapt.* III, 17, 22; VII, 51, 99 (*PL* 43, 149 and 241). 'Columba tenet, columba dimittit': *De bapt.* III, 18, 23 (*PL* 43, 150), taken up again in *In Ioan. ev.* CXXI, 4 (*PL* 35, 1958).
29. Augustine never tired of commenting in this way on the gift of the keys and the power to bind and loose in Mt 16:19ff.; see especially *In Ioan. ev.* CXXIV, 7 (*PL* 35, 1976). See also A.-M. La Bonnardière, 'Tu es Petrus. La péricope Mt 16, 12–23 dans l'œuvre de S. Augustin', *Irénikon*, 34 (1961), 451–499.
30. *Sermo* 295, 2 (*PL* 38, 1349).
31. *Sermo Guelf.* 16, 2; ed. G. Morin, *Anal. Agostin.*, I (Munich, 1917), p. 62.
32. There is the well-known text in *De jud.* 21: 'Ecclesia quidem delicta donabit; sed ecclesia spiritus per spiritalem hominem, non ecclesia numerus episcoporum'.
33. *De bapt.* III, 18, 23 (*PL* 43, 150). It is within this context that Augustine explains the logion on blasphemy against the Spirit; see his *Sermo* 71 (*PL* 38, 445ff.). It would be interesting to compare this with Simeon's explanation: see his *Cat.* XXXII (113, 238ff.); *Ethical Treatise* V (129, 111).
34. See my 'Introduction générale aux Traités antidonatistes' in the *Œuvres de Saint Augustin*, 28 (Paris, 1963), pp. 97–115.
35. Cyprian, *Ep.* LXX, 1 (ed. W. von Hartel, p. 767).

5

THE HOLY SPIRIT IN THE
PRAYER OF THE WESTERN CHURCH
DURING THE MIDDLE AGES

There was a kind of 'classical' period in the history of the Church during the centuries between the First Council of Nicaea (325) and the deaths of Gregory the Great (†604) and St Isidore (†636). It was during this period that the brilliant and holy Fathers of the Church were teaching and writing, and the great Councils defined the Church's faith in the Trinity and its Christology and promulgated the canons which provided the basis for the Church's discipline. It was also the time of the first appearance of several of the liturgical texts that were later collected and published in the classical sacramentaries of the Church.

THE LITURGY

Although there were great differences between the liturgy of the East and that of the West both in form and in expression, the reality and genius underlying them were, at the deepest level, the same. In both, the liturgy was a celebration of the 'mystery'. In other words, it was in the liturgy that believing Christians professed their faith as a community in words and gestures and the grace that God had given to men in the economy of revelation and above all in Jesus Christ and his Passover was made present in the lives of men. This act of making present was and is the work of the Lord, who is Spirit in the sense described by Paul (2 Cor 3:17). It takes place, in other words, through the inseparable action of the incarnate Son in glory as the supreme celebrant of the liturgical celebration and of his Holy Spirit, communicated as the fruit of his baptism and his Passover. The whole of the liturgy expresses and brings about a movement of God towards us and of us towards God. This movement passes from the Father through the Son in the Spirit and returns in the Spirit through the Son to the glory of the Father, who takes us, as his children, into communion with him. The Spirit is therefore invoked in every liturgical action, to be active and present in the liturgy.

I do not intend to examine this process in the missals, sacramentaries and

104

euchologia of the various rites,[1] not only because the results would fill a large volume, but also because this approach would only bear fruit if it were followed by each individual in his living experience. I would like to begin by saying a few words about the three sacraments of initiation: baptism, confirmation and the Eucharist.

The Holy Spirit is certainly given at baptism. He raised Jesus from the dead (Rom 1:4; 8:11), he makes it possible for the believer to enter the Lord's Passover and it is in him that believers are baptized into one body, the body of Christ (1 Cor 12:13). I shall speak later about 'baptism in the Spirit'. An important place is accorded to the Holy Spirit in the solemn celebration of baptism provided in the Gelasian Sacramentary (c. 750) for the Easter vigil. The first reference to the Holy Spirit in this liturgy is in the blessing of the water. In heavily charged Latin, the bond established between the Spirit and the water of baptism is first called to mind in a great prayer of consecration:[2]

> God, whose Spirit hovered over the waters at the origin of the world, in order to confer on them the power to sanctify. . . . Look, Lord, on the face of your Church and increase in it the number of your children, you who delight your City by the waves of your grace. . . . May it receive, by your sovereign will and from the Holy Spirit, the grace of your only Son. . . .
> May it be a living spring, a water that regenerates and purifies, so that all who receive this saving bath will be totally purified by the action of the Holy Spirit. . . .
> So I bless you (water) through Jesus Christ the only Son, our Lord, who . . . was baptized in you by John in the Jordan and who made you flow from his side with the blood. . . . May the virtue of your Spirit descend into the depths of these fonts. . . .

After the triple immersion in the triple confession of faith, the priest anoints those who have just been baptized with chrism and the bishop lays on his hand and pronounces this prayer, which is the prayer of 'confirmation':

> All-powerful and eternal God, who have deigned to regenerate by water and the Holy Spirit your servants here and who have granted them the remission of all their faults, send down on them from highest heaven your Holy Spirit the Paraclete with his gifts of wisdom and understanding, counsel and strength, knowledge and piety, fill them with the spirit of your fear in the name of our Lord Jesus Christ with whom you live and reign, one God, for ever, with the Holy Spirit.

Here, clearly, we pass from baptism to confirmation. In fact, baptism and the 'seal of the Spirit' are really two aspects and two actions in the same sacramental process.[3] In the early Church, both took place in the same celebration. Dozens of studies have been written about the bond uniting them and about the differences between them.[4] There are also very many articles and longer works on the history of the rite[5] and on the dogmatic and pastoral theology of the sacrament of confirmation.[6] There can be no doubt

105

that this sacrament is in an unstable state at present. How can the one who celebrates it claim to be able to 'give the Holy Spirit'?

I have written several times about this question, which, in my opinion, has both a doctrinal and a pastoral aspect. At the doctrinal level, confirmation is the liturgical expression firstly of a 'theo-logical' reality and secondly of an 'economic' reality. What it signifies is firstly that the Spirit exists beyond the Word and 'after' the Word (in the sense of being the third Person). Secondly, it points to the fact that Jesus received two anointings of the Spirit, the first constituting his human and divine holy being and the second constituting, or at least declaring, his quality of Messiah or minister of salvation.[7] Following this, the apostles were also constituted as the 'Twelve' by their call and their life with Jesus.[8] This, in their case, took the place of baptism. After this first constitution, they were constituted as those who were sent or 'apostles', witnesses and founders of Churches; this second constitution was brought about by Pentecost.[9] The Spirit brings about God's communication of himself by animating the body or the structure thus constituted. He is the fulfilment of the promise.

At the pastoral level, two different situations can be distinguished. In both of these situations, sacramental confirmation should, in accordance with its nature, be connected with baptism, of which it is the liturgical fulfilment. Since baptism is above all the sacrament of faith, infant baptism is problematical. There is no doubt, of course, that babies are baptized in the faith of the Church, their parents and their godparents. They are baptized with the prospect that they will be instructed in a catechetical process that ought normally to precede baptism. They ought also to be sacramentally 'confirmed' at the same time as they are baptized, but there is a need for a celebration of personal commitment in the Christian community, the people of God and the body of Christ. This commitment can best be made after puberty, between the age of about fifteen and thirty. The preparation for this celebration should occupy several weekends and take place with already committed Christians, so that it is possible for those preparing for this confirmation to see what it means to be a Christian in the Church today.[10] In the case of adults, this preparation, baptism and confirmation ought to take place within the same movement. The fundamental problem that arises here is not so much that of confirmation as that of the baptism of babies within a few days of their arrival in the world. Pascal wrote a little treatise on this subject which is worth reading.[11]

I do not wish to speak here about the third 'sacrament of initiation', the Eucharist, but would like to observe that the Greek word *teleiōsis*, 'perfection', would be more suitable in this context than the Latin word *initiare*, 'to begin'. I shall deal with the part played by the Holy Spirit in the Eucharist and the changing of the holy gifts into the body and blood of Christ as well as our communion in the Lord's body and blood in Volume III of this whole work. Those final chapters are, I believe, extremely important. We have already seen above how a spiritual space or framework for celebration is created by the Spirit by means of an exchange of a promise and a bearing witness to his presence: 'The Lord be with you'—'And with your spirit'.[12] This is a sign of the reciprocity that constitutes the full truth of the relationships between the Christian community and the minister who is the president and the pastor of that community.

This mutual relationship, which expresses the constant aspect of the activity of the Spirit, can also be found in the process of the ordination of ministers. It may even be because of this that it takes place in the celebration. There was also a theological meaning in the early tradition and practice of the Church that we need to recover. The most important moment in the process of ordination was the liturgical act, but, in the early Church, the process in fact began before the celebration.[13] The community took part in an election which, like all the acts that regulated the life of the Church, had to be 'inspired'.[14] In this election, the talents or charisms of the one elected were recognized. The consecrating bishop took up this intervention on the part of the community. In the consecration of another bishop, all the bishops present were ministers of the Spirit within the epiclesis of the entire assembly. In Hippolytus' prayer of consecration, the gift of the sovereign Spirit, *Pneuma hēgemonikon*, was besought. All the prayers of ordination ask for the Spirit to be communicated to the new minister as he was in the beginning to the apostles who were sent to the people of God as their teachers and pastors. The fine rite of placing the book of the gospels on the head of the one elected symbolizes the tongues of fire which, at the first Pentecost, inaugurated Christian preaching.[15]

> The Christian priesthood . . . is charismatic and spiritual. It is clear that it also has juridical and liturgical powers, . . . but it would impoverish the Christian priesthood if only this aspect were taken into consideration. The episcopate, the priesthood and the diaconate appear, in the early Church, as charisms for the building-up of the Church rather than as ritual functions.[16]

I have already said a few words about four of the sacraments, but it is the idea of sacrament as such, or rather the way in which it is understood that has to be considered carefully in this context. It is an idea that is applied in a flexible and analogous way to the different sacraments, but analogy is not ambiguity. It is therefore legitimate to speak in general terms of an idea of those realities that we call sacraments.

It is a fact, however, that several different values were attributed to the word *sacramentum* and that it was applied in various ways. Augustine defined the word and his definition was taken up later by Isidore of Seville (†636). The liturgy celebrated by Isidore was Hispano-Visigothic. In the *Post pridie* of the eucharistic prayer of this liturgy, the Holy Spirit was invoked over the sacrament.[17] Isidore believed that the offerings were consecrated by what he called the *oratio sexta*, which included all the prayers contained between the *Sanctus* and the *Pater noster*. He distinguished two aspects in the *oratio sexta*: the *sacrifice* or consecration of the gifts by the *prex mystica* in memory of the Passion—this is the Christological aspect—and the sanctification, which makes a *sacrament* of the action by the invisible operation of the Holy Spirit. There is, Isidore claims, a 'sacrament'—and it is at this point that he cites the text of Augustine—when 'in a celebration an act of the history (of salvation) is commemorated in such a way as to be able to perceive in it the meaning of something that is to be received holily'.[18] There is, then, in the celebration of the Eucharist—and, with the necessary modifications, also in the other 'sacraments'—a commemorative aspect, recalling a Christological act, and a sanctifying aspect, in which the commemoration receives its fruit, this aspect being the work of the Holy Spirit.[19] Christ himself only offered, in his flesh, a sacrifice that was acceptable to God thanks to the Spirit associated with the flesh that was offered.[20] For us, there is only a 'sacrament' when the liturgically celebrated commemoration is animated by the activity of the Spirit. In this systematization, which has become classical, however, it has become customary to speak of a visible sign of grace within the framework of a theology of created grace which may well presuppose uncreated grace, that of the Holy Spirit, but does not make this explicit in the definition.[21] It is important to make the present intervention of the Spirit that is implored in the epiclesis explicit in every act of salvation.

If we follow the liturgy now in the way in which it unfolds in its annual cycle, we encounter the feast of Pentecost. This is not a feast of the Person of the Holy Spirit—there is no separate feast of the Persons of the Holy Trinity—but a feast of the event of Pentecost as the conclusion of the paschal mystery. We have already seen above (p. 76) that it was constituted as a feast at the end of the fourth century. There are several fine Latin prayers still used today which go back to the Middle Ages. Among these are the hymn *Veni Creator*, composed by an unknown author in the ninth century, the twelfth-century antiphon *Veni, Sancte Spiritus*, and the sequence *Veni, Sancte Spiritus*, which was probably written by Stephen Langton and dates back to the beginning of the thirteenth century. The following translation of the hymn *Veni Creator* is as close as possible to the original Latin and is also largely based on Dom Wilmart's verse translation into French. The reader may like to join me in praying it:[22]

THE HYMN

I. Come, Creator, Spirit,
   visit the souls of your own;
   fill with heavenly grace
   the breasts that you have created.

II. You who are called Paraclete,
gift of the most high God,
living water, flame, charity
and spiritual anointing;

III. You who are sevenfold in your gift,
finger of God's right hand,
you who were rightly promised by the Father,
enrich our throats with speech.

IV. Inflame the light of our senses,
pour love into our hearts,
the weakness of our bodies
strengthen with lasting power.

V. Drive the enemy far back,
and at once grant us peace;
with you going ahead of us,
may we avoid all harm.

VI. Through you may we know the Father
and recognize the Son;
and may we always believe
in you, Spirit of both.

THE SEQUENCE

I. Come, Holy Spirit,
and send out a ray
of your heavenly light.

II. Come, father of the poor,
come, giver of gifts,
come, light of our hearts.

III. Come, kindly comforter,
sweet guest of our soul
and sweet freshness.

IV. Rest in hardship,
moderation in the heat,
relief in pain!

V. O most blessed light,
fill the innermost hearts
of those who believe in you.

VI. Without your divine power
there is nothing in man,
nothing that is harmless.

VII. Wash what is unclean,
water what is arid,
heal what is wounded.

VIII. Bend what is stiff,
warm what is cold,
guide what has gone astray.

IX. Give to those who believe in you
and who trust in you
your seven sacred gifts.

X. Give the reward of virtue,
give the end of salvation,
give lasting happiness!

The antiphon *Veni, Sancte Spiritus* appears in an antiphonary of Bamberg in the eleventh century in the first Vespers of Pentecost: 'Come, Holy Spirit, fill the hearts of your faithful and light in them the fire of your love; you who, by the diversity of all tongues, have brought the peoples together in the unity of faith'.[23]

In the tenth and eleventh centuries, the feast of Pentecost was chosen as the day for the anointing of the kings of France when there was no reason to anoint the king at some other time.[24] There seems also to have been a renewal of interest at the end of the eleventh century and during the twelfth in the Holy Spirit and the meaning of Pentecost. It was at this time that the *vita apostolica* flourished, that is, the common life led together without private property, and many institutions and churches placed themselves under the protection of the Holy Spirit.[25]

In this context, Pope Urban II, who left Champagne and became a monk at Cluny, deserves special mention. He actively promoted the way of life of the canons regular and regarded the revival of interest in them as taking place *instinctu Spiritus Sancti*.[26] To enable a secular priest to enter the religious life, Urban wrote the famous text on the two laws, *Duae leges sunt*, which is reproduced in the canonical collections and especially in the *Decretum Gratiani*. It was frequently quoted in the Middle Ages. Thomas Aquinas, for example, cited it in several of his works. The text is as follows:

There are two laws; one is public, the other private. The public law is the one that was written and made by the holy Fathers and includes the law of the canons. . . . The canons, for example, stipulate that a priest must not move from one diocese to another without a written recommendation from his bishop. . . . The private law, on the other hand, is the one that is written in the heart by the instinct of the Holy Spirit. The Apostle, for example, speaks of those who have the law of God written on the tablets of their hearts and elsewhere . . . that they are a law to themselves.

If one of these lives in his church and under his bishop in a secular manner, keeping his own goods, and if, driven by the Spirit, he wants to seek his salvation in a monastery or as a canon regular, as he is guided by the private law, there is no reason why he should be bound by the public law. The private law is, after all, superior to the public law. It is the Spirit of God who makes the law and those who are guided by the Spirit of God are guided by the law of God. And who can resist the Holy Spirit? If a man is guided by that Spirit, then, he should go freely, by virtue of our authority, and even defy the opposition of his bishop. In fact, there is no law for the righteous man—where the Spirit of the Lord is, there is freedom. And if you are guided by the Spirit, you are no longer subject to the law.[27]

I do not propose to trace the history of this text or the effects of the general principle to which it appeals. It would be possible, if one did so, to quote Bernard, Innocent III, Ignatius Loyola and a whole series of texts.[28] Research into this question would have to be undertaken systematically, and would go far beyond my ability and my present intention. The same would apply to any attempt to examine, even only cursorily, the prayers addressed to the Holy Spirit.

EVIDENCE OF FOUNDATIONS

Since the end of the eleventh century, the church of Saint-Sernin in Toulouse has been dedicated to the Holy Spirit. A village on the Rhône, originally called Saint-Saturnin and, in 1045, the site of a Cluniac priory, changed its name to Pont-Saint-Esprit. These data together with several others were provided by Etienne Delaruelle and were also confirmed by G. Schreiber. Delaruelle said: 'One has the impression that there was a great spiritual movement at that time, in which the idea of the Holy Spirit was associated with that of pilgrimage and its routes as well as with the notion of the *vita apostolica*'.[29] It is a fact that hospitals and communities of the Holy Spirit were founded above all along the routes of the great pilgrimages and especially in the south of France. Another factor, however, also played a part.

The twelfth century is notable for its renewed interest in the idea of human society and of the brotherhood of man. This renewal was often linked with a strong devotion to the Holy Spirit. Stephen of Muret founded the Order of Grandmont in 1076 and the lay brothers of this Order asked their priests to celebrate the votive Mass of the Holy Spirit for them; this information is reported by Jacques de Vitry. In 1129, Peter Abelard placed the abbey to which Héloïse had retired under the patronage of the Paraclete. In 1113, confraternities of the Holy Spirit appeared in the Auvergne and cared for the poor and for foundlings. In 1170–1185, a Heiliggeisthaus was founded in Cologne; similar houses were also founded in Lüneberg, Marseilles and Rostock, and provided for the poor.[30] In 1177, Abdenago of Pantasi founded a brotherhood of the Holy Spirit at Benevento. In 1195, Guy of Montpellier (†1208) opened a hospital of the Holy Spirit in his own town and founded a congregation of the same name in the region. Innocent III raised it to the status of an Order in 1204 and called Guy to Rome, where he founded a hospice under the patronage of the Holy Spirit.[31]

111

NOTES

1. For the Latin rite, see B. Neunheuser, 'Der Heilige Geist in der Liturgie', *Theologie und Glaube*, 35 (1943), 11–24, repr. in *Liturgie und Mönchtum*, 20 (1957), 11–33; F. Vanderbrouke, 'Esprit Saint et structures ecclésiales', *Questions liturgiques et paroissiales*, 39 (1958/3), 115–131; *idem*, 'L'Esprit Saint dans la liturgie', *Dictionnaire de Spiritualité*, IV (1961), cols 1283–1296; C. Vagaggini, *Theological Dimensions of the Liturgy* (Eng. tr.; Collegeville, Minn., 1976), chapter 7.
2. Gelasian Sacramentary, ed. H. A. Wilson (Oxford, 1894), pp. 85–87. Studies of this prayer of consecration over the water have been made by J. Lécuyer, 'La prière consécratoire des eaux', *M-D*, 49 (1957), 8–29; E. Stommel, *Studien zur Epiklese der römischen Taufwasserweihe* (Bonn, 1950); J. de Jong, 'Benedictio fontis', *Archiv für Liturgiewissenschaft*, 8 (1963), 21–46; E. Lengeling, 'Blessing of Baptismal Water in the Roman Rite', *Concilium*, 2, no. 3 (1967), 35–37, in which the author suggests a number of simplifications.
3. This is fundamentally what emerges from the works of L. Bouyer (see note 6 below), L. S. Thornton (*ibid.*) and B. Neunheuser (note 4) on the subject, and H. Küng, 'La confirmation comme parachèvement du baptême', *L'expérience de l'Esprit. Mélanges Schillebeeckx (Le Point théologique*, 18) (Paris, 1976), pp. 115–151. The basic work in this context is J. Amougou-Atangana, *Ein Sakrament des Geistesempfangs? Zum Verhältnis von Taufe und Firmung* (Freiburg, Basle and Vienna, 1974).
4. J. B. Umberg, 'Confirmatione Baptismus "perficitur" ', *ETL*, 1 (1924), 505–517; P. T. Camelot, 'Sur la théologie de la confirmation', *RSPT*, 38 (1954), 637–657; B. Neunheuser, *Baptism and Confirmation* (Eng. tr.; Freiburg and London, 1964); A. Hamman, *Je crois en un seul baptême. Essai sur 'Baptême et Confirmation'* (Paris, 1970); H. Auf der Maur and B. Kleinheyer, eds, *Zeichen des Glaubens. Studien zur Taufe und Firmung. Festgabe B. Fischer* (Zürich, 1972).
5. E. Llopart, *Las formulas de la confirmación en el Pontifical romè (Liturgica*, 2) (Montserrat, 1958), 121–180, presented by P. M. Gy, 'Histoire liturgique du sacrement de confirmation', *M-D*, 58 (1959), 135ff.; see also B. Neunheuser and J. Amougou-Atangana, *op. cit.*
6. Apart from P. T. Camelot, *op. cit.* (note 4), and the instalments of *M-D*, see A. G. Martimort, 'La confirmation', *Communion solennelle et Profession de foi (Lex Orandi*, 14) (Paris, 1952), pp. 159–201; L. Bouyer, 'Que signifie la confirmation?' *Parole et Liturgie*, 34 (1952), 3–12; *idem*, 'La signification de la confirmation', *VS (Suppl.)* (15 May 1954), 162–179; L. S. Thornton, *Confirmation. Its Place in the Baptismal Mystery* (Westminster, 1954); A. Adam, *Firmung und Seelsorge* (Düsseldorf, 1959); H. Mühlen, 'Die Firmung als sakramentales Zeichen der heilsgeschichtlichen Selbstüberlieferung des Geistes Christi', *Theologie und Glaube*, 57 (1967), 263–286; W. Breuning. 'When to Confirm in the Case of Adult Baptism', *Concilium*, 2, no. 3 (1967), 48–54; J.-P. Bouhot, *La confirmation, sacrement de la communion ecclésiale* (Paris, 1968); H. Bourgeois, *L'avenir de la confirmation* (Paris, 1972); L. Ligier, *La confirmation. Sens et conjoncture œcuménique hier et aujourd'hui (Théologie historique*, 23) (Paris, 1973), in which the author criticizes the present rite for the emphasis that it places on the anointing, whereas the essential aspect, in the author's opinion, is the laying-on of hands.
7. Hence the parallel $\dfrac{\text{incarnation}}{\text{baptism of Jesus}} = \dfrac{\text{baptism}}{\text{seal of the Spirit}}$;

   See J. Lécuyer, 'Le sacerdoce royal des chrétiens selon S. Hilaire de Poitiers', *Année Théologique*, 10 (1949), 302–325; *idem, M-D*, 27 (1951), 40ff.; *idem. Le sacerdoce dans le mystère du Christ (Lex Orandi*, 24) (Paris, 1957), chapters VIII and IX.
8. See Mk 3:14, literally translated: 'And he made twelve so that they might be with him and that he might send them to proclaim'.
9. J. Lécuyer, *Le sacerdoce, op. cit.*, chapters XI and XII, who makes use of the aspects of Easter and Pentecost. This is the line followed by Cyril of Jerusalem, *Cat. Myst.* III, 1–2

(*PG* 33, 1088ff.). See also W. Breuning, 'Apostolizität als sakramentale Struktur der Kirche. Heilsökonomische Überlegungen über das Sakrament der Firmung', *Volk Gottes. Festgabe J. Höfer* (Freiburg, 1967), pp. 132–163. See also E. Schillebeeckx, *Christ the Sacrament of Encounter with God* (London and New York, 1963), especially pp. 197ff.

10. With the help of modern psychological insights, this might best be done by presenting in a contemporary form the Thomist idea that the sacraments correspond to certain decisive aspects and moments in life. Confirmation, according to Thomas, corresponds to the time of transition from a life led for oneself to a life with and for others, in other words, a truly social life: 'antea quasi singulariter sibi ipsi vivit' (*ST* IIIa, q. 72, a. 2). See P. Ranwez, 'La confirmation constitutive d'une personnalité au service du Corps mystique du Christ', *Lumen Vitae*, 9 (1954), 17–36; J. Latreille, 'L'adulte chrétien ou l'effet du sacrement de confirmation chez S. Thomas d'Aquin', *RThom*, 57 (1957), 5–28; 58 (1958), 214–243; A. Auer, *Weltoffener Christ*, 2nd ed. (Düsseldorf, 1962), pp. 146ff.

11. Pascal, 'Comparaison des Chrétiens des premiers temps avec ceux d'aujourd'hui', *Pensées et Opuscules*, ed. L. Brunschvicg, pp. 201–205.

12. See above, pp. 36–37.

13. See B. Botte, 'L'Ordre d'après les prières d'ordination', *Etudes sur le sacrement de l'Ordre (Lex Orandi*, 22) (Paris, 1957), pp. 13, 35, 41; the Canons of Mondaye under the direction of Y. Congar and B.-D. Dupuy, *L'évêque d'après les prières d'ordination (Unam Sanctam*, 39) (Paris, 1962), pp. 739–780; L. Mortari, *Consecrazione episcopale e collegialità* (Florence, 1969); H. Legrand, 'Theology and the Election of Bishops in the Early Church', *Concilium*, 77 (1972), 31–42.

14. Election: the original text of the Roman formula of the pontiff addressing the faithful is: 'Et ideo electionem vestram debetis voce publica profiteri'; see B. Botte , *op. cit*., p. 19, note 1. Inspired: see the texts and references in my *Tradition and Traditions* (Eng. tr.; London and New York, 1966), Part One, Excursus B, pp. 119–137, esp. pp. 125ff.

15. This is the explanation given by Severian of Gabala, *c*. 400; see J. Lécuyer, 'La grâce de la consécration épiscopale', *RSPT*, 36 (1952), 389–417, especially 402.

16. B. Botte, *op. cit*. (note 13), p. 34.

17. For the history of these *Post pridie* prayers, see W. S. Porter, 'The Mozarabic Postpridie', *JTS*, 44 (1943), 182–194. For the sacramental and eucharistic theology of Isidore of Seville, see J. B. Geiselmann, *Die Abendmahlslehre an der Wende der christlichen Spätantike zum Frühmittelalter. Isidor von Sevilla und das Sakrament der Eucharistie* (Munich, 1933); J. Havet, 'Les sacrements et le rôle du Saint-Esprit d'après Isidore de Séville', *ETL*, 16 (1939), 32–93.

18. Augustine's Latin text is unfortunately almost untranslatable: 'Sacramentum est autem in aliqua celebratione cum rei gestae commemoratio ita fit, ut aliquid etiam significare intellegatur, quod sancte accipiendum est': *Ep*. 55, 2 (*PL* 33, 205).

19. Isidore, *Etym*. VI, 19, 38–42: 'Sacrificium dictum, quasi sacrum factum, quia prece mystica consecratur in memoriam pro nobis Dominicae passionis; unde hoc eo iubente corpus Christi et sanguinem dicimus. Quod, dum sit ex fructibus terrae, sanctificatur, et fit sacramentum, operante invisibiliter (Migne (*PL* 82, 255) has *visibiliter* here!) Spiritu Dei. . . . Sacramentum est in aliqua celebratione, cum res gesta ita fit ut aliquid significare intellegatur, quod sancte accipiendum est. . . . Quae ob id sacramenta dicuntur, quia sub tegumento corporalium rerum virtus divina secretius salutem eorumdem sacramentum operatur. . . . Quae ideo fructuose penes Ecclesiam fiunt, quia sanctus in ea manens Spiritus eundem sacramentorum latenter operatur effectum'; ed. W. M. Lindsay (1911); cf. *De officiis eccl*. I, 18, 4 (*PL* 83, 755).

20. After quoting Jn 1:33, Isidore says: 'carnem Christi Spiritui Sancto sociatam per mysterium passionis sacrificium Deo in odorem suavitatis accipimus': *In Lev*. c. 6, 4 (*PL* 83, 523).

21. In the Augustinian tradition, 'visibile signum invisibilis gratiae'. Via Peter Lombard and Thomas Aquinas, this definition in the Roman Catechism was reached: 'rem esse, sensibus

113

subiectam, quae ex Dei institutione sanctitatis et iustitiae tum significandae tum efficiendae vim habet': Pars II, c. i. q. 11.

22. A. Wilmart, 'L'hymne et la séquence du Saint-Esprit', *La vie et les arts liturgiques*, 10 (1924), 395–401; repr. in *Auteurs spirituels et Textes dévots du Moyen Age latin* (1932; reissued Paris, 1971), pp. 37–45.

23. R. J. Hesbert, *Corpus Antiphonalium Officii*, III (Rome, 1968), p. 528, antiphon no. 5327. The Dominicans preserved the words 'qui per diversitatem linguarum multarum gentes in unitate fidei congregasti'.

24. In the debate which followed a lecture given by E. Delaruelle, M. F. Lemarignier commented: 'Louis V was associated on the throne with Lothair and anointed on the day of Pentecost, 979 A.D. In the same way, during the reign of Robert II the Pious, Robert's sons Hugh and Henry were anointed at Pentecost in 1017 and 1027 respectively. Finally, during the reign of Henry I, the future King Philip I was consecrated at Pentecost in 1059': *La vita commune del clero nei secoli XI e XII* (Milan, 1962), p. 180.

25. See the lecture given by E. Delaruelle on 'La vie commune des clercs et la spiritualité populaire au XIᵉ siècle' in *La vita commune, op. cit.*, pp. 152ff., repr. in *La piété populaire au Moyen Age* (Turin, 1975), pp. 81–112, especially pp. 91–95.

26. See C. Dereine, 'L'élaboration du statut canonique des Chanoines réguliers spécialement sous Urbain II', *RHE*, 46 (1951), 534–565, especially 546–547.

27. Jaffé Loewenfeld, 5760; Mansi 20, 714; *PL* 151, 535. Quoted by Gratian, c. 2, C. XIX, q. 2 (ed. E. Friedberg, 829–840). Migne's text is defective. Quoted by Thomas Aquinas, *De perf. vitae spir.* c. 25; *Quodl.* III, 17; *ST* IIa IIae, q. 184, a. 6 and 8; q. 189, a. 7. See also M. Duquesne, 'S. Thomas et le canon attribué à Urbain II (c. 2, C. XIX, q. 2)', *Studia Gratiana*, I (Bologna, 1955), pp. 415–434.

28. See Bernard, *De praecepto et dispens*. 16 (*PL* 182, 885ff.); Innocent III, *Reg.* VIII, 195 and IX, 182 (*PL* 215, 774 and 1495). See also H. Tillmann, *Papst Innozenz III* (Bonn, 1954), pp. 28–31; W. A. van Roo, 'Law of the Spirit and Written Law in the Spirituality of St Ignatius', *Greg*, 37 (1956), 417–443.

29. E. Delaruelle, *op. cit.* (note 25), p. 154. See also G. Schreiber, *Gemeinschaften des Mittelalters. Recht und Verfassung. Kult and Frömmigkeit* (Münster, 1948), especially the tables.

30. For the great increase in the number of these Hospitals of the Holy Spirit towards the end of the twelfth century, see G. Schreiber in *Historische Vierteljahrschrift*, 15 (1912), 136ff.; W. Liese, *Geschichte der Caritas*, II (Freiburg, 1922), pp. 15ff.; M. Mollat, *Les pauvres au Moyen Age. Etude sociale* (Paris, 1978), p. 174; for the fourteenth century, *ibid.*, pp. 323 and 346 (Paris in 1360 and 1363), p. 333 (Brussels), p. 341 (Danzig) and p. 345 (Oporto).

31. A. Castan, 'Notice sur l'Ordre du Saint-Esprit', *Annuaire du Doubs* (1864), p. 152; M. Poête, *Etude sur les origines et la règle de l'Ordre hospitalier du Saint-Esprit* (Paris, 1890); P. Brune, *Histoire de l'Ordre hospitalier du Saint-Esprit* (Paris, 1892).

6

THE HOLY SPIRIT IN THE
WRITINGS OF THE THEOLOGIANS

I do not intend to provide, in this part of my work, a history of the theology of the Holy Spirit in the twelfth and thirteenth centuries, that is, during the first and greatest period of Scholasticism. I would, however, be giving a very incomplete picture of the experience of the Spirit in Christianity if I were not to examine, however briefly, the teachers of that period, who were so often spiritual men.

The Holy Spirit is active in history and causes new and sometimes very confusing things to taken place in it. This was certainly the case during the first half of the twelfth century, when so many new religious orders came into being.[1] This was a cause of scandal to Rupert of Deutz, for example, who did not like new questions. The Premonstratensian canon Anselm of Havelberg, on the other hand, was aware that many of his contemporaries were disconcerted and asking the question: 'quare tot novitates in Ecclesia Dei fiunt?' — 'Why are there so many new things in the Church?' and answered it, in 1149, in the following way:

> There is only one body of the Church. The Holy Spirit gives life to that body, rules it and governs it. The Holy Spirit to which that body is joined is manifold, subtle, moving, fine, pure, strong, sweet, loving what is good, penetrating, doing good without hindrance, a friend of men, benevolent, stable, certain, seeing everything, capable of everything, containing all spirits, understandable and spotless. According to the Apostle, 'there are varieties of gifts, but the same Spirit' (1 Cor 12:4). He also said: 'To each is given the manifestation of the Spirit for the common good. To one is given through the Spirit the utterance of wisdom and to another the utterance of knowledge according to the same Spirit, to another faith by the same Spirit, to another gifts of healing by the one Spirit, to another the working of miracles, to another prophecy, to another the ability to distinguish between spirits, to another various kinds of tongues, to another the interpretation of tongues. All these are inspired by one and the same Spirit, who apportions to each individually as he wills' (1 Cor 12:7–11).
>
> It would seem, then, that the body of the Church, which is one, is given life by the Holy Spirit, who is one, single in himself and yet manifold (1 Pet 4:10) in the distribution of his many different gifts. This true body of the Church, which is given life by the Holy Spirit and differentiated into diverse members at different ages and periods, began with the first righteous man Abel and will end with the last of the elect. It is always one in a single faith, but it is differentiated into diverse forms by the manifold variety of its way of life.[2]

We have already seen that Urban II ascribed the new way of life of the canons regular to the Holy Spirit. It should be added here that Anselm of Havelberg had been to Constantinople, where he had been in contact with Greek thought. Towards the middle of the twelfth century, Burgundio of Pisa translated into Latin the fifth *Theological Oration* of Gregory Nazianzen on the Holy Spirit. Greek influence was particularly strong in the sphere of anthropology and especially epistemology; but the controversy concerning the *Filioque* may have stood in the way of the diffusion of the Eastern Church's pneumatology.

Following the teaching of Augustine, the Church as the body of Christ was almost universally regarded in the West as animated by the Holy Spirit and the distribution of different gifts in the Church to different members for the common good was also attributed to the Holy Spirit.[3] The most classical author at this time was Hugh of Saint-Victor. He inspired others and was himself inspired by Augustine. He wrote his treatise *De sacramentis christianae fidei* in 1137 or a little earlier. The following extract is relevant to our theme:

> Just as the spirit of man descends from his head to give life to his members, so too does the Holy Spirit come, through Christ, to Christians. Christ is the head and the Christian is the member. The head is one and the members are many, but there is only one body consisting of the head and the members and in that one body there is only one Spirit. The fullness of that Spirit is in the head and the participation is in the members. If, then, the body is one, and the Spirit is one, the man who is not in the body cannot be given life by the Spirit. . . . The Church is the body of Christ. It is given life by one Spirit and united and sanctified by one faith. The believers are each one members of that one body and all believers are one body because of the one Spirit and the one faith. Just as, in the human body, each one of the members has its own distinct function and yet what it does for itself alone is not simply for itself alone, so too, in the body of the Church, the gifts of grace are distributed to individuals and yet what each one has for himself alone is not for himself alone.[4]

At this period of Christian history, a treatise on Christ as the Head—*De Christo capite*—and a theology of created grace had not yet been properly worked out. The idea of what was later (from about 1160 onwards) to be known as the 'mystical Body' (which would become equivalent to and synonymous with 'Church') was at this time strongly pneumatological. It was, in other words, not the *gratia Capitis*, but the Holy Spirit who made the body of which Christ was the Head. That Head had the Spirit first and he had that Spirit in its fullness. That Spirit then descended to the members. This pneumatology can also be found in the traditional connection between the three realities that testify to the truth of the title 'body of Christ': his natural, personal body, born of Mary, his sacramental body, and his body as the Church or a communion.[5] This connection can be seen as marked by the Holy Spirit who is one and the same and at work in each of these three 'bodies': as the principle of sanctification of Jesus (see Lk 1:35), of the gifts of the bread and wine, and of the believers who form the Church. This is precisely what the mysterious author known by the name of Honorius Augustodunesis taught, that is, that the third body—the ecclesial body—is connected to the first by the second, eucharistic body, which is so, *Spiritu sancto consecrante*. It is therefore possible to speak of the three 'bodies' as a single body of which the Holy Spirit is the principle of unity: 'Unde non tria sed unum corpus Spiritu Sancto coadunante recte affirmatur'.[6]

It is certain that the absence of a real epiclesis to the Holy Spirit in the Roman canon deprived any corresponding theology of a chance of developing. It is therefore all the more remarkable that the affirmation is so often found that the bread and wine are consecrated by the Holy Spirit.[7] In 1208, Innocent III required Waldensians rejoining the Church to make a profession of faith which extended to all the sacraments the affirmation that the Holy Spirit operated in them: *inestimabili atque invisibili virtute Spiritus Sancti cooperante*.[8] This was a common conviction. There is concrete evidence of it, based on living experience, in the lives of the saints and the visions that they are reported to have had.[9]

At the period which we are considering, a special place must be given to the gifts of the Holy Spirit.[10] For a long time and even when the text of Isaiah (11:2–3) was taken into account, it was believed that these gifts were discrete gifts of grace, distinguished in accordance with the subject-matter denoted by their name, and in virtue of which Christians were able to do what God expected of them. In the West especially, the number 'seven' was regarded as very important. It was understood not as indicating completeness, but rather as referring to a number of specific operations. The Vulgate translation was followed and this itself followed the Septuagint: 'Et requiescet super eum spiritus Domini: spiritus sapientiae et intellectus, spiritus consilii et fortitudinis, spiritus scientiae et pietatis; et replebit eum spiritus timoris Domini'—'And the spirit of the Lord shall rest upon him, the spirit of wisdom and understanding, the spirit of counsel and might, the spirit of knowledge and piety and a spirit of fear of the Lord shall fill him'. From the twelfth century onwards, often in the context of more active reading of the works of Augustine, the Christians of the Western Church frequently asked for the seven gifts of the Spirit, celebrated them and tried to understand them. These, like the virtues, were the principles of action according to God. They were often related to other septenaria, such as the seven women who were in disgrace and looked for a man who would take it from them (Origen had already made this comparison), the seven capital sins, the seven requests of the Our Father, the seven beatitudes and other more artificial groups of seven.

A little before 1135, Rupert of Deutz placed the different aspects of history, which formed the theme of the 42 books of his *De Trinitate*, under the headings of the seven gifts of the Holy Spirit and linked these with the seven days of creation and the seven ages of the world. The third part of his work consists of the nine books *De operibus Spiritus Sancti*. In this part, the various aspects of the history of the Church are placed under the headings of particular gifts.[11]

Gerhoh of Reichersberg copied whole pages from Rupert's work. He also quoted two hymns with quatrains of the same plan as Rupert's.[12] His *De ordine donorum Spiritus Sancti* also has the same source and the same view.[13]

Jacques de Vitry (†1240) placed the life of St Mary of Oignies under the sign of the seven gifts of the Holy Spirit. In the iconography of the end of the twelfth century and almost the whole of the thirteenth century, Christ is frequently shown as giving the seven gifts of the Spirit. The gifts with which the Messiah was filled (Is 11:2–3) are presented as being communicated to the Christian.[14] The part played by these gifts in the practice of the spiritual life was very present in men's minds at this period. A treatise consisting of 23 chapters, probably originating in England and dating from the second half of the thirteenth century, was edited some years ago by A. Wilmart. Each chapter of this treatise, from chapters XIII to XIX, deals wth one of the gifts.[15] God the Father is described in it as loving justice, the Son judges severely(!) and the Spirit is the mercy which gives confidence to the sinner, who would not be able to stand before a Father and a Son who would condemn him, if it were not for the Spirit. The same scholar also edited and published a 'Prayer to the Holy Spirit according to the Seven Gifts',[16] in which each of the gifts is related to one of the capital sins, from which it sets man free, to the opposite virtue, to the corresponding beatitude and to the fruit that it brings. This is a monastic text dating from the middle of the fourteenth century. It presupposes a theological elaboration similar to the one provided by Thomas Aquinas.

The gifts of the Holy Spirit were not distinguished from the virtues until about 1235. The first to make this distinction was Philip the Chancellor. Thomas Aquinas reduced it to a remarkably coherent system that was closely in accordance with a very real aspect of the life of the children of God. I therefore now briefly outline this theology as presented in the *Summa* in 1269–1270.

Thomas situates the Christian within the framework of the movement by which creatures move and are moved towards their end. He understands 'movement' in this context in the widest sense of the word, that is, as every kind of movement from one state to another. In this case, however, it is a *motus hominis ad Deum*, the journey or the ascent of man to God and nothing less than God. God alone is the beginning and the end. God's life is divine and can be and is communicated by grace, which is characteristic of the Holy Spirit.[17] As creator, God originally gave to each nature the principles of a behaviour which is truly its own. In the case of man, God made him free. This means not only that man determines and realizes himself and his own existence, that he is *causa sui* and that he builds himself up and fulfils himself by his actions and his *habitus* or 'haviours', but also that, if God moves him, he moves him through his own freedom and so that he may act freely.[18] In God's name, then, man has in himself the principle of his own movement and this includes his abilities, actions, 'haviours' and virtues (or vices). There are, however, also motivating forces of moral action that are external to man, and Thomas distinguishes these according to whether their influence is exercised by information or suggestion or by efficiency.[19] The demon acts on our freedom by means of suggestion and this is the basis of temptation. God, on the other hand, acts in the case of our coming or returning to him *per instructionem et per operationem*, that is, by teaching and by action.[20] This accounts for the following statement, which introduces us directly to the question that we are considering here: 'Principium exterius movens ad bonum est Deus, qui et nos instruit per legem et iuvat per gratiam'—'The principle outside us that moves us towards the good is God, who teaches us by the law and helps us by grace'.[21]

'By grace': this does not mean simply by means of the help received from actual graces, but by means of deep and lasting gifts: 'grace', the virtues and the 'gifts'. The distinction between the virtues and the gifts had been made comparatively recently in theology. In his *Sentences* (III d. 34, q. 1, a. 1; cf. *In Isaiam*, c. XI), Thomas Aquinas simply said that, with the help of the gifts, the believer was able to act *ultra modum humanum*, 'beyond the means of man'. In the *Summa*, however, he added that this was possible because he was moved by a superior principle (Ia IIae, q. 68, a. 2).

Thomas kept to the Isaian text, which does not refer vaguely to 'gifts', but speaks quite precisely about 'spirits'—*spiritus sapientiae* and so on. This, he claims, points to a movement by inspiration (q. 68, a. 1) and we are clearly in touch here with the biblical value of 'breath' which we discussed earlier in this book. Thomas had, from 1259 or 1260 onwards, an unexpected *confirmatur* at his disposal (he says at least twice: 'et etiam Philosophus'— 'even Aristotle') in *De bona fortuna*, a short treatise consisting of two chapters taken from Aristotle's works, the first from the *Eudemian Ethics* and the second from the second book of the *Magna Moralia*. Aristotle spoke of the *hormē* or the inclination or impulse of the superior appetite, and Thomas applied this idea to the divine impulse which goes beyond the use of reason.[22] This understanding of the term was, of course, clearly remote from that of the Greek philosopher himself.

As lasting realities that are distinct from the virtues, then, the gifts are these dispositions which make the Christian ready to grasp and follow the inspirations of the Spirit.[23] They are in themselves only a permanent disposition, but one which makes the disciple of Jesus permanently open to have his activity guided, beyond the power of the virtues, beyond his reason as animated by faith, beyond his supernatural prudence, by another who is infinitely superior and has sovereign freedom, in other words, the Holy Spirit.

This is a position far removed from a purely rational moral attitude, or from an attitude often imputed to Thomas, that is, a morality based on models derived from a nature of things that is established outside time. Thomas allows for the *event* of the Spirit; for him, morality is based on the saving and sanctifying will of God, according to norms which go beyond human and even supernatural reason. We are led by another, who does not act without us or violently (see above, p. 119, and below, note 18), but who goes beyond our own vision and the behaviour for which we have made provision, not only beyond the perspective of our human reason, but also beyond that revealed by our faith. These gifts are not superior to the theologal virtues. The latter unite us to God himself and can therefore have nothing above them. The gifts are at the service of those virtues, enabling them to be practised perfectly. Only God can, however, by intervening personally, give his fullness to the practice of these virtues and only he can complete the activity of one of his children. Thomas quotes Paul's words: 'Qui Spiritu Dei aguntur, hi sunt filii Dei'—'All who are led by the Spirit are sons of God' (Rom 8:14).

Thomas' aim, then, is to determine the part played by the gifts in the practice of the theologal and moral virtues. As he saw the perfect exercise of the virtues and especially of the gifts reflected in the beatitudes, he tried to make one gift of the Spirit and one of the beatitudes correspond to each of these virtues. He even attempted to attribute to each virtue, with its gift and its beatitude or beatitudes, one or other of the 'fruits' of the Spirit of which Paul spoke. He devoted one question to these 'fruits', in which he stresses the struggle of the spirit against the 'flesh', with a clear reference to Gal 5:22–23 (see *ST* Ia IIae, q. 70).

There is, of course, something a little forced and artificial in these parallels and I do not intend to discuss them in detail. They do not have an absolute value, but neither should their value be ignored, since they frequently reveal very deep insights. Thomas' understanding that the appeals and interventions of the living God go beyond all our human expectations enables us to recognize that the holiness of the Christian saints is the most perfect form of Christian life. It consists of continually going beyond supernatural, but still human, boundaries through generous responses to 'inspirations'. Consider Teresa of Lisieux.

It is the Holy Spirit who makes man holy. He is also the principle of the 'revelation' to the people of God of the thought, the plan and the will of God. I shall return later to the use that the Church Fathers and the theologians of the Middle Ages made of the categories of 'inspiration' and 'revelation'. In the past, I found that these categories were, in my opinion, used excessively,[24] but I am now able to understand better what they mean, by considering them in the light of pneumatology. I can also understand more fully the interest taken by the Scholastic theologians in the study of prophecy.[25] It is, of course, true that they studied the question of prophecy analytically and with a confidence, which we would regard as questionable, in the instruments, in other words, the concepts, that they used for that analysis. They were at least interested in ways of knowing that were not rational but linked to the activity of the Spirit. Following his fellow-Dominican Hugh of Saint-Cher, Thomas called prophecy an event: *non est habitus, sed actus*; 'prophetic enlightenment only exists in the spirit of the prophet at the moment of inspiration'. It is, in other words, a charism that is given for the benefit of others and for the community.[26]

The charism of prophecy has continued to be manifested in the Church, no longer in the form of the inspiration of the canonical books of Scripture, but in the form of God's action on souls and on the Church. Scholars have pointed to the existence of this charism in the Middle Ages[27] and have outlined the part played by it and the conditions under which it flourishes in the present life of the Church.[28] The term is understood here in the extended sense in which Thomas Aquinas used it: 'All the gifts that are related to knowledge can be included under the heading of prophecy'.[29] There are, however, many different forms of prophecy.

The first is that of *counsel, advice and warnings* of the kind given, for example, by Hildegard of Bingen (†1179), formally accepted by Pope Eugenius III and his successors.[30]

The second form of prophecy is *spontaneous preaching*. At certain periods in the history of the Church, hermits began to wander, abandoning hearth and home, giving themselves to a life of *peregrinatio* and preaching on their way. This happened particularly in the sixth and seventh centuries and again in the eleventh and twelfth centuries. It is possible to include within this category of great charismatic missionaires such people as Boniface (675–755), Bruno of Querfurt (†1009), Francis Xavier (†1552) and many other more recent figures. P. Boglioni has pointed to the important part played by hermits and monks who preached the Crusades, in this way affirming a kind of autonomy of the inspired word: 'per virtutem mortificationis pervenitur ad licentiam praedicationis'. It is well known that the Crusades took place in a climate of signs, visions and apocalyptic prophecies.[31] In the twelfth century, wandering preachers committed to poverty in accordance with the ideal of the *vita apostolica* were found all over Western Europe, calling on men to repent and to be converted to the gospel.[32]

The third form consists of *interventions in the life of the Church* in a spirit of prophecy. Women have played a remarkable part in this movement. They included, for example, Hildegard of Bingen, already mentioned above, Elizabeth of Schönau (†1164), Rose of Viterbo (1233–1251), Margaret of

Cortona (1247–1297), Bridget of Sweden (1303–1373), Catherine of Siena (1347–1380) and, of course, Joan of Arc (1412–1431). What a succession of saints! Each one had an exceptional mission, thanks to her astonishing charisms.

It has always been in troubled and controversial times that visions and prophecies have abounded, such as those of Robert of Uzès (†1296) during the pontificates of Celestine V and Boniface VIII[33], of the Franciscan John of Roquetaillade (†c. 1365),[34] of Vincent Ferrer[35] and of Savonarola. The great Western schism was a particularly favourable time for visions and prophecies of doom. This provoked a great deal of critical reaction on the part of theologians and the Fathers of the Council of Constance.[36]

The fourth form of prophecy is a *deep understanding of the saving truth* and a correspondingly truthful form of *teaching*. In the patristic and Scholastic tradition of the Church, prophecy is placed firmly within the framework of this activity of the word of God, the sacred texts and the doctrine of salvation.[37] Newman also believed in the prophetic tradition and even in the 'prophetical office', which he distinguished from the episcopal tradition.[38] Theologians who really deserve the name should surely be honoured!

*　　*　　*

It is the Holy Spirit who sanctifies, but it would clearly be impossible to follow him in his sanctifying process. It is his secret and it is as spacious as the love and mercy of the Father. In the West, theologians and spiritual writers have often described the sanctifying activity of the Spirit under the rather artificial heading of the seven gifts. It would also be impossible to retrace this history.[39] I will do no more than mention one chapter of it, because of the intensity and the insistence of the details of the activity of the Holy Spirit. This is the life of St Dorothy of Montau (1347–1394).

Her life was described by the man who was her spiritual director in her last years, John of Marienwerden.[40] The 'missions' or visits of the Holy Spirit to Dorothy are reduced to an excessively systematic account by this author, who, for example, counts the number of times when Dorothy received ten, nine, eight, seven, six, five, four or three visits! He also reduces these 'missions' to seven modes of manifestation or presence, according to different categories, which he illustrates by means of biblical texts. Despite the form of this treatise, however, the freedom of the Spirit and the generosity of grace break through, and one is conscious of a soul experiencing the fullness of that grace at a time when the Church was experiencing the drama of the Great Schism. Dorothy, a married woman who had had nine children, had been seized hold of by God. Words, a song, cries of joy and supplication and many tears figure in this account of her life, but above all one is aware of a great sweetness.

NOTES

1. See my *L'Eglise de S. Augustin à l'époque moderne (Histoire des dogmes*, III/3) (Paris, 1970), pp. 131–132.

2. Anselm of Havelberg, *Dialogi* I (*PL* 188, 1144; Fr. tr. G. Salet, *SC*, 118, pp. 43 and 45); see also M. van Lee, 'Les idées d'Anselme de Havelberg sur le développement des dogmes', *Anal. Praemonstr.*, 14 (1938), 5–35; G. Schreiber, 'Studien über Anselm von Havelberg. Zur Geistesgeschichte des Hochmittelalters', *ibid.*, 18 (1942), 5–90; M.-D. Chenu, *La théologie au douzième siècle* (Paris, 1957), pp. 235ff.; G. Severino, 'La discussione degli "Ordines" di Anselmo di Havelberg', *Bullettino dell' Istituto Storico Italiano per il Medio Evo*, 78 (1967), 75–122. H. Grundmann, *Studien über Joachim von Fiore* (Leipzig, 1927; new ed., Darmstadt, 1966), pp. 92–95, suggests that Anselm may have influenced Joachim.

3. See A. M. Landgraf, 'Die Lehre vom geheimnisvollen Leib Christi in den frühen Paulinenkommentaren und in der Frühscholastik', *Divus Thomas* (1946), 407–419; see also my book, *op. cit.* (note 1), p. 161. I am also bound to mention Peter Damian, *Liber gratissimus*, c. 15 (*PL* 145, 119; *Lib. de Lite*, p. 37) and *Opusc.* 11, '*Dominus vobiscum*', c. 5–7 (*PL* 145, 235–237).

4. Hugh of Saint-Victor, *De sacramentis*, II, pars 2, c. 1 (*PL* 176, 415); quotation based on Fr. tr. by E. Mersch.

5. See H. de Lubac, *Corpus mysticum. L'Eucharistie et l'Eglise au Moyen Age* (Paris, 1944; 2nd ed., 1949); F. Holböck, *Der eucharistische und der mystische Leib Christi in ihren Beziehungen nach der Lehre der Frühscholastik* (Rome, 1941); my own work, *op. cit.* (note 1), pp. 165ff.

6. Honorius Augustodunensis, *Eucharistion seu de Corpore et Sanguine Domini*, c. 1 (*PL* 172, 1250); see also H. de Lubac, *op. cit.*, p. 186.

7. See, for example, Paschasius Radbert (*c.* 830), *De Corp. et Sang. Domini*, c. 7, n. 1 (*PL* 120, 1284); Alger of Liège, *De sacr.* I, 17 (*PL* 180, 790D); Honorius Augustodunensis, *op. cit.* and *Gemma animae*, I, c. 105 (*PL* 172, 578); Rupert of Deutz (*c.* 1115), *De Trin. et operibus eis. In Exod. lib.* II, c. 10 (*PL* 167, 617); Gerhoh of Reichersberg, *Expos. Psalm. Ps.* XXXIII: see *Gerhohi Opera inedita*, II: *Expositio Psalmorum pars tertia et pars nona*, ed. D. and O. van den Eynde and A. Rijmersdael, II/1 (Rome, 1956), p. 168; Hildegard of Bingen, *Scivias*, lib. II, vis. 6 (*PL* 197, 526 and 528); Peter Celestine, *Sermo 39, De Coena Domini* 6 (*PL* 202, 761), who compared the consecration of the Eucharist with the incarnation.

8. Denz. 424; *DS* 793.

9. See K. Goldammer, *Die eucharistische Epiklese in der mittelalterlichen abendländischen Frömmigkeit* (Bottrop, 1941).

10. Full documentation, a bibliography and theological explanations will be found in the articles on 'gifts' ('Dons') in *DTC*, IV (1911), cols 1728–1781 (A. Gardeil) and the *Dictionnaire de Spiritualité*, III, cols 1574–1641 (G. Bardy, F. Vandenbroucke, A. Rayez, M. Labourdette and C. Bernard).

11. Rupert of Deutz, *PL* 167; *SC* 131 and 165. Books I to III: Incarnation, redemption and Sacrament of the Passion = wisdom; Book IV : Apostles = understanding (of Scripture); Book V: Rejection of the Jews in favour of the gentiles = counsel; Books VI to VIII: Martyrs, teachers and penitential monks = power against sin; Book IX: Eschatology = fear of God.

12. *Gerhohi Opera inedita, op. cit.* (note 7), II. pp. 448–450.

13. *Ibid.*, I (Rome, 1955), pp. 65–165.

14. I had intended to try, later in this study, to provide some information on the iconography of the Holy Spirit, in which Christian experience and understanding of the Spirit are also expressed. Let me here simply reproduce the following comment that appeared at the end of an article by T. Spasskij on 'L'Office liturgique slave de la "Sagesse de Dieu" ', *Irénikon*,

30 (1957), 188, note 1: 'In a stained-glass window in the cathedral at Chartres (west front, right-hand window, upper panel in the tree of Jesse), Christ is represented as surrounded by seven doves, the upper ones personifying Wisdom (*Sapientia*) and forming an integral part of him (see J. Verrier, *Vitraux de France aux XIIᵉ et XIIIᵉ siècles*, Paris, *Histoire des Arts plastiques*, n.d., Plate II). Another stained-glass window, in the Abbey of Saint-Denis, shows Christ between the Church and the synagogue. On his breast is a dove, connected by rays to six other doves (the seven gifts). With his left hand, he is unveiling the synagogue and with his right he is crowning the Church (see E. Male, *L'art religieux au XIIᵉ siècle en France*, Paris, 1947, p. 166). Finally, in one of the stained-glass rose-windows of Chartres cathedral above the windows in the great nave, there is a representation of the Virgin seated, with a medallion on her knees of Christ as Wisdom. This medallion is attached by rays to six doves surrounding the main figure, as in the window of Saint-Denis.'

15. A. Wilmart, 'Les méditations sur le Saint-Esprit attribuées à S. Augustin', *RAM*, 7 (1926), 17–63, reprinted in *Auteurs spirituels et Textes dévots du Moyen Age latin* (Paris, 1932; repub. 1971), pp. 415–456. Long sections of text are provided by the author.

16. A. Wilmart, 'Prière au Saint-Esprit suivant les sept dons', *VS (Suppl)*, 16 (1927), 323–344, repr. *op. cit.* (note 15), pp. 457–473.

17. For this view of things, see *C. Gent.* IV, 21 and 22; *Comp.* I, 147. It is this idea that governs Thomas' theology of merit.

18. *ST* Ia IIae, q. 9, a. 4 and 6; q. 68, a. 3, ad 2; IIa IIae, q. 23, a. 2, q. 52, a. 1, ad 3. To translate *habitus* as 'habit' would be misleading [the author therefore prefers the old French word *ayance*, which this translation renders by the cognate old English word 'haviour' (see *OED*)].

19. For this distinction, so often stressed by Thomas, see my 'Tradition et sacra doctrina chez S. Thomas d'Aquin', *Eglise et Tradition* (Le Puy and Lyons, 1963), pp. 157–194.

20. See *In I Sent.* d. 16, q. 1, a. 3; *ST* Ia IIae, q. 108, a. 1.

21. *ST* Ia IIae, q. 90 prol; q. 109 prol.

22. See T. Deman, 'Le "Liber de Bona Fortuna" ', *RSPT*, 17 (1928), 38–58.

23. 'Prompte mobilis ab inspiratione divina', 'a Spiritu Sancto', *ST* Ia IIae, q. 68, a. 1 and 8; q. 69, a. 1; IIa IIae, q. 52, a. 1; q. 121, a. 1, etc.

24. See my *Tradition and Traditions* (Eng. tr.; London and New York, 1966), Part One, pp. 91–94, 119–137, 174–176, text and notes.

25. B. Decker, *Die Entwicklung der Lehre von der prophetischen Offenbarung von Wilhelm von Auxerre bis zu Thomas von Aquin* (Breslau, 1940); *idem*, art. in *Angelicum*, 16 (1939), 194–244; J.-P. Torrell, 'Hugues de Saint-Cher et Thomas d'Aquin. Contribution à l'histoire du traité de la prophétie', *RThom*, 74 (1974), 5–22; *idem*, *Théorie de la prophétie et Philosophie de la connaissance aux environs de 1230. La contribution d'Hugues de Saint-Cher* (Louvain, 1977).

26. Thomas Aquinas, *De ver.* q. 12, a. 1 and 5; *ST* IIa IIae, q. 171, a. 2; q. 172, a. 4.

27. See I. von Döllinger, *Der Weissagungsglaube und das Prophetentum in der christlichen Zeit* (1871); P. Alphandéry, 'De quelques faits de prophétisme dans les sectes latines antérieures au joachimisme', *Revue de l'Histoire des Religions*, 52 (1905), 177–218; P. Boglioni, 'I carismi nella vita della Chiesa Medievale', *Sacra Doctrina*, 59 (1970), 383–430.

28. R. Grosche, *Das prophetische Element in der Kirche* (1956), reprinted in *Et intra et extra. Theologische Aufsätze* (Düsseldorf, 1958); K. Rahner, *The Dynamic Element in the Church* (Eng. tr.; London, 1964); A. Ulbyn, *Actualité de la fonction prophétique* (1966); *Concilium*, 37 (Sept. 1968); my *Vraie et fausse réforme dans l'Eglise* (Paris, 1950), pp. 196–228, 2nd ed. (1969), pp. 179–207.

29. *ST* IIa IIae, q. 171 prol. See also, for this wider meaning, q. 174, a. 6; *De ver.* q. 12, a. 2; *Comm. in Mat.* c. 7, lect. 2 and c. 11.

30. Hildegard of Bingen, *PL* 197, 95 and 104, 150 and 153.

31. P. Rousset, *Les origines et les caractères de la Première Croisade* (Neuchâtel, 1945); P.

Alphandéry and A. Dupront, *La Chrétienté et l'idée de croisade*, 2 vols (*L'évolution de l'Humanité*, XXXVIII) (Paris, 1959).

32. H. Grundmann, *Religiöse Bewegungen im Mittelalter*, 2nd ed. (Hildesheim, 1961), made a special study of this question.

33. J. Bignami-Odier, 'Les visions de Robert d'Uzès O.P. (†1296)', *Arch. Fr. Praedic.*, 25 (1955), 258–310. Robert is said to have predicted the plague of 1348.

34. J. Bignami-Odier, *Etudes sur Jean de Roquetaillade* (Paris, 1952).

35. E. Delaruelle, 'L'Antéchrist chez S. Vincent Ferrier, S. Bernardin de Sienne et autour de Jeanne d'Arc', *L'Attesa dell'Età nuova nella Spiritualità della fine del Medio Evo (Convegni*, VII) (Todi, 1962), pp. 37–64.

36. P. Boglioni, *op. cit.* (note 27), p. 420, mentions the reaction of Henry of Langenstein to the illuminism of Telesphorus of Cosaga (see Fliche and Martin, XIV, p. 510), the treatises of Bernardino of Siena, Pierre d'Ailly, Gerson and later Dionysius the Carthusian (†1471). Gerson, Henry of Gorcum and Guillaume Bouillé discussed the case of Joan of Arc and believed that the spirit of prophecy has always been present in the Church.

37. See P. Alphandéry, *op. cit* (note 27), 207ff. See also my *Vraie et fausse réforme, op. cit.* (note 28). Rupert of Deutz, for example, saw prophetism in the understanding that God gives us the words we pronounce in liturgical prayer: see *PL* 170, 12.

38. Newman, *The Via Media*, I, Lect. X, note 11, pp. 249–251.

39. See the article on 'gifts' ('Dons') in the *Dictionnaire de Spiritualité*, III, cols 1594ff., for information about Henry of Ghent, St Gertrude, Jan Ruysbroeck, Richard Rolle, Dionysius the Carthusian and, from the sixteenth to the eighteenth centuries, cols 1601ff., for Ignatius Loyola, John of Osuna and others. F. Vandenbroucke is responsible for the first part; A. Rayez for the second. See also the publication of John of Avila (1499–1569), *Sermons sur le Saint-Esprit* (Namur, 1961).

40. John of Marienwerden, *Septililium B. Dorotheae*, ed.F. Hipler, the Rector of the Seminary of Braunsberg, in *Analecta Bollandiana*, 2 (1883), 381–472; 3 (1884), 113–140, 408–448; 4 (1885), 207–251. See also H. Westpfahl, *Dictionnaire de Spirtualité*, III, cols 1640 and 1664–1668. Of particular interest is Treatise II, *De Spiritus Sancti Missione: Analecta Bollandiana*, 3, 113–140.

7

JOACHIM OF FIORE
AND THE FATE OF JOACHIMISM[1]

Born about 1135 in Calabria and possibly of Jewish origin, Joachim gave up legal work, travelled in Syria and Palestine and then entered the Cistercian order and set up the Cistercian monastery of Fiore (Flora) in 1189. He later became abbot, reformed the monastery according to much stricter monastic rules, broke with the order and founded half a dozen daughter-houses. He died on 30 March 1202. In addition to a number of minor works, he left behind a *Concordia Novi ac Veteris Testamenti*, an *Expositio in Apocalypsim*, a *Psalterium decem chordarum*, which he edited in 1184 and subsequently, a *Tractatus super quatuor Evangelia*; and a *Liber Figurarum*, which was written down by one of his disciples.

Joachim's thought was based on a vision of the *concordia* or an understanding of the relationships between the different elements of Old Testament history, New Testament history, and the past or future elements in the history of the Church. He believed that the *littera veteris Testamenti* and the subsequent *littera novi Testamenti* would inevitably be succeeded by a *tertius status*, a new era and a new order. He ascribed each of the three states thus distinguished to one of the Persons of the Trinity: 'Tres status mundi propter tres Personas Divinitatis'.[2] Just as the Spirit proceeds from the Father and the Son, he taught, so too does a 'spiritual understanding' proceed from the Old and the New Testaments.[3] The eternal gospel or the *Evangelium Regni* must succeed the gospel of Christ as preached and celebrated until that time. The people and the events featured in the gospel of Christ symbolize future realities in the age of the Spirit and in the spiritual Church. Each of the three ages has its own first inauguration, a kind of epiphany. The first is inaugurated in Adam and is confirmed in the patriarchs: it is the age of the Father and, in history, the age of the laity. The second is inaugurated in Uzziah and bears fruit in Jesus Christ: it is the age of the Son and the clergy. The third age began with St Benedict and was, according to Joachim, still to be fully manifested.

Joachim was in fact proclaiming the beginning of an age of the Spirit, of spiritual understanding and of the eternal gospel. This age was to be the age of monks, contemplatives and *viri spirituales*, all intimately penetrated by the Spirit. The time of the letter, then, was to be followed by the time of the freedom of the Spirit, a sabbath of pure praise. What had, in other words, generally been reserved for the eschatological era at the end of history was, according to Joachim, introduced into history as the object of hope and expectation. The Church's hierarchy and its sacraments would continue in this age of a religion *omnino libera et spiritualis*, but they would be spiritualized and would correspond more to the Johannine than to the Petrine type. The coming of this age was, Joachim believed, imminent: *tempus prefinitum adest* (*Conc.* V, c. 119; fol. 135b).

Joachim's writings were almost unknown during his own lifetime, but from about 1240 onwards they were widely circulated and associated with tendentious pseudepigraphical texts. The Franciscan Gerard of Borgo San Donnino edited an *Introductorius in Evangelium aeternum* in 1247 and distributed it in 1254. This work caused a great stir and was condemned on 23 October 1255 in the bull *Libellum quendam*. The minister general of the Franciscans, who was favourably disposed towards Joachimism, was replaced in 1257 by Bonaventure.

Bonaventure accepted that certain aspects of the Joachimite proclamation of a historical growth towards the eschatological reality should be applied to Francis of Assisi, who had been an eschatological spiritual man. He also attributed to Scripture a prophetic character and a seminal value with regard not only to Christ—this was also emphasized by Thomas Aquinas, who used it as the basis for a radical criticism of Joachimism—but also to the history of the Church and to the theme of man's knowledge of God within the Church. Bonaventure also included within this framework of knowledge the historical messianism or eschatology by which he was able to accept within the history of salvation the fact of Francis of Assisi. In this way, he was able to deal satisfactorily with certain principles in Joachim's theory of history, but at the same time he succeeded in retaining, in the Franciscan tradition, the absolute primacy and the central position of Christ. According to Bonaventure, there could be no relatively autonomous and new time of the Spirit. The time of the Spirit, as experienced by the Church, had to be the time of Christ.[4] This emphasis neutralizes the venom contained in Joachimism and even eliminates it altogether.

Thomas Aquinas was resolutely, severely and radically critical of Joachim's teaching.[5] He regarded Joachim as a lout playing with theology: 'in subtilibus fidei dogmatibus rudis',[6] and his theology of the Trinity in particular as wrong.[7] Thomas dissociated himself from Bonaventure in his recognition of the typological meaning of the facts contained in the canonical texts of the Old Testament, but rejection of the idea that one particular fact in the New Testament could be seen as corresponding to one particular fact in the Old. Such concordances were, in his opinion, matters not of prophecy, but of human ingenuity.[8]

Thomas did not explicitly refer to Joachim, but cited him almost literally and tacitly alluded to the second of the theses that had been criticized by the theologians of Paris. He expressed this fundamental criticism within the framework of a treatise on the 'new law' which appears to have been an original contribution of his own to thirteenth-century theology (Ia IIae, q. 106). This new law consists principally (and this word should be understood in its full sense) of the grace of the Holy Spirit given in it.[9] The sacramental signs and the rules of belief and conduct have a place in this new law, since this is required by the logic of incarnation (q. 108, a. 1), but they are secondary and at the service of the grace of the Spirit. The *status* or the régime of the New Testament is that of Christ and the Spirit together. It is a definitive *status* and no other age can be expected to follow it. It would be mere *vanitas*, lacking any content of truth, to claim anything else.

In his attempt to disclose future perspectives, Joachim in fact turned his back on the real meaning of Scripture so well disclosed by the early tradition of the Church and the liturgy, according to which the Spirit enables us to understand the Word-Son, who reveals the Father and leads men to the Father. The Thomist theme of *exitus* and *reditus*, on the other hand, was fully in accordance with this traditional meaning of Scripture.

Thomas belonged to an order in which the charisms had been present in the founder, Dominic.[10] In addition, the presence of a *gratia praedicationis* was also taken into account in the Dominican order when it was a question of sending out a friar to preach.[11] Thomas himself used the term.[12] This is an admirable apostolic charism the exercise of which in the history of the Church deserves further study. It was clearly a privilege which the Friars Preachers enjoyed, but which does not seem to have placed them at any time in a critical situation. The chapters took care that friars avoided strange readings and disordered enthusiasms.

The same cannot be said of the Franciscans, who did not avoid a grave crisis: that of the Spiritual Franciscans and the Fraticelli.[13] Joachim had proclaimed the imminence of a new age that would be inaugurated by poor and spiritual religious, although he had not himself greatly insisted on poverty, and Francis had appeared on the scene as a miracle of the evangelical ideal and the perfect image of Christ—*Christo totus crucifixus et configuratus*. Joachim had announced a return of Elijah to inaugurate the third age and a more complete revelation of the Spirit. Francis was that new Elijah, the angel of the sixth seal (Rev 7:2), the one who initiated an age of the Spirit and announced an eternal gospel (Rev 14:6). His evangelical rule of total poverty had to be followed, as he himself had said, 'without a gloss and literally'. From about 1240 onwards, the movement of strict observance, in opposition to the 'Conventuals', gathered strength and hardened after the Council of Lyons in 1274. The so-called 'Spirituals' became more numerous and influential, especially in the Marches under the leadership of Angelo Clareno and in Provence with Petrus Joannis Olivi as their leader. On the one hand, there is the striking evangelical spirit of poverty of those who wanted the Church to be poor and without any earthly domain[14] and who were prepared to suffer for their ideal, even to go to the stake. On the other hand, however, there is the disconcerting spectacle of men who fought and were excommunicated because they refused to abandon positions which seem to us now to be exaggerated and even false.

The situation became even worse during the pontificate of John XXII (1316–1334). The name 'Fraticelli' was applied at about this time to those Franciscans who first of all formed an autonomous group which insisted unconditionally on poverty, and later formed various groups of deviants and rebels. They began by insisting on following a purely spiritual rule of Christ, and from there went on to contestation and even rejection of the sacraments of the Church and of the hierarchy as led by the Pope, who came to be regarded by them as the forerunner of the Antichrist. In their preaching, the Fraticelli were passionate and basically irrational, making liberal use of apocalyptic language.

There was no real continuity between the 'spirituals' of the Franciscan or Joachimite traditions and the Brethren of the Free Spirit, but there were points of contact between them and a fundamental kind of community.[15] These Brethren were in no sense homogeneous. They began to appear from the eleventh century onwards and were loosely affiliated in anti-ecclesiastical and anti-sacramental groups and movements. Their ideas differed quite widely. This is clear, for example, from a comparison between the writings of Speroni and those of Amalric of Bène, whose mystical teaching was quite profound, but who advocated a passivity that was almost quietistic and an indifference to external rules that amounted to an almost complete lack of moral reserve, and spoke of a feeling of being in God that was almost pantheistic: 'Spiritus sanctus in nobis quotidie incarnatur'.

Although the ideas of Abbot Joachim and his followers may not have been regarded as theologically important by the theologians of Paris,[16] they certainly gave rise to human hopes and expectations and caused a stir that was to be felt for a very long time.[17] Has Joachimism ever completely died out? Certain religious foundations have seen themselves to some extent as following the tradition of the 'spiritual men' as proclaimed by Joachim.[18] For a very long time renewals in the Church have been linked with the emergence of religious orders, and thus with initiatives taken by the Holy Spirit.[19]

This, however, is not all that has to be said about Joachim and Joachimism. He introduced into the history of this world, which was for him, of course, the history of the Church, an eschatology that was characterized by the great novelty of a rule of the inner life and of freedom. Joachim in this way opened the flood-gates to admit what could well become the torrent of human hopes. This could at any time result in social protest, a polarized attempt to reform the Church, or many different searches for freedom and novelty. It could take the form of philosophies of reason, of progress, of the 'spirit'. This has, in fact, frequently happened, in many cases with an explicit reference to Joachim. Did he not, after all, say that God would do new things on earth—'facere novum super terram et renovare peccatis inveteratam ecclesiam'?[20] There have been, parallel to what Etienne Gilson called 'metamorphoses of the City of God', a series of 'metamorphoses of Joachimism' (K. Löwith, see below, note 17), which have often been forms of secularization of the Spirit. I summarize the most important.

In his *Sacrum Imperium*, Alois Dempf pointed to the connection between a re-emergence of the eschatological spirit expressed in apocalyptic language and a preoccupation with political questions. This combination clearly appeared in the form of Joachimism that flourished in the thirteenth century, with its hope of an emperor who would save the people and a *Papa angelicus*. Such a Pope appeared in the person of Celestine V, the eighty-year-old hermit from the Abruzzi who reigned no more than a few months in 1294. Then came Boniface VIII! Boniface's enemies, the Colonna, formed an alliance with the 'Spirituals'. As a loyal Ghibelline, Dante (1265–1321) remembered that, in their opposition to the temporal claims of the papacy, the emperor's supporters favoured a Church that was spiritual and poor. He therefore thought highly of 'Abbot Joachim of Calabria, who was endowed with prophetic spirit':

> il Calavrese abate Giovacchino
> di spirito profetico dotato.[21]

Joachimist hopes also abounded in the fourteenth century, especially when the Popes were at Avignon. Cola di Rienzo (1313–1354), the leader of the Roman party, was expecting 'an extension of the Holy Spirit, whose pouring out over all flesh had been promised and who was to renew the face of the earth'.[22] He even called himself a soldier and a knight of the Holy Spirit. This was clearly a case of politics animated by mysticism. A renewal of the world could only be expected as the result of a renewal of the Spirit.

The impulse given by Joachimism to the idea of renewal also had an impact on the literary figures and the philosophers of the Renaissance. Many 'prophets' proclaimed that the end of the fifteenth and the beginning of the sixteenth centuries would be a time not only of tribulation, but also of preparation for a *renovatio mundi*. It was in this climate of feeling that an edition of Joachim's works was prepared in Venice, during the second and third decades of the sixteenth century.[23]

Even more interesting in this context are the Joachimist references in the evangelization of Mexico by the Franciscans and Dominicans in the sixteenth century. This process of evangelization was characterized by a combination of an eschatological perspective, the need to convert the last people who had not yet been evangelized, and a clear reference to the early apostolate of the Church in the number of Franciscans sent in 1523 (twelve!), the whole placed within the context of a clearly Joachimist spirit.[24]

The missionaries had the task of trying to build up a millenarian reign. This is obviously another case of reducing eschatology to a historical perspective and of using apocalyptic terminology to express it.

A new time was, however, on the way—the modern era. This is, of course, a very vague term, but it does point to a relatively continuous movement in which man's reason was set free from a dogmatic framework and from dependence on positive and supernatural religion. It was this that made Michelet say: 'The great century, by which I mean the eighteenth'. It was at this time that explanation from on high was replaced by explanation from below, by natural realities and the movement of the human spirit and human society. G. B. Vico based his philosophy of history on divine providence, but he also showed providence as revealed in the development of languages, religions and laws. This movement took place within humanity, which is its own work (*Scienza nuova*, 1725). In 1780, the year before his death, Lessing published his *Erziehung des Menschengeschlechts*, in which he referred explicitly to a 'new eternal gospel'. The mistake made by the enthusiasts who had proclaimed that gospel in the thirteenth and fourteenth centuries had simply been that they had insisted that its coming was imminent, whereas in fact progress towards that new gospel was slow and it would only be gradually achieved in the history of mankind.[25]

Kant also came very close to this idea. He had already published *Was ist Aufklärung?* in 1784 and, in 1793, he published *Religion innerhalb der Grenzen der blossen Vernunft*, in which he interpreted the history of Christianity as a gradual ascent to a religion of reason, through which the kingdom of God would be realized on earth in the form of an ethical community.

Hegel (1770–1831) wanted to dismiss the Enlightenment, which he described as a 'vanity of understanding', and hoped to re-establish the harmony and even the unity that had existed between religion and reason in a philosophy of the absolute spirit. In an early work, *Der Geist des Christentums und sein Schicksal*, he proclaimed his intention to evolve a philosophy based on the Johannine promise and incorporating the idea of reconciliation and reunion between God and man and between the objective and the subjective spirit. Should we think of it as 'spirit' or as 'Spirit'? Hegel moves from one to the other:

> The spirit is the infinite return to oneself and infinite subjectivity that is not represented, but is true divinity, present, not the substantial in-himself of the Father, nor that of the Son and of Christ, who is the true one in that form in that objectivity. It is what is subjectively present and real, which is subjectively present. . . . This is the Spirit of God, God, the present, real spirit, God dwelling in his community.[26]

According to Hegel, then, the Spirit is God in his community and God has to bring about a return to the absolute Spirit. Is that Spirit the third Person—God as spirit? It is the energy of the manifestation in the three aspects of being in oneself, of externalization and of return to oneself. Hegel himself alludes to the Joachimist view in another essay:

> The Middle Ages were the reign of the Son. In the Son, God is not yet complete. He can only be complete in the Spirit. As the Son, he has put himself outside himself and there is therefore a state of being-differently which can only be transcended (*aufgehoben*) in the Spirit, in God's return to himself. Just as the state of the Son comprises exteriority in itself, exteriority was the rule of the Middle Ages. The reign of the Spirit began with the Reformation, when God became known as Spirit.[27]

Hegel's famous principle of *Aufhebung*, which he used in the sense of preserving and raising to a higher level what is suppressed or transcended, appears in the passage quoted above. There is a deep logic of movement in his thought here, and E. Benz, H. Grundmann, and H. Mottu, who quotes them, have compared the Joachimist ideas of *evacuare* and *consummare* with this powerful Hegelian concept.[28] The imperfection of the New Testament will, in other words, disappear (*evacuabitur*; 1 Cor 13:10), but this state will be transcended, recovered and taken up at the same time in the age of the Spirit, when *quod* perfectum est—'what is perfect'—will come.

Hegel's interpretation seems to me to do grave injustice to the witness of the Bible and to traditional Christian conviction. As J. Greisch has observed, it seeks to achieve an 'integration and a rational appropriation of the Spirit as the latter is expressed in the biblical texts (Rom 8, for example) and it claims to disclose the full meaning of those texts'.

The spiritual horizon was definitively widened by the philosophers of the Romantic movement in Germany such as Lessing, Hegel and Fichte. They looked in philosophy for a vision of the whole of reality to express the full depths of the spirit and man's inner experience. The current of Romantic philosophy to a great extent represented a transposition of Christian values. Its philosophy of history is certainly a transposition of Christian eschatology.

Schelling (1775–1854) followed the Romantic tradition and expressed its ideas very clearly. In his 'Essays on the Philosophy of Art', published in 1804, he said, for example: 'Christ has returned to a world above the senses and has stated that the spirit is to replace him. It is as though he has put an end to the past age. He is the last God. After him comes the spirit, the ideal principle, the soul that will rule the new world.'[29]

Schelling became acquainted with Joachim's ideas through the work of Neander, *Geschichte der christlichen Religion und Kirche* (6 vols, 1826–1852), which was also an important source for many other thinkers and theologians, including, for example, Möhler. In a work written in 1841 and published in 1842 with the significant title of *Philosophie der Offenbarung* ('Philosophy of Revelation'), Schelling took as his point of departure the apparent proclamation in the New Testament of a future going beyond itself, that is, Christ's announcement of the Spirit. The seed sowed on earth by Christianity was, in Schelling's opinion, to grow into a universal vision.

132

This process is outlined by the philosopher in his Lesson 37 in the figures of the three apostles, Peter, Paul and John. Peter is the one who gives the law; he is the principle of stability. Paul is movement, dialectics and knowledge; he was the first Protestant by virtue of his resistance to Peter's unlimited authority (see Gal 2). The true Church is not to be found in either of these two forms as such. From the time when it was founded on Peter, it moves forward through Paul towards its end, which is to become a Church of John.[30] The true Church is therefore still to come.

These ideas had a favourable reception, not only in Germany, but also in Russia, where Schelling had a considerable influence. This influence extended to the Slavophile movement and even later, in the present century, to D. S. Merezhkovski (1865–1941),[31] who inspired A. Moeller van den Bruck to write his book *Das dritte Reich* (1923), a title that inspired Hitler to try to establish a third empire, kingdom or age, whose dramatic fate we have witnessed. Hitler, after all, announced that he was settling the historical future for a thousand years—the millennium!

Modern philosophies of history may or may not refer to Joachimist themes, and may contain a great deal or only a minimum of utopian hope, but they have often been successors, even re-expressions, of Christian eschatology.[32] An 'eschatological' philosophy of the spirit is therefore a laicization of theology.[33] We obviously cannot pursue this theme here. It is however, interesting to note a direct reference to Joachim of Fiore in the theology of the 'death of God' that flourished in the nineteen-sixties. At that time, Thomas Altizer wrote:

> The radical Christian also inherits both the ancient prophetic belief that revelation continues in history and the eschatological belief of the tradition following Joachim of Floris. This tradition maintains that we are now living in the third and final age of the Spirit, that a new revelation is breaking into this age and that this revelation will differ as much from the New Testament as the New Testament itself does from its Old Testament counterpart. . . . We can learn from earlier radical Christians the root radical principle that the movement of the Spirit has passed beyond the revelation of the canonical Bible and is now revealing itself in such a way as to demand a whole new form of faith. To refuse such a new revelation of the Spirit would be to repudiate the activity of the Word which is present and to bind oneself to a now empty and lifeless form of the Word. Nor can we expect the new revelation to be in apparent continuity with the old. . . . Yet this should by no means persuade us that no new revelation has occurred. We can only judge by the fruits of the Spirit and if a new vision has arisen recording a universal and eschatological form of the Word, a form of the Word pointing to a total redemption of history and the cosmos, then we should be prepared to greet it with the full acceptance of faith.[34]

Needless to say, Joachim would have disapproved of such a use of his ideas. He did not suspect that he had opened up an issue and had initiated a movement to which so many would be able to contribute their own dreams!

NOTES

1. Many books and articles have been written about this subject. Among them are: M. Reeves, *The Influence of Prophecy in the Later Middle Ages. A Study in Joachimism* (Oxford, 1969); C. Baraut, 'Joachim de Flore', *Dictionnaire de Spiritualité*, VIII (1974), cols 1179–1201; B.-D. Dupuy, article in *Catholicisme*, VI (1966), cols 878–887 and 887–895; my *L'Eglise de S. Augustin à l'époque moderne* (Paris, 1970), pp. 209ff. My attention was unfortunately not drawn to H. Mottu, *La manifestation de l'Esprit selon Joachim de Fiore* (Neuchâtel and Paris, 1977), with its very full bibliography, until after my work had been completed.

2. Joachim, *Concordia* IV, c. 6, fol. 9a (repr. Frankfurt, 1964).

3. *ibid.*; *Tractatus super quatuor Evangelia*, ed. E. Buonaiuti, pp. 21–22.

4. For Bonaventure and Joachimism, see E. Gilson, *La philosophie de S. Bonaventure*, 2nd ed. (1943), pp. 21–27; J. Ratzinger, *Die Geschichtstheologie des Hl. Bonaventura* (Munich and Zürich, 1959); H. de Lubac, 'Joachim de Flore jugé par S. Bonaventure et S. Thomas', *Pluralisme et Œcuménisme en Recherches théologiques. Mélanges S. Dock* (Gembloux, 1976), pp. 31–49; O. Stephan, 'Bonaventuras christologischer Einwand gegen die Geschichtslehre des Joachim von Fiore', *Miscellanea Mediaevalia*, ed. A. Zimmermann, 11: *Die Mächte des Guten und Bösen* (Berlin, 1977), pp. 113–130.

5. E. Benz, 'Joachim Studien: III: Thomas von Aquin und Joachim von Fiore', *Zeitschrift für Kirchengeschichte*, 53 (1934), 52–116; an incomplete study. Thomas became acquainted with the writings of Joachim of Fiore in a monastery. See Tocco's life, *Acta Sanctorum Martii*, p. 665; *Fontes vitae S. Thomas Aq.*, ed. D. M. Prummer, fasc. 2 (Toulouse, 1913), pp. 93–94; A. Walz, 'Abt Joachim und der "neue Geist der Freiheit" in Toccos Thomasleben c. XX', *Angelicum*, 45 (1968), 303–315. I know no more than the title of B. McGian, 'The Abbot and the Doctors: Scholastic Reactions to the Radical Eschatology of Joachim of Fiore', *Church History*, 40 (1971), 30–47.

6. *In 2ma Decretal.*

7. *ST* Ia, q. 39, a. 5 and the text cited in note 6 above. Joachim's theology of the Trinity was condemned by the Fourth Lateran Council, c. 2 (November 1215; *DS* 803), although the Council stressed that it did not wish to harm the monastery at Fiore (see *DS* 807). This was the 'second decretal' on which Thomas commented. This commentary was intended for the instruction of the clergy, which had to be checked by the archdeacons.

8. 'Quamvis status novi testamenti in generali sit praefiguratus per statum veteris testamenti, non tamen oportet quod singula respondeant singulis, praecipue cum in Christo omnes figurae veteris testamenti fuerint completae; et ideo Augustinus "exquisite et ingeniose illa singula his singulis comparata videantur, non prophetico spiritu, sed coniectura mentis humanae, quae aliquando ad verum pervenit, aliquando fallitur" (*De civ. Dei* XVIII, 32). Et similiter videtur esse de dictis abbatis Ioachim': *In IV Sent.* d. 43, q. 1, a. 3.

9. *ST* Ia IIae, q. 106, a. 1 and 2; q. 107, a. 1; cf. *Comm. in Rom.* c. 8, lect. 1; *Comm. in Hebr.* c. 8, lect. 3, end. A full bibliography is provided in my 'Le Saint-Esprit dans la théologie thomiste de l'agir moral', *Atti del Congresso internazionale 1974*, 5 (Naples, 1976), pp. 9–19. The reference to the second thesis condemned by the theologians of Paris concerns the identification of the *Evangelium Christi* with the *Evangelium Regni*: see *ST* Ia IIae, q. 106, a. 4, ad 4; *Comm. in Rom.* c. 10, lect. 3; *Comm. in Col.* c. 1, lect. 2. Thomas said that it was *stultissimum*—extremely stupid—to deny that they were identical.

10. See M.-H. Vicaire, 'Charisme et hiérarchie dans la fondation de l'Ordre de Prêcheurs', *Vie Dominicaine*, 31 (Fribourg, 1972), 37–60, repr. in *Dominique et ses Prêcheurs* (Fribourg and Paris, 1977), pp. 198–221; see also Bede Jarrett, *The Life of Saint Dominic* (2nd ed., London, 1934).

11. See the *libellus* of Jordan of Saxony, Dominic's successor, 39, 69 and 77: *MOPH*, XVI (Rome, 1935), pp. 45, 57, 62; Process of Dominic's canonization, 24, 26 and 39: *MOPH*,

XVI, pp. 142, 143 and 158; Gérard de Frachet, *Vitae Fratrum*, Part 3, chapter XI: *MOPH*, I (Louvain, 1896), p. 108, see also pp. 138, 150.

12. *ST* IIIa, q. 7, a. 7; cf. the *gratia sermonis*, Ia IIae, q. 111, a. 4; IIa IIae, q. 177, a. 1; *C. Gentes*, III, 154; *Comm. in Rom.* c. 2, lect. 3; *Comm. in 1 Cor.* c. 1, lect. 2.

13. See E. Benz, *Ecclesia spiritualis. Kirchenidee und Geschichtstheologie der franziskanischen Reformation* (Stuttgart, 1934; 2nd ed., 1964). There are excellent articles on the 'Spirituels', *DTC*, XIV (1939), cols 2522–2549, by L. Oliger; 'Fraticelles', *Dictionnaire de Spiritualité*, V (1964), cols 1167–1188, by C. Schmitt. See also G. Leff, *Heresy in the Later Middle Ages: the Relation of Heterodoxy to Dissent, c. 1250–c. 1450* (New York, 2nd ed. 1967); *Franciscains d'Oc. Les Spirituels c. 1280–1324 (Cahiers de Fanjeaux*, X) (Toulouse, 1975). For the condemnation of Olivi by the Council of Vienne, see *DS* 908; of the Fraticelli by John XXII, see *DS* 910–916, 930.

14. W. C. van Dijk, *Le franciscanisme comme contestation permanente dans l'Eglise. Congrès de l'Association internationale des sciences religieuses* (Munich, 1960).

15. R. Manselli, *Spirituali e Beghini in Provenza* (Rome, 1959). Romana Guarnieri has written a remarkable article on the 'Brethren of the Free Spirit': 'Frères du libre esprit', *Dictionnaire de Spiritualité*, V (1964), cols 1241–1268, which is a summary of her study 'Il movimento del libero spirito', *Archivio italiano per la Storia della pietà*, 4 (1965), 351–708. For the condemnation of the Brethren by Boniface VIII, see *DS* 866; for the criticism of the Beghards at the Council of Vienne (1311–1312), see *DS* 891–899.

16. See, for example, Henry of Langenstein, *c.* 1392: 'qualis fuerat abbas Joachim . . . Parisiensis schola non ignorat. Ibi enim nullius est auctoritatis': *Contra vaticinum Telesphori Eremitae*, in B. Pez, *Thesaurus Anecdotorum* (Augsburg, 1721–23), 1/2, col. 521; see also M. Reeves, *op. cit.* (note 1), p. 426.

17. More or less fully documented evidence will be found in J. Taubes, *Abendländische Eschatologie* (Berne, 1947), with a simple table; Joachim von Fiore, *Das Reich des Heiligen Geistes*, ed. A. Rosenberg (Munich, 1955); K. Löwith, *Weltgeschichte und Heilsgeschehen. Die theologischen Voraussetzungen der Geschichtsphilosophie* (Stuttgart, 4th ed., 1961), Appendix I: *Verwandlungen der Lehre Joachims*, pp. 190–195; M. Reeves, *op. cit.* (note 1) and below (note 18); G. Wendelborn, *Gott und Geschichte. Joachim von Fiore und die Hoffnung der Christenheit* (Vienna and Cologne, 1974); G. Bornkamm, *Gesammelte Aufsätze*, III (see below, note 25).

18. This is especially true in the case of the Franciscans, but it also applies to the Dominicans: see Salimbene; Gérard de Frachet, *Vitae Fratrum*, ed. Reichert (*MOPH*, I), p. 13; M. Reeves, *op. cit.* (note 1), pp. 146ff., 161ff. It would be interesting to investigate the anti-intellectual reaction that existed among the Friars Preachers. Was it in some way connected with Joachimism? The Augustinian hermits of the fourteenth century had recourse to the prophetic spirit of Joachimism: see M. Reeves, 'Joachimist Expectations in the Order of Augustinian Hermits', *RTAM*, 25 (1958), 111–141, and again at the beginning of the sixteenth century, exploiting their title of 'hermits'. The Jesuits also appealed to it: see M. Reeves, 'The Abbot Joachim and the Society of Jesus', *Mediaeval and Renaissance Studies*, 5 (1961), 163–181. These two articles by M. Reeves are summarized, *op. cit.* (note 1), pp. 251–273 and 274–290.

19. See, for example, the bull announcing the canonization of St Dominic by Gregory IX, 3 July 1234: *MOPH*, XVI (Rome, 1935), pp. 190–194; Fr. tr. M.-H. Vicaire, *Saint Dominique de Caleruega d'après les documents du XIIIe siècle* (Paris, 1955), pp. 255–259. Written in the florid style of allegory and making use of striking symbolism, the bull refers to four chariots following each other: the martyrs, the monastic Order of Saint Benedict, the Order of Cîteaux *and of Fiore*, and the Order of Preachers and of Friars Minor.

20. Joachim, *Tractatus*, ed. E. Buonaiuti, p. 283.

21. *Paradiso* XII, 140–141. For Dante and Joachim, see L. Tondelli, *Da Gioacchino a Dante* (Turin, 1944); *idem, Il libro delle Figure*, I (Turin, 2nd ed., 1953), pp. 183–400. The

possibility that Dante used a Joachimist source for his vision of the Trinity has also been investigated.

22. M. Reeves, *op. cit.* (note 1), pp. 318–319, 420–421, with reference to K. Burdach's great work, *Vom Mittelalter zur Reformation* (Berlin, 1913–1929); P. Piner, *Cola di Rienzo* (Vienna, 1931). This extract from Rienzo's letter No. 58 is worth noting here: 'De vita aeterna disperare posset ecclesia, si de continuo etiam Spiritus Sancti adventu et renovacione humanarum mencium ab eodem eciam assidue desperaret. Tociens enim renovacione Spiritus indigemus quociens inveteramus et senescimus in peccatis' (p. 315).

23. See G. Toffanin, *La religione degli Umanisti* (Bologna, 1950); Gianpaolo Tognetti, 'Note sul Profetismo nel Rinascimento e la letteratura relativa', *Bullettino dell'Istituto Storico Italiano per il Medio Evo e Archivio Muratoriano*, 82 (1970), pp. 129–157. See also the collection *L'Attesa dell'Età nuova . . . (Convegni,* VII) (Todi, 1962). At the time of the Disputation of Lausanne in 1536, it was a physican, Blancherose, who took up the challenge of Viret and Farel, referring to the Joachimist theme: the age of the Father, that of the Empire, had been followed by that of the Son (the Pope), and this would be followed by the age of the Spirit, that is, of goodness and charity. This third period would be that of physicians! See G. Bavaud, *La Dispute de Lausanne (1536). Une étape de l'évolution doctrinale des Réformateurs romands* (Fribourg, 1956), pp. 34–35.

24. See A. López, 'Los doce primeros apóstoles de Méjico', *Semana de Missiología de Barcelona*, II (Barcelona, 1930), pp. 201–226; J. L. Phelan, *The Millennial Kingdom of the Franciscans in the New World* (Los Angeles, 1956); M. Bataillon, 'Evangélisme et Millénarisme au Nouveau Monde', *Courants religieux et Humanisme à la fin du XVe et au début du XVIe siècle* (Paris, 1959), pp. 27ff.; G. Gaudot, *Utopie et Histoire du Mexique. Les premiers chroniqueurs de la civilisation mexicaine (1520–1569)* (Toulouse, 1977).

25. Lessing, *Die Erziehung des Menschengeschlechts,* §86–89, in *Sämtliche Schriften,* ed. K. Lachmann, XIII (1897), pp. 433–434: '§86. The time of a *new eternal gospel* will come, the time that has been promised to us in the elementary books of the new covenant. §87. Some of the enthusiasts *(Schwärmer)* of the thirteenth and fourteenth centuries may have seized hold of a ray of this new eternal gospel. Their only mistake was to have proclaimed that its appearance was imminent. §88. Their idea of the *three ages of the world* may not have been an idle fancy; certainly they had no bad programme when they taught that the new covenant ought to be *declared obsolete* as the old covenant had been. They preserved the same economy of the same God. Expressed in my language, that is the same plan of general education for the human race. §89. But they acted too quickly. They believed that they could, without enlightenment *(Aufklärung),* without preparation, make their contemporaries, who had barely ceased to be children, into men worthy of their *third age'*. See also K. Löwith, *op. cit.* (note 17), pp. 136ff., 190ff.; G. Bornkamm, 'Die Zeit des Geistes', *Geschichte und Glaube,* Part I *(Gesammelte Aufsätze,* III) (Munich, 1968), pp. 90–103.

26. Hegel, *Vorlesungen über die Philosophie der Religion,* posthumous publication (1832); Fr. tr. J. Gibelin, *Leçons sur la Philosophie de la Religion* (Paris, 1954), Part III, 'La Religion absolue', chapter V, p. 173. See also *Die Phänomenologie des Geistes* (1806); Fr. tr. J. Hippolite, *La Phénoménologie de l'Esprit* (Paris, 1941), Chapter VII, pp. 284–290. See also C. Bruaire, *Logique et religion chrétienne dans la philosophie de Hegel* (1964) and A. Chapelle, *Hegel et la religion* (3 vols, 1966).

27. Hegel, *Vorlesungen über die Philosophie der Weltgeschichte,* posthumous publication (1837), ed. G. Lasson, IV (Leipzig, 1920), p. 881. Hegel believed that the Reformers devalued works and despised the world and in this way enclosed themselves within an abstract form of interiority, with the result that it was not possible for them to realize a society that was reconciled in the unity of the universal and the particular, of the inner and the outward realities. It was therefore not possible for Christianity to accomplish its vocation and the state had to carry out this failed mission!

28. H. Mottu, *op. cit.* (note 1), pp. 109–110 and 132.

29. F. W. J. Schelling, *Werke,* Part 5, Vol. V (Stuttgart, 1859), p. 452.

30. F. W. J. Schelling, *Sämtliche Werke*, II. Abteilung, Vol. IV, 2nd half (1858), pp. 298–344. See also K. Löwith, *op. cit.* (note 17), pp. 191–193. For the theme of the three apostles, see my article 'Eglise de Pierre, Eglise de Paul, Eglise de Jean. Destin d'un thème œcuménique', *The Ecumenical World of Orthodox Civilization. Russian and Orthodoxy*, III: *Essays in Honour of George Florovsky*, ed. A. Blane (The Hague and Paris, 1973), pp. 163–179.

31. Merezhkovski believed that a contrast between the Father and the Son—a theme that recurs in the work of Merleau-Ponty—led to an expectation of the Spirit.

32. See E. Hirsch, *Die Reich-Gottes Begriffe des neueren europäischen Denkens* (Göttingen, 1921); E. Gilson, *Les métamorphoses de la Cité de Dieu* (Louvain, 1952); H. Kesting, 'Utopie und Eschatologie. Zukunfterwartungen in der Geschichtsphilosophie des 19. Jahrhunderts', *Jahrbuch für Rechts- und Sozialphilosophie*, XLI (1954–55), pp. 202–230; see also H. Desroches's studies of utopian socialism and forms of messianism. Ernst Bloch saw Joachim as a forerunner of socialism; see his *Erbschaft dieser Zeit* (Frankfurt, 1962), pp. 133ff.; *Atheismus im Christentum* (Frankfurt, 1968), pp. 217, 292. Joachim was also the prophet of openness to the future: see K. Löwith, *op. cit.* (note 17), pp. 136ff.

33. E. von Hartmann (1842–1906) followed a pantheistic course in his *Philosophie des Geistes* (1882).

34. Thomas Altizer, *The Gospel of Christian Atheism* (Philadelphia, 1966), p. 27, with reference to William Blake, Hegel and Nietzsche.

8

PNEUMATOLOGY IN THE
HISTORY OF PROTESTANTISM

THE REFORMERS

In this section, we shall consider Luther and Calvin.[1] Both kept to the classical teaching of Nicaea and Constantinople (381) and even to the Creed *Quicumque* with regard to the Trinity. Both had to fight on two fronts. On the one hand, they had to combat entrenched 'Catholic' positions which were rightly or wrongly identified with a need to regard the 'Church', or rather the 'hierarchy', as absolute. On the other hand, they had to fight against 'enthusiasts' who appealed to the Spirit in their claim that they were furthering the reforming movement. The enthusiasts whom Luther had to resist were the *Schwärmer* Storch, Müntzer and Karlstadt, and those whom Calvin opposed were the Anabaptists. Both Reformers kept to a middle road, or rather a synthesis, and each in his own way insisted on a close relationship between an external 'instrument' of grace—Scripture—and the activity of the Spirit.

Andreas Karlstadt (originally Bodenstein) had been Luther's friend and had even awarded him his doctor's degree in 1512.[2] He held the same doctrine as Luther on justification by faith alone, but he was much more radical and, while Luther was absent in hiding in the Wartburg, he conducted a fanatical campaign at Wittenberg against images, the Real Presence in the Eucharist, and infant baptism (1524). The break with Luther became wider when Karlstadt wrote and published in March 1525 his *Anzeig etlicher Hauptartikel christlicher Lehre* in reply to the treatise that Luther had just published in the same year: *Wider die himmlichen Propheten, von den Bildern und Sakrament.* The false 'heavenly prophets' mentioned in the title by Luther were Storch and Müntzer. The latter had been active at Zwickau and then at Allstedt.

Not only historians of the left wing of the Reformation, but also Marxist historians and theoreticians have been interested in Müntzer.[3] He was not a 'spiritual' who could be compared with what might have survived from the mysticism of the Brethren of the Free Spirit. As against the theological reformation that took place at Wittenberg, he strove to achieve a popular reformation. He proclaimed the end of the last empire of this world and the disappearance of priests, monks and irreligious lords. He claimed to be the Daniel of the new rule. Since the princes of the world would not follow him, the poor would be chosen. Müntzer claimed that he had assimilated the ideas of Joachim of Fiore—in fact he had read the pseudo-Joachimist commentary on Jeremiah[4]—but, whereas Joachim had proclaimed an age of contemplatives, Müntzer joined the peasants in revolt. When they were defeated at Frankenhausen, he was taken prisoner and hanged on 27 May 1525. His ideas persisted in the Anabaptist movement which was inaugurated at Zwickau in 1521, but that movement became so diversified that it would be impossible to examine it here.

Luther called the Zwickau prophets, the Anabaptists and the sacramentarians *Schwärmer*, fanatical enthusiasts.[5] He described them thus in 1537:

> In these things that refer to the external word of the mouth, it is important to insist firmly on this: that God only gives his Spirit or grace through or with the previously existing external word. This is our safeguard against the enthusiasts, in other words, those spirits who flatter themselves that they have the Spirit independently of the word or before it and who consequently judge, interpret and extend Scripture or the word of the mouth according to their will. This is what Müntzer did and what is done today by very many people who want to be judges discerning between the spirit and the letter, and who do not know what they are saying or teaching. Papism is also pure enthusiasm, since the Pope claims to 'keep all laws in the casket of his heart' and since everything that he decides and commands with his Church is spirit and must be regarded as just, even if it goes beyond Scripture or the spoken word and is contrary to them. . . . That is why we have the right and we are obliged to insist that God is only able to enter into a relationship with us men through the external word and the sacraments. Everything that is said of the Spirit independently of this word and the sacraments is the devil![6]

The same idea occurs in Luther's writing two years later:

> When we were taught by the gospel that some external thing could not save us because it was a question of simple creatures which the devil had often used for sorcery, even great and learned men (Karlstadt) concluded from this that baptism, as external water, the word, as external and human speaking, Scripture, as external letters made in ink, and the wine and the bread, as baked by the baker, were only external, perishable things. And they began to shout: Spirit! Spirit! It is the Spirit who must act—the letter kills! It was in this way that Müntzer called us, the theologians of Wittenberg, learned in Scripture (*Schriftgelehrte*; scribes), while he himself claimed to be learned in the Spirit (*Geistgelehrter*).[7]

Luther defined quite clearly the rôle that he attributed to the Spirit, as closely related to the gospel and to faith in Jesus Christ as saviour through listening to and clinging to that Word that is preached according to Scripture. It was, according to Luther, through the Word that men were introduced into the Church as the community of those who were sanctified by the Spirit on the basis of faith.[8] In Luther's opinion, the purest example of this process by which the Christian was made was to be found in Mary. He outlined this idea in his commentary on the Magnificat:

In order to understand this holy canticle, it is necessary to note that the Virgin Mary speaks after having had a personal experience through which the Holy Spirit enlightened and taught her. No one can understand either God or his word if he has not been directly enlightened by the Holy Spirit. The activity of the Holy Spirit has to be experienced and felt, and it is by having these experiences that one is taught by the Holy Spirit. If one has not been through that school, words remain no more than words. The holy Virgin, who was so small, so poor and so despised, by having the experience—which God created in her—of such great things, learned from the Holy Spirit that great knowledge that God only wanted to manifest his power by raising up what was lowly and debasing what was exalted.[9]

For Luther, Scripture was self-explanatory and made Christ the saviour recognized; but in order to do this, it required the activity or the witness of the Spirit in men's hearts.[10] It was, however, Calvin who elaborated this theme and he did so with a special emphasis of his own.

It was not, according to Calvin, simply a question of being enlightened by the Holy Spirit in order to understand Scripture. This undoubtedly played a part,[11] but that was also a classical datum in the writings of the Fathers and throughout the Middle Ages. Like Luther, Calvin believed that it was the condition of faith in the Word that constituted the Church, but, whereas Luther maintained that the principle enabling us to discern an apostolic and inspired Scripture is whether it speaks of Jesus Christ, Calvin taught that it was the inner witness of the Holy Spirit that made it possible for us to discern what was the word of God, and therefore inspired, and what was not.

Like Luther, Calvin also had to fight on two fronts. On the one hand, he defended the baptism of infants, the holiness of the Church, the relationship between the Old and the New Testaments and the importance of Scripture against the Anabaptists (those 'furious beasts who are driven by a frenzied lack of restraint to ramble on about spiritual regeneration'). On the other hand, he also had to oppose what he believed to be the Roman position (which was not and still is not that position, even though certain statements made by the Church give the impression that it is), namely that the authority of Scripture is granted by the Church. He was concerned—and rightly concerned—to attribute the authority of Scripture not to the Church, but exclusively to God and therefore to attribute (re)cognition of Scripture to God's activity in us. This was, in his opinion, necessary so that certainty of faith should be totally based in God. The following statement appears in Calvin's *Institutes* of 1539:[12]

We must regard the authority of Scripture as higher than human reasons, factors or conjectures. This is because we base that authority on the inner witness borne by the Holy Spirit. For I know that, in its own majesty, Scripture has sufficient to make it revered, but it only really begins to touch us intimately when it is sealed in our hearts by the Holy Spirit. Because we are enlightened in this way by the virtue of Scripture, we no longer believe either in our own judgement or in that of others that Scripture is from God. Beyond all human judgement, we have no doubt at all that it was given to us from God's own mouth by the ministry of men. It is as if we have sight of the very essence of God in it.[13]

Article IV of the La Rochelle Confession of Faith of 1571, which is that of the French Reformed Church, is in accordance with this fundamental argument.[14] I have criticized this argument elsewhere because it contains the risk of attributing to a feeling or instinct experienced by the subject an ability to discern which Calvin himself attributed firmly to the Holy Spirit. It is, after all, possible to identify the inner witness borne by the Spirit with the voice of man's conscience and ultimately even with his reason. This has in fact happened in history.[15]

The doubtful way in which Calvin applies the inner witness of the Holy Spirit to the discernment of the canonical Scriptures as distinct from those which are not authentic, in the way we discern 'light from darkness, white from black and sharp from sweet', is not of particular interest to us in our present context. What is, however, interesting is the general principle which forms the basis of his ecclesiology (see B. C. Milner) and according to which 'God works doubly in us: within us through his Spirit and outside us through his word' and by the sacraments. The terms that Calvin liked to use in this connection were 'joined by a mutual bond', 'united with' and 'the instrument of'. Such terms are the hallmarks of a sound pneumatology and ecclesiology, even if they are not enough to define all the realism of the presence of Jesus in the Eucharist. This is because for Calvin, that presence was brought about by the Holy Spirit in the recipient, through bread being united with him as a sign and a pledge from God, whilst remaining ordinary bread. As we shall see later, the soundness of a pneumatology can be judged by a Christological reference to the Word, the sacraments, the ecclesial institution, provided always that such a reference fully recognizes and respects the place and rôle of the Spirit.

Has this balance always been preserved in the many different movements that have resulted from and have been more or less directly and legitimately associated with the Reformation of the sixteenth century? It would, of course, be quite impossible to discuss all of these Protestant movements. A selection has to be made and in this chapter I shall confine myself to George Fox and the Quakers, Pietism, the Camisards, and Edward Irving and his followers. Pentecostalism, as a phenomenon that resulted from the holiness movements, which in turn were a product of Methodism, will be mentioned in Volume II.

GEORGE FOX AND THE SOCIETY OF FRIENDS (QUAKERS)[16]

The events and ideas preceding the emergence of Quakerism have been studied in detail by a number of scholars.[17] We can briefly outline them here.

There were in the first place still strong influences from Eckhartian mysticism, the Free Spirit movement, the writings of Nicholas of Cusa and Jacob Boehme (via John Everard; see Sippell, note 16 below). Anabaptists and Schwenckfeldians were still spreading their ideas, which included a criticism of the sacrament and an emphasis on the primacy of the spirit rather than the letter. There was also a prevalent conviction that inner, personal inspiration took precedence over the teaching authority of doctors. Finally, in England especially, religion was seen to be based on a personal inner light, at least according to such groups as the Familists, the Ranters[18] and the Seekers. However, predecessors and influences do not explain a man like George Fox.

He was born in July 1624 and, even as a child, was struck by the seriousness of things and of the inner life. He left his family on 9 September 1643 and, convinced by his own experience that God loved him and illuminated him inwardly, he began to lead a wandering life dedicated to listening to God and to communicating to men, in season and out of season, a message that was full of a powerful inner flame, namely that there is a divine light and that every man is able to experience it. This experience was true Christianity. There was no need for external worship. Fox rejected the sacraments and the established ministry. True worship did not take place in temples or churches, which Fox called 'steeple-houses'. Not even Scripture could, in Fox's opinion, be regarded as the Christian norm. There was no other principle of worship and no other rule than the Holy Spirit, who revealed himself in the inner light and who baptized with the true baptism. The only cult which Fox practised or believed to be acceptable was listening to God in silence. The believer's inner prayer was formed, according to Fox, in that silent listening and only a word of revelation, which one or other of those present at the meeting might be inspired to communicate, would break the silence.

The Friends believe, then, that there are no sacraments and no ministry and that God speaks through and in all men. Even the history of the Bible as a sequence of events is of less value than the experience of the inner presence of God. They are convinced of the sacred character of each man, and that each man is capable of a personal, direct and autonomous relationship with God. It is this conviction that provides the basis for their rejection of violence and their active and boundless help of others. They are active in their struggle for the rights of man as established in God (Sippell particularly stresses this aspect of Quakerism). In 1947, the Friends were awarded the Nobel Peace Prize.

The lives of the Quakers as illuminated by the presence of God can only be admired, but certain misgivings are aroused by the absolute assurance with which Fox ceaselessly identified his own person, his activity and his words with God's cause. He also made little distinction between the inner light of the human conscience and the Holy Spirit; there is in fact no Quaker theology of the Holy Spirit as the third Person. He has no sense of the Church[19] and the absolute individualism of his inspiration imposes a terrible limitation on his life, which was in every way quite heroic.

The Quaker position cannot be justified by recourse to the New Testament. The Spirit does not, in Scripture, have that autonomy with regard to the word that is given and received externally. The apostolic mission has certain conditions of truth. Even from the point of view of pure Christian experience, the whole aspect of the sacraments, doctrine and the Church as a community is an inalienable element of the gifts by means of which God establishes communion with us.

PIETISM[20]

Pietism released those subjective and lyrical elements which had inspired early Lutheranism, but which Luther himself had later banished. The Pietist remained obedient to the institutional Church, but regarded it as necessary to give individual life to the faith of all believers, to commit them fundamentally to the everyday Christian struggle, to stimulate their understanding of personal responsibility and to enlighten them so that they would become true sons of God and betrothed to Christ. Those ardent Christians who were visited in this way by the Spirit would meet in small groups, discuss the Bible, communicate their intimate experiences to each other and regard themselves as the leaven of the Church. These little cells were animated by an intense moral ferment, a deep feeling and a sharp spirit of self-awareness; regional differences were especially marked in them.[21]

In his concluding statement above, R. Minder means by 'regional differences' the elements distinguishing Spener, the Alsatian Pietist who became a minister at Frankfurt and Leipzig and who was a moralist rather than a mystic, Francke, the North German from Lübeck who became the systematic organizer of the movement at Halle, and Zinzendorf, the great Silesian representative of mysticism in the Pietistic movement.

The words 'Pietist' and 'Pietism' refer to the book published in 1675 by Philipp Jakob Spener—*Pia Desideria*.[22] Spener had studied at Strasbourg and Basle. He had visited Geneva and had read the works of Luther, but, just as a mysticism based largely on feeling had asserted itself in a climate of dialectical Scholastic theology in the fourteenth and fifteenth centuries, so too did Spener want to go beyond a Lutheran orthodoxy that was too rigidly committed to pure formulae and give new life to the personal experience of faith. He accepted the teaching of the theologians of the conscience and especially that of Tauler (the *Theologia Deutsch*) and extended Luther's idea of justification by faith alone into an experience of rebirth in an active love of God and one's neighbour.[23] When he was in Frankfurt, from 1666 to 1686, he had groups of Christians meeting in his own home and then in other houses. These came to be known as *collegia pietatis* and at them members let themselves be permeated with the spiritual message of Scripture. He

143

refrained from being a reformer, but he did introduce at least one principle of renewal into the Church in his conviction that the minister had neither a monopoly nor a totality of charisms. The Spirit, he believed, was active in all Christians and in all groups of true Christians. All that was necessary was to let him be active. Without him, all that Scripture contained was a dead letter, a text like any other, not the word of God and his active presence, nourishing man's life and soul. What Spener repeated again and again to his 'basic communities'—for that was, after all, what his groups were—was the Pauline text: 'Let the word of Christ dwell in you richly, as you teach and admonish one another in all wisdom and as you sing psalms and hymns and spiritual songs (= songs inspired by the Spirit)' (Col 3:16).[24] The ecclesiological implications of this text are obvious.

Some of the strange manifestations that occurred in the Cévennes (see following section)—visions, sweating blood or tears of blood, and inner speaking—also occurred in Pietist circles, for example, in Halle at the beginning of the eighteenth century.

Nikolaus Ludwig, Graf von Zinzendorf (1700–1760), can certainly be described as a Pietist on the basis of his evident fervour for Jesus as saviour.[25] He went far beyond Pietism, however, in his unfailing affirmation of salvation by faith alone, as against a process of sanctification through experiences and spiritual progress, and his missionary zeal, which led the intimate pious groups to burst out into the world. His complex personality, his actions in the world and his ecumenical activity, however, do not come within the scope of this present study.

The word 'pietism' is often used today in a much wider sense, pointing to a sentimental kind of fervour and an indifference to exact teaching and demanding study.[26] In addition to this, the modern neo-Pentecostalism or Renewal in the Spirit has sometimes been described as pietistic.

THE 'PROPHETISM' OF THE CEVENNES[27]

I have put 'prophetism' between inverted commas, not because I want in any way to detract from the heroism of those Protestants who were defending their faith and their freedom of conscience, but because the spectacular manifestations of 'prophetism' which accompanied the revolt in the Cévennes were rather suspect.

The history of this movement cannot be understood without some knowledge of the dramatic circumstances of the period. Louis XIV was at that time pursuing a policy of bringing Protestants into the Catholic Church. The Edict of Nantes was revoked in 1685 and this was followed by the dragoons of Villars, the exodus of thousands of Huguenots, forced conversions to Catholicism, but in the Cévennes, the Church of the desert (see Rev 12:6) and armed resistance. From Holland, Pierre Jurieu encouraged the people of the Cévennes and even filled them with extravagant hopes, proclaiming the end of the papal empire in 1689 and the return of the exiles in 1710, and then in 1715. Literally released from his chains, he published in 1686 *L'Accomplissement des prophéties ou la délivrance de l'Eglise* and, in 1686–1689, *Lettres pastorales adressées aux fidèles de France qui gémissent sous la captivité de Babylone*. From 1689 to 1702, Jurieu went so far as to act as an employee of the Admiralty in England to stir up civil war in France. His fiery messages aroused a strong echo in the Cévennes and the Camisard uprising began in 1702. It was accompanied by a mixture of apocalyptic excitement—there were constant references to Joel 2:28–29—and military realism. The part played by a more or less unhealthy prophetism should not be exaggerated, but, in addition to demonstrations of biblical and prophetical exaltation on the part of those who conducted God's war, there were also scenes in which it is difficult to disentangle an intervention of the Spirit from a very unwholesome exaltation. The prophets, who were often very young, struck their heads, rolled on the ground, foamed at the mouth, fell to the ground as though in a cataleptic seizure, were shaken by convulsions and trembling and either uttered words in an unknown language[28] or 'prophesied' resistance, God's help and even a continuation of pitiless fighting and killing. After the Camisard uprising was over, Protestantism was restored under the leadership of Antoine Court, 'who was very severe with the prophets, whom he had seen at close quarters'.[29]

EDWARD IRVING[30]

A circle dedicated to apocalyptic and eschatological ideas existed in London during the first third of the nineteenth century. It had been founded and was led by the banker Henry Drummond. This 'school of prophets' was joined, in 1825, by the Scottish revivalist preacher Edward Irving, who was born in 1792 and had become a Presbyterian minister in 1815. The members of this circle lived in an atmosphere of charisms and in expectation of the imminent return of Christ. It was learnt in 1830 that certain ordinary people of Clydebank had received the gift of speaking in tongues. This was at once seen as a response to the prayers of the London revivalists, who without delay sent a delegation to Scotland. When its members returned, the London community also began to speak in tongues.

Because of Christ's expected return, the decision was taken to restore to the Church its Pentecostal purity and its early structure, including the functions of apostles, prophets, evangelists, pastors and teachers (see Eph 4:11). On 7 November 1832, Drummond appointed, by means of 'prophecy', the first apostle. This was not Irving, who died soon after, on 8 December 1834, in Glasgow, but John Bate Cardale. The Catholic Apostolic Church had come into existence. Its later history and the

'New Apostolic' secession do not come within the scope of our present research.

*　　*　　*

I am well aware of the fact that some of the data that I have provided concerning pneumatology in Reformed Christianity have been outrageously partial and oversimplified. I do not claim to have outlined the theology of the Spirit of those individuals and communities that have developed one—I have, for instance, not even mentioned Karl Barth or Emil Brunner—nor have I attempted to show what the activity of the Spirit was in those Protestant individuals and communities. It is, however very important to say something here, in conclusion, about what Emile G. Léonard regarded as a striking aspect of the Protestant believer—his individual expectation of divine intervention and his expectation of a revival of the Church.

The life of the Protestant communities has always been punctuated by 'revivals' going back to the activity of the Holy Spirit. Such revivals include, for example, the Methodist revival led by John Wesley in Great Britain from about 1729 onwards and in the United States from 1735 onwards,[31] the French revival movement of 1830,[32] the 1858 revival in the United States, the revival in Wales in 1905[33] and the activity of the Missionary Brigade in the Drôme region of France from 1922 onwards. This is, of course, no more than a bare list of names. It would be impossible for me to embark on a general study of the phenomenon known as 'revival' here.[34] I will therefore conclude by quoting a few lines written by a young Protestant preparing for the ministry, Yann Roullet, which were published in an article a year after he had been executed on 2 September 1944 in the concentration camp of the Struthof in Alsace:

> The Spirit of God goes before us. He acts or does not act ahead of us. May I call on that Spirit with all my strength and may he overwhelm my parish! Then I shall speak among the cypresses and beside the tombs and will receive a reply. It is probably needless for this revival or recall—who knows what to call it?—that believers should 'speak in tongues' or be shaken by convulsions. . . .[35]

NOTES

1. For Luther, see R. Prenter, *Spiritus Creator. Studien zu Luthers Theologie* (Munich, 1954); K. G. Steck, *Luther und die Schwärmer* (Zürich, 1955); P. Fraenkel, 'Le Saint-Esprit dans l'enseignement et la prédication de Luther, 1538–1546', *Le Saint-Esprit* (Geneva, 1963); M. Lienhard, 'La doctrine du Saint-Esprit chez Luther', *Verbum Caro*, 76 (1965), 11–38.
   For Calvin, see J. Pannier, *Le témoignage du Saint-Esprit. Essai sur l'histoire du dogme dans la théologie réformée* (Paris, 1893); A. Lecerf, *Introduction à la Dogmatique réfor-*

mée, II (Paris, 1938), pp. 173–240; M. Neeser, 'Raison, révélation et témoignage du Saint-Esprit dans la tradition protestante', *RTP* (1943), pp. 129–144; E. Grin, 'Expérience religieuse et témoignage du Saint-Esprit', *Et. Théol. et Rel.* (1946), 327–244; T. Preiss, *Le témoignage intérieur du Saint-Esprit (Cahiers théologiques*, 13) (Neuchâtel and Paris, 1946); W. Krusche, *Das Wirken des Heiligen Geistes nach Calvin* (Göttingen, 1957); G. W. Locher, *Testimonium internum. Calvins Lehre vom Heiligen Geist und das hermeneutische Problem* (Zürich, 1964); B. C. Milner, Jr, *Calvin's Doctrine of the Church* (Leiden, 1970); J. L. Klein, 'L'Esprit et l'Ecriture', *Et. Théol. et Rel.*, 51 (1976), 149–163.

2. For Karlstadt, apart from articles in dictionaries, see H. Barge, *Andreas Bodenstein*, 2 vols (1905); K. Müller, *Luther und Karlstadt* (1907); E. Hertzsch, *Karlstadt und seine Bedeutung für das Luthertum* (1932); R. J. Sider, *Andreas Bodenstein von Karlstadt. The Development of his Thought, 1517–1525* (Leiden, 1974).

3. M. M. Smirin, *Die Volksreformation des Thomas Müntzer und der grosse Bauernkrieg*, 2nd ed. (Berlin, 1952; tr. from Russ.); Norman Cohn, *The Pursuit of the Millennium. Revolutionary Millenarians and Mystical Anarchists of the Middle Ages*, 3rd ed. (London and New York, 1970), pp. 234–251; H. Fast, *Der linke Flügel der Reformation (Klassiker des Protestantismus*, IV) (Bremen, 1962), pp. vii–xxxiv; T. Nipperdey, 'Theologie und Revolution bei Münzer', *Archiv für Reformationsgeschichte*, 54 (1963), 145–181; E. Bloch, *Thomas Münzer, théologien de la révolution* (Paris, 1964; the original German book appeared in 1921, then in 1960); B. Töpfer, *Das kommende Reich des Friedens. Zur Entwicklung chiliastischer Zukunfthoffnungen im Hochmittelalter* (Berlin, 1964); W. Elliger, *Thomas Müntzer. Leben und Werk* (Göttingen, 1975); R. Schwarz, *Die apokalyptische Theologie Müntzer und die Taboriten* (Tübingen, 1977).

4. Thomas Müntzer, *Schriften und Briefe*, ed. G. Franz and P. Kirn (Gütersloh, 1968), p. 398; quoted by E. Bloch, *op. cit.*, p. 134.

5. P. Wappler, *Thomas Müntzer und die Zwickauer Propheten* (1908); N. Cohn, *op. cit.* (note 3), pp. 252–280; U. Gastaldi, *Storia dell'Anabattismo.* I: *Dalle origine a Münster (1525–1535)* (Turin, 1972). There is an immense bibliography: see H. J. Hillerbrand, *A Bibliography of Anabaptism, 1520–1630* (Elkhart, Ind., 1962).

6. Schmalkaldic Articles, III, 8: *Bekenntnisschriften* (Göttingen, 1952), pp. 453–454; *WA* 50, 245ff., Fr. tr. P. Jundt.

7. *Von den Konziliis und Kirchen*, 1539; *WA* 50, 646. In the Formula of Concord of 1577, the following definition of *Schwärmer* appears: 'Those who expect a heavenly illumination from the Spirit without any preaching of the Word of God are called enthusiasts'.

8. See the commentary on the third article of the Creed in the Little and the Great Catechism. According to the latter, 'Just as the Father is called creator and the Son is called saviour, so too must the Holy Spirit, because of his work, be called sanctifier. How does this sanctification take place? . . . In the first place, the Holy Spirit enables us to enter his holy community, the bosom of the Church, where he leads us to Christ by preaching. For neither you nor I would know anything of Christ, nor would we be able to believe in him or have him as Lord if the Holy Spirit did not place it in our hearts by the preaching of the gospel. The work is accomplished and Christ has gained a treasure for us by his passion, death and resurrection. If that work were to remain hidden, however, and if no one were to know anything about it, it would have been useless. So that this treasure should not remain buried, but so that we might benefit from it and enjoy it, God had the Word proclaimed and gave the Holy Spirit through it in order to bring and to communicate to us this treasure and this salvation. Sanctification is synonymous with leading to the Lord Christ to receive his benefits and what we would not have been able to obtain through our own efforts. . . . The Holy Spirit has a community of his own in this world. That community is the mother who gives birth to every Christian and feeds him by the Word of God which the Holy Spirit reveals and has proclaimed. He enlightens and inflames hearts so that they will grasp the Word, accept it, cling to it and remain faithful to it. Wherever he does not have the Word proclaimed and it does not penetrate into hearts so that it is understood, all is lost. . . .

Wherever Christ is not preached, the Holy Spirit is not at work—he who creates the Christian Church and who calls and brings together the members of that Church, outside of which no one can come to Christ.' Gerhard Sauter, *Kirche—Ort des Geistes* (Freiburg, 1976), pp. 59–106, has applied Luther's teachings to the present situation in the Church, but one is bound to ask whether this theology, which is dominated by its emphasis on Christ and the Word, can really be regarded as fully pneumatological. For this question, see M. Kwiram, 'Der Heilige Geist als Stiefkind? Bemerkungen zur Confessio Augustana', *TZ*, 31 (1975), 223–236, who has gathered together all the declarations. This, however, leaves me anxious for more.

9. *WA* 7, 538.
10. Paraphrase of the Magnificat; see *WA* 7, 546, 548; Letter to Spalatin in *WA, Briefwechsel* I, p. 57 ; *Traité du serf arbitre* (Fr. tr. in series *Je sers*) (1936), p. 110; Comm. on Galatians (1531) in *WA* 40, 574, 578.
11. The *Christianae Religionis Institutio* or 'Institutes' of 1536, final French edition of 1560 (*Institution chrétienne*), IV, c. 14, §8, end. See also J. Pannier, *op. cit.* (note 1), p. 75, and p. 125 for the First Catechism and the Confession of Faith of 1537. For Calvin's struggle against the Anabaptists, see 'Contre la secte phantastique et furieuse des libertins qui se nomment spirituels' of 1545, *Opera Calvini* in the *Corpus Reformatorum*, VIII.
12. In its Fr. tr. of 1541, reproduced in the Guillaume Budé collection, I, pp. 65ff. See also J. Pannier, *op. cit.*, pp. 82ff.
13. *Inst.* of 1541, *Opera Calvini* in *Corpus Reformatorum*, III, p. 368. See also Pannier, *op. cit.*, p. 106.
14. 'We know that these books are canonical and therefore a certain rule for our Faith, not so much because of the common consent and agreement of the Church as because of the inner persuasion and witness of the Holy Spirit, which enables us to discern them from other books of the Church. However useful the latter may be, it is not possible to base any article of Faith on them.'
15. See my *Vraie et fausse réforme dans l'Eglise* (1950), pp. 482–503, or in the later edition (1969), pp. 432–459; there are, at the end, references to liberal and rationalist interpretations. See also S. Castellion, quoted by Pannier, *op. cit.* (note 1), p. 116.
16. An immense number of books have been written about George Fox, the Quakers and the history of Quakerism. The following is a selection: George Fox's *Journal*, first pub. 1694 and frequently re-edited; see especially *The Journal of George Fox. A Revised Edition* by J. L. Nickalls, with an Epilogue by H. J. Cadbury and an Introduction by G. F. Nuttall (Cambridge, 1952); Robert Barclay, *An Apology of the True Christian Divinity, being on Explanation and Vindication of the Principles and Doctrines of the People called in Scorn, Quakers*, numerous editions, the Latin text dating back to 1676; (another) Robert Barclay, *The Inner Life of the Religious Societies of the Commonwealth* (new edition, 1876); J. R. Harris, ed., *New Appreciations of George Fox. A Tercentenary Collection of Studies* (1925); T. Sippell, *Werdendes Quäkertum. Eine historische Untersuchung zum Kirchenproblem* (Stuttgart, 1937); R. Knox, *Enthusiasm. A Chapter in the History of Religion* (Oxford, 1950), pp. 139–175, which consists mainly of anecdotes, stressing the eccentricities of the Quaker movement; P. Held, *Der Quäker George Fox, sein Leben, Werken, Kämpfen, Leiden, Siegen* (Basle, 1953); L. Eeg-Olafsson, *The Conception of the Inner Light in Robert Barclay's Theology. A Study in Quakerism* (Studia Theol. Lundensia, 5) (Lund, 1954); H. van Etten, *George Fox, fondateur de la Société chrétienne des Amis* (Paris, 1923); *idem, Le Quakerisme* (Paris, 1953).
17. See in note 16 especially R. Barclay (2); T. Sippell; R. Knox, *op. cit.*, pp. 139–142, 168–175.
18. See Norman Cohn, *op. cit.* (note 3), pp. 287–330, Appendix: 'The Free Spirit in Cromwell's England: The Ranters and their Literature'. There is evidence of the movement from 1646 onwards. It referred to three ages—those of the Father, the Son and the Spirit, which will be poured out over all flesh.
19. Lindsay Dewar, *The Holy Spirit and Modern Thought. An Inquiry into the Historical,*

Theological and Psychological Aspects of the Christian Doctrine of the Holy Spirit (London, 1959), pp. 154–157, 211–214.

20. There is an immense bibliography of Pietism. See, for example, the dictionaries. I would mention only A. Ritschl. *Geschichte des Pietismus*, 3 vols (Bonn, 1880); F. E. Stuffler, *The Rise of Evangelical Pietism* (*Numen*, Suppl. IX) (Leiden, 1965).

21. R. Minder, *Allemagnes et Allemands*, I (Paris, 1968), p. 113.

22. P. J. Spener, *Pia Desideria*, ed. Kurt Aland (Berlin, 1964). For Spener, see J. Wallmann, *aphilipp Jakob Spener und die Anfänge des Pietismus* (Tübingen, 1970); H. Bauch, *Die Lehre vom Wirken des Heiligen Geistes im Frühpietismus. Studien zur Pneumatologie und Eschatologie von Campegius Vitringa, Ph. J. Spener und Albrecht Bengel* (Hamburg, 1974): L. Hein, 'Ph. J. Spener, ein Theologe des Heiligen Geistes und Prophet der Kirche', *Die Einheit der Kirche. Festgabe Peter Meinhold* (Wiesbaden, 1977), pp. 103–126.

23. Spener was thus very close to Catholic piety: see J. Lortzing, 'Der Pietismus lutherischer Prägung als rückläufige Bewegung zum Mittelalter', *Theologie und Glaube* (1942), pp. 316–324. For Spener, it was thanks to Tauler that Luther became what he was: *Pia Desideria* (1964 ed.), p. 74. He wrote a preface to an edition of Tauler's sermons in 1681.

24. *Pia Desideria* (1964 ed.), p. 56.

25. There is a French *Vie* of Zinzendorf by F. Bovet in 2 vols (Paris, 1860). See also Erich Beyreuther, *Nicolas-Louis de Zinzendorf,* Fr. tr. E. Reichel (Geneva, 1967).

26. According to J. Baubérot, 'The adjective "pietist" is now used to describe a believer who is contaminated by moralism, an almost morbid distrust of theological criticism and intellectualism as a whole, and a total lack of political interest. The faults of Pietism seem to have been stressed much more than its positive qualities': see his article 'Piétisme', *Encyclopaedia Universalis*, 13 (Paris, 1972), p. 57. G. Gusdorf has traced the influence of Pietism on eighteenth-century philosophical movements: *Dieu, la nature et l'homme au siècle des Lumières* (Paris, 1972), pp. 59–142; *idem, Naissance de la conscience romantique au siècle des Lumières* (Paris, 1976), pp. 244–275.

27. Original documents include Maximilien Misson, *Le théâtre sacré des Cévennes ou Récit des merveilles récemment opérées dans cette partie de la Province de Languedoc* (London, 1707); new ed. by Ami Bost, *Les prophètes protestants* (Paris, 1847); C. Bost, *Mémoires inédits d'Abraham Mazel et d'Elie Marion sur la guerre des Cévennes* (Paris, 1931); *Histoire des troubles des Cévennes ou de la Guerre des Camisards sous le règne de Louis le Grand*, new impression of the 3-vol. ed. of Villefranche, 1760 (published under the name of 'Patriote françois et Impartial'), 2 vols (Marseilles, 1975). Histories include H. Hennebois, *Pierre Laporte, dit Rolland, et le prophétisme cévenol* (Geneva, 1881); R. Knox, *Enthusiasm* (Oxford, 1950), pp. 356–371, who emphasizes above all the extravagant aspects of the movement and who accepts Brueys' fable, according to which a certain Du Serre trained children to imitate prophetic trances; A. Ducasse, *La guerre des Camisards. La résistance huguenote sous Louis XIV* (Paris, 1946), who is not objective; C. Almeras, *La révolte des Camisards* (Paris, 1959); E. Le Roy Ladurie, *Paysans de Languedoc*, 2 vols (Paris, 1966), pp. 330ff., for the apocalypse according to Jurieu. Finally, a work by a friend now dead, C. Cantaloube, *La Réforme en France vue d'un village cévenol* (Paris, 1951), chapter XII, pp. 205ff.; *idem*, article in the encyclopaedia *Catholicisme*, II (1950), cols 442–443. Historiography: P. Joutard, *La légende des Camisards* (Paris, 1977).

28. 'Speaking in tongues', which occurred sporadically among the mystics—I have already called attention to certain cases and I deal at some length with this phenomenon in Volume II in the section on the present-day Renewal—appeared among the 'prophets' of the Cévennes: Morton T. Kelsey, *Tongue Speaking* (London, 1973), pp. 52ff. J. V. Taylor, *The Go-Between God* (London, 1972), p. 219, notes that this phenomenon is not to be found either in Zinzendorf or in Wesley. One of Wesley's preachers, however, wrote in his diary on 8 March 1750: 'This morning the Lord gave me a language I knew not of, raising my soul to him in a wondrous manner'.

29. C. Cantaloube, article in *Catholicisme*, *op. cit.* (note 27), col. 443.

30. To the bibliography in my article 'Irvingiens' in the encylopaedia *Catholicisme*, VI (1967), cols 113–114, should be added R. Knox, *op. cit.* (note 16), pp. 550–558; C. Gordon Strachan, *The Pentecostal Theology of Edward Irving* (London, 1931).

31. The witness of the Holy Spirit, according to Wesley, enables light to be distinguished from darkness in order that we may know that we are children of God (cf. Rom 8:16), not, as in the case of Calvin, that we should know who is and who is not inspired: see Wesley's *Collected Works*, I, pp. 211ff. The Spirit is recognized by his fruits; see pp. 213ff.

32. Léon Maury, *Le réveil religieux* (Paris, 1892). For the problems raised in theology by a Wesleyan rather than a Calvinist influence, see J. Cadier, 'La tradition calviniste dans le Réveil du XIXe siècle', *Et. Théol. et Rel.*, 28 (1952/4), 9–28.

33. Once again, as during the time of the Camisards in the Cévennes, appeal was made to Joel 2:28–29. See H. Bois, *Le Réveil du pays de Galles* (Toulouse, n.d.; the preface is dated December 1905); J. Rogues de Farsac, *Un mouvement mystique contemporain. Le réveil religieux au pays de Galles (1904–1905)* (Paris, 1907). Compare J. Chevalier, *Essai sur la formation de la nationalité et les réveils religieux au pays de Galles, des origines à la fin du VIe siècle* (Lyons and Paris, 1924).

34. See C. G. Finney, *Lectures on Revivals of Religion* (new ed., London, 1910); H. Bois, *Quelques réflexions sur la psychologie des Réveils* (Paris, 1906); *Concilium*, 89 (1973; 'Religious Revival').

35. Yann Roullet, 'Découverte d'une paroisse', *Protestantisme français* (Collection *Présences*), by M. Boegner *et. al.* (Paris, 1945), pp. 107–135, especially p. 130.

THE PLACE OF THE
HOLY SPIRIT IN CATHOLICISM SINCE
THE COUNTER-REFORMATION

The close bond between the Holy Spirit and the life of the Church has always been not only experienced, but also affirmed throughout the centuries. Who could ever provide a balanced account of the holiness of so many of its members or describe the infinite variety of the forms assumed by that holiness? We know too that the Middle Ages saw the Holy Spirit as continuing to 'inspire' the Church's councils and teachers, the most important canonical decisions and even the election and activities of the ministers of the people of God.[1] The Church's life has always been seen as overshadowed by the Spirit *Dominum et vivificantem*. This is particularly true of the Church's faithfulness to the faith it has received from the apostles. The Fathers of the Church were especially convinced of this. Irenaeus expressed this conviction perhaps more clearly than the others. He showed faith dwelling in the Church as its proper place and supported by the testimony of the prophets, the apostles and the disciples. He described that faith as something that 'always makes us young again and, under the influence of the Spirit, like a costly drink contained in a precious vase, even renews the vase that holds it'. He goes on to say that 'in this gift the intimacy of the gift of Christ, that is to say, the Holy Spirit, is contained' and concludes by stressing that 'where the Church is, there is also the Spirit of God and where the Spirit of God is, there are also the Church and all grace. And the Spirit is truth.'[2]

I have already given this text from Irenaeus in the chapter on the early Church and another quotation, this time from Hippolytus, is also worth repeating here: 'The Holy Spirit conferring on those whose faith is correct the perfect grace to know how those who are at the head of the Church must teach and preserve everything'.[3] It is clear from this text that the charism of teaching was and is not automatically guaranteed to those in authority in the Church. The Spirit is guaranteed to pastors insofar as they are pastors of the *Church*, recognized by the Church as having the grace that dwells in it and as appointed or given by God himself.[4] This guarantee of faithfulness, of which the Spirit is the principle, is given to the *Church*. It is such a firm guarantee that to admit that the Church is capable of error is to impute a failure on the part of the Spirit.[5]

This was such a deep conviction that it was hardly thought necessary to express it. It is possible, however, to provide evidence of its existence.[6] The situation was different when the Church's faithfulness in its teaching and life was radically questioned, especially by the sixteenth-century Reformers. From that time onwards, in reaction to them, more and more statements were made about the unfailing faithfulness of the Church's Tradition because of the presence of the Holy Spirit who was promised to the Church by the Lord. The first apologists who were critical of Luther all reacted in this way. In 1523, for example, John Fisher insisted that the promise of the Spirit was not made simply to the apostles, but to the Church, until the end of the world.[7] The following statement was made at the 1528 Council of Sens:

> The universal Church cannot fall into error, being led by the Spirit of truth dwelling in it for ever. Christ will remain with the Church until the end of the world. . . . (The Church) is taught by the same one Spirit to determine what is required by the changing circumstances of the times.[8]

In Germany, Luther's opponents also concluded that the Church was guided by the Spirit: the Franciscan Conrad Schatzgeyer from 1522 onwards, Cochlaeus from 1524 onwards, the Dominican Mensing in February 1528, and Gropper in 1538. In 1533, John Driedo of Louvain published a treatise *De Ecclesiasticis Scripturis et Dogmatibus*, in which he demonstrated the inner mutual relationship between Scripture and the Church on the basis of the complementary activity in both of the same Spirit—'utrobique et unus et idem Spiritus loquens et docens'—and cited Jn 14:26 and 16:16, 13. Driedo's pupil Albert Pighi returned to the same argument in 1538 and 1544. Alphonse de Castro did the same in Paris in 1534. At the Council of Trent, the legate Cervini, the Fathers and the theologians justified, by appealing to the constant activity of the Spirit, the faithful handing down of the apostolic traditions and the trust that should be placed in those traditions as in the canonical Scriptures. The Council spoke only of apostolic traditions, but, in line with what had been taught by the Fathers, the other councils and the theologians of the Middle Ages, the activity of the Spirit was extended to doctrinal and ethical pronouncements made by the 'Church': 'In the general councils, the Holy Spirit has revealed to the Church, according to the needs of the times, many truths which are not explicitly contained in the canonical books' (Claude Le Jay; Girolamo Seripando; Pietro Bertano). Insofar as Christians were at that time aware of development in dogma, they tended to attribute this too to the help of the Holy Spirit.[9]

It is obvious that these statements, which are in themselves reasonable and traditional, concealed a tendency and even a temptation to give an absolute value to the Church as an institution by endowing its magisterium with an almost unconditional guarantee of guidance by the Holy Spirit. In opposition to the Reformation, there was an insistence on the fact that the letter of the Scriptures was not enough in itself and that there was a need for authentic interpretation. But whereas the Reformers attributed that interpretation to the Holy Spirit, the theologians of Trent ascribed it to 'the Church', since it was, they believed, in the Church that the Spirit was living, the Church itself that was the living gospel:

> There is no gospel if there is no Church. It is not that it is not possible to have Scripture outside the Church. . . . But the living gospel is the Church itself (*sed vivum Evangelium ipsa est Ecclesia*). Outside the Church, it is possible to have parchments or papers, ink, letters and characters, with which the gospel was written, but it is not possible to have the gospel itself. The apostles, who were filled with the Spirit, when they provided the creed, did not say: 'I believe in the Bible' or 'I believe in the gospel', but 'I believe in the holy Church'. It is in the Church that we have the Bible, that we have the gospel and that we have authentic understanding of the gospel, or rather, the Church itself is the gospel, written not with ink, but by the Spirit of the living God and not on tablets of stone, but on tablets of flesh of the heart.[10]

This was the beginning of a developing process that can be described as an affirmation of the part played by the Church and its authority and therefore, in the nineteenth century at least, a pervading sense of the primacy of the magisterium of the Church.[11] Thomas Stapleton (†1598), an Englishman who taught at Louvain, was undoubtedly most representative of this way of thinking. The reference to the help given by the Holy Spirit allowed him to attribute an almost unconditional value to authority as such and he insisted that, 'in questions of faith, believers should consider not *what* is said, but *who* says it'.[12]

Bossuet, whose teaching was followed in the French Imperial Catechism of 1806, defined the Catholic Church as the 'assembly or society of believers spread over the whole earth' and united by the Holy Spirit, who animates the Church, 'in which he has placed all his graces'. On the other hand, nineteenth-century catechisms, which followed and quite closely copied each other throughout the century until well into the twentieth, declared, for example: 'The Church is the society of believers established by our Lord Jesus Christ, spread over the earth and subject to the authority of its legitimate pastors' (Paris, 1852) and 'The Church is the society of Christians subject to the authority of its legitimate pastors, the leader of whom is the Pope, the successor of St Peter' (Paris, 1914).[13]

The magisterium itself refers to the Holy Spirit as the guarantee of its teachings and decisions,[14] including, for example, the definitions of the Mariological dogmas of 1854 and 1950. The only biblical references to which an appeal could be made in these teachings were quite remote; the basis for them was found in the faith of the Church, with the reservation that it was animated by the Spirit. This also accounts for the emergence of such doubtful formulae defining the magisterium as the *fons fidei*[15] and others such as 'Ecclesia sibi ipsi est fons'.[16] I have spoken elsewhere about the inflated emphasis that has been placed on the magisterium. The Reformers may have, if not exactly misunderstood, at least minimized the part played by the Church in the relationship between the believer and Scripture, but that is no reason for putting the magisterium in the place of the Holy Spirit to whose 'testimony' they appealed. Certain Catholic statements have fallen into this error. One one-sided emphasis should not be replaced by another. It is far better to integrate, recognize and make a place for all the gifts by which God communicates to us the truth of his Word.[17]

In his encyclical of 1897 on the Holy Spirit, *Divinum illud munus*, Leo XIII wrote: 'Hoc affirmare sufficiat, quod cum Christus Caput sit Ecclesiae, Spiritus Sanctus sit eius Anima', that is, 'if Christ is the Head of the Church, the Holy Spirit is its soul'.[18] This affirmation, which was quoted in the Encyclical *Mystici Corporis* of 1943, is far-reaching. Taken literally, it clearly points to an ecclesiological monophysitism. It is distasteful to Protestant Christians, because it seems to given an absolute value to the acts and structures of the Church. It also gave rise to a heated discussion among Catholic theologians about the uncreated soul and the created soul of the Church.[19] To go into this question would take us too far from the theme of this work, but it is worth noting here that the Augustinian text quoted by Leo XIII does not say exactly the same thing as the Pope aimed to say. The latter says: The Holy Spirit *is* the soul of the Church of which Christ is the Head. Augustine, however, said: What the soul does in our body, the Holy Spirit does in the Church; what the soul is for our body, the Holy Spirit is for the Body of Christ, which is the Church.[20] The statement, then, is functional and not ontological. This is an important difference, which was understood by Vatican II, which also took care to attribute the comparison to the Fathers.[21] I witnessed this prudent and precise way of speaking and know that it was intentional. I shall return later to the pneumatology of Vatican II.

The Holy Spirit has been very much alive in Catholicism since the Counter-Reformation and the restoration after the French Revolution. But what has been the situation with regard to ecclesiology in the past three or four hundred years? Bellarmine, who was the dominant theologian of this period, was above all a spiritual author and he was an Augustinian on the question of grace. Pneumatology is lacking in his teaching about the Church. Petavius (†1652) is famous for his theology of the personal relationship between the righteous soul and the Holy Spirit, but this theology lacks an ecclesiological extension. At the beginning of the nineteenth century, Möhler provided, in his book *Die Einheit* (1825), a radically pneumatological ecclesiology, but he later refused to prepare a new edition of this work, and what was preserved of his teaching is taken from his later book *Symbolik* (1832), with its resolutely Christological ecclesiology, in which the Church is

154

seen as a 'continued incarnation'. This idea dominated the Roman school throughout the nineteenth century.[22]

M. J. Scheeben (†1888) combined Christological views with a pneumatological reflection, both of which he took to extreme conclusions or at least to extreme formulations. Examples of this can be found in his arguments concerning the character of baptism and ordination as giving the Church its structure, and his attribution of a special function to the Spirit in animating that Church. His analysis of the status of knowledge and Tradition in the Church is successful, but he is less successful when he calls the Church a 'kind of incarnation of the Holy Spirit'.[23]

The same formula is also found in Manning's writings, and I propose to deal at rather greater length with the Englishman's teachings about the Holy Spirit and the Church because he seems to me to be highly representative of the Catholic approach to the Spirit at the time that we are studying here. When he was still Archdeacon of Chichester, Manning (1808–1892) experienced a kind of conversion to the Holy Spirit. An ordinary believer who had read a volume of his sermons asked him why he spoke so little about the Holy Spirit.

> From that day I have never passed a day without acts of reparation to the Holy Ghost. I bought every book I could find on the work of the Holy Ghost and studied them. After five or six years I reached the last step to which reason alone could lead me, namely that the unanimous witness of the universal Church is the maximum of historical evidence for the revelation of Christianity. But the historical evidence is only human and human evidence is fallible after all. Then, and not before, I saw that the perpetual presence and office of the Holy Ghost, etc., raises the witness of the Church from a human to a Divine certainty. And to Him I submitted in the unity of the one Faith and Fold. Since then the Holy Ghost has been the chief thought and devotion of my whole soul.[24]

To confine ourselves to external order and the public sphere, Manning's intention was expressed above all in two books. In 1865, he published *The Temporal Mission of the Holy Ghost, or Reason and Revelation*,[25] the sub-title reflecting the author's concern, as confided to us in the above statement. Then, in 1875, the seventh edition of *The Internal Mission of the Holy Ghost* appeared.[26] In this book, Manning sets out a highly structured doctrine of the Spirit in the following order: grace, the theologal virtues, the gifts of the Holy Spirit (Manning's main source here was the treatise by Dionysius the Carthusian), the fruits of the Spirit, the beatitudes, and a final chapter on devotion to the Holy Spirit. The Mystical Body is mentioned frequently, but the author does not speak about the charisms in the sense of a 'pneumatology'. At the beginning of the book, he summarizes the contents of his previous book in the following way:

> I have pointed out how the Church or the mystical Body of Christ is in its structure imperishable and in its life indefectible, because it is indissolubly united to the

155

Holy Ghost, the Lord and Life-giver; I have shown also how, because it is indissolubly united to the Spirit of Truth, it can never fail in the knowledge of the perfect revelation of God; and how, because its knowledge can never fail, its voice is also always guided by the continual light and assistance of the Spirit of Truth. It can therefore never err in enunciating or declaring the revealed knowledge which it possesses.

Manning was looking for an absolute rock of truth and because of that he became a Roman Catholic. He at once committed himself to the cause of papal infallibility and wanted the definition of this teaching to be almost excessively extensive.[27] He was convinced that the Holy Spirit was connected in an indefectible manner to the Mystical Body and that the union between the two was similar to the hypostatic union. After quoting Eph 2:22 in chapter I of his earlier book, *The Temporal Mission,* Manning had this to say about this union:

The union therefore of the Spirit with the body can never be dissolved. It is a Divine act, analogous to the hypostatic union, whereby the two natures of God and man are eternally united in one Person. So the mystical body, the head and the members, constitute one mystical person.

Clearly this is passing rather quickly over the historicity of the life of the Church.[28] I do not want to stress too much this excessive and, as such, untenable position. I feel justified in having given rather a lengthy analysis because Manning's very forceful approach is characteristic of the situation in which the Holy Spirit was placed in Catholicism of the period we are considering here. At that time, the Spirit was seen, on the one hand, as the principle of holy living in the souls of individuals—this was the 'internal mission'—and, on the other, as guaranteeing acts of the institution, especially its infallible teaching.[29] This certainly does not constitute a pneumatology.

By pneumatology, I mean something other than a simple dogmatic theology of the third Person. I also mean something more than, and in this sense different from, a profound analysis of the indwelling of the Holy Spirit in individual souls and his sanctifying activity there. Pneumatology should, I believe, describe the impact, in the context of a vision of the Church, of the fact that the Spirit distributes his gifts as he wills and in this way builds up the Church. A study of this kind involves not simply a consideration of those gifts or charisms, but a theology of the Church. If, by the Church, we meant, even without saying so explicitly—although many have affirmed it!—the institution, the clergy, the hierarchy or the magisterium, then Manning's earlier work would suit our purpose admirably. He speaks of the Mystical Body, of the whole body, but what he has principally in mind is the infallibility of the magisterium and above all the infallibility of the Sovereign Pontiff as the 'organ of the Spirit in the Church and in the world'. The Spirit, according to Manning, only makes the structures that have resulted from the incarnation present and active, and this is probably why he and even Scheeben spoke about the activity of the Spirit in incarnational terms.[30] There is also very little about the Holy Spirit in the otherwise remarkable and very useful study of the Mystical Body of Christ by E. Mersch. The encyclical *Mystici Corporis* of 1943 contains a profound theology of the Holy Spirit, but it never reaches the point where it becomes a full pneumatology because it is restricted by its concentration on the institution.

There is no separation of the activity of the Spirit from the work of Christ in a full pneumatology. Everything that I have said so far points to the impossibility of making such a division. A pneumatology of this kind, however, goes beyond simply making present the structures set up by Christ; it is the actuality of what the glorified Lord and his Spirit do in the life of the Church, in all the variety of forms that this activity has assumed in time and space. This is, I think, the meaning of the rather hermetic statement by Nikos Nissiotis, who has criticized the Catholic Church on more than one occasion for what he calls its 'Christomonism': 'A true pneumatology describes and comments on life in the freedom of the Spirit and in the concrete communion of the historical Church, the essence of which is neither in itself nor in its institutions'.[31]

In the final chapter of this volume we shall examine how the Second Vatican Council initiated precisely this kind of pneumatology, the truthfulness of which will emerge gradually throughout the work.

NOTES

1. References to various studies and an abundance of texts will be found in my *Tradition and Traditions* (Eng. tr.; London and New York, 1966), Part One, Excursus B, pp. 119–137.
2. Irenaeus, *Adv. haer.* III, 24, 1 (Fr. tr. F. Sagnard, *SC* 34, pp. 399ff.). See also above, pp. 71–72, note 30.
3. Hippolytus, Prologue to the *Apostolic Tradition* (Fr. tr. B. Botte, *SC* 11, p. 26).
4. This is the meaning of the famous statement by Irenaeus: 'charisma veritatis certum secundum beneplacitum Patris', *Adv. haer.* IV, 26, 2 (ed. W. W. Harvey, p. 40). See R. P. C. Hanson, *Tradition in the Early Church* (London, 1969), pp. 159ff.
5. This was formally stated by Tertullian, *De praescr.* 28, 1–3 (*SC* 47, pp. 124–125), c. 200 A.D.
6. See, for example, Cyril of Jerusalem, *Cat. Myst.* XVI, 14 (*PG* 33, 937); John Chrysostom, *De S. Pent. Hom.* 1, 4 (*PG* 50, 458; Fr. tr. under the direction of M. Jeannin by M. C. Portelette, *Œuvres complètes de S. Jean Chrysostome*, III (Bar-le-Duc, 1869), pp. 263–264). See also Augustine and many of the texts in my book, *op. cit.* (note 1). It is useful in this context to cite the terms in which the Seventh Ecumenical Council (787; Nicaea) begins and justifies its definition of the cult of images: 'Following the royal way and pursuing the divinely inspired teaching of our holy Fathers and the tradition of the Catholic Church—for we know that it is of the Holy Spirit, who dwells in the Church. . . .': Actio VII: Mansi, 13, col. 370; *DS* 600.
7. *Assertionis Lutheranae confutatio* (1523)—there is no modern edition. For the history summarized in this chapter, see my book, *op. cit.* (note 1), pp. 156–176; J. Ermel, *Les*

sources de la Foi. Concile de Trente et Œcuménisme contemporain (Tournai, 1963); G. H. Tavard, *Holy Writ or Holy Church: The Crisis of the Protestant Reformation* (London and New York, 1959).

8. Mansi, 32, col. 1158D-E.
9. M. Hofmann, *Theologie, Dogmen und Dogmenentwicklung im theologischen Werk Denis Petau's* (Frankfurt and Munich, 1976), pp. 177 and 533.
10. Cardinal Hosius (†1579), *Opera omnia* (Cologne, 1584), I, p. 321, cf. p. 551; II, pp. 169, 244, 246, 398, 399, on the article 'Credo sanctam Ecclesiam catholicam' as containing the whole of faith. It was quite common to make a contrast between the 'vivum cor Ecclesiae' and the 'mortuae chartaceae membranae Scripturarum': see Staphylus, *In causis Religionis sparsim editi libri* (Ingolstadt, 1613), p. 24.
11. I have retraced this history in my book, *op. cit.* (note 1), chapter 6, pp. 177–221. E. Dublanchy's article 'Eglise' in *DTC*, IV, Part Publication XXXII (1910), cols 2108–2224, is characteristic of this tendency to confine ecclesiology to the magisterium.
12. This is the title that Stapleton gave to chapter V of Book X of his *De Principiis fidei doctrinalibus* (1572). See also H. Schützeichel, *Wesen und Gegenstand der kirchlichen Lehrautorität nach Thomas Stapleton* (Trier, 1966).
13. See E. Germain, 'A travers les catéchismes des 150 dernières années', *Recherches et Débats*, 71 (1971), 108–131.
14. See Clement XIV, Breve *Dominus ac Redemptor*, suppressing the Society of Jesus (21 July 1773): 'Divini Spiritus . . . adiuti praesentia et afflatu'. A more serious case was Pius IX's Bull *Ineffabilis Deus*, on the dogma of the Immaculate Conception (8 December 1854): 'Catholica Ecclesia, quae a Sancto semper edocta Spiritu columna est ac firmamentum veritatis' (*Collectio Lacensis*, VI, col. 836); see also Leo XIII, Encyclical *Divinum illud munus*, on the Holy Spirit (9 May 1897) (*DS* 3328); Pius XII, Constitution *Munificentis-simus*, defining the dogma of the Assumption (1 November 1950): 'Universa Ecclesia in qua viget Veritatis Spiritus, qui quidem eam ad revelatarum perficiendam veritatum cognitionem infallibiliter diriget' (*AAS*, 42 [1950], 768; *Denz.* 3032; not in *DS*).
15. This term is found, for example, in C. Pesch, *Compendium Theologiae dogmaticae*, I, No. 301, and in J. V. Bainvel, *De Magisterio vivo et Traditione* (Paris, 1905), p. 56.
16. See H. Dieckmann, *De Ecclesia* (Freiburg, 1925), II, note 670; J. Deneffe, *Der Traditions-begriff* (Münster, 1931), pp. 147–148. It was also unfortunately used by Pius XII, in his allocution on the centenary of the Gregoriana (7 October 1953; *AAS*, 45 (1953), 685); 'Sub tutela ductuque Spiritus Sancti sibi fons est veritatis'.
17. I appreciate the truth of the following statements, but I would have liked the Holy Spirit to have been given his rightful place: Pius XII, Encyclical *Humani generis* (*AAS*, 42 [1950], 569; *DS* 3886): 'Una enim cum sacris eiusmodi fontibus Deus Ecclesiae suae Magisterium vivum dedit'; Vatican II, Constitution on Revelation, *Dei Verbum*, 10: 'Munus autem *authentice* interpretandi verbum Dei scriptum vel traditum soli vivo Ecclesiae Magisterio concreditum est'; the word italicized by me is very important.
18. *AAS*, 29 (1896–97), 650; *DS* 3328.
19. References in U. Valeske, *Votum Ecclesiae*, I (Munich, 1962), p. 161, note 17; my book *Sainte Eglise* (Paris, 1963), pp. 503, 643.
20. Augustine, *Sermo* 267, 4 (*PL* 38, 1231), cited by Leo XIII and Pius XII; *Sermo* 268, 2 (*PL* 38, 1232–1233).
21. Constitution on the Church, *Lumen Gentium*, 7, 7: 'Dedit nobis de Spiritu suo, qui unus et idem in Capite et in membris existens, totum corpus ita vivificat, unificat et movet, ut Eius officium a sanctis Patribus comparari potuerit cum munere, quod principium vitae seu anima in corpore humano adimplet', with reference to Leo XIII, Pius XII, Augustine, John Chrysostom, Didymus and Thomas Aquinas. See also *Ad Gentes divinitus*, 4.
22. See my *L'Eglise de S. Augustin à l'époque moderne* (Paris, 1970), pp. 417–423, 428–433. For Scheeben, see pp. 429, 433–435.
23. This formula will be found in Scheeben's *Dogmatik*, III, §276, no. 1612.

24. Taken from autobiographical notes edited in 1890 and published in E. S. Purcell's *Life of Cardinal Manning, Archbishop of Westminster* (London, 1895), II, pp. 795–796.

25. *The Temporal Mission of the Holy Ghost or Reason and Revelation* (London, 1866). My quotation (above, p. 156) will be found on p. 61.

26. H. E. Manning, *The Internal Mission of the Holy Ghost* (London, 7th ed., 1875). My quotation (above, pp. 155–156) will be found on p. 3.

27. 'The definitions and Decrees of Pontiffs, speaking ex cathedra, or as the head of the Church and to the whole Church, whether by Bull, or Apostolic Letters, or Encyclicals, or Brief, to many or to one person, undoubtedly emanate from a divine assistance, and are infallible' (*The Temporal Mission*, pp. 81–82). In 1865, Manning had, in view of the proposed Vatican Council, suggested the following text: 'Vivae vocis oraculum a Summo Pontifice prolatum circa fidem, mores vel facta ut aiunt dogmatica seu circa veritates fidei morumque questionibus circumstantes infallibile esse' (Mansi, 49, col. 171). He excluded, however, the idea of infallibility inherent in the Pope's person.

28. According to Quirinus (that is, Döllinger), Manning said that the definition of papal infallibility would be a 'victory of dogma over history': see *Römische Briefe vom Konzil* (Munich, 1870), p. 61.

29. The following recent studies are interesting in that they reveal this tendency: P. Nau, 'Le magistère pontifical ordinaire au premier concile du Vatican', *RThom*, 62 (1962), 341–397; J. J. King, 'The Holy Spirit and the Magisterium Ecclesiae', *American Ecclesiastical Review*, 148 (1963), 1–26; C. Larnicol, 'A la lumière de Vatican II. Infaillibilité de l'Eglise, du corps épiscopal, du Pape', *Ami du Clergé*, 76 (1966), 246–255, 257–259, especially 254b.

30. Despite his thesis on the distinctive and personal gift and indwelling of the Holy Spirit, Scheeben attributed the anointing of Christ's humanity to the Logos and believed that the Spirit was only the means. See his *Dogmatik*, V, §222; *Mysterien des Christentums*, §51, 5.

31. See the symposium *Le Saint-Esprit* (Geneva, 1963), p. 91.

ADDITIONAL NOTE

FORGETTING THE HOLY SPIRIT

The Holy Spirit has sometimes been forgotten. It is not difficult to find examples of this. Karl Adam's *Das Wesen des Katholizismus* (1924) was rightly held in high esteem during the first half of this century. Yet we find in it: 'The structure of Catholic faith may be summarized in a single sentence: I come to a living faith in the Triune God through Christ in His Church. I experience the action of the living God through Christ realizing himself in His Church. So we see the certitude of the Catholic faith rests on the sacred triad: God, Christ, Church.'[1]

There is at present a desire and even a need for a short formula of Christian faith. Several have already been suggested, and some of these have been collected and discussed by J. Schulte in his *Glaube elementar. Versuche einer Kurzformel des Christlichen* (Essen, 1971). Regrettably, in the formulae suggested by G. Scherer, by groups of students and of mothers there is an insistence on man and on Christ as a 'man for others', but a rather disturbing

159

absence of any reference to the Holy Spirit and the Church. On the other hand, however, the brief formulae suggested by readers of the French journal *Informations Catholiques Internationales*, 471 (1 January 1975), p. 12 were remarkably Trinitarian.

In an article in *L'Aurore*, published on 2 March 1978 and entitled 'Attention! Hiéroglyphes!', Fr Bruckberger, a passionate critic of the French bishops and modern religious teaching, attempted to 'define briefly (for my readers) what is essential in Catholic faith'. He spoke firstly of 'God' and then of Christ, who has 'risen into heaven, where he reigns with his body, soul and divinity, at the right hand of his Father'. He then continues: 'Is that all? Not at all! How would we be able to console ourselves for such a physical absence? He has, of course, left us with the account of his life, and the Scriptures bear witness to him. He has also left us with the Church which, through its sacraments, embodies us in the Christian life and enables us to share in the divine life.' Fr Bruckberger concludes by enlarging on the gift of the Eucharist. Of course, too much stress should not be laid on the content of a newspaper article. Nevertheless, the total omission of the Holy Spirit, the Paraclete, and the immediate passage from Christ to the Church and the sacraments are significant.

SUBSTITUTES FOR THE HOLY SPIRIT

In a suggestive but very short article, without any references, P. Pare noted that there has always been a teaching about the Holy Spirit in the Western Church, but little of it has entered its living faith or its liturgy.[2] (This would need to be checked; in the meantime the criticism is welcome.) The liturgy of the Western Church, Pare points out, is centred on the eucharistic presence and therefore on the incarnation and the redemption, and the relationship between the second and the first Person. Rome, Pare suggests, appears to have replaced the Holy Spirit and let him be overshadowed by the Pope, the Virgin Mary and the cult of the Blessed Sacrament. This criticism is certainly exaggerated, as this present book shows in its own way. Nonetheless, Pare is criticizing something not entirely fanciful: here is some evidence for it. I shall confine myself to references to the three realities mentioned by Pare himself: the Eucharist, the Pope and the Virgin Mary.

M. J. Scheeben, whose work we have already mentioned, attempted to explain in depth the doctrine of the infallibility of the pontifical magisterium as defined by the First Vatican Council in 1870.[3] He compared this dogma with the one defined in 1854 on the Immaculate Conception of Mary, saying

160

that Mary and the Pope were two closely related 'seats of wisdom'. He connected the meaning of this with the mystery of the Eucharist and believed that 'the Eucharist, Mary and the Holy See are the most important links (*die vorzüglichsten Bindeglieder*) by which the Church is established, maintained and shown to be true, total, firm and living communion with Christ'.[4]

One of the most fervent advocates of the dogma of infallibility at the Council was Mgr Mermillod. In a sermon that he gave in Rome in January 1870, he declared: 'There are three sanctuaries: the crib, the tabernacle and the Vatican. There are three (a word is missing here): God, Jesus Christ and the Pope. What do we want? We want to give you Jesus Christ on earth. We have seen him at Bethlehem in the form of a child. We see him today in the form of an old man.'[5] Despite the great and genuine respect that I have for Mgr Mermillod, I regard these words as perfectly ridiculous, which excuses them from being blasphemous. Mermillod, who was made a cardinal by Pius IX, preached a sermon on the theme of the three incarnations of our Lord—in Mary's womb, in the Eucharist and in the Pope.[6]

Fr R. Plus, whose books on spirituality were so widely read in the first half of this century, devoted three consecutive chapters in one section of one of his books to this theme: Mary, the Pope, the Mass.[7] Possibly under the influence of Fr Plus, the directors of the Apostolate of Prayer and the Eucharistic Crusade chose for their congress in June 1945 the general theme: 'The Apostolate of Prayer in the service of Christ by devotions to the Sacred Heart, the Eucharist, the Blessed Virgin and the Pope'.[8]

Mgr Lépicier, who also became a cardinal, spoke of Abyssinia, where he had been working as a missionary, as a country 'in which the great Catholic devotion to those "three white things" ' (as he called them in preaching to the natives)—'the Host, the Virgin Mary and the Pope—flourished magnificently'.[9] The same rather imaginative theme of the 'three white things' was taken up by the Canadian Association Mariale in Paris at their church of Saint-Michel.[10]

For Mgr Marcel Lefebvre, the 'three white things' are 'The three main gifts that God has given us: the Pope, the most holy Virgin and the eucharistic sacrifice'.[11]

I now propose to consider each of these three realities in turn. It will become apparent that there is an element of truth and depth in an assimilation of the function of each of them to the Holy Spirit, but certainly not in any way that might encroach on the place occupied by and the part played by the Spirit.

1. *The Eucharist*

P. Pare undoubtedly had the spirituality of the (Real) Presence in the Eucharist in mind when he wrote his article. I do not wish to suggest any particular reference in this context, but I am bound to point out that the part played by the Holy Spirit in the Eucharist—not only in the change of the bread and wine into the body and blood of the Lord, but also in our communion—has hardly been developed. The Eucharist is seen and experienced in an essentially Christological perspective: the intimate presence in the Eucharist is the presence of Christ. This does not meant that it is not authentic or that it does not produce the fruits of grace! I shall be dealing with the pneumatological aspect of the Eucharist in Volume III of this book.

2. *The Pope*

The following remarks on the papacy do not detract in any way from what I have already said in the preceding chapter and what I shall say in Volume II, namely that there is a close link, based on God's faithfulness, between the Holy Spirit and the apostolic ministry. The Popes themselves have explicitly taught that the Holy Spirit is present and active in our personal lives and in the Church: it is sufficient to cite the encyclicals *Divinum illud munus* of Leo XIII (9 May 1897) and *Mystici Corporis Christi* of Pius XII (29 June 1943). Many of the Church's most official statements, however, have insisted forcibly on the external, visible and jurisdictional principles of unity, such as the magisterium and, above all, the papal authority. Here are four relatively recent examples:

> The Catholic Church is one with a unity that is visible and perfect throughout the whole world and among all peoples, with a unity, the beginning, the root and the indefectible source of which is the supreme authority and the 'excellent principality' of blessed Peter, the prince of the apostles and of his successors in the Roman throne.[12]

> So that the episcopate should be one and undivided and so that, through the close mutual relationship of the pontiffs, the universal multitude of believers might be preserved in the unity of faith and communion, setting blessed Peter above the other apostles, he established in his person the lasting principle and the visible foundation of each unity. The eternal temple was built on its strength and the loftiness of the Church reaching up to heaven rose on the firmness of that faith.[13]

> The one who made (the Church) unique also made it one . . . 'one body and one spirit' (Eph 4:4) . . . with a concord so great and so absolute among men that it is the agreement and the harmony of minds that form the necessary foundation. . . . For this reason, Jesus Christ established in the Church a living authentic and permanent magisterium that he provided with his own power and instructed with the spirit of truth.[14]

> Together with those sacred sources (Scripture and tradition), God has given to his Church a living magisterium to throw light on and explain those matters that are contained in the deposit of faith only in an obscure and so to speak implicit manner.[15]

The Popes who were responsible for the above texts have also spoken of the Holy Spirit.[16] Although I fully appreciate the part played by the Church's magisterium, I do not think that it can be denied that the Popes have for a very long time insisted on it as the principle of unity in the Church. In this matter, Vatican II was much more explicit in giving the Holy Spirit his rightful place.[17]

In this section I refrain from discussing the many expressions of excessive devotion to the Pope, some of which border on idolatry, like those which speak of a presence of Christ under the pontifical species, in a way analogous to that presence under the eucharistic species. A great deal could be written about this question, but it has no place in our present discussion, since it is an unedifying aspect of past history in the Church.

3. *The Virgin Mary*

This is a very large subject. On the one hand, it is necessary to acknowledge the criticisms that have been made of Catholic teaching about Mary and recognize their possible correctness. On the other, however, it is very important to remain conscious of the deep bond that exists between the Virgin Mary and the Spirit, and consequently of a certain common function despite the absolute disparity of the conditions.

The criticism is very serious. It is made mainly by Protestants and can be summarized as follows:[18] Catholics attribute to Mary what really belongs to the Holy Spirit and, in extreme cases, they give her a place that should be occupied by the Paraclete. We Catholics do indeed attribute to her the titles and the function of comforter, advocate and defender of believers in the presence of Christ, thought of as a fearsome judge. Mary's maternity is such that, thanks to her, we are not left as orphans. She reveals Jesus, who in turn reveals the Father. She forms Jesus in us[19] and thus performs a rôle which should properly be attributed to the Spirit.

Mary has also been called the 'soul of the Church'—this title has also been applied to the Holy Spirit. Many spiritual men and women have, of course, spoken of Mary's presence in their souls and have claimed that she has guided their lives and that they have experience of this that is similar to an experience of the presence and inspiration of the Spirit.[20] Elsie Gibson has said: 'When I began the study of Catholic theology, every place I expected to find an exposition of the doctrine of the Holy Spirit, I found Mary. What Protestants universally attribute to the action of the Holy Spirit was attributed to Mary.'[21] It is, in fact, hardly possible not to react as Elsie Gibson did when we read this text by Bernardino of Siena, quoted in an encyclical letter by Leo XIII, who was, a few years later, to write a fine encyclical on the Holy Spirit, *Divinum illud munus*: 'All grace that is communicated to this world comes to us by a threefold movement. It is dispensed according to a very perfect order from God in Christ, from Christ in the Virgin and from the

Virgin in us.'[22] Bernardino adds to this that Mary has at her disposal 'a certain jurisdiction or authority over the temporal procession of the Holy Spirit, to such an extent that no creature has ever received the grace of any virtue from God except through a dispensation of the Virgin herself'. This is clearly unacceptable.

Even if we reject this unacceptable statement, however, the matter is not closed. There is a deep relationship between Mary, the mother of God, and the Holy Spirit. That relationship derives from the mystery of salvation, the Christian mystery as such.[23] This is surely why, in the Latin liturgy, a prayer to the Holy Spirit was included with each commemoration of the Virgin Mary, just as Paul was always commemorated with Peter. It is, of course, true to say that certain Catholic spiritual writers expose themselves to criticism by attributing to Mary an immediate effectiveness in grace and the spiritual life and, in extreme cases, by ascribing to Mary what is inalienably the work of God and the Holy Spirit.

The part played by Mary is situated within that played by the Holy Spirit, who made her the mother of the incarnate Word and who is the principle of all holiness and of the communion of the saints. Mary has a pre-eminent place in the Christian mystery as the model of the Church and of universal intercession. This is the work of the Spirit in her. That is why Christians try to model their lives according to the image of Mary, who welcomed Christ and gave him to the world, and they pray to her so that this may be accomplished in them. They expect this from Christ himself, acting through his Spirit, but they are convinced that Mary co-operates in their activity by virtue of being a model of intercession. This accounts for their experience of Mary embracing in a warm and concrete realism their experience of the grace of Christ and his Spirit. The communication of Christ is, after all, accompanied by a memory of Mary, and the Christian mystery would lack an important dimension if it excluded or passed over the part played by Mary. Mary is the first recipient of grace and the first to have been associated with the sovereign action of the Spirit in Christ. Protestants are right to reject an attribution to Mary of what belongs only to God, but they are wrong if they remain closed to the witness borne by Catholic and Orthodox Christians to the benefit in their lives in Christ of a discreet Marian influence.

I am, of course, aware how inadequately I have dealt with this question in these few pages. I would like to quote in its entirety the extremely dense section devoted to the rôle of the Holy Spirit in the Virgin Mary in Paul VI's Apostolic Exhortation *Marialis cultus* of 22 March 1974. Here at least is the prayer of Ildefonsus of Toledo (†667) quoted therein: 'I pray to you, I pray to you, holy Virgin: that I may receive Jesus myself from that Spirit who enabled you to conceive Jesus. May my soul receive Jesus through that Spirit who enabled your flesh to conceive that same Jesus. . . . May I love Jesus in that Spirit in whom you adore him yourself as your Lord and in whom you contemplate him as your Son.'[24]

164

NOTES

1. Karl Adam, *The Spirit of Catholicism* (Eng. tr.; new ed., London, 1932), p. 51.
2. P. Pare, 'The Doctrine of the Holy Spirit in the Western Church', *Theology* (August 1948), 293–300.
3. M. J. Scheeben, 'Die theologische und praktische Bedeutung des Dogmas von der Unfehl-barkeit des Papstes, besonders in seiner Beziehung auf die heutige Zeit', series of articles in *Das ökumenische Concil vom Jahre 1869*, II, pp. 503–547; III, pp. 81–133, 212–263, 400–418.
4. M. J. Scheeben, *op. cit.*, III, p. 102.
5. J. Friedrich, *Geschichte des Vatikanischen Konzils*, III (Nördlingen, 1887), p. 587; quoted by Lord Acton, *Briefwechsel Döllinger-Acton*, ed. V. Conzemius, II (Munich, 1965), p. 77.
6. A. Dansette, *Histoire religieuse de la France contemporaine*, I (Paris, 1946), p. 414.
7. R. Plus, *Face à la vie*, 2nd series (Toulouse, 1926), pp. 93–94: section VII: 'Fêtes et dévotions', chapters CXII, CXIII, CXIV.
8. *Doc. cath.* 942 (8 July 1945), col. 481.
9. Alverne, 'La visite apostolique de Mgr Lépicier en Erythrée et Abyssinie', *L'union des Eglises*, 10 (January/February 1928), 415.
10. A. Richard, 'Faut-il incarner l'Eglise? Les trois blancheurs', *L'Homme nouveau* (7 March 1976).
11. Mgr Lefebvre, homily at Ecône 18 September 1977, on the occasion of the thirtieth anniversary of his episcopal consecration: pub. in *Le coup de maître de Satan. Ecône face à la persécution* (Martigny, Switzerland, 1977), pp. 30–41.
12. Pius IX (the Holy Office), in a letter dated 16 September 1864, rejecting the aims of the Association for the Promotion of the Reunion of Christendom: *AAS*, II (1919), 372; *DS* 2888.
13. Vatican I, Constitution *Pastor aeternus* (18 July 1870), Prologue: *DS* 3051. At the council itself, Mgr Dupanloup and Mgr Ginoulhiac remarked that the Pope was not the principle of unity in faith; Christ was. (Is this Christomonism?) See Mansi 51, 955B and 957C respectively.
14. Leo XIII, Encyclical *Satis cognitum* (29 June 1896): *DS* 3305.
15. Pius XII, Encyclical *Humani generis* (12 August 1950): *DS* 3886;
16. Leo XIII mentions the Spirit explicitly in *Satis cognitum*: *AAS*, 28 (1895–96), 715.
17. See the Constitution on the Church, *Lumen Gentium*, 7, 3: 'The same Spirit, giving the body unity through himself and through his power and through the internal cohesion of its members . . .'; 12, 1; 27, 3: 'The Holy Spirit unfailingly preserves the form of government established by Christ the Lord in his Church'; Constitution on the Church in the Modern World, *Gaudium et spes*, 40, 2; Decree on the Church's Missionary Activity, *Ad Gentes*, 4; 15, 1: 'The Holy Spirit, who calls all men to Christ by the seeds of the word and by the preaching of the gospel, stirs up in their hearts the obedience of faith . . . gathers them into one people of God'.
18. The most detailed and most fully documented expression of this criticism will be found in Lucien Marchand, 'Le contenu évangélique de la dévotion mariale', *Foi et Vie*, 49/6 (September/October 1951), 509–521.
19. A. C. Placi, quoted by R. Laurentin, *RSPT*, 50 (1966), 542, note 139.
20. As in the cenacle of Montmartre (10 January 1953).
21. Elsie Gibson, 'Mary and the Protestant Mind', *Review for Religious*, 24 (Mary 1965), 396–397, quoted by L. J. Suenens, *A New Pentecost* (London, 1977), pp. 197–198.
22. Leo XIII, Encyclical *Iucunda semper* (1894): *AAS*, 27 (1894–95), 179. Complete texts and a criticism of them will be found in H. Mühlen, *L'Esprit dans l'Eglise* (Paris, 1969), II, pp. 149ff. I can add other texts and data to these, including the following which, despite its anecdotal nature, is still significant. I have in front of me a calendar for 1955 from the Libreria Editrice Vaticana. On one page, there are two pictures: on one side, Pius XII, on

the other, the Assumption of the Blessed Virgin. Thursday 19 May, 'Ascensione N.S.'; six days later, Sunday 29 May, there is no sign of Pentecost and all that I can see is 'S. Maria M[ediatrice]'.

23. Apart from Mühlen, *op. cit.* (note 22), who is critical, see R. Laurentin, 'Esprit Saint et théologie mariale', *NRT*, 89 (1967), 26–42; L.-J. Suenens, *op. cit.* (note 21), pp. 196–197. See also the *Société française d'Etudes Mariales*, 25 (1968): 'Le Saint-Esprit et Marie, I: L'Evangile et les Pères'; 26 (1969): 'II: Bible et Spiritualité' (mainly documentary studies); Mariological Congress at Rome (1975). R. Laurentin has written about almost every aspect of this question in his very informative bulletins in *RSPT*, 50 (1966), 542; 54 (1970), 287–290; 56 (1972), 438, 478–479; 58 (1974), 296, note 110; 60 (1976), 321, note 37, 322, note 44, 452–456; 62 (1978), 277ff. Laurentin has also touched on the same question in his *Catholic Pentecostalism* (London, 1977), pp. 195–200: 'Mary, Model of the Charismatic'.

24. Ildefonsus, *De Virginitate perpetua Sanctae Mariae*, 12 (*PL* 96, 106).

10

THE PNEUMATOLOGY OF VATICAN II[1]

[*Note:* I have used the following initials in this chapter when referring to the documents of Vatican II: *AA* = *Apostolicam actuositatem*, Decree on the Apostolate of the Laity; *AG* = *Ad Gentes*, Decree on the Missions; *CD* = *Christus Dominus*, Decree on the Bishops' Office; *DV* = *Dei Verbum*, Constitution on Revelation; *GS* = *Gaudium et spes*, Constitution on the Church in the Modern World; *LG* = *Lumen Gentium*, Constitution on the Church; *PO* = *Presbyterorum ordinis*, Decree on the Ministry and Life of Priests; *SC* = *Sacrosanctum Concilium*, Constitution on the Liturgy; *UR* = *Unitatis redintegratio*, Decree on Ecumenism.]

During the Second Vatican Council (11 October 1962–8 December 1965), the Orthodox, Protestant and Anglican 'observers' frequently criticized the texts that were discussed for their lack of pneumatology. Many of these 'observers' have continued to criticize the Catholic Church for this lack since the Council, but it is debatable whether this criticism is still justified. It was certainly justified at the time. This is clear from a study of the way in which the text of *Lumen Gentium*, developed—see (note 1 below) the article by Mgr Charue and the comments by C. Moeller—or a reading of the excellent Constitution on the Liturgy, the only document that remained almost unchanged after the work of the preparatory commissions. It would be tedious to go through every document and every conciliar discussion in search of references to the Holy Spirit. There are at least 258 of them in the conciliar texts! An enumeration of them would not, however, be sufficient as a basis for a pneumatology. They might only be used, as a commentator—unjustly, in my opinion—observed, to 'give a sprinkling of the Holy Spirit' to a text that was basically not pneumatological. I propose therefore to try to draw attention to the elements of true pneumatology that were present at the Second Vatican Council and have since then been active in the Catholic Church.

1. The Council preserved the Christological reference which is fundamentally biblical and the essential condition for the soundness of any pneumatology. The pneumatology of the Council is not pneumatocentric. It stresses that the Spirit is the Spirit of Christ;[2] he carries out the work of Christ and builds up the Body of Christ. Again and again, the Holy Spirit is

called the principle of the life of that Body, which is the Church.[3] The Council also preserved—and did well to preserve, since it contained an important truth—the idea that the Holy Spirit guarantees the faithfulness of Tradition and the truth of the solemn pronouncements of the magisterium.[4]

2. The idea of the Mystical Body was not, however, put forward by the Council as the only definition of the Church, as a resolution at Vatican I, Cardinal Franzelin and Pius XII had all proposed, nor was the theme of a 'continuous incarnation', which dominated the nineteenth and the first half of the twentieth centuries, followed at the Council. Mühlen is quite right in noticing this. In *Lumen Gentium*, there is a comparison between the visible and the spiritual, and the human and the divine, aspects of the Church and the union of the two natures in Christ. This comparison is made for the purpose of attributing to the Holy Spirit the task of animating the Church as an event here and now: 'Just as the assumed nature inseparably united to the divine Word serves him as a living instrument of salvation, so, in a similar way, does the communal structure of the Church serve Christ's Spirit who vivifies it by way of building up the body' (*LG* 8, 1). The Spirit, then, is not an impersonal force—the creed, after all, describes him as 'Lord'. He remains the Spirit of Christ. The Council took up the New Testament idea that we have already encountered in Irenaeus, of the ecclesial function of sanctification as a participation in Christ's anointing by the Spirit:

> When the fullness of time had come, God sent his Son, the Word made flesh, anointed by the Holy Spirit. . . . (*SC* 5).

> In order that we might be unceasingly renewed in him (cf. Eph 4:23), he has shared with us his Spirit who, existing as one and the same being in the head and in the members, vivifies, unifies and moves the whole body (*LG* 7, 7). Christ has . . . filled it (the Church) with his Spirit (*LG* 9, 3).

> The Lord Jesus, 'whom the Father has made holy and sent into the world' (Jn 10:36), has made his whole Mystical Body share in the anointing of the Spirit with which he himself has been anointed (*PO* 2; reference in a footnote to Mt 3:16; Lk 4:18; Acts 4:27; 10:38).

> God consecrates priests so that they can share by a special title in the priesthood of Christ. Thus, by performing sacred functions they can act as the ministers of him who in the liturgy continually exercises his priestly office on our behalf by the action of his Spirit (*PO* 5, 1).

3. The Council went beyond what Mühlen called a 'pre-Trinitarian monotheism'. Whereas the idea of God that predominated in Vatican I was not explictly Trinitarian, the teaching contained in several of the documents of the Second Vatican Council is based on a Trinitarian view of the 'economy' of creation and grace. This applies firstly to the principle that the Father's initiative led to the mission of the Word, the Son, and that of the

Spirit (see *LG* 2–4; *AG* 2–4; *GS* 40, 2) and secondly to the consequence that the Church is called the people of God, the Body of Christ and the Temple of the Spirit (see *PO* 1; *AG* 7, 3 and 9, end). What is more, in accordance with the admirable formula of Cyprian that inspired me in *Chrétiens désunis*, the Church is also shown by Vatican II to be the 'people made one with the unity of the Father, the Son and the Holy Spirit'.[5] Even better, the Council also called the Church one, 'the highest exemplar and source of this mystery' being 'the unity in the Trinity of Persons, of one God, the Father and the Son in the Holy Spirit' (*UR* 2, 6).

Because of this Trinitarian view, the Church is seen to be a community of worship in spirit and in truth, in accordance with the logic of *ab*, *per*, *in* and *ad*—from the Father, through the Son, in the Spirit, to the Father—so well outlined by C. Vagaggini.[6] The intention of the conciliar document on the liturgy is essentially practical, with the result that this theology is developed very little in it. It is, moreover, more Christological than pneumatological. The Spirit, however, has a place in the other conciliar documents which refer to the doxological function of the Church (see, for example, *PO* 2 and 5) and especially in the review of the sacramental rites that the Council required and that has been carried out since the Council ended. This return of the Spirit to our liturgical celebrations calls for a detailed study.[7]

There has, of course, never been any serious problem with regard to baptism. What is more, I have already spoken about baptism from the point of view of Scripture and I shall return to this question when I discuss 'baptism in the Spirit'. The new ritual of confirmation includes the fourth- and fifth-century Eastern formula, 'The seal of the gift of the Spirit', combining the two ideas of the seal and the gift, both of them pneumatological.

A contrast has sometimes been made between the Latin Church's theme of the priest playing, at the level of the sense, the part of Christ and acting *in persona Christi*, and the Eastern practice of the priest invoking the Spirit, who is the Person who is acting. It cannot be denied that there are two theological traditions and two liturgical styles, but it would be superficial to separate them or place them in opposition to each other. The two quotations above from *Presbyterorum ordinis* show that they are closely associated. The renewed ritual of the ordination of priests includes the prayer: 'Make your servants here present priests of Jesus Christ through renewing them by your Holy Spirit' and, for bishops, restores the consecratory prayer from Hippolytus' *Apostolic Tradition*.

The part played by the three Persons is developed in a very remarkable way in the renewed rite of the sacrament of penance or reconciliation. This is particularly clear in the unfortunately little-known long text of the formula of absolution:

> Jesus Christ . . . poured out his Holy Spirit on the apostles so that they would receive the power to remit sins. Through our ministry, may Jesus Christ himself deliver you from evil and fill you with the Holy Spirit.

The Holy Spirit, our helper and defender, has been given to us for the remission of sins and in him we can approach the Father. May the Spirit illuminate and purify your hearts, so that you will be able to proclaim the wonders of him who has called you from darkness into his wonderful light.

The most important achievement of the Council in this sphere was undoubtedly the introduction of epicleses into the new eucharistic prayers, the second of which is taken almost word for word from the prayer of Hippolytus, which is the earliest liturgical text in existence. There was no epiclesis in the pre-conciliar Roman canon. It would have been easy to introduce one; a reference to the Holy Spirit could have replaced the reference to blessing in the two prayers of consecration of the gifts and of sanctification of the faithful: 'Bless and approve our offering. . . . Let it become for us the body and blood of Jesus Christ . . .' and 'Then, as we receive . . . the sacred body and blood of your Son, let us be filled with every grace and blessing'. It would be sufficient to see uncreated Grace as the principle of created grace. The other eucharistic prayers, however, each include two epicleses, one with the consecration or sanctification of the gifts in mind, and the other so that the Spirit will sanctify, fill and unite believers in Christ, within a framework of absolute praise in the communion of saints. The Spirit, then, is given as the place, the climate and the active agent of the sacrament of the body and blood of the Lord. I shall deal at greater length in Volume III with the pneumatology of the Eucharist, a subject of the greatest concern to me.

4. One of the most important ways in which the Holy Spirit has been restored to the pneumatological ecclesiology of the Council was in the sphere of charisms.[8] This meant that the Church is built up not only by institutional means but also by the infinite variety of the gifts that each person 'has the right and duty to use in the Church and in the world for the good of mankind and for the upbuilding of the Church . . . in the freedom of the Holy Spirit who "breathes where he wills" (Jn 3:8): at the same time, they must act in communion with their brothers in Christ and especially with their pastors' (AA 3). A new theology, or rather a new programme of 'ministries', giving the Church a new face that is quite different from the one that the earlier pyramidal and clerical ecclesiology presented, has developed since the Second Vatican Council on the basis of these charisms used for the common good and the building up of the Church. I have discussed this question elsewhere and shall not repeat here what I have already said. I will show in Volume II why it is important and under what conditions it is possible to call the Spirit, who makes the Church by these means, 'co-institutive' of the Church. Going beyond all legal provisions, the Holy Spirit is entrusted with the task of making sure that 'the form of government established by Christ the Lord in his Church' is unfailingly observed (LG 27, 3).

170

The Spirit 'blows where he wills'. He is an 'event'. The Council recognized this aspect of the Holy Spirit and placed it within its proper context. The social structures are, for example, at the service of the Spirit (*LG* 8, 1). He makes the gospel a contemporary reality and enables men today to understand the Word of God (*DV* 8, 3; 23). He prompts developments in the religious life (*LG* 44 and 45) and, in the case of apostolic or missionary initiatives, 'often anticipates the action of those whose task it is to rule the life of the Church' (*AG* 29, 3). It is also to the Spirit that the Council attributed the perpetual renewal that the Church has to undergo if it is to be faithful to its Lord—as we might well expect from the Council of the *aggiornamento* (*LG* 9, end; cf. 8, 3; *GS* 21, 5; 43, 6; *PO* 22, 2). The Council was also anxious that ecumenical endeavour should continue, 'without prejudging the future inspiration of the Holy Spirit' (*UR* 24, 2). The whole ecumenical movement, the Council believed, came in the first place from the Holy Spirit (*UR* 1, 2; 4, 1), who is also at work in the other Christian communities.[9]

5. At the same time as giving a higher value to the charisms and in conjunction with this renewed emphasis, the Council also reassessed the importance of the local churches. Karl Rahner was of the opinion that the most valuable new element introduced by the Council was the idea of the local church as the realization of the one, holy, Catholic and apostolic Church.[10] It was defined as such by the Council (*LG* 26, 1; *CD* 11, 1) and both these definitions include an affirmation that the people of God called and gathered together in this way is in fact called 'in the Holy Spirit'. The Church as a whole is presented as a communion of churches, with the Holy Spirit as the principle of that communion. This is very clear from the conciliar texts (see, for example, *LG* 13; 25; 49; *AG* 19, 3; *UR* 2, 2 and 6; *Orientalium Ecclesiarum* 2). A theology of the catholicity of the Church that seeks to express some of the aspects of the Orthodox *sobornost'* is outlined in *Lumen Gentium* 13: 'In virtue of this catholicity each individual part of the Church contributes through its special gifts to the good of the other parts and of the whole Church. Thus through the common sharing of gifts and through the common effort to attain fullness in unity, the whole and each of the parts receive increase.' The 'sacred Tradition' is preserved by the 'entire holy people united with their shepherds' (*DV* 10, 1), who share in the prophetic functions of Christ. The Council even went so far as to state: 'The body of the faithful as a whole, anointed as they are by the Holy One (cf. Jn 2:20, 27), cannot err in matters of belief. Thanks to a supernatural sense of the faith which characterizes the people as a whole, it manifests this unerring quality. . .' (*LG* 12, 1). As Ignace Ziadé, the Maronite Archbishop of Beirut, said: 'The Church is the mystery of the pouring out of the Spirit in the last times'.[11]

6. If the fullness that must be recapitulated in Christ is preceded by a material preparation in the history of this world, then the Spirit must already be active in history. Several times in different documents, the conciliar Fathers speak of the Spirit of the Lord 'who fills the whole earth' (*PO* 22, 3; *GS* 11, 1), 'who . . . directs the unfolding of time and renews the face of the earth (and) is not absent from this development' (*GS* 26, 4) and who works on man and turns him towards God (*GS* 41, 1). The same constitution on the Church in the Modern World also insists that the Spirit makes a new creature of the Christian (*GS* 22, 4; 37, 4), but neither this affirmation nor the others referring to the Spirit are developed in the document.

It is therefore possible to say that there are signs of a true pneumatology in the teachings of the Second Vatican Council. The Council provided the texts, but the truth of that pneumatology has to be confirmed in the life of the Church. The whole people of God knows that it has the task of building up the Church and that lay people have to contribute their gifts or charisms to this task. The local churches are still looking for ways of life that are peculiar to them. The chapter on conciliarity that was opened by Vatican II has not yet been brought to an end. There have been many crises, but there have also been generous initiatives. The Catholic Renewal which began in Pittsburgh in the U.S.A. in 1967 and which has spread throughout the world is clearly part of this living pneumatology, since the Spirit is undoubtedly experienced in that movement, at least according to the testimony of those who follow it. Is it perhaps the response to the expectation of a new Pentecost that Pope John XXIII expressed more than once in connection with the Council?[12] It is at least part of that response, but the total response is much greater and much more mysterious. The entire life of the Church is unfolding in the breath of the Spirit of Pentecost.

Pneumatology, like ecclesiology and theology as a whole, can only develop fully on the basis of what is experienced and realized in the life of the Church. In this sphere, theory is to a great extent dependent on praxis. Paul VI brought to a close the Council inaugurated by John XXIII and repeated his predecessor's desire for a new Pentecost. Some years after the close of the Council, he was able to say: 'The Christology and especially the ecclesiology of the Second Vatican Council should be followed by a new study and a new cult of the Holy Spirit, as an indispensable complement of the conciliar teaching'.[13] With these words, then, I will close this volume, since they to a very great extent justify the attempt that I make in the rest of this work to provide such a pneumatology.

NOTES

1. See especially G. Barauna, ed., *Vatican II. L'Eglise de Vatican II* (*Unam Sanctam*, 51b) (Paris, 1966), especially the contributions by O. Rousseau, pp. 39–45, C. Moeller, pp. 102–104, M. Philippon, P. Smulders, B. van Leeuwen, and H. Schürmann, pp. 541–557, on the spiritual charisms; C. Moeller, article in *Theological Issues of Vatican II* (Notre Dame, Indiana, 1967), pp. 125–126; H. Cazelles, 'Le Saint-Esprit dans les textes de Vatican II' in H. Cazelles, P. Evdokimov and A. Greiner, *Le mystère de l'Esprit-Saint* (Paris, 1968), pp. 161–186; H. Mühlen, *L'Esprit dans l'Eglise*, II (*Bibl. Œcum.*, 7) (Paris, 1969), pp. 9–114; A. Charue, 'Le Saint-Esprit dans "Lumen Gentium"' and J. G. Geenen, 'Ecclesia a S. Spiritu edocta. Heilige Geest en Heilige Kerk in de transmissie der Openbaring volgens de dogmatische Constitutie "De divina Revelatione" van Vaticaan II', *Ecclesia a Spiritu Sancto edocta. Mélanges théologiques. Hommage à Mgr Gérard Philips* (Gembloux, 1970), pp. 16–39 and 169–199 respectively.

2. 'Communicando Spiritum *suum*': *LG* 7, 1; 'Spiritus *Christi*': *LG* 8, 1; 'Spiritum *Christi* habentes': *LG* 14, 2, etc.

3. Some twenty texts can be quoted here: see *AA* 3, 2; 29, 3; *CD* 11, 1; *LG* 21, 2, etc.

4. See, for example, *LG* 25, 3; 43, 1; *DV* 8, 9 and 10. The 'help of the Holy Spirit', however, extends even further: see *GS* 44, 2.

5. *LG* 4; in a note, there is reference to Cyprian, *De orat. Dom.* 23, Augustine and John Damascene.

6. C. Vagaggini, *Theological Dimensions of the Liturgy* (Eng. tr.; Collegeville, Minn.. 1976), chapter 7.

7. There is an outline in *Notes de Pastorale liturgique*, 133 (April 1978), 19ff.

8. Simple, but important references will be found in *LG* 4; 7, 3; *AG* 4; 23, 1; 28, 1. More formal and dense texts: *LG* 12; *AA* 3, 4. See also H. Schürmann, *op. cit.* (note 1).

9. *LG* 15; *UR* 3, 2 and 4; 4, 9. H. Mühlen, *op. cit.* (note 1), pp. 175–242, has used these texts as the basis for a very positive assessment of the value of the non-Catholic communions as Churches. The theological problem is to know whether the Spirit makes use of all his ecclesial effects when the ecclesial sacrament is imperfect. It is, however, quite true that the pneumatic ecclesiology of the local Churches enables us to assess the other Churches more positively: see P. J. Rosato, 'Called to God in the Holy Spirit. Pneumatological Insights into Ecumenism', *Ecumenical Review*, 30 (1978), 110–126.

10. K. Rahner, 'The New Image of the Church' (Eng. tr.), *Theological Investigations*, X (London, 1973), pp. 3–29, especially pp. 7ff.

11. I published Mgr Ziadé's intervention of 1963 in *Discours au Concile Vatican II* (Paris, 1964), pp. 37–42; see also pp. 31–36, where Cardinal Suenens' intervention on the charismatic dimension of the Church appears. Suenens also said: 'The time of the Church, which passes through the centuries to the parousia, is the time of the Holy Spirit'. Both these texts are very significant and had a deep influence on the Council.

12. See the official collection *Acta et Documenta Concilio œcumenico Vaticano II apparando*, Series I (*Antepreparatoria*), Vol. I: *Acta S. Pontificis Ioannis XXIII* (Vatican City, 1960), p. 24, the discourse at Pentecost, 17 May 1959; the Council was convoked as to a new Pentecost. In the summer of 1959, there was the following prayer for the Council, addressed to the Holy Spirit: 'Renova aetate hac nostra veluti Pentecostem mirabilia tua' (p. 48). See also the letter of 28 May 1960 to Cardinal Alfrink with a broadcast of the celebration of Pentecost in mind (p. 87); and John XXIII's discourse on the day of Pentecost, 5 June 1960: 'È infatti nella dottrina e nello spirito della Pentecoste che il grande avvenimento del Concilio Ecumenico prende sostanza e vita' (p. 105).

13. General audience on 6 June 1973: see *Doc. cath.*, 1635 (1 July 1973), p. 601. In the Apostolic Exhortation *Marialis cultus* (22 March 1974), there is also, after a pneumatological discussion of the mystery of Mary (26), an invitation to 'think more deeply about the activity of the Spirit in the history of salvation' (27).

SOME UNUSUAL TERMS

AGE (Gr. AEON) A period regarded not only as a certain length of time, but also as a certain rule or a certain state at the spiritual level. It is variously translated: as 'this world' or 'this age' (2 Cor 4:4) or as 'the world to come' or 'the age to come' (Heb 6:5).

CIRCUMINCESSION (CIRCUMINSESSION) This is a translation of the Greek *perichōrēsis* and points to the divine Persons' being one within the other, their interpenetration, their mutual interiority; see Jn 10:38; 14:10; 17:21.

DOXOLOGY (DOXOLOGICAL) Act or a formula of praise, as, for example, at the end of the eucharistic prayer or of a psalm recited chorally.

ECONOMY (ECONOMIC) The unfolding of what God does in the history of the world to make his plan of salvation known and to have it realized.

EPICLESIS (EPICLETIC) Invocation of the Holy Spirit or a celebration including such an invocation.

EPITIMIA(I) Practice or practices suggested or imposed by a spiritual father in the Eastern Church, corresponding to some extent to what we would know as the 'penance' indicated by a confessor.

HEGUMENOS The head or superior of a monastery in the Eastern Church.

HESYCHASM (HESYCHAST) The school of spirituality, originating in Sinai in the fourth century, which can be summarized as silence, solitude and recollectedness (returning to within).

KENOSIS Emptying oneself: see Phil 2:7. A renunciation of the manifestation of oneself in glory or in obvious splendour.

MODALISM Error in the dogma of the Trinity according to which the Word or the Spirit are seen as simple modes by which divinity is manifested.

PROCESSION In the theology of the Trinity, the way in which one Person is derived from the other consubstantially within the unity of the same divinity.

174

'HE IS LORD
AND GIVER OF LIFE'

To the Abbess
and the Sisters of Pradines

CONTENTS

CONTENTS

CONCLUSION

'IN THE UNITY OF THE HOLY SPIRIT, ALL HONOUR AND GLORY'

vii

ABBREVIATIONS

AAS   *Acta Apostolicae Sedis*
Anal. Greg.   *Analecta Gregoriana*
Anal. S. Ord. Cist.   *Analecta Sacri Ordinis Cisterciensis*
Arch. hist. doctr. litt. M. A.   *Archives d'histoire doctrinale et littéraire du Moyen Age*
ASS   *Acta Sanctae Sedis*
Bib   *Biblica*
Bibl. Augustin.   *Bibliothèque augustinienne*
BullThom   *Bulletin thomiste*
CSEL   *Corpus Scriptorum Ecclesiasticorum Latinorum*
DB   *Dictionnaire de la Bible*
Doc. cath.   *La documentation catholique*
DS   H. Denzinger, rev. A. Schönmetzer, *Enchiridion Symbolorum*
DTC   *Dictionnaire de théologie catholique*
ETL   *Ephemerides Theologicae Lovanienses*
GCS   *Griechische christliche Schriftsteller*
Greg   *Gregorianum*
Jaffé   P. Jaffé *et al.* (eds), *Regesta Pontificum Romanorum*
JTS   *Journal of Theological Studies*
Mansi   J. D. Mansi (ed.), *Sacrorum Conciliorum nova et amplissima Collectio*
M-D   *La Maison-Dieu*
MGH   *Monumenta Germaniae Historica*
MScRel   *Mélanges de science religieuse*
NRT   *Nouvelle Revue Théologique*
Or. Chr. Anal.   *Orientalia christiana analecta*
Or. Chr. Period.   *Orientalia christiana periodica*
PG   Migne, *Patrologia Graeca*
PL   Migne, *Patrologia Latina*
RAM   *Revue d'ascétique et de mystique*
RB   *Revue biblique*
RHE   *Revue d'histoire ecclésiastique*
RHPR   *Revue d'histoire et de philosophie religieuses*
RomQuart   *Römische Quartalschrift*
RSPT   *Revue des sciences philosophiques et théologiques*
RSR   *Recherches de science religieuse*
RSV   Revised Standard Version
RThom   *Revue thomiste*
SC   *Sources chrétiennes*
Schol   *Scholastik*
ST   *Summa Theologica*

TDNT   G. Kittel and G. Friedrich (eds), *Theological Dictionary of the New Testament* (Eng. tr.)
ThSt   *Theological Studies*
TQ   *Theologische Quartalschrift*
TZ   *Theologische Zeitschrift*
VS   *La Vie spirituelle*
WA   Luther, *Werke,* Weimar edition
ZKT   *Zeitschrift für katholische Theologie*
ZNW   *Zeitschrift für neutestamentliche Wissenschaft*

PART ONE

THE SPIRIT ANIMATES THE CHURCH

INTRODUCTION

In his first homily on Pentecost, John Chrysostom had this to say about the Holy Spirit. It forms a good introduction to what I have to say in this part of my work and draws attention to its traditional character.

Where are those who blaspheme against the Spirit now? If he does not remit sins, then our reception of him in baptism is in vain. If, on the other hand, he does remit sins, then the heretics blaspheme against him in vain. If the Holy Spirit did not exist, we would not be able to say that Jesus is Lord, since 'no one can say "Jesus is Lord" except by the Holy Spirit' (1 Cor 12:3). If the Holy Spirit did not exist, we believers would not be able to pray to God, but we say in fact: 'Our Father, who art in heaven' (Mt 6:9). Just as we would not be able to call on our Lord, so too would we not be able to call God our Father. Who proves this? The Apostle, saying: 'Because you are sons God has sent the Spirit of his Son into our hearts, crying "Abba! Father!"' (Gal 4:6). That is why, when you call on the Father, you should remember that the Spirit must have touched your soul so that you would be judged worthy to call God by that name. If the Holy Spirit did not exist, the discourses about wisdom and knowledge would not be in the Church, since 'to one is given through the Spirit the utterance of wisdom and to another the utterance of knowledge according to the same Spirit' (1 Cor 12:8). If the Holy Spirit did not exist, there would not be pastors or teachers in the Church, since 'the Holy Spirit has made you guardians, to feed the Church of the Lord' (Acts 20:28). Do you see that this still takes place by the action of the Spirit? If the Holy Spirit did not exist in the one who is the father and teacher of us all, when he ascended to that holy throne and gave peace to all of you, you would not have been able to reply to him with one voice: 'And with your spirit'. That is why you are able to say these words not only when he ascends to the altar, but also when he converses with you or prays for you; and when he stands at that holy table and is on the point of offering that fearful sacrifice, it is then that you as initiated ones know that he does not touch the offerings before he has implored for you the grace of the Lord or before you have replied: 'And with your spirit'. This response reminds you that the one who is there does nothing by himself and that the gifts that are expected are in no way the works of man, but it is the grace of the Spirit that has descended on all of you that brings about this mystical sacrifice. There is no doubt that a man is present there, but it is God who acts through him. Do not therefore cling to what strikes your eyes, but think of grace which is invisible. There is nothing that comes from man in all the things that take place in the sanctuary. If the Spirit were not present, the Church would not form a consistent whole. The consistency of the Church manifests the presence of the Spirit (*De S. Pent. Hom.* 1, 4 (*PG* 50, 458–459)).

3

1

THE CHURCH IS MADE
BY THE SPIRIT

However far we go back in the sequence of confessions of faith or creeds, we find the article on the Church linked to that on the Holy Spirit: 'I believe in the Holy Spirit, in the Holy Church, for the resurrection of the flesh'.[1] About 200 A.D., this deep unity was expressed in the following way by Tertullian: 'Since both the witness of faith and the guarantee of salvation have the safeguard of the three Persons, the reference to the Church is of necessity added. Where the three, the Father, the Son and the Holy Spirit, are, there too is the Church, which is the body of the three Persons.'[2] It is therefore not surprising to find that the First Council of Constantinople (381) added to the Nicene Creed, after the words 'and in the Holy Spirit': 'Lord and giver of life, who proceeds from the Father, who is co-adored and conglorified with the Father and the Son, who spoke through the prophets' and the article on the Church: 'One, holy, catholic and apostolic'.

Augustine, who did not know the text that was attributed to that Council, always linked the Church with the Holy Spirit, of whom the Church was the temple.[3] This was undoubtedly the meaning of the confession of apostolic and baptismal faith, with its Trinitarian structure. If, in other words, creation is attributed to the Father, then the redemption is the work of the Word made flesh and sanctification is the work of the Holy Spirit.[4] The third article includes the Church, baptism, the remission of sins, the communion of saints (both holy things, *sancta*, and holy people, *sancti-sanctae*), the resurrection and the life of the world to come.

In the West, however, the preposition *eis* or *in* has usually been omitted before *ecclesiam* and this fact has often been accorded a religious or theological significance. It is, in other words, possible to believe *in* God, to accept him as the end of one's life, but it is not possible to believe in the same way *in* the Church.[5] When the great Scholastic theologians, then, came to consider the formula 'Credo in Spiritum Sanctum . . . et in unam . . . Ecclesiam' in the Niceno-Constantinopolitan Creed, they provided the following commentary: I believe in the Holy Spirit, not only in himself, but as the one who makes the Church one, holy, catholic and apostolic. This is fundamentally the teaching of Alexander of Hales,[6] Albert the Great (*In III Sent*. d. 25, q. 2, a. 2, c), Peter of Tarantaise (*ibid*.), Thomas Aquinas,[7] Richard of

Mediavilla (*In III Sent.* d. 25, a. 1, q. 2) and others. This fine passage occurs, for example, in a treatise by Albert the Great:

> There is reference to 'the holy Church', but every article of faith is based on eternal and divine truth and not on created truth, since every creature is vain and no creature has firm truth. This article must therefore be traced back to the work of the Holy Spirit, that is, to 'I believe in the Holy Spirit', not in himself alone, as the previous article states, but I believe in him also as far as his work is concerned, which is to make the Church holy. He communicates that holiness in the sacraments, the virtues and the gifts that he distributes in order to bring holiness about, and finally in the miracles and the graces of a charismatic type (*et donis gratis datis*) such as wisdom, knowledge, faith, the discernment of spirits, healings, prophecy and everything that the Spirit gives in order to make the holiness of the Church manifest.[8]

The Church is undoubtedly an object of faith—we believe that it is one, holy, catholic and apostolic. We trace these attributes, however, back to their cause, which is divine and of the order of grace. The Catechism of the Council of Trent, as it is usually called, a text which does credit to its authors, unites these two aspects of belief and faith:

> It is necessary to believe that there is a Church that is one, holy and catholic. So far as the three Persons of the Trinity are concerned, the Father, the Son and the Holy Spirits, we believe in them in such a way that we place our faith *in* them. But, changing our way of speaking, we profess to believe the holy Church, and not *in* the holy Church. By this difference of expression, then, God, who is the author of all things, is distinguished from all his creatures and, in receiving all the precious good things that he has given to the Church, we refer them back to his divine goodness.[9]

What we *see* of the Church is everything that is made of the material of this world. This is what unbelievers, politicians and sociologists also see. But we *believe* that God acts in that Church according to the plan of his grace. The Church therefore is—as Jesus himself was[10]—both a terrestrial reality and part of history on the one hand, and the work of God, the 'mystery' that is only known to faith, on the other. God, however, works in what is terrestrial and historical in such a way that transcendence is presented in what is visible and offered to rational man's perception. The Church is the sign and at the same time the means of God's intervention in our world and our history. Apologetics has made its own use of this truth, and it is worth what it is worth: no more—but no less either. The four attributes listed in the Creed have been used in apologetics as 'marks' to make the Church known and to enable its truth to be discerned.

This course was followed with varying success for a long time in apologetics,[11] but I would prefer to discuss this question not at this level, but at the level of faith. There is no real opposition or even break between the two: faith in the Holy Spirit who makes the Church one, holy, catholic and

6

apostolic is in fact faith in the fulfilment of God's promise *in the Church*, which, according to the Dogmatic Constitution on the Church, *Lumen Gentium*, promulgated by the Second Vatican Council, consists of 'a divine and a human element'. The same document also has this to say about the Church as a complex and concrete reality:

> Just as the assumed nature inseparably united to the divine Word serves him as a living instrument of salvation, so, in a similar way, does the communal structure of the Church serve Christ's Spirit, who vivifies it by way of building up the body (cf. Eph 4:16). This is the unique Church of Christ, which in the Creed we avow as one, holy, catholic and apostolic. After his resurrection our Saviour handed her over to Peter to be shepherded (Jn 21:17) (*Lumen Gentium*, 8).

The Church, then, is historical and visible and its 'founder' is Jesus, who is always living and active in it and is its lasting foundation. The Spirit gives life to the Church and enables it to grow as the Body of Christ. Both in its life and in its origin, the Church is the fruit of two 'divine missions', in the exact and very profound sense in which Thomas Aquinas uses this phrase. I propose to enlarge on this question in the rest of this chapter.

The 'Two Missions'
The Spirit as the Co-instituting Principle of the Church

'When the time had fully come, God sent forth his Son, born of a woman, born under the law, . . . so that we might receive adoption as sons' (Gal 4:4). There is ample evidence in all the gospels of the theme of the mission of the Son by God, but the gospel of John insists most firmly on this theme and places it in the mouth of Jesus himself (see Mt 10:40; Mk 9:37; 12:6; Lk 9:48; 10:16; Jn 3:17, 34; 5:37; 6:57; 7:28; 8:42; 10:36; 17:18; 20:21). In these texts and in those concerned with the sending of the Spirit, the two verbs *pempein* and *apostellein* are used more or less indiscriminately.[12]

'God has sent the Spirit of his Son into our hearts' (Gal 4:6). Jesus proclaims this sending in the gospel of John as having been brought about by the Father in his name (14:26) or even by him (15:26; 16:7; Lk 24:49). It will later be apparent that the Spirit is the Spirit of the Son, but at present we should note that he descended on Jesus at the time of his baptism—although the verb 'to send' is not used in this context—and that the heavenly voice declared at that time: 'Thou art my beloved Son' (Mk 1:11; Mt 3:17: 'This is my beloved Son'). The mission of the Spirit was also made manifest at Pentecost (Acts) and is seen in Paul's letters to be co-extensive with the life of the Church and of Christians.

The Scholastic theologians interpreted these data at great depth in a theme known as the 'divine missions'. Thomas Aquinas treated this theme as a link between his theology of God in himself and his theology of the activity of God placing a world outside himself and bringing men made in his own

7

image back to himself.[13] I shall here consider two aspects of his working-out of this theme. The first is his idea of mission and the second the connection with the Trinitarian processions.

'Mission' presupposes a connection with the one who sends—the Father, who is the Principle without a beginning, sends, but cannot be sent—and a connection with those to whom the one sent is sent. This is so whether the one sent begins to be near or with those to whom he is sent, not having been there originally, or whether he comes there in an entirely new way, being already there. The Word, then, was already in the world from the beginning (Jn 1:10), but he also came into the world (1:11, 14). The Spirit was also already there (see Gen 1:2) and he also came.

The fact that the Word and the Spirit *come* does not mean that they move. It means that they make a creature exist in a new relationship with them. This means that the procession that situates them in the eternity of the Uni-Trinity culminates freely and effectively in a created effect. The human individuality brought about by the Spirit in Mary's womb was at the same time assumed by the Word, the Son, and began to exist through the Person of that Son.[14] This mission was visible because the Word, the Son, who was an expression of the being of God the Father (Heb 1:3), was a human appearance of God. It was not a mere theophany, but the personal and substantial reality of the Word made flesh: 'I came from the Father and have come into the world' (Jn 16:28).

There are, on the other hand, invisible missions of the Word in the effects of grace through which God expresses himself and makes himself known. In the same way, there are also invisible missions of the Spirit in the effects of grace by which God gives himself in order to make himself loved and to make us love all the things of his love: '*God's* love has been poured into our hearts through the Holy Spirit which has been given to us' (Rom 5:5).

The Church, as an organism of knowledge and love, is entirely dependent on these missions. It is the fruitfulness, outside God, of the Trinitarian processions. We *see* the Church in the manifestations of its ordained ministry, its worship, its assemblies, works and undertakings. We *believe* that the profound life of that great body, which is both scattered and one, is the culmination and the fruit, in the creature, of the very life of God, the Father, the Son and the Holy Spirit. Cyprian's statement on the Church as the 'people whose unity comes from the unity of the Father, the Son and the Holy Spirit',[15] which was taken up again by the Second Vatican Council, expresses the hidden reality that we affirm in faith. From the infinite diversity of mankind and the many different peoples, God, who is three times holy, gathers for himself and unites a people who form his people. This idea can also be extended to the authentic unity, holiness, catholicity and apostolicity that is sought and that exists in the ecumenical movement—insofar as this is God's, it is also dependent on the Trinity and is the fruit or the term, outside God, of the processions of the Word and the Spirit.

What are the visible missions of the Spirit? There are comings of the Spirit accompanied by tangible or visible signs which manifest those missions (or the Spirit himself). These include the wind, the dove, tongues of fire, miracles, speaking in tongues and various tangible or visible phenomena of the mystical life. The Holy Spirit is not substantially or existentially connected with these realities, which are only signs or manifestations of his coming, his activity and therefore his eternal procession. They may even be ambiguous. The manifestations at Pentecost (Acts 2:13) were misunderstood, and mystical phenomena have at least external parallels in the purely 'psychical' or 'carnal' order.

Irenaeus expressed the derivation of the Church from the two missions, that of the Word and that of the Breath, in a poetical manner in the image of the two hands of God. He applied this image especially to the fashioning of man in God's image—one is at once reminded here of the carving on the south portal of Chartres Cathedral—but this was only the beginning of the economy that the Father brought about 'according to his good pleasure' through his Word, the Son, and his Spirit, Wisdom.[16]

> God will be glorified in the work fashioned by him, when he has made it resemble and conform to his Son. For, by the hands of the Father, that is, through the Son and the Spirit, man is made into the image and likeness of God.[17]

> During all this time, man, fashioned in the beginning by the hands of God, I mean by the Son and the Spirit. . . .[18]

Irenaeus, that great and beloved writer, also showed the apostles as instituting and founding the Church by communicating to believers the Spirit that they had received from the Lord: 'That Holy Spirit that they had received from the Lord is shared among and distributed to believers; in this way they instituted and founded the Church'.[19] Towards the end of the fourth century, Didymus the Blind of Alexandria wrote that all progress in the truth was attributable to 'that divine and magnificent Spirit, the author, leader and promoter of the Church'.[20] This must mean that the Spirit did not come simply in order to animate an institution that was already fully determined in all its structures, but that he is really the 'co-instituting' principle. This is clear from countless data and formal declarations.

Suppose we begin with the sacraments. Christ gave to certain actions a signification of grace, but sacramental rites were determined by history. The thirteenth-century Franciscan theologians Alexander of Hales and Bonaventure attributed the definitive institution of the sacraments of confirmation, ordination, marriage and the anointing of the sick to the Holy Spirit, that is, to the active *inspiratio* of the Spirit in the Church and its councils.[21] This question preoccupied those Catholic theologians and apologists who had to reply to Luther's criticisms and who could find scriptural support for baptism, the Eucharist and penance alone. They thought that Christ had determined the communication of sacramental grace, but that the form taken by the sacramental signs was determined and even modified by the Church, subject to the guidance and inspiration of the Spirit.[22]

Is it not possible to say the same about forms of the ministry that comes from the apostles? If it is true that the Twelve were instituted by Jesus—with the co-operation of the Holy Spirit (Acts 1:2)—did the succession in their ministry not begin with the initiative of the Holy Spirit, at least in the historical form of a mono-episcopacy?[23] Neither Trent nor Vatican II attributed the institution of different degrees of the sacramental ministry to Jesus himself. In the actual naming and institution or ordination of ministers, it is clear that the Spirit intervenes. The New Testament bears witness to this in a way that suggests rather than states clearly (see Acts 13:1–3; 20:28; 1 Tim 1:18; 4:14; 2 Tim 1:6ff.). The testimony borne by history, on the other hand, is clear: the Spirit inspires the choice of ministers and enables them to exercise their function by encouraging the qualities required. Ordination is an imploration and a communication of the Holy Spirit. It is an anointing by the Spirit. It is noteworthy that, in the liturgy, the Holy Spirit is invoked especially in connection with the three sacraments conferring 'character', which give structure to the people of God, that is, baptism, confirmation and ordination.[24]

The difference that has sometimes been emphasized between instituted functions and phenomena of a 'charismatic' type is in accordance with certain historical facts. It is in the nature of things that there should be some tension between the two. There are examples of this at almost every period of history. It would be a very questionable undertaking to try to reduce this to a systematic opposition in principle. Such a position was favoured in history by an unavowedly confessional and polemical inspiration—when Catholics insisted emphatically on the substantial rather than on the functional, on the institutional and juridical rather than on the present reality and the freedom of grace, Protestants excluded all trace of 'pre-Catholicism' from the New Testament and set free charisms against the instituted ministry.[25]

This, however, is not biblically, historically or theologically of lasting value. Although not everyone possessing the gifts of the Spirit is instituted as a minister, those who are instituted do in fact possess such gifts. In this context, it is worth comparing Acts 6:3; 16:2 with the texts from Acts and the pastoral epistles cited above and 1 Cor 16:15–16 with 1 Thess 5:12–13. Clement of Alexandria made this comment on the activity of the apostle John: 'After the death of the tyrant, John left Patmos and returned to Ephesus. In response to their request, he visited the neighbouring people, on the one hand in order to appoint bishops among them and, on the other, in order to form and constitute churches and to choose as "clergy" those who had been pointed out by the Spirit.'[26] Those who presided at the Eucharist during the period of the apostles and the martyrs were charismatics, prophets or teachers (Acts 13:1–2; *Didache* IX and X; XIV, 1; XV, 2). There were also many believers who had confessed their faith under torture, and these similarly presided at the Eucharist.[27] Those in whom the qualities of men of God were found continued to be ordained.[28] Scholastic theologians described the episcopate as a 'state of perfection' and the bishops as men who gave themselves totally to God and to their fellow-men.

Theologically, if the false opposition is accepted and a sharp division is made between charism and institution, the unity of the Church as the Body of Christ is destroyed and the claim is made that everything can be regulated and conducted, on the one hand without spirituality and exclusively in the name of power and, on the other, anarchically, in the name of the Spirit. In the first case especially, the theology of ordination would be falsified and the ministry would be seen simply as a transmission of 'power'. The essential element of pneumatology would also be eliminated from ecclesiology, and it is precisely this element that I am attempting at least to suggest in this work.

The opposition between charism and institution is generally speaking not emphasized today. It is widely recognized that there are two types of activity and that, although they are different in the way in which they present themselves and in their style, they lead to the same end, which is the building up of the work of Christ. They are, in other words, complementary.[29] Until quite recently, there has been a tendency to make the charisms subordinate to institutional authority and even to reduce them to that level.[30] Now, however, quite the opposite tendency is making itself felt and some theologians are claiming that the Church should have a charismatic structure, with the institutional element playing a secondary, supplementary part.[31] What is required, however, is to recognize that each type of gift and activity has its place in the building up of the Church.

Some years ago, I suggested a view of these matters that now needs to be revised. My intention was to call attention to the truth and importance of the mission of the Holy Spirit as something more than a simple replacement for Christ. I worked, however, too exclusively in a context of dualism and made too radical a distinction between the institution as derived from Christ and free interventions on the part of the Spirit. I stressed on the one hand the apostolate and the means of grace of which Jesus had established the principles and which were accompanied by the activity of the Spirit and, on the other, a kind of free sector in which the Spirit alone was active.[32] As a result, I was criticized both by Protestant exegetes and by Catholic theologians, each from their own point of view.[33]

I still think that what I called, perhaps rather awkwardly, a free sector is something that really exists. Its existence is, after all, recognized in the encyclical *Mystici Corporis* of Pius XII. After speaking about the powers of the bishops as an institution in succession to the institution of the apostles, that encyclical went on to say: 'But our divine Saviour also governs and directs the Church in a direct manner, either by the enlightenment that he gives to pastors or by raising up men and women saints for the edification of everyone'.[34]

These are, of course, only examples, but this 'invisible and extraordinary' direction has appeared in history in many and infinitely varied forms and manifestations. My mistake was that I followed Acts more closely than the Pauline epistles and I wanted to give the Holy Spirit his full worth. As a result I was not sufficiently conscious of the unity that exists between the activity of the Spirit and that of the *glorified Christ*, since 'the Lord is the Spirit and where the Spirit of the Lord is, there is freedom' (2 Cor 3:17). According to Paul, the glorified Lord and the Spirit may be different in God, but they are functionally so united that we experience them together and are able to accept the one for the other: 'Christ in us', 'the Spirit in our hearts', '(we) in Christ', 'in the Spirit'—all of these are interchangeable. The Lord became a 'life-giving spirit' (1 Cor 15:45). According to John, it is in and through the Spirit (Paraclete) that Jesus comes back and does not leave us orphans (see Jn 14:3, 18).

This activity of the Lord with and through his Spirit[35] cannot be reduced to a mere making present of the structures of the covenant proposed by Christ while he was on earth, that is, before he ceased to be visibly and tangibly present. It is the source of a new element in history. At the same time, however, it is always a question of doing the work *of Christ* and of building up the Body of *Christ*, in such a way that, as P. Bonnard has pointed out, the interventions in question must always be in accordance with the gospel and the apostolic kerygma. As we have already seen and as we shall see in greater detail later, a sound pneumatology always points to the work of Christ and the Word of God.

NOTES

1. This is the title of a little book by P. Nautin: *Je crois à l'Esprit Saint, dans la Sainte Eglise, pour la résurrection de la chair*. It has the sub-title: *Etude sur l'histoire et la théologie du Symbole (Unam Sanctam, 17)* (Paris, 1947).
2. Tertullian, *De bapt.* 6 (*CSEL* 20, p. 206; Fr. tr. F. Refoule, *SC* 35 (1952), p. 75).
3. Augustine, *De fid. et symb.* X (*PL* 40, 193); *De symb. ad cat.* 6, 14 (*PL* 40, 635); *Enchiridion* LVI (*PL* 40, 258–259). The first treatise dates from 393 and the last from 421.
4. J. A. Jungmann, 'Die Gnadenlehre im apostolischen Glaubensbekenntnis', *Gewordene Liturgie* (Innsbruck and Leipzig, 1941), pp. 173–189.
5. This history has been traced by J. P. L. Oulton, 'The Apostles' Creed and Belief concerning the Church', *JTS*, 39 (1938), 239–243; S. Tromp, *Corpus Christi quod est Ecclesia*, I, 2nd ed. (Rome, 1946), pp. 97ff.; H. de Lubac, *La Foi chrétienne. Essai sur la structure du Symbole des Apôtres* (Paris, 1969), chapters IV to VI.
6. Alexander of Hales, *Summa* lib. III, pars III, inq. 2, tract. 2, q. 2, tit. I, No. XVI (Quaracchi ed., IV (1948), p. 1131).
7. Thomas Aquinas, *In III Sent.* d. 25, q. 1, a. 2, ad 5, attributing the statement to Leo and Anselm; *ST* IIa IIae, q. 1, a. 9, ad 5, quoting Leo—actually Rufinus, *In Symb. Apost.* 36 (*PL* 21, 373). See also *Comp.* I, c. 147.

8. Albert the Great, *De sacr. Missae* II, c. 9, art. 9 (ed. A. Borgnet, XXVIII, p. 65); cf. *In III Sent*, d. 21, a. 6ff. See also J. de Ghellink, 'L'explication du Credo par S. Albert', *Studia Albertina (Beiträge Suppl.*, Vol. 4) (Münster, 1952), pp. 148ff.
9. Catechism of the Council of Trent, Prima Pars, art. 9, no. 23; tr. based on Fr. tr. by H. de Lubac, *op. cit.* (note 5), p. 169.
10. Hence John's theme of 'he saw and believed'. See O. Cullmann, 'Eiden kai episteusen', *Aux sources de la Tradition chrétienne. Mélanges Maurice Goguel* (Neuchâtel and Paris, 1950), pp. 52–61. For John, believing was a way of seeing and of perceiving the meaning and the deep reality of what was seen corporeally. This profound interpretation was done thanks to the Holy Spirit (p. 58).
11. G. Thils, *Les notes de l'Eglise dans l'apologétique catholique depuis la Réforme* (Gembloux, 1937); see also my *L'Eglise une, sainte, catholique et apostolique (Mysterium Salutis*, 15) (Paris, 1970).
12. See K. H. Rengstorf, 'apostellō (pempō)', *TDNT*, I, pp. 398–406. Rengstorf says that, at the most, *pempein* means simply sending as such, or the fact of sending, whereas *apostellein* points to a precise sending or mission, even a commission, 'bound up with the person of the one sent': see pp. 398 and 404.
13. *ST* Ia, q. 13; *In I Sent.* d. 14, a. 16. See H. Dondaine, *La Trinité*, II (Paris, 1946), pp. 423–454 (bibliography). This theological teaching can be found as early as Augustine: see J.-L. Maier, *Les missions divines selon S. Augustin (Paradosis*, XVI) (Fribourg, 1960). It appeared even earlier, in Origen: see G. Aeby, *Les missions divines. De S. Justin à Origène (Paradosis*, XII) (Fribourg, 1958).
14. The phrase 'he descended from heaven' simply expresses the fact that the (fully human) humanity that the Person of the Word made to exist remains *in* this world and *of* this world. Something very similar (but only similar) is true of the Eucharist.
15. Cyprian, *De orat. dom.* 23 (*PL* 4, 553; *CSEL* 3, p. 285). *Lumen Gentium*, 4 also contains references to Augustine and John Damascene. This *theo*-logy of the Church was also developed in a remarkable way by C. Journet, *L'Eglise du Verbe incarné. Essai de théologie spéculative*, II: *Sa structure interne et son unité catholique* (Paris, 1951).
16. J. Mambrino, 'Les deux mains du Père dans l'œuvre de S. Irénée', *NRT*, 79 (1957), 355–370. For the Holy Spirit as Wisdom, see *Adv. haer.* IV, 20, 1 and 3 (*SC* 100, pp. 627 and 633); *Dem.* 5 and 10 (*SC* 62, p. 36 and 1a, note 8, p. 46).
17. *Adv. haer.* V, 6, 1 (*SC* 153, p. 73).
18. *Adv. haer.* V, 28, 4 (*SC* 153, p. 361).
19. *Dem.* 41 (*SC* 62, p. 96 and 1a, note 4).
20. Didymus, *Enarr. in Ep. 2 S. Petri*, 3, 5 (*PG* 39, 1774).
21. J. Bittremieux, 'L'institution des sacrements d'après Alexandre de Halès', *ETL* (1932), 234–251; F. Scholz, *Die Lehre von der Einsetzung der Sakramente nach Alexander von Hales* (Breslau, 1940); J. Bittremieux, 'L'institution des sacrements d'après S. Bonaventure', *Etudes Franciscaines* (1923), 129–152, 337–355; H. Baril, *La doctrine de S. Bonaventure sur l'institution des sacrements* (Montreal, 1954); V. Fagiolo, 'L'istituzione del sacramento del matrimonio nella dottrina di S. Bonaventura', *Antonianum*, 33 (1958), 241–262.
22. A. Poyer, 'Nouveaux propos sur le "salva illorum substantia" ', *Divus Thomas*, 57 (1954), 3–24, who quotes, among others, John Fisher, Clichtove, Pustinger, Contarini, Gropper, Johann Eck, Albert Pighi, as well as Salmeron and others at Trent.
23. At the Council of Constantinople (869–870), the patriarchs Elias of Jerusalem and Nilus of Alexandria attributed the institution of the patriarchate to the Holy Spirit: see Mansi, 16, 35A and 317E; *PG* 132, 1097C. E. Ruckstuhl, 'Einmaligkeit und Nachfolge der Apostel', *Erbe und Auftrag*, 47 (1971), pp. 240–253, says, on p. 247: 'It must be recognized that the monarchical episcopal office is closely associated with the office of the apostle in the New Testament and was in succession to it, although there was a considerable delay in time. May we therefore call the office of the bishop a pneumatic creation that is analogous to that of the apostle?'

24. See F. Vandenbroucke, 'Esprit Saint et structure ecclésiale selon la liturgie', *Questions liturgiques et paroissiales* (1958), pp. 115–131; M. D. Koster, *Ekklesiologie im Werden* (Paderborn, 1940); *idem*, various articles.
25. After the discovery of the *Didache*, A. von Harnack took this stand in *Die Lehre der zwölf Apostel* (Leipzig, 1884). A similar position was taken by R. Sohm, who was, however, in disagreement with Harnack with regard to the place of law in the Church; see his *Kirchenrecht*, I (Leipzig, 1892). More recently, H. von Campenhausen followed this argument in *Kirchliches Amt und geistliche Vollmacht in den ersten drei Jahrhunderten* (Tübingen, 1953). U. Brockhaus provides an excellent historical account and criticism of this phenomenon in *Charisma und Amt. Die paulinische Charismenlehre auf dem Hintergrund der frühchristlichen Gemeindefunktionen* (Wuppertal, 1972). See also H. Legrand, *RSPT*, 59 (1975), 669–671.
26. Clement of Alexandria, *Quis dives salvetur*, verses 208–210 (*PG* 9, 648; ed. O. Stählin, 3, p. 188).
27. C. Vogel, 'Le ministère charismatique de l'Eucharistie: Approche rituelle', *Ministères et célébration de l'Eucharistie* (*Studia Anselmiana*, 61) (Rome, 1973), pp. 181–209; O. Casel, 'Prophetie und Eucharistie', *Jahrbuch für Liturgiewissenschaft*, 9 (1929), pp. 1–19. Recently H. Legrand has contributed to our understanding of this question in 'La présidence de l'Eucharistie selon la tradition ancienne', *Spiritus*, 69 (1977), 409–431.
28. See John Chrysostom's treatise on the priesthood; G. Hocquard, 'L'idéal du pasteur d'âmes selon S. Grégoire le Grand', *La tradition sacerdotal* (Le Puy, 1959). pp. 143–167; see also above, Volume I, p. 69.
29. See, for example, W. Bertrams, 'De constitutione Ecclesiae simul charismatica et institutionali', *Questiones fundamentales Iuris canonici* (Rome, 1961), pp. 260–299; C. García Extremeño, 'Iglesia, Jerarquía y Carisma', *La Ciencia Tomista*, 89 (1959), 3–64; E. O'Connor, 'Charisme et institution', *NRT*, 96 (1974), 3–19; E. Iserloh, *Charisma und Institution im Leben der Kirche dargestellt an Franz von Assisi und die Armutsbewegung seiner Zeit* (Wiesbaden, 1977).
30. I have found signs of this not only in the apologetical treatises *De Ecclesia*, but also, for example, in J. Brosch, *Charismen und Ämter in der Urkirche* (Bonn, 1951); F. Malmberg, *op. cit.* below (note 33).
31. G. Hasenhüttl, *Charisma, Ordnungsprinzip der Kirche* (Freiburg, 1970); H. Küng, *The Church* (London, 1967), pp. 179–191. Küng makes a distinction between temporary and permanent charisms within a structure of the Church that is fundamentally charismatic.
32. Y. Congar, 'The Holy Spirit and the Apostolic Body, Continuators of the Work of Christ', *The Mystery of the Church* (Eng. tr.; London, 1960), pp. 147–186. This can be compared with W. Kasper, *Dogme et Evangile* (Casterman, 1967), pp. 88–90, who speaks of an activity of the Spirit in the Church, first as the 'Spirit of Christ' and then as 'active in the freedom which is peculiar to him'.
33. The Protestant exegetes include P. Bonnard, 'L'Esprit et l'Eglise selon le Nouveau Testament', *RHPR*, 37 (1957), 81–90; M.-A. Chevallier, *Esprit de Dieu et paroles d'homme* (Neuchâtel and Paris, 1966), p. 212, note 3. The Catholic theologians include F. Malmberg, *Ein Leib—ein Geist. Vom Mysterium der Kirche* (Freiburg, 1960), pp. 192ff.
34. *AAS*, 35 (1943), 209–210; no. 38 in Tromp's edition.
35. Thomas Aquinas, *Comm. in Eph.* c. 2, lect. 5: 'Quidquid fit per Sanctum Spiritum etiam fit per Christum'; *ST* Ia, q. 32, a. 1, ad 3: 'Salus generis humani quae perficitur per Filium incarnatum et per donum Spiritus Sancti'.

2

THE HOLY SPIRIT MAKES THE CHURCH ONE

HE IS THE PRINCIPLE OF COMMUNION

The Spirit is given to the Church. He was promised to the apostles, but he was promised to them with the new people of God, of whom they were the first-fruits, in mind.[1] He was given first to the apostles (Jn 20:22) and then to the whole of the early community at Pentecost.[2] There are two significant terms in this context: *epi to auto*, gathered together or in the same place,[3] and *homothumadon*, of one mind or unanimous.[4] Möhler's comment on this expresses something of the deep inspiration of his work:

> When they received the strength and the light from on high, the leaders and members of the new-born Church were not scattered in different places, but gathered together in the same place and in one heart. They formed a single community of brothers. . . . Each disciple therefore was filled with the gifts from on high only because he formed a moral unity with all the other disciples.[5]

The Spirit, the principle of unity, therefore presupposes an initial unity, which he himself is already bringing about, unobserved, and which is a unity of consent to be together and of movement in this direction. Augustine was thinking of this unity when he spoke of *fraterna caritas, caritas unitatis, pacifica mens* and the love of peace, of mutual harmony and unity, the opposite of the partisan, sectarian and schismatic spirit.[6] He was therefore able to say, on the one hand, that it is necessary to be in the Body of Christ in order to have the Spirit of Christ[7] and, on the other, that one has the Spirit of Christ and lives in that Spirit when one is in the Body of Christ.[8] This is of decisive importance, since, if the Spirit is received when believers are *together*, it is not because there is one body that there is only one Spirit—it is rather because there is only one Spirit of Christ that there is only one body, which is the Body of Christ. The Spirit *acts* in order to enable men to enter that Body, but he is *given* to the Body and it is in that Body that we receive the gift of the Spirit. 'By the one Spirit we were all baptized into one body' (1 Cor 12:13; Eph 4:4). 'The Spirit is given to the Church, into which the individual is received by baptism.'[9] The Church Fathers never ceased to affirm, explain and sing of this.[10]

The Holy Spirit is given to the community and individual persons. H. B.

15

Swete observed how often Christ said, in chapters 14 and 16 of the gospel of John, 'will give *you*', 'will teach *you* all things', 'will guide *you* into all the truth' and so on. This 'you' repeated again and again points both to the community and to individual persons. The Church is in no sense a great system in which, as Arthur Koestler said of another system, the individual is simply the sum of a million divided by a million. It is a communion, a fraternity of persons. This is why a personal principle and a principle of unity are united in the Church. These two principles are brought into harmony by the Holy Spirit.

Persons are the great wealth of the Church. Each one is an original and autonomous principle of sensitivity, experience, relationships and initiatives. What an infinite variety of possibilities is contained in each individual! There are signs of a purely material kind of this individuality—each person's fingerprints are, for example, distinctive. If it is true that no two trees are identical throughout the whole world, what are we to say about mankind in space and time? And how many languages are there in the world? It has been estimated that there are some 5,000. And in each one the possible expressions and combinations are really infinite. This is a sign of man's skill and intelligence and therefore also of the number of initiatives open to him.

In the modern era, excessive emphasis has been given in the Catholic Church to the rôle of authority and there has been a juridical tendency to reduce order to an observance of imposed rules, and unity to uniformity. This has led to a distrust of expressions of the personal principle. It has also led to the development of a system of supervision that has been effective in maintaining an orthodox line and framework, but this has been achieved at the price of marginalizing individuals who have had something to say, and often even reducing them to silence and inactivity. Sometimes those persons have said what they had to say, but they have usually done so in irregular and unfavourable conditions.

Individual persons, however, want to be the subjects of their actions. This demand is felt all the more strongly when the individual leaves a situation of sociologically solid religious practice and enters a situation of personally accepted faith. This situation is especially difficult today. No one would deny that the categories and structures of theology and philosophy within which Christianity has expressed itself since the Middle Ages, including the documents issued by the magisterium, especially during the six pontificates from Pius IX to Pius XII, have become devalued. (This is a question that would be worth examining more closely.) Many Christians, including theologians, however, have been trying to reconstruct and re-express their faith in different categories, which are culturally and philosophically remote from the long Catholic tradition, but in accordance with the modern age. How is it possible not to speak of this as a break-up or a shifting of territory on the part of theology? It has even been called a Protestantization of Catholicism and the establishment of a policy of free inquiry. It is obvious that, in the spirit of

16

the world, the demon, he who is opposed to the kingdom of God, is trying to gain something from this movement in theology, and sometimes comes close to succeeding.

Nothing less than the Spirit *of God* is needed to bring all these different elements to unity, and to do so by respecting and even stimulating their diversity. Not, however, at any price. This activity of the Spirit was something which greatly impressed many of the Church Fathers, as early as Irenaeus and Origen.[11] The Spirit supports the pastoral hierarchy of the Church and through it guides Christian communities, but he does much more than this. He does not bring about unity by using pressure or by reducing the whole of the Church's life to a uniform pattern. He does it by the more delicate way of communion. The Church is not only the enclosure or 'sheepfold' (*aulē*), but also the 'flock' of individual sheep (*poimnē*), each of which the shepherd calls by its own name (Jn 10:1–3, 16).

H. B. Swete had this to say about the communion—or fellowship as he often called it, in the Anglican tradition—of the Holy Spirit:

> The communion of the Holy Spirit is not to be identified with our fellowship with Christ, although the former is inseparable from the latter. The Son was sent into the world, the Spirit into the heart (cf. Gal 4:4–6). The fellowship of the Spirit with the human spirit is immediate and direct. He who searches the deep things of God (1 Cor 2:10ff.) enters also into the depths of our inner man. Our bodies become his shrine (1 Cor 6:19; cf. 3:16); but his presence is out of sight, in the *penetralia* of our spirits, where he throws his searchlight upon our unspoken thoughts and desires. His purpose is to carry forward the work of the divine philanthropy begun in the incarnation, to make it bear on the centre of our being, regenerating and renewing the springs of our life (Tit 3:4–6).[12]

The Spirit, who is both one and transcendent, is able to penetrate all things without violating or doing violence to them. It was with good reason that the book of Wisdom said of the Spirit: 'The Spirit of the Lord has filled the world and that which holds all things together knows what is said' (1:7) and of wisdom itself, which has the same part to play: 'In her there is a spirit that is intelligent, holy, unique, manifold, subtle, mobile, . . . all-powerful, overseeing all and penetrating through all spirits' (7:22–23).

The Spirit, then, is unique and present everywhere, transcendent and inside all things, subtle and sovereign, able to respect freedom and to inspire it. That Spirit can further God's plan, which can be expressed in the words 'communion', 'many in one' and 'uniplurality'. At the end, there will be a state in which God will be 'everything to everyone' (1 Cor 15:28), in other words, there will be one life animating many without doing violence to the inner experience of anyone, just as, on Mount Sinai, Yahweh set fire to the bush and it was not consumed.[13] The Spirit is therefore an eschatological reality. He is the Promised One, of whom we here below have only the *arrha* or earnest-money (see Rom 8:23; 2 Cor 1:22; 5:5; Eph 1:14). He is the extreme communication of God himself, God as grace, God *in us* and, in this sense,

17

God outside himself. This idea will be further developed in Volume III of the present work. This communication and interiority do not lead to a merging together. It is rather a state of indwelling—God dwells in us and we dwell in him. There is no confusion of persons.

This is the way in which there is a realization of that mutual interiority of the whole in each which constitutes the catholic sense: *kath' holou*, being of a piece with the whole. The Spirit enables all men to be one and unity to be a multitude.[14] He is therefore the principle of the communion of the saints[15]— these terms form part, it should be noted, of the third article of the Creed, that referring to the Holy Spirit—and indeed the principle of communion as such. This communion consists in living and behaving as a conscious member of an organic whole and therefore, to quote Möhler's excellent phrase, 'as thinking and desiring in the spirit and the heart of all' (see note 5 below). The Scholastic formulae are less poetical than Möhler's, but in no sense less profound. Cajetan (†1534), in a commentary on Thomas Aquinas, spoke of 'agere ut pars unius numero populi'—'behaving as part of an undivided people'—and added that the Holy Spirit had provided the only really decisive reason for behaving in this way by having the article on the one holy Church and the communion of saints placed among the other articles of faith (see *Comm. in IIam IIae*, q. 39, a. 1).

This communion of saints (*sancta* as well as *sancti* and *sanctae*) brought about by the Holy Spirit transcends both time and space. This is, after all, in accordance with the nature of the Spirit, already expressed in the texts of the book of Wisdom, and with the condition of the Spirit as an eschatological gift, the supreme and ultimate gift of God as Grace. The Spirit is anticipation (*arrha*: see above), prophecy (see Jn 26:13), and also memory. As memory, he makes the actions and words of the Word made flesh into a present and penetrating reality (see Jn 14:26; 16:13–15). In the Church, then, he is the principle of that presence of the past and the eschatological future in the here and now, of what can be called the 'sacramental era'.[16]

This is also one way in which the Spirit makes the Church *one*, in all the dimensions in which we confess it to be such and which are the dimensions of God's plan of salvation: from Abel the righteous man to the last of the chosen people, the Church of earth and the Church of heaven, the Head and the members, since the same Spirit is in all things. It is the Spirit who, in God, places the seal, in love, on the unity of the Father and the Son from whom he proceeds.[17]

It was the Spirit who sanctified Jesus' humanity from the moment of his conception (Lk 1:35) and at his baptism, with his messianic ministry in view (4:27; Acts 10:37–38), through his resurrection (Rom 1:4: the 'Spirit of holiness') and who, as the Spirit of Christ and by the diversity of his gifts, makes it possible for one Body, which is the Body of *Christ* (1 Cor 12:12–13) to exist.

'There are varieties of gifts, but the same Spirit' (1 Cor 12:4). The Spirit was in Jesus during his life on earth. Since the time of his glorification, the Spirit has been communicated jointly by 'God' and by the Lord in order to form Christ in each believer, and to make all believers, together and with each other, his Body. This is the rôle that the Church Fathers were speaking of in their theme of the Spirit as the soul of the Church or the soul of the Body of Christ. This soul does not form a substantial whole with the body in which it dwells and which it animates. It continues to be transcendent, while at the same time being immanent with regard to that body. In this sense, Hans Küng was right to say that the Spirit is not the 'Spirit of the Church', but always the Spirit of God, and C. Journet and S. Tromp were also right to make a distinction between the uncreated soul, which is the Holy Spirit, and a created soul, consisting of the whole complex of gifts of grace.[18] These positions are quite justified, but the most important affirmation is that which claims that the Holy Spirit himself plays, in the Church, the part played in the body by the soul. Perhaps a better way of expressing this idea is that the identically and personally same Spirit, *idem numero*, is both in the Head, Christ, and in his Body, the Church or its members, that is, us as believers. This idea is quite traditional. It was known to Thomas Aquinas, taken up again by Pius XII and included in the Second Vatican Council's Constitution on the Church.[19] With his habitually strict form of thinking and expressing his thoughts, Thomas Aquinas looked for the principles uniting believers to each other and to God. He recognized that there were some which had only a 'specific' unity—the gifts of grace, of which each person has his own. All these, however, have a common source, however different they may be, and that is charity which is, because of its object, not only one, but also unique, and which has, as its cause and its source of strength, the same Holy Spirit, who is *unus numero in omnibus*, personally identical in all men and in them the transcendent principle of unity. A similar inspiration prompted Gregory of Nyssa to interpret Jesus' statement: 'The glory which thou hast given me I have given to them' (Jn 17:22) as referring to the Holy Spirit.[20]

Is the Church a person?

If this is really the principle of the Church's unity, it is impossible to avoid asking whether the Church is a person. The person 'Church' cannot be reduced to the mere total of the individuals who compose the Church. It has its own reality to which can appropriately be ascribed such specific properties as unity, holiness, catholicity, apostolicity and indefectibility ('Look not on our sins, but on the faith of your Church'). The Holy Spirit, who brings about precisely these properties in the Church, was promised to the Church. Should we therefore say that the Church has a created personality which is peculiar to it, or should we rather say that Christ is the 'I' of the Church[21] or that the Spirit is its supreme personality or its transcendent 'I'?[22] This can be accepted at least in one sense, which we are bound to define more precisely.

19

If Christ is the 'I' of the Church, how can the Church be his bride? And if the Holy Spirit is the 'I' of the Church, how can it be the Body of Christ?

The unity that is peculiar to the Church has its reality in the Church itself, but it has its foundation in God. In Scripture, the Church is again and again related to the absolute oneness of God, Christ and the Holy Spirit.[23] It is also related to the 'mystery of the will' of God (Eph 1:9ff.; 3:3, 9) and to his 'purpose' or *prothesis* (Rom 8:28; Eph 1:9, 11; 2 Tim 1:9), in other words, his plan of salvation. The person-Church is the one, total reality envisaged by this plan and it is at the same time the term of that plan. That reality and that term are the one 'mystical' Body of Christ and the fruit of the two 'missions' of which I spoke in the previous chapter, that of the Word, the Son, the visible mission of the incarnation and the invisible missions, and that of the Holy Spirit, the visible mission of Pentecost and the invisible missions. In relation to the mystical Body, however, these two missions have a different condition.

By appropriation—and we shall see later on the reality to which this applies—the Holy Spirit is the subject who brings about everything that depends on grace or, as C. Journet said, the supreme and transcendent effective personality of the Church.[24] He is not consubstantial with us. In Christ, on the other hand, the Word, the Son, assumed a humanity that is consubstantial with our humanity—that at least is how the Council of Chalcedon defined it. He united it to himself in a unity that is personal and substantial. Since that time, God has ceased to govern his creation at the natural and the supernatural level exclusively from his heaven and on the basis of his divinity—he governs it also in and through that man, Jesus Christ, assumed in his glory. The humanity of Christ, made entirely holy by the Spirit, has since then been the instrumental cause, not the inert cause, as a thing would be, but the intelligent and free cause, in other words, the voluntary organ of the communication of grace. He gives grace, he gives the Spirit voluntarily, since he is constituted as the Head in this sphere.[25] Since that time, the Lord Jesus and the Holy Spirit have *together* been the authors of the Body, in other words, of the Church in its unity, but Christ is the author as the Head of that Body, homogeneous with its members, in a way that is absolutely his own and strictly personal. That is why the Church is the Body, not of the Holy Spirit and not even of the Word, but of Christ.

In the concrete, everyday life of believers

The communion of which I have spoken in this chapter is an authentic reality, but it is so sublime in the sense in which I have discussed it that, if I were to leave it at that level, it could remain a pure ideal between earth and heaven and have no place in our concrete, everyday life.

The sociologist Jean Séguy asked, in a precise and well-documented study:[26] How is it that the Catholic Church in the United States, which was, in the nineteenth century, the least segregrationist Church in the country, now has so few black members and the latter belong for the most part to the Baptist and Methodist churches? Séguy himself provides the answer to this question. There was, he says, a communion at the level of faith and liturgical practice in the Catholic Church, but there was no trace of what he calls sociological communion—what I would call an effective and concrete *human* communion. Black and white Catholics communicated and received communion at the same altar, but they returned to their places with their hands together and their eyes lowered and left the church without speaking to each other, without shaking hands and even without exchanging a glance. In other words, the mystical communion of which the Holy Spirit is the sovereign principle calls for a concrete, human and personal relationship.

Let us very briefly consider a few examples. An engineer of fifty, who was baptized when he was twenty-three, said: 'The Church is cold and lacking in any kind of brotherliness. Two Scouts, two men from the same school or the same Army unit are more brotherly than two Catholics.' As a second example, there is a statement made by a nun, who was baptized when she was twenty-one: 'In the parish, I suffered a great deal from a lack of welcome on the part of the parishioners. It never seemed to me that the parish was a community.'

There are, however, some much more positive statements, such as this one, made by a married woman, who was also baptized when she was twenty-one: 'Baptism and first communion were for me belonging to Christ and because of that my admission—no, much more than that, my integration into the Church. I really became part of the "family" of the Church and was able to share its happiness, its riches and its aspirations. I began a new life. I can still see myself on the first Sunday after my baptism in the middle of the people in the parish. I was conscious of a very deep joy. I was delighted to belong to the people of God and I don't think that I have ever sung more fervently!' Another married woman with a family, baptized when she was twenty-three, spoke in the same way: 'The Church for me is a family. In the family of the Church, as in a human family, people are at one with each other and dependent on each other. We are all sinners and we have to accept each other as such.' This was the immediately affecting aspect of the solidarity among Christians. One teacher, however, who had been baptized at the age of twenty-five, reviewing the path that he had followed, commented: 'Those who were helping me on my way to the Church in fact helped me most of all in an entirely unconscious way and this made me very sensitive to their *invisible* solidarity'.

If I were to attempt to express this Christian solidarity and to make it visible, I would say on reflection that the charity that the Holy Spirit places in our hearts is not only sublime, but also very concrete. The concrete aspect of Christian love is strikingly expressed in 1 Cor 13:4–5: 'Love is patient and kind; love is not jealous or boastful; it is not arrogant or rude. Love does not insist on its own way; it is not irritable or resentful.' This concrete, practical aspect of love is included in what I have said above about the charity that forms the basis of the communion of saints. And the principle of that charity is the Holy Spirit of God. The most ordinary and concrete aspect of it forms an integral part of the most sublime element.

NOTES

1. See Jn 14:26; 15:26; 16:12–13. For the most part, the Church Fathers applied these promises to the apostles: see *DTC*, I, cols. 2124–2125. Almost all modern exegetes, however, believe that they apply to the Church as a whole as well as to the apostles: see E. Dhanis, *Greg*, 34 (1953), 207.
2. See J. Capmany, 'La communicación del Espíritu Santo a la Iglesia—Cuerpo místico, como principio de su unidad, según S. Cirilo de Alejandría', *Revista Española de Teología*, 17 (1957), 173–204.
3. Acts 1:15; 2:1; 2:47. For the part played by this term in the ideal of unity held by the early Church, see P. S. Zanetti, *Enôsis—epi to auto*. I: *Un 'dossier' preliminare per lo studio dell'unità cristiana all'inizio del 2° secolo* (Bologna, 1969); for *epi to auto*, see pp. 154ff.
4. Acts 1:14; 2:1; 2:46; see also 4:24; 5:12; 15:25; Rom 15:6.
5. J. A. Möhler, *Symbolik*, § 37; see also his *Einheit*, § 63, in which he spoke of the divinity of Christ confessed 'at the Council of Nicaea, where, for the first time, all Christians were visibly assembled in the persons of the representatives of their love': see *Unam Sanctam*, 2 (Paris, 1937), p. 205. A similar idea can also be found in Peter Chrysologus (†c. 450): 'Deo non singularitas, sed accepta est unitas. Spiritus Sanctus apostolis in unum congregatis ubertate tota sui fontis illabitur': *Sermo* 132 (*PL* 52, 653); cf. *Sermo* 139 (*PL* 52, 574).
6. See my note 'Pax chez S. Augustin' in *Œuvres de S. Augustin. Traités antidonatistes*, I (1963), pp. 711ff.; see also S. Tromp, *Corpus Christi quod est Ecclesia*, I, 2nd ed. (Rome, 1946), pp. 135ff.
7. Augustine, *Ep.* 185, 9, 42 and 11, 50 (*PL* 33, 811 and 815); *In Ioan. ev.* XXVI, 6, 13 (*PL* 35, 1612–1613). See also Origen: 'It is only in the community of believers that the Son of God can be found and that is because he only lives in the midst of those who are united': *Comm. in Mat.* XIV, 1 (*PG* 13, 1188).
8. *In Ioan. ev.* XXVII, 6, 6 (*PL* 35, 1618), etc.
9. R. Bultmann, *Theology of the New Testament*, I (Eng. tr.; New York, 1951), p. 160. This theme was developed by L. S. Thornton in *The Common Life in the Body of Christ* (Westminster, 1943), pp. 137–142.
10. J. A. Möhler, *Einheit*; P. Nautin, *Je crois à l'Esprit Saint dans la sainte Eglise* (Paris, 1947); H. J. Jaschke, *Der Heilige Geist im Bekenntnis der Kirche. Eine Studie zur Pneumatologie des Irenäus von Lyon* (Münster, 1976), § 23, pp. 265–277.
11. See Irenaeus, *Adv. haer.* I, 10, 1–5 (*PG* 7, 551ff.); Origen, *De Prin.* I, 4, 3 (*PG* 11, 122–123; ed. P. Koetschau, pp. 18–19); see also Theodoret, *Eranistes* I (*PG* 83, 80C-D).
12. H. B. Swete, *The Holy Catholic Church* (London, 1915), pp. 182–183.
13. See my article, 'Le ciel, buisson ardent du monde', *VS*, 618 (January–February 1976), 69–79.
14. It would be well here to read the little work of Peter Damian, *Dominus vobiscum* (*PL* 145, 231–232; partial Fr. tr. in *M-D*, 21 (1950/1), 174–181).
15. See P. Bernard's excellent texts of the Greek Fathers in 'Communion des saints', *DTC*, III (1908), col. 440. See also Augustine, *Sermo* 142, 7 (*PL* 38, 782); *Sermo* 267, 4 (*PL* 38, 1231); Albert the Great, *In III Sent.* d. 24 B, a. 6 (ed. A. Borgnet, 28, pp. 257–258); Thomas Aquinas, *ST* IIIa, q. 68, a. 9, ad 2; a. 12, ad 1; q. 82, a. 6, ad 3, who is not at all

original in this case, shows that the Spirit brings about in the body the communication of spiritual good things and that it is through him that, in baptism, babies are included in the faith of the Church confessed by their sponsors and their parents.

16. For this, see my *Tradition and Traditions* (Eng. tr.; London and New York, 1966), Part Two, pp. 257–270, esp. p. 260, notes 1 and 2 (with bibliography). In these pages which I wrote in 1960, however, the pneumatological aspect, although it is very important, has been rather overshadowed by the Christological aspect.

17. It is possible and indeed necessary to develop this idea further. See, for example, B. de la Margerie, 'La doctrine de S. Augustin sur l'Esprit Saint comme communion et source de communion', *Augustinianum*, 12 (1972), 107–119. One text can be quoted: 'The Father and the Son wanted us to enter into communion with each other and with them through what is common to them and wanted to join us together as one through that Gift that they both possess together, namely the Holy Spirit, God and the Gift of God. It is in him that we are reconciled with the Deity and that we enjoy the Deity': *Sermo* 71, 12, 18 (*PL* 38, 454). This text can be compared with one by Cyril of Alexandria: 'Since we have all received the same unique spirit, that is, the Holy Spirit, we are all in a certain sense merged together with each other and with God. Although we are many and separate and although Christ has made the Spirit of the Father and his own Spirit dwell in each one of us, that Spirit is still one and indivisible. He thus reduces to unity the different spirits of each one of us through himself and makes them all appear one in him': *Comm. in Ioan*. XI, 11 (*PG* 74, 561).

18. H. Küng, *The Church* (London, 1967), pp. 173ff. See also C. Journet, articles in *Nova et Vetera, VS, RThom* (1936), 651–654, and his final explanation in 'L'âme créée de l'Eglise', *Nova et Vetera* (April 1946), 165–203; *idem*, 'Note sur la distinction de deux âmes de l'Eglise, l'une créée, l'autre incréée', *ibid*. (July 1946), 284–300; *idem, L'Eglise du Verbe incarné*, II (Paris, 1951), pp. 565–579. Journet's position and above all his vocabulary were criticized by E. Mura, *RThom*, 41 (1936), 233–252 and by E. Vauthier, P. Liégé and others. See my *Sainte Eglise. Etudes et approches ecclésiologiques* (Paris, 1963), pp. 503ff., 647ff. See also S. Tromp, *Corpus Christi quod est Ecclesia*, III: *De Spiritu Christi Anima* (Rome, 1960), pp. 36ff., 107ff. and fundamentally the whole of this volume by Tromp, who had previously published two collections of patristic texts: *De Spiritu Sancto Anima Corporis mystici*, 1: *Testimonia selecta e Patribus Graecis*; 2: *Testimonia selecta e Patribus Latinis*, 2nd ed. (Rome, 1948 and 1952).

19. Thomas Aquinas, *In III Sent*. d. 13, q. 2, a. 1, ad 2; q. 2, a. 2; *De ver*. q. 29, a. 4; *Comm. in ev. Ioan*. c. 1, lect. 9 and 10; Pius XII, Encyclical *Mystici Corporis*, 54 and 77 ad sensum (*AAS*, 35 [1943], 219 and 230); Vatican II, Dogmatic Constitution on the Church, *Lumen Gentium*, 7, 7. See also S. Tromp, *Corpus Christi quod est Ecclesia*, *op. cit*., III, pp. 119ff.; G. W. H. Lampe, *Christ, Faith and History* (Cambridge, 1972), pp. 111ff.

20. Gregory of Nyssa, *Hom. 15 in Cant*. (*PG* 44, 1117A).

21. I have listed texts of this kind in my article 'La personne "Eglise" ', *RThom*, 71 (1971), 613–670. To these should be added P. Faynel, *L'Eglise* (Paris, 1971), I, pp. 189ff., 190–191.

22. For E. Klemroth, for example, the Holy Spirit was the 'supra-empirical "I" of the Church': see his *Lutherischer Glaube im Denken der Gegenwart* (Berlin, 1953), p. 137.

23. See Eph 4:4–6; 1 Cor 8:6; 12:6ff.; 10:1ff. (one bread); 2 Cor 11:2 (betrothed to one man); Jn 10:16 (one flock because there is one shepherd). This is also the sequence, although the realities are different, in the Creed: we believe 'eis hena Theon, eis hena Kurion, eis hen hagion Pneuma, eis hen baptisma, eis mian hagian katholikēn Ekklēsian'.

24. C. Journet, *L'Eglise du Verbe incarné*, *op. cit*. (note 18), II, pp. 96, 232–234, 490, 508. See also Thomas Aquinas, *Comp*. I, 147.

25. Thomas Aquinas, *ST* IIIa, q. 8, a. 1, ad 1; see also Eph 1:23; Col 1:15–20.

26. J. Séguy, 'Constitutions ecclésiastiques, rites liturgiques et attitudes collectives. A propos de la ségrégation religieuse des Noirs aux Etats-Unis', *Archives de Sociologie des Religions*, 6 (No. 11) (1961), pp. 93–128.

23

3
THE HOLY SPIRIT IS THE
PRINCIPLE OF CATHOLICITY

I have not been able to speak about the unity of the Church without mentioning its catholicity. That unity is in fact the unity of many 'according to the whole' and it is this that points to the aspect of catholicity. What is more, unity has, by its very vocation, a universal extension, and this is also incontestably an aspect of the mark of catholicity. It is also not possible to deprive Christ, despite his particular mission in his own time and his own country, of his value as the light of the world and the Lord of all (see Jn 8:12; 12:32, and the whole of Paul). It is quite possible to speak in Christ's case of a concrete universal element, but the reality of Christ as man-God goes far beyond any purely philosophical approach to the question. The same applies to the Church, although the difference between Christ and the Church has to be borne in mind here. The treasure of the Church is contained in an earthly vessel, and the continuity between Christ and the Church is formed on the one hand by what comes to the Church from him institutionally—words, baptism, the Eucharist, the apostolic mission and so on—and, on the other, the Spirit communicated by him to the Church. All that we have of that Spirit who is to renew all things at present, however, is the 'earnest-money'. That earnest-money is quite substantial, since, even though the Spirit does not at present develop the fullness of that activity by which he will enable God to be 'everything to everyone', he is even now the eschatological gift that is substantially present to the Church and active in the Church. He makes the Church catholic, both in space, that is, in the world, and in time, that is, in history.

Mission in Human Space

During the earthly life of Jesus, the Spirit dwelt in him and was active through him. This means that the Easter appearances of the Lord involved a mission (see Mk 16:15–18; Mt 28:18–20; Gal 1:16) and a promise and then the effective gift of the Spirit, whose coming was the beginning of the apostolic mission and testimony (see Lk 24:46–49; Acts 1:6–11; Jn 20:21). As we have already seen, this is an essential theme in the Acts of the Apostles. As soon as the Lord had ascended to the Father, the Spirit was in the Church as a power spreading faith and love.

This meant leaving the purely Jewish sphere. It is worth noting that this task was left mainly to a thirteenth apostle who had not known Christ according to the flesh and who was called by the Lord who was Spirit. Paul brought about not merely the entry of gentiles into the new people of God—there had already been Cornelius and his household—but the transition to the Greek and Graeco-Roman world. This was the beginning of pluralism in the Church at a socio-cultural level. Many other cultural groups were to enter the Church as they encountered the apostolic preaching in time and space. What an adventure of faith! The Graeco-Roman world was, of course, relatively homogeneous. The 'barbarian' Ostrogoths and Visigoths were converted in the fourth and fifth centuries. There followed the slow, constant, but never complete process of 'alienation' between the Western and the Eastern parts of the Church, the Greeks and later the Slavs on the one hand, and the Latin or Latinized Christians on the other. There were the great waves of missionary activity—the heroic Irish period between the sixth and the eighth centuries, the embassies or missions in Asia in the thirteenth century, the great voyages of discovery and the conquests of the sixteenth century, accompanied by missionary settlements about which it is not possible to speak in simple terms, but which certainly resulted in the establishment of Christianity in Central and South America. Finally, there was the encounter with Asia, with its great number and variety of men, nations, cultures and religions, and with Africa, where a condescending and even scornful missionary attitude has gradually been replaced by a better knowledge and a more positive appreciation.

What interests us most in all this is the encounter of peoples, languages, cultures and religions. For a very long time, the 'other' was not sufficiently recognized as different and diverse, and the profound values concealed by that diversity were not appreciated. It is in fact only quite recently that we have come to understand this, and sometimes this understanding has been accompanied by doubt about our own values and an overestimation of the 'other' and its exotic aspects—the grass is always greener in the other field. Catholic Christianity has for centuries encountered different cultures and religions, but now the need is to encounter, recognize and welcome them in a new way. This is because men are brought much more closely in contact with each other—by travel, exchanges of various kinds, the press and television, it is possible for every man to be present to every other man. It is also because a much better and more authentic knowledge of other cultures and religions is possible, and there is a greater desire to know them. Finally, it is because we have been cured (although not all of us equally) of a certain haste inspired by imperialism in politics, apologetics and even apostolic zeal. The Church today is called to be the Church of the peoples in a new way.

The Church was established in the world by Pentecost, which gave it a vocation to universality, which was to be achieved not by means of a uniform extension, but by the fact that everyone understood and expressed the marvels of God in his own language (Acts 2:6–11). Through the mission and gift of the Holy Spirit, the Church was born universal by being born manifold and particular. The Church is catholic because it is particular, and it has the fullness of gifts because each has his own gifts. The Church overcame Babel, not by a return to a uniformity that existed before Babel, but by proclaiming an implantation of the same gospel and the same faith in varied and diverse cultural soils and human spaces.[1] This process is marked in the Church of today by the emphasis placed on two different but closely related orders of reality:

1. First are the charisms, that is, the talents of which the Holy Spirit makes use *pros to sumpheron*, 'for the common good', so that the community of the Church will be built up.[2] There is no law in the whole of the New Testament and the Christian tradition that is more strongly affirmed than this law of mutual service and mutual building up.[3] There are many gifts of the Spirit—a multiplicity of gifts—and Paul's list is neither systematic nor exhaustive. They are gifts made to persons, but those persons are not monads with individual autonomy. They belong to a people, a tradition, a culture and a sociological group, to which their gifts are in a sense appropriated. The Church's catholicity calls for these gifts to be gathered together and exchanged, and for the different parties contributing them to be aware of the whole and of its unity. This is illustrated at the level of mutual aid by St Paul's collection, *koinōnia tēs diakonias*, a sharing or service for the benefit of the saints.[4] At the level of mutual contributions of knowledge and of a revelation of the wealth of Christ, as well as of spiritual help and reciprocity, it is illustrated in an exemplary and typical way in the theory and practice of catholicity expressed in the Dogmatic Constitution on the Church, *Lumen Gentium*, 13.

2. The second order of reality is that of the local and particular churches. No firmly established terminology can be found either in the documents of Vatican II or in many other texts. I believe, however, that the following distinction is clear and quite well justified. The *local* Church is the Church of God in a certain place, and the excellent definition of the diocese provided by the Second Vatican Council can be applied perfectly to that Church.[5] The *particular* Church is the Church which presents a particular aspect, for example, in language (Basque, perhaps) or in the recruitment of its members (soldiers, for instance). It may perhaps be a diocese, part of a diocese, a group of dioceses or even a patriarchate (the Armenian Church, for example). This rediscovery and reassessment of local or particular Churches is the work and fruit of the Second Vatican Council and, as Karl Rahner called it, its most novel contribution. The Council is conscious that these Churches have been made by the people called and gathered together in the Holy Spirit—the Spirit is for those Churches the principle both of

26

unity and of their own gifts or talents. It is the task of the Spirit to contain and resolve this fertile tension between the particular and unity. Unity and pluralism are both necessary—pluralism in unity and unity without uniformity.

In an article on liturgy, S. Monast took as his point of departure a gesture made by Pope Paul VI at the ordination of 172 missionaries of different nationalities and languages at the feast of Pentecost, that of giving each missionary, as a sign of unity, a Latin missal.[6] The gesture was indisputably excellent in itself. Monast, however, who was himself a missionary among the Aymaras in the Andes, asked 'Shall I use this missal with my Aymaras? What meaning would it have for them, even if it were linguistically possible, for me to translate the prayers of the Roman missal into their language?' He expressed his doubts and went on to discuss the related terms 'cult' and 'culture', concluding that, if a liturgy is to live, it has to be the liturgy of a *people*. At the same time, however, it has also to be the liturgy of the Church and therefore to translate and express the faith of the apostles. This, then, is clearly a question of unity with diversity, a problem of communion and a matter concerning the Holy Spirit.

The Holy Spirit makes the Church Catholic in History

It is a frequently asserted theological truth that the Holy Spirit ensures that the Church will be faithful to the faith of the apostles. This affirmation is a consequence of the apostolicity of the Church. It will be discussed in the following chapter and we shall see then that there is a close relationship between apostolicity and catholicity, just as there is between catholicity and unity. Rather like the functions of Christ himself, the marks of the Church exist one within the other. Christ's priesthood is royal and prophetic, his prophetism is priestly and royal, and his royalty is prophetic and priestly. In the same way, the unity of the Church is apostolic, holy and catholic, its catholicity is holy, one and apostolic, its apostolicity is catholic, one and holy, and its holiness is apostolic, catholic and one.

The Church gives its faith to the Word of God, to which the inspired Scriptures bear witness. Throughout the centuries, the Church's life has been a meditation on the Scriptures. The need for the Scriptures to be read in the same spirit and through the same Spirit under whose influence they were written has been stressed again and again in the history of Christianity.[7] The only really adequate way of reading and interpreting Scripture is to do so subject to the movement of the Spirit. Scripture is one of those places where the close connection that exists between the Spirit and the Word, the Paraclete and Christ, is revealed. The whole of Scripture speaks of Christ.[8] This deep meaning of Scripture, however, is only disclosed when we are converted to the Lord, who acts in us as the Spirit (see 2 Cor 3:16–18). Origen was sometimes excessively subtle in his interpretations of Scripture, but he brought to the study of the Bible something more than a perspicacious spirit—with a heart in which the Spirit of Jesus dwelt, he read the whole of the Christian mystery in the sacred books.[9]

I have used the words 'Christian mystery'. Christ is the principle and the centre of that mystery, but he came 'for us men and for our salvation' and he does not operate without Christians, not even without all who are called (see Rom 8:28–30). This is what enables us to read Scripture 'spiritually'. In other words, a 'spiritual' reading of Scripture is what is done in the communion of the Church and the Holy Spirit. By inspiring Scripture and by throwing light on believers' reading of it, the Spirit is simply making sure that the text will be without error and those who read it will be orthodox.

This, of course, is a reduction of the part played by the Spirit in the understanding of Scripture. Such a reduction may have been sufficient at a time when the Church was adopting a tight and rather narrow defensive posture against the Higher Criticism. Progress in the study of biblical and patristic sources has now made it possible for us to have a much wider view. The Christian mystery is God's revelation and communication of himself through his Son, Jesus Christ, in the Holy Spirit, who is undoubtedly, in the words of Irenaeus of Lyons, the *communicatio Christi*—'communion with Christ'.[10] This is the 'spiritual sense' of Origen and the Church Fathers.[11] It is also what the Second Vatican Council meant when it dealt with the question: How to interpret Scripture.[12] The Council fully recognized the historical, cultural and human conditioning of the sacred texts, their literary genres and so on. It also regarded Scripture to some extent as a sacrament, like the Church itself and, by analogy, the incarnation. It then claimed, 'since holy Scripture must be read and interpreted according to the same Spirit by whom it was written', that 'no less serious attention must be given to the content and *unity of the whole of Scripture*' and that '*the living tradition of the whole Church* must be taken into account along with the harmony which exists between elements of the faith'.

If Scripture is, as far as its content is concerned, the communication of the mystery of Christ, which is the work of the Holy Spirit, then it is clear how, given the necessary assumptions, the Church's Tradition, the Eucharist and even the Church itself have become assimilated to it, since, because of the activity of the same Spirit, the content is fundamentally the same. This is not simply the teaching of Origen or St Ambrose.[13] It also forms part of a realistic, yet spiritual view of what is involved. It can also be explained on the basis of Jn 6 or that of the traditional theme, which was taken up again by Vatican II, of the two tables—the table of the Word and that of the sacrament.[14] Both tables are Christ given to us so that we shall live, and this requires the activity of the Holy Spirit. Each of these realities has an external aspect, which it is possible to consider alone—it is possible to see nothing in Scripture but a literary text, nothing in Tradition but a human history, nothing in the Eucharist but a ceremony and nothing in the Church but a sociological phenomenon. Each, however, also has a deep spiritual aspect, to which God is committed through his Spirit.

The Spirit makes the Word present, taking the letter of Scripture as the point of departure. He enables the Word to speak to each generation, in every cultural environment and in all kinds of circumstances. He helps the Christian community at different times and in different places to understand its meaning.[15] Is this not what Jesus promised?[16] Did the first witnesses and the first Christian Churches not experience this?[17] Has the Church not always been aware of this and affirmed this when it has spoken about its Tradition?[18] Is it not a point of wide ecumenical agreement today?[19] At certain periods during the history of the Church, notably during the Counter-Reformation and the Catholic restoration after the French Revolution, theologians have especially stressed the guarantee that the Spirit gives to the Church and have interpreted the Church in terms of authority and the magisterium, a guarantee that it cannot err in its teaching. Although I would not wish to overlook this aspect, I would prefer to stress here the part played by the Spirit in making knowledge present in continuity with what has gone before, and to insist on the fact that the whole Christian community, including its pastors, are helped by the Spirit. 'You are not to be called "rabbi", for you have one teacher and you are all brethren' (Mt 23:8). The teaching of the Second Vatican Council here is very firm:

> The holy people of God shares also in Christ's prophetic office. It spreads abroad a living witness to him, especially by means of a life of faith and charity. . . . The body of the faithful as a whole, anointed as they are by the Holy One (cf. Jn 2:20, 27), cannot err in matters of belief. Thanks to a supernatural sense of faith which characterizes the people as a whole, it manifests this unerring quality when, 'from the bishops down to the last member of the laity' (Augustine), it shows universal agreement in matter of faith and morals. For, by this sense of faith which is aroused and sustained by the Spirit of truth, God's people . . . clings without fail to the faith delivered to the saints (cf. Jude 3), it penetrates it more deeply by accurate insights and applies it more thoroughly to life.[20]

This 'anointing' of faith, which comes from the 'Holy One', in other words, the Holy Spirit, takes place in history. A very common practice among the Fathers of the Church, which continued until the period of the Council of Trent and even later, was to describe the effectiveness of the Spirit in the Church by the words *revelatio (revelare), inspiratio (inspirare), illuminare, suggestio (suggerere)* and related terms. I have provided a documentation on this subject which could be extended almost indefinitely.[21] I also gave Thomas Aquinas the credit for having broken with this practice and limited or reserved the word *revelatio* to what we know now as 'revelation', by giving the word a much more precise meaning. I am still convinced that it is not really possible to place at the same level on the one hand the revelation or inspiration of the Spirit at the apostolic, constitutive

29

period of the Church's foundation and, on the other, the continuing activity of the Spirit in the life of the Church that was founded at that time. The fundamental concern of the theologians who spoke in the older way, however, was to show revelation as an event in the present, occurring in the Church as an act of faith. It is also a constant feature in the liturgical use of biblical texts. In the liturgy, they are taken out of their historical setting and divorced from their strictly exegetical meaning so that they may have a contemporary relevance as God's revelation and communication of himself. St Bernard justified this use of the Bible by insisting that the Bride of Christ enjoyed the Spirit of Christ.[22] The disadvantage of Thomas Aquinas' more precise use of the term 'revelation' was that it came to be seen as a completed event which had simply to be interpreted and elaborated by theologians. This resulted in a tendency to see God's act of revelation, religious truth, dogma and faith notionally, and it is only relatively recently that this conception has been called into question.[23] Nonetheless, theologians and the magisterium state now as in the past that the Holy Spirit is active in the Church, enlightening it and guiding it, in accordance with the Lord's promise. In view of the criticisms expressed by Protestant theologians, who also suffer from a positivism of the inspired text of Scripture, it is necessary both to avoid equating the Church's Tradition with the Word of foundation, and to join with our sister-churches in the East[24] and insist that the Church's Tradition is the very life of the Church as the Body of Christ, animated by the same Spirit who spoke through the prophets.

This brings us at once to the question: Does he still speak through the prophets? Who would dare to say that he does not? But, if he does, who is it who prophesies? One reply to this question is that the proposal of an objective revelation or the communication of the Word implies a corresponding 'spirit of revelation' in the subjects who are to receive it.[25] Because of this, God is constantly active revealing himself in men who are called to believe or who are living by faith. It is, however, necessary to go further than this and ask whether God does not speak today in events and in the lives of men. This is certainly a question that modern man asks again and again.

Inner inspirations and even what John of the Cross called 'substantial words', which, in the course of a fervent spiritual life, bring about what they say, such as 'Walk in my presence' or 'Be at peace', have always been recognized in Christianity. Private revelations have also played a part in the history of the Church.[26] It has long been thought that the lives of the saints form a commentary in action on the Scriptures[27] and Pope Pius XII went so far as to say, in connection with Teresa of Lisieux, that the lives of the saints were God's words.[28] It has also always been believed that, as the Church is guided by the Holy Spirit in its life, the Church's way of acting, the *usus Ecclesiae*, was a very precious 'theological locus', especially sacramentally. Thomas Aquinas often referred to this. The sense of faith or *sensus fidei*— the term *sensus fidelium* is often used, less precisely, to point to the feeling of

Christians themselves—can also be included among the 'theological loci'. God also makes certain aspects of faith known to this *sensus*.

All this is very interesting and even important, but it is confined to the purely Christian sphere, while the questions that we are asked as Christians go beyond that sphere. They are concerned with an experience of the world as such through which Christians may be able to know God in a new way. Is the activity of the Spirit involved in this experience? I would like to point to three aspects of that involvement.

1. The members of Catholic Action, at all levels, but especially the Young Christian Workers, have always reflected, in teams, about aspects of life in the environment in which they live. They see in these God's appeal to them and attempt to understand and respond to that appeal in the light of the gospel. J. Bonduelle said some years ago that, in this 'examination of life', as he called it, it was possible to recognize a 'sign of the Spirit', which he illustrated by quoting the well-known text of Joel applied by Peter to the pouring out of the Spirit at Pentecost (Acts 2:17–21).[29] The very facts of the secular world seem to say something concerning God and they do this thanks to the Holy Spirit.

2. In 1963, John XXIII published his Encyclical *Pacem in terris*, and two-and-a-half years later the last document to be produced by Vatican II appeared—*Gaudium et spes*, the Pastoral Constitution on the Church in the Modern World. Both documents, but especially the second, gave an essential place to the idea of the 'signs of the times' in the Church's understanding of itself in its relationship with the world that is both natural and historical:

> To carry out such a task (that is, the task of continuing, subject to the impulse of the Holy Spirit, the work of Christ himself) the Church has always had the duty of scrutinizing the signs of the times and of interpreting them in the light of the gospel. . . . The people of God believes that it is led by the Spirit of the Lord who fills the earth. Motivated by this faith, it labours to decipher authentic signs of God's presence in the happenings, needs and desires in which this people has a part along with other men of our age.[30]

These 'signs of the times' are not always clearly defined, but they are sufficiently clear. They are to be found in the situation in which the Church, as the people of God, has to carry out its mission. This situation somehow conveys the presence and plan and therefore the activity of God. The changing situation of the world is described, together with a number of facts, in *Gaudium et spes*, 4–10, and all these facts point to change in the world and a change in attitude in the Church. Several of these facts are also mentioned in other conciliar documents.[31] Many of them go back to the movement of Christianity itself, but more generally they are characteristic in a broad sense of the movement of the secular world.

31

However useful and indeed necessary the work of sociologists may be, these indications should not be interpreted purely sociologically, but rather in the light of the gospel, inspired by faith and led by the Holy Spirit. At the least, these broad facts point to developments in the history of mankind which provide the Church, or, more precisely, its catholicity, with its matter. These developments in the history of the first Adam have to be evangelized and therefore first recognized, and they also give a topicality to the Church's message, matter to its mission, and new ways of proclaiming the gospel.[32] At the most, the events taking place in the world that stimulate the consciousness of Christians, enabling them to hope and to act energetically, can be seen as a genuine 'word' of God. The Word can be identified with the 'economy' of God in action in these events. A reaction in the name of positive revelation as attested in the inspired Scriptures is then met with the response that a 'hermeneutical' approach rather than a purely exegetical one is required; in other words, we have to be conscious of the meaning of God's activity in history for us here and now. I do not deny that God acts in the history of the secular world or that historical events and movements can tell us something of what God wants for us and therefore of what he is. What is difficult, however, is the interpretation of those events. Interpretation is able to go further than mere conjecture and personal conviction only if the meaning of the facts is tied to and illuminated by the positive revelation of God's plan with Jesus Christ at its centre. And here we need to bear in mind that the salvation and the kingdom that God's plan envisages include the whole of creation and are God's response to creation's groaning and its hope (see Rom 8:20–24).

3. Nowadays, priests, catechists and others prefer not to take an established text or confession of faith as their point of departure, but very often base their instruction on facts and on life itself. Let me give three different examples, admittedly taken out of their context:

> The Christian . . . must listen to God actually speaking in his life and in the world. God addresses us through every event.[33]

> The ways in which God is revealed to us are: the world, the individual in his relationships with others, and the community, which safeguards the gospel in history.[34]

> Like all our contemporaries, we have less and less faith in the virtue of institutions and the intangibility of dogmas and we are referring more and more to our immediate experience in our search for the meaning of things and of human relationships.[35]

It is possible that these statements simply point to a new development in teaching the faith, a very valid one as such. They may, however, also indicate a tendency to neglect, at least for a time, the acquired and generally accepted datum of positive revelation or the data of a specific religious space, and to look for God or 'Jesus of Nazareth' in human events and relationships. I would not be able to accept, in such an approach pushed to its logical extreme, that listening to the Word of God as reported in the gospel and handed down in the Tradition of the Church can be entirely replaced by an interest in the world and one's fellow-men. This does not, however, mean that I reject the fact that God also speaks to us through events and other human beings. My task here is to try to define more precisely the part played by the Holy Spirit in that area.

The Holy Spirit as the 'Unknown One beyond the Word'

This description of the Spirit originated with Hans Urs von Balthasar[36] and it indicates admirably the unity that exists between the two realities and the tension that accompanies that unity. It also points to the freedom and the mysterious activity that characterize the Holy Spirit. Finally, it suggests that he acts *forwards*, in a time or space that has been made open by the Word.

All that we know about the Spirit is in accordance with this description. In Scripture, he is always characterized by symbols expressing movement, such as wind and breath, living water, the flying dove, tongues and so on. The New Testament attributes such characteristics to the Spirit as the power of new beginnings, freedom and openness to recognizing the other. Christian Duquoc, who has drawn attention to these New Testament aspects of the Spirit,[37] has shown that the Absolute is not, according to the New Testament, the metaphysical Perfectly Solitary One who is closed in on himself, but a kind of 'ecstatic one'. According to Dionysius, love is 'ecstatic', the Father ex-pressing himself in the Word and constituting him as 'different' and the Spirit breaking the self-sufficiency of the 'face to face' of the first two Figures. In the work that God places outside himself through the two missions of the Word and the Spirit, the Spirit is 'the energy which exorcizes the spell of the past or the origin and projects forwards towards a future, the principal characteristic of which is its newness'.

The theme of the Fourth Assembly of the World Council of Churches at Uppsala in August 1968 was: 'Behold, I make all things new' (Acts 21:5). Mgr Ignatius Hazim, the Orthodox Metropolitan of Latakia, who had been asked to make the opening address, described in a striking way this work of God carried out by his Spirit:[38]

> The newness of creation cannot be explained by the past—it can only be explained by the future. It is clear that the activity of the living God can only be creative. The wonder of God, who reveals himself to Abraham, Isaac and Jacob, is, however, that his creative act comes from the future. It is prophetic. God 'comes' into the world as though he were coming to meet it. He goes ahead and he calls, upsets, sends, causes to grow and sets free. . . .
> The paschal event, which came once and for all time, has to become ours today—but how? It can only become ours through the one who brought it about in

33

the beginning and will bring it about in the fullness of time—the Holy Spirit. He is himself Newness, at work in the world. He is the presence of God-with-us, 'bearing witness with our spirit' (Rom 8:16). Without him, God is distant, Christ is in the past and the gospel is a dead letter, the Church is no more than an organization, authority is domination, our mission is propaganda, worship is mere calling to mind, and Christian action is a slave morality.

In him, however, and in indissoluble combined activity, the cosmos is raised up and groans giving birth to the kingdom, man struggles against the flesh, the risen Christ is present, the gospel is the force of life, the Church is the fellowship of the Trinity, authority is a service that sets free, our mission is a Pentecost, the liturgy is a commemoration and an anticipation, and human activity is deified.

The Holy Spirit . . . gives birth. He speaks through the prophets. . . . He takes us towards the second coming. 'He is Lord and giver of life' (Niceno-Constantinopolitan Creed). It is through him that the Church and the world call out with their whole being: 'Come, Lord Jesus!' (Rev 22:17–20).

It is this energy of the Holy Spirit that introduces a new dynamism into our horizontal world. . . . We need a prophetic theology which is able to detect the coming of the Lord in history. . . . Is the Holy Spirit not urging us to hasten the coming of the creative Word, Christ the Saviour, so that he will 'guide us into all the truth', since it is he who will 'declare to us the things that are to come' (Jn 16:13)?

The Holy Spirit makes the Easter event of Christ present with the eschatological destiny of creation in mind. He also makes Christ's Revelation present. He thrusts the gospel forward into the period of history that has not yet come. After all, if it is true that Christ was only born once, only spoke once, only died once and was only raised from the dead once, then this 'once' should be welcomed and should take root and bear fruit in a humanity which has existed throughout the centuries in so many places and in such an infinite variety of cultures. There must be a link between what has already been given and the unexpected, between what has been acquired once and for all time and what is always new. This link is forged by the Holy Spirit, the Spirit of Jesus, Jesus as Spirit, who is also both the 'Spirit of truth' and 'freedom'.[39]

In the Bible, 'truth' is an eschatological reality. It is, in other words, the end towards which all things are destined by God. In the concrete, this means that, however true and venerable they may be, the forms that we know are not the last word about the ultimate realities that they express. Dogmas are not yet perfect. The Church is, in its structures, an open system. The Word is the form and the Spirit is the breath. Jesus instituted the Eucharist and proclaimed a gospel. The Spirit makes them present here and now in what is new in the history of the world. He joins the first Adam who multiplied and invented to the eschatological Adam, the Omega of the world who is also its Alpha and the Omega and Alpha of the Church. The Spirit does this, both in the truth of the One who only brings all that Christ has said to mind (Jn 14:26) and who takes what is Christ's (16:14) and in the freedom of the One who blows where he wills (3:8). As we have already seen, the Spirit is the 'co-instituting' principle. In a sense, then, God has really told and given us everything in Jesus Christ[40] and yet there is also something new and something takes place in history.

The Spirit, however, is the Spirit of *Jesus Christ*. He does no other work but that *of Jesus Christ*. There is no time of the Paraclete that is not the time of Jesus Christ, contrary to what Joachim of Fiore, who misinterpreted the original and correct idea that he had of history as open to hope and newness, seemed to believe. The catholicity of the Church is the catholicity *of Christ*.[41] The soundness of any pneumatology is its reference to Christ.

In the power of Christ and the Holy Spirit, then, the Church is able to be completely open to accomplish its catholicity, which is also the catholicity of Christ. This task can only be carried out in mystery, because it is not possible to distinguish clearly between what is for God and what is not. We shall see later that only the Spirit knows what word is formed within men's hearts. Throughout history, men have claimed to know and to be able to say who was for God and who was not, and those periods in which they claimed this knowledge most persistently were the least tolerant and often the most cruel. Those were periods of 'Christianity', but not of catholicity. In our own age, we are, as we have seen, called in a new way to an encounter of peoples, cultures and religions. The first words of the Declaration on the Non-Christian Religions of Vatican II are, significantly, *Nostra aetate*—'In our times'. This Declaration, however, goes on, in the second paragraph, to say expressly that Christ is 'the way, the truth and the life' (Jn 14:6). He is the Alpha and the Omega of this new and wider catholicity which the 'Unknown One beyond the Word' enables mysteriously to develop to greater and wider maturity.

NOTES

1. Decree on the Church's Missionary Activity, *Ad Gentes divinitus*, 4. It is possible to amplify what is said in this conciliar statement, within the spirit of the Council: '(At Pentecost) that union (of all peoples in the catholicity of faith) was (prefigured) by the Church of the new covenant, which speaks all tongues, which lovingly understands and accepts all tongues and which thus overcomes the divisiveness of Babel'. See also H. Legrand, 'Inverser Babel, mission de l'Eglise', *Spiritus*, 63 (1970), 323–346; *idem*, 'Parce que l'Eglise est catholique, elle doit être particulière', *Cahiers Saint-Dominique*, 127 (April 1972), 346–354.
2. 1 Cor 12:7; see also K. Weiss, *'sumpherō'*, *TDNT*, IX, p. 77. For the meaning of this, see 1 Pet 4:10.
3. For the New Testament, see the articles *'diakoneō'* (II, pp. 81ff.), *'doulos'* (II, pp. 261–279) and *'oikodomē'* (V, pp. 144–147) in *TDNT*; see also L. Deimel, *Leib Christi* (Freiburg, 1940), especially pp. 89ff., but also *passim*; P. V. Dias, *Vielfalt der Kirche in der Vielfalt der Jünger, Zeugen und Diener* (Freiburg, 1968). For the Tradition of the Church, see the theme of *subministratio ad invicem*, which was dear to Thomas Aquinas, but which will also be found in many other theological works, including, for example, J. A. Möhler, *Einheit*, §§ 26, 30, 31 and Appendix XIII.

4. 2 Cor 8:4. See also, for the deep meaning of this collection, L. Cerfaux, 'S. Paul et l'unité de l'Eglise', *NRT*, 53 (1926), 657–673; E. B. Allo, 'La portée de la collecte pour Jérusalem dans les plans de S. Paul', *RB*, 45 (1936), 529–537. G. Dieter has written a study in German (Hamburg, 1965); K. F. Nickle, *The Collection: A Study in Paul's Strategy* (London, 1966).
5. Dogmatic Constitution on the Church, *Lumen Gentium*, 23, 1 and 26; Decree on the Pastoral Office of Bishops, *Christus Dominus*, 11.
6. S. Monast, 'Une liturgie, œuvre du peuple', *Spiritus*, 50 (September 1972), 300–307, with reference to J. Dournes, *L'offrande des peuples* (*Lex Orandi*, 44) (Paris, 1967).
7. It is clear from the many references taken from Christian authors throughout the centuries that this principle has been affirmed again and again: Hippolytus, Methodius and Origen: see H. de Lubac, *Histoire et Esprit. L'intelligence de l'Ecriture d'après Origène* (Paris, 1950), p. 315, note 144 and p. 316, note 148; Origen, *In Num., Hom.* XVI, 9 (ed. W. A. Baehrens, 153; *PG* 12, 702); Gregory Thaumaturgus (*PG* 10, 1093A); Jerome, *In Gal.* 5, 19–21 (*PL* 26, 417A); Augustine, *Contra mend.* 15 and 26–27 (*PL* 40, 506); Isidore of Seville, *Etym.* VIII, 5, 70 (*PL* 82, 305); Abelard, *Sic et Non, Prol.* (*PL* 178, 1339B); Richard of Saint-Victor, *De erud. hom. int.* II, 6 (*PL* 196, 1305A-B); William of Saint-Thierry; Stephen of Tournai, *Epist.* 251 (*PL* 211, 517); Thomas Aquinas, *Comm. in Rom.* c. 1, lect. 6; c. 12, lect. 2; *Quodl.* XII, 26; *ST* IIa IIae, q. 173, a. 1; q. 176, a. 2, ad 4; *Contra Gent.* III, 154, post gradum; John Duns Scotus, *Opus Oxon.* IV, d. 11, q. 3, n. 15 (ed. L. Vives, XVII, 376); Eckhart, *Book of Divine Consolation*, Part Two: *Meister Eckhart* (Eng. tr.; paperback ed., London, 1963), p. 130 (Fr. tr. quoted by de Lubac, *op. cit.*, pp. 315, note 144). At the time of the Reformation: Johann Eck, *Apologia de conventu Ratisboni*, art. 9; Ambrosius Catharinus, *Claves duas ad aperiendas Scripturas* (Lyons, 1543), p. 32; Alphonsus de Castro, *Adv. omnes haereses*, lib. I, c. 4. In the present century: Benedict XV, Encyclical *Spiritus Paraclitus* (15 September 1920) (*Enchiridion Biblicum*, 469); Vatican II, Dogmatic Constitution on Revelation, *Dei Verbum*, 12.
8. See Jn 5:39, 46; 12:41; Lk 24:25–27; Acts 10:43. When he was inspired by the Spirit, David spoke of Christ as his Lord: see Mt 22:43; Mk 12:36.
9. See H. de Lubac, *op. cit.* (note 7), pp. 274, 303–304, 316–317, for Origen's texts on understanding the Scriptures by conversion to the Lord. See also *Entretien d'Origène avec Héraclide*, Fr. tr. J. Scherer, *SC* 67 (1960), p. 91. See also my *Tradition and Traditions* (Eng. tr.; London and New York, 1966), Part Two, p. 395 and the relevant note.
10. Irenaeus, *Adv. haer.* III, 24, 1 (*PG* 7, 966; ed. W. W. Harvey, II, 131; Fr. tr. A. Rousseau and L. Doutreleau, *SC* 211, pp. 472 and 473).
11. For Origen, see H. de Lubac, *op. cit.* (note 7), pp. 297ff., 304 and note 58; for the others, *see idem, Exégèse médiévale. Les quatre sens de l'Ecriture* (Paris, 1959).
12. Dogmatic Constitution on Revelation, *Dei Verbum*, 12.
13. For Origen, see H. de Lubac, *op. cit.*, pp. 366ff.; Ambrose, *Comm. in Luc.* I, 6, 33 (PL 15, 1763); see also Ephraem Syrus, *Diat.* XXII, 3 (Fr. tr. L. Leloir, *SC* 204 (1966), p. 396).
14. See my study 'The Two Forms of the Bread of Life: in the Gospel and Tradition' (orig. pub. in *Parole de Dieu et Sacerdoce. Etudes présentées à Mgr Weber* (Tournai, 1962), pp. 21–58; Eng. tr. in *Priest and Layman* (London, 1967), pp. 103–138. See also Dogmatic Constitution on Revelation, *Dei Verbum*, 21; Decree on the Religious Life, *Perfectae Caritatis*, 6; Decree on the Ministry and Life of Priests, *Presbyterorum ordinis*, 18.
15. C. Molari, 'The Hermeneutical Role of the Church Community on the Basis of the Judaeo-Christian Experience', *Concilium*, 113 (1978), 93–105. For the function of the Spirit as *memoria* for faith, see R. Pesch, *Freiheit in Gesellschaft* (Freiburg, 1971).
16. See Jn 14:15ff., 26; 15:26; 16:13–15. See also Volume I of this work, p. 58.
17. See Jn 2:22; 12:16; 13:7; 16:12ff. See also F. Mussner, *Le langage de Jean et le Jésus de l'histoire* (Paris and Bruges, 1969); A. M. Hunter, *According to John* (Philadelphia and London, 1968).
18. I have provided details and references, firstly in my book, *op. cit.* (note 9), Part One,

pp. 49. 169ff., 194ff.; Part Two, pp. 338–347; and secondly in Volume I of this work, pp. 151ff.

19. I am reminded here of the Faith and Order Conferences at Edinburgh in 1937: see A. Guimond, *Les exigences doctrinales de l'unité de l'Eglise* (Rome, 1972), pp. 50ff.; and at Montreal in the summer of 1963: see L. Vischer, *Foi et Constitution, 1910–1963* (Neuchâtel and Paris, 1968), pp. 172–185. See also the Malta report on the dialogue between the Catholic Church and the World Lutheran Federation: *Doc. cath.*, 1621, 18–25 (3 December 1972), pp. 1072–1073.

20. Dogmatic Constitution on the Church, *Lumen Gentium*, 12, 1. For the interpretation of 1 Jn 2:20, 26 and similar texts, and a theological interpretation, see M.-E. Boismard, 'La connaissance dans l'alliance nouvelle d'après la première lettre de S. Jean', *RB*, 56 (1949), 365–391; I. de la Potterie, 'L'onction du chrétien par la foi', *Bib*, 40 (1959), 12–69; repr. in *La vie selon l'Esprit, condition du chrétien* (Paris, 1965), pp. 107–167; my *Lay People in the Church* (Eng. tr.; London, 1957), pp. 259ff.

21. See my book, *op. cit.* (note 9), Part One, pp. 119–137, text and notes. For Thomas Aquinas, see *ibid.*, pp. 93, 124; for the situation at the time of the Reformation, Trent and later, see pp. 174–176 and the relevant notes. Since I wrote that book, a monograph dealing with one of the most important theologians of the twelfth century has shown that 'in the theology of Hugh (of Saint-Victor), revelation is not first and foremost a body of teaching to which nothing can be added, nor is it limited to a strictly supernatural sphere. ... It is an event rather than a doctrine': see L.-J. Bataillon's review, *RSPT*, 62 (1978), 259, of C. Schütz, *Deus absconditus, Deus manifestus. Die Lehre Hugos von St. Viktor über die Offenbarung Gottes* (Rome, 1967).

22. Bernard, *In vig. nat., Sermo* 3, 1 (*PL* 183, 94); see also, for the Church as Bride possessing the Spirit of her Bridegroom, *In Dom. Palm., Sermo* 2, 5 (*PL* 183, 253); *In Cant., Sermo* 73, 6 (*PL* 183, 1136–1137); *In festo Petri et Pauli, Sermo* 2, 5 (*PL* 183, 410). See also C. Bodard, 'La Bible, expression d'une expérience religieuse chez S. Bernard', *Saint Bernard théologien (Anal. S. Ord. Cist.)* (Rome, 1953), pp. 24ff.

23. See, for example, W. Kasper, *Dogme et Evangile* (Paris, 1967) and *Renouveau de la méthode théologique* (Paris, 1968). The Council used a concept of 'truth' which respected the notional value of the term, but to some extent accepted the biblical meaning of faithfulness on God's part to his plan of salvation: see *RSPT*, 54 (1970), 329ff.

24. See my book, *op. cit.* (note 20), Part One, chapter III, esp. pp. 87ff.

25. Eph 1:17; 1 Cor 2:10; for the reality, see 2 Cor 4:3–6; Mt 16:17. See also my books *La Foi et la Théologie* (Paris, 1962), pp. 16ff., and *op. cit.* (note 9), Part Two, pp. 386ff.

26. See my article on 'La crédibilité des révélations privées', *VS* (Suppl) (1 October 1937), 29–48; repr. in *Sainte Eglise* (Paris, 1963), pp. 375–392. For a discussion of mystical visions, see *Nouvelles de l'Institut Catholique de Paris* (February 1977).

27. See Augustine, *Contra mend.* 15, 26–27 (*PL* 40, 506); Gregory the Great, *In Ezech., Hom.* 1, 10, 38 (*PL* 76, 901); Thomas Aquinas, *Comm. in Rom.* c. 1, lect. 5; c. 12, lect. 3; *Comm. in Heb.* c. 12, lect. 1.

28. A. Combes, *Sainte Thérèse de Lisieux et sa mission* (Paris, 1954), p. 212, note 4.

29. See J. Bonduelle, article written in 1960 and repr. in *La révision de vie. Situation actuelle* (Paris, 1964), p. 39. See also J.-P. Jossua, 'Chrétiens au monde. Où en est la théologie de la "révision de vie" et de l'"événement"?', *VS* (Suppl), 71 (November 1964), 455–479. There is an echo of this movement in the Decree on the Ministry and Life of Priests, *Presbyterorum Ordinis*, 6, 2.

30. Dogmatic Constitution, *Gaudium et spes*, 4, 1 and 11, 1. For this idea, see also Paul VI, audience given on 16 April 1969; *Doc. cath.*, 1539 (4 May 1969), pp. 403–405; M.-D. Chenu, 'Les signes des temps', *NRT* (January 1965), 29–39, repr. in *Peuple de Dieu dans le monde* (Paris, 1966), pp. 35–55; *idem*, 'Les signes des temps. Réflexion théologique', *Vatican II. L'Eglise dans le monde de ce temps (Unam Sanctam, 65b)* (Paris, 1967), pp. 205–225; P. Valadier, 'Signes des temps, signes de Dieu?', *Etudes*, 335 (August-

September 1971), 261–279, who criticized or rather rejected Chenu's position; L. Léves-que, 'Les signes des temps', *Science et Esprit* (October-December 1968), 351–362; R. Coste, *Théologie de la liberté religieuse* (Gembloux, 1969), pp. 354ff. It is also important to recognize that the idea of the 'signs of the times' has a history or a pre-history. W. Kahle has shown that the 'signs of the times' were observed by nineteenth-century German Protes-tants in the 1830 and 1848 revolutions and the wars. In 1855, C. C. J. von Bunsen published *Die Zeichen der Zeit*: see W. Kahle, 'Die Zeichen der Zeit. Ein Beitrag zur Theologie und Geistesgeschichte des 19. Jahrhunderts', *Zeitschrift für Religion und Geis-tesgeschichte*, 24 (1972), 289–315.

31. The liturgical movement, which is like a passage of the Holy Spirit in his Church: see the Constitution on the Liturgy, *Sacrosanctum Concilium*, 43; the ecumenical movement: see the Decree of Ecumenism, *Unitatis redintegratio*, 4, 1; the solidarity of all peoples and nations: see the Decree on the Apostolate of the Laity, *Apostolicam actuositatem*, 14, 3; the recognition of religious freedom, e.g. in legislation: see the Declaration on Religious Freedom, *Dignitatis personae humanae*, 15, 3. Priests and lay people must be alert to the signs of the times: see the Decree on the Ministry and Life of Priests, *Presbyterorum Ordinis*, 9, 2; 6, 2.

32. This last aspect is developed in *Gaudium et spes*, 44, and in many of M.-D. Chenu's writings.

33. Michel Quoist, *Prayers of Life* (Dublin and Melbourne, 1963), p. v.

34. Nuns quoted by P. Régamey, *Redécouvrir la vie religieuse. La rénovation dans l'esprit* (Paris, 1974), p. 161.

35. From a paper read in November 1973 during the fifteenth Semaine des Intellectuels Catholiques. This did not propose a 'programme', nor did it contain a declaration. It was simply a critical questioning.

36. H. U. von Balthasar, 'Der Unbekannte jenseits des Wortes', *Interpretation der Welt. Festgabe R. Guardini*, ed. H. Kuhn (Würzburg, 1966), pp. 638–645, reprinted in *Spiritus Creator. Skizzen zur Theologie*, III (Einsiedeln, 1967), pp. 97ff.

37. C. Duquoc, *Dieu différent* (Paris, 1977). pp. 106ff.; for what follows, see pp. 120ff.

38. The text will be found in *Irénikon*, 42 (1968), 344–359, or *Foi et Vie* (November-December, 1968), 8–23. See also J.-B. Metz, 'Gott vor uns', *Ernst Bloch zu Ehren* (Frankfurt, 1965), pp. 227–241. Although I would not wish to raise him to the status of a Father of the Church, I would also like to cite André Gide in this context: 'If I had to formulate a creed, I would say: God is not behind us. He is to come. We have to look for him not at the beginning, but at the end of the evolution of all beings. He is terminal, not initial. He is at the supreme and ultimate point towards which the whole of nature is moving in time. And, since time does not exist for him, it is a matter of indifference to him whether this evolutionary process of which he is the summit follows or precedes or whether he guides it by calling it or by driving it forward': *Journal*, 30 January 1916, p. 333.

39. 'Spirit of truth': Jn 14:17; 15:26; 16:13; 1 Jn 4:6; Freedom: 2 Cor 3:17; combination of both: Jn 8:32.

40. John of the Cross, *The Ascent of Mount Carmel*, II, Part 8, chapter 20.

41. See Eph 4:10,13; 1:23. Elsewhere I have quoted Tennyson's fine poem on 'The Christ that is to be' (end of Poem CV in *In Memoriam*).

38

4

THE SPIRIT KEEPS THE
CHURCH 'APOSTOLIC'

'Apostolic' means 'relating to the apostles' or 'in conformity with the apostles'. The word therefore indicates a reference to or a conformity with the origins of Christianity. This idea is quite correct, but it needs to be amplified, since it is only half the truth. The other half is a reference to eschatology. Christ is Alpha and Omega, the beginning and the end, the one who is, who was and who is to come, the Pantocrator (see Rev 1:8; 21:6; 22:13). Apostolicity is the mark that for the Church is both a gift of grace and a task. It makes the Church fill the space between the Alpha and the Omega by ensuring that there is a continuity between the two and a substantial identity between the end and the beginning. It can therefore be conceived by reference to the end as well as by reference to the beginning. This truth is, thank God, the object of profound ecumenical agreement, whilst Protestant, Orthodox and Catholic theologians can all preserve their own distinctive emphases;[1] see also the Appendix to this chapter.

It is a question of combining the Alpha of God's intention with the Omega in such a way that his intention and his gift are identical throughout history, throughout the development and hazards of which it has been, is and will be the place. It is a question of preserving the messianic and eschatological way of living in community that was received from the Lord until he comes again. At the level of individual life, the first generations of Christians called this 'keeping the seal of baptism shining'.[2] It is, however, also a question of the Church as such. The means available to this faithfulness that is based above· all in the faithfulness of God are:

1. The essential elements of the Church as an institution as given by Jesus: the Word, the sacraments, the ministry of the Twelve and, at a deeper level, the establishment of the Twelve (Mk 3:14) as the beginning of the new people of God, just as the twelve sons of Jacob-Israel had been the beginning of the old people of God.[3] As they were at the beginning, those Twelve will also be at the end, judging the faithfulness of the tribes of the new Israel to the rules that applied at the beginning (see Mt 19:28; Lk 22:30; cf. 1 Cor 6:2; Rev 20:4). We have, as Newman urged, to watch until he returns. This eschatological aspect of the Church's apostolicity has a clear place in the last judgement. Scripture speaks of it in terms of a distinction between

the sheep and the goats (Mt 25:32) or between what has been built on the foundation with gold, silver or precious stones and what has been built with wood, hay or stubble and will therefore be burnt (1 Cor 3:12–15). The apostles, then, will judge whether what reaches the end or the Omega, the last letter of the alphabet through which history has passed, is in conformity with what was given at the Alpha, that is, at the beginning to which they were, are and finally will be witnesses.

2. The mission which has been given once and which is all-embracing ('all nations') and guaranteed ('I am with you always, to the close of the age) (see Mt 28:19–20). Apostolicity is the identity, almost the oneness, of this apostolic mission throughout the centuries until the end, while the men who carry out this mission die one after the other and are replaced by others.[4] This mission is also the mission of Christ, or at least it is a sharing in the mission of Christ.

3. At an even deeper level than the mission of Christ, there is Christ himself as 'consecrated and sent into the world' (Jn 10:36). This Johannine reference points to the fact that it is not so much Christ in himself or in his constitution as man-God—however much that may be the essential condition for the authenticity of the rest—as Christ as the one who is sent and who is for us: *propter nos et nostram salutem*. That Christ is the one who was anointed and sanctified by the Spirit for his mission as the Messiah and Saviour: at the time of his conception (Lk 1:35), when he was baptized, throughout the whole of his activity and especially during his struggle against the Prince of this world, and finally, in a way that was decisive for what was to follow, in his resurrection, glorification and enthronement as Lord. His humanity as the Servant who was obedient to death and crucifixion was established from that time onwards in the full state of a *humanity of the Son of God*, that is, a humanity that is powerful enough to communicate to us, through the Holy Spirit, the quality of sons of God. He is the eschatological Adam, the one who leads us to the God who is 'everything to everyone' by acting as the 'Spirit who gives life'. All this can be reduced to a system of the kind that is now known as a 'Christology of the Spirit',[5] but this kind of Christology is in no sense Adoptionist. It is firmly based on the classical Christology of the Word made flesh, the Chalcedonian Christology of the two natures and the hypostatic union. The 'life-giving spirit' of 1 Cor 15:45 is the same as the Word made flesh of Jn 1:14, as the one who was conceived in Mary by the Holy Spirit (Lk 1:35) and the one whom 'God anointed with the Holy Spirit and with power' and who 'went about doing good and healing all that were oppressed by the devil, for God was with him' (Acts 10:38).[6]

4. Just as they were sent, the Son and the Spirit were also given, but the title 'Gift' can be more particularly applied to the Holy Spirit, as we shall see in

40

Volume III of this work. Their mission as a gift is the movement by which the eternal and divine processions freely have a term in the history of the world. The same Spirit who is in God, as a Person proceeding by means of love—the love that is common both to the Father and to the Son—is also in Christ, the incarnate Son, sanctifying him, and in us, in other words, in the Church.[7] The Spirit is therefore the ultimate principle, that is, the supreme and fulfilling principle of the identity of the supernatural and saving work of God.

In the case of the Church as such, I propose now to discuss the part played by the Holy Spirit in bringing about and maintaining the continuity and even the identity between the Alpha and the Omega, in the category of testimony. I will consider this question within an authentically biblical perspective.

1. I have derived a great deal of help here from a posthumous work by Ragnar Asting published in 1939.[8] The Hebrew of the Old Testament is very valuable to our understanding of this question, since the New Testament authors wrote in Greek, but their categories of thought were Hebrew. The verb *'ûdh*, which means 'to bear witness', 'to testify', expresses the idea of repetition and this involves the idea of affirmation and a commitment of the will. The Ark and the Tabernacle of the exodus were called 'of testimony', because they were the places from which Yahweh revealed his will. God's law was also called his 'testimonies' (see Ps 119). This testimony is also, like the Word of God (examined by Asting, *op. cit.* (note 8 below), pp. 6–299), *vorwärtsgerichtet*, 'directed forward' and not 'backwards-looking', *zurück-schauend*. The Greek words *marturein, martur*, on the other hand, come from an Indo-European root meaning 'to remember', 'to think' or 'to reflect'. The Latin word *memor* is also derived from the same root. In other words, the witness reports and testifies to what he has already seen.

The New Testament expressed in Greek the content of the Hebrew concept. It does not express the meaning that we attach to the word 'martyr', that is, suffering and even death for a cause. One is not a martyr because one dies. On the contrary, one suffers and dies because one is a witness, testifying to and affirming the reality of God's will and commitment as expressed in his covenant and in Jesus Christ, who was the first faithful witness (see 1 Tim 2:5–7, 6–13; Rev 1:5; 3:14). This Christian witness refers to Christ's death and resurrection and to his status as Lord. It is always 'directed forwards', *vorwärtsgerichtet*, since, beyond the affirmation that these things in fact took place, it also proclaims their saving value and their present and effective reality for the world. That is why God also bears witness himself together with his witnesses. He is active in and through their testimony.

It is true, however, that the idea of the eye-witness, that is, the one who has already seen and who remembers and testifies, is also encountered in the Old Testament.[9] There are also undoubted cases of this in several texts in the

New Testament (see, for example, Lk 16:19ff.; 24:48; Acts 1:21–22; cf. 4:13; 3:15; 10:39, 41; 13:31). To these examples can be added the testimony of John the Baptist in the gospel of John, although he bears witness to a fact by affirming in it the dynamic realization of God's plan. There are also cases, as Asting pointed out (*op. cit.* (note 8 below), p. 626), in Paul's epistles, in 1 Pet 5:1, and so on. All this is, of course, normal, since God's intervention to save man and his revelation came in Jesus Christ. Testimony is not simply prophetic—it is also apostolic and bears witness to what has already come. Asting himself recognized this,[10] even though he stressed what was 'directed forwards', in other words, the dynamic affirmation of contemporary importance that looked ahead to fulfilment. In the messianic and eschatological age which began with the mission and gift of Jesus Christ and the Holy Spirit, both values of 'witness' are to be combined. The first is the recollection and attestation of what has already taken place; the second is a dynamic affirmation of the present effectiveness of those realities and their fulfilment in the apostolic mission brought about by the facts themselves, until they are eschatologically consummated (see, for example, 1 Jn 1:1–2).

2. In the Johannine discourses of Jesus, the latter speaks of two 'missions', in which his work will be carried out after his departure. The first is that of the apostles (Jn 13:16, 20; 17:18, which looks forward to 20:21) and the second is that of the Paraclete, the Spirit of truth (Jn 14:16, 26; 15:26). These two missions together bear the weight of that testimony which is, as we have seen, a recollection and an affirmation of what took place in the past and, at the same time, a looking forward to the future:

> When the Paraclete comes, whom I shall send to you from the Father, even the Spirit of truth who proceeds from the Father, he will bear witness to me; and you are also witnesses, because you have been with me from the beginning (Jn 15:26–27).

> You are witnesses of these things. And behold I send the promise of my Father upon you (Lk 24:48–49).

> You shall receive power when the Holy Spirit has come upon you; and you shall be my witnesses . . . (Acts 1:8).

> And we are witnesses to these things and so is the Holy Spirit whom God has given to those who obey him (Acts 5:32).

The relationship between the Spirit and those who are sent can be seen at work in the Acts of the Apostles and the Pauline epistles. Before sending them, the prophets and teachers of Antioch lay hands on Saul and Barnabas, who are also said to have been sent on their mission by the Holy Spirit (Acts 13:3–4). In the same way, Paul appointed elders in Lystra, Iconium and Antioch (Acts 14:23), but when he addressed the elders of the church of

Ephesus, he told them: 'Take heed to yourselves and to all the flock, in which the Holy Spirit has made you overseers' (Acts 20:28). Again, Ananias and Sapphira thought that they were only deceiving the apostles, whereas they had lied to the Holy Spirit (Acts 5:2, 3, 9). Finally, it is also worth quoting the formula of the synod of Jerusalem in this context, because it has been interpreted as pointing to a decision made by the Holy Spirit and the apostles: 'It has seemed good to the Holy Spirit and to us' (Acts 15:28).[11]

Those sent preached the kerygma 'through the Holy Spirit' (1 Pet 1:12) and their words were powerful 'in the Holy Spirit' (1 Thess 1:5; Acts 4:31, 33; Heb 2:3–4), but they were first strengthened by the Spirit in the truth (Jn 16:8–13; 1 Jn 5:6). The Church was born and increased because of preaching and the help given by the Holy Spirit (see Acts 6:7; 4:33; 9:31) and the apostolic ministry was a 'ministry of the Spirit' (2 Cor 3:4–18).

Some of Paul's activities were concerned with the institution—the word and the sacraments, or the ministry of the two tables of the bread of life. In this, the Holy Spirit acted with him, achieving in the souls of men what he celebrated externally. The Church is also built up, however, by unexpected interventions which are sometimes hidden and at others revealed to the senses. These include various encounters, inspirations and events. The experience is so generalized that it is pointless to give examples. It is, however, possible to point to a few such interventions in the ministry of the apostles. The Spirit, for example, prevents Paul from going to Asia (Acts 16:6–7), but later, at least according to Codex D, he leads him there and then prompts him to head for Macedonia (19:1; 20:3). Then Paul, anxious to reach Jerusalem, stopped in Miletus, where he delivered his farewell address to the elders of Ephesus: 'And now, behold, I am going to Jerusalem, bound in the Spirit . . . the Spirit testifies to me in every city that imprisonment and afflictions await me' (20:22–23). In his freedom as the Lord who gives life, the Spirit is therefore also involved in the apostolate and does the work of the gospel.

3. The Spirit is also given to the Church as its transcendent principle of faithfulness. Paul—if Paul was indeed the author—exhorted Timothy: 'Guard the truth that has been entrusted to you by the Holy Spirit who dwells within us' (2 Tim 1:14). It has become almost a commonplace to denounce an early form of 'catholicization' of apostolic Christianity in the pastoral epistles.[12] *Charisma* is used in those letters only in respect of Timothy (see 1 Tim 4:14; 2 Tim 1:6). Jesus had promised the Spirit to his disciples as an exegete or a living and sovereign master.[13] In the second and third centuries, the Church Fathers were conscious of a 'tradition' or communication of the Holy Spirit which ensured the unity of faith in the scattered churches:

The barbarians possess salvation, which is written without paper and ink by the

Spirit in their hearts (see 2 Cor 3:3) and they scrupulously preserve the ancient Tradition.[14]

As disciples of that (Christ) and witnesses of all his good works, his teaching, his passion, death, resurrection and ascension to heaven after his resurrection according to the flesh, the apostles, with the power of the Holy Spirit, sent by him to the whole of the earth, realized the appeal of the gentiles . . . purifying their souls and their bodies by means of the baptism of water and the Holy Spirit, that Holy Spirit that they received from the Lord. It was by sharing him and distributing him to believers that they established and founded that Church.[15]

No one will refute all that (asserted by the philosophical sects) except the Holy Spirit sent into the Church. Having received him first, the apostles communicated him to those who had right faith. We, who are their successors, who share in the same grace of the priesthood and teaching and who are thought to be the guardians of the Church, do not close our eyes and do not suppress the word.[16]

The 'tradition/transmission' of the Spirit, which enables the Church to be faithful to and united in its faith, is tied to the function of the bishops. There is evidence of the process described in the pastoral epistles at the beginning of[17] and during the second century: 'It is necessary to listen to the presbyters (bishops) who are in the Church. They are the successors of the apostles and, with the succession of the episcopate, they have received the certain charism of truth according to the good pleasure of the Father.'[18] Since Irenaeus wrote these words, there have, throughout the centuries, been dozens of testimonies to the Church's consciousness of having been helped and 'inspired' by the Holy Spirit, who was promised and given to the Church so that it would be unfailingly faithful to the faith received from the apostles. This has been affirmed again and again as applying to the whole Church[19] and especially to the ecumenical councils 'assembled in the Holy Spirit',[20] to the pastoral government of the Church in general[21] and in particular to the magisterium of the Bishop of Rome.[22] All this goes back ultimately to the Church's apostolicity.

The presence of the Holy Spirit inspiring the Church was frequently presented as automatic and occurring as a matter of course in the predominantly juridical ecclesiology that resulted from the Church's conflict with the secular power, the Counter-Reformation and the reaction to the French Revolution. This is one of the most formidable obstacles in the ecumenical debate and I would like to make three comments which, I believe, go to the root of the problem.

1. We profess to believe that it is the Church that is apostolic and to believe in the Holy Spirit as the one who makes the *Church* apostolic. It was to the Church, assembled and unanimous in the company of the apostles, that the Spirit came at Pentecost. The first community of 120 members was extended by the addition of new members, who joined the earliest nucleus.[23] The

44

apostolicity of the Church is a communion with the apostles, and with and through them a communion with the Father and his Son Jesus Christ (1 Jn 1:3, 7). The Holy Spirit is the principle of that communion (2 Cor 13:13) and 'to each is given the manifestation of the Spirit for the common good' (1 Cor 12:7).

This universal apostolicity is fundamentally an apostolicity of faith, but it is also an apostolicity of service, witness, suffering and struggle. The 'apostolic succession', in the technical sense of this term, has to be placed within the context of this apostolicity, that is, of this communion extended in time. It is, after all, possible to speak of an apostolic succession in the case of all believers, but only in the wider context of the faithful transmission of faith.[24] It is only within this communion that the 'apostolic succession' in the strict sense of the term, in other words, the succession of the bishops, can take place. This is the profound meaning of the episcopal consecration carried out by several bishops in the midst of the people, who bear witness to the fact that the bishop elect is in the catholic and apostolic faith.[25] What is more, since the Church is also 'apostolic' even in heaven (Rev 21:14), the communion of saints in heaven is also involved in the ordination of ministers (in the litany of the saints).

2. There is therefore, in principle, no automatic, juridical formalism in this question, since the 'hierarchical' function exists within the communion of the *ecclesia*. One ultimate thesis that is almost universally maintained—I only know of two exceptions in the whole domain of theology—is the one which claims that a heretical Pope would cease to be Pope, since he would, as a heretic, have left the communion of faith.

In concrete, this means that the Spirit must actively intervene in the case of any activity that is related to the sacramental or 'hierarchical' institution, whether it has to do with the Word, the pastoral government of the Church or the sacraments in the widest sense of the word, that is, those acts which are concerned with the general sacramentality of the Church. In a study written some thirty years ago and therefore in the categories and the vocabulary of that period—it was, after all, hardly possible to do otherwise—J. de Bacchiochi showed that the visible aspect or 'pole' in the sacramental act, which was connected with the 'apostolic succession' and the historical decisions of the incarnate Word, had to be received and therefore complemented inwardly in the theologal life of the subject at the 'spiritual' or 'prophetic' level or 'pole' at which the influence of the Holy Spirit who was sent by Christ was felt in the soul.[26]

Both poles are necessary. Without the coming of the Spirit, there is only a rite, but the necessity for the act by the ordained minister points to the need for the institution by Christ. In this way, the two 'missions' of the Word and the Breath, the 'Unknown One beyond the Word' or the free Gift according to grace are united and complement one another. That is the function of the epiclesis, of which I shall have more to say in Volume III of this work. Every action performed by the ministry calls for an epiclesis. Orthodox Christians are right when they say that the life of the Church is entirely epicletic. I am therefore in complete agreement with Walter Kasper in his claim that 'the Church is the specific place in which God's saving work in Jesus Christ is made present by the Holy Spirit. Ecclesiology is a function of pneumatology. In modern theology, on the other hand, one often gets the impression that pneumatology has become a function of ecclesiology; the Spirit has become the guarantor of the Church as an institution and pneumatology has become the ideological superstructure on top of ecclesiology.'[27]

We have left behind, or at least are leaving behind, the latter sort of ecclesiology.

3. The Spirit not only keeps the Church faithful to the faith of the apostles and the structures of the covenant, but also helps the Church, so that, when it is called on to confess, affirm and define that faith, it can do so in a confident and even, we have to say, an 'infallible' way. This was the conviction of the Church even before the disturbingly heavy term 'infallible' came to be used.[28] When the Church is called on to declare whether the Holy Spirit is substantially God, whether Jesus Christ had a human will, or whether his body and blood that were offered in sacrifice are really given to us in the Eucharist, it is inevitably helped to confess the truth.

This attribute has, of course, been wrongly used, just as the term 'magisterium' has been misused since the time of Pius IX.[29] 'Infallibility' can only really be applied to certain acts and to judgements made by the Church when it is called on to make a declaration about points concerning the substance of the religious relationship as it has been revealed and offered to us by God in Jesus Christ. The concept which is most suitable to express the whole of the Church's attempt throughout history to profess the saving truth is, however, 'indefectibility'.[30] The Church has, in its pastoral magisterium, approached truth in different ways. It has made mistakes. It has fallen short and has been forgetful of its task. It has been frustrated and has experienced critical moments. These all form part of its historical conditioning—its witness is always conditioned by the historical nature of knowledge, language and expression. The Holy Spirit helps the Church *ne finaliter erret*—so that error will not ultimately prevail (see Mt 16:18).

Protestants may agree with this, and indeed many have stated that they are in agreement with this position.[31] They have constantly stressed that it is not the Church itself that is the primary subject of this indefectibility, or possibly of this infallibility, but the Holy Spirit, and we can gladly accept even this insistence, provided we can also say that grace is *given*. Orthodox Christians also agree within their own theological context, as expressed by the terms *sobornost'* or 'communion' (see section 1 above, pp. 44–45) and epiclesis (see section 2 above), and an apostolicity and a life in the truth which are inseparable from the doxological existence of the Church and from its life in holiness.[32] I shall deal with the latter question in the next chapter. As I have already pointed out, the marks of the Church are not only inseparable from each other—they are also contained within each other. The apostolicity of the Church, in other words, is holy and catholic.

NOTES

1. Certain Protestant theologians, such as W. Pannenberg and K. Barth, have seen apostolicity as identical with mission; with each new generation, believers take their place with the first witnesses and receive authority, power and order to carry out the apostolic mission. J. D. Zizioulas is representative of the Orthodox position. At the end of this chapter, I append a brief survey of the teachings of Pannenberg and Zizioulas on apostolicity.
2. *The Shepherd of Hermas*, Fr. tr. by R. Joly, § 93; Pseudo-Clement, 2 Cor VIII, 6; see also the inscription of Abercius, line 9 of his epitaph. In the classical patristic period, see also John Chrysostom, *Baptismal Catechesis* I, 44 (ed. A. Wenger, SC 50, p. 131); Augustine, *De symb. ad cat.* 7, 15; *Sermo* 352, 2–8 (seal restored by penance).
3. It is possible to compare the canonical exactness of the rules of the 'apostolic succession' with the care taken for the succession and the authenticity of heredity within the tribe of Judah in the course of history: see the explanation that W. Vischer has given for the sharp practices of the patriarchs to prevent their wives from being taken away from them in *Das Christuszeugnis des Alten Testaments*, I, 6th ed. (Zürich), p. 157, or even the episode of Tamar in Gen 38: see Vischer, *ibid.*, p. 200.
4. This accounts for the fairly frequent quotation (from Augustine onwards) of Ps 44:77 (Vulgate): 'pro patribus tuis nati sunt tibi filii'. See also the chapter on apostolicity in my *L'Eglise une, sainte, catholique et apostolique (Mysterium Salutis*, 15) (Paris, 1970), especially pp. 216ff.
5. W. Kasper, *Jesus the Christ* (Eng. tr.; London and New York, 1976), has, for example, provided a synthesis of this. See also P. J. Rosato, 'Spirit Christology: Ambiguity and Promise', *ThSt* 38 (1977), 423–449.
6. The main texts in the New Testament which form the basis for this section are those relating to the life of Jesus on earth, studied in J. D. G. Dunn, *Jesus and the Spirit. A Study of the Religious and Charismatic Experience of Jesus and the First Christians as Reflected in the New Testament* (London, 1975). For Jesus at Easter and the glorified Jesus, see Rom 1:4; 8:11; 1 Cor 15:45; 1 Pet 3:18; 1 Tim 3:16.
7. For the Spirit as *idem numero* or 'identically the same' in Christ and in us, see above, p. 23, note 19. For the Spirit filling us with love with which God himself loves us, see Volume I, pp. 86–87, for the admirable prayer of William of Saint-Thierry. See also Albert the Great: 'illud autem *unum* quod Pater coelestis habet in Filio naturali (the Word, the Son) et in filio per adoptionem (ourselves) est Spiritus, quia ipse nos diligit Spiritu Sancto et nos eum et nos invicem nos diligimus Spiritu Sancto'; see his *Comm. in Ioan.* 8, 41 (ed. A. Borgnet, XXIV, 360); see also *Comm. in Luc.* q. 35 (Borgnet, XXII, 667).
8. R. Asting, *Die Verkündigung des Wortes im Urchristentum. Dargestellt an den Begriffen 'Wort Gottes', 'Evangelium' und 'Zeugnis'* (Stuttgart, 1939): for 'testimony', see pp. 458–712.
9. See, for example, Gen 31:50 (Asting, *op. cit.*, p. 476); Is 43:9ff.; 44:8, although the active meaning is emphasized here; cf. 55:4 (Asting, pp. 490ff.); Job 16:19.
10. See Asting, *op. cit.*, pp. 597, 601, 607, 626, 671ff., 685.
11. The French *Traduction Œcuménique* prefers: 'The Holy Spirit and we have decided . . .'.

Some scholars believe that the decision attributed to the Spirit was not the one about the decree borne by the apostles, the elders and the brethren, but the initiative concerning Cornelius (see Acts 10:44–47; 15:8).

12. See J. D. G. Dunn, *op. cit.* (note 6), pp. 347ff., who provides references to earlier studies.

13. Jn 14:16ff., 26; 16:13ff. See J. Michl, 'Der Geist als Garant des rechten Lebens', *Vom Wort des Lebens. Festschrift M. Meinertz*, ed. N. Adler (Münster, 1951), p. 147; J. J. von Allmen, 'L'Esprit de vérité vous conduira dans toute la vérité', O. Rousseau *et al.*, *L'Infaillibilité de l'Eglise. Journées œcuméniques de Chevetogne, 25–29 September 1961* (Chevetogne, 1963), pp. 13–26.

14. Irenaeus, *Adv, haer.* III, 4, 2 (*PG* 7, 855; ed. W. W. Harvey, II, 15; *SC* 211, p. 47).

15. Irenaeus, *Dem.* 41 (*SC* 62, p. 96).

16. Hippolytus, *Philosophoumena* I, praef. 6.

17. Ignatius of Antioch, *Smyrn.* VIII and IX, 1.

18. Irenaeus, *Adv. haer.* IV, 26, 2 (*PG* 7, 1053; Harvey, II, 236; *SC* 100, p. 719). The meaning of this *charisma veritatis certum* has been widely disputed. There have been three main interpretations: (1) a grace of infallibility or at least of orthodoxy, received at ordination with the succession: see L. Ligier, 'Le ch. ver. cer. des évêques. Ses attaches liturgiques, patristiques et bibliques', *L'homme devant Dieu. Mélanges H. de Lubac* (Paris, 1964), I, pp. 247–268. In favour of this interpretation, there are its harmony with a much wider context and the connection that it appears to make between consecration and the grace that is the effect of that consecration. More recently, J. D. Quinn has based a similar interpretation on a study of the Latin text, which is the only one that we have: *ThSt*, 39 (1978), 520–525. There are, however, certain objections to this interpretation: (a) there is no parallel to this formal statement; (b) it presupposes a kind of automatism which is excluded by other texts: see *Adv. haer.* III, 3, 1; IV, 26, 5; (c) Irenaeus' theology of Tradition calls for an objective meaning of *veritas*. (2) Several scholars, such as D. van den Eynde (*Normes de l'enseignement* (1933), p. 187) and H. von Campenhausen, have suggested that *charisma veritatis* indicates the spiritual gift of truth, in other words, Tradition in the objective sense. (3) A study of the ways in which Irenaeus used the word *charisma* and in which it was used after him has led some scholars to understand it as personal spiritual gifts. According to E. Flesseman-van Leer, *Tradition and Scripture in the Early Church* (Assen, 1954), pp. 119–122; R. P. C. Hanson, *Tradition in the Early Church* (London 1962), p. 159, and others, the meaning is: obey the presbyters whom *God* has called to the episcopate, which was and is obvious from the fact that their consecration has been preceded and accompanied by spiritual gifts, and especially the gift of unfailing faithfulness to the Tradition of the apostles: cf. *Adv. haer.* IV, 26, 5.

19. I have already cited the important text of Irenaeus, *Adv. haer.* III, 24, 1 (*SC* 211, p. 473). Thomas Aquinas appealed to Jn 16:13 to support his affirmation that the Church cannot err in matters of faith; see *ST* IIa IIae, q. 1, a. 9; *Quodl.* IX, 16. For this theme in Scholastic theology generally, see my *L'Eglise de S. Augustin à l'époque moderne* (Paris, 1970), pp. 244, 232. Statements by theologians writing during the second half of the sixteenth century on the Holy Spirit dwelling in and animating the Church have been brought together by M. Midali, *Corpus Christi mysticum apud D. Bañez eiusque fontes (Anal. Greg., 116)* (Rome, 1962), pp. 153–188. See also the Dogmatic Constitution on the Church, *Lumen Gentium*, 12; the Constitution on the Church in the Modern World, *Gaudium et spes*, 11; 43, 6, etc.

20. I quoted a number of statements made at ecumenical councils in my *Tradition and Traditions* (Eng. tr.; London and New York, 1966), Part Two, pp. 346–347; Part One, p. 172, note 3: Trent. See also H. du Manoir, 'Le symbole de Nicée au concile d'Ephèse', *Greg*, 12 (1931), 126–129. For patristic texts, see John Chrysostom, *Adv. Iud.* 3, 3 (*PG* 49, 865); Cyril of Alexandria, *Ep.* 1 (*PG* 77, 16B); 17 (*PG* 77, 108C-D)); 53 (*PG* 77, 292D-293A); Celestine I, letter to the Council of Ephesus (Mansi IV, 1283-84; *PL* 50, 505–506); Leo the Great, letter on Chalcedon, *Ep.* 103 (*PL* 54, 988–989) and on Nicaea,

Ep. 104, 3 (*PL* 54, 995–96) and 106, 2 (*PL* 54, 1003–04); Fulgentius, *Ep.* 6, 3 (*PL* 67, 923); Pope Vigilius, *Ep.* 15 (*PL* 69, 56); *De tribus cap.* (*PL* 69, 72), etc.

21. See Volume I, pp. 151ff. See also the Dogmatic Constitution on the Church, *Lumen Gentium*, 21, 2; 24; Decree on the Bishops' Pastoral Office, *Christus Dominus*, 2, 2; K. Hardt, *Die Unsichtbare Regierung der Kirche* (Würzburg, 1956).
22. L. Merklen, 'La continuité pontificale', *Doc. cath.*, 739 (3 March 1935), 515–530. There are many examples given.
23. See Acts 2:41, 47; 5:14; 11:24; 17:4. The Fathers often described the Church as a kind of expansion or enlargement from the apostles; see the texts and references in my book, *op. cit.* (note 4), p. 188.
24. Protestant theologians often speak about a wider apostolic succession applying to all believers: see, for example, the report of the European Section of the Faith and Order Commission of the World Council of Churches in preparation for the Montreal Conference and the report of that Conference, in *Verbum Caro*, 67 (1963), 301; 69 (1964), 1–29. Thomas Aquinas also spoke of oral traditions kept 'in observatione Ecclesiae per successionem fidelium': see *ST* IIIa, q. 25, a. 3, ad 4. Luther wrote 'alia et alia est ecclesia et tamen semper eadem in successionem fidelium': *WA*, 4, 169[30]. Jean Guitton also recorded these words of Pope Paul VI: 'The layman is, like the bishop, a successor of the Apostles': *The Pope Speaks* (Eng. tr.; London, 1968), p. 253.
25. In the early Church, pastors were appointed 'with the consent of the whole Church': see Clement of Rome, 1 Cor XLIV, 3; *Didache* XV, 1. See also H. Legrand, 'Theology and the Election of Bishops in the Early Church', *Concilium*, 7 (September 1972), 31–42; J. Remmers, 'Apostolic Succession: an Attribute of the Whole Church', *Concilium*, 4, no. 4 (1968), 20–27; my 'Apostolicité de ministère et apostolicité de doctrine' (first pub. 1967; later repr. in *Ministères et Communion ecclésiale* (Paris, 1971), pp. 51–94); H. Küng, *The Church* (London, 1967), pp. 355ff.
26. J. de Bacciochi, 'Les sacrements, actes libres du Seigneur', *NRT*, 73 (1951), 681–706. For the early Church, see my *Ecclésiologie du Haut Moyen Age* (Paris, 1968), pp. 113–116.
27. W. Kasper, *An Introduction to Christian Faith* (London, 1980), pp. 138–139.
28. B.-D. Dupuy, 'Le magistère de l'Eglise, service de la parole', *L'Infaillibilité de l'Eglise, op. cit.* (note 13), 53–98.
29. See my two notes, published in *RSPT*, 60 (1976), 85–112.
30. See my articles 'Infaillibilité et indéfectibilité', *ibid.*, 54 (1970), 601–618, repr. in *Ministères et Communion ecclésiale* (Paris, 1971), pp. 141–165; and 'Après *Infaillible?* de Hans Küng: bilans et perspectives', *RSPT*, 58 (1974), 243–252. See also Dogmatic Constitution on the Church, *Lumen Gentium*, 39, where the Church is said to be '*indefectibiliter* sancta'.
31. See J. J. von Allmen, *op. cit.* (note 13); J. Bosc, 'L'attitude des Eglises réformées concernant l'Infaillibilité de l'Eglise', *ibid.*, pp. 211–222, with quotations: the Scottish Confession of Faith and C. XVI of Calvin's *Institutes*, IV, 8, 13; L. Ott, who was K. Barth's successor at Basle, *Die Lehre des I. Vatikanischen Konzils. Ein evangelischer Kommentar* (Basle, 1963), pp. 161–172; the comments of several American Lutherans, *Irénikon*, 51 (1978), 251.
32. E. Lanne, 'Le Mystère de l'Eglise et de son unité', *ibid.*, 46 (1973), 298–342, compared the Vatican declaration *Mysterium Ecclesiae* of 24 June 1973 with the Encyclical of the Orthodox bishops of the United States, published at the end of March 1973. Both documents have a similar content, but the Orthodox text places the Church's magisterium and its charism of truth within a context of doxology and holy life to a far greater extent that the Roman document does.

APPENDIX
TWO THEOLOGIES OF APOSTOLICITY
W. Pannenberg and J. D. Zizioulas

W. Pannenberg, 'Apostolizität und Katholizität der Kirche in der Perspektive der Eschatologie', *Theologische Literaturzeitung*, 94 (1965), 97–112. The text of this article has also been published in R. Groscurth (ed.), *Katholizität und Apostolizität*, supplement to *Kerygma und Dogma*, 2 (Göttingen, 1971); and a French translation in *Istina*, 14 (1969), 154–170.

The apostles are not, Pannenberg stresses, simply witnesses. They are also men who have been sent out on a mission for the unfolding of history until the eschatological era and also with that era in view. Faithfulness to the testimony is therefore not only directed back into the past – it is also orientated towards the future eschatological era and consequently towards a fulfilment in the whole of history. Fundamentally, apostolicity and dynamic catholicity are the same. This is more or less my position. Pannenberg, however, has connected this with his idea of revelation as history (see his *Revelation as History* (Eng. tr.; London, 1979). God, in other words, reveals himself in history. That is, as we have seen in the case of the Church's catholicity, fairly obvious, but it is a significant step forward in Protestant theology, in that Pannenberg has gone beyond *Scriptura sola* and a too narrow positivism of scriptural revelation.

J. D. Zizioulas, 'La continuité avec les origines apostoliques dans la conscience théologique des Eglises orthodoxes', *Istina*, 19 (1974), 65–94.

According to Zizioulas, the task of the Christian mystery and the meaning of apostolicity are to realize the 'one and the many'. This can be conceived in accordance with two patterns – a historical and an eschatological pattern.

According to the historical pattern, the apostles were sent and therefore scattered in the world in order to spread the gospel there. This pattern is found in the texts of Clement of Rome. The apostles are thus taken individually. Their succession is historical and ensures a reference to an event in the distant past. This succession is also conceived juridically.[1]

According to the eschatological pattern, the apostles are gathered around the Lord and call the scattered people together to one place (*epi to auto*). This 'one place' (*epi to auto*) is expressed on earth in the celebration of the Eucharist (1 Cor 11:18), which points to the eschatological assembly (see the *Didache* and Ignatius of Antioch). Continuity is therefore conceived not as a continuity of historical transmission, but as a presence. Zizioulas believes that this presence providing continuity is

50

founded on the Spirit, who is the eschatological Gift, and in a pneumatological constitution of Christ and Christology that enables us to be included in him and therefore united as a body with him.

This continuity of presence takes the historical continuity of transmission and memory to a deeper level, and Zizioulas finds this realized in the eucharistic epiclesis which follows the account or the anamnesis. He therefore speaks of the epicletic nature of the life of the Church, by virtue of which it aspires to be what it is already and has to receive this at the present time from God. This present reception is brought about by the Holy Spirit.

Zizioulas suggests that there is another aspect, referring to ordination and the consecration of bishops. This is, in his opinion, not simply a historical (and juridical) transmission of apostolicity which is individual in nature (the logic of the 'one sent' or šāliāḥ), but an insertion into the eschatological and eucharistic community. The same applies to the *charisma veritatis certum* conferred at the consecration of a bishop. That is connected with the entire community. Only those bishops – but all those bishops – who are pastors of an *ecclesia* take part in a council of the Church.

Zizioulas does not think that only one of these patterns should be realized at the expense of the other. In the Eucharist, the epiclesis does not make the historical account unnecessary. How would it be possible for the Spirit to be present if there were not the historical reality of the 'economy'? What would be present, or be being actualized? The Fathers called what related to the consummation or the 'mystery' of Christ 'mystical', but they also stressed the fact that the Christ of the 'economy' was involved, not a heavenly being who had not been given in the economy.[2] The Omega truly comes from the Alpha. I would, however, stress this more than Zizioulas does. To be sure, he follows his own perception, which is very rich and profound, and I am fundamentally in agreement with it. Because of the originality of his approach, I have tried to present it as it stands. I reached my own position, however, before reading his article, which in fact owes a great deal to studies made before my own. I hope to have conveyed an idea of the enrichment, possibly the corrections, that an Orthodox insight can bring to our Western thought, however valuable and convincing this may be.

NOTES

1. This idea is effectively in accordance with the way in which the mediaeval theologians thought of the apostles as scattered and at the head of provinces in which they had founded particular churches. See my study, 'Notes sur le destin de l'idée de collégialité épiscopale en Occident au Moyen Age (VIIᵉ–XVIᵉ siècles)', *La Collégialité épiscopale. Histoire et Théologie (Unam Sanctam*, 52) (Paris, 1965), pp. 99–129, especially pp. 115ff. Since writing that article, I have enlarged my documentation.
2. See L. Bouyer, 'Mystique', *VS* (Suppl) (May 1949), 3–23.

5

THE SPIRIT IS THE PRINCIPLE
OF THE CHURCH'S HOLINESS

I was tempted to entitle this chapter 'the principle of holiness *in* the Church', but that would have pointed more to the sanctification of persons and this is a question that I shall consider in Part Two of this volume. In this chapter, I shall deal with the Church as such.

I must begin by repeating that the properties of the Church are not to be seen in isolation. They interpenetrate each other. The Church's oneness is holy. It is different from the phenomenon described by sociologists and is to be found at the level of faith. The Church's apostolicity is also holy. It is the continuity of a mission and a communion which begin in God. Finally, the catholicity of the Church is holy and different from, for example, a multi-national or world-wide expansion.

Nothing is said about a holy Church in the New Testament. The texts that come closest to this theme are Eph 5:26 and 27, in which the Church is seen as the Bride of Christ, and the reference to God's holy temple (1 Cor 3:16ff.). The members of the Church are, however, called 'saints' (see, for example, Rom 12:13; 1 Cor 1:2; 6:1, 2; 14:33; Phil 1:1; 4:21, 22; Col 1:1, 4; Eph 4:12; Acts 9:13, 32, 41; 26:10, 18; Rev 13:7), a 'holy priesthood' and a 'holy nation' (1 Pet 2:5, 9) and a 'holy temple' (Eph 2:21). The adjective 'holy' is the first that was attributed to the Church, although it was not used very frequently until Hippolytus expressed the third baptismal question in the following way: 'Do you believe in the Holy Spirit in the holy Church for the resurrection of the flesh?'[1] This takes us back to the turn of the second and third centuries A.D.

The Church, then, is a bride and a temple, but strictly speaking every believing soul is a bride, and every believer is a temple; this is in the New Testament[2] and is proclaimed again and again by the Fathers. At least since Origen, whose influence was very great, but even before him – Hippolytus, for example—the Fathers and other early authors said that 'every soul is the Church'.[3] Every soul is a bride and every soul is a temple. The liturgy passed from one to the other and from the singular to the plural, using the singular first.[4] For the earliest Christian writers, the Church was the 'we' of Christians.[5]

The Church as the Temple

In his commentary on the 'holy catholic Church' in the Creed, Thomas Aquinas said: 'The Church is the same as an assembly (*congregatio*) and "holy Church" must therefore be the same as an "assembly of believers" and each Christian is a member of the Church itself'. He then goes on to explain this attribute of holiness and says:

The Church of Christ is holy. The temple of God is holy and that temple is you (1 Cor 3:17). Hence the words *sanctam Ecclesiam*. The believers of that assembly (*congregatio*) are made holy in four ways. In the first place, just as a church is, at the time of its consecration, materially washed, so too are the believers washed by the blood of Christ: Rev 1:5: 'he loved us and washed us from our sins in his blood'; and Heb 13:12: 'Jesus, in order to sanctify the people through his own blood'. . . . In the second place, by an anointing: just as the Church is anointed, so too are the believers anointed in order to be consecrated by a spiritual anointing. Otherwise, they would not be 'Christians', since 'Christ' means the 'Anointed One'. This anointing is the grace of the Holy Spirit: 2 Cor 1:21: 'he who has anointed us is God'; 1 Cor 6:11: 'You were sanctified in the name of the Lord Jesus Christ (and by the Spirit of our God)'. In the third place, by the indwelling of the Trinity, since where God dwells, that place is holy: Gen 28:17: 'Truly, this place is holy!'; and Ps 93:5: 'holiness befits thy house, O Lord'. In the fourth place, because God is invoked; Jer 14:9: 'Thou, O Lord, art in the midst of us and thy name is invoked over us'. We must therefore take care, since we are sanctified in this way, that we do not, though sin, defile our soul, which is God's temple; as the Apostle says, 1 Cor 3: 'If anyone destroys God's temple, God will destroy him'.[6]

In connection with the theme of the Church as the holy temple, Thomas is not dealing with this idea as such, but simply quotes 1 Cor 3:16–17. He does not quote other New Testament texts, such as Jn 2:19–22, in which the Body of Christ, the Church, is called the temple or house in which spiritual worship is given to God. Two of the most important texts are:

Through him (Christ in his suffering) we both have access *in one Spirit* to the Father. So, then, you are no longer strangers and sojourners, but you are *fellow-citizens with the saints* and members of the household of God, built upon the foundation of the apostles and prophets, Christ Jesus himself being the corner-stone in whom the whole structure is joined together and grows into *a holy temple in the Lord;* in whom you are also built up into it for *a dwelling-place of God in the Spirit* (Eph 2:18–22).

Like living stones be yourselves built into a spiritual house, to be a holy priest-hood, to offer spiritual sacrifices acceptable to God through Jesus Christ (1 Pet 2:5).

In these texts, what is stressed is spiritual worship and above all the fact that we have access to the Father: 'Our fellowship with the Father' (1 Jn 1:3). Jesus himself said: 'The hour is coming, and now is, when the true worshippers will worship the Father in spirit and truth. . . . God is spirit and those who worship him must worship in spirit and truth' (Jn 4:23–24). To say that God is spirit is not so much a statement about his nature as about the truth of our religious relationship. The fact that Christian worship must be spiritual does not mean that it cannot be sensible, corporeal: it means that it must proceed from faith and express the theologal reality of faith, hope and charity.[7] That is the work of the Holy Spirit (see Phil 3:3; Jude 20). It is only through the Spirit that it is possible to profess that 'Jesus is Lord' (1 Cor 12:3). The anointing, which is the effect and the mark of the Spirit in us, is an anointing of faith.[8] It is therefore a question of the originality and the truth of *Christian* worship. It is the act in which the Church is most perfectly itself. The Church is the holy temple in which, through the strength of the living water that is the Holy Spirit, faith is celebrated in baptism and love or *agapē* is celebrated in the Eucharist.[9] How beautiful the Church's liturgy is, filling time and space with praise of God the creator and saviour— to the Father through the Son, in the Spirit. When our praise ceases here, it begins a little further to the west, as the sun rises. It goes around the world without interruption, 'uniting all things in him, the Christ, . . . in whom you also, who have heard the word of truth, the gospel of your salvation, and have believed in him, were sealed with the promised Holy Spirit, which is the guarantee of our inheritance until we acquire possession of it, to the praise of his glory' (Eph 1:10, 13).

Temple and house suggest the idea of dwelling or habitation. The New Testament speaks of an indwelling, not simply of 'God', that is, the Father and the Son, but explicitly of the Spirit (Jn 14:15–17; 1 Cor 3:16–17; 6:19; 1 Jn 4:12–13). The Scholastic theologians, and Thomas Aquinas especially, also affirmed this,[10] although certain difficulties are encountered in the way in which Thomists have attempted to explain this indwelling.[11] It is ultimately a question of a substantial indwelling, on the basis of supernatural faith and love, of God in his Tri-unity, as the term or object of knowledge and love. This applies quite well to individual persons,[12] but how can it be applied to the Church as such?

The difficulty does not really exist. In the first place, as Thomas himself was careful to point out, the Church is the assembly of believers. If each soul is the Church, then the latter is even more clearly characterized as the house of God in which the believers are present as 'living stones' (Eph 2:20–22; 1 Pet 2:5). And if it is on the basis of charity that God (the Spirit) dwells fully, then only the Church, as the Body of Christ, is certain always to have a faith that is fashioned by charity,[13] since every individual person is able to fail in this. It was to the Church that the promises were made, and by 'Church' what is meant is not simply the assembled believers or what H. de Lubac called the *ecclesia congregata*, but also the *ecclesia congregans*, the essential elements of the apostolic institution, that is, its function and its teaching ministry together with its sacraments. Is this not the fundamental meaning of the promises contained in Mt 16:18–19; 28:19–20, taken together with

Jn 14:16? The Church, which is the house of the living God, is the sacrament of salvation for mankind. It is not simply liturgy offered to God, but also a sign of God's love for men and of his kingdom. Even the structures that are also known as 'churches' have this part to play in our towns and villages.

The Church as the Bride

Let me begin by quoting the most important New Testament texts that are in some way related to the theme of the Church as the bride. In passing, it should also be pointed out that this theme also occurs in the Old Testament.[14]

> I betrothed you to Christ to present you as a pure bride to her one husband (2 Cor 11:2).

> Husbands, love your wives, as Christ loved the Church and gave himself up for her, that he might sanctify her, having cleansed her by the washing of water with the word, that he might present the church to himself in splendour, without spot or wrinkle or any such thing, that she might be holy without blemish. . . . No man ever hates his own flesh, but nourishes it and cherishes it, as Christ does the Church, because we are members of his body. For this reason, a man shall leave his father and mother and be joined to his wife and the two shall become one flesh (Eph 5:25–27, 29–31).

> He saved us, not because of deeds done by us in righteousness, but in virtue of his own mercy, by the washing of regeneration and renewal in the Holy Spirit, which he poured out upon us richly through Jesus Christ our Saviour, so that we might be justified by his grace and become heir in hope of eternal life (Tit 3:5–7).

This last text does not refer to a bride or bridegroom, but it completes and explains what Ephesians contains implicitly, namely that the Spirit plays a part in baptismal purification and regeneration, and it also refers explicitly to an eschatological fulfilment.

The Fathers of the Church frequently contemplated the mystery of the wedding between Christ and the Church (mankind), and this theme was often celebrated in the liturgy.[15] Tradition has the task of gathering these data of revelation, harmonizing them and deepening Christian understanding of them. I have studied that Tradition with great love. This is how it sees the mystery of that wedding. In the first place, it sees it as an election of grace, by means of a choice and an appeal and by means of an anticipatory love. The Word, the Son, decided to marry human nature through his incarnation. This aspect of election is stressed by the Fathers together with the aspect of purification.[16] Christ assumed soiled human nature and purified it, by making it his betrothed or bride. He based this purification on his baptism, which is the sacramental foundation of our baptism, and on his death on the cross. Both these realities communicate his Spirit to the Church, the new Eve. On the basis of baptism and the gift of the Spirit in the first place, and secondly on the basis of the Eucharist, in which Jesus nourishes the Church with his own spiritualized body, the Church as the bride becomes the Body of Christ and with him forms, spiritually and mysteriously (or mystically), 'one flesh'. This aspect of mystery, which is also essentially Pauline (see P. Andriessen, note 14 below), was developed by Augustine especially and, some forty years ago, Claude Chavasse gave special attention to it. In the seventeenth century, Bossuet also wrote splendidly about the complementary nature of the two terms—bride and body.[17]

The wedding has been celebrated and the Church is the bride, but she is not yet the perfectly pure bride inaugurated by baptism. She is tempted, in her sinful members, to join other bridegrooms (see 1 Cor 6:15ff.). The union that should be consummated in one spirit (or Spirit) is still imperfect. The Church must also experience an Easter event of death and resurrection in the power of the Spirit. Her wedding will only be perfect eschatologically. She aspires to that perfection. She only possesses the first-fruits of the Spirit, as earnest-money. His groaning in us towards the end of God's plan (Rom 8:26–30) also aspires to that consummation. This ultimate revelation is wonderfully expressed in the Apocalypse:

> The Lord our God the Almighty reigns! Let us rejoice and exult and give him the glory, for the marriage of the Lamb has come and his Bride has made herself ready; it was granted her to be clothed with fine linen, bright and pure, for the linen is the righteous deeds of the saints (Rev 19:6–8).

> And I saw the holy city, new Jerusalem, coming down out of heaven from God, prepared as a bride adorned for her husband (Rev 21:2).

> The Spirit and the Bride say: 'Come!' (Rev 22:17).

According to the Bible, the truth of all things is found at the end, but it is envisaged at the beginning. What is seen as fulfilled in the last chapters of the last book in this final 'unveiling' or 'Apocalypse' was already in mind in the first chapters of the first book, the book of 'beginnings' or 'Genesis':

> In the beginning . . . the Spirit of God moved over the face of the waters. . . . And God said, 'Let us make man in our image, after our likeness'. . . . So God created man in his own image . . . male and female he created them. . . . God said, 'It is not good that man should be alone; I will make him a helper fit for him'. . . . So the Lord God caused a deep sleep to fall upon the man . . . and the rib which the Lord God had taken from the man he made into a woman and brought her to the man. . . . Therefore a man leaves his father and his mother and cleaves to his wife and they become one flesh (Gen 1:1; 1:26, 27; 2:18, 21–24).

From the time of Tertullian onwards at least, the Fathers of the Church and the early Christian writers have been unanimous in seeing this as a prophetic announcement of the wedding between Christ, the new Adam, and the Church, the new Eve, when, from the pierced side of Jesus, fallen into the deep sleep of death, came water and blood, the sacraments, baptism and the Eucharist, which built up the Church: the marriage of the Cross and the marriage of the Lamb![18]

The Struggles of the Holy Church of Sinners

We are living between Genesis and the Apocalypse, subject to the rule of the Spirit, who is given to us now (only) as *arrha* or earnest-money or as first-fruits. There is always a struggle in our personal lives between the Spirit and the flesh, but the Church as such is also involved in this struggle because it is so carnal. Do I need to stress this? Christians are conscious of the weight of the flesh in the Church, but the Church does not admit it often enough.[19] People's confidence is inhibited by the mass of historical faults and the inadequacies of the Church. The Church, the bride of Christ who is 'gentle and lowly in heart' (Mt 11:29), has often been proud and hard in history. As the disciple of the Son of man who had 'nowhere to lay his head' (Mt 8:20), the Church has often sought a comfortable settled life and wealth. The Church's soul is the Holy Spirit, the 'Unknown One beyond the Word', but it has often misinterpreted the signs of the times and has remained attached to formal practices and to fixed structures of power. Paul stressed that Christians are ministers, not of the letter of the law, but of the Spirit (2 Cor 3:6). That is our task, but we hardly dare to confess it, because we know how many times we have failed in it.

But why should we go on listing these grievances? Surely we should engage, as Jacques Leclercq said, in a 'struggle for the spirit of Christ in the Church',[20] so that the Church, as the messianic people of God, may respond fully to what Bernard called *quod tempus requirit*—the appeals and demands of history, a history that is completed by the kingdom of God. Purity and fullness are the two great themes which call for and give rise, in the Church, to reforms and new creations. They point to a dividing line that is sometimes dramatic, but always open, between ideal and reality, and to what J. B. Metz has called an inexhaustible 'eschatological reserve'.

We possess the Spirit only as *arrha*, earnest-money, or as first-fruits, but he is always the 'Promised One'.[21] He is always ahead of us and calls us, as Mgr Ignatius Hazim so rightly said. He draws us on towards the eschatological inheritance of the kingdom of God. Instead of the words: 'Thy kingdom come' in Lk 11:2, several manuscripts have: 'May thy Spirit come upon us and purify us'. This reading was preferred by some of the Church Fathers.[22] The Spirit thus furthers the cause of the gospel. He encourages great initiatives to renew the Church, missions, the emergence of new religious orders, great works of the mind and heart. He inspires necessary reforms and prevents them from becoming merely external arrangements, so that they are able to lead to a new life according to the spirit of Jesus.

We can 'grieve' the Spirit (Eph 4:30) or 'quench' him (1 Thess 5:19). We can even 'resist' him (Acts 7:51). On the other hand, we can also listen to the

Spirit and co-operate with him so that we can 'reflect the glory of the Lord' and be 'changed into his likeness', by the Lord 'who is the Spirit' (2 Cor 3:18). The Church, then, is a sign of the presence of God. It is a 'hagiophany', revealing the reality and the presence of another world, an anticipation of the kingdom in which God will be 'everything to everyone' (1 Cor 15:28). A few years ago, Malcolm Muggeridge was given the task of preparing a television programme on Mother Teresa of Calcutta for the BBC. He expected it to be a pathetic failure, but it excited world-wide interest. Here is his account of this revelation of the power of God in the Spirit:

> Discussions are endlessly taking place about how to use a mass medium like television for Christian purposes, and all manner of devices are tried, from dialogues with learned atheists and humanists to pop versions of the psalms and psychedelic romps. Here was the answer. Just get on the screen a face shining and overflowing with Christian love; someone for whom the world is nothing and the service of Christ everything; someone reborn out of servitude to the ego and the flesh and into the glorious liberty of the children of God. . . . It might seem surprising, on the face of it, that an obscure nun of Albanian origins, very nervous—as was clearly apparent—in front of the camera, somewhat halting in speech, should reach English viewers on a Sunday evening as no professional Christian apologist, bishop or archbishop, moderator or knockabout progressive dog-collared demonstrator ever has. . . . The message . . . was brought . . . 'in demonstration of the Spirit and of power; that your faith should not stand in the wisdom of men, but in the power of God'.[23]

It is the Holy Spirit who causes this radiation of holiness. Even the most intelligent addresses do not produce a spiritual harvest in the world. Such a crop is produced by souls who are hidden in God, who are totally abandoned and lost to the world and who give themselves unconditionally to God: souls such as Seraphim of Sarov or Charles de Foucauld. The facts are evident: it is lives like these that change the lives of others, because they radiate holiness.

Dare I move on from this brief discussion of the revelation of God's holiness in the lives of Christian believers to mention a hagiophany in and through beauty? According to Irenaeus, Athanasius, Cyril of Alexandria and other Church Fathers, the incarnate Word reveals the invisible Father and the Spirit reveals the Word, Christ. Going further, we can say that the saints reveal the Spirit, that is to say, they reveal God as gift, love, communication and communion. The Christian iconography of the East and the West has frequently expressed this radiation in the apostles and the holy men and women of the Church (see, for example, F. Ostlender's article, cited below, note 24). Many monuments and church buildings reveal the presence of the Spirit—one has only to think of Chartres Cathedral or Le Thoronet, for example. Singing is also an expression of the Spirit in beauty. The Spirit is made audible as sweetness and harmony in the spiritual flight of Gregorian

58

chant, the blending of voices in the intonation of the psalms, the polyphony of the Orthodox liturgies and even in the spontaneous singing at meetings of the Renewal movement. All this is surely 'peace and joy in the Holy Spirit' (Rom 14:17).

The Communion of Saints[24]

This term, which has enjoyed great favour among Catholics, comes from the so-called 'Apostles' Creed', a document of the Western Church. It is not until a little before 400 that the presence of this formula is attested. Contrary to what some scholars believe,[25] it is not in apposition to the formula *sanctam Ecclesiam* and explaining its meaning.[26]

With what or with whom do we claim to be united, when we profess our faith, and in what or in whom are we participating? Does the word *sanctorum* refer to a neuter plural, the *sancta*, or to a masculine, the *sancti* (not forgetting the *sanctae*)? The earliest explanations favour the saints, that is, the community of the blessed anticipated in the Catholic Church. This was the interpretation of Niceta of Remesiana; it was given a more precise definition later in the fifth century by Faustus of Riez, who applied it to the martyrs. Later still, and especially in the Middle Ages, theologians spoke of a participation in holy things (*sancta*), in other words, the sacraments, and above all the Eucharist.[27] In the Niceno-Constantinopolitan Creed, baptism is mentioned at the point where the so-called Apostles' Creed speaks of the communion of saints. In reality, however—and the biblical Greek word *koinōnia*, translated by the Latin *communio*, requires us to see the matter in this light—it means the participation in the good things of the community of salvation together with the other members of that community.

How can this participation be applied and extended? In order to answer this question, we have to ask another: What is the principle of this participation? All those who have written about this matter have replied: charity. This is certainly the divine principle of participation, 'because God's love has been poured into our hearts through the Holy Spirit which has been given to us' (Rom 5:5). All authors agree that this is the love by which God loves himself. John of the Cross said, for example: 'The soul loves God not through itself, but through God himself, because it loves in this way through the Holy Spirit, as the Father and the Son love each other and according to what the Son himself says in the gospel of John: "that the love with which thou hast loved me may be in them, and I in them" (Jn 17:26)'.[28] If this love, which is uncreated grace, is really to be our own, it must produce in us an effect or a created grace, namely charity. It is to that charity that Thomas Aquinas, following a unanimous tradition, attached that unity through which a communication of spiritual good things took place between believers. What is in one member of the community is there for the benefit of another member, just as the health of one member benefits the health of the

whole body: 'propter communicantiam in radice operis, quae est charitas'—
'by virtue of the communication of everyone with everyone else, through the
root of their actions, charity'.[29]

Because the principles of the Church's unity are so real and firmly based, it
is possible for us, in Karl Rahner's magnificent phrase, to believe beyond this
world and to love as far as God's world, even with and into his heart. That is
why the communion of saints extends as far as the blessed in heaven and
includes our own dead who have passed beyond the veil that hides them
from our sight.

Thomas—although he, like most Scholastic theologians, sometimes gives
the impression of concentrating on physical things—can be taken as a sure
guide here. His true attitude is clear from the way in which he establishes a
foundation for merit in the communion of saints. He takes as his principal
text the promise made by Jesus to the Samaritan woman: 'The water that I
shall give him will become in him a spring of water welling up to eternal life'
(Jn 4:14).[30] Only God, through the Spirit who is what is grace and gift in him,
is able to be, in us, the radical principle of that eternal life that is the
communication of his own life. By receiving us as his sons, he receives
himself, having given himself to us and having dwelt in us. As we have
already seen, so that this may really be our own, he brings it about by a gift
that we call grace or charity.

This gift, with its radical principle, the Holy Spirit, is present in all the
members of the communicational Body of Christ and therefore allows an
intercommunication of spiritual energy to take place between them. In this
context, Thomas declares: 'Not only are the merits of the passion and the life
of Christ communicated to us, but also all the good that the saints have done
is communicated to those who live in charity, since all are one: "I am a
companion (= participant) of all who fear thee" (Ps 119:63). The one who
lives in charity is therefore the participant of all the good that is done in the
world.'[31]

As a man of the Middle Ages, Thomas insists on the satisfaction that can
be offered for another person, and even stresses the importance of
indulgences.[32] Prayer for the departed is based, he claims, on the fact that
'death . . . cannot separate us from the love of God in Christ Jesus our Lord'
(Rom 8:38–39), and he bases the effectiveness of that prayer on the unity of
charity.[33] That unity makes a bond between the Church on earth and the
Church beyond the veil. The liturgy of the Church expresses the conviction
that these two parts of the same people of God are united in praise and
concelebrate the same mystery, above all in the Eucharist. We enter into the
holy action of the Eucharist only in unity with the angels and the blessed who
acclaim that God is three times holy. Even more importantly, our sovereign
celebrant is Jesus Christ himself, our High Priest (Heb 8:2), and we call on
the Spirit to concelebrate with us. 'May the Lord Jesus and the Holy Spirit
speak in us and may he sing in hymns through us'—these words are taken

from the early anaphora of Serapion.[34] It is the supreme realization here on earth of the communion of the saints, but the holiness of men living in the Spirit also contributes to it.[35] We are, in Christ and as members of his Body, of profit and value to each other (see 1 Pet 4:10). Thomas even applies this pneumatological theology of the communion of saints to the baptism of babies. It is true, he claims, that they do not personally possess faith, but the faith of the whole Church is of profit to them, because that Church lives, through the activity of the Holy Spirit, in the unity and the communion of spiritual good things.[36] What, then, should we not dare to believe and profess if the Holy Spirit, personally and identically the same, is in God, in Christ, in his Body and in all the members of that Body?

NOTES

1. See P. Nautin, *Je crois à l'Esprit Saint dans la sainte Eglise pour la Résurrection de la chair. Etude sur l'histoire et la théologie du Symbole (Unam Sanctam*, 17) (Paris, 1947).

2. The soul as bride: 2 Cor 11:2; the soul as temple: 1 Cor 3:16ff.; 6:19; 2 Cor 6:16. See also 2 Tim 1:14.

3. This was a very common theme; see the texts in H. de Lubac, *Catholicisme (Unam Sanctam*, 3) (Paris, 1938), especially pp. 151ff.; C. Chavasse, *The Bride of Christ* (see below, note 15); E. Dassmann, 'Ecclesia vel anima. Die Kirche und ihre Glieder in der Hoheliederklärung bei Hippolyt, Origenes und Ambrosius von Mailand', *RomQuart*, 61 (1966), 121–144.

4. There are many examples of this in the Hispano-Visigothic liturgy; see R. Schulte, *Die Messe als Opfer der Kirche* (Münster, 1959), pp. 71, 72, 75; see also Peter Damian's small but profound treatise, *Dominus vobiscum*, which appeared in partial Fr. tr. in *M-D*, 21 (1950–51), 174–181.

5. K. Delahaye, *Ecclesia Mater chez les Pères des trois premiers siècles (Unam Sanctam*, 46) (Paris, 1964).

6. Thomas Aquinas, *Collationes de 'Credo in Deum'*, Lent 1273, art. IX (*Opera*, Parma ed., XVI, pp. 147–148).

7. In accordance with the New Testament and in the tradition of Augustine: *Ench.* 3, Thomas defined worship in general as a *protestatio fidei* and saw external worship as the expression of the inward worship of the three theologal virtues: see *ST* Ia IIae, q. 99, a. 3 and 4; IIa IIae, q. 93, a. 2; q. 101, a. 3, ad 2. Also in the Augustinian tradition, Hugh of Saint-Victor and William of Auxerre saw the sacraments as sacraments of faith: see J. Gaillard, *RThom*, 59 (1959), 5–31, 270–309, 664–703; L. Vilette, *Foi et sacrements*, 2 vols (Paris, 1959 and 1964).

8. 2 Cor 1:21–22; 1 Jn 2:20, 27. See I. de la Potterie, 'L'onction du chrétien par la foi', *Bib*, 40 (1959), 12–69, repr. in *La vie selon l'Esprit, condition du chrétien (Unam Sanctam*, 55) (Paris, 1965), pp. 107–167; see also Dogmatic Constitution on the Church, *Lumen Gentium*, 12.

9. This is P. Nautin's interpretation of the texts of the apostolic Fathers and Irenaeus of Lyons: *op. cit.* (note 1), pp. 49–50.

10. See Thomas Aquinas, *In III Sent.* d. 13, q. 2, a. 1, ad 2; q. 2, a. 2; see *Collationes de 'Credo in Deum'*, *op. cit.*, (note 6). E. Vauthier, 'Le Saint-Esprit, principe d'unité de l'Eglise d'après S. Thomas d'Aquin. Corps mystique et inhabitation du Saint-Esprit', *MScRel*, 5 (1948), 175–196; 6 (1949), 57–80, criticized me for having neglected the idea of the

indwelling of the Holy Spirit in the Church in my interpretation of Thomas' ecclesiology. Since that time, however, I have frequently considered these questions and the relevant texts. Thomas in fact rarely deals with the theme of indwelling and even more rarely with that indwelling in the Church as such. The truth of my statement can be seen in his *Comm. in 1 Cor*, c. 3, lect. 3, in which the theme of the indwelling of the Spirit in the Church is simply omitted.

11. See, for example, C. Journet, *L'Eglise du Verbe incarné*, II (Paris, 1951), pp. 510–565.

12. In his *Summa*, Thomas mentions the indwelling of the Spirit (through charity) very briefly five or six times. He always says 'in man' or 'in us': see *ST* Ia, q. 43, a. 3, 5; Ia IIae, q. 68, a. 5; IIa IIae, q. 19, a. 6; q. 24, a. 11; IIIa, q. 7, a. 13.

13. See Thomas Aquinas, *In III Sent*. d. 25, q. 1, a. 2, ad 4; *ST* IIa IIae, q. 1, a. 9, ad 3. There are many texts in which he deals with faith animated by charity as the substance of the mystical Body; see *Comm. in Gal*. c. 6, lect. 4, end; *Comm. in Ioan*. c. 7, lect. 7; *In IV Sent*. d. 9, q. 1, a. 2, sol. 4; *ST* IIa IIae, q. 124, a. 5, ad 1; IIIa, q. 80, a. 2, 4.

14. See, for example, Hos 2:4–20; Ezek 16 and 23; Is 61:10; 62:4–5; Song; Ps 45. For the New Testament, see R. A. Batey, *New Testament Nuptial Imagery* (Leiden, 1971); P. Andriessen, 'La nouvelle Eve, corps du nouvel Adam', *Aux origines de l'Eglise (Recherches Bibliques*, VII), ed. J. Giblet (1965), pp. 87–109.

15. See, for example, S. Tromp, 'Ecclesia sponsa, virgo, mater', *Greg*, 18 (1937), 3–21; *idem*, *Corpus Christi quod est Ecclesia*. I: *Introductio Generalis* (Rome, 1937; 2nd ed. 1946), pp. 26–53; O. Casel, 'Die Taufe als Brautbad der Kirche', *Jahrbuch für Liturgiewissenschaft*, 5 (1925), 144–147; *idem*, 'Die Kirche als Braut Christi nach Schrift, Väterlehre und Liturgie', *Die Kirche des lebendigen Gottes (Theologie der Zeit)* (Vienna, 1936), pp. 91–111; H. Engberding, 'Die Kirche als Braut in der Ostsyrischen Liturgie', *Or. Chr. Period*., 3 (1937), 5–48; F. Graffin, 'Recherches sur le thème de l'Eglise-Epouse dans les liturgies et la littérature de langue syrienne', *L'Orient chrétien*, 3 (1938), 317–336; C. Chavasse, *The Bride of Christ. An Enquiry into the Nuptial Element in Early Christianity* (London, 1940). I have also made a special study of Augustine's and Bernard's writings on this theme; the latter often quotes 1 Cor 6:17.

16. The first marriage rite in the Greek world was the bridal bath: see P. Stergianopoulos, *Die Lutra und ihre Verwendung bei der Hochzeit und im Totenkultus der alten Griechen* (Athens, 1922); O. Casel, *op. cit*. (note 15); J. A. Robilliard, 'Le symbolisme du mariage selon S. Paul', *RSPT*, 21 (1932), 243–247; J. Schmid, 'Brautschaft (Heilige)', *Reallexikon für Antike und Christentum*, II, cols 528–564.

17. Bossuet, 'IV⁰ Lettre à une demoiselle de Metz, XXIX–XXXVI': *Correspondance*, I *(Grands Ecrivains de France)* (Paris, 1909), pp. 68–71.

18. There are hundreds of texts: see S. Tromp, 'De nativitate Ecclesiae ex Corde Iesu in Cruce', *Greg*, 13 (1932), 489–527.

19. See, nonetheless, the Dogmatic Constitution on the Church, *Lumen Gentium*, 8, 3, end; 15; Pastoral Constitution on the Church in the Modern World, *Gaudium et spes*, 43; Decree on Ecumenism, *Unitatis Redintegratio*, 4, 5 and 6; Paul VI, Encyclical *Ecclesiam suam*, 6 July 1964; *AAS*, 56 (1964), 628–630, 649; and Paul VI's addresses to his audiences on 10 August 1966 and 7 May 1969, when he quoted my own book and the *ecclesia semper reformanda*: see *Doc. cath*. (1969), p. 506.

20. This is the title of a chapter in Leclercq's *La vie du Christ dans son Eglise (Unam Sanctam*, 12) (Paris, 1944), pp. 90–111. I would also mention some of my own books and articles in this context: *Vraie et fausse réforme dans l'Eglise (Unam Sanctam*, 20) (Paris, 1950; 2nd ed., 1969); 'Comment l'Eglise sainte doit se renouveler sans cesse', *Irénikon*, 34 (1961), 322–345, reprinted in *Sainte Eglise* (Paris, 1963), pp. 131–154; *Power and Poverty in the Church* (Eng. tr.; London, 1964); 'L'application à l'Eglise comme telle des exigences évangéliques concernant la pauvreté', *Eglise et Pauvreté (Unam Sanctam*, 57) (Paris, 1965), pp. 135–155.

21. For the *arrabōn* or earnest-money, see 2 Cor 1:22; Eph 1:14; 5:5; the first-fruits, see

Rom 8:23; see also Heb 6:4. For the 'Promised One', see Lk 24:49; Acts 1:4; 2:33; Gal 3:14; Eph 1:12.

22. An allusion to this will be found in Tertullian, *Adv. Marc.* IV, 26; it appears formally in Gregory of Nyssa, *De orat. Dom.* 3 (*PG* 44, 1157C); Evagrius, *Traité de l'oraison*, 58, ed. I. Hausherr (Paris, 1960), p. 83; Maximus the Confessor (*PG* 90, 884B).

23. Malcolm Muggeridge, *Something Beautiful for God* (London, 1971), pp. 31–32. The quotation from Scripture at the end of this passage is from 1 Cor 2:4–5.

24. F Kattenbusch, *Das Apostolische Symbol* (Leipzig, 1894 and 1900); P. Bernard in *DTC*, III (1908), pp. 450–454; H. B. Swete, *The Holy Catholic Church* (London, 1915), which has the subtitle *The Communion of Saints. A Study in the Apostles' Creed*; F. J. Badcock, ' "Sanctorum communio" as an Article of the Creed', *JTS*, 21 (1920), 106–126; my own article (Fr. orig. pub. in *VS* (January 1935), 5–17), 'Aspects of the Communion of Saints: some remarks on the way we communicate in holy things' (Eng. tr.), *Faith and Spiritual Life* (London, 1969), pp. 122–131; S. Tromp, *Corpus Christi quod est Ecclesia*, I, *op. cit.* (note 15), pp. 152ff.; F. Ostlender, 'Sanctorum communio. Ihr Wesen, ihre Aufgabe und Bedeutung in der altchristlichen Kunst', *Liturgisches Leben*, 5 (1938), 191–203, with 33 reproductions; *Communion des Saints (Cahiers de la VS)* (Paris, 1945); W. Elert, 'Die Herkunft der Formel Sanctorum communio', *Theologische Literaturzeitung*, 74 (1949), 577–586; J. N. D. Kelly, *Early Christian Creeds* (London, 1950), pp. 388–397; C. Journet, *L'Eglise du Verbe incarné*, II, *op. cit.* (note 11), pp. 554ff., 659ff.; A. Michel, *La Communion des Saints* (*Doctor Communis*, IX) (Rome, 1956); A. Polianti, *Il mistero della Comunione dei Santi nella Rivelazione e nella teologia* (Rome, 1957); R. Foley, 'The Communion of Saints. A Study in St. Augustine', *Bijdragen*, 20 (1959), 267–281; P.-Y. Emery, 'L'unité des croyants au ciel et sur la terre. La communion des saints et son expression dans la prière de l'Eglise,' *Verbum Caro*, 63 (1962); E. Lamirande, *La Communion des Saints (Je sais, Je crois)* (Paris, 1962); S. Benkö, *The Meaning of Sanctorum Communio* (*Studies in Historical Theology*, 3) (Eng. tr.; London, 1964); J. M. R. Tillard, 'La Communion des Saints', *VS*, 113 (No. 519: August-September 1965), 249–274; J. Mühlsteiger, 'Sanctorum communio', *ZKT*, 92 (1970), 113–132, who deals with the question from the historical point of view.

25. Even the Roman Catechism, the so-called Catechism of the Council of Trent, has this: see Part I, art. 9, 4 (Fr. tr. in *Cahiers de la VS, op. cit.* (note 24)), which also provides a good authentic commentary.

26. This is clear from several creeds or explanations of the creed; see J. Mühlsteiger, 'Sanctorum communio', *op. cit.* (note 24), pp. 123ff.

27. See, for example, Ivo of Chartres, Peter Abelard and Thomas Aquinas, who provides a characteristically Scholastic explanation, with a brief account of the seven sacraments: see his *Collationes de 'Credo in Deum', op. cit.* (note 6), art. X, in the edition cited, pp. 148–149.

28. John of the Cross, 'The living flame of love', 3; see Lucien-Marie de Saint-Joseph's Fr. tr. quoted by C. Journet, *op. cit.* (note 11), pp. 532, 551.

29. *In IV Sent.* d. 45, q. 2, a. 1, q^a 1. John Chrysostom's fine text is also worth quoting in this context: 'Charity shows you your neighbour as another you and teaches you to enjoy his good as though it were your own and to endure his sufferings as your own. Charity gathers a great number together into a single body and transforms their souls into as many dwelling-places of the Holy Spirit. It is not in the midst of division, but in the union of hearts that the Spirit of peace dwells. . . . Charity makes each one's good common to all': *De perf. car.* (*PG* 56, 281).

30. *ST* Ia IIae, q, 114, a. 3 and 6; *Comm. in Rom.* c. 8, lect. 4; *Comm. in Ioan.* c. 4, lect. 2; see also *Contra Gent.* IV, 21 and 22; *Comp.* I, 147; see also my article 'Mérite', *Vocabulaire œcuménique* (Paris, 1970), pp. 233–251.

31. Thomas Aquinas, *Collationes de 'Credo in Deum', op. cit.* (note 6), art. X, p. 149.

32. 'Actus unius efficitur alterius charitate mediante, per quam omnes unum sumus in Christo'

(Gal 3:28); *In IV Sent.* d. 20, a. 2, q. 3, ad 1; d. 45, q. 2, a. 1, sol. 1.

33. See *Quodl.* II, 14; VIII, 9.

34. *Sacramentarium Serapionis*, XIII, 7; see F. X. Funk, *Didasc. et Const. Apost.*, II (Paderborn, 1905), p. 173. For Christ as the sovereign celebrant—a theme which was taken up again in the Constitution on the Liturgy of Vatican II, see, for the Fathers, J. Lécuyer, *Le sacerdoce dans le mystère du Christ* (Paris, 1957), pp. 289ff.; for the High Middle Ages, my *Ecclésiologie du Haut Moyen Age* (Paris, 1968), p. 109 for the Western Church and p. 330 for the Eastern Church. Bede, *Expos. in Luc.* (*PL* 92, 330), presented the Church as invisibly united by the Holy Spirit around its pontiff.

35. 'Per virtutem Spiritus Sancti, qui per unitatem charitatis communicat invicem bona membrorum Christi, fit quod bonum privatum quod est in missa sacerdotis boni, est fructuosum aliis': *ST* IIIa, q. 82, a. 6, ad 3.

36. 'Fides autem unius, imo totius Ecclesiae, parvulo prodest per operationem Spiritus Sancti qui unit Ecclesiam et bona unius alteri communicat': *ST* IIIa, q. 68, a. 9, ad 2. Thomas does not say that the Holy Spirit unites the child who, in principle, does not yet possess charity, to the Church, but that the faith of the Church is there for the profit of the child. Cajetan commented on this: 'Intellige Ecclesiae merita prodesse infanti et iuxta articulum communionis sanctorum et particulariter tam orando pro infante tam applicando eumdem sacramento ex corde puro et caritate plena'.

PART TWO

THE BREATH OF GOD
IN OUR PERSONAL LIVES

In October 1963, at the Second Vatican Council, the schema on the Church was being discussed. I was having lunch with two Orthodox observers, who said: 'If we were to prepare a treatise *De Ecclesia*, we would draft a chapter on the Holy Spirit, to which we would add a second chapter on Christian anthropology, and that would be all'.

Clearly, in the Orthodox tradition, Christian anthropology includes a whole theology of man's image being reshaped not only by an ascesis which corresponds to the activity of the Spirit and which works together with the Spirit, but also by the sacraments in which the Spirit acts to sanctify man. My Orthodox friends were nevertheless making a suggestion full of meaning and very illuminating for Western Christians. The first two divisions in this volume—'The Spirit animates the Church' and 'The Breath of God in our personal lives'—have been made for the sake of clarity. These two aspects should not be confused. The Church, however, at least the *Ecclesia congregata*, is the 'we' of Christians; for this reason the two parts should not be completely separated. There are inevitably some repetitions. Some of the themes in this second part were anticipated in the first, and the substance of Part One is completed in Part Two.

This Part Two forms a single whole, but, because I have wanted to develop certain points, some of them specialized, more fully, and for the sake of the structure of the book, I have divided it into chapters.

1

THE SPIRIT AND MAN
IN GOD'S PLAN

God, the Principle and End of our Sanctification

This is not a Platonic, but a biblical concept. God is not the 'eternal celibate of the centuries', but love and goodness.[1] He places beings outside himself in order to bring them back to himself, so that they can participate in what he is in his sovereign existence, in other words, in the beginning and the end of their existence. He places outside himself beings who are similar to himself. Because they are like him, those beings are capable of knowing and loving freely, capable of giving themselves freely and returning to him equally freely. He animates them with a movement and therefore with a desire that is an echo in them of his own desire that he has revealed to us as his Spirit. It is in this context that we can place the idea that was so dear to many spiritual writers of the French school, namely that the Spirit has no intra-divine fruitfulness of his own, because he is the end of the processions from the Father and the Son, and is therefore made fruitful outside God, in the incarnation of the Word and the sanctification of men.[2]

The Spirit is the principle of love and realizes our lives as children of God in the form of a Gift, fulfilling that quality in us. It was he who brought about in Mary the humanity of Jesus and anointed and sanctified him for his messianic activity. Through his resurrection and glorification, Jesus' humanity was made by the Spirit a humanity of (the Son of) God. During his life on earth, Jesus was the temple of the Holy Spirit, containing all men with the intention and the power to accept them as children of God.[3] After the Lord's glorification, the Holy Spirit has that temple in us and in the Church and he is active in the same way in us, enabling us to be born *anōthen* (from above and anew: see Jn 3:3) and to live as a member of the Body of Christ. He himself consummates this quality in our body, in the glory and freedom of children of God (see Rom 8:21–23).

This work of the Spirit in Christ and in us constitutes the mystery which Paul regarded as a plan formed in God 'before the foundation of the world' (Eph 1:4; 3:11; Jn 17:24), in other words, at the level of the intra-divine life, the word 'before' referring to priority not in time, but in the order of God's plan. According to Paul, that plan remained hidden or was kept secret for centuries (see Rom 16:25–26; Col 1:26). It has been revealed to man in his

67

reading or hearing the announcement made by the apostles, the prophets and Paul himself. It is concerned with God as love, in other words, with God in his communication of himself and as grace. This, then, goes back to the mystery of God himself. Before the foundation of the world, the Father conceived his Son, the Word, as having to become human through the Holy Spirit and Mary, the daughter of Zion, and as having to assume a humanity that would begin again and at the same time complete the humanity that had come from Adam, because it would be a humanity of the 'first-born of many brethren' (Rom 8:29).

What is necessary and what is free in God should, it is true, not be confused, but, on the one hand, both are identified in him and, on the other, there is no difference, according to Paul, between Christ and the Son, pre-existing before the incarnation. Finally, the economic Trinity, that is, the revelation and the commitment of the divine Persons in the history of salvation, is the same as the immanent Trinity, that is, God as three and one in his absolute nature. (We shall consider this more fully in Volume III.)

The depths of this mystery are beyond our understanding now; we shall only penetrate as far as them in the world to come, and even then our understanding will never be complete. Here, in this life, all that we can do is to rely on Scripture and stammer a few sentences.[4] Christ is the image of the invisible God[5] and man was—and still is—made in God's image. In Luke's genealogy of Jesus, Jesus is described as the son of . . . , the son of . . . , the son of Adam, the son of God. Both the man who came from this earth and the Christ, the Son of God, come *from God*, as though there was in God a humanity, the expression of which was temporal—in the case of Adam, at the beginning, but in the case of Christ, in the fulfilment of time—but the idea of which is co-eternal with God. The mystery, then, is not simply that Jesus Christ is God. It is first and foremost and even more radically that God is Jesus Christ and that he is expressed in two images, each made for the other, the image of man and that of Jesus Christ. The latter, whose state was divine, became assimilated to and united with men at the lowest point of their destiny and was then raised up to the highest point, taking men with him, since 'only he who has descended from heaven, the Son of man', has ascended to heaven (Jn 3:13) and, to ascend with and in him, we must be born anew in him of (water and) the Spirit (Jn 3:5).

By one Spirit we were all baptized into one body (1 Cor 12:12).

He has saved us, not because of deeds done by us in righteousness, but in virtue of his own mercy, by the washing of regeneration and renewal in the Holy Spirit, which he poured out upon us richly through Jesus Christ our Saviour, that we might be justified by his grace and become heirs in hope of eternal life (Tit 3:5–7).

The Spirit, then, is the principle realizing the 'Christian mystery', which is the mystery of the Son of God who was made man and who enables us to be born as sons of God. Catholic theologians speak of 'grace'. In so doing, they run the risk of objectivizing it and separating it from the activity of the Spirit, who is uncreated grace and from whom it cannot be separated. Only God is holy, and only he can make us holy, in and through his incarnate Son and in and through his Spirit: 'God chose you from the beginning to be saved, through sanctification by the Spirit and belief in the truth' (2 Thess 2:13); 'You were sanctified, you were justified in the name of the Lord Jesus Christ and the Spirit (spirit) of our God' (1 Cor 6:11; cf. Rom 15:16; Heb 2:11). Yet our co-operation in this process of sanctification is required—it is possible for us neglect the gift and make it in vain (see 1 Thess 4:3, 7–8; Rom 6:22; Heb 10:29).

The Spirit is the Absolute Gift
promised in fullness eschatologically,
possessed as earnest-money in this present life

In his Pentecost address, quoting Joel, Peter stressed the eschatological character of the gift of the Spirit (Acts 2:16ff.). This eschatological aspect is also implicit in the title of 'Promised One' that is given to the Holy Spirit. It is also clear from the connection made by Paul between Christ's resurrection and glorification and the activity of the Spirit in power (Rom 1:4, 8, 10–11). In his letter to the Ephesians, Paul also said: 'You have believed in him and were sealed with the promised Holy Spirit, which is the guarantee (= earnest-money) of our inheritance until we acquire possession of it, to the praise of his glory' (Eph 1:13–14). Elsewhere, he also says:

> We ourselves, who have the first-fruits of the Spirit, groan inwardly as we wait for adoption as sons, the redemption of our bodies (Rom 8:23).

> While we are still in this tent, we sigh with anxiety; not that we would be unclothed, but that we would be further clothed, so that what is mortal may be swallowed up by life. He who has prepared us for this very thing is God, who has given us the Spirit as a guarantee (= earnest-money) (2 Cor 5:4–5).

As we have already seen (p. 57), several of the Church Fathers retained the reading of Lk 11:2 found in a number of manuscripts: 'May thy Holy Spirit come upon us and purify us' in preference to: 'Thy kingdom come', because they were convinced that the kingdom of God was brought about by the gift of God's Spirit. The East shared this conviction with the West. Nicholas of Flüe wrote on 4 December 1482 from his hermitage to the people of Berne: 'May the Holy Spirit be your last reward'.[6] Much later, Seraphim of Sarov (†1833), who became a *starets* at the age of sixty-six, after many years spent in austere solitude as a hermit, said: 'The real aim of our Christian life is that we should be overcome by the divine Spirit. Prayer, fastening, almsgiving, charity and other good works undertaken in the name of Christ are the means by which we acquire the divine Spirit.'[7] It is worth noting in this context that Seraphim places the Spirit at the end, as the aim of

Christian life, but that he also stresses the place of ascesis and man's co-operation or synergy. Simeon the New Theologian, perhaps the greatest of the Byzantine mystics, taught very much the same:

> Whether he has already received the grace of the Spirit or whether he is waiting to receive it, no one will leave the darkness of the soul and contemplate the light of the most holy Spirit without trials, efforts, sweat, violence and tribulation. 'The kingdom of God has suffered violence and men of violence take it by force' (Mt 11:12), for 'through many tribulations we must enter the kingdom of God' (Acts 14:22). The kingdom of God is, in fact, a participation in the Holy Spirit. It is he of whom it is said: 'The kingdom of God is in the midst of you' (Lk 17:21), so that we are bound to apply ourselves to the task of receiving and possessing the Holy Spirit. . . .
>
> Our father (= Simeon the Elder) worked in such a way that he went far beyond many of the early Fathers. He suffered so many trials and temptations that he may be compared with many of the illustrious martyrs. In this way, having received the gift of the Paraclete, he obtained glory and a constant peace of soul from God. Like a tank filled with water, he received the fullness of Christ our Lord and was filled with the grace of his Spirit, who is living water (Jn 4:10). (Here follow quotations from Jn 4:14 and 7:39a.) The Apostle also said: 'Now we have received not the spirit of the world, but the Spirit who is from God, that we might understand the gifts of God's grace' (1 Cor 2:12).[8]

These texts are typical of the Eastern spiritual tradition, in which a strong sense of God's initiative is combined with an equally powerful conviction of human freedom.[9] It is, however, not possible to claim that the Western Catholic tradition is very different, although an experience of the Spirit as light may certainly have developed more strongly in the East. This idea is quite prominent in the writings of Simeon, and it is difficult to read Seraphim of Sarov's famous dialogue with Motovilov and not be moved. I would like to conclude this chapter by quoting it:

> 'All the same, I do not understand how one can be sure of being in the Spirit of God. How can I recognize for certain his manifestation in me?'
>
> 'I have already told you', said Father Seraphim, 'that it is very simple. I have spoken to you at length about the state in which those who are in the Spirit of God find themselves. I have also explained to you how to recognize his presence in us. . . . What more do you still need, my friend?'
>
> 'I must have a better understanding of all that you have said to me.'
>
> 'My friend, at this moment both of us are in the Spirit of God. . . . Why do you not want to look at me?'
>
> 'I cannot look at you, my Father', I replied. 'Your eyes are flashing lightning; your face has become more dazzling than the sun, and it hurts my eyes to look at you.'
>
> 'Do not be afraid', he said, 'at this moment you have become as bright as I am. You are also now in the fullness of the Spirit of God. Otherwise you would not be able to see me as you see me.'
>
> Then leaning towards me, he whispered in my ear:

70

'Thank the Lord God for his infinite goodness towards us. As you have observed, I have not even made the sign of the cross. It was enough for me simply to have prayed to God in my thoughts, in my heart, saying within me: "Lord, make him worthy to see clearly with his bodily eyes this descent of your Spirit with which you favour your servants when you deign to appear to them in the magnificent light of your glory". As you see, my friend, the Lord at once granted the prayer of the humble Seraphim. . . . How grateful we should be to God for this inexpressible gift that he has given to both of us! Even the desert Fathers did not always have such manifestations of his goodness! God's grace, like a mother's tender love for her children, deigned to console your bruised heart, through the intercession of the Mother of God herself. . . . Why, then, do you not want to look straight at me, my friend? Look freely and without fear—the Lord is with us.'

Encouraged by his words, I looked and was seized by pious fear. Imagine the centre of the sun in the most dazzling brightness of its noonday rays, and in that centre the face of the man who is speaking to you. You see the movement of his lips, the changing expression of his eyes, you hear his voice and you feel his hands holding you by the shoulders, but you cannot see those hands or the body of your companion—only a great light shining all around in a radius of many feet, illuminating the snow-covered field and the white flakes that are still falling. . . .

'What do you feel?' Father Seraphim asked me.

'An infinite sense of well-being', I replied.

'But what kind of well-being? What exactly?'

'I feel such calm, such peace in my soul', I replied, 'that I cannot find words to express it.'

'My friend, this is the peace of which the Lord was speaking when he said to his disciples: "My peace I give you, the peace that the world cannot give . . . the peace that passes all understanding". What else do you feel?'

'An infinite joy in my heart.'

Father Seraphim continued: 'When the Spirit of God comes down on man and wraps him in the fullness of his presence, the soul overflows with an inexpressible joy, because the Holy Spirit fills everything that he touches with joy. . . . If the first-fruits of future joy already fill our soul with such sweetness, such happiness, what are we to say of the joy that is waiting in the kingdom of heaven for all those who weep here on earth? You have also wept, my friend, in the course of your life on earth, but see the joy that the Lord sends you, to console you here below. At present, we have to work and make constant efforts so that we can "attain to the measure of the stature of the fullness of Christ". . . . Then, that joy that we feel for a little time and in part now will appear in its fullness, overwhelming our being with inexpressible delights that no one will be able to take from us.'[10]

NOTES

1. See Thomas Aquinas, *ST* IIIa, q. 1, a. 1. See also N. Rotenstreich, 'The Notion of Tradition in Judaism', *Journal of Religion*, 28 (1948), 28–36; on p. 33, this author writes: '*Bonum* reveals itself, since the very essence of *bonum* is to pass beyond its limit and to exist for the others'.

2. Bérulle, *Grandeurs de Jésus*, IV, 2 (Migne, p. 208; *Œuvres complètes* of 1644 (1940), p. 212); Louis-Marie Grignion de Montfort, *Traité de la vraie dévotion à la Sainte-Vierge* (Louvain, 1947), Part I, note 17–20. The element of truth contained in this idea can perhaps be found in Thomas Aquinas, *In I Sent.* d. 14, q. 1, a. 1; *De Pot.* q. 9, a. 9, c and ad 14.
3. Jesus described himself several times as the new Temple (see Mt 21:42, par.; Jn 1:50–51; 2:19–22). See also the admirable words of Angelus Silesius: 'When God was lying hidden in the womb of the virgin, the point contained the circle within itself': *Cherubinischer Wandersmann* (1657), III, 28.
4. Basil the Great, *Contra Eunom.* III, 7 (PG 29, 669): 'It is a characteristic of the pious man to say nothing about the Holy Spirit when the Scriptures are silent about him; this is because we are convinced that our experience and understanding of this subject are reserved for the world to come'.
5. See especially 2 Cor 4:4; Col 1:15ff.; Heb 1:3. Before the foundation of the world, because he is the mediator of creation: see 1 Cor 8:6; Col 1:15.
6. See C. Journet, *Saint Nicolas de Flue*, 2nd ed. (Paris, 1947), p. 84.
7. Quoted by R. von Walter, 'Le chrétien russe', *Irénikon*, 6 (1929), 687–720, especially 713.
8. Simeon the New Theologian, *Orat.* VII (*PG* 120, 352 and 354), which I follow here; = *Cat.* VI: Fr. tr. J. Paramelle, *SC* 104 (1964), p. 23 [followed below, p. 121].
9. See Gregory Nazianzen, *Orat.* XX, 12 (*PG* 35, 1080B): 'If you want to become a "theologian" who is worthy of God, keep the commandments and walk in the way of the law'. The greatest teacher of this 'synergy' was Maximus the Confessor (†662): see A. Riou, *Le monde et l'Eglise selon Maxime le Confesseur* (Paris, 1974), pp. 123–135. See also Volume I, p. 102, note 6.
10. This translation follows the Fr. tr. of V. Lossky, *Essai sur la théologie mystique de l'Eglise d'Orient* (Paris, 1944), pp. 225ff. [not precisely the Eng. tr. (London, 1957), pp. 227ff.]. But see Drina Gorianoff, *Séraphin de Sarov* (Bellefontaine, 1974), pp. 210ff. The biblical quotation at the end of this passage is from Eph 4:13.

2

THE GIFT OF THE SPIRIT IN THE
MESSIANIC ERA

Under the Old and the New Dispensations

Only God is holy and only God can make men holy. All that belongs to him and all that is attributed to him is holy. The history of revealed holiness therefore clearly began already under the old dispensation. God dwelt among his people Israel. He had his dwelling-place in Zion. His Spirit was active and therefore present in those who carried out his work—in the kings, prophets and pious believers who served him faithfully. It cannot be disputed, however, that the Spirit was neither given nor revealed under the old dispensation in the same way and under the same conditions as he has been under the new, that is, since the incarnation and Pentecost. It has correctly been pointed out that 'In the Old Testament the Holy Spirit is spoken of mainly as a power coming upon individuals at particular times. . . . The New Testament begins by describing how the Holy Spirit descended on Jesus and abode upon him.'[1] The prophets, after all, announced for the messianic era what the New Testament tells us had come in Jesus Christ and at Pentecost. It is not difficult to assemble the texts; I have in fact already quoted many of them in Volume I of this work. The only ones that I shall consider here are those which raise the question of a difference of status or condition between the old and the new dispensations as regards the gift of the Spirit. There is no doubt that there is a difference. Everyone agrees that there is. The question, however, is what the nature is of that difference and how it should be interpreted. It is about this that there is some difference of opinion.[2]

1. 'I tell you, among those born to women, none is greater than John, yet he who is least in the kingdom of God is greater than he' (Lk 7:28; cf. Mt 11:11); 'The law and the prophets were until John; since then the good news of the kingdom of God is preached' (Lk 16:16); 'He who sent me to baptize with water said to me, "He on whom you see the Spirit descend and remain, this is he who baptizes with the Holy Spirit" ' (Jn 1:33; cf. Mt 3:11; Acts 1:5). One economy follows another: preparation gives way to reality, prophecy to a messianic era, when the kingdom is close at hand. Although the Spirit is certainly given, the gift is eschatological and a pledge of the

73

world to come. The new aspect that is proclaimed concerns both the corporate regime of the gifts of God and the religious state of individuals.

Paul similarly makes a contrast between the evangelical ministry of the Spirit and that of Moses (see especially 2 Cor 3). The people of God exist under new conditions. A text such as: 'By one Spirit we were all baptized into one body' (1 Cor 12:13) would have been inconceivable under the old dispensation. Through the gift of the Spirit, the people of God exist as the Body of Christ and the Temple of the Spirit. This is a radically new element.

Worship is likewise transformed under the new dispensation: 'The hour is coming, and now is, when the true worshippers will worship the Father in spirit and truth' (Jn 4:23). The epistle to the Hebrews is even more instructive here. It shows that the law was unable to obtain access to the Holy of Holies and that man is now, under the new dispensation, able to enter it.[3] Christ leads us to *teleiōsis*, perfection. It is not a question simply of an objective and collective situation as such. It is rather a question of the personal state of believers in their relationship with God and in their blessed state at the end. In Hebrews, the Spirit intervenes as guarantor (2:4) and even more inportantly as an element of Christian life in practice (6:4ff.; 10:29).

The pre-Christian people of Israel were sometimes called 'sons' and Yahweh was known as their 'father'. These names referred to God's special choice of these people and his consequent care of them and interventions to save them. This even led to a special intimacy between God and his people.[4] It was in this sense that Paul attributed adoption to the Israelites (see Rom 9:4). This does not mean that believers had the reality of life as sons of the kind of which Paul and John spoke. That reality presupposed the coming of the Son and the Spirit and was inconceivable without the intervention of the revelation of a Son of God.[5] Paul clearly had a good reason for associating the creation of a 'new' man with the Easter event (2 Cor 5:17).

These different data, which have a remarkable concordance, are explained in one important statement. John Chrysostom and Cyril of Alexandria regarded the affirmation in the fourth gospel: 'As yet the Spirit had not been given, because Jesus was not yet glorified' (Jn 7:39) as decisive. The interpretations of this statement, namely that Christ's glorification at Easter inaugurated a new regime in the communication of the Spirit to men, have, however, differed throughout history and I propose to review them briefly below, in the following section. (But see my study cited in note 2 below.)

2. The Greek Fathers—Irenaeus, John Chrysostom, and Cyril of Alexandria—and several of the Latin Fathers—Tertullian, Ambrosiaster and, much later, Rupert of Deutz—followed the scriptural text quite literally and made a distinction, almost an opposition, not only between the old and the new regimes, but also between the condition of grace before and that

after the coming of Christ. Before Christ, they believed, there were gifts of the Spirit, but the Spirit had not been personally given and he did not dwell substantially in believers.

Almost all the theologians working in the Western, Latin tradition—Augustine, Leo the Great, Thomas Aquinas and Thomists such as Franzelin, Pesch and Galtier—have, however, accepted a difference in regime between the two dispensations, but have insisted that the righteous in the Old Testament were personally, on the basis of their faith in Christ who was to come, subject to the same condition as later Christian believers and that, like them, they had the quality of sons and possessed a substantial indwelling of the Holy Spirit. All that the incarnation and Pentecost brought about was a wider and more abundant dissemination of that grace and that presence of the Spirit. Leo XIII and Pius XII also held this position.[6]

Attempts have been made in modern times to adapt the position of the Eastern Church, which has the merit of being closer to the facts and the biblical texts mentioned above. The Bishop of Bruges, Mgr Waffelaert, took the distinction between created and uncreated grace as his point of departure, the latter being, of course, the Holy Spirit. The righteous men of the Old Testament, he maintained, received created grace and this enabled them to act supernaturally and to acquire merit. They did not, however, possess the quality of sons and heirs of the Father, whose formal cause was the Person of the Holy Spirit as given and dwelling in his temple. Gérard Philips believed that the grace of the righteous in the Old Testament was the grace of Christ with its effect of justification,[7] but, taking up Fr de la Taille's idea of grace as a created effect brought about by an uncreated Act, he regarded that grace as going back to a time of preparation. As a result, it had to be put into effect again, if the full effects of grace were to be obtained, by means of activity connected with the historical missions of the Son and the Spirit. The difference between the righteous men of the Old Testament and Christian believers, then, was not, Philips argued, simply one of individual degree of the kind that exists between one soul and another within the mystical Body. It was a difference of 'economic' degrees and, for that reason, of 'classes'.

My own interpretation, which I have already outlined in some detail (see below, note 2), is very similar. I believe that a distinction must be made, even to the point of total separation, between certain effects of grace and grace itself, and between the supernatural righteousness granted to the patriarchs and the effectiveness of that grace in obtaining its fruits of sonship, the substantial indwelling of the divine Persons and divinization. In fact, inner righteousness was given to men who were moving from a long way off towards the realities that had been promised. We are inclined to see grace only as a created reality within us and therefore as a thing, whereas, before this takes place, it is a divine act of love and what has been created is born of that act, so that its quality, degree and mode follow from this. There is a unique plan of *charis* or grace and of various gifts *kata tēn charin*, that is, according to grace, from the patriarchs to us and from Mary to the most humble believer. Just as God now shows that he is pleased with us as members of the Body of his beloved Son, so that we are 'made to drink' of his Spirit (1 Cor 12:13), so too did he show himself to be pleased with the righteous men of the old dispensation as men who were orientated towards Christ and the promise of his Spirit. Their grace of righteousness can only be attributed to its normal effectiveness if the coming of Christ and his passion are presupposed.

One very important but at the same time mysterious episode can illustrate this: the descent of Christ into 'hell'.[8] It was necessary that the revelation of Christ and contact with him should set free, among the 'spirits in prison' (1 Pet 3:19), the potential of a grace that was otherwise unable to reach its goal. It is at least possible to understand in this light, by giving it this particular place in my interpretation, the verse in the same epistle: 'The gospel was even preached to the dead, that though judged in the flesh like men, they might live in the Spirit like God' (1 Pet 4:6). This point, however, is not a necessary part of my argument in my book published in 1958. My fundamental intention was to distinguish the part played by the decisive moments of the 'economy' and the divine interventions marking and shaping them, which were, in this case, the visible historical missions of the Son and the Spirit of God. On the basis of those missions, God himself has been given together with his gifts and men have reached him through them. These gifts have been made in abundance, but still fall short of their consummation at the end of time. In the eschatological era, there will be a new communication of the Spirit which will provide the grace, the gift and the indwelling, already part of our condition in the present messianic era, with their ultimate and definitive fruit.

3. I submitted my ideas on this subject to my fellow-Dominicans in 1954 and was subjected to quite severe criticism. What, they asked, was a grace that does not make us sons and does not reach the Father? It was simply a title and ineffective. Could justification and the possession of the divine Persons be separated in that way? A radical division of this kind did violence to the substantial unity of grace which was closely related to the unity of faith. It was the great insight of both Augustine and Thomas to recognize this twofold unity. God had pursued the same aim through both dispensations; whatever the understanding and the experience of the righteous men of the old dispensation might have been, their faith in Christ as saviour and their knowledge of the Spirit had been implicit. Thomas had pointed out that the grace received by the righteous men of the Old Testament had not reached its final end, which was spiritual and physical glory, and that it was necessary for the obstacle of the *reatus poenae* which came from the sin of nature to be overcome by the passion of Christ. But could this limitation be extended to

76

the other immediate and normal effects of sanctifying grace—sonship, God's substantial and objective indwelling, and our effectively reaching that same God?

There was also criticism of my use of biblical texts. It was possible to understand them differently and there were other texts, such as: Our fathers 'all ate the same spiritual food and drank the same spiritual drink, for they drank from the spiritual rock which followed them, and the rock was Christ' (1 Cor 10:3–4).

4. It is not easy to give a satisfactory summary of what is still valuable in my interpretation. Justice must be done, however, to Scripture. We can at least conclude the following: (1) the New Testament contains a revelation and therefore the possibility of a knowledge and a consciousness of what constitutes grace; (2) the economy of salvation is historical. It is punctuated by facts and divine initiatives, which, as soon as they take place, change what comes after them. I am bound, in this context, to quote the words of Gregory of Nyssa about the series of ascents that God places in the hearts of his servants: 'For the one who runs towards the Lord, there is no lack of space. The one who ascends never stops, going from beginning to beginning, by beginnings that never cease.'[9]

It is inconceivable that the incarnation of the Son, Christ's Easter and glorification and the coming of the Spirit who was promised should have changed nothing and should have brought nothing new. Until that time, something was lacking and the gift of the Spirit was not complete. It is still not complete, of course, since in the present era we only have the first-fruits of the Spirit. We have, however, already entered into the condition of sons because of the twofold creative mission of the Church. When we reach the state of glory—spiritual glory in our vision of God and bodily glory through the resurrection—we shall live by the same grace as here on earth, but that grace will be brought about in a different way. It will therefore have new effects or bear new fruit. My position in this question is therefore one which follows Mgr Philips' fairly closely: there is a new putting into effect, however imperfect that may still be, of gifts made *kata tēn charin*, according to grace, according to a unique plan that is historical, an 'economy'.

NOTES

1. Lesslie Newbigin, *The Household of God: Lectures on the Nature of the Church*, 2nd ed. (London, 1964), p. 104. See also my book, cited below (note 2), pp. 269ff. This theme is frequently encountered in patristic texts: see Gregory Nazianzen, *Orat.* XLI, 11 (*PG* 36, 444C); John Chrysostom, *Comm. in 2 Cor. Hom.* 7, 1 (*PG* 61, 443); Cyril of Alexandria, *Comm. in Ioan.* V, c. 2, on Jn 7:39: 'There was an abundant illumination of the Holy Spirit in the holy prophets. . . . In those who believe in Christ, however, there is not simply an illumination. I am not afraid to affirm that it is the Spirit himself who dwells and remains in

us. That is why we are called temples of God. This has never been said of the prophets'; this text is followed by quotations from Mt 11:11; Lk 17:21; Rom 8:11 (*PG* 73, 757A-B). See also Moses Bar Kipko, a ninth-century commentator on the liturgy, quoted by E.-P. Siman, *L'expérience de l'Esprit par l'Eglise d'après la tradition syrienne d'Antioche* (Paris, 1971), pp. 41–42; J. A. Möhler, *Einheit*, Appendix I; J. Lebreton, *Histoire du dogme de la Trinité*, II, pp. 598ff.

2. I have dealt with this question and have provided documentation in Appendix III on my *The Mystery of the Temple, or the Manner of God's Presence to his Creatures from Genesis to the Apocalypse* (Eng. tr.; London, 1962), pp. 262–299, to which reference should be made.

3. The impotence of the law: Heb 7:19; 9:9ff.; 10:1; 11:9–13. Free access: 4:14–16; 6:9, 10–20; 10:19–22; 12:22–24.

4. See M.-J. Lagrange, 'La paternité de Dieu dans l'Ancien Testament', *RB*, New series 5 (1908), 481–499; *Le Judaïsme avant Jésus-Christ* (Paris, 1931), pp. 459ff.; M. W. Schoenberg, 'Huiothesia: The Adoptive Sonship of the Israelites', *The American Ecclesiastical Review*, 143 (1960), 261–273; 'huios, huiothesia', *TDNT*, VIII, pp. 347–353.

5. Gal 4:5–7; Rom 8:14–17; 1 Jn 3:1. Adoption that is still imperfect: Rom 8:23; 1 Jn 3:2; Eph 1:13–14.

6. Leo XIII, Encyclical *Divinum illud munus*, *ASS* 29 (1897), 650–651; Pius XII, Encyclical *Mystici Corporis*, *AAS* 35 (1943), 206–207.

7. G. Philips, 'La grâce des justes de l'Ancien Testament', *ETL*, 23 (1947), 521–556; 24 (1948), 23–58, also published separately as *Bibl. ETL*, 4 (Bruges and Louvain, 1948).

8. See my book, *op. cit.* (note 2), pp. 279f.; to the extensive bibliography provided in that book, the following should be added: E. Biser, 'Abgestiegen zur Hölle. Versuch einer aktuellen Sinndeutung', *Münchener Theologische Zeitschrift*, 9 (1958), 205–212, 283–293; H. J. Schulz, ' "Höllenfahrt" als "Anastasis" ', *ZKT*, 81 (1959), 1–66; M. H. Lelong, 'La descente aux enfers, épiphanie aux morts', *VS*, 100 (1959), 17–28; *Lumière et Vie*, 87 (1968); H. U. von Balthasar, 'Abstieg zur Hölle', *TQ*, 150 (1970), 193–201; H. J. Vogels, *Christi Abstieg ins Totenreich und das Läuterungsgericht an den Toten: eine biblisch-theologisch-dogmatische Untersuchung zum Glaubensartikel 'descendit ad inferos' (Freiburger Theologische Studien*, 102) (Freiburg, 1976).

9. Gregory of Nyssa, *Hom. VIII in Cant.* (*PG* 44, 941C).

3

'GOD HAS SENT THE SPIRIT
OF HIS SON INTO OUR HEARTS'
(Gal 4:6)

The people of Israel were convinced that God was *with* them. This conviction was expressed in a particularly striking way in the sixth century B.C. by the priest-prophet Ezekiel, who proclaimed a restoration when the people were exiled and in a state of crisis: 'I will set my sanctuary in the midst of them for evermore. My dwelling-place shall be with them and I will be their God and they shall be my people' (37:26–27). This is a theme that recurs quite frequently in the writings of the prophets of the post-exilic restoration (see, for example, Joel 2:27; Hag 2:4–5; Zech 2:10–12) and in the priestly writings, the priestly editors using the terms *miš*^e*kān*, 'dwelling-place', and *miq*^e*dāš*, 'sanctuary':

> And I will make my abode among you and my soul shall not abhor you. And I will walk among you and will be your God and you shall be my people (Lev 26:11–12).

> And I will dwell among the people of Israel and will be their God, . . . who brought them forth out of the land of Egypt that I might dwell among them (Exod 29:45–46).

In order to indicate the transcendence of Yahweh and the tension that this involved even in his presence, his name was neither spoken nor written and one said that God had chosen Zion in order that his Name might dwell there (see Deuteronomy, for example), or one spoke of his Glory.[1] In post-biblical Judaism—the Targums, for instance—this tension and, at the same time, this connection between God's presence and his transcendence were expressed by the excellent term *šekinah*, an Aramaic or Mishnaic Hebrew word derived from the verb *šākan*, to inhabit.[2] It was in this way that the dwelling of a God who remained absolutely transcendent and above the place where he dwelt was described. God himself revealed that he was there, with his own. As G. F. Moore has pointed out, the Old Testament authors spoke of the 'Shekinah' more or less as Christians speak of the 'Holy Spirit' when they do not wish to define with theological precision the activity of the indwelling of God.[3]

When we turn to the New Testament, it is not difficult to be struck, despite the fact that constant repetition may have deadened our senses, by the power of these words:

> Do you not know that you are God's temple (*naos*) and that God's Spirit dwells in you (*oikei en humin*)? (1 Cor 3:16).

> Do you not know that your body is a temple of the Holy Spirit within you. . . . You are not your own (1 Cor 6:19).

> You are not in the flesh, you are in the Spirit, if the Spirit of God really dwells in you (*oikei en humin*). . . . If the Spirit of him who raised Jesus from the dead dwells in you, he who raised Christ Jesus from the dead will give life to your mortal bodies also through his Spirit which dwells in you (Rom 8:9, 11).

> . . . that Christ may dwell [*katoikēsai*] in your hearts through faith (Eph 3:17).

> And I will pray the Father and he will give you another Paraclete to be with you for ever (*ē meth' humōn*; subjunctive of 'to be'), even the Spirit of truth . . . ; you know him, for he dwells with you and will be in you (*par' humin menei kai en humin estai*) (Jn 14:16–17).

> If a man loves me, he will keep my word and my Father will love him and we will come to him (*pros auton*) and make our home with him (*kai monēn par' autō poiēsometha*) (Jn 14:23; cf. 15:10).[4]

> If we love one another, God abides in us (*en hēmin estin*) and his love is perfected in us. By this we know that we abide in him (*en autō menomen*) and he in us (*kai autos en hēmin*), because he has given us his Spirit (1 Jn 4:12–13).

> God is love and he who abides in love abides in God and God abides in him (1 Jn 4:16).

As we shall see, this theme of indwelling was developed to such an extent that one is inclined to read a clearly formulated doctrine into these scriptural texts. On their own, however, the terms *oikein* and *menein* do not point so far. In the gospel of John, the word 'to dwell, remain, abide', *menein*, is applied to many different constitutive elements in Christian life.[5] St Paul also speaks of sin in terms of 'dwelling' (*oikein*) (see Rom 7:17–20). The dominant idea is that of stability or indestructible firmness, although the word tends to take its meaning from the context in which it is used. Here, the context is both one of entering into a definitive relationship of covenant with God and of enjoying communion with him on the one hand and, on the other, of being in a state in which one is the true temple in which God dwells and where he is given spiritual worship.[6]

> Through him (the risen Christ) we both have access in the one Spirit to the Father. So, then, you are no longer strangers and sojourners, but you are fellow-citizens with the saints and members of the household of God, built upon the foundation of the apostles and prophets, Christ Jesus himself being the chief corner-stone, in whom the whole structure is joined together and grows into a holy temple in the Lord, in whom you are also built into it for a dwelling-place of God in the Spirit (Eph 2:18–22; cf. 1 Cor 3:10–17).

80

There are several other terms in the New Testament that are concerned with the theme of indwelling. I have sometimes tried to keep the meaning of *rûah* and *pneuma* by translating them as 'breath', but H. B. Swete pointed out that though such an association with 'wind' is known in the New Testament (see especially Jn 3:8), the comparisons that are characteristic of the Spirit are less with a temporary inspiration than with indwelling and filling.[7] The term *plērēs pneumatos*, 'full of the Spirit', is one that is used in particular by Luke, who applies it in the first place to Jesus (Lk 4:1), and spiritual writers have often regarded Jesus' heart as the first place where the Spirit was received,[8] since, after all, it was from his pierced side that water and blood flowed. However, Luke often also applies this phrase to the disciples (cf. Eph 5:18). M.-A. Chevallier comments: 'In the expression "filled with the divine breath", the gift of breath appears in the form of indwelling, for which Luke shows a great fondness'.[9]

In conformity with Scripture, then, the Fathers and later theologians preferred to stress the indwelling of God rather than simply his presence.[10] In his *Ecclesiastical History* (VI, 2, 11), Eusebius related the following story, which can be dated to about 195: Leonidas, who was later to die as a martyr, came one night to his little son, Origen, who was asleep. He uncovered Origen's breast and kissed it in the conviction that it was a temple in which the Holy Spirit dwelt, since the love of Jesus and of the Scriptures which spoke of him already dwelt in the child, who was to give evidence of that indwelling later.

Which representatives of that 'great cloud of witnesses', the later spiritual writers and mystics, should I choose? Undoubtedly John of the Cross or Jean-Jacques Olier, but also three women religious who are fairly close to us in history and who have written descriptions of their experience: Teresa of Avila (†1582), the Ursuline Marie de l'Incarnation (†1672) and the Carmelite Elizabeth of the Trinity (†1906), whose prayer: 'O my God, Trinity whom I adore' is well known in French'.[11]

These mystics describe a spiritual experience which presupposes an absolute gift, made in faith and love, and a generous and total self-abandonment to God, his activity and his inspiration of the kind that enables Paul's conviction—'It is no longer I who live, but Christ who lives in me' (Gal 2:20)—to become a reality in their lives. In their experience and in the witness that they bear, the spiritual union and the indwelling of the divine Persons are so closely connected that they are almost indistinguishable. This union has often been described as a 'spiritual marriage':

These souls no longer look for the joys and the tastes of the past; from now onwards they have the Lord himself in them and his Majesty lives in them (Teresa of Avila).

One day, at prayer in the evening, a sudden attraction seized hold of my soul. The three Persons of the blessed Trinity showed themselves once again to my soul and impressed on it the words of the most adorable incarnate Word: 'If a man loves me, my Father will love him and we will come to him and make our home with him'. That impression had the effect of those divine words. . . . And the most blessed Trinity, in its unity, took hold of my soul like a thing that belonged to it and that it had made capable of receiving its divine impression and the effects of its divine interchange. . . . From that time onwards, the effects took root and, as the three divine Persons possessed me, so did I possess them too (Marie de l'Incarnation; March 1631).

St Simeon the New Theologian, whom I could also have cited here, believed, as we have already seen in Volume I, that there has to be an experience of the Holy Spirit, who enables us to act and live. This was also clearly St Paul's conviction. For him, the Spirit acted in man's heart (see Rom 8:16; 9:1).[12] Over and above all critical questions about certainty concerning our state of grace, there is always practical evidence of the presence and activity of God in our lives. As Augustine declared: 'Interroge viscera tua: si plena sunt caritate, habes Spiritum Dei'—'Ask your inward parts; if they are full of charity, you have the Spirit of God!'[13]

If, however, we question ourselves critically or deal with the matter from the dogmatic point of view, we are bound to come to the same conclusion as the Council of Trent, namely that there can be no certainty of an infallible kind concerning man's state of grace.[14] This uncertainty does not, however, impede an experience of the activity of the Spirit in us, or a spontaneous and practical sense of certainty, without which we would never dare to partake of the body and blood of the Lord. The Holy Spirit is rightly called the 'Consoler'!

Our bodies are themselves the temple of the Holy Spirit and they form a substantial unity with our souls or 'hearts'. We must therefore take very seriously those statements which claim that our bodies can be transfigured and are able, in their own way, to reflect God's glory and the peace and joy of the Holy Spirit.[15] This aspect of the *arrha* or earnest-money of the kingdom and its manifestation in light is particularly stressed in the Eastern tradition and in particular by Gregory Palamas and Seraphim of Sarov. Another point also emphasized by Eastern Christians is that God's indwelling in our sanctified bodies is marked by their preservation—even though the body of the *starets* Zosima decomposed—and by the miracles that God works near and through them. The Western Church has, however, not lagged behind the East in this respect, and bodily effects such as transfigured faces, rays or visions of light, are attested in the West as in the East.[16]

Theologians have always considered this great supernatural reality of the indwelling in us of God who is three in one and they have, of course, considered it in their own way, that is, by asking questions and trying to formulate precise definitions. May they be forgiven for this approach! But everyone has to sing with the voice that God has given him. They have in fact asked two great questions: (1) How does this indwelling take place? and (2) Is it a personal indwelling of the Holy Spirit?

1. *How does this indwelling take place?*

There have been various explanations, some of them difficult to follow. For technical information about the different opinions, it is worth consulting specialist works or articles in encyclopaedias.[17] All that I shall do here is to outline in the simplest possible way the most common view encountered among the disciples of Thomas Aquinas. Thomas himself expressed his own view primarily in a work of his youth,[18] thus showing how important a place he gave to the Holy Spirit in his theological synthesis. I propose to discuss it under four headings:

(a) God is everywhere and nowhere. He is nowhere because he is spiritual and neither circumscribed by or settled in any place, but he is present where he is active. This is known as his presence of immensity. His activity does not make him change himself, but brings about a reality outside himself, the word 'outside' meaning simply that that reality is not himself. It is therefore a reality that is placed in a certain relationship with God, and that relationship varies according to the effects that are produced. Is grace involved here? It should not be seen as a thing or a substance, since it is we who are created or transformed according to grace, that is, according to this real relationship and therefore according to the quality of sons and heirs of the Father's goods—eternal life and glory. It is not possible to quote them all here, but it is valuable to read in this context Rom 8:14–17, 21, 29; Gal 4:4–6. The text from Galatians speaks of the two missions of the Son and the Spirit as interpenetrating and completing each other and being directed towards the same end, that of our adoption as sons of God.

(b) Because he brings this about in us and insofar as he brings it about, God becomes firmly present to us as the end of this filial relationship, that is, as the object of knowledge and love. This takes place through faith and charity, which are supernatural gifts of grace. God gives himself to us, in such a way that, although it is purely through grace and we hardly dare to confess it, we really possess him.[19] It is really God himself who is the end of that filial life of knowledge and love. This new, supernatural and deifying presence presupposes a presence of immensity and is grafted on to it.[20] God, who is already present through his activity as creator and is therefore also substantially present—since his action is himself—but only as the cause of being and working, gives himself and becomes substantially present as the object of our love and knowledge, as the end of our return to him as our Father. His presence is also personal. He is not only in us, but also with us, and we are with him.[21] We are with him insofar as it is really him!

Thomas' way of expressing this sublime reality is very similar to Cyril of Alexandria's. The latter spoke of a substantial presence and a union according to a relationship, *enōsis schetikē*, a union that places us in a new and deifying relationship with God and his Holy Spirit (see below, note 33).

(c) For Cyril and indeed for most of the Greek Fathers, this new relationship was attributed to uncreated grace, that is, to the Holy Spirit as given. The Western theologians knew that there is no created grace without uncreated grace, since grace is that gift with which God himself is given or rather, it is what God gives when he gives himself. They spoke, however, above all of the created gift, and debated whether uncreated grace preceded created grace logically and causally (in the very simultaneity of their coming). If this was so, ought it not to be admitted that God dwelt in a man who was (still) a sinner? Would sanctifying grace still be needed? It would be interesting to comment in this context on the episode of Zacchaeus (Lk 19:2–10), in which Jesus stayed with a sinner, but at the same time brought the grace of conversion to his home. However that may be, very many Fathers and later theologians, including Thomas Aquinas (see L. B. Gillon), have been convinced that uncreated grace, that is, the gift of the Holy Spirit, logically and causally precedes created grace which re-creates us according to God. The new presence and indwelling are the fruit of this simultaneous coming.[22] The witness borne by mystics here is very illuminating—they speak above all of God as acting and of coming in sovereign power to the soul in order to become one with it, to take possession of it and to be with it and in it as it is with and in him.

(d) Finally, it is important to remember the eschatological character of our divine sonship, the gift of the Spirit and the reality of God in us. Grace is, theologically, the cell from which glory grows, and we have the Spirit now only as earnest-money or *arrha*. The end will be when God is 'everything to everyone' (1 Cor 15:28) as an intimate, radiant, total and sovereign presence of a kind that does not consume the individual. Moses' burning bush is a clear image of this—it is Yahweh present and it burns, but is not consumed.[23] According to Thomas, the beatific vision does not require the mediation of created concepts. It is God's direct communication of himself, but in it the soul is adapted by him so that what takes place may be an act of its own life. On this view, the beatific vision is the supreme realization of God's indwelling and of man's possessing and enjoying God. In this life, all that we have of that supreme indwelling is a beginning that is mediated by supernatural gifts. It is worth reading Thomas' text from his first book of *Sentences* in this connection (see note 19 below).

2. *Is it a personal indwelling of the Holy Spirit?*

(a) The Eastern and the Western Churches, the Church Fathers, the theologians and the councils of the Church are all unanimous in affirming that what the divinity does outside itself is the work of all three Persons.[24] There is no activity of the nature or essence of the divinity that exists prior to or independent of the Persons. All such activity is performed by those Persons according to and through a divinity that is common to all three, not only because they are consubstantial, but also because they are inside one another. (The latter is known as perichoresis or circumincession, and I shall be discussing this question in Volume III of this work.) It is important, then, to remember that no action can be attributed to the Holy Spirit independently of the Father and the Son. Even in the 'mission' or sending of the Holy Spirit at Pentecost, the Father and the Son 'come' with the Spirit. On the other hand, it is not possible to say that the Father is 'sent'—he sends. Scripture speaks, after all, in a meaningful way!

(b) In the West at least, the fact that every action performed by God is common to all three Persons of the Trinity has given rise to the idea that an activity in creatures can only be *appropriated* to one Person, but is not peculiar to him, or his own. This clearly does not apply to the incarnation insofar as it is a personal union of a humanity with the Person of the Son, within that Person's being. If, however, it is seen as a work that has been actively caused, even the incarnation is common to the three Persons.

Although the idea of appropriation is not peculiar to Thomas Aquinas, it is usual to take his analysis as a point of departure.[25] Appropriation goes back to what Scripture tells us and to what we are able to say in an attempt to express a reality that we are incapable of defining because it has to do with the mystery of the divine Persons in the twofold work of creation and grace. It need not in any way affect what I have already said above in (a).

Certain essential attributes or activities that are really common to the three Persons are appropriated to one of those Persons, even though they may not be peculiar to that Person in a sense that would exclude the other Persons. This is because of their resemblance to the personal property characterizing that Person. This enables us to know, in a mysterious manner, what is peculiar to that Person. There is really something in that Person to justify the appropriation, but we cannot clarify it or say with certainty that there is an attribute peculiar to that one Person that would exclude the other Persons from what is appropriated to the one. This procedure has both strengths and weaknesses: it is suggestive, but at the same time it is open to criticism; it comes near to poetry, it fosters prayer; it is close to Scripture, but is not entirely satisfactory in the rational sense. One can look at it and say either, in disappointment, 'That is all it is' or, with joy, 'That is it exactly!'

It is certainly true that appropriation is used a great deal in Scripture, the liturgy and the patristic texts. The creed attributes creation to the Father, although it is clearly an action performed by the divinity of one in three Persons.[26] The fact that attributes are constantly changing their position points to the non-exclusive nature of appropriations. St Bernard criticized Peter Abelard's appropriation of power to the Father, wisdom to the Word and goodness to the Spirit, yet these are attributes which have remained classical and were upheld not only by Robert of Melun, who defended Abelard,[27] but also by Richard of Saint-Victor[28] and Thomas Aquinas. At the same time, in Scripture, Paul attributed *agapē* to the Father (see 2 Cor 13:13; Rom 15:30–31; 5:5; Gal 5:13, 22; 1 Thess 3:4) and, especially since A. Nygren's writings on this subject, this is not difficult to understand, seeing that *agapē* is love at its source, bringing goodness into being, in short, the principle of all being.[29] We have also seen that Irenaeus attributed wisdom to the Holy Spirit, and that Hermas and Justin identified wisdom with the Spirit. It would be possible to extend these comments into a methodical study of this question of attribution.

What strikes me especially is that whenever the New Testament attributes a work to one Person, it also affirms a communion of activity and describes a sort of concelebration on the part of the three Persons:

> Heb 9:14: 'the blood of Christ, who through the eternal Spirit offered himself without blemish to God';

> Tit 3:4–6: the 'goodness and loving kindness' of 'God our Saviour', who saved us and poured out his Holy Spirit on us through 'Jesus Christ our Saviour';

> Gal 4:4–6: God sent his Son to redeem us and adopt us as sons, then sent 'the Spirit of his Son into our hearts, crying, "Abba! Father!" ';

> 1 Cor 6:11: we were washed, sanctified and justified 'in the name of the Lord Jesus Christ and in the Spirit of God';

> 2 Cor 13:14: 'the grace of the Lord Jesus Christ and the love of God and the fellowship of the Holy Spirit';

> 1 Cor 12:4–6: 'there are varieties of gifts (but the same Spirit); and there are varieties of service (but the same Lord); and there are varieties of working (but . . . the same God)';

> 2 Cor 1:21–22: God establishes us in Christ and has given us the Spirit as earnest-money;

> Mt 28: 'baptizing them (all nations) in the name of the Father and of the Son and of the Holy Spirit'.

(c) Because of these data and the way in which the Greek Fathers spoke about them—a way which is very similar to the way in which Scripture deals with them—there has been a certain dissatisfaction with the category of appropriation, and several twentieth-century theologians have tried to overcome this by suggesting different approaches to the problem.[30] In particular the part played in the process of indwelling by the Holy Spirit has been questioned. As long ago as the seventeenth century, Dionysius Petavius (†1652)[31] expressed this question in terms of a dilemma: either a personal and peculiar property of the Holy Spirit (peculiar in the sense of exclusive), or a common action that is simply appropriated. Petavius believed that sanctification and indwelling were peculiar to the Holy Spirit and that they only went back to the Father and the Son because the latter were inseparable from the Spirit and followed him. In his argument, Petavius relied on the Greek Fathers and especially on Cyril of Alexandria.

P. Galtier resolutely rejected the support of the Greek Fathers.[32] He studied fourteen authors, but found that none of them attributed to the Holy Spirit a rôle of sanctification on the basis of his hypostasis that was not carried out by the Father and the Son. The Fathers were above all anxious to establish the consubstantiality of the Spirit with the first two Persons. None of the Persons did anything on his own. 'The only purpose' of the attributes applied to the individual Persons, Galtier insisted, 'is to make their personality manifest to us. This does not lead to any diversity in their activity, their will or their power' (p. 276). This may be too abrupt a conclusion to draw.[33] The truth is that the Greek Fathers were not conducting such a strictly rational search as the Latin Fathers. They approached the mystery from a different point of departure—from what Scripture had to say about the Persons. This will be elaborated in Volume III.

M. J. Scheeben (†1892) was *par excellence* the theologian of grace, and his ideas about the indwelling of the Holy Spirit in the righteous soul were widely discussed during his lifetime and continue to be discussed.[34] Although his thought is not always clear, he did not fail to recognize on the one hand the inseparability of the divine Persons in their activity outside themselves and, on the other, the part played by created grace as the internal principle of our justification and sanctification. He believed, however, that there was more, and indeed that the New Testament and the patristic texts contained more, in other words, a mission and a gift of the Person of the Holy Spirit realizing our sonship of grace and establishing us in a relation- ship which terminated in his Person as indwelling in us and taking possession of us:

> Although the substance and the activity are common to all three Persons, the possession of the substance is peculiar to each Person. Each Person possesses the divine nature in a special way and can also possess a created nature in a way that is peculiar to him and thus possess it on his own. The Son alone assumed a created nature in his physical possession. Could the Holy Spirit also not take possession of a creature in a way that is peculiar to his Person, by means of a possession that is less perfect and purely moral . . . so that the other divine Persons may possess that creature in that determined relationship, not directly, but only in him, as is the case with the Son in his humanity? . . . In his hypostatic personality and by virtue of that

personality, the Holy Spirit is the pledge by which we possess the other Persons . . .
(*Mysterien des Christentums*, §30 [cf. Eng. tr. (1946) p. 166]).

We have been made similar to the Son of God, not only because we have been
conformed to him, but also because we possess the same Spirit personally in us. . . .
That is why the Apostle was able to call the Holy Spirit 'the spirit of sonship, in
whom we cry "Abba! Father!" ' (Rom 8:15), that is to say, the Spirit brings about
our adoption as sons just as he constitutes or rather seals the relationship of
sonship that is created by that adoption [cf. *ibid*. p. 169].

This parallelism, which is almost an identification, with the physical union
of Jesus' humanity and the Person of the Son is obviously too close to be
theologically tenable. It led Scheeben to his unfortunate definition of the
Church as 'a kind of incarnation of the Holy Spirit'. His intention, however,
was not in any sense unfortunate and I hope to be able to do him justice,
since the least that can be said about Scheeben in this context is that he was
expressing dissatisfaction with the doctrine of appropriation. Nor was he the
only theologian to do this. Others have continued to do so until our own
time.[35] Karl Rahner wrote:

It would have to be proved in the strictest possible way that it was impossible for
there to be this kind of communication of the divine Persons each in his own
personal particularity and hence a non-appropriated relationship to the three
Persons. There is no way of producing such a proof. Consequently there can be
absolutely no objection to maintaining on the basis of the positive data of Revelation that the attribution of determinate relations of the recipient of grace to the
three divine Persons is not merely a matter of appropriation, but is intended to
give expression to a proper relationship in each case. In Scripture it is the Father in
the Trinity who is our Father, and not the threefold God. The Spirit dwells in us in
a particular and proper way. These and like statements of Scripture and Tradition
are first of all *in possessione*. It would be necessary to prove that they may be
simply appropriated, on the grounds that they can be understood merely as such
and that the contrary is impossible; it cannot be presupposed. So long as this has
not been achieved, we must take Scripture and the expressions it uses in as exact a
sense as we possibly can.[36]

(d) Most theologians are nowadays very open to inspiration from the Greek
Fathers, who were the first to fight for the doctrine of the Trinity. It is
valuable to quote a few typical texts here:

The Father does all things through the Word and in the Spirit and it is in this way
that the unity of the holy Trinity is safeguarded. . . . The grace and the gift granted
in the Three are given on behalf of the Father by the Son in the Spirit. Just as the
grace granted comes from the Father through the Son, so too can there be no
communication of the gift in us if it is not made in the Holy Spirit, since it is by
participating in him that we have the charity of the Father and the grace of the Son
and the communication of the Spirit himself (2 Cor 13:13).[37]

We have not been taught to say that the Father is active alone and that the Son does not act with him, or that the Son is individually active without the Spirit. But every active power coming from God to enter his creation, whatever concept or name may be used to distinguish it, comes from the Father, goes through the Son and is fulfilled in the Holy Spirit. That is why the active force is not divided among several agents, since the care that each takes of it is neither individual nor separate. Everything that is brought about, either by our providence or by the government of the universe, is brought about by the Three, without thereby being threefold.[38]

Our renewal is in a sense the work of the whole Trinity. . . . We may seem to attribute to each of the Persons something of what happens to us or of what is done with regard to the creature, but we still believe that everything is done by the Father by passing through the Son in the Holy Spirit.[39]

This coming of God to man forms the basis of the return of man in the Spirit through the Son to the Father. In this return, the Three function as one, but, both in the return and in their coming, they also function according to the order and the character of their hypostatic being. The nature, essence or being may be common to the Three, but not in the sense of being a common stock that is somehow prior—even logically prior—to the Persons. Their common essence or existence is situated only in the mutual communication of the processions and being of the Persons (their circumincession or circuminsession). The Three therefore come as one, although this operation is not threefold, but according to the order and characteristics of their hypostatic being. Their action assimilates the soul that they are sanctifying to the divinity by assimilating it to what is peculiar to each hypostasis according to a causality that is quasi-formal or exemplary.

'Quasi-formal' in this context means simply that the form does not become part of the physical composition of the recipient, but remains transcendent. We confess that the Holy Spirit is *Dominum et vivificantem*—he is Lord inasmuch as he is the principle of life. This idea of quasi-formal causality, however, and therefore the idea of assimilation to the hypostatic aspect of each Person can be based on authorities of value.[40] This was the Fathers' aim in regard to the Holy Spirit when they took up Paul's idea of the 'seal' that makes an impression on us (2 Cor 1:22; Eph 1:13–14; 4:30).[41]

Each author has to do what he can with his own insights and the resources at his disposal in considering this very difficult question. I would not like to provide a mixture of every possible element, which would result only in confusion. I would, however, like to point out that substantial agreement has been reached now, at least in certain respects: The three Persons may act together in the descending line of efficient causality, nevertheless (1) they do so according to the order of the procession and the special character of the hypostatic being of each Person.[42] (2) In the order of return established in this way, (a) the image of God as Trinity is realized in the soul in a way that is more profound and more conforming,[43] and (b) the soul thus made holy is placed in a relationship with the three Persons as the term of its knowledge of faith, of supernatural love and often of experience. This is borne out by the evidence of such mystics as Marie de l'Incarnation.[44] In this way, in its relationship of ascent back to God, the soul has a special connection with each of the three Persons, and this relationship will be fulfilled in the beatific vision.[45]

3. 'A Spirit making us adopted sons and making us cry: "Abba! Father!"' (Rom 8:15)

I do not intend to discuss our life as sons here, even in its aspect of prayer. Continuing the line I have followed in the preceding pages and applying the teaching that I have outlined there, I would like simply to ask the question: To whom is the 'Our Father' addressed?

Most believers would reply, almost without reflecting, that it is addressed to the one whom Jesus called 'my Father and your Father, my God and your God' (Jn 20:17; cf. 2 Cor 1:2–3). This is what Augustine first thought and preached.[46] In his later great work on the Trinity, however, he approached the question after much reflection and wrote:

> The Trinity is called only one God, . . . but we cannot say that the Trinity is the Father, unless we are using a metaphor (nisi forte translate) with regard to the creature, because of the adoption as sons. Scripture, after all, says: 'Hear, O Israel, the Lord your God is the only Lord'. It is impossible to understand these words if we do not consider the Son or the Holy Spirit. We quite rightly call that one Lord our Father who regenerates us by his grace. It is, however, in no sense right to give the Trinity the name of Son.[47]

This text, which was quoted by Peter Lombard (In I Sent. d. 26, c. 5), impressed the Scholastics, for whom 'God' meant the one who was invoked in the psalms and the whole of the Old Testament and was at the same time the divinity in three Persons. They did not know what Karl Rahner has so clearly pointed out, that Theos in the New Testament always refers (with only six exceptions) to the Father.[48] In short, they never failed to respect the universally held principle that all the works brought about in the created world were common to all three Persons of the Trinity. Were they, however, common to all three Persons without distinction? The Greek Fathers thought of this common character on the basis of the consubstantiality and the circumincession of the Persons, whereas in the West it was attributed to the essence or nature. This is right, but there is a risk of the direction of thought becoming less personalized. We likewise tend, when we consider our life of grace, to think in a less personalized way of the grace that makes us adopted sons, especially under its aspect of being an 'entitative' and 'accidental' reality produced in us, in other words, as created grace. As such, it is a work of God ad extra and therefore a work that is common to the three Persons of the Trinity. It is so even in Christ, and the incarnation, as a work taking place in the creature, is the work of all three Persons together.

As a result of this, a distinction is made in the *Summa Fratris Alexandri* between Christ as the Son of the Father through divine begetting and Christ as the Son of God as a creature and through created grace. Bonaventure wrote: 'Just as the Father and the Son and the Holy Spirit are a single principle of creation by virtue of the production of nature, so too are they a single Father by reason of the gift of grace . . . , Fatherhood is appropriated to the Person of the Father when we speak of his relationship with us.'[49] Albert the Great used nine arguments to prove that the Trinity was our Father, but he also said felicitously that we receive adoption as sons in accordance with the resemblance of the Son of God by nature and that its communication takes place through the Holy Spirit, who produces the image of the Son in us and leads us to call on the Father.[50]

Thomas Aquinas could not deny that, as a reality produced in us, grace went back to all the Persons of the Trinity, that is, to the divinity itself,[51] but at the same time he gave increasing emphasis to personalism. Here are some examples:

> The Holy Spirit makes us children of God because he is the Spirit of the Son. We become adopted sons by assimilation to natural sonship. As Rom 8:29 says, we are 'predestined to be conformed to the image of his Son, in order that he might be the first-born among many brethren' (*Contra Gent*. IV, 21).

> Although it is common to the whole of the Trinity, adoption is appropriated to the Father as its author, to the Son as its exemplar and to the Holy Spirit as the one who impresses in us the resemblance to that exemplar (*ST* IIIa, q. 23, a. 2, ad 3).

> Strictly speaking, sonship is related not to nature, but to the hypostasis or the Person. Adoption as sons is a shared resemblance to natural sonship (*ST* IIIa, q. 23, a. 4).

During the last Lent of his life, in 1273, when he was in Naples, Thomas wrote a commentary on the Our Father. In his explanation of this invocation of the Father, he did not consider the technical question and spoke without further definition as anyone might speak.[52] I do not believe that his point of view had in any way changed here or that he had, as E. Mersch has claimed, 'two series of texts'.[53] Thomas believed that our adoption as sons was a reality that was brought about voluntarily or freely by God as the Trinity of three Persons and that when we used the words 'Our Father' we were addressing the whole Trinity. The reality thus brought about, however, assimilates us to the eternal Son. Again and again he uses the words *similitudo, assimilare, exemplar* ('resemblance', 'assimilate' and 'exemplar' or 'model'). Now, a very positive element is stressed in this use of the idea of assimilation or similarity. It is that grace makes us resemble, not the Father or the Spirit, but the Son, or possibly the divine nature (see, for example, 2 Pet 1:4) insofar as that is hypostasized in the Son. According to the gospel of John, Jesus gives to those who believe in him what he has received from the Father.

Do the New Testament texts, that Thomas knew well and frequently quoted, call for more? We are Jesus' brothers (see, for example, Mt 18:10; Jn 20:17; Rom 8:29) and this is not a merely juridical or moral title. The title of 'sons' that has been given to us assimilates us to the eternal Son more than by way of exemplarity.[54] Is Paul addressing the three Persons generally or is he only addressing the first Person when, for example, he prays to 'the God of our Lord Jesus Christ, the Father of glory' (Eph 1:17) or 'the Father of our Lord Jesus Christ' (Col 1:3) or when he bows his knees before the Father (Eph 3:14) or gives thanks to God the Father through the Lord Jesus (Col 3:17)? When Jesus cried: 'Abba! Father!', was he addressing himself as the second of the three Persons?

Did Augustine not open up a way for us when he spoke forcefully of our unity with Christ in his Body and claimed that we form a single total Christ, one son with him and in him (see the texts quoted in the following chapter, notes 21 and 22)? A. Dorsaz followed this way earlier this century (see note 30 below). We are not, however, members of the body of Christ as a natural body united hypostatically to the Son. It is not possible to make Christians members of the Son as sons of God by nature. We are sons of God by a free decision of grace. This brings us back to Thomas' point of departure (*ST* IIIa, q. 23, a. 2), in which he quotes Jas 1:18: 'Of his own will he brought us forth by the word of truth'. The Church Fathers insisted that the Son was begotten, whereas the sons by adoption were *made*.

The Greek Fathers preserved the principle that God's works done *ad extra* were common to all three Persons, but at the same time spoke more positively about the connection between our created sonship and the uncreated sonship of Christ. They were able to do this because of two factors that were peculiar to them and also closely related to each other. On the one hand, their teaching was situated within a logical framework of participation and exemplarity and of formal and not of efficient causality.[55] Now it is on the basis of production or efficiency that our sonship should be attributed to the divinity as such. On the other hand, they believed that, when he assumed human nature, the Son of God assumed more than the *individual* humanity of Jesus and in fact assumed 'human nature', not in the sense that the hypostatic union extended to all men, but rather in the sense that the nature that each man hypostasizes individually is assumed as such by the Son of God, and that in him that nature is reconformed to the likeness of the Son, who is himself the perfect image.

This provides us with another, but equally Catholic way of constructing and expressing the mystery of our adoption as sons. The most important aspect is not the manner of explanation, but the reality itself, namely that we are truly sons in the true Son. We cry: 'Abba! Father!' and when we do this we are praying to the Father of our Lord Jesus Christ, whose holiness and grace were, in a humanity that is consubstantial with our own, a holiness and a grace of the eternal Son of 'God'.

NOTES

1. See, for example, Exod 24:16–17; 1 Kings 8:10; Ps 85:10. See also the beginning of A. M. Ramsey's excellent book, *The Glory of God and the Transfiguration of Christ* (London, 1949).

2. For the idea of *šekinah*, see J. Abelson, *The Immanence of God in Rabbinical Literature* (London, 1913), pp. 77–149; G. F. Moore, 'Intermediaries in Jewish Theology. Memra, Shekinah, Metatron', *Harvard Theological Review*, 15 (1922), 41–85; M.-J. Lagrange, *Le Judaïsme avant Jésus-Christ* (Paris, 1931), pp. 446–452; J. Bonsirven, *Le Judaïsme palestinien au temps de Jésus-Christ*, 2 vols (Paris, 1935), especially the tables; L. Bouyer, *La Bible et l'Evangile. Le sens de l'Ecriture: du Dieu qui parle au Dieu fait homme (Lectio divina,* 8) (Paris, 1951), pp. 107ff.; my own *The Mystery of the Temple* (Eng. tr.; London, 1962), pp. 11, 12, 17f., 93f., 132, 133, 297–298 note 5; A. M. Goldberg, *Untersuchungen über die Vorstellung von der Schekinah in der frühen rabbinischen Literatur* (Berlin, 1969).

3. G. F. Moore, *op. cit.*, p. 48. It is, however, very difficult to say exactly what the Talmudists themselves believed the relationship between the *šekinah* and the Holy Spirit was: see Goldberg, *op. cit.*, pp. 465–468.

4. F. Hauck, '*menō, monē*', *TDNT*, IV, p. 578: Jn 14:23 'depicts salvation after the departure of the Saviour as a permanent abiding of Christ and God in believers. (*Para* has much the same meaning as *en*, as verse 17 shows.) God's dwelling among his people is expressed cultically in the O.T. (Exod 25:8; 29:45; Lev 26:11) and is expected by promise in the last time (Ezek 37:26ff.; Zech 2:14; Rev 21:3, 22ff.). In spiritual form it has now come into the community's present.'

5. The word of God (Jn 5:38; 15:7; 1 Jn 2:14), life (1 Jn 3:15); love (1 Jn 3:17); truth (2 Jn 2), anointing (1 Jn 2:27); see F. Hauck, '*menō, monē*', *TDNT*, IV, p. 576.

6. M. Fraeymann, 'La spiritualisation de l'idée de temple dans les épîtres pauliniennes', *ETL*, 23 (1947), 378–412; my book, *op. cit.* (note 2); A.-M. Denis, 'La fonction apostolique et la liturgie nouvelle en esprit', *RSPT*, 42 (1958), 401–436, 617–650.

7. H. B. Swete, *The Holy Spirit in the New Testament* (London, 1909), pp. 328–329.

8. M.-J. Le Guillou, *Les témoins sont parmi nous. L'expérience de Dieu dans l'Esprit Saint* (Paris, 1976), p. 144, cites in particular a fine text by Stefan Fridolin, quoted in C. Richstätter, *Die Herz-Jesu-Verehrung des deutschen Mittelalters* (Munich, 1924), p. 187.

9. M.-A. Chevallier, *Souffle de Dieu. Le Saint-Esprit dans le Nouveau Testament (Le point théologique,* 26) (Paris, 1978), p. 124. Chevallier's text continues as follows: '*Plērēs pneumatos* is found in Acts 6:3, 5; 7:55; 11:24, and the same idea, but with a verb, is found in Lk 1:15, 41, 67; Acts 2:4; 4:8, 31; 9:17; 13:9; see also 13:52. Because of the formula of indwelling, the man who is filled with the breath—in this case, Jesus—remains the subject of an action and is not, as in Mk and even in Mt, moved by the breath.'

10. See Epiphanius of Salamis. *Adv. haer.* III, *haer.* 74, n. 13 (*PG* 42, 500C) and the long version of his creed (*DS* 44); Basil the Great, *Ep.* 2, 4 (*PG* 32, 229B); Cyril of Alexandria, *Comm. in Ioan.* V, c. 2 (*PG* 73, 757A-B); Augustine, *Ep.* 187 *ad Dardanum*, c. 13, no. 38 (*PL* 33, 847); Thomas Aquinas, *In I Sent.* d. 14, q. 2, a. 1; *Comm. in 2 Cor.* c. 6, lect. 3; *ST* Ia, q. 8, and q. 43, a. 3.

11. For Teresa of Avila and Marie de l'Incarnation, see G.-M. Bertrand, *Dictionnaire de Spiritualité*, VII (1971), cols 1759–1762 and 1762–1767 respectively; for Elizabeth of the Trinity, see M. M. Philipon, *ibid.*, IV, cols 590–594. There are also good bibliographies given in the dictionary. Elizabeth's prayer 'O mon Dieu, Trinité que j'adore' is reproduced in the anthology by Mme Arsène-Henry, *Les plus beaux textes sur le Saint-Esprit*, 2nd ed. (Paris, 1968), pp. 318–319. See also, in the same collection, pp. 283–288, extracts from the spiritual journal of Lucie-Christine (†1908), which can stand comparison with the texts of Marie de l'Incarnation.

12. References in J. D. G. Dunn, *Jesus and the Spirit* (London, 1975), p. 201.

13. Augustine, *In Ep. Ioan.* VIII, 12 (*PL* 35, 2043).

93

14. Council of Trent, Session VI, c. 9 and 11 and canons 13 ff. (*DS* 803–805, 823ff.). The most frequently quoted texts are Eccles 9:1; 1 Cor 4:4; 10:12; Phil 2:12; Heb 12:28–29. Many monographs have been written on this subject.
15. See V. Lossky, *The Mystical Theology of the Eastern Church* (Eng. tr.; London, 1957) and *In the Image and Likeness of God* (Eng. tr.; Oxford, 1974); M.-J. Le Guillou, *op. cit.* (note 8), pp. 105–122, including many texts.
16. St Gertrude, quoted by Le Guillou, *op. cit.*, pp. 106–107; Teresa of Avila: 'It is certain that, having received it (= the power) in this union, the soul communicates it to all those who dwell in the castle and to the body itself': *Dictionnaire de spiritualité*, col. 1761.
17. See A. Michel, *DTC*, XV/2 (1950), cols 1841–1855; R. Moretti, *Dictionnaire de spiritualité*, VII (1971), cols 1745–1757, with a full bibliography.
18. *In I Sent.* d. 14–17 (in 1254); *Contra Gent.* IV, c. 20–22 (in 1259–1260); *ST* Ia, q. 43 (in 1267). There is as yet no comprehensive study of Thomas' pneumatology. J. Mahoney of Heythrop has written a number of useful shorter studies.
19. John speaks of 'having' the Father and the Son (1 Jn 2:23; 5:12; 2 Jn 9) or of having life. I know no more than the title of H. Hanse, '*Gott haben' in der Antike und im frühen Christentum. Eine religions- und begriffsgeschichtliche Untersuchung* (Berlin, 1939). The classical theologians believed that 'possessing' God was in the first place being possessed by him: *haberi a Deo*; see Bonaventure, *In I Sent.* d. 14, a. 2, q. 1, ad 3; *Breviloquium* p. 1, c. 5, and p. 5, c. 1. Thomas Aquinas noted that God (the divine Persons) gives himself to us, though we cannot have any power over him (see *In I Sent.* d. 15, q. 3, a. 1 sol.), but he gives himself in such a way that we enjoy him (*ST* Ia, q. 38, a. 1; q. 43, a. 3). He also said: 'In the procession of the Holy Spirit in the perspective that we are discussing here, that is, as including the gift of the Holy Spirit, it is not enough for just any new relationship to exist between the creature and God. The creature must have a relationship with God as with a reality that it possesses, because what is given to someone is, in a sense, possessed by him. But a divine Person can only be possessed by us either in perfect enjoyment—this is what the gift of glory obtains—or in imperfect enjoyment—and this is so in the case of sanctifying grace; or rather the divine Person is given to us in the form of that by which we are united to him in order to enjoy him, in that the divine Persons leave in our souls, by a certain impression of themselves, certain gifts through which we formally enjoy (them), those of love and wisdom. It is because of this that the Holy Spirit is called the pledge of our inheritance': *In I Sent.* d. 14, q. 2, a. 2, ad 2.
20. See Thomas Aquinas, *In I Sent.* d. 37, q. 1, a. 2, ad 3; *Comm. in Col.* c. 2, lect. 2. Thomas distinguishes three modes or orders of union: 'secundum similitudinem' (*per potentiam, essentiam*); 'secundum esse', which is the case with Christ, through a union in hypostasis; 'secundum substantiam' (*per gratiam et operationem supernaturalem cognitionis et amoris*), which is the case with us.
21. On the one hand, then, Thomas interprets charity as friendship, which includes reciprocity, and, on the other, the formula that occurs again and again: 'they will be my people and I shall be their God', becomes in Rev 21:6–7: 'To the thirsty I will give water without price from the fountain on the water of life. He who conquers shall have this heritage and I will be his God and he shall be my son.'
22. Documentation in J. C. Martínez-Gómez, 'Relación entre la inhabitación del Espíritu Santo y los dones criados de la justificación', *Estudios eclesiásticos*, 14 (1935), 20–50; see also K. Rahner, *op. cit.* (note 36 below). For the debate in the fourteenth century, see L. B. Gillon, 'La grâce incréée chez quelques théologiens du XIVᵉ siècle', and P. Vignaux, 'La sanctification par l'Esprit incréé d'après Jean de Ripa, I Sent. d. XIV–XV', *Miscellanea A. Combes* (Rome and Paris, 1967), II, pp. 275–284 and 285–317 respectively. The great Scholastic theologians were undoubtedly embarrassed by having to criticize Peter Lombard's thesis on the Holy Spirit as charity.
23. 'Le ciel, buisson ardent du monde', *VS*, 618 (January-February 1976), 69–79. It is also worth seeing what theology has to say about charity in the state of glory; for the grace

inchoatio gloriae, see *ST* Ia, q. 8, a. 3, ad 10; q. 27, a. 5, ad 6; *In III Sent*. d. 13, q. 1, a. 1, ad 5.

24. Need I give references? Fathers of the Church: Athanasius, *Orat. II adv. Arian*. 41–42 (*PG* 26, 234ff.); *Ep. I ad Serap*. 19ff. (*PG* 26, 573ff.); *Ep. III ad Serap*. 6 (*PG* 26, 633–636); Basil the Great, *De Spir. sanct*. 37, 38, 52, 56–60 (*PG* 32, 133–140, 164–165, 172–180); *Contra Eunom*. III (*PG* 29, 660–661); Gregory Nazianzen, *Orat*. XXXIV, 14 (*PG* 36, 256A); Gregory of Nyssa, *Quod non sunt tres dii* (*PG* 45, 124–129); *Contra Eunom*. II (*PG* 45, 504–508); John Chrysostom, *Comm. in Rom. Hom*. 13, 8 (*PG* 60, 519); *Comm. in 2 Cor. Hom*. 30, 2 (*PG* 61, 608); Augustine, *De Trin*. I, 4, 7 and 5, 8 (*PL* 42, 824); *Comm. in Ioan. ev*. XX (*PL* 35, 1557–1558); *Sermo* 213, 6 (*PL* 38, 1065); Cyril of Alexandria, *Comm. in Ioan*. IV, 3 and X, 2 (*PG* 73, 588 and 74, 336); *De SS. Trin. dial*. III (*PG* 75, 801–804); *Adv. Nest*. (*PG* 76, 172A and 180B-D). Councils: Lateran of 649 (*DS* 501); Sixth and Eleventh of Toledo, 638 and 675 (*DS* 491 and 538); Friuli, 796 (*DS* 618); Florence, 1442 (*DS* 1330). Popes: Professions of faith of Vigilius, 552; Pelagius I, 561; Agatho, 680 (*DS* 415, 441, 542, 545); Leo XIII, Encyclical *Divinum illud munus*, 1897 (*DS* 3326); Pius XII, Encyclical *Mystici Corporis*, 1943 (*AAS* 35 (1943), 231; *DS* 3814).

25. Thomas Aquinas, *De ver*. q. 7, a. 3: 'To appropriate simply means to connect a thing that is common to something particular. It is certain that what is common to the whole Trinity cannot be connected to what is peculiar to one Person, if the intention is to claim that it is more suitably applied to him than to any other Person. That would destroy the equality of the Persons. What is common to all three Persons can, however, be thus connected to the extent that it bears a greater resemblance to what is peculiar to one or another Person than to what is peculiar to another. Goodness, for example, is related to what is peculiar to the Holy Spirit, who proceeds as love (and goodness is the object of love). Power is appropriated to the Father, since power is as such a beginning and it is peculiar to the Father to be the beginning of the whole divinity. And by the same reasoning, wisdom is appropriated to the Son, since it is related to what is peculiar to the Son, who proceeds, as a Word, from the Father': *De ver*. q. 10, a. 13; *ST* Ia, q. 37, a. 2, ad 3; q. 38, a. 1, ad 4; q. 39, a. 7; q. 45, a. 6. The translation above from Thomas' *De ver*. q. 7, a. 3 is based on the Fr. tr. by C. Journet. H. Dondaine has provided a clear explanation: *La Trinité*, II (Paris, 1946), pp. 409ff. A. Patfoort, *BullThom*, VIII (1947–1953), no. 3, pp. 864–877, has discussed, from the technical point of view, C. Sträter, 'Het begrip "appropriatie" bij S. Thomas', *Bijdragen*, 9 (1948), 1–41, 144–186.

26. The creed is constructed on the basis of the classical attributions: see Origen, *De prin*. I, 3, 8 (ed. P. Koetschau, p. 61): 'Cum ergo (omnia) primo ut sint habeant ex Deo Patre, secundo ut rationabiliter sint habeant ex Verbo, tertio ut sancta sint habeant ex Spiritu sancto'.

27. See R. M. Martin, 'Pro Petro Abaelardo. Un plaidoyer de Robert de Melun contre S. Bernard', *RSPT*, 12 (1923), 308–333.

28. See Richard's treatises *De Trinitate* and *De tribus appropriatis*.

29. This accounts for the part played in the Church's missionary work by the Father and the *fontalis amor* within him: see the Decree on Missionary Activity, *Ad Gentes divinitus*, 2.

30. A. Dorsaz, *Notre parenté avec les Personnes divines* (Saint-Etienne, 1921), argued, for example, on the basis of the doctrine of the mystical Body, that our being called Christ's brothers enables us to be, through grace, what Christ is by nature, that is, sons of the Father, and at the same time gives us as our own the first Person as Father and the third as life and holiness. H. Mühlen, 'Person und Appropriation', *Münchener Theologische Zeitschrift*, 16 (1965), 37–57, inferred from certain doubtful hypotheses of Thomas Aquinas that it was possible to introduce a new and equally doubtful category, which he called 'personal causality'; see also C. Sträter, *op. cit*. (note 25). I have included what is valid in Mühlen's suggestion in section (d) above, pp. 88–90.

31. For Dionysius Petavius, see the article 'Pétau' in *DTC*, XII, cols 1334–1336, and XV, cols 1851f.; *Dictionnaire de Spiritualité*, IV, cols 1305f.

32. P. Galtier, 'Temples du Saint-Esprit', *RAM*, 7 (1926), 365–413; 8 (1927), 40–76, 170–179; *idem, Le Saint-Esprit en nous d'après les Pères grecs* (*Anal. Greg.* XXXV) (Rome, 1946).

33. J. Mahé, whose article, together with its many quotations, is still valuable, said: 'The work of sanctification is not so peculiar to the Holy Spirit that it belongs exclusively to him . . . but it can be said that it belongs to him in a special way that does not apply to the other two Persons. There are three reasons for this and all are based on the Greek idea of the Trinity: (a) he is the hyphen that connects our souls to the Son and the Father; (b) he is the image of the Son and, by impressing himself on our souls, he reshapes them in the image of the Son and consequently in that of the Father; (c) he is the sanctifying virtue of the divinity; holiness is as essential to the Holy Spirit as Fatherhood is to the Father and Sonship is to the Son': see his 'La sanctification d'après S. Cyrille d'Alexandrie', *RHE*, 10 (1909), 30–40, 469–492; my quotation will be found on p. 480. See also L. Janssens, 'Notre filiation divine d'après S. Cyrille d'Alexandrie', *ETL*, 15 (1938), 233–278; B. Fraigneau-Julien, 'L'inhabitation de la sainte Trinité dans l'âme selon Cyrille d'Alexandrie', *RSR*, 44 (1956), 135–156.

34. Scheeben discusses this question particularly in his *Mysterien des Christentums*, §30, which was first published in 1865. An account of the nineteenth-century debates (especially T. Granderath) and of discussions in the earlier part of the present century (especially A. Eröss and H. Schauf) in E. Hocedez, *Histoire de la Théologie au XIXᵉ siècle*, III (Tournai, 1947), pp. 254ff.; *DTC*, XIV, col. 1273; XV, cols 1852ff.; P. Galtier, *L'inhabitation en nous des trois Personnes. Le fait. Le mode* (Paris, 1928), pp. 98–112; B. Fraigneau-Julien, 'Grâce créée et grâce incréée dans la théologie de Scheeben', *NRT*, 77 (1955), 337–358.

35. See H. Mühlen, *L'Esprit dans l'Eglise*; G. Bavaud, 'Note sur la mission du Saint-Esprit', *Freiburger Zeitschrift für Philosophie und Theologie* (1972), 120–126, according to whom it is a relationship enabling us to participate in the knowledge and the divine love personalized by the third Person.

36. K. Rahner, 'Some Implications of the Scholastic Concept of Uncreated Grace', Eng. tr., *Theological Investigations*, I (London and Baltimore, 1961), pp. 319–346; my quotation will be found on pp. 345–346. The 'kind of communication' in the text is explained in the whole article as an ontological communication of the hypostasis (or uncreated grace) by a quasi-formal causality (which finds its supreme realization in the beatific vision). Thomas Aquinas speaks of a 'causa formalis inhaerens' of our divine sonship: see *In III Sent.* d. 10, q. 2, a. 1, sol. 3.

37. Athanasius, *Ad Ser*. I, 28 and 30; Fr. tr. J. Lebon, *SC* 15, pp. 134, 138–139.

38. Gregory of Nyssa, *Quod non sint tres dii* (*PG* 45, 125C).

39. Cyril of Alexandria, *Comm. in Ioan*. X, 2 (*PG* 74, 337).

40. Basil the Great, *De spir. sanct.* XXVI, 61: 'On reflection, it seems to me that the preposition *en*, "in", has very many meanings. All the different meanings of the word are, moreover, used in the service of the idea that we have of the Spirit. We say, for example, that form is *in* the matter, that power is *in* the recipient, a permanent disposition is *in* the subject affected by it and so on. Well, insofar as the Holy Spirit perfects rational beings by consummating their excellence, he has the nature of form. And in fact the one who no longer lives according to the flesh, but lives subject to the guidance of the Spirit of God, who is called a son of God and who is conformed to the image of the Son of God is given the name of "spiritual"': *SC* 17bis (1968), p. 467, Fr. tr. B. Pruche, who comments, in a note, that it is not possible to 'make the text say that Basil attributed a rôle of formal causality to the Person of the Holy Spirit in the process of Christian deification'. According to Dionysius Petavius, *De Trin*. VIII, 5, 12 (*Opera omnia*, ed. Vivès, III, p. 474) and J. Mahé, 'La sanctification d'après S. Cyrille d'Alexandrie', *op. cit.* (note 33), 474ff., that is exactly the position of Cyril of Alexandria. According to the *Summa Fratris Alexandri* (John of La Rochelle and Alexander of Hales), 'We are bound to recognize all created grace as a likeness and disposition of the created soul making it agreeable and like to God, *quia ibi est*

forma transformans—because there is in it a transforming form—that is, uncreated grace' (Quaracchi ed., IV, p. 609). G. Philips has called this sentence a particularly happy one that is fully in accordance with his own idea of personal union with the living God; see his *L'union personnelle avec le Dieu vivant. Essai sur l'oriǵine et le sens de la grâce créée (Bibl. ETL, XXXVI)* (Gembloux, 1975), pp. 93, 277. At the same time, Philips quotes (p. 268) and praises this text of Bonaventure: 'Grace is an inflowing that comes from the supreme Light and always preserves contact with its origin, as light does with the sun': *In II Sent.* d. 26, a. 1, q. 6, end. Thomas Aquinas makes the same comparison in *ST* IIIa, q. 7, a. 13 c, and on at least one occasion calls the Holy Spirit the 'causa formalis inhaerens' of our divine sonship; *In III Sent.* d. 10, q. 2, a. 1. sol. 3. He also says: 'per dona eius ipsi Spiritui Sancto coniungimur': *In I Sent.* d. 14, q. 2, a. 1, q. 1. See also K. Rahner, *op. cit.* (note 36).

41. See Cyril of Alexandria, *Thes. assert.* 34 (*PG* 75, 689D), Fr. tr. J. Mahé, *op. cit.* p. 475: 'How is it possible to call *made* the one by whom the image of the divine essence is imprinted in us and thanks to whom the seal of uncreated nature is impressed in our souls? It is not in the manner of a painter that the Holy Spirit draws the divine essence in us, since that would make the essence separate from him. It is not in that way that he makes us in the likeness of God. God himself and proceeding from God, he impresses himself as though in wax in the hearts of those who receive him, in the manner of a seal, invisibly. By this communication and assimilation with himself, he gives his primordial beauty to human nature and remakes man in the image of God.' See also *De Trin.* VII (*PG* 75, 1088B), quoted by Mahé, pp. 483–484. For Thomas Aquinas, see his *Comm. in 2 Cor.* c. 1, lect. 5; *in Eph.* c. 1, lect. 5 and c. 4, lect. 10; *In I Sent.* d. 14, q. 2, a. 3, ad 2. It would be interesting to investigate the theme of the *sigillatio* in a pneumatological perspective. See, for example, Athanasius, *Ad Ser.* I, 23 and III, 3 (*PG* 26, 584C–585A and 629A-B); Basil the Great, *De spir. sanct.* XXVI, 64 (*SC* 17bis, p. 476). The patristic and Scholastic use of the Pauline texts obviously goes beyond the exegetical meaning of the same texts: see G. Fitzer, 'sphragis, sphragizō', *TDNT*, VII, pp. 939–953.

42. For Thomas Aquinas, see *ST* Ia, q. 34, a. 3; q. 45, q. 6 c and ad 2 (creation); *In I Sent.* d. 15, q. 4, a. 1 (return to God). See also E. Bailleux, 'Le personnalisme de S. Thomas en théologie trinitaire' and 'La création, œuvre de la Trinité selon S. Thomas', *RThom*, 61 (1961), 25–42; 62 (1962), 27–60.

43. This is a very important theme, but it would take me too far from the present subject if I were to discuss it here. There are many monographs available. I will do no more here than simply indicate the place that it occupies in Thomas' synthesis and point to the coherent nature of his approach. The anthropology of the image (Ia, q. 93), which is taken up again at the beginning of Ia IIae (Prol.) refers to the Trinity. The profound unity that exists between the two treatises is found in Thomas' philosophy and theology of spiritual being, with the two activities that characterize it—the word and love. God's image in man is realized in dependence on the missions of the Word and the Spirit and by the intensity of the acts that are in accordance with them. See S. de Beaurecueil, *L'homme image de Dieu selon S. Thomas d'Aquin. Etudes et Recherches*, VIII and IX (Ottawa, 1952 and 1955); G. Lafont, *Structures et méthodes dans la Somme théologique de S. Thomas d'Aquin* (Tournai, 1961), pp. 265–298. See also H. de Lubac, *Le mystère du surnaturel* (Paris, 1965), pp. 129ff., 240, who insisted that we are made in God's image because he destined us to that similarity (through the Holy Spirit).

44. G.-M. Oury, *Ce que croyait Marie de l'Incarnation* (Brussels, 1972), p. 149: 'The mystery of the divine life is reflected in the sanctified soul, because the mode of the relationship that the soul has with the Father, the Son and the Spirit is determined by the activities that are peculiar to the life of the Trinity'. Thomas Aquinas gives an account of this experience, for example, in his treatises *In I Sent.* d. 14, q. 2, a. 2, sol. and ad 2 (see above, note 19); *In III Sent.* d. 35, q. 2, a. 1, sol. 1 and 3; see G. Philips, *L'union personnelle, op. cit.* (note 40), pp. 170ff.; A. Gardeil, 'L'expérience mystique dans le cadre des "missions divines" ', *VS* (Suppl.), 31 (1932), 129–146; 32 (1932), 1–21, 65–76; 33 (1932), 1–28.

45. The following have explained this question in this way: John of St Thomas, *Cursus theologicus*, IV, ed. Vivès, q. XLIII, dist. 17. ad 2; A. Gardeil, *La structure de l'âme et l'expérience mystique*, II (Paris, 2nd ed., 1927), pp. 135–139; C. Journet, *L'Eglise du Verbe incarné*, II (Paris, 1951), p. 512; S. Dockx, *Fils de Dieu par grâce* (Tournai, 1948); A. Bundervoet, 'Wat behoort tot het wezen van Gods heiligende genade en inwoning volgens Sint Thomas' I Sent. d. XIV–XVII en XXXVII?', *Bijdragen* (1948), 42–58; K. Rahner, *op. cit.* (note 36); G. Philips, 'Le Saint-Esprit en nous. A propos d'un livre récent', *ETL*, 24 (1948), 127–135 (the book in question was by P. Galtier); C. Vagaggini, *Theological Dimensions of the Liturgy* (Eng. tr.; Collegeville, Minn., 1976), pp. 191–192; S. Tromp, *Corpus Christi quod est Ecclesia*, III: *De Spiritu Christi anima* (Rome, 1960), pp. 12ff. It is also possible to mention Thomas Aquinas in this context; in *In I Sent.* d. 30, q. 1, a. 2, he distinguishes the relationship between the creature and God as either 'ut ad principium' or 'ut ad terminum' and, in that case, 'secundum exemplaritatem'; he concludes: 'in infusione caritatis est terminatio in similitudinem processionis personalis Spiritus Sancti'.
46. *Sermo* 57, 11 (*PL* 38, 387), which Philips, *op. cit.* (note 40), p. 33, dates to before 410.
47. *De Trin.* V, 11, 12 (*PL* 42, 918ff.); Fr. tr. Philips, *op. cit.*, p. 34.
48. K. Rahner, 'Theos in the New Testament', Eng. tr., *Theological Investigations*, I (London and Baltimore, 1961), pp. 79–148.
49. Bonaventure, *In III Sent.* d. 10, a. 2, q. 3 concl. and ad 2 (Quaracchi ed., III, p. 238). I have quoted directly or indirectly from Alexander of Hales, Bonaventure and Albert the Great as they appear in G. Philips. *op. cit.* (note 40), pp. 89ff., 115 and 130ff. respectively.
50. Albert the Great, *Comm. in Ioan.* 3, 9 and 13 (ed. A, Borgnet, XXIV, pp. 122ff., 125ff.; see also G. Philips, *op. cit.*, p. 131: Philips clearly does not much like Albert the Great, although he credits him with a 'decisive step forward'). He vehemently refuses to grant Christ the title of Son of the Trinity or Son of the Holy Spirit, even if the words 'son of the Spirit according to grace' were added. His reason for this is irrefutable: sonship is a relation between persons. How, he argues, would it be possible to maintain that Christ is a son of himself? Anyone imagining that sonship could be attributed to 'nature' would be making himself 'ridiculous'. Albert concludes by calling Brother Alexander's opinion 'erroneous': see *In III Sent.* d. 4, a. 4, sed contra: *ridiculum*; ad 6: *erronea*.
51. Thomas Aquinas, *In III Sent.* d. 10, q. 2, a. 2, sol. 2; *ST* IIIa, q. 23, a. 2; 'Pater noster' is addressed to the whole Trinity: see *ST* Ia, q. 33, a. 3, obj. 1.
52. *Coll. in Orat. Dom.* (see *Opera*, Parma ed., XVI, p. 124; ed. L. Vivès, XXVII, p. 183).
53. E. Mersch, *La théologie du Corps mystique* (Paris and Brussels, 1944), II, p. 44.
54. E. Mersch, *ibid*, p. 25, after noting the difference in the terms used in this context by Paul (*huios*) and John (generally *teknon*) and calling attention to the well-known passages in which John indicates the difference between Jesus and ourselves (Jn 20:17; cf. 17:1–2, 26), said: 'he (John) insists even more emphatically than Paul on the union and the similarity that exists between the only Son and those who receive in him the power to become children. As he is of God (8:42, 47; 16:25), so too are they of God (1 Jn 4:4, 6; 5:19; 3 Jn 11) and just as he was begotten by the Father, so are they also begotten by the Father (see Mersch's note 9 for references and the use of the same word, *gennan*). As he dwells in the Father and the Father in him, so too do they dwell in the Father and the Father in them' (see Mersch's references, p. 26, note 1). As the world cannot know him, it cannot know them (references on p. 26, note 2). In a word, they are children only because they are connected with his sonship and by being reborn in him they are born in God (cf. 1 Jn 5:20 with 5:18; 1 Jn 5:1 with Jn 3:1–21)'. On the other hand, an anonymous author (in fact A. Michel) in *L'Ami du Clergé*, 49 (1932), 294–300, elaborated the idea that Christian grace, that is, participation in the grace of Christ, was the grace of sons, since, in Christ, it was the grace that was in accordance with a humanity united hypostatically to the eternal Son of God. I am certainly in favour of this idea, although I would wish to avoid any suggestion of continuity between the Church and the incarnation as such (see H. Mühlen) and I have

certain reservations about the correctness of what the author says about John of the Cross's statement that we breathe the Holy Spirit.

55. See my article (Fr. orig. pub. in *VS* (Suppl) (May 1935), 91–107) 'Deification in the Spiritual Tradition of the East' (Eng. tr.), *Dialogue Between Christians* (London, 1966), pp. 217–231, with a supplementary note (pp. 229ff.) on the agreement reached by many authors; Athanasius spoke, for example, of 'participation' in the Son: see his *Orat. I contra Arianos*, 16 and 56 (*PG* 26, 45 and 129). See also E. Mersch, *op. cit.* (note 53), p. 34, note 1.

4
LIFE IN THE SPIRIT
AND ACCORDING TO THE SPIRIT

Although I clearly cannot, in this context, deal in any way fully with the spiritual life, I can and must, because the spiritual life is above all a life in the Spirit and according to the Spirit, touch, in a very over-simplified way, on the main aspects of the life of a Christian.[1]

1. THE HOLY SPIRIT MAKES LIFE 'IN CHRIST' REAL, PERSONAL AND INWARD

Being a Christian is being in Christ, making Christ the principle of life and living on Christ's account. This is expressed in the letters of Paul by such well-known terms as 'Christ in us', 'Christ in you, the hope of glory' (Col 1:27) and 'we are in Christ'. Paul rejoices and is sad, he is strong and he exhorts 'in Christ' or 'in the Lord'. He also expresses the same idea in different terms, especially by using verbs with the prefix *sun*-, often created by himself—'associated (with Christ) in suffering, in death, in resurrection or in glory'—or by using genitives: having the charity *of Christ*, the patience *of Christ* or being a prisoner *of Christ*.[2]

It is the same Spirit that made Mary fruitful that makes the Church fruitful. The beginnings of the Church in the Acts of the Apostles correspond to the infancy gospel in the first two chapters of Luke. Going perhaps too far with the verbal realism of Scripture, the Fathers and others, including Thomas Aquinas and Jean Gerson, identified the *semen Dei, sperma tou Theou* or 'seed' of which we are 'born of God' (1 Jn 3:9) with the Holy Spirit.[3] R. Spitz took up the same idea recently and, in an attempt to illustrate it, used what we know today of the maintenance, despite the continuous changes that take place in our cells, of our genetic code or programme, supported biologically by the nucleic acids DNA or RNA. From the spiritual point of view, it is the Spirit of Jesus who is given to us as the principle of Christian identity until the eschatological fulfilment.[4] This 'seed of God' is also, or is rather, the word received through faith, but this only goes to show once again how intimately related the two are. They are in fact as closely united as Christ and the Spirit are when they come to us and enter us. Paul speaks of our being both 'in the Spirit' and 'in Christ' and of our knowing 'in' the Spirit and 'in' Christ, the preposition *en* here meaning

100

the same as 'through' and indicating not a place, but a principle of life and action.[5] We have already seen in Volume I that there are many different activities and situations which, Paul believed, had their cause or their reason in both the Spirit and Christ. Cyril of Alexandria, whom I have already quoted many times in this work, had this to say about this unity of the Spirit and Christ:

> Jesus called the Spirit 'another Paraclete', because he wanted to reveal him in this way in his own person and show us that the Spirit was so similar to himself and that he worked as well and achieved as effectively, without any difference, what he himself achieved that he seemed to be the Son himself. He is in fact his Spirit. Jesus therefore called him the 'Spirit of truth', describing himself as the truth.
>
> In order to show that the word 'other' should not be understood as meaning a difference, but that it was used because of the personal subsistence (for the Spirit is Spirit and not Son, just as the Son is Son and not Father) at the moment when he said that the Spirit would be sent, Jesus promised that he would come himself.[6]

There are, however, things that Paul says of Christ that he does not say of the Spirit. These things include not only everything that Jesus did in his humanity, but also situations in the lives of Christians. Paul would not, for example, have said that we are the 'temple of Christ', even though Christ dwells in us through faith (Eph 3:17), nor would he have said that we are 'members of the Holy Spirit'. As F.-X. Durrwell has observed, 'It is no longer possible to interchange the formulae *in Spiritu* and *in Christo* as soon as it is recognized that the first applies to the personal Spirit and that the second points to our identification with Christ. We are identified only with Christ and not with the Holy Spirit. ... According to Paul, there is no "body" of the Holy Spirit. The sacred host carries on a mysterious work of incarnation in us, but on the account of the Son of God, by integrating us into Christ and assimilating us to him.'[7]

This spiritual identification or 'mystical' assimilation to Christ, and this absolute credit that we give him so that he will fill our lives, are brought about by the Holy Spirit as an intimate and transcendent cause and take place, as we have seen, as the indwelling of the Spirit in us. They are also realized by faith as an attitude in us. Through his Spirit, God the Father makes Christ dwell in our hearts, that is, in the depths of our being where our lives are orientated (see Eph 3:14–17).[8] Faith is a gift of God, which he makes through pure love (Eph 2:8). It is on the basis of this (*ex*) or by means of this (*dia*) that the Spirit is given. There can be no doubt that what is involved here is living faith. There are many texts in Paul, Luke and John:

> Did you receive the Spirit by works of the law or by hearing with faith? (Gal 3:2, 5) ... that we might receive the promise of the Spirit through faith (Gal 3:14; cf. 5:5).
>
> In him (Christ) you have heard the word of truth, the gospel of your salvation and have believed in him and were sealed with the promised Holy Spirit, the guarantee of our inheritance (Eph 1:13).

And God gave them the Holy Spirit just as he did to us and cleansed their hearts by faith (Acts 15:8–9). Did you receive the Holy Spirit when you believed? (19:2).

'If anyone thirst, let him come to me and let him drink who believes in me. As Scripture has said, Out of his heart shall flow rivers of living water.' Now this he said about the Spirit, which those who believed in him were to receive (Jn 7:37–39) [for this punctuation see Volume I, p. 50].

The gift and the activity of the Spirit cannot be limited to a single aspect in the development of faith. The Spirit is active in the word (1 Thess 1:5; 4:8; 1 Pet 1:12) and in listening (Acts 16:14). He is also active in bearing witness to Jesus, both internally and externally (Jn 15:26; Acts 1:8; Rev 19:10). The anointing to which 2 Cor 1:21 and 1 Jn 2:20, 27 refer is an anointing of faith, as I. de la Potterie has, I believe, satisfactorily established.[9] It is, however, obviously connected with the action of the Spirit: 'It is God who establishes us in Christ and who has anointed us; he has put his seal upon us and given us his Spirit in our hearts as a guarantee' (2 Cor 1:21–22). The same scholar has also shown that the seed of God (*sperma Theou*) in 1 Jn 3:9 is the word of God which enables us to be born through the faith with which it is received.[10] This is also the case with 1 Pet 1:23, where the Spirit cannot be separated from our rebirth through the seed or word of God. Indeed, this anointing of faith is so much the work of the Spirit that it is an extension and a communication to believers of the prophetic and messianic anointing that Jesus received from the Spirit at his baptism.[11] This anointing is active in the whole life of faith of the one who is baptized and who bears witness, whether he be personally inspired or officially commissioned. The Spirit deepens the faith of the disciples and strengthens it. He is essentially the Spirit of truth (Jn 14:17; 15:26; 16:13).[12]

The Spirit-Paraclete plays a very important part in nourishing our faith through our reading of the Scriptures. Paul bears witness to this in a very poignant way in the contrast that he makes between the Mosaic ministry and that of the new covenant: 'To this day, when they read the old covenant, that same veil (that covered the face of Moses) remains unlifted, because it is only through Christ that it is taken away. . . . When a man turns to the Lord the veil is removed; for the Lord is the Spirit and where the Spirit of the Lord is, there is freedom' (2 Cor 3:14ff.). This was the charter for the 'spiritual' reading of the Scriptures that was practised by the Fathers. Their reading of Scripture can also be of great help to us, not perhaps in its allegorical flights, but in its sober typological interpretation of the Old Testament. We have to add the word 'sober', because not all of it is authentically typological. Both aspects of the patristic interpretation, the typological and the allegorical reading, are present, for example, in Origen's writing, but it is worth quoting from it here mainly because of the love of Christ with which he examined Scripture:

102

It is for Jesus alone to remove the veil, so that we can contemplate what was written and fully understand what was said in veiled terms.[13]

Only the Church can understand Scripture; the Church, that is, that part of mankind that has been converted to the Lord.[14]

The Church Fathers affirmed again and again that, just as the Son revealed the Father, the Spirit reveals the Son.[15] In their own vocabulary, the mediaeval theologians said the same.[16] This conviction is absolutely biblical and has a long perspective. In Scripture, the testimony of the Paraclete, which is borne together with that of the apostles but in sovereign freedom, is always related to Christ (see Jn 14:16; 15:13–16). A confession of the truth concerning Christ is a criterion of the authenticity of the action of the Spirit (see 1 Cor 12:3; 1 Jn 4:2). Only the Spirit knows what is of God (1 Cor 2:11) and only he can enable us to reach the depths of the theandric truth of Christ. As G. Martelet said, 'The Spirit has been present with Christ from the eternal beginning of his begetting as the Son and has therefore been with the Son always. He is therefore also the privileged and irreplaceable one who bears witness to him. The apostles, who were only with Christ from the time that he was baptized by John the Baptist, are *also* witnesses, but the absolute witness, if he can be called this, the one without whom the testimony of the apostles would be no more than a testimony of flesh and the letter, of the mouth and the ear, but not of the spirit, is the Holy Spirit himself. He alone, as Paul pointed out, has looked into the depths of God and is able to say what is the radical identity of Christ.'[17]

The theandric truth of Christ impels us to recognize Christ in his humanity and therefore in his socio-cultural and historical conditioning. The Christian will therefore use all available scholarly means to understand that background, but, as a believer, he will inevitably go deeper than this, bearing in mind the words of St Paul: 'Now we have received not the spirit of the world, but the Spirit which is from God, that we understand the gifts bestowed on us by God. And we impart this in words not taught by human wisdom, but taught by the Spirit, interpreting spiritual truths to those who possess the Spirit. The natural man does not receive the gifts of the Spirit of God' (1 Cor 2:12–14).

Although one hardly dares to compare oneself to Paul or to apply such a text to oneself, it is certainly possible to take one's place humbly among the 'we' of whom he speaks and in the school of the cloud of witnesses who have as human beings carried the Tradition and in this way, 'being rooted and grounded in love, . . . have power to comprehend with all the saints what is the breadth and length and height and depth . . . that (we) may be filled with all the fullness of God' (Eph 3:17–19). If we keep to this school, the fruitless ways of 'hetero-interpretation', that is, an interpretation based on ideas and norms that are alien to the divine-human reality of Christ as the centre of God's plan, will be closed to us.

Augustine brought to this Catholic Tradition the excellent theme of the inner Master, without whose secret instruction the external words and the sacred text would not yield the whole truth that they contained:

> The sound of our words strikes your ears and the Master is in them . . . , Have not all of you heard this sermon? How many of you will leave here without having learnt anything? Insofar as it depends on me, I have spoken to all of you, but those to whom this anointing has nothing to say inwardly, those whom the Holy Spirit has not instructed inwardly, will leave without learning anything. External teaching is a help and an invitation to listen. But the throne of the one who instructs our hearts is in heaven. . . . (Here follows a quotation from Mt 8–9.) . . . If the one who has created, redeemed and called you, the one who, through the faith of his Holy Spirit, dwells in you, does not speak inwardly to you, our words will sound in vain.[18]

Life 'in Christ' and subject to the action of the Spirit is a filial life

Christ is the centre and indeed the culmination of our life as Christians, but he is not the end. As the 'Son of man', the type of man, he goes beyond himself and leads us beyond himself. He is everything *ad Patrem, pros ton Patera*—towards the Father and for him. If this were not so, he would not enable us to go beyond ourselves. 'The Spirit leads us to the Son, who leads us to the Father', as the classical theologians said.[19] As we have already seen, our sonship is based on that of Jesus himself. I shall now attempt to outline the way in which this is worked out, beginning with Jesus himself.

His soul as Son, that is, his human attitude and behaviour as the Son of God,[20] can be discerned in many scriptural texts. For example, 'when Christ came into the world, he said: "Sacrifices and offerings thou hast not desired, but a body thou hast prepared for me . . . Then I said: 'Lo, I have come to do thy will, O God' " ' (Heb 10:5, 7; Ps 40:7–9). At his baptism, Jesus became conscious of these words: 'Thou art my beloved Son; with thee I am well pleased' (Mk 1:11). From then onwards, he spoke throughout his adult life about his relationship to his father in a way that had been prepared by his obedience to his earthly father (Lk 2:51). The synoptic gospels already testify to this relationship, but it is expressed in words reported by John:

> 'The Son can do nothing of his own, but only what he sees the Father doing' (5:19).

> 'My food is to do the will of him who sent me and to accomplish his work' (4:34; 6:38; cf. 10:18).

> 'I can do nothing on my own authority; . . . I seek not my own will, but the will of him who sent me' (5:30).

> 'My teaching is not mine, but his who sent me' (7:16).

> 'I can do nothing on my own authority, but speak as the Father taught me. . . . I always do what is pleasing to him' (8:28, 29).

'I have not spoken on my own authority; the Father who sent me has himself given me commandment what to say and what to speak. And I know that his commandment is eternal life. What I say therefore I say as the Father has bidden me' (12:49–50).

'I do as the Father has commanded me, so that the world may know that I love the Father' (leaving to go to the garden and to his passion) (14:31).

'Father, the hour has come' (17:1).

This, according to the fourth evangelist, was Jesus. God's plan, however, was to go from the one to the one by way of the many. 'No one has ascended into heaven but he who descended from heaven, the Son of man' (Jn 3:13)—we can only come to the Father in him. That is why God constituted, in Jesus, a unique relationship of perfect sonship with him as Father and why he calls us to enter into communion with his Son (1 Cor 1:9) 'in order that he might be the first-born among many brethren' (Rom 8:29), in a history that is co-extensive with our own, until the time when 'the Son himself will be subjected to him who put all things under him, that God may be everything to every one' (1 Cor 15:28).

Commenting on this 'the Son himself will be subjected', Augustine said that this Son is not simply our head, the Christ, but his body, of which we are the members.[21] As sons of God, we are the body of the only Son.[22] Cyril of Alexandria, who had so much to teach us about our divine sonship, said:

Christ is both the only Son and the first-born son. He is the only Son as God, but he is the first-born son by the saving union that he has constituted between us and him in becoming man. In that, we, in and through him, have become sons of God, both by nature and by grace. We are those sons by nature in him and only in him. We are also those sons by participation and by grace through him in the Spirit.[23]

Our filial life, then, is found in our obedience and our search for a loving and faithful conformity to God's will, without at the same time renouncing our intelligence and our dignity as men. It may sound old-fashioned, but it is solidly and firmly traditional, and it is also true, that God's will is made incarnate in, among other things, the responsibilities of our state of life. This is also a common denominator in Paul's exhortations.[24] The culminating point and the heart of our filial life, however, is reached when we join Jesus in his prayer to the Father: 'I thank thee, Father' (Lk 10:21; prayer subject to the 'action of the Holy Spirit'); 'Father, . . . glorify thy Son' (Jn 17:1); 'Abba! Father!' (in the garden of Gethsemane: Mk 14:36; Lk 22:42); 'Father, into thy hands I commit my spirit!' (Lk 23:46) and finally, the prayer that we all know so well: 'When you pray, say: "Father . . ."' (Lk 11:2; Mt 6:9). As a result of J. Jeremias' excellent studies, we now know that this invocation of the Father was peculiar to Jesus and that, especially in the form of 'Abba', it had a familiar note of trust and affection.[25] We also know that it is the Holy Spirit who enables us to say it and who even says it in us (Gal 4:6; Rom 8:15).

We may therefore conclude by saying that we need all this—an understanding of the mystery of Christ, a daily life of obedience and a prayer to the Father as sons—if we are to be transfigured into the image of the Son by the Lord who is the Spirit (2 Cor 3:18).

2. TODAY AND IN THE ULTIMATE FULFILMENT 'ALREADY AND NOT YET'

The best expression of the unity and tension that characterizes the status of 'already' and 'not yet', either in the kingdom of God or in 'eternal life', is found in the well-known passage in the first epistle of John: 'See what love the Father has given us, that we should be called children of God (*tekna Theou*); and so we are. . . . We are God's children now; it does not yet appear what we shall be, but we know that when he appears we shall be like him, for we shall see him as he is' (1 Jn 3:1–2).[26]

Whereas Paul speaks at the level of the 'not yet', John prefers to speak at the level of the 'already'. For Paul, our state as adopted sons is a promise and an assurance that we shall inherit the patrimony of God our Father.[27] John, on the other hand, is convinced that we already have eternal life on condition that we believe in the one whom God has sent to us.[28] Paul, however, speaks again and again of Christ in us and of the earnest-money or *arrha* of the Spirit, while John knows that we are looking forward to glory.

In the perspective of the Bible, the truth of a thing is its end or term, that towards which it is directed. 'Possessing the first-fruits of the Spirit, we sigh in ourselves, waiting to be truly treated as sons and for our bodies to be redeemed' (Rom 8:23; translation based on L. Cerfaux's French translation[29]). Those first-fruits are the pledge of our inheritance and they can strengthen our confidence (2 Cor 1:21–22; 5:5; Eph 1:13: 'You . . . who have believed in him were sealed with the promised Holy Spirit, which is the guarantee (= earnest-money) of our inheritance until we acquire possession of it'). The Spirit, given to us in fullness, will obtain for us the resurrection of our bodies as he did for Christ (Rom 1:4; 1 Pet 3:18). We shall only be fully sons of God when we are, like Christ, in the state of sons of God. It was his resurrection and glorification that ensured that state for Christ, with the result that Paul, in his sermon to the Jews (Acts 13:33), was able to claim that Jesus' resurrection was the fulfilment of the words: 'Thou art my son, today I have begotten thee' (Ps 2:7). Jesus, speaking of the state of men in the world to come, said: 'They are sons of God, being sons of the resurrection' (Lk 20:36); 'they all live to him (God)' (verse 38) in the same way that the risen Christ was living and 'the life he lives he lives to God' (Rom 6:10). That life has already begun in us, yet it is still the object of hope and expectation:

But you are not in the flesh, you are in the Spirit, if the Spirit of God really dwells in you. Anyone who does not have the Spirit of Christ does not belong to him. But if Christ is in you, although your bodies are dead because of sin, your spirits are alive because of righteousness. If the Spirit of him who raised Jesus from the dead dwells in you, he who raised Christ Jesus from the dead will give life to your mortal bodies also through his Spirit which dwells in you (Rom 8:9–11).

It is the Spirit himself bearing witness with our spirit that we are children of God, and if children, then heirs, heirs of God and fellow-heirs with Christ, provided we suffer with him in order that we may also be glorified with him. I consider that the sufferings of this present time are not worth comparing with the glory that is to be revealed to us. For the creation waits with eager longing for the revealing of the sons of God . . . because the creation itself will be set free from its bondage to decay and obtain the glorious liberty of the children of God . . . and not only creation, but we ourselves, who have the first-fruits of the Spirit, groan inwardly as we wait for adoption as sons, the redemption of our bodies (Rom 8:16–23).

The Christian can surely never grow tired of reading and re-reading that text, so rich in content! After all, we are groaning, which is quite different from complaining or whining. It is an expression of our passionate longing for the coming of the kingdom of God. Eschatologically, we shall reign with him: 'If we have died with him, we shall also live with him; if we endure, we shall also reign with him' (2 Tim 2:12). We have already seen that there is a variant of the text usually given as 'Thy kingdom come' (Lk 11:2) and that this variant: 'May thy Spirit come upon us and purify us' was followed by many of the Fathers.[30] It is also a fact that John expresses in terms of 'life' what the synoptics and Paul express in terms of the kingdom of God.[31] These two realities, in accordance with the two aspects of 'already' and 'not yet' that belong to them, can also be translated in terms of the Holy Spirit.[32]

As L. Cerfaux has pointed out, 'Rom 8, which contains Paul's most explicit doctrine of sonship, considers eschatological as a development of present sonship'.[33] Life, kingdom and Spirit have a dynamic existence in our lives here on earth.[34] The Spirit is both an appeal or a demand and the principle of holy life: 'God has not called us for uncleanness, but in holiness . . . God, who gives his Holy Spirit to you' (1 Thess 4:7–8).

Paul speaks here of purity, a theme that is closely related to that of God's indwelling and of the temple, and the personal aspect on the one hand and the communal or ecclesial aspect on the other that are associated with it.[35] I have already spoken about life in the Church in Part One of this volume and shall have to return to it later. In this chapter, it would be possible to speak about the whole *vita in Christo*. I shall deal with the most important aspects of that life in Christ later: prayer, the struggle against the flesh and our participation in Christ's passion, and life subject to the guidance of the Spirit and the 'gifts'. In Volume III I shall deal with the sacraments in their relationship with the Spirit.

The connection between our present sonship and our eschatological sonship is in the first place obviously that of the reality itself: gift of the Spirit and created grace, as we have seen, are closely linked. This connection can also be seen within the special perspective of 'merit', Thomas Aquinas especially believed that the Holy Spirit played an extremely important part in this.[36] If we are to acquire merit, we have to make use of our freedom, since, without freedom, it is difficult to see what truth there could be in a 'judgement' by God. If, however, it is eternal life that we are to merit, that is, if we are to be worthy to enter the family of God himself and be in communion with him, then the good action of our freedom must be borne up by a power of the order of God himself. That power is Christ himself. This theology was developed in the sixteenth century by Cajetan and was taken up again in the present century by E. Mersch and Cardinal Journet. It is also the Holy Spirit.

In this context, Thomas Aquinas quoted Jn 4:14: 'The water that I shall give him will become in him a spring of water welling up to eternal life' and the Council of Trent made use of the same quotation.[37] It means that the only power that can ascend again to God is one that originally comes from him. This is virtually the image of communicating vessels. Merit only exists because of grace and assumes that the Spirit is 'sent' and given in the gift of grace and that it is through his divine dynamism that we are able to return through the Son to the Father.

In the end, it is God who takes the absolute initiative insofar as he is Love and grace. We have to consent to this initiative and co-operate with it ('synergy'), but it is what carries out and carries through to its term the process described by Paul in Rom 8:29–30. Our actions, which may 'merit' eternal life, are elements in a chain of grace in which the Holy Spirit as uncreated grace takes the initiative and provides the dynamism until the ultimate victory is reached in which God is merely crowning his own gifts when he awards us a crown for our 'merits'.

The Holy Spirit and the divine charity which he pours into our hearts (Rom 5:5) are likewise the principle of the communion of saints and that of the communication of spiritual good things in which that communion is expressed. I have, of course, already spoken about this in an earlier chapter.

NOTES

1. It would be possible to quote a great number of references, but I will confine the list to two general works: L. Cerfaux, *The Christian in the Theology of St Paul* (Eng. tr.; London, 1967); I. de la Potterie and S. Lyonnet, *La vie selon l'Esprit, condition du chrétien* (*Unam Sanctam*, 55) (Paris, 1965).
2. See L. Cerfaux, *op. cit.*, pp. 358ff.
3. See Irenaeus, *Adv. Haer*. IV, 31, 2 (*PG* 7, 1069–1070; *SC* 100, pp. 792, 793), who speaks with extreme realism of a typology of Lot sleeping with his two daughters; Ambrose, *Comm. in Luc*. III, 28 (*PL* 15, 1605), brings together the word and the Spirit: 'Cui nupsit Ecclesia, quae Verbi semine et Spiritu Sancto plena, Christi corpus effudit, populum scilicet christianum'; other references will be found in S. Tromp, *Corpus Christi quod est*

Ecclesia, III: *De Spiritu Christi anima* (Rome, 1960), pp. 165ff., 228ff. In an explanation of our divine sonship. Thomas Aquinas said : 'Semen autem spirituale a Patre procedens est Spiritus Sanctus' and quoted 1 Jn 3:9: *Comm. in Rom*. c. 8, lect. 3; also, 'Semen spirituale est gratia Spiritus Sancti ': *Comm. in Gal*. c. 3, lect. 3. See also Jean Gerson's sermon 'Ambulate dum lucem habetis' (*Œuvres*, ed. P. Glorieux, V, p. 44); see also L. B. Pascoe, *Jean Gerson: Principles of Church Reform* (Leiden, 1973), pp. 45–47, 207–208.

4. R. Spitz, *Le Révélation progressive de l'Esprit Saint* (Paris, 1976), pp. 187, 191ff., 202ff.
5. The causal rather than the local meaning of *en* and its relative equivalence to *dia* are so widely recognized that it would be pointless to provide references.
6. Cyril of Alexandria, *Comm. in Ioan*. IX (*PG* 74, 257A–B and 261A; Fr. tr. A. Solignac, *NRT* (1955), 482).
7. F.-X. Durrwell, *La Résurrection de Jésus, mystère de salut*, 2nd ed. (Le Puy and Paris, 1955), pp. 257–258; 10th ed. (Paris, 1976), p. 170.
8. This is a text which St Bernard often quoted. Reacting against any physical identification of the Christian with Christ, Pius XII rejected the idea of a lengthy indwelling of Christ's humanity in us as a result of eucharistic communion: see his encyclicals *Mystici Corporis* (1943) and *Mediator Dei* (1947); see also *L'Ami du Clergé* (27 April 1950), 257ff.; (14 February 1952), 99; S. Schmitt, 'Päpstliche Entscheidung einer theologischen Streitfrage. Keine Dauergegenwart der Menschheit Christi im Christen', *Benediktinische Monatschrift* (1948); G. Söhngen. 'Die Gegenwart Christi durch den Glauben' in A. Fischer, *Die Messe in der Verkündigung* (Freiburg, 1950).
9. For the anointing of the Christian by faith, see I. de la Potterie, *op. cit*. (note 1), pp. 107–167. The text of 1 Jn 2:20, 27 is quoted in the Dogmatic Constitution on the Church, *Lumen Gentium*, 12, in connection with the *sensus fidei* of the whole people of God.
10. I. de la Potterie, *op. cit*., pp. 53ff., 56, note 1 ('Born of water and the Spirit'), 209ff. (the sinlessness of the Christian according to 1 Jn 3:6–9).
11. *Ibid*., pp. 123ff.
12. *Ibid*., pp. 85–105 (the Paraclete).
13. Origen, *Dialogue with Heraclides*, Fr. tr. J. Scherer, *SC* 67 (1960), p. 91.
14. Quoted by H. de Lubac, *Histoire et Esprit. L'intelligence de l'Ecriture d'après Origène* (*Théologie*, 16) (Paris, 1950), pp. 303, 304, 316ff. See also the very instructive little book by H. Urs von Balthasar, *Parole et Mystère chex Origène* (Paris, 1957), which first appeared as articles in *RSR*, 26 (1936), 513–562 and 27 (1937), 38–64.
15. Athanasius, *Ad Ser*. III (Fr. tr. J. Lebon, *SC* 15 (1947), pp. 163–165).
16. This is apparent from a text in one of Albert the Great's commentaries, *Comm. in Luc*. X, 22 (ed. A. Borgnet, XXIII, 45): 'The apostle clearly attributes revelation to the Holy Spirit when he says: "God has revealed to us through the Spirit" (1 Cor 2:10–13). . . . He says this because, just as man's spirit bears the thought which guides the hand of the worker in his task and bears the thought in the language that he speaks, the Holy Spirit is in the same way the one who bears the Father's Word and who therefore reveals the Father. This revelation goes back both to the Father as its origin and its author and to the Word as his form of light and formal knowledge as well as to the Spirit as the one who bears and inspires it.'
17. G. Martelet, *Sainteté de l'Eglise et Vie religieuse* (Toulouse, 1964), pp. 84–85.
18. Augustine, *Comm. in 1 Ioan*. III, 13; IV, 1 (Fr. tr. P. Agaësse, *SC* 73 (1961), pp. 211, 219; *PL* 35, 2004, 2005). For this same theme in Augustine's other writings, see *De Mag*. XI, 36–XIV, 46 (*PL* 32, 1215–1220); *Conf*. IX, 9 (*PL* 32, 773); *Sermo* 179, 1 (*PL* 38, 966); E. Gilson, *Introduction à l'étude de S. Augustin* (Paris, 1920), pp. 88–103, 137–138, 164–165, 256, note 1; J. Rimaud, 'Le maître intérieur', *Saint Augustin* (*Cahiers de la Nouvelle Journée*, 17) (Paris, 1930), pp. 53–69. For the continuation of this theme, see Gregory the Great, *Hom. in Ev*. II, *Hom*. 30 (*PL* 76, 1222); *Moral*. XXVII, 43 (*PL* 78, 424). J. Alfaro, *Greg*, 44 (1963), 180, note 357, has provided references to Prosper of

Aquitaine, Fulgentius of Ruspe, Bede, Alcuin, Rabanus Maurus, Haymo of Auxerre, Paschasius Radbert, Florus of Lyons, Atto of Vercelli, Rupert of Deutz, Hervetus, Peter Lombard, Robert Pullen, Hugh of Saint-Cher, Nicholas of Lyra and Bonaventure. For the last mentioned, see E. Eilers, *Gottes Wort. Eine Theologie der Predigt nach Bonaventura* (Freiburg, 1941), pp. 57ff., 71ff. To the above list, the following should also be added: Thomas Aquinas, *De ver.* q. 11, a. 1; *ST* Ia, q. 117, a. 1, ad 1; *Comm. in ev. Ioan.* c. 14, lect. 6, and, nearer to our own times, Bossuet, *Sermon sur la parole de Dieu* (13 November 1661) (ed. J. Lebarq, III, pp. 579–580); A. Gratry, *Les Sources*.

19. Ignatius of Antioch's 'Come to the Father' in *Ad Rom.* VII, 2 is well known, but see also Irenaeus, *Adv. haer.* V, 36, 2 (*PG* 7, 1225; *SC* 163 (1969), pp. 460, 461); Thomas Aquinas, *Comm. in ev. Ioan.* c. 14, lect. 6: 'Sicut effectus missionis Filii fuit ducere ad Patrem, ita effectus missionis Spiritus est ducere ad Filium'.

20. D. Lallement, 'La personnalité filiale de Jésus', *VS*, 47 (June 1936), 241–248; P. Glorieux, 'Le Christ adorateur du Père', *RSR* (1949), 245–269; W. Koster, 'Der Vatergott im Jesu Leben und Lehre', *Schol*, 16 (1941), 481–495; J. Guillet, 'L'obéissance de Jésus-Christ', *Christus*, 7 (1955), 298–313; W. Grundmann, 'Zur Rede Jesu vom Vater im Johannes-Evangelium (Jo 20, 17)', *ZNW*, 52 (1961), 213–230; J. Jeremias, *op. cit.* (note 25 below).

21. Augustine, *De div. quaest.* LXXXIII, q. 69, 10 (*PL* 40, 79).

22. *Ep. Ioan. ad Parth.* X, 5, 9 (*PL* 35, 2055); see also *Comm. in ev. Ioan.* XX, 5; XLI, 8 (*PL* 35, 1568 and 1696); *Enarr. in Ps.* 122, 5 (*PL* 37, 1634). To this should be added the theme of *Christus integer* and Augustine's commentary on 'Only one ascends to heaven, the Son of man'. The following quotation from his *Sermo* 71, 28 is also interesting in this context: 'Ad ipsum (Spiritum) pertinet societas qua efficimur unum corpus *unici Filii Dei*' (*PL* 38, 461).

23. Cyril of Alexandria, *De recta fide ad Theod.* (*PG* 76, 1177).

24. H. Pinard de la Boullaye, *La dévotion du devoir* (Paris, 1929), with its application, in chapter X, pp. 69ff., to Jesus' life as Son.

25. J. Jeremias, *The Prayers of Jesus* (London, 1967).

26. Col 3:3–4: 'Your life is hid with Christ in God. When Christ who is our life appears, then you will also appear with him in glory.' See also Phil 3:21. See L. Cerfaux, *op. cit.* (note 1), pp. 322–324.

27. Rom 8:19, 23–24; Eph 1:14; 1 Tim 6:12; Tit 3:7. For the theme of our future inheritance of the Kingdom of God, see 1 Cor 6:9–10; 15:50; Gal 5:21; for the theme of incorruptibility, see 1 Cor 15:50; for that of the wealth of glory, see Eph 1:18, and for that of the 'saints in light', see Col 1:12. For the inheritance of the kingdom, see also Eph 5:5; Jas 2:5. The 'already' and the 'not yet' of Paul's teaching has also been well analysed by J. D. G. Dunn in his *Jesus and the Spirit* (London, 1975), pp. 308ff.

28. See Jn 6:29, 40, 47; 1 Jn 3:1; 5:11, 13. Gregory of Nyssa interpreted the statement in Jn 17:22 as a gift of the Spirit: 'The glory which thou hast given me I have given to them': see his *In Cant. Hom.* 15 (*PG* 44, 1117).

29. L. Cerfaux, *Le chrétien dans la théologie paulinienne* (*Lectio divina*, 33) (Paris, 1962), p. 253 [the Eng. tr., *op. cit.* (note 1), p. 276, follows RSV].

30. See above, pp. 57, 63 note 22.

31. See J. B. Frey, 'Le concept de "vie" dans l'Evangile de saint Jean', *Bib*, 1 (1920), 37–58, 211–239; E. Tobac, 'Grâce', *Dictionnaire Apologétique*.

32. J. D. G. Dunn, 'Spirit and Kingdom', *The Expository Times*, 82 (1970), 36–40.

33. L. Cerfaux, *op. cit.* (note 1), p. 323.

34. E. Bardy, *Le Saint-Esprit en nous et dans l'Eglise, d'après le Nouveau Testament* (Albi, 1950).

35. See the chapter above on the holiness of the Church (pp. 52–64) and that on the indwelling of the Spirit (pp. 79–99). See also my *The Mystery of the Temple* (Eng. tr.; London, 1962), pp. 152ff.

36. See my article 'Mérite', in *Vocabulaire œcuménique* (Paris, 1970), pp. 233–251, with

110

bibliography. In addition to the references to Thomas Aquinas that I give there, this text is of interest: 'Hominis opera qui Spiritu Sancto agitur, magis dicuntur esse opera Spiritus Sancti quam ipsius hominis': *ST* Ia IIae, q. 93, a. 6, ad 1. I also quoted Albert the Great, who emphatically asserted that we can reach infinity only through the action of God; see also G. Philips, *L'union personnelle avec le Dieu vivant* (Gembloux, 1974), pp. 128–129, 271–275.

37. Council of Trent, session VI, c. 16 (*DS* 1546).

5

THE HOLY SPIRIT AND
OUR PRAYER

Prayer to the Holy Spirit was relatively uncommon in the early Church. In Volume I, I gave a few historical examples and texts.[1] One characteristic common to almost all these early prayers is that they ask the Spirit to 'come': 'Come, Creator, Spirit', 'Come, Holy Spirit' and so on. In this context, it is interesting to quote the entreaty of Simeon the New Theologian, which is so full of warmth and intensity:

Come, true light! Come, eternal life! Come, hidden mystery! Come, nameless treasure! Come, inexpressible reality! Come, inconceivable Person! Come, endless happiness! Come, light that never sets! Come, unfailing expectation of all who are to be saved! Come, awakening of those who have fallen asleep! Come, resurrection of the dead! Come, O powerful one, who always makes, remakes and transforms everything by your unique power! Come, invisible, intangible one! Come, you who never move and yet at every moment move and come to us, lying in hell—you who are above the heavens! Come, O beloved name repeated everywhere, whose being and nature we are forbidden to express or to know! Come, eternal joy! Come, imperishable crown! Come, purple of the great king, our God! Come, crystal belt studded with jewels! Come, inaccessible sandal! Come, royal purple! Come, truly sovereign right-hand! Come, you whom my wretched soul has desired and still desires! Come, only one, to one who is alone, since you can see that I am alone! Come, you who have separated me from everything and who have made me alone in this world! Come, you who have yourself become desire in me and have made me long for you—you who are absolutely inaccessible! Come, my breath and my life! Come, consolation of my poor soul! Come, my joy, my glory and my endless delight![2]

This 'Come!' is clearly a spontaneous cry of the soul. From the theological point of view, it is a call for the divine missions and particularly for the sending of the Spirit by the Father and the Son, with a shade of meaning that points to the procession of the Spirit in love. The prayer addresses the Spirit as though he were not sent, as though he were the inclination of God himself towards us moving, as it were, of its own accord.

112

'PRAY IN THE HOLY SPIRIT' (Jude 20)

The Church's Life of Praise

In the liturgy of the Church, praise and words of faith, hope and love rise continuously up to God. The Church is the holy temple—and indeed every soul is also the Church—the communion of saints, and the family of God built on the foundation of the apostles and prophets, as we are told in Eph 2:11–22. It is worth recalling verses 18–22 of that text here:

> Through him (Christ in his sacrifice) we both (Jews and gentiles) have access in one Spirit to the Father. So then you are no longer strangers and sojourners, but you are fellow-citizens with the saints and members of the household (= family) of God, built upon the foundation of the apostles and prophets, Christ Jesus himself being the chief cornerstone, in whom the whole structure is joined together and grows into a holy temple in the Lord, in whom you also are built into it for a dwelling-place of God in the Spirit.

What we have here is the worship of the new people of God, the Body of Christ and the Temple of the Holy Spirit offered to 'God' the Father. The structure of the entire liturgy of the Church is: to the Father, through the Son, in the Spirit.[3] Through the Son and in the Spirit, we have access to the Father. The word *prosagōgē* is a very strong one; it is found in Eph 3:12; Rom 5:2 and, in the verbal form, in 1 Pet 3:18. In the Epistle to the Hebrews, the verb *proserchesthai* is used for 'approaching' God.[4] We are able to approach him with boldness (*parrēsia*) because Christ, our High Priest, Lord and Head, has already entered the Holy of Holies which, as Charles de Condren pointed out early in the seventeenth century, is the bosom of the Father.[5] Everything has, in the communication of being, goodness and holiness, come from there, and everything returns there in praise that is not simply the 'fruit of lips' (Heb 13:15). That praise is indeed an offering of the whole of our lives (Rom 12:1) and brotherly love that is effective and beneficial (see Heb 13:16ff.).

This holy worship is able to reach God through Christ, the only priest of the new and definitive covenant, because we are the members of his Body—one new man—in the Holy Spirit, 'for by one Spirit we were all baptized into one body, Jews or Greeks . . .' (1 Cor 12:13; Eph 4:4). That Body is a 'holy temple in the Lord'. There is no longer any other true temple, but the one holy temple is truly a 'house of prayer for all people'.[6]

The Church's holy and precious liturgy is the place where the Spirit and the Bride say 'Come!' to the Lord (Rev 22:17). The Lord does in fact come every day to make his Easter event present for us in the Church's holy Eucharist. There is also the divine Office, the Church's hours which make time holy as the sun rises and sets, the night encloses all things in darkness and 'man goes forth to his work and to his labour until the evening' (Ps 104:23; see also verse 30: 'When thou sendest forth thy Spirit, they are created and thou renewest the face of the earth').

It is also a prayer of the seasons and the year, a cycle of mysteries made present in the celebration through which the Holy Spirit is made present for us and makes our own the incarnation, Easter, Pentecost, the Last Supper and so on. This liturgy also takes many forms—Vespers in the peace and harmony of a monastery; Mass in the parish church, where the Word and the Bread of life are shared; family prayer, a proven source of holiness and vocations; spontaneous prayer and the prayer of silence in groups in which Paul's exhortation is carried out in the 'secular city':

> Be filled with the Spirit, addressing one another in psalms and hymns and spiritual songs, singing and making melody to the Lord with all your heart, always and for everything giving thanks in the name of our Lord Jesus Christ to God the Father (Eph 5:18–20).

> Sing psalms and hymns and spiritual songs with thankfulness in your hearts to God. And whatever you do, in word or deed, do everything in the name of the Lord Jesus, giving thanks to God the Father through him (Col 3:16–17).

> When you come together, each one has a hymn, a lesson, a revelation, a tongue or an interpretation. Let all things be done for edification (1 Cor 14:26).

Individual Prayer

'When you pray, go into your room and shut the door and pray to your Father who is in secret' (Mt 6:6).

The first thing that I ask from God is that he should give me prayer: 'O Lord, open thou my lips and my mouth shall show forth thy praise' (Ps 51:15) and 'If you who are evil know how to give good gifts to your children, how much more will the heavenly Father give the Holy Spirit to those that ask him!' (Lk 11:13). In fact, 'the Spirit helps us in our weakness, for we do not know how to pray as we ought' (Rom 8:26).

We cry 'Abba! Father!' (Rom 8:15), but we say this through the Spirit, so that it is quite true to say that it is he who cries it (Gal 4:6). It is indeed difficult to say whether it is he or us. He is so deeply within us, because he has been sent 'into our hearts'[7] and, as the Holy Spirit, he is so pure, subtle and penetrating (Wis 7:22) that he is able to be in all of us and in each one of us without doing violence to the person, indiscernible in his spontaneous movement. He is above all the Spirit of freedom.[8]

The Spirit in our Prayer

The Spirit helps us to read Scripture and to meditate. *Lectio divina* is something that goes beyond any scholarly study, and meditation transcends philosophical reflection. Prayer, however, is something else again. It is a theologal activity open to every Christian who practises the spiritual life, and is not dependent on the special grace of the mystical life. Bossuet described it in the following way: 'The reading of spiritual books should never be neglected, but they should be read in a spirit of simplicity and prayer and not in a spirit of questing curiosity. When we read in this way, we let the lights and feelings that our reading reveals to us impress themselves on our souls and this impression is made more by the presence of God than by our own hard work.'[9] God's presence is more important, as Bossuet said, than our own effort, this is critical, but our prayer is neither illuminism nor quietism. We think of God—as Charles de Foucauld said, 'praying is thinking of God while loving him'.[10] During this prayer, we express words and feelings, but only for brief periods—as Tauler said, 'the time of an Our Father'.[11] Why no more than this? God himself, the Word and the Holy Spirit impress on our souls an attitude of peaceful and loving clinging which makes us dependent on them. We do not go to them—they draw us towards them and place in us a love, a quiet assent and a joyful and peaceful fullness. This comes much more from them than from us, but at the same time it points to a core within ourselves deeper than our thinking processes.

All the spiritual writers, including Bossuet, have warned that this prayer of simplicity, which is a purely theologal moment that God himself gives,[12] does not do away with the usefulness of meditation, above all not with the practice of the virtues, which such prayer in fact presupposes and requires. There are, however, certain conditions which dispose us for such a gift; they are not really specific, because they have a more general application, but they are nonetheless very valuable.

It may be too commonplace to say so, but it comes down to this: the essential presupposition is that we should really love God, not simply Jesus of Nazareth, but God himself, who has made himself known to us and who remains transcendent and unknowable. Our task is to ensure that God will be a living Person for us and the most important thought in our lives. If this is so, our lives will be offered to God and connected with him. They will form that 'spiritual worship' that was required by Jesus himself (Jn 4:24), Paul (Rom 12:1) and Peter (1 Pet 2:5).

If this is so, we shall avoid what the world offers—superficial excitement, entertainment, futile and wretched hedonism in many different forms, noise, fever, a lack of moral discipline and a thousand attractions that distract, hurt and even disintegrate us. Elijah heard Yahweh in the 'still, small voice' of the wind (1 Kings 19:12). We too need to lead disciplined lives based on a love of God's law and an attitude of strong obedience. Those who have advanced far in prayer can help us how to pray in this way. We have, in a word, to go back to our 'heart' and build up the inner man again.[13] And may God come to us!

The Spirit in our Petitionary Prayer

I do not intend to deal here with every aspect of the prayer of petition. We are promised in Scripture that it will always be heard and answered (Mt 7:7ff. par.; Mk 11:24; Jn 14:13–14; 16:23ff.; see also 1 Jn 5:14), and yet 'the memory of the prayers that have not been answered may prevent me from praying again', as Ernest Hello lamented.[14] I do not seek to justify petitionary prayer, even in the case of prayer for earthly goods, since this question has, I think, been settled. All that I shall attempt to do here is to point to the part played by the Holy Spirit in that movement in which God enables us to build a bridge between ourselves and him. In this, my point of departure will be the nature of prayer itself.

L. Beinaert made a distinction between 'prayed petition' and 'praying prayer'.[15] The first is an expression of my desire or rather, of my need. It calls for a reality of the order of earthly causes, which I have, because of my impotence, to look for in that mysterious being who is thought to be more potent, but in that search I do not really reach transcendence. 'God' is brought back to our level. This is the prayer of La Hire: 'Lord, do now for La Hire what La Hire would do for you if you were La Hire and La Hire were God'. 'Praying prayer', on the other hand, is, because of love, of the order of God and is not a mere petition, but prayer. Prayer is essentially communion with God and with his will. If Jesus had simply asked in the garden of Gethsemane: 'Let this cup pass from me', he would only have been expressing a petition. His appeal was only a prayer because he added: 'Nevertheless, not as I will, but as thou wilt'. In this way, God is recognized as God. True prayer ensures that God is God and not an extension of my arm which is too short.

Jean-Claude Sagne , who is both a theologian and a psychologist, can help us perhaps to go a step further in the direction of the Holy Spirit.[16] He has made a distinction between three aspects or moments of prayer—need, desire and petition. Conscious need leads to desire, which, if it is addressed to another who is recognized as such becomes a petition. This is where the recognition of the presence of the other begins. If I agree, in the light of this recognition, to give up my need, I will come to recognize the other fully and I will know his desire to exist totally in and through himself. I also experience love in recognizing that the other exists, with his own desire, fully in and through himself. Sagne himself goes on to say: 'In prayer, we have first to experience the dissatisfaction of our own desire, confess our own lack and recognize in faith the absent presence of God. This should lead us to desire the desire of God himself, that is, to desire what God desires and to let God desire in us. At this point, prayer appears as the mystery of God in us and an event of the Spirit, because it is the function of the Holy Spirit to be the desire of God in God himself and also the desire of God in us. The Spirit forms, deepens, expands and adjusts our desire to the desire of God by giving it the same object. The Spirit makes our desire live from the life of God himself, to the point where God himself comes to desire at the heart of our desire' (p. 94).

116

Let us once again look at some of the important texts:

Pray at all times in the Spirit with all prayer and supplication (Eph 6:18).

Come, you who have yourself become desire in me and have made me long for you (Simeon the New Theologian: see p. 112 above and note 2 below).

God's love has been poured into our hearts through the Holy Spirit which has been given to us (Rom 5:5).

The soul loves God with the will of God, which is also the soul's will and it can love him as it is loved by him, because it loves him through the will of God himself, in the same love with which he loves it; that love is, according to the Apostle (Rom 5:5), the Holy Spirit (Commentary on Rom 5:5 by John of the Cross).[17]

The Spirit searches everything, even the depths of God. For what person knows a man's thoughts except the spirit of the man which is in him? So also no one comprehends the thoughts of God except the Spirit of God. Now we have received not the spirit of the world, but the Spirit which is from God (1 Cor 2:10–12; see also Is 40:12–14; 55:8–9; Job 4:3 and *passim*; Rom 11:33–35; 1 Cor 2:16).

The Spirit helps us in our weakness, for we do not know how to pray as we ought; but the Spirit himself intercedes for us with sighs too deep for words. And he who searches the hearts of men knows what is the mind of the Spirit, because the Spirit intercedes for the saints (Rom 8:26–27).

That is the ultimate and definitive answer to our question about prayer—it reveals a new depth to us. I asked whether it is he or us in prayer. It is us, of course, but, looking forward to God who will be 'everything to everyone' (1 Cor 15:28), it is also him in us. Beyond all that we know consciously and all thoughts that we can form or formulate, the Spirit who *dwells in our hearts* is there himself as prayer, supplication and praise. He is our union with God and for that reason he is our prayer. 'We have to believe in God's love and in his saving presence in us in everything that happens in our lives.'[18] *God himself* is present as a gift and he dwells in our innermost depths—*intimior intimo meo*, 'more inward and more secret than my deepest and innermost self'. This means that the heart of the believer is, to the extent that the Spirit dwells in it, a place where God encounters himself and where there is consequently an inexpressible relationship between the divine Persons.[19] It is really the desire or longing of God himself interceding for the saints at a deeper level than their own expressed or expressible prayer. Jesus himself, after all, said: 'O righteous Father, . . . that the love with which thou hast loved me may be in them' (Jn 17:26).

NOTES

1. See Volume I, pp. 94, 108ff.
2. This prayer precedes Simeon's hymns: translation based on Fr. tr. by J. Paramelle, *SC* 156 (1969), pp. 151, 153. It is also interesting to quote this prayer by John of Fécamp, written

in 1060 (until recently attributed first to Augustine and then to Anselm; A. Wilmart has shown that it was the work of John of Fécamp): 'Come, then, O come, excellent consoler of the suffering soul. . . . Come, you who cleanse blemishes and who heal wounds. Come, strength of the weak and support of all who fall. Come, doctor of the humble and conqueror of the proud. Come, O tender father of orphans. . . . Come, hope of the poor. . . . Come, O star of sailors, port for the shipwrecked. Come, O glory of the living. . . . Come, most holy of Spirits and take me in your mercy. Let me be conformed to you': Mme Arsène-Henry, *Les plus beaux textes sur le Saint-Esprit* (Paris, 1968), pp. 204, 363, note 33.

3. I have already referred to C. Vagaggini, *Theological Dimensions of the Liturgy* (Eng. tr.; Collegeville, Minn., 1976), chapter 7, for this theme.

4. Heb 4:16; 7:25; 10:1; 11:6; 12:18; see also 10:19, where the word used is *eisodos*, entrance.

5. Charles de Condren, *L'idée du sacerdoce et du sacrifice de Jésus-Christ*, Part 3, chapter 4.

6. The important episode of the purification of the Temple, containing the quotation from Is 56:7, will be found in Mt 21:10–17; Mk 11:15–17; Lk 19:45–48; and especially Jn 2:13–16. See also my *The Mystery of the Temple* (Eng. tr.; London, 1962), pp. 120ff.

7. Gal 4:6; 2 Cor 1:22; Rom 5:5; 2:29; Eph 5:19; 3:17; Col 3:16. See also L. Cerfaux, *The Christian in the Theology of St Paul* (Eng. tr.; London, 1967), p. 296.

8. See Chapter 6 below. For another example, referring not only to him, but also to us, see Lk 21:15; cf. 12:12; Mt 10:20; Mk 13:11. Data illustrating this will be found in Acts 4:8; 5:32; 6:10; 7:55. Simeon the New Theologian, *op. cit.* (note 2), p. 153, says: 'I thank you for having become one spirit with me, without confusion, change or transformation, you who are God transcending everything, and for having become all in all for me'.

9. This quotation will be found in No. XIII of Bossuet's 'Méthode pour passer la journée dans l'oraison, en esprit de foi et de simplicité devant Dieu': *Œuvres*, ed. Lachat, VII (Paris, 1862), pp. 504–509.

10. Charles de Foucauld, *Lettre à Madame de Bondy*, 7 April 1890.

11. Johannes Tauler, Sermon 15, No. 7.

12. According to Thomas' theology, the theologal virtues call for an act of God as their 'formal object'. The object of faith is simply first, uncreated Truth and, in hope, what is expected of God is no less than God himself. In the case of charity, the text of Rom 5:5 is quite categorical. For John of the Cross and his understanding of this, see below, note 17.

13. See P.-R. Régamey's excellent account in 'Dieu parle au cœur', *Cahiers Saint-Dominique* (November 1960), 9–17 (425–433) and *Redécouvrir la Vie religieuse. La rénovation dans l'Esprit* (Paris, 1974).

14. Ernest Hello, in P. Guilloux, *Les plus belles pages d'Ernest Hello* (Paris, 1924), p. 17.

15. L. Beinaert, 'La prière de demande dans nos vies d'homme' (written in 1941), *Expérience chrétienne et Psychologie* (Paris, 1966), 333–351; *idem*, 'Prière et demande à l'Autre', *Lumen Vitae*, 22 (Brussels, 1967), 217–224.

16. J.-C. Sagne, 'Du besoin à la demande, ou la conversion du désir dans la prière', *M-D*, 109 (1972), 87–97; *idem*, 'L'Esprit-Saint ou le désir de Dieu', *Concilium* (Fr. ed. only), 99 (1974), 85–95.

17. John of the Cross, *Spiritual Canticle*, 37.

18. A. C. Rzewuski, *A travers l'invisible cristal. Confessions d'un Dominicain* (Paris, 1976), p. 368.

19. See K. Niederwimmer, 'Das Gebet des Geistes. Röm. 8. 26f', *TZ*, 20 (Basle, 1964), 252–265.

6

THE SPIRIT AND THE
STRUGGLE AGAINST THE FLESH
THE SPIRIT AND FREEDOM

The word 'flesh' can have several different meanings in Scripture.[1] It can, for example, simply point to man's state on earth—'the Word became flesh' (Jn 1:14)—and that condition is characterized by fragility and finiteness. This flesh is good in itself, but even as such it reveals the weakness and insufficiency that is present in everything that belongs to this world in comparison with the divine order. This revelation becomes dramatic when the flesh is seen in a state of tension with the Spirit, as it is in Paul's letters to the Romans and the Galatians, both of which particularly interested Luther. In that case, we are conscious of the opposition between two existential attitudes in our relationship with God (Luther's *coram Deo*), with our brothers, with ourselves and with the world. The flesh is the principle or the seat of opposition to the will of the Spirit. It is a principle of action dwelling in us, just as the Holy Spirit also dwells in us, but it does more than dwell in us, since it is our very dwelling-place, both in the neutral sense of being our simple state here on earth and in its pernicious existential sense as a propensity that goes counter to our calling as sons of God, members of the Body of Christ and temples of the Holy Spirit.

In Gal 3:1–4:12; Rom 3:21ff., this opposition is above all between the law and the promise of faith, the flesh being the Mosaic law. In Gal 5:13–6:18; Rom 7:1–8:30, the opposition is in the Christian himself, whose life is based both on the flesh and the Spirit.[2] Like J. D. G. Dunn, I believe that this tension is the result of our condition of 'already' and 'not yet'. Here we have the truth of the Christian condition, unlike that of the Jews, who were living in the 'not yet', and of the Gnostics, who influenced the Christian community at Corinth and who believed that they were 'already' in a state that went beyond the limitations and demands of the 'not yet'. The Christian, on the other hand, (already) has the Spirit. He is already a son of God. He is, however, still in the flesh, in the sense that this resists the Spirit, and he is still looking forward to the fullness of the quality of a son and to the redemption and spiritualization of his body. This, he believes, will follow in accordance with Christ, who was crucified and was dead according to the flesh, but who was raised from the dead and glorified according to the

119

Holy Spirit.[3] There are many Pauline texts pointing to this and I will only quote the most important passages:

> Walk by the Spirit and do not gratify the desires of the flesh. For the desires of the flesh are against the Spirit and the desires of the Spirit are against the flesh; for these are opposed to each other, to prevent you from doing what you would (Gal 5:16–18).

> Whatever a man sows, that he will also reap. For he who sows to his own flesh will from the flesh reap corruption; but he that sows to the Spirit will from the Spirit reap eternal life (Gal 6:7–8).

> Those who live according to the flesh set their minds on the things of the flesh, but those who live according to the Spirit set their minds on the things of the Spirit. To set the mind on the flesh is death, but to set the mind on the Spirit is life and peace. For the mind that is set on the flesh is hostile to God; it does not submit to God's law, indeed it cannot; and those who are in the flesh cannot please God. But you are not in the flesh, if the Spirit of God really dwells in you. Any one who does not have the Spirit of Christ does not belong to him. But if Christ is in you, although your bodies are dead because of sin, your spirits are alive because of righteousness. If the Spirit of him who raised Jesus from the dead dwells in you, he who raised Christ Jesus from the dead will give life to your mortal bodies through his Spirit which dwells in you (Rom 8:5–11).

The Christian should therefore set about living 'in the new life of the Spirit' (Rom 7:6). This involves him in a whole journey. And 'if we live by the Spirit, let us also walk by the Spirit' (Gal 5:25), which leads to an inner struggle. Let us consider this struggle now.

(1) It is a struggle within us between our inner propensities or the two spirits that dwell in us. The theme of the two ways was one with which the Jews were familiar. It can be found in the gospels and in the *Didache*. We know what it means in the concrete: 'Not everyone who says to me, "Lord, Lord" shall enter the kingdom of heaven' (Mt 7:21; Lk 6:46). When Paul said: 'No one can say "Jesus is Lord" except by the Holy Spirit' (1 Cor 12:3), he was undoubtedly thinking of a confession of faith and of praise of the Lord. He also spoke, however, of 'faith working through love' (Gal 5:6; cf. Rom 2:6, 10, 15–16; 2 Cor 13:4; Eph 2:8–10; Col 1:10; 1 Thess 1:3; 2 Thess 1:11) and of love fulfilling the law.[4] James was no different from Paul in urging believers to be 'doers of the word and not hearers only' (Jas 1:22).

The Spirit is also a spirit of sons, making us cry: 'Abba! Father!' This means that we cannot call on the Father of all men if we refuse to behave as brothers towards all men who are created in God's image. Relationships between man and God the Father are so closely connected with relationships between man and his human brothers that Scripture insists: 'He who does not love does not know God' (1 Jn 4:8).[5]

J. Wolinski has forcibly expressed similar ideas, especially in his commentary on a text of Origen:[6] 'The inauguration of our life as sons which begins with baptism should continue as an entire existence as sons, in the course of which the quality of sonship should be made present and should grow gradually as we perform good actions'. Origen himself claimed that 'the more one hears the word of God, the more one becomes a son of God' and goes on to say: 'provided, however, that those words fall on someone who has received the Spirit of adoption'.[7] He also insisted that one becomes the son of the one whose works one does:

> All those who commit sin are born of the devil (1 Jn 3:8). We are therefore born of the devil as many times as we have sinned. How wretched is the one who is always born of the devil, but how blessed is he who is always born of God! For I say: the righteous man is not simply born once of God. He is born again and again. He is born according to each good action through which God begets him. . . . In the same way, if you possess the Spirit of adoption, God will again and again beget you in the Son. He begets you from work to work and from thought to thought. That is the nativity that you receive and through it you become a son of God, begotten again and again in Christ Jesus.[8]

It is easy to express in terms of 'divine missions' this continuous begetting into the filial life in the actions that form the fabric of it. According to the principle of 'synergy', we make ourselves through our actions, and it is the work of God (see Gal 4:7). We know too that the greatest mystics were very remote from any kind of Quietism. In this context, it is worth recalling what Simeon the New Theologian said:

> Whether we have not yet received the grace of the Spirit or whether we have received it, we can only pass through the darkness of the soul and contemplate the light of the Holy Spirit if we suffer pain and hardship, violence, tribulation and distress (Rom 8:35). 'For the kingdom of heaven has suffered violence and men of violence take it by force' (Mt 11:12), because it is 'through many tribulations' that 'we must enter the kingdom of God' (Acts 14:22). The kingdom of heaven is a participation in the Holy Spirit—that is what is meant by the saying that the 'kingdom of God is in the midst of you' (Lk 17:21). We must therefore do all that we can to receive and to keep the Holy Spirit within us. May those who do not have continuously to suffer hardship, violence, tribulation and distress in their hearts not tell us: 'We have the Holy Spirit within us', because no one will obtain that reward without the works, the pain, the hardship and the suffering of virtue.[9]

We know from the New Testament and especially Paul, and from the experience of the saints and the spiritual writers that grace is only gained at the expense of sharing in the sufferings and the cross of Jesus, which are inseparable from his resurrection.[10] The Spirit is not often mentioned explicitly in Paul's many texts on the sufferings and tribulations of the Christian, but such sufferings form part of the tension between the 'not yet' and the 'already' and between the flesh and the Spirit. Life takes place in the weakness of the flesh and in the process of death which is the fate of the flesh (see Gal 3:1-5; Rom 15:18-19; 1 Cor 1:4-9; 2:1-5; 2 Cor 4:7-5:5; 12:9).

Paul points above all to the eschatological significance of these sufferings in the wake of what was for Jesus the conditioning of his glory by his crucifixion (see Rom 5:2ff.; 8:17; 2 Cor 4:17ff. and especially verse 10; 2 Thess 1:4ff.; 1 Pet 4:12–15, which contains an explicit reference to the Spirit). This logic, which began with Jesus' baptism, is the logic of the whole Christian life and of the action of the apostle, who, on this basis, insists that the power of God (as Spirit) is affirmed in man's distress.[11] 'God's' consolation always accompanies an experience of weakness and suffering (2 Cor 1:3–7), Paul assures us, and there is often a true *spiritual* joy (Rom 11:17; Gal 5:22). A charismatic experience occurs in the midst of all this; this is clear from what Paul says to the Thessalonians: 'Our gospel came to you not only in word, but also in power and in the Holy Spirit and with full conviction. You know what kind of men we proved to be among you for your sake. And you became imitators of us and of the Lord, for you received the word in much affliction, with joy inspired by the Holy Spirit' (1 Thess 1:5–6).

(2) Jesus was anointed by the Spirit when he was baptized with his messianic ministry in mind and was at once led by the Spirit to confront the demon in a series of temptations which referred to the two values revealed in his baptism—his quality as the beloved Son which had to prove itself in his destiny as Servant. The Christian is similarly confronted not only with flesh and blood, but also with the spirits of evil who reign between heaven and earth and with the spirit who acts among the 'sons of disobedience' (Eph 2:2; 6:11ff.). Once again, Paul does not name the Holy Spirit explicitly—the Spirit is only named in the exorcisms practised by Jesus[12]—but what can that 'strength of might' be with which the Christian should arm himself in the Lord, if not the strength of the Holy Spirit?[13]

The part played by the Spirit in the conversion of the sinner

The Paraclete whom Jesus was to send would 'confound the world with regard to sin' or 'convince the world of [RSV: concerning] sin' (Jn 16:8). All exegetes agree that this text has a universal significance. M. F. Berrouard has pointed out that 'the framework is that of a trial with the task of reviewing Jesus' historical trial and his condemnation by the world. The need is to discover on what side sin is and on what side justice, and how the first judgement should be assessed. The action of the Paraclete consists in urging the world to recognize its fault and to confess its guilt.'[14] This is all in accordance with the whole thesis of the fourth gospel, which is: Will Jesus, the Son of God and the light of the world, be received, or will he be rejected by the world, the Jews and every individual personally?

Although exegetes are in agreement about this all-embracing meaning of the text, they are divided in their interpretation. Some believe that this conviction of sin, which is the work of the Paraclete, is brought about in the consciousness of the world, while others think that it occurs in the minds of Jesus' disciples. Those who prefer the second interpretation have good arguments to support it, but why should it necessarily exclude the first? Does the Spirit not play a part in the conversion of the world? What the New Testament has to say about his function as a witness together with the apostles (see above, pp. 42–43) clearly points to the *metanoia* or conversion of the world and it is in the context of Pentecost that Luke speaks of it in his Acts of the Apostles (2:37–38).

The Holy Spirit acts within us or he penetrates into us like an anointing. He makes us, at a level that is deeper than that of mere regret for some fault, conscious of the sovereign attraction of the Absolute, the Pure and the True, and of a new life offered to us by the Lord, and he also gives us a clear consciousness of our own wretchedness and of the untruth and selfishness that fills our lives. We are conscious of being judged, but at the same time we are forestalled by forgiveness and grace, with the result that our false excuses, our self-justifying mechanisms and the selfish structure of our lives break down.[15]

Something of this kind happened to Zacchaeus. Grace came into his home, forestalling him, and at once he knew that he was a sinner. It is worth noting the boldness and at the same time the depth of understanding on the part of the Church in using this passage in Scripture (Lk 19:1–10) in the liturgy of the dedication of a church. The Church itself is a sinner forestalled by free forgiveness and is converted when the Lord comes and takes up residence in it. The Church is and always will be the coming of salvation to a house where the Lord comes to dwell, and this process begins with a conviction of injustice or sin.

Religious revivals—and it would be a pity if the 'sects' or the 'evangelistic' movements of the Billy Graham type were regarded as enjoying a monopoly in this field—have almost always begun by a call to conversion from a state of sinfulness. This was the case, for example, in Ireland in the fifth and sixth centuries.[16] It is also the case, it would appear, with the present-day movements concerned with renewal in the Spirit.

The article on the Holy Spirit in the creed is made explicit in terms of a list of the works of the Spirit—the Church, baptism and the remission of sins. It is true that the confessions of faith that were formulated in the fourth century linked the remission of sins with baptism[17] and even Peter made this connection on the day of Pentecost, according to the Acts of the Apostles (2:38). This statement was certainly in accordance with the Christological conviction that 'everyone who believes in him (Christ) receives forgiveness of sins through his name' (Acts 10:43; 13:38–39; Lk 24:47). The glorified Lord, however, acts through his Spirit and, in what is sometimes called the 'Johannine Pentecost', the 'power' to remit sins is attributed, in a view of the

Trinitarian economy, to the virtue of the Holy Spirit: 'As the Father has sent me, even so I send you' and, breathing on them (the Twelve, of whom only ten were present), Jesus goes on to say: 'Receive the Holy Spirit. If you forgive the sins of any, they are forgiven; if you retain the sins of any, they are retained' (Jn 20:21–23). It is, in other words, because the Spirit dwells in the Church that the Church is able to remit sins.[18]

In the Church's Tradition, the coming of the Spirit at Pentecost, fifty days after Easter, has been linked to the jubilee, which occurs every fifty years, after a 'week of weeks of years', as a transcendence or consummation of fullness (Exod 34:22; Lev 23:15). The year of jubilee was a year of setting free and of return to the ancestral property (Lev 25:8ff.). In the Church's liturgy, this is linked to the words of Jesus, and the gift of the Spirit is celebrated as the forgiveness of sins, because Jesus himself is the forgiveness of sins (*quia ipse est remissio peccatorum*).[19] Pentecost is also celebrated as a jubilee of remission in this hymn at Vespers:[20]

Patrata sunt haec mystice	All these things took place mystically,
Paschae peracto tempore	when the time of Easter had passed,
Sacro dierum numero	on the holy day that had been fixed
Quo lege fit remissio.	for remission to be legally enacted.
Dudum sacrata pectora	You have just filled the dedicated hearts
Tua replesti gratia.	with your grace;
Dimitte nunc peccamina	now remit their sins
Et da quieta tempora.	and grant peaceful days.

The Spirit makes us truly free[21]

The prophet Jeremiah described a new covenant in terms of fullness and warmth: 'I will put my law within them and I will write it upon their hearts' (31:31–34), and barely a generation later Ezekiel proclaimed a similar promise in the name of God: 'A new heart I will give you and a new spirit I will put within you; I will take out of your flesh the heart of stone and give you a heart of flesh. And I will put my spirit within you and cause you to walk in my statutes and be careful to observe my ordinances' (36:26ff.; 37:14).

Christians have always believed and still believe that these promises have been fulfilled in the event of Jesus Christ and the gift of the Holy Spirit, but according to the status of the 'already' and the 'not yet' that we have discussed above, that is, as earnest-money or first-fruits, and therefore in such a way that we are still waiting for their fulfilment in the literal sense of the word. As Paul said:

Where the Spirit of the Lord is, there is freedom (2 Cor 3:17)

You were called to freedom, brethren. . . . If you are led by the Spirit you are not under the law (Gal 5:13, 18).

The law of the Spirit of life in Christ Jesus has set me free from the law of sin and death. . . . All who are led by the Spirit of God are sons of God (Rom 8:2, 14).

The Spirit is the Spirit of Jesus Christ and a Spirit of adoption. He gives us not a status, but also a condition—that of sons. Adoption as sons is not simply a legal status—it is a real state, since we have in us (in our 'hearts') the Spirit of the Son who became our first-born brother. Nicholas Cabasilas expressed this idea in Trinitarian categories that were fully in accordance with the Eastern tradition when he said that 'the Father sets us free, the Son is the ransom and the Holy Spirit is our freedom'.[22] Christ, however, is more than the ransom—he is the Son. The declarations of Paul which I have quoted above and his allegory of Sarah and Hagar, Ishmael and Isaac (Gal 4:21–31) go together with Jesus' statements: 'The sons are free' (Mt 17:25–26); 'If you continue in my word (proclaiming my quality as the Son of God and letting you share in it through faith), the truth will make you free' (Jn 8:31–32); 'If the Son makes you free, you will be free indeed' (verse 36).

This freedom is not a licence dependent on whim, which is an illusory freedom or a caricature of freedom that in fact destroys true freedom if it is taken too far. According to Augustine, the Christian into whom the Holy Spirit has poured the love of God will spontaneously observe a law which can be summed up in love: 'He is not subject to the law, but he is not without a law' (*non est sub lege, sed cum lege*).[23] The content of the law is the norm for his action, but he is not subjected to the restraints of a law because he has interiorized the law. That is why it is he who determines himself from within himself and that is the very definition of freedom. Thomas Aquinas speaks about this in a strictly theological language that is nonetheless very close to that of the gospel and Paul:

> The free man is the one who belongs to himself; the slave, however, belongs to his master. Whoever acts spontaneously therefore acts freely, but whoever receives his impulse from another does not act freely. The man who avoids evil, not because it is an evil, but because of a law of the Lord's, is therefore not free. On the other hand, the man who avoids evil because it is an evil is free. It is here that the Holy Spirit works, inwardly perfecting our spirit by communicating to it a new dynamism, and this functions so well that man refrains from evil through love, as though divine law were ordering him to do this. He is therefore free not because he is not subject to divine law, but because his inner dynamism leads him to do what divine law prescribes.[24]

In his treatise on the law, Thomas says that the new law is simply the Holy Spirit himself or the proper effect of that Spirit, which is faith working through love.[25] That Spirit is so much within us—in the cry 'Father!', for example, it is the Spirit and us as well—and he is so much the weight or inclination of our love that he is our spontaneity intimately related to what is good. The decision to do the opposite is only an imperfection of a freedom insufficiently illuminated and filled with good. Christ, who could not sin, was entirely free.[26] The Holy Spirit, who is Good and Love, compels us not only by leaving us free, but also by making us free, because he compels us from within and through *our very own* movement. James, for example, was able to speak of the 'perfect law, the law of liberty' (1:25; 2:12), just as Paul spoke of the 'law of Christ' (Gal 6:2) and of our being 'slaves of righteousness . . . for sanctification' (Rom 6:18–19). Many Christian mystics have also spoken of this. At the summit of the ascent of Mount Carmel, John of the Cross wrote: 'There is no longer a path here, because there is no law for the righteous man' and Marie de l'Incarnation, seized by the action of divine Goodness, declared: 'My spirit was free and abandoned, without being able to desire or choose anything'.[27]

As Paul pointed out: 'Now we are discharged from the law, dead to that which held us captive, so that we serve not under the old written code, but in the new life of the Spirit' (Rom 7:6)[28] and 'If we live by the Spirit, let us also walk by the Spirit' (Gal 5:25). Christianity is not a law, although it contains one, and it is not a morality, although it contains one. By the gift of the Spirit of Christ, it is an ontology of grace which involves, as its fruit or product, certain attitudes that are called for and even demanded by what we are.[29] This is both extremely strong and at the same time terribly fragile. A materially defined law that is imposed as such on man produces effective results. Many of us have experienced this in the company of religious Jews, who have had no doubts about their own identity or their duty. The Spirit, on the other hand, is a law imposed not by pressure, but by appeal, as Bergson commented in his book *Les deux sources de la morale et de la religion* (1932). Paul was clearly right when he said: 'You were *called* to freedom, brethren; only do not use your freedom as an opportunity for the flesh, but through love be servants of one another. For the whole law is fulfilled in one word, "You shall love your neighbour as yourself" ' (Gal 5:13–14). In this context, Luther's words of 1520 come to mind: 'The Christian is a free man and the master of all things. He is subject to no one. The Christian is a servant and full of obedience. He is subject to all men.'

Let me, however, cite a witness who is closer to us in time. Just as Savonarola wrote his excellent commentary on the *Miserere* when he was in prison and waiting to die, so too Alfred Delp, a Catholic priest arrested by the Gestapo in August 1944 and hanged on 2 February 1945 with Goerdeler and von Moltke, wrote a meditation on the *Veni Sancte Spiritus* while he was in prison, from 11 January 1945 until the eve of his execution. With his chained hands, he wrote as a free man—liberated by the power of the Holy Spirit. His meditation is interrupted just before the final sentence: *In te confidentibus*:[30]

> The eternal hills are there, from where salvation comes. Their rescue is ready; it is waiting and it is coming. God shows it to me every day and now my whole life is bearing witness to it. All the assurance, cleverness and skill that I had in me burst

under the weight of the violence and the forces that opposed me. My months in captivity have broken my physical resistance and many other things in me and yet I have experienced wonderful times. God has taken everything in hand and I can now pray and wait for the rescue and the power that comes from the eternal hills. . . .

The man who knows how poor he is and who rejects all pride and self-sufficiency, even the pride of his rags, the man who stands before God in his nakedness and his need—that man knows the miracles of love and mercy, from the consolation of the heart and the illumination of the spirit to the allaying of hunger and thirst. . . .

Very often, during the suffering and disturbance of these last few months and bent down under the weight of violence, I have been conscious of peace and joy invading my soul with the victorious power of the rising sun. . . .

The Holy Spirit is the passion with which God loves himself. Man has to correspond to that passion. He has to ratify it and accomplish it. If he learns how to do this, the world will once again become capable of true love. We cannot know and love God unless God himself seizes hold of us and tears us away from our selfishness. God has to love himself in and through us and we shall then live in God's truth and love will once more become the living heart of the world.

There have been many men in our age who have been made strong and free in the Spirit! To mention only those who have died: Dietrich Bonhoeffer,[31] whom I did not know; Emmanuel Mounier, Father Maydieu, Paul Couturier—'Freedom has entered my life and it has the face of love'—and Edmond Michelet, whom I did know personally.

Alfred Delp had outlined a way in which a reference to the Spirit as the principle of freedom could be applied to the Church as the people of God or the messianic people. Vatican II gave special emphasis to this: 'The heritage of this people is the dignity and freedom of the sons of God in whose hearts the Holy Spirit dwells as in his temple. Its law is the new commandment of love as Christ loved us (cf. Jn 13:34).'[32] What, then, is our position with regard to this ideal? It is obvious that there is and always will be a great deal for us to do if we are to fulfil its demands at the level of the Church as an institution and as a way of life.

It is clear, for example, that Paul had a great respect for the legitimate freedom of believers. He did not try to exercise his authority by establishing a relationship between himself and his communities in which he was firmly in control and they were in a subordinate position: 'You were called to freedom, brethren' (Gal 5:13); 'Do not become slaves of men' (1 Cor 7:23); 'Not that we lord it over your faith; we work with you for your joy' (2 Cor 1:24); 'I preferred to do nothing without your consent in order that your goodness might not be by compulsion, but of your own free will' (Philem 14). This, surely, is a long way from the clerical pressure that has weighed so heavily on our pastoral attitudes in the Church—and may still be felt even now.

127

It is surely with nostalgia that we read what Augustine wrote around 390 in his treatise *De vera religione*, and again about ten years later in his reply to his friend Januarius, a text that was taken up again tranquilly by Thomas Aquinas:

> Piety begins with fear and ends in charity. That is why, when they were slaves subject to the old law, the people were held by fear and subjected to many sacred signs. They needed this so that they should long for the grace of God, the coming of which was proclaimed in the canticles of the prophets. After their coming, however, when divine Wisdom had become the man who called us to freedom, there were only very few sacred signs conveying salvation and these were set up as a social bond between Christians, that is to say, the great number of those subjected to the one God. . . .

> I cannot approve of the new practices that have been set up outside the common habits and are imposed as obligatory, as though they were sacraments. . . . Even though nothing can be found in them that is contrary to the law, they must be rejected, because they fill religion with slavery when God in his mercy wanted to establish and settle freedom on a very small number of sacraments, the purpose of which is very clear. The condition of the Jews would be much more tolerable. Although they failed to recognize the time of freedom, they were at least subjected to things established by the law of God and not to things established by human opinions.[33]

This text was frequently quoted by Catholics in the sixteenth century in an attempt to strip their religion of excrescences in which the gospel played only a minimal part.[34] Protestant Christians used the category *adiaphora* or matters of indifference which could be left to the discretion of local communities. Augustine was certainly not preaching anarchy, and Thomas Aquinas was even more certainly not.[35] Both were warning us not to make absolute what is relative, even though it is to be respected.

As Vatican II pointed out, 'the beginning, the subject and the goal of all social institutions is and must be the human person, which for its part and by its very nature stands completely in need of social life'.[36] There are facts on both sides. On the one hand, the freedom with which women and men have, under the influence of the Holy Spirit, created groups and religious communities in the Church is quite admirable. On the other hand, however, we are still a long way from opening the life of the Church, its parishes and its organizations to the free contribution of the charisms. It is true that 'God is not a God of confusion, but of peace' (1 Cor 14:33) and that the gift of manifesting the Spirit is made for the common good (1 Cor 12:7), but do we not suffer too much even now from what Alfred Delp called ecclesiastical functionalism, in which he saw the impression in the Church of the spirit of security and rigidity?

> This has given birth to a type of man who is not open to the Holy Spirit. He is a fortress that is so carefully constructed and guarded that the Spirit is so to speak

impotent and looks in vain for a breach. . . . If appeals to personal responsibility and commitment are to be heard in the life of the Church, the Lord will probably have to test by fire and steel the external apparatus and security of his Church. No one can, after all, pass through fire and not be transformed by it. The life-giving Spirit will help us to be reborn from the ashes with fresh courage and with a wider and more audacious vision. If we are to gain everything, we shall once again have to forget and give up many things. Above all, we shall have to give ourselves up. The soil will have to be ploughed again and sowed with new seed. Let us therefore love the freedom of God, do his truth and give ourselves to life.[37]

If the charisms are simply talents which we are called to place at the service of the building up of the Body of Christ, then there are personal talents, and there are also original collective gifts and resources—those of the different peoples and cultures and of historical experiences and traditions. The Holy Spirit is also at work in all of these. In the greater Church, there are countless local and particular Churches, faithful to the Spirit and respectful of Christian freedom. In this pluralism, the Church must recognize the 'signs of the times'.

There is also the freedom of the Church itself—its apostolic freedom. As Paul himself proudly claimed: 'Am I not free? Am I not an apostle? . . . For though I am free from all men, I have made myself a slave to all, that I might win the more' (1 Cor 9:1, 19). That meant becoming a Greek with the Greeks, and such openness and availability formed an essential part of the apostolic freedom. Another important aspect of that freedom is the confidence with which Paul spoke in public, the *parrēsia* which was a characteristic of Jesus himself (especially in the gospel of John) and became a characteristic of the disciples.[38] Quite frequently in the New Testament, when the courage to preach and confess Jesus Christ is discussed, this *parrēsia* or freedom is related to the Holy Spirit (see Phil 1:19ff.; 2 Cor 3:7ff., 12ff., which deals with the ministry of the Spirit; Acts 4:8, 31; 18:25ff., that is, the passage dealing with Apollos). The same boldness of language in confessing faith in Christ characterized later generations of Christians and notably the early martyrs. In the account of the persecution of Christians at Lyons and Vienne in 177, the believers there praised the courage that the Spirit gave them and, speaking of Alexander, 'a Phrygian by race and a physician by profession', they said that he was 'known to all because of his love of God and the boldness of his language (*parrēsian tou logou*), because he was no stranger to the apostolic charism'.[39]

This is all splendid evidence of apostolic freedom experienced at the level of personal commitment. The same freedom can also be considered at the level of history and therefore seen as the freedom of the Church itself, that freedom which the Church always claimed as a hierarchical and institutional authority over and against the secular power or powers. At certain periods of the Church's history, the struggle was continuous and bitter. It reached a peak during the pontificate of Gregory VII (†1085).

In the changing historical situation of the second half of the twentieth century and especially since Vatican II, this freedom of the Church has taken the form of social criticism directed at the Church's own history, certain important aspects of that history, the historical forms that Christianity has assumed and the cultural and ideological expressions based on a post-mediaeval middle-class and Western European model that have in the more recent history of the Church constituted a norm. This social criticism has also resulted in a movement to go beyond the existing model so that the gospel message can once again 'go over to the barbarians' and penetrate other areas of society where it may be welcomed. These other areas, whose authentic humanity has at last been fully recognized, have hitherto been largely prevented from receiving the gospel because of the predominantly Western bourgeois model of traditional Christianity. They include, for example, the working classes of the developed world, the poor of Latin America, Black societies and, even in Europe, many basic communities and active, creative movements and ways of community life of different kinds.

The *libertas Ecclesiae* is becoming the freedom of the Church in relation to itself in its historical and cultural forms. This freedom exists in the name of the Church's evangelical nature that is a direct result of the two missions of the Word and the Spirit. The Spirit is compelling the Church to go beyond itself. (The words of Ignatius Hazim, the Metropolitan of Latakia, are relevant in this context.) At this level, freedom presupposes an exercise of personal charisms and commitment on the part of all Christians, both pastors and lay people, who have themselves been set free by the Spirit. Thus, the second part of this volume completes the first part—the Church is an institution, but it is also and even primarily the 'we' of Christians.

NOTES

1. See L. Cerfaux, *The Christian in the Theology of St Paul* (Eng. tr.; London, 1967), pp. 446–452; E. Schweizer, '*sarx*', *TDNT*, VII, pp. 98–151; X. Léon-Dufour, 'Flesh', *Dictionary of Biblical Theology*, 2nd Eng. ed. (London, 1973), pp. 185–188; J. D. G. Dunn, *Jesus and the Spirit* (London, 1975), pp. 308ff.
2. Together with Augustine, Thomas Aquinas, Luther and many modern exegetes, I believe that Rom 7:7–25 refers to baptized Christians and to Paul himself. For a history of the exegesis of this passage, see O. Kuss, 'Zur Geschichte der Auslegung von Römer 7, 7–25', *Der Römerbrief* (Regensburg, 1957), pp. 462–485. For Augustine, see A. de Veer, 'L'exégèse de Rom. VII et ses variations', *Bibl. August.* 33 (Paris, 1974), pp. 770–778.

In opposition to W. G. Kümmel, *Römer 7 und die Bekehrung des Paulus* (Leipzig, 1929), J. D. G. Dunn, 'Rom 7, 14–25 in the Theology of Paul', *TZ*, 31 (1975), 257–273, and *op. cit.* (note 1), pp. 312ff., 444, notes, has shown that the passage deals with Paul as a Christian and the state of the Christian on earth as an inner struggle between the *pneuma* ('already') and the *sarx* ('not yet') in him and has pointed out that the struggle does not necessarily end with the coming of the Spirit, but that, on the contrary, it is then that it really begins.

3. See Rom 1:3–4; 6:4–11; 7:4; 8:3, 10–11; Gal 4:4–5; 2 Cor 4:10–14; Col 1:21; 2:12; 1 Tim 3:16a; 1 Pet 3:18. The Fathers regarded the baptism of Jesus as the type of the baptism of all believers and therefore applied to him the theme of Jesus descending into the water to submerge the old man entirely in the depths of the water; see Gregory Nazianzen, *Orat.* 39 (*PG* 36, 302).

4. Rom 13:8ff.: 'Owe no one anything, except to love one another, for he who loves his neighbour has fulfilled the law'.

5. Declaration on Non-Christian Religions, *Nostra aetate*, 5.

6. J. Wolinski, 'Le mystère de l'Esprit Saint', *L'Esprit Saint* (Brussels, 1978), pp. 131–164, especially pp. 141ff.

7. Origen, *Comm. in Ioan. ev.* XX, 293 (*PG* 14, 649B).

8. *Hom. Jer.* IX, 4 (*PG* 13, 356C–357A; Fr. tr. P. Nemeshegyi, *La Paternité de Dieu chez Origène* (Paris, 1960), p. 199; see also *SC* 232, pp. 393–395).

9. Simeon the New Theologian, *Cat.* II (*Cat.* VI; Fr. tr. J. Paramelle, *SC* 104 (1964), p. 23 [another version above, p. 70]). See also note 8 above. Others in the Eastern tradition who could be mentioned here are Mark the Hermit and Gregory of Sinai.

10. See L. Cerfaux, *op. cit.* (note 1), pp. 336–341; Dunn, *op. cit.* (note 1), pp. 326–342. For the Lutheran tradition, see the second part of R. Prenter, *Le Saint-Esprit et le renouveau de l'Eglise* (*Cahiers théologiques de l'actualité protestante*, 23–24) (Neuchâtel, 1949).

11. See 2 Cor 4:7; 12:9ff.; 13:3. See also J. Cambier, 'Le critère paulinien de l'apostolat en II Cor 12, 6ss', *Bib* 43 (1962), 481–518; S. Lyonnet, 'La loi fondamentale de l'apostolat formulée et vécue par S. Paul (2 Cor 13, 9)', *La vie selon l'Esprit* (*Unam Sanctam*, 55) (Paris, 1965), pp. 263–282.

12. Mt 12:28. See also my article 'Le blasphème contre l'Esprit', *L'expérience de l'Esprit, Mélanges Schillebeeckx* (Paris, 1976), pp. 17–29; this article also appeared as 'Blasphemy against the Holy Spirit' in *Concilium* 99 (1974/6), 47–57.

13. Eph 6:10. The word *dunamis*, which is so closely associated with the Holy Spirit, is only found here in the verb *endunamousthe*.

14. M. F. Berrouard, 'Le Paraclet défenseur du Christ devant la conscience du croyant', *RSPT*, 33 (1949), 361–389, especially 364. See also T. Preuss, 'La justification dans la pensée johannique', *La vie en Christ* (Neuchâtel and Paris, 1951), pp. 46–64 (in the 1946 text).

15. It is worth reading, in this context, A. Rabut, 'Accueillir Dieu', *VS* (August 1949), 168–177.

16. J. Chevallier, *Essai sur la formation de la nationalité et les réveils religieux au Pays de Galles des origines à la fin du VIe siècle* (Lyons and Paris, 1923), pp. 392ff, 419ff.

17. O. Cullmann, 'Les premières confessions de foi chrétiennes', *La foi et le culte de l'Eglise primitive* (Neuchâtel, 1963), pp. 73–74, quotes Cyril of Jerusalem, Epiphanius of Salamis and Nestorius. The Apostolic Constitutions and the Epistle of the Apostles, on the other hand, linked the remission of sins with faith in the Church.

18. Ambrose, *De poen.* I, 8 (*PL* 16, 468).

19. Postcommunion of the Tuesday after Pentecost in the Roman rite.

20. By an unknown author living before the tenth century (*PL* 86, 693). It used to appear in the Dominican rite, but was not included in Dom Guéranger's *Année liturgique*, although it has been restored to the new *Liturgia horarum*.

21. See H. Schlier, '*eleutheros, eleutheria*', *TDNT*, II, pp. 487–502; L. Cerfaux, *op. cit.* (note

1), pp. 452–460; S. Lyonnet, 'Liberté chrétienne et loi de l'Esprit selon S. Paul', *La vie selon L'Esprit, op. cit.* (note 11), pp. 169–195; J.-P. Jossua, 'Liberté', *Vocabulaire œcuménique* (Paris, 1970), pp. 283–297; *Lumière et Vie*, 61 (1963), 69 (1964); C. Duquoc, *Jésus, homme libre. Esquisse d'une Christologie* (Paris, 1973). Apart from Lyonnet, the following have written about Thomas Aquinas' theological systematization of this theme: J. Lécuyer, 'Pentecôte et loi nouvelle', *VS* (May 1953), 471–490; my own 'Variations sur le thème "Loi-Grâce" ', *RThom*, 71 (1971), 420–438; 'Le Saint-Esprit dans la théologie thomiste de l'agir moral', *Atti del Congresso Internazionale 1974*, 5: *L'Agire morale* (Naples, 1976), pp. 9–19 (with bibliography); Rémi Parent, *L'Esprit Saint et la liberté chrétienne* (Paris, 1976), which is a personal reflection with a philosophical slant on the part played by our human freedom in a context of a theology of the Holy Spirit.

22. Nicholas Cabasilas, *La vie en Jésus-Christ*, Fr. tr. S. Broussaleux (Amay sur Meuse, 1932), p. 54.
23. Augustine, *In Ioan. ev.* III, 2 (*PL* 35, 1397); cf. *De spir. et litt.* IX, 15: 'ut . . . sancta voluntas impleat legem, non constituta sub lege' (*PL* 44, 209).
24. Thomas Aquinas, *In 2 Cor.* c. 3, lect. 3 (ed. R. Cai, No. 112); translated by Lyonnet, who quotes *In Rom.* c. 2, lect. 3 (Cai No. 217); *Contra Gent.* IV, 22; *ST* Ia IIae, q. 108, a. 1, ad 2, as pointing in the same direction. See also J. Maritain, *Du régime temporel et de la liberté* (1933), pp. 44ff. In his treatise *Contra Gent.*, Thomas follows the theme of charity-friendship. The Spirit communicates his secrets to us through friendship, regarding us as an extension of himself (c. 21). He moves us and leads us to God by means of that contemplation which is peculiar to friendship, by the effects of his presence, which are joy and consolation, and by gentle consent to his will, which constitutes true Christian freedom (c. 22).
25. *ST* Ia IIae, q. 106, a. 1 and 2; *In Rom.* c. 8, lect. 1 (Cai Nos 602–603); *In Heb.* c. 8, lect. 2 (Cai No. 404).
26. R. Garrigou-Lagrange, 'La liberté impeccable du Christ et celle des enfants de Dieu', *VS* (April 1924), 5–20; A. Durand, 'La liberté du Christ dans son rapport à l'impeccabilité', *NRT* (September-October 1948), 811–822.
27. Marie de l'Incarnation, Relation of 1654, XXIX, *Ecrits spirituels et historiques*, ed. Albert Jamet (Paris and Québec, 1930), II, p. 271.
28. See also 2 Cor 3:3. The community of believers is a 'letter from Christ delivered by us, written not with ink but with the Spirit of the living God, not on tablets of stone, but on tablets of human hearts'.
29. See my contribution to *In libertatem vocati estis. Miscellanea Bernhard Häring (Studia Moralia*, XV) (Rome, 1977), pp. 31–40, entitled 'Réflexions et Propos sur l'originalité d'une éthique chrétienne'. See also Cerfaux, *op. cit.* (note 1), pp. 460–466, on the theme of the fruits of the Spirit.
30. Fr. tr. in *Alfred Delp, S.J.: Honneur et liberté du Chrétien. Témoignage présenté par le P. M. Rondet, S.J.* (Paris, 1958), pp. 161–200; Eng. tr. [not followed here] in *Facing Death* (London, 1962), pp. 138–179. Delp was handcuffed, but able at times to slip a hand free: *Facing Death*, pp. 11, 15.
31. I cannot resist quoting here Dietrich Bonhoeffer's fragment 'Self-discipline', which can be found at the beginning of his *Ethics* (London, 1968), p. 15 and in his *Letters and Papers from Prison*, p. 15 of paperback ed. (London, 1968):
    'If you set out to seek freedom, you must learn before all things
    Mastery over sense and soul, lest your wayward desirings,
    Lest your undisciplined members lead you now this way, now that way.
    Chaste be your mind and your body, and subject to you and obedient,
    Serving solely to seek their appointed goal and objective.
    None learns the secret of freedom save only by way of control.'
    Thomas Aquinas and Paul would both have agreed with this!

32. Dogmatic Constitution on the Church, *Lumen Gentium*, 9, 2.
33. Augustine, *De vera rel.* 17, 33 (*PL* 33, 136; Fr. tr. J. Pegon, *Œuvres de S. Augustin*, VIII (Paris, 1951), pp. 67, 69); *Ep.* 35 *ad Januarium*, 19, 35 (*PL* 33, 221; Fr. tr. H. Barreau, *Œuvres complètes de S. Augustin*, VI (Paris, 1873), pp. 480–481). See also Thomas Aquinas, *ST* Ia IIae, q. 107, a. 4; *Quodl.* IV, 13.
34. One of these was Erasmus: see A. Humbert, *Les origines de la théologie moderne* (Paris, 1911), pp. 209ff.; another was Raulin: see A. Renaudet, *Préréforme et Humanisme à Paris* (Paris, 1916), p. 170.
35. *ST* IIa IIae, q. 147, a. 3; the two texts of Augustine are quoted in objection 3 as evidence against a commandment to fast. In this text, in *Quodl.* IV, 13 and in *ST* Ia IIae, q. 108, a. 1, Thomas justifies the law, but, with great precision, refers it to its institution by ecclesiastical or temporal authorities. He therefore says: 'Hoc ipsum est de ductu Spiritus Sancti quod homines spirituales legibus humanibus subdantur': see *ST* Ia IIae, q. 96, a. 5, ad 2. See also G. Salet, 'La loi dans nos cœurs', *NRT*, 79 (1957), 449–462, 561–578.
36. Pastoral Constitution on the Church in the Modern World, *Gaudium et Spes*, 25, 1. Two articles written at the end of the last century are worth reading in this context. They are by M. B. Schwalm: 'L'inspiration intérieure et le gouvernement des âmes' and 'Le respect de l'Eglise pour l'action intime de Dieu dans les âmes', *RThom*, 6 (1898), 315–353 and 707–738 respectively. The author considers in these two articles the activity and the indwelling of the Holy Spirit.
37. *Alfred Delp, Honneur et liberté, op. cit.* (note 30), pp. 194–195, 196; *Facing Death, op. cit.*, pp. 173, 174–175. See also *Honneur et liberté*, pp. 136–142 for his lecture given in 1943. It is clear that Alfred Delp saw the Church as too firmly settled, and he experienced a terrible coming of the winnowing-fan (Lk 3:17) and the axe (Mt 3:10).
38. See H. Schlier, '*parrēsia*', *TDNT*, V, pp. 871ff.; P. Joüon, 'Divers sens de parrèsia dans le Nouveau Testament', *RSR*, 30 (1940), 239–242. Many studies have been written about *parrēsia* in the New Testament.
39. This account will be found in Eusebius, *Hist. Eccl.* V, 1, 49 (Fr. tr. G. Bardy, *SC* 41 (1955), p. 19). The term has been studied by A. A. R. Bastiensen in *Le sacramentaire de Vérone* (*Graecitas et Latinitas Christianorum Primaeva, Supplementa* III) (Nijmegen, 1970), under the sub-title 'The Church's acquisition of her freedom'. I have already cited Alfred Delp as a contemporary example of the same spirit (and Spirit) made present and would therefore refer back to the collection of his writings in note 30 above and especially to his lecture given in 1943 on trust, both the trust that we should have and that we should inspire.

7

THE GIFTS AND THE FRUITS
OF THE SPIRIT

The scriptural source of the theology of the gifts of the Spirit is the messianic text Is 11:1–2 in the translation of the Septuagint—often regarded as 'inspired'—and later in the Latin Vulgate:

> There shall come forth a shoot from the stump of Jesse and a branch shall grow out of his roots. And the Spirit of Yahweh shall rest upon him,
>   the spirit of wisdom and understanding,
>   the spirit of counsel and might,
>   the spirit of knowledge and piety
> and he shall be filled with the spirit of the fear of the Lord.

We know how attached Irenaeus, Origen and many others after them were to this septenarium.[1] These seven gifts were, however, treated as operations of grace and sometimes even as 'charisms', rather than as gifts that were specifically different from the other communications of the Spirit, in the Western Church until the thirteenth century; we can even give a precise date: 1235. According to Hilary of Poitiers and Cyril of Alexandria, the gifts pointed to the Holy Spirit acting in different ways.[2] The history of this theme has been fully traced and I would refer the reader to the numerous studies of this subject.[3]

Between 1235 and 1250, during the time of Philip the Chancellor, a theology of the gifts as specific realities of grace as distinct from the virtues and the charisms was developed. It is the vigorous and profound form given to this theology by Thomas Aquinas that I shall discuss.

It is valuable at this point to delineate the epistemological status of this theology, in other words, to define its authority. It is not a dogma, but simply a theology. Certain theologians, among them Duns Scotus, rejected the specific distinction between the gifts and the virtues. The Council of Trent was careful not to condemn Duns Scotus' position.[4] I am personally all the more inclined to stress the aspect of the theological interpretation and construction in this matter for noting, as we cannot help noting, how the saints and mystics themselves make no distinction in their own experience between the grace of the virtues and that of the gifts of the Spirit. It is their spiritual directors, biographers or interpreters who speak here of the action of the 'gifts' and who even state precisely which gift is active.[5]

134

We should also give an even more relative value to the many parallels that have been drawn between the seven gifts of the Holy Spirit and the other septenaria found in Scripture or the Church's tradition. Augustine, for example, compared the gifts with the beatitudes and the petitions in the Our Father.[6] A fantastic degree of inventiveness has been shown in the multifarious comparisons that have been made between 'sevens' in the history of Christianity,[7] and this can only serve to re-emphasize the very relative value of these parallels. There is, however, a certain homogeneity in the grace of the Holy Spirit and that of revelation as attested in Scripture, and this justifies a sober attempt to establish a relationship between the virtues, the gifts and the beatitudes. As we shall see, Thomas Aquinas provided a sound justification of the connection that was first made in 1235 by Philip the Chancellor.

Let us therefore consider Thomas' theology of the gifts.[8] It may represent a systematization, but he has, I think, given an authentic interpretation not only of the experience of Christians themselves, but also of the teaching of Paul, whose text: 'All who are led by the Spirit of God are sons of God' (Rom 8:14) he quotes again and again. The dominant idea in his theology is that only God is able to lead us to his own sphere, his own inheritance,[9] his own state of blessedness and his own glory, which is himself. Only God, in other words, can make us act divinely.

It is, however, *we* who act. In this teaching, we are once again confronted with that union between God and ourselves that we have encountered when we discussed Paul's Gal 4:6 and Rom 8:15 and when we considered merit. God is the sovereign Subject and we are really subjects of a life and of actions that are our own. Thomas criticized Augustine here[10] and rejected Augustine's and Bonaventure's theory of illumination and Peter Lombard's thesis on the Holy Spirit as charity. His concern was to ensure supernatural principles of action and a supernatural organism that are really our own, in other words, the theologal virtues and especially charity. He regarded it, however, as necessary that our actions, our virtues and even the theologal virtues of faith, hope and charity should go beyond the purely human mode of experience and our human way of practising them, which is so imperfect and exposed to chance. It is precisely because he had such an extremely lively sense of the theologal nature of the virtues that he was so conscious of the very imperfect use that we could make of them. They were *habitus* or 'haviours' [see Volume I, p. 124, note 18] which came from God, but, so that imperfection should be minimal and the virtues should be practised more fully, God, Thomas believed, had to play a part in man's practice of them and of the other virtues. He did this by creating in the soul a habitual availability—by means of the *habitus* or 'haviours'—to receive from him a movement enabling us to practise the virtues, above all charity, *supra modum humanum* (*Commentary on the Sentences*) or 'beyond the mode of man' by means of an impulse received *ab altiori principio*.[11] Thomas takes pains to stress the significance of the term *spiritus* or 'breath' as a dynamic and motivating reality.[12] The gifts of the Spirit are distinct from the virtues because they make the practice of the latter perfect. They are those permanent dispositions which make the Christian *prompte mobilis ab inspiratione divina* or *a Spiritu Sancto*, that is, at once ready to follow the movement of divine inspiration or of the Holy Spirit.[13]

This is a far cry from purely rational behaviour, or even from a form of regulation governed by a rigidly and permanently established nature, a position sometimes attributed to Thomas. Thomas recognized that human nature and the 'natural law' were to some extent determined by history, but he made room for the event of the Spirit. His ethical cosmos was a cosmos based on the will of God to save and sanctify man, using norms that transcend both human and supernatural reason. We are led by another, who does not act without us and does not use violence,[14] but who nonetheless goes beyond anything that we can see or expect. He goes beyond not only our views and expectations based on human reason, but also those that come from faith. This does not mean that the gifts of the Holy Spirit are superior to the theologal virtues, since these unite us to God himself so that nothing can be above them. No, the gifts of the Spirit are at the service of those virtues, so that they can be practised perfectly.[15] Only God, however, can give his fullness to the practice of the theologal virtues and only he can consummate the action of a child of God. This is true of the whole life of grace and of the presence to God that it establishes as the object of knowledge and love.[16] That is why Thomas attempts to show that the gifts of the Spirit are still given even in the state of blessedness.

All the more reason, therefore, for establishing the part that they play in the practice of the theologal and moral virtues. Since he regarded the beatitudes as the perfect action of the virtues and the gifts, he also tried to make one gift of the Spirit and one of the beatitudes correspond to each of the virtues. He even attempted to attribute to each virtue, with its gift and its corresponding beatitude or beatitudes, one or other of the 'fruits' of the Spirit mentioned by Paul. He devotes an entire question in his *Summa* to these fruits and in it insists on the aspect of spiritual struggle against the 'flesh'.[17]

It is, of course, always possible to find a reason for justifying such parallels. It is thus wrong to give them too much importance or, on the other hand, to attribute no value at all to them, because a great spiritual tradition has found expression in this way.

The action of the Spirit working through the gift of understanding thus perfects faith and makes it capable of a *sanus intellectus* or a certain inner penetration, the peak of which is negative in meaning. It does this by means of a keen appreciation of God's transcendence. The corresponding beatitude is that of the pure in heart (*ST* IIa IIae, q. 8). The activity of faith is also taken to a higher degree of perfection by the gift of knowledge, to which Thomas attributes the benefit of *certum iudicium* or 'sure judgement' which is not discursive, but simple and almost instinctive, *discernendo credenda a non credendis*, in other words, by this judgement it is possible to discern what has to be believed from what should not be believed. Thomas makes this correspond to the beatitude of tears.[18]

To hope, which looks forward to God's salvation, there corresponds the gift of fear, by which man is made *subditus Deo* or 'subjected to God' and the corresponding beatitude is that of the poor in spirit (*ST* IIa IIae, q. 19). To charity, the queen of the virtues, corresponds the gift of wisdom, which guarantees 'correctness of judgement concerning the contemplation or examination of divine realities' (*rectitudo iudicii circa divina conspicienda et consulenda*). The corresponding beatitude is that of the peacemakers (*ST* IIa IIae, q. 45). Prudence is clearly perfected by the gift of counsel, and the beatitude of the merciful corresponds to this (*ST* IIa IIae, q. 52). Justice, which renders to every man his due, is transcended when it is a question of what we owe to those from whom we derive our very being, and it is sustained and completed by the gift of piety, which *exhibet patri (et Deo ut Patro) officium et cultum*—'gives to the father (and to God as Father) duty and respectful attention'. Thomas attributes to this virtue the beatitude of the meek (*ST* IIa IIae, q. 121). The gift of might or power clearly helps the virtue of fortitude and goes together with the beatitude of those who 'hunger and thirst for righteousness' (*ST* IIa IIae, q. 139). Finally, there is the cardinal virtue of temperance, but Thomas seems to have been in difficulty in this case over attributing a gift of the Spirit and a beatitude to this virtue. In the end he settles for 'fear of the Lord' and either *beati pauperes* or *qui esuriunt et sitiunt iustitiam*. We realize how relative these correspondences are, to say nothing of the biblical and exegetical meanings both of the New Testament beatitudes and the Isaian text.

It is, however, interesting to note in this context how Thomas includes the presence of the gifts of the Holy Spirit in the very fabric of his minute analysis of the virtues throughout IIa IIae of his *Summa*. One has the impression, when reading his analysis, in which Aristotle and Cicero act as guides, that moral action is a matter of following the structures of nature, which are set by God, but recognized by human reason. His morality could even be called institutional—although happily we have to say that the institution calls for the event of the Holy Spirit, without which it is difficult to see how holiness of the kind that the Christian saints show in their lives is in fact the most perfect form of Christian life. It consists, as we know, of a continuous series of processes of transcendence of supernatural but human limits based on 'inspirations' that are generously listened to in generously given freedom.

Thomas also devoted a question in his *Summa*, as I have already noted above, to the fruits of the Holy Spirit. He describes them as the ultimate and delightful products of the action of the Spirit in us.[19] The comparison with plant life is interesting. The fruits are what are gathered at the end of branches growing from a vigorous stock and they are delightful to the taste. Alternatively, they are what are reaped from a crop or harvest in a field that has been cultivated and sown. In his commentary on Paul, L. Cerfaux translated the text as the 'harvest of the Spirit'[20] and the word used in Gal 5:22 is in the singular: 'The fruit of the Spirit is love, joy, peace, patience, kindness, goodness, faithfulness, gentleness and self-control'. There are other lists elsewhere in Paul's writings: 'goodness, righteousness and truth' (Eph 5:9); 'righteousness, godliness, faith, love, steadfastness, gentleness' (1 Tim 6:11); 'righteousness and peace and joy in the Holy Spirit' (Rom 14:17; cf. 15:13); and finally '(we commend ourselves . . .) by purity, knowledge, forbearance, kindness, the Holy Spirit, genuine love, truthful speech and the power of God' (2 Cor 6:6–7). These Pauline lists can be compared with the list in Jas 3:17–18.

What emerges from these texts is an ideal portrait of the Christian who is peacefully and joyfully ready to welcome, and calmly and patiently open to love his fellow-man. They are basically manifestations of the love described in 1 Cor 13:4–7, presenting the reader with a fragile imitation of Christ who was 'gentle and lowly in heart' (Mt 11:29), a man given up to God and a man for others, free, truthful, demanding, merciful, recollected and open to all men. The opposite portrait would be one of violence, aggressive self-assertion and a refusal to be available to or to accept others. The fruits of the flesh are listed in Gal 5:19–21; Rom 1:29–31.

Does this mean that the child of God necessarily preserves or acquires an element of infantilism or lacks a spirit of open commitment and combativeness? Does the religion of the Father, that is, of a God who existed before our world and transcends it, imply that the Christian is bound to be unconcerned with the history of that world and to turn away from the world? Christianity's affirmation of an incarnate God serves only to introduce a contradiction which leads to impotence, it has been claimed. This was the critical question asked by the philosopher Merleau-Ponty, whose answer, so frequently repeated, was that, in politics, the Christian was 'a bad conservative and an uncertain revolutionary'.[21]

This criticism can hardly be applied to Paul or the Christian saints, and Merleau-Ponty was too experienced and well-informed to press the question too far—because of the Holy Spirit. He said, for example: 'Pentecost means that the religion of the Father and the religion of the Son have to be consummated in the religion of the Spirit and that God is no longer in heaven, but in society and in communication with men and especially everywhere where men meet in his name. . . . Catholicism has hindered and frozen this development of religion: the Trinity is not a dialectical movement and the three Persons are co-eternal. The Father is not transcended by the Spirit and the fear of God, the law, is not eliminated by love. God is not entirely with us.'

Was Merleau-Ponty not working with a Hegelian concept of the Spirit as immanent in the community of men and above all in history and even identified with them? In Christian teaching, that immanence is real. God, through his Spirit, makes men his sons and places his law in them. That law is summed up in love and his sons are together the brothers of his Son who was made man. There is no fatherhood without brotherhood. God is not paternalistic. Transcendence and immanence go together. The Christian is open and dedicated to God, to his brothers and to the world at the same time. As we can only take hold of part of our life at a time, many of us will inevitably experience transcendence without immanence and others immanence without transcendence.[22] But the truth and the grace of the Holy Spirit unites both aspects.

I have quoted many of Paul's texts and they can seem to be extremely demanding and sublime. They are, however, also very virile and are capable of making us virile and of leading us to adulthood. I have not taken advantage of the opportunity to cite any of the sublime and often poetic formulae and accounts of spiritual writers and those who have written of their life in the Spirit.[23] I would like, however, to end this short chapter on the gifts and the fruits of the Spirit with this beautiful passage from a hymn by Simeon the New Theologian:

> How can you be both a blazing hearth and a cool fountain,
>   a burning, yet a sweetness that cleanses us?
> How can you make man a god, darkness light
>   and draw new life from the pit of death?
> How does night become day? Can you overcome gloom?
> Take the flame to our hearts and change the depths of our being?
> How are you simply one with us? How do you give us the Son of God?
> How do you burn us with love and wound us without a sword?
> How can you bear us and remain so slow to anger,
>   yet from where you are watch our smallest gestures here?
> How do you follow our actions from so high and so far?
> You servant waits for peace and courage in tears.[24]

NOTES

1. Irenaeus, *Adv. haer.* III, 17, 3 (*PG* 7, 929–930); *Dem.* 9 (*SC* 62, p. 45). See also K. Schlurtz, *Isaias 11, 2 (Die sieben Gaben des Hl. Geistes) in den ersten vier christlichen Jahrhunderten* (Münster, 1932), pp. 46–58.
2. Hilary of Poitiers, *Comm. in Mat.* 15, 10 (*PL* 9, 1007A); Cyril of Alexandria, *Comm. in Isa.* XI, 1–3 (*PG* 70, 309ff.).
3. The essential aspects of this history will be found in the articles on the gifts of the Spirit ('Dons du Saint-Esprit') by A. Gardeil, *DTC*, IV (1911), cols 1754–1779; and G. Bardy and F. Vandenbroucke, *Dictionnaire de spiritualité*, III (1954), cols. 1579–1603. More recent research has not made any really substantial additions.

4. The words 'susceptionem gratiae et donorum' occur in the sixth session of the Council of Trent and in the conciliar decree *De justificatione* (c. 7; *DS* 1528). The Council clearly wanted to leave open the question of the distinction between grace on the one hand and charity and the gifts of the Spirit on the other, which Duns Scotus had rejected. What is remarkable here is that most of the Fathers of the Council were inclined towards Duns Scotus' position: see A. Prumbs, *Die Stellung des Trienter Konzils zu der Frage und dem Wesen der heiligmachenden Gnade* (Paderborn, 1909), pp. 114ff. See also, in this connection, P. Dumont, 'Le caractère divin de la grâce d'après la théologie scolastique', *RSR*, 13 (1933), 517–552; 14 (1934), 62–95; J. A. de Aldama, 'Habla el Concilio Tridentino de los dones del Espíritu Santo?', *Estudios eclesiásticos*, 20 (1946), 241–244.

5. This is obvious from the information given in the *Dictionnaire de Spiritualité* for the sixteenth century (cols 1601–1603), the seventeenth century (col. 1605), and individual lives or souls (cols 1635–1641); see also A. Gardeil, *op. cit.* below (note 8).

6. Augustine, *De serm. Dom. in monte*, I, 4, 11; II, 11, 38 (*PL* 34, 1234 and 1236).

7. See *Dictionnaire de Spiritualité*, col. 1592. This enthusiasm for making comparisons reached a peak at the Council of Lavaur in 1368, when parallels were drawn between seven articles on God, seven articles on Christ, seven virtues (three theologal and four cardinal virtues), seven sacraments, seven gifts of the Holy Spirit, seven temporal works of mercy, seven spiritual works of mercy and seven capital vices. It is interesting to note that the beatitudes were not included here! See Mansi, XXVI, 492–493.

8. Thomas Aquinas, *In III Sent.* d. 34 and 35; *ST* Ia IIae, q. 68–70, and, in *ST* IIa IIae, the questions devoted to the gifts. Among the various studies and commentaries, I would mention only the following: A. Gardeil, *op. cit.* (note 3), and *Les dons du Saint-Esprit dans les saints dominicains* (Paris, 1903); R. Garrigou-Lagrange, *Perfection chrétienne et contemplation*, 2 vols (Paris and Tournai, 1923); M.-M. Labourdette, *Dictionnaire de Spiritualité*, III, cols 1610–1635; M.-H. Lavocat, *L'Esprit de vérité et d'amour. Essai de synthèse doctrinale sur le Saint-Esprit* (Paris, 1962); M. Philipon, *Les dons du Saint-Esprit* (1963); A. Guindon, *La pédagogie de la crainte dans l'histoire du salut selon Thomas d'Aquin* (Montréal and Paris, 1975), in which his own articles are cited; my article 'Variations sur le thème Loi-Grâce', *RThom* 71 (1971), 429–438.

9. *ST* Ia IIae, q. 68, a. 2, where Thomas quotes Ps 142:10, 'Spiritus tuus deducet me in terram rectam', and adds: 'quia in haereditatem illius terrae beatorum nullus potest pervenire nisi moveatur et deducatur a Spiritu Sancto'.

10. See E. Gilson, 'Pourquoi S. Thomas a critiqué S. Augustin', *Arch. hist. doctr, litt. M.A.*, 1 (1926), pp. 5–127. This remains a very important study.

11. *ST* Ia IIae, q. 68, a. 2. For the logic of this argument, see P. R. Régamey, 'Esquisse d'un portrait spirituel du chrétien', *VS*, 421 (October 1956), 227–258. The collection *Portrait spirituel du chrétien* (Paris, 1963) only came into my hands when I had already finished the present work, with the result that I could not, unfortunately, take its findings into account.

12. *ST* Ia IIae, q. 68, a. 1.

13. *ST* Ia IIae, q. 68, a. 1 and 8; q. 69, a. 1; IIa IIae, q. 52, a. 1; q. 121, a. 1.

14. We are free to follow or not to follow or to follow generously or reluctantly God's inspiration: see *ST* Ia IIae, q. 9, a. 4 and 6; q. 68, a. 3, ad 2; IIa IIae, q. 23, a. 2; q. 52, a. 1, ad 3. Total and constant generosity leads to heroism—as Teresa of Lisieux said: 'Since the age of three, I have never refused God anything'.

15. *ST* Ia IIae, q. 68, a. 8, c and ad 1; IIa IIae, q. 9, a. 1, ad 3.

16. This point was made by John of St Thomas, *Cursus theologicus*, I, q. 43, d. 17, a. 3, and the Carmelite Joseph of the Holy Spirit. See A. Gardeil, *La structure de l'âme et l'expérience mystique*, II (Paris, 2nd ed., 1927), pp. 232ff.; J. Maritain, *Les degrés du savoir* (Tournai, 4th ed., 1946), chapter VI, §15. John of St Thomas, *The Gifts of the Holy Spirit* (Eng. tr.; London and New York, 1951); also tr. into Fr. by Raïssa Maritain (Paris, 1930).

17. *ST* Ia IIae, q. 70, with reference to Gal 5:22–23. The grace of the Holy Spirit, which is the

main aspect of the new law, brings about in the *affectus* a *contemptus mundi*: see q. 106, a. 1, ad 1. For the connection between virtues, gifts and beatitudes, see P. R. Régamey, *op. cit.* (note 11).

18. *ST* IIa IIae, q. 9; cf. q. 1, a. 4, ad 3; q. 2, a. 3, ad 3; see also *In III Sent.* d. 24, q. 1, a. 3; q. 2, ad 3. There have been many studies; see, for example, G. H. Joyce and S. Harent, 'La foi qui discerne', *RSR*, 6 (1916), 433–467.
19. *ST* Ia IIae, q. 70: 'Ultima et delectabilia quae in nobis proveniunt ex virtute Spiritus Sancti'; cf. *Comm. in Gal.* c. 5, lect. 6.
20. L. Cerfaux, *The Christian in the Theology of St Paul* (Eng. tr.; London, 1967), pp. 461ff., who provides a useful literary analysis; A. Gardeil, *DTC*, VI (1914), cols 944–949; M. Ledrus, 'Fruits du Saint-Esprit', *VS*, 76 (May 1947), 714–733, whose article, with its 145 references, is very full—perhaps too full; C.-A. Bernet, *Dictionnaire de Spiritualité*, V, cols 1569–1575.
21. M. Merleau-Ponty, 'Foi et bonne foi', *Les Temps modernes* (February 1946), 769–782; repr. in *Sens et non-sens* (Paris, 1946).
22. Mgr Matagrin has commented: 'One of the risks of Christianity today is the split between a political Christianity without a sense of God's transcendence and a spiritual renewal without a historical incarnation': *L'Européen*, 160–161 (July-September 1976), 7.
23. Many examples will be found in M.-J. Le Guillou, *Les témoins sont parmi nous. L'expérience de Dieu dans l'Esprit Saint* (Paris, 1976); Mme Arsène-Henry, *Les plus beaux textes sur le Saint-Esprit* (Paris, 1968); Sr Geneviève, *L'Esprit du Seigneur remplit l'univers* (Paris, 1977). See also the journals of the Renewal movement in France such as *Il est vivant* and *Tychique*.
24. Adapted by Brie and Gelineau from Hymn VI (*Hymnes*, II, Fr. tr. J. Paramelle, *SC* 156 (1969), pp. 205, 207). This hymn is frequently sung in this adapted form in monasteries.

PART THREE

THE RENEWAL IN THE SPIRIT
PROMISES AND QUESTIONS

INTRODUCTION

'Do not quench the Spirit, . . . test
everything; hold fast to what is good'

(1 Thess 5:19, 21)

The story of the Renewal has been told dozens of times. The reality in question is very well known—it has its own congresses, meetings and gatherings, its own journals and publications. Events are reported in the press. I do not intend to describe its prayer meetings again: as enough has been written about it already to fill a library. Everything has already been said and often by people who have greater authority and ability than I have. Why take up the theme again? By what right? What have I to say on the subject?

I do so because, in a work of the length and breadth that I envisage for this book, it would be impossible not to speak about a religious movement of such significance placed entirely under the sign of the Holy Spirit. It is also the responsibility of theologians, however conscious they may be of their own mediocrity and their duty to be modest, to try to understand the work of God, to fit the different pieces of revelation together into the whole, and to suggest principles of discernment. The theological study of this movement is already well advanced, but some additions have still to be made, and so I venture to enter the field.

The reality involved—it does not matter very much what label we give it, and 'movement' does as well as any other—calls for attentive theological investigation. There can be no doubt that God is active in it—he is transforming lives and often working powerfully in the movement. Has he visited his people? In that case, as Peter exclaimed in similar circumstances, 'Who was I that I could withstand God?' (Acts 11:17).

The movement raises a large number of questions. It asks questions of the Church. It suggests to the Church a way to rejuvenation and renewed vitality. At the same time it also raises questions about itself. Some see it as an enterprise of the devil.[1] Bishops and theologians have warned of the risk of serious errors.[2] The truth is that it is not possible to regard this vast movement, extending over so many different countries, as completely homogeneous. As so many have done before me, I shall ask a number of critical questions. Even if I formulate them in a general way, I ask that generalizations not be made from them. Finally, why should we expect from the members of this movement a perfection not required of any religious order or Church community?

(Text written in October 1978)

145

NOTES

1. See, for example, F. Hubmer, *Zungenreden, Weissagung, umkämpfte Geistesgaben* (Denkendorf, 1972), who has reproduced in his book the Berlin declaration of the Gnadau Association in 1909. This very severe assessment was made because of certain strange and rather unhealthy phenomena which accompanied the introduction of Pentecostalism into Germany in 1906. See also J. P. Dietle, *op. cit.* in the following bibliography, pp. 230, 234.

2. Almost all Catholic studies have pointed to these risks. I have myself, for example, in 'Renouveau dans l'Esprit et Institution ecclésiale. Mutuelle interrogation', *RHPR*, 55 (1975), 143–156. See also, in the following bibliography, F. A. Sullivan, 'The Pentecostal Movement'; *Pro Mundi Vita*; F. Deleclos, 'Le renouveau charismatique'; the Malines document, etc. Above all, see J.-R. Bouchet and H. Caffarel, *Le renouveau charismatique interpellé. Etudes et documents* (*Collection Renouveau*, 5) (Paris, 1976). Finally—or perhaps first of all—see the declarations of the United States bishops, *Doc. cath*. No. 1670 (16 February 1973), 157–159, and of the Canadian bishops, *Doc. cath*. No. 1678 (15 June 1975), 569–574. H. Caffarel also made a statement in a lecture given in Rome on 5 December 1974: see *Doc. cath*. No. 1670 (16 February 1975), 162ff. There have been many replies to the little book by Bouchet and Caffarel: see especially P. T. Camelot, 'Le Renouveau charismatique', *VS* (November-December 1976), 913–930; J. Mondal, *Tychique*, 7 (January 1977), 64–71.

SELECT BIBLIOGRAPHY

Outlines of the whole movement (mainly Catholic), often with discussion

Walter Hollenweger is the author of the best outline of the whole movement: *The Pentecostals. The Charismatic Movement in the Churches* (Eng. tr.; London, 1972; Minneapolis, 1972, 2nd ed. 1973). Hollenweger, a minister in the Swiss Reformed Church, provides a fully documented account of the very varied forms of the Pentecostal movement in different countries. Because of the date of publication, there is, however, hardly any reference to the movement in the Catholic Church.

F. A. Sullivan, 'The Pentecostal Movement', *Greg*, 53 (1972), 237–266.

W. McCready, 'The Pentecostals. A Social Analysis', *Concilium*, 72 (1972), 112–116.

J. Massingberd Ford, 'Pentecostal Catholicism', *Concilium*, 79 (1972), 85–90.

Cardinal L. J. Suenens, *A New Pentecost?* (London, 1975).

R. Laurentin, *Catholic Pentecostalism* (London, 1977).

Courrier communautaire international, 9 (July-August 1976: 'Ces communautés dites charismatiques'.

VS, 600 (January-February 1974): Le mouvement charismatique'; 609 (July-August 1975): 'Prière et Renouveau'.

E. O'Connor, *The Pentecostal Movement in the Catholic Church* (Notre Dame, Indiana, 1971).

Pro Mundi Vita, 60 (May 1976): 'The Catholic Pentecostal Movement: Creative or Divisive Enthusiasm'; repr. as J. Kerkhofs (ed.), *Catholic Pentecostals Now* (Canfield, Ohio, 1977); American documentation; opinion-sounding and statistics.

F. Deleclos, 'Le renouveau charismatique dans l'Eglise catholique', *NRT*, 99 (1977), 161–170.

Histories and Accounts

K. and D. Ranaghan, *Catholic Pentecostals* (New York, 1969).

J. Randall, *In God's Providence: the Birth of a Catholic Charismatic Parish* (Plainfield, N. J., 1973).

A. Méhat, *Comment peut-on être charismatique?* (Paris, 1976).

147

Discussions and Studies

'Le Renouveau charismatique. Orientations théologiques et pastorales', *Lumen Vitae* (Brussels), 29 (1974), 367–404. This is the 'Malines document', based on the conference held there and also published separately from this number of *Lumen Vitae*: Eng. tr., *Theological and Pastoral Orientations on the Catholic Charismatic Renewal* (Notre Dame, Indiana, 1974). It is a justification of the reality that it discusses, with numerous references to the New Testament, and at the same time an instrument of theological and pastoral discernment.

J. Gouvernaire, 'Les "Charismatiques"', *Etudes*, 140 (January 1974), 123–140; a three-cornered dialogue presenting questions and elements of discernment.

A. Godin, 'Moi perdu ou moi retrouvé dans l'expérience charismatique', *Archives de Sciences sociales des Religions*, 40 (July-December 1975), 31–52; a sociological and psychological study with many references to America.

R. Quebedeaux, *The New Charismatics: the Origin, Development and Significance of Neo-Pentecostalism* (New York, 1976).

K. McDonnell, *Charismatic Renewal and the Churches* (New York, 1976).

J.-R. Bouchet and H. Caffarel, *Le Renouveau charismatique interpellé. Etudes et documents* (*Collection Renouveau*, 5) (Paris, 1976).

Protestant Studies

Foi et Vie, 4 and 5 (July-October 1973); see especially the following articles: A. Wohlfahrt, 'Espérance pour l'Eglise: choses vues', 3–20; A. Bittlinger, 'Et ils prient en d'autres langues', 97–108.

J. Dietle, 'Le réveil pentecôtiste dans les Eglises historiques. Problèmes exégétiques et ecclésiologiques', *Positions luthériennes*, 4 (October 1974), 223–287.

Publications of the Movement

Pneumathèque series, 7 bis, rue de la Rosière, 75015 Paris, France.
Il est vivant, 31 rue de l'Abbé-Grégoire, 75006 Paris, France.
Tychique, 49 montée du Chemin-neuf, 69005 Lyons, France.
New Covenant, P.O. Box 8617, Ann Arbor, Michigan 48107, USA.

A. THE POSITIVE CONTRIBUTION
OF THE 'CHARISMATIC RENEWAL' TO
THE CHARCH

Why has the Renewal in the Spirit revealed itself and spread like wildfire in the traditional churches, since 1956 in the Protestant communions and since 1967 in the Catholic Church? Has this happened because God wanted it to? This may be so, but history has shown that God's grace always acts together with human means and that men prepare the way for it. Did it come about because of John XXIII's calling the bishops to a council 'as for a new Pentecost'?[1] This too is possible, but it should not be forgotten that the Renewal is only one aspect of the immense evangelical flowering which the Church now shows to all who have eyes to see and which is taking pace in the midst of many harmful and disturbing events in the world. Is it a reaction by people at certain levels of the population who are instinctively trying to compensate for a depressed and humiliating way of life, or by believers who are seeking spiritual independence? Sociological studies and explanations point to part of the truth, and elements of these will recur; but, though valuable in certain respects, these are not so in others, and their inadequacy has been recognized. In any case, it is from the ecclesiological point of view that I seek to understand what the Renewal signifies within the changing situation of the contemporary Church, the important questions that it asks of the Church, and the positive contribution that it can make to the Church.

The amazing changes that are taking place in the world and the internal movement in the Church have led to our leaving a situation we can call 'Christendom'. Although it is unequally distributed, this is a world-wide movement. A 'Christendom' is characterized by the fact that the social and legal structures form the socially constraining framework for religious activities that are governed by a clerically dominated authority with great social power. The temporal structures are more or less completely orientated towards and subordinated to that authority. The values and expressions of such a society are part of the conditions imposed by the society itself. Although they are often fine and profound, they are also frequently hindered or shackled by those conditions.

Other conditions are imposed by the changes that are taking place now in society; the secularization (*laïcisation* is also a term used in France) of social structures is gradually modifying those conditions. Social life as such is built up without any reference to spirituality, and religion has become a personal and private affair. Relationships in society are similarly changing. Partly as a reaction against the intolerably impersonal character of urbanization gone mad and excessively rational and programmed organization, men are looking urgently for free groups where it is possible to be together with others without constraint. This search has inevitably led to the formation, at the religious level,[2] of free and spontaneous groups that govern themselves and, in prayer, to a style that is spontaneous, personal, and yet communal, open to free individual initiative and not subject to a leader appointed from outside.[3]

In modern, secularized society, with its fragmented culture, each person is looking for his own way. However weakly conscious many are of their religious need—some indeed seem to have no need at all—it is still felt. Some people find alternative paths—spiritualism, occultism, astrology, for example. Many look outside Christianity or at least outside the Church. Non-Christian Eastern mysticism, often not very authentic, has made considerable progress and many sects have sprung up outside the Church.

In the case of the Renewal, what is remarkable is that it has taken place directly within the Christian and even within the Catholic faith and, what is more, within the framework of a very categorical Trinitarian faith. If we recall that, according to the fourth gospel, Jesus' trial continues throughout history, the Holy Spirit, in the Renewal, greatly strengthens Jesus' disciples by convincing them that the world is wrong (Jn 16:8–11). They are disciples of Jesus *Christ*, of Jesus *the Lord*, and not simply of the 'Jesus of Nazareth' called on by politically orientated and secularized Christians. In addition to this, physical miracles and divine interventions in human history were eliminated from Christianity by the thinkers of the Enlightenment and later by Bultmann and his followers in demythologization, yet the Renewal claims to have experienced the direct intervention of divine power in the lives of its members and insists that God is 'living'.

The Church is not an enclosed monastery, nor is it a ghetto. It exists within the world and is affected by the changes that are taking place in the world. At a very deep level, however, it also has its own distinctive movement. This movement was decisively affirmed and defined at the Second Vatican Council, which had been preceded by decades of liturgical, mystical, pastoral and theological activity. It is not possible to discuss here every aspect of the immensely complex development leading up to the Council. It can, however, be characterized in the following way, at least in its essential tendency and as regards what concerns us here. The movement of thought that prepared the way for the Council can be described as a *re-sourcement* in the sense meant by Péguy, who coined the word—a rising up of vitality from the source into the present, rather than a simple return to the sources of Christian faith, although this also certainly took place. Theology, the official teaching of the Church, preaching and religious instruction had previously imposed a view of the Church defined first of all as a *societas inaequalis hierarchica*—'an unequal, hierarchical society'—with a clear distinction, based on divine right, between clergy and laity, between the hierarchy and ordinary believers. Then it was claimed that the Church was a *societas perfecta* or 'complete society' with all the means necessary for its own life, including its own legislative, judicial and even compulsory power. J. A. Möhler (†1838) summed up this ecclesiology in the formula: 'God created the hierarchy and in this way provided amply for everything that was required until the end of time'. It is not difficult to see the secret affinity between such an ecclesiology and a situation of Christendom. It is likewise surmised that the Renewal will be radically different. It is significant that it has established itself most firmly in countries where an Irish clergy or the ways of old France have kept the lay people very much in a state of tutelage while at the same time giving them a vigorous and forceful Catholicism.[4]

The Second Vatican Council did not deprive the ordained ministry of priests, bishops or the Pope of any of its functions, but it went beyond the hierarchical idea of that ministry and the concept of the Church as a juridical society. The order of chapters in the Dogmatic Constitution *Lumen Gentium* clearly expresses this new priority. In the first chapter of this document, the Church is seen as a mystery, within a Trinitarian perspective, in the second chapter as the people of God (who possess the priesthood of baptism and charism) und it is only in the third chapter that the Church is considered as hierarchically structured by its ordained ministries. What emerges from this is firstly that it is God who made the Church, and secondly that the fundamental aspect is what can be called the ontology of grace, based on the sacraments and the free gifts of God. The ordained ministers are called to the service of this Christian life, but the Church is first and foremost built up by that life.

With regard to that Church, the Renewal has been concerned with maintaining the supernatural quality of the people of God at the base, with giving the charisms a stronger profile, without in any way monopolizing them, and with re-introducing into the ordinary life of the Church activities such as prophecy, in what we shall see later on to be a very modest sense, and healings not only spiritual—the sacrament of reconciliation has always contributed to this—but also physical.[5] The Renewal has, at its own level and in its own way, certainly acted as a response to the pentecostal expectation expressed by John XXIII. Paul VI also declared that 'the Church needs a perpetual Pentecost'.[6] And to say this is not to underestimate what has been coming to life, growing and even flourishing everywhere in the Church.

This is, I believe, a very broad outline of the part played by the Renewal in the present changing situation of the Church and ecclesiology. I now propose to go into certain aspects of this in greater detail. These aspects include both positive contributions that the Renewal can make to the life of the Church, and certain questions that it addresses to the Church.

*   *   *

I know that it would be wrong to oppose charism and institution and to rewrite the history of the Church as a history of opposition between these two elements. The fact is that each of these two realities is the source of a different kind of order in the Church, with the result that they are often in a state of tension. That tension is normal and can even be beneficial. Grace has frequently gone beyond the fixed institutional forms of the Church. Both are required in the life of the Church. According to *Lumen Gentium*, the Spirit 'furnishes and directs' the Church 'with various gifts, both hierarchical and charismatic'.[7] The Council cannot be criticized for having preserved this duality of gifts, both kinds of which come from the same source and lead to the same end.[8] This view of the matter is theologically sound because it is deeply based on a Trinitarian understanding of God and his activity. This may be regarded as appropriation—I am of the opinion that there is more than one way of speaking in the articles of the creed. It is not possible to separate the work of the Holy Spirit, who is 'Lord and giver of life', from the creative work of the Father and the work accomplished by the Son for our salvation.[9] As I have often stressed, the soundness of a pneumatology consists in its Christology.

The Renewal introduces the vitality of the charisms into the heart of the Church. It is a long way from having a monopoly of charisms, but it bears the label of 'charismatic' and helps to make the 'charismatic' theme more widely known. The movement is not a protest against the institution. Its aim is rather to infuse it with new life. It is neither a rejection nor a criticism of the institution, and the mere fact that it has developed within the institutional Church points to the Church's existence as something other than a great apparatus of grace or a juridical or even a sacramental institution.

It has often been observed that the members of the Renewal movement neither neglect nor despise the sacraments, but, on the contrary, return to the sacrament of penance and the Eucharist with renewed enthusiasm. Their prayer meetings, however, are extra-sacramental and take place without any president, leader or ordained minister. Considered as a sociological phenomenon, the renewal is a 'self-regulating' movement (see below, note 2). It seeks and often finds the fruit of the Spirit without the mediation of a Church other than its own community of brothers and sisters and it does so simply subject to the guidance of the Spirit, for whom the community prays. It is interesting to quote Péguy, who was prevented by his marriage from receiving the Church's sacraments, in this context: 'The clergy should be distrusted. . . . Those fellows are, however, very powerful. Because they administer the sacraments, they let it be known that there is nothing other than the sacraments. They forget to tell us that there is also prayer and that prayer is at least half the reality. The sacraments and prayer, that makes two. And, whereas they hold the first, we always have the second at our disposal.'[10] Surely, then, these free prayer meetings—free because they take place in the sovereign freedom of the Spirit—are an exercise of personal initiative taken not against the Church as an institution, but simply without its mediation? Do they not point to a limitation on the part of the institutional Church in the very sphere which the Church is there to serve?

There is also the question of power. Seen as an institution or an 'establishment', the Church is, compared with, for example, the health service, the educational establishment, the press, the mass media or local or national government structures, obviously incredibly poor both in manpower and in resources. The annual balance sheet of the Catholic Church in France would probably make a pathetic impression compared with that of, say, the cinemas in Paris alone. The Church has to a great extent lost its power and hardly counts any more as a social force. This is undoubtedly good for the Church—as Pascal said, 'the Church is in an excellent state when it is only supported by God'.[11] The Church may, however, be required today to be powerful in a different way. The large-scale activity of the institution is perhaps being replaced by the more subtle action of the Church as leaven. Is it also possible that the Church is required now to be alive and active especially on the basis of its members being spiritual people? It has, of course, always been active in this way, which has long been the best aspect of its life. But perhaps God is now calling it to be like that and simply and solely like that? Is this not what Marcel Légaut has been teaching, in the best of his work, for many years?

I think all this has to be linked with a reassessment in the Church of two elements that certain circumstances in its history have caused to be regarded with great suspicion—the personal principle and spiritual experience.

By the 'personal principle', I mean the place that is accorded to the initiatives of individuals as persons and to what those persons have to say on the basis of personal conscientious conviction and motivation. It is, of course, true that the life of the Church cannot be handed over to 'private judgement' and the anarchy of irresponsible initiatives. On the other hand, however, juridicism,[12] clericalism and an emphasis on protection and safety caused in the first place by the danger of Protestantism and then by fear of rationalism and the revolutionary movements of the nineteenth century have led the Latin Catholic Church to practise—often with fearful efficiency—a pastoral policy of distrust and repression with regard to personal initiative, so that the latter has been restricted and even crushed by the principle of objectivity and by institutional rules.

The principle of objectivity is, of course, very sound and even sacred, and the institutional principle is closely connected with it. But every man is a subject who responds freely and who is always a source of free initiative, self-expression and invention. This need is expressed today in almost every sphere of human activity and in many different ways. It inevitably goes together with an ecclesiology based on the idea of the Church as a communion of persons. At its own level, the Renewal gives scope for expression to this need which, so long as the conditions of soundness which I have discussed often enough in this work are satisfied, is a very positive one.

All experience also has to be checked, tested and proved authentic. In Pentecostalism, experience is the great point of reference, the datum towards which everything is orientated. Discernment is practised in the Renewal, but experience of God plays a decisive part in this. As Cardinal Suenens has pointed out, 'many have attested that their faith was sustained by a personal experience of God and that, as faith grew, God's action became more real to them in their daily existence'.[13] There has often been a tendency to confine this type of experience to a Christian élite, but our life today is characterized by a kind of democratization of talent and knowledge. The word 'democracy' is not really suitable in this context, but it should be clear what is meant by it.

I could hardly speak disparagingly about human reason and understanding, but there are clearly aspects of man, both psychical and physical, which go beyond reason. These are precisely the aspects of man and the values which have been neglected, excluded or misunderstood in the Western Church. Even now, since the best of the aggiornamento of the Second Vatican Council, the Church has, as an institution, continued to share in the general and prevalent climate of rationalism and organization. Its liturgy is still strictly regulated and it is still extremely inclined to indulge in didactic, if not cerebral, explanations. As a result of this, the members of the Renewal tend to say, when they are asked why they belong to the movement and what benefits they derive from it: In a world that is excessively organized and totally dedicated to efficient productivity, we find in the Renewal freedom, simplicity and a certain child-likeness of heart. We find even the liturgy, the preaching and the pastoral care of our Church too external and rational. In the Renewal, we find an inner life and contact with the essence of things in its pure state.

This experience is a source of joy and it gives to the members of the movement a feeling of freedom that they are able to express almost tangibly. Peter Hocken insists that aspects of man that have been neglected in an excessively organized and cerebral religion have been brought back into play in Pentecostalism. He cites here the role of the body in hand-clapping, raised hands, cries and sounds, very rhythmical singing, dancing and the laying-on of hands. Pentecostalists attribute the use of these human resources without hesitation to the Holy Spirit, although it may, of course, be a question of something quite different—in 1 Cor 12:2, for example, Paul refers to the existence of such phenomena in pagan cults. This can also be applied to glossolalia.

A reassessment of these areas of human life that cannot be reduced to mere reason is, of course, to be welcomed. It is, however, impossible not to be to some extent apprehensive of the danger of a rather pietistic anti-intellectualism. Teaching without prophetism can easily degenerate into legalism, but prophetism without teaching can become illusory. There is a clear need for the movement and the institutional Church to question each other continuously, like the hill and the field in Barrès' novel.

This 'experiential' character of the Renewal,[14] its distance from intellectualism, the communicative power it has released, the part played in it by the body, the simplicity of its demands and its overcoming of middle-class inhibitions—all these aspects of the movement open up new and interesting possibilities for the evangelization of those who are normally not reached by the institutional Church. Walter Hollenweger has insisted on the fact that the movement has developed resources and an oral culture that are very well adapted to the twentieth century and particularly well suited to appeal to certain levels of population.[15] He was possibly thinking especially of Africa and Latin America. In Europe and North America, it is above all middle-class Christians who are involved in the Renewal—but so too are gypsies. The 'sects' are to a very great extent successful because of their manner of proselytizing and converting. We do not have to imitate them, of course, but we are bound to recognize that we lack certain forms of communication in evangelization that are in fact used by the Renewal movement. It is an all-embracing and communal form of evangelization making the newcomer an integral part of the group's life. It has a personal, immediate, spontaneous, concrete and non-conceptual character; there is no indoctrination in the charismatic form of evangelization, but a communication of an essentially attractive experience based on a personally deeply felt conviction.

The Renewal can open the way to a different kind of Christian practice which is especially valuable in communicating faith in the Lord Jesus.

This may be of help in our celebration of the sacraments of Christian initiation and especially confirmation, which has been called the 'seal of the Spirit'. Quite apart from the Renewal movement, there is a certain uneasiness with regard to the practice of these sacraments and even, in the case of confirmation, with regard to its precise status. The experience of the Spirit by Christians who have already been baptized and confirmed, often long since, points to a certain insufficiency in the practice of these two sacraments. Is it really possible to say that the Holy Spirit is given when, apparently at least, nothing happens? It has been said that nothing happens in the case of the baptism of infants, either, but here we must believe in the action of God as being deeper and more mysterious than anything of which we have evidence or tangible experience.

I would not deny the truth of this affirmation of faith, but I would like to make three points. The first is that we do find it painful to acknowledge that after confirmation it is as if nothing had happened, apart from a formal religious ceremony. Paul would not have accepted such a situation. Secondly, confirmation is 'given' in the West at an age when the child already has personal conscience and a certain conception of life. Is there, then, not a good reason for taking this seriously into consideration in pastoral practice? I shall attempt to answer this important question when I discuss confirmation in greater detail in Volume III of this work. Thirdly, infant baptism nowadays is not merely avoided by those who have no faith, but it is seriously questioned by convinced Christians for reasons by no means unworthy of consideration. Pascal had some very enlightening things to say about this subject.[16] It is hardly possible to avoid asking such radical questions about infant baptism in our present post-Christian situation. Indeed, they have already been asked again and again and received replies that are theologically and pastorally valuable. We may conclude that the baptism of babies is perfectly justified if the family environment is fully Christian, but this does not solve the problem of conscious reanimation and personal vitalization of what has been given by grace in baptism. The Renewal can make a contribution here.

In the case of the celebration of the sacrament of the 'seal of the Spirit' and the preparation that should precede its reception, the Renewal also offers a number of interesting possibilities. It would, of course, not be enough simply to take one bath of the Holy Spirit in a warm and cordial environment in order to be sure of living according to the Spirit. Life in the Spirit calls for perseverance, a daily recommitment to a generous effort and constant and repeated prayer. But if the practice of renewal in the Spirit formed part of parish life, it might well make a valuable contribution to the reanimation of the pastoral aspect of the sacraments of initiation.

*   *   *

If it formed part of parish life. . . . Is this possible? Is the Renewal bound to remain simply a movement in the Church, with its own special activities, its meetings, its conferences, its books and other publications, its adherents and its animators and leaders? Or can it perhaps become, in parishes and in the Church as a whole, a means by which the pneumatological aspect, which is an integral part of the life of all Christians individually and collectively, can be displayed and spread? I an afraid that my answer must be a negative one, since I do not believe that the Renewal, in the form in which it appears now, can be extended to the whole of the Church. I have two reasons for thinking this:

(1) The style of its meetings is not acceptable to everyone. J.-L. Leuba has pointed out that 'the gifts of the Spirit are given for the "common good"

(1 Cor 12:7), but there can be no such common good where there is no mutual consent. Every minister who is conscious of his responsibility to the gospel and of the unity of his flock in love will always avoid imposing charismatic manifestations as a *law* on his community.'[17] It is true, of course, that there are 'charismatic parishes'.[18] These are special cases, depending for their continued life on a charismatic minister or on many charismatic members, and they are parishes which Christians choose to join. Their unusual and ideal character is apparent from the very way they are projected. It should also be added that the example of the community at Corinth has often been cited in this contest—though it is not, in every respect, a good model! As far as we can ascertain, the Roman community, the community of Jerusalem and the Johannine churches did not lead the same kind of life.

(2) It would seem that, as we leave a situation of Christendom, as described at the beginning of this chapter, the Church is called upon to provide the world with manifestations of great evangelical value, even though they are very limited in scope—kinds of parables of the love of God and his kingdom. These include the religious communities of the Church, often the smaller ones rather than the larger. Taizé is a manifestation of this kind, with its resolute determination to improvise and to be 'temporary'; its council of youth is another. Yet another such parable of the kingdom of God is the Renewal. These charismatic communities may well have great value as examples, since 'God seems to want to reveal the mystery of the Christian community as he has never done so before'.[19] These communities are not subject to direction by the clergy. They are lay communities. Some have unmarried members, others consist of families. Experience has shown that they have problems, but who does not?

The movement may not be able to claim that the whole Church will eventually become 'charismatic', but it can influence the whole of the Church and, in that sense, win it over. It can point the way. It is, of course, not the only movement in the Church today that aims to renew theology and pastoral care, services and even ministries.[20] There are also, for example, the basic communities of various kinds. Together with those basic groups, the Renewal movement can contribute to a new model of the Church.

All this is of great interest to the theologian, who aims to serve the Church. He will be sufficiently orientated towards God as a *theo*logian to recognize that this new model or vision of the Church is fully in accordance firstly with the movement back to the Bible and the Church Fathers as the sources of Christian faith that has already begun, and secondly with the theological emphasis on the Trinity and on Christology seen in the light of pneumatology.

There are clear indications of the latter development in theology today. Heribert Mühlen has firmly denounced pre-Trinitarian monotheism.[21] Orthodox theologians have more than just fine promptings to offer. In

Christology, Mühlen and Walter Kasper have been following a very fruitful path.[22] They have also provided outlines of a pneumatological ecclesiology.[23] Others have done the same, although I find their attempts less satisfactory.[24]

I shall return to the theology of the Trinity and to Christology in Volume III. In the meantime, I will conclude the present chapter by welcoming the coming of a Church of charisms and ministries, of basic communities and of the sincere prayer of Christians who are dedicated body and soul to the living Lord and to being animated by his Spirit. At the same time I am aware that it is hardly possible to speak of the Renewal as a homogeneous whole that operates in exactly the same way in all its groups and manifestations. For this reason, I am devoting the following section (B) to a number of questions that I feel obliged to ask about the Renewal. However, together with very many bishops and even with the Pope himself, who have greater lights than I do, I think that it is a grace that God has given to the times we are living in.

NOTES

1. John XXIII, address delivered on 17 May 1959; see *Doc. cath.* 56 (1959), p. 770; and the Apostolic Constitution *Humanae salutis* of 25 December 1961; see *Doc. cath.* 59 (1962), p. 104. See also K. and D. Ranaghan, *Catholic Pentecostals* (New York, 1969), p. vi, and E. O'Connor, *The Pentecostal Movement in the Catholic Church* (Notre Dame, Indiana, 1971), p. 287, who quote texts relating to the Renewal. See also the address made at the end of the first session of the Council on 2 December 1962.
2. See J. Séguy, *Les conflits du dialogue* (Paris, 1973), and the very many studies that have been made of the spontaneous, informal 'basic communities'. The bibliographies of CERDIC of Strasbough and the texts of the second colloquium of CERDIC, *Les groupes informels dans l'Eglise* (Strasbourg, 1971), will be found useful in this context.
3. There is a good analysis of this new style of prayer in *Où se manifeste l'Esprit* (*Dossiers libres*) (Paris, 1977), pp. 7ff., a document written by 'A group of Christians in Lyons'.
4. A fellow-Dominican with whom I had been talking about the Renewal in Canada and who knew what it meant, told me that it was a kind of liberation and, to begin with at least, an explosion of freedom. Men—and even more so, women—had previously been living in the first place a life of piety based on fixed, obligatory, closed and very onerous spiritual exercises and in the second place in a state of fear of mortal sin and the punishment of hell. He also emphasized that confessors frequently interfered, in an indiscreet way, in certain spheres. . . . People were breathing a larger Spirit.
5. Peter Hocken in *New Heaven, New Earth? An Encounter with Pentecostalism* (London, 1976), p. 22, has rightly observed: 'I am suggesting then that what distinguishes the charismata described in 1 Corinthians as pneumatika is the particular level or zone of the human that they activate and engage. What is new in pentecostalism is not the occurrence of particular pneumatic phenomena nor the initial opening up of the pneumatic dimension in individual Christians; rather it is the organization, embodiment and expectation of all these gifts within the life of Christian communities, i.e. the articulation and organization in corporate Church life of what has over the centuries been known only spasmodically in isolated instances.'

6. Paul VI, audience on 29 November 1972: see *Doc. cath.* 69 (1972), p. 1105. See also E. O'Connor, *Pope Paul and the Spirit. Charisma and Church Renewal in the Teaching of Paul VI* (Notre Dame, Indiana, 1978).
7. Dogmatic Constitution on the Church, *Lumen Gentium*, 4; cf. 11, 2; see also the Decree on the Apostolate of the Laity, *Apostolicam Actuositatem*, 3; Decree on the Church's Missionary Activity, *Ad Gentes divinitus*, 4, 23, 1.
8. G. Hasenhüttl, *Charisma, Ordnungsprinzip der Kirche* (Freiburg, 1970), criticized the encyclical *Mystici Corporis* and the Dogmatic Constitution *Lumen Gentium* for this. In his view, 'charisms are the structure of the Church and the community is the place of those charisms' (p. 128). He did not deny the usefulness of juridical structures, but believed that they should be secondary and should help or make up for a structure that is in the first place fundamentally charismatic (p. 355; cf. pp. 231–232).
9. This point of view was forcibly expressed by J.-L. Leuba in a lecture given at Salamanca. The French text, 'Charisme et institution', has been published in the Lausanne review *Hokhma*, 5 (1977), 3–20. See also L. Boisset, *Mouvement de Jésus et Renouveau dans l'Esprit (Dossiers libres)* (Paris, 1975), 73.
10. Charles Péguy, *Lettres et entretiens, présentés par Marcel Péguy* (Paris, 1954), p. 69.
11. Pascal, *Fragment* 861.
12. See my article, 'La supériorité des pays protestants', *Le Supplément*, 123 (November 1977), 427–442.
13. Cardinal L. J. Suenens, *A New Pentecost?* (London, 1975), p. 54.
14. 'Experiential', as distinct from 'experimental', is the category used by Cardinal Suenens, *op. cit.*, p. 53, with reference to Fr Grégoire, 'Note sur les termes "intuition" et "expérience" ', *Revue philosophique de Louvain*, 44 (1946), 411–415.
15. W. Hollenweger, *The Pentecostals. The Charismatic Movement in the Churches* (Philadelphia, 2nd ed. 1973), pp. 468, 501; K. and D. Ranaghan, *op. cit.* (note 1), pp. 259–262; 'There are real possibilities there for discovering a theological methodology in an *oral* culture: one where the medium of communication—as in biblical times—is not definition, but description; not pronouncement, but story; not doctrine, but witness; not the theological *Summa*, but the hymn; not the treatise, but the television programme...': quoted by L. Boisset, *op. cit.* (note 9), 75.
16. Pascal, 'Comparaison des chrétiens des premiers temps avec ceux d'aujourd'hui'; pp. 201–208 in the small Brunschvicg edition.
17. J.-L. Leuba, *op. cit.* (note 9), 15.
18. See, for example, J. Randall. *In God's Providence: the Birth of a Catholic Charismatic Parish* (Plainfield, N. J., 1973); Michael Harper, *A New Way of Living* (Plainfield, N.J., and London, 1973), which describes the experience of the Episcopalian Church of the Redeemer at Houston, USA; F. Kohn has also written about this parish in *Il est vivant* (February-March 1976), 30–33.
19. E. O'Connor, *op. cit.* (note 1), pp. 46ff. See also Max Delespesse, *Cette communauté qu'on appelle l'Eglise* (Paris, 1968). Several such communities or groups of communities have been given publicity: Houston (see the previous note) and the most famous of all perhaps, Ann Arbor, Michigan; in France, the community of the Holy Cross at Grenoble; see *Il est vivant*, 12 (April 1977), 20–23; again in the United States, 'People of Praise', South Bend, Indiana.
20. *Tous responsables dans l'Eglise? Le ministère presbytéral dans l'Eglise tout entière "ministérielle"* (Lourdes and Paris, 1973).
21. See H. Mühlen, *Entsakralisierung* (Paderborn, 1971). This prolific author has since that time written frequently about this subject; see especially his *Morgen wird Einheit sein* (Paderborn, 1974) and *Die Erneuerung des christlichen Glaubens. Charisma-Geist-Befreiung* (Munich, 1974).
22. H. Mühlen, *Una mystica Persona* (Paderborn, 1964; 2nd ed., 1967); W. Kasper, *Jesus the Christ* (Eng. tr.; London and New York, 1976), pp. 266–268. See also P. J. Rosato, 'Spirit

Christology. Ambiguity and Promise', *ThSt*, 38 (1977), 423–449; P. J. A. M. Schoonenberg, 'Spirit Christology and Logos Christology', *Bijdragen*, 38 (1977), 350–375.

23. H. Mühlen, *op. cit.* (note 22) and many other publications, which I have reviewed in *RSPT*; W. Kasper, 'Esprit–Christ–Eglise', *L'Expérience de l'Esprit. Mélanges Schillebeeckx* (Paris, 1976), pp. 47–69; *idem*, 'Charismatische Grundstruktur der Kirche', *Glaube und Geschichte* (Mainz, 1970), pp. 356–361; *idem*, 'Die Kirche als Sakrament des Geistes', *Kirche—Ort des Geistes* (Freiburg, 1975), pp. 14–55.

24. G. Hasenhüttl, *op. cit.* (note 8); Donald L. Gelpi, *Charism and Sacrament. A Theology of Christian Conversion* (New York, 1976); the Protestant theologian J. D. G. Dunn, 'Rediscovering the Spirit, II', *Expository Times*, 84 (November 1972), 40–44, is very radical (he is a member of the Presbyterian Church).

B. CRITICAL QUESTIONS

1

WHAT TITLE SHOULD BE USED? 'CHARISMATIC'?

The word 'charism' can be understood in at least two if not three ways. (I would prefer not to use the word 'meanings' in this context, but would rather speak of two or three 'understandings' or 'extensions'.)[1]

(1) Apart from 1 Pet 4:10, the word *charisma* appears only in Paul's writings, and that sixteen times. Its use is fairly constant, even when applied once in a particular way (2 Cor 1:11). The word always goes back to *charis*, 'grace'. Greek words ending in *-ma* usually point to the result of an action. An example of this is *mathēsis*, the act of teaching, and *mathēma*, knowledge.

The term *charisma*, then, has to be understood in connection with the word *charis*, 'grace'.[2] Two or three texts throw light on this. Rom 12:6: *echontes de charismata kata tēn charin tēn dotheisan hēmin diaphora*, 'having gifts that differ according to the grace given to us'; 1 Cor 1:4, 7: 'the grace (*charis*) of God which was given to you in Christ Jesus . . . so that you are not lacking in any spiritual gift (*charisma*)'; 7:7: 'Each has his own special gift (*charisma*) from God, one of one kind and one of another'; 12:4, 11: 'There are varieties of gifts (*charismata*), but the same Spirit. . . . All these are inspired by one and the same Spirit, who apportions to each one individually as he wills'.

Charisms are gifts or talents which Christians owe to the grace of God. That grace aims at the realization of salvation, and Christians are called to put the charisms at the service of the Body of Christ. for its building up (see 1 Cor 12:7). These gifts or talents are as much from 'God' or the Lord as from the Spirit (see 1 Cor 12:4–6). When Paul speaks of 'charism of the Spirit' (*charisma pneumatikon*; Rom 1:11), he is not indulging in pleonasm. The fact that the charisms *are* 'spiritual gifts' or gifts of the Pneuma does not mean that the word 'charism' *means* 'gift of the Pneuma'.

(2) On the basis of 1 Cor 12:7: 'To each is given the manifestation of the Spirit for the common good', the charisms have often been seen as 'tangible manifestations of the presence of the Spirit'.[3] Such a definition fits the

'charismatic' Renewal. This is borne out by the briefing paper given to journalists by the organizers of the 1975 Pentecostal Conference in Rome, who described it as a place where the action of the Holy Spirit is manifested in a perceptible, tangible and visible way.[4] This does make our understanding of the term more precise, but it also narrows it down.

(3) Our understanding is narrowed down even more when the charisms are identified with speaking in tongues, prophecy (what Paul calls the *pneumatika*; see 1 Cor 12:1; 14:1) and healings or miracles, which are all, in fact, the most spectacular 'manifestations' of the gifts. They are often, unfortunately, identified in this way, even by deservedly respected authors.[5] In the same way, the great classical theologians of the Church also identified charisms with graces *gratis datae*, as distinct from sanctifying grace. This unhappy identification[6] marked out a clear and easy path which may have been rather lazily followed.

Paul did not reject the *pneumatika*, but he believed that they could be of use in the task of building up the Church only through the *charismata*, gifts given *kata tēn charin*, that is, according to saving grace, for the common good or the building up of the community.

I am inclined to see the charisms above all from the point of view of ecclesiology. It is, in other words, God who builds up his Church. In order to do this, he instituted, through Jesus Christ his faithful servant, the structures of that Church. At the same time, he continues to build it up, at all periods in history, by the gifts (*charismata*), the services or ministries (*diakoniai*) and the various *energēmata* or 'ways of working' to which Paul refer in 1 Cor 12:4–6. He does this by distributing talents and gifts to all believers. That is why I have been reluctant to accept the term 'charismatic movement' that has been applied to Catholic neo-pentecostalism and have been formally critical of it. Let me reproduce here the terms of that criticism:[7]

(1) There is a risk of attributing the charisms to a particular group, as though the whole body of believers were deprived of them, whereas, in Paul's teaching, these charisms are gifts of nature and of grace that are distributed and used by the Spirit *kata tēn charin* for the common good and the building up of the community. All believers are therefore charismatic and all are called to use their gifts for the common good. It was in this sense that the Second Vatican Council spoke of the charisms in the people of God (*Lumen Gentium*, 11) and that the conference of French bishops in 1973 had as its theme 'Everyone is responsible in the Church (and for the Church)'.[8] The members of the movement replied to this in the following way: It is true, but, just as all believers are invited to study the Bible and practise the liturgy and yet there are Bible study groups, a biblical and a liturgical movement, so too is it possible for charismatic groups to exist without other Christians being discriminated against, disqualified or excluded from this quality.

(2) Because of the prominent place occupied in public opinion and possibly in the movement itself by 'speaking in tongues', 'prophecy' and healings, there is a risk of

162

reducing the charisms to the level of extraordinary and even exceptional manifestations. This would be regrettable both for those immediately concerned and for the Church as a whole. When this question was debated at the Second Vatican Council, Cardinal Ruffini, the Archbishop of Palermo, criticized the draft text in the following way: There were charisms at the beginning of the Church's life, but there are no more today. The cardinal was thinking, when he said this, of quasi-miraculous manifestations. The following day, Cardinal Suenens replied to him in an attempt to restore the true idea of charism and to point to the abundant existence of charisms in his own church.[9] Paul in fact 'also mentions less striking charisms, such as exhortation and acts of mercy (Rom 12:8), service (Rom 12:7), teaching (Rom 12:7; 1 Cor 12:28ff.), the utterance of wisdom and knowledge (1 Cor 12:8), faith (1 Cor 12:9), discernment of spirits (1 Cor 12:10), helping and administration (1 Cor 12:28)'. The Catholic members of the movement, in France at least, claim that they do not stress extraordinary manifestations. It is, however, possible that the danger still exists.

I still regard the substance of this criticism and especially the second part of it as valid, despite Kilian McDonnell's reply to it.[10] In making it, I had a view of the whole Church in mind, and my point of departure was not a description or a justification of the movement, but an ecclesiology. The movement, however, exists and makes too many of God's good actions manifest for me not to thank God for it. What name, then, should we give to this 'movement'? This is precisely the question that is asked by the Malines document: What should the Renewal be called? The answer that the document gives is: From the sociological point of view, it would be quite legitimate to describe it as a 'movement', but the word is unsuitable in that it suggests that it is dependent on a human initiative or 'organization'. It would therefore, the document concludes, be better to avoid it.

The document continues: 'The phrase "charismatic renewal" is very widely used. It has the advantage of pointing to one of the concerns of the Renewal—the reintegration of the charisms, in all their dimensions, into the "normal" life of the Church, both at the universal and at the local level' (*op. cit.* (note 2 below), 386–387). My two objections, in an abbreviated form, follow. The document then adds: 'In certain places, the term "charismatic renewal" is avoided and preference is given to "spiritual renewal" or simply to "renewal". This choice of title certainly makes it possible to avoid some of the difficulties mentioned above. It has, however, been pointed out that it may also favour the idea of a monopoly, when there are already several forms of renewal in the Church.'

The terms 'Renewal in the Spirit' or simply 'Renewal' tend to be the most commonly used in France. They seem to me to be preferable, even though this is not the only form of renewal. It is also worth noting, at least in passing, that this term is not the same as 'Revival'. It points to a less abrupt and more continuous process that is more completely fitted into the universal life of the Church. It suggests the joy of the movement. In speaking of 'movement', it is important to add that, although some form of organization exists and is, in fact, inevitable, nothing programmed or highly organized is meant.[11]

It is possible to define the term 'charismatic' more precisely and this has in fact been done by Sr Jeanne d'Arc in her excellent notes on 'charismatic' which form part of her account of the Pentecostal Conference in Rome in 1975. I reproduce them below.

A charismatic group

When a prayer group or a community of believers is flooded with these gifts of the Spirit—prophecies, healings, works of power, striking conversions and so on, we recognize this by saying that it is a 'charismatic group' and we praise the Lord for it.

If, on the other hand, we are tempted to say: 'We want to set up a charismatic group', then the term is unacceptable. To use it would give the impression that we are whistling for the Holy Spirit and that we are able to know his intentions and make him available to us at will. It is not up to us to decide whether a meeting will be charismatic or not. That depends on the Holy Spirit alone.

A charismatic person

The same kind of remarks can be made of the adjective 'charismatic' applied to a person. If we experience the grace of meeting such a person, filled to overflowing with charisms, the gift of consolation and the gift of discernment, and powerful in works and words, we may describe him as 'charismatic'.

I am not sure, however, that it is really possible to say, as it was said, to great applause, at the Conference: 'To be charismatic is to be fully Christian'. We must take care—and we should read Paul again. To be fully Christian—this can only be measured against the fullness of charity. The whole history of the Church and its saints shows that some great saints have had very few charisms, in the sense of visible manifestations of the presence of the Spirit, and that others may have received these gifts, have spoken in the tongues of men and of angels and have had faith so as to remove mountains, but, if they have had less charity, they have inevitably have been less Christian and less holy.

Something very serious is, I think, at stake here. The whole 'charismatic movement' is involved. The danger—and it is a very real one—is not just that we shall become hypnotized, as the Corinthian Christians did, by the more spectacular gifts, but that we shall go even more seriously astray and use the term 'charismatic person' as a superlative, thus making him or her a kind of super-Christian. No, the only valid superlative is that of love.

May it please the Spirit at certain times and in certain places to release a veritable Niagara of charisms! This is a gift that fills us with praise and makes us sing of God's marvels. But all the charisms exist only for charity, which is their summit and their only criterion.

May there be a better climate in our parishes or communities, a better attitude on the part of believers, a better education in faith and a better knowledge of the charisms, so that the Spirit may be more able to fill the people of God! This would be a great blessing for the Church. There would be greater movement of life and a more joyous and powerful witness—but all this would be for charity, on this side of it, not beyond it, since there is nothing beyond love.

Charismatic prayer

There was an excellent discussion about prayer at the conference. Many attempts were made to define 'charismatic' prayer: 'Prayer that is entirely subject to the activity of the Holy Spirit'—'Prayer that is a gift from God and must be received in a spirit of attentive listening and a silence of poverty, and expressed with the whole of our being'—'Being intensely present and attentive'—'Prayer in which the Spirit reminds us that God is faithful and merciful'—'Prayer that enables us to enter God's plan and makes us conform to his will, and so is always heard and answered'—'Prayer that goes beyond our own abilities'—'Prayer that transforms and soothes us'—'Prayer which glorifies the name of Jesus and hastens his coming'.

All these statements are very fine. They contain a great deal that is spiritually deep and alive. They add up to a description of the flowering of sanctifying grace in us and of the gifts and the action of the Spirit who makes us cry 'Abba! Father!' and attunes us to his sighs that are too deep for words. But I must admit that I cannot exactly determine how this prayer is 'charismatic'. The fact that it is raised up to a high level of intimacy and love does not mean that it is necessarily charismatic.

May this prayer provide in our hearts an environment that is favourable to the emergence of a word of faith, a light for others and a prophecy for a group! May it make us more open to be moved by the Spirit and therefore to receive his charisms! All this would be of enormous benefit, but it would not necessarily transform the prayer itself into 'charismatic' prayer.

May I be forgiven for insisting, but only a very slight adjustment of the points will send the whole train along a different track and its direction is then irreversible.[12]

I personally believe that there is a charism of prayer, which is in itself an excellent gift, even though Paul does not mention it. His lists do not, however, claim to be exhaustive. The series of gifts remains open, in accordance with the abundance of grace and the needs felt in the history of salvation. A place among these gifts has, for example, been claimed for various forms of religious life[13] and for the function of a judge evaluating prudently the merits of the case.[14]

TWO CRITICAL QUESTIONS

Immediacy

The Protestant theologian Gérard Delteil has expressed what is, in my opinion, the most important critical question, at least from the practical point of view. He said: 'The charismatic form of expression seems to be to be linked to a theology of immediacy—an immediacy of the Word grasped via the text, an immediacy of God's presence grasped thorugh experience, an immediacy of relationship expressed by speaking in tongues and an immediacy that by-passes history'.[15] In other words, in the Renewal, Christians look for and find a response or a solution in a quick, immediate and personal relationship that cuts out long and difficult approaches. This emphasis on immediacy applies to the exegesis of Scripture, our understanding of social problems, our analysis of the crisis in the Church and the associated question of the rapid changes in the world, and finally our consideration of the steps to be taken towards ecumenical reunion. I shall return to the question of ecumenism later, but in the meantime would like to stress three points:

(1) I am not a rationalist. I believe that God guides our lives and intervenes in them. I have always trusted and still trust in his conduct and guidance. There is always a danger, however, that we shall fail to use the human means available to us of 'prudence' in the Thomistic sense of the word, and of decision. In the past, I encountered this kind of attitude among members of the Oxford Group which became Moral Rearmament. As J.-Y. Riocreux has said of an experience in the United States:

> God is regarded as the one who is immediately responsible for everything. Secondary causes are connected without the slightest difficulty to primary causes. Let me give an example of this. A young member of the 'charismatic renewal' was on his way to a retreat. He was hitch-hiking, but no cars were stopping. Resorting to a desperate measure, he prayed fervently: 'Lord, if you want me to go to this retreat, let me have a lift in one of the next twenty cars that go past!' This was an ultimatum that paid off! The twentieth car slowed down and stopped—and its driver was a Pentecostalist minister! How can one not see in this incident a sign from heaven?[16]

And indeed, why should we not regard it as a sign from heaven? Trust in God can go as far as that. There is, however, a general problem of balance. It is hardly possible to carry the naivety of a child so far that we make no use of the means of information and reason that God has given to man who has become adult (see 1 Cor 13:11).

(2) This applies especially to our reading of Scripture. It has often been said that there is a tendency in the Renewal towards fundamentalism. The fundamentalist approach consists of interpreting the text of the Bible literally without considering the historical context, without making sound use of criticism and without relating the text to other passages or to Scripture as a whole, and then applying it immediately to the present situation.[17] In saying this, I would not want to take back anything of what I have already written about the spiritual reading of Scripture. Intellectual effort has, however, never been despised in that kind of reading—this is evident in the works of Origen and Augustine, for example. In Pentecostalism generally, experience, above all immediate experience, takes precedence over everything else. This is not entirely true of the Renewal in our own Church, but even there a certain anti-intellectualism has been observed. I have found signs of this in Canada, both in Quebec and in Ontario. Knowledge and intelligence

are not supreme values, of course, and the Renewal fortunately brings with it the warmth of hearts that have been given to Christ. Serious religious formation is also being undertaken within the Renewal. It is, however, important to point to a possible and even real danger.

(3) Olivier Clément correctly observed that 'it is legitimate to ask, in the case of shared experience, whether it is really pneumatic or spiritual or whether it is simply psychical. Greed for psychical experience is in no way a good thing. In the Eastern Christian tradition, there is an attitude of great sobriety and vigilance. It has always been regarded as advisable not to seek the extraordinary experiences that the Spirit is able to provide.'[18] This advice is echoed in the texts that I have cited above from the great Eastern spiritual writers and especially those of Simeon the New Theologian.[19] Very much the same is taught by the saints and spiritual writers of the West.[20] I have also dealt with this question in a previous chapter on 'the struggle against the flesh'. There is no possibility of a total and definitive victory taking place here on earth.

There will, however, always be a danger that people will go looking for a psychical experience of the Spirit with an only too human attitude of greed and therefore 'carnally'. This was undoubtedly the case at Corinth and it may happen even today. It may be that someone will go to a meeting in the hope of seeing or experiencing something sensational, something extraordinary, that will make him rather superior. On the other hand, the meeting itself may be conducted, with the help, for example, of emotional and compelling singing repeated again and again, to the point of conditioning those present to expect *it* to happen—speaking in tongues or 'prophecy'.

Most members and certainly almost all leaders of the Renewal know or will eventually learn that a 'pouring out of the Spirit' implies a response to the demands made by God. Two such leaders have made this declaration:

Those of us who are engaged in political, family, cultural and other activities can hardly conceive the extent to which prayer in itself demands the total commitment of the whole person. Most of those who move in the ambit of the renewal movement regard a request to the whole community to pray for their conversion as an important step. The words and gestures (laying-on of hands) that accompany this very personal and at the same time very communitary prayer are simple, but this simplicity clothes a very important requirement: if we really commit ourselves to asking the Spirit of the Lord to come upon us, to purify us (Lk 11:13), to send us to our brothers, we will not do so in vain. For many Christians this step is not undertaken without deep fear and the expression 'baptism in the Spirit', even if it can be misunderstood, well expresses this experience of plunging in, drowning, death and resurrection.[21]

*   *   *

A Lessening of Social Commitment

Is this perhaps a consequence or an application of 'immediacy'? Many criticisms have been made of the Renewal precisely on these grounds—that it deprives its members of their commitment to social and political action. The Renewal, it is claimed, leads to a taste for intimacy. Its eschatological content points exclusively to the hereafter. Although shared prayer and brotherliness form an essential part of the Renewal and it certainly encourages commitment to life in community, it nonetheless favours a sense of personal and vertical relationship with God and therefore turns its adherents away from action in the world. This criticism is sometimes expressed by those who are so exclusively preoccupied with politics and passionate social concerns that they do not even consider the possible hypothesis that God might be able to act in the Renewal.[22] Yet, together with other contemporary realities such as Taizé and the various monastic centres with their great influence, the Renewal bears witness, I believe, to a fact of great importance—the specific character of religion. Faith is not simply a form of commitment to the life of this world, nor does it merely act to motivate that commitment. It has its own distinctive order and activities, and these are first and foremost directed towards the God who has seized hold of the believer's soul. The cry of joy directed towards God is above all a thanksgiving.

In those critical interpretations that are excessively dominated by a social or political concern, the favour shown to the Renewal by responsible ministers of the Church is seen in this light, as typically expressed by J. Chabert (*op. cit.* (note 22 below), p. 27): 'In the final analysis, the members of the hierarchy are only interested in what helps to strengthen the institution which they represent'. Are they then not interested in what may animate or give new life to faith in the Church, or in a re-awakening of the spiritual life of those who belong to the Church? Are they not concerned, in a word, with what is specifically religious? And if they are, would that be wrong? Would that be foreign to their mission?

One genuine question remains, however. It is this. The Renewal may be so firmly situated at the level of the *res* that the *sacramentum* may be underestimated. It may be so orientated towards the vertical dimension of religion, that is, the relationship with the absolute, that the horizontal aspect is neglected, if not in regard to relationships with one's immediate 'neighbour', then at least in the more extended, and in this sense more strictly social, dimension.[23] To be faithful to the gospel as a whole, man must be concerned with the vertical dimension, that is, the transcendental aspect of God, and with the horizontal dimension, man's here and now, in all the particularity of individual callings, situations and destinies.

This question arises above all in those countries which are both fundamentally religious and poor, exploited and subject to domination, for whose liberation from misery and injustice precise analyses and critical commitment are required. At least one representative of Latin American 'liberation theology' has taken up the criticisms and, one might almost say, the accusations of the Renewal that we have already encountered and examined, and done it with greater precision.[24] It is also worth mentioning a simple personal testimony that I received, one of many, in a letter at the end of the 1975 Conference: 'The charismatic movement has flourished in a most remarkable way during the past two years in the Dominican Republic. There have been countless conversions and prayer is abounding. But many people have commented that precisely where the movement has spread most, social work, road-building programmes, and the co-operatives with priests in charge (don't forget that we are in Latin America!) assisted by lay people have been set aside or at least scaled down.'

The fact that this criticism has been made again and again shows that it may be justified. Members of the Renewal have, however, replied, with facts and not simply with theoretical justifications.[25] They may be active in trade unionism and politics and, as much as other people, they have professional work in industry, research, town planning, teaching, and so on.

Although I recognize the dangers pointed out and even condemned by people like J. Chabert (see below, note 22), R. Vidales (see note 24) and others, I would dispute their interpretation of Pentecost at the level of exegesis. Vidales, for example, has said: 'The Spirit was not given to dispense the disciples from their historical responsibility, but precisely to encourage and direct their actions along the same lines as their master's commitment. The presence of the Lord, paradoxically represented as "absence", directs the Church to fulfil its central commitment—to work for the coming of justice.' I am bound to ask: Is that what the New Testament tells us? I do not in any way deny that it forms part of Christian messianism and the Church's mission,[26] but I cannot accept the possible and sinister reduction that it contains. I can no more accept it when I read Vidales' further statement: 'The oppressed *can neither believe in* nor confess *Jesus Christ*, nor can they respond freely to him, *except insofar as* they succeed in freeing themselves from all oppression. They *cannot be witnesses to the Spirit* who liberates and transforms, *except insofar as* they struggle together to win a new order of justice.'[27] The words that I (not the author) have italicized seem to me to be excessive and, as such, open to question.

The Church is not simply the Renewal, nor is it simply liberation theology. The Church is fullness. The members of the Church, however, are not making that fullness a reality and sometimes even betray it!

Three charisms have attracted a great deal of attention because of their unusual, even spectacular nature, and merit special consideration. I shall devote the next chapter to them.

NOTES

1. Among the enormous number of books and articles written about charisms, I would recommend: A. Lemonnyer, 'Charismes', *DB (Suppl)*, I (1928), cols 1233–1243; J. Brosch, *Charismen und Ämter in der Urkirche* (Bonn, 1951); H. Schürmann, 'Les charismes spirituels', *L'Eglise de Vatican II* (*Unam sanctam*, 51b) (Paris, 1966), pp. 541–573; M.-A. Chevallier, *Esprit de Dieu, paroles d'homm. Le rôle de l'Esprit dans les ministères de la parole selon l'apôtre Paul* (Neuchâtel, 1966); H. Conzelmann, 'charisma', *TDNT*, IX, pp. 402–406; H. Küng, *The Church* (London, 1967), pp. 197ff.; G. Hasenhüttl, *Charisma, Ordnungsprinzip der Kirche* (Freiburg, 1970); J. Hainz, *Ekklesia, Strukturen paulinischer Gemeinde-Theologie und Gemeinde-Ordnung* (Regensburg, 1972); J. D. G. Dunn, *Jesus and the Spirit. A Study of the Religious and Charismatic Experience of Jesus and the First Christians as Reflected in the New Testament* (Philadelphia, 1975), pp. 253ff.; B. N. Wambacq, 'Le mot "charisme" ', *NRT*, 97 (1975), 345–355; Sr Jeanne d'Arc, 'Panorama du charisme. Essai d'une perspective d'ensemble', *VS*, 609 (July-August 1975), 503–521; A. M. de Monléon, 'L'Expérience des charismes. Manifestations de l'Esprit en vue du bien commun', *Istina*, 21 (1976), 340–373.

2. Here I am following almost exactly M.-A. Chevallier, *op. cit.*, pp. 139ff. and J. Hainz, *op. cit.*, pp. 328–335. See also R. Laurentin, who defines charisms as 'freely given . . . diverse gifts bestowed upon various members for the building up of the Church', *Catholic Pentecostalism* (London, 1977), p. 51; see also *Concilium*, 109 (1978), 3–12. The Malines document also says: '. . . charism is understood to be a gift or aptitude which is liberated and empowered by the Spirit of God and is taken into the ministry of building up the body of Christ which is the Church. It is also presupposed that every Christian manifests one or more charisms. The charisms belong to a right ordering of the Church and to ministry' (Eng. tr., *Theological and Pastoral Orientations on the Catholic Charismatic Renewal* (Notre Dame, Indiana, 1974), p. 5); and further on: 'This Spirit, given to the whole Church, comes to visibility in ministries . . .' (*ibid.*, p. 12).

3. See H. Caffarel, *Faut-il parler d'un Pentecôtisme catholique?* (Paris, 1973), p. 30, who recognized that this was the narrow meaning of the word. See also Cardinal L. J. Suenens, *A New Pentecost* (London, 1975), pp. 21f.: 'These manifestations of the Spirit or charisms are . . . gifts of the Spirit recognizable by their visible presence and by their common goal . . . to build anew the kingdom of God'.

4. According to Sr Jeanne d'Arc, VS, 609 (July-August 1975), 569.

5. Leo XIII himself said: 'The charisms are only extraordinary gifts given by the Holy Spirit in exceptional circumstances and with the aim of establishing the divine origin of the Church': see his encyclical *Divinum illud munus* (9 May 1897) and his letter *Testem benevolentiae* (22 January 1899). J. D. G. Dunn quotes numerous authors writing in the Reformed tradition who have been guilty of this identification: see his *Baptism in the Holy Spirit* (London, 4th ed., 1977), p. 225, note 3. See also L. Cerfaux, *The Christian in the Theology of St Paul* (Eng. tr.; London, 1967), esp. pp. 256–261, who speaks of 'ecstatic manifestations and miracles' and thinks that the Corinthian believers were 'fleshly' and children rather than adult Christians. See also Cardinal E. Ruffini's address to the Second Vatican Council on 16 October 1963; A. Bittlinger, 'Die charismatische Erneuerung der Kirchen. Aufbruch urchristlicher Geisteserfahrung', *Erfahrung und Theologie des Heiligen Geistes*, ed. C. Heitmann and H. Mühlen (Hamburg and Munich, 1974), pp. 36–48; P.-R. Régamey, *La Rénovation dans l'Esprit* (Paris, 1974), p. 40, who understands 'charisms . . . in the strict sense of more or less passing favours, such as prophecies, miracles and extraordinary generosity in service, given by the Holy Spirit for the benefit of others, rather than those who receive them. It is possible to recognize the mark of the Spirit in these favours.'

6. I am, in this rather severe statement, criticizing only the use made of this distinction, not the distinction itself as outlined by Thomas Aquinas, for example, in *ST* Ia IIae, q. 111,

a. 1; *Comm. in Rom.* c. 1, lect. 3; *Comp. Theol.* I, c. 114. Especially in connection with the apostles, however, he observed that God generally entrusted missions that were accompanied by signs and miracles to those who were most holy; see *In I Sent.* d. 14, q. 2, a. 2, ad 4; d. 15, a. 1, qª 2; *ST* Ia, q. 43, a. 1; a. 3, ad 4; a. 4; IIIa, q. 7, a. 10, ad 2.

7. ' "Charismatiques", ou quoi?', *La Croix* (19 January 1974); 'Renouveau dans l'Esprit et Institution ecclésiale. Mutuelle interrogation', *RHPR*, 55 (1975), 143–156, especially pp. 145ff.

8. *Tous responsables dans l'Eglise? Le ministère presbytéral dans l'Eglise tout entière 'ministérielle'* (Paris, 1973).

9. See *Discours au Concile Vatican II*, ed. Y. Congar, D. O'Hanlon and H. Küng (Paris, 1964), pp. 31–36. The quotation that follows in the text is taken from H. Küng, *op. cit.* (note 1), p. 182.

10. K. McDonnell, ed., *The Holy Spirit and Power* (New York, 1975), pp. 63–73. E. O'Connor, *The Pentecostal Movement in the Catholic Church* (Notre Dame, Indiana, 1971), p. 33ff. and note 25, defends the term which provided the title for his book. Just as every believer is liturgical and biblical, he claims, and there is a liturgical and biblical movement in the Church, so too is there a charismatic or Pentecostal movement, although this does not affect the fact that every believer also has his own charism or charisms.

11. H. Caffarel, *Le renouveau charismatique interpellé* (Collection Renouveau, 5) (Paris, 1976), p. 71; *Pro mundi vita*, 60 (May 1976), p. 18ff.

12. Sr Jeanne d'Arc, *op. cit.* (note 4), 569ff.

13. J. M. R. Tillard, 'Il y a charisme et charisme. La vie religieuse', *Lumen Vitae* (Brussels, 1977).

14. See W. Bassett, 'To Judge on the Merits of the Case', *Concilium*, 107 (1977), 59–68.

15. G. Delteil, article in *L'Unité des Chrétiens*, 15 (July 1974), 5. A critical question very similar to my own will also be found in A.-M. Besnard, 'Le prisme des opinions', *VS* (January 1974), 18ff.; J.-Y. Riocreux, 'Réflexions d'un Français aux Etats-Unis', *ibid.*, 25, 27–28; K. Rahner, in an interview given on the occasion of his seventieth birthday, also said: 'There is an almost naive immediacy to God and an almost naive faith in the rule of the Holy Spirit': *Herder Korrespondenz*, 28 (1974), 91.

16. See J.-Y. Riocreux, *op. cit.*, 28. See also H. Caffarel, *op. cit.* (note 11), 75ff., 78; K. and D. Ranaghan, *op. cit.* below (note 21), p. 171.

17. J.-P. Dietle, 'Le réveil pentecôtiste ...', *Positions luthériennes*, 4 (October 1974), 236.

18. O. Clément, 'La vie dans l'Esprit selon la tradition de l'Orient chrétien', *Cahiers Saint-Dominique*, 138 (May 1973), 370–381, especially 379.

19. I have already quoted two of Simeon's texts above, pp. 70 and 121. Basil of Caesarea showed that the action of the Holy Spirit was not instantaneous, but gradual in his *De spir. sanct.* 18 (*SC* 17bis, pp. 197ff.).

20. Their teaching is so well known that it would be foolish to quote a great number of texts. It is, however, worth mentioning John of the Cross, *The Ascent of Mount Carmel*, III, chapters 29–31; *The Dark Night*, XIII and *Counsels and Maxims*, 38. Marie de l'Incarnation wrote from Quebec to her son: 'The one who is present in the most precious way of all is the Spirit of the incarnate Word when he gives that Spirit in a sublime way, as he has in fact given him to several souls whom I know in this new Church. . . . Normally he only gives him after much suffering in his service and faithful reception of his grace': see Mme Arsène-Henry, *Les plus beaux textes sur le Saint-Esprit* (Paris, 1968), p. 24.

21. G. Combet and L. Fabre, 'The Pentecostal Movement and the Gift of Healing', *Concilium*, 99 (1975), 106–110. See also K. and D. Ranaghan, *Catholic Pentecostals* (New York, 1969), chapter 7, 'Walking in the Spirit', especially pp. 214–216.

22. This is, I think, the case with 'Le mouvement charismatique: nouvelle Pentecôte ou nouvelle aliénation?', *La Lettre*, 211 (March 1976), 7–18, (M. Clévenot) 19–26; and with Arlette Sabiani, 'Non, mille fois non', *Hebdo T.C.*, 1774 (6 July 1978), 19. Many readers

sent in their reactions. It is also similar in the case of J. Chabert, 'La hiérarchie catholique et le renouveau charismatique', *Lumière et Vie*, 125 (November-December 1975), 22–32, especially 29: 'an institution built on the ruins of human hope' and 'care for structures, material and social mediations and their transformation cannot but be absent in this framework (of an almost immediate relationship with the absolute)'.

23. See Paul Ricœur's very illuminating analysis: 'Le socius et le prochain', *Cahiers de la VS* (1954); repr. in *Histoire et Vérité* (Paris, 2nd ed. 1955), pp. 99–111.

24. See Raul Vidales, 'Charisms and Political Action', *Concilium*, 109 (1978), 67–77; Enrique Dussel, 'The Differentiation of Charisms', *ibid.*, 38–55. Vidales says, p. 71: 'Religious practice effectively becomes an alienating factor within the overall framework of dependent capitalist structure, particularly amongst the traditionally exploited working classes, who have little or no historical and political consciousness and hardly any active participation in transforming the ruling system. To the extent that religious practice contributes to the maintenance of a mythical, a-historical and a-political consciousness, it sacralizes the established order and in the end becomes the one element that keeps the establishment in its place.'

25. See John Orme Mills' long note on pp. 116–117 of *New Heaven? New Earth?* (London, 1976), with reference, among others, to W. Hollenweger, *Pentecost and Politics* (Bristol, 1975); see also R. Laurentin, *Catholic Pentecostalism, op. cit.* (note 2), pp. 173–177. See also the personal witness borne in *Unité des chrétiens*, 21 (January 1976), 24–25: J.-M. Fiolet; *Il est vivant*, 11 (n.d. = 1976), 12–17: Jean, Raymonde, Michèle, Jacques and Yves.

26. See my *Un peuple messianique. L'Eglise sacrement du salut. Salut et libération* (Paris, 1975).

27. Raul Vidales, *op. cit.* (note 24), 74, 75. My italics.

2
SPECTACULAR CHARISMS
Speaking and Praying in Tongues
Prophecy · Healings

Cardinal Ruffini, in his address to the Second Vatican Council in 1963, believed, as did John Chrysostom at the end of the fourth century, that tongues had been useful at the beginning of the Church's history, but that the phenomenon had ceased now. On the contrary, however, it has in no way ceased—it is very much with us. In fact, it never ceased completely, but the evidence in the history of Christianity is neither abundant nor always very precise.[1] There is, on the other hand, a great deal of clear evidence in the past of the gift of tears. Often these have been tears of penance or 'compunction'.[2] Often, also, they have been tears of emotion, expressing great love,[3] in which case they have been a language going beyond words. In this respect, then, tears are clearly related to speaking or praying in tongues.

There have been dozens of studies of the evidence of glossolalia in the New Testament, and to date about 400 books or articles have been written about speaking or praying in tongues in the Pentecostalist or Neo-pentecostalist movement.[4] It cannot be established *a priori* that what is reported in the Acts of the Apostles about the first Pentecost, what happened at Corinth, what was personally experienced by Paul, and what is encountered now in the Renewal are identical. There has been considerable discussion about the evidence in Acts. It is certain that something quite striking happened, but did not Luke, it has been asked, reconstruct in a historical form a theology of missionary catholicity on the basis of the instances of glossolalia that were fairly common in the early Christian communities? Was it xenoglossia (speaking in foreign languages), or was it an enthusiastic manifestation of exultant praise that witnesses might have taken either as a language which they seemed to recognize or as a drunken delirium (see Acts 2:6–13)? Luke himself seems to interpreted what happened at the first Pentecost as a replica of what the Jewish tradition affirmed about Sinai, or perhaps as a reversal of Babel.

Glossolalia at Corinth was rather anarchic and at the same time overestimated as a charism. Paul himself believed that it should be controlled; he valued, but did not overvalue it. What are we, then, to say about this phenomenon among our brothers and sisters in the Renewal?

The first thing that has to be said is that it has become famous. Although it plays a relatively small part in Renewal meetings, whether they are large or small, it interests many people and has provided the subject-matter for many studies. It often occupies a considerable amount of space in more general works about the movement as a whole.[5] An extraordinary aspect of the Renewal is thus given a privileged place. In the New Testament, on the other hand, it has a relatively small place. In Acts, it appears each time that the mission which was inaugurated at Pentecost reaches a new human space—it occurs, for example, in Samaria, among the gentiles of Caesarea and among John's disciples at Ephesus. Our knowledge of glossolalia comes essentially from the case of the community at Corinth. There are allusions to it, but no descriptions of it, outside Paul's account in 1 Corinthians, but it is not found anywhere in Romans or Ephesians, which, on the other hand, provide lists of the gifts of the Spirit.[6] There is no reference at all to glossolalia in John.

Should we speak here of glossolalia, or of xenoglossia? Are these phenomena which do not correspond to any real spoken language, or are they sentences or phrases in an existing language or dialect unknown to the subject himself? Some experts claim that there have been no cases to their knowledge in which sentences or phrases of a real language have been heard and properly checked. Other scholars have provided different evidence.[7] I am inclined to agree with Peter Hocken, in his report to the English bishops, that the question is wrongly put. On the one hand, in fact, this 'language' is not a means of communication with men, but an expression of a relationship with God (1 Cor 14:2). On the other hand, it is experienced, as it was in the apostolic Church, as giving, in joy and with a feeling of fullness, a sign of the coming of the Spirit and his gifts and as strengthening the Christian's total commitment to Jesus Christ. The evidence provided by those who have this gift is categorical: they claim to have a deep sense of awakening to a communion which involves their whole person, including their body, at a level that is both below and beyond and concepts and our human words. Here is one such testimony:

> The Holy Spirit purifies and refashions certain very profound elements of the human personality that lie beyond the reach of therapeutic exploration. He reshapes us in the foundations of our personality, that basic structure which precedes even the acquisition of our mother-tongue and the first social control of our feelings and their expressions. This activity can be felt all the more strongly when the Holy Spirit makes use of the prayers that he himself gives us in the form that precedes acquired, controlled language, as in the case of praying in tongues and, by extension, praying with the prayer of the heart.[8]

Another testimony describes the phenomenon known as 'singing in tongues':

> In singing in tongues, words are pronounced expressing unity regained, perfect newness and eager anticipation. It is the language of gratuitous freedom. A deep thankfulness, the desire for which exceeds all possible expression, corresponds to

174

the abundant gift of God, who gives himself without counting the cost. It takes place when the heart overflows and can no longer find the words and phrases that it is seeking. Singing in tongues is a stammering of great abundance and thankfulness.[9]

Evidence of this kind, which cannot as such be refuted, is always to be welcomed, but two kinds of criticism have to be made of the glossolalia of Neo-pentecostalism—religious criticism and criticism based on the human sciences. My purely religious criticism of this phenomenon can be grouped under four headings:

(a) It is not possible to go beyond the clear language of Paul in 1 Cor 14:1–33. In this passage, he outlines a criticism and practical norms in accordance with three criteria. The first is the benefit to others: 'he who speaks in a tongue edifies only himself' (1 Cor 14:4). The second is the inalienable place accorded to understanding: 'I will pray with the Spirit and I will pray with the mind also. . . . Nevertheless, in church I would rather speak five words with my mind . . . than ten thousand words in a tongue' (14:15, 19). The third criterion is that the Christian should aim at an adult rather than at a childish level of understanding: 'do not be children in your thinking. . . . In thinking be mature' (14:20).

(b) In Pentecostalism, speaking in tongues is fairly generally regarded as an indispensable sign of having been baptized in the Spirit. It is not quite the same in the Renewal. This difference between the two is accompanied by another difference, which has to do with the wider ecclesiological and theological context. As Simon Tugwell has acutely observed,[10] for Pentecostalists, neither baptism of water nor the Eucharist are what they are for us, namely sacraments in the sense of acts of God, but rather actions of believers. On the other hand, speaking in tongues is brought about in us by God as the sign of baptism in the Spirit and is therefore experienced by Pentecostalists in the sense of a sacrament.

(c) In the renewal, praying in tongues is frequently identified with the inexpressible groanings (stenagmois alalētois) which Paul speaks of as being, in us, the prayer of the Spirit (Rom 8:26). I agree with K. Niederwimmer, however, in believing that what Paul is speaking about in this text is something quite different, namely a prayer of the Holy Spirit himself, a prayer that is not pronounced and therefore not audible. This is not so in the case of praying in tongues. The prayer of the Holy Spirit within us is something that does not belong to our conscious spirit, but to the presence or the indwelling of the Holy Spirit in us which I have already discussed.[11] It is, nevertheless, related to speaking, praying or singing in tongues, so long as these latter phenomena are really gifts of God, by the fact that a certain depth in our own 'heart' is involved with both.

175

(d) I have stated an important condition: 'so long as these phenomena are really gifts of God'. This critical question is certainly important, because similar phenomena have existed and still exist in the pagan world or outside the life of the Spirit. Paul was well aware of this (see 1 Cor 12:2). What is more, many psychologists have stressed the induced character of 'tongues' and the imitative and enthusiastic nature of the activity, despite the fact that a certain number of cases defy explanation. As Pascal commented, charity is what enables true miracles to be discerned. The fact that the same phenomena occur outside the life in the Spirit does not necessarily mean that they do not come from the Spirit or that they do not bear witness to his presence for our consolation and joy where there is life in the Spirit. This is clear from the fruits that are received and especially the gifts of charity, which is for Paul the supreme norm. 1 Cor 13 is in no sense a foreign body between 1 Cor 12 and 1 Cor 14—it is rather the master-light that illuminates what the apostle wants to tell his readers about the use of the gifts of the Spirit. Charity is the supreme charism.

Let us now consider the important contribution made to our understanding of glossolalia by the human sciences. Several authors have summarized the conclusions of experts in this field.[12] I shall do no more here than simply draw attention to the methods used to examine the data and the points of view from which they have been seen.

The Linguistic Sciences: In a few rare and even then doubtful cases, certain sentences or phrases in an existing language or dialect that have been recognized by observers have been uttered by a subject who has claimed ignorance of the language in question. These cases may be regarded as miraculous. Apart from them, a real language is not involved, either at the level of phonemes or at that of lexical combinations. William J. Samarin has made a systematic study of glossolalia from this viewpoint.[13]

Comparative Religion and Ethnography: Glossolalia has existed in shamanism, in pagan antiquity, in ancient Mesopotamia and in Greece (the Pythia of the oracle at Delphi), and also in Judaism during New Testament times.[14]

Sociology and Psychology: The conclusions of specialists working in this sphere have changed in the course of time. Kilian McDonnell has distinguished two periods, from 1910 to 1966 and from 1967 to 1975. The break in 1966/67 corresponds significantly to the transition from Pentecostalism proper to Neo-pentecostalism, that is, to the wider movement of the Renewal in the classical churches. It was first thought that entry into Pentecostal groups was a response to a need to escape from an insecure social situation based on economic and cultural deprivation. It is now believed that, even though this may have been the case for a time and is still the reason here and there, this is no longer strictly true. It was also thought that an important part was played by a pathological element or that the subjects were predisposed to be influenced in this way. Psychological tests have revealed that those who speak in tongues have an inclination to be dependent on a model, a leader or a group. At the same time, however, these tests have not shown in any way that members of the Renewal are, as a whole, less mature, more anxious or less adapted to living than other people.

One positive aspect of glossolalia that has been observed is that it has a 'liberating effect. From the religious point of view, it liberates man from inhibitions in regard to men and to God, that is, from human respect and from fear of approaching the God whom no words can describe. As a result, interior energies, both mystical and apostolic, are released. This is a fact of daily experience.'[15]

'Interpretation' and 'Prophecy'

Just as it is not a question of speaking a foreign language, so too is there no 'translation' in the case of 'interpretation' of tongues. This interpretation is a charism: 'The Spirit gives . . . to another various kinds of tongues, to another the interpretation of tongues' (1 Cor 12:10), although it can happen that the same person has both gifts (14:5, 13). Clearly, this interpretation cannot be checked. I have personally heard too little about it to be able to provide a valuable assessment of it, especially as what I have heard is very trivial. What is certain, however, is that the charism of interpretation is closely related to that of speaking in tongues and, since the latter does not play a large part in Renewal meetings as such, interpretation similarly has hardly any place in those meetings.

Paul attaches much more importance to 'prophecy' (see 1 Cor 14:1, 5, 39; 1 Thess 5:20). Prophets always figure in his lists of gifts and ministries and in his discussions of those matters. It is worth noting, for example, that he names them immediately after the 'apostles'.[16] The Fathers stressed the permanent nature of this gift in the Church. It has a direct bearing on its building up, whether it is seen within the ordinary framework of life in the small communities of the kind that Corinth might well have been or considered within the much wider context of the historical movement of the Church's life.

We are most conscious of this second aspect today, the prophet being seen above all as the one who opens to the Church new ways for and a new understanding of its future, the one who is able to read the 'signs of the times' and the one who goes beyond the established structures and ideas and makes gestures or creates institutions that are very promising.[17] These 'prophetic' men and women are related to the biblical prophets in that they open the way for and throw light on the accomplishment of God's plan in history.

This is not, however, exactly what we have in 1 Cor 12:10; 14:1–33, nor is it what is found in the Renewal. What is involved is the building up of persons and this leads to the building up of the Church. It is also not the habitual gift of understanding and explaining the Word of God or of teaching (*didascalia*). But nor is it, like glossolalia, an irrational form of expression. It is fully intelligible, but above all given or 'inbreathed' by the Spirit. Its effect is to make the recipient open to the truth of God and the truth of what he is himself.

The revelation that is imparted by this prophecy is not usually astonishing. The bishop and martyr Polycarp is described in a letter from his Church as an 'apostolic and prophetic teacher'[18] and we have one of his letters, which contains wise exhortation and very classical morality. In the Renewal, several cases of 'prophecy' have been recorded. These have proclaimed the future,[19] have disclosed the depths of a person's heart or have announced a precise and providential appeal. Most of them, however, have been simple, edifying exhortations: 'Prophecy exhorts, warns, comforts and corrects. . . . Prophecy can be a simple word of encouragement, an admonition, a prophetic act, or a decision for a new line of action.'[20]

Miracles and Healings

The healing of the sick or injured was, in New Testament times, a sign of the coming of the messianic era.[21] Paul listed the gifts of healing and working miracles among the charisms of the Spirit (see 1 Cor 12:9, 28–30). Was the Spirit himself not the messianic gift *par excellence*? The Acts of the Apostles are full of stories of healings and miracles. There are also many accounts of healings and miracles occurring throughout the centuries in the history of the Church, although it has, of course, to be recognized that the reality has often been exaggerated in hagiography and monastic writings as well as in the minds of the people. On the other hand, it has for centuries been maintained by many Christians that miracles, like the gift of tongues, were granted only in the early period of the Church's history.[22] Despite the fact that we are now so proud of our knowledge and our control of the elements, however, there has, in our own period, been a striking contradiction of this interpretation—miracles, appearances and, in the Renewal especially, the gift of tongues and healings.[23] What is taking place in the Renewal is of ecclesiological importance, quite apart from its pneumatological interest. In the Catholic Church, men of God have always been the instruments of healings, and the celebration of the sacrament of the sick has often resulted in noticeable improvements in health.[24] As F. Lovsky has observed, however, healings have frequently been attributed to the saints in heaven and especially to the Virgin Mary.[25] Now, with the Renewal, they have once again become an aspect of the Church here on earth and a normal, everyday feature. Attempts have even been made to avoid the sensational aspect with which they can so easily be associated.

The context of these healings in the Renewal is usually that of a prayer meeting, and the pattern followed is usually as follows: an absolute faith in Jesus who is living and whose Spirit works with power is required;[26] there is brotherly prayer in the community of the group; the one who has the gift of healing does not work alone, although there are exceptions, notably Kathryn Kuhlman;[27] finally there is a laying on of hands, which is a classic, biblical gesture, expressing the powerful action of the Spirit who is invoked; this is accompanied by prayer in faith;[28] thanksgiving, even before any improvement is observed. Basically, it is above all a question of living, with one's brethren, in a fellowship of faith and prayer and in a relationship with the living God, who transforms one's attitude, both in soul and in body, towards oneself. There are physical healings, but there have been many more healings that are spiritual, inner—psychical, if that term is preferred.

This spiritual healing gives us access to our true relationship with God. This latter is what all the Church's pastoral activity, both the Word and the sacraments, tends to secure. As J.-C. Sagne has said: 'Inner healing is . . . a healing of the psyche. It does not immediately concern the relation to God and the God-orientated life but the organization of our intelligence, our will, our memory and our emotional sensitivity.'[29] There may be hiatuses or blockages in our psyche and these may have a spiritual origin. It is important for us to be set free from these impediments. This does not usually happen suddenly, with the speed of lightning. It comes as the result of trusting prayer, in the conviction that God will bestow his gift, a brotherly, persistent prayer made in humble and peaceful practice in the life of the Church. The atmosphere of friendly welcome and joyous praise which so characterizes Renewal meetings, and tends to erase conflicts, and the freedom and power of the Spirit who is invoked in prayer should not by-pass normal human psychological development. As A. Vergote has pointed out, 'The Spirit acts by coming together with the human spirit and not by going against it or acting outside it'. The members of the Renewal and especially those who are responsible for imposing restraint on it have to exercise discernment. There have been cases, in the movement and outside it, of failure or at least of indiscreet intervention.

Physical healings of organic diseases are clearly more striking. There have been accounts that are almost incredible, but which have been supported by witnesses.[30] We should not be inflexibly sceptical or, on the other hand, childishly credulous. 'Who knows where God wants to let down his ladder?' We believe in the Holy Spirit and we believe in his power to give life. We believe in the power of prayer and faith and know that prayer is especially powerful when it is made with ardent brotherly unanimity. A messianic sign of the proximity of the kingdom of God has been given in our present century, which is critical and well provided with therapeutic means. The Church has rediscovered a forgotten form of ministry—that of healing. May God be praised for our recovery of a ministry that has so many different forms!

It should be added that there is a miraculous element in some of the cases that have been reported, but that this is in keeping with what philosophers such as Maurice Blondel and theologians have said about miracles as a manifestation of God's love of man and of the nature of his salvation, which points to the glorious freedom of the children of God and the restoration of their nature, both body and soul, in a fullness of life.

Discernment

Two aspects of discernment can be distinguished in Paul's teaching about this charism: in the first place, the special charism of discernment itself and, in the second, the general exercise of discernment, which every Christian must try to practise. In connection with 1 Cor 12:10, J. D. G. Dunn said that it is important to recognize that this gift of discernment of spirits is on a par with prophecy. It should not be regarded, he insists, as an independent gift. It provides a 'test' for the prophetic statement and a check against its abuses (see 1 Cor 14:29). It is, he concluded, the equivalent of the rôle played by the interpretation of tongues in the case of glossolalia (1 Cor 12:10; 14:27ff.).[31] It therefore clearly has its limitations. An illustration of this can be found in 1 Cor 14:29, in which Paul, having given the rules for the exercise of the *pneumatika*, speaking in tongues and prophecies—to which the Corinthians were strongly attracted (1 Cor 14:12)—invites the brethren to assess (*diakrinein*) the prophecies (1 Cor 14:29), the function of which is not to predict the future, but rather to announce, in a concrete situation, the will of God for an individual or the community. This prophetic function is, moreover, not to take place on the basis of human criteria, that is, human reason, but it must be carried out in a spiritual fashion, using the resources that come from the Spirit (1 Cor 2:13–16; 7:40).

An absolutely sovereign and objective criterion can be found in orthodox Christology (see 1 Cor 12:3; 1 Jn 4:1–3). This is an indispensable condition for authenticity, which can be expressed in the concrete as an ability to build up the Body of Christ. V. Therrien, who has specialized in this question, situated the charism of discernment within the more general framework of Christian discernment as such and then, in his detailed study of spiritual discernment, went on to say:

> It provides a source of dynamic knowledge and revelation for the service of the glory of God within a pastoral service of the people of God. The end in view is his people's freedom from influences which do not come from God and which are replaced by the lordship of Jesus as restored by the Holy Spirit. . . . Like all the charisms, charismatic discernment is an experience of actual grace. It is instantaneous, spontaneous, gratuitous, confusing, unforeseen and accidental. It is, in other words, given to be used in a situation of need. It disappears when that need disappears. . . . Charismatic discernment is a wide-reaching form of perception. . . . The climate and the conditions within which this experience takes place and

this dynamism is exercised can be defined by the following terms: peace, compassion, gentleness, merciful charity and service of the glory of God and our brethren. It can never take place in an environment of scandalized astonishment, haste, aggression, terrorism, possessiveness and oppression.[32]

Such a description cannot be read without some misgivings. What a fantastic degree of authority for a man (or woman) to have! Is there not also a need for external criteria which enable us to discern whether the Spirit has really intervened? The author, apparently aware of this, adds:

The first condition for the validity of the experience of charismatic discernment is to have recourse to other forms of discernment in order to confirm and justify charismatic discernment, because it is new and often spontaneous and confusing. ... The second condition of validity is to go back to the charismatic community and the exercise of this dynamism of service within the community.

These conditions are not, of course, always observed. There have been many recorded cases of abuse, imprudence, indiscretion and, on the other hand, unacceptable and authoritarian control.[33] These cases to some extent bring the Renewal into disrepute, but no more than mistakes and errors of judgement bring other movements or institutions into disrepute. It has, however, to be recognized that some environments are more favourable than others to abuses.

It is important in this context to consider another element mentioned by Therrien, that is, 'freedom from influences which do not come from God'. This clearly refers to the devil. In its early days, Pentecostalism had a rather simplistic, but very full demonology.[34] Even in the most Catholic branches of the Renewal, there is often a similarly simplistic way of speaking about the devil and liberation from his influence.[35] And on the fringe of the movement are an exercise of a 'ministry of deliverance' and certain practices of exorcism which give rise to a certain uneasiness.[36] I would not wish to rule out this hypothesis of demons, since there are data supporting it, but there is good reason, in this particular sphere, for sobriety and a sound demythologization.[37] Just before he died, the great spiritual writer Albert-Marie Besnard wrote to me about his worrying observation that 'members of the Renewal are more and more frequently tending to see the demon at work in everything that is no more than human'.

If 'charismatic discernment' exists, it is rare and, when it occurs, it calls for co-operation. In any case Scripture, and Paul in particular, requires all believers to exercise discernment: 'Do not quench the Spirit, do not despise prophesying, but test everything (*panta de dokimazete*), hold fast to what is good, abstain from every form of evil' (1 Thess 5:19–22; cf. Jn 4:1–6). One of the most perceptive commentators has said: 'Paul's exhortation applies

181

first and foremost to the discernment of charisms and above all to the discernment of prophecies, but it is in itself a universal principle of "spiritual prudence" '. The same author goes on to summarize his study of the act of discernment and define it as 'an act that is both unique and complex, both human and divine and both personal and ecclesial. It is both specific for a particular situation and at the same time fitted into God's one plan of salvation. It points to the building up of the brethren and is orientated towards God's glory. Finally, although it takes place in time, it also shares in the judgement at the end of time.'[38] What a programme! This is in fact the rôle of the 'discernment of spirits', which has been discussed in countless spiritual works, though no author has ever succeeded in exhausting the subject.[39] With the help of Therrien,[40] the author of the above summary, it is possible to group the criteria for the discernment of spirits under three headings:

(1) *Doctrinal or Objective Discernment*: This is basic. The first task of a believer, a brother or a 'spiritual director' is to act as a mirror in which we can see and check whether the movements of our spirit are authentic. This discernment consists of certain objective criteria: the Word of God seen as a whole and not simply certain passages of Scripture; the teaching of the Church and the masters of spirituality; the duties of our state; our observation of the commandments (see 1 Jn 2:3–5); our attitude of obedience (Teresa of Avila is an excellent model of this). All our research leads us to the conclusion that Christology is the most important condition for the soundness of any pneumatology (see below, pp. 210–211).

(2) *Subjective or Personal Discernment*:[41] This consists of an assessment of our inner tendencies on the basis of that renewal of our understanding and value-judgements of which Paul speaks in Rom 12:2 and Eph 4:23. What is the origin of these movements and where do they lead? A knowledge of what the human sciences can tell us is helpful in our attempt to discover their origin. In the last resort, however, it is our quality of life as Christians which provides the real sign of authenticity and the fruit(s) of the Spirit of which Paul speaks in Gal 5:22 play(s) a part here: 'love, joy, peace, patience, kindness, goodness, faithfulness, gentleness, self-control'. The tradition of spirituality in the Church provides an echo of this fundamental programme that has sounded throughout the centuries. There was an emphasis on peace and joy, for example, in the second century, in the writings of the Roman Hermas,[42] and at the end of the fourth century, in the homilies of Macarius the Great.[43] In the sixteenth century another classical author writing about the rules of discernment, Ignatius Loyola, attached great importance to the effects of consolation or sadness. His aim was above all to bring his readers to a mature decision in life that corresponded to God's will for us. For that reason, he is the great model to whom we return again and again.[44]

182

(3) *Discernment within the Community*: This form of discernment can be divided into two types: (a) 'A search conducted by all the members of a group for a clear consensus of God's will for the group or for one of its members in a particular case or situation. . . . The criteria for the validity of such an exercise in discernment [are] the presence of spiritual guides or competent animators: . . .'[45] The objective criterion will be what builds up the community (see 1 Cor 14:26). What is involved here is a life that forms an integral part of the greater or lesser fabric of history. For this reason, (b) a good criterion will consist in correspondence to the needs of the Church and the general tendency of its life. It is here that the 'signs of the times' have to be discerned.[46] A sense of history, a concern for events, a little prophetic perception and above all a spiritual understanding of God's work are all necessary, especially as the beginnings, in which the Spirit of God is active, are often very ambivalent and ambiguous. Our spontaneous actions have to be tested because not everything that emerges from them is necessarily from the Spirit. The Acts of the Apostles contain a certain number of new situations, through which the Church's mission had to find its way in conformity with the will of God and his plan. The solution to this difficulty was found by applying these three criteria: Experience of the Spirit, the support of scriptural evidence and the approval of the *ecclesia*.[47]

It should be clear, then, that discernment is a very complex act, calling for the exercise of many human means and of many gifts of the Spirit. The gifts which classical theology knows in the form of understanding, knowledge, counsel and wisdom all have to be used so long as the Holy Spirit gives them. He blows where he wills: one of his titles is 'counsellor'. But he does not act like the prompter in a theatre, so that we also have to use our own understanding and out own resources: 'Brethren, . . . in your thinking be mature!' (1 Cor 14:20).

NOTES

1. The following can be mentioned: Catherine de Dormans (*c.* 1110), who, according to Guibert de Nogent, bore witness to a *rotatus sermonum*: see P. Alphandéry, *Revue de l'Histoire des Religions*, 52 (1905), 186; possibly Hildegard of Bingen: see F. Vernet, *DTC*, VI, p. 2470; Elizabeth of Schönau (†1164), *Vita*, Prol. 1 (*PL* 195, 119B); Dorothy of Montau (see Volume I of this work, p. 122); Teresa of Avila, *Life*, chapter 16; Ignatius Loyola and his *loquela*, *Diary*, 11 and 22 May 1544; Marie de l'Incarnation, Relation of 1654, XXIV: 'I sang to my divine Bridegroom a canticle that his Spirit inspired me to sing'; *The Way of a Pilgrim* (Russian; between 1856 and 1861): '. . . a strong feeling came over me, urging me to withdraw within myself again. The Prayer was surging up in my heart, and I needed peace and silence to give free play to this quickening flame of prayer, as well as to hide from others the outward signs which went with it, such as tears and sighs and unusual movements of the face and lips': paperback ed. (London, 1972), pp. 78–79. I do not intend to speak here about the Cévennes Protestants of the early eighteenth century: see Morton T. Kelsey, *Tongue Speaking* (London, 1973), pp. 52ff. I also omit

any reference to Wesley's or Irving's disciples in the nineteenth century. Following K. Richstaetter, 'Die Glossolalie im Lichte der Mystik', *Schol*, 11 (1936), 321–345, however, it is possible to compare with speaking or singing in tongues what Augustine said about the *jubilus: Enarr, in Ps.* 102 (*PL* 37, 1322ff.), or St Bernard about what the ardour of love causes us to 'belch out'; *In Cant. Sermo* 67, 3 (*PL* 183, 1103D–1104A); also the comments of David of Augsburg: *De septem spir. rel.* VII, c. 15; and Jan Ruysbroeck's remarks about the *jubilus: Spiritual Notes*, liv. II, c. 25.

2. I. Hausherr, *Penthos. La doctrine de la componction dans l'Orient chrétien (Or. Chr. Anal.*, 132) (Rome, 1944); P. R. Régamey, *Portrait spirituel du chrétien* (Paris, 1963), pp. 67–116: 'compunction of the heart'.

3. See P. Adnès, 'Larmes', *Dictionnaire de Spiritualité*, IX, col. 287–303; M. Lot-Borodine, 'Le mystère du don des larmes dans l'Orient chrétien', *VS* (Suppl) (1 September 1936); repr. in *La douloureuse joie* (Bellefontaine, 1974), pp. 131–195; G. Gaucher, 'Le don des larmes aujourd'hui et hier', *Tychique*, 10 (July 1977), 33–40.

4. Cases will be found in K. and D. Ranaghan, *Catholic Pentecostals* (New York, 1969), pp. 195ff.; E. O'Connor, *The Pentecostal Movement in the Catholic Church* (1971) pp. 49–57, 121–131. R. Laurentin, *Catholic Pentecostalism* (London, 1977), pp. 213–221, has compiled a chronological bibliography on glossolalia, to which the following might be added: B. N. Wambacq, 'Het spreken in talen'. *Ons Geloof*, 30 (1948), 389–401: in 1 Cor, it is a question of ecstatic and incomprehensible speech which calls for 'interpretation'; A. Bittlinger, 'Et ils prient en d'autres langues', *Foi et Vie* (July-October 1973), 97–108, which Laurentin mentions (*op. cit.*, p. 221); A. Godin, 'Moi perdu ou moi retrouvé dans l'expérience charismatique', *Archives des Sciences sociales des religions*, 40 (July-December 1975), 31–52; J. D. G. Dunn, *Jesus and the Spirit* (Philadelphia, 1975), pp. 146ff. for Pentecost and pp. 242ff. for Corinth; see also the corresponding notes; F. A. Sullivan, 'Ils parlent en langues', *Lumen Vitae*, 31 (1976), 21–46; S. Tugwell, 'The Speech-Giving Spirit', *New Heaven? New Earth? An Encounter with Pentecostalism* (London, 1976), pp. 119–159; P. Barthel, 'De la glossolalie religieuse en Occident: Soixante-dix ans (1906–1976) de dérivations du sens', *Revue de Théologie et de Philosophie* (1977), 113–135; see also K. McDonnell, *op. cit.* (note 5 below), pp. 187–195, who provides an alphabetically listed bibliography of mainly American studies.

5. See R. Laurentin, *op. cit.*, pp. 58–99; K. McDonnell, *Charismatic Renewal and the Churches* (New York, 1976), devotes almost the whole of his book to this question. It is the most complete account of the reaction of the different churches and the studies made by specialists in the human sciences in the United States.

6. I do not think that glossolalia is implied in Rom 8:26, and Eph 5:19 and 6:18 do not, in my opinion, imply glossolalia any more than Jude 19 does. The same, I believe, applies to 1 Thess 5:19. Mk 16:17 forms part of a conclusion to the gospel; there is general agreement that it is canonical, but neither primitive nor authentic.

7. See R. Laurentin, *op. cit.* (note 4), pp. 67–77. J.-C. Sagne, *Lumière et Vie*, 125 (November-December 1975), 65, note 6, claims to have personal knowledge of at least five cases of an identification of a real language, including two in his presence. Ralph W. Harris, who is himself a Pentecostalist, has examined 60 cases and has concluded that real languages were spoken: see his *Spoken by the Spirit. Documental Accounts of 'Other Tongues' from Arabic to Zulu* (Springfield, 1973).

8. J. C. Sagne, *VS*, 609 (January-February 1975), 547. A.-M. de Monléon, 'L'expérience des charismes', *Istina*, 21, 357, also says: 'It is not a prayer based on reason or intelligence; it is a prayer of the spirit: "If I pray in a tongue, my spirit prays" (1 Cor 14:14). Praying in tongues is a prayer of the heart. . . . All the same, this form of prayer is essentially praise given by the Holy Spirit as a sign of a new invasion of his grace. It plays a very important part, among those who practise it, not only in enabling them to pray continuously with a prayer of the spirit in accordance with the Spirit, but also in enabling them to grow in

personal edification, that is, in that gradual transformation which is often invisible and intangible and in which the whole of life and the whole of their being become prayer as an expression of divine sonship (see Rom 8:26–27, 15; Gal 4:6).'

9. Ephrem Yon, *VS*, 609 (January-February 1975), 530.
10. S. Tugwell, *op. cit.* (note 4), p. 151.
11. K. Niederwimmer, 'Das Gebet des Geistes, Röm. 8, 26', *TZ*, 20 (1964), 252–265.
12. See R. Laurentin, *op. cit.* (note 4), pp. 70–79; A. Godin, *op. cit.* (*ibid.*), 42ff.; *Pro Mundi Vita*, 60 (May 1976), 26ff.; K. McDonnell, *op. cit.* (note 5).
13. W. J. Samarin, *Tongues of Men and Angels. The Religious Language of Pentecostalism* (New York, 1973); see also K. McDonnell, *op. cit.*, pp. 115–119, and bibliography, pp. 193–194.
14. See J. D. G. Dunn, *op. cit.* (note 4), p. 304; references p. 441, note 19, especially to Qumran.
15. R. Laurentin, *op. cit.*, p. 80.
16. See Rom 12:6–8; 1 Cor 12:8–10, 28ff.; 13:1–3, 8ff.; 14:1–5, 25–32; Eph 4:11; 1 Thess 5:19–22. After the apostles: Eph 2:20; 3:5; 4:11; 1 Cor 12:28. See also *Didache* XI. For the charism of prophecy, see W. J. Hollenweger. *The Pentecostals* (London. 1972; Minneapolis, 1972, 2nd ed. 1973), pp. 345ff.; J. D. G. Dunn, *op. cit.*, pp. 227–233; M. Harper, 'La prophétie: un don pour le corps du Christ', *Foi et Vie* (July-October 1973), 84–89; L. Dallière, 'Le charisme prophétique', *ibid.*, 90–96.
17. See my *Vraie et fausse réforme dans l'Eglise* (Paris, 1950), pp. 196–228; 2nd ed. (1969), pp. 179–207. Between these two editions, the following books and articles have been published: R. Grosche, *Das prophetische Element in der Kirche* (1956), repr. in *Et intra et extra* (Düsseldorf, 1958); K. Rahner, *The Dynamic Element in the Church* (Eng. tr.: Freiburg and London, 1964); P. Duployé, *La religion de Péguy* (Paris, 1965), pp. 427ff.; A. Ulryn, *Actualité de la fonction prophétique* (Tournai, 1966); *Concilium* (September 1968): various articles, by M.-D. Chenu and others, on the 'signs of the times'.
18. *Mart. Polycarpi*, XVI, 2.
19. In the Acts of the Apostles, prophetic interventions are often similar to the Old Testament type of prophecies and point to the future. See M.-A. Chevallier, *Souffle de Dieu. Le Saint-Esprit dans le Nouveau Testament*, I (Paris, 1978), pp. 166ff.
20. Malines document, *Theological and Pastoral Orientations on the Catholic Charismatic Renewal* (Eng. tr.: Notre Dame, Indiana, 1974), p. 54, which also says: 'Extreme care is used with both predictive and directive prophecy. Predictive prophecy is not to be acted upon except as tested and confirmed in other ways. . . . Neither the prophet nor his prophecy is self-authenticating. Prophecies are to be submitted to the Christian community. . . . They are also submitted to those who have pastoral responsibilities.'
21. See my *Un peuple messianique. L'Eglise sacrement du salut. Salut et libération* (Paris, 1975), pp. 110ff.; A. Mongillo, 'La guérison', *Concilium* (Fr. ed.), 99 (1974), 13–16.
22. During those very periods when accounts of miracles abounded, one type of text occurred again and again. It was to the effect that it was quite normal for there to be no more miracles; they were necessary at the beginning, as confirmation of the proclamation of the gospel, but, since its establishment, the Church has been the sign of that gospel and the evangelical promises had been transferred to the spiritual level. See, for example, Origen. *Contra Cels.* I, 9, on spiritual healing; John Chrysostom, *In Act. Apost.* (*PG* 51, 81); Augustine, *De vera rel.* XXV, 47; *De util. cred.*; *De Civ. Dei*, XXII, 8; Gregory the Great, *Hom, in Ev.*, lib. II, *Hom.* 29, 4 (*PL* 76, 1215–1216); Isidore of Seville, *In I Sent.* c. 24 (*PL* 83, 591–592); Odo of Cluny, *Collat.* I, 125; Thomas Aquinas, *In I Sent.* d. 16. q. 1, a. 2, ad 2 and 3; *ST* Ia, q. 43, a. 7, ad 6; Ia IIae, q. 106, a. 4. Modern authors could also be quoted in this context, but space forbids this. The diminishing number of miracles is noted from the second century onwards: see Justin Martyr, *Apol.* II, 6; *Contra Tryph.* 39; Irenaeus, *Adv. Haer.* II, 31, 2; 32, 4; Tertullian, *Apol.* 37. Thomas Aquinas thought that tongues had been replaced by the different voices reading the epistle and the gospel at

Mass and the nine lessons of Matins; see *Comm. in 1 Cor.* c. 14, lect. 6. The Protestant author H. E. Alexander writes: 'Signs and miracles were necessary to prove to Israel that Jesus was the Messiah, the Son of God. But as soon as the Jews had definitively rejected the gospel [references], these signs and miracles gradually disappeared. These signs—and especially speaking in tongues—were in fact gifts peculiar to the infancy of the Church (1 Cor 12:31, 11)': *La mission temporaire du Saint-Esprit pendant la disposition de grâce* (n.d., c. 1945), p. 12.

23. For healings, see W. J. Hollenweger, *op. cit.* (note 16), pp. 353ff.; Francis MacNutt, *Healing* (Indiana, 1974); M. Scanlon, *Inner Healing* (New York, 1974); O. Melançon, *Guérison et Renouveau charismatique* (Montréal, 1976); R. Laurentin, *op. cit.* (note 4), pp. 100–131.

24. The basis for this is Jas 5:12–20; *insinuatum*, as the Council of Trent said for our sacrament of the sick. See the journal *Présences*, 90 (1965), for the state of sickness, healing and the anointing of the sick; *MD*, 101 (1970), 161ff.; Donald Gelpi, 'The Ministry of Healing' in *Pentecostal Piety* (New York, 1972).

25. F. Lovsky, *L'Eglise et les malades depuis le IIe siècle jusqu'au début du XXe siècle* (Thonon, 1958). For the healing saints, see M. Leproux, *Dévotions et saints guérisseurs* (Paris, 1955); P. Jakez Helias, *Le cheval d'orgueil* (Paris, 1975), chapter III, pp. 111ff. For Lourdes, see R. Laurentin, *op. cit.*, pp. 100ff., 123ff.

26. The connection between the Spirit and power is biblical (see Lk 4:14; 24:49; Acts 1:8; 10:38; Rom 15:13–19; 1 Cor 2:4–5; 1 Thess 1:5; see also 2 Tim 1:7; Heb 2:4); see also '*pneuma*', *TDNT*, VI, pp. 397–398. For the connection between healing (miracles) and faith, see Mk 11:23–24 par.

27. What is strange and sensational here goes together with a firm affirmation of faith; see the account in A. Wohlfahrt, *Foi et Vie* (July-October 1973), 6ff.; this account also appears in R. Laurentin, *op. cit.*, pp. 107–110.

28. Human hands are a sign and a means of power: see V. E. Fiala, 'L'imposition des mains comme signe de la communication de l'Esprit Saint dans les rites latins', *Le Saint-Esprit dans la liturgie (Conférence Saint-Serge 1969)*, (Rome, 1977), 87–103.

29. For inner healing, see, in addition to R. Laurentin, *op. cit.* (note 4), H. Kahlefeld, 'Jesus as Therapist', and G. Combet and F. Fabre, 'The Pentecostal Movement and the Gift of Healing', *Concilium*, 99 (1974/6), 111–117 and 106–110 respectively; M. Scanlon, *op. cit.* (note 23); J.-C. Sagne, 'Literature on Charisms and the Charismatic Movement: Inner Healing', *Concilium*, 109 (1978), 110–115; my quotation is on p. 111; A. Vergote, 'L'Esprit, puissance de salut et de santé spirituelle', *L'expérience de l'Esprit. Mélanges Schillebeeckx* (Paris, 1976), pp. 209–223.

30. See R. Laurentin, *op. cit.*, pp. 102–105, for the Healing Service of Notre Dame, Indiana, 14 June 1974; the journal *Il est vivant*, 6–7 (February-March 1976), 26–33; *ibid.*, 15 (n.d.), 15–18, for the case of Jeanine Bévenot; Dr P. Solignac, in the Appendix to *La névrose chrétienne* (Paris, 1976; the Eng. tr. (London, 1982) lacks this Appendix), reports the apparently miraculous case of George Duc, who was healed in November 1974. See also R. Laurentin, *op. cit.*, pp. 119ff., for the charism at work.

31. J. D. G. Dunn, *op. cit.* (note 4), p. 233. The author criticizes, p. 419, note 168, the extended application of 1 Cor 12:10 in Pentecostalism and gives references.

32. V. Therrien, 'Le discernement spirituel', *Il est vivant*, 8 (June-July 1976), 16–19, 23–25, especially 23–24. Therrien is a Redemptorist and is the director of the 'Alliance' Centre in Trois Rivières (Canada). He has also written an extremely detailed study of discernment, *Le discernement dans les écrits pauliniens (Etudes bibliques)* (Paris, 1973).

33. The most serious accusations have been made by one of the pioneers of the movement in the United States, William Storey, in an interview published in *A.D. Correspondence* (24 May 1975). See also Gary McEvin, 'Les méthodes des groupes charismatiques américains vivement critiquées', *Informations Catholiques Internationales* (1 October 1975), 22–24. Kevin Ranaghan replied to William Storey (see R. Ackermann, *La Croix* (13 June 1975)),

easily refuting the accusation that the Renewal was close to schism. Edward O'Connor resigned from the National Service Committee at the end of November 1973 because he disagreed with some of the directions that it had taken and, in the French edition of his book *The Pentecostal Movement* (Paris, 1975; p. 295, note 25), he referred to certain errors made by the directors of the 'True House' community at South Bend. This community (mentioned on pp. 93ff. of the American original), was dissolved in the autumn of 1974. Finally, in *La Croix* (4 October 1978), there is a statement of opposition to the indiscretion on the part of a certain group which maintained that those who did not belong to the Renewal were not Christians. Such data, which I have not assembled for the pleasure of doing so, have to be mentioned for the sake of truth and in order to serve the church and the Renewal itself.

34. See W. Hollenweger, *op. cit.* (note 16), pp. 377ff.

35. See, for example, J. Isaac, 'Le Mal, le Christ et le Bonheur', *Cahiers Saint-Dominique*, 169 (October 1977), 20–49.

36. J.-R. Bouchet, *Le Renouveau charismatique interpellé* (Paris, 1976), pp. 41ff. For the 'ministry of deliverance', he refers to Jules Thobois, 'Possession et exorcisme', *Unité des Chrétiens*, 21 (January 1976), 20–22. A correspondent wrote to me from Canada in 1978: 'In certain charismatic groups, in Quebec at least, what is called "exorcism" is practised without rhyme or reason. Certain people, who claim to have the gift of "discernment", see possessed people everywhere and practise "charismatic" exorcism, which they distinguish from "official" exorcism.'

37. See Donald L. Gelpi, *Charism and Sacrament. A Theology of Christian Conversion* (New York, 1976), pp. 115–121.

38. V. Therrien, *Le discernement, op. cit.* (note 32), pp. 76, 292. Among other texts of Paul, see especially Rom 12:2; Phil 1:9–10; Eph 5:10.

39. The following list includes some of the many books and articles that have been written fairly recently about discernment. This list can be completed by the works mentioned in the following notes in this chapter and by those contained in V. Therrien's bibliographies, most of which relate to the Bible. A. Cholet, 'Discernement des esprits', *DTC*, IV, cols 1380–1384; J. Guillet, G. Bardy, F. Vandenbroucke and J. Pegon, 'Discernement des esprits', *Dictionnaire de spiritualité*, III, cols 1222–1291; J. B. Scaramelli, *Le discernement des esprits* (Fr. tr.; Brussels and Paris, 1910); J. Mouroux, *L'expérience chrétienne. Introduction à une théologie* (Paris, 1954), pp. 173–181 (for John), 345–365; L. Beinaert, 'Discernement et psychisme', *Christus*, 4 (1954), 50–61; Michel Rondet, 'La formation au discernement personnel et communautaire', *Forma Gregis* (1972), 175–261, repr. in *Choix et discernements de la vie religieuse* (Paris, 1974), pp. 95–221, for adaptations in the community life of female religious; J. Gouvernaire, 'Le discernement chez S. Paul', *Vie chrétienne* (Suppl), 195 (Paris, 1976); F. Urbina, 'Movements of Religious Awakening and the Christian Discernment of Spirits', *Concilium* (November 1973), 58–71. The November 1978 number (109) of *Concilium* is entirely devoted to discernment ('Charisms in the Church'). There is a bibliography of American works on the subject in Donald L. Gelpi, *op. cit.* (note 37), p. 96, note 26.

40. See V. Therrien, 'Le discernement spirituel', *op. cit.* (note 32).

41. There is a good chapter on this subject in John C. Haughey, *The Conspiracy of God: the Holy Spirit in Men* (Garden City, N.Y., 1973), pp. 118–154.

42. The Shepherd of Hermas, XI, 43, 8ff. (*SC* 39 (1958), pp. 195ff.).

43. *Hom.* 18 in *L'Evangile au désert* (Paris, 1965), pp. 152ff. These texts by Macarius and Hermas can also be found in *L'Esprit du Seigneur remplit l'univers*, texts chosen by Sr Geneviève (Paris, 1977), pp. 74–78.

44. See J. Clémence, 'Le discernement des esprits dans les Exercices spirituels de S. Ignace de Loyola', *RAM*, 27 (1951), 347–375; 28 (1952), 65–81; J. Laplace, 'L'expérience du discernement dans les Exercices spirituels de S. Ignace', *Christus*, 4 (1954), 399–404; H. Rahner, ' "Werdet kundige Geldwechsler!" Zur Geschichte der Lehre des hl. Ignatius

von der Unterscheidung der Geister', *Greg*, 37 (1956), 444–483; Leo Bakker, *Freiheit und Erfahrung. Redaktionsgeschichtliche Untersuchungen über die Unterscheidung der Geister bei Ignatius von Loyola* (Würzburg, 1970); J. C. Haughey, *op. cit.* (note 41).

45. V. Therrien, 'Le discernement spirituel', *op. cit.* (note 32), 19.
46. M.-D. Chenu, 'Les signes des temps', *NRT*, 87 (1965), 29–39, repr. in *Peuple de Dieu dans le monde* (*Foi vivante*, 35) (Paris, 1966), pp. 35–55; J.-P. Jossua, 'Discerner les signes des temps', *VS*, 114 (1966), 546–569.
47. See G. Haya-Prats, *L'Esprit force de l'Eglise. Sa nature et son activité d'après les Actes des Apôtres* (Paris, 1975), pp. 208ff. Scriptural evidence: Is 61 for the baptism of Jesus; Ps 69 and 109 for the replacement of Judas; Joel 3 for Pentecost, a promise of the gift of the Spirit for the episode of Cornelius. Approval of the *ecclesia* for this last event: Acts 11:1–8; chapter 15.

3

BAPTISM IN THE SPIRIT

Baptism in the Spirit clearly plays an important part not only in the Pentecostal movement, but also in the New Testament.[1] I shall look briefly at the way in which it is interpreted by the Pentecostalists, then go on to consider the New Testament evidence—Paul, Q, John and Luke (Acts)—before returning to the (Catholic) Renewal and its understanding of the reality.

In Pentecostalism[2]

Pentecostals generally insist on a distinction between rebirth and baptism of the Spirit. The second is experienced as a state of being filled with the Holy Spirit as the apostles were on the day of Pentecost. The key document is Acts, and the other texts are read in the light of that document, in such a way that they constitute, as it were, a 'canon within the canon'. There are, however, within this general framework, two or even three different Pentecostal positions.

Following in the tradition of the Holiness Movement, which itself began with Wesley, many Pentecostal Christians believe that there are two stages or aspects in this process: conversion, which leads to rebirth (baptism with water), and sanctification, which is tied to the baptism of the Spirit. Some of these Christians, but not all, believe that speaking in tongues is the necessary sign of baptism of the Spirit. Others—particularly the Assemblies of God— distinguish three aspects: conversion, baptism of the Spirit and sanctification, which lasts throughout life. Finally, some Pentecostals, especially those who belong to the Apostolic Church, also accept the authority of the 'apostles'.

Paul

(a) We are made Christians by the gift which is made to us of the Spirit, who is the Spirit of Jesus (see Rom 8:9, 14ff.; Gal 3:26–27;[3] 4:6; 1 Cor 12:13; Tit 3:5ff.).

(b) This life given by the Spirit is life 'in Christ'. We enter that life through faith (Gal 3:2) which is expressed and consummated by water-baptism and integration into the death and resurrection of Christ (Rom 6:3ff.; 8:1; Col 2:12). This is why there are so many Pauline texts in which the Spirit is

189

said to be given with water-baptism. Paul wanted the Corinthians to aspire to the gifts of the Spirit and especially to the gift of prophecy (1 Cor 14:1), yet these same Corinthians had been baptized with this baptism. Writing to the Corinthian Christians, Paul said:

> But you were washed, you were sanctified, you were justified in the name of the Lord Jesus Christ and the spirit (Spirit) of our God (1 Cor 6:11).

> For by one Spirit we were all baptized into one body (1 Cor 12:13).

> It is God who . . . has commissioned (= anointed) us; he has put his seal upon us and given us his Spirit in our hearts as a guarantee (= earnest-money) (2 Cor 1:21–22).[4]

> As Christ loved the church . . . that he might sanctify her, having cleansed her by the washing of water with the word (Eph 5:26).

> He saved us . . . in virtue of his own mercy, by the washing of regeneration and renewal in the Holy Spirit (Tit 3:5).

Paul describes the process by which we become Christians and members of the Body of Christ, that is, of the eschatological community to which the promise has been made that it will inherit the kingdom.[5] This process includes (a) faith in the name of Jesus (see 1 Cor 6:11; Acts 19:1–6); (b) being plunged into water; this is something to which faith in Jesus' death and resurrection leads. It is God who gives the Spirit (see 2 Cor 1:21; Tit 3:5; 1 Pet 3:21). That is why we can also speak of being plunged in the Spirit (1 Cor 12:13). All this constitutes the process of becoming a Christian. The decisive aspects are, on our part, faith and, on God's part, the gift of the Spirit.

In the second century, attention was above all directed towards the action of the *Church*: the administration of water-baptism as a public and visible act. Irenaeus stressed the unity that existed between water-baptism and the gift of the Spirit. Later there was a tendency to speak about the water being sanctified by the Spirit and about receiving the Spirit *through* the baptism by water, because it was by the Spirit that one became a Christian.[6] In Paul's teaching, these two are combined in the same simple process, although the rite of baptism cannot legitimately be regarded as the instrumental cause of reception of the Spirit. A connection between the Spirit and water has been made not only in poetry, but also in Scripture itself (see Gen 1:3; Is 44:3ff.; Jn 4:10–14; 7:37–39; Rev 22:1, 17; cf. Ezek 19:10ff.; 47; Ps 1:3; 46:5).[7] This connection has exerted a powerful influence on the Christian imagination and has had an effect on the liturgy and the theology of baptism.

The Synoptics and Q

John the Baptist protests and bears witness: 'I have baptized you with water, but he will baptize you with the Holy Spirit'. This is the basic textual reference for the Pentecostal movement.[8] In the gospels, including the fourth gospel, these texts have a particular context: the fact that groups faithful to the Baptist existed on the fringe of the Church (see Acts 19:1–6). It was therefore important to affirm the originality of the baptism that was given in the name of Christ. J.-P. Dietle has pointed out correctly that the noun 'baptism in the Spirit' was not used by New Testament authors, who used the verb 'baptize in the Spirit', always precisely in order to mark the difference between this and the baptism of John, because the verb drew attention to *the one who was baptizing*. This was Jesus, inaugurating, especially from the time of his own anointing as the Messiah and the gift of Pentecost onwards, the eschatological régime of the Spirit. Within this régime, 'baptizing' should not be identified with the rite. It points to the whole of Jesus' activity and to his mission, which was declared when he received John the Baptist's water-baptism, following by anointing by the Spirit, and which inaugurates the messianic era, which is characterized by the gift of the Holy Spirit.

In Mt 3:11 and Lk 3:16, John the Baptist says: 'I baptize you with water for repentance, but he who is coming after me . . . will baptize you in (the) Holy Spirit and fire'. This is a version of a text from the common source of both the first and the third gospels: Q. In it, John the Baptist announces, at the same time as the coming of the Messiah, the eschatological judgement, which is described in Lk 3:17 (the fire burning the chaff). In both the Old and the New Testaments and in Judaism, the last judgement and fire are closely associated.[9] Why, however, is the Spirit or Breath mentioned in Matthew and Luke in connection with the last judgement? Together with E. Schweizer and M.-A. Chevallier, I think that what we have here is a judgement by the breath of the Messiah or the Son of man; these elements are often closely associated.[10] I am also in agreement with M.-A. Chevallier's interpretation that there is a connection between baptism with water and the gift of the Spirit (see below, under *Luke: Acts*).

John

The key text in this gospel is that contained in Jesus' dialogue with Nicodemus: 'Unless one is born of water and the Spirit, he cannot enter the kingdom of God' (3:5). There have been several excellent studies to help us to understand this text.[11] Jesus himself probably did not speak of water in this context, since it would at that time only have made Nicodemus think of the baptism of John the Baptist. It is, of course, true that all the texts contain the words *hudatos kai*, 'of water and', but this only shows that the Church practised Christian baptism and has always understood the text as announcing that baptism with water. What, however, did Jesus say and what therefore is the fundamental teaching contained in this text? We can grasp it if we place the two words in question between brackets and read the text simply as: 'Unless one is born of Spirit'.[12]

191

In any case, even in the text as we have it now, the Spirit is not given as the effect of the water. There are two principles—the Spirit *and* the water—yielding the same, single result, rebirth from above. A long exegetical tradition traces 'being born of the Spirit' back to faith or the practice of the virtues. The whole dialogue with Nicodemus is an instruction with a direct bearing on the real object and the real dimensions of Christian faith. John regards the new birth of the Christian as the effect of faith in Christ and of conversion which is the consequence of faith in the gospel.[13] The text refers to 'Spirit' and not literally to faith, and this is because the author is pointing to the action of God.

There are, then, two supernatural causes—that of the Spirit and that of water-baptism, which the Church practised and still practises. There is a close bond between the two—this was clear to the evangelist, and therefore we, who read his canonical text now, are also conscious of it. John, who was one of the Baptist's disciples (see 1:37ff.), records the words of the Baptist with regard to the one who was greater than he and on whom the Spirit descended and remained as the one 'who baptizes with the Holy Spirit' (1:32, 33; cf. 3:34).

In the course of the dialogue with Nicodemus, John tells us that Jesus also baptized with water (3:22, 26),[14] or rather, that his disciples baptized (4:2). The Jesus who baptizes with water (and who was followed by the Church baptizing with water) is the same Jesus who enables man to be born from above by faith in his name (3:15–18) and baptizes in the Spirit. The fourth evangelist was anxious to make a connection between what was practised in the Church and what was said and done during Jesus' ministry on earth. It is clear that the evangelist was thinking, in 3:5, of Christian baptism, which is a baptism both of water and of Spirit. This does not mean that the rite and the water are the instrumental cause of the gift of the Spirit. This may be a theological interpretation, for which there are good arguments in the Church's tradition.[15] The text does not say this: the *kai*, 'and', points, as it does in Tit 3:5, for example, to two associated and combined causes that is all. But baptism of Spirit and baptism of water are not two distinctly separate realities.

Luke: Acts[16]

We will first look at the Lucan texts and then, after reaching a fairly general conclusion, consider the use to which Pentecostal Christians put these texts.

> They were cut to the heart and said to Peter and the rest of the apostles, 'Brethren, what shall we do?' And Peter said to them, 'Repent and be baptized every one of you in the name of Jesus Christ for the forgiveness of your sins; and you shall receive the gift of the Holy Spirit. For the promise is to you and to your children and to all who are far off, every one whom the Lord our God calls to him' (2:37–39).

This basic text is of the first importance for our understanding of Luke's theology of the gift of the Spirit. It proclaims the extension of that gift beyond Jerusalem, according to the plan of the book itself, which is concerned with the promise (1:8). According to the author of the Acts of the Apostles, a kind of Pentecost was to take place in Jerusalem (4:31), in Samaria (8:14–17) and among the gentiles (10:44–47; 15:1–7). In this first sermon, the essential elements follow in this sequence: conversion, baptism in the name of Jesus, that is, by accepting his power as Lord and saviour,[17] and the gift of the Spirit. This is reminiscent of 1 Cor 6:11, which we considered above.

The Samaritans (8:5–25) would seem to have been a special case. Philip's preaching is more 'prophetic' and 'wild' than 'apostolic' and there is also the question of the magician, Simon. The Samaritans 'believed Philip as he preached good news about the kingdom of God and the name of Jesus Christ' and they were baptized. They did not, however, receive the Spirit. To receive the Spirit, they had to have the Pentecost of Jerusalem. This was brought to them by Peter and John, who laid hands on them. It is not said whether they began to speak in tongues.[18] J. D. G. Dunn's interpretation does not strike me as acceptable. He thinks that the Samaritans and Simon (who, according to Dunn, had a very high standing among the Samaritans) did not, to begin with, have real faith in Christ; they rather believed in Philip because he worked miracles. I would also not agree with Walter Hollenweger, who believes that it is possible to be a Christian without having received the Holy Spirit. Two aspects of the case of the Samaritans are particularly striking. In the first place, it is marginal and uncertain. In the second place, the two leading apostles who came from Jerusalem to lay hands on them made them fully members of the eschatological people that had emerged out of Pentecost by means of a kind of *sanatio*.[19]

The case of Cornelius and the first gentile converts is another 'blow' struck by God in which Peter has once again to intervene (see 10:1–11:18). The connection between the word, faith, conversion, baptism, the gift of the Spirit and even, as at Pentecost, speaking in tongues is quite clear, but the initiative is taken entirely by the Holy Spirit, because it was necessary to open a door that God had until then kept closed. The Holy Spirit 'fell on' the group of gentiles gathered in Cornelius' house even before Peter had finished speaking and the gifts of the Spirit preceded their baptism, which was nevertheless required for them to be made members of the Church. This splendid story has, of course, become very well known and it is particular popular among Pentecostal Christians, partly because it seems to them to make a distinction between the baptism of the Spirit and that of water.

Very much the same applies to the case of the disciples who had been imperfectly instructed by Apollos and whom Paul found at Ephesus. They had only received John's baptism. Paul baptized them 'in the name of the Lord Jesus' and then 'when he had laid his hands on them, the Holy Spirit

193

came on them and they spoke with tongues and prophesied' (19:5–6). It would be as wrong to generalize on the basis of this single case and dissociate baptism of the Spirit from water-baptism as it would be to see in this case, and in that of the Samaritans, our sacrament of confirmation.[20] The important aspect of the story is the bond between the gift of the Spirit and the 'name of the Lord Jesus' professed at baptism. The issue is important, because it shows that pneumatology cannot be separated from Christology and soteriology.

I should like to conclude by referring to the view of J. D. G. Dunn, who is followed, with a rather important change of emphasis, by M.-A. Chevallier. We are made Christians by faith in Jesus as our saviour and by the gift of the Spirit. The Spirit is given to faith, but that faith is professed at baptism and consecrated by baptism. We do not baptize ourselves—baptism presupposes the intervention of a Christian who already belongs to the Church, and it is an act by which we become members of that Church, the Body of Christ, to which the Spirit is promised and given. Because we receive the Spirit together with our baptism with water which consecrates the confession of faith, baptism, which is the 'sacrament of faith', is also the sacrament of the gift of the Spirit.[21] 'Confirmation', as we shall see in Volume III, is only a completion of this. Dunn, however, insists on the fact that the Spirit is given *in response to faith*, to the extent that, even though he recognizes that, in Acts, faith and baptism are generally closely connected[22] and thus that baptism is normally followed by the gift of the Spirit, he maintains that 'baptism in the name of the Lord Jesus expresses commitment to Jesus as Lord, [but] the water-baptism itself does not effect entrance into the new age and Christian experience but only points forward and leads up to the messianic baptism in Spirit which alone effects that entrance' (*op. cit.* (note 1 below), p. 99). He also goes on to say: 'The view which regards [Acts] 2:38 as proof that water-baptism is the vehicle of the Spirit is one which has no foundation except in the theology of later centuries' (*ibid.*, p. 100). Kittel (see note 1 below) was even more radical in his criticism of the ecclesiastical (Lutheran) theology of baptism and concluded that, according to the New Testament, baptism was not substantially different from John's baptism of repentance!

Dunn regards the sacrament of baptism simply as a rite. In reality, however, baptism is a reality which includes conversion, the Church, an action carried out by God (by Christ through his Spirit) and a rite which refers back to the baptism of Jesus himself, all in one organic whole (see note 21 below). Many exegetes, however, have been more positive than Dunn.[23] M.-A. Chevallier, for example, has said:

Access to the eschatological reality that is represented by the breath (the Spirit) is obtained by 'conversion' to the gospel and this conversion is signified by baptism with water. The only way by which we can come to the messianic baptism of the breath is by the baptism of conversion. Luke's parallel between the outpouring at Pentecost and Jesus' baptism is also a way of establishing and emphasizing this connection between a water-baptism to be given henceforth 'in the name of Jesus' and the gift of the breath. Jesus' baptism, which is a baptism both in water and in the breath, joins together the two periods of the history of salvation that are combined in the time before the end (*op. cit.* (note 1 below), p. 198; cf. p. 207).

I am bound, together with other authors who are favourably disposed towards the charisms, to add at this point a critical reference to the use made by Pentecostals generally of the Acts of the Apostles.[24] This book is often employed by them as a 'canon within the canon', as we have already observed. (The comment was first made by Piet Schoonenberg.) In other words, it is used as a norm against which to measure the normative texts of Scripture. The texts dealing with glossolalia are above all singled out. But, apart from Pentecost itself, which is still subject to dispute, what in fact happened? Was it xenoglossia rather than glossolalia? There are only two examples in Acts: 10:46 and 19:6, the case of Cornelius at Caesarea and that of the disciples of John the Baptist at Ephesus respectively. Both of these are, so to speak, mini-Pentecosts in accordance with the plan for expansion which forms the basic structure of Luke's story. As M.-A. Chevallier has pointed out, however:

It is clearly a mistake to think that it is possible, on the basis of these data, to construct a theory that the gift of the breath is always manifested in glossolalia. This illusion has perhaps come about because, apart from rehearsing over and over again the model of the pouring out of Pentecost, Luke generally does not describe the first communication of the breath. He is usually satisfied with a reference to conversion, faith and the growth of the Church. When he mentions baptism, he often says nothing about the communication of the divine breath which, he believes, accompanies baptism. This is so in the case of the three thousand converts at Pentecost (2:41), the Ethiopian eunuch (8:38), Lydia and her household (16:15), Philip's jailer (16:33) and the group of Corinthians (18:8). He says nothing of the gift of the breath in these cases, and so he does not mention speaking in tongues. In one case, in which he mentions the gift of the breath, that of the baptism of Paul, there is no question of speaking in tongues (9:17ff.). All things considered, it would seem that, far from having thought of glossolalia as a usual sign of the communication of the breath, Luke believed that normally nothing especially remarkable happened when the breath was first communicated at baptism.[25]

It is clear that Luke was particularly interested in the Holy Spirit. At a time when it may perhaps no longer have followed as a simple matter of course that a Christian would be a missionary, he systematically developed that aspect of faith and he did so in connection with the action and interventions of the Spirit. It was on this basis that he compiled his history of the apostles, in which he made full use of visible and tangible manifestations. Sometimes he simplified things and used material representations, as in his account of the resurrection, his story of the early Church and the sudden 'fall' of the Spirit. He worked with great genius and clearly had great religious feeling. It was, however, Paul rather than Luke who provided the primary testimony and the fundamental theology.

The testimony and the interpretation of the Renewal with regard to the Baptism of the Spirit

What is involved here? Men and women are longing for the fullness of the Spirit to come into their lives and dwell and act in them. They may have read about this indwelling and activity of the Spirit and about lives that have been changed and made joyful by it and have wanted the same experience themselves. Or they may have been drawn in by a friend or have been to a meeting to see for themselves. They may at first have hesitated. They may even have been full of doubts and have resisted for a long time. Eventually, however, they have asked for hands to be laid on them and prayers to be said over them.

There is usually a certain preparation and instruction together with prayer. When the moment has arrived, several members of the group pray over the 'candidate' and lay their hands on his head or shoulders. Although the brethren, the community are mediating, it is only God who is acting. Sometimes nothing may seem to be happening to the 'candidate'. At other times an experience of peace and joy and a deep feeling for prayer ensues in a few days. At yet other times, he is invaded by the power of God, who seizes hold of his whole being—his heart, his mind and his feelings. He is perhaps conscious of a gentle inner pressure which makes tears flow. A desire to give thanks rises from his heart to his lips, and this may be expressed as praying in tongues. The Spirit is making himself manifest. His coming is powerfully experienced. We have only to read the testimonies of some of the men and women who have received the Spirit in this way:

'I was invaded by a new power of love.'

'Before, I was on the bank of a river. Now I am in it.'

'At the time nothing of which I was aware happened. I got up. I felt a bit put out. But very quickly I found inner peace and was quite sure that I had received the gift of God himself. During the time that followed, I experienced a deep certainty of faith, rather like Mary after she had been visited by the angel. It was as if I had discovered for myself the depths of my own heart, the spiritual centre of my being where God dwells. This intimate presence was like an intense but gentle fire' (*VS* (January-February 1974), 125, 126).

'A new life, I felt, was beginning for me. It consisted above all of an intense consciousness of the presence of God, but also of a new kind of prayer. At times I could hardly bear to tear myself away from that prayer. I found myself living in a climate of great trust and joy' (*ibid.*, p. 127).

'We are drawn along by the Spirit in the wake of Christ. The pouring out of the Spirit has handed us over to him. I am no longer afraid' (*ibid.*, p. 109).

'My heart was set free.'

'The whole of my being was tingling.'

'I have now begun to see more and more a vision of what life in the Spirit is like. It is truly a life of miracles, of waiting on God for his guidance and teaching, of relying on the power of the Spirit to radically change the lives of men and of being filled over and over with the creative, life-giving love of the Spirit of God' (K. and D. Ranaghan, *op. cit.* (note 29 below), p. 65).

There is a summary of the testimony of some of those who have had this experience in the Malines document:

> . . . a perception of concrete presence. This sense of concrete, factual presence is the perception of the nearness of Jesus as Lord, the realization at the personal level that Jesus is real and is a person. . . . With great frequency this sense of presence is accompanied with an awareness of power, more specifically, the power of the Holy Spirit. . . . This power is experienced in direct relation to mission. It is a power manifesting itself in a courageous faith animated by a new love which enables one to undertake and accomplish great things beyond one's natural capabilities for the kingdom of God. Another characteristic response to presence and power is an intensification of the whole prayer life, with a special love for the prayer of praise. . . . The experience has a resurrection quality about it that is joyous and triumphant. . . . The experience of the Spirit is also the experience of the cross (cf. 2 Cor 4:10). It expresses itself in a continuing *metanoia.* . . .[26]

In a very impressive testimony, a priest made the following extremely interesting suggestion:

> The Bible speaks of two actions of the Holy Spirit: the Spirit who acts 'in' (*pneuma en* in the Septuagint) and the Spirit who acts 'on' (*pneuma epi*). This distinction can be found above all in a prophetic book such as Ezekiel: The 'Spirit in' comes to cleanse (Ezek 36:25–27) and to give life (37:5–10). The 'Spirit on' seizes hold of someone for a mission, often a prophetic mission, and his coming is accompanied by visible signs. . . . The 'Spirit in' who cleanses and gives life accounts for the action of the Spirit in the initial acts of Christian life (baptism, to which must be added confirmation in the Catholic Church) and in sanctifying the believer throughout his life. The 'Spirit on', on the other hand, accounts for the sudden and visible action of the Spirit who seizes hold of someone for a special mission; Luke calls this 'baptism in the Spirit'.[27]

What is the value of this suggestion in terms of exegesis?[28] Theologically, it is interesting and even contains an element of truth. The members of the Catholic Renewal, however, interpret the term 'baptism in the Spirit' perhaps a little too facilely. Sometimes the terms is used but its content is explained—after all, the monastic life used to be interpreted as a second baptism, and Simon Tugwell has observed (see below, note 1) that it was so called because it was (ideally at least!) a way of experiencing baptism more radically and more fruitfully. At other times—fortunately—the term 'baptism in the Spirit' is avoided and other expressions are used instead: 'pouring out or outpouring of the Spirit' or 'renewal in the Holy Spirit', as the Ranaghans would seem to prefer. Whatever the case may be, it is not disputed that there is only one 'baptism' and that this baptism, given and received in faith, in the name of Jesus, communicated the Spirit. What, then, is involved here? The Ranaghans have provided a clear answer to this question:

> 'Baptism in the Holy Spirit' is not something replacing baptism and confirmation. Rather it may be seen as an adult re-affirmation and renewal of these sacraments. an opening of ourselves to all their sacramental graces. The gesture of 'laying on of hands' which often accompanies 'baptism in the Holy Spirit' is not a new sacramental rite. It is a fraternal gesture of love and concern, a visible sign of human corporeality (K. and D. Ranaghan, *op. cit.*, p. 20).[29]

> What this new pentecostal movement seeks to do through faithful prayer and by trusting in the Word of God is to ask the Lord to actualize in a concrete living way what the Christian people have already received (*ibid.*, p. 141).

> Prayer for baptism in the Holy Spirit is, most simply, a prayer in expectant faith that an individual's or community's baptismal initiation be existentially renewed and actualized (*ibid.*, p. 147).[30]

The theology of the 'divine missions' that I have discussed earlier in this work enables us to situate this new coming of the Spirit theologically,[31] assuming, of course, that the Spirit does in fact come. It is, however, difficult to doubt this when his presence is so clearly revealed by his fruits.[32]

NOTES

1. The following is a selective bibliography of works on baptism in the Spirit: G. Kittel, 'Die Wirkungen der christlichen Wassertaufe nach dem Neuen Testament', *Theologische Studien und Kritiken*, 87 (1914), 25–53; P. van Imschoot, 'Baptême d'eau et baptême d'Esprit', *ETL*, 13 (1936), 653–666; S. Tugwell, 'Reflections on the Pentecostal Doctrine of "Baptism in the Holy Spirit" ', *The Heythrop Journal*, 13 (1972), 268–281, 402–414; J. D. G. Dunn, *Baptism in the Holy Spirit* (London, 1970; 2nd ed. 1977); P. Schoonenberg, 'Le Baptême d'Esprit Saint', *L'expérience de l'Esprit. Mélanges Schillebeeckx* (*Le Point théologique*, 18) (Paris, 1976), pp. 7–96; R. Schwager, 'Wassertaufe, ein Gebet um die Geisttaufe?', *ZKT*, 100 (1978), 36–61, which I found rather disappointing; M.-A. Chevallier, *Souffle de Dieu. Le Saint-Esprit dans le Nouveau Testament*, I: *Ancien Testament. Hellénisme et Judaïsme. La tradition synoptique. L'œuvre de Luc* (*Le Point théologique*, 26) (Paris, 1978). I have not been able to obtain F. D. Bruner, *A Theology of the Holy Spirit. A Pentecostal Experience and the New Testament Witness* (Grand Rapids, 1970), who seems to have dealt especially with baptism in the Spirit.
2. W. Hollenweger, *The Pentecostals* (London, 1972; Minneapolis, 1972, 2nd ed. 1973), pp. 323–341.
3. See H. J. Venetz, ' "Christus anziehen" ', *Freiburger Zeitschrift für Philosophie und Theologie*, 20 (1973), 3–36.

4. This is, according to G. W. H. Lampe, *The Seal of the Spirit*, 2nd ed. (London, 1967), p. 4, baptism in the Spirit.

5. Apart from J. D. G. Dunn, *op. cit.* (note 1), who studies the texts one after the other, with the intention of excluding both a Pentecostal and a 'sacramentalist' interpretation, see J. K. Parratt, 'The Holy Spirit and Baptism. II: The Pauline Evidence', *The Expository Times*, 82 (1971), 266–271.

6. Irenaeus, *Adv. haer.* III, 17, 2 (*SC* 211, p. 332); V, 11, 2 (*SC* 153, p. 138); *Dem.* 41 (*SC* 62, p. 96); see also A. Benoît, *Le baptême chrétien au second siècle. La théologie des Pères* (Paris, 1953), pp. 205–208. Tertullian speaks of sanctification of the water by the Spirit (*De bapt*. IV, 1) and then says: 'non quod in aquis Spiritum sanctum consequamur sed in aqua emundati sub angelo, Spiritui sancto praeparamur': see *De bapt*. IV, 1 and R. F. Refoulé's note in *SC* 35, p. 75, note 1. The water designates baptism and the Spirit (Jn 4:10): see F. M. Braun, *Jean le théologien*, III: *Sa théologie*, 2: *Le Christ, notre Seigneur hier, aujourd'hui, toujours* (Paris, 1972), pp. 139–164.

7. For water as the symbol of the Spirit, see *Dictionnaire de Spiritualité*, VI, cols 13–19. For poetry, see especially Paul Claudel.

8. See Mk 1:8; Jn 1:33; Acts 1:5; 11:16. The statement can be regarded as authentic: see M. Isaacs, *The Concept of Spirit* (London, 1976), pp. 114–115. There is no article in any of the texts; it is only found in Jn 1:32, in the context of Jesus' baptism. J.-P. Dietle's comments will be found in his article, 'Le réveil pentecôtiste dans les Eglises historiques', *Positions luthériennes* (October 1974), 223–287, especially 250.

9. See E. Schweizer, '*pneuma*', *TDNT*, VI, p. 398, note 417. This theme has been preserved in the liturgy: 'qui venturus es iudicare mundum per ignem'. See also Georges de la Vierge, 'Le signe du feu dans la Bible', *Carmel* (1960), 161–171.

10. E. Schweizer, '*pneuma*', *TDNT*, VI, p. 399; M.-A. Chevallier, *op. cit.* (note 1), pp. 99–108, who suggests that the statement should be seen at three levels: what the Baptist in fact said, what the Christian community understood and what the editor or editors of the present text believed.

11. I. de la Potterie, ' "Naître de l'eau et naître de l'Esprit". Le texte baptismal de Jn 3, 5', *Sciences ecclésiastiques*, 14 (1962), 417–443, repr. in *La vie selon l'Esprit, condition du chrétien* (*Unam Sanctam*, 55) (Paris, 1965), pp. 31–63; F. Porsch, *Wort und Pneuma. Ein exegetischer Beitrag zur Pneumatologie des Johannesevangeliums* (Frankfurt, 1974), pp. 90, 98ff., 125ff.

12. This has been accepted not only by de la Potterie and Porsch, but also by F. M. Braun, who has quoted a number of other authors: see *RSPT*, 40 (1956), 15ff.; *NRT*, 86 (1964), 1032, note 21; 'Le Baptême d'après le IVe évangile', *RThom*, 48 (1948), 358–368.

13. Faith: Jn 1:13; 1 Jn 3:9; 5:1. Conversion: Mk 1:15; Mt 18:3 par. (becoming a child: being born).

14. For this datum and its importance in the interpretation of Jn 3:5, see C. H. Dodd, *The Interpretation of the Fourth Gospel*, 5th ed. (Cambridge, 1960), pp. 308–311; X. Léon-Dufour, ' "Et là Jésus baptisait" (Jn 3, 22)', *Mélanges E. Tisserant*, I (*Studi e Testi*, 231) (Rome, 1964), pp. 295–309; F. Porsch, *op. cit.* (note 11), pp. 50, 125–130.

15. References in I. de la Potterie, *op. cit.* (note 11), p. 33.

16. See E. Schweizer, '*pneuma*', *TDNT*, VI, pp. 413–415; J. D. G. Dunn, *op. cit.* (note 1), chapter 9 (1977 edition, from which I quote), pp. 90–102; M.-A. Chevallier, *op. cit.* (note 1), pp. 195ff.; G. Haya-Prats, *L'Esprit force de L'Eglise* (*Lectio divina*, 81) (Paris, 1975), pp. 130–138, notes pp. 267ff.

17. Further on in Acts, in 19:5, the text: 'in the name of the Lord Jesus' is found. A whole movement of faith is expressed here. See the notes in the Jerusalem Bible on Acts 2:38 and in the French *Traduction œcuménique* on Acts 2:38; 3:16; 4:12.

18. It is also not said that there was speaking in tongues when Paul was baptized, although that baptism was accompanied by the gift of the Spirit (see Acts 9:17, 18).

19. In Acts, the term *prostithēmi*, to be added, joined to, to increase, should be noted (see

199

2:41, 47; 5:14; 11:24). The Church is apostolic and is therefore only an extension of what began in Jerusalem at Pentecost (see Lk 24:47).

20. M.-A. Chevallier, *op. cit.* (note 1), 202: 'In addition to the Pentecost of the Jews in Acts 2 and that of the gentiles in Acts 10, Luke wanted to show how two special groups, the Samaritans and the disciples of John the Baptist, were able to benefit from the same eschatological outpouring and enter the one people of God. It is therefore possible to speak, by extension, of the Pentecost of the Samaritans and of that of the disciples of John, insofar as these episodes were turning-points of great importance in the missionary spread of the Church. It would go against a true exegetical interpretation of these texts to regard them as examples that could be generalized.'

21. A vitally important sequence is present here: *fides*, faith, designates simultaneously the act of faith on the part of the believer, the creed, and baptism, in which that faith is professed; this latter is traditionally the sacrament of faith: see my *Tradition and Traditions* (Eng. tr.; London and New York, 1966), Part Two, pp. 243–249, text and notes.

22. Referring to Acts 2:38, 42; 8:12ff.; 8:37 (D); 16:14ff.; 16:31–33; 18:8, Dunn adds (*op. cit.*, p. 96): 'In the case of the Ephesians [Acts 19], the sequence of Paul's questions indicates that *pisteusai* [to believe] and *baptisthēnai* [to be baptized] are interchangeable ways of describing the act of faith'.

23. Dunn mentions a great many, whose work is held in high esteem: *op. cit.* (note 1), p. 98, note 17. Haya-Prats also names several exegetes: *op. cit.* (note 16), p. 268, note 40. To these, I would add O. Cullmann: 'There is no Christian baptism without the gift of the Spirit': *Le baptême des enfants et la doctrine biblique du baptême* (Neuchâtel and Paris, 1948), p. 35; E. Trocmé: 'According to Luke, the Holy Spirit is given to everyone who receives baptism in the name of Jesus Christ and who thus becomes a member of the Church': *L'Esprit Saint et l'Eglise. L'avenir de l'Eglise et l'Œcuménisme* (Paris, 1969), p. 25.

24. W. Hollenweger, *op. cit.* (note 2), pp. 336ff.; J. D. G. Dunn, *Jesus and the Spirit* (Philadelphia, 1975), pp. 121, 191; M.-A. Chevallier, *op. cit.*, p. 209.

25. M.-A. Chevallier, *op. cit.* (note 1), pp. 213–214; see also H. Küng, *The Church* (London, 1967), pp. 164–165. The Pentecostals could have concluded that water-baptism calls for another 'baptism', that of the Spirit, but this would, of course, separate the Spirit from the baptism given in faith in the name of Jesus Christ and, as we have seen, there is no question of this at least in the New Testament. Simply as an exegete, Dunn is very critical of the Pentecostals. Hollenweger, *op. cit.*, p. 341, quotes a profession of faith used by the German Pentecostal Mülheim Association: 'The attempt to present the baptism of the Spirit as the second spiritual experience, to be fundamentally distinguished from regeneration, has no basis in Scripture'.

26. *Theological and Pastoral Orientations on the Catholic Charismatic Renewal* (Eng. tr. of Malines document; Notre Dame, Indiana, 1974), p. 22.

27. René Jacob, *Unité des chrétiens*, 21 (January 1976), 16. See also L. Fabre, *Lumière et Vie*, 125 (November-December 1975), 12.

28. Lk 3:16; Acts 11:16 have *en*; Gal 4:6 has *eis*; Acts 1:8; 2:3, 17; 8:16, 17; 10:44ff.; 11:15ff.; 19:6 have *epi*. In Acts 8:16; 10:44, the verb *epipiptō*, 'to fall on', occurs; in 19:6, the verb *ēlthe*, 'came' is used.

29. See also E. O'Connor, *The Pentecostal Movement in the Catholic Church* (Notre Dame, Indiana, 1971), pp. 117, 131ff., especially 136, 215–218. I believe that there is even more than this in the laying on of hands—it expresses a desire to communicate, at God's pleasure, a gift that has been received from him. For brotherly mediation, see K. and D. Ranaghan, *Catholic Pentecostals* (New York, 1969), pp. 148ff.

30. The same interpretation will also be found in H. Caffarel, *Faut-il parler d'un Pentecôtisme catholique?* (Paris, 1973), pp. 21ff., 53–58; J.-M. Garrigues, 'L'effusion de l'Esprit', *VS* (January 1974), 73ff.; F. A. Sullivan, 'Baptism in the Spirit: A Catholic Interpretation of the Pentecostal Experience', *Greg*, 55 (1974), 49–68; Cardinal L. J. Suenens, *A New Pentecost* (London, 1975), pp. 83ff.

31. A.-M. de Monléon, *Istina* (1976), 347, note 19, correctly cites Thomas Aquinas in this context: 'An invisible mission takes place in accordance with a growth in virtue or an increase in grace. . . . Still an invisible mission in accordance with the increase of grace is taken to occur in a special way in one who goes on to a new action or a new state of grace, as, for example, when he is raised to the grace of miracles or prophecy or when he reaches the point when he can, by the fervour of charity, expose himself to martyrdom, give up all his possessions or undertake some very difficult work' (*ST* Ia, q. 43, a. 6, ad 2).
32. E. O'Connor, *op. cit.* (note 29), devotes chapter 6, pp. 141–175, to 'The Effects of the Movement'. This chapter is subdivided into the following sections: Knowledge of God, Prayer, Love of Scripture, Transformation and Deepening, Deliverance, Physical Healings, Peace and Joy, Attitudes towards the Institutional Church, No Instant Sanctity and Durability of Effects.

4

THE RENEWAL AND ECUMENISM

The Renewal and the ecumenical movement were clearly meant to come together—not only because the same Spirit gives them to us as two ways of achieving what he wants to do with us, but also because the Renewal is in contact with and has even absorbed some of the elements of Pentecostalism (if only through reading books) and, in shared meetings, Catholics have prayed with Protestants. The leaders of the Renewal have also thought a great deal about this question. I would like to present and discuss some of these reflections and proposals of various kinds that have been made at different levels.

(1) Paul VI gave Léon Joseph Suenens the task of following the progress of the charismatic Renewal, and the Cardinal participated personally in the movement, exercising his special function of *episkopē*, concern or supervision. The result was the valuable 'Malines document', which appeared in 1974. A second publication, in 1978, was a kind of directory, consisting of eight chapters and 85 paragraphs, so that it would be easier for group study.[1] The Cardinal sees ecumenism and the Renewal as two movements brought about by the Holy Spirit, both directed towards the same end, which is the unity of the disciples of Jesus Christ on the basis of one faith and personal self-giving. On the one hand, we recognize that the Holy Spirit is at work in 'others' and in other Christian communities,[2] while, on the other, ecumenism fundamentally calls for conversion and what the Second Vatican Council called a spiritual ecumenism, using the words first employed by Paul Couturier. As Cardinal Willebrands said at the Renewal Congress held at Rome at Pentecost 1975, 'We need ecumenical activities in all sectors—contacts, dialogues and collaboration—based on the spiritual source which is conversion, holiness of life and public and private prayer'. Cardinal Suenens therefore aimed to give practical guidelines so that Catholic members of the Renewal might experience it as Catholic. He outlined all the necessary precautions and stressed that the Church and the functional charism of the bishops were the guarantee that there would be no deviation in the spread and use of the gifts of the Spirit:

> It would be wrong to succumb to a euphoric state of ecumenism and, in the warmth of newly discovered brotherhood, forget the doctrinal problems that have not yet been solved—the definition of the place and the significance of the sacramental structures and the part played by man in those structures when we speak of the

activity of the Spirit; talk of faith without defining what it contains and means; failure to define a common faith in the Eucharist and the function of the one who presides at the Lord's Supper . . . (cf. *op. cit.* (note 1 below), p. 45).

(2) The following directives were, at the suggestion of Heribert Mühlen,[3] adopted in the course of the third European Charismatic Leaders Conference, held at Craheim Castle, near Schweinfurt, in June 1975:

'There are varieties of gifts, but the same Spirit' (1 Cor 12:4). This also applies to the Churches, which are now separated because of man's fault.

1. *Finding (evaluating) oneself*
Each Church has its own established spiritual tradition and not all the gifts of grace are completely realized in each one. Each Church should therefore ask itself what inalienable vocation it has preserved from its historical origin.

2. *Openness*
Each Church should be capable of recognizing with gratitude the gifts of grace of the other Churches and of being enriched by them. Each Church will then be able to ask itself whether it has not made its own gifts of grace absolute, and to what extent it has a responsibility for the present division in the one Church of Christ. Charismatic openness to all the gifts of the Holy Spirit may in this way make the future of the Church fruitful.

3. *Welcome*
Each Church must, on the basis of its own inalienable vocation, ask itself what it can accept of what is offered by the other Churches, and it must do this by evaluating it critically, if necessary. This receptive attitude must be taken to the very limits of what is possible, since all the gifts of grace are there 'for the common good' (1 Cor 12:7).

We pray to the Lord of the Church that the dialogue between the Churches will lead to convergence and agreement. We know that this can be reached, not by human effort or even by good will, but only by an intervention by Christ who will come again (Mk 10:27; Phil 1:6).

It is not for the author of *Chrétiens désunis* to dispute that this programme is, in what it says at least, essentially in accordance with ecumenism. What it says, moreover, is no different in fact from what is already happening. Ecclesiological questions, however, have to be asked about what the text of this statement does not say. It speaks as though there were no ecclesiological truth, as though a Church of the Spirit began with 1 Cor 12. An ecclesiology, or rather a plurality of ecclesiologies, is, however, implied in the words 'what inalienable vocation it has preserved from its historical origin'. This should certainly be lived critically, since history has undoubtedly burdened the inalienable inheritance with much that is very relative, and at times with what is open to question. Ecumenical theologians are bound to undertake, on the basis of an authentic understanding of history and in dialogue with others, a very radical examination of these forms that have developed in the course of history and have, at certain times, played a very important part in dividing Christianity. This critical examination does in fact yield an ecclesiological core of great importance. Is it really possible to apply the theme of the diversity of gifts of the 'Churches', as though a Church that was indeed universal were composed of the divided Churches, in the way that a community of Christians is composed of people who all have their own gifts and who come together to build up the community by serving it in their own way? It has to be recognized that the Craheim document did not have the task of providing the theological foundations of ecumenism, but we should be clear about what is at stake even in the most generous of approaches.

It is therefore worth trying to elaborate this question of the application of the theme of the charisms to the Churches both positively and critically. Cullmann tried to do it, but limited himself to Catholicism and Protestant-ism.[4] Following the ideas that he had already developed on the structures of the history of salvation, he suggested that the harmony of the gospel keeps two forces or tendencies—concentration and universalism—in a state of balance. The grace of the Catholic Church is that it is in search of universal-ism, although there is always a danger of syncretism in the Church's open-ness to the world and its tendency to lose the purity of concentration on Christ. The charism of the Reformation, on the other hand, has been to reaffirm insistently the demands made by this concentration on the Bible, Christ and justification by faith alone.

> The spiritual *charism* of ideal Catholicism is its universal radiation and its ability to surround the gospel with external forms which can preserve it from disintegration. On the other hand, the special *danger* of Catholicism is to be found both in syncretistic identification with the world and in a juridical narrowing down at the doctrinal and institutional level.
>
> The classical *charism* of Protestantism is its concentration on one centre of radiation and the value that it places on the freedom of the Spirit. The *danger* of Protestantism is to be found, on the one hand, in a hardening and isolation of that central doctrine and, on the other, in a subjectivism without limits which has often led modern Protestantism to undermine the central foundation of Christianity and to accept in a way that is much too wide purely temporal norms that can only be partly assimilated.
>
> The ecumenical task should not be a hurried merging of the Churches, but a confronting of each Church with the duty to become fully conscious of its own charismatic character and then to purify that character and take it to a deeper level. This process of purification will inevitably go against any tendency to be exclusive. The encounter will then take place, not on the periphery, but at the centre—the ideal universalism of Catholicism must be concentrated on the central truth of the gospel and the ideal concentration of Protestantism must therefore become radiation.
>
> Each Church must live in a state of co-existence and close and peaceful collab-oration with the other. At the same time, it must deepen and purify its own special charism in such a way that it feels itself obliged to recognize the other's charism, but that it also regards the distortion of the other Church's charism as a serious warning.

204

(3) Jean-Miguel Garrigues has approached the question from within the Renewal.[5] He expresses, perhaps not a criticism, but at least a certain dissatisfaction with the theological agreements that have been reached, especially those of the mixed commissions and even more those of 'Faith and Order'. They are, he believes, intellectual conclusions which were not based on a community of prayer and express too little hope of a gift of God that moves towards fullness. Although it is doubtful whether this criticism can really be applied to the work of the Dombes group in France, it certainly pinpoints a very real question. The Renewal is a way of experiencing the same mystery of Christ that is experienced at the same time by other Christians and of experiencing it with the brethren, while receiving from it the substance of a living tradition. Many other elements, which are nevertheless connected with the authentic substance of the experience of the same mystery, have been included within this experience, and these have to be purified and so subjected to criticism. What has above all to be done is to take what is valuable in this experience to a deeper level. It is clearly sinful to accuse the other by considering only his purely human aspect and thus failing to be aware of his experience of the fullness towards which we all ought to be moving.

An echo of an experience that is, at its own level and in its more positive aspect, quite beyond dispute can be clearly heard in this approach to the question. As Mgr Pézeril has pointed out, 'God can surely have no stronger way of repudiating our disunity than by this grace, which is poured out on all of us by his Spirit and by which we invoke him, love him, sing his praises and lose ourselves in him'[6] and, I would add, by which we do all this together. Confronted with this experience, a responsible theologian who is speaking in the name of the truth that he is trying to serve nevertheless feels constrained to ask a number of questions. He feels, intervening in this way, rather like a lexicographer in the presence of an inspired poet. But what is he to do if grammar and dictionaries are his profession?

(4) Several Christians who have shared this experience have spoken of the danger of being overcome by the language and therefore by the theology of Pentecostalism.[7] The stories published by the movement were widely read and have in this way exerted a strong influence on the Catholic Renewal, although it is true, as the Ranaghans have observed, that Pentecostalism played hardly any part at all in the origins and early development of the Catholic Renewal. Whether the Renewal shares directly in this way with other Christians or not, however, its fundamental experience of the Spirit is certainly not in itself tied to the forms of the Catholic Church. On the contrary, to use an image that has been suggested, the Renewal covers all the different lakes of the divided Churches with an immense expanse of water that is common to all and is filled by the irresistible rain of the Spirit.[8]

For many members of the Renewal whom I know, there is no special problem—the Church is where they experience the Spirit. This fact is part of a much wider framework: a unity among Christians—or rather, a unity of Christians without any corresponding unity of the Churches—is happening just about everywhere. This is because the level at which the unity of the Renewal exists and the type of unity to which the Renewal points are different from those of the unity sought by ecumenism. The Renewal claims to have gone beyond the latter and in fact speaks of 'post-ecumenism'. But, like the so-called 'secular post-ecumenism', the post-ecumenism of the Renewal has not been able to overcome the problems of Church unity except by simply ignoring them and going either above or around them. I readily accept that this contains a positive aspect at the providential level of reintegration in unity, but I would hasten to add that what is needed is not only spiritual, but also visible unity. It is not possible to give a kind of autonomy to the pneumatological element without at the same time being concerned with the implications of the very necessary Christological reference.[9] If we were to use different theological categories, we would speak of a search for the *res* at the expense of the *sacramentum*—this is closely related to the question of immediacy—and of an attempt to achieve unity in grace without being concerned with the instituted means of grace.[10,11]

There is a classical procedure in theology of making a distinction between two levels, known in Latin as the *res* and the *sacramentum*. God in fact calls us to communion in his life by the mediation of visible and tangible means. These include the history of the patriarchs of Israel, the words of the inspired prophets and psalms, the incarnation—the Word of revelation does not come about simply as a human word, but also becomes flesh—and, on the basis of that incarnation, the ministry of the Twelve and those appointed to succeed them, words, baptism, the Eucharist and other messianic signs. All these have entered human history and have assumed concrete forms. These are, of course, relative, but they are the forms in which the gift of God is offered to us. In this history too, the disciples have become a people, as Israel became a people, beginning with the twelve sons of Jacob. We ourselves can only become fully disciples of Jesus if we become part of that people that is the Church, in solidarity with the apostles and the brethren. 'They devoted themselves to the apostles' teaching and fellowship, to the breaking of bread and the prayers' (Acts 2:42).

All this points to spiritual fruit. The Word is there for our faith. The gospel is there for love and the sacraments are there for grace, that is, our life as sons of God by being incorporated into Jesus Christ. The ministries of the Church are intended to further the spiritual life, our communion with God and our brethren and our offering of our lives in union with the sacrifice of Jesus himself. Existing between these two levels or dispensations, we find once more the dialectical tension between what is 'already' present (the *res*) and what is 'not yet' there (the *sacramentum*). Following J. D. G. Dunn, we have already seen that this forms part of the condition of the Spirit here below.

206

This is the normal situation and is part of God's plan. It is clear from a survey of history, however, that it is possible for each of these two levels— the spiritual level and that of the visible and tangible means—to develop autonomously. There have been ecclesiologies that have been dominated by a persistent affirmation of the means and have therefore become juridical and clerical in the extreme. There have also been ecclesiologies with an almost exclusive emphasis on the inner life and the immediacy of the spiritual fruit, more or less completely overlooking the visible and tangible means. It is well known, for example, that Luther waged war on both fronts, against those who cried '*Geist! Geist!*', 'Spirit! Spirit!' and those who could only call '*Kirche! Kirche!*', 'Church! Church!' Since his time, there have been, on the one hand, the Quakers and similar groups and, on the other, an entirely juridical and external form of ecclesiology, clearly favouring a uniform and almost monolithic Church society. The opposite tendency, emphasizing the inner life and an immediate relationship with God, is always in danger of leading to an intimate form of individualism and of forgetting the shared demands made by the people of God, the Body of Christ.

The classical theological analysis that I have summarized above may help to throw light on the relationship between the Renewal and the sort of ecumenism that aspires towards the embodiment of all Christ's disciples in a visible unity of one Church. There may clearly be a unity at the level of spiritual fruits and realities in a meeting of prayer, openness and devotion to Jesus and the Spirit, since, in such a meeting, the same Lord and the same Spirit are communicated with great intensity. A unity is therefore reached which goes beyond confessional membership and Church divisions. We have seen that, in the creed, the article in which we confess faith in the Church is connected with that on the Spirit. This means, then, that a certain Church unity is also reached in these meetings. This is already a very great deal, and we thank God fervently for it.

At the same time, however, unity has not been reached. This was sadly obvious at the Pentecost meeting between Christians of different Churches at Lyons in 1977. The Church and its particular unity consists of different elements and exists at a different level. The ultimate level may have been encountered, but the penultimate has been missed out. The Church is, we know, the beginning of the Kingdom, but it is so in the sense of being its vestibule. The Temple contains an altar of sacrifices and a holy place of incense and showbreads before the Holy of Holies is reached. The Church is not simply communion in and through the Spirit—it is also a sacrament. It is also the word and the confession of faith. It is the celebration of the Eucharist and the other sacraments. It is a community and it is ministries. It is a personal and communal discipline. In all these respects, we are not yet united. We may therefore conclude that, as such, the Renewal is not *the* solution of the monumental ecumenical problem. This problem calls for other attempts as well and, thank God, they are being made today.

It is, however, legitimate also to put the question whether unity in the spiritual realities that can be achieved by the Renewal will leave those differences and divisions that exist at the level of the 'sacrament' untouched. Here we need to let those who are active in the Renewal and at the same time belong to different Churches bear witness. My own contribution must be more modest. Each of us can only sing the song that he has been given to sing. My song is that of a theologian and I am neither proud nor ashamed of it. In this particular case, it consists of four verses:

(1) Praying together, meditating together about the Word of God and observing that those who belong to different Churches obviously have gifts of the Spirit, those who take part in ecumenical meetings and even more particularly those who are members of the Renewal are able to recognize each other as authentic Christians and as possible brothers, because they are already real brothers. They cannot dispute that there are difficulties which have not yet been resolved, but they feel that they will be transcended one day. What unites them is stronger than what separates them.

(2) The present emphasis on pneumatology is one of the factors that is currently changing the face of the Church and the significance of our membership of it as a living reality. This applies above all to the present importance given to the charisms in the sense in which Paul speaks of them, especially in Rom 12:6 and 1 Cor 12:4ff., that is, in the sense of gifts or talents which are given to each one of us and which the Holy Spirit wants to be used by us for the building up of the Body of Christ or of the communities of disciples. In the conditions that I have discussed elsewhere in this work, these charisms are used as *ministries*. The Church is, in this sense, no longer defined in terms of its priesthood, consisting of priests carrying out their task with lay people as their 'clients'. Instead, it is seen as a community that is being built up by the brotherly contributions made by all its members. This does not mean that the ordained ministry is no longer required. That ministry is still indispensable. It does, however, mean that the Church can be and is being declericalized. It also commits us in principle to a fully Trinitarian view, in contrast to the pre-Trinitarian monotheism or what A. Manaranche called the 'Jesuanism' of the past, both of which were inadequate.

(3) It is possible to transfer to the Churches and to the great traditions or spiritual families this fundamentally pneumatological and Trinitarian theology of the charisms. I would not wish to accept O. Cullmann's suggestion (see below, note 4) or the theme of a 'conciliar community' that is so favoured at present by the World Council of Churches without asking a number of questions, but I would agree with what Brother Roger Schutz said on 1 February 1977 at Zürich: 'If two people who are separated are trying to

208

THE RENEWAL AND ECUMENISM

be reconciled with each other, they have first of all to discover the specific gifts that are present in the encounter. If each one claims to have all the gifts and believes that he can contribute everything without receiving anything, there will never be any reconciliation. The same applies to reconciliation between the Churches.'

This means that the great Christian communities, which often represent distinct cultural settings, have also incorporated equally distinctive gifts of the Spirit and these have to be respected in a unity of faith, the Eucharist, ministry and mission, the bond of which is the same Spirit. In the last of the Malines Conversations held during the nineteen-twenties, Cardinal Mercier read, it may be remembered, a report by Dom Lambert Beauduin, in which the latter insisted that the 'Anglican Church should be united with Rome, but not absorbed'. Pope Paul VI more recently took up the same idea. Ecumenism has the task of trying to apply this principle by respecting at once the demands made by the true unity of the Church and the originality of the gifts of the One who distributes them 'as he wills'. The experience and the reflection that are required in the Renewal movement will, if they are deepened in a climate of humility and patience, perhaps help us to search for unity in a way that goes far beyond our human means.

(4) My deeply spiritual friend Dom Clément Lialine, towards the end of his life, attacked the heresy which he called ecclesiolatry or ecclesiocentricism. By this he meant making the Church absolute and giving a supreme value to the Church and all that concerns it, rather than to God, the Word, God's initiative and the gospel. This is a very delicate matter. Rather like prayer in relation to the perfection of the sons of God, the Church is a means consubstantial to the end in view. It is therefore not possible to oppose or separate the two. Irenaeus expressed this idea perfectly in a formula which is so balanced that it proclaims a very difficult programme: 'Ubi enim ecclesia, ibi est Spiritus Dei; et ubi Spiritus Dei, illic ecclesia et omnis gratia'—'Where the Church is, there is also the Spirit of God and where the Spirit of God is, there is the Church and all grace'.[12] Is the presence of the Spirit conditioned by the Church or does the Church have to be defined by the presence and the manifest action of the Spirit? Reformed Christians would be very happy with the second of these statements, whereas Christians of the Counter-Reformation would prefer the first. A truly Catholic synthesis calls for both. Would the Renewal not perhaps be a favourable place in which to conduct the search for this synthesis?

There are, however, certain conditions. The first is that those who belong to the Renewal should recognize that they have no monopoly of the Spirit and also that the Renewal and its activities do not form a Church for them. It is quite right that they should love the Renewal and that it should make them happy, but it would be unsound if they made it into their Church. They should above all form part of the great Catholic community with its sacraments, its pastors, its activities, its mission and its service to the world. They should fully accept its history and its life, in solidarity with their brethren who do not belong to the Renewal, but who are also animated by the Spirit and in whom the Spirit also dwells. All this is very obvious and hardly needs to be said, but there is some value in repeating it. A sound and critical rejection of any form of ecclesiolatry should find its place within an immense, deep and warm love of the Church, and experience has shown that such a love is very favourable to a life of prayer and praise.

The second condition is, as it were, the basis for the first. It is concerned with the soundness of all life in and through the Spirit. I have already criticized what my Orthodox friends call Christomonism in an article published some years ago.[13] This name is given to a theological construction that is so firmly linked to Christ that the Spirit is in danger of being forgotten. As long ago as 1934, Pastor Charles Westphal told me: 'You Catholics often give me the impression that you want to economize on the Holy Spirit'. We ought to take this comment seriously and give the Holy Spirit his rightful place. The soundness of any pneumatology, however, is dependent on its reference to Christ. The Spirit is the object of a special 'mission'. Pentecost followed the incarnation and Easter. The eucharistic consecration is brought about by the account of the institution *and* by the epiclesis. The Spirit, however, does not do any work other than that of Christ. There is only one economy of salvation and only one baptism, which is both in the paschal event of Christ and in the Spirit. Both Paul and John make the reference to Christ a criterion for the action of the Spirit:

> No one speaking by the Spirit of God ever says 'Jesus be cursed!' and no one can say 'Jesus is Lord' except by the Holy Spirit (1 Cor 12:3).

> 'The Paraclete, the Holy Spirit, whom the Father will send in my name, he will teach you all things and bring to your remembrance all that I have said to you' (Jn 14:26).

> 'When the Spirit of truth comes, he will guide you into all the truth; for he will not speak on his own authority, but whatever he hears he will speak. . . . He will glorify me, for he will take what is mine and declare it to you' (Jn 16:13–14).

> By this you know the Spirit of God: every spirit which confesses that Jesus Christ has come in the flesh is of God and every spirit which does not confess Jesus is not of God (1 Jn 4:2–3).

To accept a Christological criterion for the authenticity of a pneumatology is fundamentally to look for the way in which the actions and the fruits that are attributed to the Holy Spirit are of a piece with or at least in accordance with the work of the incarnate Word, Jesus Christ the Lord. The Spirit is the breath and he is the dynamism; he is both the inner life and the power. He makes the gift of God that comes to us in Jesus Christ personal and inward—he is 'sent into our hearts' (Gal 4:6). At the same time, he also urges the gospel forward, within the unknown context of the 'things that are to come' (Jn 16:13). The Word is the form and the face given to the communication of God's gift: the word, the teaching; the visible signs of our communion, baptism, the Eucharist and the other sacraments; the ministry of the Twelve who were appointed to undertake a universal mission (Mt 28:19–20), and the function of Peter within the apostolic college. The Spirit, together with the Word, has entered man's history and in that history they have together brought about the Church, its Tradition and the testimony of its saints. Accepting a Christological criterion for the genuineness of a pneumatology is to recognize the freedom of the Spirit to 'blow where he wills' (Jn 3:8; 2 Cor 3:17), but it is also to affirm that that freedom is at the same time the freedom of truth (Jn 8:31; the 'Spirit of truth': 16:13) and that the 'mission' or the coming of the Spirit is related and in agreement with that of the Word. It is the Spirit who makes us members of the Body of Christ (1 Cor 12:13; Rom 8:2ff.), but that Body is not the Body of the Holy Spirit—it is the Body of Christ.

To return now to the question of what the Renewal—in the Spirit—can contribute to ecumenism, we can now see that it does not leave the difficult question untouched. It experiences the truth that the Church is built up from within and that communion in love is higher than any external organization or mediation. But at the same time, it would be wrong to regard itself as achieving unity beyond and in spite of all the differences that continue to exist. The ecclesiological problem continues in the form of a Christological reference to the institution of the Lord, the *sacramentum* of the Church that he founded. This cannot simply be erased in the name of an immediate experience of the Spirit and his fruits.

The Spirit and Christ, the Word, condition each other. The Spirit is referred to the Word. He does not do away with the demands made by the Word. He makes the way open to them, so that the Word becomes present, inward and dynamically active. In a biblical meditation of great depth, Etienne Garin, a Catholic member of the Renewal, has said: 'Without the Spirit, the Word is barren, like a seed without water. Without the Word, the Spirit is blindly wandering in search of water without the seed.'[14] O great, holy and enthralling Church—you are the Body of Christ and the Temple of the Holy Spirit, the City built on the Lord's apostles and the place where the Spirit 'who has spoken through the prophets' is active!

NOTES

1. Cardinal L. J. Suenens, *Ecumenism and Charismatic Renewal: Theological and Pastoral Orientations* (Eng. tr.; Ann Arbor and London, 1978).

2. A quotation from Vladimir Soloviev appears on p. 108 of the document, *op. cit.*: 'In order to come closer to one another, we have to do two things: the first is to ensure and intensify ˅ our own intimate union with Christ; the second is to venerate, in the soul of our brother, the active life of the Holy Spirit who dwells in him'.

3. H. Mühlen has developed this programme in *Morgen wird Einheit sein. Das kommende Konzil aller Christen: Zeil der getrennten Kirchen* (Paderborn, 1974). My critical review of this book was published in *RSPT*, 59 (1975), 517–519.

4. O. Cullmann, *Vrai et faux Œcuménisme* (*Cahiers théologiques*, 62) (Neuchâtel, 1971).

5. J. M. Garrigues, 'L'Œcuménisme', *Il est vivant*, 18 (Spring, 1978), 3–6, 13–15.

6. Daniel Pézeril, in his preface to John V. Taylor, *Puissance et patience de l'Esprit* (1977), p. 12 (Fr. tr. of *The Go-Between God* (London, 1972)).

7. Not only J.-R. Bouchet, *Le Renouveau charismatique interpellé* (*Collection Renouveau*, 5) (Paris, 1976), p. 188, but also W. Storey, *ibid.*, pp. 99, 119, have pointed to this danger. Others who have referred to it are the Protestant pastor L. Dallière and the contributors to *Pro Mundi Vita*, 60 (1976). See above, pp. 147–148.

8. See Jim Brown's parable, reported by A. Wohlfahrt in *Foi et Vie* (July-October 1973), 11, and before this by G. Appia in *Réforme* (11 November 1972). See also, in the same number of *Réforme*, 67, J.-P. Gabus: 'The present movement brought about by the Holy Spirit is creating in the West *an entirely new Church* which will be neither Catholic nor Protestant, but simply evangelical or, if you like, Catholic-Orthodox-Evangelical'.

9. By 'Christological reference' I mean not only the person of the Lord Jesus, his teaching, his cross and his demanding programme, but also the introduction of these into the Church and the means of grace that come from the incarnate Word. The danger that a 'Church' will be formed from the experience of warmth and security that is shared in meetings, is by no means imaginary.

10. Paul VI pointed several times to a tendency to overestimate the charismatic aspect of the Church at the expense of its hierarchical and sacramental structures: see the references in E. O'Connor, 'Charisme et institution', *NRT*, 96 (1974), 3–19, especially 4, note 4.

11. What follows is based on my article, 'Propos sur l'Œcuménisme et Renouveau par l'Esprit', *Tychique*, 13–14 (January 1978), 81–86.

12. Irenaeus, *Adv. haer*. III, 24 (*SC* 211 (1974), p. 474).

13. See my study, 'Pneumatologie et "christomonisme" dans la tradition latine', *Ecclesia a Spiritu Sancto edocta. Mélanges théologiques. Hommage à Mgr Gérard Philips* (Gembloux, 1970), pp. 41–46.

14. E. Garin, 'Construire l'unité bien sûr, mais quelle unité?', *Tychique*, 13–14 (January 1978), 89–95, especially 91.

CONCLUSION

'IN THE UNITY OF THE HOLY SPIRIT, ALL HONOUR AND GLORY'

The two 'missions' of the Son and of the Holy Spirit, proceeding from the Father and taking place in favour of creatures, return to the Father in cosmic, universal and total praise.

A. IN JESUS, GOD GAVE HIMSELF A HUMAN HEART, PERFECTLY THE HEART OF A SON

The Father said: 'You are my beloved Son, with whom I am well pleased' and again and again Jesus said: 'You are my Father; I have come to do your will'.

Did this dialogue begin in the eternity of the life within the Trinity? Is it possible to detect in it the formula of what is known in theology as the active and the passive begetting? We can only do this on condition that we do not distinguish a duality or a trinity of consciousnesses.[1] It is, of course, true that the temporal 'missions' of the second and the third Persons are the term of the eternal processions in creatures, but the divine begetting of the Word, the Son, ends in a conscious and free humanity which has something to say to the Father, and that is: 'You are my Father; you have prepared a body for me; I have come to do your will' (see Ps 40:7; Heb 10:5–9). The Son's words can only be transferred to the Father in the 'essential' or immanent Trinity if we see the 'You are my Father' as the fruit *constituted* by the 'You are my Son', in other words, as an expression of passive begetting.[2]

We shall therefore examine only the dialogue between the Father and the holy but human consciousness of Jesus. When the Holy Spirit made Mary's capacity as a woman to be a mother active in her, what he did was to bring about in her a humanity which the Father was truthfully to address with the words: 'You are my beloved Son' (see Heb 1:5ff.). The hypostatic union that took place at that time was the personal act of the Word-Son, but the Spirit (perhaps by appropriation?) brought about the sanctification of that first human beginning, causing a son's soul and a son's love to arise in him. In the language of classical theology, this would be called the operation of

213

sanctifying grace, the absolute fullness of which was given to Jesus as the Head and the first of many brethren ('capital grace').

Ought we—and is it possible—to attribute, from that moment onwards, to the first seed of man in Mary the response 'You are my Father', the principle of which in him would be the sanctifying Spirit? The author of the Epistle to the Hebrews says: 'When Christ came into the world, he said, "Sacrifices and offerings thou hast not desired, but a body hast thou prepared for me. . . . Then I said, 'I have come to do thy will, O God' " ' (10:5ff.). This is a global proclamation about the disposition of the soul of Christ, who 'through the eternal Spirit offered himself without blemish to God' (Heb 9:14; cf. Phil 2:8). What is certain is that God aroused in Jesus a human heart that was perfectly the heart of a son and an absolute adorer. I have already discussed this to some extent above, when I spoke of Jesus' soul as Son.[3] And what should we say about his life of prayer and the nights that he spent praying in solitude?[4] At the same time, however, we have, for our own inspiration, to recall the great moments of the relationship 'You are my Son' and 'You are my Father'.

When he was twelve years old, Jesus remained behind in Jerusalem after the feast was over and the pilgrims had left. After three days of searching, his parents found him again in the Temple. He asked: 'How is it that you sought me? Did you not know that I must be in my Father's house?' (Lk 2:49). What consciousness did Jesus have of his relationship with his Father at the level of his human knowledge? As we have already seen, the substantial union that existed between his humanity and the Person of the Word, the Son, left to his human nature the normal use of his faculties. He had also to enter into his Father's plan for him on the basis not of clarity, but of obedience. This episode in Luke's gospel shows, however, that, in his understanding of his relationship with his Father, he was at that time already more advanced than his parents, despite the fact that they had some evidence of a supernatural mystery.

When he was baptized by John the Baptist, Jesus was anointed by the Spirit for his messianic work: 'When he came up out of the water, immediately he saw the heavens opened and the Spirit descending upon him like a dove; and a voice came down from heaven, "Thou art my beloved Son; with thee I am well pleased" ' (Mk 1:10–11). According to Luke, Jesus was at prayer—'Thou art my Father; I have come to do thy will'—and the Spirit descended on him and a voice from heaven said: 'Thou art my Son; today I have begotten thee' (Lk 3:22, referring to Ps 2:7). In the dispensation with the Trinity, 'the Father begets his Son incessantly, in a perpetual today'.[5] He begets him in Jesus the man in accordance with the stages of the 'economy': conception, baptism–messianic anointing (see Acts 10:38), resurrection and glorification, until the *humanity* of Jesus is invested with the sovereign condition of a humanity of the Son of God, that humanity mentioned in 1 Cor 15:45 and Phil 2:9–11.

In his prayer, through the Spirit which descended on him and the voice which applied to him the words referring to the Servants: 'My servant whom I uphold, my chosen, in whom my soul delights' (Is 42:1), Jesus quite consciously accepted obedience as a son which would impose on him the way of the Servant. He cleaved in advance to the will of his Father as expressed in the gospels by such formulae as 'It was necessary that . . .' or 'so that the Scriptures might be fulfilled'.[6] Very soon, moreover, Jesus was put to the test with regard to his obedience to the way of the Servant, and the demon contrasted that way with his condition as the 'Son of God': 'If you are the Son of God . . .'. Jesus, however, was led into the wilderness by the Spirit, with whom he was filled (Lk 4:1), with the result that his reply to the demon points to his own submission: 'You shall worship the Lord your God and him only shall you serve' (4:8).

Augustine said: 'Just as being born was, for the Son, being from the Father, so too was being sent, for the Son, knowing that he was from him'.[7] In other words, it is saying to him: 'You are my Father'. That is precisely what Jesus confessed throughout the whole of his public life:

> In that same hour he rejoiced in the Holy Spirit and said, 'I thank thee, Father, Lord of heaven and earth, that thou hast hidden these things from the wise and the understanding and revealed them to babes; yea, Father, for such was thy gracious will' (Lk 10:21).

> 'My food is to do the will of him who sent me and to accomplish his work' (Jn 4:34; cf. Mt 7:21).

> 'As the living Father sent me and I live because of the Father . . .' (Jn 6:57).

> 'My teaching is not mine, but his who sent me' (Jn 7:16)

> 'I do nothing on my own authority, but speak thus as the Father taught me' (8:28; 12:49–50; 14:10).

> 'I always do what is pleasing to him' (8:29).

> 'I do as the Father has commanded me, so that the world may know that I love the Father' (14:31).

This last statement ends with the words: 'Rise, let us go hence'. Jesus was, in other words, leaving the upper room to go to Gethsemane. Those who witnessed his agony were the same men who witnessed the transfiguration, at which the same words that were spoken at the theophany of the Father at Jesus' baptism were pronounced: 'This is my beloved Son, with whom I am well pleased; listen to him' (Mt 17:5; Mk 9:7; Lk 9:34–35).[8]

The agony in the garden was the dramatic occasion of Jesus' cry to the Father: 'Abba, Father, all things are possible to thee; remove this cup from me; yet not what I will, but what thou wilt' (Mk 14:36). This is another way of saying: 'You are my Father; I have come to do your will'. Did the Father reply to this cry? In Lk 22:42, an angel comforts Jesus, and John goes even further: ' "Now my soul is troubled. And what shall I say? 'Father, save me from this hour'? No, for this purpose I have come to this hour. Father, glorify thy name". Then a voice came from heaven, "I have glorified it and I will glorify it again" ' (Jn 12:27–28).

This brings us to Jesus' crucifixion. According to Heb 9:14, he offered himself through an eternal spirit and this text has been included in the prayer before communion in the Roman rite of the Mass: 'cooperante Spiritu Sancto'. Jesus began with the opening words of Ps 22: 'My God, my God, why hast thou forsaken me?' when he was dying (Mt 27:46; Mk 15:34), his 'You are my Father' becoming an appeal to the absent one: 'O Son without a Father! O God without God!'[9] I am personally convinced, however, that he continued this psalm or at least said some of the later verses, expressing the hope of 'You are my Father' in his heart:

> In thee our fathers trusted;
> they trusted and thou didst deliver them.
> To thee they cried and were saved;
> in thee they trusted and were not disappointed. . . .
> Since my mother bore me, thou hast been my God
> (Ps 22:4–5, 10).

In Luke 23:46, Jesus' last words are taken from another psalm (31:5): 'Father, into thy hands I commit my spirit'.[10]

The Father's response came a day and a half later and consisted of the words: 'You are my Son' said in absolutely new conditions: 'The good news that what God promised to the fathers, this he has fulfilled to us his children by raising Jesus; as also it is written in the second psalm: "Thou art my Son, today I have begotten thee" ' (Acts 13:32–33). Paul makes it clear in what way the Son was begotten on that day: 'The gospel concerning his Son, who was descended from David according to the flesh and designated Son of God in power according to the Spirit of holiness by his resurrection from the dead, Jesus Christ our Lord' (Rom 1:2–4). The same Son of God, the same Christ, after having assumed the condition of a servant and after having obeyed to the point of death on the cross—'You are my Father; I have come to do your will'—received from God, his Father, the sovereign condition of *a humanity of the Son of God* and the title of Lord (Phil 2:6–11; Acts 2:36; Rom 14:9). The same Holy Spirit, by whose power a shoot from the line of David had been brought forth, a descendant who was to be called Son of God, enabled Jesus to be born, as an eschatological gift, to the glory that was appropriate for the Son of God. Jesus was therefore able to give the same Spirit himself (1 Cor 15:45; Jn 7:37–39).

216

B. IN JESUS, WE ARE
DESTINED TO BE SONS OF GOD;
HE COMMUNICATES FILIAL LIFE TO US
THROUGH HIS SPIRIT

We are called to be sons in the Son:

Those whom he foreknew he also predestined to be conformed to the image of his Son, in order that he might be the first-born among many brethren (Rom 8:29).

He chose us in him before the foundation of the world, that we should be holy and blameless before him. He destined us in love to be his sons through Jesus Christ. . . . In him you . . . were sealed with the promised Holy Spirit, which is the guarantee of our inheritance (Eph 1:4–5, 13–14).

Because you are sons, God has sent the Spirit of his Son into our hearts, crying: 'Abba! Father!' So through God you are no longer a slave, but a son and, if a son, then an heir (Gal 4:6–7).

If the Spirit of him who raised Jesus from the dead dwells in you. . . . You have received the Spirit of sonship. When we cry, 'Abba! Father!' it is the Spirit himself bearing witness with our spirit that we are children of God and, if children, then heirs, heirs of God and fellow-heirs with Christ (Rom 8:11, 15–17).

These passages are enormously rich and we can draw certain propositions from them which it is easy and delightful to illustrate with comments made by the Church Fathers.

We are predestined in Christ. This means that God (the Father) has included us in the plan of grace that he has brought about and is still bringing about through the one to whom he said: 'You are my Son' when Jesus was conceived, baptized, resurrected and glorified.[11] We, then, are loved by the same love with which the Father loved his Son.[12]

God's effective love constitutes us as sons. There is a difference, of course, between being a Son by nature and a son by adoption[13] and Jesus in fact made this difference explicit.[14] John points to it in his gospel and epistles by using *huios* for the first and *tekna* for the second.[15] Despite this, however, we are really sons of God by adoption and by grace. We form with the Son one single being as sons.[16] He is the only Son (*Monogenēs*), but he is also the first-born of many brethren. That is why the Father is able to say, in Jesus and thanks to him, to us: 'You are my son'.

We are sons by the Holy Spirit, that is, by a communication of the Spirit of the Son (see Gal 4:6; Rom 8:14ff.). That Spirit enables us to pray: 'Abba! Father!' and he is in us like water which whispers 'Come to the Father!'[17] Thanks to Christ, 'we both have access in the one Spirit to the Father' (Eph 2:18).

If it is true, then, that the Father says to us: 'You are my son' through and in the two missions of the Son and the Spirit, how are we to respond to him and say: 'You are my Father; I have come to do your will'? We can do this by

217

praying: 'Our Father, . . . hallowed be thy name. Thy kingdom come, thy will be done, on earth as it is in heaven . . .' (Mt 6:9ff.). We can also respond to him by directing the whole of our life towards him. Life led in this way is a 'spiritual sacrifice' of the kind described by Paul in Rom 12:1, or it may be a life lived according to the Spirit, in a struggle against the 'flesh', as described in a previous chapter. Finally, it is also possible to orientate our life towards God in the same direction as the Servant who sacrificed himself and thus became a source of life for others. This applies to all believers, but more particularly, of course, to the ministers of the gospel.

Paul was conscious of the fact that this quality of sons of God, the earnest-money or guarantee of which has been placed in us by the Spirit, also has a cosmic dimension. The destiny of the world was, he believed, closely connected with ours and it too was waiting for an Easter through which it would come to share in the glory and freedom of the children of God (see Rom 8:18–25; cf. Eph 1:3–14).

This is and will be possible because the same Spirit exists in Christ, our Head, and in all his members or his Body. He is present in fullness in our Head and he has existed as such in him from the very beginning as the principle of holiness, and since Christ's 'sitting at the right hand of the Father' as the power of the Lord, who received that power from his messianic anointing (Acts 10:38), but not in the way he received the Spirit when he had been exalted to the right hand of God, as Lord, and as such able to pour it out (Acts 2:33–36; Jn 7:39). Corresponding to our own predestination to be sons in the Son who is the first-born of many brethren is the fact that it is by the same, identically the same, Spirit, *idem numero*, that we are such sons.[18] He is, however, in our Head in absolute fullness, whereas he is in us according to the measure of God's gift and according to the degree of welcome that we give him.

C. THE SPIRIT OF GOD FILLS THE UNIVERSE HE GATHERS EVERYTHING THAT EXISTS IN IT FOR THE GLORY OF THE FATHER

'The Spirit of the Lord has filled the world and that which holds all things together knows what is said' (Wis 1:7)—'Thy immortal breath is in all things' (12:1). There is clearly an echo of Stoicism in these statements, but the theme has been completely theologized. What we have here is the breath of *Yahweh*.[19] As C. Larcher has pointed out,[20] this theme has clear antecedents: the breath of God was not simply extended to man (Gen 2:7; 6:3; Job 21:3; 33:4; Ezek 37; Eccles 12:7)—it was also given to all living creatures (Ps 104:28–30; Job 34:14–15). What is more, the 'Breath of God' is also the creative Breath (Jdt 16:14; Ps 33:6; 104:30). Like Wisdom, the Spirit of God is at work everywhere.

1. *The Spirit is at work everywhere*

The Fathers were certainly convinced of this. Following the apologists, what they developed was rather the theme of the Logos who was present and active in every true thought and who made the world rational.[21] But Irenaeus believed that the gift of the heavenly Spirit was sent *in omnem terram*—'into the whole of the earth',[22] that he had been 'poured out in these latter days on the whole of mankind'[23] and that 'he descended on the Son of God who had become the Son of man and that, with him, he was therefore able to dwell in the human race, rest on men and live in the work fashioned by God'.[24]

The Christian authors living and writing before the Scholastic period agreed that the Holy Spirit was the principle of all true knowledge.[25] The mediaeval theologians were fond of quoting and commenting on a maxim first used by Ambrosiaster, which they attributed to Ambrose of Milan: 'Omne verum, a quocumque dicitur, a Spiritu Sancto est'—'All truth, no matter where it comes from, is from the Holy Spirit'.[26] Some of them believed that this was the truth about God, while others spoke of judgements involving the will. Thomas Aquinas sometimes cited the principle without any further explanation,[27] but he also made a distinction between the natural light that came from God and the light that came from the gifts of grace,[28] or else between simple present movements of the Holy Spirit *movente, sed non habito* and lights given to living faith.[29] Albert the Great accepted a much wider concept of 'grace' and, in reply to the question as to whether all truth that is the object of knowledge was inspired by the Holy Spirit, he said: yes, so long as every gift that is gratuitously given by God is called grace.[30] This was, he thought, the case with existence itself.

Today, Christians are inclined to revive this Ambrosian theme and even to extend it. There is evidence of this, for example, in the Pastoral Constitution *Gaudium et Spes*, promulgated at the end of the Second Vatican Council.[31] The Orthodox theologian Georges Fedotov believes that the Spirit is active in the dynamism of the cosmos and in the inspiration of everyone who creates beauty and is convinced that the Church should try to overcome the ambiguity in this situation by applying the criterion of the cross.[32] There is open recognition in *Gaudium et Spes*, 44, of the Church's debt to man's efforts in society and culture in the task of proclaiming the message of Christ. Although he does not explicitly refer to this text, the Protestant theologian Langdon Gilkey has expressed his conviction that the dialogue between the Church and its theologians on the one hand and the world and its cultural representatives on the other is of benefit to both and that this presupposes the presence of the Spirit in both.[33] The same principles, he believes, should also be applied with increasing urgency to our dialogue with other religions. I would certainly agree with him and in this I would also be supported even by such a firm and classically Catholic man of the Church as the nineteenth-century Cardinal Manning.[34] It would not be at all difficult to find many texts on the presence of the Spirit and his work in the life of men.[35]

An Anglican theologian, John V. Taylor, the Bishop of Winchester, has made a connection between what I have said about the active presence of the Spirit everywhere and the special character of the third Person. He calls the Spirit, understood in this sense, the 'go-between God', that is, the God who acts as a kind of broker and who penetrates subtly everywhere in order to create true relationships. The Holy Spirit, he says, is 'that unceasing, dynamic communicator and Go-Between operating upon every element and every process of the material universe, the immanent and anonymous presence of God. . . . the true ground of all mission is this creative-redemptive action at the heart of everything. . . . The Bible is consistent from beginning to end in its understanding that God works always through the moments of recognition when mutual awareness is born. It is a history of encounters.'[36]

2. *The Spirit secretly guides God's work in the world*

History is like a huge play that is not enacted on the public stage alone. Irenaeus compared the Holy Spirit to a theatrical producer, directing the drama of salvation on the stage of history in such a way that the actors, men, know him and allow themselves to be seized by him and his work. This is the fundamental meaning of this text, the original Greek of which has survived:[37]

> Everything in him (the spiritual man) is consolidated: in relation to the one almighty God, 'from whom are all things' (1 Cor 8:6), an integral faith; in relation to the Son of God, Jesus Christ our Lord, 'through whom are all things', and to his 'economies', by which he was made man—he, the Son of God—a firm adherence; and in relation to the Spirit of God, who enables us to know the truth, who *produces the 'economies' of the Father and the Son, according to each generation*, with men in view, as in the Father's will.

The Spirit is able to reveal 'the economies of the Father' to each successive generation because he is Love and because he puts into all creatures a beginning of love and hope (see Rom 5:5). One of the leading concepts of Neoplatonic thought is that Love moves the world, and Aristotle put forward the idea of the Prime Mover who was himself unmoved, but who moved all things *hōs erōmenon*, 'as loved'.[38] Spiritual men have understood that idea deeply, but differently. The Persian mystic Rūmi (†1273) described the ascending movement of all things in the following way:

> Know that it is waves of Love that make the wheel of the heavens turn. Without Love, the world would not be animated.

> How can an inorganic thing be transformed into a plant? How can vegetable things sacrifice themselves so as to be endowed with spirit?

How could the spirit sacrifice itself for that Breath, an expiration of whom made Mary pregnant? . . .

Every atom is seized by that Perfection and hastens towards it. . . .

That haste says implicitly: 'Glory be to God'.[39]

A generation later, the European poet Dante ended his *Paradiso* with the following vision:

In the depths I saw everything that is scattered in the universe, united, bound by love into a single book. . . .
I believe that I saw the universal form of that unity, because while saying it, I feel my joy opening out more fully. . . .
My spirit, suspended, looked fixedly, unmoving and with great attention, becoming more and more enflamed by the ardour of contemplation.
That light so moves one that it is impossible ever to consent to turn away from it to a different view,
because the good, which is the object of desire, gathers everything into it, and what is perfect in it seems deficient outside it. . . .
Here, my strength was not enough for the sublime vision, but already, like a wheel moving steadily round, my desire and my will were directed by the Love that moves the sun and the other stars.[40]

After these incomparable verses, dare I quote those of a canticle sung in our assemblies and coming from the sons of St Bernard? I think I may, because the words are inspired by the Bible and they express the same sublime doctrine:

Sun of justice—
he makes the universe ripe
and in our desert his Spirit
is a source of living water!

3. *The Spirit combines in a Doxology everything that is for God in the world*

'Jesus said, "Woman, the hour is coming when neither on this mountain nor in Jerusalem will you worship the Father. . . . The hour is coming, and now is, when the true worshippers will worship the Father in spirit and truth, for such the Father seeks to worship him' (Jn 4:21, 23). We are called to be true worshippers (see below, section 4), but I felt the need to write, in my book *Le mystère du Temple*, a section on the 'dimensions of the spiritual temple . . . the breadth and the depth'.[41] God in fact has worshippers everywhere. The prophets proclaimed that the peoples would go up to Jerusalem to worship him.[42] Even in their case, it was less a geographical and a material question and much more a spiritual one. It was fundamentally a proclamation of an extension of man's knowledge of God. At Pentecost, however, Jerusalem, as it were, burst out on the whole world and God knew his own (see 2 Tim 2:15). 'Can a man hide himself in secret places so that I cannot see him? says the Lord. Do I not fill heaven and earth? says the Lord' (Jer 23:24). Are we not therefore entitled to join those who have heard and expressed the secret harmonies of creation and grace—the spiritual men and the poets?

> The Word of God
> has left the lyre and the cithara,
> instruments without a soul,
> to tune the whole world, gathered into man,
> in to himself through the Holy Spirit.
> He makes use of him
> as an instrument with many voices
> and, accompanying his song,
> he plays to God
> on that instrument that is man![43]

> 'Well, it says in the New Testament that man and all creation "*are subject to vanity, not willingly*" [Rom 8:19–22], and sigh with efforts and desire to enter into the liberty of the children of God. The mysterious sighing of creation, the innate aspiration of every soul towards God, that is exactly what interior prayer is. There is no need to learn it, it is innate in every one of us!'[44]

This is not simply a 'groaning'—it is also a hymn of praise. The Bible bears witness to this cosmic hymn of praise, which the elements and those living beings that have no consciousness sing, but which man interprets. There are many well-known scriptural and other Christian texts[45] and for this reason it is interesting to look at two which are not Christian, but which nonetheless point in a very profound way to this truth:

> Have you not seen that it is before God that everything bows down—everything in the heavens and everything on earth and the sun and the moon and the stars and the mountains and the trees and the animals? (*Quran*, XIII, 13).

> Have you not seen that God—everything in the heavens and on earth proclaims his praises and also the birds while stretching out their wings? Everyone knows his prayer and his praise and God knows what they are doing (*ibid.*, XXIV, 41).[46]

4. *The Church expresses the Doxology of the Universe*

It is possible to speak to a 'kenosis' of the Spirit, who acts without revealing himself except in the acts that he secretly inspires. For we may ask where the kingdom of God is now. Where is it realized? Walter Kasper has asked this question and suggests that, according to Jesus' own words, it is not possible to point to it and say: It is here or it is there. It is rather in the midst of us in an inexpressible way (see Lk 17:21). It is found everywhere where men trust in God and in his love, even if they do not explicitly speak of God or Jesus (see

Mt 25:35ff.). That is why, he concludes, the kingdom of God is a hidden reality of which it is only possible to speak in parables.[47]

God has, however, also revealed himself. He constituted a people who, under the new dispensation of the Word, the sacraments and the gift of the Spirit, were to be called the Church.[48] Within the great domain of everything that belongs to God and is for God in this world, the Church is the illuminated zone consisting of the people who know and confess him, and who form what Peter Berger and other sociologists have called a 'cognitive minority'. This is true, so long as this is not an attempt to define a reality that is above all a sacramental and doxological communion. Because it is such a reality, the Church not only experiences its own obedience in faith and its own praise, but also gathers into that praise 'all the prayers that are not even said'[49] and all the 'undeciphered' and 'unrevealed' comings of the Spirit[50] together with all those 'sacred points' which, unknown even to most souls, say *Pater noster* in themselves.[51]

The Church gathers all this together and offers it up. But it is hardly possible to say that it is extraneous to the Church. It already belongs to the Church—as Paul Evdimokov has insisted, 'we know where the Church is, but it is not for us to judge and to say where it is not'.[52] The Church is more than their ideal space. It is their real homeland and it is in a mysterious sense their mother. How I love Psalm 87, which sings of the City of God:

> Among those who know me I mention Rahab and Babylon;
> behold, Philistia and Tyre, with Ethiopia—
> 'This one was born there', they say.
> And of Zion it shall be said,
> 'This one and that one were born in her'.

The Church, who knows God and seeks his glory, wants to share that knowledge in order that God's glory may be increased. The many reasons leading to the Church's missionary activity and above all the intention to gather the whole human race into one people of God, one Body of Christ and one Temple of the Holy Spirit were all discussed at the Second Vatican Council and the conclusion was reached, in the document on the Church's mission, that 'the plan of the Creator, who formed man to his own image and likeness, will be realized at last when all who share one human nature, regenerated in Christ through the Holy Spirit and beholding together the glory of God (see 2 Cor 3:18), will be able to say "Our Father" '.[53]

This is clearly an eschatological perspective. Does the Church not ask God for itself: 'As this broken bread, once dispersed over the hills, was brought together and became one loaf, may your Church be brought together from the ends of the earth into your kingdom'?[54] Even now, however, we are gathering together all that, in the world, is for God. Or rather, we offer that sheaf that has been bound together invisibly by the Holy Spirit. All the Eucharistic Prayers end with this doxology:

Through him,
with him,
in him,
in the unity of the Holy Spirit,
all glory and honour is yours,
almighty Father,
for ever and ever. Amen.

And in French the priest may continue: 'Unis *dans le même Esprit,* nous pouvons dire avec confiance: Notre Père . . .', 'United *in the same Spirit,* we can say with confidence: Our Father . . .'.

Two specialists in the liturgy have suggested their own interpretations of the doxology. J. A. Jungmann believed that 'in the Holy Spirit' was the equivalent of Hippolytus' 'in the holy Church'.[55] Dom B. Botte, however, traced the history of this formula, which first appeared in 420, and has concluded that it is an essentially Trinitarian formula, expressing the unity of the divine Persons and their common glorification.[56] I do not intend to go into this debate here, but would simply say that, as a Christian and a priest, I say the words of this doxology every day with great intensity and I personally interpret it in this way: The Holy Spirit, who fills the universe and who holds all things in unity, knows everything that is said and gathers together everything that, in this world, is for and tending towards God (*pros ton Patera*). He ties the sheaf together in a hymn of cosmic praise through with and in Christ, in whom everything is firmly established (Col 1:15–20).

After this doxology, we believers, who know the Father and the one whom he has sent, together with Christ make once again present among us the invocation that he taught us and that the Spirit enables us to pray: 'Abba! Father! You are my Father!' In this way, the Eucharist, which is a great thanksgiving, is made fully present. That, at least, is my own daily Mass over the world.

God brings about for himself in the world sons—in a mysterious way and by the grace of his Spirit. The same grace of the same Spirit enables those sons to reply—often in a language without words, but he knows everything that is said: 'You are my Father! Glory to you!'

NOTES

1. K. Rahner, *The Trinity* (Eng. tr.; London and New York, 1970), p. 76, note 30: 'Hence within the Trinity there is no reciprocal "Thou". The Son is the Father's self-utterance which should not in its turn be conceived as "uttering".'
2. This is not everything that is to be said about the divine life within the Trinity; see the Note following this chapter for an insight into that life.
3. See above, pp. 104–105, and for what follows on Jesus' consciousness and knowledge, see Volume I, pp. 17–18.

4. It is hardly possible to understand Jesus without taking his prayer into consideration; see my *Jesus Christ* (Eng. tr.; New York and London, 1966), pp. 86–106.
5. Origen, *Comm. in Ioan*. I, 39, 204, (ed. E. Preuschen, *Orig. W.*, IV, p. 37), following a quotation of Ps 2:7, this is also quoted by Clement of Rome (*1 Cor* XXXVI, 4), Justin Martyr, Methodius and others.
6. See my book, *op. cit.* (note 4), p. 78, text and notes 17, 18. These formulae occur mainly in connection with the passion.
7. Augustine, *De Trin*. IV, 20, 29: 'Sicut natum esse est Filio a Patre esse, ita mitti est Filio cognosci quod ab illo sit'.
8. John combines an equivalent of the agony with an evocation of Jesus' glorification by the Father (12:27–28). For the parallel between the baptism scene and the transfiguration, see L. Legrand, 'L'arrière-plan néotestamentaire de Lc 1, 35', *RB*, 70 (1963), 162–192.
9. L. Chardon, *La Croix de Jésus* (Paris, 1937), p. 158.
10. J. Guillet said of this text: 'Committing one's spirit into God's hands does not mean, for the one praying in Ps 31, dying; on the contrary, as the following couplet shows, it means: "You will deliver me, O Lord, faithful God" and help me to find life and peace again': see his *Thèmes bibliques* (*Théologie*, 18) (Paris, 1951), p. 227.
11. One of the great patristic insights is that Christ does not go without Christians. This is, of course, a biblical theme: see especially the verbs with *sun-* in Paul's letters and the dynamism of the mystery of Christ in John. For the Fathers, see Cyprian, *Ep*. LX, 13 and LXVIII, 5 (ed. W. von Hartel, pp. 711, 754); Athanasius, *Contra Arian*. I, 50; II, 69–70; Gregory of Nyssa, *Contra Eunom*. II (*PG* 45, 533). See also T. J. van Bavel, *Recherches sur la Christologie de S. Augustin* (Fribourg, 1954), pp. 74–102; R. Bernard, 'La prédestination du Christ total', *Recherches Augustiniennes*, III (1965), pp. 1–58.
12. See Rom 8:28–30, 39; 2 Cor 5:19; Eph 4:32; Jn 17:23: 'thou hast loved them even as thou hast loved me', and 26: 'that the love with which thou hast loved me may be in them, and I in them'.
13. By adoption: Gal 4:5; Rom 8:15, 23; Eph 1:5. See also E. Schweizer, '*huiothesia*', *TDNT*, VIII, p. 399.
14. 'My Father and your Father': Jn 20:17. Augustine: 'Dicimur filii Dei, sed ille aliter Filius Dei'; *Enarr. in Ps*. 88, 7 (*PL* 37, 1124).
15. *Huios*: see the various concordances; *tekna*: Jn 1:12; 11:52; 1 Jn 3:1, 2; 5:2.
16. 1 Cor 1:9: *eis koinōnian tou huiou*; Gal 3:25–29; Athanasius, *Contra Arian*. II, 59: 'The Father is really only the Father of the Son and nothing created is really his Son. It is therefore clear that we do not in ourselves become sons, but the Son in us. . . . Therefore the Father, before those in whom he sees his Son, declares that they are his sons and says: I have begotten you and this verb "beget" refers to the Son, while the verb "make" refers to creatures' (*PG* 26,273; based on Fr. tr. by E. Mersch; Cyril of Alexandria, *De recta fide ad Theod.*: 'Christ is both the only Son and the first-born son. He is the only Son as God; he is the first-born son by the saving union that he has established between us and him when he became man. By this, we, in and through him, have been made sons of God, both by nature and by grace. We are sons by nature in him and only in him; we are sons by participation and grace through him in the Spirit' (*PG* 76, 1177; based on Fr. tr. by E. Mersch); Augustine, *De div. quaest.* LXXXIII, q. 69 (*PL* 40, 79); *In Ioan. ev.* XLI (*PL* 35, 1696); *In ep. ad Parth*. X (*PL* 35, 2055). See also E. Mersch, *Le Corps mystique du Christ*, 2nd ed. (Brussels and Paris, 1936), II, pp. 86ff.
17. Ignatius of Antioch, *Ad Rom*. VII, 2 (and 116) (ed. F. X. Funk, I, p. 260). Is this an echo of Jn 4:14? See also Athanasius, *Ad Ser*. I, 25: the Son, through his incarnation, 'ennobles the whole of creation in the Spirit by making it divine, by making it son, and he takes it to the Father' (*PG* 26, 589).
18. 'Idem numero Spiritus', Encyclical *Mystici Corporis*, *AAS* 35 (1943), 219. See also above, p. 23, note 19.

19. See M. E. Isaacs, *The Concept of Spirit. A Study of Pneuma in Hellenistic Judaism and its Bearing on the New Testament (Heythrop Monographs)* (London, 1976).

20. C. Larcher, *Etudes sur le Livre de la Sagesse (Etudes bibliques)* (Paris, 1969), p. 362, note 1.

21. See Irenaeus, *Adv. haer.* III, 18, 1 (*PG* 7, 932; *SC* 211/2, p. 342: 'semper aderat generi humano'); *Dem.* 34 (*SC* 62, p. 87: 'according to his invisible state, is poured out among us in the whole of this universe'); Clement of Alexandria, *Protrept.* 112, 1 (*GCS* Clem. I, p. 79); *Strom.* VI, 6, 44, 1 (II, p. 453); 13, 106, 3 and 4 (II, p. 485). See also W. Bierbaum, 'Geschichte als Paidogogia Theou: Die Heilsgeschichtslehre des Klemens', *Münchener Theologische Zeitschrift*, 5 (1954), 246–272. For the *Semina Verbi*, see also A. Luneau, *L'histoire du salut chez les Pères de l'Eglise. La doctrine des âges du monde* (Paris, 1964), pp. 89 (Justin Martyr), 113ff. (Clement). Later the Fathers were more critical: pp. 148–149 (Basil the Great), 157 (Gregory Nazianzen), 240 (Hilary of Poitiers), 281. The same teaching was taken up again by Pius XII in his encyclical *Evangelii praecones* of 2 April 1951, 58 and 62; broadcast message of 31 December 1952; address of 29 November 1957: *AAS*, 49 (1957), 906–922; and by John XXIII in his encyclical *Mater et Magistra*: *AAS*, 53 (1961), 444; see also the Dogmatic Constitution on the Church, *Lumen Gentium*, 16, and the Pastoral Constitution on the Church in the Modern World, *Gaudium et Spes*, 57, 4.

22. *Adv. haer.* III, 11, 8 (*SC* 211, pp. 168, 169); 17, 3 (pp. 330, 331).

23. *ibid.*, III, 11, 9 (pp. 171, 172).

24. *ibid.*, 17, 1 (pp. 330, 331).

25. See Isidore of Seville, *Sent.* I, 15, 4 (*PL* 83, 569); Beatus, *In Apoc.* I, ed. H. A. Sanders (Rome, 1930), p. 44; Walafrid Strabo, *De exordiis*, pr. (*PL* 144, 919; *MGH*, Cap. II, p. 475); Pope Zacharias, in 743 (Jaffé, 2270); Pope Zosimus, quoted by Prosper of Aquitaine, *Contra Collatorem*, 5 (*PL* 51, 228A); Peter Abelard, *Theologia* (*PL* 178, 1221C). A cosmic view of the part played by the Spirit was sometimes suggested— Abelard thought, for example, that the soul of the world to which the philosophers referred might point to the life-giving activity of the Spirit in the universe, at least *per involucrum* or 'by envelopment': see M.-T. d'Alverny, 'Abélard et l'astrologie', *Pierre Abélard. Pierre le Vénérable (Cluny 2–9 juillet 1972)* (Paris, 1975), pp. 611–628. This was why Abelard was accused, at the Council of Sens in 1140, of making the Holy Spirit into the 'soul of the world': see *DS* 722.

26. *PL* 17, 245. Z. Alszeghy, *Nova Creatura—La nozione della grazia nei commentari medievali di S. Paolo* (Rome, 1956). p. 196, refers to Hervetus of Bourg-Dieu (*PL* 181, 939ff.); Peter Lombard (*PL* 191, 1650); Peter the Chanter, John of La Rochelle and Peter of Tarantaise, *Dilucidatio* (Antwerp ed., (1617), 215a).

27. Thomas Aquinas, *Comm. in Tit.* c. 1, lect. 3, end; *Comm. in ev. Ioan*, c. 8, lect. 6.

28. *ST* Ia IIae, q. 109, a. 1, ad 1.

29. *Comm. in 2 Tim.* c. 3, lect. 3.

30. Albert the Great, *In I Sent.* 2, 5 (ed. A. Borgnet, XXV, 39); II, d. 25, c. 6 (Borgnet, XXVII, 433). For Albert, the Holy Spirit was *in omnibus*: see *De grat. Cap.*, ed. I. Backes, *Florilegium Patristicum*, XL (Bonn, 1935), p. 20. In other words, no man is without some grace.

31. *Gaudium et Spes*, 41, 1 speaks of the Spirit's task in helping men in their religious need; in 38, 5, the document refers to the gifts of the Spirit leading men to salvation; and finally, in 26, 4 and 42, 4, every movement towards justice and unity in the world is attributed to the activity of the same Spirit.

32. G. Fedotov, 'De l'Esprit Saint dans la nature et dans la culture', *Contacts*, 28 (No. 95: 1976), 212–228.

33. Langdon Gilkey, 'L'Esprit et la découverte de la vérité dans le dialogue', *L'expérience de l'Esprit. Mélanges Schillebeeckx (Le Point théologique*, 18) (Paris, 1976), pp. 225–240, especially pp. 231–232.

34. In the Dedication of *The Internal Mission of the Holy Ghost* (London, 1875), Manning says: 'It is true to say with S. Irenaeus, *Ubi Ecclesia ibi Spiritus*,—Where the Church is there is the Spirit, but it would not be true to say, Where the Church is not, neither is the Spirit there. The operations of the Holy Ghost have always pervaded the whole race of men from the beginning and they are now in full activity even among those who are without the Church.'
35. Two contributors to *Concilium* have, for example, spoken about this: Y. Raguin, 'Evangelization and World Religious', *Concilium*, 114 (1978), 47–53; W. Dwyer, 'The Theologian in the Ashram', *ibid*., 115 (1978), 92–101, whose article deals with Kabīr, a mystical poet of the fifteenth century.
36. John V. Taylor, *The Go-Between God* (London, 1972), p. 64.
37. *Adv. haer*. IV, 33, 7ff. (*SC* 100, pp. 818 and 819, which contain the Fr. tr. on which the above rendering is based). I have followed the explanation of the expression: *tas oikonomias . . . skēnobatoun* given by H. J. Jaschke, *Der Heilige Geist im Bekenntnis der Kirche. Eine Studie zur Pneumatologie des Irenäus von Lyon im Ausgang vom altchristlichen Glaubensbekenntnis* (Münster, 1976), p. 51. The precise meaning of the verb translated as 'produces' is 'to produce on the stage'.
38. Aristotle, *Physics*, VIII.
39. Rūmi, *Mathnawi*, V, 39ff.: see Eva de Vitray Meyerovitch, *Mystique et Poésie en Islam. Djalâl-ud-Din Rûmi et l'Ordre des Derviches Tourneurs*, 2nd ed. (Paris, 1972), p. 184, note 5.
40. Dante, *The Divine Comedy: Paradise*, XXXIII.
41. Y. Congar, *The Mystery of the Temple, or the Manner of God's Presence to his Creatures from Genesis to the Apocalypse* (Eng. tr.; London, 1962), pp. 188ff.
42. See Is 2:2–3 (= Mic 4:1–3); 56:6–8; 60:11–14; Zech 8:20ff.; 14:16. See also *The Mystery of the Temple, op. cit.* (note 41), esp. pp. 77ff.
43. Clement of Alexandria (†c. 211–216), quoted by M.-D. Chenu, *Peuple de Dieu dans le monde* (Paris, 1966), p. 34.
44. *The Way of a Pilgrim* (Eng. tr.; paperback ed., London, 1972), p. 47. R. Laurentin's statement may perhaps be too optimistic, since the world always presents us with an ambiguous image: 'The Spirit changes the tragic, hopeless groaning of creation (Rom 8:19–23) into the ineffable groaning of hope (8:26). It is not the Spirit who groans but he brings to a new stage of awareness both man and his human environment in their anxious yearning for salvation': *Catholic Pentecostalism* (London, 1977), p. 158.
45. They can also be found in the liturgy; for example: 'Father, you are holy indeed, and all creation rightly gives you praise' (Eucharistic Prayer No. 3).
46. See also Eva de Vitray Meyerovitch, *op. cit.* (note 39), p. 192.
47. W. Kasper, *Jesus the Christ* (London and New York, 1976), p. 100.
48. See the Dogmatic Constitution on the Church, *Lumen Gentium*, 9.
49. Charles Péguy, *Le mystère des saints innocents* (NRF duodecimo ed., p. 51):
'I can see the fourth fleet. I see the invisible fleet.
And it is all the prayers that are not even said, the words that are not even pronounced,
But I can hear them. Those obscure movements of the heart, the obscure good movements, the secret good movements
Which rise unconsciously, are born and unconsciously ascend to me.
The one in whom they have their seat may not even be aware of them. He knows nothing—he is only their seat,
But I gather them up, says God, I count them and weigh them,
Because I am the secret judge.'
50. Maurice Clavel, *Ce que je crois* (Paris, 1975), p. 234: 'A young Christian whom I met, a member of the Charismatic Renewal who had been a ringleader in the riots of May 1968, told me, shrugging his shoulders: "May? A Pentecost without the Spirit at the most!" I replied, still faithful to my doctrine and thinking of the passage, which was also a doctrine:

"With an undeciphered Spirit, from whom they suffered". He said: "If you like, but in that case really unrevealed!".'

51. Paul Claudel, 'Cantique de Palmyre', *Conversations dans le Loir-et-Cher* (Paris, 1935), p. 731: 'There are many souls, but there is not one with whom I am not in communion by that sacred point in it which says *Pater noster*'.

52. P. Evdokimov, *L'Orthodoxie* (Paris, 1959), p. 343.

53. Conciliar Decree on the Church's Missionary Activity, *Ad Gentes divinitus*, 7, 3.

54. *Didache* IX, 4; see also X, 5: 'Gather it (the Church) from the four winds, sanctified, into your kingdom'.

55. J. A. Jungmann, 'In der Einheit des Heiligen Geistes', *Gewordene Liturgie* (Innsbruck, 1941), pp. 190–205; *Missarum Sollemnia* (Freiburg, 1948), II, p. 321; 4th ed., pp. 329–330 and *Nachtrag*, pp. 592–594; *The Mass of the Roman Rite* (abridged Eng. tr.; New York, 1959), pp. 457–458; 'In unitate Spiritus Sancti', *ZKT*, 72 (1950), 481–486.

56. B. Botte, *M-D*, 23 (1950), 49–53; *idem, L'Ordinaire de la Messe* (Paris, 1953), pp. 133–139. Certain additional references can be found in P. Smulders, *Dictionnaire de Spiritualité*, IV, col. 1275.

A NOTE ON
'YOU ARE MY FATHER' IN THE ETERNITY
OF THE INTRA-DIVINE LIFE

It would be wrong to postulate a reciprocity between the divine Persons of the Trinity that might lead to our acknowledging a plurality of consciousnesses and might be tainted with tritheism. This wrong interpretation is sometimes suggested, at least in forms of expression, when psychological findings with regard to intersubjectivity are applied to God. But this does not close the discussion. For, without separating them and even without making a distinction between them, the New Testament, for example, speaks of Jesus the man and Saviour because of his death on the cross and of Jesus existing 'in the form of God'.[1] If Christ is present in this way in the eternity of the Trinity, he must also, in these conditions, be the image of 'God' (that is, of the Father) and return to him the reflection of his own similarity. The least that can be said is that it was part of the eternal plan of God that Jesus the man should be his image, that is, God revealed as man: Christ the 'lamb without blemish or spot' who was 'destined before the foundation of the world, but made manifest at the end of times for our sake' (1 Pet 1:19–20).

If, however, this was God's eternal plan, does it not imply that the Son, the perfect uncreated image of the Father, was conceived eternally by that Father as due to be the perfect created image of God in a created world? Does it not mean that the Son, the Word, was conceived and begotten eternally as *incarnandus* and *immolandus*, due to be made flesh and sacrificed? It is in *that* Son, the Word, that the adventure of the world can be understood and that 'all things hold together' (Col 1:17). If this is really the situation, is the perfect human response of Jesus Christ: 'You are my Father; I have come to do your will' not to some extent at least present in the eternally begotten Word?

Let us stay a little longer with the life of God within the Trinity. What is the part played by the Spirit in a possible reciprocity between the Father and the Son, the Word? In Volume III of this work, we shall see that certain Orthodox theologians, such as Paul Evdimokov, say that the Word was begotten *a Patre Spirituque*. The order of the processions which makes the Spirit the third Person (without making God three, since the Persons are consubstantial) makes it, I feel, impossible to speak as Evdimokov does. In the Augustinian view of the Spirit as the bond of love between Father and Son, which has had very little influence of Eastern theology, 'the Father directs a fatherly love towards the Son and takes delight in the one whom he begets as his equal, and he does so in the way that is appropriate, that is to say by spirating that love [the Spirit]. The Son also takes delight in the Father, but as a son, in being born of him.' This way of putting it runs the risk of slipping from an essential love that is common to all three Persons to a so-called 'notional' love that is characteristic of the third Person, the Spirit. The author who made the above statement, E. Bailleux, however, goes on to say: 'Whereas the Father desires [but is this by his essential will?] to be the principle of the Son, the reciprocal opposite cannot be true, nor is this necessary for a real reciprocity of love. It is by spirating the Spirit as a son that the Son turns towards his principle and takes delight in the Father, by wishing to be what he in fact is personally, the principle without principle and the unbegotten.'[2] It is therefore by this spiration of the Spirit—by the Father as the first and absolute source, that is, *principaliter*, and by the Son, the Word, depending on the Father—that a reciprocity of love between the first two Persons of the Trinity occurs, and that reciprocity is the Spirit, within the firm consubstantiality of the three Persons. This means that there is a reciprocity of love between the absolute principle, the Father (who loves the Son: see Jn 3:35; 5:20), and the one who proceeds from him by pure begetting, both in dependence as a son and in equality of being, let alone in reality of substance.

NOTES

1. Jesus Christ was 'in the form of God' (Phil 2:6); he plays a part in creation (1 Cor 8:6; Col 1:15); he is the image of God (2 Cor 4:6; Col 1:15; Heb 1:3); he is 'before Abraham' (Jn 8:58); he had the glory with the Father 'before the world was made' (17:5, 24). See P. Benoît, 'Préexistence et Incarnation', *RB*, 77 (1970), 5–29. According to some readings, the Lamb in Rev 13:8 was sacrificed 'before the foundation of the world', though the Jerusalem Bible and the French *Traduction Œcuménique* translate this verse differently [as does RSV].
2. See E. Bailleux, 'L'Esprit du Père et du Fils selon S. Augustin', *RThom*, 77 (1977), 5–29, especially 20.

THE RIVER OF THE WATER OF LIFE (REV 22:1) FLOWS IN THE EAST AND IN THE WEST

In memory of Patrice Kučela
who was perhaps the most gifted of my students
and who was killed by the Gestapo in Prague,
when his country was subjected to tyranny.

'Arise, O Jerusalem, stand upon the height . . .
and see your children gathered from west and east
at the word of the Holy One!'

(Bar 5:5)

CONTENTS

CONTENTS

CONTENTS

PART TWO

THE HOLY SPIRIT AND THE SACRAMENTS

ix

ABBREVIATIONS
USED IN THIS BOOK

AAS   Acta Apostolicae Sedis
Acta Acad. Velehrad.   Acta Academiae Velehradensis
Anal. Greg.   Analecta Gregoriana
Année théol. august.   Année théologique augustinienne
Arch. Franc. Hist.   Archivum Franciscanum historicum
Arch. Fr. Praed.   Archivum Fratrum Praedicatorum
Arch. hist. doctr. litt. M.A.   Archives d'histoire doctrinale et littéraire du Moyen Age
Arch. Hist. Pont.   Archivum historiae pontificiae
Bibl. August.   Bibliothèque augustinienne
Bibl. Byzant. Brux.   Bibliotheca Byzantina Bruxellensis
Bibl. de philos. contemp.   Bibliothèque de philosophie contemporaine
Bibl. ETL   Bibliotheca Ephemeridum Theologicarum Lovaniensium
Bibl. Œcum.   Bibliothèque Œcuménique
BLE   Bulletin de littérature ecclésiastique
BullThom   Bulletin thomiste
CNRS   Centre National de la Recherche Scientifique
CSEL   Corpus Scriptorum Ecclesiasticorum Latinorum
DACL   Dictionnaire d'archéologie chrétienne et de liturgie
Dict. Hist. Geó. Eccl.   Dictionnaire d'histoire et de géographie ecclésiastiques
Doc. cath.   La documentation catholique
DS   Enchiridion Symbolorum, ed. H. Denzinger, rev. A. Schönmetzer
DTC   Dictionnaire de théologie catholique
ECQ   Eastern Churches Quarterly
ETL   Ephemerides Theologicae Lovanienses
GCS   Griechische christliche Schriftsteller
Greg   Gregorianum
JTS   Journal of Theological Studies
Mansi   *Sacrorum Conciliorum nova et amplissima Collectio*, ed. J. D. Mansi
M-D   La Maison-Dieu
MGH   Monumenta Germaniae historica
MScRel   Mélanges de science religieuse
NRT   Nouvelle Revue théologique
Or. Chr.   Oriens Christianus
Or. Chr. Anal.   Orientalia christiana analecta
Or. Chr. Period.   Orientalia christiana periodica
Patr. Or.   Patrologia Orientalis
Patr. Syr.   Patrologia Syriaca
PG   Migne, *Patrologia Graeca*
PL   Migne, *Patrologia Latina*

RAM   Revue d'ascétique et de mystique
RB   Revue biblique
RBén   Revue bénédictine
Rev. Et. byz.   Revue des études byzantines
Rev. M.A. latin   Revue du Moyen Age latin
RHE   Revue d'histoire ecclésiastique
RHPR   Revue d'histoire et de philosophie religieuses
RSPT   Revue des sciences philosophiques et théologiques
RSR   Recherches de science religieuse
RTAM   Recherches de théologie ancienne et médiévale
RThom   Revue thomiste
RTL   Revue théologique de Louvain
SC   Sources chrétiennes
Spicil. Sacr. Lovan.   Spicilegium Sacrum Lovaniense
ST   Summa Theologica
TDNT   G. Kittel and G. Friedrich (eds), *Theological Dictionary of the New Testament* (Eng. tr.)
ThSt   Theological Studies
TQ   Theologische Quartalschrift
VS   La Vie spirituelle
ZAW   Zeitschrift für die alttestamentliche Wissenschaft
ZKT   Zeitschrift für katholische Theologie
ZTK   Zeitschrift für Theologie und Kirche

INTRODUCTION

1

THE PRESENTATION OF THIS VOLUME

I must begin this book by explaining its nature and contents and how it came to be written. Chamfort said that 'theology is to religion what casuistry is to justice', but I am not very impressed by this observation, because I know that it is not true. Theology is the cultivation of faith by the honest use of the cultural means available at the time. Bonhoeffer's remark that the only choice for the Church is between concrete statement and silence, and that the Church is lying if it only utters principles, touches me more nearly, though not to the extent that I feel his disapproval of my own work. He spoke in this way, after all, at a time when Christians were required to resist Nazism. He also criticized Karl Barth in a more general way for 'positivism of Revelation', and here I would think the reference more closely applied to me, although I would point out that there is also a positivism of experience and the here and now. To each his own positivism!

One question seems to me to be very important for everyone and also for the theologian and his special task. It is the question of the country he lives in, the frame of reference within which he works and the language he speaks. As a theologian, I live in the Church of the Scriptures, the Fathers and the Councils. I am a teacher and my task is to teach. This task is reflected in my language, which is didactic. My way of life is marked by—I could almost say that it bears the stigmata of—difficulties that have for years now made it more sedentary than it once was, more restricted to papers, books and texts. This present work is the fruit of labours commenced a long time ago. Over the years, a great deal of documentation, perhaps too much, has accumulated. The work has been accompanied by love and prayer, and the sometimes too ponderous elements of scholarship have been transformed every day into praise and worship.

I have been told that my language is not the language of today and will not be understood by contemporary readers. A friend asked me if I could not go on to publish an outline of the whole which would be accessible to people like him, ordinary people of the kind described by Chesterton—if God had not loved them he would not have made so many of them. I would like to satisfy him and I may try to do so, though I cannot be sure that I shall succeed. However true these comments may be, they have not prevented me from writing, nor have they convinced me that my task is vain. After all, the suggestion that I should 'speak the language of today' raises the immediate question: Which language of today? And would it be more easily understood? All language is related to man and to whatever relationships he has, and that of the Fathers of the Church is related to God and his mystery. It not only calls for a great intellectual effort to move into the country inhabited by the Fathers—it even requires a religious conversion. And is their language really so remote from the language of today? Their writings are certainly being widely read, questioned and heeded again today. In this volume, however, I have had in mind above all the theological dialogue between Orthodox Christianity and Roman Catholicism.

This dialogue is, fortunately, to begin with the subject of the sacraments and of the Church as a 'mystery', that is, as the great sacrament. These realities of grace have remained common to Orthodox and Western Catholics at a deep level. Sooner or later, however, and probably sooner, we shall again come up against difficulties concerning the theology of the Holy Spirit as such and the theology of the part that he plays in the sacraments that have not been overcome in a thousand years of confrontation. I shall try to deal with some of them in the present volume and I have, for this purpose, divided it into two parts. In the course of his meeting with Pope John Paul II on 29 November 1980 in Istanbul, the Ecumenical Patriarch Dimitrios I spoke of the 'serious theological problems contained in essential chapters of the Christian faith'. He was probably thinking here of the problems with which I deal in this volume. The Bishop of Rome, on the other hand, spoke of 'disagreement not so much at the level of faith as at the level of expression', and in so doing confirmed the conclusion reached in several very serious studies and even in my own modest efforts.

Before proceeding to this Volume III, I should like to express my gratitude to those who have helped me so much, either by obtaining the books that I needed or by typing the manuscript. I would like to thank especially Fr Nicolas Walty and Mme Nicole Legrain, without whom this book would never have appeared, any more than Volumes I and II.

2

GREEK AND LATIN
TRINITARIAN THEOLOGY

The mystery of the Trinity only came to be suitably formulated after many tentative expressions, errors and half-truths, a large number of them running into dead-ends, had been hazarded by some of the most clear-thinking and most Christian authors in each successive period in the early history of the Church. This history has been fully written[1] and I shall not attempt to rewrite it here. I am more concerned with pneumatology, but this is, of course, inseparable from the mystery of the Tri-unity of God himself.

These very imperfect and tentative expressions conceal an intention that is much firmer than the expressions themselves. Justin Martyr made no distinction between the Logos and the Spirit, yet he gave his life for the Christian faith. It took at least two further centuries of more or less successful attemps for a satisfactory vocabulary to emerge, that of one substance and three hypostases or persons. Even such a heroic defender of orthodox faith as Athanasius did not distinguish between *ousia* (essence) and *hypostasis*.[2] Basil the Great was still hesitant on this point. This very vocabulary itself was also a source of difficulties between the Greek East and the Latin West. The literal translation of *hypostasis* into Latin was *substantia*, but the problem arose as to whether one should speak of 'three substances' in the way that the Greeks spoke, quite rightly, of 'three hypostases'. This difficulty troubled Jerome and it appeared again in the Middle Ages.[3]

The faith that was not only professed in the doxology but also lived was, however, fundamentally the same both in the East and in the West. There were, of course, differences in approach, in the theological articulation of the mystery, even at the level of its dogmatic expression, and in intellectual categories and vocabulary. However deep these differences were, however, I am convinced that the Trinitarian faith of the eastern part of the Church was the same as that of the western part.[4] I knew, liked and admired Vladimir Lossky (†1958), who had outstanding ability as a dogmatic theologian in the highest sense of the word, but I told him again and again that I could not agree with his conviction that the *Filioque* was not only the origin of all the differences between the Greek Orthodox and the Roman Catholic Church, but also an article causing an insurmountable opposition between the two branches of the Church and an unbridgeable distance between them. Lossky became less obstinate on this point as he got older, but he had in the meantime, unfortunately, won over a large number of followers.[5]

As I have indicated, there are differences between the East and the West. Their approach and their way of articulating the mystery of the Tri-unity of God are different. It is a precondition of any effort to make manifest the deep community of faith that exists between the two parts of the Church and to express that community in a satisfactory way that this different approach should be recognized and accepted. My own personal experience, both from reading and from contact with individuals and communities, leads me to agree with several experts, including Mgr Szepticky, the Metropolitan of Lwow: 'the East differs from the West even in questions in which they do not differ at all';[6] or T. de Régnon: 'we ought to regard the Greek and the Latin Churches as two sisters who love and visit each other, but who have a different way of keeping house and who therefore live apart'.[7]

It was above all de Régnon († 26 December 1893) who gave a new impetus to Trinitarian studies, more precisely to studies devoted to an improved understanding of the Greek Fathers compared with the Latin Fathers.[8] We all owe a great deal to this scholar, who came to the extremely valuable conclusion that the dogmatic structures of the East and the West are different, but express the same intention in faith. The East and the West agree in faith. At the same time, however, de Régnon simplified the difference between the theologies, with the result that many theologians, especially Orthodox scholars, have since taken his most clear-cut formulae as they stand. It is interesting to quote some of these here:

> Latin philosophers focused first on nature in itself and then traced it back to the supposit, whereas the Greeks first focused on the supposit and then entered into it in order to find nature. The Latins regarded the personality as the way in which nature was expressed, while the Greeks thought of nature as the content of the person. These are contrary ways of viewing things, throwing two concepts of the same reality on to different grounds.
>
> The Latin theologian therefore says: 'three persons in God', whereas the Greek says: 'one God in three persons'. In both cases, the faith and the dogma are the same, but the mystery is presented in two different forms.

> If we think first of the concept of nature and the concept of personality is then added to it, the concrete reality has to be defined as a 'personified nature'. This is seeing nature *in recto* and the person *in obliquo*. If, on the other hand, we think first of the concept of the person and the concept of nature comes later, then the concrete reality must be defined as 'a person possessing a nature'. This is seeing the person *in recto* and nature *in obliquo*. The two *definitions* are true and complete and both are adequate to the object in mind, but they are the result of two different views, and that is why the logical deductions from them follow opposite paths.
>
> The Scholastic theology of the Latin Church followed one of these ways, while the dogmatic theology of the Greek Church continued on the other path. The consequence is that the two theologies express the same truth, just as two symmetrical triangles may be equal, but cannot be placed one on top of the other.[9]

De Régnon had clearly perceived an authentic and fundamental truth here, and we shall see later how closely it corresponds to the reality. Similar comments were made more recently by the historian of doctrine J. N. D. Kelly, whose conclusions are closer to the original texts and at the same time less systematic.[10] De Régnon's insights have unfortunately often been even further simplified and hardened to the point of becoming misleading caricatures. A few examples will illustrate this:

> What characterizes all these constructions is their initial impersonalism. This is present at the very birth of the hypostases and it points to the ontological primacy of the ousia over the hypostasis. It is not characteristic of the Cappadocian Fathers, for whom the hypostases existed as such, but it is characteristic of Augustine's teaching and that of all Catholic theologians, with their initial *deitas* in which the hypostases exist as relationships of origin, through mutual opposition. This Catholic doctrine of the procession is simply an impersonal subordination-ism, in which the *deitas* or deity is the primordial metaphysical basis and, in this sense, the sufficient foundation or the cause of the hypostases.[11]

> For Augustine, on the other hand, the processions can be reduced to attributes of the one essence of God.[12]

> Latin theology has yielded to this influence and has abandoned the level of theological personalism, becoming a philosophy of the essence.[13]

> The doctrine of the *Filioque* . . . confines the Trinity of the persons within the unity of nature by making them relations based on essence. . . . (If the Father and the Son are a single principle of spiration) there are no longer two distinct hypostases, but impersonal substance instead.[14]

It is important first of all to understand the logic by which the Greeks on the one hand and the Latins on the other theologically (or dogmatically) elaborated their common faith in the mystery of the Trinity, and then to consider the attempts that have been made to resolve this irritating difference between their ideas concerning the procession of the Holy Spirit. Before going on to this question, however, I propose to conclude this Introduction by commenting, however schematically, on the different approach and development of theology in the East and the West and then recalling the history of the whole teaching about the Spirit. This mere reminder will enable me to discuss in a synthetic form the significance of each theology.

The contrast or at least the differences between these two theologies of the Trinity are the consequence of two different ways of approaching the mystery and of 'doing theology'. The Greeks inherited two rules from the Fathers and attempted to synthesize them. On the one hand, they made use of the resources of human reason. In opposition to Julian the Apostate, who had forbidden Christians to teach in the schools of grammar and rhetoric and to send their children to the public schools, the three 'hierarchs', Basil of Caesarea, Gregory Nazianzen and John Chrysostom, had insisted on and practised the use of rational resources. These resources were employed in the training of theologians rather than in the elaboration of revealed data. On the other hand, they had actively combated the wretched heresy of Eunomius and the Anomoeans [see below, p. 29], which proposed an entirely homogeneous and easy knowledge of God who, it claimed, could be known in the same way as other objects of our human reason. In opposition to this teaching, the Cappadocian Fathers affirmed that God was unknowable. We are able, they taught, to know something of him on the basis of his activity, but he himself always transcends every representation, which is always confined to the created order. John Chrysostom wrote a treatise on the unknowability of God (*SC* 28 (1951)) and Gregory of Nyssa's writings on the inaccessibility of God to the created mind, even when that is illuminated by faith, are classical.[15]

Reason, then, was put to good use in the theology of the Trinity—this is abundantly clear from the writings of Athanasius, Basil the Great and the two Gregorys. It was employed above all to refute heresies and to expose their errors of interpretation. In the positive treatment of the mystery, however, one simply had to follow Scripture, the Fathers and the Councils. The practice followed in the East is well summarized in the nineteenth canon of the Council 'in Trullo' (692), which is usually regarded as belonging to the Sixth Ecumenical Council (the Third Council of Constantinople): 'The Church's pastors must explain Scripture in accordance with the commentaries of the Fathers'.[16]

The situation changed with regard to our subject, the procession of the Holy Spirit, when the Patriarch Photius published his *Mystagogic Discourse on the Holy Spirit* (*PG* 102, 280–392) about 886. Photius did not confine himself to scriptural arguments and references to patristic or papal texts—he also made extensive use of his critical reason. Since his time, the debate between Orthodox and Catholic Christians over the dogmatic construction of the mystery has at least partly consisted of rational theological argument. The Greek theologians could on occasion be as competent and as subtle in their reasoning as their Latin counterparts. Their theological attitude and temperament, however, remained different. The Catholic dogma of the *Filioque* is based on dogmatic reasoning, but in the first place it goes back to scriptural data. Augustine, for example, spoke of the *Filioque* because the New Testament attributes the Spirit both to the Father and to the Son. At the same time, he also made it a rule in Latin theology that an *intellectus fidei* or an 'understanding of faith' should be sought through reasoning and meditation and therefore, if necessary, outside Scripture. Anselm and Thomas Aquinas devoted their metaphysical brilliance to developing this theology.

In the fourteenth century, therefore, in the face of the predominant Scholastic theology of the West and the humanistic attitude of, for example, Barlaam, and then when translations of the great Latin theological writings began to appear in Greece, intense discussions took place about the theological method and the place and structure of the syllogism, as well as whether it should consist of two premises of faith, or one of faith and one of reason.[17] Over and against these views, Gregory Palamas (1296–1359) defended both the unknowability of the divine essence and the reality of a supernatural and mystical knowledge of God that was quite different from a rational or intellectual knowledge. The Greek theologians of this tradition found the rationality of the Latin Scholastics an unacceptable intrusion on the part of created reason into the mysteries of God. The best example of a serious criticism of Latin theology by the Greeks who accused their Western counterparts of rationalizing the mystery of God's being by a mistaken use of the syllogism will be found in the treatise written by Nilus Cabasilas, the Archbishop of Thessalonica (†1363). This was edited some years ago by Emmanuel Candal.[18] Nilus discussed (and believed that he had refuted) fifteen syllogisms on which the theology of the *Filioque* was supposedly based. This is the impression that many Greek theologians still had at the Council of Ferrara (Florence) in 1438–1439.[19] The Latin theologians, on the other hand, thought that the Greeks' opposition to their arguments was attributable to a lack of intellectual power.[20]

I should like to make my own the testimony of Pope Paul VI in support of the position that the above observations have a significance for us today, even though they are concerned with past history; that I have a very high regard for the Eastern way of doing theology, and that I should like to place myself in a tradition common to both East and West. What Pope Paul VI said on his return from a journey—or pilgrimage—to Turkey, where he visited Istanbul (Constantinople) and Ephesus among other places, was as follows:

> The East is a master, teaching us that we, as believers, are not only called to reflect about the revealed truth, that is, to formulate a theology which may rightly be described as scientific (see *DS* 3135ff.), but also obliged to recognize the supernatural character of that revealed truth. That character does not entitle us to interpret that truth in terms of pure natural rationality and it requires us to respect, in the texts, the very terminology in which that truth was stated with authority (*DS* 824 [442], 2831 [1658]). The East provides us with an example of faithfulness to our doctrinal inheritance and reminds us of a rule which is also our own and which we have often reaffirmed recently, at a time when so many attempts are being made—many of them full of good intentions, but not always with happy results— to express a new theology that is in accordance with present-day attitudes. This rule was expressed by the First Vatican Council, which looked for progress in 'understanding, knowledge and wisdom' in the Church's teaching, on condition that that teaching remained what it had always been (see *De fide* IV; Vincent of Lérins, *Commonitorium*, 28: *PL* 50, 668).

> During our journey, we wanted to assure the East that the faith of the Councils that were celebrated on this blessed soil and that are recognized by the Latin Church as ecumenical is still our faith. That faith forms a very wide and solid basis for studies destined to restore perfect Christian communion between the

Orthodox and the Catholic Churches in that single and firm teaching that the Church's magisterium, guided by the Holy Spirit, proclaims as authentic.[21]

NOTES

1. J. Lebreton, *Histoire du dogme de la Trinité*, I and II (as far as Irenaeus), 6th ed. (Paris, 1927–1928); G.-L. Prestige, *God in Patristic Thought*, 2nd ed. (London, 1952); J. N. D. Kelly, *Early Christian Doctrines*, 5th ed. (London, 1977); G. Kretschmar, 'Le développement de la doctrine du Saint-Esprit du Nouveau Testament à Nicée', *Verbum Caro*, 88 (1968), 555. In addition to these works, the following may also be mentioned: H. B. Swete, *On the History of the Doctrine of the Procession of the Holy Spirit from the Apostolic Age to the Death of Charlemagne* (Cambridge, 1876); *idem*, *The Holy Spirit in the Ancient Church* (London, 1912); T. Reusch, *Die Entstehung der Lehre von Heiligen Geiste* (Zürich, 1953); H. Opitz, *Ursprünge frühchristlicher Pneumatologie* (Berlin, 1960).

2. See G. Bardy, *DTC*, XV, cols 1666–1667. See also Epiphanius of Salamis, *Haer.* 69, 72.

3. Volume I, pp. 75–76, 82 note 23; Prestige, *op. cit.*, pp. 187ff., 235ff.; T. de Régnon, *op. cit.* below (note 8), I, p. 216, with Faustus of Riez' excellent text of 480. For Anselm, see below, pp. 101–102, note 8; Thomas Aquinas, *Contra Err. Graec.*, I, prol.

4. Richard of Saint-Victor, confirming that some in fact spoke of three substances and one essence, while others spoke of three subsistences and one substance, wrote in his *De Trin.* IV, 20 (*PL* 196, 943C): 'Sed absit ab eis (Graeci et Latini) diversa credere, et hos vel illos in fide errare! In hac ergo verborum varietate intelligenda est veritas una, quamvis apud diversos sit nominum acceptio diversa.' Alexander of Hales said in this context: 'idem credunt (Graeci et Latini) sed non eodem modo proferunt': see below, pp. 174ff.

5. See H.-M. Legrand's article in *RSPT*, 56 (1972), 697–700.

6. Quoted by G. Tsébricov, *L'esprit de l'Orthodoxie* (*Irénikon*, Collection No. 7) (1927), p. 9.

7. T. de Régnon, *op. cit.* below (note 8), III, p. 412.

8. T. de Régnon, *Etudes de théologie positive sur la Sainte Trinité*, 4 vols (Paris, I and II 1892, III and IV 1898).

9. *Ibid.*, I, pp. 433–434 and 251–252 respectively. See also I, pp. 276, 305, 309, 387–388, 428ff.; IV, pp. 128, 143.

10. Kelly, *op. cit.* (note 1), says, for example (p. 136): 'Western Trinitarianism . . . had long been marked by a monarchian bias. What was luminously clear to the theologians representing it was the divine unity; so mysterious did they find the distinctions within the unity that, though fully convinced of their reality, they were only beginning, haltingly and timidly, to think of them as "Persons". In the East, where the intellectual climate was impregnated with Neo-Platonic ideas about the hierarchy of being, an altogether different, confessedly pluralistic approach had established itself.' He is referring to the third century, that is, before Athanasius and the Cappadocian Fathers on the one hand and Augustine on the other.

11. S. Bulgakov, *Le Paraclet*, Fr. tr. C. Andronikof (Paris, 1946), pp. 67–68; see also pp. 118 ff.

12. J. Meyendorff, *Russie et Chrétienté*, 4th series, 2nd year (1950), 160.

13. S. Verkhovsky, *ibid.*, 195.

14. V. Lossky, quoted by O. Clément, 'Vladimir Lossky, un théologien de la personne et du Saint-Esprit', *Messager de l'Exarchat du Patriarche russe en Europe occidentale*, 8th year, 30–31 (April–September 1959), 137–206, especially 194. This number of the journal was devoted to Vladimir Lossky and appeared one year after his death.

15. See Gregory of Nyssa, *Life of Moses*, II, 163–164 (*SC* 1, 1955 ed., pp. 81–82). For the apophatism of the Fathers, see J. Hochstaffl, *Negative Theologie, Ein Versuch des patristischen Begriffs* (Munich, 1976). Examples of apophatism among the Latin Fathers and even among the Scholastic theologians can, however, also be found in dozens of texts.
16. C. J. Hefele and H. Leclercq, *Histoire des Conciles*, III/1 (Paris, 1913), p. 566.
17. The history of this movement will be found, exhaustively documented, in G. Podskalsky, *Theologie und Philosophie in Byzanz. Der Streit um die theologische Methodik in der spätbyzantinischen Geistesgeschichte (14./15. Jh.); seine systematischen Grundlagen und seine historische Entwicklung (Byzantinisches Archiv*, 15) (Munich, 1977), pp. 124 ff.
18. E. Candal, *Nilus Cabasilas et theologia S. Thomae de Processione Spiritus Sancti. Novum e Vaticanis codicibus subsidium ad historiam theologiae Byzantinae saeculi XIV plenius elucidandam (Studi e Testi*, 116) (Vatican, 1945).
19. J. Gill, *The Council of Florence* (Cambridge, 1959), p. 223, writes: 'One noteworthy difference can be remarked between the Greek and Latin methods as illustrated by Mark Eugenicus and Montenero. Though Mark showed that he understood and was at home in the philosophical explanation of the mystery of the Blessed Trinity, he did not bring that into his arguments except when pressed by an opponent. When he was putting forward his own proofs he was content to quote his scriptural or patristic authority and add comments which amounted to little more than a repetition of the words of his texts. The Latin orator on the other hand almost invariably argued from the passages that he quoted to the conclusion that he claimed must follow from an acceptance of the truth enunciated in the quotation.'
20. See, for example, this text by the former Master General of the Order of Preachers in his famous report to the Council of Lyons in 1274: 'Perit apud eos pro magna parte scientia cum studio, et ideo non intelligunt quae dicuntur eis per rationes, sed adhaerent semper quibusdem conciliis et quibusdam quae tradita sunt eis a praedecessoribus suis, sicut faciunt quidam haeretici idiotae, ad quos ratio nihil valet': Humbert of Romans, *Opus tripartitum*, Pars II, col. 11, in Edward Brown, *Appendix ad Fasciculum rerum expectandarum et fugiendarum* (London, 1690), II, p. 216.
21. Paul VI, audience of 2 August 1967: see *Doc. cath.*, 64, No. 1500, 1580.

PART ONE

THE HOLY SPIRIT
IN THE DIVINE TRI-UNITY

I

KNOWLEDGE OF THE TRINITARIAN MYSTERY

1

THE SOURCES OF OUR KNOWLEDGE OF THE HOLY SPIRIT NECESSITY AND CONDITIONS FOR A DOGMATIC AND THEOLOGICAL EXPRESSION

Our first source of knowledge is obviously Revelation itself, of which the conciliar document *Dei Verbum* had this to say: 'This plan of revelation is realized by deeds and words having an inner unity: the deeds wrought by God in the history of salvation manifest and confirm the teaching and realities signified by the words, while the words proclaim the deeds and clarify the mystery contained in them'.[1] There are, in other words, certain data with a revelatory value and, together with them, inspired words which disclose their meaning.

These data are those of the whole economy of grace, in the first place those contained in the Old and New Testaments, and then those of the whole history of salvation, including the modern period. I have drawn attention to a great number of these in the first two volumes of this work, as I have also to the corresponding texts. The texts in question are pre-eminently those of Scripture, but also those of the witnesses to Tradition, texts which are of secondary importance, but nonetheless very rich: the writings of the Fathers, the saints and the theologians of the Church and the Church's liturgy, all bearing witness to the Holy Spirit in different ways. I have already quoted many such witnesses and shall quote others in this volume. Together they constitute the great Christian family of which we acknowledge that we are members.

There are numerous statements in Scripture, some of them remarkably dogmatic in character and others substantially theological. Scripture often speaks of the Spirit and even of 'God', however, in images, and these were

3

taken up again by the Fathers, who frequently commented on them. It is
worth recalling some of the principal ones here:

Breath, air, wind: this is the very name of the Spirit.
Water, and especially living water.[2]
Fire, tongues of fire (Acts 2:3; Is 6:6): 'The great symbols of the Spirit—
water, fire, air and wind—belong to the world of nature and do not have
definite shapes; above all they call to mind the idea of being invaded by a
presence and of a deep and irresistible expansion'.[3]
Dove: see especially Volume I, pp. 16–17.
Anointing, chrism.[4]
Finger of God: especially in Lk 11:20, the parallel text, Mt 12:28, having
'Spirit'.[5] In the Old Testament, the finger of God is the instrument and the
sign of God's power (Ex 8:15) and even of his creative power (Ps 8:3; in
33:6, it is the 'breath of his mouth'). It is also the sign of the authority
employed by God in his initiative—the tablets of the Law were, for example,
written by his finger (Ex 31:18; Deut 9:10). In Christianity, God's law is
written by his Spirit in our hearts.[6] God's power, then, is expressed by his
arm and his hand, the extremity of which touches man. This touch is clearly
both strong and delicate: in his great painting of the creation of Adam in the
Sistine Chapel, Michelangelo provides a wonderful representation of this.
In the gospel, this is, it has been suggested, the expression of a participation
in God's holiness through a powerful, yet delicate touch.[7]
There are also other names given to the Holy Spirit which are less graphic,
but more open to speculation. They include:
Seal: the Spirit with whom the Father anointed Christ at his baptism
(Jn 6:27; Acts 10:38) and who has since then anointed and marked Christ-
ians (2 Cor 1:22; Eph 1:13; 4:30). This 'seal' represents something final and
definitive. The Spirit is the Promised One, the eschatological Gift. In God,
he is the fulfilment of the communication of the deity. Athanasius said that
the seal that marks us can only be the Spirit, God himself.[8]
Love: see Thomas Aquinas (*C. Gent.* IV, 19; *ST* Ia, q. 37 and parallel
texts).
Gift: see below, the chapter on St Augustine; see also Thomas Aquinas, *ST*
Ia, q. 38 and parallel texts. This title is so important that a whole chapter will
be devoted to it in this volume (see below, pp. 144–151).
Peace: see Jn 20:19, 21; cf. verses 22–23; see also Rom 14:17: 'peace and
joy in the Holy Spirit'.
To these images can be added those used in the liturgy. In this context, the
section in Volume I, pp. 104–111 should be re-read; the hymn *Veni Creator*
and the sequence *Veni, Sancte Spiritus* are there translated. A number of
texts of the Fathers and the spiritual writers can also be added, as, for
example, when St Simeon the New Theologian compares the Holy Spirit to
the key which opens the door (Volume I, pp. 97–98) or when St Bernard

compares him to a kiss exchanged between the Father and the Son (Volume I, pp. 90, 92 note 16).

The fact that the mystery of God has often and even preferentially been revealed in images of this kind can be justified in many different ways. The Alexandrian theologians (Origen and others), Pseudo-Dionysius and even Thomas[9] saw in it less a value of revelation than a veil concealing it, an *occultatio*. In that case, I would go so far as to speak of the 'kenotic' conditions of God's self-revelation and self-communication. (I shall discuss this later.) It is in any case worth recalling that the crudest comparisons are often the best, because they preclude any idea of reaching the mystery itself. In my view, however, the fact that God is revealed above all in images has a much deeper reason. It is this: the most material images are metaphors which do not in any sense claim to express being in itself, that is, the quiddity of what they are speaking about; they only express behaviour and what that represents for us. God is a rock, Christ is a lamb, the Spirit is living water. This does not mean that God is a mineral, Christ is an animal, or the Spirit is a liquid with a known chemical formula. It does, however, mean that God is, for us, firmness, Christ is a victim offered for us, and the Spirit is a dynamic bearer of life. Revelation, in other words, by being expressed in images, is essentially an expression of what God is *for us*. It also, of course, discloses something of what God is in himself, but it only does this secondarily and imperfectly. What he is is his secret. 'I know what God is for me', St Bernard said, 'but *quod ad se, ipse novit*—what he is for himself, he knows.'[10]

This fact of a revelation of a 'theology', that is, of the eternal and intimate mystery of God, in the 'economy', that is, in what God has done for us in his work of creation and grace, forms the basis of the thesis that I shall examine later [pp. 11–17] in connection with the question of the identity of the economic Trinity and the immanent Trinity.

This is particularly true in the case of the Holy Spirit. He is affirmed as the subject of certain actions in the New Testament, but not, as some exegetes have insisted, to the extent that he is no more than an impersonal power. At the same time, however, subject of actions as he is, he is certainly revealed without a personal face. The incarnate Word has a face—he has expressed his personality in our human history in the way persons do, and the Father has revealed himself in him. The Spirit does not present such personal characteristics. He is, as it were, buried in the work of the Father and the Son, which he completes. 'We do not usually spend too much time thinking about the breath that supports the word.'[11]

Vladimir Lossky and Paul Evdokimov have spoken of the Spirit's kenosis as a person. He has, as it were, emptied himself of the characteristics of a private or particular person. This is why those who have written about the Holy Spirit have frequently called him the 'unknown' or the 'half-known' one.[12] Already in his own time, Augustine noted that the Holy Spirit had hardly ever been discussed and his mystery had not been examined.[13]

5

However many theological difficulties there may still be surrounding our knowledge of the third Person, we are now, thank God, in a position to provide a more balanced account. These difficulties have often been discussed by theologians of the Western Church. They include a lack of words and concepts to express the term, in us, of the act of love, whereas for the act of understanding we have the expression 'mental word'.[14] There is also the fact that 'spiration' does not really express the relation that is constitutive of the Person (of the Holy Spirit) as 'fatherhood' and 'sonship' do for the first two persons.[15] 'Holy Spirit' is not, in itself, a relative, but an absolute name. In itself, it would be equally suitable for the Father or the Son, or even for the divine essence.[16] In other words, it is only by virtue of an 'accommodation' authorized by Scripture that it has come to be used as the name of the third Person.[17] In short, our knowledge of the Person known as the 'Holy Spirit' is limited and beset with difficulties.

It is clear, then, that we moved straightaway to a certain level of conceptualization and intellectual construction in our understanding of the Spirit. One is bound to ask whether this is legitimate or even possible. Did theologians themselves not confess that when speaking of God himself they ought to follow the rule of remaining as closely as possible to the scriptural ways of speaking? This was a rule in theology even before theologians knew of Pseudo-Dionysius, who formulated it very decisively: 'It is important to avoid applying rashly any word or any idea at all to the super-essential and mysterious Deity apart from those divinely revealed to us in the holy Scriptures'.[18] This was certainly one of the reasons why those advocates of the divinity of the Holy Spirit, Athanasius and Basil, and even the First Council of Constantinople of 381, avoided giving the title 'God' to the Spirit. Cyril of Jerusalem had this to say about the Spirit: 'In the matter of the Holy Spirit, let us say only those things that have been written. If anything has not been written, let us not stop to investigate the fact. It is the Holy Spirit himself who dictated the Scriptures, he who has also said of himself everything that he wanted to say or everything which we are capable of grasping. Let us therefore say what he has said and let us not be so bold as to say what he has not said.'[19]

Cyril, who was a pastor and a catechist, was quite faithful to the rule which he himself professed. Later theologians, however, who were likewise saints, did not hesitate to go beyond the scriptural texts, at least materially. Thomas Aquinas, who often quoted the text of Pseudo-Dionysius, sometimes in objection to the term *Filioque*, commented that it was Pseudo-Dionysius himself who broke his own rule most frequently.[20] The rest of this present volume will be full of terms and concepts that are not found as such in Scripture. I would therefore ask once again: is it legitimate to use them and, if so, why?

It is justified in the first place by the fact that the scriptural statements and even the images that I have mentioned above have a very full dogmatic content. There is no need for speculation. All that is required is to consider and weigh the meaning of the words, and one is at once involved in theology. Examples of this are: 'The Spirit of truth, who proceeds from the Father' (Jn 15:26); 'He will take what is mine. . . . All that the Father has is mine; therefore I said that he will take what is mine and declare it to you' (16:14–15); 'All mine are thine and thine are mine' (17:10). The whole of Christian experience in the world over nineteen centuries points to the fact that there is something to be intellectually penetrated in the profession of one's faith, that there is coherence and substance in the faith, and that these can be understood, that there is great benefit and joy in looking for these elements, and that faith itself emerges from the search nourished and strengthened.[21]

We have to try to establish a coherence between the images that are found in Scripture. Each term may have several meanings and needs to be interpreted. What is not expressed by one image or idea has to be completed by another image.[22]

It would be impossible to confine ourselves exclusively to Scripture. The Arian and Semi-Arian creeds, the Antiochian creed of 341 and others were composed only of scriptural terms as far as the article on the Holy Spirit is concerned.[23] The Arians' objection to the *homoousios* of Nicaea was that it could not be found in Scripture, and it was for the same reason that the Macedonians rejected the attribution of the title of God to the third Person. However, it was these interpretations, which were held with great stubbornness and therefore became 'heretical', which obliged the Catholic theologians to evolve formulae and expressions sufficiently precise to exclude error. Hilary of Poitiers, who bore witness to and championed the Trinitarian faith (†367), greatly lamented the need for this: 'We are forced . . . to express things that cannot be expressed, . . . we are driven to extend the weakness of our discourse to things that cannot be said, we are constrained to do what is deplorable because the others have also done what is deplorable—what should have been kept in the inner sanctuary has to be exposed to the danger of a human formulation'.[24]

The greatest theologians of the Western tradition may not have had such a strong feeling as Hilary did of being forced to do the impossible, but it is clear that they had to discuss matters of faith and to develop an adequate vocabulary precisely because of the existence of heresies.[25] We have inherited the results of their thought and debate. In this sense, we are what Maurice Blondel called the 'adults of Christianity'. We are bound to use the language that they have evolved and express ourselves in the concepts that they have developed. I shall try to do this in this volume, while at the same time preserving the sense of the mystery that exists far beyond our hesitant efforts. It is possible to outline the mystery and to mark out its contours, but it is not possible to penetrate into it.

The ardent professions of 'apophatism' that we have inherited from the

Greek Fathers are well known, but it is sometimes forgotten that many comparable testimonies can also be found in the writings of the Latins. I have personally compiled a list that could fill several pages. Let me give only one example—a verse written by Adam of Saint-Victor (†1192) that was sung by our forebears in the Middle Ages:

Digne loqui de personis	To speak worthily of the Persons
vim transcendit rationis,	transcends the power of reason
excedit ingenia.	and goes beyond our understanding.
Quid sit gigni, quid processus	What is 'being begotten'? What
me nescire sum professus:[26]	is 'processing'?
	I profess that I do not know.

*   *   *

Faith in the mystery of the Trinity, then, goes beyond any theological terms and constructions that can be formulated by man. It is therefore clear that it is possible for several different Trinitarian theologies to exist, and even several dogmatic formulae and constructions dependent on these theologies. T. de Régnon studied the writings of the Greek and the Latin authors on the Trinity with a close attention that has proved extremely valuable to those who have come after him. His conclusion was that the Western and the Eastern Church share the same faith, although they have approached the mystery from different points and along different ways. This is also what I believe. I go so far as to think that the difference between the two great cultures—the East and the West—forms part of a historical structure of humanity that can be regarded as providential.[27] It is true, of course, that this whole matter cannot be divided neatly into two, in the way that the continent and the islands of the New World were divided between Portugal and Spain, by Alexander VI's Bull *Inter caetera divinae* (1493), according to whether they were situated to the east or the west of a certain meridian. No, there is rather a different attitude of the spirit between Eastern and Western Christians, the first being more symbolic and the second more analytical in their thinking, and this different spirituality has manifested itself in the thought, liturgy and art of the East and the West and in the entire theological approach to the same Christian mysteries. Those who are familiar with the situation will not disagree with me here. This present volume will illustrate yet again the fact that there is both a duality in the unity and also, I believe, a unity within the duality. We can conclude this chapter by quoting Goethe:

Gottes ist der Orient,	The East is God's,
Gottes ist der Okzident;	The West is God's;
Nord und südliches Gelände	Both North and South
Ruht im Frieden Seiner Hände.[28]	Rest in the peace of his hands.

NOTES

1. Dogmatic Constitution on Revelation, *Dei Verbum* (1965), 2.
2. See Is 44:3–4; Jn 4:10; 7:37–39; Volume I, pp. 49–51; Volume II, p. 108. T. de Régnon, *Etudes de théologie positive sur la Sainte Trinité*, IV (Paris, 1898), pp. 389ff., quotes the following patristic texts: Irenaeus, *Adv. haer.* III, 17, 2–3; IV, 14, 2; Athanasius, *Ad Ser.* I, 19; Cyril of Jerusalem, *Cat.* XVI, 11 and 12; Didymus, *De Trin.* II, 6, 22 (*PG* 39, 553).
3. J. Guillet, 'Esprit de Dieu', *Vocabulaire biblique*, 2nd ed. (1971), col. 391.
4. See Is 61:1 (Lk 4:18); Acts 10:38; Volume I, pp. 19–21; T. de Régnon, *op. cit.*, pp. 401–406, has quoted several excellent texts: Irenaeus, *Adv. haer.* III, 18, 3; Athanasius, *Ad Ser.* I, 23; Basil the Great, *De spir. sanct.* 12; Gregory of Nyssa, *Adv. Mac.* 15 and 16 (*PG* 45, 1320). See also de Régnon, *op. cit.*, pp. 413–421, on 'perfume, aroma and quality'.
5. The Fathers frequently made this compelling comparison: see Augustine, *Contra Faustum* 30 (*PL* 42, 270); *Ep.* 55, 16 (*PL* 33, 218ff.); *Serm.* 156, 13; etc.; Cyril of Alexandria, *Comm. in Luc.* XI, 20; Martin of Leon, *Serm.* 32 (*PL* 208, 1203); Gregory the Great, *In Ezech.* I, 10, 26 (*PL* 76, 891), made a comparison with Mt 7:33.
6. 2 Cor 3:2–3. See also Augustine, *De spir. et litt.* 16, 28; 17, 29–30; 21, 36 (*PL* 44, 218–219, 222).
7. J. Leclercq, 'Le doigt de Dieu', *VS*, 78 (May 1948), 492–507, who quotes a large number of patristic texts.
8. Athanasius, *Ad Ser.* I, 23 (*PG* 26, 584C–585B; *SC* 15 (1947), pp. 124ff.).
9. Thomas Aquinas, *ST* Ia, q. 1, a. 9, ad 2; IIIa, q. 42, a. 3.
10. St Bernard, *De consid.* V, 11, 24 (*PL* 182, 802B); *Serm. 88 de diversis* 1 (*PL* 183, 706), in which this is applied to the Holy Spirit; *In die Pent., Serm.* 1, 1 (*PL* 183, 323).
11. J. R. Villalón, *Sacrements dans l'Esprit* (Paris, 1977), p. 424.
12. Mgr Gaume († 1879) subtitled his book on the Holy Spirit 'Ignoto Deo'; in 1921, Mgr M. Landrieux published his *Le divin Méconnu* (Eng. tr.: *The Forgotten Paraclete*, London, 1924); Victor Dillard wrote a book on the Holy Spirit in 1938 entitled *Au Dieu inconnu*; in 1965, Pastor A. Granier wrote *Le Saint-Esprit, ce méconnu*; E. H. Palmer began his *The Holy Spirit* (Grand Rapids, 1958) with the words 'The Unknown God' (p. 11) and L. Wunderlich published (St Louis, 1963) *The Half-known God: The Lord and Giver of Life*.
13. Augustine, *De fid et symb.* 9, 19 (*PL* 40, 191).
14. Thomas Aquinas, *ST* Ia, q. 37, a. 1.
15. *Comp.* I, 59; *In I Sent.* d. 10, q. 1, a. 4 ad 1; *ST* Ia, q. 40, a. 4.
16. *ST* Ia, q. 36, a. 1 ad 2.
17. *ST* Ia, q. 36, a. 1, c and ad 1; see also Augustine, *De Trin.* V, 14; XV, 19.
18. Pseudo-Dionysius, *On the Divine Names*, 1 (*PG* 3, 585; Fr. tr. M. de Gandillac (Paris, 1943)). Before Pseudo-Dionysius was translated into Latin, this rule was already observed in the Western Church: see, for example, Bede, *Super par. Salom.* II, 23 (*PL* 91, 1006A–B); Alcuin, *Ad Fel.* VII, 17 (*PL* 101, 230B); *Adv. Elipand.* IV, 11 (*PL* 101, 295A).
19. Cyril of Jerusalem, *Cat.* XVI, 2 (*PG* 33, 920A; quoted and Fr. tr. J. Lebon, *SC* 15, p. 70, note 1); cf. XVI, 24 (*PG* 33, 952). References to other Fathers will be found in H. de Lubac, *La Foi chrétienne* (Paris, 1969), p. 117, note 2. See also Hugh of Saint-Victor, *De sacr.* III, pars 1, c. 4 (*PL* 176, 376A).
20. Thomas Aquinas, commentary on the text of Pseudo-Dionysius: see J. Kuhlmann, *Die Taten des einfachen Gottes* (Würzburg, 1968), p. 21. Thomas quotes Pseudo-Dionysius (in support of an objection) in *In III Sent.* d. 25, q. 1, q. 3, ad 2, 3, 4; *De ver.* q. 14, a. 6; *De pot.* q. 9, a. 9, ad 7; q. 10, a. 4, obj. 12; *Contra Err. Graec.* c. 1; *ST* Ia, q. 29, a. 3, ad 1; q. 32, a. 2, ad 1; q. 36, a. 2, obj. 1; q. 39, a. 2, ad 2; IIa IIae, q. 4, a. 1; IIIa, q. 60, a. 8, ad 1. Quotations of this rule in early Scholastic writings will be found in A. Landgraf, *Dogmengeschichte der Frühscholastik*, I (Regensburg, 1952), p. 20.
21. Thomas Aquinas often quoted the words of Augustine: 'huic scientiae attribuitur illud

9

tantummodo quo fides saluberrima gignitur, nutritur, defenditur, roboratur': *De Trin.* XIV, 1, 3 (*PL* 42, 1037); see his *ST* Ia, q. 1, a. 2; IIa IIae, q. 6, a. 1, ad 1.

22. Thomas Aquinas, *ST* Ia, q. 42, a. 2, ad 1, in reaction to Arius, who developed twelve senses or modes of 'begetting'.

23. H. B. Swete, *The Holy Spirit in the Ancient Church* (London, 1912), pp. 166ff.

24. Hilary, *De Trin.* II, 2 (*PL* 10, 51).

25. See Augustine, *De Trin.* VII, 9 (*PL* 42, 941–942); Thomas Aquinas, *Contra Err. Graec.* prol.; *De pot.* q. 9, a. 8; q. 10, a. 2.

26. Adam of Saint-Victor, *Seq. XI de sancta Trin.* (*PL* 196, 1459).

27. On the basis of the understanding that the ancient world had of things, it is possible to ask whether God's work did not often follow a pattern of unity within duality: see my *Ecclésiologie du Haut Moyen Age* (Paris, 1968), pp. 262ff.

28. Goethe, 'Talisman', *West-östliche Divan*, 3.

2

THE 'ECONOMIC' TRINITY AND THE 'IMMANENT' TRINITY

Karl Rahner has provided the most original contemporary contribution to the theology of the Trinity.[1] In it, he deals with several aspects of the question and especially with the idea of 'person'—I shall be returning to this later—but his essential argument, which he calls his *Grundaxiom*, is that the 'economic' Trinity *is* the 'immanent' Trinity and vice versa.

By 'economy' is meant the carrying out of God's plan in creation and the redemption of man or the covenant of grace. In it, God commits and reveals himself. One of Rahner's intentions and one of his main concerns in his Trinitarian theology is to establish a relationship, and even a unity, between the treatises which the analytical genius of Scholasticism and modern teaching present successively, but without showing their mutual coherence. We attribute 'creation' to 'God', for example, but at the same time we continue to have a fundamentally pre-Trinitarian notion of that 'God'. We obviously attribute 'redemption' to Jesus Christ, but he is 'God' and we do not place the Word as such into that 'God'. In addition, despite the exegetical studies that have been written about this question, the relationship between creation and redemption, which is a relationship that is closely connected with the Word made flesh, is seldom developed. The eschatological end of that relationship has also to be taken into account. What part does the Holy Spirit play in all this? The treatise on grace was written without reference to the treatise on the Tri-unity of God. Was that grace not a participation in the divine *nature*? Where, then, was the reference to the Persons? Was there also a reference to the uncreated grace which is the Holy Spirit?

It is, however, true to say that Scripture, the Creed and the ante-Nicene Fathers spoke the language of the Economy.[2] The Creed is Trinitarian only within this framework. Rahner brings them together when he affirms his 'fundamental axiom' that the *Trinity that is manifested in the economy of salvation is the immanent Trinity and vice versa*.

Three reasons justify and throw light on that fundamental principle:

(a) The Trinity is a mystery of salvation. If it were not, it would not have been revealed to us. Our recognition of this fact enables us to establish a relationship and even a unity between the treatises which have to a great extent lacked this. This implies, however, that the Trinity in itself is also the Trinity of the economy.

11

(b) There is at least one case of fundamental importance in which this affirmation must be made—the incarnation. 'So there is at least one "sending", one presence in the world, one reality in the economy of salvation which is not merely appropriated to a certain divine person, but is proper to him. Thus it is not a matter of saying something "about" this particular divine person in the world. Here something takes place in the world itself, outside the immanent divine life, which is not simply the result of the efficient causality of the triune God working as one nature in the world. It is an event proper to the Logos alone, the history of one divine person in contrast to the others.'[3]

(c) The history of salvation is not simply the history of God's revelation of himself. It is also the history of his communication of himself. God himself is the content of that self-communication. The economic Trinity (the revealed and communicated Trinity) and the immanent Trinity are identical because God's communication of himself to men in the Son and the Spirit would not be a self-communication of God if what God is for us in the Son and the Spirit was not peculiar to God in himself. In this, there is an echo of an anti-Arian argument concerned with our deification that calls for the communication of God himself in the economy. At the same time, a reality is ascribed to the 'appropriations', since the three ways in which the economy manifests that God is with us and communicates himself to us correspond to the three modes of relationship in which God subsists in himself.

There has been a wide measure of agreement with Rahner's positions, which were already those of Karl Barth in Protestant theology. If it is merely a question of the knowledge that we have of the Tri-unity of God, there is no real problem, since that knowledge is measured by the economy within which it is given to us.

On the other hand, we also know that the 'divine missions' of the Word and the Spirit are the processions of those Persons insofar as they result in an effect in the creature. In their case, then, the economic Trinity *is* in fact the immanent Trinity. This is what brings about an absolutely supernatural, theologal and even divine effect in the spiritual life of true believers and in the Church as such. The Church lives, in the conditions of the flesh, from communication with God. It is one and holy because of God's oneness and holiness. The Fathers did not hesitate to say this[4] and I have discussed this question already in Volume II of this work. The Father does not himself 'proceed' and thus he is not 'sent'. He is communicated in the economy as the absolute source of all procession, mission and work *ad extra*. 'The Father is the incomprehensible origin and the original unity, the "Word" his utterance into history, and the "Spirit" the opening up of history into the immediacy of its fatherly origin and end'.[5] 'There is only one outward activity of God, exerted and possessed as one and the same by Father, Son and Spirit, according to the peculiar way in which each possesses the God-head'.[6]

I accept Rahner's teaching, but would like to add two comments which limit its absolute character.

(A) 'The economic Trinity is the immanent Trinity and vice versa [*umgekehrt*].' The first half of this statement by Rahner is beyond dispute, but the second half has to be clarified. Can the free mystery of the economy and the necessary mystery of the Tri-unity of God be identified? As the Fathers who combated Arianism said, even if God's creatures did not exist, God would still be a Trinity of Father, Son and Spirit, since creation is an act of free will, whereas the procession of the Persons takes place in accordance with nature, *kata phusin*.[7] In addition to this, is it true to say that God commits the whole of his mystery to and reveals it in his communication of himself?[8] It seems to me to be obvious that we cannot simply affirm the reciprocity of Rahner's fundamental axiom when we read the statements that result from a purely logical proposal to develop and affirm this reciprocity. This is precisely what Piet Schoonenberg has done in his presentation of a number of theses as an extension of Rahner's. But these are the conclusions he comes to:[9]

(11) In the theology of the Trinity too, the Father should not be seen simply as the 'first Person' or as the origin and source of divinity; he should also and above all be seen as our Father in Christ. The economic fatherhood of the history of salvation is the intra-divine fatherhood and vice versa.

(12) The Son should be seen not only as intra-divine, but also and above all as the man Jesus Christ. The Logos is not simply the intra-divine Word—he is never presented in Scripture as the intra-divine response—but also and above all as the Word which reveals and which gives life in the history of salvation, the Word which became flesh and fully man in Jesus Christ. The economic sonship of the history of salvation is the intra-divine sonship and vice versa.

(13) The Holy Spirit is not only the intra-divine link between the Father and the Son, but also and above all 'gift' and 'power of sanctification' in the history of salvation. These titles were given to him by the Fathers in order to characterize his being as a Person. The Spirit of God who is active in the history of salvation is the intra-divine (Spirit) and vice versa.

(14) The communications or 'missions' of the Son and the Spirit are revealed as intra-divine 'processions'. These intra-divine 'processions' are known to us only as missions. The missions are processions and vice versa.

(15) The relations between the Father, the Son and the Spirit are accessible to us only in their relations with us. The economic relations of the history of salvation are intra-divine and vice versa. That is why the Father, the Son and the Spirit must be characterized first by their relationships with us and then by their relationships with each other.

These theses are classical insofar as we remain at the level of knowledge derived from revelation, that is, from the manifestation of God. The problem, however, is concerned precisely with the 'vice versa' or the 'reciprocity', the *umgekehrt*, in other words, to the extent to which the latter implies a transition from knowledge to ontology. He does not in fact do this formally, but he does profess an apophatism, that is, the impossibility of affirming or denying anything, where the intra-divine life is concerned.

(7) The immanent Trinity, vice versa, is the economic Trinity. It is accessible for us only as the economic Trinity. The fact that God is, apart from his communication of himself in the history of salvation, Trinitarian, can neither be presupposed as a matter of course nor denied.

(24) The fact remains that Jesus Christ and the Father personally face each other and that the Holy Spirit prays to the Father in us and calls to the Son and therefore also personally faces them. According to Scripture, then, the Father, the Son and the Holy Spirit face each other as Persons *in* the history of salvation. It follows from thesis 23 that this is possible only *through* the history of salvation. The immanent Trinity is a Trinity of Persons through the fact that it is an economic Trinity.

In God himself, the Father, the Son and the Spirit are only modes of the Deity. There are 'Persons' or personal relationships only in the economy (see thesis 28). For us at least, God is three-personal only in the economy. 'Through the history of salvation', Schoonenberg insists, 'there is a Trinity in God himself; through his own saving action, God himself becomes three-personal [*driepersoonlijk*], that is, three Persons.'[10]

This depends on the fact that Schoonenberg's understanding of the word 'person' is quite contemporary and therefore includes the person's human mode of existence and contains the ideas of consciousness, freedom and interpersonal relationships (see thesis 18). Applying this understanding of 'person' to Christ, Schoonenberg attributes a pure human personality to him and points out with insistence that speaking about Christ's pre-existent divine Person runs the risk of damaging the reality of the human personality. Because our knowledge is limited by the economy of salvation, which is its only source, we cannot know what that is in God himself. Schoonenberg therefore leaves the mystery of the immanent Trinity open, but unknown and even unknowable. This clause is a saving one and it leaves the author's orthodoxy intact.

Is it, however, permissible to act as Schoonenberg has done here and place oneself outside the whole Christian tradition of reflection based on the inspired evidence of Revelation? Jesus himself pointed to the distance between being a son through grace and a Son by nature: 'My Father and your Father, my God and your God' (Jn 20:17). And how can there be a communication of the three Persons if they are not three Persons to begin with? Rahner does not overlook this. He says, for example: 'The "immanent" actual possibility of this threefold way of being given is, despite God's free gratuitous trinitarian self-communication, forever given in God, belonging therefore necessarily and "essentially" to him'.[11]

(B) God's communication of himself, as Father, Son and Holy Spirit, will not be a full self-communication until the end of time, in what we call the beatific vision. Thomas Aquinas' thesis on this matter is well known—he describes it as a vision without created *species*, that is, God himself as the objective form of our understanding. This is, however, an heroic, an almost untenable thesis, and it has been widely disputed. The Eastern Church does not accept it as it is, although there have been many Orthodox statements about the beatific vision of God. Almost all of these, however, insist that the divine essence is unknowable and make a distinction between what cannot and what can be communicated (the 'energies' that emanate from the divine essence).

On the other hand, no Western theologian has ever maintained that we can know or understand God as he understands himself. John of the Cross, for example, applied the image of the 'distant islands' to the beatific vision. There is no participation in the aseity, the *Ipsum esse* or what makes God God. There is a very great difference between Eastern and Western theological constructions of the reality, but it would be a mistake to regard the two as dogmatically incompatible. Here, however, we are above all concerned with the perception that God's communication of himself will be complete only in the eschatological era.

This self-communication takes place in the economy in accordance with a rule of 'condescendence', humiliation, ministry and 'kenosis'. We have therefore to recognize that there is a distance between the economic, revealed Trinity and the eternal Trinity. The Trinity is the same in each case and God is really communicated, but this takes place in a mode that is not connatural with the being of the divine Persons. The Father is 'omnipotent', but what are we to think of him in a world filled with the scandal of evil? The Son, who is 'shining with his glory and the likeness of his substance', is the Wisdom of God, but he is above all the wisdom of the cross and so difficult to recognize that blasphemy against him will be pardoned. Finally, the Spirit has no face and has often been called the unknown one.

It is important in this context to recall certain essential elements in Christian thought and especially the theme of 'condescendence' and the theology of the cross. Before Luther, the latter is found above all in the writings of Maximus the Confessor, who declared: 'The Lord, who wanted us to understand that we should not look for natural necessity in what is above nature, wanted to bring about his work by means of opposites. He therefore fulfilled his life by his death and accomplished his glory by means of dishonour.'[12] It was, however, Luther who originated the term *theologia crucis*. He taught that God is not accessible to us through human logic. He reveals himself by hiding himself.[13] He does his own work under the species or by means of the opposite: justice, grace and life by a way of judgement and death. True knowledge of God is that which approaches him in this way and which finds its *opus proprium* in an *opus alienum*.

15

Salvation, in other words, is in the cross, on which Jesus was treated as accursed.[14]

There is nothing in anything that has been said above that contradicts Rahner's 'fundamental axiom'. Rahner also says : 'What Jesus is and does as man reveals the Logos himself; it is the reality of the Logos as our salvation amidst us'.[15] All these things—condescendence, humiliation, kenosis, the cross and the fact that life is stronger than death, but that love is manifested in accepting death[16]—reveal who the Word is, and the Word himself reveals who the Father is: 'He who has seen me has seen the Father' (Jn 14:9).[17]

There is powerful evidence that this 'economy' does not in any way conceal the 'theology' in the manner in which the episode of the washing of the feet is introduced in the fourth gospel: 'Jesus, knowing that the Father had given all things into his hands and that he had come from God and was going to God' (Jn 13:3). It was because he was conscious of being the expression of the Father that Jesus performed this act of humble love and service. This act was typical of God himself. The economic trinity thus reveals the immanent Trinity—but does it reveal it entirely? There is always a limit to this revelation, and the incarnation imposes its own conditions, which go back to its nature as a created work.

If all the data of the incarnation were transposed into the eternity of the Logos, it would be necessary to say that the Son proceeds from the Father and the Holy Spirit—*a Patre Spirituque*.[18] In addition, the *forma servi* belongs to what God is, but so does the *forma Dei*. At the same time, however, that latter form and the infinite and divine manner in which the perfections that we attribute to God are accomplished elude us to a very great extent. This should make us cautious in saying, as Rahner does, 'and vice versa'.

I shall be speaking later about Palamism and pointing, at the level of a theologoumenon, to a possible construction of faith. For this reason, it is possible to ask what Gregory Palamas' reaction to Rahner's thesis would have been. The first thing that strikes me is that the idea that the Trinity is a mystery of salvation would have been acceptable to Palamite theology, in which that salvation would have been interpreted in the Eastern tradition as a deification or *theōsis*. The idea of God's communication of himself would also have been accepted, so long as that self-communication was situated within the order of uncreated energies. As those energies manifest the Persons of the Trinity, there would be a revelation of the Tri-unity of God through them.

It was undoubtedly in such conditions that the Archimandrite Kallistos Ware, in his defence of the difference between essence and energies when criticized by R. Williams (who had criticized V. Lossky and Gregory Palamas for having left our level of knowledge and moved to the plane of intra-divine ontology), replied: 'This self-revelation is a real sign of the eternal being of God. If we did not believe it, how would we be able to move from the "economic" level of the Trinity to that of the eternal distinctions in the Trinity?'[19] Only a few pages earlier on in the same journal, however, Amphilokios Radovic had observed that the distinction between the essence and the energies implied a distinction, and even a radical difference, between the existential origins of the Persons and the economic manifestation of those Persons: 'On the basis of the manifestation of the Trinity in the world, we cannot come to any conclusions about God's mode of eternal existence'. The identification of the order of eternal existence of the hypostases with the order of the economy is fundamental to the Latin position.[20] What is clear is that this identification between the two calls for the *Filioque* or at least for an equivalent *per Filium* at the level of the eternal procession. This was one of the reasons why Karl Barth thought that it was necessary to preserve the *Filioque*, in the name of scriptural evidence. According to Palamite thinking, however, God may be partly revealed in the economy by his activity, but he remains absolutely hidden in his essential being.

NOTES

1. K. Rahner, 'Remarks on the Dogmatic Treatise "De Trinitate" ', *Theological Investigations*, 4 (Eng. tr.; London and Baltimore, 1966), pp. 77–102; *idem, The Trinity* (Eng. tr.; London, 1970), first pub. in German as part of *Mysterium Salutis* (Einsiedeln, 1967). To this should be added the preface (untranslated) to the book by Mario de França Miranda, *O Mistério de Deus em nossa vida* (São Paulo, 1975), pp. 7–13. This book is a study of Rahner's thesis discussed in this chapter.

2. In ante-Nicene writings, this is often balanced by a subordinationism, the Word being regarded, because of the influence of Stoicism, as the one through whom God carried out his creation and therefore as a mediator of that creation. This idea was systematized in Arianism, according to which the Son had a beginning, in the same way that a creature has a beginning. Athanasius and the Cappadocian Fathers affirmed, against this thesis, that if the Son was a creature in this way, he could not deify us, and that he could be our Saviour in the full sense only if he was God and communicated the life of God to us, in other words, if he was consubstantial with the Father. The same idea was also applied to the Spirit. By insisting in this way on consubstantiality, in other words, on the intra-divine aspect, the anti-Arian writers and the First Council of Nicaea to some extent diverted men's minds from the question of the economic Trinity.

3. K. Rahner, 'Remarks', *op. cit.*, pp. 88–89. Rahner has developed the idea that God is the subject of a history, namely the history of salvation, in the incarnate Word: 'Current Problems in Christology', *Theological Investigations*, 1 (Eng. tr.; London and Baltimore, 1961), pp. 149–200; and in *Problèmes actuels de christologie*, ed. H. Bouëssé (Bruges and Paris, 1965), pp. 15–33, 401–409.

4. See Cyprian, *De cath. Eccl. unit.* 7; *De orat. dom.* 23 (*PL* 4, 553; ed. W. von Hartel, p. 285); Origen, *In Jesu Nave, Hom.* VII, 6; Epiphanius of Salamis, *Anc.* 118, 3: 'One is the unity of the Father, the Son and the Holy Spirit, one substance, one lordship, one will, one Church, one baptism, one faith' (*GCS*, Epiph. 1, p. 146); Augustine, *Sermo* 71, 20, 33 (*PL* 38, 463ff.); John Damascene, *Adv. Icon.* 12 (*PG* 96, 1358D); see also the Dogmatic Constitution on the Church, *Lumen Gentium*, 4.

17

5. K. Rahner, *The Trinity, op. cit.* (note 1), p. 47.

6. *Ibid.*, p. 76.

7. Athanasius, *Contra Arian.* I, 18 (*PG* 26, 49); II, 31: 'Even if God had not decided to create, he would nonetheless have had his Son' (*PG* 26, 212B); John Damascene, *De fide orthod.* I, 8 (*PG* 94, 812–813).

8. My criticism has also been made, for example, by G. Lafont, *Peut-on connaître Dieu en Jésus-Christ?* (Paris, 1969), pp. 220, 226; B. Rey, *RSPT* (1970), 645.

9. P. Schoonenberg, 'Trinität—der vollendete Bund. Thesen zur Lehre von dreipersönlichem Gott', *Orientierung*, 37 (Zürich, 1973, fascicle of 31 May), 115–117, especially 115. Schoonenberg presented these theses as a continuation and a justification of his book *Hij is een God van Mensen*; Eng. tr., *The Christ* (London and Sydney, 1972).

10. This formula is taken from an article, in Dutch, on 'Jesus Christ, the same today', in *Mélanges W. H. van der Pol* (Roermond and Maaseik, 1967) and analysed and criticized by J. Coppens in *ETL*, 45 (1969), 127–137. The following statement also appears in the same article: 'The presence of God as the Word becomes the personal Son of the Father because, from the beginning, it includes the whole human existence of Jesus Christ and constitutes that existence (and not because it fills the already existing man). The presence of God as the Spirit becomes the personal Paraclete because, in a parallel manner, it bears and constitutes the community of believers. God becomes the Father, the first Person of the Trinity, because he produces in Jesus a Son of the same nature and spreads a Spirit in the Church of the same being (*wezensgelijk*).'

11. K. Rahner, *The Trinity, op. cit.* (note 1), p. 74. This transposition means that we have to speak more precisely, because of the need to respect the absolute consubstantiality of the 'Persons' in the immanent Trinity. Similarly, both Rahner and Schoonenberg speak personally in the case of the economy and modally in the case of the eternal Trinity.

12. See Maximus' 'Questions and Difficulties' (*PG* 94, 793); quoted in Fr. tr. by J.-M. Garrigues, *Maxime le Confesseur. La charité avenir divin de l'homme* (Paris, 1976), p. 160.

13. Luther, *Commentary on Galatians*, 1525: *Works*, XV (Geneva, 1969), pp. 282–295.

14. Writings of 1518: *Asterici*; marginal gloss on Heb.; Resolutions and especially the Heidelberg Disputation, 22 and 24: *Works*, I (Geneva, 1957), pp. 121ff. See also J. E. Vercruysse, 'Luther's Theology of the Cross in the Time of the Heidelberg Disputation', *Greg*, 57 (1976), 523–548.

15. K. Rahner, *The Trinity, op. cit.*, p. 33; 'Remarks', *op. cit.*, p. 94.

16. This aspect was emphasized by E. Jüngel, 'Das Verhältnis von "ökonomischer" und "immanenter" Trinität', *ZTK*, 72 (1975), 353–364.

17. See my 'Dum visibiliter Deum cognoscimus', *M-D*, 59 (1959/3), 132–161; Eng. tr. in *The Revelation of God* (London and New York, 1968), pp. 67–96.

18. See K. Barth, *Church Dogmatics*, I. 1 (Eng. tr.; Edinburgh and New York, 1936), pp. 554–556.

19. K. Ware, 'Dieu caché et révélé. La voie apophatique et la distinction essence–énergie', *Le Messager de l'Exarchat du patriarche russe en Europe occidentale*, 89–90 (1975), 45–59, especially 56.

20. This was the explicit reaction of A. Radovic: see his 'Le "Filioque" et l'énergie incréée de la Sainte Trinité selon la doctrine de S. Grégoire Palamas', *ibid.*, 11–44, especially 15–17 and 19. This can also be compared with what the monk Hilarion says, *ibid.*, 81–82 (1973), 19–25, namely that the Roman Catholic view is, in his opinion, tied to an identification of the temporal missions with the eternal processions; Hilarion rejects this idea in the name of the distinction between the procession of the hypostases and the uncreated energies.

II

THE STAGES IN THE DEVELOPMENT OF A THEOLOGY OF THE THIRD PERSON

Three great stages in this development can be distinguished: the period before the Arian crisis, the period of the crisis itself and the period of systematic constructions.

BEFORE THE ARIAN CRISIS

This was a time of slow and difficult gestation. We who are so used to firm dogma and authoritative interpretation of biblical texts have difficulty in understanding why there was such a long period of hesitation and why such apparently strange paths were followed. The theological question of the Spirit was only really approached in good conditions when light had been thrown on the relationship between the Son, the Word, and the Father.[1]

First came the Christian apologists, using the philosophical data fairly widely accepted in their times and therefore more inclined to speak about the Word than about the Spirit. They confessed the Trinitarian faith and the fact that the Logos and the Spirit (Wisdom) were eternally in God before he projected them into creation and time in order to manifest himself there. They believed that the Spirit spoke in the prophets, that he was united with the souls of those who lived in justice and that he came or flowed from God.[2] No other more precise definition of the procession of the one who, as Justin claimed, was revered by Christians in the third place[3] is to be found in the early apologetic writings.

Irenaeus was less an apologist than a man, a Doctor, of the Church. Conscious of the fact that the Spirit of God flowed constantly from the divine being,[4] he acknowledged the existence of the immanent Trinity. At the same time, however, he developed above all the part played by the Trinity in the economy, calling the Word and the Spirit (Wisdom) the two hands of God (cf. Volume II, p. 9) working together to fashion his creatures. According to Irenaeus, the Word, having become visible, revealed the Father, and the

19

Spirit was the one 'through whom the prophets spoke and the Fathers learned what concerns God, the righteous were led in the way of justice, and who was poured out at the end of time in a new way . . . in order to renew man over the whole of the earth with God in mind'.[5]

Tertullian (c. 160–c. 220) believed that the Spirit came *a Patre per Filium*, 'from the Father through the Son',[6] and that he 'came third from the Father and the Son (*a Deo et Filio*), just as the fruit from the branch comes third from the root, the channel led from the river comes third from the source, and the glowing point of light at the end of the ray comes third from the sun'.[7]

Is there a lowering in rank in the fact that, according to Tertullian, there is a passage from one Person to another in the economic existence of the Trinity? Does this imply subordinationism? The question has often been considered, but no certain answer has been provided.[8] The Spirit is the 'vicar' of the Son who, from his seat at the right hand of the Father, sent *vicariam vim Spiritus Sancti, qui credentes agat*.[9] At the same time, however, Tertullian also believed that the Son and the Spirit were *consortes substantiae Patris*.[10] The Three are one in *status, substantia* and *potestas*,[11] but they are not one individual or one person (*unus*), but rather the same reality: *unum . . . ad substantiae unitatem, non ad numeri singularitatem*.[12]

Tertullian wrote this, of course, long before the Council of Nicaea, and his idea of the economy led him to make certain statements that could easily be misunderstood. He was moving in the direction of an orthodox theology in the Trinity, but lacked the means to express it properly. He was, however, responsible for 'those well-known formulae: *Trinitas, tres personae, una substantia*, which he coined and which have become commonplaces in the Trinitarian doctrine, together with the other, more imaginative terms: *Deum de Deo, lumen de lumine*, which we still use when we profess our faith'.[13]

Origen (c. 185–254) was one of the greatest geniuses in the history of Christian thought, and a better metaphysician than Tertullian. His cultural climate was that of Middle Platonism, with the result that it is possible to find two kinds of statements in his writings. On the one hand, he teaches a theology of the three co-eternal hypostases and the eternal procession of the Spirit from the Father through the Son.[14] On the other hand, in connection with the Platonic idea of a graduated hierarchy, his work contains a number of subordinationist themes and formulae.[15] These subordinationist ideas can be found especially in his teaching that only the Father is *ho theos* or *autotheos*, whereas the Son is *deuteros theos* or God in second place.[16] The Son and the Spirit are connected with the Father, who is the 'source of divinity', but they are not alone in being co-eternal with him—a great number of spiritual beings are also co-eternal with the Father. On the other hand, however, Origen used the term *homoousios* at least with the meaning of a community of nature and affirmed the eternal existence of three *hypostases*,[17] the eternal begetting of the Son and the eternal procession of the Spirit[18] through the Son.[19] In this way, he anticipates the ideas that can be found later in the great classical Greek patristic and other writings. It must be admitted, however, that the Arians also found support in the writings of Origen, whom Prestige called 'the common father of Arianism and of Cappadocian orthodoxy'.[20]

The confession of faith under the name of Origen's disciple Gregory Thaumaturgus (†between 260 and 270) is fundamentally orthodox; it contains the following words about the Holy Spirit: 'And one Holy Spirit, who takes his subsistence from God (*ek Theou tēn huparxin echōn*) and who appeared (was revealed) to men by the Son; image of the Son; perfect (image) of the perfect one, life, cause of the living, holy source, holiness leading to satisfaction, in whom God the Father, who is above all and in all, is manifested and God the Son who is through all'.[21] This elaborate vocabulary has led other scholars to doubt whether this text should be attributed to Gregory Thaumaturgus, and Abramowski has suggested that it is the work of Gregory of Nyssa.

Pope Dionysius of Rome suspected that the teaching of his namesake Dionysius of Alexandria, another of Origen's disciples, contained a danger of tritheism ('three hypostases') and in 262 reacted strongly in favour of the monarchy of the Father. We owe to him this excellent statement:

> It is necessary for the divine Word to be united to the God of the universe and for the Holy Spirit to have his dwelling-place and his habitation in God. And it is above all necessary for the Holy Trinity to be recapitulated and brought back to one as to its peak; by this I mean that one all-powerful God of the universe. It is necessary to believe in God the Father almighty and in Christ Jesus his Son and in the Holy Spirit (quotations from Jn 10:30 and 14:10 follow here). It is in this way that we may be sure of the divine Trinity and at the same time of the holy preaching of the monarchy.[22]

NOTES

1. The most recent analysis has been written by F. Bolgiani, 'La théologie de l'Esprit-Saint. De la fin du Ier siècle après Jésus-Christ au concile de Constantinople (381)', *Les quatre fleuves*, 9 (1979), 33–72.
2. Athenagoras, *Supplicatio* (in 177), X (see *SC* 3 (1943), p. 94), who uses the word *aporroia*

for 'flowing from': cf. Wis 7:25. He also says (*SC* 3, pp. 92–93): 'The Son being in the Father and the Father being in the Son through the unity and power of Spirit', although the last word is without the article, so that it does not refer to the third Person, but rather to the divine nature.

3. Justin, *I Apol*. 4, 1; Athenagoras, *op. cit.*, speaks of a 'distinction in rank' in this context.
4. Irenaeus, *Adv. haer*. V, 12, 2; the quotation is from Is 57:16 (*SC* 153 (1969), pp. 145ff.). For the Holy Spirit in Irenaeus, see A. d'Alès, 'La doctrine de l'Esprit-Saint chez S. Irénée', *RSR*, 14 (1924), 426–538; A. Benoît, 'Le Saint Esprit et l'Eglise dans la théologie patristique des quatre premiers siècles', *L'Esprit Saint et l'Eglise* (Paris, 1969), pp. 131–136; H.-J. Jaschke, *Der Heilige Geist im Bekenntnis der Kirche. Eine Studie zur Pneumatologie bei Irenäus von Lyon im Ausgang vom altchristlichen Glaubensbekenntnis* (Münster, 1977).
5. *Dem*. 6 (*SC* 62, p. 40). A little further on, *Dem*. 7 (*SC* 62, pp. 41–42), Irenaeus enlarges on the revelatory function of the Spirit, saying that he reveals the Son, who in turn reveals the Father. The 'from the Father through the Son in the Spirit' is the principle of a return 'in the Spirit through the Son to the Father'.
6. Tertullian, *Adv. Prax*. 4 (*PL* 2, 159; *CSEL* 47, p. 232). According to J. Moingt, this *per Filium* concerns not the intra-divine procession, but the order of the economy, the Spirit being sent and poured out by the Son: *Théologie trinitaire de Tertullien*, III (*Théologie*, 70) (Paris, 1966), p. 1057.
7. *Adv. Prax*. 8 (*PL* 2, 163; *CSEL* 47, p. 238). According to P.-T. Camelot, 'Spiritus a Patre et Filio', *RSPT*, 30 (1946), 31–33, the idea of the *Filioque* is not present in this text of Tertullian's. Other scholars have, however, thought differently, especially B. de Margerie.
8. B. Piault, 'Tertullien a-t-il été subordinatien?', *RSPT*, 47 (1963), 337–369. J. Moingt, *op. cit.* (note 6), pp. 1071–1074, banished the idea of subordinationism by recalling that Tertullian made no distinction between God in himself and God as he exists for us.
9. *De praescr*. 13, 5 (*PL* 2, 26).
10. *Adv. Prax*. 3 (*PL* 2, 158; *CSEL* 47, p. 231).
11. *ibid*., 2 (*PL* 2, 156; *CSEL* 47, p. 229).
12. *ibid*., 25 (*PL* 2, 188; *CSEL* 47, p. 276).
13. Piault, *op. cit.* (note 8), p. 204.
14. H. B. Swete, *The Holy Spirit in the Ancient Church* (London, 1912), pp. 61–65.
15. See S. Bulgakov, *Le Paraclet* (Paris, 1946), pp. 22–23; J. N. D. Kelly, *Early Christian Doctrines*, 5th ed. (London, 1977), pp. 132–136, gives a more balanced and more fully documented account.
16. Origen, *Contra Cels*. V, 39 (*SC* 147 (1969), p. 118, including the long footnote 2); *Comm. in Ioan*. VI, XXXIX, 202 (*SC* 157 (1970), p. 280). Later on, Thomas Aquinas said: 'The Arians, of whom Origen was the source': *ST* Ia, q. 34, q. 1, ad 1.
17. *Comm. in Ioan*. II, X, 75 (*SC* 120, p. 257). According to G. L. Prestige, *God in Patristic Thought*, 2nd ed. (London, 1952), p. 179, Origen was the first Father to define the Persons of the Trinity using the term *hypostasis*: see *Contra Cels*. 8, 12.
18. *De Prin*. II, 1 (*PG* 11, 186).
19. Swete found this in Origen's commentary on Rom 8:9–11 (*PG* 14, 1098)—the Spirit proceeds from the Father and receives from the Son; he is also the Spirit of the Father or of Christ. Or in the commentary on Jn 1:2, 'nothing was done without him'. The Spirit has a *genesis* depending on the Word: see *Comm. in Ioan*. II, 75 and 79 (*SC* 120, pp. 254ff.; *PG* 14, 128).
20. G. L. Prestige, *op. cit.* (note 17 above), p. xiv.
21. *PG* 10, 985. According to M. Jugie, there is here a dependence on the part of the Spirit with regard to the Son: *De processione Spiritus Sancti* (Rome, 1936), pp. 104–106. See also L. Abramowski, *Zeitschrift für Kirchengeschichte*, 87 (1976), 145–166; A. Arunde, 'El Espíritu Santo en la Exposición de fe de S. Gregorio Taumaturgo', *Scripta Teol*. (Pamplona), 10 (1978), 373–407.

22. *DS* 115. In his reply defending himself against the suspicion of tritheism, of which he was accused by his namesake Dionysius of Rome, Dionysius of Alexandria formulated the well-known statement: 'We extend the unity into a trinity and summarize the trinity in a unity'; this is quoted by Athanasius in *Sent. Dionys.* (*PG* 25, 505A).

(A) IN THE GREEK PART OF THE CHURCH

1

THE CRITICISM OF ARIANISM ADVANCES IN THE THEOLOGY OF THE TRINITY

In these chapters, I shall first discuss, in a perhaps over-simplified form, the contribution made to the Trinitarian doctrine by the great doctors of the Church Athanasius, Epiphanius of Salamis, Basil the Great, Gregory Nazianzen and Gregory of Nyssa, and Cyril of Alexandria. I shall then examine John Damascene's theology of the Trinity and after that look at the intervention of the Patriarch Photius. This should place me in a position where I can survey the whole Greek approach to the mystery of the Tri-unity of God. I shall also include at the end [Chapter 5] a brief account of the theology of Gregory Palamas.

It would have been desirable to discuss the work of the Latin doctors and the Councils and pontifical pronouncements of the Western branch of the Church in parallel with that of the East, and in its chronological place. I have, however, chosen to follow a theological rather than a historical course and shall therefore consider the contribution made by the Latin Church afterwards, when I shall try to identify the points at which the same faith is expressed by both East and West, but explained in ways that are at least partly different.

Arius[1] was a priest in charge of the church of Baucalis in Alexandria. In 318 he began to preach a doctrine denying the divinity of Christ in a very radical way. His systematic teaching was largely based on subordinationism of a kind that formed part of the inheritance of Origen, Dionysius of Alexandria and Eusebius of Nicomedia. The mystery of the divine being was realized only in the Father, who alone was 'God'. The Son was a creature (no distinction was made in Arian teaching between being begotten and being created); he therefore had a beginning and there was therefore a time when he did not exist. He was, admittedly, the first among creatures and God had created the other, inferior creatures through him. In support of these arguments, Arius used a certain number of biblical texts in which such expressions as 'God has created me (Wisdom)' and 'he (Christ) was made' occur.

Athanasius (†373) is identified, in the history of Christian doctrine, with the Nicaean cause. He was a simple priest when he went with his bishop to the council (325). He became Bishop of Alexandria in 326 and carried on a tireless combat against Arianism. This struggle led to as many as five periods of exile from Alexandria: 335–337, to Trier; 339–346, to Rome; 356–362, in the desert, where he wrote his four letters to Serapion, probably in 359; 362–364, also in the desert; and for the last time for a few months in 365–366.

When he accepted Serapion's request to defend the divinity of the Spirit,[2] Athanasius had already actively championed the divinity of the Son and the *homoousios* of Nicaea, as a formula that affirmed the identity of substance between the Son and the Father. In that defence, he made use of the following arguments: God (the Father) can never be without his Word. As he is eternal, the Word also belongs eternally to him. We are called to be sons and to be deified. That is only possible if Christ, the incarnate Son, is truly and fully God: 'The Word would never have been able to deify us if he had only been divine by participation and had not himself been the deity by essence, the true image of the Father'.[3]

Athanasius applied to the Spirit what he had said of the Son. Although he quotes the text of Jn 15:26, he speaks of the relationship between the Spirit and the Father only through his relationship with the Son. He defends the divinity of the Spirit entirely on the basis of his Christology.[4] There is, he teaches, a relationship between the Spirit and the Son similar to that between the Son and the Father, 'because the state that we have recognized (as that) of the Son with regard to the Father is, we shall find, precisely that which the Spirit has with regard to the Son'.[5] Applying the linear and dynamic idea of 'from the Father through the Son in the Spirit' to this relationship, Athanasius says: 'the Father is light, the Son is its brilliance and the Spirit is the one through whom we are illuminated' and 'the Father is the source and the Son is the river, so that we can say that we drink the Spirit'. He applies that to everything that is concerned with the communication of the divine life.[6] The Spirit does this because he is consubstantial with the Father and the Son.[7]

What relationship of origin does this teaching presuppose between the Spirit and the Son? Athanasius does not speculate about the eternal and intra-divine relationships, but only speaks about them in the context of the activities of the divine Persons within the economy of salvation. All the same, however, J. Lebon has, with as much discretion as precision, drawn attention to three texts which might constitute a statement about the dependence in origination of the Spirit in the Son. It is particularly the use of the preposition *para* which gives force to these texts:

Everything that the Spirit has, he has from the Son (*para tou Logou*).[8]

. . . his gift (the Spirit), who is said to proceed from the Father because, from the

Son (*para tou Logou*) who is confessed (as coming) from the Father, he shines out and is sent and is given.[9]

For the Father creates all things through the Word in the Spirit, since where the Word is, there is also the Spirit, and the things created by the intermediary of the Word have from the Spirit through the Word (*para tou Logou*) the power of being.[10]

There are many indications and even formal evidence of the fact that the Greek Fathers thought that the Son, the Word, played a part in the eternal being of the Spirit. They kept to Scripture and never applied to the role of the Son the verb *ekporeuomai* which is employed in Jn 15:26 to speak of the procession of the Spirit from the Father. In fact, they did not ask this question in the polemical form in which it has been asked in the controversy between Greek and Latin theologians from the time of Charlemagne, and especially from the time of the Patriarch Photius onwards. Sergey Bulgakov was right in this matter, although the path that he chose to follow in his attempt to bypass the contentious posing of the question has not found much favour. It is, however, impossible to deny that there are numerous indications in the writings of the fourth- and fifth-century Greek Fathers of the Church of a dependence on the part of the Spirit with regard to the Son in the life of the eternal Trinity.

Didymus the Blind, who was head of the catechetical school at Alexandria from 340 until 395, continued Athanasius' struggle on behalf of the divinity of the Holy Spirit. His treatise *De Spiritu Sancto*, which influenced Ambrose of Milan, has come down to us only in Jerome's Latin translation. There can be little doubt that Jerome left his mark on the text and was probably responsible for such expressions as 'a Patre et me, hoc enim ipsum quod subsistit et loquitur, a Patre et me illi est' and 'procedens a Veritate' or 'neque alia substantia est Spiritus Sancti praeter id quod datur ei a Filio'.[11] These expressions have, however, been integrated into the context, which is entirely devoted to a commentary on biblical texts.

The almost complete Greek text of his treatise on the Trinity, *Peri Triados*, has, however, been preserved, Showing that the Spirit is from God (the Father), Didymus quotes the text of Tit 3:4–6: 'he has poured out that Spirit on us' and asks when God did that. It was, he replies to his own question, when Christ said 'Receive the Holy Spirit'. He then adds: 'It is right to say "he has poured out", since he in fact poured it out like water coming substantially from him'.[12] Once again, then, the context is that of the 'economic' Trinity, but the statement is general. It is also quite isolated, since Didymus only speaks of the procession *a Patre* in the rest of the chapter.[13]

Epiphanius, who began life as a monk, but later became Bishop of Salamis (367–403), was hardly a genius, but he has handed down to us an abundance of writings. In his *Ancoratus* of 374 he sometimes simply quotes Jn 15:26 on the Paraclete who proceeds from the Father and receives from the Son,[14] and at others says that he is (which means 'has consubstantial being') from the Father and the Son.[15] He is clearly referring here to the intra-divine being that is eternal, but he neither speculates nor suggests any explanation concerning the 'procession' of the Spirit. This dependence of the Spirit on the Son is identified with the fact that he receives from him. Epiphanius also says: 'the Spirit who (is) from the two, as Christ himself bears witness to this by saying: "who proceeds from the Father" (Jn 15:26) and "he will take (receive) from me" (Jn 16:14, 15)'.[16]

NOTES

1. G. L. Prestige, *God in Patristic Thought*, 2nd ed. (London, 1952), pp. 129–156: chapter VII, 'Subordinationism'; J. N. D. Kelly, *Early Christian Doctrines* (London, 1977), pp. 226–231; E. Boularand, *L'hérésie d'Arius et la foi de Nicée*, 2 vols (Paris, 1972).

2. P. Galtier, *Le Saint-Esprit en nous d'après les Pères grecs* (Rome, 1946), pp. 117–133; J. N. D. Kelly, *op. cit.*, pp. 231–237, 240–247; J. Meyendorff, 'La Procession du Saint-Esprit chez les Pères orientaux', *Russie et Chrétienté* (1950), pp. 158–178. The fundamental text here is Athanasius, *Lettres à Sérapion sur la divinité du Saint-Esprit*, Fr. tr. J. Lebon, *SC* 15 (1947).

3. *De Syn*. 51. The one who sanctifies is not the same nature as those whom he sanctifies; he is holy in himself: see *Ad Ser*. I, 23 (*PG* 26, 584B) and 25 (*PG* 26, 589). The same argument can also be found in Basil the Great, *De spir. sanct*. 26 (*PG* 32, 185; *SC* 17, pp. 230ff.), etc.

4. Sergey Bulgakov criticized Athanasius for his dyadic rather than triadic doctrine: see *Le Paraclet* (Paris, 1946), pp. 29–34.

5. *Ad Ser*. III, 1 (*PG* 26, 625B; *SC* 15,   p. 164); see also *Ad Ser*. I, 21 (*PG* 26, 580B; *SC* 15, p. 120).

6. *Ad Ser*. I, 19 (*PG* 26, 573Cff.; *SC* 15, pp. 116ff.).

7. *ibid.*, 27 (*PG* 26, 593C; *SC* 15, p. 133ff.): 'He has nothing that is common or proper in his nature or substance, to the creatures, but he is proper to the substance and divinity of the Son, through which, belonging also to the Trinity . . .'; I, 25 (*PG* 26, 589A; *SC* 15, p. 128): 'But if the Son, because he comes from the Father, is proper to the substance of the latter, then the Spirit, because he is said to come from God, must be proper to the Son according to the substance'.

8. *Contra Arian*. III, 24 (*PG* 26, 376A); see J. Lebon, *SC* 15, p. 74, note.

9. *Ad Ser*. I, 20 (*PG* 26, 580A: *SC* 15, p. 120). H. B. Swete, *The Holy Spirit in the Ancient Church* (London, 1912), p. 92, thought that this *eklampsis (resplendit)* that the Spirit has from (*para*) the Word could not be regarded as implying anything less than an essential dependence.

10. *Ad Ser*. III, 5 (*PG* 26, 632C; *SC* 15, p. 169).

11. Didymus, *De spir. sanct*. 34, 36 and 37 (*PG* 39, 1064A, 1064–1065, 1065–1066) respectively.

12. 'Eu de kai to *execheen*, hate hudōr ex autou homoousiōs ekporeuthen': II, 2 (*PG* 39, 456).

13. See *PG* 39, 460B: 'apo tou henos Patros kath' enōsin tēs heautou theotētos esti gennēsis kai ekporeusis'.

14. Epiphanius, *Anc.* 6 (*PG* 43, 25C), 7 (*PG* 43, 28A), 11 (*PG* 43, 36C), 67 (*PG* 43, 137B), 73 (*PG* 43, 153A), 120 (*PG* 43, 236B); *Panarion, Haer.* LXII (*PG* 41, 1056). Epiphanius said of the 'procession' of the Son: *ek Patros proelthōn*: *Anc.* 19 (*PG* 43, 52B), 43 (*PG* 43, 93C).

15. *Anc.* 8 (*PG* 43, 29C), 9 (*PG* 43, 32C), 67 (*PG* 43, 137B), 70 (*PG* 43, 148A), 71 (*PG* 43, 148B), 72 (*PG* 43, 152B), 75 (*PG* 43, 157A); *Panarion, Haer.* LXIX, 54 (*PG* 42, 285D).

16. *Anc.* 67 (*PG* 43, 137B); *Panarion, Haer.* LXII, 4 (*PG* 41, 1053D).

2
THE CAPPADOCIAN FATHERS
THE FIRST COUNCIL OF
CONSTANTINOPLE
(381)
JOHN DAMASCENE

It proved very difficult to formulate faith in the consubstantial divinity of the Son, the incarnate Word in Jesus, and the Spirit. A multiplicity of errors and deviations arose. Sabellius, who came to Rome shortly before 220, believed that what was involved was merely two projections or modes of action of 'God' (that is, the Father). His teaching was therefore a form of 'modalism'. Aetius and Eunomius thought that only the Father was *agennētos* and that the Son and the Spirit were not the same substance or even of a similar substance. These two Arians and their followers were known as Anomoeans. Eunomius (*c*. 335–393), a disciple of Aetius, regarded the Spirit as a creature of the Son and the Son as a creature of the Father, who was *agennētos*. The Spirit was the third, not only in rank and dignity, but also in nature. Treatises attacking this teaching (*Contra Eunomium*) were written by Basil the Great and by his brother, Gregory of Nyssa. The divinity of the Spirit was called into question by Christians of various parties during these dramatic years. The so-called Pneumatomachi or 'fighters against the Spirit', together with Macedonius and Eustathius of Sebaste (*c*. 361 onwards), based their teaching on the fact that the Spirit is not called 'God' in Scripture, which refers to the Spirit quite often as a power subordinate to God, and consequently placed the Spirit between God and the creatures.

The orthodox teachers of the Church opposed these deviations from the truth. They included Athanasius, who wrote his letters to Serapion (357 onwards), and, when he returned to Alexandria, held a council there in 362. The faith of Nicaea implied that the Spirit belonged fully to the holy Triad and had the same divinity as the Father and the Son.[1] There were also interventions from Hilary of Poitiers, Epiphanius, Didymus and Cyril of Jerusalem. In Rome, Pope Damasus proclaimed the Spirit 'increatum atque unius maiestatis, unius usiae, unius virtutis cum Deo Patre et Domino nostro Jesu Christo'.[2] A council held at Iconium (*c*. 375) extended the faith of Nicaea to the Holy Spirit in terms that were employed at the same time by Basil, the Bishop of Caesarea, who was a friend of Amphilochius, the Bishop of Iconium.[3]

It was at this time that Basil wrote his treatise on the Holy Spirit. We have already considered the circumstances in which this treatise was written (see Volume I, p. 74). Basil continued in the direction indicated by Athanasius, insisting that the Spirit belonged, both in equality and in dignity, to the holy Triad. He took as his point of departure two data that no one could seriously refute. The first was baptism in the name of the Father, the Son and the Holy Spirit. Faith should be confessed in the form in which one was baptized, and one should praise as one confesses one's faith.[4] On the other hand, as Athanasius had already said, if the Spirit is not consubstantial with the Father and the Son, he cannot make us conform to the Son and therefore cannot unite us to the Father. He cannot, in other words, deify us.[5] The Spirit, who is the image and the reflection of the Son, reveals the Son to us and incorporates us into him. It is in this context that Basil uses this formula, which is so difficult to interpret:

> He is called the 'Spirit of Christ' because he is intimately united to him by nature. Also: 'Anyone who does not have the Spirit of Christ does not belong to Christ' (Rom 8:9). Because of this, only the Holy Spirit can worthily glorify the Lord, since 'he will glorify me' as Christ himself has said (Jn 16:14), not as creation, but as Spirit of truth, who makes the truth shine in him, and as Spirit of wisdom, who reveals Christ in his own majesty as Power of God and Wisdom of God. As the Paraclete, he expresses in him the goodness of the Paraclete who sent him and in his own dignity reveals the greatness of the One from whom he came (*tēn megalosunēn emphainei tēn tou hothen proēlthen*).[6]

Note the important part played in this text by 'manifestation'. Basil repeats Athanasius' statement that the Spirit has a relationship with the Son similar to that which the Son has with the Father[7]—he is the image or the expression (*rēma*) of the Son.[8] This manifestation and assimilation clearly place us within the order of the economy and God's action in and for his creatures, but the word used—*proēlthen*—points to intra-divine relationships between the Persons. The Spirit proceeds from the Father: in chapter 16 of his treatise (*PG* 32, 136C; *SC* 17, p. 177), Basil goes back to the *para tou Patros ekporeuetai* of Jn 15:26, although a little later, in chapter 18 (*PG* 32, 152B; *SC* 17, p. 195), he also uses *proelthon* for the procession *a Patre*, as does Epiphanius (see above [p. 28, note 14]). Basil does not give the exact place occupied by the Son in the intra-divine 'coming from' of the third Person. A passage in his *Adversus Eunomium* would seem to situate it in the sense of the *Filioque*. This text was vehemently discussed at the Council of Florence.[9] In a critical study of the original text, one scholar has concluded that an explanatory scholion, reproduced in the margin by a copyist but originally borrowed from Eunomius, must have been introduced into the text of Basil's treatise and handed down in certain manuscripts. Basil must have been criticizing this scholion, which read: the Spirit is third, that is, subordinate and inferior to the Word in nature. This is a Neo-Platonic idea that was combated by the Cappadocian Fathers.[10]

Basil was not very philosophically minded. He made use of the already accepted distinction between *ousia* and *hypostasis*, which he explained in the following way: '*Ousia* and *hypostasis* can be differentiated in the same way as common (*koinon*) and the particular (*to kath' ekaston*), as, for example, in the case of "animal" and a "particular man" '.[11] Each hypostasis is the *ousia*, and so Basil attached the unity of the hypostases to the identity of nature, but at the same time taught that each hypostasis was distinguished by a special characteristic or *idiazon*.[12] This characteristic consisted of the fact that two of the Persons came from a first Person who did not come from any other. Or, put better, each hypostasis was marked by a special property or *idiotēs*—that of fatherhood, sonship or the power of sanctification.[13] This last *gnoristikē idiotēs* corresponds to what Thomas Aquinas called 'notion'. It marked the Spirit as the one who sanctified and who fulfilled in the perfection of communion with the deity.

Basil died on 1 January 379. The struggle that he had been conducting was taken up by his brother Gregory, Bishop of Nyssa (†394 or later).[14] Like Athanasius and Basil, Gregory also based his thesis on the Trinitarian baptismal formula[15] and concluded, as they had done, from the fact of our deification that the Spirit was fully divine. He went further than they had, however, and developed this classical argument into a theologal anthropology, teaching that the formation (*morphōsis*) of the Christian and his perfection (*teleiōsis*), of which Christ was the model, were the work of the sanctifying Spirit.[16] The Spirit was therefore consubstantial with the Son and the Father; he was of the same nature (against Macedonius and Eunomius); a unity of nature (*phusis, ousia*), but a distinction between hypostases.[17] The action attributed to the Spirit by Scripture required him to be God, Gregory argued on the eve of the First Council of Constantinople in May 381, and as such to receive the same honour as the Father and the Son.[18] The progress of the Council and the text of its creed were both guided by this thought. Jaeger has shown clearly that Gregory played a decisive part in the Council.[19] He brought together the various statements that insisted on the unity of nature in the Trinity and the conviction, so strong in the East, of the monarchy of the Father, saying: 'of one and the same Person of the Father (*prosōpon*), by whom the Son was begotten and from whom the Spirit proceeds. That is why we speak strictly of only one God and of only one cause of those who depend on him as on their cause.'[20] He also illustrated this theology by various meaningful images. He spoke, for example, of a lamp which communicates its light to another lamp and through that lamp to a third. The Spirit shone in this way, Gregory taught, eternally through the Son.[21] He also used the comparison of a source of power, of that power itself and of the spirit of that power.[22]

The Word therefore appears as the intermediary between the Father and the Spirit in Gregory's teaching, in which he clearly has biblical formulae in mind: the Spirit proceeds (comes) from the Father and receives from the Son, with the result that he is from God and he is from Christ.[23] This implies a certain dependence on the part of the Spirit, in his being, with regard to the Son. What Gregory does not say, however, is *ek tou Huiou* or *apo tou Huiou*—Jaeger has shown that the *ek* in certain manuscripts of *De Orat. Dom.* 3 is an interpolation.[24] At the end of Book I of his *Contra Eunomium*, however, he wrote (in 380) that the Son was always with the Father and that he, Gregory, taught the same thing about the Spirit, the only difference being in the order (*taxis*), 'since, just as the Son is united to the Father, having his being from him (*ex autou*), but is not after him (in time) in his hypostasis, the Spirit is also united to the monogenous one, for, in the hypostasis, the Son is conceived before the Spirit only in respect of the cause (*kata ton tēs aitias logon*)'.[25] Does this word *aitia*, 'cause', apply in this text to the monogenous Son or to the Father? This might be implied in such a passage.[26] A very valuable statement is made, however, at the end of his *Quod non sint tres dii*:

> If we should be accused, by not making a difference with regard to nature (*phusis*), of confusing the hypostases, we would reply: In confessing a divine nature without difference or variation, we are not denying a difference with regard to the situation of cause and caused (*kata ton aition kai aitiaton*). It is only in this way that we can understand that the one is distinguished from the other—being the cause is quite different from being caused. And we perceive in what is caused a new distinction between what comes immediately (*prosechōs*) from the first, and what comes through the intermediary of what comes immediately from the first. In this way, the property of being monogenous remains unambiguously with the Son, and there can be no doubt that the Spirit is from the Father, the middle position of the Son preserving for him the property of being monogenous, and the Spirit not being deprived of his natural relationship with the Father.[27]

This is not, of course, the same as the *Filioque* of the Latin Church, since the Eastern Christians have never spoken of the Father and the Son as forming a single principle of active spiration, even if it has been emphasized, as Augustine and Christians in the West did, that this goes back *principaliter* to the Father. The Greeks did not like speculating or arriving at greater precision on the basis of deductions. It is, however, hardly possible to deny that the Son played a part in the intra-divine existence of the Spirit, although that part was not of a causal nature. Gregory of Nyssa, however, uses the formula, either literally or with the same meaning, *ek tou Patros dia tou Huiou ekporeuetai*: the Spirit comes from the Father through the Son.[28]

Gregory's namesake of Nazianzus was born about 330 and was consecrated Archbishop of Constantinople on 27 November 380. He resigned from that office in June 381, however, and retired to his birthplace, where he died in

389 or 390.[29] He is called 'the Theologian' by the Eastern Church. Like his friend Basil, he showed that the Spirit had all the qualities of God and that his activities were those of God.[30] Unlike Basil, who did not in fact say the word, Gregory Nazianzen explicitly stated that the Spirit *is* God.[31] In his affirmation of consubstantiality, he insisted on the monarchy of the Father, who was, according to Gregory, 'without a beginning', *anarchos*:

> The name of the one who is without a beginning is Father; the name of the beginning is Son; the name of the one who is with the beginning is Holy Spirit.[32]

> Each is God by reason of consubstantiality; the Three are God by reason of monarchy.[33]

> Nature is one in the Three; it is God. What makes their unity, however, is the Father, on whom the others depend, not in order to be confused or mixed, but in order to be united.[34]

Gregory Nazianzen also makes use of comparisons. These include the source, the stream and the river on the one hand, and the sun, the ray and the light on the other.[35] He points out, however, that every comparison is insufficient. He also stresses our (his) inability to penetrate into and define precisely the nature of the processions and the difference between them, although we are acquainted with that difference through the very terms used by the sovereign theologian, Christ himself.[36] It is enough to affirm, as mysteriously different, the begetting by and the procession from the one who alone is *agennētos*.[37] Gregory ventures, however, to provide a comparison here. Eve, he says, was taken from Adam by means of an immediate coming out and that is the way in which the Spirit proceeded. Seth, on the other hand, came from Adam (and Eve!) by means of begetting (see Gen 4:35).[38] This is certainly a strange comparison—if it is taken further, then it would have to be said that the Son was begotten *a Patre Spirituque*, which would contradict the idea of the *taxis*, the order of the three Persons in their perfect consubstantiality.

The Cappadocian Fathers definitively established the distinction between the common *ousia* (substance or nature) and the hypostases, which they also sometimes called 'persons', *prosōpa*. The hypostasis is what has distinctive consistency and a concrete existence; it is what Aristotle called the *protē ousia*, the concrete being in which alone a concrete substance can exist. It is characterized by its *idiotēs*, which is known by its *gnōrismata*. Kelly has pointed out that 'for Basil these particularizing characteristics are respectively "paternity" (*patrotēs*), "sonship" (*huiotēs*) and "sanctifying power" or "sanctification" (*hagiastikē dunamis*; *hagiasmos*). The other Cappadocians define them more precisely as "ingenerateness" (*agennēsia*), "generateness" (*gennēsis*) and "mission" or "procession" (*ekpempsis*;

ekporeusis). . . . Thus the distinction of the Persons is grounded in their origin and mutual relation . . . and hence they come to be termed "modes of coming to be" (*tropoi huparxeōs*).'[39] The hypostatic characters are in this way 'derived from relationships of origin'.[40]

All the Greek Fathers, however, believed that this 'mode of coming to be' of the Word and the Spirit is inexpressible.[41] All that man can do, they insisted, is recognize, respect and affirm it. The Son, the Father's Word, was begotten *huiokōs*, filially, and the Spirit was begotten *pneumatikōs*, as Spirit, according to Didymus of Alexandria.[42] The analyses made by the Latin Fathers, which are fundamentally in agreement with the teaching of the Greeks, seemed to the latter to be a rational elaboration which lacked discretion and went beyond what could properly be said about the inexpressible mystery of the divine processions.

The struggle and the work of the Cappadocian Fathers resulted in the article on the Holy Spirit in the creed which the Council of Chalcedon attributed to the First Council of Constantinople.[43] In this creed, the Holy Spirit was not called 'God' or said to be 'consubstantial with the Father'; he was, however, said to be 'Lord, who gives life, who proceeds from the Father (*ekporeuomenon*), who is adored and glorified with the Father and the Son, who has spoken through the prophets'. To these words were added the words: 'in the one, holy, catholic and apostolic Church'. The Council followed the example of the Greek Fathers and used the words employed by Jesus in Jn 15:26, but replaced *para* with *ek*, assuming that the two prepositions were equivalent. At the same time, the Council said nothing about the part played by the Son in the Spirit's coming to be. It could have used the formula taken from Jn 16:14 and so frequently cited by the Fathers: *kai ek tou Huiou lambanon*, 'and receiving from the Son'. On the other hand, it could also have followed the example of, for example, Epiphanius, Pseudo-Cyril (*PG* 77, 1140B), John Damascene (*PG* 94, 821B) and Pope Zacharias (†752), and spoken of *en Huiō anapauomenon*, 'reposing in the Son'.

Fifty years later, nothing was said about the question by the Council of Ephesus, even though the opportunity presented itself in the Council's condemnation of the teaching of Nestorius, who limited the part played by the Spirit in the fact of Christ to a sanctificaton of his pure humanity. Against this, Cyril of Alexandria showed that the Spirit was not unrelated to the incarnate Son at the level of essence. In his ninth anathema, written before the Council, he condemned anyone who should say that the Lord Jesus Christ was glorified by the Spirit as though by an alien power, instead of acknowledging the Spirit by whom he accomplished the signs of his divinity (*theosēmeias*) as being proper to him (*idion*).[44]

This brings us to Cyril (†444), who was Bishop of Alexandria for more than thirty years. His leading part in the Christological debate has been extensively studied. In pneumatology, he merits particular attention as regards the indwelling of the Holy Spirit in the righteous and the fact that, in his being as the third Person, the Spirit depends on the Son.

I have discussed the first of these questions in Volume II (pp. 85–90, and 95–98 notes 24–45) and have provided a bibliography there. The Greek Fathers insisted not only on the community of action *ad extra* of the divine Persons, but also on the mark, in this action, of what is the property of each hypostasis in the Tri-unity of God. The Spirit, as the image of the Son, brings about our sonship by grace and, as the virtue of sanctification of the deity, he also brings about our sanctification.

With regard to the second question, there can be no doubt that the most impressive statements are to be found in the writings of Cyril.[45] His first intention was to oppose Nestorius and to show that the Spirit rightly belonged to the incarnate Word. Within this perspective of the incarnation, he from time to time had the 'economy' in mind,[46] but what is remarkable is that he based that economy on the eternal Tri-unity—the evidence is abundant.[47] The same applies to the formulae relating to the Spirit as proper to the Son (*idion*),[48] coming from him (*ek*),[49] the Spirit as proceeding from the Son (*proïenai* or *procheitai*)[50] and proceeding from the two (*ex amphoin*), that is, from the Father and the Son[51] or from the Father through the Son.[52]

All these statements point to the same context. The latter can be expressed in a precise form in Thomistic categories in the following way: the Spirit is sent by the Father and by the Son and this 'mission' is based on the eternal processions, of which it is the term in the creature, by bringing about the 'economy'. This economy is that of the incarnation of the Word and is therefore Christological. The mission of the Spirit is to bring about the (mystical) Body of Christ. The sanctification of the humanity of Christ by the Spirit is the beginning of our sanctification and it is extended to his (mystical) body.[53] In this action, which makes us into the body of Christ, making us 'con-corporeal' with Christ, the Eucharist or 'mystical eulogy' brings about a corporeal unity, just as the Spirit brings about a spiritual unity.

I have already referred to Cyril's ninth anathema against Nestorius. Theodoret of Cyrrhus came to the rescue of Nestorius and, in a pitiless criticism of Cyril's statements, had this to say about the relationship between the Spirit and the Son: 'If he says that the Spirit is proper to the Son insofar as he is consubstantial and proceeds from the Father (*kai ek Patros ekporeuomenon*), we would agree with him and regard that pronouncement as orthodox. But if he claims that this is so because the Spirit has his existence either from the Son or through the Son (*hōs ex Huiou ē di' Huiou*), then we reject that sentence as blasphemous and impious, since we believe the Lord, who said: "the Spirit of truth who proceeds from the Father".'[54]

Cyril did not deal with the question to which later controversies gave such prominence, but simply reaffirmed that 'the Spirit is the Spirit of the Son just as he is the Spirit of the Father. . . . The Holy Spirit proceeds from God the Father, as the Lord said, but he is not alien to the Son, since the latter has everything (in common) with the Father, as he said himself when he spoke of the Holy Spirit' (here Cyril quotes Jn 16:14).[55] J. Meyendorff said: 'It is interesting to note that, after that incident, which took place about 430, Cyril did not give up either his theology or his vocabulary. In his later works, expressions such as "coming from the two" (*ex amphoin*) are still to be found. This makes it possible for us to say that these expressions had for him a quite different meaning from the one they had for Augustine.'[56] To say 'different' is probably correct, but to say '*quite* different' is, I think, too much. Cyril was dealing with the Nestorian heresy and developed his own, relatively simply, uncomplicated vocabulary. Augustine used his own concepts. It is certainly not possible to misunderstand Cyril's repeated statements about the Spirit's dependence on the Son with regard to being, but he did not develop this theology as Augustine did, because he was not preoccupied with it. As G. M. de Durand has pointed out recently: 'Cyril's principal preoccupation was to draw attention to the unfailing link between the Spirit and the divine essence. Flowing physically from the Father through the Son (*De Trin. Dial.*, ed. J. Aubert, 423a) or poured out by the Father from his own nature (634b–c), the Spirit is at the same level as they are and cannot be a creature. The Son who distributes such a gift as his own (492a and d; 494c) also cannot be a creature. It was probably because of this limited and quite narrow intention in most of the texts, that of determining the nature of the Spirit and not his precise relationship with the other Persons, that Photians and Latinophrones were able to refer almost endlessly to such passages.'[57]

*   *   *

John was born about 700 at Damascus and was therefore known as John Damascene or John of Damascus. He was a monk at St Sabas, between Jerusalem and the Dead Sea, from 726 until he died in 749.[58] His main work, *Pēgē gnōseōs*, the 'Fount of Wisdom', consists of three parts, dealing with philosophy, heresies and orthodox faith respectively. The third part, translated into Latin as *De fide orthodoxa* in the twelfth century, was widely read during the Scholastic period in the West. In the East, it was used as a handbook of theology in the Byzantine schools and universities. It can certainly be regarded as a faithful expression of the faith of the Church, since John Damascene was not a very original writer. In his Trinitarian teaching, he virtually repeats two-thirds of a treatise *De Sacrosancta Trinitate* by an unknown author writing at the end of the seventh or the beginning of the eighth century. This treatise was printed at the end of the works of Cyril of Alexandria, and the author is, for that reason, called Pseudo-Cyril.[59] This

36

author was also influenced by Basil of Caesarea and Gregory Nazianzen. John Damascene owned his use of the idea of *perichōrēsis* in the theology of the Trinity to Pseudo-Cyril especially.[60] The following is an example of his writing on the Trinity:

> These hypostases are within each other, not so that they are confused, but so that they contain one another, in accordance with the word of the Lord: I am in the Father and the Father is in me. . . . We do not say three gods, the Father, the Son and the Holy Spirit. On the contrary, we say only one God, the Holy Trinity, the Son and the Spirit going back to only one Principle, without composition or confusion, quite unlike the heresy of Sabellius. These Persons are united, not so that they are confused with each other, but so that they are contained within each other. There is between them a circumincession without mixture or confusion, by virtue of which they are neither separated nor divided in substance, unlike the heresy of Arius. In fact, in a word, the divinity is undivided in the individuals, just as there is only one light in three suns contained within each other, by means of an intimate interpenetration.[61]

The opportunity clearly presents itself at this point to say a few words about this reality which is so difficult to define. The fourth gospel frequently speaks of the existence of the Father in the Son and of the Son in the Father[62] and such an important factor as this 'in-existence' was bound to have a deep effect on the minds of Christians. Although the words *perichōrēsis* and circumincession may not occur as such in the writings of the earliest Fathers of the Church, the idea certainly does.[63] It was first applied in Christology[64] and Maximus the Confessor was the first to use the word *perichōrēsis* to express the oneness of action and effect resulting from the union of the two natures in Christ.[65] It was first employed in Trinitarian theology by Pseudo-Cyril, who was followed by John Damascene.

Perichōrēsis in the theology of the Trinity points to the in-existence of the Persons within each other, the fact that they are present to each other, that they contain one another and that they manifest each other. This in-existence is based on the unity and identity of substance between the three, even in the teaching of the Greek Fathers.[66] If this teaching were to go no further than this, however, it would simply indicate the identity of God with himself, and no more than this. This is reflected in the very differences that exist within God himself, that is, in the Persons who hypostatize the same substance. They are in or within each other—in Greek *en* and in Latin *circuminsessio*; John Damascene speaks of it in this way—and each one is turned towards the other and is open and given to the other (*eis*; *circumin-sessio*). They are inconceivable without each other. Sergey Bulgakov insisted that the hypostases were always Trinitarian.[67] An interesting datum with a bearing on the delicate problem of consciousness in God can be derived from the concept of circumincession, and I shall touch on this question when we come to consider the idea of 'person'.

To return to John Damascene, it is clear that he begins by speaking of

'God' (*De fide orthod*. I, 3, 4 and 8) and, though it is not long before he is speaking of the Father, the Son and the Holy Spirit, he is still concerned primarily, to begin with at least, with 'God' as the absolute being. There is a certain ambivalence about this name, and Bulgakov criticizes John for this.[68] It is quite possible that his procedure may have strengthened Thomas Aquinas in his own approach to the question, which Orthodox theologians have seen as a perfect example of the Latin tendency to stress the essence rather than the hypostases. It is certainly true that we know, in faith, that God is Father, Son and Spirit, but is it not legitimate, if we follow the economy of revelation, to speak first of all of 'God' as the one who is and who will be what he will be (Ex 3:14)?

The one 'God' is also the Father, and John soon goes on to discuss the monarchy of that Father as the Father by nature (and not by a free decision) of his monogenous Son and the *proboleus*[69] or 'producer' of the very Holy Spirit (*De fide orthod*. I, 8; *PG* 94, 809B). The Spirit is not another Son—he does not proceed by begetting, but *ekporeutōs* or by 'procession' (*PG* 94, 816C). which is another mode of coming to be or mode of subsistence, *tropos tēs huparxeōs*.[70] Both are beyond our understanding and neither can be explained. John ventures a fairly common comparison, however, that of Eve coming from the side of Adam (the Spirit) and of Seth, who was born through being begotten (see above, p. 33 and below, note 38). The three hypostases have everything in common except their 'hypostatic properties' (*De fide orthod*. I, 8; *PG* 94, 824B, 828D) of being *agennētos, gennētos* and *ekporeuomenon*. This teaching became classical in Eastern triadology. It would be wrong to regard this teaching as diametrically opposed to what was worked out in the Western Church, even if precise concepts and logical connections were much further developed in Latin theology, where they were so developed in terms of relationships of origin. John Damascene spoke of *pros allēla scheseōs* and wrote: 'We have learnt through faith that there is a difference between begetting and proceeding, but faith tells us nothing about the nature of that difference'.[71] Many of the Western theologians said the same.[72] John Damascene, on the other hand, thought of the modes of subsistence of the one who was begotten and the one who proceeds only with reference to the unbegotten one, the Father, and his monarchy (see *De fide orthod*. I, 8, 12; *PG* 94, 824A-B, 829A and C, 849A).

It is at this point that the question concerning the relationship between the Spirit and the Son arises. Here John Damascene reproduces Pseudo-Cyril's text (*PG* 77, 1145A) and says: 'We do not say that the Son is the cause, nor do we say that he is Father. . . . We do not say that the Spirit comes from the Son (*ek tou Huiou*), but we do say that he is Spirit of the Son.'[73] 'The Spirit is Spirit of the Father . . . but he is also the Spirit of the Son, not because he comes from him (*ouch hōs ex autou*), but because he comes through him (*all' hōs di' autou*) from the Father, since the Father is the only cause (*monos*

38

aitios ho Patēr)'.[74] The Spirit is united to the Father by the Son.[75] He is called Spirit of the Son because he is manifested and given by him.[76] This, of course, is an economic aspect of the Spirit, but it becomes clear at the end of chapter 12 of the treatise that this is based on the immanent reality of the Tri-unity: 'Through the Word, the Father produces the Spirit, who manifests him (*dia logou proboleus ekphantorikou Pneumatos*). . . . The Holy Spirit is the power of the Father making the secrets of the deity known and proceeding from the Father through the Son in a way that he knows, but which is not begetting. . . . The Father is the source of the Son and the Holy Spirit. . . . The Spirit is not Son of the Father, he is the Spirit of the Father, as proceeding from him (*ekporeuomenon*), . . . but he is also Spirit of the Son, not as (proceeding) from him, but proceeding through him from the Father. Only the Father is cause (*aitios*).'[77]

The *per Filium* of John Damascene is not the *Filioque*. In the material sense, John's texts are a denial of the procession of the Spirit 'from the Father and from the Son as from a single principle'. They do, however, give the Son a certain place in the eternal state of the Spirit. J. Grégoire has vigorously analysed John's terms and formulae within their original doctrinal context, trying to make clear in this way what they aimed to establish, and against whom. He has in this way been able to define quite precisely the meaning of the procession of the Spirit from the Father in the sense of John's 'through the Son'. He has said, for example, that 'His hypostatic property, the procession, is only accessible and understandable—insofar as it can be made intelligible—by reference to the Son, just as the breath can only be accessible by reference to the word. The Spirit can therefore reveal the Father, his cause, by the procession, only through the Son and our understanding cannot pass directly from the Spirit to the Father' (*op. cit.* (note 58 below), pp. 750–751).

J. Grégoire also says, a little later in his article: 'If the Spirit comes from the Father by procession and remains in him, unlike our breath which disappears into the air, this must be by "penetrating" the Son until he remains and dwells in him at the same time as he does in the Father. The procession must therefore be *dia Huiou* (as John Damascene claims) or else the Spirit must rest *in* the Son (as the Pseudo-Cyril says). This *dia Huiou* is the dynamic expression—one is almost tempted to say the "genetic" expression—of the *perichōrēsis*, the interpenetration and the dwelling of the hypostases in each other being the static expression, the eternal "result" of the procession *dia Huiou*' (*op. cit.*, p. 753).

The subject-matter and the quality of Grégoire's work is in my opinion so important that I would like to summarize it here in his own words, given at the conclusion of his article (*op. cit.*, pp. 754–755):

1. The Father is the only cause in the Trinity; this causality cannot be divided or shared. The category of 'secondary cause' is completely absent in the teaching of John Damascene.

2. John's theology of the Trinity is dominated by the ideas of *nous, logos* and *pneuma*. It expresses in a single movement the fact that the Spirit reveals the Word and the Word reveals the Father.

3. The procession is not begetting and the Spirit is not the son of the Son.

4. The Spirit rests in the Word and accompanies him, that is, he participates indissolubly in his activity by making him manifest. He is the revelation and the image of the Son.

5. The procession of the Spirit goes back to the begetting of the Son; at the level of the *perichōrēsis*, the Spirit comes from the Father through the Son and is poured out in him.

6. In the divine activity, the Son provides the basis of the work that is wanted by the Father and the Spirit perfects it.

In John's teaching, then, there is no separation between economy and theology; these are completely integrated into a single vision. There is also no polemical element in his writing except possibly against Arianism and Manichaeanism (and perhaps against Islam). There is certainly no argument directed against the *Filioque* or the theology of Cyril of Alexandria or Theodoret of Cyrrhus. He is neither a filioquist nor a monopatrist. He is not a filioquist because, in his teaching, the causal category does not and cannot apply to the eternal relationship between the Spirit and the Son. He is not a monopatrist because, in his theology, an essential presupposition for the procession is the begetting of the Word and the procession refers entirely to that begetting.

The synthetic treatment of this subject by John Damascene on the basis of the contribution made by Athanasius and the Cappadocian Fathers provided Greek theologians with their basic concepts. These included the distinction between substance and hypostasis, the monarchy of the Father and the distinction between the begetting of the Son and the *ekporeusis* of the Spirit, as by two modes of coming into being and of subsistence establishing themselves as such in their difference. They also included the relationship between the Spirit and the Word, the Son (of whom he is the Spirit), either in the form of coming from the Father through the Son, or in the form of a resting of the Spirit in the Son, or by the fact that the Spirit expresses the Son and is the image of the Son, or, finally, at the level of the 'economy', by the fact that the Spirit is communicated by the Son and makes him known.

This is a suitable point, in view of the fact that the term plays such an important part in the triadology of the Eastern Church, to say a few words about *ekporeusis*, which is the noun derived from the verb used in Jn 15:26: 'Hotan de elthē ho paraklētos hon egō pempsō humin para tou patros, to pneuma tēs alētheias ho para tou patros ekporeuetai'—'When the Paraclete comes, whom I shall send to you from the Father, the Spirit of truth who proceeds from the Father, he will bear witness to me'. The verb *ekporeuomenai* appears in the present tense in this text, but, in view of the context, it has to be interpreted in the sense of a *futurum instans*.[78] The verb is derived from a root *poros*, which means a 'crossing' or a 'ford', and from the verb *poreuō*, to cause to cross or pass over. It means 'to come or go out' and examples of its use are: to come or go out like a word from a man's mouth, like water from the temple (Ezek 47:12), to go out of a town (Mt 20:29; Mk 10:46; 11:19), to come out of tombs (Jn 5:29); demons come out of those who are possessed and judgement comes out of the mouth of God (Rev); flashes of lightning come out of God's throne (Rev 4:5) and water comes out of the throne of God and the Lamb (Rev 22:1). In the text in question (Jn 15:26), the verb is in the middle voice, suggesting a reference to the subject of the action: 'the Spirit himself comes out of the Father'.[79]

According to the text, the Spirit 'comes out from near the Father' (*para*), as in the first half of the verse. The context is not that of a statement about the inner being of the Triad. It is rather a pronouncement about the sending by the Son to bear witness. As A. Wenger pointed out, 'the Son sends the Spirit on behalf of the Father and the Spirit will leave from near the Father—that is the meaning which should be given to the repetition of *para*, which should not be understood in the first case as meaning the temporal mission and in the second as pointing to the eternal procession'.[80] If this interpretation is correct, all that we have here is the eternal procession as the prerequisite for the economic mission. But, as J. Giblet has said, 'the two aspects are reached conjointly and understood together'.[81]

It is therefore not possible to say with certainty that the text of Jn 15:26 is as dogmatically significant as the Greek theologians have claimed, especially since there are other equivalent Greek verbs which also express the idea of procession and which can in fact be found in Greek patristic writings. Examples are: *proerchesthai, proïenai, procheisthai* and *pephēnenai*.[82] In this case, Tradition clearly accompanies Scripture. Both the Greek Fathers, most of whom read *ek* instead of *para*, and the Council of 381 regarded the text of Jn 15:26 as expressing the procession of the Spirit *a Patre*.[83] Both Augustine and Thomas Aquinas also saw the text in the same light and Augustine came very close to the Greeks with his *principaliter*. As V. Rodziensko has observed, he would never have said that the Spirit proceeds from the Father and the Son as from a single source *principaliter*. This term was reserved for the Father, with the result that it is necessary to distinguish the titles of origin in 'as from a single source'. It is a pity that the verb *procedere* was used indiscriminately here. A distinction should have been made in the terms themselves.

*   *   *

John Damascene was born in Syria. If we go back several centuries in the history of the Church in that country, we see that a very lyrical form of liturgy was developed there in continuity with the Semitic origins of Christianity, at least until the Eastern Church's liturgy as a whole came strongly under

41

Byzantine influence. The Syrian office was composed not only of psalms, which did not play such a dominant part as in the West, but also of hymns (*madrashē*), responses and *sedrē* (long prayers). The theology which is contained in this liturgy and can be deduced from it and the sacramental celebrations of the Syrian Church is made explicit in homilies, catechetical instructions and commentaries on Scripture, produced in considerable quantities between the fourth and the eighth centuries.[84] The principal authors are, in the fourth century, Aphraates, a Persian (†345), Ephraem Syrus of Nisibis (†373), Cyril of Jerusalem (†386), John Chrysostom (†407), Theodore of Mopsuestia (†428); a little later, Isaac of Antioch (fourth to fifth century), Narsai (†507), Philoxenus of Mabbug (fifth to sixth century), Jacob of Sarug (†521) and Severus of Antioch (†538).

As in the case of the Greek Church, to which John Chrysostom also belonged, both liturgical celebrations and theology in Syrian Christianity are full of Trinitarian evocations and doxologies. These are characterized by a deeply paschal or rather pentecostal spirituality: what the Holy Spirit has done for Christ in his conception, baptism and resurrection, he causes to function in the Church and the lives of Christians. He is life itself and he is life-giving. He is invoked especially in the celebration of the sacraments of initiation—baptism, the Eucharist and the *myron* or anointing with holy oils. In all three cases, the epicleses are very similar.[85] One special feature of the liturgy in the ancient patriarchate of Antioch is that baptism by water was preceded by anointing with oil. This was to indicate that faith had to precede reception into the Church, and the New Testament attributes this to a spiritual anointing by the Spirit.[86] Later an anointing with the *myron* was added after baptism; this has sometimes been interpreted as a form of the sacrament of confirmation.

The Holy Spirit was regarded as active in the Eucharist, not only through the epiclesis, but also in communion, of which he was seen to be the *res*. It is interesting in this context to consider some of the remarkably powerful formulae of Ephraem Syrus: 'The Fire and the Spirit are in our baptism; in the bread and the cup are also the Fire and the Spirit',[87] Isaac of Antioch: 'Come and drink, eat the flame which will make you angels of fire and taste the flavour of the Holy Spirit', or Matins of the second Sunday after Pentecost: 'Here is the body and blood which are a furnace in which the Holy Spirit is the fire'.[88]

According to the Syrian Church, the whole life of the Church, including that of its ordained ministers and its faithful, came from a Pentecost that was extended in time,[89] and even the order of the Church was attributed to the Spirit: 'It was he who said to the apostles at Pentecost: "Go and teach and baptize in the name of the Father, of the Son and of the Holy Spirit and lo, I am with you until the end" (Mt 28:19–20)'.[90]

The theology of the third Person was not developed speculatively to any great extent. The dynamic pattern of the 'economy' was fairly closely followed. 'The truth', Ephraem Syrus declared, 'comes from the Father through the Son and gives life to all through the Spirit.'[91] In other words, the Spirit was seen as life and as life-giving. In the case of the intra-divine life, the formula that was so much used by the Eastern Fathers was also popular in the Syrian Church: 'Father who begets and is not begotten, Son who is begotten and who does not beget, Spirit who proceeds from the Father and receives from the Son. They are three holy Persons and three distinct properties.'[92]

This theology was developed by Bar Hebraeus (†1286). According to E. P. Siman, 'The Spirit, who was caused by the Father by means of procession and not by means of begetting, is a Person who is consubstantial with the Father and the Son by the fact that the three Persons are a single essence and a single nature. That Person, Life, proceeding from the Father, also receives from the Son (Jn 16:14–15) the mode of revelation to creatures. Thus for Bar Hebraeus, who was the greatest witness to the theological tradition in the Syrian Church, the Holy Spirit is life. All life exists through that life. It proceeds from the Father and comes through the Son into the world, animating all things and giving life and deifying men and, through them, the whole cosmos.'[93]

NOTES

1. Athanasius, *Tomus ad Antioch*. 3 (*PG* 26, 797); cf. his letter to Jovianus (*PG* 26, 816 and 820).
2. See Damasus' letter *Ea gratia* to the Eastern Christians, *c.* 374 (*PL* 13, 351; *DS* 145 and 147); see also the very detailed text of 375, *Fides Damasi* (*PL* 13, 358ff.).
3. *PG* 39, 95ff.
4. Basil, *De spir. sanct.* 10 (*PG* 32, 112ff.); Fr. tr., ed. with intro. and notes by B. Pruche, *Traité du Saint-Esprit* (*SC* 17, pp. 149ff.). See also *Ep.* 159 (*PG* 32, 621A). The following monographs and articles are also valuable: H. Dörries, *De Spiritu Sancto. Der Beitrag des Basilius zum Abschluss des trinitarischen Dogmas* (Göttingen, 1956); B. Pruche, 'L'originalité du Traité de S. Basile sur le Saint-Esprit', *RSPT*, 32 (1948), 207–224; *idem*, 'Autour du Traité sur le Saint-Esprit de Basile de Césarée', *RSR*, 52 (1964), 204–232. Finally, the whole of *Verbum Caro*, 89 (1968). For Eunomius, see M. Spanneut's article in *Dict. Hist. Géo. Eccl.*, XV (1963), cols 1499–1504.
5. Athanasius, *Ad Ser.* I, 25 (*PG* 26, 589; *SC* 15, pp. 128ff.); Basil, *De spir. sanct.* 26 (*SC* 17, pp. 230ff.); see also B. Pruche's Introduction, pp. 64–77; *PG* 32, 185).
6. Basil, *De spir. sanct.* 18 (*PG* 32, 152C; *SC* 17, pp. 195–196). The question of the interpretation of this passage is discussed by B. Pruche on pp. 82ff. This aspect of manifestation makes it, in my opinion, difficult to translate as 'by the means of whom the Holy Spirit *proceeds*' the phrase which forms the transition from the Son to the Spirit in Basil's anaphora: 'par' hou to Pneuma to hagion *exephanē*', as B. Capelle has it in 'La procession du Saint-Esprit d'après la liturgie grecque de Basile', *L'Orient syrien*, 7 (1962), 69–76.
7. *De spir. sanct.* 17 (*PG* 32, 148A; *SC* 17, p. 188), which goes back to Athanasius, *Ad Ser.* I, 21; III, 1 (*PG* 26, 580B and 625B; *SC* 15, pp. 120 and 164).
8. *Adv. Eunom.* V (*PG* 29, 723 and 731). According to J. Lebon, *Le Muséon*, 50 (1937),

61–84, however, Books IV and V of the *Adv. Eunom.* were written by Didymus of Alexandria.

9. This is the text in the *Adv. Eunom.* III, beginning, which was disputed at Florence: see J. Gill, *The Council of Florence* (Cambridge, 1959), p. 199:

TEXT UPHELD BY THE LATINS	TEXT UPHELD BY THE GREEKS
Even if the Holy Spirit is third in dignity and order, why need he be third also in nature? For that he is second to the Son, *having his being from him and receiving from him and announcing to us and being completely dependent on him,* pious tradition recounts; but that his nature is third we are not taught by the Saints nor can we conclude logically from what has been said.	Even if the Holy Spirit is third in dignity and order, why need he be third also in nature? For that he is second pious tradition *perhaps* recounts; but that his nature is third we are not taught by Scripture nor can we conclude from what has been said.

10. M. van Parys, 'Quelques remarques à propos d' un texte controversé de Basile au concile de Florence', *Irénikon*, 40 (1967), 6–14. L. Lohn has written the history of this controversial text in his 'Doctrina S. Basilii de processionibus divinarum Personarum', *Greg*, 10 (1929), 329–364, 461–500. Lohn is in favour of the Latin text.

11. *Ep.* 214, 4 and 236, 6 to Amphilochius (in 376) (*PG* 32, 789 and 884). See also *Ep.* 38, written to Gregory of Nyssa, his brother, in 369–370 (*PG* 32, 325ff.).

12. *De Spir. sanct.* 18 (*PG* 32, 149B; *SC* 17, pp. 192–193).

13. *De Spir. sanct.* 25 (*PG* 32, 177B; *SC* 17, p. 222); *Ep.* 214, 4 and 236, 6 (*PG* 32, 789 and 884); *Adv. Eunom.* II, 28 (*PG* 29, 637).

14. W. Jaeger, *Gregor von Nyssa's Lehre vom Heiligen Geist* (Leiden, 1966; published posthumously, ed. H. Dörries). More general works are: H. U. von Balthasar, *Présence et Pensée. Essai sur la philosophie religieuse de G. de Nysse* (Fr. tr.; Paris, 1942); J. Daniélou, *Platonisme et théologie mystique. Essai sur la doctrine spirituelle de Grégoire de Nysse* (Paris, 1944); J. Quasten, *Initiation aux Pères de l'Eglise*, III (Paris, 1963), pp. 365–420; M. Canavet, *Dictionnaire de Spiritualité*, VI (1967), cols 971–1011.

15. Gregory of Nyssa, *Refutatio Confessionis Eunomii: Opera*, ed. W. Jaeger, II, pp. 312ff,; *Ep.* V: *Opera*, VIII/2, pp. 32ff.

16. This theme has been developed by W. Jaeger in 'Paideia Christi', *Humanistische Reden und Vorträge* (Berlin, 1960), pp. 250–265; *Early Christianity and Greek Paideia* (Cambridge, Mass., 1961); *op. cit.* (note 14), chapter V, pp. 101ff. See also the studies by M. Lot-Borodine (1932–1933) and J. Gross (1938).

17. *Orat. cat.* c. 3ff. (*PG* 45, 17ff.); *De comm. not.* 176ff.

18. *Adv. Maced.* (*PG* 45, 1301ff.); *Opera*, III/1, pp. 89ff.

19. W. Jaeger, *op. cit.* (note 14), pp. 70ff. For the council and the creed attributed to it by the Council of Chalcedon, see A. M. Ritter, *Das Konzil von Konstantinopel und sein Symbol. Studien zur Geschichte und Theologie des II. ökumenischen Konzils* (Göttingen, 1965); G. I. Dossetti, *Il Simbolo di Nicea e di Costantinopoli* (Rome, 1967); see also the introduction to *Conciliorum Œcumenicorum Decreta*, ed. J. Alberigo *et al.*, 3rd ed. (Bologna, 1973).

20. *De comm. not.* (*PG* 45, 180C).

21. *Adv. Maced.* 6 (*PG* 45, 1308); see also his *Contra Eunom.* I (*PG* 45, 416C, 396D). The same image will be found in Gregory Nazianzen, *Orat. theol.* V (*PG* 36, 136).

22. *Adv. Maced.* 13 (*PG* 45, 1317).

23. *Adv. Maced.* 2 and 10 (*PG* 45, 1304, 1313B). These include the classical references to Jn 15:26 and Rom 8:9.

24. W. Jaeger, *op. cit.* (note 14), pp. 122–153.

25. *Contra Eunom.* I (*PG* 45, 464).

26. See his *Contra Eunom.* I (*PG* 45, 416).
27. *PG* 45, 133. In this context, it is worth noting that Basil had already spoken of the distinction between the Father and the Son in terms of *aition* and *to ek tou aitiou*: see his *Ep.* 52 (*PG* 32, 393C); *Contra Eunom.* II, 22 (*PG* 29, 621B).
28. H. Dörries, in W. Jaeger, *op. cit.* (note 14), p. 149, refers back to Gregory of Nyssa, *Opera*, ed. W. Jaeger, III/1, p. 56; VIII/2, p. 76.
29. Gregory Nazianzen's works will be found in *PG* 35–38. His *Theological Orations* (*Orat. theol.*) have appeared in a Fr. tr. by P. Gallay, published as *Discours théologiques* in the series *Les grands écrivains chrétiens* (Lyons, 1942) and then, in collaboration with M. Jourjon, in *SC* 250 (1978); *Orat.* 1–3 repub. in new Fr. tr. by J. Bernardi in *SC* 247 (1978). See also J. Plagnieux, *S. Grégoire de Nazianze, théologien* (Paris, 1952); J. Rousse, *Dictionnaire de Spiritualité*, VI (1967), cols 932–971; S. Harkianekis, 'Die Trinitätslehre Gregors von Nazianz', *Klēronomia* (Thessalonica) (January 1969), 83–102.
30. *Orat.* 31 (= *Orat. theol.* V), 29 (*PG* 36, 165B–168B); 41, 9 (*PG* 36, 441).
31. *Orat.* 31 (= *Orat. theol.* V), 10 (*PG* 36, 144A).
32. *Orat.* 42, 15 (*PG* 36, 476B). This is the farewell oration to the Council.
33. *Orat.* 40, 41 (*PG* 36, 417); cf. *Orat.* 31, 14 (*PG* 36, 148D–149A).
34. *Orat.* 42, 15 (*PG* 36, 476B).
35. *Orat.* 31 (= *Orat. theol.* V), 32 (*PG* 36, 169; *SC* 250, p. 398).
36. We should not try to find how the Spirit proceeds from the Father: *Orat.* 20 (*PG* 35, 1077). It is no more possible to explain what 'proceed' (*ekporeuetai*; Jn 15:26) means than it is possible to explain the *agennēsia* of the Father or the begetting of the Son: *Orat.* 31, 7ff. (*PG* 36, 140ff.). For the inexpressible nature of the begetting of the Son and the use of Is 53:8b in this sense, see G. M. de Durand, *RSPT*, 53 (1969), 638–657.
37. *Orat.* 30 (= *Orat. theol.* IV), 19 (*PG* 36, 127C); 31 (= *Orat. theol.* V), 7–8 (*PG* 36, 140ff.); 39, 12 (*PG* 36, 348); Sermon at Epiphany, 381 (*PG* 35, 347). It was Gregory Nazianzen who made the terms *ekporeuton, ekporeusis* acceptable.
38. *Orat.* 31 (= *Orat. theol.* V), 11 (*PG* 36, 144–145), 35 (*PG* 36, 348C); *Carmen dogm.* III (*PG* 37, 408). This comparison was also used by Gregory of Nyssa (*PG* 44, 1329C), Pseudo-Basil, *Adv. Eunom.* IV (*PG* 29, 681B), Didymus, *De Trin.* II, 5 (*PG* 39, 504C–505A), Pseudo-Cyril, *De sanct. Trin.* 8 (*PG* 77, 1136D), John Damascene, *De fide orthod.* I, 8 (*PG* 94, 816C–817A) and Photius, *Q. Amphil.* 28 (*PG* 101, 208C).
39. J. N. D. Kelly, *Early Christian Doctrines*, 5th ed. (London, 1977), pp. 265–266. For *tropos tēs huparxeōs*, see Gregory of Nyssa (*PG* 45, 404C); 'Father' is the name for a relation: see Gregory Nazianzen, *Orat.* 29 (= *Orat. theol.* II), 16 (*PG* 36, 96); 31 (= *Orat. theol.* V), 9 (*PG* 36, 292 and 293). 'Between the three, everything is identical, except the relationship of origin': *Orat.* 41 (*PG* 36, 441C).
40. S. Bulgakov, *Le Paraclet* (Paris, 1946), p. 37.
41. A. Malet, *Personne et amour dans la théologie trinitaire de S. Thomas d'Aquin* (Paris, 1956), p. 18, quotes Basil, *De spir. sanct.* 18, 46 (*PG* 32, 152B), Gregory Nazianzen, *Orat.* 31, 8 (*PG* 36, 141), Cyril of Alexandria, *Contra Iulian.* IV (*PG* 76, 725) and John Damascene, *De fide orthod.* I, 8 (*PG* 94, 820A and 824A). Together with B. Pruche, *Traité, op. cit.* (note 4), p. 195, it is also possible to add Athanasius, *Ad Ser.* I and IV (*PG* 26), Didymus, *De Trin.* 2, 1 (*PG* 39, 438C) and to compare them with Augustine, *De Trin.* XV, 27, 48, 50 and 45 (*PL* 42, 1080A, 1095B, 1097A and 1092B).
42. Didymus, *De Trin.* II, 2 (*PG* 39, 464C).
43. *DS* 150 or *Conciliorum Œcumenicorum Decreta*, *op. cit.* (note 19).
44. *DS* 260. See also P. Galtier, 'Le Saint-Esprit dans l'Incarnation du Verbe d'après S. Cyrille d'Alexandrie', *Problemi scelti di Teologia contemporanea* (Rome, 1954), pp. 383–392.
45. H. B. Swete, *On the History of the Doctrine of the Procession of the Holy Spirit* (Cambridge, 1876), pp. 148–152; M. Jugie, *De Processione Spiritus Sancti ex Fontibus Revelationis et secundum Orientales dissidentes* (Rome, 1936), pp. 138–143; J. Meyendorff, 'La Procession du Saint-Esprit chez les pères orientaux', *Russie et Chrétienté* (1950), 159–178,

especially 163–165; H. du Manoir, *Dogme et spiritualité chez S. Cyrille d'Alexandrie* (Paris, 1944), pp. 221–256.

46. Cyril of Alexandria, *Adv. Nest.* IV, 1 (*PG* 76, 173).
47. See Cyril's *Thes.* (*PG* 75, 585A): 'Jesus breathed on his disciples, saying: "Receive the Holy Spirit", so that we shall be formed again in the first image and shall appear conformed to the Creator through participating in the Spirit. Thus, as the Spirit who is sent to us makes us conformed to God and as he proceeds from the Father and the Son, it is clear that he is of the divine *ousia*, proceeding essentially (by essence) in it and from it.' See also *Thes.* (*PG* 75, 608A–B), in which Cyril says (after quoting 2 Cor 5:17), 'Since when Christ renews us and makes us enter a new life, it is the Spirit who is said to renew us, as the psalmist says: "Send forth thy Spirit and they will be created and thou wilt renew the face of the earth" (Ps 104:30), we are bound to confess that the Spirit is of the *ousia* of the Son. It is by having his being from him according to nature and by having been sent from him to the creature that he brings about the renewal, being the fullness of the holy Triad.'
48. *Comm. in Ioel.* XXXV (*PG* 71, 377D): 'idion autou te, kai en autō, kai ex autou to Pneuma esti kathaper amelei kai ep' autou noeitai tou Theou kai Patros'; *De recta fide ad Theod.* XXXVII (*PG* 76, 1189A); *De SS. Trin. Dial.* VII (*PG* 75, 1093A): 'to Pneuma labōn, alla to ex autou te kai en autō, kai idion autou'; *Comm. in Ioan.* II (*PG* 71, 212B): 'pros ton idion autou kai par autou kata phusin procheomenon Pneuma'. See also *PG* 74, 301, 444, 608; 75, 600, 608, 1120. The Spirit *proeisi* from the Son; see *PG* 75, 585A, 608B, 612B–C; 76, 1408B, 308D.
49. See the texts listed in note 48 above. Cyril also says *dia* or *ek*: see Swete, *op. cit.* (note 45), p. 150; Meyendorff, *op. cit. (ibid.)*, p. 163, note 7.
50. *Adv. Nest.* IV, 1 (*PG* 76, 173A–B).
51. *De recta fide ad Reg. Or. alt.* LI (*PG* 76, 1408B); *De ador.* I (*PG* 68, 148A); see also *PG* 74, 585; 76, 1408.
52. *De ador.* I (*PG* 68, 148A); *Adv. Nest.* IV, 3 (*PG* 76, 184D); see also *PG* 74, 449, 709 (the commentary on St John).
53. See his *Comm. in Ioan.* XI, 11 (*PG* 74, 557). See also H. du Manoir, *op. cit.* (note 45), pp. 290ff., 315.
54. Reproduced by Cyril in his *Apol. contra Theod. pro XII cap.* (*PG* 76, 432C–D).
55. *Apol. contra Theod*, (*PG* 76, 433B–C).
56. J. Meyendorff, *op. cit.* (note 45), 165. Jugie, *op. cit. (ibid.)*, p. 142, and du Manoir, *op. cit. (ibid.)*, p. 224, give these references, apart from the preceding one: *Explic. XII cap.* (*PG* 76, 308D): 'idion echōn to ex autou'; *Apol. XII cap. contra Or.* (*PG* 77, 356–368).
57. G. M. de Durand, Introduction to Cyril, *Dialogues sur la Trinité*, I (*SC* 231) (1976), p. 66.
58. For a good bibliography, see J. Nasrallah, *Saint Jean de Damas, son époque, sa vie, son œuvre* (Harissa, Lebanon, 1950). Studies include J. Bilz, *Die Trinitätslehre des Johannes von Damaskus* (Paderborn, 1909) and especially J. Grégoire, 'La relation éternelle de l'Esprit au Fils d'aprés les écrits de Jean de Damas', *RHE*, 64 (1969), 713–755.
59. G. L. Prestige, *God in Patristic Thought*, 2nd ed. (London, 1952), pp. 263–264 and 280; see also B. Fraigneau–Julien, 'Un traité anonyme de la Sainte Trinité attribué à S. Cyrille d'Alexandrie', *RSR*, 49 (1961), 188–211, 386–405.
60. For the term *perichōrēsis*, see T. de Régnon, *Etudes sur la Sainte Trinité*, I (Paris, 1892), pp. 409–427; Chollet, *DTC*, II (1905), cols 2527–2532; A. Deneffe, 'Perichōrēsis, circuminsessio, circumincessio', *ZKT*, 47 (1923), 497–532; G. L. Prestige, '*Perichōreō* and *perichōrēsis* in the Fathers', *JTS*, 29 (1928), 242–252; *idem, op. cit.*, pp. 290–299; B. de la Margerie, *La Trinité chrétienne dans l'histoire* (Paris, 1975), pp. 244ff.
61. *De fide orthod.* I, 8 (*PG* 94, 829; de Régnon's translation, p. 417); see also I, 14 (*PG* 94, 860). The comparison with the three suns can also be found in Gregory Nazianzen and Pseudo-Cyril: see Fraigneau–Julien, *op. cit.* (note 59), p. 200.
62. See Jn 10:30 and 38; 14:11 and 20; 17:21; see also, less clearly expressed, 8:29. This mutual in-existence forms the basis of the unity of purpose between the Father and the Son

and between the Father and the Spirit (see Rom 8:27; 1 Cor 2:10–11). Jesus will send the Spirit, but he will send the Father's Promised one (Lk 24:49; Acts 2:33); the Father will send the Paraclete, but only at the request and in the name of the Son (Jn 14:16, 26).

63. There are only a few texts: Athenagoras, *Supplication* X, 5: 'Father and Son are one; the Son is in the Father and the Father is in the Son'; Hilary of Poitiers, *De Trin*. IX, 69; Gregory of Nyssa and Cyril of Alexandria, quoted by Prestige, *op. cit*. (note 59), pp. 287–288, 289–290; Augustine, *De Trin*. VI, 10, 12 (*PL* 42, 932): 'Each (of the divine Persons) is in each one and they are all in each one, and each one is in all, and all make only one'; Fulgentius of Ruspe, *De fide ad Petrum*, c. 1, n. 4 (*PL* 65, 674A–B; *c*. 508), who is quoted in the Decree *Pro Iacobitis* of 1442 (*DS* 1331). The German mystic Gertrude (†1302) also expressed her experience of the Trinity in these terms: 'The three Persons together radiated an excellent light, each appearing to send its flame through the other, and yet they were all with each other': see W. Oehl, *Deutsche Mystiker*, II, p. 90.

64. See Gregory Nazianzen, *Ep*. 101 (*PG* 37, 141C).

65. Maximus, *PG* 91, 88A and 85C–D.

66. T. de Régnon, pursuing his excessively simple idea of the difference between the Greeks and the Latins, was convinced that this was a Latin and not a Greek concept. But the very texts that he quotes—Cyril of Alexandria, Pseudo-Cyril and John Damascene—all speak of a unity and identity of substance or essence!

67. In *Le Paraclet, op. cit*. (note 40), p. 134, Bulgakov says: 'They should be conceived not on the basis of themselves alone, but on the basis of their Trinitarian unity; they are defined and radiated not only thanks to their own light, but also thanks to the light that they reflect and that comes from the other hypostases'.

68. S. Bulgakov devotes pp. 50–58 of *Le Paraclet* to John Damascene. This section of his book is precise and well-documented, but critical.

69. The term *proboleus* is not biblical and was relatively new when John Damascene used it. It can be found in Pseudo-Cyril, c. 7 (*PG* 77, 1132C) whom John copied, and it originated with Gregory Nazianzen, *Orat*. 23, 7; 29, 2 (*PG* 35, 1169A and 36, 76B).

70. *De fide orthod*. I, 8 (*PG* 94, 811A and 828D); I, 10 (*PG* 94, 837C); here, in an attempt to define more precisely what expresses what is different rather than the common nature, John says that the fact of being without a cause or unbegotten, of being begotten or of proceeding 'expresses the mutual relationship between the persons and their mode of subsistence'.

71. *De fide orthod*. I, 8 (*PG* 94, 824A; cf. 820A).

72. See Augustine, *Contra Maxim*. II, 14, 1; Anselm of Havelberg, *Dial*. II, 5. See also P. Vignaux, *Luther commentateur des Sentences* (*liv*. I, *dist*, XVII) (Paris, 1935), pp. 95ff.: he quotes first the hymn of Adam of Saint-Victor, *Sequentia XI de S. Trinitate* (*PL* 196, 1459): 'Quid sit gigni, quid processus, me nescire sum professus'—'What is "being begotten"? What is "processing"? I profess that I do not know'; see above, p. 8. Robert Holcot, Gregory of Rimini and Gabriel Biel all held the same position.

73. *De fide orthod*. I, 8 (*PG* 94, 832–833, with the long note, no. 28, by J. Aubert); *De hymno Tris*. (*PG* 95, 60); *In sab. sanct*. (*PG* 96, 605); see also J. Meyendorff, *op. cit*. (note 45), 171.

74. *De fide orthod*. I, 12 (*PG*, 94, 849B).

75. *De fide orthod*. I, 13 (*PG* 94, 856B). The *dia* was also taken up by Tarasius at the Seventh Oecumenical Council (Nicaea II): *PG* 98, 1461. A list of the *dia tou Huiou* will be found in J. Grégoire, *op. cit*. (note 58), 753–754, note 1.

76. Quotations from Rom 8:9 and Jn 20:29 in *De fide orthod*. I, 5, 8 (*PG* 94, 833A); see also his *In sab. sanct*. 4 (*PG* 96, 605B). John also uses the classical formula of Athanasius and says that the Spirit is the image (*eikōn*) of the Son as the Son is the image of the Father: *De fide orthod*. I, 13 (*PG* 94, 855B).

77. *De fide orthod*. I, 12, end (*PG* 94, 849). This chapter 12 of the treatise on orthodox faith, Migne observes (*PG* 94, 845–846), is missing from several early manuscripts, but it is in

accordance with the teaching of undisputed texts and those who oppose the *Filioque* do not hesitate to quote it as authoritative.

78. F. Hauck and S. Schulz, '*Poreuomai, eisporeuomai, ekporeuomai*', *TDNT*, VI, pp. 566–579, although the authors devote hardly two lines to our verse. See also F. Porsch, *Pneuma und Wort. Ein exegetischer Beitrag zur Pneumatologie des Johannesevangeliums* (Frankfurt, 1974), pp. 273–274.

79. V. Rodziensko insists on this aspect to such an extent that he lets it bear an almost excessive theological weight of freedom of action; he says, for example, that the Pneuma 'makes himself to go out from the only Father': ' "Filioque" in Patristic Thought', *Studia Patristica*, II (Berlin, 1957), pp. 295–308.

80. A. Wenger, 'Bulletin de spiritualité et de théologie byzantine', *Rev. Et. Byz.*, 10 (1953), 162; see also F. Porsch, *op. cit.* (note 78). Wenger finds it possible to say: '*para* usually denotes a relationship between two persons already existing', but is this strictly true?

81. J. Giblet, 'La Sainte Trinité selon l'Evangile de S. Jean', *Lumière et Vie*, 29 (1956), 95–126; 671–702, especially 673.

82. This comment is by M. Jugie, *op. cit.* (note 45), p. 139. Cyril of Alexandria used *procheitai* and *ekporeuesthai* as equivalents; see his *Ep.* 55 (*PG* 77, 316D–317A). He used *ekporeuetai* only once for the procession of the Son *a Patre*: *Comm. in Ioan.* V, 26 (*PG* 74, 420A).

83. The difference that they stressed from the term 'begetting' was, they felt, sufficient to distinguish the second from the third Persons; this difference to a great extent came from the response that they had to make to the objection that, if there was a second procession, there would be two Sons and the Word would have a brother. See Athanasius, *Ad Ser.* I, 15 (*SC* 15, pp. 109ff.).

84. See the bibliography in Emmanuel-Pataq Siman, *L'expérience de l'Esprit d'après la tradition syrienne d'Antioche* (*Théologie historique*, 15) (Paris, 1971). See also P. Rancillac, *L'Eglise, manifestation de l'Esprit chez S. Jean Chrysostome* (Dar-el-Kalima, Lebanon, 1970); F. Heiler, *Die katholische Kirche des Ostens und Westens*, I: *Urkirche und Ostkirche* (Munich, 1937).

85. E. P. Siman, *op. cit.*, pp. 227–229, has made a synopsis of these texts.

86. See I. de la Potterie, 'L'onction du chrétien par la foi', *Bib*, 40 (1959), 12–69, reproduced in *La vie selon l'Esprit, condition du chrétien* (Paris, 1965), pp. 107–167; E. P. Siman, *op. cit.*, pp. 74ff., 131ff.

87. Ephraem's 'Hymn of faith'; quoted by E. P. Siman, *op. cit.*, pp. 105, 223.

88. Isaac of Antioch, quoted by E. P. Siman, *op. cit.*, pp. 107, 224.

89. I will confine myself to only two texts out of the great number. They are quoted by E. P. Siman, *op. cit.*, pp. 56 and 57: 'We worship you, Lord God, Holy Spirit Paraclete, you who console us and pray in us. . . . It is you who have sealed the covenant with the Church, the spouse of the Word, the Son of God, and who have placed in her the treasures of your graces and your virtues. It is you who have taught the world the mystery of the adorable and very holy Trinity and who have led us to worship it in Spirit and truth' (*sedrē* of Terce; First Sunday after Pentecost); 'It was on Sunday that your spouse, the holy Church, triumphed and became majestic, since the covenant of her nuptials was concluded by the coming of the Holy Spirit Paraclete over her and by her spread in every region and every country, thanks to the twelve Stewards (of the Spirit)' (Sixth Sunday after Pentecost).

90. Quoted by E. P. Siman, *op. cit.* (note 84), p. 204.

91. Ephraem's 'Hymn on faith', quoted by E. P. Siman, *op. cit.*, p. 188.

92. Quoted by E. P. Siman, *op. cit.*, p. 275.

93. See E. P. Siman, *op. cit.*, p. 276.

3

THE FILIOQUE
AS PROFESSED BY THE LATIN FATHERS
AND THE COUNCILS BEFORE IT BECAME
A SUBJECT OF DISUNITY

In this question, it is important to do what Pope Leo III took care to do when he received Charlemagne's envoys, that is, to make a distinction between two things—the teaching itself and its inclusion as a formula in the creed.

THE TEACHING

All the New Testament texts that speak of a relationship between the Spirit and the Son are concerned with the economy. This includes even Jn 15:26: 'But when the Paraclete comes, whom I shall send you from the Father, even the Spirit of truth, who proceeds from the Father, he will bear witness to me', which is, of course, the reference *par excellence* in favour of the procession from the Father alone. Apart from the fact that the word 'alone' is not found in this text and that the creed refers to it only by making two small changes,[1] what is involved here in an immediate and explicit way is the temporal mission of the Paraclete.

The passages in the New Testament which speak of the relationship between the Spirit and the Son are concerned with the *incarnate* Word and the economy of grace. What is more, they also speak of a very close relationship that is concerned with the essential element. If we are indeed sons and are able to call God 'Father', that is because we have received the 'Spirit of *his* Son'.[2] Christ's sonship is eternal and the Spirit must be eternally from the *Son*. The texts to which the Latin Fathers appealed again and again are Jn 16:14–15 and 20:22,[3] which are directly concerned with the economy of grace. At the same time, as Swete has observed, it is not unreasonable to make an extrapolation. Since the Spirit belongs eternally to the divine essence, it is normal for the only Son, who has, as the Word, been with God from the beginning, to be in a relationship that is outside time with the Spirit of God.[4] It is not possible to say any more from the exegetical point of view. We have already seen that the Greek Fathers, and especially the

49

Alexandrians, believed that there was a connection and even a dependence that was eternal, but that they did not define this very precisely.

We should note one other text, namely Rev 22:1: 'Then he (the angel) showed me the river of the water of life, bright as crystal, flowing from the throne of God and of the Lamb (*ekporeuomenon ek tou thronou tou Theou kai tou Arniou*)'. This living water is the Spirit (Jn 4:10ff.; 7:37–39; Rev 21:6), proceeding from the throne of God and from the Lamb. The Lamb points to the Son in his commitment to our salvation. We are clearly still concerned with the economy here, although now at the stage of its eternal fulfilment. Scripture, as strictly limited to New Testament texts, does not therefore do away with our problem. As we shall see, it is extremely important to note that the West professed the *Filioque*, through its Fathers and its councils, at a time when it was in communion with the East and the East was in communion with the West.

The Latin Fathers[5]

Of the cloud of witnesses to this conviction, I will deal mainly with those mentioned by the Fifth Ecumenical Council, the Second Council of Constantinople (553), and called by that Council, together with the Greek Fathers, holy Fathers and doctors of the Church, whose teaching as a whole should be followed: Hilary. Ambrose, Augustine and Leo.[6]

Hilary of Poitiers (†366) said that the Spirit was *Patre et Filio auctoribus confitendus* (*De Trin.* II, 29; *PL* 10, 69), which clearly points, not to a procession, but to the witness borne by the Father and the Son. Hilary did, however, think that the *de meo accipiet* of Jn 16:14 might have a meaning equivalent to 'receiving—and therefore proceeding—from the Father' (see below, note 3), although his most certain position on the Spirit was *a Patre per Filium*.

In 381, the year of the First Council of Constantinople, Ambrose materially formulated the statement: 'Spiritus quoque Sanctus, cum procedit a Patre et Filio',[7] but, as the Benedictine editor acknowledged, before Swete and Jugie, this referred to the temporal mission of the Spirit. Ambrose seems to include the communication of the divine life itself, however, in the *de meo accipiet*.[8]

Ambrose was not a speculative thinker. In the case of Augustine, however, we are no longer left in any doubt. He not only unequivocally affirms the *Filioque* on several occasions, but also justifies, on the basis of the New Testament evidence, that the Spirit is both Spirit of the Father and Spirit of the Son and, from 393 onwards, provides a theological foundation for this in the idea of 'communio quaedam consubstantialis Patris et Filii, dilectionem in se invicem amborum caritatemque'.[9] The treatises on this subject that followed are works both of laborious scholarly research and of rich and fervent contemplation. The main works are the *De Trinitate*, Books IV and

V, the *Tractatus XCIX in Ioannem*, reproduced at the end of *De Trinitate* XV, 27, and, in 427–428, the *Contra Maximinum*, Maximinus being the bishop of an Arian community. Augustine's teaching, written in a full and eloquent Latin, had a decisive influence on thinking in the Western Church, whether it was read in his own texts or in the versions of Fulgentius of Ruspe (†533), who wrote in a more pedagogic and almost scholarly style (*PL* 65).

The evidence provided by Leo the Great is clear, but brief, and contains no further theoretical development.[10] This is not much, but numerous holy and learned bishops of the Church should be added: Eucherius of Lyons (†454), Faustus of Riez (†485), Avitus of Vienne (†523) and Fulgentius of Ruspe, whom I have mentioned above; likewise several priests, such as Gennadius of Marseilles (†495) and Julian Pomerius of Arles (†498), the Roman deacon Paschasius (†512), and highly educated laymen, such as Boethius (†c. 525) and Cassiodorus (†c. 570). At a slightly later period, the question was discussed by various doctors of the Church such as Gregory the Great, who was revered by the Greeks (†604), and Isidore of Seville (†636). Texts by all these authors and many others can be read in the works listed in note 5 below.

Texts by the Greek authors who assumed or stated that the Spirit was dependent in his eternal subsistence on the Son can also be found in the same works as well as in other books. The most important of these Greek Fathers were, of course, Epiphanius and Cyril of Alexandria. I have already discussed their contribution to this debate as well as that provided by those Fathers, notably Gregory of Nyssa, Maximus and John Damascene, who spoke of a procession from the Father through the Son.

The Councils and the Creeds[11]

A place of honour must be given here to the Councils of Toledo. Their insistence on the need to profess a Trinitarian faith and especially on the importance of the procession of the Holy Spirit *a Patre et a Filio* can be explained by the situation that had been brought about, first by the heresy of Priscillianism at the end of the fourth century, and then by the arrival of Arian invaders at the beginning of the fifth century. The Priscillianists combined the figures of the Trinity in a single Person, and the Arians regarded the Spirit as a creature of the Son, who, they believed, was himself created. The First Council of Toledo (440 and 447) is itself disputed and has therefore to be left out of account.[12] We begin on firm ground with the Third Council of Toledo in 589, at which King Recared renounced Arianism, in the name of his people, and professed the Catholic faith. Although it is doubtful whether the Niceno-Constantinopolitan creed with the addition of *et Filio* was recited there, it is certain that Recared professed 'Spiritus aeque Sanctus confitendus a nobis et praedicandus est a Patre et a Filio procedere et cum Patre et Filio unius esse substantiae',[13] in other words, 'We must equally confess and preach that the Spirit proceeds from the Father and the Son and that he is of one and the same substance with them'. The Council therefore was opposed to any form of Priscillianism or Arianism and declared that the Son was in no way inferior to the Father. The intention was to affirm the consubstantiality of the Spirit with the Father and the Son.

It is also possible in this context to quote the Fourth Council of Toledo (633), for which Isidore of Seville, who presided over it, composed the beautiful prayer *Adsumus*, with which all the assemblies of the Second Vatican Council began.[14] The Sixth Council (638) also produced an excellent and well-developed text.[15] Developed texts were also formulated at the Eighth Council (653) and the Eleventh (675). Fulgentius of Ruspe played a part in the formulation of these latter texts, and Vladimir Lossky declared that he was able to accept them.[16] At the Sixteenth Council of Toledo in 693, the Spirit was professed to be 'ex Patre Filioque absque aliquo initio procedentem' and was especially called a 'Gift'.[17]

Similar professions of faith were also made during the same period of a hundred years in other parts of the Christian world. An excellent documentation was provided by J. A. de Aldama (*op. cit.* (note 12 below), pp. 124–131) and more recently by J. Vivès (*ibid.*). The creed *Quicumque vult*, which was at one time attributed to Athanasius, was in fact composed between 440 and 500 in Augustinian circles in the south of Gaul.[18] In England, the Synod of Hatfield confessed in 680 'Spiritum Sanctum procedentem ex Patre et Filio inenarrabiliter'.[19] At the same time, however, nothing was added, in Rome, to the Niceno-Constantinopolitan text, even though the Popes were personally in favour of the *Filioque*.

It should not be forgotten that the East was in communion with the West at the time when the latter professed that the Spirit proceeded from the Father and the Son, although it is true that some people in Byzantium were unhappy about this. There is evidence of this in a letter written by Maximus the Confessor to the Cypriot priest Marinus in 655. Pope Martin I had apparently said in his synodic letter that the Spirit also proceeded from the Son, and this scandalized those who had been condemned in Rome for their Monothelitism, so that they were not slow to take revenge. This was Maximus' response:

> Those of the Queen of cities (Constantinople) have attacked the synodic letter of the present very holy Pope, not in the case of all the chapters that he has written in it, but only in the case of two of them. One relates to the theology (of the Trinity) and, according to them, says: 'The Holy Spirit also has his *ekporeusis (ekporeuesthai)* from the Son'. The other deals with the divine incarnation.
>
> With regard to the first matter, they (the Romans) have produced the unanimous evidence of the Latin Fathers, and also of Cyril of Alexandria, from the study he made of the gospel of St John. On the basis of these texts, they have shown that they have not made the Son the cause (*aitian*) of the Spirit—they know in fact that the Father is the only cause of the Son and the Spirit, the one by begetting and the

other by *ekporeusis* (procession)—but that they have manifested the procession through him (*to dia autou proïenai*) and have thus shown the unity and identity of the essence. . . .

They (the Romans) have therefore been accused of precisely those things of which it would be wrong to accuse them, whereas the former (the Byzantines) have been accused of those things of which it has been quite correct to accuse them (Monothelitism). They have up till now produced no defence, although they have not yet rejected the things that they have themselves so wrongly introduced.

In accordance with your request, I have asked the Romans to translate what is peculiar to them (the 'also from the Son') in such a way that any obscurities that may result from it will be avoided. But since the practice of writing and sending (the synodic letter) has been observed, I wonder whether they will possibly agree to do this. It is true, of course, that they cannot reproduce their idea in a language and in words that are foreign to them as they can in their mother-tongue, just as we too cannot. In any case, having been accused, they will certainly take some care about this.[20]

Maximus the Confessor's explanation throws a good deal of light on the situation. He himself believed that the Spirit proceeded from the Father *dia mesou tou Logou*, 'by means of the Logos'.[21] The Spirit proceeded, in his view, ineffably from the Father and consubstantially through the Son.[22] It will be necessary to return to this question later, or rather to recognize, with all due explanation, that there was never any intention to say anything else.

THE ADDITION OF THE *FILIOQUE* TO THE CREED

The history of this addition is so well known that all that I need to do here is summarize the principal points.[23] The teaching was widely accepted, but it would seem that the text of the creed was not changed in any way, even at the Third Council of Toledo in 589. The addition did not, in any case, come from Spain, but from England, through the offices of Alcuin, who went from York in 782 to the court of Charlemagne.[24] There can be little doubt, however, that he himself received it from Spain. At that time, the creed was recited during Mass in Gaul and in Spain. The *Filioque* was probably added during the last decade of the sixth century in those places and it was accepted in good faith that it came from Nicaea-Constantinople—so much so that even before the time of the fiery Humbert of Silva Candida in 1054, the *Libri Carolini* of 790 or thereabouts were able to accuse the Greeks of having suppressed it there![25]

The Second Council of Nicaea (787), which canonized the cult of images, also received the confession of faith of the Patriarch Tarasius, who professed that he believed 'in the Holy Spirit, Lord and giver of life, proceeding from the Father through the Son'.[26] Charlemagne protested through a capitulary which he sent to Pope Hadrian I, who replied by guaranteeing that Tarasius' formula was in conformity with the teaching of the holy Fathers.

Charlemagne, however, persisted, maintaining that *per* did not have the same meaning as *ex*.[27] In 794, he convoked a council at Frankfurt, which was to condemn the teachings of the Council of Nicaea of 787 with its cult of images and to proclaim the *Filioque*. Frankfurt—the ford of the Franks—became a line of demarcation and division. The addition to the creed was justified at a synod held in Friuli (Venezia Giulia) in 796 by the argument that it was necessary to affirm full consubstantiality in opposition to heretics. Pope Leo III, who succeeded Hadrian I, however, defended the Council of Nicaea and denounced the Council of Frankfurt.

Frankish monks of the Mount of Olives at Jerusalem had introduced the singing of the creed into the Mass, with the addition of the *Filioque*, in the form in which they had heard it in the palace at Aix-la-Chapelle. They were, as a result of this, accused of heresy by a Greek monk of Mar Sabas at Christmas 808. They consequently appealed to the Pope, who in turn wrote to the emperor. The latter called on the theologians to justify the Western teaching and practice in opposition to the Greeks and, at a council convoked at Aix-la-Chapelle in November 809, decreed that the *Filioque* was a doctrine of the Catholic Church and had to be retained in the creed that was sung at Mass. He also sent two trusted prelates to Pope Leo III to win his support for these decisions. We have the account of this audience.[28] The Pope agreed about the doctrine, but refused to change or add anything to the creed. In confirmation of his position, the text of the creed, engraved in Greek and Latin without the addition, was hung up in St Peter's [see next chapter].

Rome, a city in which traditions are carefully preserved, remained faithful to this practice for a long time. That is why Photius did not criticize Rome for making the addition and appealed to the example of Nicholas I and John VIII, the Popes who were his contemporaries. The controversy about the addition of the *Filioque* clause was unleashed when Cardinal Humbert accused the Greeks in 1054 of having suppressed the clause.[29]

The creed was not in fact introduced into the Mass in Rome until 1014, during the pontificate of Benedict VIII, and it certainly included the Latin interpolation then. Henry II was to be crowned emperor and he was astonished that the creed was not chanted at Mass. The explanation he was given was that the Roman Church had no need to express its faith because it had never fallen into heresy! Henry insisted on the creed, however, and had his way.[30] A new tradition was created.

The question of the insertion of the *Filioque* into the creed was raised with some determination by the Greeks at the Council of Ferrara-Florence in 1438–1439. If communion was to be re-established betweeen East and West, they insisted, the clause had to be suppressed. The question is still with us, and its importance should not be underestimated. I shall deal with it when I come to discuss the attempts made to reach an understanding from Florence to the present.

NOTES

1 The text of Jn 15:26 has 'ho para tou Patros ekporeuetai', with the verb in the present, whereas the creed has 'to ek tou Patros ekporeuomenon', thus replacing *para* with *ek* and placing the verb in the form of a participle, which makes it express the eternal procession. See H. B. Swete, *The Holy Spirit in the New Testament* (London, 1909), p. 304, note 2. I do not in any sense criticize this approach. A.-M. Dubarle has shown that the Greek Fathers established the eternal relationship of the incarnate Word with the Father (God) from his part in the economy and has concluded from this that a similar approach is legitimate in the case of the Spirit: 'Les fondements bibliques du "Filioque" ', *Russie et Chrétienté* (1950), pp. 229–244. In the same volume, pp. 125–150, Mgr Cassien discusses the biblical teaching regarding the procession: 'L'enseignement dans la Bible sur la procession du Saint-Esprit'.

2. Gal 4:6; 'Ex hoc ergo Spiritus Sanctus nos facit filios Dei in quantum est Spiritus Filii Dei': Thomas Aquinas, *Contra Gent*. IV, 24.

3. Hilary of Poitiers thought that *de meo accipiet* (Jn 16:14) might possibly have the same meaning as *a Patre procedere*: *De Trin.* VIII, 20 (*PL* 10, 250–251). As we shall see, Augustine and later Anselm believed that the breathing on the disciples in Jn 20:22 implied the procession of the Spirit *a Filio*.

4. H. B. Swete, *op. cit.*, pp. 304–305.

5. H. B. Swete, *On the History of the Doctrine of the Procession of the Holy Spirit* (Cambridge, 1876); A. Palmieri, 'Filioque', *DTC*, V (1913), cols 2309–2343; see also cols 762–829; M. Jugie, *De Processione Spiritus Sancti* (Rome, 1936), pp. 196–232; P. T. Camelot, 'La tradition latine sur la procession du Saint-Esprit "a Filio" ou "ab utroque" ', *Russie et Chrétienté* (1950), pp. 179–192.

6. Mansi, 9, 201–202.

7. Ambrose, *De Spir. Sanct.* I, 11 (*PL* 16, 762).

8. See the passages in *De Spir. Sanct.* II, 5 and 11; III. 1 (*PL* 16, 783, 800, 810), and in *Comm. in Luc.* VIII (*PL* 15, 1876); these are quoted by Swete, *op. cit.* (note 5), p. 121.

9. Augustine, *De fid. et symb.* IX, 19 (*PL* 40, 191), in which he alludes to certain predecessors, especially Marius Victorinus in his hymn to the Trinity (*PL* 8, 1146; *SC* 68, p. 620): see Volume I of this work, p. 77.

10. In his sermon at Pentecost 442, Leo says: 'Spiritus Sanctus Patris Filiique . . . Spiritus . . . cum utroque vivens et potens, et sempiterne ex eo quod est Pater Filiusque subsistens' (*PL* 54, 402; *SC* 74 (1961), p. 150; sermo 63). The letter to the Bishop of Astorga, Turibius, which says 'ab utroque processit' (*PL* 54, 680; *DS* 284) is, at least according to K. Künstle, *Antipriscilliana* (Freiburg, 1905), pp. 118 and 126, a forgery made after the Council of Braga in 563. According to J. A. de Aldama, *op. cit.* (below, note 12), p. 54, note 34, it is authentic. De Aldama quotes several authors who are in favour of it.

11. H. B. Swete, *op. cit.* (note 5), pp. 160–176; Jugie, *op. cit.* (note 5), pp. 115–120; F. Cavallera, *Thesaurus Doctrinae catholicae ex documentis Magisterii ecclesiastici* (Paris, 1920), pp. 284ff.

12. F. Cavallera, No. 533 and 560, according to the *Libellus Pastoris* (Mansi, 3, 1003–1004); K. Künstle, *op. cit.*, pp. 43ff.: 'Paraclitus a Patre Filioque procedens'. J. A. de Aldama, *El símbolo Toledano I. Su texto, su origen, su posición en la historia de los símbolos* (*Anal. Greg.*, VII) (Rome, 1934), concluded that there were two editions. The first was a shorter version, made by the Council of 400; the second and longer edition was the work of Bishop Pastor, in 447, and contained two references to the term *Filioque*. See J. Vivès, ed., in collab. with T. Marín and G. Martínez. *Concilios Visigóticos e Hispano-Romanos* (Barcelona and Madrid, 1963); for this first creed, see p. 26.

13. *DS* 470; this reference is not found in Denz.; see also Vivès, *op. cit.*, p. 109.

14. Mansi, 10, 615–616; *DS* 458; Vivès, p. 187. For the *Filioque* in Isidore of Seville, see H. B. Swete, *op. cit.* (note 5), pp. 172–173.

15. Mansi, 10, 661ff.; *DS* 490; Vivès, p. 234.

16. Mansi, 11, 131ff.; *DS* 525–541 (for the Spirit, see 527); Vivès, *op. cit* (note 12), p. 348; see also J. Madoz, *Le symbole du XIe Concile de Tolède* (Louvain, 1938).
17. Mansi, 12, 67; *DS* 568–570; Vivès, p. 489; see also J. Madoz, *El símbolo del concilio XVI de Toledo* (*Estudios Onienses*, I, vol. 3) (Madrid, 1946).
18. *DS* 75–76, with the introduction; J. N. D. Kelly, *The Athanasian Creed 'Quicumque vult'* (London, 1964).
19. Mansi, 11, 177B.
20. Maximus, letter to Marinus, *PG* 91, 136; Mansi, 10, 695ff.; Swete, *op. cit.* (note 5), pp. 183–186; Jugie, *op. cit.* (note 5), pp. 182–186; Fr. tr., apart from one or two words, by J. M. Garrigues, *Istina* (1972), 363–364. There is evidence of the fact that the procession of the Holy Spirit continued to be a controversial point between the Greeks and the Latins in what we know of the Synod held at Gentilly in 767: see Swete, *op. cit.*, pp. 198ff.
21. Maximus, *Quaestiones et dubia, Interr.* XXXIV (*PG* 90, 813B).
22. *Quaestiones ad Thalassium*, LXIII (*PG* 90, 672C).
23. Swete, *op. cit.*, (note 5), pp. 196–226 with the texts in an appendix, pp. 227–237; Jugie, *op. cit.* (note 5), pp. 234–258; *idem*, 'Origine de la controverse sur l'addition du Filioque au Symbole. Photius en a-t-il parlé?' *RSPT*, 28 (1939), 369–385; see also below, note 29; E. Amann, *L'époque carolingienne* (*Histoire de l'Eglise, VI*) (Paris, 1947); B. Capelle, 'Le pape Léon III et le Filioque', *L'Eglise et les Eglises, Mélanges Dom Lambert Beauduin* (Chevetogne, 1954), I, pp. 309–322; R. G. Heath, 'The Schism of the Franks and the Filioque', *Journal of Ecclesiastical History*, 23 (1972), 97–113; R. Haugh, *Photius and the Carolingians. The Trinitarian Controversy* (Belmont, Mass., 1975).
24. B. Capelle, 'Alcuin et l'histoire du Symbole de la Messe', *Travaux liturgiques de Doctrine et d'Histoire* (Louvain, 1962), II, pp. 211–221.
25. See Jugie, *op. cit.* (note 5), p. 238, note 2. H. Sieben, *Die Konzilsidee der Alten Kirche* (Paderborn, 1979), pp. 306–343, has examined the basis on which the Second Council of Nicaea in 787 was received in the East and in Rome and has suggested the reasons why the Frankish Church rejected it (the *Libri Carolini* and the Council of Frankfurt in 794).
26. Mansi, 12, 1122; reception by the Council, col. 1154.
27. *Libri Carolini* III, 3 (*PL* 98, 1117).
28. See *PL* 102, 971ff.; *MGH, Concilia* II/1, pp. 239ff. Swete has reproduced this text, *op. cit.* (note 5), pp. 233ff. See also B. Capelle, *op. cit* (note 23).
29. See M. Jugie, *op. cit.* (note 23). V. Grumel has critically examined point by point Jugie's argument eliminating Photius from the controversy about the addition: 'Photius et l'addition du Filioque au symbole de Nicée-Constantinople', *Rev. Et. Byz.*, 5 (1947), 218–234.
30. This is according to an eye-witness, Berno: *De officio missae*, 2 (*PL* 142, 1061–1062).

4

THE PATRIARCH PHOTIUS
THE ERA OF CONFRONTATION
AND POLEMICS

The age of confrontation between East and West began before Photius. The letter written to the Second Council of Nicaea in 787 (which approved the cult of images) by the Patriarch Tarasius, who professed the procession of the Spirit *ek tou Patros di' Huiou*,[1] had caused great scandal at the court of Charlemagne. The emperor had sent a capitulary to Pope Hadrian I, as we have already seen, protesting against this teaching. He had also criticized it in the *Libri Carolini* and had finally had it condemned by the Council of Frankfurt in 794.[2] The *Filioque* was by this time included in the creed and chanted in the churches of the Empire. A few years later, at the end of 808, this practice gave rise to a serious incident, when a Greek monk in the monastery of Mar Sabas noticed that the liturgical books used in a Frankish monastery on the Mount of Olives included the *Filioque*. The monk, John, proclaimed the heresy of the books and conducted a campaign against the Frankish monks, who, as we have seen, appealed to the Pope, who, in his turn, wrote to the emperor.[3] Charlemagne convoked a synod at Aix-la-Chapelle in 809, with the aim of approving and justifying, through his own bishops, the practice already accepted in his own chapel and in his empire. He sent a delegation to the Pope to win him over not only to the doctrine—of which the Pope was already convinced—but also to the inclusion of the *Filioque* in the text of the creed. Leo III, however, refused to comply with the second request and insisted on retaining the pure text. In order to make his own position public, he had the text without the *Filioque* engraved in Greek and Latin on two silver scrolls and these were hung on each side of the entrance to the high altar or Confessio in St Peter's.[4] This took place in 810.

Ten years after Leo III had defined his position as being in favour of the teaching, but against the addition of the *Filioque* to the text of the creed, Photius was born.[5] This extremely gifted man led a life full of tensions and dramatic episodes. He was enthroned as Patriarch of Constantinople on 25 December 858, throught the favour of Bardas, the uncle of the Emperor Michael III. He was, however, twice deposed and relegated to a monastery, in 868–878 and in 886–897. (He died on 6 February 897). He was

57

excommunicated and deposed by Pope Nicholas I in 863 and he himself excommunicated the Pope in 867. He was condemned by a council which was regarded in Bellarmine's accredited list of councils as the Eighth Ecumenical Council (869–870), but this same council was condemned to oblivion by Pope John VIII.[6] Another council, over which the legates of the same Pope John VIII presided and which our Orthodox friends would like the Western Church to call the Eighth Ecumenical Council, solemnly annulled the measures taken against Photius. It is probable and even almost certain that the creed was proclaimed at that council without the *Filioque*,[7] which was at that time the practice in Rome. Photius himself died in communion with the Roman See. He was canonized by the Orthodox Church at a time when that Church was also in communion with Rome and the West.[8]

Nevertheless, from 867 onwards Photius condemned the *Filioque* in a series of texts and formulated the doctrine of the procession of the Holy Spirit from the Father alone: *ek monou tou Patros*.[9] He did not understand the homogeneity of the Latin idea of the mystery of the Trinity, according to which the distinction between the Persons in their perfect consubstantiality is derived from their relationship and the opposition of their relationship— the Father and the Son are relative to one another—and that relationship is one of origin and procession. Photius, however, believed that the Persons were distinguished by personal properties that could not be communicated. Their properties were, in his opinion, sufficient to characterize them. The Father was *anarchos*, without principle or beginning. The Son was begotten, and this referred him to the Father as such. The Spirit proceeds from the Father as *aitia*, the cause and the only cause both of the Spirit and of the Son.[10]

Photius regarded the monarchy of the Father as the principle both of the Spirit and of the monogenous one, and as the principle of their consubstantiality.[11] Whereas the Greek Fathers saw this monarchy as moving dynamically in a straight line, from the Father through the Son in the Spirit, however, Photius adopted a scheme consisting of two branches: Father$<{}^{Son}_{Spirit}$.[12] He also either passed over in silence or eliminated numerous patristic texts which were open to the idea that the Son played a part in the eternal coming of the Spirit to consubstantial being.[13] In his view, there were only two possibilities—an activity that is common to the three Persons and goes back to their nature, or one that is strictly personal.[14] To admit, as the Latins did, that the procession of the Spirit came both from the Father and from the Son, as from a single principle, was to withdraw that procession from the hypostases and to attribute it to their common nature. In those conditions, it would be wrong to dissociate the Spirit from that common nature, because he also possesses the same nature as the Father and the Son—thus he would proceed from himself, which would be clearly absurd.[15]

The Latin construction is only tenable if the Persons are distinguished by an opposition in relationship, but the spiration does not allow for such an opposition in relationship between the Father and the Son. It can therefore be common to them. We do not, for that reason, do an injustice to the hypostatic order and favour the divine nature, because that nature is hypostatic in its existence and the hypostases are constituted by their *subsistent* relationships—the Father *is* fatherhood and the Son *is* sonship or begottenness. What is more, in that unity of the principle of active spiration, the Father is the first principle (*principaliter*). It is necessary to admit that this is not sufficiently apparent—the word 'procession' is not clear. The Father and the Son seem to be at the same level, whereas they are in fact not, since 'the Father is greater than I'. The Father is the absolute and primordial origin.[16]

It cannot be denied that the teaching of the Fathers and of John Damascene was narrowed down and hardened in the theology of Photius. Although, as Sergey Bulgakov has pointed out, 'there is no unanimous and homogeneous patristic doctrine of the procession of the Holy Spirit',[17] and there are openings in the direction of a procession *per Filium* and even *Filioque*, Photius enshrined pneumatology in a form of expression which put out of the question an agreement with the West or even with those Latin Fathers whom the Orthodox Christians accept as their own. As a result of this, confrontation and polemics have all too often prevailed over an attempt to reach agreement. But—as I shall be happy to show—the victory of confrontation has not been total, nor is it definitive. We must, however, take Photius' arguments seriously—the more so because the Greek Church has taken over his theology—without at the same time losing sight of those Fathers whose work Photius himself tended to leave aside.

NOTES

1. Mansi, 12, 1122 D.
2. The *Libri Carolini*, which were composed *c.* 790, are attributed either to Alcuin or to Theodulf of Orléans. There is a bibliography in my *Ecclésiologie du Haut Moyen Age* (Paris, 1968), p. 281, note 115. For the text, see *PL* 98; *MGH, Concilia* II, *Supplementum* (Hanover, 1924). For the debate about *ex* and *per*, see cols 1117f., p. 110. For the profession of the *Filioque* at the Council of Frankfurt, see Mansi 13, 905; *MGH, Concilia* II, *Concilia Aevi Karolini* (Hanover, 1896), p. 163. The history of this period has been retraced by H. B. Swete, *On the History of the Doctrine of the Procession of the Holy Spirit* (Cambridge, 1876), chapter IX, pp. 196–226, with the appendix, pp. 227–237, containing the text of the letter of the Jerusalem monks to Leo III, the Pope's letter to the emperor, the Pope's profession of faith, the emperor's letter to the Pope and the account of the dialogue between the Pope and the emperor's envoys. See also M. Jugie, *op. cit.* (note 5 below), pp. 261–277; B. Capelle, 'Le pape Léon III et le "Filioque" ', *1054–1954. L'Eglise et les Eglises (Mélanges L. Beauduin)* (Chevetogne, 1954), I, pp. 309–322, who shows that the text given as Pope Leo III's profession of faith is in fact Alcuin's; R. G. Heath, 'The Schism of the Franks and the Filioque', *Journal of Ecclesiastical History*, 23 (1976), 97–113.

3. *PL* 129, 1257f.; *MGH, Epistolae* V, pp. 64–66 (for the monks' letter); *PL* 129, 1259f.; *MGH, op. cit.*, pp. 66–67 (for the Pope's letter to Charlemagne).
4. Anastasius Bibliothecarius, *Hist. de vitis Pontif.* (*PL* 128, 1238). This fact was borne out by Peter Damian in the second half of the eleventh century: *De proc. Spir. sanct.* 2 (*PL* 145, 635); and in the twelfth century by Peter Abelard and Peter Lombard: see Swete, *op. cit.* (note 2), p. 224, note 1. The account of the conversations between Charlemagne's envoys and the Pope can be found in *PL* 102, 971ff,; *MGH, Concilia* II, *Concilia Aevi Karolini*, Pars I, pp. 240ff.
5. Cardinal Hergenröther's study is still of fundamental importance: *Photius Patriarch von Konstantinopel*, 3 vols. (Regensburg, 1867–1869); see also F. Dvornik, *The Photian Schism: History and Legend* (Cambridge, 1948). Photius' argument is outlined and then disputed and rejected in L. Lohn, *Doctrina Graecorum et Russorum de Processione Spiritus Sancti a solo Patre*, Pars I: *Photii temporibus* (Rome, 1934); M. Jugie, *De Processione Spiritus Sancti* . . . (Rome, 1936), pp. 282–386. See also J. Slipyi, *Die Trinitätslehre des byzantinischen Patriarchen Photios* (Innsbruck, 1921); E. Amann, 'Photius', *DTC*, XII, cols 1536ff.; R. Haugh, *Photius and the Carolingians* (Belmont, Mass., 1975).
6. See F. Dvornik, *op. cit.*, esp. App. I, pp. 435–447; J. Alberigo *et al.*, eds, *Conciliorum Œcumenicorum Decreta* (Bologna, 1973), pp. 157–158. For the Council of 869–870, see D. Stiernon, *Constantinople IV* (*Histoire des conciles œcuméniques*, 5) (Paris, 1967).
7. V. Grumel, 'Le "Filioque" au concile photien de 879–880 et le témoignage de Michel d'Anchialos', *Echos d'Orient*, 29 (1930), 257–264. Even more important is the article by M. Jugie, 'Origine de la controverse sur l'addition du Filioque au Symbole', *RSPT* 28 (1939), 369–385—but see also note 29, p. 56 above.
8. See F. Dvornik, 'Le patriarche Photius: père du schisme ou patron de la réunion?' *La Vie intellectuelle* (December 1945), 16–28.
9. Photius, encyclical letter to the Bishops of the Eastern Church, 867 (*PG* 102, 721–741); letter to Walpert, the Metropolitan of Aquileia, probably 882 (*PG* 102, 793–821); *Amphilochia*, q. 28, between 867 and 876 (*PG* 101, 205–209); *The Mystagogy of the Holy Spirit*, which was composed in exile after 886 and is the most important text (*PG* 102, 263–400).
10. *Mystagogy*, 20 (*PG* 102, 300A).
11. *ibid.*, 53.
12. M. Jugie, *op. cit.* (note 5), p. 297, quotes *Contra Man.* III, 17 (*PG* 102, 168B) and *Amph.* q. 188 (*PG* 101, 909B) here. The diagram is generally attributed to Photius.
13. The texts in question are either those which speak of *dia tou Huiou, per Filium*, or those which show the Spirit to be united to the Father through the Son—see Athanasius, *Contra Arian.* III, 24 (*PG* 26, 373)—or those which attribute to the Son everything that the Father is or has except for his fatherhood—see L. Lohn, *op. cit.* (note 5), no. 69, pp. 59–60—or those which contain a commentary on the *de meo accipiet*, 'he will receive from me' (Jn 16:14), inclining towards a dependence of being—see L. Lohn, *op. cit.*, no. 76, pp. 64–65. Photius understands this as 'de meo *Patre*'; letter to the Metropolitan of Aquileia, 15 (*PG* 102, 808–809); *Mystagogy*, 22, 23 and 29 (*PG* 102, 301, 304, 312).
14. Letter to the Bishops of the Eastern Church, 22 (*PG* 102, 732); M. Jugie, *op. cit.* (note 5), p. 290.
15. Letter to the Bishops of the Eastern Church, 12 (*PG* 102, 728); *Mystagogy, passim*; see M. Jugie, *op. cit.*, p. 291, note 1.
16. Several of the Fathers explained this 'greater than I' by the fact that the Father is the begetter and the principle: see T. de Régnon, *Etudes de théologie positive sur la Sainte Trinité*, III (Paris, 1898), pp. 166ff.; *Œuvres de S. Augustin*, 15: *La Trinité*, I (Paris, 1955), pp. 574–575; Hilary of Poitiers, *Tract. super Ps.* 138, 17 (*PL* 9, 801).
17. S. Bulgakov, *Le Paraclet* (Paris, 1946), p. 110.

A NOTE ON THE
THEOLOGY OF GREGORY PALAMAS

We must now turn to a very important subject which would call for a much more developed treatment if I were to deal with it as such. As regards the theme of this book, it is necessary to speak about Palamite theology, but it is sufficient to do so relatively succinctly. I have, in this, made considerable use of the many indispensable texts and excellent analyses available.[1]

Gregory Palamas (1296–1359) became a monk on Mount Athos about 1316 and there experienced Hesychastic spirituality, in which the body is very closely associated with the spirit in the search for recollection and concentration. In Hesychastic prayer, a breathing technique is used to enable the prayer to descend from the head and find its way to the heart. The particular prayer used is the 'Jesus Prayer': the words 'Lord Jesus Christ, Son of God, have mercy on me' are said again and again in time with the breathing until they become a continuous prayer of the heart. Hesychasm eventually fitted into the pattern of Church and social life of the empire and became a reforming movement, working for the humble and the poor and for the independence and transcendence of the Church.

In the meantime, a monk from Calabria, Barlaam, attacked the Hesychasts' claim that it was possible to know God, their practice of prayer, and their theology of the divine light of Mount Tabor. Palamas replied to these attacks, and his defence of the Hesychastic positions forms the basis of Palamite theology. Two synods took place in 1341. Barlaam's teachings were condemned by the first in June and those of Akindynos by the second, which met in August. Despite the approval of these synods, Palamas became involved in the vicissitudes of ecclesiastical politics which led at times to his being excommunicated and the triumph of his enemies and at other times to the confirmation of his teachings. In 1347 he was made Archbishop of Thessalonica, but did not take up his see until 1350. Years of struggle and frequently dramatic episodes followed. He died on 14 November 1359 and was canonized by the Church of Constantinople in 1368. His teaching had by this time already been approved, by a council that met in 1351.[2]

Palamas was almost completely forgotten for several centuries—so much so that T. de Régnon published his four great volumes in 1892–1898 without even referring to him, even in those passages where he was commenting on the term 'energy' (IV, pp. 425ff., 476ff.). In the nineteen-thirties and forties, however, there was a wonderful revival of interest in him and his theology. Broadly speaking, Eastern theologians have come to recognize in Palamism a clear expression of the genius and the tradition of their Church. It is therefore of great importance for the theme of this book.

It is also relatively simple. In the first place, there is the whole context of Eastern apophatism, according to which it is not possible either to know God or to express any positive idea of him, the deepest knowledge of him being purely experiential or mystical. At the same time, God calls us to become deified. This is such a fundamental datum in the teaching of the Greek Fathers that they constantly used it as proof of the divinity of the Son and the Spirit in their controversy with the Arians. It is within this context that should be placed the Hesychastic experience of communion with God and of a knowledge, through experience, of his light. According to the Greek tradition, then, there is, in God, a secret essence that cannot be known or shared and a radiation which, once it has been experienced and shared, ensures our deification. This accounts for the distinction that Palamas makes *in God*—without impairing the simplicity of God—not only between the essence and the hypostases, but also between the hypostases, the divine essence that cannot be known or shared, and the uncreated energies of God. These energies are God, not in his being in himself, which is not accessible to creatures, but in his being for us. The energies must be available for us to share in them, and they must be God as uncreated, or else we could never be deified. The Palamists are unable to accept that the created grace of the Scholastic theologians of the West and the intentional union of the Thomists, the depth and realism of which they do not fully understand, can bring about a true deification of man, and the direct vision of the divine essence without any created *species*, as affirmed by Thomas Aquinas, is, in their view, contrary to the unknowable character of that essence.

These uncreated energies are therefore what surround the essence of God that cannot be communicated to man—*ta peri auton* (or *autou*).[3] Scriptural terms for these are, for example, the glory, the face or the power of God. The light that transfigured Christ on Mount Tabor was the uncreated splendour that emanates from God. It was always with Christ because of his divinity, but it remained invisible to carnal eyes—the apostles were only able to perceive it miraculously because their bodily eyes were illuminated by grace. This perception of the divine light is, in the opinion of the Hesychasts and the Palamists, the peak of all spiritual experience, and this idea is very closely associated with the very fundamental decision not to separate the body from the highest spiritual life.

What, then, is the relationship between these energies and the hypostases or Persons of the Trinity? According to Sergey Bulgakov, 'Palamas hardly touches on the complex and important question of the relationship between the energies and the hypostases (except in a few isolated sentences that are lacking in precision)'.[4] The texts and the studies that have been published since Bulgakov said this enable us to make a better reply to our question. The divine energies are 'inhypostatized'.[5] The eternal and uncreated activity that flows from the divine essence is possessed, put to work and manifested by the divine Persons and communicated by them to our persons.[6] The energetic manifestations of God follow the order (*taxis*) of the Persons—from the Father, through the Son, in the Spirit.

In the particular case of the Holy Spirit, the part played by the latter in the economy of salvation was made manifest at Pentecost, when, however, no incarnation of the hypostasis of the Spirit or communication of the essence of God took place. But the manifestation of his Person by the energies confirms a dependence with regard to the Son. 'The grace is therefore uncreated and it is what the Son gives, sends and grants to his disciples; it is not the Spirit himself, but a deifying gift which is an energy that is not only uncreated, but also inseparable from the Holy Spirit' (*Triad*, III, 8).

At this point Palamas goes back to a statement by Gregory of Cyprus, the Patriarch of Constantinople (†1290),[7] and recognizes that the *Filioque* may possibly have a meaning in the order of energetic manifestation, that is, that the holy Spirit, not as hypostasis but as inhypostatizing the energy, is poured out from the Father, through the Son (*dia tou Huiou* or even *ek tou Huiou*). Vladimir Lossky discovered this openness as early as 1945, but he kept to the idea of an eternal manifestation of the Spirit through the Son.[8] His disciple O. Clément, however, went further than this and said:

If the 'monarchic' character of the Father as the unique principle of the Son and the Spirit is an absolutely incommunicable hypostatic character, is his character as the divine source (of the essence and energies)—to use a Latin theological term, his 'fontal' privilege—not communicated to the Son and then from the Father and the Son to the Spirit, the source of our deification? And would it not be this participation in the divine source, the rhythm that makes first the Son and then the Spirit the source with the Father, that is indicated by a certain Latin (and Alexandrian) *Filioque*?[9]

It may be because I am not sufficiently well informed, but I have to admit that I am not quite clear what Palamas thinks about his attribution to the energies or to the Person of the Holy Spirit. When he says, for example, ' "The new spirit and the new heart" of Ezek 36:26 are created things, . . . whereas the Spirit of God given to the new heart (Ezek 27:5) is the Holy Spirit',[10] is he speaking about the uncreated energies or the Person of the Holy Spirit? Again, when he says that the energies are nothing but the Holy Spirit, but that they are not the divine essence,[11] is he referring to the energies inhypostatized in the Holy Spirit or to the third Person of the Trinity? This may, of course, have to do with the fact that Palamas gives the name of Holy Spirit both to the uncreated energies and to the hypostasis. He says, for example: 'When you hear him (that is, Cyril of Alexandria) say that the Holy Spirit proceeds from the two, because he comes essentially from the Father through the Son, you should understand his teaching in this sense: it is the powers and essential energies of God which pour out, not the divine hypostasis of the Spirit'.[12] What the Fathers called *energeia* is the supernatural action of God, which is his Spirit—Father, Son and Spirit are the first subject, his power and his act.[13] Or else they spoke of the energies of the Spirit and meant by this his gifts, given to believers, but caused by him.[14]

This at once gives rise to the question—widely discussed by Palamas' opponents[15]—of the continuity between the statements made by the Fathers and Palamas' systematic treatment of the subject. This whole question would be well worth examining in depth and with scholarly objectivity.[16] It would, in my opinion, certainly be possible to dispute the meaning of the texts of the Cappadocian Fathers and John Damascene that have been quoted in favour of Palamas' thesis.[17] The ante-Nicene Fathers, and in particular Athanasius, always denied that there could have been any procession in God other than that of the Persons. According to them, apart from the hypostases, only creatures proceeded from God. In opposition to Eunomius, according to whom the term *agennētos* adequately expressed the essence of God, the Fathers stressed the unknowable aspect of that essence. God, they believed, could only be known by his properties and works, and Basil of Caesarea called these his 'energies', which, he claimed, 'descend towards us, while his substance remains inaccessible'.[18]

The Fathers frequently expressed this distinction by using the terms *kat' auton* (God in himself) and *ta peri auton* or *peri autou* ('about him', in other words, what can be known and said about him, that is, on the basis of his properties and his activity) or *peri tēn phusin*.[19] André de Halleux, who is a considerable expert in this field, has, however, defended the interpretation of *peri auton* which is favourable to Palamas.[20] From the philological point of view, he is clearly right, since *peri* followed by the accusative certainly means 'around' or 'in connection with'. The question as to what theological or metaphysical conclusion should be drawn from the term, however, still remains. Did the Fathers postulate a kind of corona of divine energies which were active *ad extra*, which could be shared and which were ontologically and really distinct from the divine essence and the hypostases? E. von Ivanka, who is also a considerable expert, disputes this (see note 16 below). The problem has, in my opinion, not yet been fully cleared up, and I am in no position to decide. I am, however, impressed by the formal decision reached by so many Greek and Slav Orthodox theologians, who are in the best position to judge and interpret the writings of those who have borne witness to their own tradition.

We must now consider the question whether Palamism can be accepted by Western Catholicism or whether it is irreconcilably contrary to our teaching—and to our faith? The negative and critical position has been held, with varying shades of emphasis, by M. Jugie, S. Guichardan (see note 1 below), E. Candal[21] and those who contributed to the 1974 number of *Istina* (see also note 1 below). On the other hand, there have been as many specialists in this sphere who have regarded it as possible to reconcile Palamism with the Catholic faith.[22] I say quite deliberately the 'Catholic faith', because, if we are thinking of the *theology* of Augustine or Thomas Aquinas, we are bound to admit that, after reading Palamas openly and sympathetically and after recognizing very wide possibilities of agreement, there are still many great divergences. This ground has been covered to a great extent by Cardinal Journet on the basis of Jean Meyendorff's excellent book.[23] The distinction between faith and theology is quite fundamental—so much so that T. de Régnon referred to it again and again throughout the four volumes of his work on the Trinity.

Cardinal Journet has pointed out first of all that there is no opposition between Palamism and the Catholic faith with regard to the following articles: the natural and the supernatural order, Christ and the Eucharist, the Church as a mystical reality, the Virgin Mary and the saints. There are divergencies in the case of that very ambiguous term 'original sin', the immaculate conception of Mary, and the procession of the Holy Spirit from the Father *and the Son* through the same spiration. The question of the real distinction between the essence and the divine energies, however, still remains, and this distinction is required by the affirmation of the full truth of our deification. The doctrine of the light of Mount Tabor is only an application of that distinction. I believe, together with Cardinal Journet, J.-M. Garrigues, G. Philips and, ultimately, also J. Kuhlmann (*op. cit.* (note 22 below), pp. 43–57), that this difference comes from the idea of participation. Let us look at this question more closely.

Kuhlmann and Journet have both compared the same Pseudo-Dionysian texts as interpreted by Thomas Aquinas (and Maximus the Confessor) on the one hand and by Palamas on the other. To 'participate' means to 'take part', *partem capere*. Palamas interprets this as taking part in God entitatively and ontologically, but this participation cannot be in his essence, which cannot be communicated—it must be in the energies which emanate from that essence and which surround it. This, however, makes it possible for us to be deified in a literal and absolute sense—we become God and therefore we become, by grace, uncreated.[24] From the philosophical point of view, this Palamite idea of participation is clearly elementary and material,[25] one might almost say Neo-Platonic. The interpretation provided by Thomas Aquinas (and Maximus the Confessor), on the other hand, is Aristotelian, although it has taken from Plato a note of exemplarism. Maximus and Thomas comment on Pseudo-Dionysius' *Divine Names* in the following way: God, as a sovereign artist, lets his creatures participate, not in his divinity as such, which would be as impossible for us as it was for Palamas, but in the likenesses of his perfections of being—this is the exemplarism of the divine ideas—and through the efficient causality which confers existence. Thomas comments on *The Divine Names* II, 4 as follows:

> God is manifested by the effects that come from him. It is the Deity itself which to some extent proceeds in these effects, when it pours a likeness of itself into things according to their capacity, in such a way, however, that its excellence and its singularity remain intact in itself; these are not communicated to us and they remain hidden from our sight.[26]

This expresses the same sense of God's transcendence as I welcome and admire in the teaching of Gregory Palamas, but the concepts used by Thomas are, of course, quite different. The participation of which Thomas speaks is in a likeness of God's perfections and is realized in existence by the efficient causality of the absolute Being. There is no distinction in God himself between the divine essence that cannot be shared and the energies that are communicated, not even when it is a question of our *supernatural* participation. To the extent to which that participation includes created realities such as grace, charisms and gifts of the Holy Spirit, those realities have a status that is similar to that of natural realities. Participation, then, is not in perfections which are God's common perfections. It is rather in the divine nature as a principle of activities with God himself in view (see 2 Pet 1:3–4). The divine causality of grace produces in us principles of existence and action which enable us to attain the reality of God himself, that is, the Tri-unity, as the object of the life of the spirit, of knowledge and of love. These principles of action are limited (because they are created) in their entitative being, but they are effectively open to the infinite aspect of God himself, which they can attain without exhausting (*totum, non totaliter*). This is the effect of grace, of the theologal virtues and of the light of glory. And just as grace is that supernatural gift with which God himself is given, the indwelling in us of the divine Persons follows the gift of grace, with the enjoyment of their presence (see Volume II of this work, pp. 83–84). This explanation, however, is as such not really dogmatic, but rather theological.

I do not dispute the underlying intention of Palamas' teaching, but find myself in disagreement with the concepts that he uses and his metaphysical mode of expression. Even if it is admitted that he is supported by several of the Fathers in his distinction *a parte rei* between the divine essence and the energies, he still only presents us with a theologoumenon in the precise sense in which this term has been defined by B. Bolotov: 'The opinions of the Fathers of the *one* and *undivided* Church are the opinions of those men among whom are found those who have rightly been called *hoi didaskaloi tēs oikoumenēs*. . . . But, however widely accepted it may be, a theologoumenon does not constitute a dogma.'[27]

Does Palamas' teaching constitute a dogma in the Orthodox Church? Certain Eastern Christians think so, including, for example, Professor Karminis and Archimandrite [now Bishop] Kallistos Ware (*op. cit.* (note 1 below), 58). Considerable importance has obviously also to be attached to the Council of Constantinople of 1351 and its decisions that were incorporated into the synodicon to be read on the First Sunday of Lent, the so-called Feast of Orthodoxy. (Are they still read then?) At the Council of Florence in 1439, the Greeks regarded the distinction between the divine energies and the uncreated character of the light of Mount Tabor as their teaching. Nowadays, Palamism is almost universally accepted by Orthodox theologians. But does all this evidence point to a dogma? There are strong reasons for doubting it.[28]

Did the Roman Catholic Church dogmatically condemn the Palamite theses at any time? J. Kuhlmann does not think so. He has examined the dogmatic statements concerning the vision of God.[29] Although the Latin participants at the Council of Florence regarded the Palamite thesis as heretical, no formal condemnation was pronounced by the Council itself. The Fathers of the Council spoke of 'intueri clare ipsum Deum trinum et unum sicuti est', but did not say 'per essentiam'. Palamas might have agreed with that formula by seeing it as pointing to a vision of energies *which are God*. The Constitution *Benedictus Deus* of 1336 speaks of seeing 'essentiam divinam visione intuitiva et etiam faciali', and Kuhlmann's comment on this is that all that was intended was to oppose a vision of something created. Palamas may, however, have disputed the vision of the divine essence, but he certainly admitted participation in the divine nature (2 Pet 1:4), not *kata phusin*, but *kata charin*, that is, through grace. Kuhlmann has therefore concluded that, as far as Palamism is concerned, there is no obstacle to re-establishing communion with the East. Is he being too optimistic here? Mgr Gérard Philips, who was the king-pin in the Theological Commission of Vatican II, has come to the same conclusion. This is, in my opinion, a firm guarantee.

NOTES

1. D. Stiernon has published a bulletin containing 303 items on Palamism in *Rev. Et. byz.* 30 (1972), 231–341. This alone shows that the subject is so full and technical that only specialists can deal adequately with it. For the works of Palamas, see J. Meyendorff, *Introduction à l'étude de Grégoire Palamas* (*Patristica Sorbonensia*, 3) (Paris, 1959), Appendix I, pp. 331–399 [the Eng. tr. (see below) lacks the Appendixes]. For our particular subject, only the following need to be consulted: *PG* 150, 809–828: *Chapters against Akindynos*; 909–960: dialogue *Theophanes*; 1121–1126: *Capita CL physica, theologica, moralia et practica*; 1225–1236: *Hagioritic Tome*; *PG* 151, 424–449: *Homilies* 34 and 35 on the Transfiguration and the Light of Tabor; see also J. Meyendorff, ed., *Pour la défense des saints hésychastes* (*Spicil. Sacr. Lov.*, 29) (Louvain, 1959: 2nd ed. 1973).

Studies and analyses of Palamas include: I. Hausherr, 'La méthode d'oraison hésychaste', *Or. Chr. Period.* 9 (1927), 97–210; M. Jugie, 'Palamas et Palamite (Controverse)', *DTC*, XI (1932), cols 1735–1776, 1777–1818; *idem, Theologia dogmatica Christianorum Orient. ab Ecclesia cath. diss.*, II (Paris, 1933), pp. 47–183; S. Guichardan, *Le problème de la simplicité divine en Orient et en Occident aux XIVᵉ et XVᵉ siècles. Grégoire Palamas, Duns Scot, Georges Scholarios* (Lyons, 1933); B. Krivocheine, 'The Ascetic and Theological Teaching of St Gregory Palamas', *ECQ*, 3 (1938–1939), 26–33, 71–84, 138–156, 193–215; V. Lossky, *The Mystical Theology of the Eastern Church* (Eng. tr.; London, 1957), especially pp. 67ff.: 'Uncreated Energies'; *idem*, 'The Procession of the Holy Spirit in the Orthodox Triadology' (Eng. tr.), *ECQ*, 7, Supplementary Issue (1948), 31–53, also tr. in *In the Image* . . . (see below), chapter 4, pp. 71–96: 'The Procession of the Holy Spirit in Orthodox Trinitarian Doctrine'; *idem, In the Image and Likeness of God* (Eng. tr.; London and Oxford, 1975), especially chapter 3: 'The Theology of Light in the Thought of St Gregory Palamas'; C. Lialine, 'The Theological Teaching of Gregory Palamas on Divine Simplicity', *ECQ*, 6 (1946), 266–287; C. Kern, 'Les éléments de la théologie de Grégoire Palamas', *Irénikon*, 20 (1947), 6–33, 164–193; J. Meyendorff, *A Study of Gregory Palamas* (Eng. tr. of *Introduction, op. cit.*; London, 1964): an original and fundamental work, and, at a less technical level, but more synthetic, S. *Grégoire Palamas et la mystique orthodoxe (Coll. Les Maîtres spirituels)* (Paris, 1959); *idem*, 'the Holy Trinity in Palamite Theology', *Trinitarian Theology: East and West* (Brookline, Mass., 1977), pp. 25–43; E. Boularand, 'Grégoire Palamas et "La Défense des saints hésychastes" ', *RAM*, 36 (1960), 227–240; O. Clément, *Byzance et le Christianisme* (Paris, 1964); R. Miguel, 'Grégoire Palamas, docteur de l'expérience', *Irénikon*, 37 (1966), 227–237; Amphilokios Radovic, ' "Le Filioque" et l'énergie incréée de la Sainte Trinité selon la doctrine de S. Grégoire Palamas', *Messager de l'Exarchat du Patriarche russe en Europe occidentale*, 89–90 (1975), 11–44; Kallistos Ware, 'Dieu caché et révélé. La voie apophatique et la distinction essence-énergie', *ibid.*, 45–59. A double number of the journal *Istina* on 'Orient et Occident. La Procession du Saint-Esprit' appeared in 1972 and a series of articles on Gregory Palamas in 1974, of which the editorial, 257–259, is especially valuable; see also in that number (19) J. P. Houdret, 'Palamas et les Cappadociens', 260–271; J.-M. Garrigues, 'L'énergie divine et la grâce chez Maxime le Confesseur', 272–296; J. S. Nadal, 'La critique par Akindynos de l'herméneutique patristique de Palamas', 297–328; M. J. Le Guillou, 'Lumière et charité dans la doctrine palamite de la divinisation', 329–338. The articles in this number of *Istina,* together with several other publications, give the impression of being a combined attack. For a Catholic reply, see A. de Halleux, 'Palamisme et tradition', *Irénikon*, 48 (1975), 479–493. Finally, for the epistemological debate, see G. Podskalsky, *Theologie und Philosophie in Byzanz. Der Streit um die theologische Methodik in der spätbyzantinischen Geistesgeschichte (14./15. Jahrhundert), seine systematischen Grundlagen und seine historische Entwicklung (Byzantinisches Archiv, 15)* (Munich, 1977), which contains an exhaustive documentation and a full bibliography. See also below, notes 15 to 20, for Palamas and the Fathers, and note 22 for the reception by Catholic theologians of Palamism.

2. J. Meyendorff, *A Study, op. cit.*, pp. 94–97; for the text see *PG* 151, 717–762.

3. See below, notes 19 and 20.

4. S. Bulgakov, *Le Paraclet* (Paris, 1946), p. 236.

5. See J. Meyendorff, ed., *Pour la défense des saints hésychastes, op. cit.* (note 1), III, 1, 18, pp. 591–593.

6. J. Meyendorff, *A Study, op. cit.* (note 1), pp. 216ff.; *idem*, 'The Holy Trinity in Palamite Theology', *op. cit. (ibid.)*, 31–33, 38–39, in which the author quotes an article by Edmund Hussey, 'The Persons–Energy Structure in the Theology of St Gregory Palamas', *St Vladimir's Theological Quarterly*, 18 (1974), 22–43. In this context, it is also worth quoting from O. Clément, *Byzance et le Christianisme, op. cit.* (note 1), p. 46: 'This energy is not an impersonal radiation subsisting in itself. It is rather an expansion of the Trinity and

expresses *ad extra* the mysterious otherness of the Trinity in its unity. It is a "natural procession" from God himself, bursting or flashing out, like a flash of light, of the Father through the Son and in the Holy Spirit. It reveals the "interpenetration" or perichoresis of the divine Persons, who "interpenetrate each other in such a way that they possess only one energy" '. See also A. de Halleux, 'Palamisme et Scolastique', *op. cit.* below (note 22), 425, who refers to Palamas, *Capita CL physica, op. cit.* (note 1), 75 and 107 (*PG* 150, 1173B and 1193B).

7. Gregory's treatise on the *ekporeusis* of the Holy Spirit (*PG* 142, 269–300) has been analysed by O. Clément, 'Grégoire de Chypre "De l'ekporèse du Saint-Esprit" ', *Istina*, 17 (1972), 443–456.

8. V. Lossky, 'The Procession of the Holy Spirit', *ECQ, op. cit.* (note 1), 48–49; *In the Image and Likeness of God, op. cit.* (*ibid.*), pp. 90–93. In his article 'Vladimir Lossky, un théologien de la personne et du Saint-Esprit (Mémorial Vladimir Lossky)', *Messager de l'Exarchat du Patriarche russe en Europe occidentale*, 30–31 (April–September, 1959), 137–206, O. Clément referred to this openness on Lossky's part and, on pp. 192 and 178, points to expressions of it, taken from classes given on 10 November and 17 November 1955: 'The *Filioque* can be justified at the level of manifestation—the Holy Spirit manifests the common nature of the Trinity and proceeds from the Father and the Son not as a Person, but as a function. His function is essentially to make manifest. He manifests the nature of the Father and the Son (which is also his own)'; 'In this *taxis* (of manifestation), it is possible to say, if need be, that the Spirit proceeds from the Father and the Son. The Son shows in himself what the Father is; the Spirit shows what the Father is and what the Son is, insofar as they are the same principle, but a principle to which the Spirit himself belongs and which he manifests.'

9. O. Clément, *op. cit.* (note 7), p. 450. Amphilokios Radovic, *op. cit.* (note 1) shows that Palamas affirmed the procession of the Holy Spirit only from the Father, but that the Spirit also receives the divine essence from the Son (pp. 27ff.); he devotes pp. 42–43 to Gregory of Cyprus. In this context, it is also worth quoting Paul Evdokimov, *L'Esprit Saint dans la tradition orthodoxe* (Paris, 1969), p. 63: 'The distinction between essence and energy is the first of the possible solutions of the *Filioque* in the light of the Eastern tradition. It postulates the distinction and identity of the Spirit (*to Pneuma* with the article) as hypostasis and of Spirit (*Pneuma* without the article) as energy. At the level of the common essence, the Spirit as hypostasis proceeds from the Father alone, although conjointly with the Son on whom he rests. As divine energy, Palamas teaches, "the Spirit is poured out from the Father through the Son and, if one wants, from the Son" [quoted by J. Meyendorff, *Introduction, op. cit.*, p. 315 (= *A Study, op. cit.*, p. 230)]. The solution, then, is to be found in the distinction between the hypostasis of the Holy Spirit and the energy that it manifests *ex Patre Filioque*.'

10. Quoted by J. Meyendorff, *A Study, op. cit.*, (note 1), p. 164.

11. *Against Akindynos*, II, 17, quoted by J. Meyendorff, *A Study, op. cit.*, p. 225.

12. *Apodictic Treatises*, quoted by J. Meyendorff, *A Study, op. cit.*, p. 230.

13. See the many texts, together with full commentaries, in T. de Régnon, *Etudes de théologie positive sur la Sainte Trinité*, IV (Paris, 1898), pp. 425–465. This is, in particular, what is found in Athanasius, *Ad Ser.* I, 19, 20 and 31; III, 5. See also G. L. Prestige, *God in Patristic Thought*, 2nd ed. (London, 1952), pp. 257ff.

14. This seems to me to be the case in the *Const. Apost.* V, 20, 4, with regard to Pentecost: 'We have been filled with his energy and have spoken in new tongues', and in Maximus the Confessor, *Q. ad Thal.* 63 (*PG* 90, 672); *Theol. Polem.* 1 (*PG* 91, 33). In his anti-Monothelite struggle, Maximum spoke of divine energy in the sense of the active faculty of a nature or essence. For him, however, it was the creative causality and not the energies in the sense in which Palamas distinguished them from the essence and the hypostases; that, at least, is how J.-M. Garrigues interprets it; *op. cit.* (note 1).

15. J. S. Nadal, *op cit.* (note 1).

16. All that we have at present is this partial study: E. von Ivanka, 'Palamismus und Vätertradition', *L'Eglise et les Eglises*. *Mélanges Lambert Beauduin* (Chevetogne, 1954), II, pp. 29–46, who concluded that the texts in question do not speak of a real distinction in God himself, but of a distinction made by our spirit, which can only think in distinctions; see also J. P. Houdret, *op. cit.* (note 1). This conclusion is of crucial importance.

17. G. Florovsky, 'Grégoire Palamas et la patristique', *Istina*, 8 (1961–1962), 115–125, especially 122 (only Basil of Caesarea, *Ep.* 234 *ad Amphilochium*, and John Damascene, *De fide orthod.* I, 14); G. Philips, *op. cit.* below (note 22), 254.

18. Basil of Caesarea, *Contra Eunom.* I, 4 (*PG* 29, 544); *Ep.* 234 *ad Amphilochium* 1 (*PG* 32, 869 A–B).

19. See, for example, Gregory Nazianzen, *Orat.* 38, 7 (*PG* 36, 317B); 45, 3 (*PG* 36, 525C); Maximus the Confessor, *Centuries on Charity*, IV, 7 (*PG* 90, 1049A); *First Century on Theology and the Economy*, 48 (*PG* 90, 1100D); John Damascene, *De fide Orthod.* I, 4 and 10 (*PG* 94, 800C and 840).

20. A. de Halleux, *op. cit.* (note 1), 484: 'The contrast that the Cappadocian Fathers expressed by the words *kat' auton* and *peri auton* cannot be translated as that between God as he is in himself and what we are able to know about him. When it is followed by the accusative, the preposition *peri* usually means "around" and not "about" in this sense. By *peri auton*, the Fathers therefore meant what is "around" or what surrounds the essence of God, the radiation of light coming from the dark nucleus of the essence. . . . This *peri auton* is not what God reveals of his *kat' auton*, that is, the essence as we are able to know it, the simple perceived as many. It is rather a flowing that is distinct in God himself from the inaccessible source of his being.'

21. Many publications are listed in D. Stiernon's bulletin on Palamism, *op. cit.* (note 1).

22. I would mention here, in chronological order and for the most part in accordance with D. Stiernon's very valuable bulletin, *op. cit.*, to which the page numbers in brackets refer: G. Habra, 'The Source of the Doctrine of Gregory Palamas on the Divine Energies', *ECQ*, 12 (1957–1958), 244–252, 294–303, 338–347 (311); P. Bossuyt, 'Hesychasmus en katholieke theologie', *Bijdragen* (1964), 229–238 (306); M. Strohm, 'Die Lehre von der Einfachheit Gottes. Ein dogmatischer Streitpunkt zwischen Griechen und Lateiner', *Kyrios*, New Series, 7 (1967), 215–228; *idem*, 'Die Lehre von der Energeia Gottes', *ibid.*, 8 (1968), 63–84; 9 (1969), 31–41 (309–311); J. Kuhlmann, *Die Taten des einfachen Gottes. Eine römisch-katholische Stellungnahme zum Palamismus* (*Das östliche Christentum*, New Series, 21) (Würzburg, 1968) (294–299), with reference to a criticism by B. Schultze, *Or. Chr. period*, 36 (1970), 135–142; G. Philips, 'La grâce chez les Orientaux', *ETL*, 48 (1972), 37–50, reprinted in *L'union personnelle avec le Dieu vivant. Essai sur l'origine et le sens de la grâce créée* (*Bibl. ETL*, XXXVI) (Gembloux, 1972), 241–260 (I shall be returning to this article by G. Philips, because his position has not received the attention that it deserves); A. de Halleux, 'Palamisme et Scolastique', *RTL*, 4 (1973), 409–422; *idem*, 'Orthodoxie et Catholicisme: du personnalisme en pneumatologie', *ibid.*, 6 (1975), 3–30; *idem*, 'Palamisme et tradition', *op. cit.* (note 1). See also the following note.

23. C. Journet, 'Palamisme et thomisme. A propos d'un livre récent', *RThom*, 60 (1960), 429–452.

24. J. Meyendorff, *A Study, op. cit.* (note 1), pp. 176–177.

25. Thus, according to Palamas, if man were to participate in God's essence, he would himself become omnipotent and there would consequently be an infinite number of divine hypostases: *Capita CL physica*, 108–109 (*PG* 150, 1193C–1196A). This accounts for G. Philips' comment, *op. cit.* (note 22), p. 253: 'Palamas sees "participation" as a division into almost materialized pieces, each participant possessing a fragment of the whole, which is clearly absurd. In his view, everything that can be shared can also be divided (*Cap.* 110; *PG* 150, 1196C; *Theoph.* 944 A).'

26. Thomas Aquinas, *In lib. de Divinis Nominibus expositio*, Turin ed., p. 46, No. 136, translated by Journet, *op. cit.* (note 23), p. 448. On p. 449, Journet has also translated

Thomas' commentary on XI, 6 (*PG* 3, 956) (Thomas, *op. cit.*, p. 346, no. 934), and that of Maximus, *Scholia in lib. de Div. Nom.* XI, 6 (*PG* 4, 401). J. Kuhlmann, *op. cit.* (note 22), pp. 43–57, has compared Thomas' and Palamas' commentaries on the *Divine Names*, XI, 6 (*PG* 3, 953ff.). For the idea of participation in the likeness, see also Thomas' fine passage *ST* IIIa, q. 23, a. 2 ad 3.

27. B. Bolotov, 'Thèses sur le "Filioque" ' (Fr. tr.), *Istina*, 17 (1972), 261–289, especially 262 and 263.

28. For the 'non-dogmatic' character in the strict sense of the distinction between essence and energies, despite the Council of 1351 and the Sunday anathemas of the Feast of Orthodoxy, see M. Jugie, *Theologia dogmatica*, *op. cit.* (note 1), pp. 132ff., who gives texts and summaries. What I. K. says, for example, in *Or. Chr. Period.*, 17 (1951), 488, is: 'Is it a true dogma? Is it now still held as such in all the Eastern Churches? As for the Russian Church, it is well known that that Church ceased to affirm this from the eighteenth century onwards. In 1767, that Church radically changed the office of the Sunday of Orthodoxy and removed every trace of Palamism from it.' See M. Jugie, *op. cit.*, pp. 176ff.

29. J. Kuhlmann, *op. cit.* (note 22), pp. 108–125, for the Council of Florence (*DS* 1305); pp. 126–135 for the Constitution *Benedictus Deus* of Benedict XII, 29 January 1336 (*DS* 1000–1001).

6
EASTERN PNEUMATOLOGY TODAY

Now that we have considered the patristic sources of the Eastern tradition, we are in a position to provide a conspectus of the present state of pneumatology in the Eastern Church. In this synthesis, I shall leave aside Sergey Bulgakov's *Le Paraclet* (1946), not because the book is not interesting—quite the reverse!—but rather because it is too personal a work to be really representative of the Orthodox tradition.[1] There are, however, many more classical studies available.[2]

They are all deeply indebted to Greek patristic literature, but they contain an element that is not present in the Fathers. Although their tone may be irenical, they incorporate the data of the anti-Latin polemics. The result is that these works are at the same time a very positive expression of deep insight into the Eastern theological tradition and a criticism of Latin theological or dogmatic constructions. They almost all go back to the difference that T. de Régnon observed, namely that the point of departure for the Latin Fathers was the divine nature, whereas for the Greeks it was the hypostases. De Régnon unfortunately extended this penetrating insight into a simplification that no longer expressed the full reality of the situation. I shall try, in what follows, to avoid this over-simplification and to keep to the fundamental truth of the insight.

The Orthodox first affirm the three Persons or hypostases. Their point of departure, it would seem, is a difference between the essence or substance and the hypostases of a kind that enables them to speak in two different ways about the divine Persons, according to whether they are regarded as hypostases or are seen in their relationship to the divine essence. In Latin dogmatic theology, on the other hand, the hypostases are really identical with the divine essence. This means that, as far as the Holy Spirit is concerned, dependence on the Son in respect of the divine essence also implies dependence on him with regard to the hypostasis. In Orthodox dogmatic theology, however, it is possible to claim a hypostatic dependence on the Father alone and at the same time a reception of the divine essence also from the Son. After the abortion—or rather the still-birth—of the union discussed at the Council of Lyons in 1274, the Patriarch of Constantinople, Gregory of Cyprus (†1290), wrote:

> How could we affirm dogmatically that, because the Spirit is of the essence of the Son, he is from him, as from a cause? . . . We say in fact that the Holy Spirit has his essential *ekporeusis* from the Father and that he exists from his essence. Because,

on the other hand, the Father and the Son do not have a different essence, but have a single and the same essence, we of necessity confess that the Spirit is also from that essence. That, because he is of the essence of the Son, he is also from his hypostasis, no reason could persuade us to confess it, insofar as it has not been established that the essence and the hypostasis are the same principle.[3]

The divine hypostases are affirmed as such without any apparent need for an explanation by means of an opposition in relationship, as is the case in Latin theology. In the latter, Son implies Father and Father implies Son. In the community and unity of substance, the hypostases are distinguished by the mutual relationship which opposes them by affirming them. That relationship is and can only be a relationship of origin, or of principle or beginning and end. On the one hand, spiration of the Spirit does not bring about any opposition in relationship between the Father and the Son and, on the other hand, the Spirit proceeding from the Father can be distinguished hypostatically from the Son only if he has a relationship of procession or origin with that Son. He is, in many scriptural texts, Spirit of the Father and Spirit of the Son and for this reason he must be confessed as proceeding from the two by a single common act of active spiration.

The Orthodox reject this theology for the following reasons:

1. The hypostases must be affirmed for themselves and as such because they are affirmed by revelation and in the formula of baptism. To distinguish the Spirit from the Son, it is sufficient to keep to biblical terms, according to which the Son comes from the Father by begetting. The Spirit, on the other hand, comes by 'procession' or *ekporeusis*. It is enough for there to be two different modes of coming from the Father. The relationships are not what define the persons—they follow and are constituted by the persons, like inseparable properties.[4] The Latins have developed reasons and make inferences from logical necessities, whereas it is sufficient—and indeed necessary—to revere the mystery, to accept it and to defend it as it is given to us, without attempting to rationalize it.[5]

2. Since the time of Photius, the Orthodox have continued to object to the procession of the Spirit 'from the Father and the Son as from the same principle and by a single act of spiration', claiming that the Father and the Son, who are distinguished in their hypostases, can only spirate the Spirit through a common nature. A hypostasis cannot, however, come from a common nature—a hypostasis can only come from a hypostasis. If the Spirit proceeded from a common nature, he must have proceeded from himself, because he also shares in that common nature, but that, the Orthodox theologians maintain, is absurd.

The Latins have, of course, been replying to this objection for centuries. The fact that it has been raised again and again shows how what is intellectually effective in one theological construction of faith can continue to be

73

remote from another theological construction and even alien to it. The Orthodox are convinced that we have deduced the hypostases from the divine nature or essence; our idea of the hypostasis as a subsistent relationship does not appeal to them. We recognize for our part that the way in which the Scholasticism that has, as H. Clérissac put it, 'run to seed' has reasoned with an almost tactless lack of caution and beyond what the eye can see about the data of the mystery of the Trinity[6] may well have encouraged Eastern Christians to think that there has been excessive rationalization about the Trinity in the West. This, however, should not prevent us from trying to understand the great value of what saints and geniuses such as Thomas Aquinas have attempted to express in their use of such terms as 'subsistent relationships'.

It would be wrong to think that the Greek Fathers knew nothing about or simply neglected the question of consubstantiality through the divine essence. On the contrary, the Cappadocians affirmed the common essence before insisting on the specific aspect of the hypostases. Basil the Great (*Ep*. 38; *PG* 32, 325ff.), Gregory of Nyssa and Pseudo-Dionysius all did this. It is true that they insisted on the monarchy of the Father, claiming that only he was *archē*, the original and originating principle, but so did the Latin Fathers (see below, pp. 134–137). It is from the Father that the one substance of the deity is communicated, by begetting in the case of the Son and by procession in the case of the Spirit.[7] Gregory Nazianzen said: 'The divine nature is one in the three, but what makes their unity is the Father, on whom the others depend'.[8] Because it is a positive affirmation, I welcome what Paul Evdokimov said about this question, although I cannot welcome what he appears to exclude: 'For the Greeks, the principle of unity is not the divine nature, but the Father, who establishes relationships of origin with regard to himself as the one source of every relationship'.[9]

The unity of the three is also brought about by their being within each other, that is, by their *perichōrēsis* or circumincession. In their affirmation of the persons or hypostases without justifying the difference between them in terms of relationships of origin—although what I have said in the preceding section shows that this does not have to be so absolute—the Orthodox emphasize that, for the Greek Fathers, 'the relations only serve to *express* the hypostatic diversity of the Three; they are not the basis of it. It is the absolute diversity of the three hypostases which determines their differing relations to one another, not *vice versa*.'[10]

So far as these different relationships are concerned, there are not only different relationships of origin, but also different relationships of manifestation and reciprocity.[11] It is one of the most valuable aspects of the Orthodox view of the Tri-unity that the interaction of the Persons is so clearly envisaged, because they are affirmed together and the dependence of the Son and the Spirit with regard to the Father does not point to any immediate priority in the case of the latter. Each Person is always

Trinitarian. This is clearly expressed by Athanasius, for example, who said: 'As the Father has given all things to the Son, the Father again possesses all things in the Son and, as the Son possesses them, the Father again possesses them'.[12] With this datum, that the relationships are always Trinitarian, Paul Evdokimov was even able to say that 'In the act of begetting, the Son receives the Holy Spirit from the Father and therefore, in his being, he is eternally inseparable from the Holy Spirit, so that he is born *ex Patre Spirituque*. In the same way, the Holy Spirit proceeds from the Father and rests on the Son, and this corresponds to *per Filium* and *ex Patre Filioque*.'[13]

If it were simply a question of the birth of the Word made flesh in time, there would be no problem, but we have a discussion of eternal being. The formula can therefore be disputed, because it does not respect the order of the Persons in their eternal being and the fact that, as Basil the Great pointed out, the Spirit is numbered together with the others, but third. Athanasius can also be quoted in this context.[14] Nonetheless, we should welcome this idea of the in-existence of the hypostases one within the other, the idea, in other words, of exchange and reciprocity. It points to the fact that there is a Trinitarian life that does not simply consist of processions or relationships of origin. The Fathers and the Orthodox tell us again and again that the Spirit is received in the Son or that he takes from the Son and, in so doing, they are providing a foundation for relationships of reciprocity, the relationships, in other words, of the *perichōrēsis*. S. Verkhovsky had this to say about the *perichōrēsis*:

> I am sure that the doctrine of the *perichōrēsis* is the best commentary on *di' Huiou*. The Holy Spirit proceeds from the Father with the Son. . . . It is therefore possible to say, although in a hypostatic sense, that the Holy Spirit is for the Son because he is sent by the Father as his hypostatic Spirit, his Life or his Love in the Son. He is the living revelation of the Father to the Son. The Holy Spirit, who is sent by the Father, rests in the Son as an anointing. It is also possible to say that the Holy Spirit, who proceeds from the Father, leaps out towards the Son in order to find in him that Truth, that 'hypostatic Idea of God' that is, for the Holy Spirit, *quasi forma* of his existence as a Person. By receiving in him the hypostatic Wisdom, the Holy Spirit becomes the Spirit of Wisdom, his active Image. He therefore no longer remains in the Son, but comes from him by revealing him and in order to reveal him . . . that principle of the Orthodox triadology that all relationships in God are always Trinitarian. As a result of this, if the Holy Spirit is the revelation of the Father, he is also that revelation both for the Father and for himself and for the Son. If he is a manifestation of the Son, he is also that manifestation for the Son, for himself and for the Father. When the Holy Spirit reveals the Son, then, he reveals him to the Father, and that revelation is also a manifestation of the Son's infinite love for the Father. Thus it is possible to say that the Holy Spirit returns to the only one who has spirated him and he is the union not only of the Father with the Son, but also of the Son with the Father. The real meaning of *dia tou Huiou* is therefore not simply 'with'. It is also 'for' or 'after' (in the sense of the order of the hypostases) or 'from' the Son, but above all 'through' the Son, because the Holy

Spirit, in his inexpressible circumincession, proceeding from the Father, passes into the Son and through the Son while at the same time being reflected in him.[15]

This long text, which would be difficult to express in clear Latin theological concepts, indicates the main aspects of the in-existence/reciprocity of the Spirit in the divine Tri-unity. It also provides an interpretation of the 'through the Son' (*di' Huiou*), which the Council of Florence brought close to the meaning of the Latin *Filioque*. Most contemporary Orthodox Christians interpret it, not at the level of the origin of the third hypostasis, but at that of the eternal and immanent manifestation in the first place and then at that of the voluntary and economic manifestation. Gregory of Nyssa, for example, speaks of the Spirit shining eternally through the Son.[16] V. Lossky and other authors whom I have cited have interpreted this within the framework of the Palamite distinction between the essence of the hypostases and the energies.[17] As for the hypostatic procession, they believe that the Spirit comes from the Father alone. There is, however, *in God* and eternally, a procession of the common divinity which is brought about in the Holy Spirit 'through the Son'. In other words, 'in the order of natural manifestation (that is, the common manifestation outside the essence), the Holy Spirit proceeds from the Father through the Son, *dia Huiou*, after the Word, and this procession reveals to us the common glory of the three, the eternal splendour of the divine nature'.[18] 'From all eternity, the Father is "the Father of glory" (Eph 1:17), the Word is "the reflection of his glory" (Heb 1:3) and the Spirit is "the Spirit of glory" (1 Pet 4:14).'[19]

Do the patristic texts that I have cited not call for more than this? Are they not an undefined opening or a beginning, in the sense of pointing to the part played by the Son in the hypostatic existence of the Spirit? I am not alone to think that they are, although it is difficult to say exactly to what extent and in what sense. Probably not in the sense of *a Patre Filioque tanquam ab uno principio*, that is, 'from the Father and the Son *as from a single principle*'.

NOTES

1. S. Bulgakov provides first a number of interesting notes on the pneumatology of the Fathers, and then a personal reflection. He believed that it was necessary to go beyond the debate between the East and the West and, in order to do that, the problem of the origin of the hypostases had to be left aside. In his opinion, 'the divergence expressed by the two traditions—*Filioque* and *dia tou Huiou*—is neither a heresy nor a dogmatic error. It is a difference of theological opinion. There is no dogma about the relationship between the Holy Spirit and the Son': *Le Paraclet* (Paris, 1946), pp. 140–141. His aim was to work out a theology of the Trinity on new foundations and to analyse the inner dynamism of God who is Spirit and Love, and the correlation between the three hypostases who are situated within that absolute and living Subject. God is therefore 'one Person in three hypostases', who reveals himself in Wisdom identified with his *ousia* (this is sophiology, the object of discussion in its own right). An Orthodox theologian like V. Lossky could obviously only

reject this gnosis, since Lossky became the champion of Palamism and, as a member of the Confraternity of St Photius, regarded the *Filioque* as the radical cause of the differences between East and West—differences which he took so far that reconciliation is in danger of being made impossible (I have personally criticized him for this). On the other hand, another of my Orthodox friends, Paul Evdokimov, was more open and favourable to the insights of Bulgakov (whom I met on two occasions).

2. V. Lossky, *The Mystical Theology of the Eastern Church* (Eng. tr.; London, 1957); *idem, In the Image and Likeness of God* (Eng. tr.; London and Oxford, 1975), chapter 4; J. Meyendorff, 'La procession du Saint-Esprit chez les Pères orientaux', and S. Verkhovsky, 'La procession du Saint-Esprit d'après la triadologie orthodoxe', *Russie et Chrétienté* (1950), pp. 158–178 and 197–210 respectively, and the resulting discussions, pp. 193–196 and 219–224 respectively; P. Evdokimov, 'L'Esprit Saint et l'Eglise d'après la tradition liturgique', *L'Esprit Saint et L'Eglise. L'avenir de l'Eglise et de l'Œcuménisme. Symposium de l'Académie Internationale des Sciences religieuses* (Paris, 1960), pp. 85–111; *idem, L'Esprit Saint dans la tradition orthodoxe* (*Bibl. Œcum.*, 10) (Paris, 1969). See also numerous articles in *Le Messager de l'Exarchat du Patriarche russe en Europe occidentale*.

3. Gregory of Cyprus, 'On the *ekporeusis* of the Holy Spirit' (*PG* 142, 272); Fr. tr. O. Clément in *Istina* (1972), 446. Maximus the Confessor's letter to Marinus of Cyprus can also be mentioned in this context.

4. In this context, it is worth recording Karl Rahner's far-reaching comment: 'It has not been proved that a relationship that is peculiar to a person and a relationship that results in the constitution of a person are necessarily the same': *Mysterium Salutis*, I (Fr. tr.; Paris, 1971), p. 33 [the Eng. tr. (*The Trinity*, London, 1970, p. 26) is less clearly expressed].

5. 'The positive approach employed by Filioquist triadology brings about a certain rationalization of the dogma of the Trinity, insofar as it suppresses the fundamental antinomy between the essence and the hypostases. One has the impression that the heights of theology have been deserted in order to descend to the level of religious philosophy. On the other hand, the negative approach, which places us face to face with the primordial antinomy of absolute identity and no less absolute diversity in God, does not seek to conceal this antinomy but to express it fittingly, so that the mystery of the Trinity might make us transcend the philosophical mode of thinking. . . .' These words come from V. Lossky, *In the Image and Likeness of God, op. cit.*, p. 80; he also says, *ibid.*, p. 88: 'By the dogma of the *Filioque*, the God of the philosophers and savants is introduced into the heart of the Living God, taking the place of the *Deus absconditus, qui posuit tenebras latibulum suum*. The unknowable essence of the Father, Son and Holy Spirit receives positive qualifications. It becomes the object of natural theology: we get "God in General," who could be the god of Descartes, or the god of Leibnitz or even perhaps, to some extent, the god of Voltaire and the dechristianized Deists of the eighteenth century.' Surely this is going too far!

6. An attempt should be made—as I have done—to read M. Schmaus' monumental and massive work (over 1,000 pages), *Der Liber Propugnatorius des Thomas Anglicus und die Lehrunterschiede zwischen Thomas von Aquin und Duns Scotus*, II. Teil: *Die trinitarischen Lehrdifferenzen* (Münster, 1930). The effort merits admiration, and one is bound to appreciate the serious contribution made by the authors studied to the discussion of the arguments. It is certainly not to be despised, but the reasoning and the discussion of terms and concepts obscure the underlying theological insights almost completely.

7. See Athanasius, *Contra Arian*. I, 45; IV, 1 (*PG* 26, 105B, 468B–C); Basil the Great, *De spir. sanct*. XVIII, 47 (*PG* 32, 153B–C); Gregory Nazianzen, *Orat*. 2, 38, 40, 41 (*PG* 35, 445; 36, 417B); Gregory of Nyssa, *De comm. not*. (*PG* 45, 180C); John Damascene, *De fide orthod*. I, 8 (*PG* 94, 829A–C); . To these can be added the images expressing a dynamic linear diagram—the arm, hand and finger (Didymus); the root, branch and fruit (John Damascene); the source, river, sea or water that is drunk (Athanasius, John Damascene), and several others.

8. Gregory Nazianzen, *Orat.* 42, 15 (*PG* 36, 476B).

9. P. Evdokimov, *L'Esprit Saint dans la Tradition orthodoxe*, *op. cit.* (note 2), p. 46.

10. These words are by V. Lossky, *In the Image and Likeness of God*, *op. cit.* (note 2), p. 79. He continues: 'Here thought stands still, confronted by the impossibility of defining a personal existence in its absolute difference from any other, and must adopt a negative approach to proclaim that the Father—He who is without beginning (*anarchos*)—is not the Son or the Holy Spirit, that the begotten Son is neither the Holy Spirit nor the Father, that the Holy Spirit, "who proceeds from the Father," is neither the Father nor the Son. Here we cannot speak of relations of opposition but only of relations of diversity.'

11. P. Evdokimov, *L'Esprit Saint dans la tradition orthodoxe*, *op. cit.* (note 2), p. 41: 'According to Eastern Christians, the relationships between the Persons of the Trinity are not of opposition or separation, but of diversity, reciprocity, reciprocal revelation and communion in the Father'. This is a suitable point at which to point out a serious misunderstanding. Our Orthodox friends often speak of 'relationships of opposition' as a principle by which the Latins distinguish between the hypostases. Thus, in addition to Evdokimov, *op. cit.*, pp. 41, 42 and 65, and *L'Orthodoxie* (Paris 1959), pp. 137–138, Elie Melia, *Russie et Chrétienté* (1950), 223, and Vladimir Lossky, nine times in chapter 4 of *In the Image and Likeness of God*, *op. cit.* have also spoken of this. Is this due to a slip or an omission in reading? But such omissions often point to an unconscious inclination of the mind. To speak of 'a relationship of opposition' instead of 'opposition in relationship' (as in the case of Father–Son or Son–Father) could mean that, for the Latins, the persons are pure relations in essence, but this would point to a lack of understanding, both of the idea of subsistent relationships and of the way in which the Latins think of the diversity of the persons in the unity and simplicity of the divine Absolute.

12. Athanasius, *Contra Arian.* III, 36 (*PG* 26, 401C). For the permanently Trinitarian character of the relationships, see S. Bulgakov, *op. cit.*, (note 1), p. 70, note 67; P. Evdokimov, *L'Esprit Saint dans la tradition orthodoxe*, *op. cit.* (note 2), pp. 42, 70, etc.

13. P. Evdokimov, *ibid.*, pp. 71–72. The formula *Spirituque* can also be found on pp. 77 and 78 and in the last and unfinished work by the same author, 'Panagion et Panagia', *Bulletin de la Société française d'Etudes Mariales*, 27th year (1970), 59–71, especially 62–63. See also below, pp. 158, 164 note 25.

14. Athanasius, *Contra Arian.* III, 24; 'The Son does not participate in the Spirit in order to come about in the Father. He does not receive the Spirit, but rather distributes him to all. It is not the Spirit who unites the Son to the Father; the Spirit rather receives from the Logos' (*PG* 26, 373).

15. S. Verkhovsky, *Istina* (1950), 206–207.

16. Gregory of Nyssa, *Contra Eunom.* I (*PG* 45, 336D, 416C).

17. V. Lossky, *In the Image and Likeness of God*, *op. cit.*, pp. 90–95. Jean Meyendorff, *op. cit.* (note 2), pp. 169ff., keeps as a whole to the order of economic manifestation and communication, even in the texts of Cyril of Alexandria; cf. P. Evdokimov, 'L'Esprit Saint et l'Eglise', *op. cit.*, (note 2), p. 91.

18. Cf. V. Lossky, *In the Image and Likeness of God*, *op. cit.*, p. 93.

19. Cf. *ibid.*, p. 94.

(B) THE WEST AND THE REVELATION OF THE TRI-UNITY OF GOD[1]

It is not my intention to write a history of Christian doctrines, and this means that I do not have to attempt to be complete. I am simply looking for the theological view and possibly for the dogmatic construction that has been formed by Latin Catholicity. For this purpose, it should be sufficient (though still a monumental work) to present: (1) Augustine, who so determined the subsequent development in the West: (2) Anselm; (3) Richard of Saint-Victor and Bonaventure; and (4) Thomas Aquinas. It will then be possible for us to compare, with a full knowledge of the data, the theological approach of Greeks and Latins, that is, of Orthodox Catholics and of Roman Catholics. My ultimate aim, however, is to put forward a theology of the third hypostasis and I hope to do that under the sign of the freedom of grace and the Gift.

That is, of course, an enormous and perhaps excessive plan, but it is one that I regard as necessary in the name of theological honesty. I am all too aware of my own shortcomings. I have only been able to carry out this work in an environment of prayer and the celebration of the mysteries of faith—in other words, in a theological and doxological climate, and in the communion of saints.

NOTES

1. H. B. Swete, *The Holy Spirit in the Ancient Church. A Study of Christian Teaching in the Age of the Fathers* (London, 1912), pp. 295ff.; T. Camelot, 'La tradition latine sur la Procession du Saint-Esprit "a Filio" ou "ab Utroque" ', *Russie et Chrétienté* (1950), 179–192; P. Smulders, 'L'Esprit Saint chez les Pères', *Dictionnaire de Spiritualité*, IV, cols 1272–1283.

1

AUGUSTINE

Here we shall consider, although not exclusively, Augustine's *De Trinitate*, which he began in 399 and handed over to the public in 419.[1] He was not the first Christian in the West to write about the Trinity and the Holy Spirit. He knew the writings of Tertullian and had read the treatise on the Trinity by Hilary of Poitiers (†366),which he quotes. There can also be no doubt that he knew Marius Victorinus, who was greatly influenced by Plotinus (see Volume I, p. 77). He had heard Ambrose of Milan and had probably read his *De Spiritu Sancto* (*c*. 381), which was in many places inspired by Basil the Great and literally by Didymus the Blind and which transfers into Latin thought an exegesis of several passages in the Bible originally made by the Greek Fathers. As far as the latter are concerned, Augustine knew or may have known, in translation, Origen's *De principiis* and Didymus' *De Spiritu Sancto* and the references that he makes to their vocabulary show that he must have had access to the writings of Basil the Great and, at a relatively late period, to those of Gregory Nazianzen, although it is impossible to say exactly to what extent.[2]

Augustine's *De Trinitate* is less dominated than the writings of Athanasius and the Cappadocians by immediate polemics against the fourth-century heretics, although his adversaries were the same as theirs—the Arians and Eunomius. Arianism still had its followers and was at times favoured by those in authority. Augustine had it consciously in mind.[3] He also attacked Sabellius, who affirmed unity in the deity to such a degree that he went so far as to obscure the distinction between the hypostases, whereas the Arians made a distinction between the Word and the Spirit in such a way as to deny their consubstantiality with 'God'. The essential problem was to combine the identity with the distinction of the Persons. This is just how Augustine expressed it.[4] He declared his intention in these words: 'to undertake, with the help of the Lord and as far as we can ourselves, a justification (*reddere rationem*) of this affirmation: the Trinity is one true God and it is exactly true to say, believe and think that the Father, the Son and the Holy Spirit are of one single and the same substance or essence' (*De Trin.* I, 2, 4). A few lines later, he states more precisely the means that he intends to employ. These are firstly the authority of Scripture—he does this in Books I to IV of *De Trinitate*—and then a rational process of discussion—he does this in Books V to VII.

Augustine was sometimes very prolix, but the words that he uses in this context—*dicatur, credatur, intelligatur*—outline a programme. Like the Greek Fathers, he takes as his point of departure what Scripture says, that is, the texts and the terms employed. Later, Thomas Aquinas was to do the same. To a very great extent, the treatises on the Trinity consist of a search for a way of speaking. Is it possible to say this or that, is it wrong to utter a certain sentence? Then, after making sure of the truth by faith, reasoning continues on the basis of the terms chosen. What is sought is an understanding of what is believed.

The Theology of the Relationships

In his *De Trinitate*, then, Augustine takes biblical texts as his point of departure and shows that they disprove the Arian construction (Books I to IV). Then he goes on to consider the problem of an intellectually valid agreement between unity and diversity (Book V). It is necessary, but at the same time sufficient, to distinguish between absolute and relative terms. The terms 'Father', 'Son' and 'Holy Spirit' distinguish the Persons, and they are 'relative' terms, that is, terms of relationship, expressing an *ad aliquid*. *Relative dicuntur ad invicem*, they affirm the Persons by opposing one to the other. Augustine says what the Greek Fathers so often said—the Son is not the Father and the Father is not the Son, but the Father has never been without the Son; one term implies the other. But this 'relative' or 'relational' diversity can exist and does in fact exist within the same substance or, as Augustine preferred to say, 'essence'.

The absolute terms point, on the other hand, to the one substance that is common to all the Persons. 'Good' and 'all-powerful' are such absolute terms. They apply to each of the Persons without diversifying or multiplying the substance—the Father is God; he is also good and he is all-powerful; he is also Creator. The Son is also all this, and so is the Holy Spirit. This does not, however, make three gods or three creators. The Father, the Son and the Spirit are each one Person, and any person affirms himself for himself: *ad se dicitur (not ad aliud)* (*De Trin.* VII, 11). If, however, I search for how or of what it is made, I find inevitably that it consists of a relational opposition—*relative dicitur*, that is, the Son exists by his relationship with the Father and therefore by a relationship of origin or procession. The Persons of the Trinity are therefore, according to the aspect by which they are considered, both relational and absolute. As I. Chevalier pointed out, 'the substance of the Father comes from his being God, not from his being Father; his property as Father, on the other hand, comes from his being in relationship (*ad Filium*). Hence the identity of substance, despite the plurality of relationships; hence also the reality of the relationships which would not exist without that substance.'[5] Augustine did not know or use the term, but he had the fundamental idea of what Thomas Aquinas later called a 'subsistent relationship'.[6] In the same way, even before Thomas, he also expressed the fact that the Father, the Son and the Holy Spirit were one with regard to each other: *alius*, but *non aliud*; each was a different subject, but not of a different substance.[7] This had already been said by Gregory Nazianzen.[8]

It is worth noting in this context that the Greek Fathers recognized the distinction between the hypostases in terms of their relationships, or rather their characterization by correlative terms. In his treatise against Eunomius, for example, Basil accused the latter of translating the relative diversity between the Father and the Son into a diversity of substance.[9] Gregory of Nyssa followed his brother Basil in his defence of the unity of nature and repeated what Basil had said, namely that the words 'Father' and 'Son' are relative terms.[10] In the same way, Gregory Nazianzen stated that 'Father' and 'Son' were names not only of a relationship, but also of a relationship of origin.[11] Augustine only knew of this after 417. To the Cappadocian Fathers, we can also add Maximus the Confessor (†662): 'The name "Father" is neither a name of essence nor a name of energy. It is a name of a relationship and it tells us how the Father is with regard to the Son and how the Son is with regard to the Father.'[12]

In his study of the possible dependence of Augustine on the Greek Fathers, in which he stressed their real agreement in this whole question of relationships,[13] I. Chevalier also noticed certain important differences and commented on them:

The two terms (*schēsis, oikeiōsis*) which Basil uses to characterize the divine begetting do not represent for him the same hierarchy of ideas that they do for Augustine and the Scholastic theologians. For the Greek doctor, what was in question was the community of nature which exists between a father and a son as a result of begetting. It is this relationship of origin as the only cause of difference between the Father and the Son which, far from destroying their identity, confirms it and explains it. But Basil does not mean to say that, because the unity and identity of the essence of God are presupposed, the immanent begetting can only result in a distinction of relationships. His point of departure is the relationship established by this begetting, and from this he ends up by way of the relationship with the community of nature, whereas Thomas Aquinas, for example, takes the simplicity of God as his point of departure and goes on from that to purely relative terms of procession. This last point of view is also that of Augustine. Although we must take care not to exaggerate it, and above all not to build it up into a system characteristic of 'the Latin mind', we cannot ignore this difference. The part played by the idea of relationship is somewhat changed in it. Basil notes these relationships, but, as it were, granted their divine subjects and above all their source, the begetting *ex ipsa natura* and the procession, he deduces from these the unity of the divine essence. Augustine notes the divine identity and then, since the processions have been revealed, deduces from these the relationships. What we have, then, are the same truths seen from different points of view. There is, surely, nothing surprising in this!

In the case of the Greeks, however, the result is that the idea of relationship is presented in a more realistic and, it could be said, more vital form. It is important to emphasize that the *schēsis* is not seen from a static point of view, that is, as a constitutive principle of the divine hypostasis. This idea is seen rather as a means of expressing the mystery of the divine life, those immanent processions from the one and the return to that one-principle from which those modes of subsistence which are the divine Persons, whose whole reason for existing is to be directed towards each other and who safeguard the unity of the divine essence, eternally come and circulate within each other. These two points of view still come to the same conclusion, namely that the three divine hypostases are distinguished by their properties and the latter are distinguished by differences in origin, which are oppositions of relationship within an essential identity. 'Between the three, everything is identical, apart from the relationship of origin.'[14]

Olivier du Roy has expressed the difference between Augustine and the Greeks in an even more radical way.[15] T. de Régnon tirelessly repeated his own argument, namely that, whereas the Greeks took the Persons as their first data and then showed that they were consubstantial in their unity of nature on the basis of the 'monarchy' of the Father, Augustine and the Latin Fathers took the unity and unicity of 'God' as their starting-point and from that unity of the sovereign divine Being went on to affirm the plurality of the Persons. It cannot be denied that there is an element of truth in what de Régnon maintained, but close examination reveals the emptiness of his formula that the Greeks saw the Persons *in recto* and the unity of the divine essence *in obliquo*, whereas the Latins considered the unity *in recto* and the Persons *in obliquo*. Du Roy does not deny the validity of de Régnon's insight, but points to another origin of difference in the case of Augustine, who undoubtedly had a powerful influence on later Latin theology. Augustine discovered the Trinity in the works of the Neo-Platonists before he discovered the incarnation in the letters of Paul. His approach was not purely theoretical. It was rather the beginning of a very deep existential conversion. As a priest and bishop, dedicated to meditating on the Scriptures and to studying and analysing them with the aim of defending the Christian faith, Augustine kept at heart to his original direction, which differed from that of the Greek Fathers, who spoke of a Tri-unity connected with its economic revelation.[16] Augustine, on the other hand, was fundamentally concerned with a *Deus-Trinitas* thought of in a static manner, independently of the incarnation and the economy of salvation. Du Roy therefore says: 'Augustine's special contribution to Western theology consists of this representation of God who is one in his essence and who deploys the Trinity of his inner relationships in the knowledge and love of himself. This was the logical conclusion of a Neo-Platonism applied to a deep reflection about faith before being converted.'[17]

It is quite certain that Arianism made Christian thinkers apply their minds to a different set of considerations. Before Arianism emerged, the Trinity was seen in its revelation and its economic commitment, at the risk of inclining towards subordinationism. Arianism and Nicaea turned their thoughts towards the unity and consubstantiality of the three Persons. In the case of Augustine, this tendency, which was justified by the persistent influence of Arianism, may have been inherited from and reinforced by his Neo-Platonic past and his own deeper existential approach. Even his reflection about the 'missions' of the Word and the Spirit did not improve the chances that he might consider the economy.[18] He was somewhat hampered by the question of theophanies, which the Arians used very effectively, and he therefore turned to the visible missions of the Word and the Spirit and then to the invisible missions, describing them theologically, on the one hand as a value of manifestation and knowledge and, on the other, by means of their connection with the processions. Even Hilary and Ambrose, whose works Augustine had read, went back from the temporal to the eternal procession. Augustine said: 'Sends, the One who begets; sent is the One who is begotten' (De Trin. IV, 20, 28). The missions reveal a divine Person in his eternal origin. According to Augustine, 'As for the Son to be born is to be from the Father, so for the Son to be sent is to be known in his origin from the Father. In the same way, as for the Holy Spirit to be the gift of God is to proceed from the Father, so to be sent is to be known in his procession from the Father. What is more, we cannot deny that the Spirit also proceeds from the Son. . . . I cannot see what he could otherwise have meant when, breathing on the faces of the disciples, the Lord declared: "Receive the Holy Spirit" (Jn 20:20).'[19]

Augustine's thoughts about the theophanies in the first place and then about the divine missions were guided on the one hand by the affirmation of the unity and consubstantiality of God and, on the other, by his related desire to deepen and intensify the image of the Deus-Trinitas in the souls of believers. The soul is more God's image when, because of the knowledge that the Word communicates to it and the love that the Spirit places in it, it makes present the resemblance to the one of whom it is the image. The missions make possible an increase in faith and love.[20]

This theory of the relationships which make the Persons different within the substance or essence without dividing the latter is simple, grand and satisfactory. Nonetheless, it does involve a difficulty in characterizing the Holy Spirit. 'Father' and 'Son' are correlative, terms which comprise an opposition in a reciprocal relationship. If, however, the Spirit is the Spirit of the Father and the Son, as Scripture testifies, how does he affirm two Persons by a reciprocal relational opposition? What correlative term has the Spirit from which he proceeds and which points to a hypostasis? From Photius onwards, the Orthodox have continued to stress this difficulty in opposition to the Filioque. But on this view, which is based exclusively on the terms of

Jn 15:26, the theory of relationships does not fit easily, since, if the Spirit is in a relationship of procession only with the Father, he must be his Son. How, in that case, can he be distinguished from the monogenous one?[21]

Augustine was aware of this difficulty. In his reply to it, he made use of his theology of the Holy Spirit in which he attributed the personal title of Gift to the latter. I shall set out this theology briefly here, since it seems to me to be true and very profound. Augustine notes that 'Spirit' (holy Spirit) can be applied either to the Father or to the Son or can point to the third Person. He has this to say about the third Person:

> There is no need for anxiety (after this remark) about the absence, it would seem, of a term that corresponds to him and points to his correlative. We speak of the servant of the master or of the master of the servant, of the son of the father or of the father of the son, since these terms are correlative, but here we cannot speak in that way. We speak of the Holy Spirit of the Father, but we do not speak in the reverse sense of the Father of the Holy Spirit; if we did, the Holy Spirit would be taken to be his son. In the same way, we speak of the Holy Spirit of the Son, but not of the Son of the Holy Spirit, since, in that case, the Holy Spirit would be seen as his father.
>
> In many relatives, it is not possible to find a term that expresses the reciprocal connection between the relative realities. For example, is there a term that is more manifestly relative than 'pledge' (*pignus*)?[22] A pledge clearly refers to the thing of which it is the pledge[23] and a pledge is always a pledge of something. If we speak of the pledge or guarantee of the Father and the Son (2 Cor 5:5; Eph 1:14), can we speak in the reverse sense of the Father and the Son of the pledge? At least, when we speak of the gift of the Father and the Son, we obviously cannot speak of the Father and the Son of the gift. In order to have a reciprocal correspondence in this case, we must speak of the gift of the giver or the giver of the gift. In this latter case, then, it has proved possible to find a term that is in use, in the other case, not.[24]

It is true that the Father and the Son are not brought together in Scripture under the same title of 'giver', but Scripture does speak of the mission or sending of the Spirit by the Father and by the Son. It is on that basis that it is possible to call the Spirit 'Gift'—Augustine always quotes Acts 8:20, also Rom 5:5 and Jn 4:7—and both the Father and the Son 'givers'. It is therefore on the basis of the economy that Augustine constructs his theology of the eternal procession of the Spirit from the Father and the Son (see note 19), that is, not as 'Father' and as 'Son,' but as 'giver'. I have already said that I think that this theology is very profound. It is also Christian. But it does not, of course, satisfy the Orthodox, who have a different understanding of the Trinity and its homogeneity.

The Filioque

This teaching did not originate with Augustine. It had already been expounded in one form or another by Tertullian, Hilary, Marius Victorinus and Ambrose. Augustine deals with this question only in his *De Trinitate*.

We have to bear in mind that he borrowed a great deal from his commentary on St John and that it is difficult to date with certainty the composition of any particular book in his great work. To begin with, he does no more than simply affirm that the Spirit is the Spirit of the Father and the Son (*De Trin*. I, 4, 7; 5, 8; 8, 18). His point of departure is the fact that the Spirit is said to be both Spirit of the Father (Mt 10:28; Jn 15:26) and Spirit of the Son (Gal 4:6; Jn 14:26; 20:22; Lk 6:19; cf. Rom 8:15). The Spirit, then, is common to both. Thus, if the Spirit is said by Scripture to proceed from the Father (Jn 15:26), it cannot be denied that he also proceeds from the Son (*De Trin*. IV, 20, 29; V, 11, 12; 14, 15). The Son, however, has this faculty of being the co-principle of the Spirit entirely from the Father. Augustine stresses this fact very forcibly, either by using his term *principaliter*[25] or in formulae which could be taken to mean *a Patre solo*.[26] Whichever way he chooses, it is the equivalent of a *per Filium*.

The Spirit, then, is from the Father and the Son. Augustine reflects about this datum, often within the context of his ordinary preoccupations, such as the need to answer certain questions, to reply to the Donatists, or to throw light on the spiritual life of believers and their life in the Church. He says, for example: 'Scripture enables us to know in the Father the principle, *auctoritas*, in the Son being begotten and born, *nativitas*, and in the Spirit the union of the Father and the Son, *Patris Filiique communitas*. . . . The society of the unity of the Church of God, outside of which there is no remission of sins, is in a sense the work of the Holy Spirit, with, of course, the co-operation of the Father and the Son, because the Holy Spirit himself is in a sense the society of the Father and Son. The Father is not possessed in common as Father by the Son and the Holy Spirit, because he is not the Father of the two. The Son is not possessed in common as Son by the Father and the Holy Spirit, because he is not the Son of the two. But the Holy Spirit is possessed in common by the Father and the Son, because he is the one Spirit of the two.'[27]

Augustine was naturally loving and always gave priority to charity. As a pastor and teacher living in the midst of Donatists, he elaborated an ecclesiology at two levels, that of the *sacramentum* and that of *unitas-charitas-Columba*, in which the Spirit was the principle of life, unity and effectiveness to save. Even in his early writings, he called the Spirit *charitas*.[28] This idea emerges from the first evidence of his interest in a theology of the Holy Spirit. It can be found, for example, in his preaching and his commentaries on Scripture.[29] It is clearly present in *De Trin*. VI, 5, 7. Augustine concludes: 'They are three, the one loving the one who has his being from him, the other loving the one from whom he has his being, and that love itself'.

He also showed that, in God, that *charitas* is substantial, because 'God *is* charity' (1 Jn 4:16). This gives rise to a question: the Father is charity, the Son is also charity, and the *Deus-Trinitas* is also charity. Since it is substantial, then, how is it peculiar to the Spirit and characteristic of his Person? This question is not answered until the last book of the treatise (XV, 17, 27ff.). The answer is first of all related to the economy—it is the Spirit who gives us charity (XV, 17, 31 to 19, 35)—and then the answer is given at the intra-divine level (XV, 19, 36ff.), the Spirit being the substantial communion of the Father and the Son, *communio amborum*, because *communis ambobus*. Being common to the Father and the Son, he receives as his own the names that are common to both of them (XV, 19, 37).

Before concluding his treatise on the Trinity with a humble prayer, Augustine replies to the following difficulty: 'If the Holy Spirit proceeds from the Father and the Son, why does the Son say: the Spirit proceeds from the Father (Jn 15:26)?' In answering this question, he repeats the reply that he had already given a little earlier in his commentary *In Ioan. ev.* XCIX, 8–9, namely that the Father communicates to the Son all that he is, apart from his being Father. Thus, all that the Son has comes from the Father and is from the Father. This reminds us inevitably of the *principaliter* discussed above. Just as he said: 'My teaching is not mine, but his who sent me' (Jn 7:16), when he said 'the Spirit proceeds from the Father' the Son did not mean: 'He does not proceed from me'. There are therefore good reasons to believe that the Spirit also proceeds from the Son. It is clear, however, that the Orthodox could not declare themselves satisfied with this.

A Note on Augustine's Theology of the Trinity and the Eastern Tradition

In anticipation of a conclusion which I shall be in a better position to maintain at the end, when the situation has been fully examined, I can say now that what we have here are two theological constructions of the same mystery, each of which has an inner consistency, but a different point of departure.

Augustine's aim was to guarantee the perfect consubstantiality of the three Persons. He made sure of this by making the distinction between them consist in the relationship which opposes them correlatively to each other and which is a relationship of procession. The relationship between the Father and the Son does not give rise to any questions—it is clear, and our own experience provides a striking analogy. The Spirit is distinguished relationally from the two in the unity of the divine essence only by proceeding from the two as their common Spirit. If he did not proceed from the Son, he would not be distinguished from him by that relationship which safeguards the divine equality and consubstantiality. As H. B. Swete, who, as a historian, was not disposed to speculate, said: 'the Western *Filioque*, as Augustine states it, is almost a necessary inference from the Homoousion'.[30]

An initial difference, not to say difficulty, comes from the vocabulary. The same Latin verb, *procedere*—although Augustine also says *exire* (*De Trin.* V, 14, 15)—is used to translate the *proeimi* or the *erchomai* of Jn 8:42 and the *ekporeuomai* of Jn 15:26, although the Greeks make a distinction between these terms in that the second, which is reserved for the 'procession' of the Holy Spirit, refers to the Father as the original source. From the time of Gregory Nazianzen—who did not give the matter any polemical emphasis—the Greeks have on many occasions remarked that the Latin lacks the subtlety of the Greek. In theological Latin, the word 'procession', means the fact of coming from another, in the more general sense. It therefore includes the sense of the Greek *ekporeusis*, but does not express the shade of meaning given to this word as a procession from an original and absolute principle.

The Greeks thought of and justified consubstantiality in terms of the monarchy of the Father,[31] the *perichōrēsis* and the Trinitarian character of all the relationships. In itself, the monarchy of the Father is not opposed to the Spirit's also deriving from the Son. This is clear from the various images that we have previously considered: the images of the arm, the hand and the finger (Didymus), the root, the branch and the fruit (John Damascene) and the source, the river and the water, as well as others. All these images illustrate a theology of the procession of the Spirit from the Father through the Son. It has to be recognized, however, that the Latin vocabulary fails to express the value that the Greeks rightly place on the *ekporeuetai* of Jn 15:26. Having said that, we can also say with Pusey in the nineteenth century that we in the West also condemn the heresy for which we have been criticized since the time of Photius, because the real meaning of the *Filioque* is quite different.

As we have already seen, the Greek Fathers were familiar with the category 'relationship'. This applies particularly to Gregory the Theologian. The concept, however, plays only an occasional part in their writings,[32] whereas, in the work of Augustine and Thomas Aquinas, it helps to justify the diversity of the hypostases in the unity of substance. The Greeks appeal to the particular character of each hypostasis as different from that of another.[33] They do this within a theological climate that is more apophatic than that of the Latins, although these too do not lack the apophatic sense.[34]

The idea of the Holy Spirit as communion between the Father and the Son is exceptional in the East. In the patristic period, it is only to be found in the writings of Epiphanius of Salamis.[35] Gregory Palamas was, however, also familiar with it and said, for example: 'The Spirit of the Word is like a love (*erōs*) of the Father for the mysteriously begotten Word, and it is the same love that the beloved Word and Son of the Father has for the one who begot him. That love comes from the Father at the same time as it is with the Son and it naturally rests on the Son.'[36] We should not therefore be surprised to find Sergey Bulgakov writing in this century: 'if God, in the Holy Trinity, is Love, then the Holy Spirit is Love of that love'.[37] No more surprising is the profound comment of Paul Evdokimov on the Person in the centre of the Andrei Rublev's wonderful icon; the Holy Spirit, he says, 'is in the middle of the Father and the Son. He is the one who brings about the communion between the two. He is the communion, the love between the Father and the Son. That is clearly shown by the remarkable fact that the movement comes from him. It is in his breath that the Father moves into the Son, that the Son receives his Father and that the word resounds.'[38]

These pieces of evidence are not sufficient, of course, to form a theological tradition, but they do create a link and point to an openness. 'The walls of separation do not reach as high as heaven!'

The Images of the Trinity[39]

Augustine continued, in Books VIII to XV of his *De Trinitate*, to look for an understanding of what Christians believed and he did this on the basis of the images of the Triad that could be found in the human spirit and its activity. It was, for him, certainly not a question of deducing a Trinity of Persons philosophically from the structure of man's spirit, as Hegel, Günther and perhaps also Gioberti have claimed to do. For Augustine, it was a search in faith, one which becomes deeper by an existential conversion to be conformed once again to the image of God by thinking of him and loving him. (The stages are: *credere Deo, credere Deum, credere in Deum, credendo in Deum ire*.) Augustine therefore analysed a series of triads, moving from more external ones to more intimate ones and from simple psychological analysis to an expression of supernatural experience. The following summary has been provided by Fulbert Cayré (*Bibl. August.* 16, p. 587):

1. *amans, amatus, amor* (*De Trin.* VIII, 10, 14; cf. IX, 2, 2);
2. *mens, notitia, amor* (IX, 3, 3);
3. *memoria, intelligentia, voluntas* (X, 11, 7);
4. *res (visa), visio (exterior), intentio* (XI, 2, 2);
5. *memoria (sensibilis), visio (interior), volitio* (XI, 3, 6–9);
6. *memoria (intellectus), scientia, voluntas* (XII, 15, 25);
7. *scientia (fidei), cogitatio, amor* (XIII, 20, 26);
8. *memoria Dei, intelligentia Dei, amor Dei* (XIV, 12, 15).

A little later, Cayré observes, Augustine wrote his *De Civitate Dei* and, in Book XI, 24–28 of this work there are six similar triads.[40] Each time and in related terms, Augustine finds in the structure of the soul (see A. Gardeil, note 39 below) and in the way in which it is supernaturally actualized an image of the Holy Triad: three in the unity of the same substance; one stable consciousness of self, one act of knowledge and one movement of love. To make God, the Christian God, present in these three aspects is to experience a conversion and restore the image.[41] It is also being able to perceive how the manifestations of the Persons in the economy and the three whom we confess in the baptismal formula are one inseparable Trinity.[42] In this way, the personalization and the consubstantial unity of the *Deus-Trinitas* are united.

In this case too, the way followed by Augustine has hardly any parallel in the East, apart from the theme of man's re-formation in the image and likeness of God.[43] In this case too, however, there is once again a parallel in the East in the work of Gregory Palamas, who drew attention to the analogy of the Holy Triad in the soul, with the *nous*, the *logos* and the *erōs*.[44] There can be little doubt that Gregory had read Maximus Planudes' translation of Augustine.

Augustine was very conscious of the distance separating the image from the model. Both his *Sermo* 52 and Book XV of his *De Trinitate* end with his expressing his feeling of inadequacy and with an appeal to prayer, thanks to which God may himself give man an experience and a knowledge of his mystery. Again and again Augustine expresses his awareness of the fact that the similitudes are dissimilar.[45]

In the same Book XV, Augustine looks back at what he has already written and expresses the feeling that he has spoken more about the Father and the Word than about the Holy Spirit. He therefore resolves to devote several chapters (17–20 and 26–27) to the latter. I too have the feeling that I have discussed Augustine's Trinitarian theology more than his pneumatology. One is, of course, contained within the other. As there are so many excellent texts, several of which I have quoted in Volume II of this work, I shall only consider two groups.

A.-M. La Bonnardière noted that 'from 387 to 429, Augustine quoted at least 201 times the verse of St Paul: "God's love has been poured into our hearts through the Holy Spirit which has been given to us" (Rom 5:5). His quotations of this verse were relatively rare until 411 (51 in all), but they became very frequent in the decade 411–421, which was the period in which he was engaged in controversy with the Pelagians over the question of grace, and they continued afterwards in his works of controversy with Julian of Eclanum.'[46] In fact the criticism which the Bishop of Hippo made of the Bishop of Eclanum was as follows: 'You would like to make the grace of Christ consist in his example and not in his life. You say that man is made righteous by imitating him, and not by the help of the Holy Spirit who leads him to imitate him, that Spirit whom he has poured out so abundantly on his own.'[47] The Spirit is the principle of all life according to the grace that Augustine continued throughout his Christian life to preach, discuss and further.

For the edification of his people and in his struggle against the Donatists, Augustine developed and defined more precisely the part played by the Spirit in the Church. There are dozens of texts to be found in his works, each one more magnificent than the last. There are, for example, those in which he shows how the Spirit brings about in the mystical Body of Christ what the soul brings about in our body. S. Tromp listed 83 of these texts, either as extracts or as references.[48] There is also the ecclesiology that Augustine developed in his controversy with the Donatists at two levels, that of the *sacramentum*, that is, the signs and institutions that the Donatists had in common with the Catholics, and that of the *res*, that is, the spiritual fruit that saves, which the Donatists did not have, the principle of which is the Holy Spirit.[49] The Spirit, for Augustine, was not only the principle of unity. He was also the principle of that catholicity which consists of the variety of gifts in the communion of the same Body.[50]

NOTES

1. See the *Œuvres de S. Augustin*, 15: *La Trinité*, Fr. tr. M. Mellet and T. Camelot, with an introduction by E. Hendrikx; 16, Fr. tr. P. Agaësse, with notes by J. Moingt (Paris, 1955); a full bibliography of works published up to that date will be found in these volumes, which give column references to *PL* 42. Apart from the works listed in note 29 on Volume I, p. 83, and articles mentioned below, see O. du Roy, *L'intelligence de la foi en la Trinité selon S. Augustin. Genèse de sa théologie trinitaire jusqu'en 391* (Paris, 1966); J. Verhees, 'Die Bedeutung des Geistes im Leben des Menschen nach Augustinus frühester Pneumatologie', *Zeitschrift für Kirchengeschichte*, 88 (1977), 161–189. I consider principally, but not exclusively, the *De Trinitate* in this section of my book. Arranged in terms and themes, a mass of other Augustinian texts dealing with the Holy Spirit will be found in the articles of F. Cavallera and these, however material they are, or rather, precisely because they are material, can be of great use in this respect: 'La doctrine de S. Augustin sur l'Esprit Saint à propos du "De Trinitate" ', *RTAM*, 2 (1930), 365–387; 3 (1931), 5–19.
2. I. Chevalier has concluded from a careful study: 'It is certain that Augustine read Athanasius', Basil's and Gregory Nazianzen's works on the Trinity as well as Epiphanius' *Recapitulation*, but it is probable, or simply possible, that he also knew the latter's *Panarion* and *Ancoratus* and the two works on the Trinity by Didymus the Blind': *S. Augustin et la pensée grecque. Les relations trinitaires* (Fribourg, 1940), p. 160.
3. *De Trin.* V, 3, 4; 6, 7; VI, 1, 1; see also *Contra sermonem arianorum* (418–419); *Collatio cum Maximino* and *Contra Maximinum*.
4. *In Ioan. ev.* 39; *De Civ. Dei* XI, 10; *De Trin.* I, 2, 4; 3, 5; 5, 8; VI, 6, 8; VIII, proem.; XV, 3, 5; *Enarr. in Ps.* 68; *Ep.* 170, 238.
5. I. Chevalier, *op. cit.* (note 2), p. 63, commenting on the following text, which resists translation: 'Quidquid est Pater quod Deus est, hoc Filius, hoc Spiritus Sanctus. Cum autem Pater est, non illud est quod est, Pater enim non ad se, sed ad Filium dicitur: ad se autem Deus dicitur. Itaque eo quod Deus est, hoc ipso substantia est . . . secundum substantiam tibi dixi hoc esse Filium quod Pater est, non secundum id quod ad aliud dicitur' (*Enarr. in Ps.* 68, 5; *PL* 36, 845): 'All that the Father is in that he is God, the Son is, the Holy Spirit is. But when one takes him as Father, he is not what he is thus, but he is taken in his relationship to the Son. It is in his being in itself that he is called God. Thus, from the fact that he is God, he is substance . . . and it is according to the substance that I have said that the Son is what the Father is, not according to what he is described in relationship to another (another thing).'
6. Thomas Aquinas, *De Pot.* q. 9, a. 1 and 2; *ST* Ia, q. 29, a. 4. It is clearly because of his Thomist training that I. Chevalier, *op. cit.*, p. 76, spoke of 'a double character of relationship—a character of inhering in, expressing the need of a subject in order to exist at all, and a character that is specific (*ad*), expressing an entering into a relationship with another'. But this is certainly Augustine's idea.

7. Augustine, *De anima et eius origine*, II, 5 (*PL* 44, 509); see the references in I. Chevalier, *op. cit.* (note 2), p. 62.
8. Gregory Nazianzen, *Orat.* 31 (*PG* 36, 141ff.); the Son is not the Father, but he is *what* the Father *is*. The Holy Spirit is not the Son, but he is *what* the Son *is*.
9. Basil, *PG* 29, 588C–589A; Fr. tr. in I. Chevalier, *op. cit.* (note 2), p. 131.
10. See Gregory of Nyssa, *Quod non sint tres dii* (*PG* 45, 133C) and other references in I. Chevalier, *op. cit.*, p. 103; see also T. de Régnon, *Etudes de théologie positive sur la Sainte Trinité*, I (Paris, 1892), pp. 77–78.
11. See Gregory Nazianzen, *Orat.* 29 (*PG* 36, 96); 31 (*PG* 36, 140C and 141C); I. Chevalier, *op. cit.*, pp. 146–147; de Régnon, *op. cit.*, I, pp. 76–77.
12. Maximus, *Ambigua* 26 (*PG* 91, 1265C-D).
13. Chevalier goes so far as to say, *op. cit.* (note 2), p. 174: 'The famous axiom "In God all is one, except where there is an opposition of relationship" is Greek as much as Latin in all its parts. Although it is not stated in exactly the same form and although it does not play precisely the same part as it does in Augustine, it is familiar to both. The Greek doctors always taught that the persons are distinguished by their properties, but that those properties should be seen as mutual relationships. They rejected as absurd the fact that they might be accidents. It is no more than a single step from this to the synthesis, subsistent relationship, but they did not make that step.'
14. Gregory Nazianzen, *Orat.* 34 (*PG* 36, 253A); 20 (*PG* 35, 1073A); 31 (*PG* 36, 165B); 41 (*PG* 36, 441C); quoted in I. Chevalier, *op. cit.*, pp. 168–169.
15. O. du Roy, in his difficult, but very suggestive thesis, *op. cit.* (note 1).
16. O. du Roy adopted an attitude that was opposite to that of A. Malet in *Personne et Amour dans la théologie trinitaire de S. Thomas d'Aquin* (Paris, 1956); Malet's claims are taken up by M.-J. Le Guillou in *Istina*, 17 (1972), 457–464, and *Le Mystère du Père* (Paris, 1973). The Cappadocians apparently abandoned the ante-Nicene view of the economy, according to Le Guillou, and taught a primacy of essence. G. Lafont, *Peut-on connaître Dieu en Jésus-Christ?* (Paris, 1969), pp. 67ff., and L. Scheffczyk, *Mysterium Salutis*, V (Fr. tr.; Paris, 1970), pp. 252, 261, have a similar attitude.
17. O. du Roy, *op. cit.* (note 1), p. 458.
18. Augustine discusses the 'missions' in *De Trin.* II, 5, 7–10; IV, 18, 24 to 20, 29; see also I, 22, 25; II, 7, 12–13; 12, 22; III, proem. 3 and 1, 4. See also J.-L. Maier's monograph, *Les Missions divines selon S. Augustin* (*Paradosis*, XVI) (Fribourg, 1960).
19. *De Trin.* IV, 20, 29. This link between the temporal mission and the eternal procession of the Spirit, with reference to the text of Jn 20:22, can also be found in *De Trin.* XV, 26, 45; *De Gen. ad litt.* 10, 5; *De Civ. Dei*, XIII, 24; *In Ioan. ev.* XCIX, 7 and CXXI, 4; *Contra Maxim.* II, 14, 1; see Cavallera, *op. cit.* (note 1) (1931), 17; Maier, *op. cit.* (note 18), p. 152. Only the Father is not sent 'quoniam solus non habet auctorem a quo genitus sit vel a quo procedat': *Contra serm. arian.* 4, 4 (*PL* 42, 686).
20. For faith, *De Trin.* IV, 20, 28; for charity, *In Ioan. ev.* LXXIV, 3.
21. In the colloquium that took place in 1950 between Orthodox and Catholic Christians, S. Verkhovsky reaffirmed that 'the Son and the Spirit as hypostases coming from the Father are sufficiently distinguished, so that there is no need to affirm an opposition of relationship between them'. H. Dondaine's response to this was: 'The Son is distinguished from the Father because he is a hypostasis coming from the Father. In the same way, the Holy Spirit is distinguished from the Father. How does that distinguish the Son from the Holy Spirit?': see *Russie et Chrétienté* (1950), 223.
22. 'Pledge' or 'guarantee' is one of the names for the Holy Spirit in the New Testament: 'You ... were sealed with the promised Holy Spirit, which is the guarantee (*arrabōn*) of our inheritance' (Eph 1:14). In 2 Cor 1:22 and 5:5, *arrabōn tou Pneumatos*, the genitive is a genitive of apposition: see H. Behm, '*arrabōn*', *TDNT*, I, p. 475; cf. Rom 8:23, *aparchē tou Pneumatos*. Augustine's texts on *pignus* have been gathered together by F. Cavallera, *op. cit.* (note 1) (1930), 370.

23. 'Ad id quippe refertur cuius est pignus'; is it not possible and even necessary to translate this as 'a pledge refers to that from which it comes as a pledge (to the being of which it is the pledge)'? Otherwise the sentence says the same thing twice.

24. *De Trin*. V, 12, 13. I. Chevalier said, for example (and I give in brackets what he placed in notes): 'By the character of his procession, which is holiness, love or gift, the Holy Spirit on the one hand ensures the unity of spirit of the Father and the Son and, on the other hand, the same Holy Spirit is distinguished from each of them (*De Trin*. VI, 5, 7; XV, 17–20). If there is a relative meaning, it is that he takes his origin from the Father and the Son. He proceeds as a Gift and the latter are a single Giver. The Giver and the Gift are, then, essentially relative (V, 14, 15; 15, 16; 16, 17). That Gift and that giving are, like the Giver, eternal (V, 15, 16; 16, 17). The relationships that result from the second procession are therefore no more accidents than the relationships of the Son and the Father': *op. cit.* (note 2), pp. 79 and 81.

25. *De Trin*. XV, 17, 29 and 26, 47; *Sermo* 71, 26 (*PL* 38, 459); see the crit. ed. in *RBén*, 75 (1965), 94. The term *principaliter* can be found in Tertullian, *Adv. Prax*. 3. The following is the first of these texts: 'God the Father, the only one from whom the Word is begotten and from whom the Holy Spirit proceeds as from his original principle (*principaliter*). I say "as from his original principle", because it is proven that the Holy Spirit also proceeds from the Son. But it is also the Father who gives him'; cf. *De Trin*. IV, 20, 29: 'totius divinitatis, vel, si melius dicitur, deitatis, principium est Pater'; *De vera rel*. 31, 58: '(Filius) non de seipso est, sed primo summoque principio, qui Pater dicitur: ex quo omnis paternitas' (*PL* 34, 148).

26. Apart from the text quoted in the preceding note, it is also possible to cite from *De fid. et symb*. IX, 19 (in 393): 'nulli debere sed Patri ex quo omnia, ne duo constituamus principia sine principio'; *Contra Maxim*. II, 14 (428): 'cum de illo (Spiritus) Filius loqueretur ait "de Patre procedit", quoniam Pater processionis eius est auctor qui talem Filium genuit et gignendo ei dedit ut etiam de ipso procederet Spiritus Sanctus'.

27. *Sermo* 71, 18 and 33 (*PL* 38, 454 and 463–464); crit. ed. P. Verbraken, *RBén*, 75 (1965), 82 and 102. Augustine worked at this text intensely, because he was treating in it the *difficillima quaestio* of blasphemy against the Holy Spirit; it was written about 417.

28. *De quant. anim*. 34, 77 (388 A.D.): 'in quo omnia, id est incommutabile principium, incommutabilem sapientiam, incommutabilem charitatem, unum Deum verum' (*PL* 32, 1077); *De mus*. VI, 17, 56 (389); 'qua inter se unum et de uno unum charissima, ut ita dicam, charitate junguntur' (*PL* 32, 1191); *De fid. et symb*. IX, 19–20 (393), where Augustine reported the opinion of those (Marius Victorinus) for whom the Spirit was the Deity, or the charity that was common to the Father and the Son. Valuable in this context is the rather complicated, but very rich study written by J.-B (= O.) du Roy, 'L'expérience de l'amour et l'intelligence de la foi trinitaire selon S. Augustin', *Recherches Augustiniennes* II: *Hommage au R.P. Fulbert Cayré* (Paris, 1962), pp. 415–445.

29. See the reference and texts quoted in F. Cavallera, *op. cit.* (note 1) (1930), 382 ff.

30. H. B. Swete, *The Holy Spirit in the Ancient Church* (London, 1912), p. 353.

31. See Gregory Nazianzen, *Orat*. 42, 15 (*PG* 36, 476).

32. This was observed by W. Ullmann in 'Das Filioque als Problem ökumenischer Theologie', *Kerygma und Dogma*, 16 (1970), 58–76, especially 64; the article as a whole is disappointing in view of what the title suggests.

33. See Gregory Nazianzen, *Orat*. 25 (*PG* 35, 1221): what is peculiar to the Father is that he cannot be born, to the Son his being begotten, and to the Spirit his procession (*ekporeusis*); Gregory of Nyssa, *Contra Eunom*. I, 22 (*PG* 45, 355ff.): 'In his uncreated nature, the Holy Spirit is united with the Father and the Son and is, on the other hand, distinguished from them by the marks that are peculiar to him (*tois idiois gnōrismasin*). His most characteristic mark is that he is nothing of what is rightly thought peculiar to the Father and the Son—he is neither unbegotten nor monogenous, but he is simply what he is. One with the Father in that he is uncreated, he is distinguished from him in that he is not Father. One with the Son, since both are uncreated and derive their substance from the God of all things, he differs

from the Son in that he is not monogenous and has been manifested by the Son'; Leontius of Byzantium (†c. 543), *De sectis*, 1 (*PG* 86, 1196): 'These three Persons differ from one another in no way, except for their properties. . . . The Son and the Spirit differ only in this, that the Son is begotten of the Father and the Spirit proceeds from him. We do not have to look for how the one is begotten and the other proceeds'; Anastasius of Sinai, *Hodēgos* (*PG* 89, 60).

34. V. Lossky has himself pointed to this in the case of Augustine: 'Les éléments de "Théologie négative" dans la pensée de S. Augustin', *Augustinus Magister*, I (Paris, 1945), pp. 575ff.
35. The Holy Spirit is *sundesmos tēs Triados*: see Epiphanius' *Anc.* 7 (*PG* 43, 28B).
36. Gregory Palamas, *Cap.* 36 (*PG* 150, 1144D–1145A).
37. S. Bulgakov, *Le Paraclet* (Paris, 1946), p. 74. Augustine is quoted. The theme is connected with Bulgakov's personal construction.
38. P. Evdokimov, 'L'icône', *VS*, 82 (1956), 24–27, especially 36.
39. M. Schmaus, *Die psychologische Trinitätslehre des heiligen Augustinus* (Münster, 1927); A. Gardeil, *La structure de l'âme et l'expérience mystique* (Paris, 1927); F. Cayré, 'Le mysticisme de la sagesse dans les Confessions et le De Trinitate de S. Augustin', *Année théolog. august.*, 13 (1953), 347–370; G. B. Ladner, 'St. Augustine's Conception of the Reformation of Man in the Image of God', *Augustinus Magister*, II (Paris, 1954), pp. 867–878; P. Verbraken, 'Le sermon LII de S. Augustin sur la Trinité et l'analogie des facultés de l'âme', *RBén*, 74 (1964), 9–35.
40. The last three triads are: 4. *sumus, novimus, diligimus* (*De Civ. Dei* XI, 26 and 27); 5. *essentia, notitia, amor* (XI, 28); 6. *aeternitas, veritas, caritas* (XI, 28). Complete tables either of the most diverse triads or of the Trinitarian images and comparisons in the works of Augustine will be found in the French translation, *Bibl. August.* 15, p. 571 and in O. du Roy, *op. cit.* (note 1), pp. 537–540.
41. G. B. Ladner, *The Idea of Reform. Its Impact on Christian Thought and Action in the Age of the Fathers* (Cambridge, Mass., 1959), pp. 185–203.
42. In *De Trin.* XV, 7, 12; 17, 28; 20, 37, Augustine insists on the fact that each of the three Persons is memory, understanding and love, because they are only one substance. In his *Sermo* 52 (*PL* 38, 354–364; see also P. Verbraken, *op. cit.* (note 39)), Augustine shows that the three Persons reveal themselves *separabiliter* in the economy, while acting *inseparabiliter*. Then, treading on very delicate ground as a teacher, he explains this by the analogy of our soul, our activity and our experience. At the level of the economic revelation, he seems to go beyond simple appropriation (*De Trin.* XV, 21).
43. This is found above all in Gregory of Nyssa; see G. B. Ladner, *op. cit.* (note 41), pp. 96ff.; H. Merki, *Homoiōsis Theō* (Fribourg, 1952).
44. Gregory Palamas, *Cap.* 35–39 (*PG* 150, 1144–1147). See also the *Confession* of Gennadius Scholarios (*c.* 1450): spirit, reason and will. Other approaches to this theme can also be found—in Gregory of Nyssa, for example, who said: 'The one therefore who sees himself sees in himself the object of his desires . . . looking at his own purity, he sees the archetype in the image': *Beatitudes*, 6 (*PG* 44, 1272); Photius: 'God, in his pre-eternal counsel, decreed to place the logos in man so that man would approach in his own structure the enigma of Theology': *Amph.* CCLII.
45. For *similitudo dissimilis*, see *Ep.* 169, 6; *De Trin.* I, 1; V, 8; VIII, 5 and 6; XV, 5; 16; 20; 23 and throughout.
46. A.-M. La Bonnardière, 'Le verset paulinien Rom. V, 5, dans l'œuvre de S. Augustin', *Augustinus Magister*, I (Paris, 1945), pp. 657–665, especially pp. 657 and 658.
47. *Opus imperfect. Contra Julianum* II, 146 (*PL* 45, 1209). In what follows, Rom 5:5 is quoted. The Spirit gives charity: *De Trin.* XV, 18, 32.
48. S. Tromp, *De Spiritu Sancto anima Corporis mystici*. II: *Testimonia selecta e Patribus latinis* (Rome, 1952). See also F. Hofmann, *Der Kirchenbegriff des heiligen Augustinus* (Munich, 1933), pp. 148–173. It is also possible to quote passages from Augustine's *Sermo* 71, for example, 71, 33 (*PL* 38, 463–464); see above, note 27.

49. See my general introduction to Augustine's anti-Donatist treatises, *Bibl. August.*, 28 (Paris, 1963), pp. 109–115. The following text is relevant here: 'Isti autem (donatistae) . . . non sunt desperandi: adhuc enim sunt in corpore. Sed non quaerant Spiritum Sanctum nisi in Christi corpore, cuius habent foris sacramentum, sed rem ipsam non tenent intus, cuius illud est sacramentum. . . . Extra hoc corpus, neminem vivificat Spiritus Sanctus': *Ep.* 185, 50 (*PL* 33, 815).
50. For example, *Sermo* 267, 4 (*PL* 38, 1231); 268, 2 (*PL* 38, 1232–1233); *De Trin.* XV, 19, 34.

Augustine's profound thought and valuable work provided material for the reflection of Christian teachers in the Middle Ages. In the theology of the Trinity, he opened two great ways, each of which was followed further in mediaeval thinking. The first of these took up the analysis of the activities of the spirit, understanding and love, and was followed above all by Anselm and Thomas Aquinas. The second way followed the theme of God-charity and the Spirit as the mutual love between the Father and the Son. This was the way which attracted, with individual differences, Achard and Richard of Saint-Victor, Bonaventure and the Franciscan school.

2

ANSELM (1033 – 1109)

Anselm wrote his *Monologion c.* 1070 as Abbot of Bec. During one of his exiles, he took part in a council held at Bari in 1098 with the bishops of the Greek rite of Apulia, Calabria and Sicily. In 1100, when he was at Canterbury, where he died as Archbishop on 21 April 1109, he finished a treatise *De Processione Spiritus Sancti*. His theology of the third Person of the Trinity, which had an undoubted influence on early and high Scholastic thought, is to be found in these two treatises.[1]

Anselm's point of departure is Augustine's psychological analogies, since it is clear that Augustine was his master,[2] but he dealt with them as a born metaphysician and used arguments which strictly inter-linked and were expressed in precise and sober language, the only beauty of which is its exactness. In the *Monologion*, he declares his intention: to understand, by the use of reason, what he believes. He does this in accordance with a statement made elsewhere: 'I thank you, because what I already believed by your grace I now understand by your illumination, to the point that, if I refused to believe it, my understanding would force me to recognize it'.[3]

Anselm believed that the fact that the spirit, and therefore the *summus spiritus* as well, could produce an act of intellectual understanding and therefore a word—he did not make a distinction between the act and its term[4]—and that, in knowing itself, it could love itself, could be traced back to a nature and a necessity of what the spirit was. It was, in his view, a simple and absolute perfection, like goodness or wisdom. As a result, it was necessary to affirm it in God. In us it was, of course, no more than a likeness of what was perfect in God.[5] This was enough for Anselm to state, as a necessary reason, the existence in the *summus spiritus* or *summa natura* of a memory, an understanding and a love of itself, in which he saw the Father, the Son and the Holy Spirit.

This intellectual understanding or Word is the Son because he comes from the supreme spirit as his image and likeness and therefore *nascendo, sicut proles parentis*.[6] This is the beginning of a plurality within the unity of God. The *parens* and his *proles* are a single supreme spirit, *unus spiritus*, distinguished from each other and made two by the relationship which makes one Father and the other Son: 'Sic sunt oppositi relationibus, ut alter numquam suscipiat proprium alterius; sic sunt concordes natura, ut alter semper teneat essentiam alterius'.[7] Their essence is identical, but they are distinguished in that one essence by the pure relationship of the one who begets and the one who is begotten.

As early as the *Monologion* (chapter 49 onwards), Anselm states that the supreme spirit loves himself because he is memory and understanding of himself; that the Father loves himself, the Son loves himself, and that they love each other (*Mon.* 51). That love is simply what the Father and the Son are, that is, the *summa essentia* (*Mon.* 53). It is a single, unique love (*Mon.* 54). It is not 'son' and it does not verify the quality of likeness that is brought about by the Word (*Mon.* 55). Only the Father is *genitor* and *ingenitus*. The Son is *genitus*, and the Spirit, who is the love of the two, is neither *genitus* nor *ingenitus* (*Mon.* 56). Thus Memory, Understanding and Love are identical *essentialiter*, that is, through and in the divine essence (*Mon.* 60), and they are one in each other (*Mon.* 59—although Anselm does not use the term, he is clearly speaking of circumincession). They are identical in *summa essentia* and yet they are not confused because, in that identity of essence and activities, there is a *genitor*, a *genitus* and a *procedens* (*Mon.* 61).

When he speaks of the Spirit, Anselm always uses this term, which is biblical and which comes close to the practice of the Greek Fathers. The *quomodo sit*, that is, the manner of that procession, the intimate being of the three whose existence can be deduced by reason, goes beyond our understanding, however, and cannot be expressed (*Mon.* 64–65). Anselm therefore concludes that there is 'a unity because of the unity of essence; a trinity because of the three I know not what (*trinitatem propter tres nescio quid*)' (*Mon.* 79; see Schmitt, *op. cit.* (note 1 below), I, p. 85). It is therefore hardly possible to say 'three Persons' because persons exist separately from each other—they are, in other words, individual substances. It is only because it is necessary to speak and because usage authorizes one to speak that, having expressed oneself clearly about the unity of the absolute essence, one can speak at all about an essence and about three Persons or substances.[8]

Dealing with the procession of the Holy Spirit, Anselm speaks at some depth in the treatise that resulted from his participation in the Council of Bari. In *De processione Spiritus Sancti*, he no longer tries, as he did in the earlier treatise, to understand what he believes by drawing attention to the inner consistency and logical necessity of the affirmations of faith. He takes as his point of departure what the Western Church has in common with the Greeks in faith in God and his Tri-unity in order to lead them to agreement with the West in the article on the procession of the Holy Spirit 'a Patre *et Filio*'. There are two possible ways which can be followed in this, and Anselm in fact follows each in turn. The first is the way of logical argument (the two very long and difficult chapters which open *De Processione Spiritu Sancto*). The second way is that of the implications of the scriptural texts. Anselm does not appeal to the Fathers, because the Greeks were ignorant of the writings of the Latin Fathers and he himself apparently did not know the Greeks.

The logical argument, which is extremely complicated and abstract, can, I think, be summarized as follows. The Father, the Son and the Spirit are equally God. Hence, there is a rigorous logic of identity. There can only be a difference by opposition of relationship of origin or of procession. That and that alone is what limits the identity. The latter, left to itself, would require the Father to be the Son and the Spirit, because they are also the one God, but to this is opposed the fact that it is not possible to be the one from whom one has one's being. The Son is from the Father by mode of begetting, *nascendo*, and the Spirit is from him by mode of procession, *procedendo*. That is the opposition of relationship which establishes the differences within the unity of God. Anselm did not create the definition of the Persons by relationships—we have already found that in Augustine and the Greeks. He is the origin of the axiomatic formula which, although it is not strictly speaking a dogma, is nonetheless more than a theologoumenon: 'in Deo omnia sunt unum, ubi non obviat relationis oppositio'.[9]

In this one divinity, the Spirit is not from nobody, *a nullo*, he is from God, *a Deo*. He is *God from God*, from that God who is Father, Son and Spirit. He cannot be 'a se ipso, quoniam nulla persona a se ipsa potest existere'.[10] He is therefore from the Father and the Son, not as Father and Son, but as God, the divine essence—'secundum eandem deitatis unitatem'—and therefore, in this respect, not distinct from each other.[11] The Spirit, then, proceeds from the Son at the same time as he does from the Father, as from the same principle.

Anselm also insists that he proceeds *equally* from the two as from the one principle. This is necessary, because he proceeds from the two according to the essence that is common to both. Here, Anselm meets Augustine's *principaliter a Patre*. He does not deny this, but explains it within the framework of his own teaching, in which the begetting of the Son and the procession of the Spirit are seen within the context of an identity of essence and an equality of divinity:

Ex eo enim quod pater et filius unum sunt, id est ex deo, est spiritus sanctus, non ex eo unde alii sunt ab invicem. . . . Et quoniam pater non est prior aut posterior filio, aut maior aut minor, nec alter magis aut minus est deus quam alter, non est spiritus sanctus prius de patre quam de filio.[12]

The Holy Spirit comes from that in which the Father and the Son are one, that is, from God, not from that in which they differ from each other. . . . And because the Father is neither before nor after the son, neither greater nor lesser, and because the one is neither more nor less God than the other, the Holy Spirit is not from the Father before [being from] the Son.

Si ergo dicitur quod spiritus sanctus principaliter sit a patre, non aliud significatur, quam quia ipse filius de quo est spiritus sanctus, habet hoc ipsum ut spiritus sanctus sit de illo, a patre (Schmitt, II, p. 213).

If, then, it is said that the Holy Spirit comes from the Father as the principle, nothing more than this is meant: the Son himself, from whom the Spirit comes, has it from the Father that the Spirit comes from him.

It is important not to transfer to God what *principaliter* implies for God's creatures. In God, Anselm teaches, everything is not so much 'aequale vel simile sibi et coaeternum quam idem sibi ipsi' (Schmitt, II, p. 214). There is nothing wrong with this teaching, but it does not really contain the traditional idea of the monarchy of the Father and it is a long way from the Greek understanding of the mystery.

This same distance is also reflected in Anselm's treatment of the *a Patre per Filium*. The bishops who took part in the Council of Bari must have spoken to him about this question, but he was clearly unaware of the important place that this formula had in Greek patristic literature. He himself says that he could not see what the formula could mean (Schmitt, II, pp. 201ff.). He says: 'As the Father and the Son do not differ in the unity of the deity and as the Holy Spirit only proceeds from the Father as the deity, if that deity is similarly in the Son, it is not possible to see how the Spirit would proceed from the deity of the Father through the deity of the Son and not (immediately) from that same deity of the Father, but from his fatherhood, and that he proceeds through the sonship of the Son and not through his deity—but that idea is clearly stupid' (Schmitt, II, p. 202).

After this, Anselm, probably not knowing that the comparison can be found in the Greek Fathers, whose linear plan it expresses, critically examines the image of the source which, through the river, produces a lake.

The lake, he comments, certainly comes from the river and in the same way the Spirit comes from the Son. If, however, it is insisted that the lake strictly speaking comes only from the source and not from the channel between the source and itself, Anselm's reply is: that is true in the material order, but in the case of God it is not possible to speak of the Son differently from the way in which we speak of the Father, because he is *in* the Father and is in no way different from him in essence. And if the source, the channel and the lake are three, the same water is in all three, that is to say, the divine essence or the deity itself.[13] Gregory Nazianzen's comments about this comparison are very similar to Anselm's. All this is quite true, but nonetheless, Anselm's approach to the mystery of the Trinity is different from that of the Eastern tradition.

Anselm's aim, in taking as his point of departure in his theology of the Trinity what the Orthodox have in common with the Western tradition, was to take the Greeks to the point where they might confess what they had hitherto rejected, namely the procession of the Spirit *a Patre Filioque tanquam ab uno principio*. In chapters 4 to 7 of *De Processione*, he pursues his intention and his argument no longer by reasoning, but by interpreting a number of New Testament texts. These are Jn 20:22 and 16:13, reinforced by Mt 11:27 and Jn 10:30. In chapter 11, he shows that the Son is also affirmed in Jn 15:26: 'Who proceeds from the Father'. I shall not discuss this exegesis in detail, but go on to chapter 13, in which Anselm deals with the question of the addition of the *Filioque* clause to the creed. He deals with it very quickly and without realizing how important it is—as has frequently been the case in Western Catholic circles until our own time!

I would like on the other hand, to draw attention to a more favourable element in Anselm's treatise. He does not use the word *procedere* as a generic term, but as an expression of the coming to be of the Spirit or of Love, whereas he uses *gigni* or *nasci* for the Son.[14] These are two different ways of being 'God from God'. He does not, however, regard the difference between these two modes of origin as sufficient to form a basis for distinguishing between the Son and the Spirit. In his view, it is necessary to go back to the opposition of relationship of origin; the Spirit is distinct from the Son because he proceeds from him. This was also Thomas Aquinas' view, whereas Duns Scotus held a position that was close to that of the Greeks. This is, however, not a strictly dogmatic question.

Anselm was above all a speculative theologian. He did not develop his pneumatology within the framework of the history of salvation; indeed, he did not refer to the latter at all. He moves immediately from the activity of God in the economy to the eternal procession, for example, in the case of Jn 16:13, 'he will not speak of himself'. Even his prayers and meditations are not pneumatological. They do not even mention the Holy Spirit. He has, however, great dynamism, although he has certain limitations. Like Augustine (see Volume I, p. 78), he tends to block together the essential and the notional. He is interested in the divine essence and does not take the hypostases as his point of departure. The notion of 'person' seems to have perplexed him. He does not, therefore, make a very clear distinction between their principle *quo*, their nature, and their principle *quod*, the person, in the processions. However much we have to admire him, there is always a feeling that there is a need to go beyond his thinking. He would himself have agreed with that sentiment.

*　　*　　*

It is not because they have the same name that I add a note at this point on Anselm of Havelberg (†1158). It is rather because of the content of his dialogue with Nicetas of Nicomedia. The whole of Book II of his *Dialogi* deals with the Holy Spirit, and in it he discusses the theology of the Latins with its supporting scriptural texts and arguments. Nicetas complies a little too easily and is above all anxious to affirm the monarchy of the Father. He finds the term 'proceed' an obstacle, while Anselm stumbles over *ekporeusis*. Each refers to the Fathers of his own tradition, although Anselm declares that he reveres the Greeks as he does the Latins and respects every orthodox Christian who has received the gift of the Spirit (*Dial.* 24; *PL* 186, 1204).

NOTES

1. I follow in this section the critical edition of S. Schmitt: for the *Monologion*, I (Seckau, 1938), pp. 5–87; for the *De Processione Spiritus Sancti*, II (Rome, 1940), pp. 177–279. The following studies of Anselm's work are worth consulting: B. Bouché, *Le doctrine du 'Filioque' d'après S. Anselme de Cantorbéry. Son influence sur S. Albert le Grand et S. Thomas d'Aquin* (this is a duplicated thesis I have not been able to read) (Rome, 1938); R. Perino, *La dottrina trinitaria di S. Anselmo nel quadro del suo metodo teologico e del suo concetto di Dio* (*Studia Anselmiana*, 29) (Rome, 1952); C. Vagaggini, 'La hantise des *rationes necessariae* de S. Anselme dans la théologie des processions trinitaires de S. Thomas', *Spicilegium Beccense*, I (*Congrès international du IXe centenaire de l'arrivée d'Anselme au Bec*) (Le Bec-Hellouin and Paris, 1959), pp. 103–139; P. del Prete, *Il concilio di Bari nel 1098* (Bari, 1959).

2. *Mon.* Prol. (Schmitt, I, p. 8, 1. 8f.). The editor gives, at the foot of his pages, Augustine's similar texts.

3. *Prosl.* 4 (Schmitt, I, p. 104); cf. *Ep. de Inc. Verbi*, VI (Schmitt, II, p. 20).

4. 'Cum idem sit illi sic dicere aliquid quod est intelligere': *Mon.* 32 (Schmitt, I, p. 51). Thomas Aquinas makes a distinction here: see *De ver.* q. 4, a. 2 c and ad 7.

5. *Mon.* 65.

6. *Mon.* 39–41. In *Mon.* 42, Anselm asks why Christians speak of the Father and the Son and not of the Mother and the Daughter; this is, he says, because the father comes before the mother in the causality of begetting.

7. *Mon.* 43 (Schmitt, I, p. 60).

8. 'Potest ergo hac necessitatis ratione irreprehensibiliter illa summa et una trinitas sive trina unitas dici una essentia et tres personae sive tres substantiae': *Mon.* 79 (Schmitt, I, p. 85). This equivalence between 'Person' and 'substance' came to Anselm from what he knew of

the Greeks: 'Quod enim dixi summam trinitatem posse dici tres substantias, Graecos secutus sum, qui confitentur tres substantias in una persona eadem fide, qua nos tres personas in una substantia. Nam hoc significant in deo per substantiam, quod nos per personam': *Mon.*, Prol. (Schmitt, I, p. 8). See also *Ep. de Inc. Verbi*, XVI (Schmitt, II, p. 35); *Ep.* 83 *ad Rainaldum* (Schmitt, III, p. 208), in which the following interesting text can be found: his *Monologion* had been criticized by those who 'nesciebant enim sic non dici proprie de deo tres personas quomodo tres substantias, quadam tamen ratione ob indigentiam nominis proprie significantis illam pluralitatem quae in summa trinitate intelligitur, Latinos dicere tres personas credendas in una substantia, Graecos vero non minus fideliter tres substantias in una persona confiteri'.

9. This axiom is not to be found as such in Anselm's work, but its meaning and use can be found: see *De proc. spir. sanct.* 1 (Schmitt, II, p. 180, 1. 27; 181, 1. 2–4; 183, 1. 3). It can only be found, in connection with the Council of Florence, in the decree of 4 February 1442 for union with the Copts: see J. Alberigo *et al.*, *Conciliorum Œcumenicorum Decreta*, 3rd ed. (Bologna, 1973), p. 571; *DS* 1330. According to Heribert Mühlen, the axiom was applied in that case to a tritheism which the Monophysites who were opposed to the definition of Chalcedon had adopted in the sixth century from John Philoponus. Its dogmatic implication would therefore be limited: see H. Mühlen, *Der Heilige Geist als Person in der Trinität, bei der Inkarnation und im Gnadenbund; Ich-Du-Wir*, 3rd ed. (Münster, 1966), p. 314. 'It is not of faith', H. Dondaine told the Orthodox: *Russie et Chrétienté* (1950), 223. It is, however, a commonly accepted principle in Catholic theology. Is it not possible to find the equivalent in Greek patristic thought in the following text from Athanasius, *Contra Arian.* I, 22: 'Because they are one and the divinity is itself one, the same things can be said of the Son that are said of the Father, although it cannot be said that he is Father'; see also *De decr.* 23.

10. *De proc. spir. sanct.* 2 (Schmitt, II, p. 188). It is astonishing that Anselm does not explain how this statement applies or does not apply to the Father. He does not, however, have the monarchy of the Father in mind, but only the divinity. In the case of the latter, the Father is only Father when the Son is affirmed, and that through his relationship as *genitor* to the *genitus*.

11. *Mon.* 54 (Schmitt, I, p. 66): 'non ex eo procedit in quo plures sunt pater et filius, sed ex eo in quo unum sunt. Nam non ex relationibus suis quae plures sunt . . . sed ex ipsa sua essentia quae pluralitatem non admittit, emittunt pater et filius pariter tantum bonum'; *De proc. spir. sanct.* 1 (Schmitt, II, p. 183): 'non est filius aut spiritus sanctus de patre nisi de patris essentia'. See also below, pp. 109, 114 note 7, and p. 120.

12. *De proc. spir. sanct.* 14 (Schmitt, II, p. 212); cf. *ibid.* 9 (Schmitt, II, p. 204).

13. *De proc. spir. sanct.* 9 (Schmitt, II, pp. 203–205). The comparison can also be found, for example, in John Damascene (*PG* 94, 780). For Gregory Nazianzen, see *Orat.* 31 (= *Orat. theol.* V), 31 (*PG* 36, 169). Anselm's explanation was explicitly rejected by Abelard, but not for a good reason—it would not be *simul* and would presuppose a *successio temporis*: *Intro. ad Theol.* II, 13 and *Theol. Christ.* IV (*PL* 178, 1071 and 1287).

14. See, for example, *De proc. spir. sanct.* 1 (Schmitt, II, p. 178, 1. 3ff.; p. 179, 15ff.; p. 180, 15ff.; etc.). Again and again *nascens* and *nascendo* are found for the Word, the Son, and *procedens* and *procedendo* for the Spirit: see Schmitt, II, p. 179, 12ff.; p. 185, 3ff.: 'habent utique a patre esse filius et spiritus sanctus, sed diverso modo: quia alter nascendo, alter procedendo'.

3

SPECULATIVE TRIADOLOGY CONSTRUCTED IN FAITH AND UNDER THE SIGN OF LOVE

[*Note*: the numbered notes are collected at the end of each of the two sections in this chapter.]

A. RICHARD OF SAINT-VICTOR

For half a century, the abbey of Saint-Victor in Paris was a centre of intense theological speculation in a climate that was marked by an astonishing trust in the power of reason, an acute intellectual curiosity, an intense religious and doxological life and a deep interest in love or charity. G. Dumeige has considered a large number of texts relating to this interest on the part of the Victorines.[1] The leading members of Saint-Victor were Hugh (†1141), Achard (†1171), Richard, Walter, Adam, Godfrey and Andrew.

Richard, who died in 1172, wrote a remarkable treatise *De Trinitate* late in life.[2] It has been demonstrated that he was directly indebted to his abbot, Achard,[3] for it, and more distantly to Augustine and Anselm. Like the latter, he believed that it was possible to find the 'necessary reasons' to support the affirmations of faith in a reflection made in faith. He was conscious of the inadequacy of our concepts and of all that we can say with regard to the transcendent mystery of God, and we today are less convinced of the effectiveness of his reasons, but he developed and repeated them with what was intended to be vigorous consistency.

Whereas Anselm took as his point of departure *id quo nihil maius cogitari potest*, 'that than which it is not possible to conceive anything greater', Achard said: *Deo nihil pulcrius et melius esse vel cogitari potest*—'nothing better or more beautiful than God can exist or be conceived of'. Richard's point of departure was: *id quo nihil est maius, quo nihil est melius*, that is, 'a being, greater or better than whom there is nothing'.[4] Unlike Achard, he did not appeal to the *summum* of beauty, although he often made use of the aesthetic argument. To Anselm's teaching, he added the *summum* of goodness, that is to say, the *summum* of a value, not of a purely ontological reality.

In Book III of his treatise on the Trinity, Richard deduces the plurality, or more precisely the Trinity of the Persons in the unity of the divine substance. It is valuable to quote his own summary of his argument. He begins by showing that it is necessary for there to be a plurality in God, through the existence of a second Person who, in order to be the term of a perfect love, will be the *condignus* or equal of that love:

In God, the supreme and absolutely perfect good, there is total goodness in its fullness and perfection. Where there is a fullness of total goodness, however, there is necessarily true and supreme charity. . . . It is never said of anyone that he possesses charity because of the exclusively personal love that he has for himself—for there to be charity, there must be a love that is directed towards another. Consequently, where there is an absence of a plurality of persons, there cannot be charity.

You may say: 'Assuming that, in this true divinity, there is only one Person, that Person might be able to have and in fact would have charity with regard to his creatures'. Yes, but with regard to a created person, it would be impossible for him to have a sovereign charity, because it would be a disorder in that charity to love sovereignly what is not sovereignly lovable.[5]

Richard gave a character that was personal, and not purely essential to charity by conceiving it in the form of friendship, which in itself presupposes an interpersonal relationship. The perfect one, the deity, has everything, Richard taught, from himself.[6] He is *innascibilis*.[7] Richard showed that what perfect love implies is that there is one who is personally over and against that perfect presence and who is the Son.[8] He also deduces, in the name of the same perfect love, a third, who is *condilectus*:

Sovereign charity must be perfect in every respect. To be sovereignly perfect, it must be of such an intensity that there can be nothing more intense and of such a quality that there can be nothing better. . . . In true charity, the supreme excellence is to want another to be loved as one is loved oneself. . . . The proof of consummate charity is the desire for the love with which one is loved to be communicated.[9]

The procession of the second and the third Person can therefore be understood thanks to the concept of perfect love or charity, and by making a distinction in that love. There is, for example, the love that is simply given. This gratuitous love is the Father.[10] There is the love which is received (*debitus* or due to another) and which gives (*gratuitus*). That love is the Son.[11] The love that is purely received (*debitus*) is the Spirit.[12] He enjoys the privilege of a love that is exclusively due and he loves those who give everything to him perfectly. Each divine Person is therefore equally love that is sovereign but possessed in a distinct way which corresponds to his mode of existence.[13] In this context, Richard uses a precise vocabulary and works out a distinctive concept of 'Person'. He is critical of the definition given to the term by Boethius—'an individual substance of reasonable nature'[14]—and replaces it by a different definition: 'one who exists in himself alone, according to a certain mode of reasonable existence'[15] and who is distinguished from everyone else by a property that cannot be communicated.[16] Richard therefore defines the person in terms of being, but does so within a personalistic and not within a purely ontic perspective. The person is not a *quid*, but a *quis* (see *De Trin.* IV, 7). He also uses the term *existentia* for the person; this word expresses both the nature or essence (*sistere*) and the origin (*ex*) of the person. It can, Richard insists, be applied suitably to the divine Persons each of whom has, within the community of substance, his own mode of subsistence.[17] In this way, then, Richard affirms the unity of the divine essence and the plurality of the divine Persons. It would be futile to ask whether he affirms the one or the other first, whether he is more Greek than Latin, according to the difference between the two traditions emphasized in such an over-simplified way by T. de Régnon. The fact that he begins by outlining the essential attributes of God does not make him into an 'essentialist' any more than it does John Damascene. What is certain, however, is that his idea of the person is very close to that of the Greeks.[18]

Although he does not engage in polemics or even in debate with the Greeks, he parts company from them on the question of the procession of the Holy Spirit from the Father and the Son. He says, for instance: 'If the two (the Father and the Son) possess the same power in common, it must be concluded that it is from both that the third Person of the Trinity received his being and has his existence'.[19] In the Trinity, he claims, the third Person proceeds both from the one who was born and from the one who cannot be born (*innascibilis*).[20] This does not mean that the Spirit is, according to Richard, what he was for Augustine—the love of the Father and the Son for each other.[21] The Spirit is, according to Richard, the particular and incommunicable mode of existence of the divine substance, which is Love. This special way of existing which characterizes the divine Persons consists in a manner of living and realizing Love. That Love is either pure grace, or it is received and giving, or it is purely received and due. This can then be expressed equally well in terms of procession and therefore also in terms of origin. Beginning with the one who is *innascibilis*, there is an immediate procession, that of the Love-Son, and one that is simultaneously immediate (from the Father) and mediate (from the Son), that of the *Condilectus* or the Spirit.[22]

No other Person proceeds from the Spirit, but it is through the latter that God as Love is given to the believer and takes root in him. The Spirit therefore merits the name of 'Gift':

> The Holy Spirit is given by God to man at the moment when the due (*debitus*) love that is found in the divinity is breathed into the human soul. . . . Insofar as we enable the love that is due (*debitum*) to our creator to go back to him, we are quite certainly configured into the property of the Holy Spirit. It is precisely for this end that he is given, that he is breathed into man, so that the latter may be, to the full extent of what is possible, configured into him. For the rest, this gift is sent to us, this mission is given to us at the same time and in the same way by the Father and by the Son. It is, after all, from the one and from the other that the Spirit has everything that he possesses. And because it is from the one and from the other that he has his being, power and will, it is right to say that it is they who send and give him, who has received from them the power and the will to come from them into us and to dwell in us.[23]

105

Richard does not make use of the principle formulated by Anselm: 'in Deo omnia sunt unum ubi non obviat relationis oppositio'.[24] He does not make an inference from the relationship between the Father and the Son, the Giver and the Gift, in order to distinguish between the Persons. He too distinguishes between them by means of the principle of origin, but in so doing he only uses an analysis of love in its absolute perfection and the distinctions that are contained within that love.

Despite appearances, Richard does not base his ideas on a pure deduction from sacred metaphysics. They presuppose not only revelation—taking expressions of faith as a point of departure—but also spiritual experience, and indeed Richard refers explicitly to this.[25] He justifies the fact that he bases his teaching on the human experiences of love in its most intense state by quoting at least ten times a Pauline text: 'The invisible nature of God . . . can be clearly perceived in the things that have been made' (Rom 1:10). This frequent quotation is all the more remarkable because of the paucity of quotations in the treatise as a whole. This appeal to human experience does not, however, mean that Richard also looked for the life of the Spirit in history or in the economy of salvation. He gives us a theology of the third Person of the Trinity, but not a full 'pneumatology'.

NOTES

1. After I had written this chapter, I read Jean Leclercq's *Monks and Love in Twelfth-Century France* (Oxford, 1979). The author is principally concerned in this remarkable and suggestive study with Bernard, and this is right, but he also cites the Victorines. The new religious orders in the twelfth century found recruits among adults who were acquainted with the expressions of human love. These men developed a spirituality in which love played a new part and was studied with a new richness and delicacy. It became a special theme in spiritual reflection.

   In Volume I, pp. 86–87, I quoted the fine prayer of William of Saint-Thierry (†1148), who said that God loves himself in and through us with the same love with which he loves himself. For his theology of the Trinity, see M.-J. Le Guillou, 'Guillaume de Saint-Thierry: l'équilibre catholique de la triadologie médiévale', *Istina*, 17 (1972), 367–374.

   Bernard can also be placed within this context. He spoke of 'caritas, quae Trinitatem in unitate quodammodo cohibet et colligat in vinculo pacis': *De diligendo Deo* XII, 35 (*PL* 182, 996). In his commentary on the verse of the Song of Songs, 'May he kiss me with a kiss of his mouth', he suggests that this kiss is the Holy Spirit and adds: 'It is enough for the spouse to be kissed by a kiss of the bridegroom, even if she is not kissed by his mouth. It is not a trivial matter or an everyday thing to be kissed by a kiss. It is simply being penetrated by the Holy Spirit. If it is the Father who kisses, the Son is the one who is kissed and it is not out of place to see in that kiss the Holy Spirit, who is the unchangeable peace of the Father and the Son, their firm bond, their unique love and the inseparable unity': *Sermo 8 in Cant.* 2 (*PL* 183, 811).

2. See *PL* 196, 887–902 (which is not complete or perfect); J. Ribaillier, *Richard de Saint-Victor, De Trinitate. Texte critique* (Paris, 1958); *idem*, crit. ed., in *Richard de Saint-Victor, Opuscules théologiques* (Paris, 1967), of the brief text *Quomodo Spiritus Sanctus est amor Patris et Filii* and another text, *De tribus Personis appropriatis in Trinitate*, which is partly

reproduced in *De Trin*. VI, 15; G. Salet, *Richard de Saint-Victor, La Trinité* (Latin text, Fr. tr. and notes; *SC* 63) (Paris, 1959). There are several studies, including T. de Régnon, *Etudes de théologie positive sur la Sainte Trinité*, II (Paris, 1892), pp. 233–335; A.-M. Ethier, *Le 'De Trinitate' de Richard de Saint-Victor* (*Publ. de l'Inst. d'Etudes méd. d'Ottawa*, IX) (Paris and Ottawa, 1939); F. Guimet, 'Notes en marge d'un texte de Richard de Saint-Victor', *Arch. hist. doctr. litt. M. A.*, 14 (1943–1945), pp. 361–394; *idem*, ' "Caritas ordinata" et "amor discretus" dans la théologie trinitaire de Richard de Saint-Victor', *Rev. M. A. latin*, 4 (1948), 225–236; G. Dumeige, *Richard de Saint-Victor et l'idée chrétienne de l'amour*) (*Bibl. de philos. contemp.*) (Paris, 1952), which contains a bibliography with 101 items.

3. M. T. d'Alverny, 'Achard de Saint-Victor, *De Trinitate, de unitate et pluralitate creaturarum*', *RTAM*, 21 (1954), 299–306; J. Ribaillier, *De Trinitate*, *op. cit.* (note 2), pp. 27–33; J. Chatillon, *Théologie et spiritualité dans l'œuvre oratoire d'Achard de Saint-Victor* (Paris, 1969).

4. *De Trin*. I, 11 and 20; V, 3.

5. *De Trin*. III, 2; G. Salet, *op. cit.* (note 2), p. 169. There is an implicit quotation of Gregory the Great here: 'Minus quam inter duos caritas haberi non potest. Nemo enim proprie ad semetipsum habere caritatem dicitur, sed dilectio in alterum tendit ut caritas esse possit': *Hom. in Ev.* I, *Hom.* 17 (*PL* 76, 1139). Quoting the same passage, Abelard saw it as realized by the extension of God's love to creatures; *Theol. Summi Boni* III, 3; ed. H. Ostlender (Münster, 1939), p. 103. Richard is replying to his statement here.

6. *De Trin*. V, 7 and 8.

7. *Innascibilis* is a commonly used word: see *De Trin*. V, 7, 8 and 19; VI, 2, 3, 5, 6 and 8.

8. *De Trin*. V, 7; VI, 5; begotten, VI, 16; the image of the Father, which the Spirit is not, *because*, like the Father, he produces a different Person, he is charity that gives: VI, 11, 18 and 20. Thinking of the first procession within the framework of love and not as a procession of intellectual understanding, Richard did not connect 'image' with 'Word'. He shows, however, that the second Person is 'Word' (VI, 12) within a personalistic perspective of communication.

9. *De Trin*. III, 11: G. Salet, *op. cit.* (note 2), p. 191; cf. III, 19; V, 20.

10. *De Trin*. V, 16 and 17.

11. *De Trin*. V, 16 and 19.

12. *De Trin*. V, 16 and 18. The distinction between the three conditions of love is expressed in III, 3 and V, 16.

13. *De Trin*. V, 20 and 23.

14. *De Trin*. IV, 21; Boethius, *Liber de persona et duabus naturis*, 3 (*PL* 64, 1343). Thomas Aquinas accepted Boethius' definition after correcting it and explicitly quoted Richard: *ST* Ia, q. 29, a. 3, ad 4.

15. *De Trin*. IV, 24; G. Salet, *op. cit.* (note 2), p. 285.

16. *De Trin*. IV, 17 and 20; in this final chapter of his treatise, Richard affirms the identity of meaning in the difference between the terms used by the Greeks and the Latins: see below, p. 175.

17. *De Trin*. IV, 12 and 19, where this formula can be found concerning two distinct Persons in God: 'Quamvis enim utrisque sit unus modus essendi, non tamen utrisque est unus modus existendi'. There is another excellent statement in IV, 20: 'nihil aliud est persona ista quam dilectio summa alia proprietate distincta'.

18. G. Salet quoted John Damascene in this context, *op. cit.* (note 2), p. 254, note 1: 'The word hypostasis has two meanings. It can mean simply existence, in which case it has exactly the same value as ousia. . . . On the other hand, it can also mean that existence which is in itself and subsists in its individuality, in which case it points to the numerically distinct individual—Peter, Paul or a certain horse': *Dial.* 42 (*PG* 94, 612).

19. *De Trin*. V, 8; G. Salet, *op. cit.*, p. 321.

20. *De Trin*. V, 13; G. Salet, *op. cit.*, p. 377; see also *De Trin*. VI, 13, end.

21. In his brief treatise or letter *Quomodo Spiritus Sanctus est amor Patris et Filii* (*PL* 196, 1011–1012); see J. Ribaillier, *Opuscules*, *op. cit.* (note 2), pp. 164–166. Richard takes as his point of departure the Augustinian view which had been brought to his attention by the question asked by his correspondent and which was not exactly his own. Ribaillier, *op. cit.*, pp. 159–160, has shown that, although the two views are different, they do not contradict each other. *De Trin.* III, 19 indicates an openness on Richard's part to the idea of mutual love. The latter is explictly discussed in *De tribus appropriatis*: ed. Ribaillier, *op. cit.*, p. 184.
22. *De Trin.* V, 6–10.
23. *De Trin.* VI, 14; G. Salet, *op. cit.* (note 2), pp. 413 and 417.
24. The only place where a 'relationship of opposition' is possibly called to mind—and then only remotely—is *De Trin.* V, 14, but even here it is only between receiving and giving, or giving and receiving.
25. *De Trin.* III, 3; G. Salet, *op. cit.*, pp. 171ff., translates this text as: 'Let everyone reflect about this and, without the slightest doubt, he will indisputably recognize that there is nothing better or more agreeable than charity'. What he says in *De Trin.* III, 16 about the sweetness of friendship presupposes personal experience.

B. ALEXANDER OF HALES AND BONAVENTURE

Both these theologians continued in the tradition of Richard of Saint-Victor and their triadology is deeply indebted to his teaching. As members of the high Scholasticism of the thirteenth century, they continued to develop, within faith itself, a rational and consistent discourse about faith. Bonaventure taught that 'fullness' was the source and that 'first' meant the 'principle' and therefore the beginning of a communication, and this teaching was based not on the rational content of the concepts, but on faith itself. Those concepts, however, seen in the light of his affirmations about faith, gave his theological vision grandeur and coherence. I have already spoken in Volume I of this work (pp. 87–88 with the bibliography p. 91 note 7) about the theme of the Spirit as the link of mutual love between the Father and the Son,[1] and I shall later on discuss the theology of the *innascibilis*, that is, of the Father as the source of the divinity (see below, pp. 135–136).

Alexander of Hales (†1245) dealt briefly with the Trinity in his *Glossa* on the Sentences, but nonetheless outlined quite clearly the course that he was to follow and that his disciples were to follow after him. This amounted to an accord between John Damascene on the one hand and Augustine on the other, John representing the Greek and Augustine representing the Latin tradition, John speaking of God's relationship with his creatures and Augustine of the inner life of God.[2]

This is, however, clearly unsatisfactory. The questions *Antequam esset frater* reveal a truly irenical intention in their treatment of the 'controversy between the Greeks and the Latins about the procession *ab utroque*'.[3] It is possible that they contain an echo of dialogues that really took place ('concedebant . . .'). The Greeks maintain, Alexander's argument runs, that the Spirit is the Spirit of the Son, but that he does not proceed from him. As the *responsio pro illis*, in accordance with the teaching of John Damascene, whom Alexander quotes frequently, the Spirit is the Father's love for the Son and proceeds from the Father to the Son, but he is the Son's love for the Father without proceeding from the Son to the Father. That is why the Greeks call him, Alexander says, the Spirit of the Son and do not say that he proceeds from the Son to the creature. They do not say that he proceeds *simpliciter* from the Son, because he does not proceed from the Son to the Father.[4] Alexander is therefore conscious of *utriusque positionis concordia*.[5] It was sufficient in his opinion to affirm with Augustine the inner procession of the Spirit *a Filio*, but not *in Patrem*, and with John Damascene the procession *ad creaturas*. But is this question really so simple? Has Alexander reached the real facts in the debate?

There is a change of style in his *Summa Theologica*, in which his pneumatology is presented in a more systematic way, and which was continued by his disciple John de la Rochelle. The divine life is seen as a good that is communicated, since good is naturally and essentially something that is diffusive of itself.[6] This takes place, according to Alexander, in two ways—by mode of nature, which is the begetting of the Son, and by mode of love or gift, which is the procession of the Spirit. Alexander quotes Richard of Saint-Victor frequently here (c. 1). He also makes use of Richard's idea of the *condilectus* in his reply[7] to the Greek objection, namely that, if the Spirit proceeds from the Father and the Son, this procession takes place either from the common essence—but he shares in that common essence—or in accordance with the difference between the Father and the Son—but then *non conveniunt in aliquo*: they have no common fund. Alexander's reply to this objection is that the Spirit does not proceed from the Father and the Son either in accordance with their unity (in essence) or in accordance with their difference, but rather in accordance with the fact that, although they are different, they are still one, that is to say, insofar as they are, as Father and Son, God. Their unity is one of essence as hypostatized in the Father and in the Son in a personal way.

*   *   *

Bonaventure's triadology is constructed on a very conceptual basis, but always in faith.[8] He attempted to decipher the mystery of God in three books. In the first he dealt with nature, in the second with the soul and in the third with revelation. The third book throws light on the other two, since it is itself read under an inner light or illumination that enables us to sense God *altissime* and *piissime*, in other words, in accordance with the most sublime, the most religiously profound and fervent way one can think.[9] The work is certainly constructed on the basis of intellectual concepts, but the criteria of the most sublime, the most profound and the most fervently religious things one can think are always followed. This can be detected in the following summary from Bonaventure's *Itinerarium mentis ad Deum*, which he wrote in 1259:

See and note well—the best is simply the best that can be conceived. It is such that it cannot validly be conceived as not existing, because it is better to be than not to be and it is also such that it cannot validly be conceived other than threefold and one. 'Whoever says "good" says "diffusive of itself" ', so that the sovereign good is sovereignly diffusive of itself. A sovereign diffusion can only be present and intrinsic, substantial and hypostatic, natural and voluntary, full of grace and necessary, without restriction and perfect. If, then, there were not eternally in the sovereign good a present and consubstantial fertility and a hypostasis of equal dignity, as the fertility by mode of begetting and spiration is, so that it is from an eternal principle that is in eternity doubly principle, with the result that there is a Beloved and a loved Companion [*dilectus* and *condilectus*], begotten and an outcome of spiration, in other words, Father, Son and Holy Spirit, there would never have been a sovereign good, because that good would not have diffused itself sovereignly. Diffusion of a temporal kind in the creature is no more than a point in the centre of a sphere in comparison with the immensity of eternal goodness. It is therefore possible to conceive of a greater diffusion, namely that in which the principle of diffusion communicates the whole of its substance and nature to another. There would therefore not be a sovereign good if this did not exist in the idea that is conceived of it and in reality.

If you can, then, with the eye of your spirit, seize hold of (*contueri*) the purity of the goodness which is the pure act of the principle of charity that loves with a gratuitous love and a due (love) and (a love) that is a mixture of the two, which constitutes the fullest diffusion by mode of nature and (by mode) of will—it is a diffusion by mode of the Word, in whom (God) says all things, and by mode of Gift, in whom the other gifts are given—then you will see through the sovereign communicability of the good that it is necessary for the Trinity of the Father, the Son and the Holy Spirit to exist. In them, by reason of the supreme goodness, there must be supreme communicability and, by reason of that supreme communicability, there must also be a sovereign consubstantiality and, by virtue of that sovereign consubstantiality, there must also be a sovereign configurability and, because of (all) that, a sovereign co-equality and, for that reason, a sovereign co-eternity and, as a result of all that, a sovereign co-intimacy, by virtue of which the one is necessarily in the other through a sovereign circumincession, the one functions with the other through the totally undivided substance, virtue and functioning of the blessed Trinity itself.[10]

This synthesis is dominated and inspired by two great values. In the first place, the idea that the supreme good is diffusive of itself comes from Pseudo-Dionysius[11] and expresses the primacy that is recognized in Neo-Platonism to value and the supreme good over being. It is simply a question of seizing hold of this property of the good in its supreme degree, in other words, in supreme or sovereign love. In the second place, there is also Richard of Saint-Victor's application of the idea of love to the intra-divine life, for which he may or may not have been indebted to Pseudo-Dionysius, in its supreme form of altruism or friendship. Bonaventure took from Richard the ideas of *dilectus condignus* and *condilectus*, the distinction between gratuitous love, due or received love, and the mixture of the two.

To this he added the theme of communication or emanation by mode of nature and by mode of will and liberality. It was this theme, together with that of the *condilectus*, which enabled Bonaventure to justify the existence of the third Person of the Trinity as 'necessary'.[12] The Spirit is therefore, for Bonaventure, Love and Gift. He also defines this Love more precisely. In what sense, he asks, is this title 'Love' personal to the Holy Spirit, since love must, after all, be attributed to all three Persons?[13] Love exists in God in the essential and in the notional sense, that is, as the personal name of the Spirit, It is, he claims, in this second sense that the Spirit is the mutual love of the Father and the Son.[14] For that is what he is. Bonaventure comes back again and again to this point, which is fundamental for him:

> Love has the perfection of its delectable value and of its value of union and uprightness from its character of reciprocity. As a consequence of this, we have either not to speak of a person in God who proceeds by mode of love or, if there is such a procession, it must be by mode of reciprocal charity.[15]

> The love that the Holy Spirit is does not proceed from the Father insofar as he loves himself, nor does he proceed from the Son insofar as he loves himself, but he proceeds insofar as the one loves the other, because he is a *nexus* (a bond or link).[16]

If there is a first procession by mode of nature and a second procession by mode of will and liberality, Bonaventure taught, it is that the principle of both is essentially the Source of being. The idea of hierarchy and that of communication predominated in Bonaventure's thinking; in every sphere, there is a first who is for that reason the principle of communication or emanation, in his own words, 'primum, ergo principium':[17]

Ratione primitatis persona nata est ex se aliam producere; et voco hic primitatem innascibilitatem ratione cuius, ut dicit antiqua opinio, est fontalis plenitudo in Patre ad omnem emanationem, ut infra patebit.	By reason of his quality of first, one person is, by nature, inclined to produce another. I call here a 'quality of first' the *innascibilitas*, the fact that he cannot be born, by virtue of which, as an early view states, there is in the Father the fullness of a source from which everything emanates, as we shall see later.[18]

These words go back to a passage in Bonaventure's distinction 27, in which he discusses and justifies his decision about the question whether God begets because he is Father—this was to be Thomas Aquinas' position—or whether he is Father because he begets. But in that case, what is the reason for his begetting? Bonaventure claims that it is because he is first and distinguished by the fact that he cannot be born (*innascibilitas*). For Thomas, this *innascibilitas* is a negative quality that cannot positively describe anyone. Bonaventure, however, says:

It is, on the contrary, important to stress that this *innascibilitas*, under a negative form, is a perfect and positive reality. The Father cannot be born because he does not proceed from another. Not to proceed from another is to be the first, and primacy is a noble affirmation. In fact, 'first', seen in the formal sense of 'first', is such a positive affirmation that, as we shall see, the position of second follows the position of first. He is first and therefore he is the principle; he is the principle and therefore there is, in act or in potency, a term that proceeds from that principle (*Quia primum, ideo principium; quia principium, ideo vel actu vel habitu est principiatum*). Once it is admitted that the sense of primacy is always the sense of principle for things of the same order, we must conclude that, if the Father begets and produces by 'spiration', this is because he is the first with regard to every emanation, either by begetting or by spiration. And because being first in the order of begetting, that is to say, being *innascibilis*, at the same time includes being first in the order of spiration, that is to say, *improcessibilis*, we must say that he begets because he is the God who cannot be born. There is no value in asking why he is *innascibilis*, because this *innascibilitas* implies primacy and we have to stop at the first. . . . This is what will be said below, at the beginning of my twenty-ninth distinction, in the sentence: *Pater est principium totius divinitatis quia a nullo*. I have already touched on this truth in several other passages.

Quod movet ad hoc dicendum—what prompts me to maintain this doctrine is the early statement made by the great teachers who said that the Father's *innascibilitas* pointed to a flowing fullness (*fontalem plenitudinem*). A flowing fullness is, after all, a productive fullness. It is clear, however, that this flowing fullness is not attributed to the Father because he produces the creatures, since that is an act which is common to all three Persons. Nor is it attributed to him because he produces the Holy Spirit, because that act is common both to him and to the Son. This flowing fullness in the Father, then, affirms the active begetting in the same Person. If his *innascibilitas*, then, is his flowing fullness, it is clear that. . . .

Movet etiam communis opinio—what also prompts me is the common opinion, according to which this *innascibilitas* is peculiar to the Father. What is peculiar to the Father, however, characterizing him in the most excellent way, cannot be a notion that is purely negative. In this respect, the idea of *innascibilitas* is more suitable for the essence and the Holy Spirit. This notion nonetheless points to something—but neither to an absolute reality, since nothing that is absolute is a personal priority, nor to anything relatively positive which refers to the producer. This *innascibilitas* therefore has a positive relationship with a term that is produced. In accordance with our way of understanding, however, the first mode of production is by begetting. The position of *innascibilitas* therefore leads to the position of begetting. . . .

Movet etiam verbum Hilarii—what also prompts me is the statement mady by Hilary in the twelfth book of the Trinity, in which he says that the Father is the 'author' of the Son. It is clear that by 'author' here he does not mean the creator, but the one who begets. He is the author, then, by what constitutes authority in the Father. But the supreme authority in the Father has *innascibilitas* as its reason. Thus, it is by reason of innascibility that the hypostasis of the Father begets. This is what Hilary seems to be saying in the twelfth book of the Trinity, if his words are interpreted in depth, and the same applies to the fourth book.

Movet etiam verbum Philosophi—what also prompts me are the words of the philosopher, who speaks of principles that are all the more powerful the more they are first, who says that the first cause has more influence than the others and who claims that the cause which is absolutely and simply the first has a sovereign influence. If, then, we see, in the order of those causes between which there is an essential connection, that primacy confers a sovereign influence on the first cause and an influence that is in proportion to their essential rank on the second causes, the same reasoning must be applied when there is an order of persons and we must affirm that primacy in the first person is the reason for producing the others. And because *innascibilitas* connotes primacy, it also connotes the flowing fullness with regard to all personal production. A sign of this can be found in the hierarchy of kinds. The first kinds are the principles of the lower kinds. Those that are so much the first that it is necessary to stop there have an infinite power, like the point with regard to the line or the unit with regard to the numbers; the same applies to the divine essence insofar as it is the first with regard to the creatures. It is possibly because the divine essence is the first that it is omnipotent. And because all essence is posterior to the essence of the three Persons, it is impossible for one Person to produce something without the others. Therefore, although the ability to produce persons should not be extended to an infinite number, as I have shown above, if the impossible supposition is made that a thousand persons were produced, it would be necessary for all of them to proceed immediately from the Person of the Father. The first cause functions not only immediately in all mediate production, but also in the processions of the Persons.[19]

Bonaventure provides four more reasons in the text that follows. If I were asked what Bonaventure's position was in his teaching about the Trinity, I would say that he is certainly in the Augustinian tradition, not only in his idea of the Spirit as the bond of love between the Father and the Son, but also in his psychological analysis of the image of God in the *mens*. But Bonaventure, who outlined this in his *In I Sent.* d. 3, did not make it the principle of organization of his synthesis, which is indebted to Richard of Saint-Victor, Alexander of Hales and John Damascene and is ultimately closer to Greek thought, not so much in its style, which is clearly Scholastic, but rather in its great and decisive values.

Examples of this are his description of the monarchy of the Father, expressed in such concepts as *primitas*, *innascibilitas*, fertility and 'ideo principium quia primum'[20] and his definition of the Person as the 'supposit of a reasonable nature that is distinguished by a property'.[21] This property is, of course, the relationship, but Bonaventure does not, as Thomas Aquinas was to do, make use of the principle singled out and expressed by Anselm, namely that in God everything is one, except where there is an opposition of relationship. The Persons are distinguished by their different properties, each of which is identical with their origin and therefore with the relationship. They cannot be distinguished by anything absolute. It is, however, indisputable that, in his affirmation of the unity of the divine substance, Bonaventure keeps close to the idea of the communication of life from one Person to another. This sense of mystery is also clear from the fact that he may have been the first in the West to give a place to the circumincession (which he spelt in this way). We have already seen this in the passage that is quoted above from his *Itinerarium* (p. 110, and below, note 10), but he speaks of it elsewhere as well.[22] It points to a mysterious but admirable aspect of the life of the Trinity as a life of *Persons* in unity of nature.

NOTES

1. Alexander of Hales, *ST* I, pars 2, inq. V, tract. II, sect. II, q. 3, memb. 3 (Quaracchi ed. (1924), pp. 460ff.). Alexander says in this context: 'Magistri concedunt hanc "Pater et Filius diligunt se Spiritu Sancto", sed dissentiunt in determinatione ablativi'. Bonaventure also asks how this ablative should be interpreted and replies: 'quasi effectus formalis' and 'aliquo modo in ratione formae': *In I Sent*. d. 32, a. 1, q. 1 (Quaracchi ed. (1924), p. 560). Odo Rigaldus also spoke in the same way: see Volume I, p. 91 note 7.
2. Alexander of Hales, *Glossa in quatuor libros Sententiarum. In librum primum (Bibl. Franciscana Scholastica Medii Aevi*, XII) (Quaracchi, 1951), dist. XI; pp. 135ff.
3. Alexander of Hales, *Quaestiones disputatae 'Antequam esset frater' (Bibl. Franciscana Scholastica Medii Aevi*, XIX) (Quaracchi, 1960), q. 8, memb. 1, 2 and 3; pp. 67ff.
4. *Ibid.*, memb. 1, nos 16 and 18; pp. 71 and 72.
5. *Ibid.*, memb. 3, nos 29–35; p. 75.
6. *ST* I, pars I, inq. II, tract. I, q. 1 (Quaracchi ed., pp. 436ff.). T. de Régnon discussed Alexander's triadology exclusively on the basis of the *Summa Theologica*, insofar as the text was known at the time: *Etudes de théologie positive sur la Sainte Trinité*, II (Paris, 1892), pp. 338–431.
7. *ST* I, c. 5; pp. 452–453. He returns to it again in Pars II, inq. II, tract. III, sect. II, q. 1, tit. II, a. 3; pp. 602ff.: 'sunt unum in spirando'; see also a. 6; pp. 696–697: 'spiratio convenit Patri et Filio secundum hoc commune quod est unitas naturae sive rationis naturae, quae non est unitas naturae absolute vel essentialiter dictae, sed relative dicitur'. He also quotes a text of Isidore of Seville, *In Sent. V*, 15, 2 (*PL* 83, 569), who himself quotes Jn 17:22: 'ut sint unum sicut et nos unum sumus'. I do not know how the Greek Fathers commented on this text.
8. Bonaventure stresses this from the very beginning: see *In I Sent*. d. 2 (Quaracchi ed., I, p. 24): 'sicut fides dicit'; see also d. 3; p. 93.
9. *De myst. Trin*. q. 1, a. 2 (Quaracchi ed., V, pp. 51ff.).
10. *Itin*. VI, 2 (Quaracchi ed., V, pp. 310–311).
11. Pseudo-Dionysius, *De coel. hier*. c. 4, 1 (*PG* 3, 177); *De div. nom*. c. 4 § 5 and c. 5 § 20 (*PG* 3, 593, 720); see Bonaventure, *In I Sent*. d. 2, q. 2 (Quaracchi ed., I, p. 53).
12. *In I Sent*. d. 2, q. 4 (Quaracchi ed., V, p. 57); d. 10, a. 1, q. 1 (Quaracchi ed., V, p. 195); and q. 2 (Quaracchi ed., V, p. 197). See also J.-F. Bonnefoy, *Le Saint-Esprit et ses dons selon S. Bonaventure* (Paris, 1929), pp. 26–28.
13. *In I Sent*. d. 10, a. 2, q. 1 (Quaracchi ed., V, p. 201). T. de Régnon provided the following translation of this text, *op. cit.* (note 6), p. 549: 'The word "dilection" can be understood in the context of God as referring to the divine essence, the notional act or the Person. It can be used with reference to the essence, since each Person loves himself. It can be applied to the notional act, since the Father and the Son agree with each other to produce the Holy Spirit, "concordant in spirando spiritum sanctum", and that agreement is a love or "dilection". Finally, it can be employed in the personal sense, because the one who is produced by way of perfect liberality can only be love or "dilection". An example of this can be found in the affection of creatures, through which a bridegroom and his bride love

each other. They love one another with a "social" love so that they can live together. What is more, they love one another with a "conjugal" love so that they can procreate a child. If that child were produced by the agreement of wills alone, it would be "love". In fact, the child is only the "loved one", although it may be called "love" by virtue of a kind of emphasis. In God, however, it is truly "love", because it has the characteristics of love and hypostasis. It has the character of love because of the immediate procession from a very liberal will by means of perfect liberality. It has the character of hypostasis because, being distinguished from its productive principle and not being able to distinguish itself from it essentially, it is distinguished from it personally.'

14. *In I Sent.* d. 32, a. 1, q. 1 and a. 2, q. 1 (Quaracchi ed., pp. 552 and 562).

15. *In I Sent.* d. 10, a. 1, q. 3 (Quaracchi ed., p. 199).

16. *In I Sent.* d. 13, a. unic., q. 1, No. 4 (Quaracchi ed., p. 231); d. 10, a. 2, q. 2 (Quaracchi ed., p. 202).

17. 'Ideo principium quia primum': *In I Sent.* d. 7, a. un. q. 2 (Quaracchi ed., p. 139). For this *primitas* as a very important category in Bonaventure's thought, see *De myst. Trin.* q. 8 (Quaracchi ed., V, p. 114); and the *Lexique S. Bonaventure* (Paris, 1969), under the entry 'Primitas'. Another idea that is much favoured by Bonaventure is that of *reductio ad unum primum*. He also makes use of this idea in his ecclesiology. See, for example, *De myst. Trin.* q. 2, a. 1 (Quaracchi ed., V, p. 61); *In II Sent.* d. 37, a. 1, q. 3, fund. 3 (Quaracchi ed., II, p. 867).

18. *In I Sent.* d. 2, q. 2 (Quaracchi ed., p. 54). This is an opening statement, made on the threshold of the *De myst. Trin.*

19. *In I Sent.* d. 27, q. 1, a. 1, q. 1 ad 3; tr. T. de Régnon, *op. cit.* (note 6), pp. 484ff. Further relevant quotations are: 'innascibilitas quae idem est in Patre quod primitas, cum primum et principium sint idem': d. 11, a. un. q. 2 (Quaracchi ed., p. 215); 'auctor dicit in Patre fontalem plenitudinem, quia ipse non est ab alio sed alii ab ipso, et inde dicit, ut credo, eandem notionem quem dicit innascibilis, sed differenti modo': d. 13, dub. IV (Quaracchi ed., p. 240). See also below, pp. 135–136. Bonaventure believed that this *innascibilitas* implied fertility, that there was no antecedent or father and that it could give being to another: see, for example, the long *retractatio* in the prologue to *In II Sent.*, reproduced in the scholion of the editors; *In I Sent.* d. 27, p. 1 to 2 (Quaracchi ed., pp. 472ff.).

20. See the previous note. The Holy Spirit proceeds *prius a Patre origine* and *auctoritate*: *In I Sent.* d. 12, a. un. q. 1 and 2.

21. *In I Sent.* d. 23, a. 1, q. 1 (Quaracchi ed., p. 409); d. 25, a. 1, q. 1 (Quaracchi ed., p. 436); in q. 2, Bonaventure accepted Boethius' definition; d. 34, a. un. q. 1 (Quaracchi ed., p. 587), where he also says *hypostasis*.

22. *In I Sent.* d. 19, q. 1, a. un. q. 4 (Quaracchi ed., p. 349); *Coll. in Hexameron* XXI, 19 (Quaracchi ed., V, p. 434). Peter Lombard wrote an excellent chapter on this question, but did not use the word. It is also worth noting, in this context, the comment made by William of Saint-Thierry, that we cannot name one of the Persons of the Trinity without implying another—the Son calls for the Father, and the Spirit as Gift calls for a Giver. This, William thought, was evidence that the Persons were related to each other and that they existed within each other.

4

THOMAS AQUINAS[1]

According to Thomas Aquinas, it is impossible to prove or understand by human reason the mystery of the Tri-unity of God. All that can be grasped by reason alone is the existence and the attributes of God the creator. God acts as creator through his nature, which is common to the three Persons, while revealing the latter only in traces, like the traces of a man whose face and voice remain unknown.

Thomas' theology is thus based on faith and his thinking is done in faith.[2] He did so with an exceptional use and mastery of the resources of reason, which was formed in the Aristotelian school and Scholastic disputation. He was firmly convinced of the value and the consistency of the truth that human reason was able to deduce from the reality of creation. He applied the rules of that reason and observed the demands made by it in elaborating his theological arguments, within the framework of affirmations of faith and on the basis of certain scriptural statements. This gives his work an impression of overriding rationality. This impression is particularly powerful, for example, in a text such as question 10 of *De Potentia*. It is, however, at the same time impossible to avoid being struck by his masterly knowledge and use of Scripture, and of the writings of the Fathers, although it has to be admitted that his knowledge of the Greek patristic texts was incomplete.[3]

A whole book could be written on his pneumatology. Such a book would contain at least four chapters: (1) the great principles of the theology of faith in the Trinity; (2) the procession of the Holy Spirit *a Patre et Filio tanquam ab uno principio*; (3) the theme of the Spirit as the mutual love of the Father and the Son (see Volume I of this work, pp. 88–90); (4) the part played by the Holy Spirit in the life of the Christian and of the Church. The last chapter has not been greatly studied, except for the question of the indwelling of the Holy Spirit and that of the gifts of the Spirit. I have already dealt with these questions in Volumes I and II.[4] Later in this volume, I shall look at the part played by the Spirit in the sacraments. Thomas Aquinas' consideration of the rôle of the Holy Spirit in the whole economy of grace and in his view of the Church has, however, still to be discussed with the full and precise attention that it deserves.[5]

Any attempt to present him as an 'essentialist', that is, as being conscious of and as affirming first of all the common divine essence, and only secondarily the Persons in that essence, would be to betray the balance of his theology. Such an interpretation should no longer be possible since the appearance of the studies by A. Malet, H. F. Dondaine, E. Bailleux, M.-J. Le Guillou and others.[6] This interpretation has all too frequently been based on the fact that Thomas' study of the Trinity of Persons in the *Summa* is preceded by a study of the divine essence. Surely, however, it is hardly possible not to proceed in this way from the point of view of teaching? Is this procedure not justified by the economy of revelation itself? Did John Damascene not begin with the unity of 'God'? Thomas had a very lively sense of the absolute character of God, his transcendence, his independence and his sufficiency.[7] In his mystery, which is both necessary and absolute, God knows and loves himself. He communicates his goodness with sovereign freedom in the free mystery of creation and of the 'divine missions' through which creatures, who are made 'in his image', are included in that life of knowledge and love and are in this way 'deified'.

Through the Word of God and in faith, we know that there are three Persons in the unity of the divine substance. Thomas accepts this article of faith from no other source than the faith, but, as a theologian, he attempts to understand it: 'utcumque mente capere' (*Contra Gent.* IV, 1). God descended to us in the forms and words of our world, and we have to use the same instruments in order to re-ascend to him.

In a very resolute way, Thomas follows the path traced first by Augustine and especially by Anselm. He is aware of the path followed by Richard of Saint-Victor and Bonaventure, and he criticizes it cautiously.[8] He retains the idea of the Holy Spirit as Love and Gift and affirms that these titles are correctly bestowed on the Spirit (*ST* Ia, q. 37 and 38). He also preserves the idea that the Spirit is the mutual love of the Father and the Son. He does not, however, make these ideas the principle by which the mystery of the holy Triad should be understood *theologically* or that on which a *theological* construction should be erected. The principle that he prefers is the structure of the spirit itself, which includes knowledge and love of itself.[9] He does not, however, deduce these faculties or these acts from the essence of God, nor does he see in this structure the equivalent of Anselm's *rationes necessariae*. He is familiar with the work of Anselm and follows him, but rejects the idea of 'necessary reason'.[10] For him, what affirms the Triad of Father, Word-Son and Spirit is faith. The best way of approaching this mystery of faith intellectually, he claims, is through our knowledge of the structure of a spiritual being. This being exists in three ways—in its being as reality, in its thought as a known 'object' and in its will as a loved 'object'. Thinking and will are immanent functions which remain in the subject as its life. The term of these functions, the intellectual expression or the mental word, and the impression made in the one who loves by the act of loving are also immanent.

There are two 'processions' in God, but the term 'procession' is used in a very general sense by Thomas and, in his teaching, points simply to the fact that one reality comes from another.[11] From the theological point of view, these processions can be understood on the model of the functioning of the

117

spirit—as emanations or communications of the nature of that spirit by mode of intellectual understanding and by mode of will.[12] The mode of will clearly produces dynamic movement, and Thomas stresses the fact that the very name 'spirit' indicates a movement or an impulse.[13] He makes a similar comment with regard to the gifts of the Holy Spirit and the text of Isaiah in which they are listed.[14]

These emanations of the divine nature do not, Thomas believes, take place in the same way as the human faculties emanate from man's essence, from which the faculties are really quite different. The divine processions in fact constitute Persons who are both really identical with the essence of God and at the same time different from each other. This is the whole problem of the Trinity—it is one in the absolute sense and at the same time several. These several Persons are identical with the absolute one and yet really different from each other, to the point of being Persons, that is, a spiritual reality existing in itself in a way that cannot be communicated. The solution to these aporias can be found in the ideas of *relationship, relationship of origin*, with the *opposition* between the two terms that this idea implies, and *subsistent relationship*.

The Son is not the Father and the Father is not the Son. But the Father is God and the Son is God. Each is everything that the other is, apart from that character which describes it by reference to another and which in this way also distinguishes it within the unity of both.[15] What defines the Person, then, is the relationship which both unites and opposes that Person to the other. This opposition is an opposition of the relationship itself—to say Father is to say Son and vice versa. The unity is in the communication of the entire good of the nature (or the essence or substance) of God. This communication takes place by means of the fact that one Person is the origin of the other—the Father is the origin of the Son as the spirit is similarly the origin of the word in which it is expressed. What constitutes the Person, then, according to Thomas, is his relationship of origin.[16] Through that relationship, the Person is *really* distinguished from the Person who is correlative to him. But in God, these relationships are *really* identical with the sovereignly simple essence and this means that they have that quality of 'subsistent relationships' that Thomas defines and employs in his triadology.[17] As H. F. Dondaine pointed out,[18] 'the divine Person is the divine and subsistent relationship regarded as distinctly subsistent. In other words, it is the relationship of origin insofar as that relationship enjoys in God the prerogatives of substance and insofar as it is absolute, while at the same time being intra-divinely incommunicable.'

Thomas' theology of the Person and the relationship of origin is also applied to the second procession, the one that takes place in God by mode of will or love. The procession of the Holy Spirit is not only *ex Patre*, from the Father, but also *ex Filio*, from the Son. Thomas deals with this question in his *Summa* in a dialectic and highly rationalized way. In other writings, he provides proofs derived from Scripture and the Fathers.[19] The scriptural texts that he uses are those that had been employed for centuries by the Latins, but their value as proofs is heightened by rational explanations. The Spirit is, for example, the Spirit of the Son (or of Christ) (Rom 8:9; Gal 4:6). The Spirit is sent by the Son (Jn 15:26), but the 'mission' of a Person is linked to his procession. 'He will take what is mine' (Jn 16:14)—this declaration that the Spirit will receive from Jesus is followed by the decisive reason: 'All that the Father has is mine; therefore I said that he will take what is mine'. The Greeks, as we have seen, thought that these texts referred to the economy and not to the eternal relationships, but Thomas shows that they cannot be applied to the humanity of Christ, but only to his divinity. He is above all concerned to provide reasons for this.

His main reason is derived from the essence of the Trinitarian theology elaborated by Anselm. The divine Persons are distinguished not by an absolute perfection, but only by a mutual opposition in their relationships. If these relationships are not opposed, there is no question of different Persons. The Father produces the Son by begetting and the Spirit by spiration, but, as begetting and spiration are not opposed, this duality of relationships does not bring about a duality of Persons in the Father. In the same way, these two processions or modes or proceeding are not opposed, so that they are not in themselves sufficient to distinguish the Son from the Spirit as two different Persons. In God, the only relationships that are really opposed are those of origin, which are opposed as the beginning or principle and the term. Consequently, if the Holy Spirit is to be personally distinguished from the Son, there must be a relationship of origin between them, in other words, the Spirit must proceed from the Son at the same time as he proceeds from the Father. Thomas is categorical and even almost rough in his affirmation of this, saying: If the Spirit did not proceed from the Son, he would not be distinguished from him![20] He thus decisively rejects Photius' triadology.

Thomas was, however, more positive in his acceptance of the theme of *per Filium* than Anselm had been before him.[21] The Father is the *auctor*, the absolute principle, from whom the Son is able to perform the 'spiration' of the Spirit.[22] The Word begotten by God the Father is not an ordinary conception. In his very reality as Word, he is a Word from whom Love proceeds—as Thomas himself said, he is 'Verbum non qualecumque, sed spirans amorem'.[23] Thomas is, however, more anxious to affirm the unity of the hypostases than to stress their order. He does not fully recognize the implication of the *dia tou Huiou* on which the Greeks insisted so much, but he does sense the complementarity of the two formulae.[24] Although he accepts the *per Filium*, he, like Anselm, is anxious to exclude any inequality. The Father, as *auctor*, communicates the faculty of spiration to the Word, but he does so by making him a single and identical principle, along with himself.

119

The Greeks, however, have been raising objections to the Western teaching and asking critical questions since the time of Photius. Nilus Cabasilas[25] asked such questions in the fourteenth century and they were asked a century later at Florence by Mark Eugenikos. The identical objections are raised by my Greek friends and contemporaries, and it is at this point that we must consider them. They can be summarized as follows: If the Spirit also proceeds from the Son, then either he proceeds from two principles or else he proceeds from the essence that is common to the Father and the Son, but in that case he would also proceed from himself, because that essence is also common to him. This situation is clearly absurd, the Greeks claim, unless the divine essence is not shared by all three Persons and the two first Persons have a reality that the third lacks.

These objections are, of course, justified within the perspective of Eastern triadology and within the context of the Greek vocabulary applied to the Trinity. The hypostases and the monarchy of the Father are aspects of great importance in the Orthodox triadology. One hypostasis proceeds only from another hypostasis, who communicates the fullness of the divine nature or essence to him. The terms *ekporeusis*, *aitia* and *archē* are only applied in the East to the Father and they express above all the *first* origin. The Latins were wrong to translate them as *processio*, *causa* and *principium* respectively, in the belief that these words had the same meaning as the Greek words, when in fact they can be applied more widely to include the Son with the Father.[26]

The Latin theologians, especially Thomas Aquinas, but before him Alexander of Hales (see above), have provided reasons for their belief. It is not enough to say that 'the spiration comes from the divine nature insofar as it is common to the Father and the Son',[27] because it does not come from that nature, but from supposits or Persons who have in common a nature that exists only in a hypostatized form. Thomas follows the logic of the principle according to which the divine Persons are distinguished from each other only by a relationship of opposition and goes on to distinguish, in the properties, those which are identical with the Persons because they are constitutive of those Persons—fatherhood and sonship—and those which, not being constitutive (because they do not include a relationship of opposition), can be common to several Persons. This is so in the case of active spiration, in which the Father and the Son are not, as such, opposed. Thomas' insistence on these relationships and their opposition leads him to make a further subtle, but very important definition, namely that the Father is not, *as Father*, the principle of the Spirit, because he is only the Father of the Son. He is, the Greeks claimed, the principle of the Spirit as *archē* and has the title of *proboleus*.[28] The Latins, on the other hand, maintained that the Spirit proceeds not from God his Father, but from God who is Father,[29] or else that he proceeds from the Father as *auctor* or absolute Principle. They also claim that, in the equal status of the *virtus spirativa*, there is also an order—just as the Persons in the Trinity are equal, yet proceed from each other, the Father being the Principle without principle and the Son receiving from him his faculty which enables him to produce the Spirit in a simple and unique act of spiration that is common to both.

The Latin theologians, including Thomas, based their reasoning on the principle that the Father gives the Son all that he has apart from his quality of being Father. He therefore also gives him the faculty of spiration. The Father does not, however, give the Son the faculty to beget, nor does he give the Spirit the faculty of spiration. Even if the Father gives the Son the faculty of spiration with him, he does not communicate to him the nature to be *principaliter* at the origin of the Spirit. As Thomas pointed out, 'the essence and the dignity of the Father and the Son are identical, but in the Father they exist according to the relationship of the one who gives, whereas in the Son they exist according to the relationship of the one who receives'.[30] The Latins were therefore careful to preserve the full truth of the monarchy of the Father, although they did not make it the axis of their theological construction, as the Greeks did in their triadology.

The Holy Spirit proceeds by mode of will or love. The personal names that he receives are Love and Gift (see *ST* Ia, q. 37 and 38). Thomas also pursued the theme of the Spirit as the mutual love of the Father and the Son at every stage of his life and in all his writings (see Volume I, pp. 88–90).

There is, then, a procession in God in accordance with will and love. This procession enables the Holy Spirit to exist eternally. The latter is therefore hypostatically Love. The word 'love', however, at once evokes the idea of an impulse or a movement towards a good. In man, it is because of a lack and the need to acquire what we do not have, except in friendship, which is a communication with the other, whereas in God that love is a superabundance and a great generosity. God is Love, *agapē*. He is the source of Love, a Love that gives itself in grace. His love does not try to satisfy a hunger, but to arouse and communicate being.[31] If the Spirit, then, is hypostatic Love in God—and his name 'Spirit', Thomas believed, points to an impulse (see note 13 below)—everything that is gift, grace and the communication of being and good must be traced back to him as manifesting his property as a Person.

It is in this line of love of self (and of all things in himself) by God that Thomas looks for a theological understanding of what he believes through faith regarding the third Person. Secondly, he considers essential love of the kind that is common to the three Persons. This accompanies the first procession. The Father experiences it with regard to the Son and the Son experiences it with regard to the Father. In this question, Thomas goes back to the theme of mutual love and sees the Holy Spirit as the link between the two Persons—the *nexus amborum* or *amor unitivus duorum*.[32] All those who have considered pneumatology in the context of the mutual love of the Father and the Son have always quoted scriptural texts in which Jesus speaks of the love of the Father for him and of his love for the Father.[33] These texts have the incarnate Word in mind. The 'I' of these texts is certainly that of the eternal Son, but one in whom human consciousness and freedom must be acknowledged. It is therefore a metaphysical 'I', but an 'I' who is also psychologically human.

The theme of the Spirit as the mutual love of the Father and the Son has been widely discussed in recent works on triadology and in spiritual books. It is not difficult to explain and it can easily be applied to other forms of expression. It is in accordance with human experience and it has strong echoes in the psychological study of interpersonal relationships. It also quickly arouses a warm response. On the other hand, however, it presents certain difficulties to the theologian. Above all, it takes anthropomorphic expressions to the limit of doctrinal precision. Also, it goes back to a different way of thinking from that of the Eastern Orthodox. But we should have no illusion about this—Thomas' way of thinking may be more accessible than that of the Eastern Christians because it is more dogmatic, but it is not the same as theirs either.

According to Thomas, then, the Spirit proceeds by mode of will and love. He is uncreated, hypostatic Love and he deserves to be called Love and Gift. In that case, he clearly is, by appropriation, the principle of what God freely produces outside himself as a participation of his goodness. Thomas develops this idea in three very dense and rewarding chapters in his *Contra Gentiles*—I shall come back to these below—and in a short chapter in his *Compendium theologiae* which is a gloss on the third article of the creed. The text of the latter is as follows:

> The second effect caused by God is the government of the world and in particular of those creatures who are gifted with reason and to whom he has given grace and whose sins he has remitted. All this is called to mind in the creed, on the one hand when we confess the Holy Spirit as God—this means that all things are ordered to the end of divine goodness, since it is God's function to order his subjects to their end (the Spirit is called 'Lord')—and, on the other hand, it is clear that he gives movement to all things—he is called the 'giver of life'. In the same way, just as the movement that passes from the soul to the body is the life of the body, so too is the movement with which God animates the world a kind of life of the universe. It was suitable that the effects of divine Providence should be situated close to the Holy Spirit, since the whole of divine government is dependent on divine goodness, which is appropriated to the Holy Spirit, who proceeds as love. For what is of the effect of supernatural knowledge, which God brings about in men through faith, we say 'the holy Catholic Church', since the Church is the assembly of the faithful; for what is of the grace that he communicates to men, we say 'the communion of saints'; for what is of the remission of faults, we say 'the remission of sins'.[34]

What is stated in the rational and rather barren style of this *Compendium* is set out more explicitly in:

(1) The very rich biblical chapters of *Contra Gentiles* IV. These are chapter 20: 'the effects attributed to the Holy Spirit with regard to the whole of creation', that is, everything that exists of goodness, movement towards the end, and life; chapter 21: 'the effects attributed to the Holy Spirit with regard to the creature gifted with reason, as regards what God grants to us or lavishes on us', that is, everything that is given through love to a friend; chapter 22: 'the effects of the Holy Spirit through whom God enables his creature to return to himself', that is, according to what a life of friendship, a filial life, a life in freedom includes. I dream of an eloquent translation of these three chapters with a commentary and notes, pointing out especially the use that Thomas has made of so many magnificent biblical texts elsewhere in his writings. . . .

(2) Part IIa of the *Summa*. Thomas describes the general structures of Christian action in Part Ia IIae and studies the composite parts of that action in IIa IIae. He shows that it is a supernatural form of human activity sustained by the law of God and the grace of the Holy Spirit and that the principal aspect of this Christian law is grace itself, which operates in such a way that the law is a law of freedom (see Volume II, pp. 124–126). It is a life as children of God.[35] Grace places charity in us and Thomas defines this as friendship.[36] This friendship means that the Trinity dwells in us (see Volume II, pp. 79–90). Thomas' sense of the theologal character of faith, hope and charity was exceptionally acute, with the result that he believed that these virtues, which make us children of God, could only be practised according to their divine demands if there were impulses from the Holy Spirit. This constitutes his theology of the gifts, to which the fruits of the Spirit and the beatitudes, which are the supreme acts of forms of Christian life, correspond. I have spoken about these in Volume I, pp. 117–121, and Volume II, pp. 134–139. Finally, there is the question of merit, the principal agent of which is the Holy Spirit (see Volume II, p. 108).

(3) All this actively concerns the life of the Christian, which is personal, but not simply individual. Thomas is conscious of the believer as a member of the Church and sees charity as a virtue of the common good of the City of God.[37] That City is also the Church, which Thomas sees as unified, sanctified and animated by the Holy Spirit.[38] Unfortunately it is not possible for me to discuss in detail here the many scattered, but quite consistent indications in his writings that form part of his pneumatology. This is all the more regrettable, since this question has not yet been studied as exhaustively as it should have been.

*   *   *

Many of the later, less successful imitators of the great thirteenth-century theologians of the Western Church, some of whom were very active and vigorous workers, elaborated and discussed the great questions of Trinitarian theology with an excessive reliance on philosophical concepts and arguments. M. Schmaus[39] analysed and partly edited this copious body of writing in which these sublime questions were discussed with great confidence in the unlimited scope of theological reasoning: Does the Father beget because he is Father or is he Father because he begets? Are the two processions, begetting and spiration, to be distinguished by their term or by their principle or beginning? If the Father and the Son love each other through the Spirit, can this 'through the Spirit' be regarded as a 'formal effect'? What is the principle by which (*quo*) of spiration? What is the difference between begetting (generation) and spiration? Would the Spirit be different from the Son because of an absolute quality if he did not proceed from him? In the thirteenth and fourteenth centuries, there were two traditions or schools. One was in the path followed by Thomas Aquinas. The other was the tradition of Henry of Ghent and Duns Scotus, and before that of Bonaventure and, before him again, up stream, Richard of Saint-Victor.

NOTES

1. The most important texts are: *In I Sent*. d. 3 to 31; *Contra Gent*. IV, 1 to 28; *Contra Err. Graec*. (1264); *De Pot*. q. 8 to 10; *ST* Ia, q. 27 to 43; see H. F. Dondaine's translation, with commentary, 2 vols (Paris, 1943). Apart from T. de Régnon, *Etudes de théologie positive sur la Sainte Trinité*, II (Paris, 1892), the following studies are valuable: H. F. Dondaine, 'La théologie latine de la procession du Saint-Esprit', *Russie et Chrétienté* (1950), 211–218; M. T. L. Penido, ' "Cur non Spiritus Sanctus a Patre Deo genitus". S. Augustin et S. Thomas', *RThom* (1930), 508–527; *idem*, 'Gloses sur la procession d'amour dans la Trinité', *ETL*, 14 (1937), 33–68; for the discussion that followed this article, see *BullThom* (1937–1939), 135–139 and 547–549; A. Malet, *Personne et amour dans la théologie trinitaire de S. Thomas* (*Bibl. thomiste*, XXXII) (Paris, 1956); J. Pelikan, 'The Doctrine of the Filioque in Thomas Aquinas and its Patristic Antecedents. An Analysis of Summa Theologica Part I, q. 36', *S. Thomas Aquinas. Commemorative Studies*, I (Toronto, 1974), pp. 315–336. See also Volume I, pp. 88–90, 91–92 notes 9 to 14, and 118–121, 124 notes 17 to 26.
2. Thomas frequently stated and justified this, for example, in *In I Sent*. d. 3, q. 1, a. 4; *Contra Gent*. I, 3 and 9; IV, 1; *De Pot*. q. 9, a. 5 and 9; q. 10, a. 1; *ST* Ia, q. 1, a. 8, ad 2; q. 32, a. 1; q. 45, a. 6. See also *Quodl*. IV, 18: 'quomodo sit verum'.
3. In his Trinitarian theology, he only really cites Pseudo-Dionysius and John Damascene. There is a vague and general reference to the 'doctores Graecorum' in *ST* Ia, q. 35, a. 2 c. and ad 4. His references to the Greek Fathers in *ST* Ia are concerned with anthropology and the work of the six days of creation: see G. Bardy, 'Sur les sources patristiques grecques de S. Thomas dans la 1ʳᵉ partie de la Somme théologique', *RSPT*, 12 (1923), 493–502. Thomas thought very highly of Gregory Nazianzen: q. 61, a. 3 c. end. There is also a general comment in *Contra Err. Graec*. I, 10.
4. For the indwelling of the Spirit, see Volume II, pp. 82–90; for the gifts, see Volume I, pp. 117–121, and Volume II, pp. 134–139.
5. M. Grabmann, *Die Lehre des heiligen Thomas von der Kirche als Gotteswerk* (Regensburg, 1903), has some interesting observations; references in my article, 'Vision de l'Eglise chez S. Thomas d'Aquin', *RSPT*, 62 (1978), 523–542, especially 532–536.
6. A. Malet, *op. cit.* (note 1), and 'La synthèse de la personne et de la nature dans la théologie trinitaire de S. Thomas,' *RThom*, 54 (1954), 483–522, and 55 (1955), 43–84; E. Bailleux,

'Le personnalisme de S. Thomas en théologie trinitaire', *ibid.*, 61 (1961), 25–42; *idem*, 'La création, œuvre de la Trinité selon S. Thomas', *ibid.*, 62 (1962), 27–60; M.-J. Le Guillou, *Le Christ et l'Eglise. Théologie du mystère* (Paris, 1963); *idem*, *Le Mystère du Père* (Paris, 1973). *Contra Err. Graec.* I, 4 criticizes all the formulae in which the procession of the Persons is linked with the divine essence.

7. May I record the evidence of my personal experience here? We had to begin our theological studies with *De Deo uno* because of the way in which Thomas' treatises to be studied were distributed at the time. This coincided with our reception of minor orders. The benefit that we derived from this was a very lively sense of the absolute nature of God.

8. Thomas criticizes Richard's argument with regard to the communication of good, which is necessary to God's perfect state of blessedness. See *De Pot.* q. 9, a. 5, videtur quod non 24; *ST* Ia, q. 32, a. 1, ad 2. For a criticism of Bonaventure's construction on the basis of God's *innascibilitas*, see *ST* Ia, q. 33, a. 4, ad 1.

9. See *Contra Gent.* IV, 19, 23, end, 26; *De Pot.* q. 10, a. 1 and 2; *ST* Ia, q. 27, a. 1, 3 to 5; q. 37, a. 1. In the enigmatic *Comp.* I, 50, we read: 'Deus in esse suo naturali existens, et Deus existens in intellectu, et Deus existens in amore suo unum sunt'.

10. See C. Vagaggini, 'La hantise des *rationes necessariae* de S. Anselme dans la théologie des processions trinitaires de S. Thomas', *Spicilegium Beccense*, I (*Congrès internationale du IXᵉ centenaire de l'arrivée d'Anselme au Bec*) (Le Bec-Hellouin and Paris, 1959), pp. 103–139. I do not believe that an 'obsession [*hantise*] with the *rationes necessariae*' is a good category, since it is a question of rationality of faith and in faith. The fact that the sending out of a word by intelligence is treated as a simple perfection shows us, subject to the presupposition of faith, that there is a procession in God of a Word, the Son, but it does not enable us to infer the fact, since we do not know the positive mode by which this perfection is realized in God or the way in which God is this perfection in the absolute unity of his substance. Is it a simple attribute? Is it a hypostasis? Or is it a subsistent relationship? It is, however, true to say that, when grounds of fittingness (*convenientia*) are taken from the formal structure of realities, they come close to the proof of existence.

11. See *De Pot.* q. 10, a. 1; a. 4 ad 13: *procedere* has the advantage of being the 'verbum communissimum eorum quae ad originem spectant', although this excludes an understanding of the meaning and the importance that *ekporeuesthai* had for the Greeks, despite the fact that Thomas was very near to an understanding of this in his *In I Sent.* d. 12, q. 1, a. 2, ad 3. See also *Contra Err. Graec.* II, 16; *ST* Ia, q. 36, a. 2, c. end.

12. In *De Pot.* q. 10, a. 2, Thomas uses this formula in place of the one that appears in the *Sentences*: 'per modum naturae, per modum voluntatis'. Logically enough, the theme of 'Son' was given priority over that of 'Word' in the *Sentences*. The Greek Fathers had also tended to follow the theme of 'Son', although they had also stressed the theme of 'image'. Thomas shows very rigorously that the Word proceeds in God in accordance with a process of begetting—the second Person is the Son because he is the Word and he is the Word because he is the Son; see *Contra Gent.* IV, 11; *ST* Ia, q. 27, a. 2; q. 34, a. 1 and 2. See also Gregory Nazianzen, *Orat.* 30 (= *Orat. theol.* IV), 20 (*PG* 36, 129A).

13. See *Contra Gent.* IV, 19, in which Thomas uses the word *inclinatio* again and again; see also IV, 20: 'amor vim quandam impulsivam et motivam habet'; *ST* Ia, q. 27, a. 4, c. end and q. 36, a. 1: 'nomen spiritus impulsionem quamdam et motionem significare videtur'.

14. *ST* Ia IIae, q. 68, a. 1: Isaiah speaks not of 'gifts', but of 'spirits', which means that they are *ab inspiratione divina*.

15. As Maximus the Confessor said, *Amb.* 26 (*PG* 91, 1265C-D), 'the name of Father is neither a name of essence nor a name of energy, but rather a name of *schēsis*, that is, of relationship, and it says how the Father is towards the Son and how the Son is towards the Father'.

16. *De Pot.* q. 8, a. 1. Thomas believed that the relationship logically preceded the origin and that it was what defined the Person. Consequently, in a discussion in which Bonaventure, taking as his point of departure the ideas that we have outlined above, held a different view,

Thomas said: 'quia Pater est, generat', in other words, he is not the Father because he begets, but he begets because he is the Father. This is, of course, a very subtle distinction. It is a question which preoccupied the Scholastic theologians, not because of the words themselves, but because of the need to establish order in our human ways of thinking and speaking. It is the famous *modus significandi*. It means that the subsistent Person, with all that constitutes it (the relationship), is absolutely first. It is logically first and precedes its act: see *ST* Ia, q. 40 and the explanations provided by H. F. Dondaine. In the relationship itself, if what it is in God is considered, the *esse in*, which makes it subsistent, logically precedes the *esse ad*, which distinguishes it from another Person by opposing it relationally.

17. *De Pot*. q. 8, a. 1, ad 4; a. 2; a. 3, ad 7 and 9; a. 4; q. 9, a. 4; a. 5 ad 13; q. 10, a. 1 ad 12; a. 2, ad 1; *ST* Ia, q. 28, a. 2; q. 29, a. 3 and 4; q. 40, a. 1; q. 42, a. 5. This real identity between relationship and substance, two terms which seem to be situated at the extreme end of reality, is possible because 'substance' in God is not in a genus: see *De Pot*. q. 8, a. 2, ad 1.

18. Fr. tr. H. F. Dondaine, *op. cit.* (note 1), I, p. 245; *In I Sent*. d. 23, a. 3, c. See also A. Malet, *op. cit.* (note 1).

19. Thomas did this before his rational argument in *Contra Gent*. IV, 24, but after that provided in *De Pot*. q. 10, a. 4. See also the second part of the *Contra Err. Graec.*, where several of the patristic texts quoted are known to be, at least in part, unauthentic. Thomas refrained from using them in his *Summa*.

20. *In I Sent*. d. 13, q. 1, a. 2; *De Pot*. q. 10, a. 5, a very well developed article; *ST* Ia, q. 36, a. 2; *Comm. in ev. Ioan*. c. 15, lect. 5, No. 7. See also *Contra Gent*. IV, 25, where Thomas deals with the Greek rejection of the *Filioque* with a vivacity which shows that he had not really grasped their reasons.

21. *De Pot*. q. 10, a. 5; the *a Filio* is established in the body of the article; cf. *ST* Ia, q. 36, where the *a Filio* is established in art. 3.

22. See below, p. 136, for Thomas Aquinas' acceptance of Augustine's *principaliter* and of the theme of *auctor*.

23. *In I Sent*. d. 27, q. 2, a. 1; *ST* Ia, q. 43, a. 5, ad 2; *Comm. in ev. Ioan*. c. 6, lect. 5, No. 5.

24. In his *De Processione Spiritus Sancti* (*PG* 161, 397C-400A), John Bessarion observes that *ex Filio* means equality and not order, whereas *per Filium* points to order rather than to equality and sees in these two different and yet complementary aspects the anxiety of the Latins and the Greeks respectively.

25. Cabasilas rejected the possibility of proving the procession from the Son by means of syllogisms and studied and criticized fifteen such syllogisms. These have been examined by E. Candal, *Nilus Cabasilas et theologia S. Thomae de Processione Spiritus Sancti* (*Studi e Testi*, 116) (Vatican, 1945): Cabasilas' treatise is edited on pp. 188–385. See also the criticism of Thomas Aquinas' syllogisms in *Contra Gent*. IV, 24, by Cabasilas and the reply made by the translator, Demetrios Kydones, in M. Rackl, 'Der heilige Thomas von Aquin und das trinitarische Grundgesetz in byzantinischer Beleuchtung', S. Szabó, ed., *Xenia Thomistica* (Rome, 1925), III, pp. 363–389.

26. V. Grumel pointed this out in his article 'S. Thomas et la doctrine des Grecs sur la procession du Saint-Esprit', *Echos d'Orient*, 25 (1926), 257–280. This is an excellent article, which has lost nothing of its value with the passage of the years.

27. This is T. de Régnon's formula, *Etudes de théologie positive sur la Sainte Trinité*, I (Paris, 1892), pp. 308–309.

28. *Proboleus*—see above, pp. 38, 47 note 69; John Damascene, *PG* 94, 849A. This question has been discussed by A. de Halleux, 'La procession de l'Esprit Saint dans le symbole de Constantinople', *RTL*, 10 (1979), 34. According to this author, in Gregory Nazianzen, *Orat*. 31, 6, 'the Father is understood as divine nature and as the source of divinity before being seen as a pole of personal opposition', and with the creed of 381, 'the title of God, which is necessary because of the Johannine text (15:26), does not point here to the first

Person in his personal uniqueness, but only to him as the source of divinity': *op. cit.*, pp. 33–34.

29. T. de Régnon, *op. cit.* (note 27), IV (Paris, 1898), p. 275.
30. *ST* Ia, q. 42, a. 4, ad 2.
31. See Thomas' frequently repeated axiom: 'amor Dei creans et infundens bonitatem in rebus', *ST* Ia, q. 20, a. 2, 3 and 4; q. 23, a. 4; Ia IIae, q. 26, a. 3, ad 4, *Tabula aurea*, 'amor', No. 21.
32. *ST* Ia, q. 36, a. 4, ad 1; q. 37, a. 1, ad 3; q. 39, a. 8.
33. The Father loves the Son: see Jn 3:35; 5:20; 10:17; 17:23, where the evangelist is clearly speaking of the incarnate Christ; 17:24, where he presupposes the pre-existence of Christ (see Volume II, pp. 229, 230 note 1); 17:26. The Son loves the Father: see Jn 14:30; 15:10, where the evangelist is speaking of the incarnate Son.
34. *Comp.* I, 147.
35. See E. Bailleux, 'Le Christ et son Esprit', *RThom*, 73 (1973), 373–400. For our life as sons, see Volume II, pp. 90–92 and 104–106.
36. *ST* IIa IIae, q. 23. It is surprising that Thomas does not name the Spirit in this text as the mutual love of the Father and the Son; but see *Contra Gent.* IV, 21 and 22. For his moral teaching in the perspective of charity, see H. D. Noble, *L'amitié avec Dieu. Essai sur la vie spirituelle d'après S. Thomas d'Aquin* (Tournai, 1929).
37. See *Quaest. disp. de virtutibus in communi*, a. 9; *de caritate*, a. 2; *Comm. in I Cor.* c. 13, lect. 4; *Comm. in Eph.* c. 2, lect. 6.
38. See above, note 5; see also below, Part Two, and Volume II, Part One.
39. M. Schmaus, *Der Liber Propugnatorius des Thomas Anglicus und die Lehrunterschiede zwischen Thomas von Aquin und Duns Scotus*, II: *Die trinitarischen Lehrdifferenzen (Beitr. zur Gesch. der Phil. und Theol.*, 29) (Münster, 1930), xxvii–666 and iv–334 pages!

5

DOGMATIC DEFINITIONS IN PNEUMATOLOGY A NEED FOR HERMENEUTICS

There are different norms of faith and it is important to weigh them. They include canonical Scriptures, conciliar definitions, professions of faith, liturgy, the teachings of the ordinary magisterium and those of the 'authentic' doctors of the Church, and finally the experience of Christians themselves and the witness borne by spiritual men.

The professions of faith, which can be found, for example, in the collection of A. and G. L. Hahn and at the beginning of Denzinger and Schönmetzer, are sober expressions of the 'economic' activity of the third Person—the remission of sins, the resurrection of the body and eternal life. The Spirit has spoken through the prophets. He is the giver of life and he dwells in the saints.

It is, of course, not possible for me to study the ancient liturgies here, but it is possible to state that they express doxologically the faith of baptized Christians. In the ante-Nicene Church, these liturgical expressions of faith preceded theological expressions.[1] In the anaphora of the liturgy of St Basil, for example, the reference to the Spirit is linked to the mention of the Word by the words: 'by means of whom (the Word) the Holy Spirit manifests himself'.[2] Finally, we have already seen how rich is the pneumatology contained in the Syrian liturgy [above, pp. 41–43].

I have already spoken about the First Council of Constantinople, held in 381 (see Volume I, pp. 74–75, and above, p. 34). It was at Constantinople that the article on the Holy Spirit was completed in opposition to the Pneumatomachi and Macedonius:[3] we believe 'in the Holy Spirit, the Lord and giver of life, coming from the Father, co-adored and conglorified (with the Father and the Son), having spoken through the prophets'. The Council wanted to affirm the consubstantiality and therefore the divinity of the Spirit without in fact using these words and therefore retained the economic context of the text of Jn 15:26, to which it refers.[4] Its intention was not to define precisely the mode of procession followed by the Spirit, the mystery of which it revered. Both 'filioquism' and 'monopatrism' were alien to the spirit of Constantinople. No Latin bishop had been called to the Council, nor was any Latin bishop present at it; it was convoked by the emperor

128

Theodosius I. It described itself as 'ecumenical' because it was of the empire, but, if it was 'received' by the West, it was not described as such before the end of the fifth century by the Western Church.[5] This text is, in any case, absolutely normative. It expresses our faith.

A decree which begins with a profession of faith insisting on the relationship between the Spirit and Christ and which appeared at about the same time is attributed to Pope Damasus. According to the *Decretum Damasi*, the Spirit is not simply the Spirit of the Father, but also the Spirit of the Son. Christ himself said: 'he proceeds from the Father' (Jn 15:26) and 'he will receive from me and declare it to you' (16:14).[6] This was the Roman faith, as expressed later by Pope Pelagius I when he addressed King Childebert in 557.[7] Rome did not in fact adopt the *Filioque* until the eleventh century.[8]

It was introduced into the profession of faith in the seventh century, however, by the national Councils of Toledo. Such national councils, however, assume an importance which goes far beyond their local character when, on the one hand, they deal with faith, as is the case here, in order to combat dogmatic errors and, on the other, the teaching that they promulgate has already been widely 'received' by other Churches.

It is generally agreed that the Roman councils over which the Pope presided have increased authority by virtue of the fact that the Roman Church and its pontiff are a kind of mirror or epitome of Catholicity. Louis Bouyer, for instance, said: 'The Church has always recognized that partial councils could, in certain cases, express the *mens ecclesiae* in a definitive manner. This must, to some extent, be the case with all the councils convoked by the Pope and confirmed by him after a considerable episcopal representation has met.'[9]

This comment can certainly be applied to the Fourth Lateran Council, which was of great importance for the whole Latin Church in the thirteenth century. Its chapter on the 'Catholic faith', *Firmiter credimus*, was received as a fourth creed.[10] According to this conciliar statement, the Spirit is *ab utroque*.

It is customary to include the five Lateran Councils and the two Councils of Lyons among the so-called 'ecumenical' councils. I have mentioned elsewhere, as the decisive studies of the question by V. Peri have shown, that there is no official list with overriding authority of the 'ecumenical councils' of the Church, apart from the first seven which were common to both the Eastern and the Western Churches.[11] The application of the description 'ecumenical' not only to Lateran IV, but also to Lyons II of 1274 can therefore be called seriously into question. In any case, this qualification of 'ecumenical' is very difficult to define adequately. Paul VI published an important *actum* of the Apostolic See in 1974 which authorized this questioning of the term. In his letter written on 5 October of that year to Cardinal Jan Willebrands, *Lugduni, in urbe Galliae nobilissima*,[12] he described the Second Council of Lyons as the 'sixth of the general councils held in the

West'. The other five are, of course, the four Lateran Councils and the First Council of Lyons, held in 1245. The Pope also took note of the fact that the 'reception' of the union of Lyons was absent in the East.

In Lyons, on 6 June 1274, the logothete read, in the name of Emperor Michael VIII, a profession of faith that had been sent by the Pope. This profession stated that the Holy Spirit proceeded *ex Patre Filioque*.[13] In the sixth session of the same Second Council of Lyons, on 17 July, the Catholic teaching was proclaimed: 'The Holy Spirit proceeds eternally from the Father and the Son, not as from two principles, but as from a single principle, not by two spirations, but by a single spiration'.[14]

There was no debate at Lyons. The Byzantine emperor was represented, but it is not possible to say that the Greek Church was really represented. The situation was quite different at the Council of Florence, as we shall see. This council really deserves to be given the title of 'ecumenical council' and in fact it is often included in the list as the eighth (see note 11 below). The union that was reached there—I give the text of this below [p. 186], recognizing at the same time both its serious implications and its limitations—was denounced in the East.[15] The text of the Council of Florence is therefore not a link between the two parts of the Church. It has, however, served as a basis for a later union, such as that of Brest, which was prepared by a profession of faith compiled in 1575.[16]

Louis Bouyer went on to say this, not directly about Florence, but about councils held and accepted since the eleventh century in the West:

> It is no less true to say that, even when they can be regarded as infallible and, for that reason, unchangeable, their decisions, because they were taken in the absence of a considerable part of the episcopate, that part which would have represented a very venerable theological tradition, may still call for later additions and augmentations which would not have been necessary in the case of an ecumenical council in the earliest and fullest sense of the word.
>
> ... The whole of the West may and indeed should ask the East to accept these councils at least provisionally and in a favourable sense, as a positive element that is essential if the questions involved are to be reconsidered together more broadly and more profoundly. At the same time, the West should offer the East the same promise—that the councils and decisions which the Eastern Church unanimously regards as equally important will be seriously considered in the West.

There is no doubt at all that the procession of the Holy Spirit from or through the Son as well forms part of the Roman Catholic expression of faith in the Trinity. It is taught by the ordinary universal magisterium of the Church and professed in the creed. But it is the *Latin* expression of that faith. It is more or less formally supported by a few Greek Fathers such as Cyril of Alexandria. It is not the Greek expression of Trinitarian faith. Bonaventure said of John Damascene, *graecus erat*—he spoke in Greek! An Eastern Christian could say of Augustine, Anselm, Thomas Aquinas and Bonaventure himself—they thought and spoke as Latins. The same applies to the

Second Council of Lyons and, at Florence, a Greek point of view was reduced to a Latin point of view, without the other Greek points of view having been really effectively taken into consideration. At least, as we have already seen, a door is left relatively open for Palamism.

An Anglican author once said: 'Rome cannot change, but she can explain'. The Roman Catholic Church cannot be asked to deny its teaching about the part played by the Son in the eternal procession of the Spirit. It can, however, reasonably be expected to recognize that the Western formulae do not express everything that the Catholic Church believes,[17] that certain points of doctrine are a matter, not absolutely of faith as such, but of theological explanation,[18] and that it is possible for other expressions of the same faith to exist, taking different insights as their point of departure and using other instruments of thought. There is a need to invite Orthodox theologians to engage in an analogous critical hermeneutical examination of their own doctrines. In other words, we must re-create the situation of the Church Fathers, who were in communion with each other while following different ways, and admit the possibility of two constructions of dogmatic theology, side by side, of the same mystery, the object of the same faith.

NOTES

1. H. B. Swete, *The Holy Spirit in the Ancient Church* (London, 1912), pp. 151–159. A. de Halleux, *op. cit.* (note 3 below), 9, says, with reference to G. Kretschmar's studies: 'There was a clear break in the fourth century between spontaneous, charismatic or sacramental experience of the Holy Spirit as a Person and as a divine and Christological gift, and a reflected form of pneumatology'.

2. B. Capelle has the translation 'proceeds' here: 'La procession du Saint-Esprit d'après la liturgie grecque de S. Basile', *L'Orient syrien*, 7 (1962), 69–76. I have criticized him about this. According to him, the text is by Basil himself.

3. *DS* 150; G. L. Dossetti, *Il simbolo di Nicea e di Constantinopoli. Edizione critica* (Rome, 1967); A.-M. Ritter, *Das Konzil von Konstantinopel und sein Symbol* (Göttingen, 1965); J. Ortiz de Urbina, *Nicée et Constantinople* (*Histoire des Conciles œcuméniques*, 1) (Paris, 1963); A. de Halleux, 'La procession de l'Esprit Saint dans le symbole de Constantinople', *RTL*, 10 (1979), 5–39.

4. An indication of this is to be found in the preservation in the text of the mode of the present particle, *ekporeuomenon*, instead of the aorist, as in the case of *gennēthenta* with regard to the Son; this would have stressed the eternity of the *ekporeusis*: see A. de Halleux, *op. cit.*, 34–45.

5. J. Ortiz de Urbina, *op. cit.*, pp. 223–240.

6. *DS* 178. The date of this decree is perhaps 382.

7. *DS* 441.

8. See above, p. 54. The profession of faith which Leo IX sent to the Patriarch Peter of Antioch on 13 April 1053 contains the *Filioque* (see *DS* 682), but the Roman Council of 680 said only: 'ex Patre procedentem' (see *DS* 546).

9. See L. Bouyer, *L'Eglise de Dieu, Corps du Christ et Temple de l'Esprit* (Paris, 1970), Excursus II, pp. 678–679.

10. *DS* 800; see also Y. Congar, 'S. Thomas et les archidiacres', *RThom*, 57 (1957), 657–671; R. Foreville, *Latran I-III. Latran IV* (*Histoire des conciles œcuméniques*, 6) (Paris, 1968).

11. Documentation and a bibliography will be found in my article, '1274–1974. Structures ecclésiales et conciles dans les relations entre Orient et Occident', *RSPT*, 58 (1974), 355–390.

12. *AAS* 66 (1974), 620–625.

13. *DS* 853.

14. *DS* 850.

15. See below, pp. 185–188. The text will be found in *DS* 1300. To this should be added the decree of 4 February 1442, *Decretum pro Iacobitis* (*DS* 1330–1331), in which the principle of Anselm and Thomas Aquinas figures, namely: 'in Deo omnia sunt unum ubi non obviat relationis oppositio'. This decree is a statement of classical Scholastic theology.

16. *DS* 1968.

17. This is, the *principaliter a Patre*. The Orthodox Christians, on the other hand, could perhaps recognize that the creed does not express the relationship between the Spirit and the Son.

18. This can be seen in the principle of Anselm, included only in the *Decretum pro Iacobitis* (see above, note 15).

III

THEOLOGICAL REFLECTIONS

1

THE FATHER,
THE ABSOLUTE SOURCE OF DIVINITY

Mian gar isasin Huiou kai
Pneumatos ton Patera aitian
Maximus the Confessor, letter to
Marinus of Cyprus, 655 (*PG* 91, 136)

THE GREEK FATHERS

The first insight into the mystery of the Trinity is that concerning its origin in the monarchy of the Father. That is the import of the well-known text of Dionysius of Alexandria (*c.* 230): 'We extend the monad without dividing it in the Triad and at the same time we recapitulate the Triad without diminishing it in the monad'.[1] This insight continued to play a decisive part in the theology of the Greek Fathers even after the time when, in opposition to Arianism, they insisted on the consubstantiality of the three Persons on the basis of identity of *ousia* or *phusis*. There is evidence of this in these texts of Gregory Nazianzen and John Damascene:

> The Father is the principle of the goodness and the divinity that we contemplate in the Son and the Spirit.[2]

> There is one single nature in the three and that is God. The union is the Father, from whom proceed and to whom return those who follow (that which follows).[3]

> The Father is the source by begetting and procession of all the good hidden in that source itself.[4]

The description of the Father as 'source of divinity', *pēgē tēs theotētos*, can be found in Origen,[5] and Pseudo-Dionysius speaks of *pēgaia theotēs*, 'divinity-source', or in Latin *fontana deitas*,[6], which will recur later. Tertullian included 'source' among a list of images[7] and Athanasius, Basil, Cyril of Alexandria and John Damascene called the Father the 'source' of what proceeded from him.[8]

Pēgē, source, is not the only image of the Father. There is also *archē*,

133

principle or beginning: *tēs theotētos archē*, 'Principle of divinity'.[9] The Father is the Principle without any other principle or beginning apart from itself; he is, in other words, *anarchos*. It was necessary to explain this term because the Arians both used and misused it, saying that the Father was the only *anarchos*, the only one without a beginning, whereas the Son had a beginning—there was a time when he was not. There was a need to overcome the ambiguity of the term—the Son was without any beginning, because he was consubstantial with the Father, but he was not without a principle, since he proceeded from the Father, who was the only *anarchos* in this sense.[10]

The Arians also seem to have misused another term taken from Neo-Platonism—*agennētos*, the one who cannot be born, *innascibilis*. Only the Father was, in their opinion, *agennētos*, just as only he was *anarchos*. The begotten Son had a beginning; he had been created before the centuries.[11] Eunomius believed that *agennētos* was a definition of God, since a knowledge of God's name meant a knowledge of his nature.[12] This is why the Fathers at first rejected the term *innascibilis* (Athanasius) or at least avoided it and disputed its application to God (Basil). After Basil had shown, however, that it could not be applied to the *ousia*—which included the Son—but could only be applied to the *hypostasis*, the Fathers used it and made this *innascibilitas* a characteristic of the Father. Those who employed it include, among the Greeks, Basil himself,[13] Gregory Nazianzen,[14] Gregory of Nyssa,[15] Epiphanius of Salamis[16] and John Damascene[17] and, among the Western Fathers, Hilary of Poitiers, writing in his difficult Latin and preceding the Greeks (†366).[18]

THE LATIN WEST

Clearly Augustine must be mentioned first, because he had such a deep influence on Western thinking and, although he did not initiate the idea, continued to be the major source in the question of the *Filioque*. He said, for example: 'The Father is the principle of all divinity or, to be more precise, of the deity, because he does not take his origin from anything else. He has no one from whom he has his being or from whom he proceeds, but it is by him that the Son is begotten and from him that the Holy Spirit proceeds.'[19] Later in the same treatise, he reaffirms this conviction: 'The Son has all that he has from the Father; he therefore has from the Father that the Holy Spirit (also) proceeds from him'.[20] This 'also' is my insertion, not Augustine's. Augustine, on the contrary, expresses the monarchy of the father in the following words: 'It is not in vain that God the Father is called the one by whom the Word is begotten and from whom the Holy Spirit principally proceeds. I have added *principaliter*, "principally", because the Holy Spirit also proceeds from the Son. But it is the Father who gave it to him.'[21] This *principali-*

ter has a very strong import—it expresses the idea of the first and absolute source. In his translation in the *Bibliothèque augustinienne*, Fr Agaësse renders this as 'proceeds as from his first principle' (*De Trin.* XV, 17, 29) or as 'proceeds originally [*originairement*]' (XV, 26, 47). As I have already said and as I shall say again later, this *principaliter* should lead to a difference in the way of stating the affirmation of the procession of the Spirit 'from the Father and the Son as from one principle'. Despite my respect for and devotion to Anselm, I regret that he had so little regard for this *principaliter*.

If the Councils of Toledo received the *Filioque* from Augustine, then they also took from him the statements 'Fons ergo ipse (Pater) et origo totius divinitatis' and 'Patrem, qui est totius fons et origo divinitatis'.[22]

These formulae were not very much in favour in the Carolingian period, which was preoccupied with the affirmation of the *Filioque*. It is interesting to note, however, that Ratramnus of Corbie takes up the *principaliter* again and refers to Augustine's *De Trin.* XV, 17.[23]

Bernard, on the other hand, makes an almost Eastern statement: 'Fontem assigna Patri, ex qua nascitur Filius et procedit Spiritus Sanctus'—'Attribute the source to the Father; from it the Son is born and from it the Spirit proceeds'.[24] Bernard's friend William of Saint-Thierry returned insistently to the *principaliter*: 'The Father, who takes his origin from no one else, is the origin of the divinity'.[25] Richard of Saint-Victor was responsible for this excellent statement: 'In Patre origo unitatis, in Filio inchoatio pluritatis, in Spiritu Sancto completio Trinitatis'.[26]

Both Albert the Great (†1280) and Bonaventure (†1274) were influenced by Pseudo-Dionysius, who used the expressions *pēgaia theotēs ho Patēr*, translated into Latin as *fontana deitas*, and *theogonos theotēs*, translated as *deitas deigena*.[27] Albert commented favourably on these formulae and presented the Son and the Spirit as a 'pullulatio deigenae deitatis'. These are Dionysian terms.[28]

Of all the great thirteenth-century teachers. Bonaventure worked out a theology that was most clearly inspired by the idea of the Father as the absolute source.[29] That theology is a reflection of his own warm nature and his use of striking images. It is influenced by Richard of Saint-Victor and at the same time by the Greek Fathers.[30] He takes as his point of departure the fact that the Father is *innascibilis* (the *agennētos* of the teaching of the Greek Fathers).[31] This fact results in a fullness of the source: 'Innascibilitas dicit in Patre plenitudinem fontalitatis sive fontalem plenitudinem'—it 'places in the Father a fullness that is characteristic of a source'.[32] This *plenitudo fontalis* is equivalent to *primitas*, and *primus* means *principium*: 'quia primum, ideo principium'.[33] The fact that the Father is first means that he has a propensity to communicate himself: 'ratione primitatis persona nata est aliam producere'.[34]

There are two modes of communication in God according to Bonaventure—communication by nature and communication by generous free will. As such, the fullness of the source cannot be communicated, because it is peculiar to the Father. The Father, however, communicates to the Son the capacity to communicate the divine nature, by means of generosity. Being the *auctor* is connected with being the *plenitudo fontalis*. The Father is the only *auctor*. The Son is not the *auctor* of the Holy Spirit, because he receives his fertility from another, that is, the Father. Bonaventure's *auctor* is here the equivalent of Augustine's *principaliter*, and it may even be more expressive. Alan of Lille (†1203) had written: 'Pater auctor Filii; Spiritus auctoritate Patris procedit a Filio'.[35] Albert the Great is very insistent on the *principaliter*, which he identifies with the *auctoritas processionis*. He attributes this—and justifies and defines more precisely this attribution—to the Father.[36]

Turning now to Thomas Aquinas, we find that he too, in his *Sentences*, calls the Father the only *auctor*, whereas he called the Son the *principium* of the Holy Spirit.[37] In his *Summa*, he explains how a statement of Hilary of Poitiers saying that the Spirit 'a Patre et Filio auctoribus confitendus est' should be interpreted.[38] He traces Augustine's *principaliter* back to this datum of *auctoritas* on the only occasion when he quotes it, that is, in his first book of *Sentences*, the quotation having been taken from the work of Peter Lombard (see *In I Sent*. d. 12, q. 1, a. 2, ad 3). He does not use this term in the *Summa*. According to *ST* Ia, q. 36, a. 3, ad 2, he does not do so because he is afraid of suggesting that the Spirit proceeds more from the Father than from the Son or proceeds from the Father before he proceeds from the Son.

In a number of texts which reveal an insight into the divine reality rather than a concern for conceptual precision, Bonaventure shows that the *auctor* is equivalent to the *fontalis plenitudo* or the *innascibilitas* of the Father.[39] The Father's supreme authority comes from his *innascibilitas*, which in itself means *primitas* and therefore firstly *esse principium* and secondly being *principians*.[40] In this context, Bonaventure quotes Hilary of Poitiers. The Son is not the *auctor* because he receives his fertility from another. The Father, on the other hand, as the original or flowing fullness, practises to perfection the two modes of communication, that is, by nature and by generosity. Because he is not the original source, the Son cannot practise communication by nature—he does not, for example, beget—but he can and does receive from the Father the ability to practise communication by generosity.

Thomas does not follow Bonaventure here. Without in fact naming him, he even criticizes him. He was, of course, familiar with the *fontana deitas* of Pseudo-Dionysius.[41] He accepts this idea in the sense in which Augustine spoke about the Father as the 'principium totius divinitatis'.[42] It is therefore not correct to say, as Nilus Cabasilas did, that the Latins unite or merge together the Father and the Son in the state of the source (*fontalitas*).[43] Pseudo-Dionysius' text, especially when it goes on to speak of 'pullulationes, sicut flores, sicut divina lumina', undoubtedly provides a number of excellent images, but it is not possible to base a rational argument on it. As Pseudo-Dionysius himself admits: 'locutiones illae sunt symbolicae; et ideo ex eis non procedit argumentatio'.[44]

Thomas, then, believed that *innascibilitas* was a property of the Father, but not a personal notion enabling us to know the Person positively as such.[45] He reacted, however, against an interpretation of the character 'unbegotten' that would identify it with this *innascibilitas* in such a way that would give this property not a simply negative value, but a positive value, characterizing the quality of the Father as 'a nullo esse, esse principium aliorum, esse fontalis plenitudo'. For Bonaventure, *innascibilis* did not characterize the Father simply in the negative sense, that is, it did not simply describe him as having his being from no one else—it also characterized him positively, as having the ability to give being to another. The term, in other words, is negative only in appearance. Thomas was open to the reality of the mystery of the Father expressed in this way, but he preferred to speak of that mystery by respecting the vigour of our concepts, since they are inadequate but valuable means of our talk about God. Even Cyril of Alexandria and Augustine had perceived that 'unbegotten' and 'Father' were not synonymous.[46]

Here I conclude my investigation; for the rest, I would simply quote L. Cognet on the subject of Cardinal Bérulle (†1629): 'Bérulle believed that the Father was essentially the principle in the life of the Trinity. This is an idea to which he returned again and again, even outside the *Grandeurs de Jésus*. He saw in the Father the "source of divinity" (68). This idea occurs frequently in patristic writings and especially in the Greek Fathers. Bérulle was able to remember the teaching of his master at the Sorbonne, Philippe de Gamaches, who had called the Father *fons et origo divinitatis* (69). Bérulle also characterized this function of the Father by calling it the "fontal deity" (70). He atributed this expression to Pseudo-Dionysius; it is true that Dom Goulu, in his seventeenth-century translation of the *Corpus dionysiacum*, spoke of the "fontal and originating deity" (71) and these terms may have inspired Bérulle. Elwhere, using a rather strange pleonasm, he spoke of the "fontal source of the divinity" (72).'[47]

*   *   *

I agree with Thomas Aquinas in his assessment of the *innascibilis*, but I have to admit that Bonaventure's insights continue to attract me. Beyond the concepts, with which he deals in a masterly way, there is the reality of the living God as perceived by the religious soul in the prayer that accompanies his *lectio divina*, that is, his meditation on the Scriptures and the liturgy in which the mysteries are celebrated and experienced.

What is particularly striking is that God is presented in the biblical revelation both as transcendent and as immanent, both as beyond and above everything and as with and for us, in other words, as given and handed over to us.

● God appeared to Jacob in the place that was to be called Bethel. He appeared to him in a prophetic dream (see Gen 28). Waking, Jacob 'was afraid and said: "How awesome is this place!" ' (28:17). This is the *terribilis est locus iste*, 'This is a place of awe', of our Masses for the dedication of a Church, a heartfelt cry expressing our consciousness of the transcendence of the most high God. But, in the Old Testament story, a ladder is placed on the earth with its top reaching up to heaven, and angels go up and down it. An interchange is established between the most high God and here below. God has come down to us and will come to us in Jesus Christ, God-with-us (Jn 1:51).

A second example is Moses on Horeb (Sinai). God manifests himself there to Moses as a flame in the heart of the bush which is burnt without being consumed (see Ex 3). God calls to Moses, but, when he comes, tells him: 'Do not come near; put off your shoes from your feet, for the place on which you are standing is holy ground' (Ex 3:5). So we have 'come' and 'do not come near'—Moses may come because God has come near, but he may not come near because God continues to be sublime, the most high, beyond and above everything and all men. But Moses asks God: 'What is your name? Who are you?' and God calls himself both absolutely transcendent and at the same time the companion of our destiny in human history on this earth. Immediately after calling himself 'I am' or 'I will be (who I will be)', he adds: 'Yahweh, the God of Abraham, the God of Isaac and the God of Jacob has sent me to you' (Ex 3:15). Augustine pointed to the unity that exists between these two names.[48] Confronted with the sublimity of the 'I am who I am', man can only be conscious of the distance caused by his smallness and ignorance. But that is what God is in and for himself. From that distance, however, he has come to us and made himself near to us—he is the God of Abraham, Isaac and Jacob: '*Ego sum qui sum* ad Me pertinet. *Deus Abraham . . .* ad te pertinet'. The absolute Being, the eternal, transcendent one, has entered with us into our history: 'I will be with you', in other words, 'I will be Jesus Christ'.[49]

This revelation on Mount Sinai is renewed in the same place, after the making of the golden calf. Yahweh refuses to accompany the rebellious people of Israel, lest he should have to exterminate them on the way (Ex 33:3). This is a sign of his transcendence. Moses, who has beseeched him to make himself known to him, sees only his back, because, as he says, 'you cannot see my face . . . my face shall not be seen' (Ex 33:20, 23)—another sign of his transcendence. Yet, when he comes down and makes himself known as he passes by, he is 'Yahweh, a God merciful and gracious, slow to anger and abounding in steadfast love and faithfulness'.[50] Because he is such a God, he will go with his people. He is able to go with them without exterminating them, because he is merciful and therefore close to them, as he is still close to us in our misery.

The God who revealed himself twice on Mount Sinai is the same God whom we invoke in the psalms—the God who is so sublime, yet so pre-occupied with me that he is 'my God'. The God who is 'enthroned upon the cherubim' manifests himself to those who believe in him and 'comes to save them' (Ps 80:2). It is true to say that 'the exaltation of God was not his exile. He who dwells in the high and holy place, dwells no less with him that is of a contrite and humble spirit . . . he is lofty enough to think nothing beneath him, great enough to count nothing too small to be his concern.'[51]

There is the case of the prophet Isaiah, who, in 740 B.C., the year when King Uzziah died, had a vision of the Lord Yahweh 'sitting upon a throne, high and lifted up. . . . Above him stood the seraphim. . . . And one called to the other and said: "Holy, holy, holy is Yahweh Sabaoth" ' (Is 6:1ff.). The prophet was aware that he was confronted with the transcendent God, for he said: 'Woe is me, for I am lost; I am a man of unclean lips and I dwell in the midst of a people of unclean lips; for my eyes have seen the King, Yahweh Sabaoth!' (6:5). This is, of course, very similar to Jacob's 'How awesome is this place', but at once one of the seraphim purifies Isaiah's unclean lips with an ember taken from the altar. Isaiah becomes God's messenger among his people and for that people, in him, Yahweh Sabaoth becomes the 'holy one of Israel', which is a very frequent expression in the book of Isaiah.

We too sing every day that 'holy, holy, holy', but, even though we are conscious that we are 'mystically representing the cherubim', as the Eastern liturgy expresses it, we add: 'blessed is he who comes in the name of the Lord', since, in Jesus Christ, Yahweh made himself Emmanuel, God-with-us, for ever.

The Wisdom writings also provide examples of God's transcendence and immanence. The fact that statements from these writings have often been applied to the Holy Spirit and that some of them speak explicitly of the Spirit (see Volume I, pp. 9–12) makes this even more interesting. These texts, which express a much more elaborate theoretical thought than those considered so far, say that it is because God is transcendent and immense that he can, through his Wisdom and his Spirit, be with and in all things. In this context, the following texts are particularly relevant: Job 37 to 39; Sir (Ecclus) 1:3; 24:5–6; Wis 1:7 (the Introit for the Mass of Pentecost); 7:22–26; 8:1. Precisely because he is transcendent, God can be given to us and become close and intimate.

Finally, there is God the Father—but when we invoke him by this tender and close name, we add 'who art in heaven'—who has sent us his Son, his Word, his image, and his Holy Spirit, who is the Gift above all. 'No one has ever seen God' (Jn 1:18; 6:46)—a source is not seen; all that is seen is the river that flows from it. 'God', the unbegotten fountain of divinity, is invisible.[52] He made himself visible in his Son who became man, the *Unigenitus* who became *Primogenitus in multis fratribus*. He comes to dwell in our hearts through his Holy Spirit. These are the 'divine missions' which are, in the creature, the outcome of the intra-divine 'processions', a communication of the very mystery of God.[53] The one who exists before everything—everything that has a beginning—entered time. The Absolute entered what is relative and exposed to risk.

Why did this happen? Because that Absolute *is* Love. 'God is Love' (1 Jn 4:8 and 16). We know that, in the New Testament, 'God', with only two or three exceptions, means the Father. *Agapē*—love flowing like a source, love initiating being and life—is attributed to God as a hypostatic mark, that is, as a personal characteristic (see 2 Cor 13:13; 1 Cor 13:11). The Father is the subject of this *agapē* (see 1 Jn 2:15; Jn 3:14; Eph 2:4). He is often the subject of the verb *agapan*, which means 'to love with *agapē*'.[54] This is intimately concerned with his plan of love and with his gift of mercy for the world, but its truth is to be found first of all in the mystery of the intra-divine life. Maximus the Confessor (†662), who forms a link between the East and the West, said: 'God the Father, moved by an eternal love, proceeded to the distinction between the hypostases'.[55] His Son is therefore called his beloved Son—*agapētos*.[56] This love is obviously the essential love that is hypostatized in the Father, the first Person, the Principle without a principle and the source of divinity.

NOTES

1. See Athanasius, *De sent. Dion.* 17.
2. Gregory Nazianzen, *Orat.* 2, 38 (*PG* 35, 445) and 20, 6 (*PG* 35, 1072C).
3. *Idem*, farewell discourse at the Council, 15 (*PG* 36, 476B).
4. John Damascene, *De fide orthod.* I, 12 (*PG* 94, 848).
5. Origen, *Comm. in Ioan.* II, II, 20 (*SC* 120, p. 121).
6. Pseudo-Dionysius, *De div. nom.* II, 7 (*PG* 3, 645B): 'The divinity-source is the Father. Jesus and the Holy Spirit are so to speak the divine buds and like the flowers of that divinely fertile divinity'.
7. Tertullian, *Adv. Prax.* 8 (*PL* 2, 163; *CSEL* 47, 238).
8. Athanasius, *Contra Arian.* I, 19 (*PG* 25, 52); Basil the Great, *Hom. contra Sab.* 4 (*PG* 31, 609); Cyril of Alexandria, *Comm. in Ioan.* I, 1 (*PG* 73, 25); John Damascene, *op. cit.* (note 4). See also T. de Régnon, *Etudes de théologie positive sur la Sainte Trinité*, III (Paris, 1898), pp. 164–165.
9. Gregory Nazianzen, *op. cit.* (note 2). The Son is 'ek tēs archēs tou Patros': see Basil the Great, *Hom.* 24, 4 (*PG* 31, 605).
10. Gregory Nazianzen, *Orat.* 25, *In laudem Heronis Philos.* 15 (*PG* 35, 1220; Fr. tr. in T. de Régnon, *op. cit.*, IV (Paris, 1898), p. 257); see also *Orat.* 20, 6 (*PG* 35, 1072C); 30, 19 (*PG* 36, 128); 39, 12 (*PG* 36, 348).
11. Arius, *Thalia*, quoted by Athanasius, *De syn.* 15 and 16 (*PG* 26, 705 and 708); see T. de Régnon, *op. cit.*, III, p. 202, who devotes pp. 185–259 to this idea of *innascibilis*.
12. Gregory of Nyssa, *Contra Eunom.* (*PG* 45, 929).
13. Basil, *Ep.* 125, 3 (*PG* 32, 549); *Adv. Eunom.* II, 28 (*PG* 29, 637).
14. Gregory Nazianzen, *Orat.* 25, 16 (*PG* 35, 1221); 31 (= *Orat. theol.* V), 8 (*PG* 36, 141).
15. Gregory of Nyssa, *Contra Eunom.* I, 1 (*PG* 45, 369).
16. Epiphanius, *Anc.* 7 (*PG* 43, 28).
17. John Damascene, *De fide orthod.* I, 8 (*PG* 94, 828D); 10 (*PG* 94, 837); 13 (*PG* 94, 856).

18. Hilary, *De Trin*. IV, 6, 15; 33 (*PL* 10, 90; 108; 120); *De syn*. 60 (*PL* 10, 521). See also P. Smulders, *La doctrine trinitaire de S. Hilaire de Poitiers* (Rome, 1944).
19. Augustine, *De Trin*. IV, 20, 29 (*PL* 42, 908); this is a text frequently quoted, for example, by Peter Lombard, *I Sent*. 29, Bonaventure, Thomas Aquinas and even by Leo XIII, in his encyclical *Divinum illud munus* of 9 May 1897 (*DS* 3326).
20. *De Trin*. XV, 26, 47 (*PL* 42, 1094).
21. *De Trin*. XV, 17, 29 (*PL* 42, 1081); 26, 47 (*PL* 42, 1095; *principaliter*); *Contra Maxim*. II, 14 (*PL* 42, 770). The word also occurred in Tertullian; see *Adv. Prax*. III, 3. Tertullian used it to affirm the monarchy of the Father in begetting the Son.
22. The Eleventh and the Sixteenth Councils of Toledo respectively (675 and 693); see Mansi XI, 132 and XII, 640; J. Vivès, ed., *Concilios Visigóticos e Hispano-Romanos* (Barcelona and Madrid, 1963), pp. 346 and 489; *DS* 525 and 568.
23. Ratramnus, *Contra Graec. opp*. III, 3 (*PL* 121, 282). See. W. Schulz, *Der Einfluss Augustins in der Theologie und Christologie des VIII. und IX. Jahrhunderts* (Halle, 1913), p. 56.
24. Bernard, *In vig. nat., Sermo* 4, 9 (*PL*, 183, 104D).
25. William of Saint-Thierry, *Enigma fid.* (*PL* 180, 430D–431A, 435D, 439B). See also J. M. Déchanet, *Guillaume de Saint-Thierry. L'homme et son œuvre* (Bruges and Paris, 1942), pp. 99–110.
26. Richard of Saint-Victor, *De trib. approp.* (*PL* 196, 992); see J. Ribaillier, *Richard de Saint-Victor. Opuscules théologiques* (Paris, 1967), p. 184.
27. Pseudo-Dionysius, *De div. nom.* II, 7 (*PG* 3, 645B); cf. II, 5 (*PG* 3, 641D): 'monē de pēgē tēs huperousiou theotētos ho Patēr'.
28. See F. Ruello, 'Le commentaire inédit de S. Albert le Grand sur les Noms divins. Présentation et aperçus de théologie trinitaires', *Traditio*, 12 (1956), 231–314. This commentary has been edited since the time of F. Ruello's article by P. Simon, *S. Alberti Magni Operum omnium*, XXXVII, *Pars I* (Münster, 1972). The commentary on the text quoted above (see note 27) will be found on pp. 82ff.; it is emphatically 'Scholastic'.
29. See O. González, *Misterio trinitario y existencia humana. Estudio histórico teológico en torno a San Buenaventura* (Madrid, 1966); A. de Villalmonte, 'El Padre plenitud fontal de la deidad', *S. Bonaventura 1274–1974* (Grottaferrata, Rome, 1974), IV, pp. 221–242; see also T. de Régnon, *op. cit.* (note 8), II (Paris, 1892), pp. 435–568.
30. A. de Villamonte, 'Influjo de los Padres Griegos en la doctrina trinitaria de S. Buenaventura', *XIII Semana Española de Teología* (Madrid, 1954), pp. 554–577.
31. See *In I Sent.* d. 27, q. 2, ad 3 (Quaracchi ed., I, pp. 470–472); d. 28 (Quaracchi ed., pp. 495–505); *In II Sent.* proem. (Quaracchi ed., II, pp. 2–3); *Breviloquium*, p. 1, c. 3 (Quaracchi ed., V, p. 212).
32. *In I Sent.* d. 29, dub. 1 (Quaracchi ed., I, p. 517); *Breviloquium, op. cit.*: 'Cum enim proprium sit Patris esse innascibilem sive ingenitum . . . innascibilitas in Patre ponit fontalem plenitudinem'. Bonaventure refers to Hilary of Poitiers and the Greek Fathers.
33. References in A. de Villalmonte, *op. cit.* (note 29), 236, note 26. The formula is taken from Aristotle, *Post. Anal.* I, c. 2,
34. *In I Sent.* d. 2, q. 2, concl. (Quaracchi ed., I, p. 54). See also A. de Villalmonte, *op. cit.*, 231, note 21.
35. Alan of Lille, *Reg. theol.* 3 (*PL* 210, 625) and 53–54 (*PL* 210, 647).
36. Albert, *In I Sent.* d. 12, a. 5 (ed. A. Borgnet, XXV, p. 359); see also a. 6 (Borgnet, p. 361). For the application of this *principaliter* to the procession of the Holy Spirit *a Filio*, see d. 13, a. 6 (Borgnet, p. 379).
37. Thomas Aquinas, *In I Sent.* d. 29, q. 1, a. 1 sol. end: 'Nomen auctoris addit super rationem principii hoc quod non est esse ab aliquo; et ideo solus Pater auctor dicitur, quamvis etiam Filius principium dicatur notionaliter'. See also d. 12, q. 1, a. 2, ad 3; a. 3, ad 1; *ST* IIIa, q. 21, a. 3: 'ut ostenderet Patrem suum esse auctorem a quo et aeternaliter processit'; see also *De Pot.* q. 10, a. 1, ad 9 and ad 17.

141

38. *ST* Ia, q. 36, a. 4, ad 7. See also Hilary of Poitiers. *De Trin*. II (*PL* 10, 69). In this text, however, Hilary deals with the witness to the Father and the Son which is expressed in the baptismal confession of faith and not with the intra-divine procession.
39. Bonaventure, *In I Sent*. d. 13, dub. 4 (Quaracchi ed., I, p. 240).
40. *In I Sent*. d. 27, p. 1, q. 2, ad 3 (Quaracchi ed., pp. 470–471). This important text is translated in T. de Régnon, *op. cit*. (note 8), II, pp. 484ff. See also *In II Sent*. prol.
41. Not only in Thomas' commentary on Pseudo-Dionysius' *De div. nom*., but also in *In I Sent*. d. 11, q. 1, a. 1, obj. 1; d. 28, q. 1, a. 1.
42. *In I Sent*. d. 28, 1. 1, a. 1; *In III Sent*. d. 25, q. 1, a. 2; ed. Moos, no. 36: 'fons totius deitatis'; *Comm. in Eph*. c. 4, lect. 2: (super omnes) 'appropriatur Patri, qui est fontale principium divinitatis'; *ST* Ia, q. 39, a. 5, obj. 6 and ad 6; see also *In I Sent*. d. 29, expos. textus.
43. Folio 72ᵛ of the Greek manuscript in the Vatican Library: see E. Candal, *Nilus Cabasilas et theologia S. Thomae de Processione Spiritus Sancti* (*Studi e Testi*, 116), (Vatican, 1945), p. 86.
44. *In I Sent*. d. 11, q. 1, a. 1, ad 1. The saying 'symbolica theologica non est argumentativa' can be found no less than six times in Thomas' writings.
45. *In I Sent*. d. 26, q. 2, a. 3; d. 28, q. 1, a. 2; *ST* Ia, q. 32, a. 3; q. 33, a. 4, the ad 1 of which refers to Bonaventure word for word. See also q. 40, a. 3, ad 3; Basil the Great, *Adv. Eunom*. I, 15 (*PG* 29, 545).
46. Cyril of Alexandria, *De sanct. Trin. Dial*. II (*PG* 75, 720); Augustine, *De Trin*. V, 6 (*PL* 42, 914), quoted by Peter Lombard, *I Sent*. d. 28. Gregory Nazianzen, on the other hand, said: 'the quality of the Father is non-begotten': *Orat*. 25, 16 (*PG* 75, 1221B), but this was in comparison with the Son, who is begotten. See also Hilary of Poitiers, *De Trin*. IV, 6 (*PL* 10, 90).
47. L. Cognet, *La spiritualité moderne*, I: *L'essor, 1500–1650* (Paris, 1966), p. 332. The notes given in brackets in the text refer to: (68) Bérulle, *Œuvres*, CLXXXII, §7, col. 1242 in Migne's edition; probably *c*. 1624; (69) *Philippi Gamachi, Summa theologica* (Paris, 1634), I, p. 270; (70) Bérulle, *Grandeurs*, V, §3 and VI, §2, cols 230 and 246 respectively; J. Dagens made a slight mistake when he said that Bérulle applied these words to the divine essence: see *Bérulle et les origines de la restauration catholique* (Paris, 1952), pp. 307 and 353; (71) *Les œuvres du divin S. Denys Aréopagite* (Paris, 1629), folio 146ᵛ; (72) *Grandeurs*, VII, §3, col. 267.
48. Augustine, *Enarr. in Ps*. 101, *Sermo* 2, 10 (*PL* 37, 1311); *Enarr. in Ps*. 134, 4 and 6 (*PL* 37, 1341–1343); *Sermo* 6, 4 and 5 (*PL* 38, 61); *Sermo* 7, 7 (*PL* 38, 66).
49. An article which I wrote a long time ago may be useful here: 'Dum visibiliter Deum cognoscimus', *M-D*, 59 (1959/3), 132–161; Eng. tr. in *The Revelation of God* (London and New York, 1968), pp. 67–96.
50. Ex 34:6; cf. Ps 86:15; 103:8; 145:8; Joel 2:13; Neh 9:17; Jon 4:2.
51. G. F. Moore, *Judaism*, I (Cambridge, Mass., 1972), p. 442. Compare also the statement by Gregory the Great in connection with the Scriptures, taken up in the Middle Ages and frequently quoted by Luther: 'est fluvius, ut ita dixerim, in quo et agnus ambulet et elephas natet': *Moralia* (*PL* 75, 515); even more pertinent is his other pronouncement: 'Omnipotens Deus, qui nec in magnis tenditur nec in minimis angustatur': *Comm. in Ezech*. (*PL* 76, 957B); see also this statement from the *Imago Primi Saeculi* (*Societatis Jesu*) of 1640: 'Non coerceri a maximo, contineri tamen a minimo, divinum est'.
52. Col 1:15; 1 Tim 1:17; 6:16; Rom 1:20.
53. See Volume II, pp. 79–90. See also the Decree *Ad Gentes divinitus*, on the Church's Missionary Activity, 2, which claims that the latter flows from the 'fountain of love within God the Father', *ex fontali amore Dei Patris*. See also below, note 56.
54. See Jn 3:35; 15:9; 17:23–26; 8:12; 14:21 and 23; Rom 5:8; 8:39; Eph 2:4; Jude 1. A. Nygren showed the nature of *agapē* to be love as the source, without antecedent; I assume that his ideas on this subject are known and accepted. He was rightly criticized for

unilateralism and excessive systematization, but these faults have since been corrected. His insight is still illuminating. See also 1 Jn 4:10; Rom 5:8; 8:32.

55. See Pseudo-Dionysius, *Scholia on the Divine Names*, 2 (*PG* 4, 221). See also Origen, *Comm. in Rom.* IV, 9 (*PG* 14, 997B–C): 'Paul speaks of the Spirit of charity (Rom 4:30) and God is called Charity (1 Jn 4:8) and Christ is called the Son of Love (Col 1:13). If there is a Spirit of charity and a Son of love and if God is Charity (Love) it is certain that the Son and the Spirit come from the source of the paternal deity'; Gregory of Nyssa, *De anim. et res.* (*PG* 46, 96C): 'Love is the very life of the divine nature', *hē te gar zōē tēs anō phuseōs agapē estin.* This can be compared with the Decree of Vatican II, *Ad Gentes divinitus*, cited above (note 53): 'Hoc autem propositum (Patris mittentis Filium et Spiritum Sanctum) ex "fontali amore" seu caritate Dei Patris profluit, qui, cum sit Principium sine Principio, ex quo Filius gignitur et Spiritus Sanctus per Filium procedit'—'this decree (of the Father sending the Son and the Holy Spirit) flows from that "fountain of love" or charity within God the Father. From him, who is the Origin without Origin, the Son is begotten and the Holy Spirit proceeds through the Son.'

56. Mk 1:11 and par.; Mt 12:18; 17:5; 2 Pet 1:17; Col 1:13.

2

A THEOLOGICAL MEDITATION
ON THE THIRD PERSON

The Spirit is without a face and almost without a name. He is the wind who is not seen, but who makes things move. He is known by his effects. He is the one who produces everything that I have discussed in Volume II. He is the one who *is given* in order to produce everything that can be summarized as the community of the sons of God, the universal body of the only Son made man. He is, above all, the Gift. The Word or the Son of God has also, of course, been given to us (see Jn 3:16; Rom 8:32), but it is only the Spirit who is called 'Gift'. There is abundant evidence of this in Scripture and the writings of the Fathers in the East and the West.

The Spirit is presented by Jesus, and then by Peter and Paul, as what the Father had promised.[1] He is not the only object or content of God's promise, since Jesus, as the Saviour and as the risen Lord, was also promised,[2] but it was the Spirit who raised him (Rom 1:4, 8:11). Eternal life[3] is also our inheritance, and with regard to this the Spirit who is given here and now has the function of *arrha* or earnest-money (see Eph 1:14). The eschatological era has already commenced since Jesus' exaltation (Acts 2:33) resulted in the gift of the Spirit, and that era leads to total salvation, the kingdom of God.

The Spirit is the one who completes all things and who brings a perfection in which we can rest in peace. This creation calls for a renewal which will pass from persons to nature itself and from man to the cosmos (see Rom 8:1–25). The Spirit will be and is already given to us as *arrha* or as a pledge. He is the agent of that fulfilment of creation in God by a new creation, the first-fruits of which he has affirmed in the resurrection and glorification of Jesus Christ, the *eschatos Adam* (see 1 Cor 15:20–28 and 42–50). The Spirit, then, is the Gift par excellence. He is often called in Greek *dōrea*, which contains the meaning 'formal donation' as opposed to *dōron*, which means either a 'present' in the wider sense or a cultic 'offering'.[4] Let me give some examples of the use of this word in the New Testament:

Simon is condemned because he thought he could buy the 'gift of God' with silver, whereas that gift, the Spirit, is 'given by the laying on of hands by the apostles' (Acts 8:20).

Jesus says to the Samaritan woman: 'If you knew the gift of God' (Jn 4:10). That

Gift is salvation by faith, the living water of the Spirit, 'welling up to eternal life' (4:14).[5]

Peter proclaims on the day of Pentecost: 'Repent and be baptized every one of you in the name of Jesus Christ for the forgiveness of your sins and you shall receive the gift of the Holy Spirit' (Acts 2:38). The words 'Holy Spirit' are, in Greek, in the 'epexegetical' genitive—the gift is the Holy Spirit himself.

At Caesarea, in the house of Cornelius, who had just been converted, 'the gift of the Holy Spirit was poured out even on the gentiles' (Act 10:45). In this case too, the gift is the Spirit accompanied by the signs that point to his coming. The disciples had received the same gift on the day of Pentecost (11:17).

'It is impossible to restore again to repentance those . . . who have tasted the heavenly gift and have become partakers of the Holy Spirit . . . if they then commit apostasy' (Heb 6:4–6).

There are many other New Testament texts containing the verbs *didōmi*, to give, or *lambanō*, to receive, which have the Spirit as their complement and which could be added to the above list. (I include them in a note below, so as not to overburden the text.[6]) All these cases where 'gift' or 'to give' is used with reference to the Spirit give an impressive density to the theme of the Spirit as the eschatological Gift and the agent of the fulfilment of God's plan and work.

The Fathers reflected this revelation in their writings. Dionysius Petavius observed that the description 'Gift (of God)' was less often used by the Greek than by the Latin Fathers.[7] The theme is, however, undoubtedly present in their work, although they use different terminology. It can be found especially in the dynamic diagram Father→Son→Spirit, which is developed above all by Athanasius and Basil the Great in their affirmation of the monarchy of the Father and, against the Arians, the consubstantiality of the three Persons. 'The Father, through the Son and the Holy Spirit, gives all good things'—*ta panta charizetai*.[8] 'It is the Father himself who does everything and gives everything through the Word in the Spirit'—*energei kai didōsi ta panta*.[9] It was only occasionally that the Greek Fathers attributed the title of Gift to the Spirit. Pseudo-Justin, for example, spoke of *tou Theou dōrean*—'the Gift of God (the Father)'[10]—and Irenaeus spoke of 'that drink that the Lord received as a "gift" from the Father and also gave to those who participate in him, by "sending the Holy Spirit over the whole world" '.[11] Athanasius used the word *dōrea* in the following text:

Just as the Son is the only begotten one, so too is the Spirit, who was given and sent by the Son, equally one and not many . . . for, just as the Son, the living Word, is unique, so too must his living sanctifying and illuminating effectiveness be unique, perfect and full, as well as his donation (*kai dōrean*), who is said to have proceeded from the Father, because, through the Son, who is confessed (as proceeding) from the Father, he shines and is sent and is given (*kai didotai*).[12]

Cyril of Alexandria also pointed out that 'the good donation (*dosis*) and the perfect gift (*dōrēma teleion*) are nothing other than obtaining a participation in the Holy Spirit'—*metalachein hagiou Pneumatos*.[13] Basil the Great used the word 'Gift' for the Spirit, although the Pneumatomachi concluded from this use that the giver was honoured, but not the gift.[14] The Spirit is called *dōrea* at the beginning of the anaphora in the Greek text of the liturgy of St James.[15]

In the West, it was above all Augustine who developed the theme of the Spirit as Gift, although he claimed that he owed this to Hilary of Poitiers, who in turn owed a great deal to the East in his teaching about the Trinity. It is interesting to quote the main text on the Spirit as Gift in Hilary's *De Trinitate*:

> He (the Christ) commanded (his disciples) to baptize in the name of the Father and the Son and the Holy Spirit, that is, by confessing the Author, the only Son and the Gift (*Doni*). There is only one author of all things, since there is only one God, the Father, from whom all things come, and only one Son, our Lord Jesus Christ, through whom all things are, and only one Spirit, the Gift, in all things. All are therefore ordered according to their virtues and their merits—only one power, from which all things come, only one Son, through whom all things come, only one Gift (*munus*) of perfect hope. Nothing is absent from such a consummate perfection, within which there are, in the Father and the Son and the Holy Spirit, infinity in the Eternal, beauty in the Image and activity and enjoyment in the Gift (*usus in munere*).[16]

Augustine quotes these last lines of Hilary's text in *De Trin.* VI, 10, 11, and interprets the terms used. In his text, he makes these terms express not the logic of the divine economy, but an intra-Trinitarian process: 'The inexpressible embrace (*complexus*) of the Father and the Image does not take place without enjoyment (*perfruitione*), without charity and without joy. This dilection, this pleasure, this felicity, this happiness—if any human word can suitably express it—was called in a very concise way "enjoyment" (*usus*) by Hilary and, in the Trinity, this is the Holy Spirit. He is not begotten, but is the sweetness of the begetter and the one who is begotten. He overwhelms with his generosity and his abundance all creatures according to their capacity, so that they retain their respective ranks and rest in their places.'

As early as his treatise *De vera religione*, Augustine called the Holy Spirit by the personal name of *Donum* or *Munus*.[17] This name 'Gift' is personal because it is relative and it relates not only to the creatures who benefit from the Gift, which is something that could not be verified freely and in the course of time, but also to the Giver.[18] The Giver is the one who sends the Holy Spirit, mission and gift being identical: it is the Father and the Son. They are eternally Giver. The Spirit is sent by both in time, but proceeds eternally from both as the Spirit who is common to both, as their Love and as their substantial Communion.

What is given to us, then, according to Augustine, in the Holy Spirit is God himself, hypostatized as Gift: 'ipse (Spiritus) proprie sic est Deus ut dicatur etiam Dei donum'.[19] God gives nothing less than himself.[20] On this basis, Augustine develops a very great and profound teaching about the Spirit. We love God, he teaches, but we also love each other. The Church, as the Body of Christ, is one because of what—and here we should say because of the one who—in God is Love and Communion.[21] We have been made fully happy and we reach the fullness of our being as men because we enjoy God—*frui Deo*—by the same reality of which Augustine, speaking here of the intra-divine life in the text of *De Trin*. VI, 11, 12, which I have already quoted above, said: 'this dilection, this pleasure, this felicity, this happiness'. At present, of course, we have the Spirit only as *arrha* or earnest-money. The Gift is communicated to us as a *pignus* or 'pledge'.[22]

Peter Lombard (*I Sent*., d. 18), and the classical theologians of the Western Church re-used the biblical and Augustinian theme of the Holy Spirit as Gift, and Thomas Aquinas gave special emphasis in his teaching to two personal names of the third Person: Love (*ST* Ia, q. 37) and Gift (q. 38.)[23]

*   *   *

I shall now try to contemplate and, as far as possible, to express the mystery of the Spirit as the absolute Gift. May he be gracious enough to illuminate, support and guide me in this attempt, since 'no one comprehends the thoughts of God except the Spirit of God' (1 Cor 2:11)!

(1) The Greek Fathers continually repeated the formula: 'from the Father, through the Son, in the Spirit'—*ek Patros, di' Huiou, en Pneumati*. This is a statement of the dynamism in which the Spirit is that in which—or the one in whom—the process is completed. To this statement can be added their numerous quotations, in a Trinitarian sense, of a doxology taken from certain New Testament texts: Rom 11:36, which is given in the Vulgate as 'Quoniam ex ipso et per ipsum et in ipso sunt omnia: ipsi gloria in saecula',[24] 1 Cor 8:6, which speaks of the Father and the Son,[25] and Eph 4:6, applied to the Father who is above all, the Son through whom everything is and the Spirit who is in all.[26] These texts are often merged together in the writings of the Greek Fathers and used in a doxological form that is of a liturgical type. The same is found, for example, in Augustine and in a canon of the Second Council of Constantinople (the Fifth Ecumenical Council: 553): 'God the Father, from whom all things are, is one; the Lord Jesus Christ, through whom all things are, is one; and the Holy Spirit, in whom all things are, is one'.[27]

Here we have an economic order, but one expressing the order of the immanent Trinity. According to that order, the Spirit is the one through whom God's communication of himself is completed. His economic attributes are sanctification or the ability to make perfect.[28] He is the completion, the *telos* or *teleiōsis*, in the Tri-unity of God.[29] I have quoted the Greek

Fathers here, because this attribute is in accordance with their linear pattern, but, as I have indicated above, the same can be found in Augustine's theme of the Spirit as the link of love between the Father and the Son. The Father and the Son remain in the Spirit and set the seal on their communication of life in him, Richard of Saint-Victor, an original disciple of Augustine in the twelfth century, said, for example: 'In Patre origo unitatis, in Filio inchoatio pluritatis, in Spiritu Sancto completio Trinitatis'—unity has its origin in the Father, plurality begins in the Son, the Trinity is completed in the Holy Spirit.[30]

(2) God is a Triad. His unity is not limited to only one mode of subsistence or to only one 'figure'. As Karl Barth has said, 'in equal Godhead the one God is, in fact, the One and also Another, . . . He is indeed a First and a Second . . . because in the same perfect unity and equality He is also a Third . . . the One who makes possible and maintains his fellowship with himself as the one and the other'.[31] An Other who is the perfect Image of the Father comes (or proceeds) by begetting from the Father. The Father and the Son are for each other, they are relative to each other. The Spirit is the one in whom they are united, in whom they receive each other, in whom they communicate with one another, and in whom they rest. Does God, then, remain tied to what psychologists have called a narcissistic structure, which they have further described as the essential foundation for love of self? Taking human experience as his point of departure, Christian Duquoc has pointed to a very deep aspect of *theo*-logy which calls on us to go beyond a static attitude that is not suited to the concept of the *living* God:

> The 'Trinitarian symbolism' not only sets aside the image of narcissistic self-contemplation as an ideal of perfection—it also equally strongly rejects the idea of a 'face to face' which is sufficient in itself, and points to a life or a communion that is both differentiated and open. The Spirit makes it impossible for such a self-sufficient 'face to face' between the two first figures to take place. The Christian tradition has accorded to the Spirit a creative and dynamic rôle and, in this sense, he is the one who gives rise to other differences. He makes the divine communion open to what is not divine. He is the indwelling of God where God is, in a sense, 'outside himself'. He is therefore called 'love'. He is God's 'ecstasy' directed towards his 'other', the creature.[32]

This text makes the transition to the economy, but it does so as the continuation of a *theo*-logy in which the Spirit is shown to be an opening to communion between God and man. He is the communion between the Father and the Son, but he is first of all the Breath of God. The Son is the Image, but he is first of all the Word coming from the mouth of the Father and accompanied by the Breath, and therefore accompanied by a power that sets things in motion. The life of God is, according to Duquoc, 'ecstasy, because each divine "figure" only exists in his relationship with the other "figures" and those figures are different because of that relationship'.[33] If

148

this is so, then the Holy Spirit is, as his name indicates, a going out, an impulse, an 'ecstasy'. That is why, if the Spirit is, in God, the term of the substantial communication that goes out from the Father, it is suitable, though not necessary, that this movement should continue, no longer by mode of substantial transference, but by mode of free and creative will. The *Spiritus creator* is the one who creates the *communicatio Spiritus Sancti*. As Walter Kasper has said, 'There is in God something that is most intimate, the unity of a freedom which transcends itself, and, at the same time, something that is most external, the freedom and the possibility of self-communication in God in a new way, that is to say, outside himself. The Spirit is therefore the bond of unity not only in God, but also between God and creation, a unity of love.'[34] God, in other words, can exist, as it were, outside himself.[35] Not only the possibility of this is there—there is also the inclination. God is Love and he is Grace. Love and Grace are hypostatized in the Spirit.

Grace is a synthesis of generosity, freedom and power. For the most high God, it is also the possibility of being not only with the lowliest, but also with the most wretched of creatures. Grace even makes God prefer what is wretched to what is sublime.

This is the fact of 'God'. Revealing himself, as we have seen, as the One who is, he also adds that he is the God of Abraham, Isaac and Jacob.[36] 'Who is like Yahweh our God, who is seated on high, who looks far down upon the heavens and the earth?' (Ps 113:5–6). Hannah's canticle (1 Sam 2:1–10) and the Magnificat (Lk 1:46–55) also point to this. It was the Spirit who came down on Mary and inspired her thanksgiving: the one who is mighty has looked down on me, his humble servant; he has 'filled the hungry with good things' and so on. In other words, the almighty God comes above all to the weak, lowly and poor.

What is the situation with regard to Jesus, the Son of God? Although his condition was divine, he came in the form of a servant. Nothing is more eloquent than the words which John uses to describe the washing of the disciples' feet: 'Jesus, knowing that the Father had given all things into his hands and that he had come from God and was going to God, rose from supper, laid aside his garments . . .' (Jn 13:3–4).

The Spirit is the water which flows towards the lowest, because he is grace, and can spring up into eternal life because he is grace from on high. He is implored as riches and as Gift, in the name of what is wretched and lacking. We ask him to come to us in the sequence *Veni, Sancte Spiritus*:

> Come, father of the poor. . . .
> Rest in hardship,
> moderation in the heat. . . .
> Water what is arid,
> heal what is wounded.
> Bend what is stiff,
> warm what is cold. . . .

In this context, I would also like to quote a prayer by Søren Kierkegaard (†1855), despite its rather excessive paradoxes and its Lutheran pessimism about man's fate:

> It is in a fragile vase of clay that we men carry the holy one, but you, O Holy Spirit, when you dwell in a man, you dwell in what is infinitely inferior—you, spirit of holiness, dwell in impurity and dirt, you, spirit of wisdom, dwell in foolishness, you, spirit of truth, dwell in deceit!
>
> Oh dwell in me for ever!
>
> O you, who do not look for the comfort of a desirable residence, something that you would certainly look for in vain, you who create and regenerate and make your dwelling-place for yourself—dwell in me for ever! Dwell in me for ever, so that you will, one day, end by being pleased with that dwelling-place that you have prepared for yourself in the impurity, wickedness and deceitfulness of my heart![37]

Grace is, by definition, free. Jesus compared the Spirit with the wind that 'blows where it wills': 'you hear the sound of it, but you do not know whence it comes or whither it goes'.[38] We have evidence every day of the freedom of God's grace in the inspirations, the charisms and the movements that appear again and again in our history. We also experience ourselves the paradox of the gratuity of God's gift on the one hand, as the prophet Isaiah said: 'Every one who thirsts, come to the waters, and he who has no money—come, buy and eat! Come, buy wine and milk without money and without price!' (Is 55:1)—and on the other hand, of what Dietrich Bonhoeffer called the 'price of grace'.

(3) God, as it were, outside himself is God in us—God in his creatures. He is in us in his activity and the movement by which he directs and inspires history.[39] He is there, in us, above all by the gift that he makes of himself. As Augustine said, God gives us nothing less than himself.[40] This gift is in accordance with a deep desire that is present in our nature, if it is true that we are made in God's image. We are therefore destined to become children of God by receiving the Spirit of his Son.[41]

Do we grasp the realism of such a statement? We receive the reality of the Spirit who has made Jesus' humanity a humanity of the Son of God: on this earth, in obedience and in the prayer 'Abba, Father!' and then, through the resurrection, in glory. The image of God comes more intimately alive in the leading of our filial life which the Spirit brings about in us and through which we return to the Father.

It is important to give its fullest realistic sense to the theologal character of this life. It is our life and it is firmly rooted in us because of the gifts that are really ours, but its principle and its term are, in a very real sense, God. We are sons of God (1 Jn 3:1–2). We are really deified! God is God not only in himself, but also in us! He is God not only in heaven, but also on earth! The Holy Spirit, who is the term of the communication of the divine life *intra Deum*, is the principle of this communication of God outside himself and beyond himself.[42]

150

According to Orthodox theology, which was systematically formulated in Palamism, this is the work of the uncreated energies which are God insofar as he is open to participation. This would then be the sense in which to interpret the texts of the Fathers which speak of a participation *in the Holy Spirit* by attributing directly to that Spirit the process of our deifying sanctification. We have, of course, encountered many such texts in the course of our reading. This does not, however, presuppose a personal presence that is distinctively and especially that of the Holy Spirit. Dionysius Petavius' thesis about this question has been criticized very effectively by Paul Galtier, but, in spite of this criticism, it continues to reappear, because it has to be admitted that the feeling expressed by the texts is stronger than the explanations that have been given of them.

According to our classical theology, God is present through his creative power in the things that he sets in being and moves. This creative power is that of the three consubstantial hypostases, according to the order in which they process from the Father. In the communication of covenant and grace, God gives himself in a new way to the creatures made in his image, through the gifts that enable them to reach him in a very real way as the reality towards which their knowledge and love are directed. The divine Persons are made present by means of the gifts of grace, the effect of the invisible movements of the Word and the Spirit, as partners in a spiritual communion. Sometimes—witness the experience of the great mystics—their presence is felt in a life of knowledge and love of great intensity. Christ and the Holy Spirit in fact become the life of these mystics.

Is this a deification'? It will be, in the perfect possession of heaven. In it, God will become 'everything to everyone' (1 Cor 15:28). He himself will become our peace, our joy and our 'everything'. Peace and joy will become ours, but they will also be his. We shall in the fullest sense be children of God. Here on earth we only taste the first-fruits, but does our theological talk about the divine missions and created grace suffice to do justice to the terms in which the mystics and the spiritual writers have spoken about the transforming union—iron which becomes fire in contact with a source of intense heat, air which glows when the sun penetrates it, and so on?[43] The Orthodox think that Latin theology does not express a true *deification*. All the same, based as it is on the very profound teaching about the divine missions, Western theology sees the communication of grace as a prolongation, in the created world, of the eternal processions. This doctrine thus takes its place, as H. F. Dondaine has suggested, 'among the most spacious ideas of mediation between the finite and the Infinite'. Through the missions of the Word and the Spirit and with their effects of grace, God, as the Trinity, is really able to exist outside himself.

151

NOTES

1. Lk 24:49; Acts 1:4; 2:33 and 38; Gal 3:14; Eph 1:13.
2. Acts 13:23 and 32; 26:6.
3. 1 Jn 2:25; Heb 4:1; 9:15; 10:36; 2 Tim 1:1.
4. *Dōron* is used in a way which most closely approaches the cases in which *dōrea* is applied to the Spirit in Eph 2:8, which refers to salvation as a gift from God; cf. *dōrea* in Rom 5:15 and 17; 2 Cor 9:15.
5. The well of Jacob, beside which the conversation wih the Samaritan woman took place, was sometimes called 'gift': see A. Jaubert, *Approaches de l'évangile de Jean* (Paris, 1976), p. 59, who says that the water of the well represents the Holy Spirit in certain rabbinical texts: p. 60, note 13, and p. 144. On the other hand, there is also a connection between 'our father Jacob gave us the well and drank from it himself and his sons' (4:12) and 'whoever drinks of the water that I shall give him' (4:14): see C.-J. Pinto de Oliveira, *RSPT*, 49 (1965), 82–83.
6. *Didōmi*: Acts 5:32: 'We and the Holy Spirit whom God has given'; 8:18; 15:8: 'God . . . gave them the Holy Spirit just as he did to us'; Lk 11:13; Rom 5:5: 'through the Holy Spirit which has been given to us'; 2 Cor 1:22: 'he has given us his Spirit in our hearts as a guarantee' (= as *arrha* or earnest-money); similarly 5:5; Eph 1:17; 1 Thess 4:8: 'God, who gives his Holy Spirit to you'; 2 Tim 1:7; Jn 3:34: 'It is not by measure that he (God) gives the Spirit'; 4:14, which can be compared with Rev 21:6; 14:16: 'I will pray the Father and he will give you another Paraclete'; 1 Jn 3:24 and 4:13: 'By this we know that we abide in him and he in us, because he has given us of his own Spirit'.

   Lambanō: Acts 1:8: 'But you shall receive'; 2:33; 2:38; 8:15: Peter and John 'prayed for them that they might receive the Holy Spirit', which can be compared with 8:17 and 19; 10:47; 19:2; 1 Cor 2:12: 'We have received . . . the Spirit which is from God'; 2 Cor 11:4; Gal 3:2 and 14: 'that we might receive the promise of the Spirit through faith'; Jn 7:39: 'he said this about the Spirit, which those who believed in him were to receive'; 14:17: the world cannot receive him; 20:22: 'he breathed on them and said to them: "Receive the Holy Spirit" '.
7. Dionysius Petavius, *Dogmata Theologica. De Trinitate*, VIII, c. 3, §3; see also T. de Régnon, *Etudes de théologie positive sur la Sainte Trinité*, IV (Paris, 1898), p. 475 and pp. 466–498, where the author deals with the Holy Spirit as a Donation.
8. Cyril of Jerusalem, *Cat*. XVI, 24 (*PG* 33, 953).
9. Athanasius, *Ad Ser.* III, 5 (*PG* 26, 633; *SC* 15, p. 171); see also Basil the Great (*PG* 32, 133C).
10. Pseudo-Justin, *Coh. ad Graec.* 32 (*PG* 6, 300).
11. Irenaeus, *Adv. haer.* III, 17, 2 (*PG* 7, 930; ed. W. W. Harvey, II, 93; Sagnard, pp. 306 and 307).
12. Athanasius, *Ad Ser.* I, 20 (*PG* 26, 580; *SC* 15, pp. 119–120, Fr. tr. J. Lebon).
13. Cyril of Alexandria, *De sanct. Trin. Dial.* III (*PG* 75, 844; *SC* 250, p. 237).
14. Basil, *De spir. sanct.* XXV, 58 (*PG* 32, 173A–B; *SC* 17, p. 218).
15. Liturgy of St James, ed. B. C. Mercier, *Patr. Or.* XXVI/2 (Paris, 1946), pp. 198–199.
16. *De Trin.* II, 1 (*PL* 10, 50); cf. II, 29 (*PL* 10, 70A). It is very difficult to translate this word *usus*. In other passages, it is clear that Hilary employs it in the sense of the welcome that we give to the Gift or the usefulness that God is or could be for us as given in the Holy Spirit: see *De Trin*. II, 33–35 (*PL* 10, 73–75). For this meaning of Hilary's text, see P. Smulders, *La doctrine trinitaire de S. Hilaire de Poitiers* (*Anal. Greg.*, 32) (Rome, 1944), pp. 270–278. For the way in which Augustine employed the word *usus*, see O. du Roy, *L'intelligence de la foi en la Trinité selon S. Augustin* (Paris, 1966), pp. 320–322. Du Roy quotes Ambrose, p. 320, note 3: 'Sanctificatio autem Spiritus donum munusque divinum sit': *De spir. sanct.* I, 7, 83, but he observes that Ambrose did not make it a title or a name of the Spirit.

17. See the texts in F. Cavallera, 'La doctrine de S. Augustin sur l'Esprit Saint', *RTAM*, 2 (1930), 368–370. With the passage of time, the word *donum* was used by Augustine rather than *munus*. When he wanted to speak of the mission of the Holy Spirit, however, he tended to use *datio*. See J. L. Maier, *Les missions divines selon S. Augustin (Paradosis*, XVI) (Fribourg, 1960), p. 168.
18. Augustine, *De Trin.* V, 11, 12 and 15; see also Volume I, pp. 79–80, 84 notes 39 to 42. For this theology taken over word for word by the Sixteenth Council of Toledo in May 693, see *DS* 570.
19. *Ench.* 40 (*PL* 40, 252)
20. *De fid. et symb.* 9, 19 (*PL* 40, 191); *Bibl. Augustin.*, 9, pp. 56ff.: 'ut Deum credamus non seipso inferius donum dare'; cf. *Sermo* 128, 4 (*PL* 38, 715): 'donum dat aequale sibi, quia donum eius Spiritus Sanctus est'; *Enarr. in Ps.* 141, 12 (*PL* 37, 1840): 'quid dabit amanti se, nisi se?'.
21. *De Trin.* XV, 19, 35: 'The Spirit is the gift of God as given to the one who, through him, loves God'; cf. *Sermo* 71, 12, 18 and Fénelon: 'It is the love that God has for us which gives us everything, but the greatest gift that he can give us is to give the Love that we should have for him'; quoted by F. Varillon, *Fénelon et le pur amour* (1957), p. 101. See also Volume I, pp. 86–87: the prayer of William of Saint-Thierry.
22. See above, p. 92, note 22. All the theology summarized here will be found in Augustine's *De fid. et symb.* 9, 19.
23. Thomas speaks of the created gift and the uncreated Gift and makes use in this context of the categories *uti* and *frui*, which come from Augustine.
24. O. du Roy, *op. cit.* (note 16), pp. 479–485 has an appendix on the quotations from Rom 11:36 in Augustine's work. He finds that there are 46 of these and that the text is often combined with that of 1 Cor 8:6 and also frequently applied formally to the three Persons, sometimes with a doxological emphasis.
25. This text is often compared with Rom 11:36 (see Augustine, *De Trin.* I, 6, 12) or merged with it in patristic writings. For Origen, see Cécile Blanc's Fr. tr. of his *Commentary on St John, SC* 120 (1966), p. 252, note 1. For Cyril of Alexandria, see the Introduction to G. M. de Durand's *Dialogues sur la Trinité*, I, *SC* 250 (1976), pp. 74ff.
26. See Irenaeus, *Adv. haer.* V, 18, 1 (*PG* 7, 1173; *SC* 153, p. 374); *Dem.* 5; Hilary of Poitiers, *De Trin.* II, 1 (*PL* 10, 51): 'unus est enim Deus Pater, ex quo omnia; et unus unigenitus Dominus noster Jesus Christus, per quem omnia; et unus Spiritus, donum in omnibus'. See also Athanasius (note 28 below).
27. *DS* 421; O. du Roy, *op. cit.* (note 16), p. 484, compared this with Justinian's confession of faith in 551–553: see Mansi, 9, 540.
28. Athanasius, *Ad Ser.* I, 14 (*PG* 26, 565B; *SC* 15, pp. 107–108): 'The grace which (coming) from the Father through the Son is completed in the Holy Spirit (*en Pneumati hagiō plēroumenē*) is one; the divinity is one and there is only one God who is over all and through all and in all'; Basil the Great, *De spir. sanct.* XVI, 38 (*PG* 32, 136B; *SC* 17, p. 175); Gregory Nazianzen, *Orat.* 34, 8 (*PG* 36, 249A): the Father is *aitios*, the Son is *dēmiourgos* and the Spirit is *telepoios*; we have already seen that both Basil and Gregory made the ability to 'sanctify' the characteristic property (*gnōristikē idiotēs*) of the third Person; Gregory of Nyssa, *Quod non sint tres dii* (*PG* 45, 129): 'every action comes from the Father, progresses through the Son and is completed in the Holy Spirit (*en tō Pneumati tō hagiō teleioutai*)'; Didymus the Blind, under the name of Basil, *Contra Eunom.* V (*PG* 29, 728): *teleiourgon*; John Damascene, *De fide orthod.* I, 12 (*PG* 94, 136): the *telesiourgikē dunamis* is given to the Holy Spirit.
29. T. de Régnon, *op. cit.* (note 7), IV, p. 120, provides an excellent documentation: Basil the Great, *De spir. sanct.* XVIII, 45 (*PG* 32, 152A; *SC* 17, p. 194): 'the Holy Spirit is connected by the one Son and by the one Father and by himself he completes the blessed Trinity' (*di' heautou sumplēroun tēn poluhumnēton kai makarian Triada*); Gregory Nazianzen, *Orat.* 31 (= *Orat. theol.* V), 4 (*PG* 36, 137A; *SC* 250, p. 283): 'What kind of

divinity is it if it is not complete? . . . Something would be absent from it if it was without holiness. And how would it have it if it did not have the Holy Spirit?'; Cyril of Alexandria, *Thes.* (*PG* 75, 608): 'The Holy Spirit is the completion of the Trinity (*sumplērōma*), . . . completing the Holy Trinity (*sumplērōtikon tēs hagias Triados*). Finally, see Thomas Aquinas, *Contra Err. Graec.* II, 30.

30. Richard of Saint-Victor, *De trib. approp.* (*PL* 196, 992).
31. K. Barth, *Church Dogmatics*, IV. 1 (Eng. tr.; Edinburgh and New York, 1956), pp. 202–203.
32. C. Duquoc, *Dieu différent* (Paris, 1977), pp. 121–122. See also O. Clément, 'A propos de l'Esprit Saint', *Contacts*, 85 (1974), 87; and the mystic Adrienne von Speyr: H. Urs von Balthasar, *Adrienne von Speyr et sa mission théologique. Anthologie* (Paris, 1978), p. 108.
33. C. Duquoc, *op. cit.*, p. 120.
34. W. Kasper, *Kirche, Ort des Geistes* (Freiburg, 1976), p. 34.
35. H. Mühlen, *Morgen wird Einheit sein* (Paderborn, 1974), p. 128: 'the Pneuma is God's being outside himself'; *idem, Die Erneuerung des christlichen Glaubens. Charisma-Geist-Befreiung* (Munich, 1974), p. 186.
36. See above, p. 142, note 48.
37. Based on Fr. tr. of Kierkegaard quoted in Sr Geneviève, *Le trésor de la prière à travers le temps* (Paris, 1976), p. 119.
38. Jn 3:8. See also the parallels: Eccles 11:5; Prov 30:4; Sir (Ecclus) 16:21.
39. The Pastoral Constitution *Gaudium et spes,* on the Church in the Modern World, 11, 1; 38, 1; 26, 4, pointed to this fact.
40. See Augustine's *De fid. et symb.* 9, 19 (*PL* 40, 191; *CSEL*, 41, 22): we have scarcely learnt only one thing about the Holy Spirit, 'nisi quod cum Donum Dei esse praedicant, ut Deum credamus non seipso inferius Donum dare'.
41. Rom 8:14ff.; Gal 4:5–6; Athanasius, *Contra Arian.* III, 24 (*PG* 26, 373).
42. This idea was shared by Bérulle, Louis-Marie Grignion de Montfort and others: see Volume II, pp. 67, 72 note 2. See also A. Stolz, *De SS. Trinitate* (Freiburg, 1941), pp. 88ff.; *Anthropologia*, p. 71.
43. For a purely literary and historical study of these formulae and their prehistory in Aristotle, the Stoics and Alexander of Aphrodisias, see J. Pépin, ' "Stilla aquae modica multo infuso vino, ferrum ignitum, luce perfusa aer". L'origine des trois comparaisons familières à la théologie mystique médiévale', *Miscellanea André Combes*, I (Rome and Paris, 1967), pp. 331–375.

THE MOTHERHOOD IN GOD AND THE FEMININITY OF THE HOLY SPIRIT

The question of the femininity present in God, or even of the femininity of God, is raised insistently nowadays, in reaction to an overwhelming, centuries-long, male dominance. In every language, the word for 'God' is masculine. In triadology we always speak of his 'Son'. The Word was made flesh—in the masculine form.

These are, of course, indisputable facts, but one will not insist on them too much if it is remembered how careful the canonical Scriptures are to avoid attributing sex to God. Israel was surrounded by religions with female deities,[1] but there was no goddess alongside the one living God in its own belief and practice. In obedience to his word and to the revelation of Jesus Christ, we call God 'Father', but this does not mean that he has a female partner, a bride or mother, alongside him. If we were not afraid of anthropomorphism, we would say, together with Bérulle, that, in the begetting of the Word, God 'performed the functions of father and mother, begetting him in himself and bearing him in his womb'.[2] Thomas Aquinas observed that Scripture attributed to the Father, in begetting the Word, what, in the material world, belonged separately to a father and a mother, but that there was no reason in this case to speak of a mother in God because he was pure Act, whereas in the process of begetting, the mother represents what receives passively[3]—this is, of course, an idea no longer acceptable to modern physiology. The Word of God remains.

On the other hand, however, 'God created man in his own image, in the image of God he created him, male and female he created them' (Gen 1:27). If this is true, then there must be in God, in a transcendent form, something that corresponds to masculinity and something that corresponds to femininity.

In fact, there is no lack of feminine characteristics in the God of the biblical revelation, and these are emphasized by the vocabulary of Scripture itself. In the first place, there is the theme of tenderness. This is, of course, not a uniquely feminine attribute: there is a paternal tenderness, and, in Scripture, God, as father, is tender (see Ps 103:13; Is 63:16). Sometimes tenderness is attributed simply to Yahweh (see Ps 25:6; 116:5; Ex 34:6). It is, however, indisputably feminine in many of the texts of the prophets and especially in the very concrete image incorporated into the term itself:

When Israel was a child, I loved him and out of Egypt I called my son. . . . Yet it was I who taught Ephraim to walk, I took them in my arms, but they did not know that I healed them. I led them with cords of compassion, with the bands of love. . . . How can I give you up, O Ephraim! How can I hand you over, O Israel! . . . My heart recoils within me, my compassion grows warm and tender (Hos 11:1–4, 8).

Is Ephraim my dear son? Is he my darling child? For as often as I speak against him, I remember him still. Therefore my heart yearns for him; I will surely have mercy on (tenderness for—*raḥam*) him (Jer 31:20).

But Zion said: 'Yahweh has abandoned me, the Lord has forgotten me'. Can a woman forget her sucking child, that she should have no compassion on the son of her womb (*mereḥem*)? (Is 49:14–15).

As one whom his mother comforts, I will comfort you (Is 66:13).

The word used in Hebrew for 'tenderness' is *raḥamîm*, 'bowels', 'entrails', which is the plural of *reḥem* (*raḥam*), 'womb', matrix.[4] Tenderness, then, is feminine. God has the disposition and the love of a mother. Jesus had the same disposition—he is often shown in the gospels as [literally translated] 'moved in his bowels'.[5] Feminine qualities, activities and attitudes, such as feeding with milk, gentleness, love and so on, are celebrated in Christ, giving rise to the devotion to 'Christ our Mother'.[6] This was especially an ideal for the superior of a monastic community—the abbot, the father, should be maternal. This ideal was followed in detail by the great abbots and Cistercian monks of the twelfth century—Bernard, Aelred of Rievaulx, Guerric of Igny, Isaac of Stella, Adam of Perseigne, Hélinand of Froidmont and William of Saint-Thierry.[7] These are, however, psychological attitudes rather than *theo*-logy. The Holy Spirit is not mentioned at all in the monastic texts in this context. The idea of maternity in God does recur in a somewhat curious form in the writings of the English mystic Julian of Norwich, at the beginning of the fifteenth century. She saw three attributes in the Trinity: fatherhood, motherhood and lordship. It is, however, rather the theme of wisdom that she relies on in attributing motherhood to the second Person.[8]

Wisdom is, as the *šekinah*, Presence or Indwelling of God, a mode of being or action on the part of God and especially with reference to the world, to men, and to Israel. It is a feminine attribute and it is loved and sought like a woman (Sir 14:22ff.). Wisdom is a bride and a mother (Sir 14:26ff.; 15:2ff.). She is the source of fertility, intimacy and joy. In the New Testament and theological tradition, Wisdom is appropriated to the Word, Christ.[9] In the Old Testament, on the other hand, Wisdom is often identified with the Spirit (Wis 9:17) and many of the ante-Nicene Fathers thought of it as representing the Holy Spirit.[10]

G. Quispel recently suggested a new interpretation of the well-known text about the woman in Rev 12. She is, he thinks, the Holy Spirit accompanying the Christian community in its flight from persecution and seeking refuge at Pella, as the *šekinah* accompanied the people of God into exile. The birth of the male child would correspond to the baptism of Jesus, at which the Spirit is presented as *genetrix* in the *Gospel of the Nazarenes*.[11]

In Christian reflection, the feminine character of God is ultimately attributed to the Holy Spirit. The fact that the words *rûaḥ* or *ruho* are feminine in Hebrew and Syriac respectively has often been used as evidence of this. We shall see later that this may play a part, but, apart from the fact that the Syriac *meltha*, 'word', is also feminine, the word *rûaḥ* is often masculine in both languages; in Syriac, it is always masculine when it refers to the third Person.[12] Furthermore, Jerome noted that 'Spirit' is feminine in Hebrew, neuter in Greek and masculine in Latin, and interpreted this as a sign of God's non-sexuality.[13]

Nonetheless, it is in the linguistic and cultural domains of Judaism and the Syriac world that the Holy Spirit is most frequently called 'mother'.[14] In the climate of Judaeo-Christianity, this occurred especially in the *Gospel of the Hebrews* or the *Gospel of the Nazarenes*, which are mentioned by Clement of Alexandria, Origen and Jerome.[15] In Jerome's quotations, we read of the coming of the Spirit on Jesus at the time of his baptism, with the words: 'You are my beloved Son'. In the *Odes of Solomon*, which originated in Syria, the Dove-Spirit is compared to the mother of Christ who gives milk, like the breasts of God. Finally, within the framework of Judaeo-Christian Ebionism, Elkesai saw in a vision an immense angel, who gave him a book: 'This angel was immense, ninety-six miles high, and "was accompanied by a feminine being whose dimensions were of the same scale. The masculine being was the Son of God, the feminine was called the Holy Spirit." '[16] In the Syrian liturgy, the Spirit is compared to a merciful mother, and Aphraates, a Syrian writing in Persia about 336–345, said that 'the man who does not marry respects God his father and the Holy Spirit his mother, and he has no other love'.[17] R. Murray quotes these words from the *Homilies* of Macarius: after the fall, men 'did not look on the true, heavenly Father, or the good, gentle kind Mother, the grace of the Spirit, nor the sweet and longed-for Brother, the Lord'.[18]

Methodius of Olympus (†c. 312) evinces, if not speculation, at any rate an insight the depth of which we should not ignore on account of certain surprising statements.[19] As A. Orbe has shown, these insights did not come from the Gnostics, but from a very early common tradition, according to which the making of Eve was interpreted in the light of Christ and the Church.[20] God took Eve from Adam's side and gave her to him as his spouse. The Spirit of truth similarly came from the breast or the side of the Logos on the cross (Jn 16:13). The septiform Spirit (Is 11:2) came in this way to form the Church, his bride. That Church is the life and unity of the Spirit, especially in the pure souls of virgins, who are brides *par excellence*. Christ, the new Adam, and the Church-Spirit are the spiritual Adam and Eve. There is therefore, in this view, a real typological continuity or even identity. The Church-Spirit is Eve and it is the bride or spouse.

This idea was taken up again in the nineteenth century by M. J. Scheeben (†1888), who explicitly quoted Methodius as well as a rather different text by Gregory Nazianzen, in this way merging together two different themes, thereby not making his own thought any clearer.[21] In order to find some clarity and respect the course of history, I shall return to Scheeben later and say something now about the third- and fourth-century Fathers.

They had to reply to the difficulty raised since the third century, and again later by the Arians and Macedonius, namely: how could the Spirit proceed from the Father and not be the Son, that is, not proceed by begetting? If he does not proceed by generation, how can he be of the same essence? A. Orbe has brought together a great deal of evidence (see note 19 below). There are differences between individual authors, but the general consensus appears to be that Eve had a different origin ánd a different mode of coming into existence from Adam. She did not come by begetting. She is therefore not a daughter, although she is of the same nature as Adam. The same applies to the Spirit after the Son.[22] There was a certain amount of assimilation of the Spirit to Eve, but only in order to justify his consubstantiality in that his mode of coming into existence is not that of begetting, but there is no insistence on his feminine character, except in Methodius.

Gregory Nazianzen (†389–390) was similarly preoccupied with this question, but he introduced a third term into the discussion. Eve, he maintained, was taken from Adam by means of a coming out or immediate procession. It was in this way that the Spirit also proceeded. Seth, however, came out of Adam (and Eve!) by begetting, as a son.[23] John Damascene's teaching was very similar to Gregory's, although he replaced Seth with Abel: 'There was in Adam the one who was not born, in Abel the one who was begotten, in Eve the one who proceeded'.[24] It is clear that Gregory was only interested in showing that there could be an identity of nature despite different modes of coming into existence or of proceeding. He was not interested in the femininity of the Spirit, whom he compared to Eve only in their similar modes of procession. If his teaching in this case were to be taken to its ultimate conclusion, it would be necessary to say that the Son, who comes about by begetting, proceeds *a Patre Spirituque*. This teaching has, in our own time, been upheld by Paul Evdokimov, within the framework of a subtle and very profound triadology.[25] This is, however, not what Gregory wanted to say; his comparison was taken up again by several Greek writers, some of whom replaced Seth with Abel.[26]

The Greeks, then, were not concerned with a comparison between the Trinity and a family consisting of father, mother and child, save in the purely material sense. That idea was, however, current—Augustine came across it and rejected the image of the father, mother and child as false and unworthy of God, although he believed that the creation of Eve pointed to a mode of procession that ensured the consubstantiality of a son or a daughter, without the need for begetting.[27] He did not, however, concern himself in any way with the femininity of the Spirit. For him, woman, in the image of God that is realized in the individual person, represented the *ratio inferior*!

It is clear that Thomas Aquinas also came across the analogy of the family. He opted for Abel rather than Seth and obviously believed that this could illustrate the procession *a Patre et Filio*. The Son here is prefigured by Eve. Thomas does not refer at all the Holy Spirit's possible femininity:

> The Holy Spirit proceeds from the Father immediately insofar as he has his being from the Father, and mediately insofar as he has it from the Son. It is in this sense that we say that he proceeds from the Father and through the Son. It is in this way that Abel proceeded from Adam immediately, because Adam was his father, and mediately, because Eve was his mother and proceeded from Adam. To tell the truth, this example, taken from a material source, is badly chosen to represent the immaterial procession of the divine Persons.[28]

Thomas' criticism has not deterred a considerable number of contemporaries, attracted by the analogy based on interpersonal relationships, from gladly using the image of the family in connection with the Trinity.[29] In this comparison, the Holy Spirit is seen as the child. This has nothing to do with the theme of his femininity. Let us return at this point of Scheeben.

In *The Mysteries of Christianity* (see also below, note 21), Scheeben tried to establish a link between the Spirit and woman. He was familiar with the teaching of the Greek Fathers and noted first that, in man, the child (the son) came third, as the fruit of the union between the father and the mother, whereas, in God, the Son proceeded as the second Person, as the immediate and exclusive fruit of the Father. This is because, whereas there is a duality in the creature, a distance between the act and power, the active and the passive principles, God is pure act as the fertile Father. But Scheeben re-introduced the Holy Spirit between the Father and the Son as the bond of love between the two and as the expression of the unity of nature between them (Paul Evdokimov's 'manifestations' or, better still, the idea suggested by Gregory of Cyprus and Gregory Palamas), since he is the fruit of their love. Scheeben thus re-found a relationship here between the procession of the third Person and the creation of the first woman, Eve. It is at this point that he quotes Methodius of Olympus and suggests the following relationship:

$$\frac{\text{Adam}}{\text{Eve}} = \frac{\text{Christ}}{\text{Church-Spirit}}$$

Scheeben likewise brought together, in his *Dogmatik* (see also note 21 below), the Christological reality of the Church and the account of the origin of man, which is a very early tradition (see below, note 20) and in accordance with Jerome's quotations from the *Gospel of the Hebrews* (see below, note 15). He compared the procession of the Word, the Son, with the production of Adam and the procession of the Holy Spirit with the production of Eve. In the case of man, he insisted, man, who is *virtus et sapientia*, and woman, who is *suavitas et caritas*, are thus like Christ and the Holy Spirit. In the economy, the relationship between Christ and the Church corresponds to the relationship between Adam and Eve, and the Holy Spirit—the Church-Spirit—is the substantial unity of believers.

In an original, but ponderous attempt to base the difference and the relationship between the sexes on the intra-divine mystery of the Trinity, H. Doms relied a great deal on Scheeben's study.[30] The duality and complementary unity of action that we have noted and stressed between Christ and the Holy Spirit are reflected in the duality and the dynamic and symphonic unity of man and woman in society and the Church.[31] In the Church especially, but also in society as a whole, a pre-Trinitarian monotheism or a 'Christomonism'—in other words, a neglect of the Holy Spirit and of pneumatology—has led to the predominance of a patriarchal type and of an emphasis on masculinity.[32] The Church is consequently now confronted with a twofold task—on the one hand, it has to become more fully both masculine and feminine and, on the other, it has to preserve feminine values without keeping women in the 'harem' of passive and charming qualities from which they wish to emerge to be treated simply and authentically as persons.

There is an obstacle here that attempts to develop a 'theology of woman' have encountered. I would mention two of these, both by German-speaking Christians which, with varying degrees of basis, develop such a theology, in the light of the Holy Spirit. The first is by Mother Maura Böckeler and the second by Willi Moll.

(1) Maura Böckeler expounds a vision of the whole economy of grace, illustrating her reflections with numerous quotations from the Fathers, the liturgy and Hildegard of Bingen.[33] The intra-divine mystery of the three Persons has a parallel in the signs culminating in that of Rev 12. First there is Wisdom, in which the Breath accompanies the Word as Eve is given to help Adam. According to the author, then, as in the Fathers (see below, note 20) and in Methodius of Olympus, several passages of whom the author cites under the name of Pseudo-Gregory (of Nyssa), the origins are the sign of the Trinitarian mystery and Eve is the image of the Spirit. The Word calls for a response, the *Wort* for an *Antwort*. That response is love: the Spirit returns to the Father and completes the Triad, and consecrated virginity returns the praise of the cosmos to God. Eve fell, but the response of the virgin was taken up by Mary and then in the new Eve, the Church, which gives a body to love and to the Holy Spirit. Methodius is quoted again here, this time under his own name (*The Banquet*, III, c. 8): the Logos who became man received, by the thrust of the lance when he was on the cross and at Pentecost (*op. cit.* below (note 33), p. 400), when the Church was born, his opposite, the new Eve, the Church, that is, the Spirit in a human existence. Woman, then, is the great symbol of the response of love given to God. In God, that response is the Holy Spirit.

160

(2) Willi Moll tried to establish the specific character of the masculine person in the fatherhood of the first divine Person. The specific character of woman was based, according to Moll, on the Holy Spirit, in his property of Love in the three tasks or situations that are peculiar to woman as a *virgin*, that of welcoming or receiving, as a *spouse* or bride, that of union—the Spirit is the great 'and' of God, the copula that unites—and as a *mother*, that of communicating life.[34] Do these three characteristics, exemplified in the highest and most perfect way in Mary, really throw light on a theology of the Holy Spirit and of the femininity in God which would belong to him? Certainly, tradition recognizes in the Spirit a certain maternal function.

In Gen 1:2, the Spirit is shown, in a sense, as God's *rûaḥ* hatching the egg of the world.[35] He is likewise at the principle of the second creation, as if realizing the Father's plan in a maternal manner—the Word, the Son, is begotten in our humanity (Lk 1:35), in his messianic function, the dove descending on Jesus when the Father's voice declares: 'You are my beloved Son',[36] and in his new creation, when he was raised and glorified in the condition of a humanity of the Son of God (Rom 1:4, together with Acts 13:33; Phil 2:6–11; Heb 5:5).

The Spirit, however, exercised and continues to exercise this motherhood with regard to Christ, our Head, in the first place and then with regard to the Church as Christ's body and members. For the Church, Pentecost was what the Annunciation was for Christ. The Spirit has never ceased to form Christians. In an article written in 1921, but frequently quoted ever since. A. Lemonnyer described 'the maternal part played by the Holy Spirit in our supernatural life'.[37] Firstly, he said:

> Of all the divine Persons, he is the one who is, in a more special way, 'given' to us. He is *par excellence* the Gift of God and he has that name. In the Trinity, he is Love, and that is also one of his names. These titles, however, are more suitably applied to the mother than to any other person. To some extent, they define what a mother is. No one on earth is 'given' to us in exactly the same way as our mother is and she personifies love in its most disinterested, most generous and most devoted form.

What Lemonnyer showed, however, above all in his article was that, in the imperfect state of the divine life in ourselves in our condition of faith, we are still living in the supernatural order as children and, what is more, as children picked up out of the gutter and called to live as children of the king. The part played in our upbringing by the Holy Spirit is that of mother—a mother who enables us to know our Father, God, and our brother, Jesus. The Spirit also enables us to invoke God as our Father and he reveals to us Jesus our Lord, introducing us gradually to his inheritance of grace and truth. Finally, he teaches us how to practise the virtues and how to use the gifts of a son of God by grace. All this is part of a mother's function. The mother fashions her child's mind by her daily presence and a communication more of feeling than of the intellect. That is, as I have shown elsewhere, the part played by Tradition in the Church.[38] The Spirit, who is the transcendent subject of that Tradition, completes the contribution made by the Word by making it interior and present here and now in the course of time. He does this by an intimate educative activity and a kind of impregnation and, so that the seal may be set on this work, his maternal and feminine part is combined with the function of the Father and that of the Son.

As I observed in Volume I of this work (pp. 163–164) the maternal function of the Holy Spirit has often been replaced in recent Catholic devotion by the Virgin Mary. The value of this may perhaps be ambiguous, but it forms part of the deep Christian mystery.[39]

NOTES

1. Inanna of Sumer, Ishtar of Akkad (see Jer 44:19), Astarte of the Phoenicians (see Judges 2:13), Cybele of the Phrygians, Isis of the Egyptians, Anath of the Canaanites, who is associated with Yahweh in the Elephantine papyri, as well as Gaia and Demeter of the Greeks. I pass over here the invocations and forms of worship of God as mother in non-Christian religions, such as Ramakrishna Paramahamsa celebrating the divine mother, Kali.

2. Bérulle, *Les Grandeurs de Jésus*, X, §2, ed. J. P. Migne (Paris, 1856), col. 355.

3. Thomas Aquinas, last chapter of *Contra Gent*. IV, 9; *Comp*. I, 39. The idea that fatherhood precedes motherhood in causality is the reason that Anselm gives us a justification for speaking of Father and Son and not of Mother and Daughter, although there is no sex in God. It is interesting to note in this context that Bonaventure rejected the Aristotelian idea that the woman was a passive principle, and the male was the only active principle: *In III Sent*. d. 4, a. 3, q. 1. Modern physiology and recent developments in the rôle of woman in society have led theologians nowadays to reconsider the question of God's maternity and femininity. In Anita Röper, *Ist Gott ein Mann? Ein Gespräch mit Karl Rahner* (Düsseldorf, 1979), Rahner accepts the attribution, in a transcendent and analogical way (*simpliciter diversum!*), of the function of motherhood, together with that of fatherhood, to God, but does not accept that we should call him man and woman. He also observes that, in a patriarchal society such as our own, the mother's status is secondary and subordinate. There is constantly a risk that controversial characteristics may be introduced into our speaking about God. Anita Röper, on the other hand, wishes in fact to transcend the representations of a patriarchal society and the results that these involve for the situation of woman in the Church.

4. The *Vocabulaire biblique* refers to Gen 43:30—Joseph is moved in the presence of his brethren—and 1 Kings 3:26—the real mother of the child is moved with tenderness after Solomon's judgement. To these can be added Prov 12:10.

5. The verb used is *splagchnizomai*: see Mt 9:36; 20:34; Mk 1:41; 6:34; Lk 7:13.

6. A. Cassabut, 'Une dévotion médiévale peu connue, la dévotion à "Jésus notre Mère" ', *RAM*, 25 (1949; *Mélanges Marcel Viller*), 234–245.

7. Caroline Walker Bynum, 'Jesus as Mother and Abbot as Mother: Some Themes in Twelfth-Century Cistercian Writings', *Harvard Theological Review*, 70 (1977), 257–284; this article has a very full bibliography and promises a second article on this subject by the same author.

8. 'The great power of the Trinity is our Father, the deep wisdom our Mother and the great love our Lord': Julian of Norwich, *Revelations of Divine Love*, tr. Clifton Wolters (Harmondsworth, 1966), p. 165.

9. Wisdom is the Son who reveals the Father: see E. Wurz, 'Das Mütterliche in Gott', *Una Sancta*, 32 (1977), 261–272. *Ibid.*, 273–279, G. K. Kaltenbrunner, 'Ist der Heilige Geist weiblich?', applies these texts to the Spirit together with other common themes and several quotations from modern poets.

10. Especially Theophilus of Antioch, Irenaeus and the Clementine *Homilies*. For the theme of Wisdom and the Holy Spirit, see Volume I, pp. 9–12. The *šekinah* is also identified with the Holy Spirit: see Volume II, p. 79. In the Zohar, I, 91–93, it has a feminine aspect— God will be united to this *šekinah* as man and woman are united. The motherhood of the *šekinah* is developed in Shmuel Trigano's very complex book, *Récit de la disparue* (Paris, 1978). Finally, it is also present in the Cabbala.

11. Professor Quispel made this suggestion at the Patrological Congress at Oxford in 1979, in a paper entitled 'The Holy Spirit as Woman in Apocalypse 12'. He kindly let me have the text of this paper before its publication.

12. K. Albrecht provided a list of texts in which *rûaḥ* is masculine: *ZAW*, 16 (1896), 42ff. For the Syriac, see E.-P. Siman, *L'expérience de l'Esprit par l'Eglise d'après la tradition syrienne d'Antioche* (*Théol. hist.*, 15) (Paris, 1971), p. 212, note 89.

13. *Comm. in Isaiam* XI, in which Jerome comments on Is 49:9–11 (*PL* 24, 419B). According to Gregory Nazianzen, God is neither masculine nor feminine: *Orat.* 31 (= *Orat. theol.* V), 7 (*PG* 36, 140–146; *SC* 250, pp. 288–289).

14. I only know the title of P. A. H. de Boer's brief account, *Fatherhood and Motherhood in Israelite and Judean Piety* (Leiden, 1974). I have, on the other hand, read R. Murray's *Symbols of Church and Kingdom. A Study in Early Syriac Tradition* (Cambridge, 1975), pp. 312–320, 'The Holy Spirit as Mother'.

15. J. Daniélou, *The Theology of Jewish Christianity* (London, 1964), pp. 22–23. The quotations from Jerome, *Comm. in Is.* IV and *Comm. in Mich.* II (*PL* 24, 145 and 25, 1221) are especially interesting, since they have to do with the coming of the Spirit on Jesus at the time of his baptism and the proclamation 'You are my beloved Son'.

16. *Elench.* IX, 13; see Daniélou, *op. cit.*, p. 65.

17. References will be found in E.-P. Siman, *op. cit.* (note 12), p. 155. See also Aphraates, *Dem.* XVII, *De virginitate et sanctitate* (*Patr. Syr.* I, p. 839).

18. R. Murray, *op. cit.* (note 14), p. 318.

19. Methodius of Olympus, *The Banquet (Symposium)* III, c. 8, §69–75 (*SC* 95, pp. 106–110 (Greek), pp. 107–111 (Fr. tr)). See also A. Orbe, 'La procesión del Espíritu Santo y el origen de Eva', *Greg*, 45 (1964), 103–118, especially 110ff. I hesitate to suggest it here, because the meaning is obscure, but the verse of Synesius of Cyrene († after 412), in which the Spirit, in the feminine (*Pnoia*), is presented as mother, sister and daughter (!), 'so that there was a pouring out from the Father to the Son', would seem to have to do with the part played by the Spirit in the incarnation: 'She has her place in the middle, God from God through the Son who is God, and it is also by this sublime pouring out of the immortal Father that the Son also came to be': *Hymn* II (at one time IV), ed. and Fr. tr. C. Lacombrade in the Budé collection (1978), p. 63.

20. For evidence of this tradition, see Anastasius of Sinai, *Hexaemeron*, I and VII (*PG* 89, 860B-C and 961D).

21. M. J. Scheeben, *The Mysteries of Christianity* (Eng. tr.; St Louis and London, 1946), pp. 181ff.: Appendix I, following §31; *Dogmatique*, Fr. tr. P. Bélet, II (Paris, 1880), nos 1019ff. (pp. 685ff.) and III (Paris, 1881), nos 375 (pp. 241ff.) and 445ff. (pp. 296ff.).

22. In chronological order, these authors are Methodius of Olympus, who situated the Son between Adam and Eve (*PG* 44, 1329C–D); Ephraem Syrus (†373), *Diat.* XIX, 15 (*Patr. Syr.* 145, p. 199); Gregory Nazianzen (see below, note 23); Procopius of Gaza († *c.* 529), *Comm. in Gen.* 1, 26 (*PG* 87, 125); Anastasius of Antioch (mid-sixth century), *Orat.* I, 13

(*PG* 89, 1318B–D); Anastasius of Sinai (mid-seventh century), *Hexaem.* X (*PG* 89, 1059A–B).

23. Gregory Nazianzen, *Orat.* 31 (= *Orat. theol.* V), 11 (*PG* 36, 144ff.).

24. John Damascene, *De duabus Christi vol.* 18, 30 (*PG* 95, 167).

25. In *La femme et le salut du monde. Etude et Anthropologie chrétienne sur les charismes de la femme* (Paris, 1958), p. 216, P. Evdokimov spoke of *a Patre Spirituque* exclusively with regard to the manifestation. In *L'Esprit Saint dans la Tradition orthodoxe* (Paris, 1969), pp. 71–72, 77, 78, and in his last work, 'Panagion et Panagia', *Bulletin de la Société française d'Etudes Mariales*, 27 (1970), 59–71, especially 62–63 (this text repr. in *La nouveauté de l'Esprit* (Bellefontaine, 1977), pp. 259–262), however, he spoke of the eternal procession of the Son, in which the Holy Spirit, he believed, had a 'begetting function' which could also be found in the conception of Christ by Mary. He situated this function within the context of a very profound understanding of the relationships, always Trinitarian, never dyadic, between the divine Persons, both *ad intra* and *ad extra*.

26. See above, p. 45, note 38.

27. Augustine, *De Trin.* XII, 5 and 6 (*PL* 42, 1000ff.); F. K. Mayr, 'Trinität und Familie in Augustinus, De Trinitate XII', *Revue des Etudes Augustiniennes*, 18 (1972), 51–86.

28. Thomas Aquinas, *ST* Ia, q. 36, a. 3, ad 1; q. 93, a. 6, ad 2.

29. See, for example, Taymans d'Epernon, *Le mystère primordial* (Tournai, 1950), p. 57; S. Giuliani, 'La famiglia a l'immagine della Trinità', *Angelicum*, 38 (1961), 257–310; H. Cafferel, 'Notre Dieu, la Sainte Trinité', *L'Anneau d'Or*, 138 (1967), 440, 443–444; B. de Margerie, *La Trinité dans l'histoire* (*Théol. hist.*, 31) (Paris, 1975), pp. 370ff.

30. H. Doms, *Du sens et de la fin du mariage* (Tournai, 1937), pp. 29ff.

31. This is clearly why P. Evdokimov, *La femme et le salut du monde*, *op. cit.* (note 25), p. 16, said: 'If woman is ontically connected with the Holy Spirit, that bond only has universal validity and special application if man, for his part, is also ontically connected with Christ. The two together, in a mutual relationship, fulfil the requisite task. . . . The creation, together with man, of the whole new reality of masculine and feminine forms the body of the royal priesthood.'

32. See F. K. Mayr, 'Patriarchalisches Gottesverständnis? Historische Erwägungen zur Trinitätslehre', *TQ*, 152 (1972), 224–255; *idem*, 'Die Einseitigkeit der traditionellen Gotteslehre. Zum Verhältnis von Anthropologie und Pneumatologie', *Erfahrung und Theologie des Heiligen Geistes*, ed. C. Heitmann and H. Mühlen (Munich, 1974), pp. 239–252. There are suggestions as to how this can be applied to temporal society in my articles 'La Tri-unité de Dieu et l'Eglise', *VS*, 128 (August–September 1974), 687–703; 'La supériorité des pays protestants', *VS* (Suppl), 123 (November 1977), 427–442.

33. M. Böckeler, *Das grosse Zeichen. Apok. 12, 1. Die Frau als Symbol göttlicher Wirklichkeit* (Salzburg, 1941, but published after the war).

34. W. Moll, *Die Antwort der Liebe. Gedanken zum christlichen Bild der Frau* (Graz, 1964); *idem*, *Vater und Väterlichkeit* (Graz, 1962).

35. L. Bouyer, *Woman and Man with God* (Eng. tr.; London and New York, 1960), p. 189, gives references to a Jewish exegesis of this text.

36. Mk 1:10–11; Lk 3:22. See also notes 15 and 19 above.

37. A. Lemonnyer, *VS*, 3 (1921), 241–251, repr. in *Notre Vie divine* (Paris, 1936), pp. 66–83, and also pub. separately in the collection *Lectures chrétiennes*, 3rd series (Paris, 1941).

38. Y. Congar, *Tradition and Traditions* (Eng. tr.; London, 1966), Part Two, pp. 348–375, esp. p. 373, which deals with a formal expression of the feminine aspect; for the Holy Spirit as the transcendent subject of Tradition, see pp. 338ff.

39. See A. M. Greeley, *The Mary Myth. On the Femininity of God* (New York, 1977).

4

TOWARDS A
PNEUMATOLOGICAL CHRISTOLOGY

In recent years, many Christological studies have been written. At the same time there has also been reflection and books and articles about the Holy Spirit and pneumatology.[1] There are even signs that a beginning has been made in formulating a Christology based on the intervention of the Holy Spirit in the mystery of Christ. The first move in this direction should perhaps be attributed to Heribert Mühlen, who has worked assiduously to establish a firm connection between the mystery of the Church and, not the incarnation as such, but the baptism of Jesus, as anointed by the Holy Spirit in order to carry out his messianic ministry.

This type of Christology in no sense contradicts the classical Christology that has been developed since Chalcedon. What it in fact does is to develop certain important aspects to which both the New Testament and Church Fathers such as Irenaeus have borne witness, but which have not been sufficiently developed in the classical Christology based on the incarnate Word. It has two important preconditions:

(1) Christology should not be separated from soteriology: 'qui propter nos homines et propter nostram salutem'. The incarnation has an aim and that aim is Easter, the resurrection and eschatological fulfilment. The *katabasis* is there with an *analēpsis* or *anabasis* in view. In Pars IIIa of his *Summa*, Thomas Aquinas shows Christ as 'the way by which we can, by rising again, achieve the blessed state of eternal life' (Prol.) and considers the *acta et passa* of Christ, that is, the facts of his life which are the data of the history of salvation.

It is in fact almost true to say that Christology must be situated *within* soteriology, which embraces it. P. Smulders has shown how the need to define the formal constitution of Christ in precise terms as the Word made flesh has in the past led to a neglect of Christ's saving and messianic work in the history of man's salvation. This happened, according to Smulders, even at the Council of Chalcedon. It was only the crisis caused by Monothelitism and the solution provided by the Councils held in the Lateran in 649 and at Constantinople in 680–681 that threw a clearer light on the fact that, in the truth of his human nature, Christ had been called to realize himself and his mission as Messiah and Saviour by acting consciously and in freedom.[2] In view of the important issue at stake, I do not regret my criticism of Luther's Christology, written for the fifteenth centenary of Chalcedon, even if I am now inclined to supplement and correct it in certain respects.

(2) God's work takes place in human history. It is achieved in a series of events situated in time, which, once they have happened, contribute something new and bring about changes. There are *kairoi*, times that are auspicious and favourable for a given event (see, for example, Mk 1:15; Gal 4:4; Eph 1:10). On the other hand, according to non-historical theology and even for Thomas Aquinas, Christ possessed everything from the time of this conception and, in what are reported in Scripture as institutive events, there is simply a manifestation *for others* of a reality that is already there. The theophany at the baptism of Jesus is an example of this.[3] We hold that the historical stages punctuated by events pointing to God's work are true qualitative moments in his communication of himself to and in Jesus Christ. There were successive events in which the Spirit descended on Jesus as Christ the Saviour. This is clear from the New Testament texts, as we read and interpret their teaching.

The hypostatic union is a metaphysical fact by means of which a human nature subsists through the Person of the Son of God. It clearly requires the man who is thus called into existence to be holy. In Scholastic theology, this is the work of the Holy Spirit, who follows the presence of the Word, and of sanctifying grace, which follows the grace of the union as its consequence (see *ST* IIIa, q. 7, a. 13). That grace, which is given in its absolute fullness to Christ, is both his personal grace and his grace as the Head (*gratia capitis*).[4] In the New Testament, the coming and the action of the Spirit made the fruit conceived by Mary 'holy', that is, realizing the will of 'God' (= the Father) perfectly (see Lk 1:35).

This will of God, which Irenaeus called the 'Father's good pleasure', was that the man Jesus should live perfectly in obedience as the Son (Heb 10:5–9). The way that the Father wanted him to follow was the way that led, through the cross, to glory. It was, in other words, not the way of (beatific) vision, but the way of obedience. That obedience consisted in going where God wanted him to go without knowing where it led (see Heb 11:8). It was the way of prayer—for how is it possible not to see Jesus' own life of prayer and the prayer that he himself taught us (see Mt 6:9–11) within the context of his whole 'mission' and the history of salvation? It was also the way of *kenōsis* and of the suffering Servant (Phil 2:6–8). It was, then, in this way that Jesus acted as a son.

What consciousness did he have, in his human soul, of his quality of Son of God? This is something that is hidden from us. The hypostatic union left his human soul, which was consubstantial with ours, in his human condition of

166

kenōsis, obedience and prayer.[5] The Spirit, who sanctified him in that condition (see Lk 2:40 and 52), however, enabled him to understand more and also more deeply than the teachers of the law (2:47) and even than his mother, to whom he replied: 'Did you not know that I must be in my Father's house?' (2:49). What consciousness of himself and of the fatherhood of God is concealed within this reply?[6] The 'I' is that of the eternal Son, but it is at the level of the 'me', the objectively conscious content (or the content that is qualified to be conscious) of his experience, which may be called 'personality'. Jesus only realized his relationship with the Father in and through the acts of his spiritual life as a son, the Spirit being the source of these in him. These acts include his prayer, his clinging in love to the Father's plan for him, and the 'works' that the Father gave him to fulfil.[7]

The decisive event was the one that accompanied Jesus' baptism by John the Baptist. This event was a theophany of the Trinity. The Spirit descended and remained on Jesus as he came out of the water of the Jordan. According to the three synoptic gospels, a voice was heard—that of the Father—quoting the messianic psalm (2:7): 'You are my son, today I have begotten you'. Luke cites this psalm as it is (3:22), but Matthew (3:17) and Mark (1:11) combine it with a few words from the first song of the suffering Servant (Is 42:1). According to Mark (1:11), the words are addressed to Jesus: 'Thou art my beloved Son; with thee I am well pleased'. In all three synoptics, the same words occur in the theophany of the transfiguration, although in the latter there is no manifestation of the Spirit.[8]

The event in the Jordan marks the beginning of the messianic era. The period of John the Baptist is over and that of Jesus begins.[9] The fact that Luke has John the Baptist put in prison before Jesus' baptism and the theophany is no doubt intentional—it points to this end and beginning. The Spirit who descends on Jesus anoints him as Messiah or the 'Christ' (see Acts 10:38). He then leads him out into the desert and makes him begin his messianic activity: 'The time is fulfilled and the kingdom of God is at hand' (Mk 1:15; cf. Acts 1:22). That time was to be a time of a new humanity, in the image and in the wake of Jesus, the son and servant, through the Spirit.[10] Jesus is proclaimed the Son of the Father. He had always been that Son since the time of his conception—Luke, who has the words 'today I have begotten thee' in his account of the theophany, knew very well that Jesus had been Son and Lord since his conception (see Lk 1:35, 43, 76; 2:11, 26, 49). This is what Jesus was in himself, as the *Unigenitus a Patre*. He was to become this and be proclaimed this for us, as the *Primogenitus in multus fratribus*. This event brought about no change in Jesus himself, but it denoted a new *kairos* in the history of salvation. Jesus himself entered a new era, that of which Peter speaks in Acts 10:38. It was disclosed to Jesus by the voice 'from heaven'. At the same time, he also entered in a new way into his consciousness of being the Son, the Messiah and the Servant (see Lk 4:18). This is also borne out by his temptation in the desert and his first proclamation at Nazareth, to which he was led by the Spirit who had come down on him (Lk 4:1).

Jesus' temptation has a precise bearing on what he was told at the time of his baptism in the Jordan—it was a test of his quality of Son and Servant. The tempter says to him: 'If you are the Son of God'. The tempter knows only one temptation—the desire to be god (see Gen 3:5)—and therefore suggests to Jesus: If you are the Son of God, work miracles, use your power. Jesus, however, knows that he is the Servant and that he has come to do the Father's will (Heb 10:5–9). Through the Spirit, he follows the way of the Servant and Son (Lk 4:18ff.), choosing the apostles (Acts 1:2), driving out demons (Mt 12:28; Lk 11:20) and bringing the kingdom of God close and present as a kingdom of mercy and salvation (see Lk 10:9–11, 21ff.). Finally, he offers himself as Servant (Mk 10:45) and does so through the Spirit (Heb 9:14; cf. 9:8).[11]

The second decisive event leading to a new acquisition of Jesus' quality of son by virtue of an act of 'God' through his Spirit is, of course, Jesus' resurrection and glorification. Let us consider the essential New Testament texts:

> The gospel concerning his Son, who was descended from David according to the flesh and designated Son of God in power according to the Spirit of holiness by his resurrection from the dead, Jesus Christ our Lord (Rom 1:3–4).[12]

For to what angel did God ever say:

> 'Thou art my Son,
> today I have begotten thee' (Ps 2:7)?

Or again:

> 'I will be to him a father,
> and he shall be to me a son' (2 Sam 7:14)?

And again, when he brings the first-born into the world, he says:

> 'Let all God's angels worship him' (Deut 32:43 Gk) (Heb 1:5–6).[13]

> This Jesus God raised up. . . . Being therefore exalted at the right hand of God, and having received from the Father the promise of the Holy Spirit, he has poured out this which you see and hear. For David did not ascend into the heavens, but he himself says:
> 'The Lord said to my Lord, Sit at my right hand. . . .' (Ps 101:1)
> (Acts 2:32–35; Peter's address on the day of Pentecost).[14].

> And we bring you the good news that what God promised to the fathers, this he has fulfilled to us their children by raising Jesus; as also is written in the second psalm:

'Thou art my Son,
today I have begotten thee' (Ps 2:7)
(Acts 13:32–33; Paul's address at Antioch in Pisidia).

What is sown is perishable, what is raised is imperishable. It (the body) is sown in dishonour, it is raised in glory. It is sown in weakness, it is raised in power. It is sown a physical body, it is raised a spiritual body. . . . Thus it is written, 'the first man Adam became a living being'; the last Adam became a life-giving spirit (1 Cor 15:42–45).

The above texts have been called the texts of 'Christology of exaltation'.[15] This is a historical Christology, according to which there are two states in the destiny of Jesus-Christ. The first is the state of *kenōsis*, that of the Servant, and this culminated in the cross and the 'descent into hell'. The second is the glorious state, that of the resurrection and 'sitting on the right hand of God'. In the first of these two states, Christ received the Spirit and was sanctified by him. He also acted through the Spirit. In the second state, he is 'seated at the right hand of God; he is assimilated to God and can therefore, even as a man, give the Spirit'.[16] He is penetrated by the Spirit to such an extent that Paul could even say that 'the Lord is the Spirit' (2 Cor 3:17). The communication of divinity took his humanity, united without separation to the Person of the Word, to the condition of a *humanity of the Son of God*. This divinity communicated to him bestowed on him not only glory, but also the power to make sons by giving the Spirit, since it is the Spirit who places the life of Christ in us, who makes us sons in the divine Son and who dedicates us to resurrection after him (see Rom 8:9–11 and 14–17; Gal 4:6; 1 Cor 12:13).

Both the Church Fathers and the Scholastic theologians insisted that Christ gave the Spirit as God, but that as man he received it.[17] I would agree that this is correct from the ontological point of view. If, however, we are to think historically and in the concrete, with the New Testament, we are bound to say, together with Basil the Great, that 'the Spirit was first of all present to the Lord's flesh when he made himself the "anointing" of that flesh and the inseparable companion of the Word, as is written: "He on whom you see the Spirit descend and remain is my beloved Son" and "Jesus of Nazareth, whom God has anointed with the Holy Spirit". Then all the activity of Christ took place in the presence of the Spirit. He was with him. . . . He did not leave him even after his resurrection from the dead. When the Lord, to renew man and to give him what he had lost, namely the grace received from the breath of God, breathed on the faces of the disciples, what did he say? "Receive the Holy Spirit".'[18] Thomas Aquinas, whose understanding of the organic union between the soul and the body was different from that of Augustine, believed that Christ's humanity was an 'organ' of his divinity for the purpose of giving the Holy Spirit.[19]

Both the Fathers and the Scholastic theologians also used various images to express that communication of the Spirit by Christ, who was inseparably

169

both God and man and who was, by virtue of his two natures, the Head of his Body, the Church. The image of anointing in Ps 133:2—'like the precious oil upon the head, running down upon the beard of Aaron, running down on the collar of his robes'—was tirelessly evoked and applied to the Holy Spirit.[20] From the Head, the oil of the Holy Spirit was communicated to the Body. The Scholastic treatise *De gratia Capitis* was not confined to a theology of created grace—it was open to an intervention by the Spirit.[21] The same Spirit who was given to Christ and who dwelt in him and moved him also dwelt in and moved his followers, the members of his Body.[22] What took place 'mystically', that is, through the Spirit, was the formation of a single filial being which prayed 'Our Father'.

This is the prayer that Jesus taught us. In a sense, its meaning is contained in the word 'our': Jesus and we are one being in this prayer. We are not, of course, 'sons' at the same level as Jesus, nor is God his Father and ours in the same way. The risen Christ, after all, said to Mary Magdalen: 'I am ascending to my Father and your Father, to my God and your God' (Jn 20:17). Jesus clearly expresses both the community and the difference between himself and us.[23]

Jesus is Son on several accounts. He is Son by eternal generation: 'begotten, not made'. He is therefore the *monogenitus* or *monogenēs*.[24] In a theology of the economy of salvation, however, we must take very seriously the texts in which Ps 2:7—'You are my son, today I have begotten you'—is applied to history. It is so applied, in the first place, as we have already seen, to the annunciation by the angel: 'he will be called the Son of God' (Lk 1:35). Later, it is applied to the theophany at Jesus' baptism (Mt 3:17; Mk 1:10; Lk 3:22) and to the resurrection and exaltation of Christ (Acts 13:33; Heb 1:5; 5:5). These are all moments when Jesus became—and was not simply proclaimed as—the 'Son of God' in a new way, that is, not from the point of view of his hypostatic quality or his ontology as the incarnate Word, but from the point of view of the plan of God's grace and the successive moments in the history of salvation. That point of view, then, is the one according to which Jesus was destined to be *for us*. He was to be the Messiah and Saviour as the Servant, and Lord as raised to God's 'right hand'. As Peter said on the day of Pentecost: 'God has made him (*epoiēsen*) both Lord and Christ, this Jesus whom you crucified' (Acts 2:36). This means that, from then onwards, Jesus was seen no longer as the *monogenēs*, but rather as the *prōtotokos*, that is, the first-born to divine and glorious life, with regard to the multitude of brothers who are called and predestined by God to be conformed to his model. There is one begetting—and even two—of Jesus as the first-born Son, that is to say, with us in mind and including us in the divine sonship. Like him in his humanity, we too shall only be fully sons through the glorious transfiguration of the resurrection, but, again like him, we are already sons according to the first-fruits of this life, 'amid sighings'.[25]

For us as for Jesus himself, the quality of sonship is, in both its stages, the work of the Spirit. The Spirit is not only the third in the intra-divine life, although he is equal in consubstantiality—he is also, in the economy of salvation, the agent of sonship as the effect of the grace and reality of holy living. The whole of our filial life is animated by the Spirit (see Rom 8:14–17; Gal 4:6).

In the case of Jesus, it is important to avoid Adoptianism. He is ontologically the Son of God because of the hypostatic union from the moment of his conception. Because of that too, he is the Temple of the Holy Spirit and is made holy by that Spirit in his humanity. We have, however, as believers, to respect the successive moments or stages in the history of salvation and to accord the New Testament texts their full realism. Because of this, I would suggest that there were two moments when the *virtus* or effectiveness of the Spirit in Jesus was actuated in a new way. The first was at his baptism, when he was constituted (and not simply proclaimed as) Messiah and Servant by God. The second moment was at the time of his resurrection and exaltation, when he was made Lord.

The Son is conceived eternally (= here and now) as due to become incarnate and due to be the first-born of many brothers whom he is to conform to his own image through the Spirit. That takes place in our history as the times (*kairoi*) come to fulfilment (see Gal 4:4; Eph 1:10). Parallel to this truth concerning the Son is one concerning the Father—he is eternally the 'Father of our Lord Jesus Christ'.[26] There is, of course, a distinction between the essential mystery of God in his Trinitarian life and the free mystery of his plan of grace. In God, however, his freedom and his essence are really identical. We affirm that identity in our own inability to represent it and to understand it. We can only revere that mystery and make it the object of our praise.[27]

NOTES

1. The most important recent studies concerned with this subject are: H. Mühlen, *Una mystica Persona. Eine Person in vielen Personen* (Paderborn, 1964); J. D. G. Dunn, 'Rediscovering the Spirit', *Expository Times*, 84 (1972–1973), 9–12; W. Kasper, *Jesus der Christus* (Mainz, 1974); Eng. tr., *Jesus the Christ* (London and New York, 1976); *idem*, 'Esprit-Christ-Eglise', *L'expérience de l'Esprit. Mélanges E. Schillebeeckx* (Paris, 1976), pp. 47–69; *idem*, 'Die Kirche als Sakrament des Geistes', *Kirche, Ort des Geistes* (Freiburg, 1975), pp. 14–55; P. J. Rosato, 'Spirit Christology. Ambiguity and Promise', *ThSt*, 38 (1977), 423–449; P. J. A. M. Schoonenberg, 'Spirit Christology and Logos Christology', *Bijdragen*, 38 (1977), 350–375.

2. P. Smulders, 'Développement de la christologie dans le dogme et le magistère', *Mysterium Salutis*, 10 (Fr. tr.; Paris, 1974), pp. 235–350; cf. K. Adam, 'Jesu menschliches Wesen im Licht der urchristlichen Verkündigung', *Wissenschaft und Weisheit*, 6 (1939), 111–120, especially 116ff.

3. If Jesus possessed the sovereign attribute of kingship from the beginning, however, he only

171

received its *executio* eschatologically: see the sermon edited by J. Leclercq in *RThom*, 46 (1946), 152–160 and 572.

4. Thomas Aquinas, *ST* IIIa, q. 7 and 8; see also C.-V. Héris, *Le mystère du Christ* (Paris, 1928).

5. C.-V. Héris, 'Problème de christologie. La conscience de Jésus', *Esprit et Vie*, 81 (1971), 672–679; H.-M. Féret, 'Christologie médiévale de S. Thomas et christologie concrète et historique pour aujourd'hui', *Memorie Domenicane* (1975), 107–141, especially 128ff. and 135ff.; see also my *Christ, Our Lady and the Church: A Study in Eirenic Theology* (Eng. tr.; London, New York and Toronto, 1957), esp. pp. 51ff., 96 note 11.

6. The first two chapters of Luke's gospel reflect the situation and the categories of the Old Testament—messianic times began with the arrest of John the Baptist and the baptism of Jesus (Lk 3:19ff.): see J. D. G. Dunn, *Baptism in the Holy Spirit*, 4th ed. (London, 1977), pp. 31ff.

7. B. Sesboüé, *RSR*, 56 (1968), 635–666, quotes J. Maritain, *De la grâce et de l'humanité de Jésus* (Bruges, 1967), pp. 97 and 107; C. Duquoc, *Christologie*, I (Paris, 1968), pp. 327–328.

8. Mt 17:5; Mk 9:7; Lk 9:35. There is a parallel between the scene of Jesus' baptism and that of his transfiguration: see J. Legrand, 'L'arrière-plan néotestamentaire de Lc 1, 35', *RB*, 70 (1963), 162–192.

9. J. D. G. Dunn, *op. cit.* (note 6), pp. 25ff.

10. What the event in the Jordan was for Jesus, the event at Pentecost was for his disciples: see J. D. G. Dunn, *op. cit.*, pp. 40–42; in Jn 1:33, the descent of the Spirit on Jesus denotes him as the one who was to baptize in the Spirit; see also Mk 1:8. For Jesus as the new Adam, see J. D. G. Dunn, *op. cit.*, p. 29.

11. According to C. Spicq, *Epître aux Hébreux* (Paris, 1952–1953), pp. 258–259, and the majority of exegetes, verse 14 does not deal with the Holy Spirit, but with the nature of Christ, who is divine. See, however, *DTC*, V, col. 222, and A. Vanhoye, *De epistola ad Hebreos, Sectio Centralis* (c. 8–9) (Rome, 1966), p. 158.

12. M. E. Boismard, ' "Constitué" Fils de Dieu (Rom 1, 4)', *RB*, 60 (1953), 5–17, showed that this 'constitution' of Jesus as 'Son of God' was the same as his enthronement as the Messiah and the ruler of the nations. This can be compared with Rom 1:4; 1 Tim 3:16: 'he was manifested in the flesh, justified in the Spirit'; 1 Pet 3:18: 'put to death in the flesh, but made alive in the Spirit'.

13. This text, which can be applied to the incarnation (see W. Michaelis, 'prōtotokos', *TDNT*, VI, p. 880), can be better understood if it is seen as referring to the enthronement of the First-born: see Ps 89:28; Col 1:15ff. The invocation of the angels and their bowing down, which recurs in Heb 2:5, suggests the situation of Lord; cf. Eph 1:18–22; Phil 2:9–11; Heb 5:5.

14. See Acts 5:30–31, in which Peter replies to the Sanhedrin: 'The God of our fathers raised Jesus whom you killed by hanging him on a tree. God exalted him at his right hand as Ruler and Saviour.'

15. See R. Schnackenburg, 'La christologie du Nouveau Testament', *Mysterium Salutis*, 10 (Fr. tr.; Paris, 1974), pp. 55–64.

16. See M. Gourges, *A la droite de Dieu. Résurection de Jésus et actualisation du Ps 110:1 dans le Nouveau Testament (Etudes bibliques)* (Paris, 1978), pp. 163ff., 209ff.

17. Augustine, *De Trin.* XV, 46 (*PL* 42, 1093); Cyril of Alexandria, *Comm. in Nahum 2:27*, II, 35 (*PG* 71, 777–780); *Comm. in Luc.* 4, 1 and 18 (*PG* 72, 525 and 537); *Comm. in Ioan.* 17, 18–19 (*PG* 74, 548B); *De recta fide, Or. alt.* 34, 35, 50 (*PG* 76, 1381 and 1405).

18. Basil the Great, *De spir. sanct*, XVI, 39 (*PG* 32, 140; *SC* 17, pp. 180–181); see also Irenaeus, *Adv. haer.* III, 9, 3 (*PG* 7, 872A).

19. *ST* Ia IIae, q. 112, a. 1, ad 1 and 2; IIIa, q. 8, a. 1, ad 1, in which Thomas replies to Augustine's text quoted above. For Thomas, it was a question of giving the Spirit insofar as he was the principle of grace and gifts: see *ST* Ia, q. 43, a. 8. In his commentary on

1 Cor 15, lect. 7 (see R. Cai, no. 993), Thomas says: 'sicut Adam consecutus est perfectionem sui esse per animam' (and therefore he was only a living soul), 'ita et Christus perfectionem sui esse inquantum homo per spiritum Sanctum' (and therefore he can be the Spirit who gives life).

20. See, for example, Origen, *Contra Cels*. VI, 79 (*PG* 11, 1417D); Athanasius, *Exp. in Ps.132* (*PG* 27, 524B-C); *Orat. III contra Arian*. 22 (*PG* 26, 369); Jerome, *Tract. in Ps. 132* (ed. G. Morin, CCL, 58, 277; Augustine, *Enarr. in Ps. 132*, 7–12 (*PL* 37, 1753ff.); Prosper of Aquitaine, *Expos. in Ps. 132* (*PL* 51, 381–382); frequent examples in mediaeval theology.

21. If Christ is the Head, then the Holy Spirit is the Heart, from which the Head receives the impulse and the warmth of life; see Thomas Aquinas, *De ver*. q. 29, a. 4, ad 7; *ST* IIIa, q. 8, a. 1, ad 3. For Thomas' teaching about this datum, see M. Grabmann, *Die Lehre des heiligen Thomas von Aquin von der Kirche als Gotteswerk* (Regensburg, 1903), pp. 184–193.

22. Thomas Aquinas, *In III Sent*. d. 13, q. 2, a. 1, ad 2; *Comm. in ev. Ioan*. c. 1, lect. 10, no. 1.

23. Jesus 'always says "my Father" or "your Father", but never "our Father". The prayer which according to Matthew begins with the last phrase is not spoken by Jesus with the disciples, but is part of the prayer he taught them to pray': O. Cullmann, *The Christology of the New Testament* (Eng. tr.; London, 1959), p. 289. John reserves the title of *huios* for Jesus, when it is a question of his relationship with the Father, and calls Christians *tekna*.

24. This term is peculiar to the Johannine writings: see Jn 1:14, 18; 3:16, 18; 1 Jn 4:9.

25. Rom 8:29–30. See also W. Michaelis, '*prōtotokos*', *TDNT*, VI, p. 877.

26. See Rom 8:11 and 16–25. For the meaning, see Col 3:3–4; 2 Cor 3:18; 1 Jn 3:1–2; Eph 1:5 and 13–14.

27. See Paul's formula in Rom 15:5; 2 Cor 1:3; Eph 1:3. It is worth quoting Louis Bouyer here: 'it is in time that he makes himself man, i.e. it is in a definite moment of time that our humanity is assumed. But as far as he is concerned he assumes it eternally. Thus the Father eternally generates his Son, not only as before his incarnation but also as the Word made flesh': *The Eternal Son* (Eng. tr.; Huntington, Ind., 1978), p. 401.

IV
CONTRIBUTIONS TO AN AGREEMENT

1
UNITY OF FAITH BUT A DIFFERENCE OF THEOLOGICAL EXPRESSION GREEKS AND LATINS IN THE UNDERSTANDING OF WESTERN THEOLOGIANS

Difficulties were encountered from the fourth century onwards in the translation of Greek terms into Latin. *Hypostasis* was rendered as *substantia*, but whereas the Latins believed in one *substantia*, the Greeks spoke of three *hypostases*. A synod held at Alexandria at the beginning of 362, after Athanasius had returned from exile, declared that the Latins meant *ousia* when they spoke of *substantia* and that there was no question of tritheism in the Greeks' speaking about three hypostases.[1] Jerome went no further than an acceptance of the fact that *substantia* and *ousia* were equivalent to each other and he was consequently scandalized when he was asked to declare that there were *tres hypostases*. Did this mean, he asked, that he was to accept *tres substantiae*?[2] His mistrust of the term 'hypostasis' continued into the Middle Ages in the West, when his hypochondriacal statement about this question: 'nescio quid veneni in syllabis latet' was frequently cited.

Thus orthodox thinking was dogged by a problem of terminology. Augustine bore witness to this in his treatise on the Trinity: 'Essentiam dico, quae *ousia* graece dicitur, quem usitatius substantiam vocamus. Dicunt quidem et illi *hypostasim*; sed nescio quid volunt interesse inter *ousiam* et *hypostasim*: ita est plerique nostri qui haec graecio tractant eloquio, dicere consueverint *mian ousian, treis hypostaseis*, quod est latine unam essentiam, tres substantias.'[3] Augustine preferred 'essence' to 'substance' in order to express the unity of the divine nature[4] and ended by speaking of 'one essence and three substances'.[5]

Anselm, who supported the *Filioque* in opposition to the Greeks living in southern Italy at the Council of Bari of 1098, made the following declaration at least four times: 'Latinos dicere tres personas credendas in una substantia. Graecos vero non minus fideliter tres substantias in una persona confiteri.'[6]

The formula used by the Apulian Greeks expressed the Trinitarian faith no less than that used by the Latins.

Abelard was familiar with the passage in *De Trinitate* in which Augustine discussed the difference in vocabulary between the Greeks and the Latins, the first speaking of 'one essence, three substances' and the second of 'one essence or substance, three persons'. Augustine had recognized the identity of meaning despite the difference between the terms, and Abelard added this gloss: 'We do not intend to speak against the Greeks here and there is no doubt that they do not differ from us with regard to the meaning, but only in their use of words; they unfortunately employ the term "substance" instead of "person", yet they do not refuse to speak of *ousia*, that is, of the substance in the sense of essence and not of what is peculiar to the person'.[7] In illustration of this, Abelard used the term *homoousion* and cited the well-known passage of Jerome on the dangers of the word 'hypostasis'.

This important question of terminology also concerned Richard of Saint-Victor, whose *De Trinitate* dates from a little before 1172. Here is his text.

> Perhaps my readers would like me to explain how the different formulae should be understood and how it is possible to make them agree with each other. Some speak of 'three substances and one essence', while others speak of 'three subsistences and one substance' and others again of 'three persons and one substance or essence'. There seems to be a clear opposition and an absolute contradiction between the Latins, who speak of one substance in God, and the Greeks, who speak of three. I am, however, far from thinking that their beliefs are disparate and one or the other party is erring in faith! We need to grasp the one truth in the diversity of formulae (*in hac ergo verborum varietate intelligenda est veritas una*): the words used by one party and the other are understood in different senses.[8]

It was relatively easy to reach agreement when it was only a question of vocabulary, since it was always possible to find equivalents, although the words themselves involved the use of categories of thought and therefore theological constructions. Thomas Aquinas explicitly formulated this rule governing equivalents and applied it himself to various statements about the theology of the Trinity.[9] This question became much more difficult when dogmatic judgements and statements became involved, as, for example, in the case of the article on the procession of the Holy Spirit. Even in that particular case, however, some remarkable declarations were made by Latin theologians in the Middle Ages. Hugh of Saint-Cher, whose commentary on the *Sentences* appeared at the same time as the texts of Alexander of Hales, *antequam esset frater*, said, for example:

> Is the controversy between ourselves and the Greeks real, or is it simply about words? It would seem that it is real, since they deny the procession of the Holy Spirit, which we affirm. There could in fact be no greater controversy that one concerned with an opposition in affirmations. It can, however, be seen to be only about words from the fact that they agree that the Holy Spirit is the Spirit *of the*

175

Son, that is, *a Filio*, which is the same thing as proceeding from the Son. The contradiction, then, is purely about words. We may conclude by saying that they contradict themselves when they say that the Spirit does not proceed from the Son, yet at the same time that he is *a Filio* or of the Son, and they are mistaken in their belief that proceeding from the Son and being *a Filio* is something different, when it is in fact the same thing. We are therefore not really opposed to them. The opposition is simply one of words. They do, however, really contradict themselves.[10]

Hugh clearly loaded the dice in his own favour when he affirmed that for the Greeks to speak of the Spirit *of the Son* was to say that the Spirit was *a Filio*. What is interesting for us, however, in his text is his attempt to bring about an agreement between the Greeks and the Latins. There is also an echo of Hugh's attempt in this direction—a very prudent echo—in Thomas Aquinas' statement: 'et quidam eorum (the Greeks) *dicuntur* concedere quod sit a Filio vel profluat ab eo, non tamen quod procedat'.[11]

From the time of Anselm onwards, the Latins were convinced that what the Greeks believed in agreement with the Latins in the case of the Holy Spirit logically implied that the Spirit also proceeded from the Son, despite the fact that this was denied by the Greeks themselves. Thomas also thought that 'if the expressions that are used by the Greeks are carefully examined, it will be seen that they differ from us more in words than in meaning'— *inveniet quod a nobis magis differunt in verbis quam in sensu*.[12] He adds that they in fact profess either that the Spirit is the Spirit *of the Son*, or that he proceeds from the Father *through the Son*.[13] This argument by implication from what is professed as belief, would appear to be also that of Thomas of Sutton at the beginning of the fourteenth century: 'Although the Greeks explicitly deny the procession of the Holy Spirit *a Filio*, they concede it implicitly in its antecedent'. There cannot, in other words, be a difference in origin without the principle being different.[14]

The Franciscans in particular felt that the Greeks and the Latins both had fundamentally the same faith in the Trinity and that they differed only in their theological constructions and modes of expression. Was this perhaps because of Robert Grosseteste, who taught at the Franciscan house in Oxford from 1224 onwards and who wrote a commentary on the works of the Pseudo-Areopagite?[15] His text can be read in Duns Scotus. Although it is less probable, it may be because many Franciscans were sent to Constantinople and Nicaea from 1231 onwards, particularly Haymo of Faversham in 1234.[16]

Alexander of Hales wrote a commentary on the *Sentences* of Peter Lombard *c.* 1225. He dealt in it with the question of the differing opinion between the Greeks and the Latins concerning the procession of the Holy Spirit. He believed that the Latins, as represented by Augustine, and the Greeks, as represented above all by John Damascene, both of whom he quotes a great deal, had different points of departure, consisting of two different levels or aspects in the created analogies of the sending out of the Word and the Spirit.[17] Augustine, he thought, considered the *inner* structure of the spirit and therefore maintained that it was from the *mens* that the *cogitatio* or word proceeded and the latter was followed by the spiration of the *affectus*. The Damascene, on the other hand, according to Alexander considered the *external* word, so that the point of departure was the intellect, followed by the word, which emerged as a word with a breath, which was connected in an immediate way to the intellect. The Spirit, then, was *Spiritus Verbi, non a Verbo*. These were, then, two different ways of representing the *proportio* or relationship between the Spirit and the Word.

This attempt to harmonize two different theologies met with some success. M. Roncaglia quotes, on p. 194 of his work (*op. cit.*, note 16 below), a text from the University Library of Münster (cod. 257), in particular a treatise *De fide* by an unknown author, which is worth translating:

> It has been said that the Greeks are mistaken in claiming that the Spirit proceeds only from the Father. . . . If they are mistaken in this, then it is an error in an matter of faith. Others have expressed themselves differently. The Latin doctors, they say, have come to know the Trinity differently from the Greeks. The first have come to understand it from considering the image and the trace of the Trinity in the creature. Augustine therefore came to know the Father, the Son and the Spirit through this triad: the spirit, knowledge and love. The first is like the father, the second his child, and the third the Spirit that proceeds from both. The Latins, observing that love, which they call inner spirit, proceeds from understanding as from the Father and from knowledge or the inner word, therefore say that the same applies to the uncreated Trinity and that the Spirit consequently proceeds from both.
>
> The Greeks, on the other hand, came to a knowledge of the Trinity through the external intellect and word and the external spirit and here I call 'spirit' the breathing in and out of air. There is first the intellect, then the word, and the word expressed in the breath is like the vehicle of the word. The intellect forms the word by breathing and is itself manifested in the breathed word. This is the position adopted by John Damascene. . . . He says that our word is not without the spirit-breath, although the latter does not come from the substance of the word. That is why the Greeks have insisted that, just as our external spirit-breath depends only on the intellect which forms it, in the uncreated Trinity, the Holy Spirit similarly comes from the Father alone as from the one who breathes (out) and the Word also comes from the same Father as from the one who pronounces, that is, begets him. There is therefore no contradiction between the Greeks and the Latins, each of whom express themselves quite consistently (*proportionaliter*). This is the solution provided by Alexander and Pagus.[18]

When John de la Rochelle edited the first part of the *Summa Alexandri* from 1256 onwards, basing his edition on Alexander's teaching and as far as possible on his text, he made use of the same ideas, although he did so with a precision that can later be found in other theological works. 'Proceed' can be understood in two different ways—either as a purely local proceeding, that is, as a movement *ab aliquo in aliquid*, or in a simply causal way, that is, *in exitu causati a causa*. Two terms have to be postulated in the case of the first—an *a quo* and an *ad quem*. This was the way in which the Greeks understood *procedere* and it presupposed that the Spirit proceeded from one Person into another. If he had proceeded from the Son, he would have had to proceed from him to the Father, and this was clearly untenable. He therefore did not proceed from the Son. The Latins, on the other hand, thought of 'proceed' in the causal sense: *ab aliquo exire, quamvis non in aliquam*. They were therefore able to maintain that the Spirit proceeded from the Father and from the Son, 'velut amor a notitia et mente'.[19]

This idea that there were two ways of understanding the procession of the Holy Spirit can also be found in the work of Bonaventure[20] and Odo Rigaldus[21] although it must be admitted that the value of this idea is not increased by its frequent occurrence. Thomas Aquinas appears not to have made use of it. It would also be difficult to find really significant Greek references to illustrate it. It is fundamentally a reconstruction. This also applies to the way in which Odo Rigaldus presented the course of the controversy, which is of value as pointing to the opinions of a magister of Paris, rather than as a historical summary:

> We agree that the Holy Spirit proceeds from the Son. And I believe that those among the Greeks who were really learned and understood the question have never denied it. This is clear from the texts quoted by the Master (*I Sent.* d. 11). Those who, on the other hand, were outraged, at the period when the addition was made to the creed, because they had not been summoned, refused to accept it, although we do not believe that even they denied that it was true. Less cultured men (*simpliciores*) who came later, having heard that their élite refused to concede it, simply denied it. In this way, the situation went from bad to worse. Their main reason for maintaining their position was that they saw the procession as going from one person to another (*esse ab aliquo in aliquem*). . . .
>
> It is, however, important to note that the Latins made a distinction in the statement *Spiritus Sanctus procedit a Filio*. If the preposition *a* means that the Son has the *auctoritas* of the procession of the Spirit, then the Latins accept it no more than the Greeks. If, on the other hand, it does not point to that *auctoritas*, then the Latins accept it and this may be what the Greeks meant to say.

In his commentary on the same distinction (11) in 1250–1251, Bonaventure is more interesting and more profound[22]. He distinguished between three levels or aspects. The first was the aspect of faith in divine revelation as contained in Scripture, about which Greeks and Latins were agreed. The second aspect was that of explicitation, that is, of the knowledge and use of categories and terminology, and it was this aspect that had given rise to the difference between the Greeks and the Latins. The third was that of the profession of the teaching in a formula and that was the controversy.

What is common to both Greeks and Latins is the scriptural basis of the procession, according to which the Spirit is the Spirit of the Son and is sent by the Son. There is, however, also the *ratio intelligendi*. The Greeks understood the procession as a local movement *ab uno in alium*, whereas the Latins saw it simply as a causal process, *unius ex alio*. What is more, the Greeks understood spiration as a *flatus exterioris*, while the Latins regarded it as the spiration of an inner love. Where Scripture says that the Spirit proceeds as a bond and as fellowship, the Greeks interpreted 'bond' as a mean between the two, whereas the Latins understood it as the term in which the two were united. In these various exercises in theological reasoning, the Latins made use of more spiritual and therefore more true ideas.[23] They were therefore able to understand Scripture better. The Greeks, on the other hand, were less open, since they had closed their own approach to a full development of its meaning and had limited that meaning to the purely temporal procession of mission of the Holy Spirit.

The controversy came fully into the open when the Latins introduced this article into the profession of faith. They did it with good reasons and legitimately—the teaching was correct and it was necessary to oppose error with the authority that the Roman Church had at its disposal. The Greeks were opposed to this addition because of ignorance, pride and obstinacy. Their ignorance had been revealed at three levels—they lacked an understanding of Scripture, they did not use the correct concepts, and they were not open to the illumination that was required for a true profession of faith. They were proud men who thought that they were well informed, but were offended because they had not been summoned and had therefore rejected what had been discovered by others. Finally, their obstinacy made them invent reasons to justify their own position. They consequently accused the Latins of having themselves incurred the excommunication that applies to those who tried to change the creed. The Latins had, however, not changed the creed. They had simply made more explicit and perfect what it had already contained.

There was a question about the text of John Damascene, *De fide orthod*. I, 8 (*PG* 94, 832): 'We do not say that the Spirit comes from the Son, although we call him the Spirit of the Son'. John was very highly regarded by the Scholastics of the West. Alexander of Hales explained a similar text by saying that John Damascene wanted to avoid saying that the Spirit proceeded from the Son *in Patrem*.[24] Alexander was deeply irenical and attempted to reconcile Augustine and John by saying that the first had dealt with the inner life of God, whereas the second was speaking of God's relationship with his creatures.[25]

Bonaventure was less accommodating. Like Thomas Aquinas, he said of John Damascene *non est in ista parte ei assentiendum*, adding 'I understand that he was writing at the time when the controversy first emerged. There is no need to support him in this because he was simply Greek. Nonetheless, he expressed himself subtly. He did not say that the Spirit did not have his being from the Son. What he said was: we do not say that he had it from him.

The Greeks did not in fact confess this truth, but nor did they deny it.'[26]

Duns Scotus was more favourable not only to John Damascene, but also to the Greeks as a whole. In his *Lectura* on the *Sentences*, a work that he wrote as a young man at Oxford in the last years of the thirteenth century, he refers to Robert Grosseteste's note on John Damascene but comments: 'In hac quaestione (that of the procession of the Spirit from the Son, *a Filio*) discordant graeci vario modo a latinis'.[27] Later on, however, in his *Ordinatio Oxoniensis* or *Opus Oxoniense*, he was more cautious: 'In ista quaestione *dicuntur* graeci discordare a latinis, sicut *videntur* auctoritates Damasceni sonare' and quoted the whole of Grosseteste's note. Because it is of such great interest, I translate it here:

> If two learned scholars, one Greek and the other Latin, both really loving the truth and not their own way of expressing it from their individual point of view, were to discuss this opposition, they would end by finding that it is not a real one, but one based on words. Otherwise, either the Greeks or ourselves, the Latins, are really heretical. But who would dare to accuse of heresy such an author as John Damascene and such saints as Basil, Gregory the Theologian, Cyril and other Greek Fathers? In the same way, who would impute heresy to blessed Jerome, Augustine and Ambrose, Hilary and the skilled Latins? It is therefore probable that, despite these different modes of expression, there is no real disagreement between the thought of these Fathers who are opposed to each other. There is more than one way of expressing oneself. One man expresses himself in one way and another way is derived or comes from another man. If we were to understand and distinguish the great number of modes of expression, it would appear that there is no disagreement in meaning or intention between these opposing terms. However, since the Catholic Church has declared it as having to be held as faith, it is necessary to maintain that the Holy Spirit proceeds *ab utroque*.[28]

Duns Scotus was very open to the Greek way of expressing the mystery and therefore defended pluralism in this question. The following important statement is very interesting in this respect:

> It should be understood in this debate that there are two articles which are of the substance of faith and these are discussed in the first book of *Sentences*. The first article is that there are only three Persons and one God. The second is that these Persons do not exist of themselves alone, but one Person produces another and those two produce a third. We are not permitted to think differently about these two articles. It is, however, possible to think differently about whether the Persons are constituted by relationships or by their mode of being, so long as we respect the articles mentioned above. It is permitted to discuss and to seek (*exerceri*), because I am not bound by faith to any particular true assertion.[29]

In fact, Duns Scotus kept close to the teaching of Bonaventure and several other theologians, according to whom the Person in God is constituted, not by relationships, but by something absolute, namely the (first) substance or supposit that is distinguished by a certain property. That property is identical with the relationship in question. But 'person' connotes in the first place a substance or supposit.[30] The Greek way of distinguishing the Holy Spirit from the Word—not by their relationship, but by the different mode of processing—was therefore seen by Duns Scotus to be acceptable. Thomas Aquinas did not accept this judgement.

Thomas regarded it as impossible to distinguish the Spirit from the Son if he did not proceed from him and if they did not both proceed from the Father.[31] This was the position that was in general held by the Dominican school. The question continued, however, to be disputed.[32] From the time of Robert Grosseteste onwards—he was not a Franciscan, although he taught them—the Franciscan school continued generally to maintain a different position from that held by Thomas and, before him, by Anselm. Those who opposed Thomas in this included William of Ware,[33] John Peckham,[34] Matthew of Aquasparta,[35] Petrus Johannis Olivi and, of course, John Duns Scotus. Outside the Order of Friars Minor, there were Praepositinus, William of Auvergne, Henry of Ghent[36] and James of Viterbo.

All these theologians regarded the procession of the Holy Spirit from the Father *and the Son* as a dogma of the Church. Many of them did not hesitate to describe the Greeks not simply as teaching error, but as heretics. In using this word, however, we should remember that the idea of heresy was wider in its meaning at that time than it is today.

NOTES

1. Athanasius, *Tomos ad Antiochenos*; see also H. B. Swete, *The Holy Spirit in the Ancient Church* (London, 1912), p. 173.
2. Jerome, *Ep.* 15, 3–4, written to Pope Damasus in September 374 (*PL* 22, 356–357).
3. Augustine, *De Trin.* V, 8, 9–10 (*PL* 42, 917).
4. *De Trin*, VII, 5, 10 (*PL* 42, 942).
5. *De Trin*. VII, 4 and VIII, proem. (*PL* 42, 939ff., 947).
6. See the critical edition of Anselm by S. Schmitt: *Mon.*, prol. (Schmitt, I, p. 8) and 79 (p. 86); *Ep.* 83 (III, p. 208) and 204 (IV, pp. 96–97); *Ep. de Inc. Verbi*, XVI (II, p. 35). Anselm's position was very similar in the case of the celebration of the Eucharist—whether it was unleavened or leavened, it was still bread!
7. See Abelard, *Theol. Christ*. IV (*PL* 178, 1268). The first sentence of this text is found, after an appeal to Augustine, *De Trin*. VII, 4, in the *Theol. Summi Boni* III, 1, No. 7: see H. Ostlender, *Peter Abaelards Theologia Summi Boni* (*Beiträge zur Geschichte der Philosophie und Theologie des Mittelalters*, XXXV, 2–3) (Münster, 1939), p. 77.
8. Richard, *De Trin*. IV, 20 (*PL* 198, 943); see the crit. ed. of J. Ribaillier (Paris, 1958), p. 184; Fr. tr. G. Salet, *SC* 63 (1959), pp. 273 and 275.
9. Examples are: *hypostasis–substantia: Contra Err. Graec.* I, prol.; *ST* Ia, q. 30, a. 1, ad 1 and q. 39, a. 3, ad 2; *causa–principium: ST* Ia, q. 33, a. 1, ad 1 and 2; *De Pot.* q. 10, a. 1, ad 8, in which Thomas generalizes: 'aliquid enim inconvenienter in lingua latina dicitur quod propter proprietatem idiomatis convenienter in lingua graeca dici potest'. See also my article 'Valeur et portée œcuméniques de quelques principes herméneutiques de S. Thomas d'Aquin', *RSPT*, 57 (1973), 611–626. For Thomas' respect for the Greek Fathers: 'quia praesumptuosum est tantorum doctorum expressis auctoritatibus contraire'; *ST* Ia, q. 61, a. 3: 'quamvis contrarium non sit reputandum erroneum propter sententiam

Gregorii Nazianzeni, cuius tanta est in doctrina christiana auctoritas ut nullus unquam eius dictis calumniam inferre praesumpserit, sicut nec Athanasii documentis, ut Hieronymus dixit'. .

10. Text edited by M. Schmaus in *Der Liber Propugnatorius des Thomas Anglicus und die Lehrunterschiede zwischen Thomas von Aquin und Duns Scotus*, II. Teil: *Die trinitarischen Lehrdifferenz (Beiträge zur Geschichte der Philosophie und Theologie des Mittelalters*, XXIX) (Münster, 1930), p. 314.

11. *ST* Ia, q. 36, a. 2; cf. *Contra Err. Graec.* II, c. 9.

12. *De Pot.* q. 10, a. 5 c.—a very important article.

13. The Spirit of the Son: *De Pot.* q. 10, a. 5, ad 14; *ST* Ia, q. 36, a. 2; cf. *Contra Err. Graec.* II, 1. The Spirit proceeding through the Son: *De Pot.* q. 10, a. 4, c. end; *ST* Ia, q. 36, a. 3; *Contra Err. Graec.* II, 8.

14. Thomas of Sutton, *Quaest. disp.* 9; M. Schmaus, *op. cit.* (note 10), p. 95.

15. The Franciscans would seem to have owed their fundamental arguments in the debate with the Greeks, the principal concern being that they should believe that the Spirit was the Spirit of the Son, to Robert Grosseteste, in his note added to the *Ep. ad Trisagion* of John Damascene; see the evidence of Duns Scotus, *Oxon.* I, d. 11, p. 1 (ed. L. Vivès, *Opera*, IX, p. 325); Robert Grosseteste, MS. British Museum Royal 6, E. V, fol. 109 and 7 F. 2, fol. 72ᵛ–73ʳ; M. Roncaglia, *op. cit.* (note 16 below), p. 239; Oxford, Magd. cod. 192, fol. 215, quoted in the edition of the *Lectura* of Duns Scotus.

16. See M. Roncaglia, *Les Frères Mineurs et l'Eglise grecque orthodoxe au XIIIᵉ siècle (1271–1274)* (Cairo, 1954). The report by Haymo of Faversham (in 1234) was edited by G. Golubovich in *Arch. Franc. Hist.*, 12 (1919), 418–470.

17. Alexander of Hales, *Glossa in quatuor Libros Sententiarum*, lib. I, d. XI (Quaracchi ed. (1951), pp. 135ff.).

18. Münster, Universitätsbibliothek Cod. 257, fol. 72d–73c, quoted by Roncaglia, *op. cit.*, p. 195. For John Pagus, see the brief reference by P. Glorieux in *Répertoire des Maîtres en Théologie de Paris au XIIIᵉ siècle*, I (Paris, 1933), pp. 328–329.

19. Alexander of Hales, *ST* I, pars I, inq. II, tract. unicus, q.1, tit. II, c. IV (Quaracchi ed., p. 450). In his reply to the sixteenth objection, Alexander uses the idea expressed above to make a distinction between the inner word (and spirit) favoured by Augustine and the Latins and the external word of John Damascene and the Greeks.

20. Bonaventure, *In I Sent.* d. 11, art. un., q. 1, reply to the first objection.

21. Odo Rigaldus, *Utrum Spiritus Sanctus sit Patris et Filii ita quod ab utroque, vel sit Filii non tamen procedens a Filio, sicut volunt Graeci. Solutio.* This text was edited by Roncaglia, *op. cit.* (note 16), p. 215 in accordance with the Paris MS. BN lat. 14.910, but an integral edition of the whole question was prepared by M. Schmaus, *op. cit.* (note 10), pp. 281–286, especially p. 284, where our text appears.

22. Bonaventure, *In I Sent.* d. XI, art. un., q. 1 (Quaracchi ed., I, pp. 211ff.). J. Ratzinger commented on this article in 'Offenbarung, Schrift und Überlieferung. Ein Text des heiligen Bonaventura und seine Bedeutung für die gegenwärtige Theologie', *Trierer Theologische Zeitschrift*, 67 (1958), 13–27.

23. It is interesting to record a more favourable statement. In the question as to whether the personal name may be applied to God, Bonaventure raised this objection: 'vocabula nostra debent respondere Graecis, ut unitas fidei ostendatur; sed Graeci non utuntur vocabulo *prosopon* in divinis, quod est idem quod *persona*; ergo cum ipsi proprius habeant vocabula quam nos, nec nos debemus uti': *In I Sent.* d. 23, a. 1,q. 1, arg. 4 (Quaracchi ed., I, p. 405). In his reply to this objection, Bonaventure says that the word 'person' is used because of the lack of other terms; the Greeks have their own word, 'hypostasis', but we cannot say 'substance', because it is synonymous with 'essence'.

24. Alexander of Hales, *Quaestiones disputatae 'Antequam esset frater'*, q. 8, membr. 1, Nos. 16 and 18 (*Bibl. Franciscana Scholastica Medii Aevi*, XIX; Quaracchi ed. (1960), pp. 71 and 72).

25. *Glossa in quatuor Libros Sententiarum*, Lib. I, d. XI (*Bibl. Franciscana Scholastica Medii Aevi*, XII; Quaracchi ed. (1951), pp. 135ff.).
26. Bonaventure, *op. cit.* (note 22 above); cf. d. XXXI, a. 1, q. 2 ad 1, (Quaracchi ed., I, p. 542), in which the same explanation can be found: *fuit Graecus*. The finer interpretation is that he simply thought in Greek, with all its limitations. For Thomas Aquinas, see *ST* Ia, q. 36, a. 2, ad 3; *De Pot*. q. 10, a. 4, ad 24. For the introduction of John Damascene's texts to the Scholastics, see J. de Ghellinck, 'L'entrée de Jean de Damas dans le monde littéraire occidental', *Byzantinische Zeitschrift*, 21 (1912), 448–457; P. Minges, 'Zum Gebrauch der Schrift "De fide orthodoxa" des Johannes Damaszenus in der Scholastik', *TQ* (1914), 225–247. In the *Summa* alone, Thomas quotes him more than 200 times. For the Scholastic theologians, he was a very valuable authority. Peter Lombard said, for example: 'Ioannes Damascenus inter doctores Graecorum maximus, in libro quem de Trinitate scripsit, quem et papa Eugenius transferri fecit': *I Sent.*, d. 19. Albert the Great was anxious to show that he agreed with Augustine: see *In I Sent.* d. 27, a. 7 (ed. A. Borgnet, XXVI, pp. 46–47). Duns Scotus insisted that John Damascene was not heretical in his article on the procession of the Holy Spirit: 'Damascenus reputatur doctor authenticus et catholicus adeo ut liber suus translatus fuerit mandato papae de graeco in latinum, propter quod non videtur quod liber suus contineat aliqua opposita traditioni ecclesiae Romanae, et tamen ipse posuit ibidem non quod Spiritus Sanctus sit a Filio, sed quod est Filii': quoted by M. Schmaus, *op. cit.* (note 10), p. 374, note 199.
27. Duns Scotus, *Lectura in librum primum Sententiarum* (D. VIII-XLV), *Opera omnia*, XVII (Vatican, 1966), p. 128 = d. 11, q. 1.
28. *In I Sent.* d. XI, q. 1; *Opera omnia* (Paris, 1893), IX, p. 325. I have not been able to consult the most recent edition, the *Opera omnia*, V, pp. 2–3.
29. *Lectura*, d. II, No. 164 in the Vatican edition of the *Opera omnia*, XVI, pp. 166–167.
30. Duns Scotus, *Lectura*, d. XXVI; Vatican ed., *op. cit.*, pp. 328ff., in which William of Auvergne and Robert Grosseteste are given, in a note, as antecedents. Bonaventure, *In I Sent.* d. XXV, a. 1, q. 1 and q. 2, ad 3 (Quaracchi ed., pp. 436–437 and 441).
31. Thomas Aquinas, *In I Sent.* d. 13, q. 1, a. 2; *De Pot*. q. 10, a. 5; *ST* Ia, q. 36, a. 2; *Comm. in ev. Ioan.* c. 15, lect. 5.
32. See pp. 253ff. of M. Schmaus' enormous study, *op. cit.* (note 10 above). According to the list given in a Munich manuscript, it was the thirteenth of the articles on which the *magistri* disagreed: see A. Dondaine, 'Un catalogue des dissensions doctrinales entre les Maîtres parisiens à la fin du XIIIᵉ siècle', *RTAM*, 10 (1938), 374–394.
33. See the texts of William of Ware in J. Slipyj, *De principio spirationis in SS. Trinitate. Disquisitio historico-dogmatica* (Lwow, 1926).
34. The text of John Peckham will be found in M. Schmaus, *op. cit.* (note 10), pp. 295–296.
35. Matthew of Aquasparta, *Quodl.* II, q. 3; see M. Schmaus, *op. cit.*, pp. 291–292.
36. Henry of Ghent, *Quodl.* V, q. 9 (Paris, 1518), fol. 167.

2
ATTEMPTS AT AND SUGGESTIONS
FOR AN AGREEMENT

The procession of the Holy Spirit from the Father *and the Son* was, for the Latins, an article of faith or a dogma. It had been professed by the Church's councils at least since the beginning of the seventh century, and before that by the Fathers of the Church, the Popes and the creed *Quicumque*. What is more, this had taken place during a period when the East and the West had—sometimes only with great difficulty—been in communion. After this communion had been broken, this same article of faith was proclaimed in the West by successive councils. These included Bari of 1098,[1] the Fourth Lateran Council of 1215,[2] the Second Council of Lyons in 1274, when the delegates of the Greek basileus chanted this passage in the creed twice, once in Greek and once in Latin,[3] and finally the Council of Ferrara-Florence in 1438–1439. We shall be returning to this last council later in this chapter.

The centuries in which East and West have been divided, but never totally separated, have been marked by efforts to re-establish communion and attempts at elucidation and agreement.[4] Unfortunately, however, on both sides, the main consideration has almost always been to reduce the other side to one's own level.[5] The Greeks put forward their own formula and the Latins proposed theirs—each formula was given as an absolute which excluded the other.[6] In particular, the numerous conferences held in the East by the Dominicans and the Franciscans, while providing an opportunity for the formulation of precise statements which are of interest to theologians, resulted in a hardening of the situation rather than a reduction of the difficulties between East and West. An abortive attempt to reach agreement has always involved the risk of creating a greater distance between the two sides. Was this the case with Ferrara-Florence? That is a possible view, especially considering the aversion that the Greeks still feel, even nowadays, for it. I have studied this council very carefully and asked searching questions about it. It seems to me that, as far as the article of faith that interests us here is concerned, Ferrara-Florence was at once a very serious confrontation between East and West, and (too brief) an attempt to look for a possibility of communion in diversity.

The Council of Florence

The debate began at Ferrara in 1438 on whether the addition of the *Filioque* clause to the creed was justified. I shall consider this extremely important point after I have summarized the whole debate and evaluated the agreement reached on the doctrinal question.[7]

The doctrinal discussion proper began on 2 March 1439 at Florence. It was at first concerned mainly with terminology: the meaning of the word 'procession'. Mark Eugenikos' definition was *huparktikē proodos*—a 'substantial going out or emanation'. A little later, it became necessary to clarify—once again—the relationship between 'substance' and 'hypostasis'. Then there was a long discussion about the real meaning of the texts of Basil the Great and Athanasius (see above, pp. 30, 44 note 9).[8]

The Greeks were anxious to safeguard the unity of the source of divinity, the Father from whom everything proceeded. The Latins replied to this by claiming firstly that the Son's spiration of the Spirit was derived entirely from the Father and secondly that the Holy Spirit proceeded from the two (*duo spirantes*) as from a single principle (*unus Spirator*). They did not want to say that the Son had a different function from that of the Father with regard to the Spirit proceeding *a Patre per Filium*. To claim this would have been to compromise on the one hand the real identity of the hypostases and the divine substance and, on the other, the community of essence of the Father and the Son. For this reason, then, it seemed important to them to interpret the *a Patre per Filium* in the sense of 'a Patre et Filio tanquam ab uno principio'.[9] They believed that an affirmation of the procession of the Spirit *a Patre solo* did violence to the divine unity by destroying the real identity of the hypostases and the divine substance because it attributed to the Father something, apart from fatherhood, that the Son did not have.

Obviously, this Latin theological construction of the mystery of the Trinity was alien to the Greek mind. They thought that it introduced a non-personal principle into the reality of the Triad. Instead of a Triad, the Latins, they believed, were postulating two dyads: Father→Son and Father-Son→Holy Spirit. The Greeks wished to recognize only relationships between the Persons, within which the Father was the Principle or beginning, the Cause, the Author and the Source. In fact, the Latins also recognized that, as Mgr Sergey, who was the Bishop of Yamburg and Rector of the Ecclesiastical Academy at St Petersburg at the beginning of the present century and became the second head of the restored Patriarchate of Moscow in 1925, pointed out in 1903 [see Appendix to this chapter, pp. 190–191].

A door was opened to possible agreement at Florence on 19 March when the Greeks presented the text of the letter written by Maximus the Confessor to Marinus, a priest in Cyprus, declaring that the Latins acknowledged that the Father was the only Cause of the Son and the Spirit.[10] Since John of Montenero had also produced texts by the Latin Fathers showing that the *Filioque* had the same meaning as *per Filium* as well as texts by Basil, Epiphanius, Didymus the Blind and Cyril of Alexandria saying much the same as the Latin texts, Isidore of Kiev and Bessarion of Nicaea declared their agreement.[11] It was, in other words, not a question of 'Latinizing', but rather of following the saints of the Church. The Fathers could not have been mistaken, nor could they have been opposed to each other, because the Holy Spirit had spoken in them.[12]

These ideas gradually came to be accepted and on 12 April Bessarion made his magistral dogmatic pronouncement, which was in fact a full pneumatological treatise.[13] Maximus the Confessor's letter to Marinus was taken as the basis for union (on 17 April 1439), since the holy Fathers of the Church clearly in no way explicitly denied a relationship of eternal existence between the Holy Spirit and the Son. The Greek Fathers and the Patriarch Tarasius, whose work was also cited, used the formula 'through the Son' and a number of other formulae which were quite close to the *Filioque*. They could, it was argued, not be regarded as heretics and the formula 'through the Son' could only point to a contribution from the Son, received from the Father, to the 'procession' of the Spirit. Interpreted in this sense, it was seen as equivalent to *ex Filio*, explained, as the Latins did, *tanquam ab uno principio*.[14]

Union was achieved on this basis, proclaimed on 6 July 1439 and accepted by the emperor and thirty-nine Eastern Christians—bishops, procurators, deacons and superiors of monasteries.[15] The text of this decree on the procession of the Holy Spirit is as follows:

> In the name of the holy Trinity, the Father, the Son and the Holy Spirit, with the approval of this sacred universal Council of Florence, we define that this truth of faith must be believed and received by all Christians and that all must profess, namely, that the Holy Spirit has his being eternally from the Father and the Son, that he has his essence and his subsistence both from the Father and from the Son together, and that he proceeds eternally from both as from a single principle and by a single spiration. We declare that what the holy doctors and Fathers say, that is, that the Holy Spirit proceeds from the Father through the Son, is intended to mean that the Son is also, according to the Greeks, the cause and, according to the Latins, the principle of the subsistence of the Holy Spirit, as the Father is. And since everything that belongs to the Father, the Father gives to his only begotten Son by begetting him, apart from being Father, the Son has it eternally from the Father, by whom he is eternally begotten, that the Holy Spirit proceeds from him. We define, moreover, that the explanation (or explicitation) of those words *Filioque* has been lawfully and reasonably added to the creed in order to declare the truth and because of the urgent need.[16]

The essential aspect of this historic text is that the two formulae, the *Filioque* and the *per Filium*, had come to be regarded as equivalent or at least as possibly equivalent. This was also the basis of later unions, such as that achieved at Brest in 1596.[17] I find it difficult to understand that the formula that the Son is, together with the Father, the *cause* of the procession of the Holy Spirit was attributed to the Greeks, since the latter had always reserved this term for the *Father*.[18] I find it equally difficult to understand why the verb *ekporeuesthai* was used in the Greek text of the act of union in the sentence 'he proceeds (*procedit*) eternally from both as from a single principle and by a single spiration', whereas this verb was reserved by the Greeks for the procession of the Holy Spirit from the Father as from his first origin.[19] Finally, to affirm that *per Filium* is equivalent to *ex Filio* does not express the shade of meaning that exists between two expressions that go back to two quite different theological constructions of a mystery believed in the same way and confessed in the doxology. As Bessarion pointed out, however, *ex* meant equality and not order, whereas *per* pointed to the order of the Persons and not their equality. In accepting the *per Filium*, on the other hand, the Latins provided a critical gloss on it as tending to suggest that the Son was inferior or impossibly instrumental.[20]

In fact, the Florentine act of union did not simply stop at declaring an agreement of intent between two different expressions stemming from two different theological approaches to the same faith. It reduced the Greek expression to the fundamentally Western meaning of its Latin equivalent: *per Filium* is Catholic if it is interpreted in the sense of *Filioque*. This may be so, but then let us take this equivalence seriously and agree with André de Halleux, who said:[21] 'After having affirmed for such a long time that the *di' Huiou* was the equivalent of the *Filioque*, would it not be possible to agree in return that the *Filioque* goes back to the *di' Huiou*, in other words, to recognize the fundamental authenticity of monopatrism?' After having analysed the advantages and the disadvantages of the two formulae, M. Jugie (*op. cit.* (note 4 below), p. 12), provided a meaningful suggestion: 'Omnibus accurate perpensis formula Graecorum praeponenda videtur, quatenus et principii unitatem subindicat, et ordinem personarum in luce ponit, et Patris monarchiam directe exprimit'—'After having considered everything very carefully, the formula of the Greeks seems preferable, inasmuch as it demonstrates the unity of principle, sheds light on the order of the Persons and directly expresses the monarchy of the Father'.

The formula 'to recognize the fundamental authenticity of monopatrism' has, however, to be defined more precisely. The formula 'through the Son', taken on its own, could express forgetfulness or denial of the part of the Son in the eternal production of the Spirit. The Son would only be, in that case, a transitional stage in the act of spiration of the one Father. Karl Barth rightly objected to this interpretation, but he failed in this to understand and perhaps even to show sufficient knowledge of the Eastern tradition.[22] This was undoubtedly the price that Barth had to pay for taking Jesus Christ as his point of departure in all his theology, for working Christologically. With greater recognition than he had of the value expressed by the *di' Huiou*, we can more easily accept the fact that each formula is the complement of the other.

Florenced was too great a victory for the Latins—and the papacy—for it to be a full council of union.[23] The Orthodox are wrong to reject it so completely, because the debate on the pneumatological question was both free and serious. It is not difficult, however, to understand their dissatisfaction and their reluctance to accept the conclusion *in the form in which it was expressed*.[24] The indefeasible deposit of Florence is twofold: (1) the intention to recognize that the two formulae were compatible and even equivalent—I would willingly say, that they were complementary; (2) the principle on the basis of which this intention was pursued, namely that the Fathers of the Church, inspired by the Holy Spirit, held, in communion, both formulae. Any new attempt to approach this question should take this as a point of departure and as a basis for discussion.

NOTES

1. Mansi, 20, 947–992.
2. *DS* 800; the first decretal, *Firmiter*, a theological reference to the thirteenth century; *DS* 805: the decretal *Damnamus*.
3. The Emperor's profession of faith on 6 June 1274; see *DS* 853; and the Constitution *De summa Trinitate et fide catholica*, sixth session, 17 July 1274: see *DS* 850, with its repeated insistence on the *tanquam ex uno principio*.
4. There have been very many special studies. Among the most useful are W. Norden, *Das Papsttum und Byzanz. Die Trennung der beiden Mächte und das Problem ihrer Wiedervereinigung bis zum Untergang des byzantinischen Reiches (1453)* (Berlin, 1903); M. Viller, 'La question de l'union des Eglises entre Grecs et Latins depuis le concile de Lyon jusqu'à celui de Florence (1274–1438)', *RHE*, 17 (1921), 260–305, 515–532; 18 (1922), 20–60; R. J. Loenertz, 'Autour du traité de Fr. Bartélémy de Constantinople contre les Grecs', *Arch. Fratr. Praed.*, 6 (1936), 361–378; *idem*, 'Les dominicains byzantins Théodore et André Chrysobergès et les négociations pour l'union des Eglises grecque et latine de 1415 à 1430'; M. Jugie, *De Processione Spiritus Sancti ex fontibus Revelationis et secundum Orientales dissidentes* (Rome, 1936); A. Dondaine, ' "Contra Graecos". Premiers écrits polémiques des Dominicains d'Orient', *Arch. Fratr. Praed.*, 21 (1951), 320–446; M. Roncaglia, *Les Frères Mineurs et l'Eglise grecque orthodoxe au XIIIᵉ siècle (1231–1274)* (Cairo, 1954); E. Herman, 'Neuf siècles de schisme entre l'Eglise d'Orient et d'Occident', *NRT*, 76 (1954), 576–610; F. Stegmüller, 'Bonacursius contra Graecos. Ein Beitrag zur Kontroverstheologie des XIII. Jahrhunderts', *Vitae et Veritati. Festschrift für Karl Adam* (Düsseldorf, 1956), pp. 57–82; *1274 année charnière. Mutations et continuités. Colloque Lyon-Paris, 30 Septembre–5 Octobre 1974* (CNRS, 1977); C. Capizzi, 'Fra Bonagrazzia di San Giovanni in Persicato e il concilio unionistico di Lione (1274)', *Arch. Hist. Pont.*, 13 (1975), 141–206.
5. See G. Alberigo, 'L'œcuménisme au Moyen Age', *1274 année charnière, op. cit.* (note 4 above); this essay was also published in *RHE*, 71 (1976), 365–391.
6. Although it was admitted at Florence that the Greeks should not pronounce the *Filioque* formula, since there was agreement concerning the doctrine itself, Pope Nicholas III later wanted to impose the formula on them: see *DTC*, V, cols 2340–2341.
7. Between 1940 and 1971, the Pontifical Oriental Institute published ten volumes of the *Concilium Florentinum: Documenta et Scriptores*. In addition to this, the critical works of Mark Eugenikos were edited by L. Petit in *Patr. Or.*, 17, pp. 307–524, and Sylvester Syropoulos' memoirs were translated and edited by V. Laurent in *Concilium Florentinum*, IX (Rome, 1971). See also J. Gill, *The Council of Florence* (Cambridge, 1959);

idem, Constance et Bâle-Florence (Les conciles œcuméniques) (Paris, 1965); J. Decarreaux, *Les Grecs au Concile de l'union Ferrare-Florence (1438–1439)* (Paris, 1970); A. Leidl, *Die Einheit der Kirchen auf den spätmittelalterlichen Konzilien von Konstanz bis Florenz* (Paderborn, 1966); H. Mühlen, 'Das Konzil von Florenz (1439) als vorläufiges Modell eines kommenden Unionskonzils', *Theologie und Glaube*, 63 (1973), 184–197; H. J. Marx, *Filioque und Verbot eines anderen Glaubens auf dem Florentinum. Zum Pluralismus in dogmatischen Formeln* (Steyl, 1977).

8. Basil the Great: see above, pp. 30, 44 note 9; see also J. Gill, *The Council of Florence, op. cit.* (note 7), pp. 194ff. For the use of patristic texts, see E. Boulerand, 'L'argument patristique au concile de Florence, dans la question de la procession du Saint-Esprit', *BLE*, 63 (1962), 162–199.

9. See Mansi, 31 A, 971, and the declaration made by the Latins on 1 May, Mansi, 31 A, 974–975; see also 'Florence', *DTC*, V, 1 col. 40.

10. Mansi, 31 A, 877 (Greek) and 878 (Latin); see also J. Gill, *The Council of Florence, op. cit.*, pp. 212f. see also above, pp. 52–53.

11. Mansi, 31, col. 886.

12. See *Concilium Florentinum*, Series B, V/2 (Rome, 1953), p. 426: 'Sancti non discrepant, sed idem Spiritus Sanctus locutus est in omnibus sanctis. . . ; ita comperietur sanctos nunquam dissentire'. This section, 'Quae supersunt Act. Graec.', is ed. by J. Gill.

13. Mansi, 31, cols 893–968; *PG* 161, 543–612; E. Candal, ed., *Concilium Florentinum*, VII/1 (Rome, 1961); J. Gill, *The Council of Florence, op. cit.* (note 7), pp. 240–241.

14. Mansi, 31, col. 1002.

15. J. Gill, *The Council of Florence, op. cit.*, pp. 293f. Mark Eugenikos refused to sign. The Patriarch of Constantinople, Joseph II, died on the very day that had been chosen for the union, 8 June: see Mansi, 31, col. 1007. He left a paper in which he clearly subscribed to this union and recognized the Pope as the 'vicar of Christ': see *Concilum Florentimum, op. cit.*, pp. 444–455; J. Gill, *The Council of Florence, op. cit.*, p. 267. Final consent was delayed for a month by the request made by Eugenius IV that, before union was agreed, the Greeks should accept five points: his primacy, purgatory, unleavened bread, the addition of the *Filioque* clause to the creed and consecration of the Eucharist using the words of institution. These points were hastily discussed.

16. *DS* 1300–1302.

17. *Or. Chr.*, 3 (1924), 150. The procession of the Holy Spirit 'non ex duobus principiis, nec duplici processione, sed ex uno principio velut ex fonte, ex Patre per Filium procedere' (§1).

18. See Gregory of Nyssa, *Adv. Eunom.* I (*PG* 45, 416C); Maximus the Confessor, *Ep. ad Mar.* (*PG* 91, 136); John Damascene, *De fide orthod.* I, 8 and 12 (*PG* 94, 832 and 849).

19. See M. Jugie, *op. cit.* (note 4 above), p. 15. Maximus' text, which is the basis of the agreement, was much more satisfactory. Maximus not only insisted that the Father was the only *aitia*, but also, in speaking of the Spirit's dependence on the Son, used the verb *proïenai*.

20. See Thomas Aquinas, *ST* Ia, q. 36, a. 3 and parallel texts; *Contra Err. Graec.* II, 8. See also J. Gill, *The Council of Florence, op. cit.* (note 7), pp. 240ff. The Greeks also discussed more fully whether *ex* and *dia* were equivalent.

21. A. de Halleux, 'Orthodoxie et Catholicisme: du personnalisme en pneumatologie', *RTL*, 6 (1975), 3–30, especially 30, note.

22. K. Barth, *Church Dogmatics*, I. 1 (Eng. tr.; Edinburgh and New York, 1936), pp. 551–552.

23. This emerges even more clearly when the decree *Pro Armenis* of 22 November 1435 is read: see *DS* 1310ff. This text is taken from Thomas Aquinas, sometimes literally: see his *De art. fid. et Eccl. sacr.* It is not a dogma, but merely theology and, what is more, only one theology.

24. It is important to point to the serious limitations of the Council of Florence, which was not

189

an ideal council of union. The Orthodox, however, have almost always failed to be fair—and sometimes to be well-informed—with regard to the positive achievements of the Council. The history of the Council by Syropoulos—and this emerges especially clearly from the title of the first edition, prepared by the Anglican scholar R. Creyghton, *Vera Historia Unionis non verae* (The Hague, 1660)—is full of elements that are very valuable from the historical point of view, but at the same time passionate and one-sided. It has, however, continued to be regarded by many as the leading work on the Council. A passionate attack against Florence, written by Ivan N. Ostroumoff in Moscow in 1847, has been translated and published in English by Basil Popoff: *The History of the Council of Florence* (Boston, 1971). This publication concludes with a criticism of attempts made by Patriarch Athenagoras to open the way to ecumenism.

APPENDIX

Mgr Sergey published an article entitled 'What separates us from the Old Catholics?' in 1903 in the Russian-language journal *Tserkovniy Vestnik*. A French translation appeared in 1904 in the *Revue internationale de Théologie*, 12, 159–190. A more complete text of this article will be found in *Istina*, 17 (1972), 290–292. The following extract from the text is of direct interest to our subject:

Like the Old Catholics, we also have to bear in mind, in our mutual relationships, the difference that has existed for a thousand years between our two cultures and our intellectual development. This difference has continued to have an effect on our lives since the time of separation. Many words and terms which are used by both sides in fact have for each side a special meaning, very dear to each, which is not acceptable to the other side. If we are both absolutely convinced of the identity of our faith, we will end our debate about words and terminology and grant each side the right to use the term that it is accustomed to use.

Thus, when we deny the *Filioque*, we defend the 'monarchy' as the unity of the source in the Trinity and as an element that is quite necessary for any definition of the truth of the divine unity. For us, or rather for the Greek mind, to accept that the Son is, together with the Father, the true cause of the Holy Spirit is equivalent to accepting two principles of divinity, something both logically and psychologically impossible. In their defence and preservation of this truth in opposition to the Latins, the Greeks are prepared to add these words to the creed from 'the Father alone', so as to define the dogma decisively and beyond dispute, with no possibility of an interpretation other than their own.

The Old Catholics have inherited quite a different tradition. They have worked out a completely different system in order to understand God. For them, to say that the Son and the Holy Spirit are, in their eternal procession, quite independent of each other and that they are not in contact with each other is equivalent to doing violence to the very 'monarchy' that is so energetically defended in the East. The Eastern and the Western Christian each has his own point of view. Each sees through his own glasses of special and different colours, and cannot in any way understand the other's point of departure and way of thinking, or at least can do so only after making a great effort and renouncing all his own ideas.

That is why, when we are completely certain that the Old Catholics, when they take the *Filioque* out of their creed, are not simply going through a formality and trying to make rough canonical ways smooth but are really expressing a faith in the Trinity that is as orthodox as that of the holy Church, we shall not ask them to sign the formula *a Patre solo*. We shall, on the contrary, leave them their *Filioque* in the certain conviction that this formula is indispensable to the Western mind to express the same idea that we stress by means of our formula *a Patre solo*.

It is interesting to compare this passage by Mgr Sergey with the report made by Mgr Basile Krivocheine in the name of the Russian Orthodox Church to the conference held in Belgrade in 1966 with representatives of the Church of England; see *Istina*, 13 (1968):

Certain essential elements of the doctrine of the *Filioque* can be found in the writings of Church Fathers in the West long before the Roman Church became separated from the Orthodox Church (in St Augustine, for instance). What is more, this question is concerned more with theology than directly with faith itself. For this reason, the Orthodox Church cannot insist on the acceptance by Western Christians of the full teaching of the Fathers about the procession of the Holy Spirit as a precondition for the reunion of the Western with the Eastern Church. In this, Orthodox Christians are simply following the example of St Basil the Great, who did not insist that the divinity of the Holy Spirit should be recognized (only the fact that he was not created) as a precondition for reunion with the Orthodox Church on the part of those who accepted the Nicene creed. Disagreements of this kind, as St Basil the Great wrote, can be easily overcome later, after reunion, in the course of life together over a long period and study together without polemics. If that course were followed, it would have to be understood that there is no place in the creed for the *Filioque* clause; otherwise, the opinion of a Western theologian would be placed at the same level as the teaching of the universal Church.

3

RELATIONSHIPS AND DISCUSSIONS BETWEEN ORTHODOX AND NON-ROMAN CATHOLIC COMMUNIONS

A. ORTHODOX AND OLD CATHOLICS

After breaking away from the Roman Catholic Church in 1871, the Old Catholics tried to establish links, and if possible intercommunion, with other Churches whose structure was basically 'Catholic'. The Orthodox Church was very interested in this group of Western Christians who had emancipated themselves from papal authority.[1] One of the direct outcomes of this contact was a conference held at Cologne and Bonn in 1874–1875. This was attended by twenty-two bishops and priests of the Orthodox Church, American and English representatives of the Anglican Church, and a number of Old Catholics, including Döllinger (who refused to be described as 'Old Catholic'), Reusch and others. Altogether, 120 Christians came to the conference.[2] The question of the *Filioque* was at the heart of the discussions.

The Old Catholics and the Anglicans agreed that the addition had been made to the creed in an illicit and one-sided way and without any prior decision on the part of an ecumenical council. The following conclusions regarding doctrinal questions were reached by those taking part:

1. We agree totally that we should accept ecumenical creeds and decisions made by the early, undivided Church in matters of faith.
2. We agree totally that we should recognize that the addition of the *Filioque* was not made in a way that was in conformity with the rules of the Church.
3. We are in agreement with all the aspects of the representation of the teaching about the Holy Spirit suggested by the Father of the undivided Church.
4. We reject every representation or mode of expression containing any acceptance of the idea of two principles, *archai* or *aitiai* in the Trinity.

We accept the teaching of John Damascene about the Holy Spirit as summarized in the following paragraphs, in the sense of the teaching of the early, undivided Church:

1. The Holy Spirit comes from the Father (*ek tou Patros*), as from the principle (*archē*), the cause (*aitia*) and the source (*pēgē*) of divinity (*De rect. sent.* 1; *Contra Man.* 4).

192

2. The Holy Spirit does not come from the Son (*ek tou Huiou*), because there is only one principle (*archē*) and one cause (*aitia*) in the divinity through which everything that is in that divinity is produced (see *De fide orthod*.: 'ek tou Huiou de to Pneuma ou legomen, Pneuma di' Huiou onomazomen').

3. The Holy Spirit comes from the Father through the Son (*De fide orthod*. I, 12: 'to de Pneuma to Hagion ekphantorikē tou kruphiou tēs theotētos dunamis tou Patros, ek Patros men di' Huiou ekporeumenē'; *ibid*.: 'Huiou de Pneuma, ouch hōs ex autou, all' hōs di' autou ek tou Patros ekporeuomenon'; *Contra Man*. 5: 'dia tou logou autou ex autou to Pneuma autou ekporeuomenon'; *De hymno Trisag*. 28: 'Pneuma to Hagion ek tou Patros dia tou Huiou kai logou proïon'; *Hom. in Sabb. S.* 4: 'tout' hēmin esti to latreuomenon . . . Pneuma Hagion tou Theou kai Patros, hōs ex autou ekporeuomenon, hoper kai tou Huiou legetai, hōs di' autou phaneroumenon kai tē ktisei metadidomenon, all' ouk ex autou echon tēn huparxin').

4. The Holy Spirit is the image of the Son, who is himself the image of the Father (*De fide orthod*. I, 13: 'eikōn tou Patros ho Huios, kai tou Huiou to Pneuma'), proceeding from the Father and dwelling in the Son as his radiating power (*De fide orthod*. I, 7: 'tou Patros proerchomenēn kai en tō logō anapauomenēn kai autou ousan ekphantikēn dunamin'; *ibid*., I, 12: 'Patēr . . . dia logou proboleus ekphantorikou Pneumatos').

5. The Holy Spirit is the personal procession coming from the Father, who is of the Son, but not coming from the Son, because he is the Spirit from the mouth of the divinity, expressing the word (*De hymno Trisag*. 28: 'to Pneuma enhupostaton ekporeuma kai problēma ek Patros men, Huiou de, kai mē ex Huiou, hōs Pneuma stomatos Theou, logou exaggeltikon').

6. The Holy Spirit is the medium between the Father and the Son and he is connected to the Father through the Son (*De fide orthod*. I, 13: 'meson tou agennētou kai gennētou kai di' Huiou tō Patri sunaptomenon').

This pneumatological teaching is clearly Catholic, but it is only one expression of the mystery of the Spirit; there are others, not only in the West, but also in the East. It can, however, be regarded as a suggested synthesis of the common Greek tradition.

At Florence, the Greeks' *per Filium* was reduced to the *Filioque*. The Old Catholics who attended the Bonn conference did the opposite. The Russian Holy Synod, however, appointed a commission to continue the work and strengthen relationship with the Old Catholic Church in 1892. Two historians were given the task of preparing a report. Each did it in his own way. We shall examine B. Bolotov's work below. The other historian, A. L. Katansky, presented the *a Patre solo* as *the* teaching of the Orthodox Church. The Old Catholics also appointed a commission. Its members unfortunately decided to call the Son the 'secondary cause' of the procession of the Holy Spirit,[3] something that neither Thomas Aquinas nor the theologians at the Council of Florence would ever have allowed themselves to say. B. Bolotov died at the age of forty-six in 1900, after having caused a great controversy in Russia' with his theses.[4] Even nowadays, they were accepted categorically by such theologians as Sergey Bulgakov and Paul

Evdokimov,[5] but vehemently rejected by Vladimir Lossky, who has said that it is not the historian's duty 'to judge dogmatic values as such'.[6]

Bolotov distinguished three levels of doctrinal statements—the level of dogma formulated in the creeds and at ecumenical councils, that of individual theologies, and, between these two levels, that of the theologoumena, expressions of faith formulated by one or more Fathers at the time when the Church was undivided and accepted by that undivided Church. Bolotov published a systematic and well-documented study, which concluded with twenty-seven theses. I give below the most important elements of these theses:[7]

(1) The Russian Orthodox Church regards as a dogma that has to be believed only the following truth: the Holy Spirit proceeds from the Father and is consubstantial with the Father and the Son. The other aspects, insofar as they do not have the same meaning, should be regarded as theologoumena.

(2) The fact that the idea that the Holy Spirit proceeds, comes or shines from (*ekporeuetai, proeisi, eklampei*) the Father through the Son is frequently found in patristic texts, its occurrence in the treatise on *Orthodox Faith* by John Damascene, above all its introduction into the synodicon of Tarasius of Constantinople, the orthodoxy of which has been confirmed not only by the East, but also by the orthodox West in the person of the Roman pontiff Hadrian, and even by the Seventh Ecumenical Council, give to this idea of procession such importance that theologians cannot simply regard it as the private opinion of a Father of the Church, but are bound to accord it the value of an ecumenical theologoumenon, so to speak, with authority everywhere in the orthodox East.

(3) The opinion that the expression *dia tou Huiou* implies nothing but a temporal mission of the Holy Spirit in the world leads to violent distortions (*Verdrehungen*) of some patristic texts.

(4) At least we cannot find fault with this interpretation, according to which the expressions frequently found in the teaching of the Fathers of the Church of the Holy Spirit's coming through the Son and his shining or manifestation from the Father through the Son contain an indication of a mysterious aspect in the activity, the life and the eternal relationships of the Holy Spirit with the Father and the Son, an aspect that is also known as the Holy Spirit's dwelling and remaining in the Son (*meson, anapauomenon*).

(5) This aspect is the imaginative expression of the identity of nature (*sumphues*) between the Spirit and the other two Persons and of that incomprehensible truth, revealed in the gospel, that the Holy Spirit is the third and the Son is the second Person of the Holy Trinity.

(6) This doctrine is not identical in meaning with that which is revealed in the words *ek tou Patros ekporeuetai*, if these words are interpreted in the strict sense of the technical terms *ekporeutos* and *ekporeuetai*.

(7) As a result of this, the Holy Spirit proceeds from the Father alone, in the strict sense of the word *ekporeutos*. This thesis, however, is not a dogma, but only a theologoumenon.
. . .
(11) The formula *ex Patre et Filio*, as found in the writings of St Augustine, is not

identical in its terminology, nor even in its meaning, with the teaching of the Eastern Fathers.

. . .

(13) The difference in opinion between Western and Eastern Christians is not so much in the words *ex Patre Filioque* as in the Augustinian idea that is connected with it, namely of a single spiration by the Father and the Son, according to which both form the single principle of the Holy Spirit. This idea is unknown to the Eastern Fathers; as we know, none of them ever said that the Son was *spirans* or *sumproboleus*.

(14) Even as a private opinion, we cannot recognize the Western *Filioque* as equivalent in authority to the Eastern *di' Huiou*.

. . .

(19) Within God's unfathomable plan, however, no protest was made by the Eastern Church at the time of St Augustine against the view suggested by him.

(20) Many Western Christians who preached the *Filioque* to their flocks lived and died in communion with the Eastern Church, and no objection was raised on either side.

(21) The Eastern Church honours the Fathers of the early Western Church as it honours its own Fathers. It is therefore quite natural that the West should regard the individual opinions of those Fathers as holy.

. . .

(25) Photius and those who followed him remained in communion with the Western Church without obtaining from that Church an explicit and conciliar denial of the *Filioque*, even, as far as we know, without asking for it.

(26) It was therefore not the question of the *Filioque* which caused the division in the Church.

(27) The *Filioque*, as an individual theological opinion, ought therefore not to constitute an *impedimentum dirimens* for the re-establishment of communion between the Eastern Orthodox and the Old Catholic Churches.

The interchange between Orthodox and Old Catholics in the matter of the Holy Spirit has continued until the present time. During the discussions in September 1966 in Belgrade, the representatives of the Orthodox Church observed that the promise made in 1931 and 1932 to withdraw the *Filioque* clause from the creed had been kept only in part. The Old Catholics had only done so subject to the reservation that the true elements of the doctrine expressed by the clause might always be retained as a free, private opinion, and this did not satisfy the Orthodox. The latter, or at least the Greeks among them, asked for a simple and total denial of the Latin construction of the mystery which, they claimed, could not claim to be regarded as equivalent to the 'through the Son' of the Eastern Fathers.[8]

In their proposal to refer to an earlier state of affairs in which there had not yet been any opposition between the teachings of the Churches, the Old Catholics seem, however, to be weakening their links with the Western tradition that has begotten them and sustains them.[9] Is it possible to go back to a situation preceding the events of history? Do we not have to accept the inheritance of our fathers? The International Conference of Old Catholic

Bishops, which comprises the pastors of the Churches belonging to the Union of Utrecht, made the suppression of the *Filioque* in the creed official for all those Churches in 1969, claiming that the addition of this clause had not been made in a canonical manner, that it had an inadequate theological foundation, and that it had contributed to the disunity of the Churches. At the conference held in August 1975 at Chambésy, the Old Catholics simply adopted the Orthodox position.[10]

B. ORTHODOX AND ANGLICANS

For a long time, the Anglicans have wanted as much as the Old Catholics to enter into relationships and, if possible, into communion with the Orthodox Churches. They have a deep sympathy for the religious spirit of the East and this sympathy goes back far into the past. The *Filioque*, however, forms part of the Catholic inheritance that has been preserved in the Church of England and appears in several official doctrinal texts.[11]

The pneumatological question has been discussed in the course of several approaches made by members of the Church of England to the Orthodox Church. Between 1716 and 1725, for example, the Nonjurors attempted to establish relationships and intercommunion with the Patriarchate of Constantinople.[12] The first article raised for discussion was apparently that of the *Filioque*.[13] After this, there were only personal exchanges for a long time.[14]

Together with the Old Catholics, the Anglicans took part in the Bonn Conference of 1875 and the Conference in Belgrade in 1966. I have already discussed these above. Between the two conferences, F. V. Puller visited and had conversations with Mgr Evlogy in Russia in May 1912. Puller kept to Tarasius' profession of faith (see above, pp. 53 and 57), namely that *Filioque* and *dia tou Huiou* were equivalent, which his Russian Orthodox hosts accepted.[15] Mgr Evlogy told Brilliantov, who was questioning Puller, that he authorized him to say that, despite the different formulae, the teaching was the same. These words were printed in the official bulletin of the Holy Synod.

It is interesting in this context to look at the different positions adopted at the two Lambeth Conferences in 1920 and 1930.[16] Reference was made back to the Bonn Conference of 1875. The Anglicans were still prepared to suppress the *Filioque*, but they insisted that this term, in which their Church had for centuries confessed its faith, was quite open to a true meaning. They encountered resistance on the part of the Orthodox on this point.[17]

Progress is inevitably slow and difficult in a question in which the Churches preserve their faith in the formulae of creeds and their liturgical celebration. In their recent conferences with Eastern Christians, the Anglicans have once again committed themselves to suppress the *Filioque* in the creed, irrespective of the merits or demerits of its doctrinal content.[18]

NOTES

1. For one member of the Orthodox hierarchy at least—Mgr Anthony, the Archbishop of Finland, has been quoted—it was a question of 'obtaining a foothold in the middle of the Romano-Germanic world' and of thus 'giving a terrible blow to the heart of Roman Catholicism': see the Old Catholic *Revue internationale de Théologie*, 5 (1897), 111.
2. For the history of this question, see A. Palmieri, 'Filioque', *DTC*, V, cols 2331–2342. For the text of the Bonn Conference, see H. Reusch, *Bericht über die vom 10. bis 16. August 1875 zu Bonn gehaltenen Unionskonferenz* (Bonn, 1875). For the conference itself, see E. B. Pusey, *On the Clause 'And the Son' in regard to the Eastern Church and the Bonn Conference* (Oxford, 1876); E. Michaud, 'L'état de la question du "Filioque" après la Conférence de Bonn de 1875', *Revue internationale de Théologie*, 3 (1895), 89–99.
3. The text will be found in *Revue internationale de Théologie*, 5 (1897), 1 and 2.
4. A. Palmieri, 'Filioque', *op. cit.* (note 2); see also M. Jugie, *Theologia dogmatica Christian. Orient. ab Eccl. cath. diss.*, II (Paris, 1933), pp. 467–478.
5. S. Bulgakov, *Le Paraclet* (Paris, 1946), pp. 99ff., 116, 137; P. Evdokimov, *L'Esprit Saint dans la tradition orthodoxe* (Paris, 1969), pp. 74–75.
6. See V. Lossky, *In the Image and Likeness of God* (Eng. tr.; London and Oxford, 1975), p. 72. This comment is reminiscent of the remark attributed to Cardinal Manning at the First Vatican Council, although it is more moderate.
7. The German text of Bolotov's report will be found in *Revue internationale de Théologie*, 6 (1898), 681–712; Fr. tr. in *Istina*, 17 (1972), 261–289. I give here the same extract that Fr Malvy gave, under the pseudonym of 'Valmy', in his 'Bulletin de Théologie russe', *Etudes*, 101 (1904), 856–879, especially 866–867. See also M. Jugie, *op. cit.* (note 4), p. 460.
8. See the preparatory report by S. Karmiris of Athens in *Istina*, 13 (1968), 404–424, and the Declaration of the Inter-Orthodox Theological Commission, *ibid.*, 425–432, especially 428.
9. This is at least what I have found in an article by U. Küry, 'Die Bedeutung des Filioque-Streites für den Gottesbegriff der abendländischen und der morgenländischen Kirche', *Internationale Kirchliche Zeitschrift*, 33 (1943), 1–19.
10. See *Irénikon*, 47 (1975), 514–515.
11. In the Niceno-Constantinopolitan Creed, the *Quicumque* Creed, the litany, the Ordinal and the fifth of the Thirty-Nine Articles. The Church of England, however, leaves its ministers a great deal of freedom in their interpretation of the doctrines contained in these and other texts.
12. The documentation has been edited by L. Petit in Mansi, 37 (Paris, 1905), cols 369–624.
13. The Nonjurors were prepared to suppress the *Filioque* in the creed. On the doctrinal question, they noted that *dia* and *per* were not equivalent; they justified the procession *a Filio* by using the same texts, both biblical and patristic, that the Scholastic theologians had employed, although they did not make use of Scholastic arguments and syllogisms. In suggesting a basis for union (Mansi 37, cols 387–388) they simply adopted the Orthodox position.
14. The most interesting episode among these personal contacts is provided by William Palmer of Magdalen College, Oxford; for the whole of Palmer's mission, see S. Tyszkiewicz, 'Un épisode du Mouvement d'Oxford, La mission de William Palmer', *Etudes*, 136 (1913), 43–61, 190–210, 329–347. In a letter of exposition to Khomiakov, he expressed astonishment that all that the Orthodox Christians wanted the Catholics to do was to take the word *Filioque* out of the creed, while leaving them free to retain their teaching: see Birkbeck, *op. cit.*, below, p. 49. Khomiakov justified this practice, saying that it was not heretical and had never been condemned as contrary to Scripture by any council, but that it was simply an opinion that the Eastern Church regarded as wrong. The mistake that the Latins had made was to have added a purely human opinion to the truth of the creed: see W. J. Birkbeck, *Russia and the English Church. Containing a Correspondence between M. W. Palmer and*

M. Khomiakoff in the Years 1844–1854 (London, 1895; 2nd ed., 1917), pp. 60ff. It is interesting to note the open attitude of the Russian Orthodox: see, for example, in other contexts, Mgr Sergey, Mgr Evlogy to F. V. Puller, and Mgr Basile Krivocheine. Professor N. O. Lossky, the father of Vladimir Lossky, though that the opposition between the Catholics and the Orthodox in the question of the *Filioque* could be overcome by a further evolution of dogma: see his Russian-language *Questions of Russian Religious Consciousness* (Berlin, 1924), pp. 325ff.; quoted by Clément Lialine, *De la méthode irénique* (Amay, 1938), p. 24 and note. Sergey Bulgakov thought that the difference expressed in the two traditions between the *Filioque* and the *dia tou Huiou* was 'neither a heresy nor a dogmatic error, but a difference between theological opinions'; there was, in his view, 'no dogma concerning the relationship between the Holy Spirit and the Son' and he even went so far as to accept the *Filioque* for the West at least: see *op. cit.* (note 5), pp. 140–141. Finally, see also V. Soloviev's questions in the appendix to this chapter.

15. See *DTC*, V, col. 2336; M. Jugie, *op. cit.* (note 4), II, pp. 479ff.
16. For the 1920 Lambeth Conference, from the Anglican side, see *Terms of Intercommunion suggested between the Church of England and the Churches in Communion with Her and the Eastern Orthodox Church* (London, 1921), especially sections VII and VIII; these details will also be found in G. K. A. Bell, *op. cit.*, below, pp. 80–81. For the Orthodox side, see the report made by their delegation to the Conference in G. K. A. Bell, *Documents on Christian Unity*, I (London, 1924), pp. 64–65. For the 1930 Lambeth Conference, see the *Report of the Joint Commission* (London, 1932), pp. 14, 32–33.
17. See the *Report of the Joint Commission*, *op. cit.*, p. 14.
18. See *Irénikon*, 48 (1975), 362, for the work of the mixed sub-committees, July 1975; *Irénikon*, 49 (1976), 507–508, for the session held at the highest level at Zagorsk in July and August 1976; see also K. Ware and C. Davey, eds, *Anglican-Orthodox Dialogue. The Moscow Agreed Statement* (London, 1977), pp. 87ff.

APPENDIX

Below I give the first four questions of the nine asked by Vladimir Soloviev (†1900): see M. d'Herbigny, *Un Newman russe. Vladimir Soloviev* (Paris, 1911), p. 196:

Do the canons of ecumenical councils that stipulate that the faith of Nicaea should be preserved intact have the meaning or the letter of the Niceno-Constantinopolitan creed in mind?

Does the word *Filioque* added to the early text of the Niceno-Constantinopolitan creed inevitably contain a heresy? If it does, which ecumenical council condemned this heresy?

If this addition, which appeared in the creed of the Western Churches in the sixth century, and which was known in the East in the middle of the seventh century, contains a heresy, how is it that the last two ecumenical councils, the sixth in 680 and the seventh in 787, did not condemn this heresy and did not anathematize those who had accepted it, but, on the contrary, continued in communion with them?

If it is impossible to affirm with certainty that this addition (*Filioque*) is a heresy, is every orthodox Christian not free to follow, in this question, the opinion of Maximus the Confessor, who, in his letter to the priest Marinus, justified this addition and gave it an orthodox meaning?

4

SOME SUGGESTIONS FOR AGREEMENT

All those who have studied the question in the Eastern and the Western traditions have agreed that there is a difference in content in the terms *ekporeuesthai (ekporeusis)* and *procedere (processio)*. The fact that this difference was not observed early enough is at the origin of two parallel but not wholly corresponding movements in the two traditions. *Ekporeuesthai* pointed to the origin and could only be applied to the Father. On the Latin side, the same meaning was approached if Augustine's *principaliter* was added to the *procedere*. This is really contained in the *Filioque tanquam ab uno principio*, since the single principle is that of the Father and it is only in the Son as received from the Father. But *that* is precisely what is not *expressed*. Hence the criticism of the Orthodox Christians that has been repeated until the present time, despite the responses made to that criticism, that the West has sought to affirm two principles of the Holy Spirit. The formula *per Filium* would, in this respect, be more satisfactory. How would it be if Thomas Aquinas' formula in the *Summa*—'duo spirantes, *unus Spirator*—were accepted? More than one Latin Catholic theologian has noted the inherent weakness in the Latin formula and has from time to time, tried to remedy it.[1] How can the different state of the *duo spirantes* be expressed in the one 'spiration'?

Paul Henry, who has specialized in the theology of the Trinity, has made the suggestion that the *Filioque* should be abandoned and replaced by a different formula which might better express the reality, for instance *ex unione Patris et Filii procedit*.[2] This formula, however, expresses neither the *principaliter* nor the monarchy of the Father.

Juan-Miguel Garrigues has suggested a way of agreement which merits the greatest attention.[3] He has shown that the West has, since Tertullian, had a theology of the three consubstantial Persons in terms of procession, or a theology of an order of procession from the Father, in consubstantiality. The problem to which the Cappadocian Fathers had to find a solution against the teaching of Eunomius, that of a theology of subordinate participation, smacking of a hierarchical emanation characteristic of Platonism, was unknown in the West. The Cappadocians were led to make an antinomical distinction in God between the divine essence and the hypostases. This meant that there was a possibility of speaking in a differentiated manner of the procession of the third hypostasis and his participation in the common divine substance. According to Cyril of Alexandria, Gregory of Cyprus, Gregory Palamas and others, the Spirit has his hypostatic existence from the Father alone, but his substantial existence (*huparchein*) from the Father and the Son according to his mode of existence as the third Person in the divine consubstantiality. Garrigues says: 'In their hypostatic name, which cannot be communicated, the Son and the Spirit are only in a relationship with the Father, who is, so to speak, the origin of their own personal originality. To the extent that the hypostasis is manifested in a mode of existence (*tropos tēs huparxeōs*), according to which it enhypostatizes the essence (the Latins and the Alexandrians say: according to which it proceeds in the essence), the divine Persons manifest an order according to which they are for one another the conditions of the consubstantial communion.' Finally, he suggests this formula as one which might satisfy both the Eastern and the Western Churches: 'I believe in the Holy Spirit, the Lord and giver of life, who, issued from the Father (*ek tou Patros ekporeumenon*), proceeds from the Father and the Son (*ex Patre Filioque procedit; ek tou Patros kai tou Huiou proïon*)'.

In the course of my study, I have been struck by the fact that, if I am not mistaken, the Greeks think of the hypostatic being as an absolute and autonomous value, after which they see the consubstantiality acquired through the dependence of origin on the monarchy of the Father and expressing itself in the triadic relationships of circumincession. Does this amount to speaking, in a differentiated manner, of the Father as the only source of the hypostasis of the Spirit and the Son as the condition of his full consubstantiality? Several of the Fathers would seem to support this view. Hilary of Poitiers, for example, wrote during his exile in the East:

> 'Everything that the Father has is mine; that is why I told you: "the Spirit will take what is mine and declare it to you" ' (Jn 16:15). Therefore he who is sent by the Son and proceeds from the Father, receives from the Son. And I wonder whether receiving from the Son and proceeding from the Father are the same. If we believe that there is a difference between receiving from the Son and proceeding from the Father, it is nonetheless certain that receiving from the Son and receiving from the Father are the same.[4]

According to Hilary, then, the Spirit proceeds from the Father and receives from the Son. And what the Father gives to the Son is 'everything', that is, the divine substance or essence. The Spirit therefore completes and manifests the unity of the consubstantial Trinity. Maximus the Confessor, for example, said:

> Just as the Holy Spirit exists by his nature according to the essence of God the Father, so too does he exist by his nature according to the essence of the Son insofar as he proceeds essentially from the Father through the begotten Son.[5]

> They (the Latins of Rome) have shown that they have not made the Son the cause

200

of the Spirit. They know, in fact, that the Father is the only cause of the Son and the Spirit, of the first by begetting and of the second by *ekporeusis* (original procession). They have, however, pointed to the procession through him (*to dia autou proïenai*) and have shown in this way the unity and identity of the divine essence.[6]

Both Gregory of Cyprus[7] and Gregory Palamas[8] outlined the terms by which, if this interpretation is correct, the Spirit receives his hypostatic being by *ekporeusis* from the Father and has his consubstantial being from both the Father and the Son.

Is this expression of the mystery acceptable as a suggestion for possible agreement between East and West? It would hardly seem to be acceptable to the Latins. Is there a difference between receiving hypostatic being and receiving consubstantiality? Would it not be more useful to develop the theme of the monarchy of the Father on the basis, for the Latins at least, of Augustine's *principaliter* as accepted and explained by Thomas Aquinas?[9] This idea could perhaps be taken to the point where, with a different terminology, the equivalence with the *dia tou Huiou* might be such that the formula of the Florentine union could be reversed and Monopatrism could be recognized as true at the same time as and to the same extent as Filioquism. This is what André de Halleux suggested.[10]

The ideal solution would be a vocabulary that of itself expressed the fact that, in the *tanquam ab uno principio*, the Father is the original source and the Son is associated or a participant. In the absence of such a vocabulary, however, it is desirable that the Latin formulation should be completed by the Greek. The Greeks express this by the difference between the verbs *ekporeusthai* and *proïenai*. The Latin only has the verb *procedere* to cover the meanings of both Greek verbs. The aspect of the Son that is recognized in the procession of the Spirit is his eternal being. There are many statements of this by the Greek Fathers, tinged, it must be stressed, with an apophatism that refuses to be drawn into more precise definitions, but this is sufficient.

What we have to aim at and what can, in fact, be reached is a recognition both of the unity of faith on both sides of Catholicity and of the legitimate difference between the two dogmatic expressions of this mystery. Each expression is consistent in itself, and each is impossible in the categories and vocabulary of the other side. In the course of ten centuries of discussion, neither side has succeeded in convincing the other or in persuading it to accept its point of view. There is no chance that this goal will be reached in the future. In fact, we may say quite unambiguously that this is not a goal to be pursued.

Both Eastern and Western Christians are baptized in a common faith. For both, 'the Spirit is confessed as the third Person-hypostasis of the one divine nature-essence and consubstantial with the Father and the Son'.[11] Both confess the Father as the Principle without principle or beginning of the whole divinity. Both profess the Son as not unrelated to the Father in the production of the Holy Spirit.

201

The expressions of this faith, however, are different, especially in the matter of the third of these points. There are two main causes for this:

(1) The Latin vocabulary cannot adequately convey the important shades of meaning contained in the Greek terminology. *Causa* is not exactly *aitia*; *principium* is wider in its use than *archē*; *procedere* does not render *ekporeuesthai* very well. This was not always sufficiently taken into account in the past. Each side was so certain of itself and had so little curiosity about the other's views that it only wanted to reduce those to its own ideas and formulae. More than half a century ago, V. Grumel wrote: 'What was above all required, but no one thought of doing it, was for each side frankly and loyally to explain the terms that it used and for this to be followed by mutual tolerance, leaving each Church free to retain its traditional way of expressing dogma, leaving intact the unity of faith in a diversity of languages and formulae'.[12]

(2) A different principle is used by each to establish the distinction between the Persons. For the Greeks, the difference is found in the modes of procession from the Father, that is, by begetting or generation and by *ekporeusis*. This affirms the distinction between the hypostases. Criticism by the Latins has never seriously disturbed the Eastern Christians, who have always steadfastly refused to regard the application of our rules of logic to the mystery of God as legitimate. In the West, however, we have always been conscious of the principle that, in God, everything is common, apart from what is distinguished by an opposition in relationship. I have already pointed out that this principle is not a defined article of faith. It does, however, express a very acute sense of consubstantiality within the Trinity.

In the debate about the ways in which each tradition is expressed, we must, if we are to deal satisfactorily with the difficulties and respond positively to each other's demands, find out why a given Father or teacher of the Church—who was often a saint inspired by the Spirit—approached a given question in a certain way and why he formulated in precisely that way a datum of a faith that is basically shared by both sides. We then have to recognize that we have in this way achieved an inadequate expression of the mystery, which has not been equally illuminated in all its aspects. We are therefore open to criticism from another teacher in the Church, but our work may in this way be completed.

I would conclude this section with a statement by Mgr Damaskinos of Tranoupolis, who is the Director of the Orthodox Centre at Chambésy. His words may seem fanciful, but they echo my own thoughts: 'It is both possible and necessary to explain, on the one hand, the formulations of the Greek Fathers and, on the other, those of the Latin Fathers, including the *Filioque*, and, while respecting the originality of each, to draw attention to the ways in which they are in agreement. From the fourth century onwards, the *Filioque* came to form part of the Western tradition, but it was never regarded as an obstacle to union until that union was ended for other reasons.'[13]

NOTES

1. One of these theologians was V. de Buck, who was appointed by the Jesuit General to be theologian at the First Vatican Council: see his 'Essai de conciliation sur le dogme de la procession du Saint-Esprit', *Etudes religieuses*, 2 (1857), 305–351, which is based on the agreement between the Orthodox confessions of faith and an assessment of the monarchy of the Father, 'unicum fontem Trinitatis'. M. Jugie, *De Processione Spiritus Sancti* (Rome, 1936), pp. 8–12, agreed that the power of spiration 'non esse eodem titulo eodemque modo in Filio sicut in Patre' and that 'formula Graecorum [per Filium] praeponenda videtur'. See also A. de Halleux, 'Pour un accord œcuménique sur la procession du Saint-Esprit et l'addition du Filioque au Symbole', *Irénikon*, 51 (1978), 451–469.
2. P. Henry, 'Contre le "Filioque" ', *Irénikon*, 47 (1975), 170–177.
3. J.-M. Garrigues, 'Procession et ekporèse du Saint-Esprit. Discernement de la tradition et réception œcuménique', *Istina*, 17 (1972), 345–366, and his earlier essay, 'Le sens de la procession du Saint-Esprit dans la tradition latine du premier millénaire', *Contacts*, 3 (1971), 283–309.
4. Hilary, *De Trin.* VIII, 20 (*PL* 10, 251A).
5. Maximus, *Q. ad Thal.* LXIII (*PG* 90, 972C–D).
6. See Maximus' letter to Marinus (*PG* 91, 136). See also B. Bolotov's seventh thesis, 4: 'the thesis of the *ek monou tou Patros ekporeuetai* should not be used to deny, for example, the thesis *ek monou tou Patros ekporeuetai, di' Huiou de proeisin*'.
7. Cited by O. Clément, 'Grégoire de Chypre, "De l'ekporèse du Saint-Esprit" ', *Istina*, 17 (1972), 442–456.
8. Cited, in J.-M. Garrigues, 'Procession et ekporèse', *op. cit.* (note 3), 365.
9. Thomas Aquinas, *In I Sent.* d. 12, q. 1, a. 2. There is also an excellent passage in T. de Régnon, *Etudes de théologie positive sur la Sainte Trinité*, IV (Paris, 1898), p. 103.
10. A. de Halleux, 'Orthodoxie et Catholicisme . . .', *RTL*, 6 (1975), 3–30, and *op. cit.* (note 1), which ends with these words: 'The Roman Catholic Church will be able to restore the creed (to its original state) and recognize the fundamental truth of Monopatrism as soon as the Orthodox Church also recognizes the authenticity of the *Filioque*, interpreted in the sense of the traditional *di' Huiou*'.
11. A. de Halleux, *op. cit.* (note 1), 458.
12. V. Grumel, 'S. Thomas et la doctrine des Grecs sur la procession du Saint-Esprit', *Echos d'Orient*, 25 (1926), 257–280, explained these questions of terminology very lucidly; my quotation is taken from page 279 of this article.
13. Mgr Damaskinos, 'Réflexions et perspectives au sujet du rétablissement de la communion sacramentelle', *Oriente Cristiano*, 15 (1975), 7–25; quoted in *Irénikon*, 48 (1975), 219.

5

SHOULD THE *FILIOQUE*
BE SUPPRESSED IN THE CREED?

As I have, with the passage of time, come to learn more about this question, my attitude has changed, I admit. It is a question that has been asked for a long time. The Latins' answer to it was easy, perhaps too easy. They were, it would seem, not sufficiently aware of the full gravity of the question. Anselm, Thomas and Bonaventure all declared that when Ephesus forbade any change to be made in the faith that had been formulated at Nicaea,[1] that meant a change that would make belief different or contrary. Every council, however, always defines more precisely a point of faith that is challenged at the time—Chalcedon, for example, justified the addition made to Nicaea by the Fathers of the First Council of Constantinople. If the clause *a Patre et Filio* was true, after all, why should it not be declared? It was when this point of doctrine was denied that the *Filioque* was added to the creed by a certain council in the West, with the authority of a Roman pontiff, as one who convokes and confirms councils.[2] These answers to the question were not without value, even if the last point was based on a principle that was contested by the Greeks.

From the very beginning of the Council of Union at Ferrara, the Greeks declared that they were prepared to accept union, but only on condition that the Latins were equally prepared to suppress the *Filioque* in the creed. Unity of faith would in fact be restored in this way.[3] This shows the great importance of this question. The Orthodox have continued to insist on the same question until the present time, although it is being asked nowadays in a very different climate of opinion and with a very different set of implications from 1438. At Ferrara and Florence, at that time, in the spirit of the chief protagonist of the Greek conditions, Mark Eugenikos of Ephesus, to have agreed to suppress the *Filioque* would, for the Latins, have been to admit a doctrinal error.[4] Nowadays, on the other hand, the suppression of the *Filioque* is discussed in an atmosphere which recognizes that two different expressions of a common faith may be compatible and equivalent to each other.

At Florence, as in the mediaeval treatises,[5] the Latins declared that the *Filioque* made no change in faith, but simply explicitated it more clearly. The prohibition at Ephesus against the introduction of a different faith, *hetera pistis*, implied a prohibition of a contrary faith, not of a more perfect

204

formulation. The Greek reply to this was that when a doctrinal point was made more precise by a council, that council formulated its own definition—it did not introduce it into the creed. Ephesus, for example, did not add *theotokos*, 'Mother of God' to 'born of the Virgin Mary' in the creed.

The Greeks, however, had a view of the creed rather different from that of the Latins. In the Eastern Church, converts were expected to profess their faith in the unchangeable form of the creed, which the Church also proclaimed doxologically in the liturgy. The Latins had a more intellectual and a more external view of the creed as a formula of faith or belief promulgated by a council or the Pope, the decisive point here being the authority promulgating it. If we go back to the prohibition formulated by the Council of Ephesus, for example, we can see how this came about in the history of the council itself. It wanted to avoid accepting as the official profession of faith of the Church one or other of the many creeds that existed at the time, Since this would have opened the door to accepting doubtful or even heretical formulations.[6] Both the Council of Ephesus and the later councils of the Church up to the Second Council of Nicaea thought of *hetera pistis* as a teaching that was contrary to that of Nicaea. From the historical point of view, then, the Latins were right.

The situation is quite different when viewed from the point of view of the Church. The one-sided introduction of the *Filioque*, without consulting the Eastern Church, into a creed of ecumenical value was not only a way of behaving that was canonically illicit, but also an action which devalued the unity of the Christian family. Khomiakov called it 'moral fratricide'. There was also a certain touch of contempt for the Eastern Christians in the Carolingian period. It is true, of course, that the Eastern Christians held the Council in 381 without calling a single Latin bishop, an action which caused Ambrose to complain about the *communio soluta et dissociata*.[7] The West recognized its own faith in the text of Constantinople and 'received' the Council as 'ecumenical', but there are many examples of refusal to accept a decision because of a failure to participate in it. The Monophysites, for example, used the Nicene prohibition against making any new definition of faith as an argument against Chalcedon.[8] I think, however, that the Latins, including Anselm and Thomas Aquinas, have all too lightly shrugged off the Greek criticism that they were neither called nor consulted.

Ecumenism consists to a very great extent of repairing the damage that has been done in the past. If this task is to be done properly, a knowledge of the history of the period is incomparably useful.

As we have already seen, the Old Catholics and the Anglicans have decided to suppress the *Filioque* in the creed.[9] The Theological Commission of the World Council of Churches, 'Faith and Order', organized two meetings on 25–29 October 1978 and on 24–27 May 1979, at Klingenthal in Alsace, with the task of discussing precisely the question with which we are concerned here. There were Roman Catholics among the participants.

There was a unanimous vote in favour of the following resolution, which is clearly not a decision of the Church, but has its own importance: 'The original form of the article of the Niceno-Constantinopolitan creed on the Holy Spirit . . . (the text of this article follows) . . . should be recognized by all as the normative form of the creed and be re-introduced into the liturgy'.[10] Many Catholic theologians have also pronounced in favour of this suppression.[11] The formula is already not obligatory for Eastern-rite Catholics.[12] On 31 May 1973, the Greek Catholic hierarchy decided to suppress the formula in the Greek text of the creed.[13] As far as I personally am concerned. I would say categorically that I am in favour of suppression. To suppress the *Filioque* would be a gesture of humility and brotherhood on the part of the Roman Catholic Church which might have wide-reaching ecumenical implications. I can, however, only see this happening under two conditions, both of which are necessary if the suppression is to have a sound basis:

(1) Together with recognized and authoritative representatives of the Orthodox Churches, the non-heretical character of the *Filioque*, properly understood, should be made clear and recognized, as should the equivalence and complementarity of the two dogmatic expressions, 'from the Father as the absolute Source and from the Son' and 'from the Father through the Son'. This was the path followed at Florence. It is still a valid course, though, if it were retraced today, it would take place in a different climate, one in which the Eastern tradition and its depth would be fully respected. The Orthodox should not, for their part, go beyond the implications in the 'from the Father alone' of the monarchy of the Father and the demands made by the New Testament texts.

(2) The Christian people on both sides should be prepared for this so that it may be done in the light, in patience, with respect for each other's legitimate sensibilities, and in love. We should 'love one another so that we are able to profess with a single heart our faith in the Father, the Son and the Holy Spirit, the one consubstantial and indivisible Trinity'.[14]

NOTES

1. This prohibition will be found in canon VII of Ephesus: see J. Alberigo *et al.*, *Conciliorum Œcumenicorum Decreta*, 3rd ed. (Bologna, 1973), p. 65. For the use of this text in polemics, see M. Jugie, 'Le décret du concile d'Ephèse sur les formules de foi et la polémique anticatholique en Orient', *Echos d'Orient*, 30 (1931), 257–270.
2. See Anselm, *De proc. spir. sanct.* 13 (ed. S. Schmitt, *Opera*, II, pp. 211–212); Bonaventure, *In I Sent.* d. 11, a. un., q. 1 (Quaracchi ed., I, pp. 211–213); Thomas Aquinas, *De Pot.* q. 10, a. 4; *ST* Ia. q. 36, a. 2, ad 2: 'Sed postea insurgente errore quorumdam, in quodam concilio in Occidentalibus partibus congregato expressum fuit auctoritate Romani Pontificis'. This vague comment by Thomas, who was usually so precise, is very surprising.

It comes from a *Contra Graecos* by a Dominican in Constantinople in 1252: see A. Dondaine, *Arch. Fratr. Praed.*, 21 (1951), 390ff. It was commonly believed that every council formulated a confession of faith: see my article 'St Thomas Aquinas and the Infallibility of Papal Magisterium', *The Thomist*, 38 (1974), 87, notes 15 and 16, for references.

3. H. J. Marx has written an exhaustive study: *Filioque und Verbot eines anderen Glaubens auf dem Florentinum. Zum Pluralismus in dogmatischen Formeln* (Steyl, 1977).

4. See J. Gill, *The Council of Florence* (Cambridge, 1959), pp. 261ff. For the dramatic events following the council, see pp. 349ff.

5. Bonaventure, *In I Sent.* prol., a. 2: 'est additio distrahens, et est additio complens . . . in qua additum est consonum' (Quaracchi ed., I, p. 23).

6. See H. J. Marx, *op. cit.*, pp. 203ff. The addition of the *Filioque* seems to be in no way scandalous in itself—with the reservation that it is a one-sided approach—if it is seen in the context of the whole history of the Church's creeds: see the preface by J. Gribomont to G. L. Dossetti, *Il Simbolo di Nicea e di Constantinopoli* (Rome, 1967).

7. Ambrose, *Ep.* 13, 6 (*PL* 16, 953): 'Cohaerere communionem nostram cum Orientalibus non videmus' (No. 5) and 'postulamus ut ubi una communio est, commune velit esse iudicium concordantemque consensum' (No. 8)—these are golden rules!

8. See *Or. Chr. Period.*, 18 (1952), 55.

9. This was the last promise made by the Anglicans to the mixed Commission that met at Pendeli in July 1978: *Episkepis*, 195 (15 September 1978), 13. It was approved by the Lambeth Conference in 1978: see the *Report of the Lambeth Conference, 1978*, pp. 51ff.

10. *SOEPI* (Geneva, June 1979).

11. See H. J. Marx, *op. cit.* (note 3); A. de Halleux, *Irénikon*, 51 (1978), 469, which contains his report to the Klingenthal Commission.

12. This decision was made by Benedict XIV in his bull *Etsi pastoralis* (26 May 1742).

13. This decision can be explained and justified by a knowledge of the fact that the terms *ekporeuesthai* and *procedere* are not identical and by the agreement between the two formulae as confirmed by the declaration made by Maximus the Confessor, and by the dialogue between Anselm of Havelberg and Nicetas of Nicomedia. The text of this pastoral instruction will be found in *Les Quatre Fleuves*, 9 (1979), 75–78, which deals with 'God as revealed in the Spirit'.

14. Invitation and introduction to the recitation of the creed in the liturgy of St John Chrysostom.

6
DID THE *FILIOQUE*
HAVE AN ECCLESIASTICAL
IMPACT?

Vladimir Lossky thought that the *Filioque* was the cause of all the conflicts between Orthodoxy and Roman Catholicism, conflicts amounting, in his view, to as many doctrinal errors in the West. The *Filioque* was especially linked to consequences in the sphere of ecclesiology. André de Halleux has provided a very precise survey of the whole, with references to Lossky's work (here given in brackets):[1]

> The Spirit is here reduced to the function of a link between the two other Persons and one-sidedly subordinated to the Son in his very existence, in contempt of the genuine perichoresis. He thereby loses, together with his hypostatic independence, the personal fullness of his economic activity [Lossky, pp. 243–244]. The latter is henceforth seen as a simple means of serving the economy of the Word, both at the level of the Church and at that of the person. The goal of the Christian way of life therefore becomes the *imitatio Christi*, no longer a deification by the Holy Spirit [Lossky, pp. 166, 192–193]. The people of God are subjected to the body of Christ, the charism is made subordinate to the institution, inner freedom to imposed authority, prophetism to juridicism, mysticism to scholasticism, the laity to the clergy, the universal priesthood to the ministerial hierarchy, and finally the college of bishops to the primacy of the Pope. Creative and renewing source as he is, the Spirit was nevertheless expropriated by the Catholic Church, which made that Spirit the supreme guardian of the dispensation set up by Christ in favour of his Vicar. The Orthodox Church, on the other hand, has preserved the mutual subordination and the fertile tension between the economy of the incarnation and that of Pentecost [Lossky, pp. 156–157, 164, 166–167, 184–185; Clément, pp. 201–204].

Olivier Clément, who was Lossky's friend and disciple, took up the same themes.[2] When I spoke with Lossky some years ago, I made him very happy and even confirmed his teaching by making him acquainted with this Thomistic text: 'Those who maintain that the Vicar of Christ, the Pontiff of the Roman Church, does not enjoy the primacy of the universal Church, are committing an error which is similar to that which consists of saying that the Holy Spirit does not proceed from the Son. In fact, Christ, the Son of God, consecrates *his* Church and places *his* mark on it by his character and his seal, that is, by the Holy Spirit. . . . In the same way, the Vicar of Christ, as a faithful servant, keeps the Church subjected to Christ by the exercise of his primacy and his administration (*providentia*).'³ It is not difficult to cite other more recent texts with the same import.⁴

It is possible to criticize the Western Church for a certain lack of pneumatology, as I have already done in this work and elsewhere.⁵ On the one hand, however, I hope that my second volume to some extent makes up for this lack, while, on the other, I think it accords with the New Testament to protect with the utmost fidelity the reference of pneumatology to Christology. This is a condition of soundness for any life in the Spirit, any Renewal in the Spirit. It is something that we Catholics have in common with our Protestant friends, not simply because they are also Western Christians, but rather because they, like us, also follow the evidence of the Bible. Karl Barth, for example, has said:

> In all its aspects, the message of the New Testament implies, in the most indisputable way, that the Holy Spirit (and with him everything that makes the Church and Christians what they are) proceeds from Christ and from nowhere else. . . .
>
> This brings us to the very root of the theme which, within the framework of the doctrine of the Holy Spirit, led the Church to accept the *Filioque* into the creed (see I. 1, Eng. tr., pp. 546–557). The Church's conviction that the Holy Spirit should be recognized as the Spirit of Jesus Christ was such that it was obliged to affirm this and define it by saying: the Holy Spirit not only exists for us, he also exists from all eternity; he forms part of the hidden being of the Trinitarian God who manifests himself to us through revelation; he is the Spirit of the Father and the Son. Because he is the eternal bond which unites the Father and the Son, the Holy Spirit also creates the bond between the Father and all whom the Son has called in this world to be his brothers. The reason why no one can come to the Father except through the Son has to be found in the eternal mystery of God's being, because the Spirit through whom the Father draws men to himself is from all eternity also the Spirit of the Son, and it is through him that we are able to share in the divine sonship of Christ. If Western Christianity was right to recognize that the Holy Spirit to which revelation bears witness is none other than the Spirit of Christ and if the Western Church has really proclaimed the eternal God in the way in which he is pleased to encounter us, we should unhesitatingly declare our solidarity with that Church in the struggle that it has conducted to have the *Filioque* accepted.
>
> It is therefore possible for us to understand how Western Christian thinking came to be dominated throughout the whole of the Middle Ages by that sacramental and ecclesiastical objectivism which was so stubbornly—and victoriously—defended by the Popes, notably against Franciscan Spiritualism and its proclamation of the 'third age', that of the Spirit.⁶

Barth develops a criticism of spiritualism of the Joachimist type which, while appealing to the Holy Spirit, was to terminate in a humanism of man, expressing merely himself and his feelings. I have already discussed and criticized this in Volume I, pp. 126–133. The Orthodox can, of course, show that their own pneumatology does not in any way encroach on their sacramental and ecclesiastical objectivism and they can provide justifications of the titles 'Spirit of Christ' and 'Spirit of the Son'. Their theology is in this respect consistent and balanced. They are no more proof than we are against various forms of 'spiritual' teaching insufficiently closely linked to the Person of Christ, the Word and Son.[7] I would agree that a theological construction of the Triadic mystery in which the procession of the Spirit is linked to the Person of the Word, the Son, favours a tendency of thought which relates personal inspiration more closely to defined forms, but I am convinced that the whole body of consequences to which Lossky drew attention is too much his own reconstruction to be really precise.

The *Filioque* is contained in several of the Reformers' Confessions of Faith.[8] It is clear that the Reformers were able to keep the *Filioque* without subjecting 'the charism . . . to the institution, inner freedom to imposed authority, prophetism to juridicism, mysticism to scholasticism, the laity to the clergy, the universal priesthood to the ministerial hierarchy', as Lossky has maintained.

Once again, we can, in this context, go back to André de Halleux for quotations which I have known for a long time: 'It is valuable to recall, for the sake of those who are very impressed by the anti-Filioquist conclusions of Lossky and his school, the words of an Orthodox theologian who was particularly allergic to juridicism and the Roman Catholic insistence on infallibility, Sergey Bulgakov, who said, in *Le Paraclet* (Paris, 1946), p. 124: "For many years, as far as we have been able, we have looked for traces of this influence (of the dogmatic difference in the life and the teaching of the two Churches) and we have tried to understand what was at stake, what this difference really meant and how and where it was manifested in practice. I have to admit that I have not succeeded in discovering this. In fact, I would go so far as to deny it" '.[9]

This, of course, is precisely why Bulgakov disputed the claim that the *Filioque* constituted a real dogmatic difference between East and West. On p. 141 of his book, we read, for example: 'The two sides . . . cannot in practice prove that there is a difference between them in their veneration of the Holy Spirit, despite their disagreement about the procession. It is very strange that a dogmatic difference that is apparently so important should have had no practical repercussions, especially when, in most cases, a dogma has such an influence on practice that it determines the religious life of the community. In the present case, however, even the most extreme presentations of schismatic thought have so far not been able to apply this pseudo-dogma to the life of the Churches or to point to any practical consequences. It is possible to say that no important heresy concerning the Holy Spirit has ever been known in the life of either the Eastern or the Western Church, yet such heresy would have been inevitable if there had been a dogmatic heresy.' Paul Evdokimov has also commented in similar terms.[10]

It is just as possible to deny that the *Filioque* expresses a subordination of the Spirit to the Son or a conditioning of the Spirit by the Word as it is to accept it and be glad of it. At the same time, it is also possible to ask whether the decision to reject it would not lead to consequences which might be regarded either positively or critically, according to the Church community and tradition to which one belonged.[11] In the final analysis, then, the quarrel about the ecclesiological consequences of the *Filioque* is of doubtful value.

NOTES

1. A. de Halleux, 'Orthodoxie et Catholicisme: du personnalisme en pneumatologie', *RTL*, 6 (1975), 13–14. 'Lossky' in this quotation refers to V. Lossky, *The Mystical Theology of the Eastern Church* (Eng. tr.; London, 1957)—pp. 174–175 could be added to de Halleux's references; 'Clément' refers to O. Clément, 'Vladimir Lossky, un theologien de la personne et du Saint-Esprit', *Messager de l'exarchat du patriarche russe en Europe occidentale*, 8 (1959), 137–206.

2. O. Clément, *L'Eglise orthodoxe* (Paris, 1961), p. 50: 'Filioquism, according to which the "fontal" privilege which is peculiar to the Person of the Father alone is also shared by the Son, thus placing the Spirit, in his hypostatic existence, in a position of dependence on the Son, has certainly contributed to an increase in the authoritarian and institutional aspect of the Roman Church. The Trinitarian theology of the Orthodox Church, on the other hand, teaches that procession and begetting condition each other. . . . That is why there is also a mutual conditioning in a reciprocity of service between sacrament and inspiration, the institution and the event, the economy of the Son and that of the Spirit.'

3. *Contra Err. Graec.* II, 32 (Leonine ed., p. 87); cf. II, prol., where Thomas traces heresies back to betrayals in the sphere of Christology; see also Bonaventure, *De perf. evang.* q. 4, a. 3, n. 12 (Quaracchi ed., V, p. 197).

4. See, for example, B. de Margerie, *La Trinité chrétienne dans l'histoire* (Paris, 1975), p. 242.

5. See Volume I, pp. 152–154 and 156–160; see also my 'Pneumatologie ou "Christomonisme" dans la tradition latine?', *Ecclesia a Spiritu Sancto edocta. Mélanges théologiques G. Philips* (*Bibl. ETL*, XXVII) (Gembloux, 1970), pp. 41–63.

6. K. Barth, *Kirchliche Dogmatik*, I/2, pp. 272–273; Eng. tr. [not followed here], *Church Dogmatics*, I. 2 (Edinburgh and New York, 1956), p. 250. See also other Protestant texts cited in my study above (note 5), p. 63, note 90. To these can be added O. Henning Nebè, *Deus Spiritus Sanctus. Untersuchungen zur Lehre vom Heiligen Geist* (Gütersloh, 1939), pp. 60ff. who regarded the *Filioque* as the doctrine that prevented the theology of the Holy Spirit from falling into a kind of immanentism.

7. It is possible to see a parallel to Joachimism in the great Hesychastic movement in the Eastern Church: see L. N. Clucas, 'Eschatological Theory in Byzantine Hesychasm, a Parallel to Joachim da Fiore', *Byzantinische Zeitschrift*, 70 (1977), 324–244.

8. The sixteenth-century Reformers preserved the *Filioque* not only by retaining the Niceno-Constantinopolitan creed in its Western form and the so-called Athanasian creed, but also in the credal documents composed at the time of the Reformation: see, for example, the Lutheran Schmalkaldic Articles of 1537, I and II, the Formula and Book of Concord (1577 and 1580), and the *Solida Declaratio* VIII, 73. See also G. Hoffmann, 'Der Streit um das Filioque in der Sicht lutherischer Theologie', *Luthertum* (1941), 56ff. In the case of the confessions of faith of the other Reformed Churches, it is interesting to note that Zwingli accepted the *Filioque*: see G. W. Locher, *Die Theologie Huldrych Zwinglis im Lichte seiner Christologie* (Zurich, 1952), II, p. 110. Calvin's Confession of Faith of La Rochelle (1559), the Genevan Catechism of 1542, no. 91, and the Scottish Confession

(1560), art. 12, have nothing of interest to contribute to our particular subject. The Belgic and the Second Helvetic Confessions, on the other hand, both express the procession *ab utroque*: see the *Confessio Belgica* (1561), art. IX, and the *Confessio Helvetica Posterior* (1566), art. III. It would obviously not be possible to compile a list here of Protestant theologians who have written about this subject.

9. A. de Halleux, *op. cit.* (note 1), 3–30, especially 15, note 30.
10. P. Evdokimov, *L'Esprit Saint dans la tradition orthodoxe* (Paris, 1969), p. 76.
11. Karl Barth, whose Christological emphasis was dominant, as I have noted, in his theology, suggested a clear defence of the *Filioque*: *Church Dogmatics*, I. 1 (Eng. tr.; Edinburgh and New York, 1936), pp. 546–557. Speaking of the Russian theologians and philosophers, he said: 'It is possible that their way of thinking, in which philosophy and theology, reason and revelation, tradition and direct illumination, Spirit and nature, pistis and gnosis tend to be confused, should be explained by other, more immediate causes. . . . It is, however, not possible to prevent ourselves from making a connection between the stubborn denial of the *Filioque* and the way in which that idea is expressed, the manifestations of which it is all too easy to interpret as a consequence or a sign of that denial' (tr. based on Fr. tr.; cf. *ibid.*, p. 551). These comments are suggestive, but it is possible to question them. On the one hand, the Russians, of all the Orthodox, are the most open to the *Filioque*. On the other hand, the points mentioned by Barth depend, in my opinion, on a theology of the natural and the supernatural, which is in turn linked to an anthropology based on the image of God.

7

NINE THESES IN CONCLUSION

(1) Trinitarian faith is the same in the East and the West. Baptism is the same. The Christian, as Basil the Great pointed out, believes as he was baptized and praises as he believes. The experience of all the saints and all believers is the same, with the special marks that form part of the gifts of God. The action of the Spirit is similar. The Fathers are shared by both groups of Christians.

(2) The Tri-unity of God is a mystery which goes beyond all created understanding and expression. As Hilary of Poitiers said (*De Trin.* XII, 55): 'I possess the Reality although I do not understand it'.

(3) The East has remained closely attached to the terms expressed in Jn 15:26 and 16:14ff. Its theological construction of the mystery is quite consistent, but it also has its limitations.

(4) Several of the Greek Fathers have claimed that the Word, the Son, has a share in the production of the Holy Spirit, which cannot be reduced to the economic order. That share has, however, not been defined more precisely or systematically.

(5) If the Palamite theology of 'energies' is accepted, that function is situated not in the procession, but in the energetic manifestation of the Spirit. In the first place, however, Gregory Palamas accepted that, 'proceeding' from the Father alone, the Spirit also receives his consubstantiality from the Son. In the second place, the energetic manifestation is uncreated; it is God.

(6) The *Filioque* is necessary in the Latin Church's approach to the mystery, so that firstly the hypostatic distinction of the Spirit with regard to the Son, and secondly the Son's consubstantiality with the Father will be safeguarded.

(7) Historically, the *Filioque* was introduced as a measure against Arianism, by Augustine and by the Hispano-Visigothic councils. It was retained and expressed in the West at a time when there was communion between East and West and councils were even held in common.

(8) The *Filioque* did not cause any difficulties. The first evidence that we have of this is contained in Maximus the Confessor's letter to the priest Marinus. Maximus explains and accepts the *Filioque* in this letter in the sense of *dia tou Huiou*, without prejudice to the monarchy of the Father.

(9) It is in that direction that we must go. The Council of Florence, to which intelligent recourse must be had, traced the *per Filium* back to the *Filioque*, in an attempt to avoid making the Son a mere passage through which the Father's power of spiration flowed. It is necessary to combine the truth invested in the two formulae by showing that they are complementary. Conditions are favourable to this at the present time. The ideal solution would be to call a new council to complete the creed, for example, by re-using the terms of Jn 15:16 and 16:14–15, but also by avoiding all ambiguity.

The Roman Catholic Church could, under the conditions that I have outlined, suppress the *Filioque* in the creed, into which it was introduced in a canonically irregular way. That would be an ecumenical action of humility and solidarity which, if it was welcomed in its really 'genuine' sense by the Orthodox Church, could create a new situation which would be favourable to the re-establishment of full communion.

PART TWO

THE HOLY SPIRIT AND THE SACRAMENTS

1

THE 'SEAL OF THE GIFT OF THE SPIRIT'
SOME THOUGHTS ABOUT THE
SACRAMENT
OF 'CONFIRMATION'

In this chapter, I do not intend to discuss the present rite of this sacrament, although I may allude to it, its historical development, which is sufficiently well known,[1] or, apart from a few incidental references, the question of the minister who celebrates it. I intend to reflect on the significance of this sacrament. This chapter of sacramental theology is intended as a chapter of pneumatology. In the Apostolic Constitution *Divinae consortes naturae*, published on 15 August 1971, establishing the renewed rite of confirmation in the Latin part of the Church,[2] we read, for example: 'The sacrament of confirmation is conferred by anointing with sacred chrism on the forehead, by the imposition of the hand and by these words: "Accipe signaculum doni Spiritus Sancti" '. In note 20 of this Constitution, there are several references in ancient Christian tradition, all of them Eastern, to this formula 'the seal of the gift of the Spirit'. Paul VI also wrote about it, saying: 'As far as the words that are pronounced at the time of anointing with chrism are concerned, we have certainly assessed the dignity of the venerable formula used in the Latin Church at its true value. We have, however, concluded that it was necessary to give preference to the early formula of the Byzantine rite, in which the gift of the Spirit himself is expressed and the pouring out of the Spirit on the day of Pentecost is recalled.' This noteworthy declaration by the Pope is very close to my own concerns.

(1) *Uneasiness about Confirmation*

Confirmation is one of the sacraments of Christian initiation and is situated between baptism and the Eucharist. The unity of this initiation with these three stages would even seem to be the object of an ecumenical agreement.[3] Whether they are directly connected with baptism or separated from it by an interval of time, the rites of confirmation make the sacrament itself a simple completion of baptism, its final stage rather than a new and different sacrament. The classical statement that there are seven sacraments[4] can certainly

217

be interpreted in this way.[5] Even those who keep to the distinction between the two sacraments—and the fact that they are administered separately would seem to make this distinction necessary—are anxious to stress the close connection between them. There is, however, also the difference between them, in that the second completes the first. That is why a believer who had only been baptized in an emergency had later to be taken to the bishop so that his initiation would be completed.[6]

The urgent question that arises in this context is: What does confirmation add to the grace of baptism? Christian baptism is, of course, baptism in the Spirit (Mk 1:8; Jn 1:33; 1 Cor 6:11; 12:13; Tit 3:5). It confers regeneration or rebirth and introduces the recipient into the life of Christ himself, that is, into his body (Rom 6:4ff.; 1 Cor 12:13; Gal 3:27). This is certainly stated in the Church's liturgies and the writings of the earliest Fathers.[7]

The Spirit, then, is given in baptism. Why is it therefore necessary to add another sacrament in order to give the Spirit? It is not possible to be confirmed without having been baptized, but it is possible to be baptized, that is, it is possible to receive the gift of the Spirit and of Christian life, without confirmation. What does confirmation bring? An increase in grace? This would not be specific enough. The seal placed on what the baptism has brought about? This is what many early texts and the Church's liturgy itself say. This Spirit has already been given, the grace of the gift is sealed liturgically. There is a single process, the different aspects of which are detailed in the liturgy by its ritual expression of them one after the other, including the baptism with water. It is only in this way that we can answer the difficult question asked by Protestants, namely: does confirmation not violate baptism and simply add a kind of useless repetition to the sacrament already administered?

And what is the situation when, in the Western Church, the two aspects have been separated and the second reserved for the bishop? It causes a certain uneasiness when it is said that children who are confirmed at the age of six, eight or twelve are given the Holy Spirit. Is it possible to measure the enormity of such a statement? It is all the more difficult to make such a claim when, in the vast majority of cases, nothing new seems to take place. It is, of course, said—quite correctly—that the supernatural reality takes place in secret and cannot be experienced immediately, and that in baptism too nothing seems to happen. Nonetheless, a certain dissatisfaction remains, and Christians who are already committed to the Christian way of life are troubled by the sacrament of confirmation. Doubts about the age at which this sacrament can most suitably be given, partly because it has become separated chronologically from baptism, likewise indicate the unstable state in which confirmation is situated.[8] The mere fact that these and other questions are still being asked again and again shows that the suggested replies have not proved satisfactory.

(2) *The meaning of Confirmation is derived from the Mystery of Christ*

This explanation is based on a relationship of analogies, but the fundamental structure which is indicated thereby is a combination of the Christological and the pneumatological aspects of the same mystery. There are two ways of approaching this structure and they are so alike that two authors, L. S. Thornton and J. Lécuyer, develop both of them in turn. The relationship can in fact be set out diagrammatically:

$$\frac{\text{Christ in his Pasch}}{\text{Pentecost}} = \frac{\text{baptism}}{\text{confirmation}}$$

Apart from Thornton and Lécuyer, this is also what P. Fransen and E. Schillebeeckx did.[9] The two sides of the equation are closely connected—Pentecost is the fiftieth day of the feast of Easter and is its fullness and completion. Baptism absorbs us into the death and resurrection of Jesus (Rom 6:3–11), and confirmation means life through the fruit of the Pasch, which is the sending of the Spirit by the Lord. This relationship of the two aspects of the same mystery has undoubtedly inspired the Church's liturgy. It can, for example, be found in the celebration of the Eucharist.

Thornton and, even more emphatically, Lécuyer have also referred to the two comings by which the Spirit firstly made Jesus exist as the Word of God and the son of Mary and secondly made him exist as the Christ, by anointing him at the time of his baptism with his messianic function in mind.[10] In the first case, the Spirit came to Mary to give existence to a son who was the Son of God. In the second case, he came to Jesus so that, when he was baptized and emerged from the water and prayed, he was consecrated for his mission (see Volume I, pp. 17–21). In the same way, baptism makes us be conceived and born as sons of God within the Church, and confirmation enables us to participate in Christ's messianic anointing. God created a body, then gave it breath.[11] 'Christ' means 'anointed'. In the writings of the Fathers and in the liturgy, we cannot be fulfilled as 'Christians' unless our spiritual anointing is expressed visibly and tangibly. Cyril of Jerusalem saw in the anointing of the Christian the antitype of Christ's own anointing.[12]

It has even been suggested—quite rightly—that, at confirmation, it should be stated that the candidate participates in those offices of Christ himself that were so frequently mentioned during the Second Vatican Council—the offices of king, priest and prophet.[13] The last-mentioned office is particularly important in the case of confirmation. In considering this, we are led to reflect about the connection between confirmation and the Church.

(3) *Confirmation in the building up and the mission of the Church*

In its description of the common priesthood of the people of God as expressed in the sacraments, the Second Vatican Council declared: 'Bound more intimately to the Church by the sacrament of confirmation, they (believers) are endowed by the Holy Spirit with special strength. Hence they are more strictly obliged to spread and defend the faith both by word and deed as true witnesses of Christ.'[14] *Perfectius Ecclesiae vinculantur*. This conciliar statement is concerned with individuals and is therefore not explicitly ecclesiological. No one would nowadays try to discover, by sound and critical exegesis, the sacrament of confirmation in the two episodes in the Acts of the Apostles, of the Samaritans who were evangelized and baptized by Philip and on whom Peter and John laid their hands (Acts 8:14–17), and of the Ephesian disciples of John whom Paul had baptized in the name of the Lord and on whom he also laid hands (19:1–6).[15] These texts nonetheless contain a meaningful analogy with the sacrament of confirmation, because what takes place in these episodes is a Christian initiation in two stages, marked by two closely linked rites. The very strong ecclesiological significance of the two episodes therefore rightly enables us to understand the ecclesiological meaning of confirmation itself. What takes place in the sacrament is that the baptized persons who are confirmed are fully fitted into the apostolic community of the Church. They are able to become full members of the Church when those who are called to bear the Church's apostolicity have publicly accepted them.

The fact that, in the West at least, confirmation has normally been administered by a bishop, as writers as early as Hippolytus and Cyprian[16] have attested, can be connected with this aspect of the sacrament. Christian initiation at this stage is so much a part of the Church that it has to be carried out and sealed by a leader of the Church, that is, by one who above all bears the Church's apostolicity, representing its unity and catholicity.[17]

This being vitally fitted into the Church can be understood by means of the Church's sacramental structure. M. D. Koster suggested this mode of understanding when he presented the Church as the corporation of Christians organized according to the sacramental characters of the baptized, the confirmed, deacons, priests and bishops,[18] each of these degrees corresponding to a ministry in the whole people of God. Confirmation pointed to the ministry of bearing witness and to participation in the prophetic nature of Christ, which consisted in particular in proclaiming and confessing faith in Christ, to the point, if necessary, of martyrdom.

There can be no doubt that the Holy Spirit is given especially in order to encourage the witness that should be borne to Jesus Christ in space and time.[19] In the Bible, the Holy Spirit is clearly connected with bearing witness—he provides the power, the dynamism and the continuity for this task.

The consecration and the grace of confirmation have also been characterized as a participation in the prophetic mission for which Christ himself was also consecrated.[20] In the heyday of Catholic Action, many members of the movement believed that the sacramental basis of their 'Action' was to be found in confirmation.[21] Others took a wider view and saw confirmation as a basis and a source for the apostolate of the laity.[22] The latter, however, derives from the fact of a Christian and the state of being a Christian. The Second Vatican Council observed that the lay apostolate results from all the elements that contribute to Christian existence: 'Incorporated into Christ's Mystical Body through baptism and strengthened by the power of the Holy Spirit through confirmation, they (the laity) are assigned to the apostolate by the Lord himself. They are consecrated into a royal priesthood and a holy people. . . . For the exercise of this apostolate, the Holy Spirit who sanctifies the people of God . . . gives to the faithful special gifts as well (cf. 1 Cor 12:7).'[23]

(4) *Confirmation in the growth of the baptized person*

The baptismal gift is a gift of fullness because, through faith and the anointing of the Holy Spirit, it is a communion in the mystery of Christ with eschatological salvation in mind. It is what Irenaeus called, in a well-known text, the *communicatio Christi*. This fullness must be made present and developed, according to the good pleasure of the Lord indeed, as Irenaeus said, but also according to the degree of development of our conscious understanding and our entry into human society and the history of the world.

It is at this point that we can most suitably look at Thomas Aquinas' very remarkable theology of confirmation.[24] It is firmly situated within the Western practice of reserving the celebration of the sacrament for the bishop and separating it by an interval of time from the baptism conferred universally on infants, locating it *tempore juventutis vel pueritiae*.[25]

Thomas distributes the sacraments according to the stages in the life of man and the needs experienced at certain times. Baptism corresponds to birth, and confirmation to the period at which the child is no longer content to live *quasi singulariter, sibi ipsi* or *secundum seipsum*, in a way in which he is only conscious of himself and refers everything to himself, but *incipit communicare actiones suas ad alios*, in other words, when he begins to communicate with others, to feel part of a society in which others also exist and each person has the task of contributing to the life of that society, in history and, of course, in the Church.

Thomas connected the new aspect of this stage in human life with Pentecost and especially with the life of the apostles that was initiated at that time. It was then that they received the Holy Spirit as the grace of the apostolate—for the mission in which they were to bear witness and to evangelize.[26] It is not difficult to apply these ideas to contemporary data, but if we follow Thomas' own brief note, it also becomes obvious that his thinking goes very far. What he says is: 'sicut episcopus confirmat puerum contra pusillanimitatem'.[27] 'Small-mindedness' has a precise meaning in Thomas' teaching.[28] It can be defined as the fault, possibly even the sin, of acting at a level below one's full potential and not letting one's gifts bear fruit. It is contrasted with 'great-mindedness' (*magnanimitas*), which is the virtue by which man realizes himself by committing himself.[29]

This Thomistic teaching about the place of confirmation in the growth of the baptized Christian is certainly very interesting and can be borne out and developed by modern psychology. There is an age when the child moves from an egocentric stage to a social stage, or at least a pre-social stage. At this point, he goes beyond the limited, protected environment in which he has hitherto lived *quasi singulariter, sibi ipsi* and is able to recognize the other person as different. This also coincides with a growth in personal consciousness and discernment. In Western Europe, this stage would seem to be reached when the child is seven or eight years old.[30]

These data obviously have to be transferred into the framework of ages of faith and of a Christian life open to the influence and impulses of the Holy Spirit. In that case, confirmation can be seen as the sacrament marking responsible entry into the communal and missionary life of the Church, following the *Praxeis tōn Apostolōn* reported by Luke. In this context, it is also possible to quote the Epistle to the Hebrews, according to which, we can, with 'our bodies washed with pure water', 'hold fast to the confession of our hope without wavering' and 'consider how to stir up one another to love and good works' (Heb 10:23–24).

(5) The two Sacraments of Baptism and Confirmation and the two missions of Christ and the Spirit

For a long time now,[31] I have thought that both the pair of sacraments, baptism and confirmation, and the twofold aspect of story and epiclesis in the celebration of the Eucharist are an expression, at the level of liturgical symbolism, of the double mission of the incarnate Word and the Spirit, with the aim of achieving the same task of saving communion with the mystery of God or deification. The work in question is the realization of the Body of Christ, his body as communion or Church and his sacramental body, after his physical or natural body. This was the work both of the Word, who assumed an individual human nature, and of the Holy Spirit, who sanctified the fruit that he had brought about in the womb of the Virgin Mary. Since then, we have had two closely combined aspects.

Jesus entered the water, identifying himself with those who repent, and, while he was praying, the Spirit came down on him. In the same way, Christians are plunged into the water as into his death (Rom 6:3) and the Spirit is given. This is a baptism of water and the Spirit, introducing the believer into the body which is the Body of Christ (1 Cor 12:12–13; see also Volume II, pp. 189–195). In the one single process of initiation, which is consummated in the sacrament of the body and blood of the Lord, a symbolic aspect, which completes the act of baptism and seals the gift received in it, the sacrament of the 'seal of the gift of the Spirit', has been distinguished from the baptism strictly so called. I believe that this is the liturgical expression of the two missions of the Word, the Son, and of the Holy Spirit, who are closely associated in the task of accomplishing the same work.

(6) *Suggestions for sacramental practice*

There has been a good deal of controversy about the sacrament of confirmation, as is clear from the discussions about the age at which it should be administered (see above, and note 8 below). It is obvious that two views, each with its own logic and truth, are in conflict with each other and would, moreover, seem to be irreconcilable.

The first is a theoretical or theological view. According to this view, there are three sacraments of initiation, and confirmation is simply the seal of baptism. It is so closely connected with baptism, in fact, that it is given with it, and in the early texts, it is sometimes very difficult to distinguish confirmation from the rite of baptism. In the East and in Spain, for example, practice conforms with this principle, and confirmation is administered to infants. It cannot be denied that the problem with regard to the baptism of infants is a very real one. The theological justifications that have been suggested are perfectly valid, but they do not solve the problems that have arisen in connection with the demands of evangelical truth as regards the present situation and what the facts demonstrate.[32]

The second view is pastoral, combining a concern for the truth of gestures and a knowledge of the possibility of personal commitment according to the age of the baptized person. This view has led to a search for a different way of administering the sacrament. This consideration is justified and indeed is almost a necessary consequence of the Western practice of separating confirmation from baptism and administering it at the age of reason, that is, at about seven years old,[33] and very often after first communion (see R. Levet, note 8 below). It is also frequently linked to completing a stage in religious education (the 'catechism'), itself often linked to requiring sufficient discernment and knowledge. In the present age, increasingly conscious of the individual and of personal responsibility, this view (which formed part of Erasmus' suggestions for reform) is inescapable. Not only in the practice of confirmation, but also in the view that we have of its function, it emerges clearly as a personal ratification of the baptismal commitment that we accepted in the faith of our parents and the Church, although we did not play an active part at the time.

If it is a question of honouring that, it is not enough simply to celebrate confirmation at the age of seven or eight or 'during the first years of school (and therefore before the child has received the Eucharist)'.[34] Should it be later still? The synod of German bishops in 1976, for example, suggested the age of twelve, while the Catechetical Congress at Munich in 1928 suggested fifteen, and A. Exeler, about eighteen.[35] If the logic of this option is to be fully respected, I would say confirmation should undoubtedly take place after puberty, when the young person's ways of feeling and perceiving reality are so fundamentally changed, the way is opened to an autonomous understanding of himself, and he is on the inevitable threshold of adult life.

In my opinion, both the first and the second views outlined above contain truths that should be respected. Their perspectives are so diverse that they do not contradict each other. Each deals with a different aspect. I have often expressed my own attitude towards this question. It is that both truths should be given a place and the special attributes of each respected.

Confirmation is linked to baptism as its seal. If infants are baptized, the sacramental seal of the gift of the Spirit should also be conferred to them. The problems involved in doing this are no greater than those raised by infant baptism. The essential problem, after all, is that of infant baptism itself. There are very good reasons for administering infant baptism when the child's environment is Christian. Baptism is, of course, the 'sacrament of faith' and it calls for religious education, but catechesis can be given afterwards. I can, however, understand why parents delay the baptism of their children. They do so not for the wrong reason of letting the children choose for themselves when they are older, but because they feel that baptism requires knowledge and personal consciousness on the part of the child. They prefer therefore to present the child to the Church, enrol him as a catechumen and let him come to know and pray to Jesus and the God of Jesus Christ.

There should also be a personal act of commitment to the service of Jesus Christ, in the Church, in the presence of witnesses, made at the beginning of adolescence or on the threshold of adult life. For this to take place properly, there must be a ceremony and a choice of texts. The best arrangement would be for it to take place within the framework of the Eucharist, celebrated within the community. An environment of prayer is absolutely necessary. It calls for careful preparation, either in a course lasting for three weekends or in a retreat lasting for several days and should include exchanges with other, already committed Christians, who are able to manifest what commitment to the service of one's fellow-men in the Church means today. All this could take place in religious centres of various kinds. In this way, a beginning would be made in the training of committed, adult Christians. There would perhaps only be a few of them—those who really believed—but something would be happening.

I would very much like to see the members of the Renewal take part in such days of preparation and in the ceremony of confirmation. They would bring to it their vital conviction that 'Jesus lives' together with a warmth and a feeling of joy. It would be a feast of the Holy Spirit. With or without 'baptism in the Spirit', it would be the making real, to an adult personal consciousness, of the grace received unawares in the sacraments of baptism and confirmation.

NOTES

1. D. L. Greenstock, 'El Problema de la Confirmación', *La Ciencia Tomista*, 80 (1953), 175–228, 539–590; 81 (1954), 201–240; J. Lécuyer, 'La confirmation chez les Pères', *M-D*, 54 (1958), 23–52; E. Llopart, 'Las formulas de la confirmación en el Pontifical romè', *Liturgica*, 2 (Montserrat, 1958), 121–180; P. M. Gy, 'Histoire liturgique du sacrement de confirmation', *M-D*, 58 (1959), 135–145; B. Neunheuser, *Baptism and Confirmation* (Eng. tr.; Freiburg and London, 1964); L. Ligier, *La confirmation. Sens et conjoncture œcuménique hier et aujourd'hui* (*Théol. hist.*, 23) (Paris, 1973); K. F. Lynch, *The Sacrament of Confirmation in the Early-Middle Scholastic Period*, I (London, 1957).

2. *AAS* 63 (1971), 657–664.

3. I am thinking here of the report made by the 'Faith and Order' Commission of the World Council of Churches on baptism, confirmation and the Eucharist: 'Baptême, Confirmation et Eucharistie', *Istina*, 16 (1971), 337–351.

4. This is affirmed by both the Orthodox and the Roman Catholic Churches. See, for example, the profession of faith made by Michael Palaeologus (6 June 1274) (*DS* 860); the Decree *Pro Armenis* (22 November 1439) (*DS* 1310); the Council of Trent, Session VII (3 March 1547), canons 1 and 3 (*DS* 1601 and 1603); the profession of faith of Pius IV (1564) (*DS* 1864); the profession of faith given to the Eastern-rite Catholics by Benedict XIV (16 March 1743) (*DS* 2536). The weakness of these statements is that they contain nothing concerning the analogical, non-uniform and inadequately equal character of the sacraments.

5. See, for example, K. Rahner, *The Church and the Sacraments* (Eng. tr.; Freiburg, Edinburgh and London, 1963), who has pointed out that baptism and confirmation can be seen as two degrees of the one sacrament, just as the diaconate, the presbyterate and the episcopate are degrees in holy orders. See also S. Amougou-Atangana, *Ein Sakrament des Geistempfangs? Zum Verhältnis von Taufe und Firmung* (Freiburg, 1974), p. 279; Hans Küng, 'La confirmation comme parachèvement du baptême', *L'Expérience de l'Esprit. Mélanges Schillebeeckx* (*Le point théologique*, 18) (Paris, 1976), pp. 115–150.

6. The Council of Elvira (in 306), canons 38 and 77 (Mansi, 2, 12B and 18C; *DS* 120): by the laying-on of hands; the Council of Laodicea, canon 48 (Mansi, 2, 571): by anointing with chrism.

7. See J. B. Humberg, 'Confirmatione baptismus perficitur', *ETL*, 1 (1924), 505–517; G. W. H. Lampe, *The Seal of the Spirit* (London, 1951); B. Neunheuser, *op. cit.* (note 1); *idem*, 'Taufe im Geist. Der heilige Geist in den Riten der Taufliturgie', *Archiv für Liturgiewissenschaft*, 12 (1970), 268–284; P. T. Camelot, 'Sur la théologie de la confirmation', *RSPT*, 38 (1954), 637–657, especially 643ff.; *idem*, *Spiritualité du baptême* (*Lex orandi*, 30) (Paris, 1960), pp. 237–256.

8. See R. Levet, 'L'âge de la confirmation dans la législation des diocèses de France depuis le concile de Trente', *M-D*, 54 (1958/2), 118–142, based on an analysis of more than 600 documents; G. Biemer, 'Controversy on the Age of Confirmation as a Typical Example of Conflict between the Criteria of Theology and the Demands of Pastoral Practice', *Concilium*, 112 (1978), 115–125.

9. L. S. Thornton, *Confirmation. Its Place in the Baptismal Mystery* (Westminster, 1954); P. Fransen, 'De gave van de Geest', *Bijdragen*, 21 (1960), 403–424; E. Schillebeeckx, *Christ the Sacrament of Encounter with God* (Eng. tr.; London and New York, 1963), pp. 197–210. See also W. Breuning, 'When to Confirm in the Case of Adult Baptism', *Concilium*, 2, no. 3 (1967), 48–54; *idem*, *op. cit.* below (note 15).

10. J. Lécuyer, 'Le sacerdoce royal des chrétiens selon S. Hilaire de Poitiers', *L'année théologique*, 10 (1949), 302–325; 'Essai sur le sacerdoce des fidèles chez les pères', *M-D*, 27 (1951), 7–50, especially 40ff.; 'La grâce de la consécration épiscopale', *RSPT*, 36 (1952), 380–417, especially 390–391; 'Mystère de la Pentecôte et apostolicité de la mission de l'Eglise', *Etudes sur le sacrement de l'ordre* (*Lex orandi*, 22) (Paris, 1957),

pp. 167–208; *Le sacerdoce dans le mystère du Christ* (*Lex orandi*, 24) (Paris, 1957), in which Lécuyer relates the incarnation and Easter to baptism in chapters VIII and IX and the Jordan and Pentecost to confirmation in chapters XI and XII; 'Théologie de l'initiation chrétienne chez les Pères', *M-D*, 58 (1959/2), 5–26.

11. Adam (Gen 2:7); the dry bones of Ezekiel (Ezek 37). See Cyprian, *Ep*. 754, 7, 5.

12. Cyril of Jerusalem, *Cat. myst*. III, 1 (*PG* 33, 1088ff.; *SC* 126 (1966), pp. 122 (Greek) and 123).

13. Adolf Adam, *Firmung und Seelsorge* (Düsseldorf, 1959), pp. 52–54; E. J. Lengeling, 'Die Salbung der christlichen Initiation un die dreifache Aufgabe des Christen', *Zeichen des Glaubens. Studien zu Taufe und Firmung. Balthasar Fischer zum 60. Geburtstag* (Freiburg, 1972), pp. 429–453. Lengeling himself summarizes the results of his study in the following words: 'The trilogy of the post-baptismal anointing of "confirmation" can be found in the West Syrian, Jacobite, Byzantine, Armenian, Coptic and Ethiopian liturgies and in the Western non-Roman liturgies (the *Missale Gallicanum* and Peter Chrysologus), but also in the Roman post-baptismal anointing which, both structurally and because of its content, can be compared with the anointings of the "confirmation" type found in other liturgies which are the forerunners of the typically Roman anointing on the forehead in the sacrament. Textual evidence of this trilogy includes the prayer of anointing with chrism, the preface to the consecration of the chrism, texts in the Roman Catechism and in the writings of recent authors and, since 1969, the present form of the anointing. It is therefore not exclusively the work of Vatican II, but there is evidence, in the rite of baptism itself, of a very early and universal tradition.' Among the 'recent authors' to whom Lengeling refers in the above passage on p. 452 of his article, I would count myself, especially in my book *Lay People in the Church* (Eng. tr.; London, 1957).

14. Dogmatic Constitution on the Church, *Lumen gentium*, 11, with a note containing references not only to Thomas Aquinas, but also to Cyril of Jerusalem and Nicholas Cabasilas.

15. Not only H. Conzelmann, *Die Apostelgeschichte* (Tübingen, 1963), pp. 54ff., but also many Catholic authors have insisted on the fact that the Spirit of the charisms is given. References will be found in E. J. Lengeling, *op. cit.* (note 13), p. 128, note 26, and W. Breuning, 'Apostolizität als sakramentale Struktur der Kirche. Heilsökonomische Überlegungen über das Sakrament der Firmung', *Volk Gottes, Festgabe J. Höfer* (Freiburg, 1967), pp. 132–163, especially p. 155, note 57 and, for our theme, pp. 152ff.

16. See Hippolytus, *Trad. apost*. 22, 23 (*SC* 11, pp. 50–53); Cyprian, *Ep*. 73, 9, 2 (*PL* 3, 1115; ed. W. von Hartel, p. 784). See also the Council of Elvira (note 6 above). In the East, the priest gives the sacrament, but uses *myron* consecrated by the bishop (or patriarch). Hence we read in the Dogmatic Constitution on the Church, *Lumen gentium*, 26, 3, that the bishops are the '*original* ministers of confirmation' (*ministri originarii confirmationis*). In the Latin Church, the sacred oils are also blessed by the bishop, and a simple priest administers confirmation only when the bishop commissions him to do so. It is always desirable for the sacrament to be celebrated by a minister who, because of his title, points to the diocesan authority.

17. This aspect was stressed by L. Bouyer, 'La signification de la confirmation', *VS* (Suppl), 29 (15 May 1954), 162–179, especially 175–177; also by J.-P. Bouhot, *La confirmation, sacrement de la communion ecclésiale* (Lyons, 1968).

18. M. D. Koster, *Ekklesiologie im Werden* (Paderborn, 1940); *idem, Die Firmung im Glaubenssinn der Kirche* (Regensburg and Münster, 1948). F. Vandenbroucke also showed, in 'Esprit Saint et structure ecclésiale selon la liturgie', *Questions liturgiques et paroissiales*, 39 (1958), 115–131, that the liturgy speaks of the Holy Spirit above all in connection with the three 'character' sacraments, that is, baptism, confirmation and holy orders.

19. This is clear in Acts: see G. Haya-Prats; and in John. See Volume I, pp. 44–47, 57–59; Volume II, pp. 24–35.

20. See A.-G. Martimort, 'La Confirmation', *Communion solennelle et Profession de foi* (*Lex orandi*, 14) (Paris, 1952), pp. 159–201.
21. V. M. Pollet, 'De Actione Catholica', *Angelicum* (1936), 453, note 1; E. Sauras, 'Fundámento sacramental de la Acción católica', *Revista española de Teología*, 3 (1943), 129–258; Damasus Winzen, 'Anointed with the Spirit', *Orate Fratres*, 20 (1945–1946), 337–343, 389–397, especially 394. Pius XI took note of the connection between Catholic Action and confirmation, but did not make it the sacrament of the movement: see his letter of 10 November 1933 to the Patriarch of Lisbon.
22. See D. Winzen, *op. cit.* (note 21); J. R. Gillis, 'The Case for Confirmation', *The Thomist*, 10 (1947), 159–184; Max Thurian, *La confirmation. Consécration des laïcs* (Neuchâtel and Paris, 1957). There are many more books and articles on this subject.
23. See the Decree on the Apostolate of the Laity, *Apostolicam actuositatem*, 3.
24. Thomas Aquinas, *ST* IIIa, q. 72 and par. For this theology, see J. R. Gillis, *op. cit.* (note 22), 159ff.; P. Ranwez, 'La confirmation, constitutive d'une personnalité au service du Corps mystique du Christ', *Lumen Vitae*, 9 (1954), 17–36; J. Latreille, 'L'adulte chrétien, ou l'effet du sacrement de confirmation chez S. Thomas d'Aquin', *RThom*, 57 (1957), 5–28; 58 (1958), 214–243; Adolf Adam, *Weltoffener Christ* (Düsseldorf, 1960; 2nd ed. 1962), pp. 146ff.; R. Bernier, 'Le sacrement de Confirmation dans la théologie de S. Thomas', *Lumière et Vie*, 51 (1961), 59–72.
25. This is Thomas' phrase: see *ST* IIIa, q. 72, a. 8, c and ad 2. For him, *In IV Sent.* d. 40, expos. textus, *pueritia* extended from seven to fourteen, and *juventus* from twenty-one to fifty! Etienne Gilson has pointed out that he apparently took this idea from Isidore of Seville.
26. *ST* IIIa, q. 72, a. 2, ad 1; *In IV Sent.* d. 7, q. 1, a. 2, sol. 2. The apostles already had 'Spiritum Sanctum in munere gratiae quo perficiebantur ad ea quae ad singulares personas eorum pertinebant, tamen in die Pentecostes acceperunt Spiritum Sanctum in munere gratiae quo perficiebantur ad promulgationem fidei in salutem aliorum'.
27. *Comm. in Ep. ad Eph.* Prol., where Thomas is dealing with children between the ages of seven and fourteen.
28. *ST* IIa IIae, q. 133.
29. *ST* IIa IIae, q. 129ff.; see also R.-A. Gauthier, *Magnanimité. L'idéal de la grandeur dans la philosophie païenne et dans la théologie chrétienne* (*Bibl. thom.*, 28) (Paris, 1954). See also my book, *op. cit.* (note 13), pp. 391ff. The whole of chapter VI of Part Two of that book is a development of what I am merely suggesting here.
30. I am not competent to judge in this case and I lack information. I have therefore consulted Jean Piaget and, in the *Encyclopaedia Universalis*, VI, p. 223, the article 'Enfance'; also P. H. Maucorps and R. Bassoux, *Empathies et connaissance d'autrui* (Paris, 1960); R.-F. Nielsen, *Le développement de la sociabilité chez l'enfant* (Neuchâtel and Paris, 1961); F. Tilmann, 'Um den rechten Zeitpunkt der Firmungspendung', *Diakonia*, 1 (1966), 285–291.
31. I have thought this for a long time, at least since 1949: see *RSPT*, 452.
32. It is useful in this context to read P.-A. Liégé, 'Le baptême des enfants dans le débat pastoral et théologique', *M-D*, 107 (1971), 7–28, and to re-read Pascal, 'Comparaison de chrétiens des premiers temps avec ceux d'aujourd'hui', small Brunschvicg edition, pp. 201–208.
33. See also the *Cordex iuris canonici*, canon 788.
34. See Hans Küng, *op. cit.* (note 5), p. 146.
35. References will be found in G. Biemer, *op. cit.* (note 8), 117–118.

2
THE EUCHARISTIC EPICLESIS

Relatively late in the history of Christianity, a controversy developed concerning the consecration or conversion of the bread and wine into the body and blood of Christ. Although the controversy was apparently about the moment of consecration, it was in reality concerned with the agent of that consecration: the priest as the representative of Christ in the sacramental action in which Christ's words were re-used, or the Holy Spirit as invoked in the epiclesis? This is, however, the wrong way of postulating the problem, since it gives the wrong emphasis to this controversial question.

This controversy dates from the first half of the fourteenth century, the first witness to it being that great and greatly loved master, Nicholas Cabasilas.[1] The Latins had criticized the fact that the Greeks had added prayers for the consecration of the sacred elements after the words of institution, which brought about the consecration. Whenever the question was approached in this way, that is, whenever the question was about the precise moment of the eucharistic transformation, to the exclusion of every other consideration, conflict was inevitable.[2] What the Latins did in the case of the words of institution, the Greeks did in the case of the epiclesis, and the same climate of controversy persisted. It was perpetuated at Florence, with Mark Eugenikos. We must get away from this area of controversy. It is not too difficult to do so.

A list of all the books and articles that have been written on this question of the epiclesis would fill several pages and would include studies of the whole problem, monographs and discussions of various aspects.[3] I shall not provide a history of the question here, since it is not difficult to find that elsewhere. It is, however, necessary to go into details in some respects and to quote a number of texts if we are to understand what is at stake and to appreciate the depth of the issues involved. Paul Evdokimov, for example, wrote: 'It would seem that, in the ecumenical dialogue, the question of the epiclesis is as important at present as that of the *Filioque*, since it is above all in the light of the epiclesis that the *Filioque* can be correctly resituated within the whole problem'.[4]

The Epiclesis cannot be separated from the whole of the Eucharistic Prayer or Anaphora
The meaning of the Anaphora

'Epiclesis' (*epiklēsis*) means 'invocation'. The term has come to have the

228

limited and technical meaning of an invocation for the sending of the Holy Spirit after the account of the institution, but this is too particular a significance that has been attributed to it in the course of the discussions about this subject. Even in the work of those Fathers of the West Syrian tradition who witness to the most formal epicleses, this 'invocation' applies to the whole of the anaphora.[5] It is this anaphora that we have to consider here. Those excellent scholars, Le Quien and Combefis,[6] certainly insisted on this. In his study of the question, Louis Bouyer cited and explained the whole of the eucharistic prayers and in this way broke free of the discussions concentrated on particular elements treated in detail.

Although they are very diverse in their formulation, these eucharistic prayers are homogeneous in their spirit and have a very clear sense of the whole.[7] Their common aim is to realize the Christian mystery, that is, to extend to the Body of Christ, the Church, the salvation, deification and membership as sons that Christ himself has gained for us through his incarnation, his death, his resurrection and glorification through the Spirit, and finally the gift of Pentecost. The Eucharist is the synthesis, communicated sacramentally and spiritually, of what God has done for us in and through Jesus Christ—as we sing in the office of the Feast of Corpus Christi, 'memoriam fecit mirabilium suorum'. This simple yet immense fact is expressed in the five aspects of the eucharistic prayer outlined below:

(1) An analogy, even a continuity, exists between the Eucharist and the incarnation. This is clearly revealed in Justin Martyr's description of the Eucharist[8] and in Irenaeus' repeated statements, against the Gnostics, about the coming of the Lord in the flesh, linking this to the Eucharist, the 'unity of the flesh and the spirit . . . in which the earthly and the heavenly realities are intermingled'.[9] Gregory of Nyssa makes use of this analogy to point to our communion with the immortality of God through the Eucharist.[10] The great teachers of the Eastern Church who supported the veneration of icons, such as Germanus I of Constantinople (†738), insofar as the treatise quoted below was written by him, and the Syrian Christians are particularly categorical. Germanus first draws attention to the anamnesis—Christ's incarnation, suffering and death, resurrection and glorious second coming—and then goes on to say, speaking of the incarnation:

'From the womb, before the dawn, I have begotten you' (Ps 110:3). Once again he (the priest) pleads (*parakalei*) that the mystery of the Son may be accomplished (*teleiōsai*) and that the bread and the wine may be begotten (*gennēthēnai*) and transformed into the body and blood of Christ and God and that the 'today I have begotten you' will be accomplished (Ps 2:7). In this way, the Holy Spirit, invisibly present by the pleasure of the Father and the will of the Son, demonstrates the divine energy and, by the hand of the priest, consecrates and converts the holy gifts that are presented into the body and blood of our Lord Jesus Christ, who said: 'For them I consecrate myself, that they may also be consecrated in truth' (Jn 17:19).

How does this happen? 'He who eats my flesh and drinks my blood abides in me, and I in him' (Jn 5:56).[11]

The Eucharist, then, is like a begetting every day of Christ, body and blood. Just as the incarnation came about through the action of the Holy Spirit, so too should the consecration and sanctification of the gifts sanctify believers and incorporate them into Christ. Theodore of Mopsuestia traces the eucharistic epiclesis back to the action of the Spirit in the resurrection of Christ.[12]

(2) As Louis Bouyer emphasized, the epiclesis is closely connected with the anamnesis. In the anaphora, thanks are given ('Eucharist') for the good things of creation and for the history of salvation. In the eucharistic prayer of John Chrysostom, the account of the institution is introduced as follows: 'When he had come and had accomplished the whole economy of salvation which was for us, the night when he handed himself over . . .'. This is followed by the account of the institution, which is in turn followed by the anamnesis: 'Mindful . . . of everything that has been accomplished for us—of the crucifixion, of his burial, of his resurrection on the third day—we offer these things that come from you'. Then, after a brief acclamation by the people, the epiclesis begins, with the words: 'We offer you this spiritual sacrifice'. It is thus inserted into the anamnesis.

The same applies to Hippolytus' *Apostolic Tradition*: 'Mindful of his death and resurrection, we offer you the bread and wine . . . and we ask you to send your Holy Spirit upon the offering of your holy Church'.[13] In the Roman canon, which was established in its essential aspects in the fourth century, we also find, after the account of the institution, 'Unde et memores (the anamnesis), offerimus . . .', a little later, 'Supplices te rogamus', which has frequently been regarded as the equivalent of an epiclesis. It is certainly true to say that the eucharistic prayer forms a single whole. What has to be accomplished in the believers through the action of the Holy Spirit comes from the sacrament-sacrifice, which is the commemoration of the actions and gifts of salvation, for which thanks are given.

(3) It is not possible, even though both may occur, to contrast an epiclesis for the consecration of the eucharistic gifts and an epiclesis asking for those present to be sanctified, that is, that the sacrifice-commemoration may have the fruits of grace. The two are in fact combined in certain formulae, such as the one contained in the *Apostolic Constitutions*. There are also several Greek patristic texts referring to an action of the Spirit with the aim of making the 'eucharisted' gifts something that sanctifies believers.[14] These epicleses follow the anamnesis immediately. What we have here is a movement that extends the mystery of Christ who has died and risen again to the believers—it envisages the people's communion as part of the consecration

of the gifts. That is also why several epicleses ask the Spirit to *sanctify* the bread and the wine, as in the liturgy of St James and that of St Mark.[15] Did Paul not already speak of it (see Rom 15:16; 1 Tim 4:5)? What the Eucharist has in mind is our deification through our union with the Spirit-filled flesh of Christ. For his part, Christ blessed, sanctified and filled with his Spirit the bread and the wine at the Last Supper.[16]

(4) It would be quite wrong to isolate the epiclesis which follows the anamnesis. There are in fact epicleses not only in the anaphora, before the account of the institution—as in Egypt[17]—but also before the epiclesis in the anaphora, even in the Roman rite. Avvakum believed that those of the prothesis consecrated the gifts. There is, for example, the dialogue between the priest and the deacon at the end of the 'great entrance' in the Byzantine liturgy. The liturgies of John Chrysostom and Basil the Great present it today in the following way:

> *Priest*: The Holy Spirit will come upon you and the power of the Most High will cover you with his shadow.
>
> *Deacon*: The Holy Spirit himself will concelebrate with us all the days of our life.[18]

(5) An epiclesis asking for the gifts to be consecrated, even after the account of the institution, was developed when the orthodox teachers of faith insisted, in opposition to Macedonius and the Pneumatomachi, on the personality and the divinity of the Spirit. Gregory Dix thought that the epiclesis was not authentically due to Hippolytus. Whatever may be the case, it is certainly not an epiclesis of consecration. It was apparently added during the second half of the fourth century, in the text of Addai and Mari.[19] J. Quasten has likewise shown that, before the First Council of Constantinople in 381, the descent of Christ into the water of baptism was invoked, whereas, after the Council, it was the coming of the Spirit that was invoked.[20] Louis Bouyer was therefore able to say:

> It is easy then to understand that at a time when it was thought necessary to stress the equal divinity and personality of the Spirit in the second half of the fourth century, and probably, as we shall see, in Syria, there developed what at first was merely a subordinate clause making up the first epiclesis: an express invocation of the descent of the Spirit, today, upon the eucharistic celebration, parallel to the invocation of the Son in the incarnation in order that its effect might be fulfilled in us (*op. cit.* (note 3 below), p. 184).

This was done especially in Western Syria—Antioch and other centres—during the second half or the last third of the fourth century. It is at this time and place that the texts of the so-called 'consecratory' epicleses appear.

The Fourth-Century Epicleses
Consecration by them or by the words of institution?

The three essential texts are:

The *Mystagogic Catecheses* of Cyril of Jerusalem (written *c*. 350) or of his successor, John II (*c*. 390 in that case):

> Just as, before the sacred epiclesis of the adorable Trinity, the breed and wine of the Eucharist were ordinary bread and wine, but, after the epiclesis, the bread becomes the body of Christ and the wine the blood of Christ. . . .[21] After having been sanctified ourselves by these spiritual hymns (the Trisagion), we implore the God who loves men to send the Holy Spirit on to the gifts placed here, so as to make the bread the body of Christ and the wine the blood of Christ, since everything that the Holy Spirit touches is sanctified and transformed.[22]

The liturgy of Basil the Great:

> We sinners also . . . dare to approach your holy altar and, bringing forward the symbols (*prosthentes ta antitupa*; S. Salaville: 'the antitypes') of the holy body and blood of your Christ, we implore you and invoke you, Holy of Holies, through the benevolence of your goodness, to make your Holy Spirit come down on us and on these gifts that we present to you; may he bless and sanctify them and present to us (*anadeixai*) (in) this bread the precious body itself of our Lord, God and Saviour Jesus Christ and (in) this cup the precious blood itself of our Lord, God and Saviour Jesus Christ, poured out for the life of the world, *changing them by your Holy Spirit*.[23]

The last words of this text, that I have italicized, do not appear in Brightman's classical edition and, according to H. Engberding, whom Bouyer follows, they were added to Basil's text. The word *antitupos* gives rise to a problem of interpretation. John Damascene (†749), who was writing within the context of the polemics with the iconoclasts, understood it to refer to the bread and wine before they had been sanctified by the epiclesis. This interpretation gave the epiclesis the meaning of a prayer of consecration to the exclusion of the words of institution.[24] Cyril of Jerusalem used the word *antitupos* in his sacramental catechesis in order to express a relationship between the visible sacramental reality and the spiritual reality that is made present by the sacrament. For example, baptism, according to Cyril, represented the passion of Christ (*Cat. myst.* II, 6), the anointing with chrism pointed to the anointing of Christ by the Spirit (*Cat. myst.* III, 1), and the bread and wine consecrated and received in communion pointed to the body and blood of Christ (*Cat. myst.* V, 20). In the seventeenth century, Bossuet translated this as 'the figures of the sacred Body and the sacred Blood'. The word *anadeixai* is also problematical. Bouyer translated it as '(may he) present to us', but S. Salaville said 'may he make of this bread', claiming that it was equivalent to *poiēsai, poiein* and other similar words. The meaning of consecration is therefore quite clear, but it does not neces-

232

sarily exclude the words of institution. Here now is the third important text, taken from the liturgy of John Chrysostom, in the version that is most used:

> Calling therefore to mind . . . and offering you what is yours from all that is yours, in everything and for everything. . . . We offer you this spiritual and bloodless worship and we invoke you, imploring you to send your Holy Spirit of us and on these gifts that are presented and to make of this bread the precious body of your Christ, changing it by your Holy Spirit (Amen) and of what is in this cup the precious blood of your Christ, changing it by your Holy Spirit (Amen), so that they may be, for those who partake of them, for the soberness (S. Salaville: 'purification') of the soul, the remission of sins, the communication of your Holy Spirit, the fullness of the Kingdom, free access to you (*parrēsia*; S. Salaville: 'the pledge of trust') and not judgement or condemnation.[25]

It is worth noting in this context that the earliest Eucharists always either contain the words of institution or else refer to the words spoken by Jesus; Paul does this in 1 Cor 11:23ff., as do Justin Martyr ('the prayer of the word that comes from him', i.e. Christ), Irenaeus (*Adv. haer.* V, 2, 3) and Tertullian (*Adv. Marc.* IV, 40). These words constitute the Eucharist. It is, to tell the truth, not certain that Jesus himself consecrated the bread by saying 'This is my body'. He may have consecrated it by blessing (God) and have given the *consecrated* bread to his apostles, saying: 'This is my body given up for you'. The Scholastics, beginning with Peter Comestor (see P.-M. Gy, note 39 below), were acquainted with this question, but they said that Christ gave it to his Church to 'do this' in memory of him, using *his words*. The institution, then, is connected with the repetition of the account of the institution itself and the words of that institution. This is already clear from St Paul. The Orthodox, on the other hand, believed that it was no more than an account and that it was therefore necessary to add the epiclesis.[26] The Scholastics agreed that it was no more than an account, and that it was necessary for the celebrant to have the *intention* of speaking *in the name of and as in the person of Christ*.[27]

There was (and there is), in fact, only *one* Eucharist—the one celebrated by Jesus himself the night he was betrayed. Our Eucharists are only Eucharists by the virtue and the making present of *that* Eucharist. John Chrysostom throws a very clear light on this problem: 'The words "Increase and multiply", although they were only said once, continue to have an influence and to give you the power to procreate children. The same applies to the words: "This is my body". Although they were only spoken once, they give, and will continue to give until the end of the world, their existence and their virtue to all sacrifices.'[28]

It is quite correct to speak of the words of *institution*. The real question is: how are we to know by what means and by what mediation the words of institution will be effectively applied, now, to the bread and wine of this particular celebration?[29] This was the question asked by Nicholas Cabasilas in his argument for the epiclesis, after he had quoted John Chrysostom's text.[30] His reply was, of course, that it is through the prayer of the priest, in other words, the epiclesis. The Latins' reply was: it is through the words of institution said by the priest with the intention of doing what Christ instituted and what the Church celebrates. The truth, to which both the liturgies and very many authors testify, precludes maintaining the latter to the exclusion of the former.[31] The consecration of the sacred gifts is the act of Christ, the sovereign high priest who is active through his minister *and* through the Holy Spirit. The clearest evidence is undoubtedly provided by John Chrysostom, who asserts the consecration by the Spirit who was invoked in the epiclesis as vigorously as that by the priest pronouncing the words of Christ, or by John the Sabaite in his seventh-century *Life of Barlaam and Josapha* (see note 31 below). This twofold unity of divine action in the sacrament can be connected without difficulty to certain great constants and, in that sense, certain great laws that are effective in God's work, for example:

> —the frequent bond between the word and the Spirit: see Ps 33:6; Is 59:21; see also my observations in Volume I, pp. 57–58, and Volume II, pp. 42–43, on bearing witness; see also Acts 4:19–21; 1 Tim 4:5;
> —the fact that, in order to make his work after his departure present, Jesus deploys the joint mission of the apostolic ministry and of the Holy Spirit;[32]
> —the existence of the two missions, which nonetheless do the same work; to accomplish this, not only was the incarnation followed by Pentecost, but also Jesus Christ himself, the Word made flesh, was sanctified and guided by the Spirit: see above, p. 165–171;
> —the Trinitarian structure of the whole economy of salvation, which is reflected both in the creed, as a summary of faith, or in the anaphoras, most clearly in the liturgy of St James. As Gregory of Nyssa and Cyril of Alexandria pointed out, 'all grace and every perfect gift comes to us from the Father through the Son and they are completed in the Holy Spirit'.[33] Bessarion applied this Trinitarian structure to our eucharistic question.[34] S. Salaville saw it as the key to open the door to an understanding of the meaning of the epiclesis (*DTC*, V, cols 293ff.). There is also a parallelism between the creed and the anaphoras.[35]

The meaning of the celebration in the West
The ordained celebrant is himself a sacramental reality

This is, if not a dogma, at least a commonly accepted and official doctrine in the Catholic Church. In the West, then, the consecration of the bread and wine is accomplished by the words of the account of the institution spoken by a priest with the intention of doing what Jesus himself did. The Church has celebrated this from its very beginning (see below, pp. 239–240). The priest therefore acts not through his personal quality or energies, but *in persona Christi* or *in nomine Christi*, taking the place or playing the part of Christ, in his name.[36] This idea has antecedents of a very firm kind in the biblical notion of the *šaliaḥ*, the messenger commissioned by an authority that he makes present by representing, and also in the idea so well known in the early centuries of Christianity that the bishop (the priest) was the image of the Father or the image of Christ in the midst of the Christian community and over and against the people.[37] The most important value in the earliest texts is one of conformity or *model*; it is an iconic value. Together with this, however, there is a value of authority and power. This is found in the teaching of those excellent and well-loved martyrs Clement of Rome, Ignatius of Antioch, Irenaeus and Cyprian. The power comes from the Spirit (see the prayer for the consecration of a bishop in Hippolytus), but it also includes an authority that comes from that of the apostles and is ultimately received from Christ (see Irenaeus and Cyprian). The bishop (the priest) is therefore, in the community, in a sense the incarnation or at least the sacrament of Christ.[38]

I am aware of the fact that, from the twelfth century onwards, when the theology of the sacraments had been stabilized by the early Scholastic theologians and the sacrament of ordination had been defined as the power to consecrate the Eucharist, but above all as a result of accepting Thomas Aquinas' idea of the instrumental causality of the words spoken by the priest *in persona Christi*, the concept of the priest as the representative of Christ, playing the part of Christ, had become somewhat isolated, hardened and material. Thomas believed that the priest would consecrate the bread if he pronounced only the words 'This is my body', but, of course, on condition that he has the intention of fulfilling the sacrament.[39] The Catholic position cannot be traced back to this thesis, which has been widely disputed and which I, for my part, also reject.

The true perspective of the *in persona Christi* is sacramental. The priest who celebrates the Church's act of worship is himself a sacramental reality, that is to say, he represents, at the level of what can be seen, a spiritual reality. He is that reality in accordance with the fullness that is realized by the Church's worship. That fullness is defined, for example, in the papal encyclical *Mediator Dei* of 20 November 1947 and in the conciliar Constitution on the Liturgy, *Sacrosanctum Concilium*, 7, as the 'full public worship performed by the Mystical Body of Jesus Christ, that is, by the Head and his members'. It is in accordance with this organic reality with its two aspects that the priest represents Christ. He represents not only Christ, the sovereign high priest, in whose person he acts, but also the *ecclesia*, the community of Christians, in whose person he acts also. He therefore acts *in persona Christi* and *in persona Ecclesiae*. One of these aspects cannot be isolated from the other—the one is contained within the other. An insistence on the Christological aspect—this has occurred in the West—means that the *in persona Ecclesiae* is situated within the *in persona Christi*, which is consequently seen as the basis and the reason for the first. *Mediator Dei* presents the teaching in this way. If, on the other hand, the pneumatological aspect is emphasized, as the Eastern tradition loves to do, the *in persona*

Christi is more easily seen as situated within the *in persona Ecclesiae*. There is no denial here of the fact that the priest has received, through his ordination, the 'power' to celebrate the Eucharist and therefore to consecrate the bread and wine. The Eastern tradition teaches as firmly as the Western Church that only the priest can do this, but this does not mean that he can do it alone, that is, when he remains alone. He does not, in other words, consecrate the elements by virtue of a power that is inherent in him and which he has, in this sense, within his control. It is rather by virtue of the grace for which he asks God and which is operative, and even ensured, through him *in the Church*.

It is worth recalling at this point the meaning of the exchange of words between the one who presides over the celebration and the assembled people: 'The Lord be with you'—'And with your Spirit'. This does not mean simply 'and with you'. It means 'with the grace that you received through ordination for the common good; we are asking now for that grace to be made present in this celebration'.[40] The 'power' received at ordination and the making present of the gift of the Spirit, the ordained celebrant and the community-or the *ecclesia* are united in the celebration of the Eucharist. In the Eastern rite, the epiclesis is spoken in the plural, indicating clearly that the whole community invokes the Spirit. The Roman canon, however, also has 'Memores offerimus' and 'Supplices te rogamus' in the plural. We are not so very far apart.

Several Orthodox theologians whom I have known and loved have, however, severely criticized the *in persona Christi*. This, for example, is what Paul Evdokimov had to say about this question.

> If the very deep reason for the conflict (which keeps the Eastern tradition apart from that of the West, the essential aspect of which is not the eucharistic epiclesis alone, but rather the epiclesis as an expression of the theology of the Holy Spirit) is to be grasped, it is important to recognize that, for the Greeks, the canon of the liturgy is a whole that is inseparable from the one Mystery. It cannot be broken down into different elements so that one central point can be, as it were, isolated. For the Latins, the *verba substantialia* of the consecration, the institutional words of Christ, are pronounced by the priest *in persona Christi*, which bestows on them a value that is immediately consecratory. For the Greeks, however, a similar definition of the priestly action—*in persona Christi*—which identifies the priest with Christ is absolutely unknown. Indeed, it is quite unthinkable. For them, the priest invokes the Holy Spirit precisely in order that the words of Christ, *reproduced and cited* by the priest, acquire all the effectiveness of the speech-act of God.[41]

It seems to me that we Western Christians have, by certain theological statements that we have made, prepared the way for and even caused a misunderstanding here. Statements, for example, such as *sacerdos alter Christus* have to be understood in their true sense, which is spiritual and functional, not ontological or juridical. What I have said here has been part

236

of an attempt to allay suspicions and to come closer to a truth which is, I believe, common to both East and West. For the rest, many Orthodox also invest the *in persona Christi* with meaning. Here I would like to quote a number of contemporary authors; for earlier writers, I would refer to S. Salaville's article (*DTC*, V, cols. 253ff., 257), though I would cite in addition a text by John Chrysostom and another by Severus of Antioch. I begin with these:

> Christ is there. . . . In fact, it is not a man who makes the gifts that are offered become the body and blood of Christ, but Christ himself, who was crucified for us. The priest stands there, *schēma plērōn* (*figuram implens*: 'fulfilling a role as figure') and saying the words, but the power and the grace are God's.[42]

> The priest who stands at the altar fulfils the function of a mere minister there. Pronouncing the words as in the person of Christ and taking the action that he is performing back to the time when the Saviour instituted the sacrifice in the presence of his disciples. . . .[43]

> I find it difficult to place a statement such as this (made by Paul Evdokimov): unlike what takes place in the Catholic Church, the Orthodox priest does not act *in persona Christi*, but *in nomine Christi*. I wonder whether this is not merely a linguistic quibble. The whole of Paul's writings and the whole of the Orthodox tradition provide evidence that *in persona Christi* and *in nomine Christi* are equivalent to each other. . . . The one who acts *in nomine Christi* acts through the power of the Spirit bestowed at the time of ordination. He acts effectively *in persona Christi* for the fulfilment of the *oikonomia* of the mystery.[44]

> Like an icon, the priest must be transparent to the message that he bears without identifying himself with it. He must know how to be there without imposing his presence. If the priest enters the sanctuary, behind the iconostasis, this is neither a right nor a privilege, since only Christ has the right to be there. The priest is there as an icon, *in persona Christi*.[45]

> In the Eucharist, the eternal priesthood of Christ is continuously manifested in time. The celebrant, in his liturgical action, has a twofold ministry: as the icon of Christ, acting in the name of Christ for the community, and also as the representative of the community, expressing the priesthood of all believers.[46]

> The bishop is not simply the successor of the apostles and Jesus Christ himself, whose vicar he is. He is also the sacramental image (or icon) of the Saviour. That image is most fully revealed in the liturgical celebration and in presiding over the eucharistic assembly. Over and against the Church, then, the bishop has a place that is similar to that occupied by Christ himself.[47]

The liturgical expression of the Mystery in the two original traditions

Finally, we can say that the epiclesis confronts us less with a sacramental question, that is, with a problem as to the 'form' of the sacrament of the Eucharist, and much more with a question of Trinitarian *theo*-logy, or rather with a question of liturgical expression of the economy in which the mystery of the Tri-unity of God is revealed to us and is communicated to us.

The Orthodox rightly tell us that the anaphora forms a whole, from which one element, the account of the institution, for example, or the epiclesis, cannot be isolated and treated separately. No Orthodox would think of the consecration as taking place simply through the epiclesis.[48] It is, however, possible to ask whether consecration would take place if the epiclesis were omitted. . . .

In the West, unfortunately, too much and indeed almost exclusive attention has been given since the High Middle Ages to the words of Christ. This has resulted in the rest of the anaphora being devalued and the sense of the unity of the eucharistic prayer as a whole being endangered.[49] This emphasis undoubtedly came about as a result of Scholastic theology, since the sense of unity seems to have been present in the contemplative monastic communities of the twelfth and thirteenth centuries. Until the Middle Ages, no attempt was made to define the precise moment of consecration and even theologians gave considerable value to other moments than the account of the institution. Peter Lombard, for example, thought that an excommunicated priest could not consecrate the bread and wine because he was placed outside the Church and therefore could not say '*we* offer you . . .', and the angel of the *Supplices te rogamus*—the epiclesis!—would not accept the offering of such a priest to take it up to the heavenly altar.[50] Whatever hypotheses may have been suggested in the past, we now tend once more to see the anaphora as a whole. The fact that a prayer is said after the account of the institution does not necessarily mean that the consecration takes place after it. It is interesting to quote Bossuet here:

The spirit of the liturgies and, in general, of all consecrations does not lead us to concentrate on certain precise moments. On the contrary, it makes us consider the whole of the action in order to understand the entire effect. An example will make what I mean clearer. In the priest's consecration, hardly any scholars doubt any more, since the discovery everywhere of so many ancient sacramentaries, that the most important part is the laying on of hands with the prayer that accompanies it (however, after it, the bishop anoints the priest's hands, then makes him touch the chalice and, even after the new priest has celebrated, passes on to him the power to remit sins). Is it possible for anyone to say that a man is a priest without having received this power, which is so inseparable from this character? After all, what is said to him is: 'Receive it'. . . . Why, unless it is that on these occasions the things that are celebrated are so great, have so many different aspects and so many varied relationships, that the Church cannot say everything . . . in one place, and distributes its activity, however simple it may be in itself. . . . (Bossuet here adds the examples of the celebration of confirmation and the anointing of the sick.) . . . All this is an effect of human language which can only be explained bit by bit. . . .
(XLVII) If this doctrine is applied to the prayer used by the Greeks, there will be no further difficulty. After the words of our Lord, the priest asks God if he will

change the gifts into his Body and Blood. This can be either the application of the thing to be done or the more special expression of the thing done. Nothing else can be concluded from the precise terms of the liturgy. . . . In this mystical language of the liturgies and in general in the sacraments, an expression is often given after what may have been done before, or rather, in order to say everything, an explanation is given in succession of what may have all taken place at the same time, without looking into the precise moments. In that case, we have seen that an expression is given of what may have been done already, as though it was done when it was expressed, with the result that all the words of the sacred mystery are related to each other and the entire activity of the Holy Spirit is visible.[51]

What led to the desire to state exactly when the consecration took place, at least from the time of Innocent III onwards, was the principle according to which the conversion of the bread and wine or their transubstantiation must be instantaneous.[52] A 'progressive', 'gradual' or 'dynamic' change in which the body and blood of the Lord might be there a little, then a little more and finally totally, was not envisaged.

This teaching is beyond dispute when applied to the *res et sacramentum*, the reality itself or the 'presence' of the body and blood. It seems less convincing if it is seen from the point of view of the liturgical rite and the celebration as such. There are several cases in which the precise moment of effectiveness is not adequately stated. These cases include, for example, the consecration of the holy oils on Maundy Thursday, or the laying on of hands as the 'form' of the ordination of priests, in which a number of priests impose their hands after the bishop and the celebration lasts quite a long time. There is also the case of concelebration in the Eucharist itself. Thomas Aquinas raised two objections to the latter.[53] The first was that, if there are several celebrants, there would be several consecrations. His reply to this is that this would not be so, since all the celebrants have the intention of bringing about one consecration. His second objection is this: the words of consecration can never be spoken simultaneously if there are several celebrants; the consecration is complete when some of them finish saying the words, with the result that the others do nothing. We should note in passing how far removed such considerations are from the Orthodox understanding of the situation. In the East, there is concelebration even when one concelebrant only intervenes at one moment of the celebration, or when the concelebrants say nothing at all. Thomas' reply to this was to cite Innocent III: priests concelebrating (on the day of their ordination) must refer their intention (to consecrate the bread and wine) to the moment when the bishop says the words of institution. For Thomas, then, the intention of the celebrant is what determines the matter.

Is it therefore not possible to return now to the question that was asked above (pp. 233–234): how can the words pronounced by Christ himself at the Last Supper be applied to this bread and this wine (see notes 28 and 29 below)? The Scholastic theologians gave a very decisive importance to the intention, as we have seen. Is it consequently not possible to say that it is the intention of the priest celebrating *according to the rite of his Church* that determines the change of the bread and wine into the body and blood of the Lord by the application of the words of institution pronounced once only by Christ? In the Eastern rite, the priest's conviction and intention are closely connected with the saying of the epiclesis, in which the Spirit is asked to make the words of the account of the institution effective. This means that the words are only effective through the coming of the Spirit invoked in the epiclesis.[54] It does not mean that the conversion of the holy things only takes place, as Prince Max of Saxony believed,[55] after the epiclesis has been pronounced. My position is very similar to that of S. Salaville. Not only I, but many others who have studied this question, have had to rely on his learning.

Poor Prince Max's intention at least was right. He wanted to recognize the existence and the legitimacy of two different liturgical ideas, both concerned with the same reality, the celebration of the holy Eucharist as received from the Lord. Since his time, there have been very many remarkable liturgical studies—the lion's share produced in the West—and this notion of two liturgical ideas, two styles of liturgy has become commonplace. It would not be difficult to write a great deal about it, but, so as not to lengthen an already long chapter and to keep to the central theme of our subject, at the risk of appearing excessively schematic, I will summarize my ideas in two columns:

Eastern Rite

(1) The Eastern liturgies, which were developed in the controversial climate of the fourth century, are fundamentally Trinitarian.[56]

(2) The style is that of an epiclesis; this is noticeable in the celebration of various sacraments:

baptism: 'N. is baptized';

anointing with chrism: 'the seal of the gift of the Spirit';

Eucharist: epiclesis;

penance: 'May God forgive you'; 'Heal your servant';

ordination of ministers: 'May the grace of the Holy Spirit raise you to the order of deacon (priest, bishop)';

Western Rite

(1) The West was less affected by the fourth-century debates. Its inspiration is therefore more Christological.[57]

(2) The formulae used are often not deprecatory in form, although the Holy Spirit is expected in every effect of grace:

baptism: 'I baptize you';

confirmation: the renewed rite has the Eastern form (see above, p. 217);

Mass: the words of institution;

penance: 'I absolve you'; but see the formulae of the renewed rite (Volume I, pp. 169–170, and below, p. 269);

ordination: the renewed prayers are very close to those in the Eastern rite (see Volume I, p. 169, and below, pp. 268–269);

marriage: 'N. is crowned the servant of God'; the crowning has the character of an epiclesis.[58]

marriage: the bride and bridegroom are regarded as the ministers of the sacrament, which consists of the contract made sacred by God.

(3) The liturgy of the Eucharist is a dynamic whole finalized by deification. The sanctification of the elements by the Spirit therefore takes precedence over interest in a 'real presence' by an ontological transformation of the elements.[59]

(3) Attention has, at least since the end of the twelfth century, been concentrated on the 'real presence' and the cult of the Blessed Sacrament.

(4) The epiclesis is said in the plural, as a prayer of the community. The idea that the whole of the people is consecrated is expressed theologically in the profound doctrine of the *sobornost'*.

(4) Apart from a few additions of private prayers in the Middle Ages, the liturgy also speaks as 'we'. In speculative theology, however, and pastoral practice, the person of the priest (the Pope) is dominant.

(5) Interest is centred on the present descent of good things from the eschatological City, through the Holy Spirit.[60]

(5) Interest is more concerned with the historical continuity since the incarnation of the salvation that originated with Jesus Christ.

It is worth noting that, in very many of the questions that I have discussed here, the Second Vatican Council itself, as well as the attitudes, ways of thinking and explorations that prepared the way for it and the renewal in the liturgy and the Church as a whole that has followed it, have given life—or restored life—in the Catholic Church to a spirit that is in accordance with that of the Fathers and has been preserved in the Orthodox Church. The new eucharistic prayers, in particular, all contain an epiclesis before the account of the institution, asking for the gifts to be sanctified and consecrated, and an epiclesis after the consecration, asking for the fruits of the sacrament through the action of the Holy Spirit.[61] The results of this liturgical fact are already making themselves felt in theology and at the pastoral level.

*   *   *

Symbols of Life peculiar to the East

I believe that the Eastern Church has a more Platonic attitude and that it feels at ease with symbols and with a more organic and holistic approach to the world and faith. Its attitude is in striking contrast to that of the Western Church, with its more Aristotelian and analytical approach. As I commented almost half a century ago: formal and exemplary causality, and efficient and active causality![62] The value accorded to and the part played by images is particularly significant in each case, though the dogmatic pronouncements of the Second Council of Nicaea (787), with its affirmation of the veneration of icons, are common to both East and West. The Eastern Church undoubtedly has an 'iconic' approach to realities, and perceives their deep meaning in religious symbols, which are not, for it, simply objects of knowledge, but imply an intense orientation to life and important practical consequences. The most poetic liturgical texts, the most detailed rites, are living, give inspiration to thought and life—this is very evident in two eucharistic rites—the zeon and the celebration with leavened bread.

The 'Zeon' or the Eucharistic Pentecost

In the Eastern rite, the priest or the deacon pours a little boiling water into the chalice before communion, with the words: 'The fervour of faith, filled with the Holy Spirit. Amen.' Nicholas Cabasilas (†c. 1380) explained, in his treatise on the liturgy, that the liturgy, having unfolded the series of mysteries from the incarnation to the passion and the resurrection of Christ in symbols, now continues with a symbolic representation of Pentecost. 'The Holy Spirit came down after all things pertaining to Christ had been accomplished. In the same way, when the holy offerings have attained their ultimate perfection, this water is added. . . . The Church . . . received the Holy Spirit after our Lord's ascension: now she receives the gift of the Holy Spirit after the offerings have been accepted at the heavenly altar.'[63] This concluding sentence is a good illustration of Bossuet's comments quoted above on the laws governing liturgical expression.

This 'zeon' is also an excellent symbolic expression of what we shall be considering in the next chapter. I myself have experienced that, if it is expressed in this way and if it is given this meaning, the zeon is very significant. It is, however, important to point out in this context that this is *Cabasilas'* interpretation of the zeon. The zeon itself and its interpretation go back a long way in the history of the Eastern Church.[64] It was introduced about 565 during the reign of Justinian and in the context of Aphthartodocetism. In a thesis that was influenced by Monophysitism, Julian of Halicarnassus maintained that the body of Christ was in itself incorruptible and would not pass away. It had therefore remained warm after his death and had yielded warm blood at the lance thrust. In the eleventh century, Nicetas Stethatos, Cardinal Humbert's opponent, explained the zeon rite by the fact that the living Spirit had remained united with Christ's body after his death. When communion was received from the warm chalice, Christians received the warm blood flowing from the side of Christ (with the water and the Spirit; see 1 Jn 5:8) and they were filled with the Holy Spirit, who is warmth. The same explanation was also provided by the Patriarch of Antioch Theodore Balsamon in the eleventh century. A pneumatological meaning was therefore preserved at the same time as a Christological one.

Unleavened or leavened bread?

It would seem that ordinary, that is, leavened bread, was first used throughout Christendom for the celebration of the Eucharist. The first really clear evidence of the use of unleavened bread is to be found in Rabanus Maurus (†c. 856).[65] The Eastern Church has always used and still uses leavened bread. The difference between the practice in the East and the West did not become an active reason for opposition between them until the dramatic confrontation between the Roman legate, the fiery Cardinal Humbert of Silva Candida, and the Patriarch Michael Cerularius in 1053–1054. The history of the polemics, including letters and scurrilous publications, is quite complex, but recent studies have thrown a great deal of light on it.[66]

It was not Cerularius who began hostilities. Leo of Ochrida wrote a letter to the Pope which Humbert believed had come from Cerularius. The latter had first intervened in opposition to Stylichus, the governor of the Byzantine territories in the south of Italy, who had introduced the practice of unleavened bread there. The quarrel soon became bitter: consecrated hosts of unleavened bread were even profaned. On the Greek side, the fires were immediately fanned by an argument that established a relationship between the rite of the Eucharist and the theology of the incarnation. In argument against the Monophysites and the Armenians, it had been said again and again that bread without leaven was dead bread, which consequently expressed only a Christ without a soul. Peter of Antioch and Nicetas Stethatos, with whom Humbert was engaged in controversy, accused the Latins of crypto-Apollinarianism. This accusation was renewed in comparatively recent polemics.[67]

The Latins based their argument on the fact that Jesus celebrated the Last Supper 'on the first day of the feast of unleavened bread' and that he observed the Mosaic Law. Humbert emphasized the lasting benefits of this. They too had their own symbolism—the bread of the Eucharist had to be pure, white, lasting and imperishable, since the body of Christ could only appear as white and immaculate. The argument, then, was Christological.[68] As we have already seen in Volume I of this work (p. 161), this symbolism still plays an important part in the feelings of many Catholics even today.

The Greeks opposed this argument by pointing to the new covenant, the change in the Law and the priesthood and the symbolism of the resurrection, which were not expressed by 'dead', unleavened bread. The Latins, in other words, were Judaizing.

In my opinion, the debate itself is not unimportant, but I am glad of the great number of declarations, some of them very general, others made specifically in connection with this particular question, which have stated, at the time of the controversy and subsequently, that the Eucharist of the Lord is celebrated equally with leavened or with unleavened bread.[69] Outside certain unprogressive quarters, this kind of controversy is almost unknown today. Alexander Schmemann, for example, wrote: 'Almost all the Byzantine arguments against the Latin rites have lost their importance; all that remains to be discussed now are the dogmatic differences with Rome'.[70] In my opinion, the main divergence is without doubt the *Filioque*. I have tried to deal with this question irenically.

NOTES

1. See Nicholas Cabasilas, *A Commentary on the Divine Liturgy*, tr. J. M. Hussey and P. A. McNulty (London, 1960); Fr. tr. S. Salaville, *SC* 4 (1943; 2nd ed., 1967). For Cabasilas, see M. Lot-Borodine, *Nicolas Cabasilas. Un maître de la spiritualité byzantine au XIVᵉ siècle* (Paris, 1958); W. Völker, *Die Sakramentsmystik des Nikolaus Kabasilas* (Wiesbaden, 1977).

2. See T. Spačil, *Doctrina theologiae Orientis separati de SS. Eucharistia* (*Or. Chr.* XIII and XIV) (Rome, 1928 and 1929). For the debate in Russia in the last quarter of the seventeenth century, see I. Smolitsch, *Russisches Mönchtum* (Würzburg, 1953), pp. 345ff., 541.

3. I would mention only the following: S. Salaville, 'Epiclèse eucharistique', *DTC*, V (1913), cols 194–300; see also the Tables, *DTC*, I, cols 1365–1372; F. Cabrol, *DACL*, V/1 (1922), cols 142–184; G. Dix, *The Shape of the Liturgy* (London, 1945); B. Botte, 'L'épiclèse dans les liturgies syriennes orientales', *Sacris erudiri*, VI (1954), 46–72, and many other articles; L. Bouyer, *Eucharist: Theology and Spirituality of the Eucharistic Prayer* (Eng. tr.; Notre Dame, Ind. and London, 1968); W. Schneemelcher, 'Die Epiklese bei den griechischen Vätern', *Die Aufrufung des Heiligen Geistes im Abendmahl* (*Beiheft zur ökumenischen Rundschau*, 31) (Frankfurt, 1977), pp. 68–94; H. A. J. Wegman, 'Pleidooi voor een tekst. De Anaphora van de apostelen Addai en Mari', *Bijdragen*, 40 (1979), 15–43; M. de la Taille, *Mysterium Fidei*, Elucidatio XXXIV, 2nd ed. (Paris, 1924), includes an impressive list of publications and shows at the same time a distressing lack of understanding of the liturgical and theological meaning of the epiclesis.

4. Paul Evdokimov, *L'Esprit Saint dans la tradition orthodoxe* (*Bibl. Œcumén.*, 10) (Paris, 1969), p. 101, note 42.

5. See J. W. Tyrer, 'The Meaning of *Epiklēsis*', *JTS*, 25 (1923–1924), 139–150; O. Casel, 'Neuere Beiträge zur Epiklesenfrage', *Jahrbuch für Liturgiewissenschaft*, 4 (1924), 173. For Cyril of Jerusalem, see J. Quasten, *Monumenta eucharistica et liturgica vetustissima* (*Florilegium Patristicum*, VII) (Bonn, 1925), p. 77, note 2; *SC* 126, p. 95, note 2. For John Chrysostom, *De sac.* III, 4, see A. Naegele, *Die Eucharistielehre des heiligen Johannes Chrysostomus* (Freiburg, 1900), pp. 136ff. For Basil the Great, see M. Jugie, 'De epiclesi eucharistica secundum Basilium Magnum', *Acta Acad. Velehrad.*, 19 (1948), pp. 202ff.

6. See S. Salaville, *op. cit.* (note 3), col. 202, who also cites contemporary authors (col. 203) who wrote in the same way.

7. This emerges clearly from J. Lécuyer, 'La théologie de l'anaphore selon les Pères de l'école d'Antioche', *L'Orient syrien*, 6 (1961), 385–412. The principal Fathers concerned are Theodore of Mopsuestia, John Chrysostom and Theodoret.

8. *I Apol.* LXVI, 2. Justin first says that the 'president of the brethren' 'eucharists' the bread and wine; he then adds in his text: 'We do not receive these gifts as ordinary food or ordinary drink. But as Jesus Christ our Saviour was made flesh through the word of God, and took flesh and blood for our salvation, in the same way the food over which thanksgiving has been offered (= the "eucharisted bread") through the word of prayer (or 'the

prayer of the Word' *or* 'word') which we have from him—the food by which our blood and flesh are nourished through its transformation—is, we are taught, the flesh and blood of Jesus who was made flesh' (tr. H. Bettenson, *The Early Christian Fathers* (Oxford, 1969), pp. 61–62).

9. Irenaeus, *Adv. haer.* IV, 18, 5; V, 2, 2 (*PG* 7, 1027 and 1124).
10. Gregory of Nyssa, *Orat. cat.* 37 (*PG* 45, 93), written in 385.
11. Germanus, *Historia ekklēsiastikē kai mustagōgikē* (*PG* 98, 436–437). See also John Damascene (†749), *De fide orthod.* IV, 13 (*PG* 94, 1140ff.); Nicephorus of Constantinople (†828), *Antirrheticus secundus*, 3 (*PG* 100, 336); see also the two Syrians, Chosroe Magnus (†c. 972) and Dionysius Bar Salibi (twelfth century), *Expositio liturgiae*, ed. H. Labourt (Louvain, 1955). The *proskomidia* of the Eastern Eucharist is an evocation of the life of the incarnate Word.
12. Theodore of Mopsuestia, *Hom. cat.* 16; ed. and Fr. tr. R. Tonneau and R. Devreesse, *Homélies catéchétiques* (Vatican City, 1949), pp. 551–553.
13. Hippolytus, *Trad. apost.* 4; Fr. tr. B. Botte, *SC* 11, who accepts the original authenticity of this epiclesis.
14. For the Apostolic Constitutions, see F. E. Brightman, *Liturgies Eastern and Western*, I: *Eastern Liturgies* (Oxford, 1896), pp. 20ff.; S. Salaville, *op. cit* (note 3), col. 205; L. Bouyer, *op. cit* (note 3), pp. 264, 266. Cabasilas 'calls the conversion of oblations and the sanctification of the faithful by the same terms (*hagiasmos, hagiazō*)': J. Gouillard in Nicholas Cabasilas, *op. cit.* (note 1), 2nd Fr. ed. (1967), p. 37. See also J. Havet, 'Les sacrements et le rôle de l'Esprit Saint d'après Isidore de Séville,' *ETL*, 16 (1939), 85–91 for quotations from Cyril of Alexandria, John Chrysostom, Gregory of Nyssa, Theodore of Mopsuestia and others; 72–85 for quotations from the Western author Fulgentius of Ruspe; 61–72, for the Mozarabic rite; some of the epicleses seem to aim at the consecration of the bread and wine, but as a whole they aim rather at a sanctification of the elements by the Holy Spirit, insofar as this makes them able to sanctify the believers. See also Boris Bobrinskoy, 'Présence réelle et communion eucharistique', *RSPT*, 53 (1969), 402–420, especially 409.
15. S. Salaville, *op. cit.*, cols 205 and 206; L. Bouyer, *op. cit.*, p. 274; for the liturgy of St James, see the edition of B. C. Mercier.
16. As a good Thomist, J. M. R. Tillard, 'L'Eucharistie et le Saint-Esprit', *NRT*, 90 (1968), 363–387, considered the function of the Holy Spirit firstly in the context of the *res et sacramentum* of the Eucharist (the presence of the dead and risen Christ) and then as the *res tantum* (the charity of unity in the Mystical Body). At the same time, however, he also saw the second in continuity with the first, as Thomas Aquinas himself did together with other Scholastics. The Fathers and the Scholastics of the High Middle Ages were even more synthetic in their treatment of the question: see H. de Lubac, *Corpus mysticum* (Paris, 1944; 2nd ed., 1949).
17. See S. Salaville, *op. cit.* (note 3), col. 206.
18. E. Mercenier and F. Paris, *La Prière des Eglises de rite byzantin*, I (Amay-sur-Meuse, 1937), p. 235. In the present text, the words of the priest and the deacon are reversed. See A. Raes, 'Le dialogue après la Grande Entrée dans la liturgie byzantin', *Or. Chr. Period.*, 18 (1952), 38–51, who attributes the text to the fifteenth or sixteenth centuries; R. F. Taft, *The Great Entrance. A History of the Transfer of Gifts and Other Preanaphoral Rites of the Liturgy of St. John Chrysostom* (*Or. Chr. Anal.*, 200) (Rome, 1975), who goes back to tenth-century manuscripts. See also Paul Evdokimov, *op. cit.* (note 4), p. 100, who stresses the fact that there are epicleses that precede the canon.
19. See H. A. J. Wegman, *op. cit.* (note 3); L. Bouyer, *op. cit.* (note 3), pp. 146ff. and, for Hippolytus, pp. 170ff.
20. J. Quasten, 'The Blessing of the Font in the Syrian Rite of the Fourth Century', *ThSt*, 7 (1946), 309–313.
21. Cyril of Jerusalem, *Cat.* I, 7; ed. A. Piédagnel and P. Paris, *SC* 126 (1966), p. 95, who, in a

footnote, observe that the epiclesis should be understood here in the wider sense as designating the whole Canon of the Mass.

22. *Cat.* V, 7; A. Piédagnel and P. Paris, *op. cit.* (note 21), p. 155, who, again in a note, draw attention to the absence of any reference to an account of the institution or of the anamnesis and point to parallels for the epiclesis taken from the theological and geographical context. See also A. Tarby, *La prière eucharistique de l'Eglise de Jérusalem* (*Théol. hist.*, 17) (Paris, 1972).

23. See L. Bouyer, *op. cit.* (note 3), pp. 295–296; S. Salaville, *op. cit.* (note 3), cols 194–195. See also H. Engberding, *Das eucharistische Hochgebet der Basiliusliturgie* (Münster, 1931). In *De spir. sanct.* 23, 65 (*PG* 32, 188B), Basil the Great speaks of the words of the epiclesis 'at the moment of consecration' and Pruche translates *epi* in this way, to avoid the precision of 'following' or 'in view of': see *SC* 17, p. 239.

24. Hence S. Salaville's very severe judgement, *op. cit.*, cols 247–252.

25. See L. Bouyer, *op. cit.*, pp. 287, 288; S. Salaville, *op. cit.*, cols 195–196.

26. Nicholas Cabasilas, *Commentary on the Divine Liturgy*, 29.

27. Duns Scotus, *In IV Sent.* d. 8, q. 2; Durandus, *ibid.*, wrote that, in the account alone, 'non significatur quod corpus *Christi* sit sub speciebus panis quem sacerdos tenet vel coram se habet, sed solum sub speciebus panis quem Christus accepit et benedixit'.

28. John Chrysostom, *De proditione Iudae, Hom.* 1, No. 6 (*PG* 49, 380); see also *Hom.* 2 (*PG* 49, 589–590); tr. based on Fr. tr. by S. Salaville.

29. See A. Chavasse, 'L'épiclèse eucharistique dans les anciennes liturgies orientales. Une hypothèse d'interprétation', *MScRel*, 2 (1946), pp. 197–206. This can be compared with Isidore of Kiev at Florence (Mansi 31, 1686–1687); see also S. Salaville, *op. cit.* (note 3), col. 258.

30. Nicholas Cabasilas, *op. cit.* (note 26); see also J. Lukman, article in Serbian on 'The Doctrine of Nicholas Cabasilas and Simeon of Thessalonica on the Epiclesis', *Bogoslovni Vestnik*, 7 (1927), 1–14, who pointed out that Cabasilas uses the word *epharmozō*, 'to harmonize, put in touch with, make a connection between'.

31. See S. Salaville, *op. cit.*, cols 232–240; for the Eastern texts, see cols 236–238 (John Chrysostom) and col. 240 (John the Sabaite).

32. See Jn 14–17 and my *The Mystery of the Church* (Eng. tr.; London, 1960), pp. 147–186.

33. Gregory of Nyssa, *Ep. ad Ablabium* (*PG* 45, 125); Cyril of Alexandria, *Comm. in Luc.* XXII, 19 (*PG* 72, 908); see also S. Salaville, *op. cit.* (note 3), col. 236.

34. Bessarion, *De sacr. Euch.* (*PG* 161, 516).

35. This suggestion was made by A. Hamman, 'Du symbole de la foi à l'anaphore eucharistique', *Kyriakon, Festschrift J. Quasten* (Münster, 1970), II, pp. 835–843. I am inclined to think that this parallelism justifies the commemoration, in the anamnesis of the Byzantine rite, of the second coming of Christ in the future; in the creed, what concerns the Son is complete before professing faith in the Spirit.

36. Texts will be found in B. Marliangeas, *Clés pour une théologie du ministère. In persona Christi. In persona Ecclesiae*, with a preface by Y. Congar (*Théol. hist.*, 51) (Paris, 1978). These include mediaeval texts, texts from the thirteenth century and from Thomas Aquinas, important theological texts from the fourteenth to the seventeenth century and finally 'magisterial' texts: see pp. 231ff.

37. B. Marliangeas does not draw attention to these aspects, because he limits himself to the themes stated in the title of his book (*op. cit.*). See, however, J. Pascher, 'Die Hierarchie in sakramentaler Symbolik', *Episcopus. Studien über das Bischofsamt. Festschrift für Kardinal M. von Faulhaber* (Regensburg, 1949), pp. 278–295, and especially O. Perler, 'L'évêque, représentant du Christ, selon les documents des premiers siècles', *L'Episcopat et l'Eglise universelle*, ed. Y. Congar and B. D. Dupuy (*Unam Sanctam*, 39) (Paris, 1962), pp. 31–66.

38. O. Perler, *op. cit.* (note 37), p. 65.

39. *ST* IIIa, q. 78, a. 1, ad 4. See, for this question, in which Thomas played a special part,

P.-M. Gy, 'Les paroles de la consécration et l'unité de la Prière eucharistique selon les théologiens de Pierre Lombard à S. Thomas d'Aquin', *Mélanges C. Vagaggini* (Rome, 1980), pp. 189–201.

40. In this context, I quoted, in Volume I, p. 43 notes 33 and 35, W. C. van Unnik, 'Dominus vobiscum: The Background of a Liturgical Formula', *New Testament Essays in Memory of T. W. Manson* (Manchester, 1959), pp. 270–305. I would add, to the references given by the author to John Chrysostom and Theodore of Mopsuestia, A. Piédagnel's note 1 on Cyril of Jerusalem's fifth *Mystagogic Catechesis* (*SC* 126, p. 150), and what J. Lécuyer has said, *op. cit.* (note 7), 390, with reference to Theodore of Mopsuestia, *Hom. cat.* 15, 37–38, in which Rom 1:9 is cited, and to John Chrysostom, *De S. Pent. Hom.* 1, 4 (*PG* 50, 458–459).

41. Paul Evdokimov, *L'Orthodoxie* (*Bibl. théol.*) (Neuchâtel and Paris, 1959), p. 250; *idem*, 'L'Esprit Saint et l'Eglise d'après la tradition liturgique', *L'Esprit Saint et l'Eglise. L'avenir de l'Eglise et l'Œcuménisme* (*Acad. Int. des Sciences Relig.*) (Paris, 1969), pp. 85–111, especially p. 108; see also *idem*, *op. cit.* (note 4), pp. 103–104. See also Cyprien Kern's book in Russian, *The Eucharist* (Paris, 1947), (reviewed by C. R. A. Wenger, *Rev. Et. byz.*, 10 (1952; pub. 1953), 163ff.); *idem*, 'En marge de l'épiclèse', *Irénikon*, 24 (1951), 166–194, especially 182ff. and, for example, 184: 'The priest always acts *in persona Ecclesiae*, imploring in the name of the assembled people and not manifesting his own power'.

42. John Chrysostom, *De prod. Iud., Hom.* 1, 6 (*PG* 49, 380). But the same author also says, *De Pent., Hom.* 1, 4 (*PG* 50, 458–459): 'The priest only places his hand over the gifts after having invoked God's grace. . . . It is not the priest who brings about whatever takes place. . . . It is the grace of the Spirit, coming down and covering it with his wings, who brings about the mystical sacrifice.'

43. See the whole text of Severus of Antioch and the reference in S. Salaville, *op. cit.* (note 3), col. 240.

44. See André Scrima, *L'Esprit Saint et l'Eglise, op. cit.* (note 41), p. 115.

45. Anthony Bloom in an interview on 2 January 1977; reported in *Le Monde*, 2–3 January 1977, p. 14.

46. An agreement reached by the Mixed Anglican-Orthodox Doctrinal Commission; Moscow Conference, 26 July–2 August 1976, No. 27: see *Istina*, 24 (1979), 73.

47. Mgr Meletios, in an address to the plenary assembly of the French bishops at Lourdes, 1978: *Unité des Chrétiens*, 34 (April 1979), 57.

48. Cyprien Kern, 'En marge de l'épiclèse', *op. cit.* (note 41), 181.

49. J. R. Geiselmann, *Die Abendmahlslehre an der Wende der christlichen Spätantike zum Frühmittelalter* (Munich, 1933). I will confine myself to one quotation, from Paschasius Radbert, *De corp. et sang. Dom.* 15 (*PL* 120, 1322): 'Reliqua (apart from the *verba Christi*) vero omnia quae sacerdos dicit, aut clerus canit, nihil aliud quam laudes et gratiarum actiones sunt, aut certe obsecrationes fidelium, postulationes, petitiones'. This text was often attributed to Augustine: by Peter Lombard, *IV Sent.* d. 8, for example, and by Thomas Aquinas and others.

50. *IV Sent.* d. 13. Thomas Aquinas here abandons the Master of the Sentences.

51. Bossuet, *Explication de quelques difficultés sur les prières de la Messe, à un nouveau Catholique* (1689), XLVI and XLVII.

52. This is clear from the way in which Albert the Great displays a lack of understanding of the meaning of concelebration: see *De Euch.* d. 6, tract. 4, c. 2, Nos 15 and 16 (ed. A. Borgnet, 38, pp. 428–429). He cites the fact of concelebration at an ordination Mass as an *objection*, whereas Thomas treats this fact as a datum.

53. Thomas Aquinas, *In IV Sent.* d. 13, q. 1, a. 2, q^a 2; cf. *ST* IIIa, q. 82, a. 2.

54. May I quote two Orthodox texts here? The first is from Nicholas Cabasilas, *Commentary on the Divine Liturgy*, 29: 'We believe that the Lord's words do indeed accomplish the mystery, but through the medium of the priest, his invocation, and his prayer'; here

Cabasilas is referring to the application of the words said by Jesus at the Last Supper, words that the priest uses again in the form of an account in order to apply them to the oblations: see section 27. The second quotation is from Paul Evdokimov, *op. cit.* (note 4), pp. 103–104: 'So that the words of Christ that he has memorized may acquire a divine effectiveness, the priest invokes the Holy Spirit in the epiclesis. The Holy Spirit makes the words of the anamnesis: "Taking bread . . . he gives it to his disciples . . saying . . . This is my body" an *epiphanic anamnesis*, pointing to the intervention of Christ himself as identifying the words said by the priest with his own words and identifying the Eucharist celebrated by the priest with his own Last Supper. This is the miracle of the *metabolē*, that is, of the conversion of the gifts.'

55. Prince Max of Saxony, 'Pensées sur l'union des Eglises', *DTC*, V, col. 276, a thesis that was sanctioned by Pius X's letter of 26 December 1910: see *DS* 3556. The mistake that Prince Max made was to separate the two aspects, thus attributing a kind of autonomy to the epiclesis; this was, of course, alien to the Orthodox conception: see above, pp. 238, 247 note 48. Ambrosius Catharinus took up a similar stance in the sixteenth century: see *DTC*, XII, col. 2432. His document was placed on the Index of forbidden books, but has since been withdrawn.

56. All the liturgies are Trinitarian—the Roman and the Eastern liturgies: see C. Vagaggini, *Theological Dimensions of the Liturgy* (Eng. tr.; Collegeville, Minn., 1976), chapter 7, esp. pp. 217ff.; the Eastern liturgies are, however, more full of Trinitarian expressions. On the other hand, their economic and Trinitarian structure called for a formal epiclesis invoking the Spirit after the thanksgiving had been addressed to the Father and the sacrifice in the upper room had been made present by the words of Christ, the sovereign high priest.

57. See my article 'Pneumatologie et "christomonisme" dans la tradition latine', *Ecclesia a Spiritu Sancto edocta. Mélanges G. Philips* (Gembloux, 1970), pp. 41–63.

58. See P. Evdokimov, *Le sacrement de l'amour* (Paris, 1962).

59. The opening sentence of Nicholas Cabasilas' *Commentary on the Divine Liturgy* is very characteristic: 'The essential act in the celebration of the holy sacred mysteries is the transformation of the elements into the divine body and blood; its aim is the sanctification of the faithful, who through these mysteries receive the remission of their sins and the inheritance of the kingdom of heaven'.

60. See J. D. Zizioulas, 'La continuité avec les origines apostoliques dans la conscience théologique des Eglises orthodoxes', *Istina*, 19 (1974), 65–94; see also Volume II, pp. 50–51.

61. See Volume I, p. 170; D. Lallement, 'Le Saint-Esprit dans les prières eucharistiques nouvelles', *Bienfaits spirituels de la nouvelle liturgie romaine de la Messe* (Paris, 1979), pp. 35–46.

62. See my article, first published in May 1935, 'La déification dans la tradition spirituelle de l'Orient d'après une étude récente'; Eng. tr., 'Deification in the Spiritual Tradition of the East', *Dialogue between Christians* (London und Dublin, 1966), pp. 217–231.

63. Nicholas Cabasilas, *Commentary as the Divine Liturgy*, 37.

64. See H. Grondijs, *L'iconographie byzantine du crucifié mort sur la croix* (*Bibl. Byzant. Brux.*, 1) (Brussels, 1941); the author has collected together in this book all the texts relating to the zeon rites.

65. K.-H. Kandler, 'Wann werden die Azyme das Brotelement in der Eucharistie im Abendland?' *Zeitschrift für Kirchengeschichte*, 75 (1964), 153–155; see also J. A. Jungmann, *The Mass of the Roman Rite* (Eng. tr.; New York and London, 1959), pp. 330–331.

66. Mahlon H. Smith III, *And Taking Bread. Cerularius and the Azyme Controversy of 1054* (*Théol. hist.*, 47) (Paris, 1978). It is also worth consulting K.-H. Kandler, *Die Abendmahlslehre des Kardinal Humbert und ihre Bedeutung für das gegenwärtige Abendmahlsgespräch* (Berlin and Hamburg, 1971).

67. See *Revue de l'Orient chrétien* (1901), 98; M. Jugie, *Theologia dogm. Christ. Orient.*, III, p. 244; IV, p. 442.

68. D. N. Egenter, 'La rupture de 1054', *Irénikon*, 27 (1954), 142–156, quoted Peter Damian: 'Christ took out of the leavened mass the azyme of sincerity that had been purified of the infection of decay. From the flesh of the Virgin which was conceived from sin came a flesh that was without sin': *Liber gratissimus*, 19 (*PL* 145, 129).

69. Cardinal Humbert himself wrote, in the name of Leo IX, to Cerularius in September 1053: 'Although you have closed the Latin churches, the Greek liturgy is still celebrated freely in Rome, since the Church knows that a diversity of practices is not an obstacle to the salvation of believers when one faith, acting through charity, recommends all men to God' (*PL* 143, 764): see C. Will, *Acta et Scripta de Contr*. (Leipzig, 1861), p. 181, containing the text as reproduced in the collections of Ivo of Chartres and Gratian. Peter of Antioch's reply to Cerularius was: 'If the Latins agreed to suppress the addition to the creed, I would not ask for anything more. I would even include the question of unleavened bread, with all the rest, among the indifferent things': see C. Will, *op. cit.*, p. 203. See also Gregory VII, *Reg*. VIII, 1: 'ipsorum fermentatum nec vituperamus nec reprobamus': Caspar, p. 513; Anselm, *Ep. de sacrificio azymi et fermentati*, 1 (ed. S. Schmitt, *Opera*, II, p. 223): 'De sacrificio in quo Graeci nobiscum non sentiunt multis rationibus catholicis videtur quia quod agunt non est contra fidem christianam. Nam et azimum et fermentatum sacrificans panem sacrificat'. Thomas Aquinas, *Contra Err. Graec*. II, 39, defended the use of unleavened bread, on the grounds that Christ employed it, and concluded: 'non autem propter hoc intendimus quod ex fermentato hos sacramentum confici non possit'.

70. A. Schmemann, *Historical Road of Eastern Orthodoxy* (New York, 1961), p. 248, quoted by M. H. Smith, *op. cit.* (note 66), p. 26, note 18.

APPENDIX
THE PART PLAYED BY THE
HOLY SPIRIT IN THE EUCHARIST
ACCORDING TO THE WESTERN
TRADITION

The effectiveness of the grace of the sacraments has always been attributed to the effectiveness of the Holy Spirit, the *virtus Spiritus Sancti*, throughout the history of the Church. This means that the sacred action celebrated in the Church's Eucharist calls for the complement of an active coming of the Spirit—though this is a complement that is not in any sense an optional extra.

What is true of all the sacraments is clearly true of the Eucharist. There is ample testimony that the consecration of the bread and wine into the body and blood of Christ is brought about by the Holy Spirit. This testimony does not, however, necessarily have in mind the existence of an epiclesis. The texts that in fact allude to an invocation (of the Spirit) may refer to the whole of the Canon or even to the whole eucharistic celebration, which includes prayers which have the value of an epiclesis. It is well known that the Roman Canon does not include an epiclesis to the Holy Spirit, and it is very doubtful whether it ever included such an epiclesis even originally. Is the prayer *Supplices te rogamus*—'Almighty God, we pray that your angel may take this sacrifice to your altar in heaven—an epiclesis? The significance of this prayer is still being debated. It is obviously a supplication, in which God is asked to accept the Church's offering and that the offering may obtain its spiritual fruit. It is in the place of an epiclesis, but it does not have a consecratory function and it is not indisputably pneumatological.

Here I now cite a number of witnesses and texts showing that the Latin West has always been convinced not only of the consecratory function of the words 'This is my body' and 'This is my blood', but also equally of the part played by the Holy Spirit. I must openly admit that I compiled this list of witnesses before reading S. Salaville's great article to which I have frequently referred in the earlier part of this chapter: 'Epiclèse eucharistique', *DTC*, V, cols 194–300. Had I consulted this article first, I should not have needed to do the work; his list is more complete, and quotes the text more fully. I am, however, also indebted to another author, Kurt Goldammer, whose dissertation *Die eucharistische Epiklese in der mittelalterlichen abendländischen Frömmigkeit* (Bottrop, 1941) has proved very valuable. Goldammer quotes many versions and descriptions of spiritual experiences, which I have not included. Also, his theological position, as a Protestant, is not one that I have wished to follow in this work.

Ambrose (†397) is the most powerful witness to testify to the consecration of the elements by the words of Christ himself, pronounced by Christ, that is, over the bread and wine: *De sacr*. IV, 14–23; V, 24; *De myst*. 52 (Fr. tr. and ed. B. Botte, *SC* 25bis (1966), who produces convincing arguments in favour of the authenticity of the treatise). Ambrose, however, knew that the Holy Spirit was invoked by priests with the Father and the Son *in oblationibus*: *De spir. sanct*. III, 16, 112 (*PL* 16, 803).

The only text of Augustine (†430), who clearly believed in the decisive part played by the *verbum* (*Sermo Denis*, 6 and other texts: see *DTC*, V, cols 241–242 for S. Salaville's comments) that I would quote here is from *De Trin*. III, 4, 10: 'The consecration, which makes it such a great sacrament, comes only from the invisible action of the Spirit of God' (*PL* 42, 874; Fr. tr. M. Mellet and T. Camelot, *Bibl. August*., XV, p. 291). Augustine might have admitted that there was an epiclesis, but its aim would have been to make the sacred gifts gifts according to Christ and capable of being received by him, not to 'consecrate' them for their conversion into Christ's body and blood: see A. Sage, 'S. Augustin et la prière "Supplices te rogamus" ', *Rev. Et. Byz*., 11 (1953), 252–265.

The Leonine Sacramentary has this Secret for the third Mass of Christmas Day: 'Lord, look with benevolence upon the offering of your people; on your altars it is not an alien fire or the blood of animals without reason that is poured. By the virtue of the Holy Spirit, our sacrifice is the body and blood of the Priest himself' (ed. C. L. Feltoe, p. 61).

Fulgentius of Ruspe, who was Augustine's disciple, replied *c*. 508 to Monimus, who had asked him why we ask for the mission of the Spirit to sanctify the gift of our oblation (*Ad Mon*. II, 6; *PL* 65, 184), that it is to obtain the gift of charity and unanimity (*Ad Mon*. II, 10; *PL* 65, 188), that is, the holy fruit of the Eucharist, what the Scholastics called the *res* of the Eucharist.

Pope Gelasius I (†496) wrote to Elpidius of Volterra about 'the way in which the heavenly Spirit whom we invoke must come to consecrate the divine mystery'[1] and a little later wrote, against the Christological errors of the period, that the bread and wine 'change into the divine reality and the Holy Spirit brings this about'.[2]

There is no explicit epiclesis invoking the Holy Spirit in the Roman rite from the time of Gregory the Great until our own century, although the *Quam oblationem* before the consecration and the *Supplices te rogamus* after the consecration certainly have the value of an epiclesis. In the practical use of this liturgy, however, this relative gap has been filled by a great number of prayers, which were sufficiently widespread to show that they must have been commonly used: see Joaquim O. Bragança, *op. cit.* (note 5 below), pp. 39–53. From a great number of examples, I have chosen this text: 'Lord, may your Holy Spirit descend on this altar, we beseech you, may he bless and sanctify these gifts offered to your Majesty and may he deign to purify all those who receive them'. Until the present century, the Missal of Pius V contained a prayer, the fourteenth-century version of which was, according to a manuscript of the period: 'Veni, sancte Spiritus invisibilis sanctificator, veni et sanctifica sacrificium istud tibi hodie praeparatum ad laudem et gloriam nominis tui. In nomine Patris et Filii et Spiritus Sancti. Amen.'

The Gregorian Sacramentary, the oldest form of which goes back to Gregory the Great (†604), has this prayer: 'The Host which is offered by several and becomes one body of Christ by the infusion of the Holy Spirit': see C. L. Feltoe, *JTS*, 11 (1910), 578; see also the edition by H. Lietzmann (Münster, 1921), nos. 116, 196.

The Hispano-Visigothic rite, which is sometimes called the Mozarabic rite, is extremely rich and even prolix, lyrical and full of patristic inspirations. Isidore of

Seville (†636)[3] regarded the sacrament as brought about 'operante invisibiliter Spiritu Dei' (*Etym.* VI, 19; *PL* 82, 255). His sixth prayer ensures the 'confirmatio sacramenti, ut oblatio, quae Deo offertur, sanctificata per Spiritum Sanctum, Christi corpori et sanguini conformetur' (*De eccl. officiis* I, 15, 3; *PL* 83, 753). It is not easy to say exactly what this *sexta oratio* included. According to Férotin, Cabrol and Séjourné, it was simply what followed the account of the institution—the *Post pridie*. In the opinion of Geiselmann and Havet, on the other hand, it was everything that came after the *illatio* (the Preface) and the Sanctus. In any case, these *Post pridie* prayers, which changed with each Mass, but had a similar structure, asked for the sanctification of the gifts and their fruit of charity and unity in the hearts of the faithful. They are addressed to the Father, the Son or the Holy Spirit, or else to the Holy Trinity. They pray that the body and blood that are offered may be sanctified by the *virtus* of the Holy Spirit, by his warmth. Colunga, and Havet, *op. cit.* (note 3 below), 61–72, thought that these prayers presupposed the consecration of the gifts by the words of institution, but there are several texts which can be opposed to this. The truth is that in the *Liber ordinum* (ed. M. Férotin, 1904) and Isidore of Seville it would be wrong to isolate a single aspect of the entire prayer that begins with the *Sanctus* and ends with the *Pater noster*, because it forms a single whole. The celebration of the Eucharist is a dynamic process which concludes in the communion of the believer, whom the Holy Spirit, transfiguring the gifts into the body of Christ, incorporated by this means into the same Christ.

Bede (†735) was close to Isidore. He believed that the sacrament was brought about by the 'ineffabili Spiritus sanctificatione' (*Hom.* 14; *PL* 94, 75).

Paul the Deacon (†799) reported a eucharistic miracle which has often been described and discussed, from which Pope Gregory benefited. The Pope apparently said: 'Our creator . . . changed the bread and wine with water, leaving them their own appearance, into his flesh and blood, at the Catholic prayer, through the sanctification of his Spirit' (*Vita Gregorii Papae*, c. 23, *PL* 75, 53).

The prayer of the Roman rite, *Summe Sacerdos*, which is attributed to Ambrose of Milan and used to appear in missals as a prayer of preparation for the celebration of the Eucharist, is in fact the work of John of Fécamp (†1078). Its language is taken from various pre-existing texts which go back to a *Post pridie* in the *Liber ordinum* of the Hispano-Visigothic rite. John of Fécamp simply transferred this prayer to the beginning of the celebration.[4] It begins with the words: 'Supreme Priest and true Pontiff, Jesus Christ, . . . who instituted this mystery in the virtue of the Holy Spirit, saying :"Each time that you do this, you do it in memory of me" '.

Many witnesses can be found in the ninth century. There is Florus of Lyons, *De actione missarum*, c. 59 and 60 (*PL* 119, 51B and 52C; ed. P. Duc, Bellay, 1937). The response to the *Orate fratres* in several missals of this period is: 'The Holy Spirit will come upon you . . .'.[5] Like the incarnation, the Eucharist is also brought about by the coming of the Spirit. Paschasius Radbert (†865) also said this (*Liber de corpore et sanguine Domini*, c. 7; *PL* 120, 1285): 'quod sane corpus, ut vera caro sit Christi, pro mundi vita quotidie per Spiritum Sanctum consecratur'. In the same treatise, c. 3 (*PL* 120, 1275–1276), he says that the consecration is brought about 'per sacerdotem super altare in verbo Christi per Spiritum Sanctum' (*PL* 120, 1279) or 'virtute Spiritus Sancti per verbum Christi' (c. 12; *PL* 120, 1310–1312). Paschasius here combines the Christological and the pneumatological aspects, the Spirit having the task of making the words of Christ effective, while those words bring about the consecration. Gottschalk (†c. 866), in his controversy with Paschasius, was not opposed to the latter in this particular case. He also used the analogy of the incarnation (*Ep.* 3; *PL* 112, 1513),[6] but he spoke more explicitly of a supplication addressed to the Holy Spirit; this was undoubtedly the *Supplices te rogamus*: 'Spiritus Sanctus, per quem ea creat et consecrat, et in quo sacerdos ista fieri supplicat' (*PL* 12, 1516). It was at this time that Pope Nicholas I wrote to the Byzantine Emperor Michael (in 860): 'Post sanctificationem Spiritus sanguis Christi efficitur' (*PL* 119, 778D).

This, then, was the generally accepted teaching. It is worth noting in this context another text that originated at the very interesting Council of Arras (1025), held to combat the first manifestations of anti-sacramental dualism. At that Council, it was said of the Eucharist, 'fit sacramentum operante invisibiliter Spiritus Dei' (Mansi, 16, 431A) and 'quae invisibiliter eodem Spiritu vivificatur quo operante in utero Virginis incarnatus est Dei Filius' (Mansi, 16, 433B).

As we shall see, this was to continue to be the teaching of theology and of the Catholic Church. The importance of that teaching was to some extent lessened by the stress laid on the effectiveness of the words of institution—made necessary by the heretical teaching of Berengar of Tours. In opposition to his one-sidedly spiritual teaching about the Eucharist, the Church insisted on the 'real presence', in other words, that what was found on the altar *after the consecration* was the true body and blood of Jesus Christ. The second profession of faith that Gregory VII obliged Berengar to make, on 11 February 1079, says: 'per mysterium sacrae orationis et verba nostri Redemptoris'.[7] The force of circumstances, however, reinforced by the juridical mentality and by the need felt by the Scholastic theologians to define this teaching precisely, led to special emphasis being placed on the exact moment of the consecration when the words of institution are pronounced by the priest.[8] This is clearly illustrated by two great authors, the classical canon lawyer Gratian in 1140, and the classical theologian of the Church Thomas Aquinas in the thirteenth century.[9] According to the latter, it is the words of institution which consecrate; the rest are not the *substantia*, but *decor sacramenti*. Thomas also believed that the mere fact that there were different liturgies proved that they were not concerned with the essence or form of the sacrament. That essence or form was to be found exclusively in the words of Christ as pronounced by the priest *in persona Christi*. Thomas was aware, however, that the water of baptism and all the sacraments were effective because of the Holy Spirit, who was their first cause (*ST* Ia IIae, q. 112, a. 1, ad 2; IIIa, q. 66, a. 11 and 12) and that, if Paul said that we were 'all made to drink of one Spirit' (1 Cor 12:13), this must also be understood in a second sense of the sacramental drink consecrated by the Holy Spirit (*Comm. in 1 Cor.* c. 12, lect. 3). But we must return to the eleventh century, the period of Berengar of Tours.

His first profession of faith, which was not acceptable, was composed in 1055 by Humbert of Silva Candida (†1061), who had in the previous year, on 16 July 1054, placed the bull excommunicating the Patriarch Michael Cerularius on the altar of the Church of Hagia Sophia. What is remarkable, however, is that, in his dialogue with Nicetas Stethatos, he attributed the change in the elements of bread and wine to the invocation of the whole Trinity.[10] He regarded all the sacraments as gifts and instruments of the Spirit, who, in one way or another, dwelt in them.[11]

Peter Damian (†1072) was even more devoted to the Holy Spirit than Humbert. He attributed the consecration of the elements to the words of institution, but the sanctifying and life-giving virtue to the Spirit (*Liber qui dicitur gratissimus*, c. 9; *PL* 145, 110). Since, he believed, simoniacal priests administered valid sacraments, the *virtus Spiritus Sancti* was able to act through the Eucharists of such priests for the benefit of those who had a good disposition. This teaching was taken up again by Cardinal Deusdedit, who died at the end of the century, although he did not name Peter Damian (*Libelli de Lite*, II, p. 322).

There is a great deal of evidence that theologians in the twelfth century were convinced that the Holy Spirit played a part in the Eucharist. Hildebert of Lavardin (or of Le Mans; †1123) affirmed, in connection with the *Supplices te rogamus*, that the gifts were made into the body and blood of Christ 'virtute Spiritus Sancti . . . per Spiritum Sanctum' (*Liber de expositione missae*; *PL* 171, 1168). Rupert of Deutz (†1135) also thought that the fire of the Spirit changed the bread and wine into the eucharistic body and blood of Christ. The Spirit who did this was the same Spirit who had made the Virgin conceive and who had driven Jesus on to offer himself as a living sacrifice (*De Trin. et operibus eius, in Exod. lib.* II, c. 10, in connection with the paschal Lamb cooked in the fire; *PL* 167, 617).

The mysterious Honorius Augustodunensis stated that the body of Christ was produced 'Spiritu Sancto consecrante' and thought that this was proclaimed in the *Quam oblationem* (*Eucharistion seu de corpore et sanguine Domini*, c. 1; *PL* 172, 1250; and *Gemma animae*, I, 105; *PL* 172, 578) respectively. Hildegard, the visionary of Bingen (†1179), frequently spoke of the priest's prayer or *invocatio* in the action of the Eucharist and claimed that the *verba sacerdotis* which invoked God in his power made the Spirit come as he had come on the Virgin Mary at the incarnation (*Scivias*, lib. II, vis. 6; *PL* 197, 516). At the end of the twelfth century, Adam of Saint-Victor (†1192) wrote, in a sequence to the Holy Spirit:[12]

Tu commutas elementa.	You change the elements.
Per te suam sacramenta	Through you the sacraments
habent efficaciam.	have their effect.

It was at this time that the formula of the profession of faith for the Waldenses, the disciples of Peter Waldo (1179–1181), and later for Bernard Prim and Durandus of Huesca (Osca), which was finally prescribed by Innocent III (1208), was first defined. We should note these significant statements: 'Sacramenta quoque, quae in ea (Ecclesia) celebrantur, inaestimabili atque invisibili virtute Spiritus Sancti cooperante' and 'Sacrificium, id est panem et sanguinem . . . in verbo efficitur Creatoris et in virtute Spiritus Sancti' (*DS* 793 and 794). On the other hand, Innocent was convinced that it was the words of institution that brought about the consecration.

It was this certainty that the Scholastic theologians attempted to express and to justify. Albert the Great, for example, asked: 'An in sacramento Eucharistiae potest dici creari corpus Christi per Spiritum Sanctum? et utrum per spiritum fiat transsubstantiatio?' (*In IV Sent.* d. 10, a. 10; ed. A. Borgnet, 29, p. 262). This question was prompted by a text of Peter Lombard, who quotes a passage by Paschasius Radbert under the name of St Augustine: 'sicut per Spiritum Sanctum vera Christi caro sine coitu creatur, ita per eundem ex substantia panis et vini idem corpus Christi et sanguis consecratur, etc.' (*De corp. et sang. Dom.* c. 4; *PL* 120, 1278). Albert believed that the consecration of the elements was brought about by the words of institution and, in the matter of transubstantiation, he attributed the effect of the love that unifies the mystical Body of Christ, which is the *res* of the sacrament, to the Holy Spirit.

Thomas Aquinas also commented on the same passage of Paschasius, still attributed to Augustine. In his gloss, he maintained that transsubstantiation was appropriated to the Son as the one who brings it about and to the Holy Spirit as the one through whom Christ is active (*In IV Sent*. d. 10, expos. textus; ed. Moos, No. 144). A little earlier in the same treatise, he raised in objection a text by John Damascene: 'the conversion of the bread into the body of Christ takes place only by the virtue of the Holy Spirit' (*De fide orthod.*, IV, 13; *PG* 94, 1139). Thomas keeps to the principle of attributing transubstantiation to the Holy Spirit as the one who is principally active, but insists that this does not exclude the action of an instrument, in this case, the words of the priest (*In IV Sent*. d. 8, q. 2, a. 3, ad 1). There is, then, a lack of complete agreement between these two passages of Thomas, but there is nevertheless agreement that the words of institution and the Holy Spirit have to be taken together. It can be added here that Thomas did not regard the *Supplices te rogamus* as a consecratory epiclesis (*In IV Sent*. d. 13, Expos. textus: ed. Moos, no. 174).

From the beginning of the fourteenth century onwards, the Latins became acquainted, in the East, with the Orthodox view of the rôle of the epiclesis. This led to a series of papal declarations in favour of the words of institution as the form of the sacrament and the moment when the elements were converted into the body and blood of the Lord:

Benedict XII: libellus *Cum dudum*, addressed to the Armenians, August 1341 (*DS* 1017).

Clement VI: letter *Super quibusdam*, addressed to the Catholicos of the Armenians, 29 September 1351 (*DTC*, V, col. 199).

Benedict XIII: instruction to the Melchite Patriarch of Antioch, 31 May 1729 (*DTC*, V, col. 200).

Benedict XIV: brief *Singularis Romanorum*, 1 September 1741 (*Collectio Lacensis*, II, 197).

Pius VII: brief *Adorabile Eucharistiae*, 8 May 1822, addressed to the Melchite Patriarch of Antioch and bishops (*DS* 2718; *DTC*, V, cols 200 and 264).

Pius X: letter *Ex quo, nono*, addressed to the apostolic delegates in the East, 26 December 1910, against the article written by Prince Max of Saxony ('Thoughts on the Union of the Churches') (*DS* 3556; *DTC*, V, col. 276).

These communications did not preclude an acknowledgement of the part played by the Holy Spirit in the bringing about of the sacrament and consecration of the gifts.

Cornelius a Lapide, the Jesuit biblical exegete (†1637), exalted the eucharistic sacrifice above the Levitical rites because of its mode of offering: 'consecration and transubstantiation are brought about by a sublime and mysterious activity of the Holy Spirit'(*Comm. in 1 Pet*. II, 5–9; based on Fr. tr. by P. Dabin).

French scholars in the seventeenth and eighteenth centuries made the Greek patristic texts and Eastern liturgies accessible on a wide scale to the West. The effect of this was apparent in the work of a great number of authors who, without prejudice to the statements made about the words of institution, continued to insist on the part played by the Holy Spirit in the transformation and the sanctification of the sacred elements. S. Salaville provides some useful references: *DTC*, V, col. 273.[13]

The eucharistic prayers introduced since the Second Vatican Council have given the epicleses back their place. Theology will in this case follow Christian practice.

NOTES

1. See A. Thiel, *Epistolae Romanorum Pontificum*, I (1868), p. 484; see also J. Brinktrine, 'Der Vollzieher der Eucharistie nach dem Brief des Papstes Gelasius (†496) an den Bischof Elpidius von Volterra', *Miscellanea C. Mohlberg* (1949), II, pp. 61–69.
2. Thiel, *op. cit.*, I, pp. 541–542. Attempts have been made to appeal to this text as a denial of the change from bread and wine into the body and blood of the Lord.
3. See the remarkable study of J. R. Geiselmann, *Die Abendmahlslehre an der Wende der christlichen Spätantike zum Frühmittelalter. Isidor von Sevilla und das Sakrament der Eucharistie* (Munich, 1933); A. Colunga, 'La epiclesis en la liturgia mozárabe', *Le Ciencia Tomista*, 47 (1933), 145–161, 289–366; J. Havet, 'Les sacrements et le rôle de l'Esprit Saint d'après Isidore de Séville', *ETL*, 16 (1939), 32–98, especially 72: 'For Isidore, the metamorphosis that occurred in the Eucharist was very complex. It did not merely consist in making the body and blood of Christ present—this was only its sacrificial aspect. This body and blood had in addition to be sanctified by the Holy Spirit, in such a way that they would themselves be sanctifying for those who received them. This was, for Isidore, the truly sacramental aspect of the eucharistic change. The whole of this complex transformation was accomplished by the *oratia sexta* or *prex mystica*, which culminated in the *Eucharistia*, the sanctifying body and blood of Christ.'
4. A. Wilmart, 'L'Oratio S. Ambrosii du Missel Romain', *RBén*, 39 (1927), 314–339; repr. in *Auteurs et Textes dévots du Moyen Age* (Paris, 1932), pp. 101–125; B. Fischer, 'Eine ausdrückliche Geistepiklese im bisherigen Missale Romanum', *Mélanges liturgiques offertes à B. Botte* (Louvain, 1973), pp. 139–142.
5. See J. O. Bragança, 'L'Esprit Saint dans l'Euchologie médiévale', *Le Saint-Esprit dans la liturgie. Conférences Saint-Serge, 1969* (Rome, 1977), p. 44; A. Raes, 'La Dialogue après la Grande Entrée', *Or. Chr. Period.*, 18 (1952), 52–88, who thought that this might have influenced the East; from the fifteenth century onwards, the following excellent formula can be found in the above-mentioned dialogue in the Orthodox Church: 'The Holy Spirit will concelebrate with you'.
6. This *Ep. ad Egilem*, printed under the name of Rabanus Maurus, was attributed by G. Morin and later by C. Lambot, *Œuvres de Godescalc d'Orbais* (1945), pp. 324–335, to Gottschalk.
7. DS 700. For the decisive influence of the Berengarian controversy on the development of the theology of the Eucharist, see H. de Lubac, *Corpus mysticum. L'Eucharistie et l'Eglise au Moyen Age* (*Théologie*, 3) (Paris, 1944, 2nd ed., 1949).
8. This is expressed in popular devotion by the 'desire to see the Host': see H. Dumoutet, *Le désir de voir l'hostie et les origines de la dévotion au Saint-Sacrement* (Paris, 1926) and *Le Christ selon la chair et la vie liturgique au Moyen Age* (Paris, 1932). It was also expressed by the institution of the Feast of Corpus Christi by Urban IV in 1264; this feast was extended to the 'whole Church' in 1311.
9. See Gratian, *De cons.* d. II, c. 55 and 61 (ed. E. Friedberg, 1334–1355 and 1337); in c. 72, however, he quotes Paschasius Radbert. See also Thomas Aquinas, *ST* IIIa, q. 78, a. 1, with an ad 4 which must make everyone who is familiar with and devoted to the liturgy feel uneasy! See also his q. 75, a. 7.

10. 'Taliter praeparatus azymus fideli invocatione totius Trinitatis fit verum et singulare corpus Christi': Humbert, *Dial.* c. 31; C. Will, *Acta et Scripta quae de controversiis Ecclesiae Graecae et Latinae saeculo XI composita extant* (Leipzig and Marburg, 1861), p. 108. See also K.-H. Kandler, *Die Abendmahlslehre des Kardinal Humbert* (Berlin and Hamburg, 1971), pp. 78–81.

11. *Adv. Sim.* II, c. 20 (*Libelli de Lite*, I, p. 163); K.-H. Kandler, *op. cit.*, pp. 42–43. It should be borne in mind that this treatise begins with a passionate invocation of the Spirit, who is the most free of all and will therefore defend the *libertas Ecclesiae* and overthrow the simoniacs and their trafficking (p. 102).

12. Adam of Saint-Victor, *Sequentia X de Spiritu Sancto* (*PL* 196, 1455).

13. I do not know what use to make of an excellent text attributed to Charles de Condren (†1641), since the first Paris edition (1677) was by Quesnel and does not contain this text except for a fragment: Part IV, XXVII, pp. 210ff. This is what can be found in *L'idée du sacerdoce et du sacrifice de Jésus-Christ par le R. P. de Condren*, rev. and augmented ed. by a Benedictine of the French Congregation (Paris, 1901), Part III, Chapter VIII, 'In which it is shown how the Holy Spirit is the fire of the sacrifice of Jesus Christ, in whatever state he is regarded', pp. 160–161: 'The liturgies of the Greek Church attribute everything to the Holy Spirit, both the change of the bread and wine into the body and blood of Jesus Christ and the oblation that this adorable victim makes of himself to God through himself, his ministers and the whole of the Church. As Cyril of Jerusalem said, referring to the liturgy of his own time, which was the fourth century: "What the Holy Spirit touches is changed and sanctified". Is it not also apparent that it is in relation to the fire which from time to time descended from heaven on to the sacrifices of our ancestors that the priest prays in this way in the early Latin liturgies: "Lord, may the Spirit of consolation, who is co-eternal with you and therefore also co-operates in your blessing, descend on these sacrifices"? This is also similar to what is said in the Roman Missal in the Secret of the Friday of the octave of Pentecost: "Lord, may this divine fire, which, through the descent of the Holy Spirit, has inflamed the hearts of the disciples of your Son Jesus Christ, consume these sacrifices that are offered in your presence".' The Paris Missal, which contains this Secret of the Friday in the octave of Pentecost, also contains a Secret for the Monday of that week, in which the Church prays that the gifts that are on the altar may be consecrated by the coming of the Holy Spirit: 'Munera nostra Domine, sancti Spiritus sacrentur adventu'. On the Tuesday of the same week, the Secret is as follows: 'Send, Lord, the Holy Spirit, that he may make these gifts into your sacrament for us'.

3

THE HOLY SPIRIT IN OUR COMMUNION WITH THE BODY AND BLOOD OF CHRIST

Many epicleses ask for the Spirit to bring about not only the consecration of the gifts into the body and blood of Christ and their sanctification, but also the fruits of the communion received by the believer. I propose to consider in this chapter the part played by the Spirit in communion.

The Fathers and the later theologians discussed this question a great deal, and they did so in such a way as to reflect the careful balance they maintained between their Christology and their pneumatology. That is precisely what is theologically at stake in this question and the response we make to it involves the way we practise communion in the Eucharist. Is the Holy Spirit implicated in communion? Why is he implicated? How?

In any examination of the evidence provided by the Church's Tradition, we are confronted by two, even three different approaches to the problem—the Alexandrian approach, the Augustinian approach, which was taken up and extended by the Scholastic theologians, and the Syrian tradition. Let us try to benefit from them all.

(1) The Alexandrian Fathers Athanasius (†373) and Cyril of Alexandria (†444) spoke about the Eucharist in the context of their struggle against Arius and later against Nestorius. In other words, they were anxious to affirm the divinity of the incarnate Word and the sanctifying and deifying power of his 'flesh'.[1] As Cyril declared, 'The body of the Lord himself was sanctified by the power of the Word who was united to him, but it was made so effective that, in the Eulogy, it can communicate its own sanctification to us'.[2]

This does not mean that these Fathers associated the power of sanctification with the incarnation as such and neglected the facts of Easter, that is, the redeeming passion and resurrection. There are many texts testifying to their concern with the latter.[3] Nor does it mean that they had a purely Christological view of the Eucharist, without any pneumatological emphasis. Cyril, for example, wrote: 'Just as the virtue of the sacred flesh makes those who receive it con-corporeal with each other, so too, it seems to me, does the Spirit, who comes to dwell in all of us, lead them to spiritual

258

(pneumatic) unity'.[4] Athanasius' gloss on the text of 1 Cor 10:3–4 is frequently quoted: 'Made to drink of the Spirit, we drink Christ'.[5] The two are inseparable and the Alexandrian Fathers did not separate them, even though they stressed the Word. They say again and again that the Father brings everything about through the Son in the Holy Spirit.

(2) A great tradition that has flourished for centuries in the West is associated with the sixth chapter of the gospel of John on the bread of life and the exposition of this text by Augustine.[6] This exposition is based on a Pauline text: 'Our fathers . . . all ate the same supernatural (spiritual) food and drank the same supernatural (spiritual) drink. For they drank from the supernatural (spiritual) Rock which followed them and the Rock was Christ' (1 Cor 10:3–4).

Augustine's argument is as follows: We all eat and drink the same Christ in the eucharistic bread and wine. The 'sacraments' as signs are different, but the reality to which they point is the same—it is Christ. The Jews of the exodus did not attain to Christ and are therefore *our* fathers only to the extent that they ate and drank 'spiritually'. This is why Augustine stressed, even for us, the need to 'understand' and, what is more, to understand 'spiritually'. It is necessary to come, in and through the sacrament, to what is signified by the sacrament. This is done through faith (in Christ).[7] That faith is the essential. Hence the famous *crede et manducasti (Comm. in ev. Ioan.* XXV, 12)—'Believe and you have then eaten (Christ)'. The man who desires life should approach, believe and be incorporated in order to be given life (XXVI, 13). Considering Christ, Augustine saw him as our Head, he considered the 'whole Christ', that is, Head and members, the whole Body, and the principle that animates it, the Holy Spirit. These ideas follow each other and combine in his thought: the living bread, the Body of Christ (Head and members), the sacrament of the Body that is on the altar. Also, on the altar there is what you are; we are the body and this is what is on the altar, Christ, but a Christ who is not without his Body, the city of saints. It is necessary to belong to that Body to live in the Spirit, which is to that Body what the soul is to our body. The Spirit, who is common to both the Father and the Son, is their love for each other.[8]

There is a constant movement from the sacramental body to the Body of the Church. In order to live from the Spirit, it is necessary to belong to the Body (of the Church). We are of the Body of the Church, firstly if we have the spirit of communion and unity, and then, if we eat the sacrament of the body, if we go beyond the visible sign of bread to reach the Reality to which it points. This is done by eating the bread in a spiritual manner. The expression *manducatio spiritualis* is not used as such by Augustine, but its equivalent is: 'panem coelestem spiritaliter manducate' (XXVI, 11); 'ut carnem Christi et sanguinem Christ non edamus tantum in sacramento sed usque ad Spiritus participationem manducemus et bibamus' (XXVII, 11).

What part, then, does the Holy Spirit play in all this? It refers back to the

Body of Christ which we form: we have to be in that Body if we are to live from the Spirit of Christ (XXXV, 13). The flesh of Christ present sacramentally on its own has nothing to offer in itself. It has to be given life by charity in our eating of it, and that is precisely what the Spirit does (XXVII, 4–6). In a word, the Spirit gives life to those who receive communion. The latter must not simply receive the sacrament, however, but must eat and drink to the point of sharing in the Spirit, through the lively faith that they have in Christ (XXVII, 11).

These Augustinian master texts had a powerful effect on the meditations of the Latins and the reflections of theologians. I do not attempt to trace the history of this influence here—all that I can do is to refer to a number of important authors and texts. The first is Prosper of Aquitaine, who was active only a few years later than Augustine himself.[9] During the early years of the sixth century, Fulgentius of Ruspe[10] saw the intervention of the Spirit in the gift of charity enabling us to preserve unanimity and to be crucified to the world. The Spirit brings about the charity of Easter in the one who receives communion.

The early Scholastic theologians were concerned with the sacrament itself as one of the Church's celebrations. Following Alger of Liège, Peter Lombard adapted a vocabulary inherited from Augustine to suit contemporary needs and distinguished two *res* in the Eucharist. By *res*, he did not mean, as Augustine had meant, Christ himself, but also an aspect of the sacrament. The first of these two *res* is the reality that is at once aimed at and contained. This is the personal body of Jesus Christ. The second is the reality aimed at but not contained. This reality is the unity of the Church in its saints.[11] Thus when Peter Lombard distinguished between 'two modes of eating', he defined these by reference to one or other *res* acquired in that eating. He spoke of *manducatio sacramentalis* and of *manducatio spiritualis*, taking place through faith and enabling the one who receives the sacrament to remain in the unity of Christ and the Church.[12] Its virtue is such that it is possible to eat (the second reality or *res*) without eating (the sacrament itself), or not to eat (the second reality) when one has eaten (the sacrament), 'quia non manducans sacramentaliter aliquando manducat spiritualiter, et e converso'.

According to H.-R. Schlette's analysis, Bonaventure took the distinction made between the two modes of eating from the point of view of the believer, 'per comparationem ad manducantem', whereas Thomas Aquinas continued in the line followed by Peter Lombard and took it in terms of the structure of the sacrament. He distinguished between a *manducatio spiritualis*, in which the *res tantum* was acquired, that is, the spiritual reality to which the sacrament finally pointed, and a *manducatio sacramentalis*, which reached the *res et sacramentum*, what we term the 'real presence'.[13] Fundamentally, however, this *manducatio* is only that of the *sacramentum*. On the contrary, the *manducatio spiritualis*, which normally presupposes the *manducatio sacramentalis*, has such a power that it can obtain the effect of the sacrament without the sacrament itself being received.[14]

This teaching about the *manducatio spiritualis* led eventually to what is now known as 'spiritual communion'.[15] This gives us altogether three modes of eating: the first is the purely external eating of the sacrament alone, the second the truly spiritual reception of the sacrament, and the third the purely spiritual eating without the real reception of the sacrament. This is what the Council of Trent and the Roman Catechism taught.[16] As J. Eichinger pointed out, however,[17] a curious inversion of the vocabulary has taken place in this process, so that now, someone who does not receive the Host does not *really* receive communion—but only receives it *spiritually*. In the past, as we have seen, *real* communion, that is, receiving the ultimate reality or *res* of the Eucharist, presupposed a *spiritual* eating.

It is interesting in this context to note the part that Thomas attributes to the Holy Spirit. In the first place, like all the Scholastic theologians, he attributes the effectiveness of all the sacraments in a general sense to the Spirit.[18] At the same time, like Augustine, he also maintains that the spiritual eating of the sacrament is a participation in the Holy Spirit. In the following passage, quoted from Thomas' commentary on the gospel of John, I show this in small capital letters:

> That man eats and drinks sacramentally who receives the sacrament, and spiritually if he goes as far as the *res* of the sacrament, which is twofold: the one is contained and signified; that is Christ who is complete, contained in the species of bread and wine; the other is signified and not contained; that is the mystical Body which is found in those who are predestined, called and made righteous. Thus, the man who is united to him through faith and charity so as to be transformed into him and to become his member eats his flesh and drinks his blood spiritually in respect of the Christ who is contained and signified. . . . It is therefore a food that is capable of making man divine and of making him drunk with divinity. In the same way, in respect of the mystical Body which is simply signified, if he participates in the unity of the Church. . . . In this relationship with the mystical Body, he will have life if he perseveres, since the unity of the Church is brought about by the HOLY SPIRIT, according to Eph 4:4: 'one Spirit and one Body', and Eph 1:14: 'the guarantee (earnest-money) of our inheritance'. That food therefore brings a great benefit, that is, the eternal life of the soul—and also of the body.
>
> Paul also adds: 'And I will raise him up on the last day'. The man who eats and drinks spiritually comes to participate in the HOLY SPIRIT, through whom we are united to Christ in a union of faith and charity and through whom we become members of the Church. The HOLY SPIRIT enables us to obtain resurrection, according to Rom 8:1. . . . If what he said: 'Whoever eats my flesh . . .' refers mystically to the body and blood, then the words are clear, since, as has been said, that man eats spiritually so far as the *res* that is merely signified is concerned who is incorporated into the mystical Body by the union of faith and charity. But charity enables God to dwell in us and, according to 1 Jn 4:16, 'he who dwells in charity dwells in God and God dwells in him'. This is precisely what the HOLY SPIRIT does,

as we are told in 1 Jn 4:13: 'By this we know that we dwell in God and God in us, because he has given us of his own Spirit'.[19]

Thomas Aquinas, then, attributed the gift of faith and charity to the Holy Spirit in communion. It is through this gift of faith and charity that the believer is united, as their member, to Christ and the Church, which Thomas calls the mystical Body. The action of the Spirit is in this way situated on and in the believer. Even in the details, this is fully within the tradition of Augustine, except for the fact that the category of *res* had been defined more precisely by Hugh of Saint-Victor and Peter Lombard.

(3) The Syrian tradition is rather different from the Alexandrian and the Augustinian traditions.[20] The image of fire is frequently used in it. According to Ephraem Syrus,

> There is fire and Spirit in Mary's womb;
> there is fire and Spirit in the river in which you were baptized.
> Fire and Spirit in our own baptism,
> in the bread and in the cup, fire and Holy Spirit.[21]

> In your bread is hidden the Spirit who is not eaten;
> in your wine dwells the Fire that cannot be drunk.
> The Spirit in your bread, the Fire in your wine,
> a remarkable miracle that our lips have received.[22]

This image of fire is also found, together with visions of fire, in the West, but there they are both connected with the consecration of the elements of bread and wine through the virtue of the Holy Spirit.[23] It seems to me that the distinctive aspect of the Syrian tradition is that the activity of the Spirit in the Eucharist is linked with his activity in the Christological economy of salvation, that is, in the conception, baptism, Last Supper and resurrection of Christ. The Spirit first came upon Jesus and filled him. Jesus himself filled the bread and the wine of the Eucharist with the Spirit. A number of texts should provide evidence of this:

> In the same way, after supper, he took the cup, made a mixture of wine and water, raised his eyes to heaven, presented it to you, his God and Father, gave thanks, consecrated it and blessed it, *filled it with the Holy Spirit* and gave it to his holy and blessed disciples, saying. . . .[24]

> He called the bread his living body, filled it with himself and with the Spirit, stretched out his hand and gave them the bread: 'Take and eat with faith and do not doubt that this is my body'. And the one who eats with faith, through it he eats the fire of the Spirit. . . . Eat all of you and eat through it the Holy Spirit.[25]

> Henceforth you will eat a pure and spotless Pasch, a perfect leavened bread that the Holy Spirit has kneaded and baked, a wine mixed with fire and the Spirit.[26]

> He wanted us no longer to see according to their nature those things (the bread and the wine) that had received the grace and the coming of the Holy Spirit, but to

take them as the body and blood of our Lord. For the body of our Lord, it was also not of his own nature that he had immortality and the power to bestow immortality, but it was the Holy Spirit who gave these to him and it was through the resurrection from the dead that he received the combination with divine nature and became immortal and the cause of immortality for others.[27]

According to the *Testament of Our Lord*, a Syrian document dating back to about 475 or even earlier, the one giving communion to his fellow-believers said: 'The Body of Jesus Christ, the Holy Spirit, for the healing of soul and body'.[28] As we have seen, at the zeon in the Byzantine rite, the deacon says: 'The fervour of faith, filled with the Holy Spirit', and the priest, putting a fragment of the bread, the Lamb, into the chalice, says: 'The fullness of the Holy Spirit'. Again and again, the Syrian authors stressed that, when we receive the body and blood of the Lord, we receive the Holy Spirit, his grace and his gift of immortality.[29]

*   *   *

To what conclusion can we come? Fervent, but reasonable, reasonable, but fervent, we take our place modestly in the assembly of believers who are celebrating and then in the line of those who are receiving communion.

The 'eucharisted' bread and wine can be taken merely *sacramentaliter* or materially, just as a thing. This attitude may be encouraged by too much insistence on the 'real presence', but in the same way the most beautiful hymns about the fire of the Spirit and the most beautiful words about the Spirit himself can also become purely ritual.

Sacramental communion, if it is to achieve what it aims to achieve, calls for an act on the part of the one receiving it which is an act of living faith and love and at the same time an act which comes from the Holy Spirit as its first cause. Rather like a packet placed in a trough and then carried along by a current of living water, my sacramental communion is taken up by the movement and the warmth with which the Spirit, who is invoked and who opens up a channel for himself in me, invests the presence of Jesus. My communion is therefore a cleaving, in abandonment and love, to what Jesus is, wants and brings about in me.

In his very illuminating study of the Eucharist, Henri de Lubac denounced the disadvantages of a movement 'from symbolism to dialectics'.[30] One of these disadvantages was the distinction that led to what de Lubac called a break in the earlier unity between the *res contenta* or 'real presence' and the *res non contenta*, the unity of the mystical Body. For Augustine, on the other hand, the bread and wine, the body and blood of Christ on the altar, 'represented and contained, in a real and physical way, his mystical Body, since the head without the body was not the head'.[31] In Scholastic theology, a bond was preserved between Christ present or 'contained' in the sacrament and his mystical Body, but this bond was to a reality that was extrinsic to what is found on the altar and to what we eat.

263

I would like to have what Thomas Aquinas meant by *res non contenta* investigated more closely. Examples concerning other sacraments would lead me to think that it means the effect to which the sacrament points (*res significata*), but what is not obtained or produced by the sacramental act alone.[32] It calls for the intervention of another energy. It is true that the sacrament of the Eucharist 'perficitur in ipsa consecratione materiae', is brought about by the consecration of the bread and wine and their 'conversion' into the body and blood of Christ.[33] In that sense, the spiritual fruit of the sacrament, which takes place in the one who receives communion, is 'extrinsic' to it. Thomas, however, knew that a sacrament was 'the sign of a sacred reality *insofar as it sanctifies men*',[34] in other words, that the spiritual fruit belonged to the sacrament and that it was its *res* or 'thing'. The bond between the Eucharist and the unity of the mystical Body was very carefully preserved in Scholastic theology. I myself have a file on this subject which would fill many pages in a book. Albert the Great would have a privileged place. But—and this brings us back to our point—if the sacrament is to have, in the life of Christians, its 'reality', that is, the fruit to which it points, what is required is an intervention on the part of the Spirit, who is, in us, the author of charity. And that charity is paschal, it is of the Church, and it is orientated towards God's work in the world and towards his kingdom.[35] Jesus is in us, but, if his sacramental presence is to have its effect, the Holy Spirit must add his breath, his fire and his dynamism.

The Eucharist follows the structure of the economy of salvation. It was, in other words, necessary for the Holy Spirit to sanctify, anoint and guide Jesus, the Word made flesh. On pp. 165–171 of this volume, I have provided an outline of what might be called a pneumatological Christology. It was necessary for the Holy Spirit to 'pneumatize' him, according to the teaching of Paul in, for example, Rom 1:4; 1 Cor 15:45; 2 Cor 3:17–18. The Christ whom we receive in sacramental communion is the Christ of Easter who has been 'pneumatized' or penetrated by the Spirit. According to the Decree on the Ministry of Priests promulgated by the Second Vatican Council, 'the most blessed Eucharist contains the Church's entire spiritual wealth, that is, Christ himself, our Passover and living bread. Through his very flesh, made vital and vitalizing by the Holy Spirit, he offers life to men.'[36]

What the Spirit has brought about in Christ in order to make him the Head of the Body, he has also to bring about in us to make us his members and to complete and sanctify his Body. The same Spirit is at work in the three realities that bear the name of the body of Christ and are dynamically linked to each other through the dynamism of the Spirit: Jesus, who was born of Mary and who suffered, died and was raised from the dead and glorified→ the bread and wine that are 'eucharisted' → the communion or Body of which we are the members. There is only one economy of grace in which the same Spirit sanctifies the body of Christ in its three states that are differentiated but at the same time dynamically linked together and this is to the glory of God the Father: 'Through him, with him, in him, in the unity of the Holy Spirit', as we say at the end of every eucharistic prayer.

NOTES

1. J. M. R. Tillard, *L'Eucharistie Pâque de l'Eglise* (*Unam Sanctam*, 44) (Paris, 1964), pp. 60ff.; A. Houssiau, 'Incarnation et communion selon les Pères grecs', *Irénikon*, 45 (1972), 457–468, especially 466.
2. Cyril of Alexandria, *Comm. in ev. Ioan*. XI, 9 (*PG* 74, 528) for Jn 17:13.
3. J. M. R. Tillard, *op. cit*. J.-P. Jossua has shown that this opposition points to a false alternative for the Latin Fathers as well: see his *Le Salut. Incarnation ou Mystère pascal chez les Pères de l'Eglise de S. Irénée à S. Léon le Grand* (Paris, 1968).
4. Cyril of Alexandria, *Comm. in ev. Ioan*. XI, 11 (*PG* 74, 561). See also *Comm. in Luc*. XXII (*PG* 72, 912): 'Giving life and uniting himself to a flesh that he made his own, the Word of God made that flesh life-giving. It was suitable for him also to unite himself in a certain fashion to our bodies through his sacred flesh and his precious blood which we receive in the bread and wine for a life-giving blessing.' This passage is quoted by Thomas Aquinas in his *Catena aurea, in Luc*. 22 and in *ST* IIIa, q. 79, a. 1.
5. Athanasius, *Ad Ser*. I (*PG* 26, 576A). It is also possible to cite Gregory of Nyssa, *In illud 'Tunc ipse Filius'* (*PG* 44, 1320D); *Antirrhet*. 42 (*PG* 45, 1224B).
6. Augustine, *Comm. in ev. Ioan*. XXVI, 12 to XXVII, 11; see *Œuvres de S. Augustin*, 72: *Homélies sur l'Evangile de S. Jean XVII–XXXIII*, Fr. tr. and notes by M.-F. Berrouard (Paris, 1977). Berrouard's notes are especially valuable. For the commentaries and the exegesis of Jn 6, there are references in J. M. R. Tillard, *op. cit*. (note 1), p. 183, note 3 and in my own study, first pub. in *Parole de Dieu et Sacerdoce. Etudes présentées à Mgr. Weber* (Tournai, 1962), pp. 21–58; Eng. tr., 'The Two Forms of the Bread of Life in the Gospel and Tradition', *Priest and Layman* (London, 1967), pp. 103–138, esp. p. 127, note 2.
7. Hence, in Augustine's teaching, the importance of this idea, which was later used by Thomas Aquinas and which can be summarized as: the ancient world, with its faith in Christ to come, and we ourselves, with our faith in Christ who has come, together make up the same church.
8. For this point, see M.-F. Berrouard, *op. cit*. (note 6), p. 832; see also Volume I, pp. 77–79, 85–90.
9. Prosper, *Sent*. 341 (*PL* 45, 1890).
10. Fulgentius, *Contra Fab*., fragment 28 (*PL* 65, 789–791).
11. Peter Lombard, *IV Sent*, d. 8 (Quaracchi ed. (1916), p. 791). For what follows, see H.-R. Schlette, *Die Lehre von der geistlichen Kommunion bei Bonaventura, Albert dem Grossen und Thomas von Aquin* (*Münch. Theol. Stud*., II, *Syst. Abt*., 17) (Munich, 1959), pp. 22ff. for Peter Lombard.
12. *Sent*. IV, d. 9 (Quaracchi ed. (1916), pp. 793ff.).
13. Thomas Aquinas, *In IV Sent*. d. 9, a. un. q^a 3; *Comm. in ev. Ioan*. c. 6, lect. 7; *ST* IIIa, q. 80, a. 1.
14. *ST* IIIa, q. 80, a. 1, ad 3.
15. There are articles on this subject by H. Moureau, *DTC*, III (1923), cols 572–574, and L. de Bazelaire, *Dictionnaire de Spiritualité*, II (1953), cols 1297–1302.
16. Council of Trent, Sessio XIII, c. 8; *Roman Catechism*, II, c. 4, q. 41, n. 1–3.
17. J. Eichinger, 'Die Lehre vom "sakramentalen" und vom "geistlichen" Empfang Christi', *TQ*, 132 (1952), 87–92.
18. Thomas Aquinas, *ST* Ia IIae, q. 112, a. 1, ad 2; for baptism, see IIIa, q. 66, a. 11, ad 1; a. 12 c and ad 3. See also Albert the Great for the Eucharist: *In ev. Ioan*. c. 6: 'Haec autem

omnia per causam non facit nisi Spiritus divinus operans in sacramento' (ed. A. Borgnet, 24, p. 281); 'Spiritus divinus operatur omne quod in sacramento est operandum' (Borgnet, 24, p. 286).

19. Thomas Aquinas, *Comm. in ev. Ioan.* c. 6, lect. 7, § 3–5; Cai, Nos 972–976.
20. See J. M. R. Tillard, *op. cit.* (note 1), pp. 83ff., and especially E.-P. Siman, *L'expérience de l'Esprit par l'Eglise d'après la tradition syrienne d'Antioche* (*Théol. hist.*, 15) (Paris, 1971); *idem*, 'La dimension pneumatique de l'Eucharistie d'après la tradition syrienne d'Antioche', *L'Expérience de l'Esprit. Mélanges Schillebeeckx* (*Le Point théol.*, 18) (Paris, 1976), pp. 97–114; I. H. Dalmais, 'L'Esprit Saint et le mystère du salut dans les épiclèses eucharistiques syriennes', *Istina*, 18 (1973), 147–154; P. Yousif, 'L'Eucharistie et le Saint-Esprit d'après S. Ephrem de Nisibe', *A Tribute to Arthur Vööbus. Studies in Early Christian Literature* (Chicago, 1977), pp. 235–246.
21. Ephraem Syrus, *De Fide*, VI, 17. I have taken these texts from the authors mentioned in the preceding note.
22. *De Fide*, X, 8.
23. K. Goldammer, *Die eucharistische Epiklese* (Bottrop, 1941), pp. 78–79, quoted Rupert of Deutz, *De Trin. et oper. eius, in Exod.* II, 10 (*PL* 167, 617) and Hugh of Saint-Victor, *Sermo* 27 (*PL* 177, 958), according to whom the fire of the Spirit cooked the Host as the paschal Lamb; on pp. 96ff., Goldammer speaks of visions of a fiery sphere above the altar and the priest at the time of the consecration. The idea of cooking in the fire of the Holy Spirit can also be found in Augustine, in connection with the sacrament of Christian initiation: see *Sermo* 272 (*PL* 38, 1247).
24. Liturgy of St James.
25. Ephraem Syrus, *Sermons for Holy Saturday*, IV, 4; *Hymni et Sermones*, I, ed. T. Lamy (Malines, 1882), pp. 415ff.
26. *Ibid.*, p. 418.
27. Theodore of Mopsuestia, *Hom. cat.* XV, First on the Mass, No. 10 (Fr. tr. R. Tonneau and R. Devreesse (Vatican City, 1949), p. 475); cf. XVI, Second on the Mass, No. 24 (*ibid.*, p. 571).
28. E. P. Siman, *L'expérience de l'Esprit par l'Eglise, op. cit.* (note 20), p. 106.
29. E. P. Siman, *ibid.*, pp. 106ff., 222–242; Theodore of Mopsuestia, *Hom. cat.* XVI, Second on the Mass, Nos 13, 22, 25 (*op. cit.* (note 27), pp. 555, 565, 573).
30. H. de Lubac, *Corpus mysticum* (Paris, 1944; 2nd ed. 1949), chapter X and the end of Part II.
31. O. Perler, *Le pèlerin de la Cité de Dieu* (Paris, 1957), p. 135.
32. Thomas Aquinas, *Comm. in 1 Cor.* c. 12, lect. 1 and c. 15, lect. 1, who says that grace is the *res contenta* of the sacraments and that the *res non contenta* is the resurrection, 'cum non statim habeat eam qui suscipit sacramenta'; *In IV Sent.* d. 26, q. 2, a. 1, ad 4: in marriage, 'unio Christi and Ecclesiam non est res contenta in hoc sacramento sed res significata'.
33. *ST* IIIa, q. 73, a. 1, ad 3.
34. *ST* IIIa, q. 60, a. 2.
35. It would be possible to comment on each of these words. Apart from J. M. R. Tillard, *op. cit.* (note 1), see my earlier works: *L'Eglise une, sainte, catholique et apostolique* (Paris, 1970), pp. 31–38; 'The Eucharist and the Fulfilment of the World in God' (Eng. tr.), *The Revelation of God* (London and New York, 1968), pp. 189–197; *Lay People in the Church* (Eng. tr.; London, 1957).
36. Decree on the Life of Priests, *Presbyterorum ordinis*, 5, §2.

4

THE LIFE OF THE CHURCH
AS ONE LONG EPICLESIS

Before I try to give an overall view, and in order to do this properly, I would like to look briefly at the other sacraments, all of which refer to the Eucharist.

The three sacraments of initiation—baptism, anointing with chrism, and the Eucharist—are celebrated thanks to an epiclesis which, in the Syrian Church, has a very similar structure in all three.[1] These sacraments, in which the faith of the subject is expressed, lead him, by progressively incorporating him into the glorified Body of Christ, towards eschatological fulfilment. The Holy Spirit is the eschatological gift through and in which we return to the Father.

(1) This initiation begins in the water, over which the Spirit hovers, as at the beginning of the world (Gen 1:2), as though he were hatching it. This connection between the Spirit and water was often stressed by the Fathers.[2] It is also a biblical theme.[3] The Spirit himself is represented by water—living water 'welling up to eternal life' (Jn 4:14). The business of the liturgy is to express in rites accompanied by words the truth of God's activity, and the water of baptism is therefore consecrated in it by invoking the Spirit in a solemn epiclesis. This water is like the womb of our mother the Church, in which the Spirit gives birth to the Body of Christ.[4] Christology and pneumatology are closely associated in the liturgy, as they are in the whole divine economy of salvation. In the Roman liturgy (there is evidence as early as the Gelasian Sacramentary), the celebrant plunges the paschal candle with its flame (representing the risen Christ) three times into the water and at the same time three times invokes the descent of the Holy Spirit, as at the baptism of Jesus himself in the Jordan.[5]

I have already considered, in Volume II, pp. 189–190, the part played by the Spirit in the act of baptism, with reference to the New Testament. It has often been pointed out by theologians that the virtue or power of the Spirit is active in this sacrament.[6] It is not simply a question of divine activity in the neophyte according to the general attribution of the effectiveness of the sacraments to the Holy Spirit. In the case of the baptism of infants, the Holy Spirit intervenes as the principle of communion which transcends the details of space and time and is able to include the infant, who is still unconscious, within the faith of his parents, his sponsors and the whole Church. This presents us with a real problem today and, what is more, one for which psychological, sociological and biological considerations have not been adequate. What is needed is an effective power of communion and a trans-supplementation of one consciousness by another in a unity that transcends human experience. This is supplied by the Spirit: 'If the faith of one person or rather of the whole Church is valuable to the infant, this is thanks to the activity of the Holy Spirit who is the bond of the Church and through whom the treasures of each person are shared by all the others'.[7]

(2) The process by which a minister—a deacon, priest or bishop—is ordained also takes place subject to the invocation of the Spirit. I have called it a process, because it begins before the act of ordination in the strict sense of the term. It begins in fact with the election or the call of the one who can no longer be called a 'candidate' in the modern sense of the word. There are prayers for this election, which is attributed to the Holy Spirit.[8]

In the ordination rite itself, according to the Apostolic Constitution of Pius XII, *Sacramentum Ordinis*, of 30 November 1947, the 'matter' is the laying-on of hands.[9] This is in itself a gesture pointing to the communication of the Spirit, but it has always been accompanied or followed by prayer.[10] It is also a gesture that was practised by the apostles and the first disciples (see Acts 6:6; 13:3; cf. 1 Tim 4:16; 2 Tim 1:6). The 'form' of ordination is the Preface which follows. Its expression is deprecative and for this reason it is clearly an epiclesis. Here is the text of the *Sacramentum Ordinis* for the ordination of deacons, followed by that for the ordination of priests:[11]

> Lord,
> send forth upon them the Holy Spirit,
> that they may be strengthened
> by the gift of your sevenfold grace
> to carry out faithfully the work of the ministry.
>
> Almighty Father,
> grant to these servants of yours
> the dignity of the priesthood.
> Renew within them the Spirit of holiness.
> As co-workers with the order of bishops
> may they be faithful to the ministry
> that they receive from you, Lord God,
> and be to others a model of right conduct.

When a bishop is consecrated, those consecrating lay their hands on the man elected and, while they do this, 'all remain silent, praying in their hearts for the descent of the Spirit. After this, one of the bishops present, at the request of all, laying on his hand on the one who is made a bishop, prays, saying: "Pour out the power that comes from you, (that) of the sovereign

268

Spirit, (that) which you gave to your beloved Son Jesus Christ and which he granted to his holy apostles who constituted the church in various places as your sanctuary, to the praise and glory of your name".' This is how Hippolytus described the consecration of bishops in his *Apostolic Tradition* (*Trad. apost.* 3). It is also the text which the Apostolic Constitution *Pontificalis Romani* of Paul VI (18 June 1968) established as the form of episcopal ordination. This Constitution refers explicitly to Hippolytus and notes that the text is still in use in the Coptic and West Syrian rites. This renewal by allowing an early source to well up again is something that I find very valuable. I also appreciate very much the allusion to Pentecost, since it is well known that many of the Church Fathers saw in Pentecost the ordination of the apostles.[12]

(3) Several of the Fathers saw a first ordination in what has wrongly been called the 'Johannine Pentecost' (Jn 20:19–23): 'Receive the Holy Spirit. If you forgive the sins of any, they are forgiven; if you retain the sins of any, they are retained.' The so-called 'power of the keys' and the sacrament of penance are entirely under the sign of the Holy Spirit. The Spirit is mentioned more than twenty times in the *Praenotanda* of the new ritual which was promulgated in December 1973. The renewed formula of absolution is not simply a declaration and it is only implicitly in the form of an epiclesis. It is, however, strikingly Trinitarian. The text is as follows:

> God, the Father of mercies,
> through the death and resurrection of his Son,
> has reconciled the world to himself
> and sent the Holy Spirit among us
> for the forgiveness of sins:
> through the ministry of the Church
> may God give you pardon and peace,
> and I absolve you from your sins
> in the name of the Father, and of the Son,
> and of the Holy Spirit.

(4) In the Latin Catholic West, the important moment in the sacramental celebration of marriage is the exchange of consent between the bride and the bridegroom in the presence of witnesses from the Christian community, normally the priest and other witnesses.[13] In the Eastern Churches, the celebration culminates in the crowning of the bride and bridegroom by the priest, his function being parallel that to the part that he plays in the celebration of the Eucharist. The crowns symbolize the descent of the Holy Spirit on the couple. The priest's gesture and the prayer that follows it correspond to the invocation of the Holy Spirit, the epiclesis, in the celebration of the Eucharist.[14]

(5) In the seventeenth and eighteenth centuries, it was suggested by a number of canon lawyers that religious profession should be seen as a contract between the professed religious and his or her institute. This was not very successful, because the reality presented greater spiritual substance.[15] Religious profession is a consecration and it is not difficult to understand why early Christians included it among the *sacramenta*, at a time when that term was less precisely defined than it is today, or even called it *ordinatio*, as Theodore of Canterbury (†698) did. Pseudo-Dionysius described the consecration of monks at the beginning of the sixth century, probably in Syria, in the following way: 'This ritual includes a prayer of consecration (or epiclesis), an oral profession in the form of a renunciation of the world, and the tonsure and clothing'.[16] Whenever the Christian mystery or our *vita in Christo* has to be made present here and now, the Spirit has to be invoked.

(6) This is particularly true of an area of Christian life which is very dear and familiar to me, that of Christian knowledge and the word of God. These also have a sacramental structure of a kind, in that they are meant to go through and beyond a visible and tangible expression, which as such is part of our world, to an insight into the Word of God himself in and through men's minds, which can be assimilated to the *res* of the sacraments.[17] Does, for example, chapter 6 of the gospel of John not present the bread of life in the two forms of faith and the Eucharist? Has the theme of the two tables at which the people of God are fed, that of the Word and that of the Eucharist, not been taken up again and again in the Church's Tradition?[18] If it is necessary, however, to have spiritual fruit to make the mystery of Christ present here and now in our lives, then it is also necessary to invoke the Holy Spirit in epicleses.

It is traditional to invoke the Spirit when the Holy Scriptures are read. It is not for nothing that they have been called *lectio divina*! We always need the Spirit to come when we read the Scriptures, Jerome declared.[19] I have already spoken, in Volume II, pp. 27–29, of the part played by the Spirit in our 'spiritual' understanding of the Scriptures. The Holy Spirit is the principle of all right knowledge.[20]

It is obvious that there is a need for the Spirit to intervene and therefore for an epiclesis in the preaching of the Word as a human activity, which is always a risk, involving the transmission of the absolute Word. God has to open the hearts of the listeners, as he opened the heart of Lydia (Acts 16:14). The anointing by faith mentioned by John (1 Jn 2:20, 27) and Paul (2 Cor 1:21) comes from the Spirit and, if the Word is to be expressed in human words and the mystery of Jesus is to be manifested in them, the Spirit has to act. Without him, there can be no spiritual event. With him, something will happen.[21] The preacher has to beseech him earnestly to come both into his poor words and into the hearts of those who hear them. What is more, he is not the only one who should pray for the Spirit—the community should pray with him: 'Pray for us also', Paul wrote to the Colossians (Col 4:3), 'that God may open to us a door for the word, to declare the mystery of Christ'.[22] The word of God, then, has a kind of sacramental structure.[23] It has its external form, its content of truth and its spiritual fruit or its *res* in our souls. It has in fact often been compared to the Eucharist.

* * *

(7) The Church as a whole is sacramental in its nature. It is, *in and through Christ*, the great and primordial sacrament of salvation. I have elaborated this teaching already in another book.[24] The whole Church—its people, its ministers, its treasure of the means of grace and its institution—is that sacrament of salvation. So far from the comings of the Holy Spirit to the Church challenging and questioning its institutional character, they establish it in its truth. The Church is, after all, an institution of a very special kind. It acts in the present on the basis of past events and in the prospect of a future which is nothing less than the kingdom of God, the eschatological City and eternal life in communion with God himself. This is undoubtedly a sacramental structure, containing a memory of the event of foundation, a prophetic sign of the absolute future, and present grace coming from the first and preparing the way for the latter. It is, however, the Holy Spirit who ensures the unity of these three aspects. 'There is a sacramental presence where the Holy Spirit enables, by means of "earthly" elements, men to live here and now from the past, present and future work of Christ, and where he makes them live from salvation.'[25]

In and for the purpose of all these activities, the part played by an intervention of the Holy Spirit and by an epiclesis is to affirm that neither the 'earthly means' nor the institution of the Church produces these by themselves. What we have here is an absolutely supernatural work that is both divine and deifying. The Church can be sure that God works in it, but, because it is God and not the Church that is the principle of this holy activity, the Church has to pray earnestly for his intervention as a grace. As an apostle, Paul was convinced that he was proclaiming the Word of God, yet he still prayed and had others pray for it (see Col 4:3; Eph 6:19). Jesus was sure that he was doing God's work, yet he too prayed before he chose his apostles (see Lk 6:12–13). In the same way, the Church does not in itself have any assurance that it is doing work that will 'well up to eternal life'; it has to pray for the grace of the one who is uncreated Grace, that is, the absolute Gift, the Breath of the Father and the Word.[26] At the level of dogmatic theology, as we have seen already in Volume II, pp. 5–6, 'I believe the holy Church' is conditioned by the absolute 'I believe in the Holy Spirit'. This dogma means that the life and activity of the Church can be seen totally as an epiclesis.

* * *

271

(8) The Spirit is the principle of unity. He is present and active every-where,[27] but he is that principle in a more formal and intense way in the Christian communions, which, alas, have been disunited for centuries. The ecumenical movement was given life and has been kept alive by him. For many decades now, there has been a growing awareness of and sensitivity to the Holy Spirit in the Christian communions. Even the Lutherans, who have always been so orientated towards the Word that their Lord's Supper does not contain an epiclesis,[28] but who have always at the same time affirmed the bond that connects the Spirit with the Word (see Volume I, pp. 139–140), agree with us now sufficiently to be able to say: 'the eucharistic action of Christ is brought about by the Holy Spirit. Everything that the Lord gives us and everything that makes us ready to appropriate it is given to us by the Holy Spirit. This is expressed in the liturgy and especially in the invocation of the Holy Spirit (the epiclesis).'[29] I would gladly quote the Reformed theologian J. J. von Allmen here (see below, note 25), but the place of the Holy Spirit in Calvinist dogmatic theology is obvious (see Volume I, pp. 138 and 141). There is no need for me to speak of the Orthodox Church in this context, as I have again and again throughout this whole work presented it, quoted its authors and, I hope, walked along with it. Not long ago, Nikos Nissiotis spoke about the Holy Spirit and the Churches in connection with 'Faith and Order' in the World Council of Churches (see below, note 26). It was, moreover, the secretary of the 'Faith and Order' Commission, Lukas Vischer, who recently suggested that the epiclesis should be seen as a sign of unity, the pledge of renewal for the Churches and a new breakthrough for ecumenism.[30]

I hope very much that this long and thankless study that is now completed will contribute to the holy work of restoring Christians to unity—a unity not of uniformity and imperialism, but of communion through the one who, distributing his charisms of every kind, wants to lead everything back to the Father through the Son.

NOTES

1. E.-P. Siman revealed this vividly in his synopsis, given in the form of a table, in *L'Expéri-ence de l'Esprit par l'Eglise* (Paris, 1971), pp. 227–229. Cyril (or was it John?) of Jerusalem compared the epiclesis of post-baptismal anointing with the epiclesis of the eucharistic gifts: *Cat. myst.* III, 3 (*PG* 33, 1092A; *SC* 126, pp. 124 and 125). See also Lufti Laham, 'Der pneumatologische Aspekt der Sakramente der christlichen Mystagogie (oder Initia-tion)', *Kyrios* (1972), 97–106.
2. See J. Daniélou, *Bible et liturgie* (*Lex orandi*, 11) (Paris, 1951), pp. 100ff., 125ff.; the second reference is to the sea and the Cloud.
3. See Volume I, pp. 49–51; Volume II, pp. 189–190, and 199 note 7. O. Cullmann thought that Jn 3:4 established a connection between the Spirit and water that was reminiscent of the connection between the Word and flesh: *Urchristentum und Gottesdienst* (Zürich, 1944), p. 50.

4. W. M. Bedard, *The Symbolism of the Baptismal Font in Early Christian Thought* (Washington, 1951); J. Daniélou, *op. cit.* (note 2), p. 69.
5. E. Stommel, *Studien zur Epiklese der römischen Taufwasserweihe* (*Theophania*, 10) (Bonn, 1951).
6. Alcuin, *Comm. in Ioan.* I, 2, n. 33 (*PL* 100, 757); Haymo of Auxerre, under the name of Haymo of Haberstadt (*PL* 118, 50); the Council of Arras, 1025, c. 1 (Mansi, 19, 427); Thomas Aquinas, *ST* IIIa, q. 73, a. 1. ad 2 and other references.
7. Thomas Aquinas, *ST* IIIa, q. 68, a. 9, ad 2. For the Holy Spirit as the principle of the communion of saints, see Volume II, pp. 59–61.
8. R. Sohm, *Kirchenrecht* (Munich and Leipzig, 1923), II, p. 264, note 3 and ff.; see also my *Ecclésiologie du Haut Moyen Age* (Paris, 1968), p. 115, note 236.
9. *AAS* 40 (1948), 5–7; *DS ch* 3860.
10. V. E. Fiala, 'L'imposition des mains comme signe de la communication de l'Esprit Saint dans les rites latins', *Le Saint-Esprit dans la Liturgie* (*Conférence Saint-Serge, 1969*) (Rome, 1977), pp. 87–103; German version of the same article, 'Die Handauflegung als Zeichen der Geistmitteilung in den lateinischen Riten', *Mélanges liturgiques offertes à D.B. Botte* (Louvain, 1972), pp. 121–138.
11. It is interesting to quote the epiclesis for the ordination of priests in the Eucology of Serapion in this context (ed. F. X. Funk, II (1905), pp. 188–190): 'We raise our hand, sovereign God of heaven, Father of your only Son, over this man and we pray that the Spirit of truth may fill him. Grant him the understanding and the knowledge of a right heart. May the Holy Spirit be with him so that he may govern your people with you, uncreated God. Through the Spirit of Moses, you have poured out your Holy Spirit over those whom you have chosen. Grant also to this man the Holy Spirit, through the Spirit of your only Son, in the grace of wisdom, growth and right faith, so that he may serve you with a pure conscience through your only Son Jesus Christ. Through him may glory and honour be given to you for ever and ever. Amen.'
12. J. Lécuyer, *Le sacerdoce dans le mystère du Christ* (*Lex orandi*, 24) (Paris, 1957), pp. 316–320.
13. P. Jounel, 'La liturgie romaine du mariage. Etapes de son élaboration', *M-D*, 50 (1957), 30–57.
14. I. H. Dalmais, 'La liturgie du mariage dans les Eglises orientales', *ibid.*, 58–69. See also P. Evdokimov, *Le sacrement de l'amour* (Paris, 1962).
15. See F. Vandenbroucke, *Le moine dans l'Eglise du Christ. Essai théologique* (Louvain, 1947), pp. 83ff.
16. F. Vandenbroucke, *ibid.*, p. 67; Pseudo-Dionysius, *De hier. eccl.* 6.
17. See my ideas in 1946: *M-D*, 16 (1948), 75–87; Eng. tr., 'A "real" Liturgy and "real" Preaching', *Priest and Layman* (London, 1967), pp. 139–150.
18. See my study first pub. in *Parole de Dieu et Sacerdoce. Etudes présentées à Mgr Weber* (Tournai, 1962); Eng. tr., 'The Two Forms of the Bread of Life in the Gospel and Tradition', *Priest and Layman, op. cit.*, pp. 103–138. The theme of the two tables occurs quite often in the documents of Vatican II: see, for example, the Dogmatic Constitutions on Revelation, *Dei Verbum*, 21; on the Liturgy, *Sacrosanctum Concilium*, 48; the Decrees on the Ministry of Priests, *Presbyterorum Ordinis*, 18; on Priestly Formation, *Optatam totius*, 8; on the Religious Life, *Perfectae caritatis*, 6 and 15.
19. Jerome, *In Mich.* 1, 10–15 (*PL* 25, 1215). According to Bonaventure, it is only possible to understand any branch of knowledge when one knows its language. In the case of eternal life, the knowledge of which is the scientia sacra, Bonaventure said: 'lingua eius est Spiritus Sanctus. . . . Non potest homo intelligere eam nisi Spiritus Sanctus loquatur ad cor eius'; *De S. Andrea Sermo*, 1 (Quaracchi ed., IX, p. 463); cf. *De S. Stephano Sermo*, 1 (Quaracchi ed., IX, p. 478b); *De S. Nicolao Sermo* (Quaracchi ed., IX, p. 473a). See also E. Eilers, *Gottes Wort. Eine Theologie der Predigt nach Bonaventura* (Freiburg, 1941), pp. 57ff.
20. There is a reference to this in my *Ecclésiologie du Haut Moyen Age, op. cit.* (note 8),

pp. 114–115. For the councils, see Isidore of Seville's *Adsumus*, composed for the Fourth Council of Toledo (633) and still in use. This prayer is a real epiclesis! See also Volume II, pp. 28–30.

21. See Gregory the Great, *In lib. I Reg. IV*, 122 (*PL* 79, 267): 'Habent ergo electi praedicatores experientiam Spiritus in se loquentis in repentina revelatione veritatis, habent in subito ardore caritatis, habent in plenitudine scientiae, habent facundissima verbi praedicatione: nam et subito instruuntur et repente fervescunt et in momento replentur et mirabili eloquii potestate ditantur'. The text of Bonaventure's *De S. Andrea Sermo*, 1, quoted above (note 19), continues: 'Nihil facimus nos praedicatores nisi Ipse operetur in corde per gratiam suam. Ut igitur possemus istam linguam intelligere et audire, rogabimus Spiritum Sanctum ut iuvat nos per gratiam suam, me ad loquendum, vos ad audiendum'. See also *In Hexaem*. Coll. IX, 7: 'Radiavit Spiritus Sanctus in cordibus praedicatorum ad omnem veritatem praedicandam et scribendam' (Quaracchi ed., V, p. 373b); *Comm. in Luc*. Proem. 3: 'Quod aliquis sit doctor idoneus eorum quae per Christum sunt suggesta, et per Spiritum Sanctum scripta, necesse est quod sit inunctus superna gratia' (Quaracchi ed., VII, p. 3b); I would also refer the reader to what I said about the *gratia praedicationis* in Volume I, p. 128.

22. Preachers have often asked the assembled people to pray at the beginning of their sermons; this could clearly become routine! Or else they ask the congregation to give 'prayerful attention': see A. Olivar, 'Quelques remarques historiques sur la prédication comme action liturgique dans l'Eglise ancienne', *Mélanges liturgiques offertes à D.B. Botte, op. cit.* (note 10), pp. 429–443, especially pp. 432–434. See also Bonaventure, in the quotations in note 21 above; see also E. Eilers, *Gottes Wort, op. cit.* (note 19), pp. 76ff., 78–79.

23. There have been many German studies and, in French, G. Auzon, *La parole de Dieu*, I (Paris, 1963), pp. 167–175.

24. Y. Congar, *Un peuple messianique. L'Eglise, sacrement du salut. Salut et libération* (*Cogitatio fidei*, 85) (Paris, 1975).

25. J.-J. von Allmen, *Prophétisme sacramental. Neuf études pour le renouveau et l'unité de l'Eglise* (Neuchâtel and Paris, 1964), p. 300.

26. See N. Nissiotis, 'Appelés à l'unité. Le sens épiclétique de la communion ecclésiale', *Lausanne 77. 50 ans de Foi et Constitution* (Geneva, 1977), pp. 45–60, especially p. 52.

27. See Volume II, pp. 218–221. Since then, this has also been said by the Pope in his encyclical *Redemptor hominis* of 3 March 1979, Nos 6 and 12.

28. See H. Geisser, 'Das Abendmahl nach den lutherischen Bekenntnisschriften', *Die Anrufung des Heiligen Geistes im Abendmahl* (*Beiheft zur ökumenischen Rundschau*, 31) (Frankfurt, 1977), pp. 119–147, especially p. 142. In the same collection of essays, W. Schneemelcher quotes a declaration made by P. Brunner, 'Zur Lehre vom Gottesdienst der im Namen Jesu versammelten Gemeinde', *Leiturgia*, I (1954), p. 349: 'dass die Epiklese nicht notwendig ist', 'that the epiclesis is not necessary': *op. cit.*, p. 68.

29. The agreement on the Lord's Supper reached by the Mixed Roman Catholic and Lutheran Commission: *Doc. cath.*, 76, No. 1755 (7 January 1979), 22.

30. L. Vischer, *Oekumenische Skizzen. Zwölf Beiträge mit einem Vorwort von Bischof O. Tomkins* (Frankfurt, 1972), pp. 46–57. Just as I was sending my manuscript to the publisher, I received the final document of the Dombes Group, *L'Esprit Saint, l'Eglise et les sacrements*; Nos 113ff., pp. 70ff., are devoted to the epiclesis.

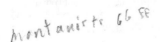